DAN BROWN

MW01671959

X, y, z

marketing

- ism's

Pubic / Private

Sector

C+mu = Sp

1000 + 20% sp = Sp

~~1000 +~~

S = 1000 + .2S

.8S = 1000

S = 1,250

S = VC + FC + P

S = 3/4

THE BUSINESS ENVIRONMENT

Steven J. SKINNER

Rosenthal Professor of Marketing

School of Management

University of Kentucky

John M. IVANCEVICH

Cullen Professor of Organizational Behavior and Management

College of Business Administration

University of Houston

SOUTH-WESTERN College Publishing

An International Thomson Publishing Company

Acquisition Editor: Randy G. Haubner
Developmental Editor: Alice C. Denny
Production Editor: Sharon L. Smith
Production House: WordCrafters Editorial Services, Inc.
Cover Design: Tin Box Studio
Cover Illustration: © Linda Bleck/SIS
Internal Design: Joseph M. Devine
Photo Research: Feldman and Associates
Marketing Manager: Stephen E. Momper

1 2 3 4 5 6 7 VH 0 9 8 7 6 5

Printed in the United States of America

Library of Congress Cataloging-in-Publication Data
Skinner, Steven J.
The business environment / Steven J. Skinner, John M. Ivancevich.
p. cm.
Includes bibliographical references (p.) and indexes.
ISBN 0-538-84627-5
1. Industrial management. 2. Business. I. Ivancevich, John M. II. Title.
HD31.S5744 1995
658—dc20 95-12729
CIP

I(T)P
International Thomson Publishing
South-Western College Publishing is an ITP Company. The ITP trademark is used under license.

PREFACE

Business as a field of interest and study has made a dramatic impact in higher educational institutions in the past two decades. In order to continue this growth more students need to be encouraged to consider a major in a business discipline or to take elective courses in the business school. Many four-year colleges now offer an introductory or survey of business course to students as an orientation for further business courses. *THE BUSINESS ENVIRONMENT* addresses the needs of these students.

The premise of this text is that the practice of business is exciting, challenging, and globally oriented. The excitement of starting your own business, investing in a company, or negotiating deals are part of the daily menu of how business is conducted in New York, Tokyo, Lima, Hong Kong, or Sydney. The challenges of learning about and conducting business are interesting and rewarding. As this book will clearly show, business transactions are sometimes simple and sometimes very complex. Commonly accepted business practices in one country are considered unethical or even illegal in another country. Business is not mysterious, but it is not always either black or white.

As we move toward the next century, the business world is becoming increasingly global. New markets are opening in Latin America, Eastern Europe, and the Pacific Rim. The global orientation of business is a part of every reader's daily life. Clothing, food, transportation, entertainment, electronics, and service industries are booming around the globe. Countries located thousands of miles from the United States are providing goods and services that have become household names. Although the United States is a powerful market economy, there are a growing number of countries that are competing head on with the United States for customers, market share, and resources.

The American economy is now dominated by service businesses, and *quality* is the initiative of many firms. Social responsibility and ethical practices are now important forces in the way business must be conducted. Diversity, total quality management (TQM), and environmental issues are highlighted in this text because they have become an important part of today's workplace. Demographic and lifestyle shifts are changing the way we shop, where we work, and how we live. Students who understand these changes will be more likely to succeed than those who do not. This is the business book that integrates these and many other current developments to help prepare students for tomorrow's business world. Current examples of practices in large, medium, and small organizations and how business issues impact people are used throughout each chapter to relate the text to the real world.

THE BUSINESS ENVIRONMENT USES AN INNOVATIVE MODULAR FORMAT

THE BUSINESS ENVIRONMENT is the first survey of business text published in both a full textbook and a modular format. The text is organized into eight modules that allow for ultimate flexibility in course content. Modules may be ordered through your bookstore in any combination and taught in your preferred sequence. The modules provide students with an integrated and practical approach to understanding current business practices. Every chapter fits logically into this integrated approach. Part 1 (**Module One**) provides an overview of the core of business—the business enterprise. It discusses the foundations of business; forms of business ownership; and small business, entrepreneurship, and franchising. Part 2 (**Module Two**) presents the business environment that surrounds the core, including the social, legal, and international environment.

Part 3 (**Module Three**) focuses on managing and organizing the business, and on the management of production and operations. Part 4 (**Module Four**) examines the management of human resources, as well as human relations and labor relations. Part 5 (**Module Five**) covers marketing strategy, including product, price, distribution, and promotion decisions. Part 6 (**Modules Six** and **Seven**) explores the financial management of business firms. Part 7 (**Module Eight**) is devoted to accounting and information systems.

There is also a **Business Plan Module** available for professors who wish to include preparing a business plan in their course work. It is also possible to order a package for your students that contains the chosen text modules and the academic version of the leading business plan software, *BizPlan Builder.* This package will be particularly useful for courses where there is strong interest in entrepreneurship and small business.

THE BUSINESS ENVIRONMENT DEVELOPS CRITICAL-THINKING SKILLS

Our textbook has several features that make it enjoyable to read and challenging to teach. The book is purposefully written to provoke critical thinking about business issues, practices, and policies. Students can use the learning tools and applications features to help them understand and use the material to critically analyze business thinking and practice.

Whenever possible, the students are asked to critically think and reflect. Instead of relying on rote memorization, we believe that critically analyzing, communicating, and reflecting are more important skills to sharpen. In each element used in the book—the chapter opener vignettes, the boxed features, and end-of-chapter cases and activities—the reader will be asked to form an opinion, to analyze, and to evaluate. Business transactions require that the manager, customer, or worker be able to communicate an opinion, analyze a situation, and evaluate an action. We believe that, by using *THE BUSINESS*

ENVIRONMENT, the critical thinking skills requirements will stretch the reader and require him or her to take and defend a position on some crucial business matters.

Critical thinking is also fostered by a comprehensive case that continues throughout the text. At the ends of Modules 1 through 5 and 7 there is a case involving Nike, Inc. The objective of the use of this integrative case is to illustrate to readers how business practices are linked and how each influences the other. The Nike case integrates each of the modules and main business functions covered in the book.

FEATURES INCLUDED IN *THE BUSINESS ENVIRONMENT*

Readers can use the following learning tools to help them understand and retain the material in the text.

- *Learning Objectives*. Each chapter begins with several clear, attainable learning objectives; questions in the test bank are keyed to these objectives.
- *Margin Notes*. Definitions of key terms are placed in the margin next to where the terms are introduced to facilitate learning. The key terms are again listed at the end of the chapter to help students identify and review important concepts.
- *Summary of Learning Objectives*. Items in the chapter summary are tied to the corresponding chapter learning objective to provide a cohesive, integrated chapter review.
- *Questions for Discussion and Review*. Students can use these questions to evaluate their understanding of the chapter. Many of these questions also require and encourage critical thinking and analysis.
- *Glossary*. Key terms and their definitions are again presented in the comprehensive glossary. Please note that the glossary is included with any combination of modules.
- *Complete Indexes*. Topics throughout all modules can be easily located with the company, name, and subject indexes that accompany any module packages.

THE BUSINESS ENVIRONMENT also offers several application features that will help students to relate the text material to their own experiences and to apply the concepts in the text to the real world of business. Questions to encourage critical thinking are included in all of these features.

TODAY'S BUSINESS WORLD

TOMORROW'S BUSINESS WORLD

- *Opening Vignette*. Each chapter begins with a current news story that introduces students to the chapter's topics.
- *Today's Business World*. Each chapter features a story that focuses on recognizable firms and contemporary topics, extending the concepts discussed in the text.
- *Tomorrow's Business World*. A futuristic application or business trend is presented to help readers think about how business will be practiced in the near, and sometimes more distant, future.

YOUR VALUES AND ATTITUDES

- *Your Values and Attitudes.* Each chapter features a short self-assessment quiz that helps students evaluate their attitudes and values concerning business.
- *Cases.* Two relatively sophisticated cases at the end of each chapter help students put business concepts into practice. Many of the case questions require critical analysis.
- *Experiential Exercises and Application Exercises.* Each chapter contains two individual and/or group projects. Working alone or collaboratively with others on relevant topics will help each reader understand business decision making from a personal perspective.

THE BUSINESS ENVIRONMENT PROVIDES EXCELLENT INSTRUCTIONAL RESOURCES

- *Instructor's Manual.* Each chapter includes a chapter perspective; the learning objectives; an outstanding annotated lecture outline that includes all key terms and definitions as well as supplemental lecture materials; notes on the chapter's boxed materials; answers to the end-of-chapter discussion questions and cases; and a list of recommended readings.
- *Test Bank.* The Test Bank contains about 3,000 questions including multiple choice, true/false, essay, and mini-cases. Each question is categorized by level of learning and chapter learning objective. The Test Bank is also available in computerized form.
- *Acetates.* Many of the acetates are original materials prepared to augment the exhibits in the text. The acetates, as well as all the other exhibits from the text, are also available on PowerPoint disks. (The PowerPoint package contains a viewing disk so the screens may be used even if you do not have PowerPoint software.)
- *Videos.* The videos, taken from a variety of sources, will assist in bringing text concepts to life in the classroom. There is one video for each text chapter and a video instructor's guide that includes additional activities.
- *Videodisc Technology.* The videodisc contains video, definitions, transparencies, and llustrations. Its flexibility and ease of use make it a dynamic tool for instructors. A compatible CAV-type videodisc player is required to use this ancillary.

ACKNOWLEDGMENTS

Many reviewers made valuable comments during the development of this product. We appreciate the helpful suggestions of the following colleagues:

Eldon Bailey, McNeese State University
Jeff Cannon, University of North Carolina
Dawna Dewire, Babson College
Larry Halpern, Boston College
Ken Hoffman, Emporia State University

Frederick J. Kelly, Seton Hall University
Gary Latanich, Arkansas State University
Jay Laughlin, Kansas State University
Dave Lemak, Washington State University
Gordon Long, Georgia College
John Loveland, New Mexico State University
Steven Burd, University of New Mexico
Joseph A. Newman, Northern Illinois University
John Palmer, James Madison University
Herman Patterson, University of Memphis
Thomas W. Sharkey, University of Toledo
Kay Stewart, Kansas State University
James B. Thurman, George Washington University
David Van Over, University of Idaho
R. Grady Wade, Georgia State University
Wayne R. Wells, St. Cloud State University
Judy Maese, New Mexico State University

We are also grateful to teaching associates who contributed to the text and ancillary package. Special thanks go to Daniel M. Ivancevich of the University of Nevada at Las Vegas for his help in developing, critiquing, and revising the accounting and MIS chapters; to Theresa Bilitski of Old Dominion University for her work on revising the finance chapters; and to Tom Duening of the University of Houston for preparing the Nike case. We also appreciate the work of David Reiter of the City Colleges of Chicago, who prepared the Instructor's Manual, and Elizabeth Elam of Saint Francis College, who prepared the Test Bank.

We have enjoyed our working relationship with the MMT Team at South-Western College Publishing. Deserving mention are Team Director Chris Sofranko, Acquisitions Editor Randy Haubner, Developmental Editor Alice Denny, Production Editor Sharon Smith, and Joe Devine and Jennifer Mayhall, who coordinated the design and photographs.

We also want to thank our immediate support team, which includes Ginger Roberts, Jacque Franco, and Ernestine Barnes. These team members again and again do so many positive things in word processing, database searches, contacting businesses, and finding materials that the authors can't imagine producing a book without their support.

Finally, our families—Moira, Aaron, and Carrie Skinner; and Dan, Jill, Dana, and Pegi Ivancevich—merit and receive our heartfelt appreciation for their support and willingness to share our lives with another textbook.

Steven J. Skinner

John M. Ivancevich

BRIEF CONTENTS

PART 1
ENTERPRISE

PART 2
THE BUSINESS ENVIRONMENT

PART 3
MANAGEMENT AND ORGANIZATION

PART 4
HUMAN RESOURCES

PART 5
MARKETING

PART 6
FINANCIAL MANAGEMENT

PART 7
ACCOUNTING AND INFORMATION SYSTEMS

CONTENTS

PART 1 ENTERPRISE

PART 2 THE BUSINESS ENVIRONMENT

PART 3 MANAGEMENT AND ORGANIZATION

PART 4 HUMAN RESOURCES

PART 5 MARKETING

PART 1

Enterprise

CHAPTER 1

Business and Economics

LEARNING OBJECTIVES

1. Comment on the study and importance of business and define it in your own terms.
2. Explain why people are the key to any business.
3. Identify the four main objectives of business.
4. Explain why profit is important to the owners of a business.
5. Describe and compare the three types of economic resources.
6. Distinguish between planned and mixed market economic systems.
7. Determine how gross domestic product (GDP) is calculated.
8. Identify some of the trends facing business leaders in the future.

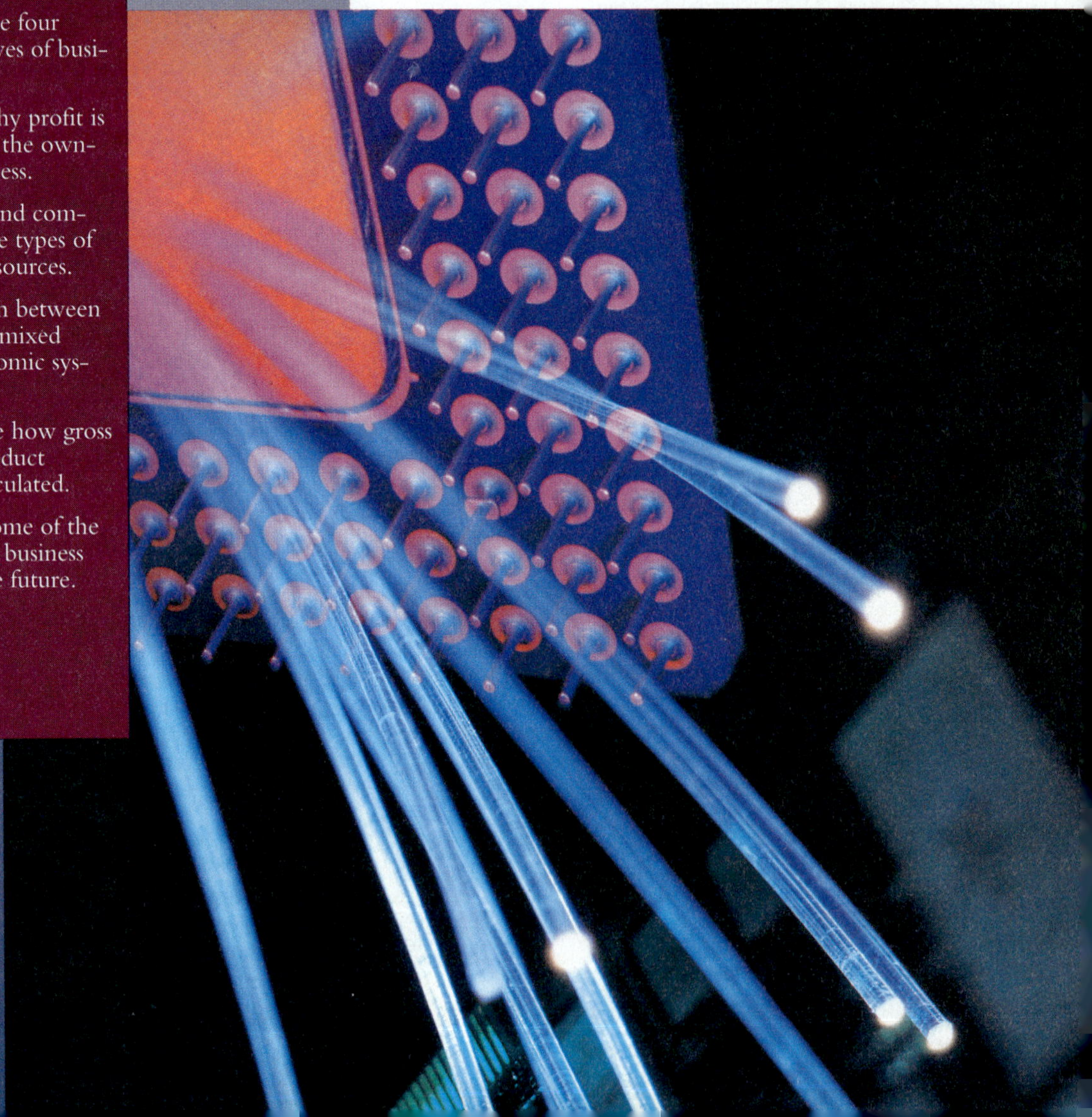

Signs of significant change in the business world are everywhere. Hungarian entrepreneurs operate McDonald's franchises in Budapest. Internet connections expand every day. American business negotiators discuss joint ventures with Chinese managers in Beijing. Individuals walk around with scuba-like masks, engaging in virtual reality simulations of business committee meetings. These changes are bringing about more opportunities for nations to conduct business, companies to negotiate business deals, and individuals to learn from each other in becoming more proficient at transacting business. The opportunities for conducting business are growing at a rapid rate all around the world.[1]

The United States is still a land of business opportunities from New York to Chicago to Houston to Los Angeles to Honolulu. There are problems, deficiencies, serious questions and issues, and many challenges facing Americans and their institutions. However, as this book will illustrate clearly, there is a lot of life left in American businesses and the U.S. economic system.[2] We believe there is enough evidence to show that the United States will continue to be a major economic power, certainly one of the top four in terms of productivity, standard of living, quality of life, and job opportunities.

By the year 2000 about 132 million Americans will be in the work force. A number of trends will be in place as the new century begins:

- The average business firm will be smaller than today's enterprise, employing fewer people.
- The changes in American and worldwide consumer tastes and needs will continue to place a special emphasis on the quality of goods and services.
- Technicians ranging from computer repair specialists to radiation therapists will replace manufacturing technicians as the worker elite.
- The key role of business will have shifted from making a product to providing a service.
- Work itself will require continuous relearning, more high-order thinking, and less routine or working a nine-to-five job.
- Different races, ethnic groups, cultures, and languages will be more valued in a more culturally diverse country.
- The information superhighway (the National Information Infrastructure) will grow in importance each day, with managers, entrepreneurs, and workers learning how to use the information it makes available.
- Quality and customer satisfaction will supersede productivity as the primary focus of business.

Some of these trends have already started. For example, in 1994 IBM employed 302,000 people, down from 406,000 in 1985, and Digital Equipment employed 98,000, down from 126,000 in 1981. In the United States in 1995, over 70 percent of the gross domestic product

was generated by the service industries. Services now dominate the economy. Job growth in the service sector is likely to continue to grow.

The nine-to-five job goes back to the factory setting. Today over 6 million people work out of their homes,[3] and over 30 million work in part-time jobs.[4] Information technology is permitting more and more workers to break away from the traditional office-type existence. Working in an airplane, bus, car pool, or at the kitchen table is becoming more commonplace.

U.S. business will need to develop workers, technology, and markets to remain a powerful force in the global marketplace. Reinventing and renewing the way business is transacted across oceans, telecommunications networks, or negotiating tables will require new ideas, new ways of performing work, and new workers.[5] Students should openly consider the tremendous range of opportunities available to them. They should ask themselves: What skills will I need to become a productive contributor to the business opportunities that are available? What do I have to learn in order to work for an employer in a global business or to operate my own business?

The way Americans conduct, negotiate, and transact business has been copied, vilified, praised, misunderstood, and debated. Without question, the American way of business can be improved; however, to borrow from the words of Mark Twain, rumors of its death have been greatly exaggerated. Actually, it works exceptionally well compared with other systems around the world. U.S. business has helped provide Americans with a relatively high standard of living in both *goods,* such as homes, cars, and clothing, and *quality of life,* such as a free public education system and a clean environment. The freedoms enjoyed by U.S. businesses and consumers are typically not appreciated until they are compared with the lack of such freedoms in Cuba, North Korea, Libya, and Iraq.

This chapter begins with a discussion of why the study of business is important. We explain how people—owners, managers, employees, and consumers—form the core of business. Next we discuss the business objectives of survival, growth, social responsibility, and profit. The discussion of profit leads to a description of economics and economic systems. We also present some challenges and issues that must be addressed both today and in the future to ensure the continuing success of U.S. business. The final section of the chapter explains how the organization and structure of the book will guide the student through the study of business.

YOUR CURRENT BUSINESS IQ

The world's largest, most powerful, and most influential economy is the U.S. economy. Much of what is known about it, however, is not fully understood or is based on conventional judgment. This is not for lack of information. Daily newspapers, television programs, movies, books, and trade publications bombard the public with business data, information, and stories. Unfortunately, the bits and pieces of information are not coherently organized and are difficult to interpret. Studying business and how it is conducted can be more informative and coherent if the field of business is presented in an accurate, straightforward, and dynamic manner.

Before we start to present the world of business, it is important to determine how much the bits and pieces of information have influenced your thoughts and thinking. Try the Your Values and Attitudes quiz about your business IQ to give you feedback regarding your current knowledge of business. By the end of the book we will have succeeded as authors—and you as students—if your knowledge about business has increased.

YOUR VALUES AND ATTITUDES

Check Your Business IQ

Directions: It is interesting to trace your progress as you learn about a subject. This quiz is designed to help you measure your business knowledge as you start the course.

Answer the questions; then turn to the Feedback section. Score one point for each correct answer.

1. What does the gross domestic product measure?
2. Name a successful U.S.-Japanese joint venture in the automobile industry.
3. What size companies create the most jobs in the United States—large, medium, or small?
4. What does liquidity mean?
5. Currently, female full-time workers' wages are what percentage of male full-time workers' wages?
6. What is a flextime work schedule?
7. What does the term ESOP mean?
8. What is a *direct* channel of product distribution?
9. What is the most powerful American brand name in the world?
10. Where is the European Union (EU) headquarters?

Feedback: How do you think you did on the quiz? The questions were not tricky, but you had to be knowledgeable about current events to score a perfect 10. Here are the answers:

1. Gross domestic product measures the market value of all final goods and services produced by resources located within the United States.
2. GM-Toyota, Ford-Mazda, and Chrysler-Mitsubishi are a few worth mentioning.
3. Small companies (under 500 employees) created about 80 percent of the new jobs between 1984 and 1994.
4. Liquidity is a measure of how quickly any item, such as a car, can be converted into cash.
5. About 70 percent and improving slowly each year. A gap still exists.
6. A work schedule that allows workers to vary their starting and quitting times. It is used by one in eight full-time workers.

7. Employee stock option plan. Nearly 10 million employees own ESOPs, which means they own part of their companies.
8. It is the movement of goods directly from the producer to the consumer. An example would be a farmer selling produce at a roadside stand.
9. Coca-Cola. It is found all over the world.
10. Brussels, Belgium.

How did you do?

0–5 You are not yet familiar with some business concepts or issues, but that's why we're here. There is some work to be done.

6–8 Not a bad beginning. With some work, you can be really knowledgeable.

9 Outstanding. Not perfect, but really a great beginning.

10 Wow, you might be one in a thousand. Don't get too excited, because a lot of areas were not included in the quiz. Take a bow, and let's go to work and learn more.

Everyone should have at least some knowledge of business. Are you ready now to start the journey toward becoming business intelligent? Why do you need to learn about business and how it is conducted around the world?

WHY LEARN ABOUT BUSINESS?

A liberal arts major, an engineer, and a business major will all eventually end up working in a business, owning a share of a business, or transacting business with an enterprise. It doesn't matter what course of study is pursued or what diploma is earned, eventually everyone must engage in some form of business activity. The person may be a worker in a business, may provide consulting expertise to a firm, or may purchase an automobile from a dealer that provides the best price.

A *business* is any activity that attempts to earn a profit by providing goods and services to others. The person who is aware of, knowledgeable about, and understands business can function better in a society built upon business enterprises than an individual who is not educated about businesses and business transactions. Learning about business through education, training, attending seminars, self-improvement, and observation can improve a person's ability to live and work in society.

Protecting and Improving Our Standard of Living

One reason to study business is to protect our way of life. Americans take great pride in being free and independent. Because of the independence, hard work, and values embodied in business institutions, Americans enjoy a comfortable standard of living. Exhibit 1.1 presents a sampling of a few standard of living indicators across four countries. The United States leads in all indicators except life expectancy, which presents an interesting dilemma to policy makers. Are Americans getting soft because they possess more goods, eat

Exhibit 1.1
Standard of Living

	Life Expectancy	Schooling Mean Years	Number of People Per: Doctor	TV	Telephone	McDonald's
U.S.	75.9	12.3	404	1.2	1.3	28,000
China	70.1	4.8	724	37.5	76.9	384,000,000
Japan	78.6	10.7	609	1.6	1.9	130,000
Hong Kong	77.3	7.0	933	4.0	1.6	95,000

Source: WETA *Asiaweek*, McDonald's

too many McDonald's french fries, or do not engage in enough physical work and exercise?

Standard of Living
A measure of how well a person or family is doing in terms of satisfying needs and wants with goods and services.

Free Enterprise
A system in which private businesses are able to start and do business competitively to earn profits, with a minimal degree of government regulation.

We need to understand the contributions of business and also learn how to maintain an acceptable standard of living for future generations. **Standard of living** describes the amount of goods, services, and quality of life that an average family or individual can achieve with its income. The standard of living of each generation of Americans has been better than that of the previous generation. How has this happened? We believe that a minimal amount of government interference and a free market business system have been the major reasons for perpetuating our way of living. This free market system, called **free enterprise,** means that private businesses are able to organize and conduct business activities competitively with minimal government regulation. As a result of this system, the productive activities of people have been as free as possible.

The Heritage Foundation has found that the freedom found in a nation is a critical factor in its relative wealth.[6] The Foundation has calculated an "index of economic freedom" for 101 nations. Just 43 nations were found to have "free" or "mostly free" economies (e.g., Hong Kong, Singapore, Bahrain, United States, Japan). The index, the first comparative analysis of its kind, measures the degree of economic freedom each country allows in such areas as trade policy, taxation policy, property rights, regulations, and foreign investment. A few of the most economically restricted (eight were identified) included Sudan, Mozambique, Cuba, and North Korea. The index provides some evidence that countries with the highest level of economic freedom also have the highest living standards.

Coping with Change

Business is dynamic—always changing. Coping with both predictable and unpredictable events can be easier, more efficient, and less traumatic if we understand business. Prices increase or decrease, products are added, needs change, services are created to meet needs, laws are passed, and unexpected events occur—for example, stock market crashes, hamburger contamination at Jack-in-the-Box, the comeback of the Big Three American automobile producers, new digital technology, and the elimination of layers of management hierarchy. Changes are occurring at a rapid rate, and coping with them is becoming an increasingly important factor in conducting business intelligently.

Understanding Mutual Dependence

Business
The exchange of goods, services, or money for mutual benefit or profit.

Over the years, people have become more and more dependent on one another. This book is about understanding mutual dependence, using the business system effectively, and being a part of business. As stated earlier, **business** is the exchange of goods, services, or money for mutual benefit or profit. Years ago, our ancestors discovered that producing everything one needs occasionally requires doing some undesirable work. They also discovered that individuals have various traits, needs, and skills. If a person specialized in a particular job, such as making shoes or growing corn, the surpluses produced could be traded for other desirable goods. Today, the business conducted in and among the United States, Canada, Great Britain, Germany, Japan, and other countries is more complicated than trading shoes for corn.

Few people today produce everything they need or use; a complex division of labor has encouraged us not to be self-sufficient. For example, you buy food at the local supermarket. You drive a car manufactured in Dearborn, MI. You use fuel pumped from oil wells in Texas. You go to schools built by carpenters, bricklayers, ironworkers, and cement workers. You watch news programs produced in Atlanta, GA. You wear clothing designed in Milan, Italy. You pitch baseballs manufactured in Haiti.

Realizing Global Opportunities

The era of business in the global marketplace requires leaders who know how to start, operate, and sustain businesses. Business negotiations, joint ventures between companies in different countries, travel across borders, investment across geographical boundaries, and working for foreign-owned enterprises are becoming commonplace. To function in such a world, each of us must understand the principles of business.

Preventing Misconceptions

Understanding business also prevents accepting misconceptions, misinformation, and inaccurate data as truths. Many people still believe that Japan has the number one economy, that the average U.S. business earns 15 percent profit, that most new jobs are created by large businesses, and that most Japanese managers have guaranteed jobs for life. Each of these assumptions is inaccurate.

PEOPLE: THE KEY TO BUSINESS

The human element is the key to any business. Business needs people as owners, managers, employees, and consumers. People need business for the production of goods and services and the creation of jobs. Whether business is transacted in Mexico, Canada, or Nigeria does not matter. Businesses may be operated differently and their objectives may differ, but the universal element in all business activities is people.

Owners

People who directly own a business, as well as those who invest money in one, do so because they expect to earn a profit. Most of the giant corporations, such as General Motors, Eastman Kodak, Dow Chemical, Du Pont, and Exxon, are owned by large numbers of people. General Motors has over 1.2 million shareholders (owners) and 745,000 employees.[7] When making decisions, the professional managers in business organizations need to consider the owners and what they expect from the business.

Managers

The person responsible for operating the business may be the owner (an owner-manager, also called an entrepreneur) or a professional manager employed by the owner. Both types of managers seek business survival, profit, growth, and social responsibility.

The owner-manager sets his or her own objectives, whereas a professional manager attempts to achieve objectives set by others. The professional manager is accountable to the owners of the business, who judge the manager's performance by how well their objectives have been accomplished over a period of time.

Many business owners are *entrepreneurs,* people who take the risks necessary to organize and manage a business and receive the financial profits and nonmonetary rewards. In Chapter 3, a more thorough discussion of entrepreneurs will be presented. Today's entrepreneurs are expected to be innovative, practical, and strong willed. This view was actually established years ago by noted Austrian economist Joseph Schumpeter. He stated:

The function of entrepreneurs is to reform or revolutionize the pattern of production by exploiting an invention or, more generally, an untried technological possibility for producing a new commodity or producing an old one in a new way, opening a new source of supply of materials or a new outlet for products, by organizing a new industry.[8]

The owner-managers who fit Schumpeter's description are too numerous to list, but they would include people such as Ted Turner (CNN), Ken Olsen (Digital Equipment Corporation), Fred Smith (Federal Express), Bob Reis (Final Technology), Frank Perdue (Perdue Chickens), Debbie Fields (Mrs. Fields Cookies), John McCormick (Visible Changes), Bill McGovern (MCI Communications), Elizabeth Fettinger (Beacon Metal Fabricators), and Barbara LaMont (WCCL-TV). Each of these entrepreneurs practices what Schumpeter described. They all personify the term *entrepreneur.*

TOMORROW'S BUSINESS WORLD

Tomorrow's Business World

The look of the U.S. work force in the years to come will be different than it is today. It will be different in terms of age distribution, gender mix, cultural diversity, inclusion of people with disabilities, and the mix of attitudes reflected. Here are a few forecasts:

- As the population ages, younger persons will manage older persons to a greater extent than ever before.
- Nontraditional workers, such as people with disabilities, retirees, immigrants, and women who are not currently in the work force, will be in demand.
- Leave policies will be revamped. There will be increasing pressure for both parents to be on leave for childbirth, child-related emergencies, and elder care.
- It will be increasingly common for men to work for women.
- Companies will establish rewards that are valued by different cultural groups and will be flexible about holidays, time off, and leaves.
- Workers will receive training to become comfortable working with persons with disabilities.

Today's portrait of diversity will be broadened in U.S. businesses. The need to effectively use and develop the skills and competencies of an increasingly diverse work force will become a major responsibility of anyone in a leadership position in a business enterprise.

Do you know much about the values, needs, and goals of individuals of another race, religious affiliation, age, or educational background? How do you plan to learn about people with different backgrounds?

Employees

Employees supply the skills and abilities needed to produce the goods or services a business sells to earn a profit. Most employees expect to receive an equitable wage or salary and to be given gradual increases in the amount they are paid for the use of their skills and abilities. To compete with other businesses, a business enterprise needs a committed and effective team of employees.

Consumers

Consumer
A person who purchases a good or service for personal use.

In the global marketplace, from Hong Kong to Monterrey to Los Angeles to Munich, the target of business activity is the consumer. A **consumer** is a person or business who purchases a good or service for personal or organizational use. Consumers everywhere want more and better goods and services. They want better automobiles, better homes, more luxuries, and better leisure equipment, and they want to pay a fair price.

Businesses attempt to satisfy consumer demands in order to earn a profit. To do so, they must determine what those consumer demands are. Because consumers continually want more and better things, new businesses are formed and existing businesses make adjustments to accommodate the demand. When a demand for products or services exists, a business can earn a profit by supplying them promptly, efficiently, and cost effectively. The uncertainty and risk involved in assessing consumer demands pose a challenge to business decision makers.

BUSINESS OBJECTIVES

Businesses must achieve their objectives to remain in operation. Business objectives include such factors as profit, survival, growth, and social responsibility.

Survival, Growth, and Social Responsibility

Survival is an obvious objective. Other objectives can be accomplished only if the business enterprise survives.

Growth is an objective because business cannot stand still. Increased market share, personal and individual development, and increased productivity are important growth objectives. The growth of Compaq Computer and Wal-Mart to multibillion-dollar enterprises is often used as an example of business success accomplished through growth.

In recent years, many businesses have recognized meeting social responsibilities as an important objective. Businesses, like each person in society, must accept their responsibilities in areas such as pollution control, elimination of discriminatory practices, and energy conservation.[9] Examples of new corporate acceptance of social responsibilities appear almost daily in the media. For example:

- Polaroid has effectively reduced toxic waste by 20 percent since 1988, established a new Marketing Environmental Group Advisory Board, and appointed a manager for its newly created Marketing Environmental Program.
- Camet Company, an affiliate of W.R. Grace, has introduced a new catalytic converter that will eliminate 50 percent of exhaust pollutants.
- Wal-Mart Stores and Kmart Corporation have requested that manufacturers supply them with more recycled and recyclable products.

Profit

Although survival, growth, and social responsibility are important objectives, the profit objective plays the major role in business. Profit, however, means different things to different people because of their values, attitudes, and perceptions.

Typically, a businessperson calculates profit by subtracting all the costs, including taxes, from the revenue received for selling a product or service in the

Kmart demonstrates social responsibility by using energy-efficient equipment, using and selling recycled and recyclable building materials and products, and participating in and donating to community environmental awareness and improvement projects.

Profit
The difference between business income (revenue) and business expenses (costs); the selling price of a product minus all the costs of making and selling it, including taxes.

market. The difference is referred to as **profit.** For example, the franchise owner of a Wendy's fast-food restaurant subtracts all expenses (for supplies, staff wages, property, advertising, and so on) from all income to determine the business profit.

Successful business organizations earn a profit because their goods and services effectively meet customers' needs and demands. Basically, profits reward a business enterprise for effectively conducting a number of activities. The business may earn a profit when it takes risks by entering a new market or by competing head-on with another business. For example, Honda invested millions of dollars in promoting and selling small cars in the United States. Today, this Japanese corporation is one of the top five sellers in the U.S. market.

Business organizations that evaluate consumer demand and then move efficiently into a market can earn substantial profits. Xerox in the photoreproduction industry, Compaq Computer in personal computers, and Domino's in the pizza business are examples of companies whose accurate assessments of consumer demands resulted in good profits.

Efficient planning, organizing, controlling, directing, and staffing can help ensure satisfactory profits. Some of the most profitable enterprises (e.g., Ethan Allen, Molly Maid, Blue Bell Ice Cream, H&R Block, and Coca-Cola) are also known as well-managed businesses. Such well-managed enterprises earn, on the average, 5 percent profit a year on total sales. Of course, business profit rates vary greatly by industry and by size and location of the business, as well as managerial effectiveness. A major cause of business failure is improper or inadequate management of people, technology, materials, and capital.

ECONOMICS: THE FOUNDATION OF BUSINESS

Understanding economics is essential to understanding business.[10] **Economics** is the study of how a society chooses to use scarce resources to produce goods and services and to distribute them to people for consumption. Economic theory is divided into two branches: microeconomics and macroeconomics. Microeconomics considers economics from the viewpoint of individuals and firms. It is the study of individual choice and how choice is influenced by economic forces. **Microeconomics** involves the study of household decision making on what to buy, business pricing decisions, and how markets allocate resources among alternatives.

Macroeconomics is the study of inflation, unemployment, business cycles, and growth focusing on the aggregate relationships in a society. Micro and macro analysis of an economy are related, and both need to be used to better understand how a country functions economically. Three issues are key to understanding economics: (1) resources, (2) goods and services, and (3) allocation of both resources and products.

Economics
The study of how a society chooses to use scarce resources to produce goods and services and to distribute them to people for consumption.

Microeconomics
Involves the study of household decision making on what to buy, business pricing decision, and how markets allocate resources among alternatives.

Macroeconomics
The study of inflation, unemployment, business cycles, and growth focusing on the aggregate relationships in a society.

Resources

A nation's resources consist of three broad areas: natural, capital, and labor. **Natural resources** are provided by nature in limited amounts; they include crude oil, natural gas, minerals, timber, and water. Natural resources must be processed to become products or to be used to produce other goods or services. For example, trees must be processed into lumber before they can be used to build homes, shopping malls, and schools.

Capital resources are goods produced for the purpose of making other types of goods and services. Some capital resources, called *current assets*, have a short life and are used up in the production process. These resources include fuel, raw materials, and paper. Long-lived capital resources, which can be used repeatedly in the production process, are called *fixed capital*. Examples include factory buildings, personal computers, and railroad cars.

Labor resources represent the human talent of a nation. To have value in the labor force, individuals must be trained to perform either skilled or semiskilled work. For example, the job of physicist requires extensive training, whereas only minimal training is needed to operate a service station's gas pumps. This collection of human talent is the most valuable national resource. Without human resources, no productive use of either natural or capital resources is possible.

Natural Resources
Resources that nature provides in limited amounts, including crude oil, natural gas, minerals, timber, and water.

Capital Resources
Goods produced for the purpose of making other types of goods and services; includes current assets (short-lived) and fixed capital (long-lived).

Labor Resources
The human talent, skills, and competence available in a nation.

Goods and Services

A nation's resources are used to produce goods and services that will meet people's wants. Wants are things people would like to have but do not absolutely need for survival. Such items as food, clothing, shelter, and medical care are *needs*; video recorders, cassettes, fashionable clothes, and luxury vacations are *wants*.[11]

A person's wants can be unlimited: As soon as one want is satisfied, another is created. Even wealthy people tend to have unlimited wants. Henry Ford was once asked how much money it would take before a person would stop wanting more. He reportedly answered, "Just a little bit more."

Allocation

All countries face the age-old economic problem of limited resources and unlimited wants. We all know, for example, that the supply of oil and natural gas in the United States is a limited natural resource.

Allocation
The process of choosing how resources will be used to meet a society's needs and wants; includes the distribution of products to consumers.

Resource Allocation. Because we live in a world in which the quantity of all resources is limited, we must make choices about **allocation**—how these scarce resources are to be used. To make these choices, we have to answer three fundamental questions:

1. What goods and services will be produced, and in what quantities? What industrial goods and what consumer goods will be produced? Apartments or new houses? Railroad cars or large trucks?
2. How will goods and services be produced, and by whom? For instance, will energy be produced from coal, natural gas, or nuclear power?
3. Who will use the goods and services? When the goods and services are divided, who is to benefit from their use? Rich or poor? Families or single people? Old or young?

Once these questions are answered, we have a basis for choosing how our resources will be used, how they will be allocated to best satisfy consumers' wants and needs. In a market economy, allocation of resources also involves other issues. Should the need for business prosperity and success be a consideration? What priority should be given to government's need for resources? In our economy, allocating resources—especially scarce resources—involves all these questions. Allocation can be very complicated, indeed.

Product Distribution. The issue of allocation is not limited to scarce resources. It also involves the distribution of goods and services to the consumer. In this context, allocation involves an exchange (e.g., money, goods, time, services) between a business and a consumer (e.g., client, customer, patron). In an ideal pattern of distribution in a market economy, the business earns a profit and the customer is satisfied with the good or service: The exchange provides mutual benefit. That is important in a market economy. A tailor able to earn a profit is likely to continue to work hard at the job. Likewise, a customer who likes the price and quality of the tailor's services will continue to use that tailor. When goods and services get to the customers who want or need them and mutual satisfaction occurs, both resources and products have been well allocated.

ECONOMIC SYSTEMS

Economic System The accepted process by which labor, capital, and natural resources are organized to produce and distribute goods and services in a society.

An **economic system** is an accepted way of organizing production, establishing the rights and freedom of ownership, using productive resources, and governing business transactions in a society. There are three basic types of systems: (1) the government can produce almost all the goods and services (a planned economy); (2) private enterprise can produce almost everything (a pure market economy, found only in textbook examples); and (3) there can be some government production and some private production (a mixed economy).

No economy is entirely privately owned, but a few (e.g., North Korea and Cuba) are almost entirely government owned. The United States is a mixed economy, with about 90 percent of production provided by the private sector.

Planned Economies: Socialism and Communism

Modern socialism has much of its roots in the ideas of Karl Marx (1818–1883), published in 1867 in *Das Kapital.* Marx believed that workers were being exploited by owners (capitalists) and forced to work for wages that barely allowed them to survive. Capitalists, who owned the means of production, were viewed as a separate, distinct class. According to Marx, capitalists made profits by paying workers less than the value of their production.

Socialism. Socialism is a system based upon government ownership. Government planning, rather than the market, is relied upon to coordinate economic activity.

Prior to major changes in 1989 and 1990, countries such as East Germany (now part of Germany), Romania, Bulgaria, and the former Soviet Union had planned economies. The governments owned productive resources, financial enterprises, retail stores, and banks. In a **planned economy,** the government is the owner because it speaks for the people. Personal property, such as automobiles, clothing, and furniture, is owned by private citizens; however, almost all housing and the means of production are owned by the government. In a planned economy, politically appointed committees plan production, set prices, and manage the economy. Each factory receives detailed instructions on how many goods to produce.

Planned Economy An economy in which the government owns the productive resources, financial enterprises, retail stores, and banks.

Today, socialism is in a state of transition. Before 1990 socialist economic systems used administrative controls or central planning to answer the questions of what, how, and for whom to produce. Recent reforms in countries such as China have reduced the central planner's power and role and increased the market's role.

Communism. Communism is a form of autocratic state socialism. A small group of nonelected officials decides what society's needs and goals are. In a pure communist economic system, the state owns most resources, including labor. A worker under pure communism has no claim to any of his earnings. Workers provide their labor in service to the government.

Resentment toward autocratic control in the former Soviet Union, East Germany, Hungary, and other countries led to demands for democracy in the late 1980s. The pure communist system has never actually existed, but it was the stated goal of many socialist countries until their demise. Today, many previously Communist Party-controlled countries hold elections and use multiparty political groups to change their political orientations.

The People's Republic of China was established as a communist state in 1949. China's famous five-year economic plans emphasized heavy industry, defense, and self-sufficiency. Wage differentials were frowned on as a way to motivate workers. In the late 1970s China opened its doors to international trade, foreign investment, and communication. Worker incentives were improved through installing bonus systems, and private enterprise was encouraged in agriculture and consumer goods. The Chinese have even developed a stock market. The People's Republic of China is moving away slowly from being a planned communist-controlled state. There is still a high degree of central planning, but there are more market incentives. Today's Business World illustrates that China has the potential to become the world's biggest economy. The Chinese are fast becoming very knowledgeable about business, trade, and competition. Profit making, which was once a dirty word, has become acceptable and encouraged.

TODAY'S BUSINESS WORLD

China Is Learning Fast About Business

China is still a tightly planned communist society. However, the government controls and planning councils are slowly shrinking. In China's vast and rapidly growing underground economy, many urban residents report to their official jobs, and knowing they can't be fired, quickly depart for second, or even third jobs in the new private sector. Almost no one reports his or her true income. Counting income from second jobs, unpaid taxes, and underground economic activity, the Chinese economy is growing at a rate of 9 percent a year. At this rate, China creates a new market as big as Argentina's market each year.

Because of the tremendous market opportunities, global firms such as Coca-Cola view China as a ripe market for business. Sales there of Coke, Sprite, and Fanta have skyrocketed by 54 percent a year, and China is now Coke's fastest-growing major market. With 13 bottling plants already in China, Coca-Cola plans to add 10 more over the next three years. Coca-Cola is now available to 900 million of China's 1.2 billion people.

The list of foreign companies doing business in China is growing daily. Examples include Johnson & Johnson, SmithKline Beecham, Procter & Gamble, and Bausch & Lomb. Avon sales personnel are selling all over southern China. Kentucky Fried Chicken will be operating in all 31 Chinese cities with a population of over 1 million by 1998. How do the Chinese, cloistered for so long, know all about Coca-Cola, Kentucky Fried Chicken, disposable contact lenses, and Contac cold capsules? They watch television, read advertisements, listen to visitors, and travel to other countries. More than 800 million Chinese now have access to television sets. There are 12 million color television sets sold each year in China, which makes it the world's largest TV market.

China opened its retail sector to direct foreign investment in 1992. Department stores and supermarkets financed through Hong Kong and Japan are going up in main cities. Foreign-branch producers are establishing distribution and sales networks.

The Communist Party has permitted foreign investment to come into China and hopes to raise the standard of living throughout the country significantly. So far, the Chinese leadership has worked with foreigners who have delivered goods and services. Chinese workers are talented, energetic, and fast learners. They are learning about business, marketing, management, distribution, quality control, and the importance of customers. There is tremendous potential for business in China. One day, China may be a strong competitor in global markets.

If you operated a business, would you attempt to conduct business in China? What risks would you consider before attempting to do any business in China?

Source: Adapted from Richard Hornik, "Bursting China's Bubble," *Foreign Affairs* (May–June 1994): 28–42; Andrew Tanzer, "This Time It's for Real," *Forbes* (August 2, 1993): 58–61; "Trick or Treat," *The Economist* (July 10, 1993): 28–29; and "The Biggest Prize," *The Economist* (January 16, 1993): 68–69.

Mixed Market Economy

Capitalism
A type of economic system characterized by private ownership of capital, competition among businesses seeking a profit, and consumers' freedom of choice.

Capitalism is an economic system based on private ownership of property and a market in which individuals decide how, what, and for whom to produce. Under a pure capitalist system, individuals are encouraged to follow their own self-interest, while market forces of supply and demand are relied on to coordinate economic activity. Markets work through a system of rewards and payments. If you work, you get paid for that work; if you want a product or service, you pay the owner or provider for it. In a capitalist economy, individuals are free to do whatever they want as long as it's legal. The market is relied upon to see that what people want to get and want to do is consistent with what is available. Under capitalism, fluctuations in prices coordinate individuals' wants.

Mixed Economy
An economy in which both the government and private business enterprises produce and distribute goods and services.

The United States is not a pure capitalist nation. It is instead a mix of free markets plus government ownership and involvement. A pure capitalist nation would have no government control or ownership of markets. In a **mixed economy,** both the government and private business enterprises produce and distribute goods and services. The government usually plays a role in supplying defense, roads, education, pensions, and some medical care.

A mixed market economy allows the freedom to start a business.[12] *Freedom of enterprise* means that businesses and individuals with capital may enter essentially any legal business venture they wish. This important feature of the market economy permits individuals to seek out profit-making business opportunities. Under the market economy, any business or individual can earn a profit by producing a useful good or service. However, businesses and individuals do not have an automatic right to profit. Profit is a reward to a business for using scarce economic resources efficiently. Consumers must consider a good or service reasonable in price, quality, and value before a profit can be made.

Competition is yet another important part of a market economy. In general, *competition* refers to the rivalry among businesses for consumer dollars. Because of competition for consumer dollars, businesses have to be aware of what consumers want to buy. If they ignore consumer wishes, they are likely to lose sales, which directly affects the level of profit. A business that consistently loses money and makes no profit will fail. Consequently, competition among businesses generally provides consumers with lower prices, more services, and improved products. The continual fare wars in the airline industry illustrate how fierce competition among businesses can become.

Exhibit 1.2 summarizes some key characteristics of the different types of economic systems.

Over time, companies can lose their stature or competitive position. Fearsome megacorporations have vanished like the dinosaurs, but in a much shorter time period. Poor decision making, improper business practices, lazy responses to competitors' actions, poor selection of top executives, inadequate training of the work force, and ignoring signals of problems have all contributed to the fading of many business enterprises.

In two decades, IBM, General Motors, and Sears, Roebuck have lost their leadership positions on the world stage. These three seemingly invincible giants are today fighting for their lives against global competitors. In this short time period, Wal-Mart has shot to the number 3 position in terms of stock market valuation, as shown in Exhibit 1.3.

Each of the fading U.S. giants appears to have miscalculated its competition. In a mixed market economy, competitors are likely to seek out the most vulnerable areas of a firm. Compaq, Honda, Toyota, and Wal-Mart were not frightened by the three "kings of the mountain" in 1972. As Exhibit 1.3 illustrates, a business shouldn't be impressed with its market position, profits, or wealth. Everything can change in only two short decades.

The U.S. economic system became mixed when the government established operating guidelines and laws for businesses to follow. For example, one important federal law requires a variety of safety rules to be followed on construction jobs. An economic system also becomes mixed when government competes directly with business. This often happens in such areas as medical research, electric power generation, and communication. The U.S. Postal Service is an example of a government-subsidized business that competes with private businesses such as Federal Express.

The U.S. Economic System. The United States has developed the world's largest economic system. The basic parts of the U.S. economy are illustrated in Exhibit 1.4. This model, a simplification of our mixed economic system, includes only the broadest parts of the economy; it does not include the government. If there's not enough of something to go around (excess demand), its price goes up. If something isn't wanted (excess supply), its price goes down.

Exhibit 1.2
Comparison of Three Economic Systems

System Features	Socialism	Communism	Mixed Market Economy
Ownership of enterprises	Basic industries are owned by government, but small-scale enterprises can be privately owned.	The government owns the means of production with few exceptions, like small plots of land.	A strong private sector exits along with public enterprises in a mixed economy. The private sector is larger than that under socialism.
What is produced	What planners believe is socially beneficial.	What central planners decide the citizens need.	What producers believe people want and will make the firm a profit.
Rights to profits	Profits officially exist only in the private sector of socialist economies.	Profits are not acceptable under communism.	Entrepreneurs and investors are entitled to private-sector profits. State enterprises are also typically expected to break even or provide a return to the government.
Management of enterprises	Significant degree of government planning exists.	Centralized management of all state enterprises is a traditional feature. Management is subject to centralized plans (5-year plans). Planning is now being decentralized.	Managed by owners or people who represent the owners.
Rights of employees	Workers have the right to choose their occupations and to join labor unions. However, the government influences many career decisions.	Employee rights were traditionally limited in exchange for a promise of no unemployment.	Workers have the right to job choice and labor union membership.
Worker incentives	Incentives are usually limited in state enterprises, but do exist in the private sector.	Incentives are emerging in communist economies (e.g., Vietnam and North Korea).	Incentives exist in the private sector. Incentives in the public sector are more limited.

Note the differences between resource markets and product markets in the exhibit. *Resource markets* are places where economic resources—natural, labor, and capital—are bought and sold. The New York Stock Exchange, where money is invested in companies, is a financial capital resource market. The employment section in local newspapers is a resource market where labor is bought and sold. *Product markets* are the thousands of markets in the United States where business outputs (goods and services) are sold to consumers (the government can be viewed as a consumer in some cases). Con-

Exhibit 1.3 *Twenty Largest Companies Worldwide, by Stock Market Valuation, in Billions*

1972		1982		1992	
1 IBM	$46.8	1 IBM	$57.0	1 Exxon	$75.8
2 AT&T	29.2	2 AT&T	52.2	2 General Electric	73.9
3 Eastman Kodak	23.9	3 Exxon	25.7	3 Wal-Mart	73.5
4 General Motors	23.2	4 General Electric	21.6	4 Royal Dutch/Shell	71.8
5 Exxon	19.6	5 General Motors	19.0	5 Nippon Tel. & Tel.	71.4
6 Sears Roebuck	18.2	6 Royal Dutch/Shell	16.9	6 Philip Morris	69.3
7 General Electric	13.3	7 Eastman Kodak	14.2	7 AT&T	68.0
8 Xerox	11.8	8 Schlumberger	13.4	8 Coca-Cola	55.7
9 Texaco	10.2	9 Toyota Motor	12.6	9 Mitsubishi Bank	53.5
10 Minnesota Mining & Mfg.	9.7	10 Amoco	11.7	10 Merck	50.3
11 Procter & Gamble	9.1	11 Chevron	10.9	11 Indus. Bank of Japan	46.5
12 Royal Dutch/Shell	9.1	12 Mobil	10.7	12 Sumitomo Bank	45.6
13 Coca-Cola	8.9	13 Sears Roebuck	10.3	13 Toyota Motor	44.1
14 Du Pont	8.4	14 Atlantic Richfield	10.2	14 Fuji Bank	41.8
15 Ford Motor	8.0	15 Hitachi	9.9	15 Daiichi Kangyo Bank	41.8
16 Avon Products	7.9	16 Proctor & Gamble	9.8	16 Sanwa Bank	37.9
17 Mobil	7.5	17 Matsushita Electric Ind.	9.6	17 British Telecom.	37.8
18 Johnson & Johnson	7.4	18 General Electric Co. (U.K.)	9.3	18 Proctor & Gamble	36.4
19 Chevron	6.8	19 Johnson & Johnson	9.3	19 Glaxo Holdings	36.1
20 Merck	6.6	20 British Petroleum	8.7	20 Bristol-Myers Squibb	35.1

Source: Carol J. Loomis,"Dinosaurs?" *Fortune* (May 3, 1993): 37, from data supplied by Morgan Stanley and Wilshire Associates.

sumers pay for goods and services with money. This type of consumer expenditure is called *retail sales.* The money businesses receive from retail sales is *revenue.*

Where do consumers get money to spend for goods and services? Exhibit 1.4 shows that consumer households supply economic resources to the resource markets. In return for money, people provide labor through work, invest in businesses (capital), and sell natural resources to businesses. The money received in payment for these economic resources is then used to purchase goods and services. Of course, businesses view money paid to suppliers of goods and services as an expense.

Two distinct types of economic resource flows are illustrated in Exhibit 1.4. The flow of economic resources and products is shown by the inner loop. It flows counterclockwise, showing that economic resources move from consumers to businesses and then return to consumers as finished goods and services. Money flow, on the other hand, is shown by the outer loop. This clockwise flow of money begins when firms pay consumers for the economic resource they purchase. Consumers use their money to purchase the goods and services produced by businesses. These two economic flows take place continuously and at the same time. As long as consumers spend all their money, the flow of money into and out of consumer households is equal. However, some money is diverted into savings, and the government needs to intervene to bring about a balance in the flows.

Exhibit 1.4.
Flow of Money and Products in the U.S. Economy

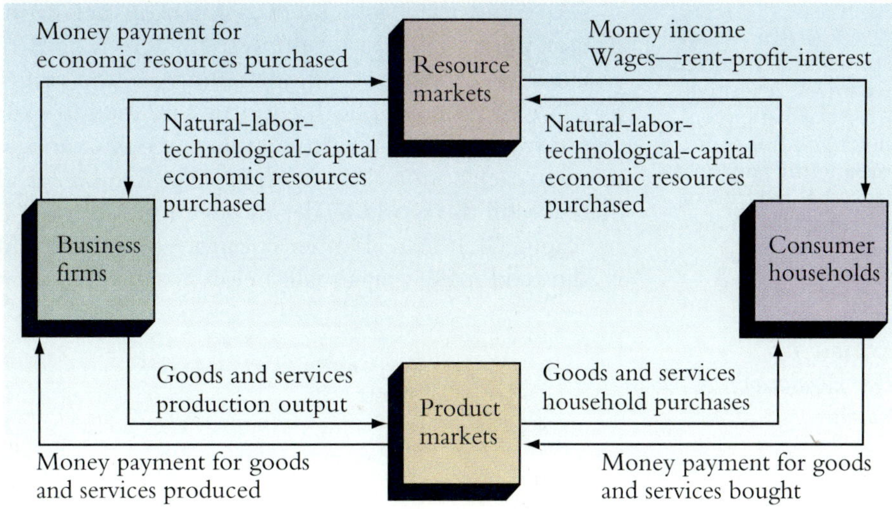

What Economic System Is Best? The most appropriate economic system for a nation depends on several things, including cultural factors and the availability of economic resources. For example, the free market system is unlikely to be appropriate for a nation that creates hurdles for individuals who want to organize their own businesses. The right of business owners to use economic resources for whatever purpose they want is the backbone of the free market system. The free market system normally works best with people who are willing and able to make their own economic decisions. In fact, the free market system encourages people to take the initiative to become better educated and to make their own decisions.

How Is the U.S. Mixed Market Economy Doing? A business generally measures how much market it has, how much profit it earns, and how much it produces or the volume of service it provides. To discuss how well an economic system is doing, a concept called **gross domestic product (GDP)** is used. GDP is the total market value of all goods and services produced in a one-year period within the boundaries of a nation. Thus, GDP excludes what products or services U.S. firms produce overseas, but it includes products and services produced by foreign companies operating in the United States.

Gross Domestic Product (GDP)
A measure of the economic activity within the physical borders of a country.

GDP figures are used to make comparisons between countries, and this enables each nation to learn how it sizes up to others. Per capita GDP is another measure to make comparisons. To arrive at per capita GDP, simply divide a nation's GDP by its total population. This gives a sense of the relative standard of living of the people in the country. Bangladesh has a per capita GDP of about $200, compared to the U.S. per capita GDP of over $22,000.[13] However, remember that GDP is a measure that values activities at the market price in a society. Renting an apartment in downtown Chicago for $1,400 a month would provide you with a one-bedroom space. In a poorer country such as Bangladesh, $1,400 a month would yield outstanding living conditions.

Purchasing Power Parity (PPP) The adjustment of relative prices. A relative market basket of consumer goods is compared to the same market basket in terms of the currencies of the two countries.

To avoid the problem in comparing per capita GDP, a **purchasing power parity (PPP)** measure is used. This is done by comparing the cost of a market basket of goods in one country to the same basket in another country. The currencies of both countries are used to make the comparisons. PPP adjusts for the different relative prices among countries by using costs and currency in each country. Using the PPP in Exhibit 1.5 illustrates that the United States is still the world leader in per capita adjusted GDP. Japan has a higher per capita GDP than all other countries except the United States, but when it is adjusted for PPP, Japan falls below four other countries.

Exhibit 1.5
The Wealth of Nations

	Per Capita GDP adjusted for purchasing power, U.S. dollars, 1990	**GDP** in billions of U.S. dollars, 1992	**Annual Growth Rate** 1987–92	**Population** in millions, 1992
U.S.	$21,571	$5,954.0	1.6%	255.5
Switzerland	20,893	241.5	1.6	6.8
Canada	20,694	568.1	1.2	27.4
Luxembourg	19,205	9.6	2.6	0.4
Germany	18,122	1,928.1	2.9	80.7
Japan	17,792	3,674.3	4.2	124.3
Sweden	17,320	247.9	0.3	8.7
Australia	17,144	286.7	2.1	17.6
Finland	16,990	111.0	0.1	5.1
Hong Kong	16,822	96.1	4.7	5.9
Belgium	16,739	219.6	3.0	10.0
France	16,681	1,336.8	2.6	57.3
Denmark	16,679	142.8	1.2	5.2
Norway	15,967	112.9	1.3	4.3
Bahamas	13,400	2.5	(2.2)	0.3
Iceland	15,589	6.7	(0.4)	0.3
Netherlands	15,543	323.2	2.9	15.2
Austria	15,475	186.0	3.5	7.9
Britain	15,374	1,051.3	0.8	57.6
Italy	15,062	1,237.7	2.3	58.0

Source: "Who's on Top," *Fortune* (July 26, 1993): 96, from data supplied by Penn World Trade and WEFA.

Economic, Social, and Technological Trends

We live in a period of extraordinary change. An important theme in this text is that it is important for each person to be knowledgeable about the business world and how business is transacted. While no one can predict exactly what will occur in the future, there are noticeable trends that individuals will have to respond to. There is no step-by-step prescription for responding, but there are some driving forces that will be discussed throughout the remainder of the text. Identifying and learning about these forces can be helpful in dealing with the future instead of being overwhelmed or controlled by what is happening in the business environment.

Demographic Trends

In 1994, 260 million Americans lived in a world of about 5.5 billion people. The population of the United States increased about 11 percent between 1980 and 1990. Forecasts indicate that by the year 2000 there will be 272 million Americans; the country will be about 13 percent African American, 9.5 percent Hispanic, 74.3 percent white non-Hispanic, and about 3.2 percent other.

The average American is getting older. In 1820 the median age of the population was only 16.7 years. In 1994 the median age was about 32. An older population is not bad for business, but changes must be made in what products and services are produced. The aging of the U.S. population also benefits those who will grow up and begin their business careers in future decades. With fewer young workers available to produce goods and services, wages and salaries are expected to rise. The downside is the cost of caring for an aging population. With fewer workers bearing the tax burden to support programs for the care of the elderly, some difficult political decisions must be made. Social Security and pension funds will have to be carefully managed to withstand the drain.

The increasing number of older workers will mean that motivations for working will change. What is motivational and stimulating to 20-year-olds may not be for 40- and 50-year-olds. Older workers may also be less willing to relocate. There will also be an increased emphasis on health care and wellness.

Diversity in the United States

The United States has always been a country of minorities, a nation of immigrants and refugees. In 1920, of 105 million Americans, 14 million were foreign born and 10.5 million were African American. In 1994, of 260 million Americans, 12 million were foreign born. As the number of minorities and immigrants increases, they will play a more significant role in the U.S. economy and workplace.

Like other Americans, minorities seek entrepreneurial opportunities. The number of nonwhite self-employed persons increased by over 50 percent in the 1980s—faster than white self-employment, which grew by over 40 percent during the same period. African-American entrepreneurs have made inroads in entertainment and media, led by long-established black-owned firms such as Motown (entertainment) and Johnson Publishing (*Ebony* magazine).

Hispanic businesses have grown significantly in recent years; the Hispanic population is expanding at four times the national rate. As Hispanics begin to gain more affluence, they draw the attention of businesses. Hispanic-owned businesses such as Goya Foods (see Case 1.2), Banco Popular de Puerto Rico, E&G Trading, and Sedano's Supermarkets are already producing goods and services geared to the needs and wants of Hispanics.

Growth of the Marketplace

In past centuries, heads of state were all-important because the relationships between countries were primarily political. Nations are now linked by telecommunications and trade. Americans made overseas calls totaling over 5

African Americans and other minorities are taking advantage of entrepreneurial opportunities in growing numbers.

billion minutes in 1990, up from 580 million in 1970. A fiber optic cable across the Pacific went into service in April 1989, linking the United States and Japan. North America, Europe, Asia, and Australia are being strung with fiber optic cable. In 1994, more than 20 million miles of fiber optic cable were in place, tripling the volume of calls that could be placed simultaneously in the 1980s.

Telecommunications will continue to link nations, people, and businesses. Just as we are becoming a global marketplace, we are moving toward a single worldwide information network. Businesses will soon have the capacity to communicate anything to anyone, anywhere in the world, by any form—voice, data, text, or image—at the speed of sound. Business students need the skills to work with computers and communications systems because the world of business requires these skills.

Developing economies will expand the global marketplace. Five hundred years ago, the world's trade center began moving from the Mediterranean to the Atlantic. It is now moving from the Atlantic toward the Pacific. Los Angeles, Tokyo, Sydney, and Hong Kong are becoming major centers of business. By the year 2000, Asia is expected to have two-thirds of the world's population, while Europe will have only 6 percent and the United States about 4.8 percent. Asia is a $3 trillion market growing at a rate of $3 billion a week.

The Pacific Rim stretches from the west coast of South America northward across the Bering Strait to Russia and southward to Australia. It includes all countries touched by the Pacific Ocean. The lifeblood of Japan, a tiny group of islands that is far from self-sufficient, is trade with the United States, Europe, and other countries. Although Japan is the Pacific Rim's economic power today, South Korea, Taiwan, Hong Kong, and Singapore (called the "Four Tigers") are also major business centers.

Eastern Europe, the Commonwealth of Independent States, Chile, and other Third World nations have begun to move toward democracy. The democratizing of these nations will have a significant impact on how business is conducted in future decades. To clean up the chaos and poor economies of Eastern Europe, more private ownership and free enterprise will be needed. Hungarians, Poles, Russians, Czechs, and Slovaks want more, better, and reliable goods and services. The opportunities for U.S. businesspeople in democratizing countries are constrained only by limits to their creativity.

Growth of the Service Sector

Overall, employment will be about 132 million in 2000, according to Labor Department projections. The service sector will create more jobs (20 million) than any other part of the economy.[14] *Services* are intangible products (e.g., insurance, airline travel, tax preparation advice) that are not physically possessed and that involve a performance or an effort. Examples of service industries include banking, transportation, retail trade, and entertainment.

Already about 70 percent of the GDP is being provided by the service sector of the economy. It is the dominant sector in terms of jobs, opportunities, and new business start-ups. The U.S. economy is depending more and more on the service sector for growth, jobs, and expansion into global markets.

The Explosion of Information Technology

The total amount of information in the world is doubling every 18 months. The microprocessor is making everything in the developed economies of the world move faster. Computing power is now increasing at a rate of 4,000 times per decade for a given unit of cost. That means that a personal computer bought in the year 2006 will be 4,000 times more powerful than one purchased in 1996.[15]

One of the most significant trends is the rapid interconnection of individual computers. Global networks of millions of personal computers, connected by fiber optic and satellite links, will eventually allow almost instantaneous around-the-clock communication to any person anywhere in the world. The Internet ("the network of networks") started in 1968. By 1994, over 20 million computers were connected through the Internet. People can interchange mail, documents, books, pictures, voice and music, and films on the Internet. Users can access databases from around the world.

The boom in information technology has led some futurists such as Alvin Toffler to speak of future economic systems as being "knowledge based." As information becomes more important in the success of businesses, the most significant resource then becomes the base of knowledge that has been acquired about the business.

The information technology explosion suggests that businesses will need to be fast, since speed increasingly means value. Information availability is what allows speed. Faster production, faster delivery, and faster service are becoming important indicators of whether a business is successful or not.

Business in All Sizes

A steady stream of warnings about the dwindling concentrations of economic power in big business has been popularized by the media. Big businesses are not as dominant as they were in the 1960s and 1970s, but they are still around and are likely to be a major source of jobs and economic influence far into the future. Big businesses are still dominant in services, where commercial banks, diversified financial companies, retailers, and transportation companies have done very well in the 1990s.

The United States rediscovered small businesses and entrepreneurs in the early 1980s. Like big business, small business is here to stay and it will continue to provide opportunities for individuals. People can select how to invest, where to work, and how to live in a society that is likely to be based on both big and small businesses. One size doesn't fit every individual. Fortunately, in the mixed market economy in which we live each of us can decide whether our future rests in working for a large or a small enterprise. Trends indicate that businesses of all sizes should prosper if leaders understand and conduct business effectively.

Environmental Responsibilities

Worldwide, the momentum of the environmental movement has created a shift in how business operates. There is a growing awareness of and concern about global environmental issues. Television showed us the effects of the Valdez oil spill, complete with oil-drenched wildlife and blackened landscapes. The thick gray-black air in Kuwait resulting from hundreds of burning oil fires was seen around the world on television. Reports about illness years after the Chernobyl nuclear accident frighten everyone.

As the public becomes more aware of and concerned about the environment, business leaders pay more attention. If a company's environmental reputation affects people's buying decisions, then environmental concern may be tied to survival of the enterprise. Business leaders in the late 1990s will have to make environmental considerations (e.g., pollution, waste, recycling) a part of product decision making. Businesses will have to do the right things routinely and by choice, not because some group or law forces them to do so.[16] Chapter 4 will discuss the environment further.

Changes in business concerns about the environment appear daily. At Wal-Mart, environmentalism is a cause; suppliers are asked to provide recycled or recyclable products. The London-based Body Shop, with 14 U.S. outlets, puts the environment at the center of its business. Its skin and hair care stores display literature on ozone depletion next to sunscreens and fill their display windows with information on issues such as global warming. Each employee must spend half a day each week on activist work. Customers get discounts if they bring their old bottles back for recycling. Sales are skyrocketing, the company gets frequent positive publicity, and the environmental theme excites Body Shop employees. They love to work for a responsible firm.

THE THEMES OF THIS BOOK

The excitement, challenges, trends, and opportunities in business are what this text intends to portray to students. The book is organized into six parts. Each of the parts projects five themes that business leaders and employers will face in making decisions and in performing their respective jobs.

Business Ethics and Responsibility

Businesses must operate in a manner that is ethical and socially responsible. Ethical decisions that go beyond legality need to be made on a regular basis

Exhibit 1.6.
Organization of Your Text

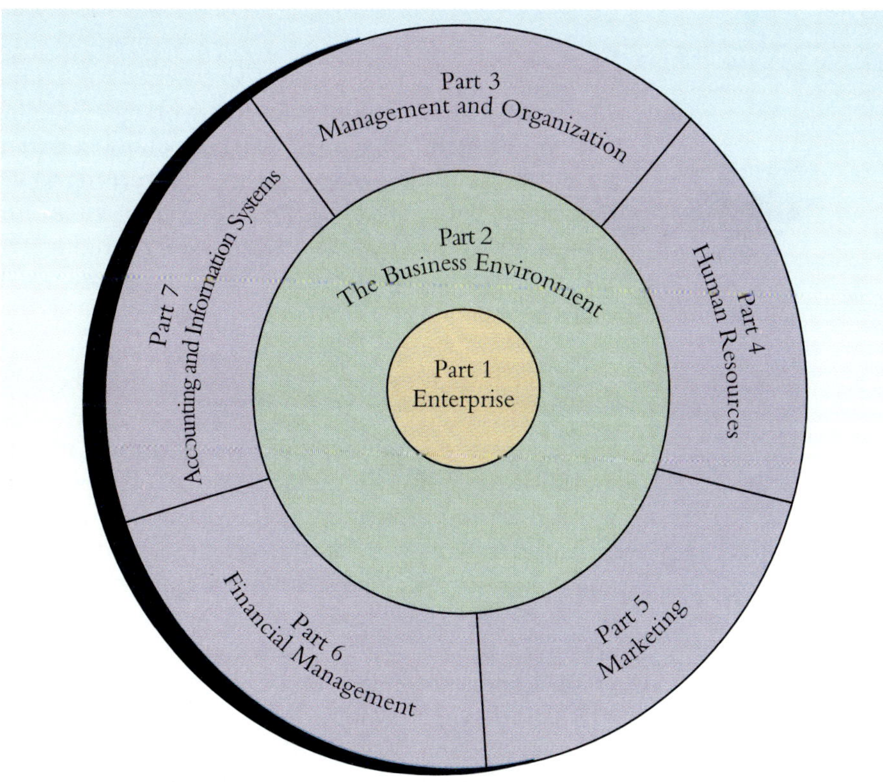

so that all parties interacting with a business benefit. Throughout this text ethical dilemmas will be presented and considered.

Business Profit

Profit is not a dirty word in this text. Business profit is earned and is one of the major reasons individuals take risks. The profit motive is the centerpiece of capitalism and is crucial in a mixed market economy. Even in a growing number of planned economies, profit making is important and is recognized as being a motivating force.

Global Markets

The U.S. consumer is richer, better educated, and more demanding of quality than ever before. But the United States is not alone. The average consumer in every industrial country fits the same profile—having more discretionary spending power, more education, and more purchasing discrimination. The emerging world middle class wants easy access to products and services unhindered by national boundaries. Businesses that are filling these demands are presented throughout the text. As will become apparent, some are doing better than others in the global marketplace.

Diversity

The most dramatic changes in the work force center around increasing diversity. Women, minorities, working couples, part-timers, two-job holders, the physically challenged, and retirees returning to work are all part of the increasingly diverse work force. The labor force employed by businesses is changing each day. The text reflects the changing make-up of the work force and the challenges that these changes create for businesses and business leaders.

The Skill Mix

The information and technology revolution has created a host of opportunities for those skilled in using a host of technologies. The worldwide shift to more market-based economies, increased educational levels, and increased technical training have produced a global work force skilled to work in high-technology-oriented jobs. The changing skill mix is a theme that is illustrated in every chapter in this text. Global competition for higher-skilled jobs is increasing.

In addition to high-tech skills, employers are interested in hiring individuals who have communication, interpersonal, teamwork, leadership, problem-solving, and flexibility skills. Also in demand are workers who are responsible, hard-working, and comfortable with diversity.

Jobs are not reserved simply for Americans, Italians, Canadians, or people in a developed society. Jobs are likely to be held by anyone from any location around the globe who can perform the best. The skill mix needed to be successful in business should become evident to each person using this text.

SUMMARY OF LEARNING OBJECTIVES

1. ***Comment on the study and importance of business and define it in your own terms.*** We need to study business because (a) we have become so interdependent on others, both individually and as a nation, (b) increasing globalization of business will bring many opportunities, (c) we strive to maintain and improve our standard of living, (d) coping with unforeseen events will be easier and less traumatic, and (e) we will be able to separate fact from fiction in business issues. Business involves the exchange of goods, services, or money for mutual benefit.

2. ***Explain why people are the key to any business.*** Business needs people as owners, managers, employees, and consumers. Businesses may be operated differently, and the objectives of business may differ, but the universal element in all business activity is people.

3. ***Identify the four main objectives of business.*** A business must first *survive* if other objectives are to be accomplished. *Growth* is an objective because business does not stand still. Businesses must accept *social responsibility* in areas such as the environment and protection from discrimination. The *profit* objective plays a major role in business. Profits reward a business enterprise for effectively or efficiently conducting a number of activities.

4. ***Explain why profit is important to the owners of a business.*** Profit is calculated by subtracting all costs, including taxes, from the revenue received from selling a product or service in the marketplace. Profit represents the owners' reward for conducting business. Profit is a motivational force that serves to attract people to own or invest in businesses.

5. ***Describe and compare the three types of economic resources.*** Economics is the study of how a society chooses to use scarce resources to produce goods and services and then distribute them to people for consumption. *Natural resources* are provided by nature in limited amounts (e.g., coal, oil, natural gas); *capital resources* are goods produced for the purpose of making other goods and services (e.g., fuel, money, factories); *labor resources* are the nation's human talent, the most valuable national resource. Each of these resources must be managed properly and coordinated to achieve goals.

6. ***Distinguish between planned and mixed market economic systems.*** In *planned economies,* such as those in Cuba, North Korea, and Vietnam, the government owns the means of production, financial enterprises, retail stores, and banks. Prior to 1985 in what was then the Soviet Union, politically appointed committees planned production (by telling factories how much of which goods to produce), set prices, and managed the economy. This is now slowly changing. In a *mixed economy* both the government and business enterprises produce and distribute goods and services. The government usually provides defense, roads, education, pensions, and some medical care. Markets are free and competitive.

7. ***Determine how gross domestic product (GDP) is calculated.*** GDP is the total market value of all final goods and services produced in an economy in a one-year period. The market value of millions of different products (e.g., cars, personal computers) and services (e.g., financial advice, airplane trips) are calculated to arrive at a total.

8. ***Identify some of the trends facing business leaders in the future.*** The challenges facing leaders include how to work effectively with an increasingly diverse work force, use technology effectively, manage the shift in emphasis from goods to services, develop strategies that are globally competitive, operate profitably while at the same time protecting the environment, and conduct business transactions with integrity and ethically correct behavior.

KEY TERMS

Business
Standard of Living
Free Enterprise
Consumer
Profit
Economics
Natural Resources
Capital Resources
Labor Resources
Allocation
Economic System
Planned Economy
Capitalism
Mixed Economy
Macroeconomics
Microeconomics
Gross Domestic Product (GDP)
Purchasing Power Parity (PPP)

QUESTIONS FOR DISCUSSION AND REVIEW

1. In a free enterprise system, should there be a limit placed on the amount of profit a business owner can earn? Explain.
2. When calculating GDP, why is the market value of the product or service calculated?
3. In considering the skill mix needed for global businesses, how can a student interested in working in a large business prepare for a career?
4. How would the incentive to produce high-quality goods be affected by a centrally planned (government) approach to quality control?
5. Do you consider the U.S. economy to be moving toward socialism? Is this good or bad for business opportunities?
6. Review a recent issue of *The Wall Street Journal* and provide examples of two business enterprise successes and two business enterprise failures.
7. Provide some specific examples of the role the U.S. government plays in the way business is conducted.
8. The service sector of the economy has grown beyond the product sector. What implications does this have for job opportunities in the next century?
9. How do you plan to improve your business I.Q.? Why is it necessary to have a business I.Q. in a mixed market society?
10. What type of government intervention occurs in the U.S., Japanese, French, and Mexican airline industries? Search out information in your library and compare it to what is shown in Exhibit 1.2.

CASE 1.1

Dell Computer Corporation: An Example of Free Enterprise

In 1995 Dell Computer Corporation of Austin, Texas, was the sixth-largest PC maker in the United States. At that time Dell had over 4,600 employees and sold over $3 billion a year in equipment.

In 1984, 19-year-old Michael Dell started what was then a mail order company. He took $1,000 of his personal savings and started his firm. He didn't finish his college education, but he does know business. Dell subsidiaries are now found in the United Kingdom, Germany, France, and Canada. The company sells PCs in 18 countries and plans to continue its move into global markets.

Dell had learned about computers as a boy in Houston and had become proficient in their technical aspects. He also possessed business sense. He reasoned that if a manufacturer receives $2,500 for a computer a customer buys for $4,000, there is a profit. The store owner keeps $1,500. Dell asked himself why. Did the owner add anything of value to the equipment? Dell concluded that the answer was no.

So Michael Dell came up with another way to sell computers. During the first few years of business, he sold directly to customers. He used direct advertising (telling people about the computer with a flyer), telemarketing (calling and telling people about the computer), and salespeople (going directly to large corporate clients).

Did Michael Dell learn how to be successful by studying business? Not in a formal sense. He is a good observer, a creative thinker, and a hard worker. He also is fortunate to be living in the United States, where everyone has the freedom to start a business. He decided to go into business, he had an idea about bypassing the retail store, and he took action. His inquisitive, fertile mind processed what he observed, and this led to action.

Early in the firm's history (in 1985), Dell made the decision not to clone IBMs. Wanting a more sophisticated machine than a stripped-down IBM, he decided to design and make his own Dell machine.

Despite his market success, Dell has some critics. He is accused of being unable to delegate, of wanting to control, and of being difficult to work for. However, others quit high-paying, secure jobs just to work with him. To these individuals, Michael Dell has vision and is a world-class business leader.

During 1995 Michael Dell faced new challenges from IBM, Apple, and Compaq and lost two of his top managers. Dell also fell behind mail-order rival Gateway 2000 Inc. in U.S. shipments. In addition, more customer complaints came in about delays and filling orders and about product quality. Dell's notebook computers and Dimension line of PCs were plagued with broken hinges and bad power supplies. The quality problems hurt sales.

In order to stay successful, Michael Dell will have to correct the quality problems and beat back the competitors. In a mixed market economy, success is not forever. Business leaders like Michael Dell have to prove themselves to their customers and employees every day. If Michael Dell is a true business leader, he will accept the new challenges and make his firm stronger.

Source: Adapted from Scott McCartney, "Michael Dell and His Company Grows Up," *The Wall Street Journal* (January 31, 1995):B1–B2; Howard Gleckman, "Meet the Giant Killers," *Business Week Enterprise* (1993):69; "Tease for Two," *The Economist* (February 26, 1994):64–65; Kyle Pope, "For Compaq and Dell, Accent Is on Personal in the Computer Wars," *The Wall Street Journal* (July 2, 1993): A1–A2; "The Education of Michael Dell," *Business Week* (March 22, 1993): 82–88; and *INC. magazine* (January 1990).

Questions for Discussion

1. How does an entrepreneur like Michael Dell view profit, from the point of view of an economist or from a business perspective? Explain.
2. How can competition alter the plans of successful business leaders such as Michael Dell?
3. What characteristics of the free enterprise system permitted Michael Dell to start and operate his business?

CASE 1.2

Goya Foods: Competition and Job Creation

More immigrants flock to the United States than to any other nation in the world. Freedom, opportunities, a high standard of living, and multicultural influences are some of the attractions. There is some backlash occurring because of perceptions that immigrants are taking jobs away from U.S. citizens because they are willing to work for lower wages. Another side of this ongoing debate is the point that a number of immigrants have been successful in starting businesses and creating jobs. Job creation and business success send the message that the United States can and does benefit from immigration.

The Unanue (you-NAN-oo-way) family is an example of successful immigration. The family patriarch, Prudencio Unanue, immigrated from his native Spain to Puerto Rico in 1904 and to New York in 1915. He started what has now become the largest Hispanic-owned food company in the United States, Goya Foods. Unanue worked odd jobs in the food industry for two decades before he started working with a Spanish importer of olives and canned sardines. He lost the job because the outbreak of civil war in Spain cut off import opportunities with Spain.

Unanue knew that foods of Spain and Puerto Rico were hard to find and purchase in the United States. So, in 1936, he and his wife, Carolina Unanue, started Goya Foods. In 1992 privately owned Goya Foods had revenues of $452 million and over 1,800 employees, making it one of the largest Hispanic-owned firms in the United States.

For decades, Goya Foods has dominated the Northeast, where it controls 80 percent of the Hispanic-foods market. It has almost 1,000 products including beans, tomato sauces, seasonings, and olive oil. Goya has expanded its product line to accommodate the needs of Hispanics of Mexican and Central American descent who enjoy many foods that are unfamiliar to Hispanics of the Caribbean. In 1992 salsa surpassed ketchup as the United States' best-selling condiment. When he began Goya Foods, Prudencio Unanue had a vision that the Hispanic food business would become a giant, and he was correct.

As immigration from Mexico and Central and South America continues, Goya Foods searches for products to sell to the new immigrants. The firm is now intent on making Goya a national brand name, but competitors are stepping into the market. Campbell Soup, Knorr, and Heinz all intend to show Goya Foods that competition in the U.S. economy can be stiff. Identifying Hispanic markets, their needs, and tastes is what Goya Foods has been built on, and it is what competitors are searching for every day.

From Unanue's experience, his family learned that there were opportunities to conduct business in the United States. They also learned that business success creates competitors. Once you achieve business success, it is important to continue working hard to stay successful. Today, 1,800 people are working hard to keep Goya Foods in front of the competition.

Source: Adapted from "Joseph A. Unanue," *Hispanic Business* (March 1994): 40; Rhonda Richards, "Goya Foods Born of a Job Lost," *USA Today* (May 10, 1993): 1E–2E; and "Unanues Make This Business a Family Affair," *USA Today* (May 10, 1993): 1E.

Questions for Discussion

1. Could Prudencio Unanue have started Goya Foods in a planned communist economy such as North Korea? Why?
2. Why would Goya Foods be classified as a product marketing firm?
3. In what ways do Goya Foods products contribute to the U.S. gross domestic product?

EXPERIENTIAL EXERCISE

Finding Business Data

Objective:

To familiarize the student with the materials available to improve a person's knowledge about business. The time required to complete the project is 2 to 3 hours.

The project is designed to have the student identify places to find relevant business information and data. If the information is not available in the city, the student will have to go outside the area or access computer databases to complete the project.

Directions:

1. Identify three separate sources (locations) of materials and data that address the following topics:

   Economics
   Business Performance (e.g., stock market valuation)
   The Great Depression
   Globalization
   Work Force Diversity
   Free Enterprise
   Business Technology

2. Select three topics and find three different sources of information in your city or town. Prepare a one-page report on each of the topics from the available sources.

3. How do you rate the sources of information in terms of currentness, ease of accessing, and completeness?

BUSINESS APPLICATION

A Values Exercise

How Does Everyone View the Business World?

"You can't judge a book by its cover" is an old saying that is becoming very important in the determination to use the talents of every single citizen to improve a country's standard of living. An older person doesn't necessarily have traditional values. A college graduate doesn't necessarily lack the background to operate a business. Today's and tomorrow's work force is characterized by a mix of values, backgrounds, and attitudes. Values and attitudes change with significant life experiences or simply with age. Backgrounds remain fixed.

Although values and attitudes vary greatly it is important for people with differing values to work effectively with each other. Participants in surveys indicate that a number of values are extremely important to men, women, old people, young people, African Americans, Hispanics, Caucasians, Asians, Southerners, Northerners, and every possible mix of the diverse demographic landscape of the United States. The most important common values are:

1. Recognition for competence and accomplishments
2. Respect and dignity
3. Personal choice and freedom
4. Pride in one's work
5. Life-style quality
6. Financial security
7. Self-development
8. Health and wellness

Questions:

1. Form into groups of four or more students and discuss these eight values. Are they the most important values among the group members?
2. In operating a business, would a manager need to know the values of his or her employees? What does the group think? Why?
3. In this chapter various countries were mentioned such as China, the former Soviet Union, Iraq, and Japan. In the group, discuss the eight values as they pertain to these four countries. Would different values emerge as the most important in other countries? Why?
4. Does the increasing diversity of the U.S. work force mean that U.S. managers/leaders will have a more difficult time learning about the values of workers than managers/leaders in India? Think about the diversity of India and of the United States. What does the group think?

NOTES

1. Christopher Farrell, "The Triple Revolution," *Business Week* (Bonus Issue, 1994): 16–25.
2. "The Final Frontier," *The Economist* (February 20, 1993): 63.
3. David Foster, "Phone from Home," *Austin American-Statesman* (April 20, 1992): C6.
4. Louis S. Richman, "The New Work Force Builds Itself," *Fortune,* (June 27, 1994): 68–76.
5. Michael Hammer and James Champy, *Reengineering the Corporation: A Manifesto for Business Revolution* (New York: HarperCollins, 1993).
6. Kim R. Holmes, "In Search of Free Markets," *The Wall Street Journal* (December 12, 1994): A14.
7. General Motors, *Annual Report,* 1994.
8. Joseph A. Schumpeter, *The Theory of Economic Development.* Translated by R. Opie. (Cambridge, MA: Harvard University Press, 1934), 74.
9. Thomas F. P. Sullivan (ed.), *The Greening of American Business* (Rockville, MD: Government Institutes Inc., 1992), 1–31.
10. William A. McEachern, *Economics: A Contemporary Introduction,* 3e (Cincinnati: South-Western, 1994), 14.

11. David D. Colander, *Economics,* 2e (Homewood IL: Irwin, 1995), 159.
12. *The Economist Guide to Global Economic Indicators* (New York: Wiley, 1994), 1; and Lawrence Mishel and Jared Bernstein, *The State of Working America* (Armonk, NY: M. E. Sharpe, 1993), 1–11.
13. David N. Hyman, *Economics,* 3e (Homewood, IL: Irwin, 1994), 654.
14. Jaclyn Fierman, "Jobs in America," *Fortune* (July 12, 1993): 34–55.
15. John L. Petersen, *The Road to 2015* (Corte Madera, CA: Waite Group Press, 1994), p. 4.
16. "Waste and the Environment: A Lasting Reminder," *The Economist* (Special Report, May 29, 1993): 1–18.

C H A P T E R 2

Forms of Business Ownership

LEARNING OBJECTIVES

1. Discuss the advantages and disadvantages of sole proprietorships.
2. Examine the advantages and disadvantages of partnerships.
3. Identify the features that should be included in a written partnership contract.
4. Explain the advantages and disadvantages of corporations.
5. Define the term *merger* and identify three types of mergers.
6. Identify other incorporated forms of business.

Use of Owner's Abilities. Jane Deleri had everything to lose or gain from her efforts. The chance of personal losses motivated her to devote time, energy, and expertise to the deli's operation, and success depended largely on the efficient use of her abilities. She had to use her own managerial abilities or pay someone else who had managerial expertise. Either way, full credit for success or blame for failure belonged to Deleri.

Tax Breaks. A major advantage of the proprietorship is that the business pays no income tax. A corporation pays taxes on profits; its owners, the shareholders, also pay taxes on their dividends. Deleri as a sole proprietor, paid no taxes on business profits. Instead, she paid taxes as an individual on all her income earned from the deli.[4]

Secrecy. Deleri filed information on income, expenses, hours worked, and other items required by income tax regulations. This information typically is not made available to the public. Information such as the special formula for her delicious Italian pastries or financial data does not have to be shared with the public because she is a sole proprietor.

Ease of Dissolving. If Jane Deleri were to decide to dissolve her business for any reason, there would be no legal complications. As long as she had paid all the outstanding bills, her decision would be all that was needed to close the deli.

Disadvantages of a Sole Proprietorship

If the sole proprietorship had only advantages, a person organizing a business would have little to consider. But the realities of business are never so simple or certain. Sole proprietorships have disadvantages too.

Unlimited Liability
Obligation of investors to use personal assets, when necessary, to pay off debts to business creditors; a disadvantage of sole proprietorships and partnerships.

Unlimited Liability. The law provides Jane Deleri's total wealth may be used to satisfy the claims of the deli. This is called **unlimited liability.** For Deleri this means almost everything she owns could be sold to pay any debts from operating the deli. For example, if the deli failed, she might have to sell her personal jewelry or automobile to pay business debts that couldn't be paid by the liquidation or sale of such business assets as deli equipment (the computer, display cases) or inventory of canned products.

Difficulty in Raising Capital. Deleri's investment in the deli was limited to personal wealth. The amount she could borrow to operate the business was also limited by her personal wealth; if she had a large estate, she would have little problem borrowing money. Generally, businesses requiring large amounts of financial capital are not formed as sole proprietorships.

The U.S. government through the Small Business Administration (SBA) has a loan program for people, like Deleri, desiring to start their own small business. Few individuals can afford $500 million to build a gas pipeline or to operate a shuttle airline on the East Coast.

Limitations in Managerial Ability. Jane Deleri must have or must obtain all the know-how needed to manage the shop. Operating a deli requires planning, organizing, controlling, marketing, financial, motivational, and customer relations skills. Rarely does an individual have this range of needed expertise. However, many of these skills can be bought. For example, she could hire an accountant to keep the books and an advertising consultant to help promote her deli goods.

Today's Business World illustrates how one owner recognized her limita-

TODAY'S BUSINESS WORLD

Recognizing a Potential Problem and Taking Action

Arguments over religion plagued Emma Colquitt's business, Cardiac Concepts, for a long time. Then a major blow-up occurred when a Hispanic Roman Catholic woman approached her operations manager with a complaint: Another worker, an African American and follower of Jehovah's Witnesses, had listened sympathetically as a customer "bashed" Catholicism.[5]

Colquitt didn't have the solution to this kind of problem, but she knew that if it continued it would hurt the business. Most of her 11 employees were women and minorities, representing half a dozen religious faiths. She needed to stop the conflict and ease the tension. Colquitt decided to hire a consultant to give her diverse work force a workshop.

As more African Americans, Hispanics, Asians, and other ethnic minorities join the U.S. labor force, diversity training is gaining popularity. The four-hour workshop is not a panacea, but it is a step toward making employees aware of the values and lifestyles of their colleagues.

The Changing Workplace

Expected growth in major ethnic minority groups of the U.S. labor force, in millions

	1988	2000
African Americans	13.3	16.5
Hispanic*	9.0	14.3
Asians and others	3.6	5.6

*Hispanic workers, who can be of any race, are also included in the other categories.

Source: *The Wall Street Journal* (September 2, 1993): B5.

Any short workshop has a limited impact. However, more and more small businesses realize that something must be done to improve understanding. Emma Colquitt was sensitive enough to the differences and misunderstandings among her employees that she took what she believed was an appropriate first step to improve the situation and ease the tension.

Is there another way that Colquitt could have solved the situation?

tions and hired an outsider to remedy a potential problem. She was brave enough to admit that she lacked the expertise to solve the problem by herself.

Lack of Stability. Death, illness, bankruptcy, or retirement of the owner terminates the proprietorship. Deleri's business could be sold to others, but the deli, as organized, would cease to exist.

Demands on Time. Although Deleri loves to bowl and attend major league baseball games, she will have trouble finding the time; the deli has to be open all day to develop a customer base. Owners such as Deleri often work 60 to 80 hours a week, especially when the business is new.

Difficulty in Hiring and Keeping Highly Motivated Employees. The sole proprietor is the business. Where can a self-motivated, high-energy employee go in the business? Workers with their own visions and goals and a high drive to succeed often have to quit the one-person business to find opportunities for personal growth.

PARTNERSHIPS

Partnership
A business owned by two or more people.

Section 6 of the Uniform Partnership Act defines **partnership** as "an association of two or more persons to carry on as co-owners of a business for profit." Other than the difference in the number of owners, a partnership is similar in many respects to a sole proprietorship. In a partnership the co-owners share everything, including the risk, hard work, assets, and profits. Some of today's large corporations, including Sears, Roebuck, Procter & Gamble, and Lever Brothers, began as partnerships.

A partnership can be based on a written contract or a voluntary and legal oral agreement. The law regards individuals as partners when they act in such a way as to make people believe they operate a business together.

General Partnership
A partnership in which at least one partner has unlimited liability; a general partner has authority to act and make binding decisions as an owner.

Limited Partnership
A partnership with at least one general partner, and one or more limited partners who are liable for loss only up to the amount of their investment.

Types of Partnerships

About 1.6 million partnerships of various types exist in the United States. The three major types are general partnerships, limited partnerships, and joint ventures. A **general partnership** is a business with at least one general partner who has unlimited liability for the debts of the business. A **limited partnership** has at least one general partner and one or more limited partners. The *joint venture* is a special type of partnership established to carry out a special project or to operate for a specific time period. Let's look at each type separately.

General Partnership. Regardless of the percentage of the business they own, general partners have authority to act and make binding decisions as owners of the business. A general partner may be liable for all the debts of the business; by contrast, the sole proprietor is always liable for such debts. Partners generally share profits and losses according to a plan specified by agreement between them.

With the authority to act as an owner, each general partner can engage the partnership in binding agreements. Unless a partnership agreement prevents a general partner from making such agreements, the partnership is responsible for all actions of each owner.

Limited Partnership. All partnerships must have at least one general partner. A limited partnership includes one or more general partners and one or more limited partners. The general partners arrange and run the business, while the limited partners are investors only. Investors receive special tax advantages and protection from liability. Limited partners legally may have no say in managing the business. If this requirement is violated, the limited partnership status is dissolved.

Limited partnerships are usually found in real estate, dentistry, and various international arrangements. In some states, a special notice must be filed in the county or district where the limited partnership has its offices.

The Boston Celtics organization is a master limited partnership.

A limited partner has limited liability, being liable for loss only up to the amount of capital invested. Thus, a limited partner who invests $30,000 in the business is liable for only that amount. In contrast, general partners have unlimited liability in the partnership.

Master Limited Partnership (MLP) A partnership that sells units traded on a recognized stock exchange.

The **master limited partnership (MLP),** used since 1981, is a partnership that sells units traded on a recognized stock exchange. The MLP has been popular in real estate and oil. It has many of the advantages of a corporation, such as unlimited life, limited liability, and transferable ownership. However, MLPs do not pay corporate taxes, because earnings are passed directly to unit holders.

The unit holders then pay taxes at the individual rate. On August 10, 1993, The Omnibus Budget Reconciliation Act of 1993 was signed into law. The 1993 tax act adds two individual tax brackets of 36 and 39.6 percent to the three existing brackets of 15, 28, and 31 percent. Thus, the highest average individual rate became 39.6 percent in 1993. It applies to taxable income over $250,000 if filed by a single person, head of household, or married people filing jointly. It also applies to married people making $125,000 if filing separately and estates or trusts of $7,500 or more.[6] For corporations the rate is 35 percent. The National Basketball Association's Boston Celtics organization is established as an MLP.

Joint Venture. Sometimes a number of individuals and businesses join together in order to accomplish a specific purpose or objective or to complete a single transaction. For example, they may wish to purchase a building in downtown Boston and resell it for a profit. This would be called a joint venture. Wheeling-Pittsburgh Steel Corporation formed a joint venture with Japan's Nisshia Steel Co. for the purpose of manufacturing steel in the United States and selling it around the world. Hewlett-Packard (U.S.) and Samsung (South Korea) have also initiated a joint venture. Under the agreement, Samsung will manufacture both microprocessor chips and computer workstations, using Hewlett-Packard's technology and software. The firms are attempting to produce a $5,000 workstation that will compete with workstations costing twice as much.[7]

International joint ventures have increased significantly since the early 1980s. Companies such as Monsanto have formed strategic partnerships with international firms such as Collegan, Genex, and Genentech.[8] There are three fundamental reasons for the growing role of international joint ventures: growing internationalism, technology's increasing complexity, and the speed of technological change.

A joint venture in the United States or abroad is something less than the ordinary partnership, which continues as a business. There is some confusion among the courts as to whether a joint venture is a partnership. We think there are enough similarities to categorize it as such. For instance, one of the joint venture partners acting within the scope of his or her authority may bind the other partner(s) in the joint venture. Also, the liabilities of the parties to a joint venture are similar to the liabilities of the partnership.

The Partnership Contract

Sound business practice dictates that a partnership agreement be written and signed, although that is not a legal requirement. Written *articles of partnership* can prevent or lessen misunderstandings at a later date. Oral partnership agreements, though quite legal, tend to be hard to recreate and are open to misunderstandings. Written articles of partnership provide proof of an agreement.

A written partnership agreement includes the following main features:

- Name of the business partnership.
- Type of business.
- Location of the business.
- Expected life of the partnership.
- Names of the partners and the amount of each one's investment.
- Procedures for distributing profits and covering losses.
- Amounts that partners will withdraw for services.
- Procedure for withdrawal of funds.
- Duties of each partner.
- Procedures for dissolving the partnership.

Like the sole proprietorship, the partnership has both advantages and disadvantages. Any person considering a partnership should carefully weigh each of the following advantages and disadvantages before closing the deal. Do some of the pluses outweigh the minuses?

Advantages of a Partnership

More Financial Capital. In the sole proprietorship, the amount of capital is limited to the personal wealth and credit of the owner. In a partnership, the amount of capital may increase significantly. A person with a good idea but little capital can look for a partner with the capital and/or credit standing to develop and market the idea.

Combined Managerial Skills. In a partnership, people with different talents and skills may join together. One partner may be good at marketing: the other may be expert at accounting and financial matters. Combining these skills could provide a greater chance of success.

Outback Steakhouse, founded in 1987, is a company that expects 1995 sales to be over $700 million as a partnership.[9] Exhibit 2.3 illustrates how the partnership was formed. Three businessmen, Basham, Sullivan, and Gannon, used different experiences, backgrounds, and goals, combined them with strong work ethics, and started a successful business.

Ease of Starting. Because it involves a private contractual arrangement, a partnership is fairly easy to start. It is nearly as free from government regulation as a sole proprietorship. The cost of starting a partnership is low; it usu-

Exhibit 2.3. *The Origins of Outback*

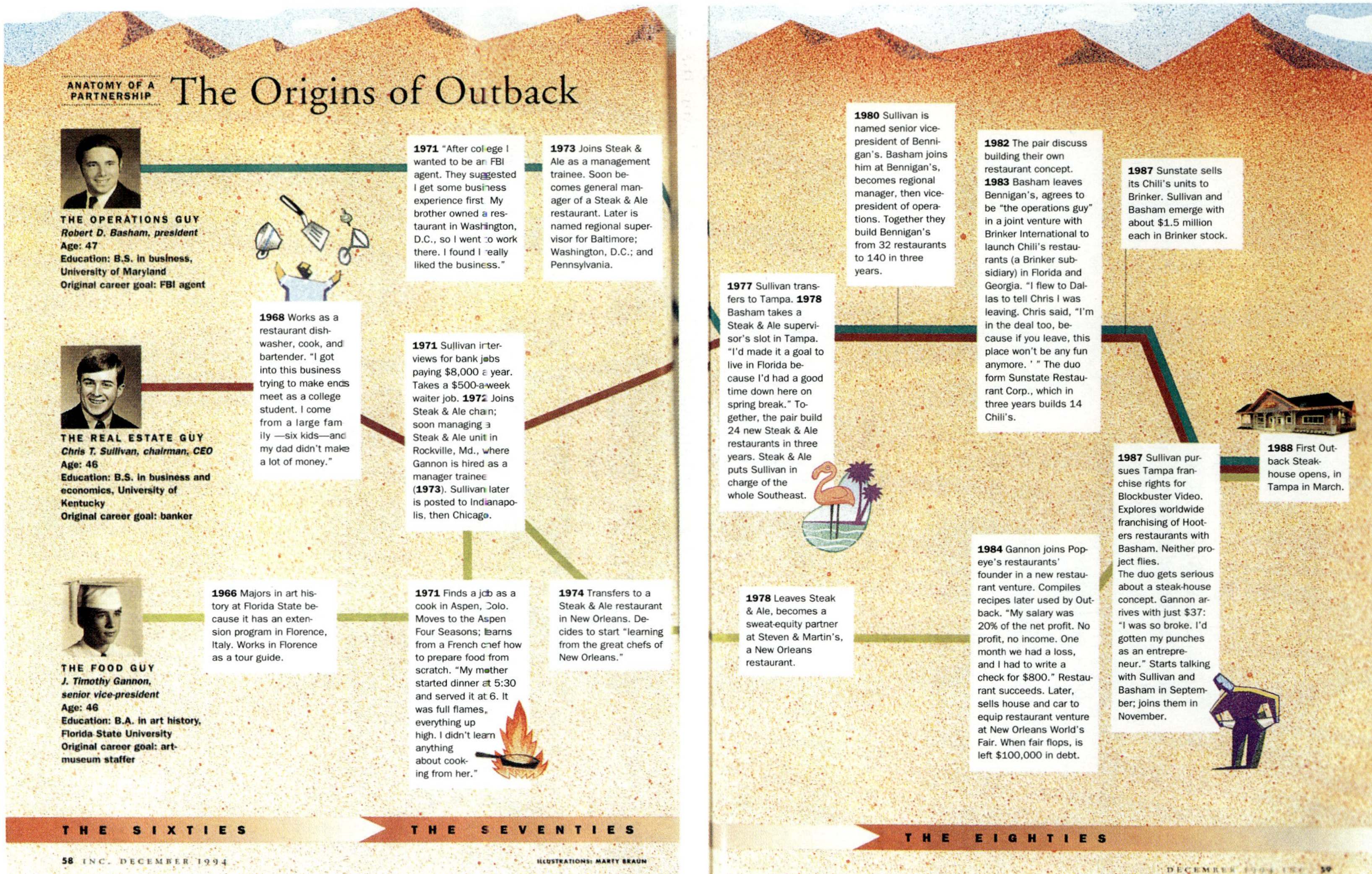

Source: *Inc.* (December 1994): 58–59.

ally involves only a modest legal fee for drawing up a written agreement, which is highly desirable. An oral agreement is sufficient but not recommended.

Clear Legal Status. Over the years, legal precedents for partnerships have been established through court cases. The questions of rights, responsibilities, liabilities, and partner duties have been covered. Thus the legal status of the partnership is clearly understood: Lawyers can provide sound legal advice about partnership issues.

Tax Advantages. The partnership has some potential tax advantages over a corporation. In a partnership, as in a sole proprietorship, the owners pay individual taxes on their business earnings, but the partnership, as a business, does not pay income tax.

Disadvantages of a Partnership

Unlimited Liability. Each general partner is liable for a partnership's debts. Suppose Jack and Jill's partnership fails with outstanding bills of $25,000. This amount must be paid by someone. If Jack lacks the personal assets to pay his share of the debt, Jill would be called on to make up the difference. This is one reason for choosing partners carefully.

YOUR VALUES AND ATTITUDES

Is This a Sound Partnership Contract?

Directions: Carefully examine the following partnership agreement and decide if it is sound, complete, and accurate.

Agreement

This partnership agreement is entered into on January 8, 1996, between Mary Richards of Spring, Texas, and Niki Stutzman of Houston, Texas, both of Harris County.

We agree that:

One: We will become equal general partners in the women's cosmetics business.

Two: We will use the name "Yellow Rose" of 1818 Milam Street, Houston, Texas 77001.

Three: Each general partner will contribute $10,000 to the partnership on January 8, 1996.

Four: All profits earned from selling "Yellow Rose" cosmetics will be divided equally by the general partners, and all losses incurred by the business will be equally shared by them.

Five: Proper accounting books will be kept by the business; a public accounting audit will be conducted each year by a firm mutually agreed upon. Profits, inventories, and losses will be accurately accounted for each year.

Six: Each partner will earn no more than $750 per month, if earnings permit this amount to be taken out of the business. No more than $9,000 per partner per year will be drawn out during the first four years of the partnership.

Seven: No new partners can be added without the full written consent of both partners.

Eight: If grievances between partners cannot be resolved, an arbitrator will be hired that is acceptable to both partners. The decision reached after arbitration is binding.

Nine: In the event of the death or retirement of a partner, the remaining partner will pay the estate or retiring partner the full amount of the original investment ($10,000), plus 1.5 times the most recent year's gross sales for all "Yellow Rose" products. The payment will be made within one year of the death or retirement of the partner.

Ten: At the termination of the partnership, a full inventory and balance sheet will be prepared by an accounting firm. All debts will be paid, and all property will be divided between the partners.

The parties have carefully reviewed the contract and have freely signed, in the presence of a witness, this document.

Witness ____________________	Partner ____________________
Date ____________________	Date ____________________
	Partner ____________________
	Date ____________________

Feedback: Well, what do you think? A fairly thorough contract? If you were Stutzman, would you sign the contract or would you make some modifications?

You should make some modifications. A review of the contract shows some key information is missing:

1. For how long will this partnership be doing business? There is no mention of the duration of the partnership.
2. Which partner is responsible for managing, marketing, handling complaints, ordering cosmetics, answering the telephone, using the word processor, paying bills, and so on? The duties of each partner need to be specifically spelled out. If a partner can't fulfill her duties, how will they be handled?

Other than these two major points, the contract is fairly thorough. It is not loaded with legalese, but it is descriptive enough to provide a clear understanding of each important point. You never want to be faced with a situation where you are in a partnership with a stranger or a friend and neither person knows the rules of the game. If you lack confidence in your ability to prepare a legal contract, spend the $100 to $500 needed to have a lawyer draw up this type of document. Be safe at the beginning.

Potential Disagreements. Decisions made by several people (partners) are often better than those made by one. However, having two or more people deciding on some aspects of the business can be dangerous. Power and authority are divided, and the partners will not always agree with each other. As a result, poor decisions may be made. Also, decision making becomes more

Having several people involved in the process often leads to better decisions.

time-consuming because agreement must be reached before action can be taken.

Investment Withdrawal Difficulty. A person who invests money in a partnership may have a hard time withdrawing the investment. It is much easier to invest in a partnership than to withdraw. The money, typically considered a "frozen investment," is tied up in the operation of the business.

Limited Financial Capital Availability. The partnership may have an advantage over the sole proprietorship in the availability of financial capital, but it does not compare to a corporation in ability to raise capital. In most cases, partners have a limited capability and cannot compete in businesses requiring large outlays. The amount of financial capital a partnership can raise depends on the personal wealth of the partners and their credit ratings. It also depends on how much they are willing to invest.

Instability. If a partner dies or withdraws from the business, the partnership is dissolved. A new partnership or some other form of business organization must be legally established.

OTHER UNINCORPORATED FORMS OF BUSINESS

Besides proprietorships and partnerships, several other forms of ownership do not require incorporation. These forms are used by people who want to join together to accomplish various objectives without going to the trouble of forming a corporation.

Syndicates

Syndicate
Two or more businesses joined together to accomplish specific business goals; a popular form in underwriting large amounts of corporation stocks.

An association of two or more businesses for a particular business purpose is a **syndicate.** In most cases, syndicates engage in financial transactions. Unlike a joint venture, a syndicate need not be dissolved after the transaction is completed. The members of a syndicate can sell their ownership interest to buyers of their choice. But in a partnership, the remaining partners can veto a new partner.

A common type of syndicate is the underwriting syndicate, a group of investment banking companies formed for the purpose of selling a large issue of corporation stocks. Managerial decisions are in the hands of the group that forms the syndicate.

Business Trusts

Business Trust
A business used to hold securities for investors; allows the transfer of legal title to a property of one person for the use and benefit of another.

A **business trust** is often used to hold securities for investors. In its simplest form, a trust allows the transfer of legal title to a property of one person for the use and benefit of another. The original name for this form of business was the Massachusetts trust, because it was created in that state when the laws did not allow corporations to buy and sell real estate.

Under the business trust, a trustee or group of trustees is legally permitted to do business. The trustees issue shares, called *trust certificates,* to investors. These shares show that the holder has transferred funds to a trustee and has the legal right to benefit from the success of the trust investments. Shareholders have no right to vote for trustees or to have a voice in management; they do have the right to sell their trust certificates to a buyer of their choice.

CORPORATIONS

Corporation
A business that is a legal entity separate from its owners.

Some businesses, such as automobile manufacturing, computer manufacturing, oil refining, and natural gas production, require millions of dollars to operate. Typically such vast sums of money are put together by attracting numerous investors. The unincorporated forms of business—the proprietorship and the partnership—do not attract investors who do not want to make decisions or to be actually involved in managing the firm. The **corporation,** by contrast, provides a form of business ownership in which owners spread over a wide geographical area can hire professional managers to operate the business. In the eyes of the law, the corporation is an artificial being, invisible and intangible. It has the legal rights of an individual: It can own property, purchase goods and services, and sue other persons or corporations.

The corporate form of business organization accounts for 90 percent of the total sales (over $9.8 trillion) of U.S. businesses. There are about 3.6 million profit-oriented corporations of all sizes. In addition, many corporations are not conducted for profit and do not have private owners or shareholders. These nonprofit corporations conduct their business in the areas of government (e.g., the U.S. Postal Service), education, health (e.g., a public-health clinic), religion, and charity (e.g., the Salvation Army).

Forming a Corporation

Charter
A state's written agreement giving a corporation the right to operate as a business.

Domestic Corporation
An enterprise organized under the laws of one state or country and doing business within that state or country.

Foreign Corporation
A business incorporated in one state or country and doing business in another state or country.

The legal status of a corporation stems from a **charter,** which is a state-issued document authorizing its formation. The individuals forming the corporation are called its *incorporators.* In 1830, New York extended the use of the corporate form to businesses; by the early 1860s, most other states also granted corporate charters. A corporation that conducts business in the state in which it is chartered is known as a **domestic corporation.** A corporation doing business in a state other than the one in which it is incorporated is called a **foreign corporation** (e.g., a New Jersey-incorporated business doing business in Oregon).

Most states require that at least three persons join together to form a corporation. The applicants fill out an application form for a charter (articles of incorporation); the form is then reviewed by the appropriate government officials. An example of such a form appears in Exhibit 2.4.

After the charter has been granted, the incorporators and all subscribers or the owners of the stock of the business meet and elect a board of directors. They also approve the bylaws of the corporation, if this is a state requirement. The board of directors then meets to select the professional managers and to make any other decisions needed to start the business.

Board of Directors elected by shareholders run business by making decisions

TOMORROW'S BUSINESS WORLD

Investing in Electric Cars

In 1990, the California state legislature told automakers that by 1998, 2 percent of their unit sales in the state must be zero-emission vehicles. Zero-emission means electric cars. The requirement climbs to 5 percent in 2001 and to 10 percent in 2003. About 2 million new vehicles are sold in California in a good year.[10] Massachusetts and New York have enacted similar sales mandates. But unless the politicians plan to reinvent physics, electric cars are not likely to be on the roads in 1998.

Ford, Chrysler, and General Motors have each spent hundreds of millions of dollars to produce an electric car, but they have not been able to produce one that provides the driving range that is acceptable to customers at a reasonable price. General Motors has developed one they call Impact that is supposed to have a range of 70 miles, but recharging the battery, the equivalent of filling up the gasoline tank, takes hours. Fiat sells a few hundred electric cars in Europe each year but the tiny cars are stuffed with batteries and have little space for passengers. GM and rival automakers are rushing to develop batteries that don't require frequent recharging and that won't raise the price of electric cars beyond most consumer's reach.

Large corporations, like the Big Three in automobiles, have financial resources, but some people believe government regulations force them to waste a lot of money. Many in the U.S. auto industry believe that California politicians are gouging U.S. corporations. The 1988 rule includes most autos produced by U.S. and Japanese corporations, but excludes a Hollywood favorite, the German-made Mercedes.

Do you think that public outcry may cause California politicians to change the zero-emission standard?

The corporation has relationships with various groups. Included in the corporations's domain of operation are shareholders, creditors, customers, and employees. Exhibit 2.5 charts the corporations's range of relationships. The actual owners of the business are the shareholders, those who have invested their money. The corporation is run by professional managers who plan, organize, control, and direct the activities needed to sell goods and/or services to customers. The managers also decide what property to purchase, what employees to hire, and where to borrow needed funds.

Types of Corporations

When we think about business corporations our attention usually centers on the giants listed annually in *Fortune's* "Directory of the 500 Largest U.S. Industrial Corporations" or "500 World's Largest Industrial Corporations." The World listing indicates that every one of the 500 firms listed has sales of over $2.7 billion annually. Exhibit 2.6 presents the largest 25 industrial firms in the world. Note that there are 8 U.S. firms, 6 Japanese firms, and 3 German firms in the list of 25.[11] Corporations come in many sizes and types, as illustrated by Exhibit 2.7.

Corporate Policymakers

A corporation's policy is established by a board of directors, which is elected by the shareholders, or owners. Directors are assumed to be free to make their own judgments on all matters presented to them. The directors do not make judgments for a single group or clique of owners—they make judgments in the best interest of *all* owners. Thus they are usually elected for their business ability. A growing number of shareholders are challenging the abilities and performance of board members. Boards have been getting smaller. Spencer Stuart & Associates canvassed 55 of the largest corporations and found that the average size of boards is about 12. There is also a trend toward adding outsiders and more foreign members instead of insiders.[12] These trends are considered positive given the need for board independence and the increasingly global economy.

Exhibit 2.4
Sample Articles of Incorporation

ARTICLES OF INCORPORATION
OF

____
(name of corporation)

We, the undersigned, of full age, for the purpose of forming a corporation under and pursuant to the provisions of Chapter 301 Minn. Statutes, known as the Minnesota Business Corporation Act, and laws amendatory thereof and supplementary thereto, do hereby associate ourselves as a body corporate and adopt the following Articles of Incorporation.

ARTICLE I

The name of the corporation is: ____________________________

Note: The corporate name must end with"Incorporated," "Inc.," or "Corporation," or contain "Company" or "Co.," not immediately preceded by "and"or "&"

ARTICLE II

The purposes of this corporation are: ____________________________

ARTICLE III

The period of duration of corporate existence of this corporation shall be: ____________________________

Note: The duration may be perpetual or for a specified period of time.

ARTICLE IV

The location of the registered office of this corporation in this state is: ____________________________

Note: Give street or post office address, city or town, county, and Zip Code number

ARTICLE VI

The amount of stated capital with which this corporation will begin business is: ____________________________

Note: The stated capital must be at least $1,000

ARTICLE VII

The total authorized number of shares of par value is: ______________
and the par value of each share is: ______________

The total authorized number of shares without par value is: ______________

ARTICLE VIII

The description of the classes of shares, the number of shares in each class, and the relative rights, voting power, preferences, and restrictions are as follows: ______________

Exhibit 2.5
The Range of a Corporation's Relationships

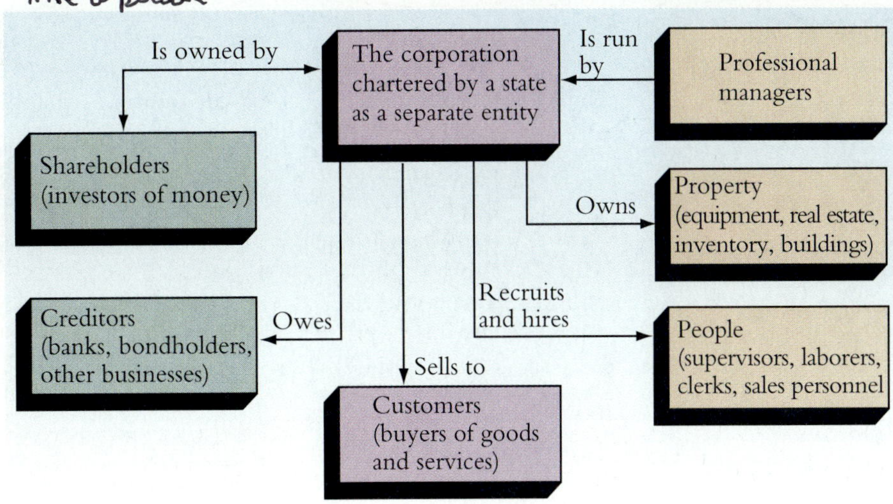

Directors are elected by the shareholders. Usually, each share of common stock entitles the shareholder to one vote (see Chapter 18 for a discussion of stock). For example, Amanda Knight owns 10 shares of Amoco voting stock and therefore is eligible to cast 10 votes. In many cases, shareholders vote by proxy. A **proxy** is a written statement, signed by the shareholder, allowing someone else to cast his or her number of votes. Usually, the proxy permits a director to cast the votes.

Proxy
A written statement, signed by a shareholder of a corporation, allowing someone else to cast his or her number of votes.

The board, once elected, must put together the best possible team of managers to run the day-to-day operations. In governing the corporation, the board of directors decides for or against recommendations submitted by the officers of the corporation. Although the board is the final authority, it usually responds to requests and recommendations made by the professional managers.

More than 47 million Americans own stock in publicly traded companies. As shareholders they have the right to inspect the books and papers of the business, to attend shareholders' meetings, to vote on certain matters (such as mergers), and to share in the profits earned. Even if Amanda Knight owns only 10 shares of Amoco, she has all these rights. Many shareholders are uninterested in the rights of ownership except for the privilege of sharing in the profits by receiving dividends. This may be just as well because, if decisions had to be based on the opinions of all owners, the business would stand still. Of all U.S. corporations, AT&T has the largest number of shareholders (over 2.5 million), General Motors has over 1 million owners, and IBM has about 700,000.

Exhibit 2.6
Twenty-Five Largest World Corporations

Rank	Corporation	Country	Sales ($ in billions)	Number of Employees
1.	General Motors	U.S.	133.6	710,800
2.	Ford Motor	U.S.	108.5	322,200
3.	Exxon	U.S.	97.8	91,000
4.	Royal Dutch/Shell Group	Brit/Neth	95.1	117,000
5.	Toyota Motor	Japan	85.3	109,279
6.	Hitachi	Japan	68.6	330,637
7.	Intl. Business Machines	U.S.	62.7	254,059
8.	Matsushita Electric Industrial	Japan	61.4	254,059
9.	General Electric	U.S.	60.8	366,736
10.	Daimler-Benz	Germany	59.1	366,736
11.	Mobil	U.S.	56.6	61,900
12.	Nissan Motor	Japan	53.8	143,310
13.	British Petroleum	Britain	52.5	72,600
14.	Samsung	South Korea	51.3	173,000
15.	Philip Morris	U.S.	50.6	173,000
16.	IRI	Italy	50.5	366,471
17.	Siemens	Germany	50.4	391,000
18.	Volkswagen	Germany	46.3	251,643
19.	Chrysler	U.S.	43.6	128,000
20.	Toshiba	Japan	42.9	175,000
21.	Unilever	Brit/Neth	41.8	302,000
22.	Nestlé	Switzerland	38.9	209,755
23.	Elf Aquitaine	France	37.0	94,000
24.	Honda Motor	France	35.8	91,300
25.	ENI	Italy	34.8	106,391

Source: Adapted from "FORTUNE Global 500," *Fortune* (July 25, 1994): 143. © 1994 Time Inc. All rights reserved.

Advantages of a Corporation

The power and presence of corporations in American business suggest that this form has certain advantages over other forms of business ownership.

Limited Liability. A person investing funds in a corporation receives shares of stock and becomes an owner. In a corporation, the liability for the shareholder equals the amount of funds invested. Thus, if the business is forced to liquidate, each owner loses only the amount of money he or she has invested.

Skilled Management Team. The board of directors has the duty of hiring professional managers, and the owners delegate their power of operating the business to these managers. Professional managers are trained and experienced career executives. They may own shares of stock in the business but usually not enough to control the corporation.

Exhibit 2.7
Types of Corporations

Type	Description	Examples
Private	Attempts to earn a satisfactory profit.	RJR Nabisco, Thrislington.
Public	Owned and run by the government.	NASA, Tennessee Valley Authority.
Closed	Stock held by only a few owners and not actively sold on the stock market.	Gallo Winery, Hallmark Cards, Weis Markets.
Open	Stock held by numerous people and actively sold on the stock market.	United Technologies, Ford.
Municipal	Cities and townships that carry out business.	Ft. Worth, Texas; Manitou Springs, Colorado.
Domestic	Incorporated in the state in which it is operating.	Georgia Pacific (Georgia) doing business in Georgia.
Foreign	Incorporated in one state and doing business in another state.	Compaq Computer (Texas) selling computers in New York.
Alien	Incorporated in one nation and operating in another nation.	Motorola (incorporated in Illinois) operating in Chiba Prefecture, Japan.
Nonprofit	Service organization incorporated for limited-liability status.	Harvard University, Boy Scouts of America.
Single individual or Family	Individually or family-owned business incorporated to escape high personal income tax rate.	Mars, Inc. (world's second largest candy maker)

Transfer of Ownership. Shareholders have the right to sell their shares of a corporation's stock to whomever they please, barring a legal restriction on some closed corporations. These shares of ownership can be sold whenever the shareholder desires and at the price the buyer is willing to pay. Thus, shareholders can freely buy and sell shares of stock. The investment flows easily and is not frozen. This right to sell shares of stock gives corporations the ability to attract large numbers of shareholders.

Greater Capital Base. As previously stated, the size of a proprietorship or partnership is limited to the amount of capital that one or several people have available and are willing to invest. Corporations, however, can attract capital from a large number of investors by selling shares of stock.

Stability. State law varies, but a corporation can usually be chartered to operate indefinitely. Shareholders' deaths, retirement, or sale of stock need not dissolve the business. The corporation's policies may be altered by the sale of large blocks of stock, but the business will go on. Nor will the death or retirement of the president of the board or the chief executive officer stop the corporation from doing business.

Legal-Entity Status. A corporation can purchase property, make contracts, or sue and be sued in its corporate name. These characteristics distinguish it most clearly from other forms of business organization. As Justice Thurgood Marshall of the U.S. Supreme Court stated, a corporation is "an artificial being." This legal status allows the shareholders to have limited liability.

Disadvantages of a Corporation

As was true with the other forms of business organization, the corporation has some disadvantages.

Difficulty and Expense of Starting. Starting a corporation involves applying for a charter from a state. Each state has its own set of laws; these must be considered before deciding where to incorporate. An attorney should be hired to complete legal forms. Attorney fees and state charter fees must be paid. The chosen state then reviews the application and issues a charter that specifies various restrictions on operations.

Lack of Control. The individual shareholder has little control over the operations of the corporation except to vote for a slate of individuals for the board of directors. The buying and selling of shares of stock is the only real control an owner has.

Multiple Taxation and Fees. In addition to an annual franchise tax in the state of incorporation, an annual payment is required by most states for the right to operate as a corporation. No such fees are charged to a proprietorship or partnership. Some states levy a corporate income tax on those monies earned within the state. At the federal level, the corporation has to pay taxes on its profits. Small corporations are taxed at 15 percent for income up to \$50,000; income \$50,000–\$75,000, 25 percent; income over \$75,000, 34 percent. The shareholders must also pay income tax on the dividends they receive through ownership. This practice of taxing corporate income and dividends is referred to as **double taxation.**

Double Taxation
Taxing a corporate owner's money twice by taxing it as income of a corporation and as dividends of the individual owner.

Lack of Secrecy. A corporation must provide each shareholder with an annual report. In a closed corporation, the few reports circulated usually won't get into the hands of nonowners. But when a large number of reports are issued, the reports become public knowledge. These reports present data on sales volume, profit, total assets, and other financial matters. Public disclosure enables competitors and other outsiders to see the corporation's financial condition.

Lack of Personal Interest. In most large corporations, management and ownership are separate. This separation can result in a lack of personal interest in the success of the corporation. If the managers are also shareholders, personal interest is enhanced. It is assumed that employees who are also owners will work harder for the success of the business, but the accuracy of this assumption is an individual matter. Most managers have pride in their work and want any business they are involved with to succeed.

Credit Limitations. Banks and other lenders have to consider the limited liability of the owners of a corporation. If the corporation fails, its creditors can look only to the assets of the business to satisfy claims. For partnerships, the creditors can rely on personal assets of the partners to pay off business debts.

Exhibit 2.8 lists the characteristics of the four types of businesses we have discussed. It will summarize the main points discussed in the chapter so far.

Mergers and Acquisitions

Over the past century, surges in merger and acquisition activity have occurred at various times. During the decade of the 1980s, mergers and acquisitions valued at over $1.3 trillion transpired.[13] In 1994 mergers valued at almost

Exhibit 2.8
Comparison of Four Major Types of Business Organizations

	Type of Organization			
Characteristic	**Sole Proprietorship**	**General Partnership**	**Limited Partnership**	**Corporation**
1. Start-up and operation	Simplest to establish and form.	Relatively easy but needs written contract.	Requires written agreement, filing of certificate, and compliance with limited partners' noninvolvement.	Laws and procedurs vary from state to state; charter required; legal and charter fees can be expensive.
2. Liability for debts and taxes	Owner has unlimited liability.	General partners have unlimited liability.	Limited partner is liable only to the amount of investment.	Shareholders are liable only to extent of investment.
3. Federal taxes on profits	Taxed at individual rates, 15, 28, 31, 36 and 39.6 percent.	Taxed at individual rates, 15, 28, 31, 36 and 39.6 percent.	Taxed at individual rates, 15, 28, 31, 36 and 39.6 percent.	Taxed at corporate rates which range from 15 to 35 percent; dividends also taxed at individual rates.
4. Termination	Easy, after debts are paid.	May be complicated; depends on contract.	Same as general partnership.	Difficult and expensive.
5. Duration of business	Terminates at death of owner.	Terminates at death or withdrawal of partner.	Sames as general partnership.	Indefinite.

Merger
Combining two or more business enterprises into a single entity.

$336 billion occurred. **Merger** refers to the joining together of two corporations to become a single corporation. An *acquisition* refers to the process in which one firm buys the assets and assumes the obligations of another company. The federal government is concerned with mergers and acquisitions if there is a reduction in competition. Mergers that reduce market competition can result in government action under the Celler-Kefauver Act and review by the Justice Department and the Federal Trade Commission (FTC).

Exhibit 2.9 presents a 10-year summary of the number of mergers that occurred in the United States between 1984 and 1993. Exhibit 2.10 provides the number of foreign company acquisitions of U.S. firms and U.S. firm acquisitions of foreign firms between 1985 and 1992.

Within and across borders mergers and acquisitions are continuing, but at a slower rate and for less amounts of money. Economic, political, and attitude differences at various times largely determine the attractiveness of merger and acquisition activity within a country and across borders.[14]

Horizontal Merger
A merger involving competitive firms in the same market.

Vertical Merger
A merger in which a firm joins with its supplier.

Conglomerate Merger
A merger involving firms selling goods in unrelated markets.

A **horizontal merger** occurs when competitive firms in the same market merge into a single firm. For example, in early 1995 aerospace/defense companies Lockheed Corp. and Martin Marietta Corp. merged to form Lockheed Martin Corp. A firm's merger with a supplier or distributor is called a **vertical merger.** In late 1993 the large pharmaceutical firm, Merck, merged with Medco Containment Services, Inc., a pharmacy benefits management company. A **conglomerate merger** joins firms selling goods in unrelated markets. There were many conglomerate mergers during the early 1980s but there have been few in more recent years. One merger you may recall was footwear manufacturer U.S. Shoe and LensCrafters, an optical retailer.

In general, the government allows mergers when the market share of the largest firms in the industry is relatively low or when new firms can enter the market easily. Government also has intervened less when mergers seem needed to meet foreign competition. Some people believe mergers bring cost and productivity advantages that can help reduce prices, making U.S. products cheaper and more competitive on the world markets.

Exhibit 2.9
Ten-Year Merger Completion Record

Year	No. of Deals	% Change	Value ($ bil)	% Change
1984	2,243	—	153.2	—
1985	1,719	−23.4%	149.6	− 2.3%
1986	2,497	45.3	223.1	49.1
1987	2,479	− 0.7	198.8	−10.9
1988	2,970	19.8	281.8	41.8
1989	3,752	26.3	316.8	12.4
1990	4,239	13.0	205.6	−35.1
1991	3,446	−18.7	141.5	−31.2
1992	3,502	1.6	125.3	−11.5
1993	4,000	14.2	170.3	35.6

Source: *Mergers & Acquisitions* (January–February 1995): 53.

Exhibit 2.10 *Foreign Acquisitions*

Foreign Acquisitions of U.S. Companies 1985 to 1992					**U.S. Acquisitions Overseas 1985 to 1992**				
Year	**No. of Deals**	**% of All Deals**	**Value ($ bil)**	**% of Total M&A Value**	**Year**	**No. of Deals**	**% of All Deals**	**Value ($ bil)**	**% of Total M&A Value**
1985	259	15.1%	$27.9	18.6%	1985	91	5.2%	$3.7	2.5%
1986	345	13.8	31.4	14.1	1986	111	4.4	3.4	1.5
1987	365	14.7	55.3	27.8	1987	162	6.5	6.9	3.5
1988	536	18.0	66.0	23.4	1988	223	7.5	11.1	3.9
1989	693	18.5	69.2	21.8	1989	347	9.2	27.1	8.6
1990	773	18.2	56.4	27.4	1990	392	9.2	20.5	10.0
1991	504	14.6	29.1	20.6	1991	402	11.7	14.8	10.5
1992	361	10.3	17.6	14.0	1992	455	13.0	13.7	10.9

Source: *Mergers & Acquisitions* (May–June 1993): 57.

OTHER INCORPORATED FORMS OF BUSINESS

The private corporation is certainly the dominant form of incorporated ownership. However, a number of other widely used incorporated forms of business have unique advantages. Let's discuss three: S corporations, nonprofit corporations, and professional service associations.

S Corporations

Special rules and regulations under the Omnibus Budget Reconciliation Act of 1983 permit what is referred to as the S corporation to use non-corporate tax rates at the request of the shareholders. This allows the shareholders to be treated as individual taxpayers. In other words, the income or loss of the corporation passes through to the individual shareholders as if they were partners.

S Corporation
A corporation with 35 or fewer owners that files an income tax return as a partnership to take advantage of lower tax rates.

To qualify as an **S corporation,** a business must meet the following requirements:

- It must be incorporated within the United States.
- All shareholders must be residents of the United States.
- Shareholders must be natural persons, estates, or trusts.
- No shareholder can be a partnership or a corporation.
- There cannot be more than 35 shareholders.
- No more than 20 percent of its income can come from passive activities (such as owning shares of stock in another corporation).

Like other forms of ownership, the S corporation has advantages and disadvantages. The primary advantage is that the shareholders' tax brackets can result in tax savings. If a corporation expects to lose money in the first years of operation and if the shareholders will have income from other sources, the S corporation is preferred. Here the losses "passed through" from the S corporation can shelter the shareholders from income tax. (Losses are limited to specific amounts.) The primary disadvantage is that the tax law governing the S corporation is very complex. Tax and legal advice is strongly recommended before and after making the S corporation choice. The best time to terminate S status is when the S corporation begins to produce very high levels of taxable income. Thus, owner(s) must be alert and up-to-date on the flow of taxable income.

Nonprofit Corporations

Nonprofit Corporation
An enterprise (e.g., university, charity, church) that is not driven by a profit-seeking motive.

There are more than 1.1 million nonprofit organizations that employ about 12 million people in the United States. Many organizations are **nonprofit corporations**; that is they are not profit-seeking enterprises. The nonprofit sector includes universities and other schools, charities, churches, volunteer organizations, credit unions, country clubs, government organizations, cooperatives, and a number of other organizations. The nonprofit enterprise is prohibited by law from distributing any earnings (paying dividends) to owners. It exists because the founders believe that the firm provides something of value (e.g., help to the homeless, research, education) that is not being provided well or at all by other enterprises. Donations, dues, and the sale of goods or services provide the funds to pay employees and finance operations.

Cooperative (Co-op)
An organization in which people collectively own and operate a business in order to compete with bigger competitors.

An organization in which a group of people (members/customers) collectively own and operate all or part of the business is a **cooperative (co-op)**. The member/customer owners pay an annual membership fee. The first formal co-op, organized by Benjamin Franklin in 1752, is still in business today. Co-ops are often found where a large number of small producers can band together to become more competitive. Such well-known brands as OceanSpray juice, Sunkist oranges, and Sun-Maid raisins are the property of food producer cooperatives that formed to market the products grown by many members.

More than 5,500 producer co-ops do business in the United States, with annual sales of over $16 billion. In addition, approximately 7,500 farmer-owned buying co-ops purchase machinery, fertilizer, seeds, materials, and so on, spending over $4 billion annually. Farm co-ops have increased their annual revenues from $25 billion in 1970 to over $60 billion today. Farmland Industries, Inc., an agricultural food marketing and manufacturing co-operative headquartered in Kansas City, MO, is the largest farmer-owned cooperative association in the United States. Other billion-dollar co-ops are Associated Milk Producers, Grain Terminal Association, and Land O' Lakes. Most farm co-ops are generally unknown to the public.

Dividends are paid to co-op members in proportion to the amount of goods that each member has bought or sold through the cooperative. These patronage dividends are considered a refund of overpayment rather than a distribution of profits.

A disadvantage of co-ops is that as they grow larger they become more visible to the public. And if the public questions their market power, they may lose their special status under the law.

The Farmland System captures profits for producers and provides markets that, without the cooperative system, would have been lost. Farmland Food's products are marketed around the world.

Professional Service Associations

Traditionally, the professional services of doctors, lawyers, dentists, and the like could be performed only by individuals, not by corporations. Impersonal corporate entities were not allowed to provide personal-care services. But in late 1969, the Internal Revenue Service agreed that organizations of professional people, structured under professional association laws, could be treated as corporations for tax purposes. Thus members could have the tax advantages of profit sharing and pension plans, not available to private persons and partnerships. They also have limited liability. Such organizations are called **professional service organizations.**

Professional Service Organization
An organization of professional people, organized under professional association laws and treated as a corporation for tax purposes.

Entrepreneurship, franchising, and small-business opportunities are discussed in the next chapter. Business students need to learn about smaller business forms and their role in the world marketplace. In fact, in the United States, most new jobs and career opportunities today are found in smaller business organizations. U.S. business has been able to create small firms, and the country's economic freedom has invigorated a sluggish economy that plodded along in the past decade (1985-1995) and lost some world market share in autos, computers, electronics, and steel to foreign competitors. By standards of many business leaders and economic forecasters in Europe and Japan, U.S. businesses are looking more efficient and more ready to compete in world markets.[15]

SUMMARY OF LEARNING OBJECTIVES

1. **Discuss the advantages and disadvantages of sole proprietorships.** The advantages are (*a*) ease of starting, (*b*) owner's control over daily operations and decisions, (*c*) owner's sole right to profits, (*d*) use of owner's abilities, (*e*) secrecy about business information, (*f*) tax breaks, and (*g*) ease of dissolving. The disadvantages are (*a*) owner's unlimited liability, (*b*) difficulty in raising capital, (*c*) limitations of owner's abilities, (*d*) lack of stability, (*e*) demands on time, and (*f*) difficulty in hiring and keeping self-motivated employees.

2. **Examine the advantages and disadvantages of partnerships.** Advantages include (*a*) more available capital, (*b*) combined managerial skills of the partners, (*c*) ease of starting, (*d*) clear legal status, and (*e*) tax advantages. Disadvantages include (*a*) general partners' unlimited liability, (*b*) potential for disagreements, (*c*) investment withdrawal difficulty, (*d*) more capital than the sole proprietorship but less than available to corporations, and (*e*) instability.

3. **Identify the features that should be included in a written partnership contract.** The main features of a written partnership agreement include the name of the business partnership, type of business, location of the business, expected life of the partnership, names of the partners and the amount of each one's investment, procedures for distributing profits and covering losses, amounts that partners will withdraw for services, procedure for withdrawal of funds, each partner's duties, and procedures for dissolving the partnership.

4. **Explain the advantages and disadvantages of corporations.** Advantages include (*a*) limitation of owners' liability to the amount of their investments, (*b*) use of skilled management team to run the corporation, (*c*) easy transfer of ownership, (*d*) greater availability of capital, (*e*) stability, and (*f*) status as legal entity. Disadvantages include (*a*) difficulty and expense in starting, (*b*) individual owner's lack of control, (*c*) double taxation, (*d*) government involvement, (*e*) lack of secrecy, (*f*) managers' possible lack of personal interest in the corporation's success, and (*g*) credit limitations.

5. **Define the term *merger* and identify three types of mergers.** A merger takes place when two or more businesses combine to form a single enterprise. There are three types of mergers: horizontal, vertical, and conglomerate.

6. **Identify other incorporated forms of business.** The corporation is not the only incorporated form of business. Four other widely used incorporated forms of business are S corporations, nonprofit corporations, cooperatives, and professional service associations.

KEY TERMS

Sole Proprietorship
Unlimited Liability
Partnership
General Partnership
Limited Partnership
Master Limited Partnership (MLP)
Syndicate
Business Trust
Corporation
Charter
Domestic Corporation
Foreign Corporation
Nonprofit Corporation
Proxy
Double Taxation
Horizontal Merger
Vertical Merger
Conglomerate Merger
S Corporation
Cooperative (Co-op)
Professional Service Organization

QUESTIONS FOR DISCUSSION AND REVIEW

1. Describe some of the advantages and disadvantages of a sole proprietorship, partnership, and corporation.
2. Why would someone consider forming an S corporation instead of a traditional corporation?
3. Explain the difference between an open and a closed corporation.
4. When a 12- or 13-year-old starts a business, is it necessary to pay taxes? Explain.
5. What factors would a manager consider in deciding whether to attempt to acquire through a merger another firm?
6. What characteristics of the sole proprietorship make it the most popular form of business ownership?
7. Why would a person be attracted to join a cooperative?
8. Why does double taxation irritate stockholders in a company?
9. Why have joint ventures between American and non-American partners become so popular?
10. What factors should you consider when deciding whether to team up with someone in a partnership form of business?

CASE 2.1

Manhattan Distributing: A Close-Up View of a Family Business

Dozens of large corporations and small businesses have had to address issues about family businesses, that is, businesses operated by family members. Anheuser-Busch, Exxon, Caterpillar, and Hallmark Cards have all tackled the family-business problem because most of their dealerships are family run. And many training programs, pamphlets, and videos are available on this subject. The video titles point to the potential problems in family-run businesses: "How In-Laws Become Out-Laws" and "Managing Nepotism Constructively."

Increasingly, corporations recognize that members of family businesses are prone to feuding over everything from the size of a brother's office to who is in charge of the marketing campaign. Fights, arguments, and clashes that annoy family members mean that efficiency suffers and profits can be lost. In a family-run business, emotions can be extremely powerful.

On the other hand, everyone knows each other in a family business. The best family businesses turn that understanding into efficiency that breeds speedier management. There is a form of telepathic relationship in a well-run family business, and time is not wasted.

Unfortunately, when trouble in a family-run business brews, it may remain below the surface for a long time before it finally explodes. Joseph Rothberg is a self-made man and founder of Manhattan Distributing Co., a St. Louis-based wine and spirits business. Under his management, the company grew to 90 employees and annual sales of over $30 million. Being a sole proprietor, Rothberg *was* the business. He hired and fired people, prepared the orders, sold the product, worked on payrolls, and purchased the delivery trucks needed to distribute the wine and spirits to St. Louis-area stores. As the business grew, it became apparent that Manhattan Distributing Co. was too big for one man to do everything.

Rothberg had no heir apparent. After thinking about selling out, he instead asked his son-in-law, Nolan, to join the business. Nolan had worked for 10 years in large corporations, and his motives for working were based on a different philosophy from Rothberg's. He didn't plan to devote every waking hour to Manhattan Distributing, while Rothberg didn't have enough hours in the day to do everything he wanted to accomplish.

Sensing their differences in philosophies, Rothberg began to isolate himself from Nolan. The elder man rarely shared major decisions or plans with his son-in-law. Nolan became frustrated, angry, irritable, cynical, and depressed. He attempted to have his spouse (Rothberg's daughter) talk to her father, but she really didn't want to become involved or take sides.

At a party, Nolan's wife overheard a friend who worked for his father in the construction business commenting, "I'll never have any say in our business unless they carry my father out feet first." He went on to mention an organization called Sons of Bosses (SOB).* Members included sons, daughters, sons-in-law, and daughters-in-law in family businesses. The friend said SOB had helped him deal with his father.

The SOB organization offers a set of practical guidelines to its members. These guidelines, which can be useful in preventing harsh, emotional conflict from bubbling over, include:

- Junior family members should acquire experience in the business elsewhere. Work for another enterprise first.
- Junior family members need to receive clear job responsibilities. Find out what your tasks are and what the founder expects you to do at work.
- Expect to work harder, longer hours in the first five years than you have ever worked.
- Discuss and reach agreement on salary and fringe benefits (perks) in advance. When will you vacation? When will discussions about raises and bonuses occur?
- Define the roles of other family members in the business. What will the relatives be doing?
- Establish a family council.
- Time is on the side of the SOB member. Be patient but firm. Be thoroughly prepared and in control of your emotions.

The family-run business can be a tremendous opportunity or a nightmare. Some families have shared success, challenge, and opportunity. Other families have split apart and don't even want to talk to each other. The SOB group hopes to improve relationships within families so that family members can enjoy the personal benefits of continuing a meaningful tradition.

Questions for Discussion

1. Why would a business's founder such as Joseph Rothberg be so emotional about how the company is run and operated?

2. Should Nolan work out a transfer-of-ownership plan with his father-in-law? Why is succession planning so important in a family-owned business?
3. Of what value to Nolan is a group like SOB?
4. Would it be informative for Joseph Rothberg to attend, as a guest, an SOB meeting? Why or why not?

*SOB was founded in 1969. In 1976 the national organization and some chapters were renamed the National Family Business Council; other chapters retained the original SOB name and are not affiliated with the national organization. For more information, contact NFBC at 1000 Vermont Avenue, N.W., Washington, DC 20005.

Source: Adapted from Sharon Nelton, "Exercise Your Political Power," *Nation's Business,* February 1993, p. 52; Leslie Brokaw, "Why Family Businesses Are Best," *Inc.,* March 1992, pp. 73–81; Sharon Nelton, "Earning One's Good Fortune," *Nation's Business,* January 1990, p. 63; John L. Ward and Gary E. Amoff, "To Sell or Not to Sell," *Nation's Business,* January 1990, pp. 63–64; "Inside the Reichman Empire," *Business Week,* January 29, 1990, pp. 32–36; Mark Robichaux, "Family Business Isn't All in the Family," *The Wall Street Journal,* November 8, 1989, pp. B1–B2; Margaret Crane, "How to Keep Families from Feuding," *Small Business Success Guide,* 1987, pp. 1–3.

CASE 2.2

A Three-Way Merger: Marvel, Toy Biz, and Avi Arad

Marvel Entertainment, Toy Biz, and toy creator Avi Arad teamed up to form a new Toy Biz as a 46 percent-owned subsidiary of Marvel. Toy Biz will have the exclusive services of Arad, who also will have a stake in the company. Marvel will contribute a working capital investment and a master license for its comic book characters, which include The Amazing Spiderman, The Uncanny X-Men, and The Incredible Hulk.

Marvel Entertainment, a producer of comic books and sports picture trading cards, had 1992 sales of $223.8 million and earnings of $32.7 million, or 55 cents a share. Toy Biz, a manufacturer and distributor of toys and games, had 1992 sales of $223.8 million and earnings of $32.7 million, or 66 cents a share. Toy Biz had 1992 revenue of approximately $65 million. Some of its toys include Caboodles, Baby Loves to Talk, BOTS, The Eliminator, and Marvel Super Hero action figures.

The unique three-way alliance is a response to the intensifying competition in youth entertainment products that is increasingly being waged on a global basis. By tightening its links with Toy Biz, a licensee since 1990, Marvel effectively brings toy making know-how in house and provides itself with a greater share in the revenue generated by toy sales. Previously, Marvel was entitled to only royalties from Toy Biz.

With this alliance, Marvel is continuing its expansion beyond comic books. Last year it purchased Fleer Corporation, a leading producer of sports trading cards and Dubble Bubble chewing gum. When rival sports card producer Topps announced plans to expand into comic books, Marvel began looking for new avenues for growth.

Toy Biz will also benefit from the companies' new relationship, since it will now have free rein to use Marvel characters in toy designs. And since both companies serve similar audiences, they should be able to target each other's markets.

Arad, who also will have an equity interest in the new Toy Biz, has worked for Ideal, Mattel, Tyco, Hasbro, Nintendo, and Sega toy companies, though never exclusively. Some of his most popular toy creations are Baby Bubbles, Roller Blade Baby, The Eliminator, and Videomation. He has expressed interest in developing toys based on Marvel's sports trading card celebrities. As new athletes reach the Big Leagues, new toys and trading cards would have to be designed each year.

Marvel noted that its alliance with Toy Biz will allow it to have more control than if it had formed a partnership with a larger, unaffiliated company. And because Toy Biz has all of its manufacturing done outside, Marvel can maintain its high-margin, low capital investment profile.

Questions for Discussion

1. Why would the management of Marvel Entertainment want to form this alliance? Who benefits the most?
2. Is a creator such as Avi Arad valuable in making this alliance work?
3. Suppose you were preparing a competitor's complaint to the FTC about this alliance. What would your complaint state?

Source: Adapted from "Sega!," *Business Week* (February 21, 1994): 66–74 and "Parlaying Strengths in the Toy Field," *Mergers and Acquisitions* (July–August 1993): 51.

EXPERIENTIAL EXERCISE

Importance of Small-Business Development

General Information

A review of the literature shows that after years of government control Eastern Europe is fascinated by Western-style small business (sole proprietorship and partnership). There is now little doubt that small businesses will play a large role in any turnaround of economies that have been stagnate for decades in Hungary, Russia, Poland, and the Czech and Slovak Republics. Exactly what model of small-business development each Eastern European nation will follow is not known at this time. The governments and citizens of each nation will have a lot to do with what happens in Eastern European economies.

1. Groups will be formed by the instructor to examine the history and current progress of various Eastern European nations regarding small-business development. The nations to be studied are:

   - Poland
   - Russia
   - Ukraine
   - Kazakhstan
   - Czech Republic
   - Slovak Republic
   - Hungary
   - Rumania
   - Lithuania
   - Latvia

2. Each group should go to the library (or contact the relevant embassy if possible) and examine historical facts, laws, government taxation policies, regulations, labor markets, and other data for each nation.
3. Prepare a 5- to 10-page report to be shared with other groups.
4. In a class discussion determine which of the nations studied has the best chance of succeeding in terms of small-business growth and economic impact. Also, decide which nation has the most similarities when compared to the United States.

BUSINESS APPLICATION

Creativity and Corporate Growth

Objectives:
To emphasize the importance of one or a few individuals in growing large corporations that have a major impact on the way we live and conduct business. Completing the application requires 3 to 4 hours.

Directions:
Look at Exhibit 2.6 and note the list of names of the 25 largest world corporations. Find in your library a list of either the *Fortune 500* Largest Domestic or World Corporations. Pick a corporation in your state (if none is available simply pick a company of interest in one of the Fortune lists) and examine its history: How did it start? Who were the founders? Conduct a background review of the founders and prepare a report on how the company has grown.

Every corporation has a story of how its founder(s) influenced its history. The dreams of George Eastman who invented his Kodak camera in his off hours while working as a Rochester (NY) bank clerk will illustrate how large corporations usually start in the mind of a creative individual.

After preparing your review the instructor will set up groups of four to five students to meet and share their studies. Groups should include individuals who studied different firms.

NOTES

1. Adapted from Robert Lenzner, Em Young, *Forbes* (September 12, 1994): 70–71; Brian Dumaine, "America's Smart Young Entrepreneurs," *Fortune* (March 21, 1994): 34–38 and "The Fall of Big Business," *The Economist* (April 17, 1993): 13, 14; and Sharon Nelton, "Early Achievers," *Nation's Business* (December 1992): 42–45.
2. John W. Wright (ed.) *The Unusual Almanac* (Kansas City, MO: Andrews and McMeel, 1993), 256–265.
3. *Statistical Abstract of the United States,* 1994 (Washington, DC: U.S. Department of Commerce, 1992), 519.
4. Kenneth J. Soderman, *Omnibus Budget Reconciliation Act of 1993* (Somerset, NJ: John Wiley & Sons, 1993), 1–120.
5. Adapted from Melissa Lee, "Diversity Training Brings Unity to Small Companies," *The Wall Street Journal* (September 2, 1993): B2.
6. *Analysis: 1993 Tax Legislation* (Washington, DC: Coopers & Lybrand, 1993), 1–129.

7. Timothy M. Collins and Thomas L. Doorley, *Teaming Up for the '90s* (Homewood, IL: Business One Irwin, 1991), 186.
8. John S. DeMott, "Strength in Numbers," *Nation's Business* (August 1993): 53–55.
9. Jay Finegan, "Unconventional Wisdom," *Business Week* (September 12, 1994): 30–38.
10. Adapted from Gabriella Stern "GM's Saturn May Market Electric Cars," *The Wall Street Journal* (March 8, 1995): A3; and Jerry Flint, "Don Quixote, Meet Alex Trotman," *Forbes* (January 3, 1994): 26.
11. "The Fortune 500 Largest Industrial Corporations in the World," *Fortune* (July 23, 1994): 143–152.
12. Catherine M. Daily and Dan R. Dalton, "Bankruptcy and Corporate Governance: The Impact of Board Composition and Structure," *Academy of Management Journal* (December 1994): 1603–1617; Joann S. Lublin, "How to Keep Director's Eyes on the CEO," *The Wall Street Journal* (July 20, 1994): B1, B6; Judith H. Dobrzynski, "Corporate Boards May Finally Be Shaping Up," *Business Week* (August 9, 1993): 26.
13. "Mergers Today, Trouble Tomorrow?" *Business Week* (September 12, 1994): 30–38 and Robert H. Rock, "Care Over Speed in 1990s Dealmaking," *Mergers and Acquisitions* (July–August 1993): 5.
14. Ann K. B. Buchholtz and Barbara A. Ribbens, "Role of Chief Executive Officers in Takeover Resistance: Effects of CEO Incentives and Individual Characteristics," *Academy of Management Journal* (June 1994): 554–579.
15. "Ready to Take On the World," *The Economist* (January 15, 1994): 65–66.

C H A P T E R 3

Entrepreneurship, Small Business, and Franchising

LEARNING OBJECTIVES

1. Define the term *entrepreneur*.

2. Identify the types of risks that an entrepreneur takes in starting a business.

3. Identify services the Small Business Administration offers to small-business owners.

4. Explain the concept of franchising.

5. Compare the advantages and disadvantages of becoming a franchisee.

Entrepreneurship often involves a great deal of risk and personal sacrifice, especially in the first couple years of operating a new business. No one should even think about going into business for themselves unless they are prepared to work long hours, endure hardships, and persevere based on a vision of future rewards.

Tae Wan Cho knows the trials and triumphs of entrepreneurship. He left his native South Korea in 1982 to seek freedom and opportunity in the United States. Cho left his wife and two daughters behind so he could focus his energies on starting a new business in the United States. What business? He had no idea. He also had no capital, no credit rating, and spoke little English.

Cho moved to Harrisonville, MO, where he lived with a friend. Reading in a trade magazine, Cho learned that there was strong sales growth in hair-care products to African Americans. This was the opportunity he was looking for, and he decided to open a store in St. Louis.

Obtaining funding to open the store was the beginning of Cho's difficulties. After his $10,000 application for a loan from a local bank was turned down, Cho borrowed $3,000 from his Harrisonville friend and $2,000 from his new landlord in St. Louis. Cho signed a lease for 500 square feet of space on the first floor of a vacant downtown building—the second floor was condemned. He called the store "King's Beauty Supply" because, he says, "King is a common and respected name in the African-American community." He painted the name on the window and opened for business.

On the first day of business Cho sold $40 worth of merchandise. The first month he rang up over $3,000 in sales. During the first winter of operation, however, Cho didn't make enough money to heat his shop and much of his merchandise froze. Cash flow was so tight that he was only able to stock two items of many products. But he made a firm decision that every penny he made would be reinvested in the business. "I spent no money on myself," he said. "I paid my bills before I ate. I had no radio, no television, no chair, no sofa, no bed. I did not turn on the heat or the air conditioning in my apartment because I knew I couldn't pay the bills. All I had was a blanket and a 10-year-old Ford Pinto."

Cho used the Pinto to pick up products, driving to Kansas City each weekend because he couldn't afford the freight charge to have it shipped. He would buy as much merchandise as the Pinto would hold, usually about $1,000 worth of shampoos, conditioners, relaxants, and gels.

For three years he lived this way. He worked 10 hours a day, seven days a week. Today, he says, whether he was selling or sweeping in the store, hauling merchandise from Kansas City, or shivering in his apartment, he was constantly thinking about the business.

When he was confident that he could make a living with his business, Cho sent for his family. Not long after they arrived, he opened a second store that his wife, Young Suk, managed. Soon, Cho was operating nine retail stores in St. Louis and selling his products wholesale all over the United States. King's Beauty Supply Distributor, Inc., generated $7 million in sales in 1993, and Cho expected sales of $8 to $10 million in 1994. From the unheated, 500-square-foot shop, the company has grown to occupy a 30,000-square-foot warehouse. The Pinto has been replaced by semitrailers that arrive daily with as much as

$100,000 in merchandise. Cho now has a $1 million line of credit at the same bank that originally turned him down for the $10,000 loan.

Cho attributes his success to hard work, a good reputation, and advertising. He said, "In the beginning manufacturers wouldn't see me because I was so small and I knew nothing about the product I was selling. So I started studying the labels, questioning the manufacturers on the phone, and talking a lot to my customers. I made it a high priority to become knowledgeable about what I was selling." His strategy worked. As his sales improved, manufacturers came calling, and brought with them advertising allowances for their products.

Summarizing his experience, Cho said, "When I started out, I had no idea that I could do this well. But I still have a long way to go and a lot more to learn."

Think about a period in your life when you made a great sacrifice for the sake of a commitment or goal. Describe what it was like, and consider whether you would be willing to make sacrifices to start your own business.[1]

Most entrepreneurs need to have a fundamental optimism and a belief that hard work and sacrifice will lead to success. Do you think these are reasonable dispositions in today's business climate? Explain.

Not all businesses are large businesses. While Fortune 500 corporations such as IBM and General Motors are the most visible, many individuals—like Tae Wan Cho, owner of King's Beauty Supply Distributor in St. Louis, MO—start out with a small business. And small businesses can grow.

This chapter discusses the entrepreneurial and small-business spirit. First, we examine entrepreneurship and the risks that entrepreneurs take. Then we examine small business. Finally, we examine franchising, looking at both the advantages and disadvantages of being in the franchise business.

ENTREPRENEURSHIP

The debate about what makes an entrepreneur continues. However, some characteristics of entrepreneurs and entrepreneurship are worth discussing because they are consistently portrayed and studied.

The Individual Entrepreneur

The entrepreneur, according to French economist J. B. Say, "is a person who shifts economic resources out of an area of lower and into an area of higher productivity and yield."[2] But Say's definition does not tell us who this entrepreneur is. Some define the entrepreneur simply as one who starts his or her own new and small business. For our purposes, we will define the **entrepreneur** as a person who takes the risks necessary to organize and manage a business and receives the financial profits and nonmonetary rewards.

Entrepreneur
A person who takes the risks necessary to organize and manage a business and receives the financial profits and nonmonetary rewards.

The man who opens a small pizza restaurant is in business, but is he an entrepreneur? He took a risk and did something, but did he shift resources to start the business? If the answer is yes, then he is considered an entrepreneur.

Ray Kroc is an example of an entrepreneur because he founded and established McDonald's. His hamburgers were not a new idea, but he applied new techniques, resource allocations, and organizational methods in his venture. Ray Kroc *upgraded the productivity and yield from the resources applied* to create his fast-food chain. This is what entrepreneurs do; this is what entrepreneurship means.[3]

Many of the sharp, black-and-white contrasts between the entrepreneur and the professional have faded to gray. Formerly, professionals such as doctors, lawyers, dentists, and accountants were not supposed to be entrepreneurial, aggressive, or market oriented. They were "above" the market-driven world. Entrepreneurs, on the other hand, were the mavericks of society. They were risk takers who aggressively sought to make something happen. Long hours were about all the two worlds had in common. However, increased competition, saturated markets, and a more price-conscious public have changed the world of the professionals. Today they need to market their skills, talents, and competencies: Lawyers advertise their services. Doctors specialize in one form of surgery. Accounting firms join with other businesses (e.g., consulting and law) to serve clients.

Entrepreneurs exhibit many different behaviors; searching for a specific personality pattern is very difficult. Some entrepreneurs are quiet, introverted, and analytical. On the other hand, some are brash, extroverted, and very emotional.[4] Viewing change as the norm, entrepreneurs usually search for it, respond to it, and treat it as an opportunity. An entrepreneur such as Ray Kroc is able to take resources and shift them to meet a need. Making the decision to shift resources works better if a person is creative, experienced, and confident.

One example of how an entrepreneur operates is Polaroid's Edwin Land. One day, as he took pictures of his daughter, she asked impatiently why they had to wait for the pictures to be developed. Her question sparked her dad's imagination. Land worked, put his ideas together, and developed the first Polaroid instant camera. He combined his experience with cameras and films with his creativity to change history.

The strong desire for personal achievement and innovation is a characteristic of individuals such as Ray Kroc and Edwin Land that apparently helps sustain them during bad times or move them beyond business failures.[5]

College buddies Dave Pitassi and Wally Klemp were 23 years old when they founded VMG Products, a diaper company in Vancouver, WA, in 1983. They lost control of it to venture capitalists who were brought in to finance VMG's expansion. "It was an extremely difficult, very emotional time," recalls Klemp. "In retrospect, I like to joke it was the best postgraduate education I ever could have paid for. When you emerge from college full of ambition and naivete, you believe you can count on people's sense of what's right. But it's not the way the business world works. People don't share the same view of what's right and fair. We learned to be careful."

In 1988, Pitassi and Klemp came to Houston to turn personal disaster into Drypers, which by October 1993 was the fastest growing private company in the United States, according to *Inc.* magazine. These two entrepreneurs dis-

Dave Pitassi and Walter Kemp, featured on the cover of Houston Magazine, *teamed up to establish Veragon Corp. to produce and market Drypers after being ousted from their previous disposable diaper venture, VMG Products.*

play a pattern of personality traits that helped them grow a successful business. Today, Klemp and Terry Tognietti are co-chief executive officers who are attempting to help Drypers gain name recognition.

Drypers captured a top spot while competing with the best and biggest consumer marketer in the United States, Procter & Gamble. In five years, the young entrepreneurs built Drypers into a $160 million business and the third-best-selling disposable diaper in the country. With financial help from Equus Capital of Houston, they bought their original company and acquired two others. Now Drypers markets diapers in 47 states and 17 countries.

Crucial to Drypers's success was Houston's offer of tax abatement, rare at the time for a business in a nondistressed area. Klemp and Pitassi also felt a kinship with the city whose boom had gone bust. "We ran into a 'can do' attitude at a time when people should have been crying in their beer," said Klemp.

The success of low-cost disposable diapers put Drypers on the front line of a fierce turf war: skirmishing with brand-name giants Procter & Gamble and Kimberly-Clark over price and product innovation while fending off a flanking action by Paragon, a private label that in 1994 sold 3.5 billion diapers a year to Drypers's 1 billion, at 5 percent to 10 percent below competing Drypers' products.

In a high-tech industry in which nearly 12,000 patents are held, Klemp points to Drypers's new smaller-scale packaging and innovative pull-on training pants. Drypers training pants are the second on the market in a category P&G has yet to enter. A key company goal is to expand its international market. To better sell in Latin America, Drypers bought a plant in Puerto Rico.

Drypers founders said rapid growth has not changed the company's team player personality. "We have an absolutely open-door management style. At any given point in time, an operator from the production floor can walk in and say, 'We have a problem.' . . . A lot of ideas get generated by the people actually making the product and the people in direct communication with retailers and consumers," said Klemp.[6]

Corporate Entrepreneurs

An enterprise need not be small or new to be entrepreneurial. General Electric Company (GE), a large multinational business, has a reputation of being entrepreneurial. GE organized the GE Credit Corporation and numerous new manufacturing businesses. These firms made money for GE; they also provided ideas and concepts that raised the company's overall level of performance.

Intrapreneur
An entrepreneurial person employed by a corporation and encouraged to be innovative and creative.

GE is one of a growing number of firms that employ and recognize intrapreneurs. An **intrapreneur** is a person with entrepreneurial characteristics who is employed within a large corporation. Companies such as 3M, Hewlett-Packard, Merck, and Rubbermaid encourage intrapreneurs. Post-it™ note pads were developed at 3M by Arthur Fry, an employee looking for a better paper for marking pages in a book. At Hewlett-Packard, researchers are urged to spend 10 percent of their workweek on personal pet projects. Intrapreneurs are usually found in enterprises that encourage experimentation, tolerate failure, recognize success, and share the wealth.

Another interesting example of experimentation in the corporate setting is the case of Francis G. Okee of Minnesota Mining & Manufacturing (3M). In 1922, he dreamed of ways to boost the sales of sandpaper, then the firm's top seller. Why not sell sandpaper to men as a replacement for razor blades? The idea (thankfully) never caught on. However, Okee, who continued to sand his own face, was still able to work for 3M. The company had a high tolerance for experimenting with creative ideas. It still does today.

Entrepreneurship is not applicable only to profit-making institutions. In health care, the traditional hospital—which appeared in Vienna in the late 1700s—has changed greatly. Today we have highly specialized centers such as the Mayo Clinic and the Menninger Institute. Entrepreneurs in health care are introducing new methods of treatment delivery to serve patients' needs.

Characteristics of Growth-Oriented Entrepreneurs

Why do entrepreneurs continue to emerge when significant risks, time, and energy are needed to be successful? Researchers studying the entrepreneurial personality have made some interesting discoveries.

Researcher Donald Sexton compared founders of high-growth firms with founders of companies that exhibited little or no growth. Sexton's findings were similar to those in much earlier studies conducted by David McClelland, a noted social psychologist. Founders of high-growth companies appear to share a distinct cluster of personal characteristics (no single trait but a pattern, or cluster). As you review these characteristics, consider whether they can be applied to you. Do you have the characteristics of an entrepreneur?

Need for Achievement
A strong desire to succeed, to grow, to accomplish challenging tasks.

Need for Achievement. Growth-oriented entrepreneurs have a high **need for achievement:** They need to succeed, to achieve, to accomplish challenging tasks. The strong desire for achievement leads to a desire for independence. Such entrepreneurs need to be free to set their own course, establish their own goals, and use their own style. The need for achievement may help explain why growth-oriented entrepreneurs are not satisfied with founding or working in one firm; they need to prove themselves again and again.

Low Need to Conform. Growth-oriented entrepreneurs listen, but they are able to ignore others' advice. Also, handling skeptics is easy for entrepreneurs. Taking the unpopular course of action, if they consider it best, is the way they do business.

Persistence. Growth oriented entrepreneurs are persistent, doggedly doing what is best for the business to succeed. They work hard on the details and relentlessly attempt to find ways to become more profitable.

High Energy Level. The capacity for sustained effort requires a high energy level. The necessary work—planning, organizing, directing, creating strategy, and finding funds—can only be accomplished on a demanding schedule. The 60- to 80-hour workweek is common.

Risk-Taking Tendency. McClelland's findings suggest that people with a high need for achievement tend to take risks. Growth-oriented entrepreneurs believe so strongly in their ability to achieve that they do not see much possibility of failure. Thus they accept risk and find it motivating.

Risks of Entrepreneurship

In launching a business, the entrepreneur usually faces substantial business risk. Well over three million new businesses are started each year, and two out of three new jobs in the economy are in small businesses. However, the failure rate among these new ventures is disturbingly high. According to research by the Small Business Administration, from 25 to 33 percent of all independent small U.S. businesses fail during the first two years of operation. Research suggests that after eight years about 54 percent of start-ups still survive in some form; 28 percent have the original owner, and another 26 percent survive with new owners.[7]

Nowhere is there a report listing the specific reasons why thousands of businesses fail each year. However experts, business practitioners, and consultants point again and again to three reasons. First, people fail because they jump into a business too quickly. They plunge into a new venture hastily, without doing their homework. They do not analyze their own strengths and weaknesses: Who am I? What do I want? What are my goals? Businesses also fail because they run out of money. If you cannot meet your payroll or pay your bills, you are out of business. Realistic planning for the money needed is critically important. Estimates of cash requirements are a top priority before starting a venture.

Third, failing to plan is an obvious mistake. A detailed business plan forces the entrepreneur to think ahead, to reflect, to decide on how to proceed. A business plan should be in writing.

These three reasons for business failure are not exhaustive. However, they are the most common and the most serious. Exhibit 3.1 captures in a concise format the main reasons for small-business failure. These reasons need to be considered when starting or operating a business.[8] The four main categories

Exhibit 3.1
Causes of Small-Business Failures

Cause	Characteristics
Planning oversights	Not able to detect market and competive changes. Poor knowledge of economics. No plans for emergency situations. Inadequate financial planning.
Poor managerial qualities	Unwillingness to work hard, long hours. Lack of ability to deal with people. Failure to delegate responsibility and tasks. Unwillingness to learn the business from the ground up.
Inefficient business methods	Poor record keeping. No credit controls. No inventory control system. Inability to hire help.
Underfinancing	Lack of funds to buy adequate stock and equipment. Lack of funds to buy merchandise. Lack of funds to hire personnel.

(planning oversights, poor managerial qualities, inadequate business methods, and underfinancing) can undermine hard work, brilliant creativity, risk taking, and distinctness.

Besides considerable business risk, entrepreneurs face significant financial risk, since they typically invest most—if not all—of their financial resources in the business. They may take a career risk by leaving a secure job for a venture with a highly uncertain future. They also incur family and social risks because the demands of starting and running a young business leave little time for attention to family and friends. The demands of entrepreneurship often strain marriages and friendships.

SMALL BUSINESS

In projecting the future of small business, entrepreneurs, and entrepreneurship, management consultant Thomas Jones asserts that risk takers and innovators will dominate the future, supplying most of the new jobs, growth, and innovation in the United States. Jones points to specific social trends that support his claim:

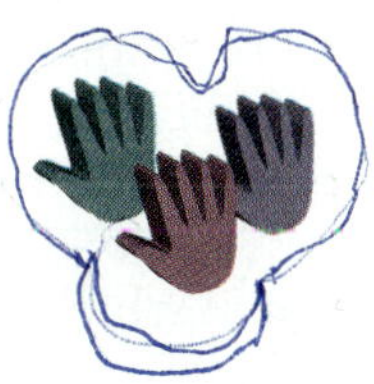

- Recent immigrants to the United States have demonstrated incredible talent, drive, and success in new business ventures. Immigrants will continue to establish themselves in their new country.
- Advances in technology and access to information allow new ventures to begin with considerably less start-up costs and lower overhead expenses. The small business can compete with higher-cost firms by being efficient.
- A glut in the professions, such as law, has forced many educated professionals to seek other career paths. Many are choosing to go into business for themselves.
- Middle-management cutbacks have put well-trained, educated men and women into the job market. Many of these managers have started their own businesses.
- Americans love their independence. This desire for freedom extends to the job one holds. The closest one can get to being independent is owning a business. Many people love to be their own boss.
- Entrepreneurship—being your own boss—is popular today. Success stories abound, and everyone wants to believe they can be a success.

The enthusiasm for small business and entrepreneurship is at an all-time high. This enthusiasm is a prerequisite for a healthy economy.

Many of the most publicized corporate giants began as small businesses and grew large through effective management.[9] For example, three engineers working out of a garage established one of the fastest-growing computer companies in the United States, Compaq Computer; Coca-Cola began when a pharmacist brewed a batch of syrup that tasted good; a restaurant owner named Colonel Sanders owned a small cafe that served "finger-lickin' good" chicken; and a salesperson named Ray Kroc discovered a tasty hamburger in California that he turned into the McDonald's burger.

Characteristics

Small Business
One that is independently owned and operated and is not dominant in its field of operation.

What characterizes small businesses? The Small Business Act of 1953 defines **small business** as "one which is independently owned and operated and not dominant in its field of operation." The act authorized the Small Business Administration (SBA) to use a number of yardsticks to identify a small business. For example, in lending money to small businesses, the SBA has established the following limits for qualifying:

- *Retailing and service.* The sales limit varies depending on the industry. In some industries, the maximum amount of sales is $3.5 million. In others, the maximum amount may be as high as $13.5 million.
- *Wholesaling.* The maximum number of employees cannot exceed 500.
- *Manufacturing.* The business must have 250 or fewer employees. If employment is more than 250 but less than 500, a size standard for a particular industry is used.
- *Special trade construction.* The maximum amount of sales is $7 million, regardless of industry.

These criteria suggest that smallness depends on your point of view. Marshall Field's (a department store company that started in Chicago) might be considered small in comparison to Sears, but compared to many other department store companies, Marshall Field's is large. Therefore, a small business is one that is not dominant (does not control a large market share) in its industry and one that can be started with a moderate investment for that industry.

Incubator
A facility in which fledgling businesses can share space, costs, services, and information while their firms grow and become strong.

A business **incubator** is a facility, office, shop, or location in which fledgling businesses can share space, costs, services, and information to grow their firms and to become strong enough to leave and operate independently. Today's Business World briefly explains some of the features of an incubator.

Smallness in business does not equate with a small contribution to the economy. Here are some facts about small businesses in the United States:

- They provide nearly 60 percent of the total employment in business.
- They account for about 43 percent of the gross domestic product of the United States.
- They account for nearly $8 of every $10 earned in the construction industry.
- More than 90 percent of all corporations are small, including farms.
- Fifty percent of all American businesses employ fewer than 10 people.

Advantages and Disadvantages

Any business venture involves potential benefits and costs. For many people, one important benefit is the personal gratification gained from operating one's own business. Business owners can exercise all their talents and can do so with some degree of independence; some also can obtain power by operating their own business. Another benefit of starting a small business is financial gain. The financial return from a successful small business can be substantial.

On the other hand, potential and actual costs can be important. The initial investment may be lost. Some risks are out of the entrepreneur's control; fashion changes, government regulations, competition, and labor problems may threaten the business. Some businesses also tend to produce irregular income; during the first six months of many potentially profitable firms, the owner may receive zero profits. Being in business for yourself also means long hours, generally leaving less time for recreation and family. These important parts of life sometimes must be sacrificed to operate a business successfully.

The Small Business Administration (SBA)

Small Business Administration (SBA) An independent agency of the federal government created in 1953 to protect the interests of small-business owners.

The **Small Business Administration (SBA),** an independent agency of the federal government, was created in 1953 to protect the interests of small-business owners. Big-business interests are promoted in Congress by well-organized lobbies, which work to create an atmosphere favorable for big business. Small businesses did not have this type of lobby power; for this and other reasons, the SBA was created.

SBA Loans. One important SBA function is to provide loans. If a small-business owner needs more money, the agency can help. The SBA does not compete with banks. Generally it will lend money to entrepreneurs only after they have been turned down by private lenders.

The SBA lends money on a term basis; that is, the money must be paid back within a specified number of years. *Direct loans* come from the agency's own funds. Loans made directly by the SBA are available only to those applicants not able to obtain financing from SBA participating or guaranteed loans. As of 1994, the maximum direct loan is $150,000. *Participating loans* supplement loans from banks. In another type of SBA loan, the *guaranteed loan,* the money comes from a bank, but the SBA guarantees to pay 90 percent of the loan if the owner defaults or can't pay. The SBA's guarantee cannot exceed $750,000. The SBA guarantees up to 22,459 loans annually, with a total value around $5.6 billion.[10]

The process for applying for and securing an SBA loan is spelled out in Exhibit 3.2. Banks often help the loan applicant fill out the right forms.

Management Assistance. The SBA provides management advice through its Management and Technical Assistance (7j) Program. Companies can remain in this program for nine years. The goal is that by the end of this time the small business will be competitive.

The SBA provides an "Answer Desk" to receive inquiries from small-business owners. The toll-free number is 1-800-827-5722. Reports and other publications also provide managerial assistance and can be requested from the SBA at 1441 L Street NW, Washington, DC 20005.

In addition, a number of universities such as the University of Houston and the University of Georgia offer advice, training, and other forms of assis-

Exhibit 3.2
SBA Loan Application Procedure

1. Assemble the information outlined below.
2. Take it to your bank and ask you banker to review the information and loan proposal. (It will be necessary for you to locate a bank that is willing to participate with SBA and make the loan since direct loan funds from SBA are quite limited and an unreliable source of financing.)
3. If the bank is willing to participate, ask the bank to forward the information to us for our review, along with their comments.

Information Needed for Loan Review

1. Brief résumé of business.
2. Brief résumé of management, setting forth prior business experience, technical training, education, age, health, etc.
3. Itemized use of loan proceeds:

Working capital	$ ________
Land	$ ________
Building	$ ________
Furniture and fixtures	$ ________
Machinery and equipment	$ ________
Automotive equipment	$ ________
Other	$ ________
Total	$ ________

4. Current business balance sheet and profit/loss statement.
5. Year-ending balance sheets and profit/loss statements for the last three years or, if the business has been in existence less than three years, financial statements for each year it has been in operation. (Copies of the financial statements submitted with the income tax returns are adequate.)
6. If the business is not in existence but is proposed, furnish a projected balance sheet of the business, showing its proposed assets, liabilities, and net worth upon commencement of operations, together with projected annual operating statements for the first three years of operation.
7. Furnish a separate personal balance sheet showing all assets owned and liabilities owed outside of the business.

The above information is what SBA loan representatives need to properly analyze a loan proposal. They may request additional information.

tance to small-business owners for free or a small fee. A list of the schools that have Small Business Development Centers can be requested from the SBA.

Women-Owned Small Business Assistance. The Small Business Administration estimates that by the year 2000 women will head about 40 percent of all small businesses. A growing number of women have decided that the "glass ceiling" in corporations or someone else's business has blocked their career progress. Other women desire the autonomy of heading their own business. The Women's Business Ownership Act of 1988 has helped many women secure loans to start their own businesses. Banks make loans of less than $50,000, and the SBA guarantees them. The SBA also has a microloan program granting from $50 to $15,000 to single mothers to start businesses.

Minority Business and the SBA. In the United States, which has about 48 million minority citizens, the number of African-American and Hispanic minority-owned businesses is disproportionately small. This may be due to lack of funds, inexperience, inability to obtain credit, or lack of interest in business. Minority small-business people tend to have a harder time finding investors.

The business community, government, and a large portion of society are promoting minority ownership. Large corporations are attempting to buy from and support minority-owned businesses. In cooperation with the U.S. Department of Commerce, the SBA has instituted programs that assist small businesses owned and managed by the socially or economically disadvantaged. The category includes but is not restricted to African Americans, Native Americans, Mexican Americans, Asian Americans, and Inuits (native Alaskans).

Small-Business Investment Company (SBIC)
A privately owned and operated company licensed by the SBA to furnish loans to small firms.

MESBIC
Minority-enterprise small-business investment company. Such a company is owned and operated by established industrial or financial concerns, private investors, or business-oriented economic development organizations.

The Small Business Investment Act of 1958 allows small firms to more easily get needed long-term capital to finance their growth. This act authorized the SBA to license **small-business investment companies (SBICs),** privately owned and operated companies that furnish loans to small firms.

SBICs dedicated to assisting small firms owned and operated by minority-group members are called **minority-enterprise small-business investment companies (MESBICs).** A MESBIC is owned and operated by established industrial or financial concerns, private investors, or business-oriented economic development organizations. Minority owners can ask for financial and managerial support from a MESBIC.

The SBA does more than lend money. It offers a starter kit for owners, sponsors local college courses and workshops, puts clients in touch with volunteers, and helps owners secure contracts with the federal government.

Exhibit 3.3 presents the 10 largest African-American-owned firms. There are about 500,000 African-American-owned companies in the United States with gross revenues of about $2.5 billion annually.[11]

Small-Business Opportunities

Three typical ways to become a small-business owner include taking over a family business by succession, buying an existing business, or starting a new business. Children of entrepreneurs often take over the family business. In many cases, the employees in small bakeries, barbershops, grocery stores, and butcher shops are the owners' children. They learn the business by working with their parents. Sometimes the children learn well and want to continue the business. In other cases, the parents force the business on the children, resulting in parent–child conflict and business failure.

Passing a business on to children is known as *succession.* Families that want to continue to run a business by passing on responsibilities need to begin succession planning while the business leader is in his or her 50s, and the chil-

Exhibit 3.3 *Ten Largest African-American-Owned Businesses*

	Company	Location	Chief Executive	Year Started	Staff	Business	Sales (000s)
1	TLC Beatrice International Holdings Inc.	New York	Jean S. Fugett Jr.	1987	5,000	International food processor & distributor	1,665.000
2	Johnson Publishing Co. Inc.	Chicago	John H. Johnson	1942	2,785	Publishing; broadcasting; TV production; cosmetics; hair care	274.2
3	Philadelphia Coca-Cola Bottling Co. Inc.	Philadelphia	J. Bruce Llewellyn	1985	1,000	Soft-drink bottler	266.0
4	H. J. Russell & Co.	Atlanta	Herman J. Russell	1952	825	Construction & development; food services	145.6
5	The Anderson-Dubose Co.	Solon, OH	Warren Anderson	1991	80	Food distributor	110.0
6	RMS Technologies Inc.	Marlton, NJ	David W. Huggins	1977	1,176	Computer & technical services	103.3
7	Gold Line Refining Ltd.	Houston	Earl Thomas	1990	51	Oil refinery	91.9
8	Soft Sheen Products Inc.	Chicago	Edward G. Garner	1964	547	Hair care products manufacturer	91.7
9	Garden State Cable TV	Cherry Hill, NJ	J. Bruce Llewellyn	1989	300	Cable TV operator	91.0
10	Threads 4 Life Corp. d/b/a Cross Colours	Los Angeles	Carl Jones	1990	250	Apparel manufacturer	89.0

Source: Adapted from "Largest African-American-Owned Companies," *Black Enterprise* (June 1993): 91.

dren are in their mid-20s or early 30s. Small-business consultants estimate that the succession process can take 10 to 15 years.[12]

Some people *buy out* an established business. The buyer and seller agree on terms involving the inventory, equipment, and price. The details of this purchase agreement should be spelled out in a legal contract between the buyer and seller.

Research also suggests that before a buyout can occur three parties need to be satisfied. Managers in the firm must feel comfortable about who is buying the firm. Institutions doing business such as suppliers and banks need to be satisfied. Employees who are operating the business must feel comfortable about the buyer. A discussion with these parties could go a long way toward making the buying of an existing business an eventual success.[13]

The third method of becoming a small-business owner, *starting* a new business, requires hard work and careful planning. Without solid planning, a new owner is likely to be swamped by the first wave of problems. Because a new business has no previous customers or business records, as an established business does, getting all the information needed to do a good job will involve hard work. The new owner must study materials about products and markets, consult with professional and business experts, and perhaps attend seminars and workshops for a quick education about managing a small business.

The result of all the study and research is the business plan. The *business plan* is a formal document of what the entrepreneur intends to do to sell enough of the firm's product or service to make a satisfactory profit. It should include basic information about the company and about the entrepreneur who intends to run it. In addition, the business plan should contain information about the market for the product or service, basic financial data, and a description of how the business will operate.

Many people imagine themselves running their own business, making the key decisions, and earning a profit. Becoming a small-business owner can provide these opportunities. The Your Values and Attitudes quiz can help you decide whether you are ready to operate your own business.

YOUR VALUES AND ATTITUDES

Are You Ready to Run Your Own Business?

Directions: Are you ready to run your own business? An important starting point in making a decision is determining your goals in life. Then you must match these goals with the benefits offered by the type of business you are considering. Other important questions to ask yourself include:

- Are you a self-starter?
- Do you like other people?
- Can you lead others?
- Are you well organized?
- Are you a decisive decision maker?
- Do you enjoy hard work and long hours?
- Do you stick with a project?
- Can you handle pressure?
- Can you communicate well?
- Do you understand planning, organizing, and controlling?
- Do you learn from past mistakes?
- Are you in excellent health?

Feedback: Operating a small business can be both challenging and rewarding. But owning or running a small business is not for everyone. A small business can be a lot of pressure, long hours, and a test of management and leadership skills. The reward is the satisfaction in running your own show and succeeding both personally and financially.

A score of at least nine yes responses indicates a strong interest in running your own business. If you answered no to four or more of these questions, you may want to think carefully before attempting to operate a small business. Of course, this is only a checklist of questions, and is only meant to help assess your own entrepreneurial potential. And even if you answered no, you can change—good communication skills can be developed, leadership skills can be acquired, and so on. If you answered yes to most of these questions, you seem to have what it takes to operate a small business.

Answering these types of questions requires honesty. Ask a few close friends or relatives how they would answer these questions about you. How does your view compare with how others see you?

Every industry has successful small businesses. Small-business owners operate manufacturing plants, salad bars, computer stores, yogurt stores, daycare centers, skating rinks, retail stores, computer production plants, construction firms, accounting offices, printing plants, record stores, and hundreds of other businesses. However, small business is more concentrated in some areas of the economy than in others.

Manufacturing. Small manufacturing businesses number in the thousands. In fact, about 30 percent of all manufacturing companies are considered small.[14] This category includes printing shops, steel fabricating shops, recreational equipment plants, clothing manufacturers, cabinet shops, furniture shops, and bakeries. The manufacturing business involves converting raw materials into products needed by society. Therefore the owner must understand production and marketing and how these business functions complement each other.

Service. The service sector is a diverse field; there are hundreds of service business opportunities. About 60 percent of all private business jobs in the United States involve selling services to consumers. **Services** are intangible products that cannot be physically possessed and that involve performance or effort. Service businesses include:

Services
Intangible products that cannot be physically possessed and that involve performance or effort.

- *Business services*—businesses that provide service to other business organizations; include accounting firms, advertising agencies, software writers, computer programmers, systems analysts, blueprint service, tax consultants, collection agencies, and so on
- *Restaurant services*—include fast food restaurants, franchised restaurants, and standard restaurants
- *Personal services*—include barber and beauty shops, baby-sitting agencies, piano teachers, laundries, and travel agencies
- *Repair services*—include automobile, jewelry, appliance, furniture, plumbing, and truck repair services
- *Entertainment and recreation services*—include racetracks, motion picture theaters, amusement parks, golf courses, and bowling alleys
- *Hotels and motels*—include the operation of hotels, motels, and recreational vehicle (RV) camps

With increased leisure time and consumer spending power, individuals, families, and other businesses are expected to increase their use of service firms.

This bicycle repair business markets its effort and performance in the service sector.

Wholesaling. Wholesaling involves selling to other sellers, such as retailers, other wholesalers, or industrial firms. Wholesale trade consists mainly of small businesses. Firms with fewer than 100 employees are responsible for more than 75 percent of the industry's employment. In fact, very small firms (those with fewer than 20 employees) have 41 percent of the total employment.

Merchant wholesalers sold over $2.0 trillion of goods in 1994. A merchant wholesaler is an independent business, such as Super Value Stores, that holds ownership to the goods it markets. Small wholesale firms also sell a wide range of products, including groceries, supplies, machinery, appliances, grain, and fruits and vegetables. These businesses serve as a link between manufacturers and retailers or industrial users. Wholesaling is discussed in detail in Chapter 15.

Retailing. Retailers are merchants who sell goods to consumers. The giants of retailing include Sears, Roebuck, Kmart, Wal-Mart, and JC Penney. Small, local retail businesses sell many of the same products as these giant corporations. Corner drugstores, shoe stores, grocery stores, restaurants, jewelry stores, and hardware stores appear in almost every populated area in the United States. Chapter 15 explores retailing further.

Home-Based Business
Business in which an individual works or conducts activities out of the home. About 22 percent of the total work force now works out of the home.

Home-based businesses. Twenty-five percent of the total U.S. work force now works at home, either full or part time. At the end of 1994 over 33 million Americans were working out of their homes. The keys to succeeding in a **home-based business** are to (1) select a business you truly enjoy, (2) do your research on the business idea, (3) prepare a thorough business plan, (4) have enough start-up money, and (5) start on a part-time basis.

TOMORROW'S BUSINESS WORLD

Small Businesses Will Cooperate in Virtual Corporations

The virtual corporation is a form of business enterprise that specializes in producing products or services that can be made available at any time, in any place, and in any variety. According to some futurists, individual consumers of the next century will not be satisfied with standardized products produced for mass markets. There are already a handful of so-called virtual products and services available to consumers today. Prescription eyeglass lenses are ground and placed in custom frames within 60 minutes by such companies as Lenscrafters and Pearle Vision Express. Polaroid gave consumers the instant camera years ago and has followed it with one-hour developing and printing of high-quality conventional photographs.

Virtual services are also available. Changing the oil in your automobile used to be a messy job, or one that would require sacrificing the vehicle to a mechanic for the better part of a day. Now you can get your oil changed in 10 minutes or less at a number of quick-oil-change shops such as Jiffy Lube. Banking can be done instantaneously and conveniently with an automated teller machine (ATM).

All of these products and services offer instant customer utility in a cost-effective way. They frequently can be produced in diverse locations and offered in a wide variety of models or formats. The only way to provide customers with virtual products and services is to maintain integrated and ever-changing data files on customers, products, and production and design methodologies. For many virtual corporations one of the primary tasks will be to develop systems that will enable the customer to take on some design responsibilities previously reserved for the company. A virtual corporation is thus best described as a pattern of networks and relationships.

Small businesses are especially well adapted for playing a role in this emerging type of enterprise. A new form of cooperation known as "teamnetting" is already being used to respond to new, more demanding markets. One small company that has succeeded with this approach is Erie Bolt of Erie, PA. A decade ago, when Harry Brown took over as CEO, sales were plummeting and employee morale was low. Today, under the new corporate name EBC Industries (of which Erie Bolt is a division), the company's sales have doubled to $7.2 million on products ranging from circus tent stakes to exotic fasteners for the aerospace industry.

One factor that was crucial in the revival of EBC was teamnetting. For EBC, teamnetting meant joining with 14 other area companies to give itself more muscle to tackle domestic and global markets. EBC and the other teamnet companies share equipment, customer lists, and other information that entrepreneurs never would have dreamed of sharing just a few short years ago.

Like EBC, Advanced Circuit Technology of Nashua, NH, maker of systems that connect electronic components, was seeking teamnet partners. The company's CEO, Joseph Roberts, and nine other regional companies who don't compete with each other formed an organization they call Team Nashua to make and sell electronic components. Roberts has personally secured contracts and shared them with team members, who are bound by confidentiality agreements not to disclose customer information to anyone except other team members.

There are potential drawbacks to managing teamnets or virtual corporations. As organizational consultant Tom Peters said, "You are trying to bring to bear the power of various autonomous people, and the autonomous small company has even more ego at stake than the average unit manager within the corporate hierarchy. The potholes in the road are large in number." Nonetheless, according to Jessica Lipnack and Jeffrey Stamps, authors of the book *The TeamNet Factor,* small businesses that cooperate under this model can accomplish more than any could acting alone.

To ensure a fair and competitive playing field, federal laws prohibit large corporations from working too closely together. Explain how small corporations can continue to prosper from business alliances and avoid becoming regulated.

What are some of the difficulties with maintaining relationships among two or more firms? Do you think these difficulties increase with the number of participants in the alliance?

Source: Adapted from John S. DeMott, "Company Alliances for Market Muscle," *Nation's Business* (February 1994): 52–53; John Byrne, Richard Brandt, and Otis Port, "The Virtual Corporation," *Business Week* (February 8, 1993): 98–103; William H. Davidow and Michale S. Malone, *The Virtual Corporation* (New York: HarperBusiness, 1992); Jessica Lipnack and Jeffrey Stamps, *The TeamNet Factor* (Essex Junction, VT: Oliver Wight Publications, 1993).

FRANCHISING

Franchise
The right to use a specific business name (Pizza Hut, Subway, H & R Block, Blockbuster, Masterworks International) and sell its goods or services in a specific city, region, or country.

Today franchising is not solely a U.S. phenomenon. A **franchise** is a business that has signed an agreement with a franchiser (e.g., McDonald's) to use the name, operating plan, and overall procedures used in the firm to sell its products or services. Thus, in starting up a business the franchisee buys a franchise unit. Visits to Hungary, Germany, Italy, Mexico, and over 70 other countries would confirm that franchises are found around the world. Today approximately 550,000 franchise units are in operation in the United States. Franchising cuts across 40 industries, ranging from motels and automobile dealers to campgrounds. Exhibit 3.4 shows how franchise sales are distributed among industries. Franchise sales in 1994 were approximately $950 billion, double the revenues earned in 1980 franchise sales. Now, more than one-third of the nations's retail revenue comes from franchised businesses, and over 8 million people are employed by franchises.

Franchising: A Brief History

An attractive way to become involved with business is to invest in a franchise. Legislation mandates that three components must be present for a franchise to exist:

1. The utilization of a uniform tradename or service mark (e.g., Dairy Queen, Subway, Blockbuster).
2. A uniform system of operations.
3. A fee of at least $500 during the first six months of business.

Exhibit 3.4 *Percentage of Franchise Sales in the U.S.**

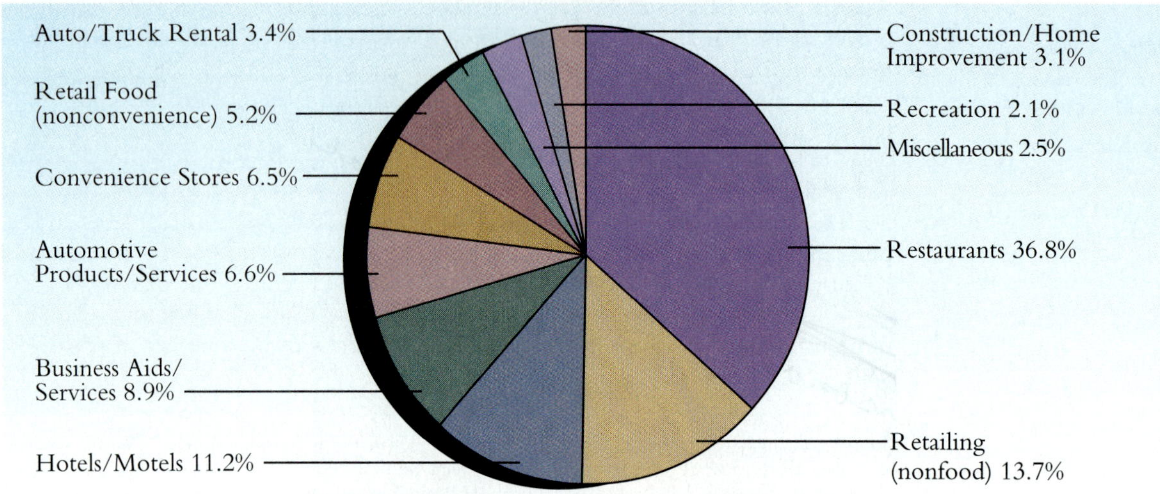

*Based on business format franchises where the franchisee receives not only a trademark and logo but also a complete system of doing business, including site selection, personnel training, and advertising.

Source: *Franchise Fact Sheet*, (New York: International Franchise Association, 1994).

With these components, a franchise relationship is established between the franchisor (the company) and the franchisee (the small-business owner). A new franchised business opens every 15 minutes in the United States. Franchising is the fastest growing method of doing business, but it is not really new. Some believe that franchising dates back to the Middle Ages (A.D. 476–1453), when it was common practice for governments to offer people a license or franchise granting them the right to do business or to establish and collect tax revenues.

The first contractual commercial franchise in the United States was Singer Sewing Machine Company in 1851. To solve the "sewing machine war," in which four manufacturers were suing one another, Isaac Singer and his attorney-partner Edmund Clark organized the Sewing Machine Combination. It became the first patent pool in the United States, dividing the distribution rights among the manufacturers. The franchisees were granted worldwide rights, territories, and exclusive rights to sell and service their machines.

Two other early franchise operations in the United States were Coca-Cola, which first supplied its syrup to franchised bottlers around 1900, and Rexall Drug Stores, which started around 1902. Other examples of early franchise pioneers included automobile dealerships and gasoline stations. Oil companies had been operating their own stations until about 1930. A few of them began to license dealers, and the practice spread from 1930 to 1935 until it became the sole method employed to distribute gasoline.[15] In the 1950s franchising spread across the United States. In fact, 90 percent of all franchise companies doing business today started in the early 1950s.

Coca-Cola, dating back to around 1900, was one of the early franchise operations in the United States, supplying syrup to bottlers.

Obvious signs of franchising's popularity are the numerous fast-food outlets lining the highways and littering shopping malls. Today there are over 75,000 fast-food restaurants in the United States, many of them franchise operations. They serve everything from special flavors of ice cream to hot dogs. McDonald's has an international network of over 8,000 restaurants that sell a billion hamburgers every five months. It is the biggest food franchise operation in the world, with sales of over $25 billion in 1994. Kentucky Fried Chicken (KFC, a subsidiary of Pepsi-Cola) has over 5,000 outlets, which have total worldwide sales of about $2.5 billion.

The Franchising Agreement

The franchise organization enters into a contractual agreement with each of its franchisees. These contracts may differ in a number of areas, such as capital needed, training provided, managerial assistance available, and size of the franchise territory. But most franchise contracts have points in common. The franchise buyer normally pays an initial fee to the company and agrees to pay the franchisor a monthly percentage of sales. In exchange, the franchisee has the right to sell a standard product or service.

In almost every franchise, the franchisee must invest some money. The amount can vary from a few thousand dollars to millions. Despite having to put money down, people still have to wait for certain franchises. Each year, more than 2,000 people apply for the approximately 150 franchises granted by McDonald's.

A McDonald's franchise can cost as much as $600,000. Although most of the fee can be borrowed from a bank, $66,000 would be the minimum cash down payment required. This payment covers landscaping and opening costs, license fee, site development fee, equipment down payment, signs, and security deposit. McDonald's Corporation does not lend money or guarantee loans. The company will provide a site, build the restaurant, and develop the parking lot. In return, the franchisee must pay 12 percent of gross sales to McDonald's and put at least 4 percent of gross sales annually into marketing and advertising.

Franchise purchasers enter the business to earn money; in fact, the owner and the company both want to earn money. Earnings are a measure of the franchise's success. To succeed, it must be well managed, provide good products or services, and obtain repeat customers.

The franchisor begins to earn money when the cash down payment is made. In some cases, a franchise fee must be paid before certain rights of operation are granted. The franchisor also requires some type of royalty payment on gross sales (the 12 percent franchisees pay to McDonald's, for example). The amount of royalty, or share of the proceeds, paid to the franchisor differs from company to company. Typically, a franchisee pays a royalty of between 3 and 15 percent on gross sales (total sales revenue).

No matter what the percentage of royalty, franchisees often dislike paying profits to someone else. It is only human nature for people to feel pain when they see part of the fruits of their labor go to someone else. Paradoxically, this pain may become more intense as franchise operation becomes more successful. The franchisee may be making many thousands of dollars, but so is the franchisor.[16]

Being involved and working hard to make the franchise a success, then being required to share the earnings deflates the ego of some franchisees. If franchisees believe the sharing of profits is unfair, this perceived inequity is also a problem. The franchisee may believe that he or she does all the work and the franchisor takes too big a share of the earnings.

Many people who consider entering into a franchise contract assume they will be their own boss. This assumption is only partially accurate. The franchisor exercises a significant amount of control over the franchisee in such areas as (1) real estate ownership, (2) territorial restrictions, (3) cancellation provisions, and (4) required exclusive handling.

Some franchise companies own the real estate, select the site of the business location, and build the facility. These companies then lease the facility to a franchisee. Exxon, Shell, Gulf, and Texaco, for example, often select the location for a service station and build it according to their specifications.

Cancellation Provision
The contract provision giving a franchisor the power to cancel an arrangement with a franchisee.

Exclusive Handling
A form of control in which a franchisor requires the franchisee to purchase only supplies approved by the franchisor.

The **cancellation provision** in a contract is a powerful control device. For instance, gasoline companies often issue operators of service stations a one-year franchise. If the company does not consider the operator successful, the franchise agreement can be canceled after that time. This provision can force operators to run the business as directed by the franchisor.

Exclusive handling means that the franchisee will only sell items, products, or services that are acceptable to the franchisor. This means that the franchisor has control over what is sold directly to customers or clients.

Advantages of Owning a Franchise

Although owning a franchise business has its problems, there are reasons why it appeals to people. A person who has never owned or managed a business needs guidance to operate successfully. This guidance can be provided by a well-run franchise organization. Also, franchisors can provide a brand name, proven products or services, and financial assistance. Today's Business World illustrates how franchising benefits firms and owners.

Guidance. A glaring weakness in small businesses is lack of managerial ability. A person with limited managerial skills may be able to get by in a large organization because he or she is just one of many managers. But no one can cover up for or "carry" a franchise manager. Many franchisors try to overcome managerial deficiencies or inexperience by providing some form of training. Kentucky Fried Chicken operates Chicken University, a training school for improving management skills.

Brand Name. The investor who signs a franchise agreement acquires the right to use a nationally or regionally promoted brand name. This identifies the local unit with a recognized product or service. Travelers recognize the Holiday Inn sign, the colors of a Pizza Hut building, and Century 21 real estate signs. National promotion brings these features and characteristics to the attention of potential consumers.

Proven Product. The franchisor can offer the franchisee a proven product and method of operating the business. The product or service is known and accepted by the public: customers will buy Baskin-Robbins ice cream, AAMCO transmissions, Athlete's Foot sneakers, and H&R Block income tax counseling.

Financial Assistance. By joining a franchise company, the individual investor may be able to secure financial assistance. Start-up costs of any business are often high, and the prospective investor usually has limited funds. The sole owner generally has a limited credit rating, making it difficult to borrow needed funds. In some cases, association with a well-established franchisor—through its reputation and its financial controls—may enhance the investor's credit rating with local banks.

TODAY'S BUSINESS WORLD

Franchisor Maturity Affects Management Style

Besides taking a long, hard look at their own personalities and skills, potential franchisees need to take a hard look at the parent company. What is its financial condition? What role does it play in assisting individual franchisees? How is it managed? More important, potential franchisees should examine the *maturity* of the franchisor. The relationship between franchisor and franchisee will depend in large part on the maturity of the franchisor's internal management processes.

Many franchising firms today prefer to use the same proven management techniques that have been successful in large corporations. Mature franchising operations will transform their entrepreneurial culture to one where professional management dominates. AlphaGraphics Printshops, based in Tucson, AZ, is one successful franchising operation that has shifted to a professional management approach. Michael Witte, chairman and CEO, said, "Professional management is a method of looking at a business using real analytical tools, such as forward planning, and benchmarking progress against established good business practices. It is also considering the needs of the franchisees and working out ways to meet those needs."

Keeping in touch with a far-flung group of franchises poses a unique set of difficulties for the franchising firm. Witte described his printing empire as "a voluntary alliance of independent businesspeople all using the same operating system and sharing the same philosophy." Managing such a loose group requires two-way communication, an open-door policy that solicits suggestions from franchisees, and an empowerment program that involves every member of the organization. Witte said, "Once we understand what our franchisees want to accomplish, then we can figure out how to help them."

McDonald's, which receives between 10,000 and 15,000 requests for franchising information each year, manages its franchises by requiring new owners to undertake a two-year training regimen that includes working without pay at a McDonald's restaurant. The parent company will only sell a franchise to people willing to commit working 12- to 18-hour days, seven days a week and who will personally manage their stores. Its professional management structure allows it to carefully screen potential franchisees and to achieve diversity goals. For example, in August 1994, 64 percent of current franchising candidates in training were minorities or women.

Deciding to become a franchise owner requires some research into the maturity of the franchisor. According to business author Roy Cammarano, entrepreneurial firms that grow into franchisors traverse four different growth phases:

1. Entrepreneurial Genius: The company is new, the founding entrepreneur is loaded with enthusiasm. It is typical in this phase for the entrepreneur to view the future from a simple, one-dimensional perspective: produce the product and sell it. During this phase, the leader has little patience, time, or energy for anything but the pursuit of more sales.
2. Benevolent Dictator: In this phase of development, entrepreneurs act like parents who tell their children—employees and franchisees—what to do and when and how to do it. As more force is used to bring everyone into conformity, employees and franchisees often rebel.

3. Dissociated Director: This phase of development is usually confusing for everyone in the company. Entrepreneurs learn that the company doesn't want to be dependent on them for every decision. Their egos suffer, and they become alienated. Dissociated directors often claim they will remove themselves from day-to-day running of the firm and bring in professional managers. They usually can't help meddling, however, and many soon go back to running the company "their" way.
4. Visionary Leader: In this phase, the entrepreneur has truly let go. Leadership and management processes are used in a corporate environment to position the company for long-term growth. Visionary leaders:

   - Live within identified values.
   - Think before acting.
   - Are consistent.
   - Communicate openly, honestly, and directly.
   - Exhibit patience.
   - Develop a participatory style of management and decision making.

Knowing the franchisor's level of maturity can prevent unwanted surprises. With all the stresses of owning a business, doing the research ahead of time is well worth the trouble.

Imagine you are an entrepreneur who has founded a firm, and that you are now selling franchises around the country. From your perspective as head of the company, what factors do you think are relevant to a decision to implement professional management techniques? Imagine you are an entrepreneur who wants to purchase a franchise. Would you prefer to buy from a franchisor who has already adopted professional management techniques, or from one who is still in the entrepreneurial stage?[17]

Disadvantages of Owning a Franchise

As does any business venture, franchising has some disadvantages. Many were mentioned briefly earlier in this chapter. Some of the more pressing negative features include costs, lack of control, and inadequate training programs offered by some unscrupulous promoters.

Costs. As already mentioned, franchisees must pay franchise fees. In return, the franchisor can provide training, guidance, and other forms of support that would otherwise cost money. Thus the franchisee pays for the opportunity to share in these forms of support. If it were possible to earn the same income independent of the franchisor, the investor could save the amount of these fees.

Exhibit 3.5 presents a few examples of the fees and start-up costs needed to secure a franchise. Fees and costs to start up a franchise can range from a small amount to over $5 million.

External Control. A person who signs a franchise agreement loses some independence. The franchisor, in order to operate all of the franchise outlets as

Exhibit 3.5
Required Investment and Number of Outlets for Selected Franchisors

Franchisor	Total Required Investment	Number of Franchised Outlets	Number of Company-Owned Outlets
H & R Block	\$5,000–\$8,00	4,868	4,087
Merle Norman Cosmetics	\$8,500–\$123,810	2,300	0
International Tours	\$103,000–\$123,00	278	3
Baskin Robbins	\$142,500–\$187,50	3,557	29
Goodyear Tire Centers	\$90,000 and up	344	941
Budget Rent-a-Car	\$165,000	2,819	558
Century 21 Real Estate	\$14,000–\$30,00	7,038	0
Aamco Transmission	\$123,000	650	0
7-Eleven Stores	\$12,500–\$304,00	3,031	3,238
McDonald's	\$220,000–\$265,000	7,077	1,544
Holiday Inn	Up to \$5,500,000	1,451	176

Source: *The 1994 Franchise Annual* (Lewiston, NY: Info Press, 1994).

a business, must exercise some control over promotional activities, financial records, hiring, service procedures, and managerial development. Although useful, these controls are unpleasant to the person who seeks independence. In the best of circumstances, the franchisee is semi-independent. In a sole proprietorship, by contrast, the owner is totally independent.

Overdependence. Often new franchises become overdependent on the franchisor, and this can lead to an inability to make timely or even simple decisions without constantly checking and asking for advice. Franchisees need to use judgement and not rely on the franchisor to check every decision about the local market.

Poor Local Reputation Can Spread. In some communities where there are multiple franchise units with different franchisee, the performance and reputation of one can affect all the units. For example, Jack-in-the-Box restaurants were affected negatively nationwide because some franchises in the state of Washington improperly cooked food, allowing the spread of E-coli bacteria and resulting in the deaths of three young children.

Franchisor Disclosure

Because of the nature of franchising in the United States, evaluating an opportunity carefully before signing an agreement is important. The large number of franchise companies makes the task difficult. The Federal Trade Commission requires every franchisor to provide buyers with a full disclosure form. The form has 20 categories of information, including a financial statement, company history review, fees, investment requirements, and a litigation history. The best investment a prospective franchisee can make is to have an attorney and an accountant review the document and provide opinions.[18] Exhibit 3.6 presents a sample of the types of questions that need to be asked and answered before signing a franchise agreement.

Legal guidelines are crucial to the continued success of franchising. Currently, 35 states have laws on franchising issues such as disclosure, registration, and franchise-relationship definitions. The most stringent state law is the Iowa Franchise Act of 1992. The Iowa law requires that franchisors disclose financial information to prospective buyers. It also stipulates that franchisors agree to pay fair market value for any franchise location they decide to close. Moreover, franchisers are barred from terminating, refusing to renew, or denying a transfer of a franchise to another owner except for "good cause."

International Franchising

Franchising has become a major export of U.S. business. There are now over 400 U.S. companies that franchise around the world. About 35,000 U.S.-franchised units operate internationally. One can find McDonald's in Russia, Weight Watchers in Spain, Burger King in Germany, Subway in Japan, Postal Instant Press in the United Kingdom, and Wal-Mart in Mexico.

The largest McDonald's in the world is in Moscow. It opened as a joint venture between McDonald's Restaurants of Canada Ltd. and the Moscow City Council. As countries around the world move toward free market business practices, franchising is likely to become a popular business start-up alternative.

Exhibit 3.6
Sample of Questions to Ask and Answer About Franchising

Since a franchise agreement can be a legally binding contract that defines the franchise relationship between the franchisor (company) and franchisee (small-business owner), it should be carefully reviewed.

1. What are the legal obligations of the franchisee? Of the franchisor?
2. Are there any legal suits currently pending or recently settled by the franchisor and other franchisees?
3. What is the financial history of the franchisor?
4. What amount of royalty must be paid to the franchisor? When?
5. Please provide me with a list of all current franchisees in my area.
6. What type of support services will the franchisor provide and how good are the services?
7. Does the franchise agreement conform to the requirements of the Federal Trade Commission?
8. Can the franchise agreement be terminated by either party? What are my (franchisee) obligations if the agreement is terminated by me? By the franchisor?

workers. Wendy Wigtil, company president, decided to pursue foreign markets as a result of a decline in the domestic market.

The first contract from a foreign buyer was an unsolicited order from a distributor at a trade show. That was in 1989, when Barnyard Babies was just three years old. When the domestic market declined shortly after that, Wigtil made a decision to pursue exporting as a central business strategy. The opportunities for small businesses to export are increasing, she says. There are more intermediaries in foreign markets today that are looking to buy American products. Her company's exports, for example, are handled almost entirely by foreign distributors.

Wigtil also points to improving foreign economies as a major factor in the increasing attractiveness of exporting. She says that, formerly, many foreign buyers requested products for trial in foreign markets. Today they are more likely to place orders. The most significant factor in her decision to pursue exports, however, has been the opening of new, untapped markets such as the former Soviet Bloc.

While foreign opportunities are tremendous, not all small businesses are poised to become successful exporters. There are several factors small businesses should consider prior to adopting an exporting strategy. First and foremost the firm must be an established, viable concern in the domestic market. Second, the firm must be able to offer a marketable product at a competitive price. Beyond these fundamentals, successful exporting requires:

- A long-term commitment.
- Perseverance and the realization that success won't come instantly.
- Ability to adapt a product or service to meet overseas expectations.
- Willingness to tap available information and resources.
- An attitude of partnership with agents in foreign markets.
- A commitment to quality.

Along with the many exporting success stories like Barnyard Babies, there are plenty of ventures that have had trouble. Most would-be exporters are naive, says management company executive John Everett, who has exported for 23 years: "They expect too much. They believe that success will be instantaneous. In fact, it takes about three years to become profitable, if all goes well." One major problem, Everett says, is that American CEOs often believe automatically that their products are superior and their prices lowest. They fail to understand that foreign countries often have equal or better technology and products of equal or better quality.

Wendy Wigtil found success in exporting because she continued to offer high-quality products at a competitive price. Currently, Barnyard Babies exports to Japan, France, and Canada and plans to expand to Brazil. Wigtil also notes that the company stands to benefit as tariffs on toys sold to Canada are reduced as a result of NAFTA. Clearly, her small company has found a long-term source of business in foreign markets.

Questions for Discussion

1. Besides those mentioned in the case, can you identify any developments that are favorable to small-business exporters like Barnyard Babies?

2. What do you think are some of the special problems small businesses face when considering exporting to developing countries such as Vietnam or China?
3. Wendy Wigtil exports primarily through distributors in the foreign country. What advantages does this provide?

Source: Adapted from Rob Norton, "Strategies for the Export Boom," *Fortune* (August 22, 1994): 124–132; Roberta Maynard, "A Good Time to Export," *Nation's Business* (May 1994): 22–32; Paul C. Hsu, "Profiting from a Global Mind-Set," *Nation's Business* (June 1994): 6; G. A. Chiaruttini, *Breaking into the Global Trade Game: A Small Business Guide to Exporting* (U.S. Small Business Administration and The Global Source, Inc., 1994).

CASE 3.2

The Rebirth of Mrs. Fields Cookies

Debbi Fields, the woman behind Mrs. Fields Cookies, could not bear to franchise. A perfectionist, Fields was afraid she would lose control. "I always feared that independent franchisees might substitute product or sacrifice quality," she says.

But too much growth nearly sank the company; now Mrs. Fields Cookies is using a newly popular franchising industry technique known as *conversion franchising* in order to build its way back. A hot industry concept, conversion franchising means changing company-owned units or independent businesses into franchises. For Mrs. Fields Cookies, it will create an instant franchise network—bringing the on-site ownership of franchisees to the formerly centralized cookie company.

Back in the roaring 1980s, Fields was opening some 70 stores a year. Fields and her husband, Randy, built a chain of nearly 800 stores that were all owned and operated by the company. By the early 1990s, growth had come to a dead stop. Over-expansion left the company saddled with massive debt. To write off \$49.5 million of those loans and restructure the rest, Fields was compelled to surrender nearly 80 percent of her company to lenders. She also gave up operational control, although she is still the largest stockholder, with 11 percent of the company.

Now Mrs. Fields Cookies plans to reinvigorate marginal stores through conversion. The company is replacing employee managers with franchisees in 250 company-owned outlets. The reorganization takes advantage of franchising's most fundamental premise, which is that highly motivated owner/operators possess an entrepreneurial drive and energy rarely found in employees.

The technique is nothing new. As far back as 1971, Century 21 used conversion franchising to unify independent real estate agents nationwide. Since then, franchisors have used conversion both to bring outside vendors into the franchise-network fold and to convert company stores into franchise outlets.

To become franchisees, independent business owners must pay initial fees and an ongoing percentage of their gross sales to the franchisor. In return, they receive pooled advertising and sophisticated management and control systems that have been proven on a national or regional level. Then there's the power and security of a proven trade name. Look at Mrs. Fields Cookies. Despite the company's recent financial problems, it offers prospective franchisees a nationally recognized brand with a built-in market. For company-owned chains, existing franchising units can recapitalize sagging financial fortunes as well as create the highest-quality manager, someone who owns the business and has the motivation to make it work.

Mrs. Fields Cookies is using technology to maintain the quality control Fields thought franchising would sacrifice. Through Randy Field's software development firm, Park City Group, the company had developed sophisticated retail management software. The software lets distant stores download sales information to the company's huge database, stored in a mainframe in Park City, UT. There, the company tracks, budgets, and monitors in-store activity, right down to the number of cookies or muffins prepared each hour.

The program can look backward in time, then project how many muffins and cookies a franchisee should prepare during the next hour of operation. It gives the company a microscope to examine every corner of operations and boost sales. Already, sales have surged 17 percent in the franchised outlets that are using the system.

After Michael Zreik bought a Mrs. Fields location in West Covina, CA, sales doubled. "It's just too difficult to manage a business from a distance," says Zreik, who bought the franchise in 1992. "I am here on location. I drive the business forward." One of his first acts as a franchisee was to meet with employees to stress the need for quality. "I laid down the ground rules," he says. "We were going to have a spotless store, superlative product, and great customer relations. Some employees left. Others bought into my dream."

He also courted new markets. "We go out of our way to introduce the product to new people," he says. "Every week, we deliver sample trays to businesses and corporations. Two days after we did that with a local bank, they called and ordered $1,000 worth of cookies for all their branches. An employee isn't going to do that kind of marketing. But an owner will."

Questions for Discussion

1. How do you think conversion franchising will work for Mrs. Fields Cookies? Why?
2. What role does top quality product and service play in the cookie business?
3. How important is it to the franchisor to have a franchise network? Explain.

Source: Adapted from Greg Matusky, "Rebirth!" *Success* (September 1993): 64–66.

EXPERIENTIAL EXERCISE

Portrait of an Entrepreneur

Activity:

This activity is designed to enhance students' understanding of the entrepreneurial personality and the motivations, challenges, and rewards of entrepreneurship.

Directions:

Each member of the class should complete the following assignment:

1. Each student should identify a successful entrepreneur in the community that they can interview. Students should concentrate on identifying a small business that is directed by its founder. The business section of recent issues of the community newspaper should be helpful in locating an entrepreneur.
2. After the entrepreneur has been identified, students should contact the person and arrange an interview.
3. Students should perform a 30- to 60-minute interview, including the following questions:
   a. What motivated you to start your own business?
   b. How would you describe yourself to a stranger? Are you self-confident, energetic, independent? Are you an optimist, a realist, a pessimist?
   c. Which personality characteristics and abilities are essential for success as an entrepreneur?
   d. How would you describe your leadership style?
   e. Describe a typical workday.
   f. What aspects of your work do you find the most satisfying? The most frustrating?
   g. Which aspects of your work are the easiest for you? The most difficult?
   h. In which of your business's activities (operations, finance, marketing, personnel) are you most involved?
   i. How much emphasis do you place on motivating employees?
   j. What important lessons have you learned from your experience in creating and running your own business?
   k. What advice would you offer to a young, prospective entrepreneur?
4. After completing the interview, students should prepare a short (1- to 2-page) synopsis.
5. Students should be asked to share and discuss their findings in class.

BUSINESS APPLICATION

The Decision to Franchise: What Are the Concerns?

Activity:

Students will analyze the concerns an entrepreneur or several entrepreneur partners may have when contemplating a move to franchise. The time required to complete the activity is 50 minutes.

Directions:

1. Divide the class into small groups of 4 to 7 members, asking each group to appoint a recorder/spokesperson for the group.
2. Provide the class with the following background and ask them to consider pertinent concerns about a decision to franchise:
    - The owner of a pizza shop has been running this successful business from five locations within the central Florida area for the past four years.
    - Some potential investors have approached the owner about selling them a franchise to allow the investors to use the good name associated with the high quality of pizza and service.
    - The amount of money the investors have offered is very attractive to the owner and will be difficult to turn down.
3. Before the owner signs an agreement to franchise, what should the owner ask the potential buyers to agree to do? Ask each group to come up with a list of conditions the potential franchise operators will have to pledge agreement to prior to letting the franchise begin.
4. Ask each group's spokesperson to tell the class about the group's list and to explain the rationale behind each item in the list.

Note: If the groups have trouble getting conversation started, the instructor might provide the class with one item for the list. For example, the owner might insist on having the pizza made from certain brand names of flour, tomato sauce, pepperoni, etc.

NOTES

1. Adapted from Cheryl Jarvis, "When Sacrifice Equals Success," *Nation's Business* (July 1994): 14–15.
2. Robert D. Hisrich and Michael P. Peters, *Entrepreneurship* (Homewood, IL: Richard D. Irwin, 1989), 9.
3. William D. Bygrave, "The Entrepreneurial Process," in *The Portable MBA in Entrepreneurship,* William D. Bygrave (ed.) (New York: John Wiley, 1994), 1–23.
4. John H. Christy, "The Americanization of Matthais Zahn," *Forbes* (March 13, 1995): 123–124.
5. John B. Miner, Norman R. Smith, and Jeffrey S. Bracker, "Role of Entrepreneurial Task Motivation in the Growth of Technologically Innovative Firm's Interpretations from Follow-Up Data," *Journal of Applied Psychology* (August 1994): 627–630.
6. Beverly Narum, "Drypers' Cry for Name Recognition," *Houston Post* (February 27, 1995): C-2; and "Drypers Fastest-Growing Success Tale," *Houston Post* (September 25, 1993): C1, C10.
7. G. Dale Meyer, Andrew L. Zacharakis, and Julio De Castro, "A Postmortem of New Venture Failure: An Attribution Theory Perspective," in Neil

C. Churchill (et al.), *Frontiers of Entrepreneurship Research* (Sharon, MA: P&R Publications, 1993): 256–269; and "The Incredible Shrinking Failure Rate," *Inc.* (October 1993): 58.

8. Jeffrey L. Seglin, "How Can You Survive the Regulators?" *Inc.* (September 1994): 62–64.
9. Edward O. Welles, "Bootstrapping for Billions," *Inc.* (September 1994): 78–86.
10. William D. Bygrave, *The Portable MBA in Entrepreneurship* (New York: John Wiley, 1994), 244.
11. Earl G. Graves, "Black Companies Need More Revenues," *Black Enterprise* (June 1993): 210.
12. Sharon Nelton, "What I've Learned—Part Two," *Nation's Business* (May 1994): 74.
13. Stanley Kaplan, "The Staying Power of Leveraged Buy-outs", *Journal of Financial Economies* (Spring 1991): 287–313.
14. Carol Steinberg, "Turnaround," *Success* (January–February 1995): 71–77.
15. Robert M. Rosenberg and Madelon Redell, *Profits from Franchising* (New York: McGraw-Hill, 1969), 12.
16. Steinberg, "Turnaround,": 71–77.
17. Adapted from Meg Whittmore, "The Second Generation," *Nation's Business,* (June 1994): 57–65; Irene Middleman Thomas, "Formula for Success," *Hispanic* (August 1994): 60; Stephen M. Pollan and Mark Levine, "Exercising the Franchise," *Business Week* (Enterprise 1993 (Bonus Issue): 171–174.
18. Philip K. Howard, *The Death of Common Sense* (New York: Random House, 1995).
19. "Franchising in Congress and State Capitols," *Nation's Business* (January 1993): 56.

Nike: The Story and the Spirit

"We try as hard as we can to build a good company, good in every sense of the word: service, produce, advertising, charitable contributions, character, and earnings per share."—Philip H. Knight, Nike CEO

There is a well-known children's story about a struggling old shoemaker who, after spying them through his shop window, gives his last crust of bread to a group of starving, shivering little birds in the dead of winter. Unbeknownst to the old man, these are no ordinary birds, but rather shoemaker elves. As the story goes, the elves are so taken by the shoemaker's act of kindness that, as the old man sleeps that night, they work feverishly preparing hundreds of fine shoes for him to sell. It is a simple story of kindness, diligence, and doing the right thing.

The story of Nike is not unlike the children's tale of the shoemaker and the elves. Hard work, diligence, and doing the right thing are trademarks of Nike and its enigmatic CEO, Philip H. Knight. But the Nike story is better than the fairy tale, because it's real. It's a real story of ingenious marketing, in-your-face risk taking, and the establishment of a global empire through a creative approach to a simple, timeless craft—shoemaking.

The story of Nike's rise to the top of its industry is filled with lessons for virtually any business enterprise. The company began small: In 1964, Knight and a partner invested in $1,000 worth of running shoes from an unknown Japanese company and sold them out of the back of a car. Thirty years later, Nike is dominant in its industry and is one of the most recognized brands in the world. In 1994, one out of every three pairs of running shoes sold in the United States was made by Nike. An independent brand-power survey conducted in 1993 found that 77 percent of American boys between the ages of 18 and 25, if they could have any brand shoe they wanted, chose Nike. Word of the arrival of a new Nike brand in local shoe stores is often a theme of schoolyard conversations weeks in advance. Young shoppers are able to name more than two dozen new Nike models, and many of them are able to refer to the six-digit Stock-Keeping-Unit number stamped on the side of the shoe boxes. Nike has become one of the most widely known cultural artifacts of the late 20th century. In fiscal 1994, Nike sold over 100 million pairs of shoes worldwide. That is nearly 200 pairs of shoes for every minute of every day. Clearly, this is not your ordinary shoe company. The story of Nike's rise from out-of-the-trunk, entrepreneurial shoe sales to global corporation is a compelling one.

The Nike Story

The Nike story began modestly enough on the running track at the University of Oregon during the late 1950s. There, a good-but-not-great middle-distance runner, majoring in journalism, named Phil "Buck" Knight, toiled away in what was then the unglamorous sport of track and field. Knight's main claim to running fame stems from the fact that he ran on a University of Oregon four-mile relay team that included a future world record holder. For the most part, however, Knight did not stand out, and he remained one of the squad runners who excelled through sheer competitive spirit and drive. Knight was the guy who was always ready for dozens of uphill 400-yard runs at 6:00 A.M. He was coached by future U.S Olympic track team coach Bill Bowerman.

It was Bowerman who planted the intellectual seed that eventually led to the development of Nike. Bowerman grew up in the country and was known as a man of few words. He did like to complain about the American Athletics Union, and also about "people who like to sit on their butts and watch life go by." When one Oregon runner asked his coach to please explain the secret of improved performance, Bowerman barely hesitated with his response: "Run faster."

Being a fierce competitor, Bowerman constantly looked for ways to improve his runners' times. He developed training protocols such as interval runs years before the technique was adopted as standard procedure in track and field training, and he spent long days pulling apart track shoes and trying to make them lighter. Watching his athletes in the mile run, Bowerman counted the number of strides they took to complete the race. With that figure in mind, he reasoned that if he could reduce the weight of their shoes by a mere ounce, he could free his runners of having to lift some 550 pounds during the course of the race. A shoe must be three things, he preached: "It must be light, comfortable, and it's got to go the distance."

Bowerman's athletes often found him busy mixing vats of tar or grinding up tires retrieved from the junkyard for experiments. Bowerman was driven by the belief that the state-of-the-art track shoes built by Adidas—the predominant athletic shoemaker of the period—were simply not good enough. Phil Knight, who was captivated by Bowerman's vision while he ran for him at the University of Oregon, would go on to write a term paper about that vision for a course in small-business management at the Stanford Graduate School of Business.

Knight's assignment in the small-business course was to imagine a new business and describe its purpose and basic marketing plan. Knight thought about Bowerman's constant griping about the inadequacy of current running shoes. In his term paper he reasoned that, just as Japanese-brand cameras had come to replace German brands, so could a low-cost Japanese producer make high-quality running shoes. The price differential, Knight wrote, would open up a niche market.

Knight's professor in the class was impressed with the idea, but Knight didn't immediately pursue it, choosing instead to complete his major in accounting. After graduation from Stanford with his MBA, Knight was headed back to Oregon and a full-time job with Coopers & Lybrand, a Big Eight accounting firm that had a Portland office. Before starting his job, however, Knight spent the summer traveling the world, including a stop in Japan. While there, he decided to take his first entrepreneurial risk, presenting himself as a shoe salesman to the managers of the Onitsuka Company, producers of running shoes that were sold under the brand name Tiger. He toured the plant and purchased several pairs of the running shoes.

Knight brought the Tiger shoes back to Oregon and showed them to Bowerman. When the ever-critical Bowerman liked the shoes, Knight knew they could be sold in the United States. With that conviction, he and his former coach took another risk; they each invested $500 in 1,000 pairs of Tiger shoes. The year was 1964. Knight, who still worked full time as an accountant for Coopers & Lybrand, began visiting high school track meets on weekends and days off to sell Tigers out of the back of his Plymouth Valiant. He called his fledgling company Blue Ribbon Sports and stored his inventory in his mother's laundry room. ("Blue Ribbon Sports," incidentally, was the name Knight arrived at on the spur of the moment when the Onitsuka managers asked him what company he represented—another daring early move.)

By the end of the first year, Blue Ribbon Sports had sold over $8,000 worth of track shoes. Knight and Bowerman plowed all of their profits back into the company, ordering another 3,500 pairs of shoes. The two entrepreneurs were persistent in their efforts to launch their small shoe company. Finally, in 1965, Knight quit his accounting position and began to run the company out of a storefront hole-in-the-wall next to the Pink Bucket Tavern in a working-class section of Portland. The company now had two full-time employees: Knight and a competitive runner from California named Jeff Johnson. Johnson, who was hired as a full-time salesman while Knight was still working as an accountant, had a degree in anthropology from Stanford. Like other competitive runners of the time, he didn't see how he could ever hold a real job and still continue to do the one thing that really mattered in life—run. His passion for running, competitive drive, and nonconformist attitude fit in well with the personalities of Knight and Bowerman.

Johnson was typical of the type of person who came to be associated with the shoe company over the early years of its growth. None had been raised in the New England-based American shoe industry. All most of them knew about shoes was how they were supposed to feel and that a good shoe could help you win the race. The rebellious, nonconformist, entrepreneurial spirit was the company's trademark from the beginning, and it was reflected in the individual personalities of the people who worked there.

Over the last few years of the 1960s, Blue Ribbon Sports grew slowly, but steadily. Knight and Bowerman continued to invest their own money, and they were able to secure a $100,000 loan from a Portland banker for new inventory. Knight had written a letter to the banker explaining how the Japanese had created a niche market for the low-price shoes. He also stated—without explaining their business connection—that one prominent track coach, Mr. Bill Bowerman of the University of Oregon, had decided to order his $6.95 running shoes "exclusively from Blue Ribbon Sports." It was another in a growing list of risky moves by Knight, who was becoming more confident each day of the wisdom of Bowerman's early vision.

In 1969, Blue Ribbon Sports sold $1 million worth of shoes. By 1971, Knight became concerned that Onitsuka might begin to sell distributorships to others, and he decided that it was time to give some of the shoes a new name and adorn them with a separate symbol or trademark. The image of Nike came to Johnson one night during a fitful dream. "Nike" is the name of the winged Greek goddess of victory. Knight didn't particularly like the idea at first, but Johnson argued that Nike implied a sporting spirit, and that some of the most memorable names in American business had only one or two syllables and included seldom-used letters such as "X" or "K." "Look at Xerox, look at Kleenex," Johnson argued. Johnson won, and the Nike brand was born.

The Nike brand name was accompanied by a distinctive symbol, resembling a half moon, that was designed by a Portland art student. It was not until the late 1970s, however, that the name Blue Ribbon Sports was retired in favor of renaming the company for the obscure word on most of the shoes. The Nike brand, and the distinctive Nike "swoosh," are now among the most recognized corporate symbols in the world, ranking near the top with Sony and Coca Cola.

During the last half of the 1970s, Nike's sales grew from $10 million to $270 million. At decade's end, one out of every three Americans owned a pair of running shoes, and half of all running shoes owned were Nikes. The *Forbes* 1982 Annual Report on American Industry marked Nike as the single most profitable company in America over the previous five years. In fiscal 1994, Nike reported net income of $298.8 million on revenues of $3.79 *billion*. The company has also actively pursued global markets, opening stores in Europe, Asia, Mexico, and South Africa. This growth is a result of risk taking, persistent hard work, and a burning competitive desire to do things differently from the rest of the shoemaking crowd—to be nonconformist. That desire is evident throughout the company. Employees call it the Nike spirit.

CRITICAL THINKING CHALLENGE

Many companies have a difficult time going from entrepreneurial start-up to a mature, global corporation. How do you think Phil Knight can keep the entrepreneurial spirit alive in his company while at the same time competing on a global scale?

The Nike Spirit

In the mid-1960s, organizational researchers began to study organizations using the anthropological concept of culture. Today, it is a commonplace to speak of an organization's culture, and a vast body of research supports the utility of applying the concept to business organizations.

Nike's culture is dominated by a rogue spirit drawn from the anti-authoritarian impulses of the company's founders. Employees have a shared determination to work day and night for the sake of the company cause. They are equally committed to never becoming so self-serious as to lose sight of the importance of having a good time. At the base of the Nike culture, however, is a relentless commitment to sports and the athletes who play them.

The sports-mindedness of the corporate culture means that employees must follow team scores. Casual conversations among employees invariably include give-and-take about recent sporting events and players' performances. Sports knowledge can even affect hiring decisions. One candidate for a job at Nike, with a Ph.D. in a relevant field of science and a law degree, had passed several rounds of grueling interviews. Finally a member of the selection committee had one final question: "Who is Deion Sanders?" "Well, I don't really know," the candidate replied. He didn't get the job.

Many of Nike's competitors refer to Nike as "the cult" and, because Knight has created a team-based culture, to Nike employees as "the family." Indeed, as Donald Katz discovered in his study of Nike, "most Nike employees clearly imagine themselves to be elite functionaries of a company cast as a movement." In his book, *Just Do It* (New York: Random House, 1994), which is the story of "the Nike spirit in the corporate world," Katz remarked, "It's not the buildings or the work environment or the products or the ads that is the story. It's the fact that some employees go out on their own and get tattooed with a Nike Swoosh."

Nike employees refer to the corporate headquarters as "the campus" and to the world outside their headquarters as "the biosphere" or "the real world." Beyond the corporate walls lies a world that Nike "enriches" through sports products and fitness. Inside the walls lies Nikeworld, where nearly everyone is fit and healthy, where no one smokes, where the company pays employees a fee if they ride bicycles or in-line skates to work, and where it's quite typical to spend a two-hour lunch at the on-campus corporate fitness facility.

The average age of a Nike employee is 31, and the majority of the 40,000 job applicants in 1992 were younger than that. One of the videos produced by Nike for orienting new employees is titled "What It's Like to Work at Nike." The video features a number of employees who enthusiastically state that working at Nike is like:

"... a factory for fun."
"... the night after finals."
"... being in a playground."
"... coming down the face of a wave."

During orientation, new employees are introduced to important Nike values, such as: Be flexible and adaptive; stay lean and mean; challenge the status quo; use structure to promote innovation; manage with courage; fight any feeling of entitlement; be humble; and live off the land.

Without having to leave the corporate campus, Nike employees can get a haircut, do their laundry, get a massage or a complete fitness evaluation, buy Nike products, and even shop in a store for items that are made to appease spouses and children who haven't seen a hard-working loved one in a while. Life inside the company is filled with the spirit and traditions of the past and present. For example, the buildings on the Beaverton campus have names such as "The Michael Jordan Building," "The Bo Jackson Fitness Center," and so on, paying homage to the athletes and others who have helped create the company's image. Statues and giant photographs of famous athletes who have endorsed Nike products are dispersed about the campus. All these symbols serve as a reminder of what the company thinks is important, and are designed to galvanize employees to work for a common goal with an enthusiasm known as the Nike Spirit.

CRITICAL THINKING CHALLENGE

The Nike organizational culture has been identified as a key factor in the overall success of the company. What do you think is the importance of corporate culture? How do you think managers can develop a corporate culture that improves overall productivity?

Source: Adapted from Philip H. Knight, "President's Letter," *Nike Annual Report to Shareholders* (May 1994); Donald Katz, *Just Do It* (New York: Random House, 1994); Ken Hamburg, "Nike's 4th Quarter Hit Not as Bad as Expected," *The Oregonian* (July 8, 1994): E1.

PART 2

The Business Environment

C H A P T E R 4

Social Responsibility and Business Ethics

Learning Objectives

1. Explain the meaning and importance of social responsibility.
2. Trace the evolution of the consumer movement and identify the rights of consumers.
3. Outline the responsibilities business firms have to employees.
4. Describe the impact of business decisions on the environment.
5. Determine the responsibility of firms to their investors.
6. Identify ways in which firms can advance social responsibility.
7. List and describe factors influencing business ethics.

On October 4, 1992, a Boeing 747 cargo plane flown by El Al Israel Airlines lost two engines and crashed into a Dutch apartment complex. All four crew members and 39 people on the ground were killed. Ten months earlier, a China Airlines 747 freighter crashed under similar conditions, killing all five aboard. Both were cargo planes carrying heavier loads than passenger jets. And in both cases, evidence pointed to the failure of a hollow steel "fuse pin" that attaches an engine to a wing. The pins broke while the planes climbed, and the engines fell off.

Problems with the pin date back to 1979, when Boeing received reports of cracks in fuse pins. In 1980, the firm introduced a stronger pin, but some airlines opted to inspect old ones rather than replace them. The China Airlines plane was using the new pin. A third-generation stainless-steel fuse pin and stronger mountings were announced in 1993. Boeing is asking all carriers to install the stronger pin, developed using powerful supercomputers and software.

An apparent design flaw also contributed to the problem. In the original design of the 747, even the breakage of a fuse pin should not have caused a crash; the engine was expected to fall away cleanly, and the plane would be able to fly on the remaining three engines. Engineers failed to realize that if the inside engine breaks away, it could knock off the same wing's outside engine, as happened in both cases mentioned earlier.

The design flaw is costing Boeing millions of dollars, but the company says that all 747s in service today are safe and all fuse pins are either new or being inspected frequently. But some critics still ask why Boeing took so long to fix the problem. According to the president of the Aviation Safety Foundation, "They waited to act until they were forced into a bad situation." Boeing maintains it acted as quickly as possible while still being thorough and using a logical engineering approach to find a solution.[1]

Do you think Boeing acted responsibly? How far should a company go to ensure safe products?

The opening example illustrates the importance of social responsibility and business ethics. A company's reputation is an important asset.[2] Individuals and organizations making purchasing decisions expect high-quality products that are safe and free of defects. But even with the best of intentions, individuals who make up organizations are not perfect, and products have flaws. And although most of us know right from wrong and understand our responsibility to society, a strong catalyst—financial pressure—can result in an ethical dilemma.

SOCIAL RESPONSIBILITY

Social Responsibility The awareness that business activities have an impact on society, and the consideration of that impact by firms in decision making.

Business firms conduct activities to produce goods and services and to generate profits. These activities greatly affect our society. **Social responsibility** is the awareness that business activities have an impact on society and the consideration of that impact in decision making. Society expects businesses to make a profit but also to obey laws, be ethical, and be good corporate citizens.[3] Besides emphasizing profits, firms concerned with social responsibility voluntarily engage in activities that benefit society. Many, for instance, take an active role in rebuilding our public education system. A socially responsible firm makes deliberate, regular efforts to increase its positive impact on society while reducing its negative impact.

TOMORROW'S BUSINESS WORLD

Environmental Concerns Are Top Priority

Social responsibility and concern for the environment will be the issue of the next century. Leaders of 172 nations met in Rio de Janeiro in 1992 at the Earth Summit. They signed *Agenda 21,* a plan for sustaining development, conserving resources, and cutting pollution. The problems are not simple:

- World population is expected to double, reaching 11 billion by 2030. Industrial output would have to quintuple to meet the needs of all these people.
- Industrialized nations make up only 25 percent of the world's population, yet they consume 70 percent of the resources. As more nations become developed and boost economic growth, resources will be scarce.
- Seven industrial countries, including the United States, are responsible for 45 percent of human-caused greenhouse gas emissions. As developing nations industrialize, worldwide pollution will skyrocket.
- Human activities are destroying the earth's soils, forests, wetlands, and grasslands. Over 40 million acres of tropical forests are destroyed each year, and the ozone layer is thinning, increasing the potential for global warming.
- Damage to the environment costs industrialized nations 1 to 5 percent of their GDP (gross domestic product). Forest damage in Western Europe is cutting GDP in that area by $30 billion a year.

- In places like Mexico City and Eastern Europe, millions of people breathe toxic air. China will soon deplete all of its harvestable forests. The Baltic Sea is dying from sewage and other pollution.

For small businesses, these environmental concerns are a two-edged sword. Increasing concerns about the environment will mean new opportunities to develop businesses dedicated to these concerns. But environmental concerns will mean new regulations, and a pressing issue will be how small businesses will be able to afford to live with such regulations, even if they are socially worthwhile. And regulations in foreign countries may be even more strict than U.S. regulations, placing an added burden on firms doing business overseas.

Source: Adapted from Emily T. Smith, Mary Beth Regan, and Patrick Oster, "One Year After Rio: The U.S. Waves a Green Flag," *Business Week* (June 14, 1993): 90–92; Special Advertising Section, *U.S. News & World Report,* 1992; and Emily T. Smith, "Growth vs. Environment," *Business Week* (May 11, 1992): 66–75.

Today many firms practice social responsibility in various ways. Warner-Lambert, Ford, Liz Claiborne, and many other companies participate in "Take Our Daughters to Work," an event sponsored by the Ms. Foundation for Women. The purpose of the event is to allow girls ages 9 to 15 to trail their mothers and fathers at work and get a glimpse of the work world.[4] Newman's Own, a food company founded by actor Paul Newman, donates all profits to charities in the United States. Working Assets Money Fund offers investors a chance to invest in a mutual fund according to their beliefs; it screens companies and excludes any with a history of environmental or discrimination violations, military contracts, or involvement in nuclear power plants. JC Penney sponsors awards for outstanding community volunteers in many areas where its retail stores are located. McDonald's has switched from

Participation in the annual "Take Our Daughters to Work" event, which affords girls an opportunity to get a look at the world of work, is one way in which firms practice social responsibility.

disposable to reusable containers for Happy Meal boxes, napkins, and paper towels. The fast-food giant also stopped using cups and containers made of polystyrene, which is not biodegradable.

Practicing social responsibility costs money. But failing to emphasize social responsibility also has its costs, whether in fines, increased regulation, negative publicity, public disfavor, or loss of customers. Consumers, special interest groups, and the general public are aware of the impact of business on society and expect firms to do more than try to make profits. Most managers today regard the costs incurred in practicing social responsibility as a necessary part of doing business.[5]

Social responsibility raises many challenging questions for business firms. To whom are we responsible? How far should we go to satisfy our customers and achieve organizational objectives? Will our decisions affect any segments of society that we have not considered? Decision makers in every type and size of firm must address many such questions, which rarely have simple answers. Business activities have an impact on consumers, employees, the environment, and those investing in the firm, as Exhibit 4.1 shows. Socially responsible firms weigh the consequences of their decisions on these different

Exhibit 4.1
Social Responsibility Concerns of Business

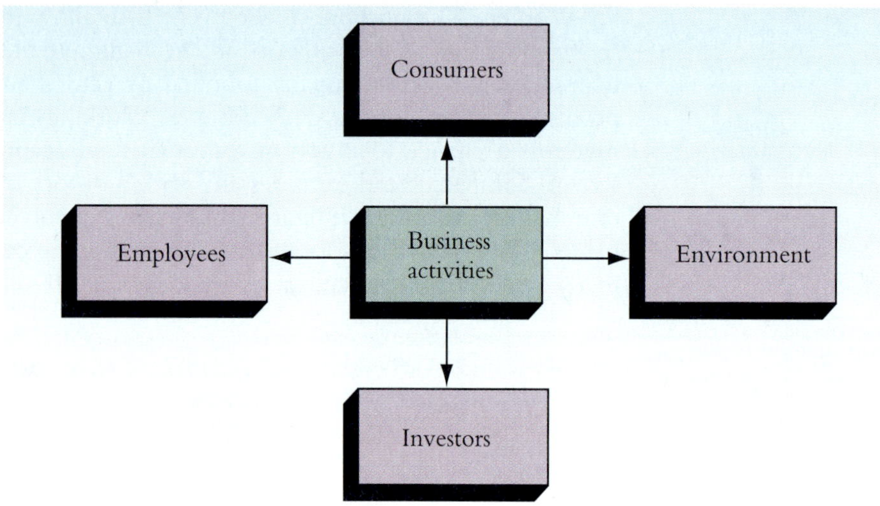

concerns. To understand how firms try to achieve an acceptable balance, let's look more closely at each of these concerns.

RESPONSIBILITY TO CONSUMERS

When you make a purchase, you cast a vote for a product and indicate your approval of the product and the company providing it. If you are satisfied with the product, you will buy and use it again and maybe recommend it to your friends.

Firms trying to succeed provide products that satisfy the needs of their customers, since dissatisfied customers eventually take their business elsewhere. But a company also needs to consider how customers view the firm itself. Increasingly customers are looking beyond a firm's goods and services, evaluating its policies and actions and taking action in the marketplace. For instance, consumers can consult a book called *Shopping for a Better World,* which rates 168 companies and more than 1,800 products according to social responsibility issues. The guide is published by the Council on Economic Priorities, a 20-year-old research group. It includes categories such as environmental protection, involvement in weapons production (especially nuclear arms), promotion of females and minorities into upper-level management, availability of employee benefits such as corporate day-care centers, and charitable contributions.

When firms engage in practices that individuals or special-interest groups oppose, consumers sometimes boycott products to convey their dissatisfaction. Groups have organized boycotts of table grapes to protest the poor working conditions of migrant farm workers; boycotts of coffee brands that include Salvadoran coffee beans to protest Salvador's policies and violent events there; and boycotts of certain fruits and vegetables to protest pesticide use.[6]

Consumerism
Activities of individuals, groups, and organizations aimed at protecting consumer rights.

Pressure from consumers and special-interest groups has prompted many business firms to adopt socially responsible policies. **Consumerism** includes the activities of individuals, groups, and organizations aimed at protecting consumer rights. Consumer groups perform many activities, including testing and reporting on the safety and performance of products and service firms, informing the public and government officials of consumer issues, and advocating legislation.

Although many people think of the consumer movement as a 1960s phenomenon, consumerism actually originated with the Industrial Revolution. The rapid growth in the production of goods between 1870 and 1900 led to poor working conditions, the sale of harmful food and drugs, and false advertising. Shocking conditions in various industries were exposed in books such as Upton Sinclair's *The Jungle,* which chronicled dangerous working conditions and unhealthy practices in the meat packing industry. Subsequently the Consumers' League was formed in New York City, followed by several other consumer groups.

The consumer movement gained momentum during the 1920s and 1930s. During the Great Depression, many consumers blamed business firms for joblessness and difficult economic times. Concern with product safety grew, and independent testing groups such as Consumer Research formed. High school classes in home economics began to emphasize consumer rights.

Interest in consumerism peaked again in the 1960s, when consumer advocates such as Ralph Nader called attention to abuses by business firms. During this time, President John F. Kennedy established the consumer "bill of rights," which includes the right to safety, the right to be informed, the right to choose, and the right to be heard. These four rights underlie many of the goals espoused by people and organizations active in consumerism today.

The Right to Safety

The most basic consumer right is the right to products that are safe to possess and use. To ensure safety of goods, manufacturers should test them and provide buyers with explicit directions for use. In 1972 the federal government created the Consumer Product Safety Commission (CPSC) to monitor the safety of thousands of products sold to consumers. Many state and local agencies also regulate product safety.

Industries in the United States have made great strides in product safety, but more progress is needed. Products that are defective or dangerous damage public confidence in a company's ability to serve society. For instance, consumers have become concerned with electromagnetic fields and their possible link to cancer, reducing the public's confidence in utility companies and certain products such as cellular phones and electric blankets. Although the evidence linking electromagnetic fields to cancer is not conclusive, many industries have yet to address public fear in a convincing manner. The cellular phone industry has spent more than $1 million on research, which has validated the findings of existing studies showing cellular phones to be safe.[7]

Automobiles, appliances, children's toys, and many other products are safer today than they once were. Product packages have also been made more tamper resistant. But instances of chemicals found in foods, such as apples treated with alar (a chemical linked to cancer) or bottled water with traces of benzene (a dangerous chemical used in cleaning fluids), illustrate that safety problems continue.

The Right to Be Informed

Consumers have the right to receive the information available about a product before they purchase it. Customers seeking a loan from a bank or other financial institution, for example, should be told of all costs and repayment terms associated with the loan. Necessary information for foods includes ingredients and detailed instructions for use. To aid shoppers making decisions in the supermarket, new FDA package labeling rules that went into effect in 1994 require food makers to adopt uniform labels for their products. The labels give consumers more information about nutrition content and limit health claims that can be made.

Consumers also have the right to know whether or not the product has any limitations or problems. In one case, regulators in Florida and a dozen other states are investigating whether Metropolitan Life Insurance Company agents sold life insurance to nurses while calling it a retirement plan.[8] Failing to describe an insurance product as insurance is not only misleading, it is prohibited by state consumer protection laws. The Food and Drug Administration requires that eye drops be labeled as such and sold in small bottles, fearing that larger bottles could be dropped in a contact lens wearer's eye. But the tiny bottles of Bausch & Lomb Sensitive Eyes Drops cost $5.65 ($5.65 per ounce), while a larger bottle of the identical Sensitive Eyes Solution costs $2.79 ($.23 per ounce).[9]

The Right to Choose

Consumers have the right to choose and make purchases from a variety of products at competitive prices. They also have the right to expect quality service at a fair price. Consumer demand for pesticide-free foods, for example, has resulted in a movement to grow vegetables and fruits without chemicals. Thousands of farmers are experimenting with different methods of crop rotation and greater use of natural materials to control insects and increase productivity. If the experiments are successful, consumers will have the choice they desire.

The Right to Be Heard

Consumers also have the right to have their opinions considered in the formation of government policies and in business firms' decisions that affect them. A number of large firms have established consumer affairs departments to address consumer concerns. Many, including Little Tykes (toys), General Electric (appliances), Nabisco (foods), and Beecham (toothpaste and other personal care products), provide toll-free telephone numbers as an easy way for consumers to ask questions, make comments, and register complaints. Small businesses may not have reason or resources to establish hot lines or hire personnel specifically for consumer relations. But small-business owners and managers can set up procedures and train employees to invite consumer comments, answer questions, and handle complaints.

Responsible firms of all sizes attempt to address customer complaints in a satisfactory manner. For instance, many consumers complained to telephone companies about huge bills racked up when their children and teenagers called national numbers prefixed by 976 and 900. Such numbers reach party-line services, recorded sports scores, weather information, and even pornography (see Case 4.1). In response to customer complaints, some telephone companies now offer an option called call blocking, which prevents a customer's phones from making a connection with any number beginning with 900 or 976.

RESPONSIBILITY TO EMPLOYEES

Like consumers, employees hold certain expectations of business firms. They expect safe working conditions, fair compensation, equal opportunities, and adequate benefits (e.g., health insurance, vacation, and time off to care for sick children). Employees also want to know what is going on in the company and want managers to be responsive to problems or complaints. Firms aware of their responsibility to the people who work for them make every effort to meet these expectations.

Safety in the Workplace

Occupational Safety and Health Administration (OSHA) A federal agency with the primary purpose of ensuring safe working conditions.

In 1970 Congress passed the Occupational Safety and Health Act, which created the **Occupational Safety and Health Administration (OSHA).** Charged with the primary purpose of ensuring safe working conditions, OSHA has established many standards with which employers must comply. OSHA covers all employees except those working for government bodies and those covered by specific employment acts such as the Coal Mine Health and Safety Act. Under OSHA regulations, firms failing to protect the health of their employees can be held criminally liable.

OSHA employs 1,000 field inspectors who make unannounced inspections of workplaces during normal working hours. Field inspectors concentrate their efforts in the most hazardous industries, such as construction and manufacturing. Firms with health or safety violations may be fined; the individuals responsible can receive prison terms. With more than 5 million workplaces to oversee, however, OSHA cannot identify every violation.

In many states, candy distributors hire young children to sell candy door to door, sometimes late at night. An 11-year-old girl was hit and killed by a car in Washington state while selling candy alone on a school night at 10 P.M., 160 miles from her home. The Labor Department in Miami fined Burger King $500,000, the largest child labor penalty in history, for letting 14- and 15-year-olds work late on school nights; the Fair Labor Standards Act of 1938 prohibits children this age from working after 7 P.M.[10]

TQM

Many firms realize that responsibility for employee safety lies with them, not with a government agency. They adopt and carry out their own health and safety programs. Managers often face a balancing act to keep the workplace safe yet continually improve efficiency. At its Camry assembly plant in Georgetown, KY, Toyota is striving to cut its injury and illness rate to half the national auto industry average. The company emphasizes safety training to avoid repetitive-motion injuries, which result from performing the same stressful arm or hand motions over and over, and other injuries. Toyota tries to match workers to jobs physically so they do not work in areas for which they are too tall or too short. It has restructured workstations to eliminate awkward motions, improved job rotation so workers do not perform the same tasks all day, and analyzed every job in the plant to determine which ones are likely to produce injuries. Levis Strauss goes one step further, insisting that its contractors, regardless of where they are located, adhere to strict standards regarding minimum age of employees, plant safety, and healthy working conditions.[11]

Equality in the Workplace

Equal Employment Opportunity Commission (EEOC) A federal agency whose purpose is to increase job opportunities for women and minorities.

Individuals also expect to be treated equally in the workplace. The Civil Rights Act of 1964 guarantees equal employment opportunities for all people, regardless of age, race, sex, religion, or national origin. This act established the **Equal Employment Opportunity Commission (EEOC),** a federal agency whose purpose is to increase job opportunities for females and minorities, who are defined by the EEOC as African Americans, Hispanics, Asian or Pacific Islanders, American Indians, or Alaskan natives. The EEOC can file legal charges against companies that discriminate in their hiring practices.

Nonetheless, some inequalities still exist. Although female and minority workers are being hired by some companies, they have generally been denied the needed experience to attain top-level positions. In some cases, females, minority workers, and people with disabilities earn less than white males, even when they perform the same work. In other cases, females and minorities continue to find it difficult to land certain jobs. For instance, female golfers find that many golf clubs hire only male pros. While women represent 22 percent of all U.S. golfers who play regularly, they account for only 6 percent of all accredited U.S. golf professionals.[12]

Sexual Harassment

Sexual Harassment Unwelcome advances and requests for sexual favors that affect a person's performance, and a hostile work environment in which employees are subjected to sexual comments, jokes, or materials.

Employees also have a responsibility to ensure a working atmosphere free of **sexual harassment,** defined by the EEOC as unwelcome advances and requests for sexual favors that affect a person's performance, and a hostile work environment in which employees are subjected to sexual comments, jokes, or materials. According to a recent Harris poll, 18 percent of all workers—31 percent of women and 7 percent of men—say they have experienced sexual harassment at work.[13] Examples of controversies that have placed sexual harassment in the limelight include the Tailhook incident in which male Navy officers harassed female officers and civilians at their national convention; professor Anita Hill's testimony at the Clarence Thomas Supreme Court confirmation hearings in the Senate and a subsequent book that claims to tell the real story; and the accusation by Paula Jones that she was harassed by President Bill Clinton when he was governor of Arkansas.

The number of complaints filed with the EEOC doubled in the five years from 1988 to 1992 and continues to rise. Many cases are settled out of court, with costly consequences for corporations. Research shows that 90 percent of Fortune 500 companies have dealt with sexual harassment complaints; such complaints cost the average large corporation $6.7 million a year.[14] The cost to victims, in terms of dignity and productivity, is unmeasurable.

Harassers are not always men, though it is estimated that nine of ten are males. In 1993, a jury awarded $1 million to a man harassed by his female supervisor in Los Angeles.[15] Often, harassment is subtle and difficult to prove. Conversely, false accusation of sexual harassment has proven difficult to defend.[16]

Many companies have policies stating exactly what is considered sexual harassment and that it won't be tolerated. But for a policy to work, employees must understand it. This requires communicating sexual-harassment guidelines to everyone and even providing training seminars or workshops on the subject. Large firms like Du Pont, Federal Express, and Levi Strauss have designed such programs.

To ensure that sexual-harassment guidelines are understood by everyone, many business firms provide training seminars or workshops.

Managing Cultural Diversity

Another major challenge facing leaders today is managing a diverse work force. In 1987, the Hudson Institute published *Workforce 2000: Work and Workers for the 21st Century*.[17] This landmark study opened the eyes of corporate America to the reality that dramatic changes are taking place in the work force. The study projected that 25 million people would join the U.S. work force between 1987 and 2000; only 15 percent of these new workers would be white males, almost 61 percent would be female, and 29 percent would be minorities (minority females were counted twice).

As a result, employers will have to train, manage, and motivate a work force composed of individuals with widely varying backgrounds and perspectives.[18] In the past, managers had to decide how to manage a predominantly white, male work force. Managing diversity requires various activities related to recruiting, hiring, and effective use of people from different cultural backgrounds.[19] Programs must be developed to promote both the awareness of cultural differences and positive attitudes toward these differences. Human resources managers must develop bias-free systems to recruit, train, and promote individuals from diverse backgrounds. Work itself will also have to be restructured, since it has been structured in terms of males in the past.[20] For instance, restructuring will include more flex time so women can have children and also advance their professions; women comprise about half the work force.

Cultural Diversity Differences between and within cultures.

Cultural diversity refers to differences between and within cultures. Any leader that sincerely values cultural diversity must make it safe for everyone in the organization to talk about these differences. This means a change for those organizations that have been denying that differences exist while meeting EEOC or affirmative action guidelines. Valuing diversity looks at the multicultural work force from a positive perspective rather than from a defensive position. Valuing diversity views people as having equal rights while being different and encourages the open discussion of these differences of gender, age, ethnicity, physical ability, and so on.[21] Diversity-awareness training programs can help bring these differences out into the open and identify the unique characteristics and talents of diverse individuals that are a resource for the organization. Valuing diversity also requires that organizations be responsible for providing products to various races and cultures. Toy companies, for instance, are manufacturing multicultural products such as ethnic doll varieties.[22]

While cultural diversity brings stimulation, challenge, and energy, it does not always lead to harmony.[23] A mix of genders, cultures, and alternative lifestyles can lead to conflict and misunderstanding. The job of the manager is to create an environment where differences are appreciated and where a group of diverse individuals works productively together. This is a formidable challenge, but organizations who meet this challenge face a brighter future. Diversity awareness will not work without the commitment of top executives, and unless it is a business objective.[24]

Other Responsibilities to Employees

The Family Medical Leave Act, which went into effect in the United States August 5, 1993, mandates unpaid leave for child care and other family and personal needs. The law covers employers with at least 50 employees; eligible employees must have worked about 25 hours a week for one year. The law provides up to 12 weeks unpaid leave after birth or adoption. It also allows unpaid leave to care for a child, spouse, or parent, or when an employee is too ill to work. Employees receive health benefits during the leave, and are given the same jobs in terms of pay and responsibilities upon returning.[25]

Some organizations also have taken active steps to train the hard-core unemployed. These are individuals with little training or few skills and a long history of unemployment. The National Alliance of Businessmen, for instance, works to train such individuals so they can find and keep jobs. This effort helps people gain dignity and become productive members of society; it also reduces the burden on the nation's welfare system and adds trained individuals to the work force. Firms can take a progressive step by providing programs or extra training to quality persons who want to work.

RESPONSIBILITY TO THE ENVIRONMENT

The public is concerned with the impact of business on the environment in the United States and around the world. Earth Day 1990 raised public concern for the environment to a new level and began what many people believe will be the decade of the environment. Socially responsible managers join consumers in this concern and take active measures to protect our environment.

Pollution Contamination of air, water, and land.

One vital environmental concern is **pollution,** the contamination of water, air, and land. Concern for the environment also involves conserving scarce natural resources and curbing the use of those which damage the environment. As with other social concerns, laws and regulations play a critical part in environmental issues. The Environmental Protection Agency (EPA), created by the national Environmental Policy Act of 1970, is the federal agency charged with enforcing laws designed to protect the environment.

Water Pollution

Water pollution is caused by dumping toxic chemicals, sewage, and garbage into rivers and streams. Toxins and pollutants from buried industrial waste can also find their way into underground water supplies. A recent concern is the liberal use of agricultural fertilizers and pesticides, which drain into water supplies. Environmental laws such as the Water Quality Improvement Act of 1970 and the Water Pollution Control Act Amendment of 1972 regulate pesticides, but prosecutions are rare. Even in California, which the EPA considers the toughest state for pesticide regulation, growers and large agribusiness firms that break pesticide laws are rarely prosecuted. Critics attribute this to the fact that in most states pesticide regulation is handled by the state department of agriculture, whose main task is to help and protect farmers. Millions of Americans have unsafe water supplies. Many other areas of the world including Japan, the former Soviet Union, Brazil, and India, are experiencing water pollution.

Air Pollution

Air pollution is caused by carbon monoxide and hydrocarbons that come from motor vehicles and by smoke and other pollutants from manufacturing plants. The Clean Air Act of 1970 and the 1977 Clean Air Act Amendment provide stringent emission standards for automobiles, airplanes, and factories. The Clean Air Act Amendment of 1990 requires that motor vehicles be equipped with Onboard Systems to control about 90 percent of refueling vapors. Devices such as catalytic converters have been developed to help control air pollution.

Much progress has been made in fighting air pollution, but with air quality below federal standards in about 60 metropolitan areas and the number of vehicles on the roads up 70 percent since 1970, environmentalists are calling for tougher regulation of auto emissions and better fuel efficiency. Automakers expect more emission controls to be required by both federal and state regulations.

Many scientists fear that the earth's ozone layer, which shields the planet from the sun's deadly ultraviolet rays, is being destroyed, with a *global warming trend* as a result. Scientists believe the major cause is chlorofluorocarbons (CFCs), used to cool refrigerators and air conditioners and to manufacture some plastic foam containers. Evidence of this threat is stronger than ever.

The National Aeronautics and Space Administration, along with scientists from several institutions, completed a study of the earth's atmosphere. They reported that the ozone layer over some regions, including the northernmost parts of the United States, Canada, Europe, and Russia, is temporarily depleted by as much as 50 percent.[26] The United States and more than 80 other nations agreed to halt the production of CFCs after 1995.[27]

Air pollution also has been attributed to *acid rain.* When sulfur dioxide is pumped into the air (often by manufacturing and power plants burning high-sulfur coal) and mixes with moist air, rain with an acid content is created. Damage to forests and lakes in the eastern United States and Canada has been blamed on acid rain.

Land Pollution

Land pollution results from strip mining of coal and minerals, forest fires, garbage disposal, and dumping of industrial wastes, including chemicals and medical supplies such as used hypodermic needles. Land pollution often results in water pollution because toxic wastes drain into water supplies. Of the 6,750,000 square miles of the earth's original forests, only about 40 percent remains. Global forest destruction extends from the Pacific Northwest of the United States to the tropical rain forests of Brazil and Malaysia.[28] If forests are not managed properly, commercial timber harvesting, fuel source use, and cattle ranching threaten to destroy forests even further. In addition, deforestation contributes to soil loss, which exceeds new soil formation by over 25 billion tons annually. Congress created a $1.6 billion Superfund in 1980 to help cover the costs of cleaning up polluted land, although criticism about inefficiencies in administering the fund has Congress looking at the program.[29] The Resource Conservation and Recovery Act of 1984 requires federal regulation of potentially dangerous solid-waste disposal. Solid waste—the term for trash and garbage discarded by homes, businesses, and factories—includes paper and cardboard, grass clippings and leaves, food wastes, metals, glass, plastics, textiles, leather, wood, and rubber.

Recycling
Reusing materials such as paper, plastic, glass, and aluminum to make other products.

Businesses and government organizations face the problems of where to dispose of solid waste and how to do so safely. Many used products and containers do not have to go to the dump; they could be recycled. **Recycling** involves reusing materials to make other products. Newspapers, office paper, cardboard boxes, aluminum, tin cans, glass and plastic containers, and even motor oil can be recycled to reduce the drain on resources and the costs of producing new products and containers, and to slow the need for more and bigger landfills. The number of landfills in the United States, once over 14,000, is expected to drop to about 1,800 in the next decade.[30] Aluminum beverage cans are the most recycled containers in the United States. Many firms conduct recycling programs within their organizations. They build the market for recycled materials by buying and using such products whenever possible. They also help educate consumers and encourage them to recycle.

Along with consumers and special-interest groups, many business firms and government bodies are trying to solve problems of garbage disposal and land and water pollution. Exhibit 4.2 shows an advertisement explaining

Exhibit 4.2
DuPont's Plastics-Recycling Program: Largest in the United States

DuPont's plastic recycling program. A major refiner in Houston, Lyondell Petrochemical, has started making gasoline from used motor oil.[31] The U.S. and Mexican governments are working together on the pollution problem inside Mexico's border with the United States, where some factories burn tires for fuel. The region has been described by the American Medical Association as a "virtual cesspool."[32] Economists working for the United Nations and the Environmental Defense Fund are trying to link countries with vastly different economies and environmental laws into a single pollution-control system.[33] The government is also learning that publicizing the names of polluters sometimes works better than laws at cutting toxic releases of U.S. manufacturers, which have fallen since the EPA began publishing the names of firms along with data on their toxic releases.[34]

These are just a few examples, and the results may seem small in comparison to the size of the problem, but they represent steps in the right direction.

It will take the ongoing participation of every individual and firm and cooperation from the governments of all nations to reverse the current threats to the environment.

Green Marketing

Although many firms openly embrace environmentalism, they are learning that to be considered an environmentalist requires moving beyond the law and ahead of the industry. Danger exists at two levels: (1) damage to local environments, such as from toxic waste dumping, which leaves the earth unable to support living organisms, and (2) damage to global systems of climate, atmosphere, and food resources, which are breaking down as a result of pollution. As the previous sections pointed out, global systems already in danger include the ozone layer, rain forests, and topsoil.

Green Marketing
Efforts by firms to move beyond the law to provide environmentally sound goods and services in areas ranging from conservation to pollution control.

Green marketing includes many areas ranging from conservation to control of pollution. For instance:

- Procter & Gamble now sells Tide Refill for powder detergents. A refill carton slips into the original box for a 50-percent waste reduction.
- Church & Dwight is testing 98-percent phosphate-free Arm & Hammer automatic dishwashing detergent in mid-Atlantic markets.
- Scott Paper is testing Scotties Recycled, a tissue made from 100 percent recycled paper, in the Midwest.
- 3M is introducing Scotch-Brite Never Rust wool soap pads made from recycled plastic fiber.[35]

Corporations that excel in green marketing hope to benefit from better relations with customers, regulators, suppliers, and other firms in their industry. Companies such as AT&T, Apple Computer, Church & Dwight, Clorox, and Digital Equipment rank high in developing products and processes that are friendly to the environment.[36] Firms that choose to ignore the environment face loss of profits and market share. Although this is difficult to prove, most experts agree that as environmental regulations tighten, forward thinking will pay off. That is why 3M decided to comply with a new federal regulation for underground storage tanks by 1992, when compliance was not required until 1998. Many firms are finding that the longer they wait to deal with regulations, the more it costs. In short, firms are realizing that green marketing adds to the bottom line. It is especially important for products having an effect on the environment that is easily seen, such as lawn and garden products, household cleaning products, and paper products.[37]

To have a successful green marketing program, a company must have the commitment of top-level management as well as an internal environment that encourages employees to act as environmentalists. Some companies have established new positions, such as vice president of environment, health, and safety. Others reward employees for reducing waste or developing new products that are less harmful to the environment. But green marketing can also be abused by firms that are not socially responsible. The popularity of environmentally sound products has led to concerns that firms may make exaggerated claims about products to show their concern for the environment.

As individuals become more committed to the environment, green products will gain a competitive edge. But because environmental claims have been used to mislead consumers, some firms are finding it difficult to launch a green marketing program successfully.[38] In addition, consumers have not responded well to some green products because of the confusing language that surrounds the products. *Recyclable, recycled, degradable, biodegradable, environmentally friendly,* and *ozone safe* are examples of terms that are often misunderstood. Successful green marketing requires being as precise as possible to enable consumers to understand the claims made in the message. Phrases like "this product contains 60 percent recycled material" should be used rather than "friendly to the environment." If a package cannot realistically be recycled, manufacturers should not call it recyclable.

As a result, some firms have retreated from making environmental claims about their products, even though they continue to develop products and packages that are better for the environment.[39] Part of the reason is that firms do not know which claims violate which state laws; to date, there are no federal standards regulating green marketing. Price is also a big concern, since green products typically cost more than competing brands, sometimes considerably more. Consumers prefer green products when they are readily available and their price and quality are similar to those of other products. But even environmentally conscious people will balk at paying quite a bit more for green products. Despite these problems, many believe that in the long run companies that demonstrate concern for the environment will be rewarded.

RESPONSIBILITY TO INVESTORS

Business firms also have a responsibility to the people who invest money in them. Many investment-related abuses have come to light in recent years. The public, government regulatory agencies, and many business leaders are concerned with problems such as mishandling of investors' funds, insider trading of stocks, and excessive compensation of executives.

Proper Management of Funds

Firms have a responsibility to manage funds properly and return a fair profit to investors. Investment scams have probably existed since people started using money. The United States saw many during the California Gold Rush in the 1800s, when scores of hapless investors bought worthless mines. In recent years, some investors have been equally unfortunate. They have discovered that their money went for gold mines or oil wells that did not exist, resorts or hotels that were never built, or new business ventures that never got off the ground. Drug chain Phar-Mor filed for bankruptcy after a massive fraud scheme, including the falsification of its books by $350 million.[40]

Unscrupulous firms today take advantage of computerized dialing and low telephone rates to reach unsuspecting consumers and trick them out of hundreds of millions of dollars each year. The Securities and Exchange Commission handles investors' complaints of hundreds of *penny stock scams*. In these scams, operators offer stock in a company for only a few dollars a share or even less. But usually the companies are mere shells, with no operations or revenues. To sell the stock to clients, the scam operator employs telephone salespersons trained to be smooth-talking and persuasive. As sales take off, the stock's value skyrockets to several dollars a share. But when investors try to collect their money, they find their holdings are worthless.

Mishandling of funds goes beyond penny stock scams. Managers have a responsibility to investigate their investments thoroughly and to present all facts and risks to investors clearly. When mismanagement causes investors to lose large sums of money, the results can be disastrous, especially for small investors who put their life savings into a risky venture on the advice of a trusted stockbroker or financial adviser. Prudential-Bache Securities, which uses the slogan "rock solid, market wise," gained the confidence of numerous investors. But when the firm marketed real estate limited partnerships the managers and account executives knew little about and the funds lost millions of investors' dollars, Prudential-Bache lost many investors and became embroiled in numerous lawsuits by investors to regain their money.[41] When investors lose confidence in a firm, they find another place to invest their money.

Access to Information

Insider Trading The practice of buying and selling stock on the basis of information gained through positions or contacts with others that is not available to other investors or the general public.

Firms have the responsibility to make financial information available to all potential investors. **Insider trading** occurs when individuals buy and sell stock on the basis of information gained through their positions or contacts with others that are not available to other investors or the general public. Such information, known only to a few insiders, gives them an unfair advantage over typical investors. Stock purchases by officers of a corporation, for instance, often precede a merger or sale that leads to temporary increases in the value of the stock.

Certain laws prohibit insider trading, and the Securities and Exchange Commission prosecutes individuals found violating them. Two widely publicized cases involve former Wall Street traders Ivan Boesky and Michael Milken. Boesky, who used insider information to accumulate a fortune of \$250 million, was fined \$100 million and sentenced to three years in prison. Milken, after pleading guilty to felonies involving his dealings with Boesky and others, was sentenced to ten years in prison and three years of full-time community work, the most severe penalty ever handed down for a white-collar crime case. He was fined \$600 million by the government and also faced hundreds of millions of dollars in civil judgments. With Milken's harsh sentence, the judge wanted to raise the penalty for white-collar crime and deter others on Wall Street from insider trading and other violations.

Executive Compensation

Executives who run firms carry tremendous responsibility and deserve to be compensated accordingly. But some people question whether executives of large corporations are now being paid too much. By orchestrating the turnaround of the Walt Disney Company, chairman Michael Eisner earned more in one year than the founder of IBM (Tom Watson Sr.) and the founder of General Motors (Alfred P. Sloan) earned in their entire careers. Exhibit 4.3 lists the 10 highest-paid chief executives in the United States.

According to a *Business Week* survey, the average total compensation for a U.S. chief executive officer (CEO) in 1993 exceeded $3.8 million.[42] The gap between executive pay and the pay others earn is widening dramatically and causing resentment. For instance, in 1960 a large-company CEO averaged an annual salary of $190,383, 41 times that of a factory worker's average pay ($4.667). In 1993, the CEO's average pay had grown to a figure of 149 times that of an average factory worker.[43] In contrast, Japanese CEOs earn an average one-fourth of the pay of their U.S. counterparts.[44] Some experts in the area of executive pay are predicting a revolt on the part of investors and consumers.

A fair compensation program should reward executives for outstanding performance. In fact, some executives might be considered underpaid when you look at the performance of their companies. Raymond J. Noorda of Novell received relatively low pay—$522,000—for a three-year period in which his company gave shareholders a 152 percent return on their investment.[45] But executive compensation is not always directly linked to performance, a fact that concerns many investors. For instance, of the chief executives included in the *Business Week* study, Heinz chairman Anthony O'Reilly gave shareholders a low return relative to his pay; he took home over $114 million in salary and stock options from 1991 to 1993 while the market price of their stock fell.[46] Although the problem has no easy solution, some suggest linking executive pay more closely to company performance and requiring full disclosure of executive earnings to investors.

Exhibit 4.3
The 10 Highest-Paid Chief Executives

	Company	**Compensation***
1 Michael D. Eisner	Walt Disney	$203,011,000
2. Sanford I. Weill	Travelers	52,810,000
3. Joseph R. Hyde, III	Autozone	32,220,000
4. Charles N. Mathewson	International Game Technology	22,231,000
5. Alan C. Greenberg	Bear Stearns	15,915,000
6. H. Wayne Huizenga	Blockbuster Entertainment	15,557,000
7. Norman E. Brinker	Brinker International	14,925,000
8. Roberto C. Goizueta	Coca-Cola	14,513,000
9. C. Robert Kidder	Duracell International	14,172,000
10. Thomas M. Hahn Jr.	Georgia-Pacific	13,680,000

* Includes salary, bonuses, and long-term compensation.

Source: Adapted from *Business Week* (April 25, 1994): 53.

ADVANCING SOCIAL RESPONSIBILITY

Many firms recognize the importance of social responsibility and take steps to see that their policies and activities make a positive impact on society. They practice social responsibility through programs of community support, self-regulation, and social audits.

Community Support

Business firms throughout the United States provide support for a wide variety of activities designed to improve their communities. Both large and small businesses contribute to the arts, build parks, donate equipment to schools, and sponsor academic scholarships. Some sponsor social programs to help the disadvantaged. For example, pharmaceutical manufacturer Lederle Laboratories recently conducted a health care program for homeless people. The program provided antibiotics for homeless individuals and funding to develop health care programs. Many community activities could not start up or continue without the support of business.

Some firms enable employees to share their time and talent with their communities. IBM, for example, lends engineers to teach in schools. Others provide company time, materials, or facilities for employees active in community organizations. Businesspeople also participate in the Rotary, Kiwanis,

Many business firms provide support for community projects as a way of practicing social responsibility. The Los Angeles marathon is one example.

Junior Achievement, and other groups that raise money for local projects or help youngsters. Firms are major contributors to charities and encourage employees to donate to organizations such as the United Way, which distributes donations among many diverse social agencies operating in an area. Through such activities, the business sector makes a significant contribution to society.

Self-Regulation

The business community can also advance social responsibility by establishing standards of conduct and ensuring that firms follow them. One of the best-known self-regulatory agencies is the *Better Business Bureau,* a nationwide organization with local branches supported by local firms. The bureau's purpose is to help consumers settle problems with specific firms. Although the Better Business Bureau does not possess strong enforcement powers, it does maintain records of consumer complaints and warns consumers through local media when a firm is engaging in deceptive or questionable practices. More than 140 bureau branches operate today in the United States. Another active self-regulatory agency is called the *National Advertising Review Board* (NARB). NARB screens national advertisements for honesty and handles complaints about deceptive ads. If a firm refuses to comply with its directives, the NARB may publicize the incident or file a complaint with the Federal Trade Commission.

Many other industries, trade associations, and professional organizations establish self-regulatory programs. For example, the U.S. cable television industry, faced with complaints about service and prices, has established standards for cable companies to follow to guarantee better service. Exhibit 4.4 lists the standards set by the National Cable Television Association.

Businesspeople generally prefer self-regulation to that imposed by the government. The guidelines established within an industry are often more realistic than those established by the government. Self-regulatory programs usually cost less to put into place than does government regulation. The main drawback of self-regulatory programs is that sometimes they are difficult or impossible to enforce. Complying with standards is often voluntary (as is the case with the cable TV industry). When firms comply with the standards, self-regulation can be an effective way to foster social responsibility. When business behaves on the assumption that if it is not illegal then it is ethical, the government eventually responds with a host of laws and regulations.[47]

The Social Audit

Social Audit
A systematic review of an organization's performance of social responsibility activities.

Some firms conduct a systematic review of their performance of social responsibility activities through a social audit. A **social audit** looks at the firm's short- and long-run contributions to society. Activities reviewed might include community involvement, product safety, and the impact of business practices on the environment.

With information from a social audit, managers can evaluate how effective the current programs are and decide whether they should initiate new

Exhibit 4.4
National Cable Television Association Standards

- Companies should state clearly on bills what services a customer is receiving and how much they cost.
- Customers should be given a month's notice when a company is going to raise rates.
- Telephone calls should be answered within 30 seconds.
- A customer should receive a busy signal less than 3 percent of the time a cable company office is open.
- A company should respond to service interruptions within 24 hours in situations not beyond its control, within 36 hours otherwise.
- If an installer or technician is running late, an attempt must be made to contact the customer to set up a new appointment.

Source: National Cable Television Association

courses of action. Some firms spend millions of dollars each year on social responsibility activities; they need to determine whether they are spending their money wisely. Although a social audit is more informal than an accounting audit, it can be a useful tool in accessing social responsibility.

BUSINESS ETHICS

Ethics
The principles of behavior that distinguish between right and wrong.

Business Ethics
The evaluation of business activities and behavior as right or wrong.

Social responsibility requires individuals engaging in business endeavors to behave in an ethical manner. **Ethics** are principles of behavior that distinguish between right and wrong.[48] Ethical conduct conforms with what a group or society as a whole considers right behavior. People working in business frequently face ethical questions. **Business ethics** is the evaluation of business activities and behavior as right or wrong. Ethical standards in business are based on commonly accepted principles of behavior established by the expectations of society, the firm, the industry, and an individual's personal values.

With unethical business practices often receiving publicity, the public sometimes believes that people in business are less ethical than others in society. But ethical problems challenge all segments of our society, including government, churches, and higher education. For instance, college basketball players bring in millions of dollars every year for universities, coaches, television networks, and sports announcers; yet many of those athletes do not receive an education. Also, universities and professors have been accused of abandoning undergraduate students while professors pursue grants, conduct research, and participate in academic politics to further their careers and promote their universities. Such situations could destroy the trust society holds in higher education and may lead to close scrutiny of university policies and practices.

Most business leaders realize their firms cannot succeed without the trust of customers and the goodwill of society. A violation of ethics makes trust and goodwill difficult, if not impossible, to maintain.[49] In thousands of companies, executives and employees act according to the highest ethical standards. Robert Haas, the chief executive of Levi Strauss, believes the organization should be an ethical creature capable of making profits and making the world a better place in which to live.[50] Unfortunately, managers in some firms behave unethically, and these instances are often highly publicized. Fiat, Italy's largest company, became involved in a highly publicized scandal when top-level executives were implicated in making payments to leading Italian politicians and their parties. The company was already facing business problems, and its share of the Italian market slumped to a record low of 44 percent.[51] Personnel executives say the major reason managers behave unethically is to obtain power and money. But significant costs result from unethical behavior, in the form of reduced sales and loss of goodwill.[52] In this section, we examine the various factors influencing ethical behavior and discuss how firms can encourage ethical behavior.

Factors Influencing Ethical Behavior

To encourage ethical behavior, executives, managers, and owners of firms must understand what influences behavior in the first place. Exhibit 4.5 presents several factors that affect individuals' behavior in business: the business environment, organizational factors, and an individuals' personal moral philosophy.

The Business Environment. Almost daily, business managers face ethical dilemmas resulting from the pressures of the business environment. They are challenged to meet sales quotas, cut costs, increase efficiency, or overtake competitors. Managers and employees may sometimes think the only way to

Exhibit 4.5
Factors Influencing Behavior in Business

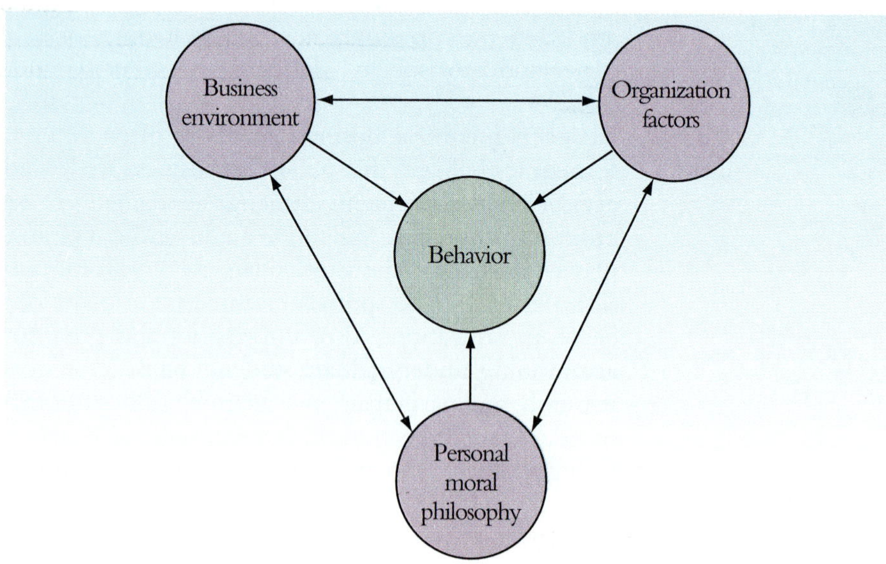

survive in the competitive world of business is by deception or cheating. In some instances, an organization may use someone else's successful work without the permission of the owner or originator. Chase Manhattan, a large New York bank, sued advertising agency J. Walter Thompson for copying an advertisement. The suit charged that J. Walter Thompson got ideas when competing with other agencies for Chase's $35 million global campaign and used them to develop advertisements for Northwestern Mutual Life Insurance Co.[53]

Conflict of interest is another common ethical problem stemming from the business environment. Often an individual has a chance to further selfish interests rather than the interests of the organization or society. To gain favor with people who make purchasing decisions for their companies, a seller may offer special favors or gifts, ranging from a meal to clothing to trips. Some offer cash—a kickback—for putting through a contract or placing orders with a company. Others offer bribes. Such illegal conduct damages the organization in the long run. In order to limit unethical behavior, business firms must begin by expecting their employees to obey all laws and regulations.

The international business environment presents further ethical dilemmas. Businesspeople and government officials in other countries and cultures often operate according to different standards than those held in the United States. Firms doing business internationally sometimes have separate ethical standards for domestic and international operations.

The Organization. The organization itself also influences behavior. Individuals often learn ethical or unethical behaviors by interacting with others in the organization. An employee who sees a superior or coworker behaving unethically may follow suit. In the Iran-Contra trial, Oliver North defended himself by saying that his actions (including shredding documents and withholding information from investigators), although unethical, were expected by his superiors. A simply stated directive from the person at the top can set the tone in an organization. In fact, an employee's perceptions of peers and superiors in an organization are often a stronger prediction of behavior than is the employee's own system of moral and ethical values.[54]

An organization can also use rewards to influence the behavior of its members. If an individual is rewarded or is not punished for behaving unethically, the behavior will probably be repeated. Likewise, the threat of punishment and the lack of reward for unethical activities encourage ethical behavior. The severity of punishment also sends a message to other individuals who might be considering similar activities. For example, the National Collegiate Athletic Association (NCAA) has placed member institutions on probation for violating recruiting rules. Teams on probation have been barred from tournament games and from having games televised and have had limits placed on scholarships. These penalties should discourage other university athletic programs from violating NCAA rules.

Moral Philosophy
The set of principles that dictate acceptable behavior.

The Individual. A person's own moral philosophy also influences his or her ethical behavior. A **moral philosophy** is the set of principles that dictate acceptable behavior. These principles are learned from family, friends, coworkers, and other social groups and through formal education. The Your Values and Attitudes will help you evaluate your moral philosophy.

YOUR VALUES AND ATTITUDES

Evaluating Ethical Behavior

Directions: Below are a number of statements that involve ethical decisions you may have to make when conducting business. Circle the number that represents your level of agreement with each statement.

	Strongly Disagree					**Strongly Agree**
1. It is OK to take supplies such as pencils and paper home from a company office.	1	2	3	4	5	6
2. I would break a company rule if my coworkers did.	1	2	3	4	5	6
3. If it meant getting ahead, I would take credit for someone else's work.	1	2	3	4	5	6
4. I would not turn in a fellow employee for breaking a company policy.	1	2	3	4	5	6
5. If I made a mistake that could hurt the company, I would cover it up to avoid being reprimanded.	1	2	3	4	5	6
6. I would not mind breaking a law to get a promotion, as long as I did not get caught.	1	2	3	4	5	6
7. I would be willing to provide customers false information to make a sale.	1	2	3	4	5	6
8. I see no problem with taking longer than necessary to do a job and then billing a client for the extra time.	1	2	3	4	5	6
9. It is OK to take care of personal business on company time.	1	2	3	4	5	6
10. I would call in sick to take a day off work.	1	2	3	4	5	6

Feedback: How are your ethical standards? Although the situations are hypothetical, they present typical business decisions. For items circled 1 or 2, you considered these behaviors unacceptable; 3 or 4 indicates you are uncertain or indifferent; and 5 or 6 suggests you believe these activities are acceptable.

Some people view the activities listed as common practices. Doesn't everyone take pens and paper home from the office? Yet many companies prohibit such actions. Some of the activities, such as misleading customers or covering up mistakes, can result in serious penalties. If you believe most of the activities are unacceptable, you have a solid ethical base from which to work. If you found most of these activities acceptable, think about them again. It may seem as though people must do such things to succeed in business. We hope that is not true.

Humanistic Philosophy
A set of moral principles focusing on individual rights and values.

Utilitarian Philosophy
A set of moral principles focusing on the greatest good for the largest number of people.

In developing a moral philosophy, individuals can follow two approaches: humanistic and utilitarian. The **humanistic philosophy** focuses on individual rights and values. Individuals and organizations adopting this philosophy would honor their moral duties to customers and workers. If a product poses harm to workers or customers, it is taken off the market. Individuals and organizations following the **utilitarian philosophy** seek the greatest good for the largest number of people. Pharmaceutical manufacturers who make the vaccine for pertussis, the deadly disease of whooping cough, adhere to this philosophy. Some children react to the killed bacteria in the vaccine, which is administered three times in the first two years of life. Reactions include fevers, persistent crying, and temporary unresponsiveness. The vaccine has been blamed for severe brain damage in a few children, although several studies dispute this. Despite these problems, because so many children benefit from the vaccine, doctors continue to administer the current version while researchers work on new pertussis vaccines. Today's Business World examines GM's philosophy in deciding not to recall pickup trucks.

TODAY'S BUSINESS WORLD

How Much a Life?

In 1993, the federal government requested that GM recall 4.7 million pickup trucks equipped with "side-saddle" gasoline tanks. But many experts think that for more than two decades the National Highway Traffic Safety Administration's (NHTSA) evaluation of the GM trucks has been mishandled. By seeking a billion-dollar recall, regulators responded to pressure from trial lawyers and the Washington, DC-based Center for Auto Safety.

GM decided to fight back. GM general counsel Harry Pearce and his colleagues took on critics at press conferences and public forums. They demanded an apology from NBC after the producers of *Dateline* admitted that a demonstration of a GM truck bursting into flames was rigged for the show. GM got the apology, and three NBC producers and the network's news division head resigned. GM refused to voluntarily recall the 4.7 million trucks.

The vehicle in question is the C/K pickup, made between 1973 and 1987. At issue is whether it is more prone than competitors' trucks to catch fire in side-impact collisions because its gas tank is located on the side of the truck outside the frame. The company maintains that the trucks are safe. Overall, their fatal-crash rate is only marginally higher than Ford or Chrysler trucks of the same class. But statistics used by the NHTSA and the Insurance Institute for Highway Safety show that fatal side-impact crashes with fires occur 2.5 times more frequently in GM's trucks than in Ford's or Chrysler's. Statistics also show that fatal side-impact collisions with fires dropped significantly in GM trucks built after 1988, when the gas tanks were moved inside the frame. GM officials, when pressed, don't deny that their trucks have a higher fatality rate in side-impact collisions that result in fires.

The real question GM faced was how much the firm should spend to save a few lives a year. By some estimates, if all 4.7 million trucks were to remain on the road for the next 10 years, 50 to 60 people would die in the pickups. As crass as it sounds, if a recall cost $1 billion, each life saved would cost GM $16 to $20 million.

Worried about weaknesses in the government's case for a recall, the Justice Department reached a surprise settlement with GM in late 1994. The agreement called for GM to spend $51 million over five years on a variety of vehicle-safety programs. To say the least, GM was satisfied, considering the potential cost of a recall. And the company continues to maintain that its trucks are no less safe than the competition in side-impact collisions.

Should a life be reduced to dollars and cents? Whom do you think GM should represent: company officials, stockholders, or customers?

Source: Adapted from Daniel Pearl and Gabriella Stern, "Driving a Bargain," *The Wall Street Journal* (December 5, 1994): A1; Andrew Evan Serwer, "GM Gets Tough with Its Critics," *Fortune* (May 31, 1993): 90–97; and Douglas Lavil and Bruce Ingersoll, "Is U.S. Recall Request on GM Trucks Driven by Safety or Politics?" *The Wall Street Journal* (April 29, 1993): A1, A4.

Encouraging Ethical Behavior

Many organizations take positive steps to encourage ethical behavior. Some offer courses in ethics and include ethics in training programs. Most courses and training seminars focus on how to analyze ethical dilemmas. The emphasis is on understanding why individuals make the decisions they do rather than on teaching ethics or moral principles.

Code of Ethics
A statement spelling out exactly what an organization considers ethical behavior.

An organization can also encourage ethical behavior through a code of ethics.[55] A **code of ethics** is a statement specifying exactly what the organization considers ethical behavior. Many firms, as well as trade and professional associations, have established codes of ethics. For instance, the American Medical Association has its own code of ethics that limits the amount and types of advertising used by doctors. By enforcing codes of ethics, rewarding ethical behavior, and punishing unethical behavior, a firm limits opportunities to behave unethically.

Whistle-Blower
An employee who informs superiors, the media, or a government regulatory agency about unethical behavior within an organization.

Employees of an organization can also encourage ethical behavior by reporting unethical practices. **Whistle-blowers** are employees who inform their superiors, the media, or a government regulatory agency about unethical behavior within their organization. Whistle-blowers often risk great professional and personal danger by reporting the unethical behavior of others. They may be harassed by coworkers or supervisors, passed up for promotions, fired, or even threatened with damage to their property or harm to themselves or their families. Nonetheless, some organizations have developed plans that encourage employees to report unethical conduct and that provide protection for whistle-blowers.

Efforts to encourage ethical behavior will be effective only with the support of top-level management. Employees base their decisions on the guidelines and examples set by their superiors. Management must set the proper tone by never compromising ethical behavior in its dealings with customers, employees, and competitors.

SUMMARY OF LEARNING OBJECTIVES

1. ***Explain the meaning and importance of social responsibility.*** Social responsibility is the deliberate effort of a firm to increase its positive impact on society while reducing its negative impact. In light of many publicized instances of corruption and illegal behavior, the public, special interest groups, and consumers are making increasing demands that business firms demonstrate social responsibility.

2. ***Trace the evolution of the consumer movement and identify the rights of consumers.*** The consumer movement began with the Industrial Revolution, when many workers faced unsafe conditions and consumers were exposed to harmful products. The movement gained momentum during the 1930s, the time of the Great Depression, and peaked again in the 1960s. During this time, President Kennedy established the consumer "bill of rights," including the right to safety, the right to be informed, the right to choose, and the right to be heard.

3. ***Outline the responsibilities business firms have to employees.*** Firms have a responsibility to provide safe working conditions, fair compensation, equal opportunities, and adequate benefits for employees. The Occupational Safety and Health Administration monitors conditions in the workplace. The Equal Employment Opportunity Commission works toward increasing job opportunities for females, minorities, and handicapped people.

4. ***Describe the impact of business decisions on the environment.*** Business decisions have a profound impact on the environment. Business activities can cause pollution, the contamination of the environment—water, air, and land. The Environmental Protection Agency sets standards and monitors compliance among business firms and industry. Socially responsible firms and consumers take active measures to reduce pollution.

5. ***Determine the responsibility of firms to their investors.*** Firms have a responsibility to provide information to investors and to act prudently in managing funds, as well as to compensate executives fairly. Recent problems, including the mishandling of investors' funds, insider trading, and excessive compensation for executives, have contributed to a loss of money and trust on the part of investors.

6. ***Identify ways in which firms can advance social responsibility.*** Firms can advance social responsibility in many ways, such as supporting programs to improve communities where they are located. Some firms and industries participate in self-regulation to encourage good business practices. Others review their performance of social responsibility activities through social audits.

7. ***List and describe factors influencing business ethics.*** Socially responsible businesspeople behave in an ethical manner. The business environment, the organization, and an individual's own moral philosophy influence ethical and unethical behavior. Firms can encourage ethical behavior through education and by developing and enforcing codes of ethics.

KEY TERMS

Social Responsibility
Consumerism
Occupational Safety and Health Administration (OSHA)
Equal Employment Opportunity Commission (EEOC)
Sexual Harassment
Cultural Diversity
Pollution
Recycling
Green Marketing
Insider Trading
Social Audit
Ethics
Business Ethics
Moral Philosophy
Humanistic Philosophy
Utilitarian Philosophy
Code of Ethics
Whistle-Blower

QUESTIONS FOR DISCUSSION AND REVIEW

1. What is social responsibility? Why is it important for businesses to act in a socially responsible manner? What is the cost of social responsibility?

2. What is consumerism? Trace the evolution of consumerism to the present. Where does the consumer movement stand today?

3. What rights are guaranteed in the consumer "bill of rights"? Give an example of each and explain how firms can see that consumer rights are guaranteed.

4. How can a firm ensure that it meets its responsibility to its employees?

5. What is cultural diversity? Why is it important to manage diversity? What skills will managers need to be successful in a diverse work force?

6. Describe the three major types of pollution. Who is responsible for protecting and preserving the environment? Can the trend toward environmental damage be reversed?

7. How can green marketing help the environment? What are some of the barriers to a successful green marketing program?

8. Describe several ways in which business firms can advance social responsibility. Find three examples of firms demonstrating social responsibility in your community.

9. What factors help determine whether a business manager will behave ethically or unethically? Give an example of how each factor might influence ethical behavior.

10. List specific actions a firm could take to encourage ethical behavior. Which do you believe would be most cost effective?

CASE 4.1

Dialing 900 Numbers

Imagine coming home from work to a $2,000 phone bill. First you place an angry call to your telephone company to say there's something wrong with your bill. Then the person at the phone company informs you that your bill is indeed correct; there really is a 900-666-PORN. When you get off the phone, you find the guilty party: your 12-year-old child.

This scenario happens over and over again. Every day more than a million people dial numbers prefixed by 900 and 976 to hear jokes, sports, news, stock reports, and much more. Estimates of annual revenue from such dial-up services exceed $300 million a year. More than $50 million is spent on dial-a-porn services that offer sexually explicit messages. Many of the callers are children and teens.

Parents and other concerned groups, the Federal Trade Commission, and Congress are proposing regulation of dial-a-porn services. Conveying pornographic messages to minors or nonconsenting adults over telephone lines is already prohibited by the Federal Communications Act. But many observers believe that banning dial-a-porn may be unconstitutional. Therefore lawmakers are considering a plan that requires phone companies to offer a free service that would allow customers to block their phones from access to 900 or 976 exchanges. The FTC has been asked by attorneys general from 18 states to toughen proposed regulations for the advertising, billing, and operation of 900 numbers. Proposals include a ban on 900-number services aimed at children under 12 years of age unless they are educational.

In many instances, telephone companies are accused of promoting pornography since they provide the 900 and 976 dial-up exchanges for companies to use. Several local telephone companies have introduced plans to block calls to porn lines because of complaints by consumers. Bell Atlantic plans to block all porn lines in Pennsylvania and Maryland. Customers could unblock the services by writing to the telephone company. New York Telephone plans to offer call blocking for a one-time charge of $5. Most local companies are dealing with customer complaints by enabling them to block access to 900 and 976 numbers. But blocking can also hurt firms offering legitimate services.

American Telephone & Telegraph Company has threatened to drop its 900 exchange if Congress requires call blocking. AT&T claims it does not have the computer software to handle such a task. Antipornography advocates do not believe blocking will be effective, since kids can simply find another telephone. Some argue that the telephone companies should refuse to call dial-a-porn services.

The law governing dial-a-porn services is unclear and varies by state. A federal appeals court in Atlanta upheld a decision by Southern Bell to disconnect dial-a-porn services in Atlanta and Miami. However, a federal district court in California stopped Pacific Bell from disconnecting porn services. Because of the large sums of money involved, this issue will not be resolved without a lengthy fight.

Questions for Discussion

1. Should the government be involved in the regulation of dial-a-porn services? Why?
2. If they can do so legally, should telephone companies refuse to carry dial-a-porn services?
3. Should telephone companies be required to block dial-a-porn or other services upon request from customers? If so, should the consumer pay a fee for blocking or should the telephone company pick up the expense?
4. Do you think it is the responsibility of the firms involved to keep children from accessing dial-a-porn services? Why or why not?

Source: Adapted from Jeanne Saddler, "Politics & Policy: Rules to Regulate '900' Phone Service Proposed by FTC," *The Wall Street Journal* (March 10, 1993): A16; "Marketing & Media: Attorneys General Seek Tougher Rules Over 900 Numbers," *The Wall Street Journal* (April 13, 1993): C13; Bob Davis, "Proposed Curbs on Dial-a-Porn Are Seen Reducing Access to All Dial-Up Services," *The Wall Street Journal* (March 30, 1988): 21; Christopher Elias, "Dialing for Cash and Controversy," *Insight* (August 15, 1988): 44–45; "Get Off the Telephone," *Time* (August 1, 1988): 25.

CASE 4.2

Environmental Problems Facing the Commonwealth of Independent States

The old Soviet Union is gone, but it won't be forgotten soon. Through 74 years of mismanagement, its Communist regime left behind a legacy of environmental damage that threatens neighboring Europe and Asia and requires billions of dollars for cleanup.

The Soviet empire once spanned one-sixth of the earth, and the environmental problems it left equal its magnitude. Says a spokesperson for the Washington, DC-based Natural Resources Defense Council, "If we don't deal with [Commonwealth of Independent States] environmental problems now, we won't have to worry about dealing with economic problems." Germany and France are pushing the world's leading industrial nations to pledge billions of dollars in environmental aid beyond the $24 billion in economic assistance they have already promised.

Russia and other former Soviet republics need help not only with cleanup but also with stopping ongoing environmental destruction. A Western diplomat in Moscow describes the Commonwealth of Independent States (CIS) as a "big polluting machine." Cars lack catalytic converters and pollute the air with leaded gasoline. Hundreds of factories pour waste into the Gulf of Finland and the Neva River, from which the Russian city of St. Petersburg gets its drinking water—contaminated by untreated sewage. CIS households, with smaller homes and fewer appliances, use 90 percent less energy than do Western households. But factories and the oil and gas industries produce vast amounts of waste products and environmental nightmares. Manufacturing, designed without the environment in mind, uses more than four times as much energy per unit of GDP as in the United States. Malfunctioning and old equipment, the lack of spare parts, poor workmanship, and shabby repairs regularly produce immense blowouts, leaks, and spills in the oil and gas industry throughout the former Soviet Union.

A horrendous disaster occurred in March 1992 near Tashkent, the capital of Uzbekistan, when drillers struck oil at a well in the Fergana Valley oil fields but could not control the flow. Oil shot hundreds of feet into the air, filling the sky with black slime and smoke for 62 days. After a month, Uzbek officials called in Oklahoma-based Cudd Pressure Control to seal off the well. Before it was finally controlled, the well had thrown out as much as 6.2 million barrels of oil, which soaked into nearby cotton fields or burned off in the air. Uzbekistan officials never said how severe the damage was, and neither did the U.S. Environmental Protection Agency, which sent a technical team to the site at the Uzbekistan government's request. Experts estimate the oil spill to be some 24 times the amount spilled by the *Exxon Valdez* in Alaska. The loss from this well alone cost the Uzbeks about $130 million, as well as untold environmental damage.

The Fergana Valley spill, although the worst reported, is but one of many disastrous incidents in recent years. One blowout near the Caspian Sea blazed for a year before it was controlled. A gas pipeline explosion several hundred miles south of Moscow resulted in the deaths of 607 people when sparks from passing trains ignited the leak. In western Siberia, a break in a rusted oil line leaked three million barrels of oil into the ground and caused 27 wells to be shut down. Moscow officials have admitted that 26,000 ruptures occurred in 1989, spilling 4.3 million barrels of oil.

Over 370,000 miles of oil and gas pipelines cross through the former Soviet Union. Many stretches of pipeline, as well as compressors, need to be repaired or replaced. Some German consultants estimate that the principal gas lines are leaking almost 10 percent of their annual production and local connecting networks are losing up to 40 percent of their load. The loss far exceeds Germany's entire yearly gas requirement. Leaking pipelines are said to have cost the former Soviet republics some $8 billion in lost oil and gas revenues in 1991.

The greatest danger to the outside world lies in the CIS nuclear energy program. Of the 37 existing reactors, which provide 12 percent of the commonwealth's energy, at least 15 are poorly designed and should be taken out of operation. The reactors' slowness to cool during emergencies can cause the core to explode, which is what happened at the Chernobyl plant in 1986. The aftermath of that explosion was felt throughout Europe. Nearly $180 million of agricultural products had to be destroyed in Finland, Sweden, and Norway. In Britain, some 1,350 miles away, the sale of sheep was banned until radioactive isotopes they may have consumed while grazing had dissipated. The radioactive contamination that fell on Europe is expected to cause about 6,000 more cancer deaths over the next 50 years. More than 2.5 million acres of farmland in the Ukraine and Belarus were never properly cleaned up, and radioactive food occasionally shows up in markets.

"Radioactive contamination is our number one problem," says Alexei Yablokov, a scientist and adviser to Russian President Boris Yeltsin. The problem sites are numerous. Around Chelyabinsk, the former Soviet Union's top-secret nuclear weapons production site, radioactive wastes have been dumped in local lakes and rivers since 1950. *The Bulletin of Atomic Scientists* estimates that you could get a lethal dose of radiation in less than an hour just by standing on the bank of the once-beautiful Karachia Lake. Officials tried to seal off the Techa River by surrounding it with barbed-wire fencing, but radioactive waste has been found where the river empties into the Arctic Ocean 100 miles away. For 30 years, the Soviet navy dumped nuclear waste in the Barents Sea in a known fishing area several hundred miles from the Norwegian coast. Because the protective barrels floated, the Soviets punctured them so they would fill with water and sink.

If other nations provide financial assistance, there will be many opportunities for companies that can help with environmental cleanup and restructuring. U.S. companies make the gas turbine power plants that should replace the deficient Russian nuclear reactors. Conoco, in bidding to develop a 100-million-barrel oil field, sent environmentalists to recommend ways to drill without harming forests. Other Western firms can provide help in disposing of nuclear and other hazardous wastes, controlling air and water pollution, and bringing nuclear reactors up to global safety standards. The Ukrainian government will be taking bids for a contract to finally bury the still-hot Chernobyl plant, now encased in a giant tomb that was never fully sealed.

Questions for Discussion

1. What was the concept of social responsibility within the Soviet Union, a socialist state?
2. How does a nation's system of government, general economic condition, and cultural traditions affect the degree of social responsibility its organizations display? Cite examples of various countries.
3. Why must governments, business organizations, and citizens of other countries of the world be concerned with changing the dreadful environmental situation in the CIS? Should other countries pay to clean up the huge mess and get industries there on the right track?

Source: Adapted from Richard C. Morais, P. Pietsch, and Christoph von Schoeller, "Blow-out," *Forbes* (July 20, 1992): 65, 68; Paul Hotheinz, "The New Soviet Threat: Pollution," *Fortune* (July 27, 1992): 110–114; and Associated Press, "Sewage Is Found Pouring into River Used for Russian City's Drinking Water," Lexington, KY, *Herald-Leader* (September 17, 1992): A8.

EXPERIENTIAL EXERCISE

Viewing Pollution Control Practices

Purpose:

To provide students with the opportunity to observe the pollution control practices of corporate plants within the college's regional area. Groups should be given three weeks for completion of task, and approximately 20 minutes for class reporting.

Directions:

1. Divide the class into four to five smaller groups, with each group expected to conduct an on-site visit/interview with a local corporate plant or other facility. The instructor should contact the local pollution control department and request the names of both companies with excellent pollution control practices and those corporations with poor pollution code violation records. Two of the class's small groups should visit companies with excellent reputations and the remaining groups should visit those with poor records of violations.
2. Each group needs to elect a leader to contact company officials, set up the interview/visit, take notes, and report back to the class at large following the plant visit.
3. During the plant visits the student groups should seek to determine information such as:
   - The types of pollution often associated with firms in the particular industry.
   - The company's pollution code violations history, both long-term and recent past.
   - The company's efforts to correct pollution control problems or to minimize the chance for pollution problems to occur.
   - Future plan for pollution control programs or practices of the company.
4. Following the plant visits each group should be provided up to 20 minutes of class time to share their information with the class.

BUSINESS APPLICATION

Codes of Ethics

Contact an organization or professional in your area to find out whether the organization or individual has a code of ethics. (Suggestions: bank, investment company, radio or television station, newspaper, real estate company, insurance agency, lawyer, physician.) Ask questions such as these:

1. Is a written code of ethics in effect at your organization or in your profession? For how long? If not, has there been any move to establish one?
2. Who established the code of ethics—someone inside the organization or perhaps an industrywide committee?
3. What issues are covered in the code of ethics? (Obtain a copy, if possible.)
4. How is the code of ethics enforced in your organization or profession?
5. What influence has the code of ethics had on the ethical behavior of employees in the organization or profession?

NOTES

1. Adapted from Stewart Toy, "That Sinking Feeling at Airbus," *Business Week* (July 18, 1994): 49–50; Mark Lewyn, Dori Jones Yang, Neal Sandler, and Stewart Toy, "Boeing: For Want of a Pin," *Business Week* (July 5, 1993): 96–97; and William M. Carley, "Mystery in the Sky," *The Wall Street Journal* (April 26, 1993): A1.
2. Christopher L. Tyner, "New Chairman Prepares the Ethics Resource Center for the 21st Century," *Ethics Journal* (Winter 1994): 1, 4–5, 7.
3. Archie B. Carroll, "The Pyramid of Corporate Responsibility: Toward the Moral Management of Organizational Stakeholders," *Business Horizons* (July–August 1991): 39–48.
4. Lori Bongiorno, "Big Ideas for Little Girls," *Business Week* (May 3, 1993): 38–39.
5. Margaret A. Stroup and Ralph L. Neubert, "The Evolution of Societal Responsibility," *Business Horizons* (March–April 1987): 22–24.
6. William Mueller, "Who's Afraid?" *American Demographics* (September 1990): 40–43.
7. David Kirkpatrick, "Do Cellular Phones Cause Cancer?" *Fortune* (March 8, 1993): 82–89.
8. Greg Steinmetz, "Met Life Got Caught: Others Sent Same Letter," *The Wall Street Journal* (January 6, 1994): B1, B6.
9. Mark Maremont, "Eyeway Robbery?" *Business Week* (February 27, 1995): 48.
10. Brian Dumaine, "Illegal Child Labor Comes Back," *Fortune* (April 5, 1993): 86–95.
11. D. Kirk Davidson, "Marketers Can't Ignore New Ethics Issue," *Marketing News* (February 27, 1995): 34.
12. Elizabeth Lesly and Lori Bongiorno, "Women Golfers Have a Handicap, All Right," *Business Week* (April 19, 1993): 94.
13. Humphrey Taylor, "Sexual Harassment in the Workplace," *The Lane Report* (July 1994): 22.
14. Anne B. Fisher, "Sexual Harassment," *Fortune* (August 23, 1993): 84–88.
15. Fisher, 84–88.
16. Julie Amparano Lopez, "Control the Damage of a False Accusation of Sexual Harassment," *The Wall Street Journal* (January 2, 1994).
17. William B. Johnston and Arnold E. Packer, *Workforce 2000: Work and Workers for the 21st Century* (Indianapolis, IN: Hudson Institute, 1987).
18. Patricia W. Hamilton, "What a Changing Work Force Means for Business," *D&B Reports* (January/February 1992): 20–23.
19. Taylor H. Cox and Stacy Blake, "Managing Cultural Diversity: Implications for Organizational

Competitiveness," *Academy of Management Executive* (August 1991): 45–56.

20. Tim Turner, "A Woman for All Seasons: An Interview with Betty Friedan," *Hemispheres* (August 1993): 19–23.
21. Charles Garfield, *Second to None* (Homewood, IL: Business One Irwin, 1992), 286–291.
22. Michael Wilke, "Toy Companies Take Up Diversity Banner," *Advertising Age* (February 27, 1995): 1, 8.
23. Faye Rice, "How to Make Diversity Pay," *Fortune* (August 8, 1994): 78–86.
24. Lee Gardenswartz and Anita Rowe, *Managing Diversity* (Homewood, IL: Business One Irwin, 1993), 4.
25. Michele Galen, "Sure, "Unpaid Leave' Sounds Simple, But . . . ," *Business Week* (August 9, 1993): 32–33.
26. Michael D. Lemonick, "The Ozone Vanishes," *Time* (February 17, 1992): 60–63.
27. Scott McMurray, "Air-Conditioner Firms Put Chill on Plans to Phase Out Use of Chlorofluorocarbons," *The Wall Street Journal* (May 10, 1992): B1, B4.
28. Nancy C. Morey and Robert V. Morey, "Business and the Environment in the 21st Century," *Business Forum* (Winter 1992): 51–55.
29. Mary Beth Regan, Joseph Weber, Chris Roush, and Kevin Kelly, "Toxic Turnabout?" *Business Week* (April 25, 1994): 30–31.
30. Tim Triplett, "Economics Meets Geology as Recycled Paper Matures," *Marketing News* (February 28, 1994): 17.
31. Caleb Solomon, "Refiner Begins Making Gasoline from Used Oil," *The Wall Street Journal* (February 11, 1993): B1–B2.
32. Dianna Solis and Sonia L. Nazzario, "U.S., Mexico Take on Border Pollution," *The Wall Street Journal* (February 25, 1992): B1, B8.
33. Jeffrey Taylor, "New Rules Harness Power of Free Markets to Curb Air Pollution," *The Wall Street Journal* (April 14, 1992): A1, A4.
34. Mary Beth Regan, "An Embarrassment of Clean Air," *Business Week* (May 31, 1993): 34.
35. Jennifer Lawrence, "Recycled Products Sprouting Again," *Advertising Age* (May 10, 1993): 12.
36. Faye Rice, "Who Scores Best on the Environment," *Fortune* (July 26, 1993): 114–122.
37. Peter Stisser, "A Deeper Shade of Green," *American Demographics* (March 1994): 24–29.
38. Gary Levin, "Green Marketing Gets Cautious," *Advertising Age* (July 5, 1993): 4.
39. Howard Schlossberg, "Reports Says Environmental Marketing Claims Level Off," *Marketing News* (May 24, 1993): 12.
40. Zachary Schiller, "Wait a Minute—Phar-Mor Is Still Kicking," *Business Week* (March 8, 1993): 60–61.
41. Chuch Hawkins and Leah Nathan Spiro, "Pru Securities Isn't Secure Yet," *Business Week* (September 7, 1992): 82–84.
42. John A. Byrne, Lori Bongiorno, and Ronald Glover, "That Eye-Popping Executive Pay," *Business Week* (April 25, 1994): 52–58.
43. Byrne, Bongiorno, and Glover, 52–58.
44. Robert Neff, "What Do Japanese CEOs Really Make?" *Business Week* (April 26, 1993): 60–61.
45. Byrne, Bongiorno, and Glover, 52–58.
46. Byrne, Bongiorno, and Glover, 52–58.
47. C.J. Silas, "The Moral Dimension of Competitiveness," *Ethics Journal* (Summer/Fall 1994): 1, 3.
48. Vern E. Henderson, "The Ethical Side of Enterprise," *Sloan Management Review* (Summer 1982): 8.
49. Vernon R. Loucks Jr., "A CEO Looks at Ethics," *Business Horizons* (March–April 1987): 4.
50. Russell Mitchell and Michael O'Neal, "Managing by Values," *Business Week* (August 1, 1994): 46–52.
51. John Rossant, "Fiat's Right Turn," *Business Week* (May 3, 1993): 38.
52. Gene R. Laczniak and Patrick E. Murphy, "Fostering Ethical Marketing Decisions," *Journal of Business Ethics* (April 1991): 259–271.
53. Laura Bird, "Thompson Is Named in Copycat Lawsuit," *The Wall Street Journal* (July 13, 1992): B3.
54. O.C. Ferrell and Larry Gresham, "A Contingency Framework for Ethical Decision Making in Marketing," *Journal of Marketing* (Summer 1985): 87–96.
55. O.C. Ferrell and Steven J. Skinner, "Ethical Behavior and Bureaucratic Structure in Marketing Research Organizations," *Journal of Marketing Research* (February 1988): 103–109.

CHAPTER 5

Business, Law, and Government

LEARNING OBJECTIVES

1. List the sources from which laws are derived.

2. Outline the court system in the United States.

3. Identify the various categories of business law.

4. Discuss how government regulates business activities to encourage competition.

5. Explain the effects of deregulation on business.

6. Describe how taxation supports the activities of government.

Until early 1992, breast implants represented a $90 million market. Dow Corning Corporation, in Midland, MI, was a major manufacturer of silicone breast implants. Since the mid-1970s, 600,000 women have received silicone implants made by Dow Corning. Although some recipients chose implantation as part of reconstruction after breast cancer surgery, about 80 percent opted to enlarge their breasts for purely cosmetic reasons.

But questions about the safety of silicone gel implants began to arise as women reported that implants erupted or leaked inside the body and caused health damage. Lawsuits bombarded implant makers, especially Dow Corning. In December 1991, a San Francisco jury agreed with an implant recipient that Dow Corning knowingly sold her a defective implant. The woman, whose suit said that leaking silicone had damaged her immune system, was awarded $7.3 million. Although the only previous verdict against the company, for $1.7 million, occurred in 1984, Dow Corning has quietly settled several cases. Considering the number of lawsuits currently outstanding, the damages could cost Dow Corning hundreds of millions of dollars, against a business that contributed less than 1 percent of the company's $1.84 billion in 1991 revenues.

The firm's legal risks are staggering:

- Hundreds of women who received implants and later suffered health problems have filed suits; damages could exceed $500 million.
- Stockholders have filed about 10 suits charging that the company failed to disclose the implants' risks; the suits seek hundreds of millions in damages.
- Dow Corning risks civil liability under food and drug laws for selling or shipping adulterated products; government action could results in fines reaching $1 million.
- Under federal criminal statutes and food and drug laws, company executives could be charged with rigging or hiding data.

Many critics believe the manufacturer was slow to respond to safety concerns. Dow Corning continued to maintain that the implants were safe. Yet officials in government probes said they had reviewed documents which seemed to show that the company had been misrepresenting its safety data on implants for more than 15 years. Highly visible in the media coverage of the controversy was a former Dow Corning engineer, Thomas D. Talcott. Talcott said that for years the company sold silicone implants that could rupture and leak, posing a serious health risk. One of the developers of the original silicone gel used in implants, Talcott quit in 1976 in protest when Dow Corning switched to a more liquid gel designed to make the implants softer. He said he feared the thinner gel could migrate through the body.

As the Food and Drug Administration began hearings on whether silicone implants should be banned, Dow Corning's CEO, Keith R. McKennon, promised to cooperate fully. He also discussed funding research and paying the medical bills of poor women whose implants could be removed. In early March 1992, the FDA's advisory committee decided that implants could remain on the market in limited use but would be tested for safety in clinical trials. On March 19, Dow Corning Corporation announced that it would stop making breast implants altogether.

How, some observers asked, could such a debacle occur at Dow Corning, long recognized as a pioneer in corporate ethics? The company was one of the first to establish an ethics program, one which many believe to be the most elaborate of any in American corporations. In 1976, Dow Corning's chairman started a Business Conduct Committee. Six managers serve three-year terms on the committee and devote up to six weeks a year to its business. Committee members audit every business operation every three years, hold reviews with employees, and report results to an Audit and Social Responsibility Committee of the board of directors. Company training programs include segments on ethics, and semi-annual surveys ask employees about ethics issues.

Since 1983, four audits failed to turn up any questions on the safety of breast implants. Nor did a three-hour audit held in October 1990 with nine employees at the unit that makes silicone implants. Yet some evidence of controversy apparently existed. Talcott, the whistle-blowing engineer, quit Dow Corning in protest in 1976, the same year the ethics program was launched. A 1977 memo by another employee, Frank Lewis, noted reports by four doctors that 52 of 500 implant procedures had resulted in ruptures.

Why didn't any of the audits turn up such internal documents? Ethics experts point out that ethics programs are not designed to deal directly with complex problems, but rather to help build an overall environment of ethical conduct. At Dow Corning, product safety issues are channeled through managers and the company's Medical Device Business Board, which had decided to conduct further safety studies on the implants. Also, ethics programs are constrained because few managers or employees are likely to discuss moral issues openly in meetings with other employees or managers, including the boss. And employees are not likely to raise concerns about safety when top managers believe such concerns are not justified. In fact, Dow Corning maintained throughout the controversy and litigation that breast implants do not pose unreasonable risks.[1]

Should breast implants be outlawed? How far should the government go in regulating business?

Businesses must operate within the boundaries of laws and government regulation. Laws are established not only to protect consumers but also to preserve competition. Government agencies enforce laws at the federal, state, and local levels. Firms that do not comply face fines and other penalties.

In this chapter, we examine the important roles of law and government in business. First we discuss business law, the sources of law, and the court system. We describe the various types of laws and specific laws affecting business. Then we examine government regulation of business, with emphasis on the laws designed to encourage competition. Next we discuss the trend toward deregulation. Finally we explain how the government uses various taxes to support its activities.

INTRODUCTION TO LAW

Law
A standard or rule established by a society to govern the behavior of its members.

A **law** is a standard or rule established by a society to govern the behavior of its members. Federal, state, and local governments, constitutions, and treaties all establish laws. So do court decisions. Laws have a direct and substantial impact on how business firms conduct various activities. In this section, we discuss some of the basic concepts of law, including the sources of law, the U.S. court system, and laws affecting business.

Sources of Law

The United States Constitution specifies how the U.S. government must operate; it is the foundation of law. Federal and state constitutions provide the framework for the various levels of government, which derive laws from three major sources: common law, statutory law, and administrative law.

Common Law. The body of law created by judges through their court decisions is known as **common law.** Based on custom, usage, and court rulings of early England, common law came to America when the first colonies were established and has become a major body of law in the United States. Judicial decisions establish precedents, or standards, that later are used in similar cases. Following precedents gives certainty and stability to many areas of law.

Common Law
The body of law created by judges through their court decisions.

Statutory Law. A law created by a federal, state, or local legislature, constitution, or treaty is called a **statute.** Most laws created today are statutes. Together the laws enacted by various legislative bodies make up **statutory law.** A statute must be drawn up in a precise manner to be constitutional. However, courts often must interpret a law's meaning. Court decisions sometimes lead to statutes being changed, clarified, or even dismissed entirely.

Statute
A law created by a federal, state, or local legislature, treaty, or constitution.

Statutory Law
As a body, the laws enacted by federal, state, and local governments, constitutions, or treaties.

Many statutes pertain to the business environment or business practices. Congress, for example, passes laws establishing tax regulations for individuals and businesses. State legislatures and city councils also pass laws regulating general and specific business practices. For instance, a toxic substances law passed in California requires that the public be warned about the dangers of any products containing toxic substances that could cause cancer or birth defects.

An important part of statutory law is the **Uniform Commercial Code (UCC),** a group of statutory laws designed to simplify interstate commerce by eliminating differences between state laws governing business. The UCC, consisting of 10 articles, covers the rights of buyers and sellers in transactions. Drafted in 1952, the UCC has been adopted in its entirety by every state except Louisiana (which has adopted about half of the code).

Uniform Commercial Code (UCC)
Comprehensive statutory laws designed to eliminate differences between state laws governing business.

Administrative Law. Regulations passed by state and federal administrative agencies are included in **administrative law.** Numerous administrative agencies enforce laws affecting business. Federal agencies with extensive powers include the Federal Trade Commission, the Consumer Product Safety Commission, the Federal Communications Commission, and the Food and Drug Administration. Exhibit 5.1 lists the major federal agencies and their responsibilities. Agencies on the state level include public utility commissions, licensing boards for various professions and trades, and other regulatory bodies. Some examples of local agencies are planning commissions, zoning boards, and boards of appeal.

Administrative Law
Regulation affecting business, passed by state and federal administrative agencies.

Exhibit 5.1
Major Government Agencies

Government Agency	Responsibility
Federal Trade Commission (FTC)	Antitrust, deceptive advertising
Interstate Commerce Commission (ICC)	Interstate rail, bus, truck, and water carriers
Environmental Protection Agency (EPA)	Pollution standards and control
Food and Drug Administration (FDA)	Consumer protection from hazardous products.
Equal Employment Opportunity Commission (EEOC)	Discrimination in employment practices
National Highway Traffic Safety Administration (NHTSA)	Vehicle safety
Occupational Safety and Health Administration (OSHA)	Safety in the workplace
Federal Communications Commission (FCC)	Radio, television, and telephone communications
Securities and Exchange Commission (SEC)	Stocks and bonds
Consumer Product Safety Commission (CPSC)	Consumer safety
Federal Aviation Administration (FAA)	Airline industry
Federal Power Commission (FPC)	Rate and sales of natural gas
Nuclear Regulatory Commission (NRC)	Nuclear power

The Court System

Jurisdiction
The right and power of a court to interpret and apply laws and make binding decisions.

The court system, or judiciary, is the branch of government responsible for applying laws to settle disputes between parties. Courts possess **jurisdiction,** the legal right and power to interpret and apply laws and make binding decisions. The major method of taking disputes to court is by filing a lawsuit. Airline passengers who get bumped from overbooked flights, for instance, can sue for damages.[2] Because of the considerable time and expense involved in going to court, many firms try to resolve their legal disputes outside the courtroom.

A dual court system operates in the United States. The federal government and each of the 50 state governments have separate court systems, as Exhibit 5.2 illustrates. The federal court system includes district courts established by Congress, federal courts of appeals, and the Supreme Court created by the U.S. Constitution. The systems established by the states include circuit courts, courts of appeals, and state supreme courts.

Federal Court System. Federal courts in the United States primarily hear cases involving questions of constitutional law; federal crimes; disputes between citizens of different states (or between a U.S. citizen and a citizen of another country) over property valued at $10,000 or more; bankruptcy, tax, postal, copyright, patent, or trademark laws; and maritime cases.

A U.S. district court is the first to hear a federal case (see Exhibit 5.2). At least one district court is located in each state. The decision resolving the case is made by a jury, or by the judge if each party waives the right to a jury trial. The losing party can appeal the case to the U.S. court of appeals for that region, one of 13 federal courts of appeals. Finally, a party may appeal the decision of a U.S. court of appeals to the U.S. Supreme Court.

The highest court of the land, the U.S. Supreme Court is composed of nine justices appointed by the president and confirmed by the Senate. Justices are appointed to the Supreme Court for life. The Court's major function is to hear cases appealed from the U.S. courts of appeals or state supreme courts. The Supreme Court decides which cases it will hear; roughly 4 percent of all appeals are heard each year. Many Supreme Court decisions affect businesses. The Court, citing first amendment freedom of speech, recently struck down a city ordinance that banned news racks containing advertising fliers from sidewalks. While the news rack ruling favored business, the same court declined to limit "excessive" punitive damages.[3] General Motors was ordered by an Atlanta jury to pay $101 million in punitive damages to the parents of a teen who died in a fiery crash in his GMC pickup truck.[4] This is an example of a punitive damage award that may have been considered excessive.

State Courts. Most state court systems have a structure similar to the federal system (see Exhibit 5.2). Cases originate in a circuit court; each county generally has a circuit court. Most states also have courts of appeals. Decisions of a court of appeals can be appealed to the state supreme court. Finally, decisions made by a state supreme court that involve a question of constitutional or federal law can be appealed to the U.S. Supreme Court.

Exhibit 5.2
The U.S. Court System

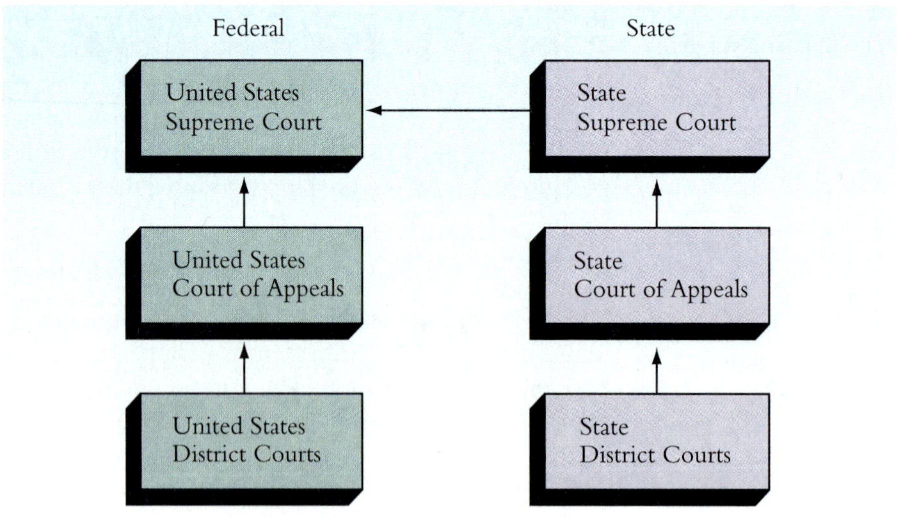

Specialized Courts. Several types of specialized courts have been created to hear certain types of cases. For example, some states have small-claims courts to hear cases involving disputes over small amounts of money, usually below $1,500. States also commonly have divorce courts, juvenile courts, and traffic courts. At the federal level, specialized courts include the U.S. Tax Court (for tax cases) and the U.S. Court of Claims (for claims against the government).

LAWS AFFECTING BUSINESS

Numerous and varied laws regulate the activities of all businesses and everyone involved in the business, from owner to manager to employee. In this section, we discuss the major business law categories, which involve torts, contracts, sales, agency, property, bankruptcy, and negotiable instruments.

The Law of Torts

Tort
A noncriminal (civil) injury to other persons or their property or reputation; results from intentional acts or negligence.

While criminal law deals with crime against society or the state, tort law is concerned with compensating the victims of noncriminal wrongs. Derived from the French word for wrong, a **tort** is a noncriminal (civil) injury to other persons or their property or reputation. Torts can be intentional or they may result from negligence. *Intentional torts* are deliberate acts by a person or business firm. For example, slander (spoken defamation of character) and libel (written defamation of character) are intentional torts. A tort results from negligence when one party fails to exercise reasonable care and causes injury to another. Negligence torts arise from carelessness rather than intentional be-

Under tort law, business firms are liable for harm caused by their products, such as those containing PCBs.

havior. A hotel, for example, may be held responsible for injuries to a guest who trips on loose or worn carpeting on the premises.

Product Liability
Area of tort law that holds business firms responsible for negligence in design, manufacture, sale, and operation of their products.

Product liability is an important part of tort law. **Product liability** involves the responsibility of business firms for negligence in design, manufacture, sale, and operation of their products. For example, workers are suing virtually every keyboard maker for selling products that cause wrist injuries, and not warning users of the potential risks.[5] Public interest groups are seeking to broaden the liability of businesses and manufacturers of such products as breast implants, automobiles, cigarettes, and guns.[6] Conversely, opponents to such reform use every available means—emotional appeals from victims of crimes, powerful lobbies for gun and cigarette manufacturers, and connections to key lawmakers—to fight the passage of product liability laws.[7] Today's Business World examines some product liability cases in the tobacco industry.

TODAY'S BUSINESS WORLD

Clearing the Air: Product Liability in the Tobacco Industry

The tobacco industry says it has never paid a dime on a suit from a smoker claiming health damage from cigarettes. In fact, few tobacco product liability cases have ever gone to trial, and only a handful have reached juries since the 1960s. But a case that reached the U.S. Supreme Court may have far-reaching effects on tobacco product liability.

The case began when Rose Cipollone, a smoker for 40 years, sued Liggett, Philip Morris, and Loriland after having a cancerous lung removed. After her death in 1984, her family pursued the lawsuit, blaming the three companies for her death. The suit claimed that the cigarette companies failed to properly warn of health risks, that they made false statements, and that they intentionally committed fraud and conspired to hide the truth about smoking. In 1988, a federal jury in New Jersey found that Cipollone was 80 percent responsible for her illness, but ordered Liggett to pay her husband $400,000, on the basis of many years of smoking (between 1942 and 1965) before warning labels were required on cigarette packages. The other two firms were absolved. In 1990, an appeals court overturned the verdict and ordered a new trial. Thomas Cipollone, Rose's son, appealed to the U.S. Supreme Court, and in an unusual move, the tobacco companies agreed that the high court should hear the case, since so many similar lawsuits were pending.

In June of 1992, the Supreme Court ruled that smokers may not file lawsuits charging tobacco companies with failing to provide adequate warnings. However, they may file lawsuits alleging that cigarette makers hid or distorted the health dangers of tobacco. The court gave the Cipollone family the option of retrying their suit.

Both tobacco companies and antismoking groups claimed the Supreme Court ruling as a victory. Plaintiffs gained a way to persuade juries that cigarette makers committed fraud or misrepresentation, and a chance to obtain punitive damages.

Says Matt Myers, counsel to the Coalition on Smoking or Health, "The decision focuses attention on what truly is the potential Achilles' heel of the tobacco industry: whether their own research showed that smoking causes disease and whether they consciously sought to conceal the fact."

But that's why the tobacco companies hailed the decision. They say they are off the hook unless someone can prove they lied to the public, and they insist they did not. Industry representatives say that smokers will have to prove that misconduct by companies led them to start or continue to smoke. "There was so much information in the public realm about the dangers of smoking that it will be very difficult to find plaintiffs who are able to persuade a jury that they either began to smoke or continued to smoke because of misleading statements from the tobacco industry," says Victor Schwartz, a product liability expert who has consulted for tobacco companies.

Antismoking forces claim that they have information that proves cigarette corporations have been deliberately covering up information for decades. In another suit, a federal judge in New York City ruled in early 1992 that tobacco companies must hand over 1,500 pages of evidence concerning the Council for Tobacco Research, an industry trade group formed in 1954 to study the health risks of smoking. The plaintiff says that cigarette makers and the council withheld important research that showed the dangers of smoking. Worse, the suit says the industry's claim that it was sponsoring independent research was a fraud, and the judge agreed. Federal prosecutors conducting a criminal probe of tobacco companies and the research council are watching the case. A recent development: Internal papers leaked from Brown & Williamson support claims that the industry knew cigarettes are addictive.

Tobacco companies may really feel the heat as the secondhand smoke controversy intensifies. One class-action suit filed by seven flight attendants in Miami seeks $5 billion against six major tobacco companies. The suit, on behalf of 60 thousand flight attendants, says that the plaintiffs suffer from lung cancer and other diseases as a result of their exposure to secondhand cigarette smoke before Congress banned smoking on flights in 1989. In June 1992, the U.S. Environmental Protection Agency issued a report reinforcing findings that environmental smoke is a known human carcinogen and is particularly dangerous to children. Antismoking lawyers predict that secondhand-smoke liability cases will proliferate if lawyers find any evidence that cigarette makers knew about and concealed the dangers. On November 5, 1992, lawyers for the estate of Rose Cipollone dropped the most prominent damage case filed against a tobacco company. With the exception of the $400,000 awarded in the case, no jury has assessed damages against a tobacco company. But evidence collected in the Cipollone case is expected to lead to even more lawsuits. And the Supreme Court's decision to permit damage suits alleging the industry hid the risks of smoking may signal more problems for the tobacco industry.

Industry insiders continue to respond to pressure by arguing that smoking is not addictive. But the pressure on tobacco companies is expected to intensify as class-action lawsuits gain momentum. In 1994, class-action lawsuits charged tobacco producers with manipulating nicotine levels in cigarettes (*Castano* v. *American Tobacco*); sought to recover the cost of treatment for all smokers (*Allman* v. *Philip Morris*); charged R.J. Reynolds with deceptive business practices in targeting children with its Joe Camel ads (*Sparks* v. *R.J. Reynolds*); and attempted to recover smoking-related health-care costs paid by state programs (*Mississippi* v. *American Tobacco et al.*). For the first time, the class action strategy may result in even deeper pockets than the tobacco companies.

Which side do you take in the tobacco issue? What regulation would you support for tobacco?

Source: Adapted from Maria Mallory and John Carey, "These Days, Where There's Smoke, There's a Lawsuit," *Business Week* (June 6, 1994): 36; John Carey, "It's Time for Regulators to Stop Blowing Smoke," *Business Week* (March 14, 1994): 34; Michael Galen, "When the Smoke Clears, Cigarette Makers May Get Burned," *Business Week* (November 23, 1992): 89; Walecia Konrad and Catherine Yang, "This Decision May Be Hazardous to Tobacco's Health," *Business Week* (July 6, 1992): 33; Joanne Lipman, "Marketers Say Ruling Spares Tobacco Ads," *The Wall Street Journal* (June 26, 1992): B3; Milo Geyelin, "Liability Suits, While Rising, May Not Prevail," *The Wall Street Journal* (June 25, 1992): A1, A10; and Maxine S. Lans, "Ruling on Cigarette Ads: What Does It Really Mean?" *Marketing News* (August 17, 1992): 15.

Strict Product Liability
Legal concept that holds manufacturers responsible for injuries caused by products regardless of whether negligence was involved.

In certain instances, product liability laws have been expanded to include cases in which the producer or marketer of the product is not proved negligent. Under **strict product liability,** the manufacturer is responsible if the injured party can show that the product was defective, that the defect caused the injury, and that the defect caused the product to be dangerous.

The Law of Contracts

Contract
A legally enforceable, voluntary agreement between two or more parties.

A **contract** is a legally enforceable, voluntary agreement between two or more parties. A contract is like a private statute, in which the parties define the considerations they owe each other. Contracts are generally part of most business transactions. They can be either express or implied. An express contract is one in which the words are actually put forth, either orally or in writing. Generally, oral contracts are just as legally enforceable as written contracts. (Some types of contracts must be in writing to be valid, such as for the sale of an interest in land.) But since the words used in an oral contract may be difficult to prove at a later time when parties are in dispute, the best policy for business firms to follow is to put all contracts in writing. An implied contract results from the actions of the parties rather than from an explicit promise. For example, when a passenger boards a train, it is implied that the passenger will have a ticket when the agent collects them and that the train will provide safe transportation to the destination. Again, since actions can be misunderstood, the best policy in business situations is for the contract to be expressed in words and written down.

To be enforceable, a contract must meet several requirements:

- *Voluntary agreement.* Both parties must accept the terms of the agreement voluntarily, free of correction, fraud, and the like.
- *Consideration.* Each party must provide something of value to the other, such as money, a product, or a promise to do or not do something.

- *Contractual capacity.* Each party must have the legal ability to enter into a binding agreement. (Generally, minors, persons with mental handicaps, and intoxicated persons do not have contractual capacity.)
- *Legality.* A contract must not involve any unlawful act.

Breach of Contract
The failure of one party to live up to a contractual agreement.

The failure of one party to live up to a contractual agreement is called **breach of contract.** For example, failure to make payments on a car loan would be considered breach of contract. The bank or other lending institution could bring legal action against the breaking party—the car owner who signed the loan—and recover damages.

The Law of Sales

Sales Law
Body of law involving the sale of products for money or on credit.

Sales law, which grew out of contract law, involves products sold for money or credit. Sales agreements are contracts subject to the requirements discussed above. Article 2 of the Uniform Commercial Code provides that some sales contracts are binding even if all the requirements for a contract are not met. For instance, a sales agreement is legally binding even if the selling price is left out of the agreement; the buyer must pay the reasonable value of the goods.

Express Warranty
Oral or written assurances made by the seller regarding a product.

Article 2 also establishes the law of warranty for sales transactions. An **express warranty** is any statement of fact or promise made by the seller to the buyer relating to the products sold, and which becomes an important part of the sales agreement. A warranty is in the nature of a guarantee, although no formal words such as warrant or guarantee need be used. If the products in fact are not as represented by the seller, the seller can be held responsible either to make the products as warranted or to give the buyer the money back. The law also imposes an **implied warranty,** not specifically expressed by the parties, ensuring that the business firm has clear title of the products it sells and that the products will serve the purpose for which they are sold.

Implied Warranty
Warranty legally imposed on the seller; ensures that the seller owns the products and that they will serve the purpose for which they are sold.

The Law of Agency

Agency
A legal relationship between two parties who agree that the agent will act on behalf of the principal.

An **agency** is a business relationship in which a principal (the person or business entity who wants a task performed) appoints an agent (the person or business entity who performs the task) to act on his or her behalf. The actions of the agent, authorized by the principal, are legally recognized as though they were performed by the principal. For example, a talent agent can enter into a contract for a client as though the client personally signed the contract. Agents are used in many diverse industries, including insurance, sports, entertainment, and real estate. Generally, agents are paid a fee or commission for their services.

Power of Attorney
A legal document authorizing an agent to act on behalf of the principal.

Because the principal is bound by the actions of the agent, it is important to put the agency agreement in writing. Generally, a legal document called a **power of attorney** is granted to authorize the agent to act on behalf of the principal. For instance, a person may grant an accountant power of attorney to act as his or her agent during a tax audit. It is the agent's duty to act in a professional manner and to exercise good judgement. The agency relationship can be terminated when the task is completed or by mutual agreement of the parties.

The Law of Property

Anything that can be owned is considered property. Property is something for which a person or business entity has unrestricted right of possession or use. There are several categories of property. **Real property** is real estate, land, and anything permanently attached to it, such as houses, buildings, and parking lots. **Tangible personal property** means physical items such as equipment, automobiles, and a store's inventory of goods. **Intangible personal property** includes property shown by documents or other written instruments, such as checks, money orders, receipts, stocks, and bonds.

Real Property
Real estate (land and anything permanently attached to it, such as houses, buildings, and parking lots).

Tangible Personal Property
Physical items, such as goods and equipment.

Intangible Personal Property
Property represented by a document or other written statement.

Three forms of intangible personal property provide legal protection for individuals or business firms. A **trademark** is a name or symbol registered with the U.S. Patent and Trademark Office. It guarantees the owner exclusive rights for 20 years and can be renewed as many times as the owner wishes. **Patents,** granted by the U.S. Patent and Trademark Office, give inventors the exclusive right to make, use, or sell their products for 17 years. Patents cannot be renewed. The number of patent suits initiated in U.S. courts has jumped significantly in recent years, many involving small investors suing large companies.[8] A **copyright,** filed with the U.S. Copyright Office, gives the creator exclusive right to publish and sell an original written work. Copyrights last for the lifetime of the author plus 50 years. Recently, recording companies have claimed that while it is legal to resell a copyrighted product, resales cut into the sales of compact disks (CDs), diminish their value, and deprive artists of royalties. This has led to a major battle between some recording companies and stores selling CDs, one the recording companies are not likely to win.[9] Many U.S. companies are also filing copyright infringement lawsuits against foreign firms. Walt Disney, Microsoft, and Harcourt Brace have filed over 25 lawsuits in China for knockoff books, pirated software, and black-market video cassettes.[10]

Trademark
A name or symbol, registered with the U.S. Patent and Trademark Office, that guarantees the owner exclusive rights to its use.

Patent
The exclusive right of an inventor to make, use, or sell the registered product.

Copyright
Protection of an individual's exclusive right to publish and sell original written materials.

The Law of Bankruptcy

Bankruptcy is a legal procedure provided for individuals and firms that cannot pay their debts. By declaring bankruptcy, the individual or firm asks to be declared legally unable to satisfy creditors and to be released from financial obligations.

Three types of bankruptcy are possible: Chapter 7, Chapter 11, and Chapter 13. Under *Chapter 7 bankruptcy,* the business firm is dissolved and the assets are sold to pay off debt. Individuals filing Chapter 7 are allowed to keep a limited amount of assets, determined by federal or state law. *Chapter 11 bankruptcy* temporarily relieves a company from its debts while it reorganizes and works out a payment plan with its creditors. *Chapter 13 bankruptcy* allows an individual to establish a plan for repaying debts within three to five years.

The Law of Negotiable Instruments

Negotiable Instrument
A written promise to pay a specified sum of money; it can be transferred from one person or firm to another.

A **negotiable instrument** is a substitute for money. It is a written promise to pay a specified sum of money; it can be transferred from one person or business firm to another. Examples of negotiable instruments include checks, drafts, and certificates of deposit. The Uniform Commercial Code specifies that negotiable instruments must meet the following requirements:

- They must be in writing and signed by the maker or drawer (the party who orders the payment of the money).
- They must contain an unconditional promise to pay a certain sum of money.
- They must be payable on demand or at a specific date.
- They must be payable to a specific person or business firm or to the bearer (the party who possesses the instrument).

Endorsement
A person's signature on the back of a negotiable instrument, making it transferable.

The payee (the one to whom the instrument is written) must endorse a negotiable instrument before it is transferred. An **endorsement** is a person's signature on the back of a negotiable instrument (see Exhibit 5.3). A *blank* endorsement is accomplished when the payee signs the back of the instrument. This type of endorsement can be unsafe because anyone can cash the instrument once it is endorsed. Restrictive and special endorsements protect the negotiable instrument should it be lost or stolen. Using the words "for deposit only" along with the signature constitutes a *restrictive* endorsement; it states what the instrument is for and is much safer than a blank endorsement. A *special* endorsement specifies to whom the instrument is payable by including the person's or firm's name on the back of the instrument along with the signature. Finally a *qualified* endorsement—using the words "without recourse"—

Exhibit 5.3
Types of Endorsements

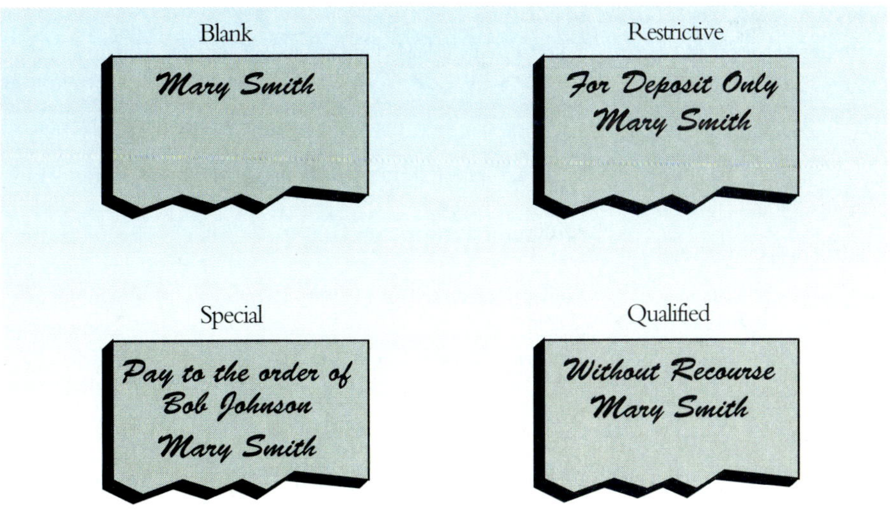

means the person who originally signed the instrument, not the endorser, is responsible for payment. The endorser does not guarantee payment if the instrument is not backed by sufficient funds.

GOVERNMENT REGULATION OF BUSINESS

The federal and state governments have enacted substantial legislation to encourage competition among business firms. Many laws, such as those outlawing monopolies, price fixing, and other practices that restrain trade, are intended to help ensure that consumers have a choice in the marketplace and that firms have the freedom to compete. For instance, the justice department recently launched an investigation of pricing in the cereal industry because prices are, according to them, way too high and controlled by four firms that dominate the industry and make huge profits.[11] In this section, we discuss federal laws designed to regulate competition among American business firms. Exhibit 5.4 summarizes these laws.

Sherman Antitrust Act

One of the first laws passed to regulate competition, the Sherman Antitrust Act (1890) declared that two or more business firms could not agree to the prices to be charged for goods. It also prohibited business firms from dividing markets among themselves and from deciding not to sell to or buy from a particular company.

Exhibit 5.4
Major Laws Designed to Preserve Competition

Law	Purpose
Sherman Antitrust Act (1890)	Prohibits contracts or conspiracies that attempt to reduce competition
Clayton Act (1914)	Prohibits specific acts that reduce competition: price discrimination, tying agreements, binding contracts, and community of interest
Federal Trade Commission Act (1914)	Prohibits unfair trade practices and deceptive advertising
Robinson-Patman Act (1936)	Prohibits price discrimination that reduces competition
Celler-Kefauver Act (1950)	Prohibits mergers that reduce competition
Antitrust Improvement Act (1976)	Provides additional time for the Federal Trade Commission and the Justice Department to evaluate proposed mergers
Gramm-Rudman Act (1985)	Requires Congress to meet annual deficit targets and to balance the federal budget by 1993

TOMORROW'S BUSINESS WORLD

Businesses See More Regulation

Contrary to what some of us might think, the majority of Americans want more regulation, especially in the areas of toxic waste disposal, exposure to hazardous substances, honesty and accuracy in advertising, and the manufacture and sale of drugs. Businesses can expect to see more regulation in the future, not less. A few current regulatory actions point to this trend:

- The Federal Trade Commission (FTC), under a broad new federal regulatory program, adopted a formula to determine what it considers reasonable rates for cable television rate. As a result, rates are expected to fall 10 percent or more.
- New Food and Drug Administration (FDA) guidelines regulate the labeling and marketing of food products. The guidelines deal with the promotional claims permitted, the definitions required, and the puffery forbidden.
- As of 1995, auto companies are not allowed to manufacture cars with air conditioners that use chlorofluorocarbons (CFCs). Congress has called for a 50 percent decrease in the production of CFCs by 1999.
- The FDA has cracked down on several industries, restraining orange-juice makers from misusing the word "fresh," pulling most breast implants off the market for safety reasons, and scrutinizing drug factories and industry marketing claims.
- The FTC recommended filing antitrust charges against the Professional Golf Association (P.G.A.) Tour, which runs most U.S. pro golf events. The focus of the investigation is the P.G.A. rule limiting members from playing in rival tournaments.

Source: Adapted from Catherine Yang, "Crying Foul on the Fairway," *Business Week* (January 23, 1995): 45; Steven W. Colford, "Food Makers Await FTC Ad Guidance," *Advertising Age* (April 18, 1994): 10; Joseph Weber and John Carey, "Strong Medicine," *Business Week,* (September 6, 1993): 20–21; Jeanne Saddler and Mark Robichaux, "Cable-TV Rates Could Fall 10% Due to Ruling," *The Wall Street Journal,* (April 2, 1993): B1, B10; Kurt Topfer, "Sunscreens to Benefit, as Health Trends Emerge," *Chemical Marketing Reporter,* (April 27, 1992): 33.

The Sherman Antitrust Act was not used for more than a decade. But in the early 1900s, with Teddy Roosevelt in the White House, the act was used to break up J.P. Morgan's railroad monopoly, John D. Rockefeller's Standard Oil, and Buck Duke's tobacco trust. Today the Sherman Act is still the basis for legal action. For example, Abbott Laboratories was charged under this act with price fixing in setting prices for its infant formula.

Clayton Act

Congress enacted the Clayton Act in 1914 to strengthen the Sherman Antitrust Act. Specifically, the Clayton Act outlawed four practices that reduce competition. These are:

- *Price discrimination,* charging one firm (usually a large one) a lower price for goods than the price other (usually smaller) firms are charged.

- *Tying agreements,* requiring a buyer to purchase unwanted products for the right to purchase desired products.
- *Binding contracts,* requiring a buyer to purchase products from a specific supplier.
- *Community of interest,* a business buying stock in a competing firm to reduce competition between the two.

Federal Trade Commission Act

The Federal Trade Commission Act (1914) established the Federal Trade Commission (FTC), a five-member committee empowered to investigate illegal trade practices. This act prohibits all unfair methods of competition. The Wheeler-Lea Amendment (1938) expanded the FTC's power to eliminate deceptive business practices, including those affecting consumers as well as competitors.

The FTC acts on its own accord to investigate a firm's business practices or on complaints made by other firms or individuals. Recent targets have included fly-by-night telemarketers who use television to help sell fraudulent products and advertisers who make unsubstantiated claims.[12] Wal-Mart, for instance, agreed to stop stating in ads that it always offered the lowest prices.[13]

Robinson-Patman Act

The Robinson-Patman Act, passed in 1936, outlaws price discrimination that substantially reduces competition. Price discounts are legal, however, if they are based on actual lower selling costs, such as discounts for large orders. The act also prohibits advertising and promotional allowances unless they are offered to all retailers regardless of size.

Celler-Kefauver Act

The Celler-Kefauver Act (1950) outlaws mergers through the purchase of assets, when the mergers tend to reduce competition. The act also makes it mandatory that all mergers be approved by the FTC and the Justice Department. The FTC denied a proposal by McKesson, the largest U.S. drug wholesaler, to take over the number four wholesaler, Alco Health Services Corporation. The merger would have given McKesson 90 percent of the market in some states.

Antitrust Improvement Act

The Antitrust Improvement Act of 1976 strengthens previous antitrust laws. The act gives the FTC and the Justice Department a longer period of time to evaluate proposed mergers. It also allows state attorneys general to prosecute firms accused of price fixing.

DEREGULATION

Deregulation
The process of reducing government involvement in the regulation of business, by eliminating legal restraints on competition.

Since the 1970s, a trend toward deregulation of business has been evident. **Deregulation** is the process of reducing the involvement of government in the regulation of business by eliminating legal restraints on competition. The goal of deregulation is to make business regulations less complex and to lower the costs of complying with them. Industries that have been most affected by the movement toward deregulation include airlines, railroads, and banking (see Exhibit 5.5).

Deregulation of business results in several benefits for business firms and consumers. Regulation costs firms and consumers billions of dollars each year; deregulation eliminates or reduces some of the costs, and the savings can be passed on to consumers. Deregulation can also increase competition, resulting in lower prices for consumers. After the airline industry was deregulated, for example, air fares dropped to the lowest levels in many years. Increased competition can also lead to better service. Since the government deregulated the banking industry, many banks are providing more services, such as discount brokerages (for purchasing stocks, bonds, and other securities) and money market accounts.

Exhibit 5.5
Major Deregulation Laws

Law	Purpose
Natural Gas Policy Act (1978)	Requires pipeline firms to transport natural gas owned by other companies
Airline Deregulation Act (1978)	Eliminates regulation of airline rates and schedules
Motor Carrier Act (1980)	Allows trucks to travel more freely and change prices more quickly
Staggers Rail Act (1980)	Gives railroads more flexibility to raise and lower rates without government approval
Depository Institutions Deregulatory Committee Act (1981) Depository Institutions Act (1982)	Permits financial instituions to complete on a more even basis for deposit accounts by paying higher interest rates and to broaden investments beyond homes and small commerical mortgages
Drug Price Competition and Patent Term Restoration Act (1984)	Allows generic drugs to reach the market sooner by awarding patents for shorter periods of time

Opponents of deregulation fear that this trend could actually reduce competition. For example, since the airline industry has been deregulated, many major carriers have gone out of business, while others continue to lose money. Many politicians and consumers believe that further deregulation will lead to some of the same problems that led to government regulation in the first place—pollution, poor working conditions, and low-quality products. The future of deregulation is uncertain, but it will depend to a large extent on the conduct of business organizations.

Do you think U.S. business needs more regulation or less? The Your Values and Attitudes quiz will help you determine your attitude toward regulation.

YOUR VALUES AND ATTITUDES

How Do You Feel about Regulation?

Directions. For each statement, circle the number that shows your level of agreement.

	Strongly Disagree					Strongly Agree
1. The government should let business regulate itself.	1	2	3	4	5	6
2. It is up to consumers to make sure the products they use are safe.	1	2	3	4	5	6
3. Firms should be able to advertise in the manner they desire.	1	2	3	4	5	6
4. Regulations and the paperwork they require cost businesses too much money.	1	2	3	4	5	6
5. The public and business firms, not the government, need to control pollution.	1	2	3	4	5	6

Feedback: Government regulation of business is a sensitive issue. It does indeed increase the amount of paperwork firms must do. It may limit business activities. Yet, without regulation, firms may not act in the interest of consumers or the public. In short, someone usually needs to police the activities of business firms, whether it be the government, businesses themselves, or another alternative.

Do you think government is the best source of regulation? If you circled 1 or 2 for most statements, you strongly think so. In which business sectors would you like to see more regulation? If you chose 3 or 4, you are neutral. Finally, if you circled 5 or 6, you strongly support less government regulation. In what realms of business should the government regulate less?

GOVERNMENT TAXATION

Tax
A payment for the support of government activities, required of organizations and individuals within the domain of the government.

Citizens of a country must pay for the services the government provides. This is accomplished through taxation. A **tax** is a payment for the support of government activities, required of organizations and individuals within the domain of the government. Revenues from taxes pay for national defense, roads, schools, social programs, medical care, regulation of business, and for government itself.

The U.S. government obtains about 95 percent of the money it needs to operate through taxes, including corporate and personal income taxes and other federal taxes. State and local governments are also financed through taxation. Taxation can be viewed as another form of government regulation, because virtually all business firms and individuals pay taxes.

Corporate Income Tax

Progressive Tax
Form of taxation in which the percentage of income paid in taxes increases as income increases.

Corporations are required to pay federal tax on their income, after deducting allowable business expenses. Corporations pay a **progressive tax,** meaning the percentage of income paid in taxes increases as income increases. In 1995, the federal tax rate for corporations was:

- 15 percent on the first $50,000 of pretax profit.
- 25 percent of the next $25,000.
- 34 percent on profits between $75,000 and $100,000.
- 39 percent on profits between $100,000 and $335,000.
- A flat federal rate of 34 percent on profits over $335,000.

Recall from the discussion in Chapter 2 that some corporate profits are actually taxed twice. The corporation must first pay a federal income tax on its profits. Then, if it distributes profits to shareholders by declaring dividends, the shareholders must pay a personal income tax on the dividends they receive.

Individual Income Tax

Individuals are subject to a personal income tax that is also progressive in nature. In 1995, five tax rates existed for single individuals. The rates are cumulative, with each new percentage added to the previous total as income increases.

- 15 percent for those with a yearly taxable income of not over $23,350.
- 28 percent of excess above $23,350 for those with annual taxable incomes from $23,350 to $56,550.
- 31 percent of excess over $56,550 for those with annual taxable incomes from $56,550 to $117,950.
- 36 percent of excess over $117,950 for those with annual taxable incomes from $117,950 to $256,500.
- 39.6 percent of excess over $256,500 for those with annual taxable incomes over $256,500.

For employees, most income tax is withheld from paychecks by employers and paid to the Internal Revenue Service (IRS). Individuals whose income comes from ownership of a sole proprietorship or a partnership must pay their income taxes to the IRS in four quarterly payments.

Every individual subject to paying income taxes must file a return with the IRS on or before April 15 of each year (unless an extension is requested and granted). If too much money was withheld from an individual's paycheck, he or she is entitled to a refund. A person may owe additional taxes if insufficient taxes were withheld. Individuals also pay state and, in many cases, local (city) income taxes.

Other Taxes

Federal, state, and local governments use several taxes other than income taxes as sources of funds. The second largest source of federal revenue is the *Social Security and Medicare tax,* which both employers and employees pay. This tax provides retirement, disability, hospital insurance, and death benefits for participants. In 1995 the Social Security tax rate was 12.40 percent of the first $61,200 earned; the employee pays half and the employer pays half. Medicare tax was 2.90 percent of all wages, also split between employee and employer. Employers also pay an annual unemployment tax of 6.2 percent of the first $7,000 of each employee's wages. This tax is used to fund benefits for unemployed workers.

An *excise tax* is a tax on the manufacture or sale of a domestic product. The government uses excise taxes to help pay for services directed at those who use the products, and sometimes to discourage the use of potentially harmful products. For instance, Americans pay an excise tax on gasoline to help finance the construction of roads and bridges. The government has also set an

An example of how state and federal taxes are used to pay for government services.

excise tax on tobacco and alcohol products to discourage their use. Before his retirement, Surgeon General C. Everett Koop urged the government to increase the excise tax on alcoholic beverages to discourage consumption of alcohol.[14] The government also places an import tax on certain foreign products entering the United States.

The majority of states obtain most of their revenues through a *sales tax* on the merchandise consumers buy; some cities levy additional sales taxes on the same products. Some states have no sales tax, while others exempt certain items such as food from being taxed. Local governments raise the majority of their operating revenues through a *property tax* on residential and commercial property, such as houses, land, buildings, machinery, and automobiles.

SUMMARY OF LEARNING OBJECTIVES

1. ***List the sources from which laws are derived.*** Laws have a substantial impact on how business firms conduct activities. The various levels of government derive laws from three sources: common law, created by judges through court decisions; statutory laws, passed by federal, state, and local legislatures; and administrative laws, enacted by federal and state administrative agencies.

2. ***Outline the court system in the United States.*** The U.S. judicial system is charged with the application of law to settle disputes between parties. The United States has a dual court system. The federal court system includes district courts, courts of appeals, and the Supreme Court. The state court system includes circuit courts, courts of appeals, and state supreme courts. Specialized state courts include small-claims, divorce, juvenile, and traffic courts.

3. ***Identify the various categories of business law.*** Several types of laws regulate business activities. These include tort law (which includes product liability) and laws governing contractual agreements, sales agreements, use of agents, property transactions, bankruptcy proceedings, and negotiable instruments.

4. ***Discuss how government regulates business activities to encourage competition.*** The most important laws designed to preserve competition are the Sherman Antitrust Act (1890), which prohibits price fixing, firms dividing markets among themselves, and boycotting certain firms; the Clayton Act (1914), which prevents price discrimination, tying agreements, binding contracts, interlocking directorates, and community of interest; the Federal Trade Commission Act (1914), which prohibits all unfair methods of competition; the Robinson-Patman Act (1936), which outlaws price discrimination that reduces competition; the Celler-Kefauver Act (1950), which outlaws mergers through the purchase of assets; the Antitrust Improvement Act (1976), which strengthens the previous laws; and the Gramm-Rudman Act (1985), passed to force politicians to meet annual deficit targets.

5. ***Explain the effects of deregulation on business.*** Since the 1970s, the United States has experienced a trend toward deregulation, or reducing government involvement in the regulation of business. Deregulation can lower the costs of regulating business and can lead to increased competition, better service, and lower prices.

6. ***Describe how taxation supports the activities of government.*** Citizens pay for the work of government through taxation. Corporations and individuals are subject to federal, state, and local taxes, including taxes on the income they earn, the property then own, and the products they purchase.

KEY TERMS

Law
Common Law
Statute
Statutory Law
Uniform Commercial Code (UCC)
Administrative Law
Jurisdiction
Tort
Product Liability
Strict Product Liability
Contract
Breach of Contract
Sales Law
Express Warranty
Implied Warranty
Agency
Power of Attorney
Real Property
Tangible Personal Property
Intangible Personal Property
Trademark
Patent
Copyright
Negotiable Instrument
Endorsement
Deregulation
Tax
Progressive Tax

QUESTIONS FOR DISCUSSION AND REVIEW

1. Why are there three separate sources of law in our government? How do these sources of law relate with one another?

2. Outline the court system of the United States. Explain the relationship between the state court system and the federal court system.

3. Why is product liability a concern of business firms? To customers? To society?

4. What requirements must a contract meet to be enforceable? Have you ever entered into a contract? If so, explain why a contract was used.

5. What is the difference between an express warranty and an implied warranty? Give an example of each.

6. In a free enterprise system such as we have in the United States, why does government regulate business? Why should the government encourage competition, and how can regulation be used to preserve competition?

7. In our free enterprise system, why is it important to limit the size of an individual company? Is it fair to break up a large successful company like Standard Oil or AT&T?

8. List the specific practices the Clayton Act outlaws and describe how each practice limits competition. Give an example of each based on real business situations.

9. What has the movement toward deregulation been intended to accomplish? Has it been successful?

10. How can government establish social policy through the use of taxes? What taxes do you pay currently? Which do you expect to pay in the future?

CASE 5.1

Name Brands Versus Counterfeits: A Tough Battle with High Stakes

We have all heard of counterfeiting. Usually it refers to people making money—printing it instead of earning it. But counterfeiting also can involve all sorts of consumer goods and manufactured products. From well-known brand names such as Calvin Klein jeans to auto parts, counterfeiters have found ways to produce goods that look authentic. In some instances, counterfeit products look better than the original!

The demand for brand-name products has helped counterfeiting grow into a very profitable business throughout the world and into a serious problem for legitimate manufacturers and consumers. Faulty counterfeit parts have caused more than two dozen plane crashes. Most counterfeit auto parts do not meet federal safety standards.

Counterfeiting hurts manufacturers in many ways. Analysts estimate that, in the United States alone, annual revenue lost runs from $6 billion to $8 billion. Perhaps even worse, consumers blame the innocent manufacturer when they unknowingly buy a counterfeit product and find it doesn't perform as expected. Sometimes even economies can suffer. For instance, when farmers in Kenya and Zaire used counterfeit fertilizers, both countries lost most of their crops.

In 1984 the U.S. government enacted the Trademark Counterfeiting Act that made counterfeiting of products a criminal offense punishable by fines and stiff jail terms. However, stopping counterfeiters does not receive high priority from law enforcement officers and prosecutors. Legitimate firms therefore have the burden of finding their own way to fight the problem. IBM, with a court order, conducted its own raids and found keyboards, displays, and boxes with its logo. The fake parts were used to create counterfeits of IBM's XT personal computer.

Some companies use secret product codes to identify the genuine article. They must change the codes periodically because counterfeiters learn the codes and duplicate them. Perhaps the most effective way for manufacturers to fight counterfeiting is to monitor the distribution network and make sure counterfeit products are not getting into the network. Some companies even hire investigators to track counterfeit products.

By copying other firms' products, counterfeiters avoid research and development costs and most marketing costs. High-tech products such as computers are especially vulnerable. As long as counterfeiting is profitable, an abundance of products are available to copy, and the laws are difficult to enforce, counterfeiters can be expected to prosper for a long time.

Source: Adapted from Ronald F. Bush, "Product Counterfeiting Self-Defense Strategies," *Boardroom Reports* (January 15, 1990): 9–10; Celia F. McAllister, "Using Stool Pigeons to Clip Software Pirates' Wings," *Business Week* (March 19, 1990): 122; Chris Brown, "IBM Crackdown Uncovers Signs of Counterfeiting Ring," *Computerworld* (July 10, 1989): 95.

Questions for Discussion

1. What type of law does counterfeiting violate?
2. Why isn't the Trademark Counterfeiting Act of 1984 effective in controlling counterfeiting?
3. What part can manufacturers play in seeing that their products are not copied?
4. Can you suggest any other remedies for the counterfeiting situation?

CASE 5.2

Do Foreign-Owned Companies in the United States Pay Taxes?

Foreign-owned companies operating in the United States make a lot of money. From 1979 to 1987, the assets of foreign corporations grew 368 percent, to $959 billion. During that same period, the receipts of these firms grew 183 percent, to $685 billion. Yet in 1986 these same companies reported a new loss of $1.5 billion. Most foreign corporations operating in the United States pay little or no tax to Washington; the revenue loss is estimated at $20 to $30 billion.

How can firms that show such growth be losing money? That is what the IRS wants to know. In 1990 it began investigating the 1989 income tax returns of foreign-owned firms. The IRS believes that if foreign companies were losing so much money, they would pull out of the U.S. market. Instead, the firms were increasing their investments. Japanese firms are thought to be major offenders. Easily the most successful foreign investors in the United States during the past decade, the Japanese have nevertheless reported decreasing income during that time. That fact prompted the IRS to launch investigations of 18 Japanese companies.

IRS officials think foreign companies are overcharging their U.S.-based firms. This strategy is sometimes referred to as transfer of payments. The corporation gains an advantage by shifting costs to a high-tax country and income to low-tax countries. For instance, a product is manufactured in Germany at a cost of $80, and then sold to an Irish subsidiary for $80. The tax rate is 48 percent, but no taxes are paid because there was no profit. The Irish subsidiary than sells the item to a U.S. subsidiary for $150, earning a $70 profit. The tax rate in Ireland is 4 percent, so $2.80 is paid in taxes. The U.S. subsidiary then sells the item at cost for $150. The U.S. tax rate is 34 percent, but no profit is earned. The Irish subsidiary then lends money to the U.S. company for future expansion. Such transfer of payments is illegal but extremely difficult to prove.

The IRS runs into several obstacles when investigating a suspected corporate tax evader. First, the agency is understaffed; in 1990 it was just beginning to examine 1987 tax returns. If the IRS does decide to audit a company, investigators are often outmatched by the troop of accountants that represent the corporation. When the IRS does decide to prosecute a case, six to eight years may pass before it reaches court.

No one knows exactly how to solve the problem. Congress may end up writing some form of legislation to enable the IRS to conduct effective global audits. But many observers fear that as long as firms devote large sums of money to the illegal practice of shifting, the IRS stands little chance of catching them.

Source: Adapted from Larry Marty and Rich Thomas, "The Corporate Shell Game," *Newsweek* (April 15, 1991): 218–249; adapted from Jeff Shear, "Profits Elude Internal Revenue at Foreign-Owned Companies," reprinted by permission from *Insight*. Copyright 1990 *Insight*. All rights reserved. Dick Janssen, "Taking the Fangs Out of This Year's Tax Bite," *Business Week* (March 11, 1991): 108–109.

Questions for Discussion

1. Should there be laws or regulations developed to address the situation described in the case?
2. What law does transfer of payments appear to break?
3. What regulatory agency would you recommend to deal with this problem?

BUSINESS APPLICATION

Filing for Bankruptcy

Jimmy Hernandez, a 28-year-old owner of a surfing gear shop in Miami, is seriously in debt and contemplating his options. For the last three years, the business has been declining and he has run up approximately $60,000 in debt. Hernandez's business has reached a cash flow crisis: So much of his cash flow goes towards paying debt that he is unable to pay his two employees or himself without getting another loan.

Hernandez believes that his business is nearly defunct and is thinking about calling it quits and filing bankruptcy to eliminate the debts he's incurred.

Questions:

1. What would you do if you were Jimmy Hernandez?
2. Do you think any financial institution would loan Hernandez more money?
3. Assume Hernandez does file for bankruptcy and is able to get out from under his debt obligations. What advantages would filing for bankruptcy offer? What disadvantages?
4. How long does a person incur the consequences of having filed for bankruptcy?
5. How might a decision to file for bankruptcy affect Hernandez 10 or 12 years from now?

EXPERIENTIAL EXERCISE

Liability Is Open to Interpretation

Activity:

Students and instructor will discuss issues related to bringing a law suit against the owner of a business. The classroom discussion will use about 20 minutes of class time.

Directions:

1. Explain to students the growing concerns of business owners over the prospects of being sued over areas such as product liability or customers being injured on the premises of the owner's store.

2. Present the following scenario to the class: You are shopping in a local grocery store and you fall down after slipping on a wet spot on the floor. After experiencing severe pain, you go see a doctor who determines you have a broken collarbone which will necessitate further medical treatment. Assuming the medical services eventually total $7,000 in costs and that you have experienced a lot of pain and suffering, would you take any kind of legal action against the store owner, such as suing for actual damages as well as pain and suffering?
3. Call on several students to share what legal action, if any, they would take against the store owner. Assuming the store owner agreed to pay for the actual medical bills, but balked at paying for anything additional, would you sue for pain and suffering? If so, how much money would you seek to obtain?
4. Ask several students if their action would be any different if an investigation determined the store's janitor had been asked to clean up the wet spot half an hour prior to your slipping on it, but the janitor went on a coffee break instead.
5. Clarify to what extent the students would seek substantive compensation for pain and suffering based on the store owner's degree of negligence. In other words, if the injury was caused by extreme carelessness would the student seek more money, even though the injury may have not been that severe.

NOTES

1. Adapted from John A. Byrne, "The Best-Laid Ethics Programs," *Business Week* (March 9, 1992): 67–69; Michele Galen, "Debacle at Dow Corning: How Bad Will It Get?" *Business Week* (March 1992): 36, 38; Tim Smart, "This Man Sounded the Silicone Alarm—in 1976," *Business Week* (January 27, 1992): 34; and Joseph Weber, "I Guess the Price of Salt Water Is Going Up," *Business Week* (April 6, 1992): 28.
2. Milo Geyelin and James S. Hirsch, "Bumped Fliers Can Sue Airlines for Damages," *The Wall Street Journal* (June 7, 1993): B1, B2.
3. Catherine Yang, "Legally, At Least, 'Business Is No Worse Off,'" *Business Week* (July 12, 1993): 34.
4. Michael J. McCarthy and Douglas Lavin, "GM Ordered by Jury to Pay $105.2 Million Over Death," *The Wall Street Journal* (February 5, 1993): A3, A6.
5. Linda Himelstein, "The Asbestos Case of the 1990s," *Business Week* (January 16, 1995): 82–83.
6. Milo Geyelin, "Product-Liability Groups Take Up Arms," *The Wall Street Journal* (January 29, 1993): B1, B3.
7. Catherine Young, "Snatching Defeat from the Jaws of Victory," *Business Week* (August 1, 1994): 76–77.
8. Richard B. Schmitt, "Discoverers Call Patent Lawyers for Recoveries," *The Wall Street Journal* (April 22, 1993): B1, B10.
9. Larry Armstrong, "What's Wrong with Selling Used CDs?" *Business Week* (July 26, 1993): 38.
10. Linda Himelstein and Pete Engardio, "See You in Chinese Court," *Business Week* (February 27, 1995): 48.
11. Brigid Schulte, "Lawmakers Try to Blow Boxtop Off Cereal Pricing," *Lexington, KY, Herald-Leader* (March 8, 1995): A1, A6.
12. Larry Armstrong and Maria Mallory, "The Diet Business Starts Sweating," *Business Week* (June 22, 1992): 32–33.
13. "Always a Slogan," *Marketing News* (June 20, 1994):1.
14. Alix M. Freedman, "Koop Urges an Excise-Tax Increase, Ad Restrictions on Alcoholic Beverages," *The Wall Street Journal* (June 1, 1989): B6.

CHAPTER 6

Global Business

1. Discuss the meaning and scope of international business.
2. Explain why firms become involved in international business.
3. Define the basic concepts of international business.
4. List the various barriers to international business.
5. Identify the ways in which international business is regulated.
6. Describe the different approaches firms take to conduct business internationally.
7. Determine how a firm can adapt to foreign markets.

It's "You Can't Beat the Feeling" in the United States; "I Feel Coca-Cola" in Japan; "A Unique Sensation" in Italy; and in Chile "The Feeling of Life." The subtle differences in these slogans reflect Coca-Cola's philosophy regarding global marketing: Plan globally and act locally. In other words, Coca-Cola has developed a fairly standardized strategy that views the entire world as a single market, but is also sensitive to local cultures. The formula has succeeded. International sales account for about 80 percent of Coca-Cola's profits.

Like many firms, Coca-Cola is finding growth difficult. Its Coca-Cola Classic and Diet Coke brands are barely maintaining U.S. market share. Some cola drinkers are switching to cheaper store brands like Wal-Mart's Sam's American Choice. Noncolas like Dr Pepper and Barq's root beer have also gained popularity, along with flavored seltzers, juice drinks, and "natural" sodas.

Changing tastes and falling market share have Coca-Cola looking to Eastern Europe for new market opportunities. From 1989 to 1994, Coca-Cola invested $450 million in eastern Germany. Former East Germans, who watched Coca-Cola commercials on West German television for years, are crazy about Coca-Cola. Germany is Coca-Cola's largest market among European Union nations, contributing $767 million in 1991 profits, more than the United States did. At 177 rubles a can (27 cents), not many Russians can afford it yet, but Coca-Cola has plans to stay in Russia for the long haul. The company is building a $15 million production plant and training facility in Moscow and plans to build a $50 million production plant in St. Petersburg.

Cultural differences have posed challenges. Horst Muller, director of Coca-Cola's operations in eastern Germany, encountered a major difficulty—finding sales representatives to handle orders, deliveries, and sales promotions. To eastern Germans, selling was a foreign idea. So he turned to his 2,100 employees, many of whom came from former East German plants that Coca-Cola bought from the state. The friendliest technicians, factory workers, and clerks headed to the West for training and emerged as an enthusiastic team of sales representatives hustling for new business. Coca-Cola sold 74 million cases of soda in eastern Germany in 1991, up from zero cases the previous year.

With this level of success, Coca-Cola expects to take on PepsiCo, which has had a stronghold in most of Eastern Europe and the former Soviet Union for years. Coca-Cola has always been stronger in Germany, and its dominance in Western Europe (where it outsells Pepsi 6 to 1) has helped bring it closer to the lucrative markets in Eastern Europe dominated by Pepsi. Industry analysts expect Coca-Cola to start shipping to Poland from its eastern German plants. Coca-Cola also has facilities planned for Bulgaria, Rumania, the Czech Republic, Slovakia, and Russia.

Success will not come easy for Coca-Cola in Eastern Europe. PepsiCo already has sixty-five bottling plants there and in the former Soviet Union. Awareness of Pepsi is higher than of any other brand. In 1991, Pepsi sold 45 million cases in the former Soviet Union alone. It has allocated $1 billion for global expansion. But as cola wars are staged on new ground, many expect Coca-Cola's superior global resources to neutralize PepsiCo's advantage in Eastern Europe.[1]

What is the worldwide appeal of cola? What other products do you think would sell well around the globe?

Like Coca-Cola, more and more U.S. firms are conducting business across national boundaries. The world is changing rapidly, and opportunities in foreign markets will play a critical role in the future of many U.S. companies.

In this chapter, we examine some unique aspects of international business. First we discuss the nature and importance of the global economy. Then we present the reasons why firms start to do business internationally. Next we introduce several concepts important to understanding international business. We explain some barriers to international business and discuss its regulation. Finally we describe different approaches to international business and discuss how a firm can adapt to foreign markets.

THE NATURE AND IMPORTANCE OF THE GLOBAL ECONOMY

In the global economy, products have to compete with similar products made anywhere else. Cars made in Tennessee compete with cars made in Japan; flowers grown in Florida compete with flowers grown in Columbia; wine bottled in California competes with wine bottled in France. The question facing firms in the United States and throughout the world isn't whether they should compete with foreign firms, but how they can survive in the global economy.

The answer to this question, of course, is complex. We know that customers are demanding better products, improved service, and lower prices, and the way to compete is through quality. Global competition means that consumers have a better choice of products and lower prices; management's common goal must be customer satisfaction. In the past decade the United States' dominance in the world economy has faltered because of the decline in competitiveness of U.S. goods. A major factor in this decline is that our economic status in the new global economy will depend upon our ability to meet new competitive standards.

TOMORROW'S BUSINESS WORLD

Business Leaders Recognize Global Interdependence

With high-capacity cables, satellites, and digital switchers, a huge corporation or a small factory can conduct business anywhere, finding customers and supplies around the globe. "In order to survive and prosper in the coming years, business leaders need to realize there really is a thing called global interdependence," says William Archey of the U.S. Chamber of Commerce. "Even a small business isn't just competing against other local small businesses, but against small businesses in other cities, in other states, in other regions and perhaps even in other countries. The notion that the small business is insulated from the world economy is dead wrong."

Today's customer is able to buy from suppliers from all over the world, says Leonard Berry of the Center for Retailing Studies at Texas A&M University. According to Berry, "Whether it's through the fax machine or the telephone, or through international catalogs or domestic arms of international companies, customers now have access to international success." In addition, Berry believes that thanks to the globalization of the media, customers are influenced by international trades and fashions to a much larger degree than many small-business owners may realize.

Even if exporting goods or services or dealing with foreign suppliers isn't an issue, it's important for small-business owners and operators to be aware of what's happening internationally. "You need to know what your foreign competitors are doing overseas," says Archey, "because they may soon be doing it next-door. There used to be a joke that a small company's idea of international trade was going from Michigan to Minnesota—in the 21st century that will change."

Source: Adapted from Catherine Arnst and Gail Edmondson, "The Global Free-For-All," *Business Week* (September 26, 1994): 118–126; and the 1992 Special Advertising Section of *U.S. News & World Report.*

Defining International Business

International Business
The performance of business activities across national boundaries.

International business is the performance of business activities across national boundaries. Every nation in the world participates in international business to some extent. Involvement in international business has increased steadily since World War II, and it's expected to continue growing. More than $2 trillion is spent annually on trade between nations. By the year 2000 a key requirement for chief executives of U.S. firms will be experience in international business. And worldwide employment will increase in nearly all U.S. firms. This growth will be due in part to the global boom and new business opportunities throughout the world.

Today Japan is one of the world's largest economic powers. Only 50 years ago the country was left devastated by American bombing raids during World War II. Tokyo was burned to the ground; atomic bombs leveled Hiroshima and Nagasaki. When the war ended, Japan's economy no longer existed. But Japan learned from the disaster. Ever since, the Japanese have invested in people. Current changes in Eastern Europe, South Korea, Vietnam, and Taiwan also suggest a global environment in which market power, not military power, will prevail. Learning how to manage organizations in this new environment will be critical to firms throughout the world.

As more and more firms begin to conduct business with foreign countries, the importance of international business will increase. Your Values and Attitudes will help you assess your thoughts about foreign firms doing business in the United States.

As part of the growing involvement of U.S. firms in international business, Levi Strauss & Co. opened its first store in Moscow, where hundreds lined up to get in.

YOUR VALUES AND ATTITUDES

Foreign Business in the United States

Directions: For each statement, circle the number that shows your level of agreement.

	Strongly Disagree					Strongly Agree
1. Foreign individuals and firms should be restricted from purchasing assets, such as banks, farmland, and hotels, in the United States.	1	2	3	4	5	6
2. Americans should purchase American-made products whenever possible.	1	2	3	4	5	6
3. The United States should limit the amount of foreign goods it imports.	1	2	3	4	5	6

4. Foreign companies should not be allowed to build factories in American cities.	1	2	3	4	5	6
5. The United States should put a high tax on all foreign goods entering the country.	1	2	3	4	5	6

Feedback: Americans often have strong feelings about foreign companies selling products in our country and competing with U.S. firms. If you strongly disagreed with most of the statements, you favor foreign firms being able to do business in the United States. If you strongly agreed with the statements, you tend to be against such business. You may echo a popular phrase of the last several years, "Buy American!"

Some Americans fear foreign competitors because they do not fully understand them—in language, culture, or social values. Some American companies have been hurt by foreign competition; you may know people who lost jobs after U.S. firms closed or moved operations overseas. Conversely some Americans have few qualms about foreign companies conducting business on U.S. soil. They, and you, may think that international business is exciting and that competition from all manufacturers of a product, regardless of country of origin, is fair to businesses and beneficial to consumers. Regardless of your position on this issue, you as a student of business have already realized that international business will continue to expand in the United States and throughout the world.

Global Opportunities

The global boom has resulted in a customer-driven world economy. Harvard University professor Rosabeth Moss Kanter says that information, the computer, and transportation advances caused the global market. She contends that many of the changes taking place in Europe today are because people in Eastern Europe wanted to go shopping. Through TV and other mass media, people can learn about lifestyles in the rest of the world. It's interesting to think that Levi Strauss and Bon Jovi—not just U.S. military strength—helped cause the Soviet bloc's breakup.[2]

A customer-driven economy means new opportunities throughout the world. For example, Russians know that their standard of living is lower than that of citizens in the West. As Russia's economy changes, demand will rise for products of all types—food, clothing, appliances, leisure items, medical care, and so on. Countless new opportunities will arise for firms to offer goods and services that meet these demands. In short, the global economy means global opportunities for firms that simply need the vision to act upon them. Argentina has experienced one of the fastest and most successful processes of privatization. The state-owned oil company, railroads, telephones, airline, utilities, and television and radio stations have been privatized. Inflation has dropped from 4,000 percent in the 1980s to 17.5 percent in 1993, while growth is exceeding 6 percent annually.[3] Foreign investors, including U.S. firms such as Motorola, AT&T, Chrysler, IBM, and Apple, are flocking to

China to invest in that country's double-digit growth.[4] China's flagrant piracy of American products ranging from pop music to computer software presents a clear risk to Western and Asian companies doing business there.[5] Western firms also are finding new opportunities in India, the world's fifth-largest economy, with a middle class of approximately 300 million people eager for new products.[6]

Taking advantage of global opportunities won't be easy. Firms throughout the world are poised to offer products to emerging markets. More competition means more choices, which drive the need for quality even higher. In 1980 there were seven primary competitors in the luxury car market. By 1990 the number rose to 15, including companies in the United States, Japan, Germany, and other European countries. Competition in other industries is following the same pattern. The increased globalization of markets has led to greater competition among corporations throughout the world and erosion in the world dominance of U.S. firms—a trend that's expected to continue.[7] Firms that supply high-quality products will be in the best position to survive and prosper in the global economy.

WHY FIRMS CONDUCT INTERNATIONAL BUSINESS

Scarcity of resources is perhaps the major reason why nations trade with each other.[8] A country with a surplus of some product may decide to sell this surplus to other nations. Such sales will enable the country to purchase other products that it may not have the ability to produce.

No nation has every raw material or resource; no nation can produce everything it needs. Most nations specialize in producing particular goods or services. The United States, for example, has developed a specialty in producing agricultural products efficiently; thus it sells food to many nations of the world. But the United States purchases much of its oil from other countries, such as Saudi Arabia, that specialize in the production of crude oil.

Absolute Advantage
When a country can produce a product more efficiently than any other nation.

A nation has an **absolute advantage** if it can produce a product more efficiently (using fewer resources) than any other nation. South Africa has an absolute advantage in the production of diamonds. Absolute advantages are rare because usually at least two countries can efficiently supply a specific product.

Comparative Advantage
When a country can produce one product more efficiently and at a lower cost than other products, in comparison to other nations.

A country has a **comparative advantage** if it can produce one product more efficiently than other products in comparison to other nations. For instance, countries with low labor costs, such as China and South American countries, have a comparative advantage in producing labor-intensive products such as shoes and clothing. Many nations become involved in international business because they have a comparative advantage. Firms sell those goods for which they have the greatest comparative advantage over other countries. The United States has its greatest comparative advantage in food products, aircraft, and coal.

Comparative advantages shift frequently. For many years, the United States held a comparative advantage in manufacturing a variety of products, such as automobiles, television sets, and appliances. Today many of these products are made in Japan, Germany, and South Korea. The United States, for instance, experienced a dramatic loss of comparative advantage in manufacturing televisions. One reason for shifts in comparative advantages is competition.

Some nations want to become self-sufficient and thus do not specialize in the production and sale of particular products. The choice of specialization or self-sufficiency is generally a political and economic issue. For instance, communist nations traditionally have strived for self-sufficiency because they feared economic dependency on other countries. Some nations also view self-sufficiency as necessary for achieving military supremacy. Of course, no country is completely self-sufficient.

BASIC CONCEPTS OF INTERNATIONAL BUSINESS

Several basic concepts are important for an understanding of international business. In this section, we discuss the concepts of exporting and importing, balance of trade, balance of payments, and exchange rates.

Exporting and Importing

Exporting
Selling domestic-made goods in another country.

Importing
Purchasing goods made in another country.

The United States is one of the world's largest exporter and importers. **Exporting** is selling domestic-made goods in another country. **Importing** is purchasing goods made in another country. Most of the video recorders purchased in the United States are imported from Japan.

No doubt you realize that the United States imports a wide variety of products: oil, automobiles, electronic equipment, clothing and shoes, iron and steel, and paper products, to name a few. But U.S. exports are on the rise, up 121 percent since 1978.[9] The major growth is in exports to Canada, Japan, Mexico, Taiwan, Korea, and Germany. The fastest-growing U.S. exports are music, video, and computer tapes; cigarettes and tobacco products; meat; pulp and wastepaper; and synthetic resins, rubber, and plastics. Exhibit 6.1 contains a list of the leading U.S. exports and imports.

Balance of Trade

Balance of Trade
The difference (in dollars) between the amount a country exports and the amount it imports.

If we export more than import we have favorable balance of trade,

Balance of trade is the result of importing and exporting. A country's balance of trade is the difference (in monetary terms) between the amount it exports and the amount it imports. A nation that exports more than it imports maintains a favorable balance of trade, or a *trade surplus*. Japan and Taiwan have a favorable balance of trade. A nation that imports more than it exports has an unfavorable balance of trade, or a *trade deficit*. The United States has reduced its trade deficit and should see a trade surplus if exports continue to grow.

Exhibit 6.1
U.S. Exports and Imports

Products	Export Value (millions)	Import Value (millions)
Foods, feeds, and beverages	$ 40,114	$ 27,879
Industrial supplies and materials	109,570	139,770
Capital goods (except automotive)	176,837	134,411
Automotive vehicles and parts	46,686	91,238
Consumer goods (nonfood)	50,386	123,003

Source: *Statistical Abstract of the United States,* (Washington, DC: U.S. Department of Commerce, Bureau of the Census 1994), 804.

Balance of Payments

Balance of Payments
The total flow of money into and out of a country.

A country's **balance of payments** is the total flow of money into and out of the country. The balance of payments is determined by a country's balance of trade, foreign aid, foreign investments, military spending, and money spent by tourists in other countries. A country has a favorable balance of payments if more money is flowing in than is flowing out; an unfavorable balance of payments exists when more money is flowing out of the country than in. For many years, the United States enjoyed a favorable balance of payments. But in recent years, more money has been leaving the country than has been flowing in.

Exchange Rates

Exchange Rate
The rate at which one country's currency can be exchanged for that of another country.

The rate at which one country's currency can be exchanged for that of another country is called the **exchange rate.** For instance, on January 16, 1995, one U.S. dollar exchanged for 1.4 Canadian dollars, for 0.64 British pounds, and for 98.4 Japanese yen.

Governments and market conditions determine exchange rates. *Devaluation* by its government reduces the value of a nation's currency in relation to currencies of other nations. If the United States were to devalue its currency, for example, the cost of American goods in foreign countries would decrease. *Revaluation* increases the value of a country's currency in relation to that of other countries. Revaluation of the dollar would increase the cost of American goods purchased in foreign countries.

Fixed Exchange Rate
An unvarying exchange rate set by government policy.

Floating Exchange Rate
An exchange rate that fluctuates with market conditions.

After World War II, during a meeting held at Bretton Woods, NH, the major industrialized nations of the world established a **fixed exchange rate.** Known as the Bretton Woods Accord, this agreement mandated that a nation pay its debts by transferring gold reserves to the reserves of creditor nations. As the U.S. balance of payments deficit began to exceed its gold reserves, President Richard Nixon took the United States off the gold standard. This led to a **floating exchange rate,** which allows the exchange rate to fluctuate with market conditions. For instance, when Americans spend U.S. dollars to buy automobiles and other products from Japan, the value of the dollars relative to the Japanese yen goes down. Today, many nations use a floating exchange rate.

BARRIERS TO INTERNATIONAL BUSINESS

Firms desiring to enter international business face several obstacles, some much more severe than others. In this section, we examine the most common barriers to effective international business: cultural, social, and political barriers, and tariffs and trade restrictions.

Cultural and Social Barriers

Understanding differences in cultures and social forces is a basic requirement for successful international business.[10] *Culture* consists of a country's general concepts and values and tangible items such as food, clothing, and buildings. *Social forces* include family, education, religion, and customs. Selling products from one country to another is sometimes difficult when the cultures of the two countries differ significantly. As noted in Chapter 4, *cultural diversity* refers to the differences that exist both within and among cultures.[11] Meanings attached to body language, time, greetings, spatial patterns, and other symbols differ significantly across cultures. When products are introduced into one nation from another, acceptance is far more likely if differences between cultures are recognized and accommodated. For example, managers of McDonald's realized that when they opened restaurants in Japan, they would have to adapt to Japanese culture. The first McDonald's restaurant was therefore located in a prestigious area in Tokyo to impress the Japanese. Had the restaurant been opened in the suburbs, the Japanese would have considered it a second-class enterprise. Understanding how Japanese consumers view locations helped McDonald's succeed in Japan.[12] Conversely, Yokohama Rubber Company, based in Tokyo, recalled auto tires with a tread pattern that resembled the Arabic word for Allah, discontinued the tires, and replaced them free of charge in Islamic nations.[13]

Some countries also have different values about spending. The Japanese have long been a people that believe in paying cash for the products they buy, although the use of credit cards has soared in Japan over the last few years. The more the Japanese borrow and spend, the more they import—meaning increased trade for countries such as the United States. Yet the Japanese as a nation still save nearly 20 percent of individual income, compared to about 4 percent saved by people in the United States.

Social forces can create obstacles to international trade. In China, for instance, a firm cannot claim in its advertisements to be number one, since the moral system there holds that everyone is equal. In some countries, purchasing items as basic as food and clothing can be influenced by religion. In many nations, individuals do not have the choices in food, clothing, and health care that we do in the United States. And some societies simply do not value material possessions to the same degree that Americans do.

Most firms know the importance of understanding the cultural and social differences between selling and buying countries. However, executives still make costly mistakes when conducting business internationally simply because they do not understand such differences. For instance, a business deal in Japan can fall through if a foreign executive refuses a cup of green tea during a visit to a native Japanese firm, or if a Japanese businessperson is put in a position where he or she must admit failure.

Political Barriers

The political climate of a country can have a major impact on international business. Nations experiencing intense political unrest may change their attitude toward foreign firms at any time; this instability creates an unfavorable atmosphere for international trade. The greatest risk for international firms is in politically unstable areas of the world such as Africa and the Middle East. Countries such as the United States, Australia, and Japan are more attractive because of their political stability.

Tariffs and Trade Restrictions

Tariffs and trade restrictions are also barriers to international business. A nation can restrict trade through import tariffs, quotas and embargoes, and exchange controls.

Import Tariff
A duty, or tax, levied against goods brought into a country.

Import Tariffs. A duty, or tax, levied against goods brought into a country is an **import tariff.** Tariffs can be used to discourage foreign competitors from entering a domestic market. Some Americans have called for high tariffs on Japanese products such as cars and stereos. The risk in imposing tariffs is that the other country could take the same action against U.S. products.

Quota
A limit on the amount of a product that can leave or enter a country.

Quotas and Embargoes. A **quota** is a limit on the amount of a product that can leave or enter a country. For many years, Japan placed strict quotas on beef and citrus imports. When Japan began to lift the quotas in 1988, it opened one of the world's wealthiest consumer markets to beef and citrus producers in countries such as the United States and Australia.

Some quotas are established on a voluntary basis. Generally, a *voluntary quota* fosters goodwill and protects a country from foreign competition. For instance, Japan set a target to buy 20 percent of its computer chips from U.S. firms. In 1992, imported chips accounted for over 17 percent of Japan's market.[14] The United States also wants auto dealerships in Japan to grow faster, Japanese automakers to buy $19 billion in parts from U.S. suppliers, and market share for American-made medical equipment to rise from its current level of 20 percent.[15]

Embargo
A total ban on certain imports and exports.

An **embargo** is a total ban on certain imports and exports. Many embargoes are politically motivated, such as the United Nations' embargo of goods to Iraq after that nation invaded Kuwait in 1990. Often, if a country places an embargo on products imported from or exported to another country, the second country retaliates with embargoes of its own. In 1994, when President Clinton ended the U.S. embargo on Vietnam, American firms found that doors that once were closed in Vietnam soon became wide open.[16]

Exchange Controls Restrictions on the amount of a certain currency that can be bought or sold in a nation.

Exchange Controls. Restrictions on the amount of a certain currency that can be bought or sold are called **exchange controls.** A government can use exchange controls to limit the amount of products that importers can purchase with a particular currency. In 1985, for example, China placed strict restrictions on foreign exchange spending.

REGULATION OF INTERNATIONAL BUSINESS

As business between nations has grown, so has the number of laws and organizations involved in the regulation of international trade. In this section, we look at major legislation and organizations that have been developed to regulate international business.

Legislation

The major U.S. laws affecting American firms engaged in international business are summarized in Exhibit 6.2 The *Webb-Pomerene Export Trade Act* of 1918 exempts U.S. firms from certain antitrust laws if they are working together to develop export markets. The Webb-Pomerene Act does not allow companies to reduce competition in the United States or to use unfair methods of competition. The *Foreign Corrupt Practices Act,* passed in 1977, prohibits American firms from making bribes to foreign officials. This law spells out the penalties for companies and individuals who are in violation: Companies may be fined up to $1 million, and individuals may receive a fine up to $10,000 and a prison sentence of up to five years. The *Export Trading Companies Act* of 1982 eliminates some antitrust barriers and allows banks to participate in joint ventures. An export trading company is an organization that attempts to create exports.

Unfortunately, many firms can take advantage of weak regulation in foreign countries. For example, products that are regulated in the United States, such as dangerous pesticides and drugs, may not be regulated in other coun-

Exhibit 6.2
U.S. Laws Affecting International Business

Law	Purpose
Webb-Pomerene Export Trade Act (1918)	Exempts U.S. firms from antitrust laws if they are acting together to develop international trade
Foreign Corrupt Practices Act (1977)	Makes bribing foreign officials to obtain sales illegal for American firms
Export Trading Companies Act (1982)	Encourages the formation of export trading companies by eliminating antitrust barriers and allowing banks to participate in such ventures

tries so firms look to those foreign markets to sell dangerous products. Third World nations are often the target of dangerous products because they have the weakest regulation, a subject explored in Today's Business World.

TODAY'S BUSINESS WORLD

Danger for Sale

The Environmental Protection Agency bans the sale of DowElanco's weedkiller Galant to U.S. farmers because it might cause cancer. But DowElanco still sells it in Costa Rica. The painkiller dipyrone was outlawed by the U.S. Food and Drug Administration over 15 years ago, but Winthrop Products sells it in Mexico. As cigarette smoking drops considerably in the United States, Philip Morris, R.J. Reynolds, and Brown & Williamson sell 3.7 billion cigarettes a year in Taiwan, a country that had wanted to prevent the import of cigarettes.

Some of the largest and most respected U.S. firms are selling dangerous products to millions of people around the world. Most of the customers live in Third World countries characterized by weak or unenforced regulation and illiterate consumers. The U.S. government does little to stop such sales. Placing a dollar figure on this trade is difficult because the federal government doesn't report shipments of banned products. But it's estimated that foreign sales of tobacco, banned pesticides, hazardous drugs, and toxic wastes total billions of dollars and involve thousands of jobs. For instance, the U.S. Cigarette Export Association says total tobacco exports amount to $5 billion annually and account for 125,000 U.S. jobs.

The controversy over exports of dangerous products by U.S. firms came to public attention in 1981. After intense public debate and congressional investigations, President Jimmy Carter signed an executive order on January 15, 1981, that forbade companies to export products that were not allowed to be sold in the United States. According to Carter, the nation had an obligation "not to export to unsuspecting nations products which we ourselves would not allow in our country." Ronald Reagan revoked Carter's order 33 days later at the beginning of his term as president. In the years that have followed, the U.S. government has virtually given exporters of dangerous products a free hand.

Critics say the export of dangerous products is highly unethical. The Bush administration maintained that as long as the products are legal in foreign countries, who is the United States to tell the rest of the world what to do? Many CEOs refuse to discuss the issue. Some justify their decisions, saying poor countries need chemicals to grow food and wipe out disease. Besides, they argue, in today's global economy purchasers can always obtain the products from other sellers, which would deprive Americans of profits and paychecks.

Should firms export products such as these? Even if legal, is this ethical?

Source: Adapted from Christopher Scanlon, "What Isn't Safe at Home Is Being Shipped Abroad," Knight-Ridder News Service, Lexington, KY, *Herald-Leader* (May 19, 1991): A1, A13; Christopher Scanlon, "Toxic Products from U.S. Threaten Third World Workers," Knight-Ridder News Service, Lexington, KY, *Herald-Leader* (May 20, 1991): A1, A5; and Christopher Scanlon, "U.S. Drug Firms Thrive on Loose Regulation, Illiteracy in Third World," Knight-Ridder News Service, Lexington, KY, *Herald-Leader* (May 21, 1991): A1, A5.

International Organizations

GATT
An international organization formed to reduce or eliminate tariffs and other barriers to international trade.

Several international organizations exist to facilitate world trade. The major ones are summarized in Exhibit 6.3.

GATT. Signed in 1947, the **General Agreement on Tariffs and Trade (GATT)** formed an international organization of 23 nations, including the

Exhibit 6.3
Organizations that Facilitate International Business

General Agrrement on Tariffs and Trade (GATT)

Formed in 1947 by 23 nations to reduce or eliminate tariffs and other barriers to international trade.
Members: 96 countrties, including the United States and Russia.

European Union (EU)

Founded in 1957 to reduce barriers among members.
Members: Belgium, Denmark, France, Germany, Greece, Ireland, Italy, Luxembourg, the Netherlands, Portugal, Spain, and the United Kingdom.

Latin American Free Trade Association (LAFTA)

Founded in 1960 to develop free trade among member nations.
Members: Argentina, Brazil, Chile, Columbia, Ecuador, Mexico, Paraguay, Peru, and Uruguay.

European Free Trade Association (EFTA)

Founded in 1960 to eliminate trade restrictions among members and develop common trade policies.
Members: Austria, Iceland, Norway, Portugal, Sweden, Switzerland, and Finland (associate member).

Organization of Petroleum Exporting Countries (OPEC)

Established in 1960 to provide oil-producing nations control over prices and reduce the oversupply of oil.
Members: Algeria, Ecuador, Gabon, Indonesia, Iran, Iraq, Kuwait, Libya, Nigeria, Qatar, Saudi Arabia, United Arab Emirates, and Venezuela.

International Monetary Fund (IMF)

Founded in 1944 to promote trade among member nations by eliminating trade barriers and increasing cooperation on financial issues.
Members: 149 industrial and developing countries.

World Bank

Founded in 1946 to lend money to underdeveloped and developing countries for a variety of projects.
Members: 149 industrial and developing countries.

President Clinton signs the 1994 GATT agreement during a ceremony at the Organization of American States in Washington.

United States. GATT works to reduce or eliminate tariffs and other barriers to international trade. Today nearly 100 countries agree to the guidelines established by GATT.

Since it was organized, GATT has sponsored several rounds of negotiations to reduce trade barriers. President John F. Kennedy, through authority granted by the Trade Expansion Act of 1962, called for the reduction of tariffs through GATT. The Kennedy Round, which began in 1964, led to a nearly 40 percent reduction in tariffs. The Tokyo Round, held from 1973 to 1979, led to a reduction of over 30 percent. Other nontariff restrictions, such as import quotas and unnecessary red tape in customs procedures, were also removed. In 1989 more than 100 countries agreed to halt foreign subsidies and institute a new system of arbitration for handling disputes between countries. In 1994, a new GATT accord adopted by 124 nations including the United States reduced tariffs worldwide by an average of 38 percent.[17]

Economic Community
An organization that facilitates the movement of products among member nations through the creation of common economic policies.

Economic Communities. An organization formed to facilitate the movement of products among member nations through the creation of common economic policies is called an **economic community.** One of the largest, the 12-nation European Union (EU), created by the Treaty of Rome in 1957, called for eliminating most trade barriers between its members (Germany, France, Italy, the United Kingdom, Spain, and Netherlands, Belgium, Denmark, Greece, Portugal, Ireland, and Luxembourg) in 1992. Historically the member nations have primarily been separate markets, unable to compete with the giant resources of Japan and the United States. With the barriers dissolved, however, competitive European companies would likely tap the unified European market. With over 340 million consumers, unified Europe would be one of the largest markets in the world.[18] The elimination of trade barriers has meant gains for Europe in several industries, including airlines, telecommunications, and financial services. However, the broad monetary and political union of the 12 nations has yet to occur.[19]

Another economic community, the Latin American Free Trade Association (LAFTA), was organized in 1960. Its purpose was to develop free trade among members, a goal yet to be achieved. The European Free Trade Association (EFTA), organized in 1960 in response to the European Community, has eliminated many trade barriers among members. Two original members of EFTA, the United Kingdom and Denmark, dropped out to join the EU. Another well-known economic community is the Organization of Petroleum Exporting Countries (OPEC). Established in 1960, OPEC exists to give oil-producing nations some control over the price and supply of oil. OPEC has been fairly successful in controlling both.

The United States and Canada signed the *Free Trade Agreement (FTA)* in 1989, providing for the eventual elimination of tariffs and other trade barriers. The agreement essentially merged the U.S. and Canadian markets and made them the largest free trade zone in the world. Trade between the United States and Canada was nearly $170 billion annually before the FTA was signed.[20] Even greater commercial activity is expected after barriers to trade are removed. Some experts predict that the two countries' GNPs could increase by 1 to 5 percent annually.

Even more far reaching is the *North American Free Trade Agreement (NAFTA),* a three-nation alliance of the United States, Canada, and Mexico signed on August 12, 1992. The United States needs resources and a source of new labor, Canada is resource-rich but small in population, and Mexico has an abundance of oil and workers but desperately needs exports to fuel its economy. The three nations combined comprise a $6 trillion market of nearly 360 million consumers.[21] Thus, the agreement made sense to many. Trade among the three nations, $237 billion a year before NAFTA, was expected by some to increase dramatically once trade barriers were removed.[22] Others feared that the agreement would mean more U.S. jobs lost to Mexico, where wages are about 10 percent of those in the United States.[23] Many economists argue, however, that lower labor costs should put U.S. firms in a better position to take on global competitors and thus should provide a long-range benefit to the economy.[24] Furthermore, they feel the treaty will keep U.S. ex-

IMF
An international financial organization that lends money to countries to conduct international trade.

World Bank
An international organization that lends money to underdeveloped and developing countries for development.

ports to Mexico booming and result in more jobs in several industries, including automobiles, textiles, and telecommunications.[25] A year after NAFTA was signed, it had increased trade among nations, although it had yet to create the number of new jobs expected.[26]

IMF and World Bank. Two international organizations have been established to help finance international trade. The **International Monetary Fund (IMF)** was founded in 1944 to promote cooperation among member nations by eliminating trade barriers. The IMF lends money to countries that need short-term loans to conduct international trade. The **World Bank** was formed in 1946 to lend money to underdeveloped and developing countries for various projects. The World Bank makes loans to member nations to fund the development of roads, factories, and medical facilities.

APPROACHES TO INTERNATIONAL BUSINESS

A firm that decides to enter international trade must select an approach. There are several choices, some requiring relatively low levels of commitment and others requiring much higher levels. Approaches to international business include exporting, licensing, joint ventures, strategic alliances, trading companies, countertrading, direct ownership, and multinational corporations.

Exporting

The simplest way to enter international business is exporting—selling domestic goods to a foreign country. It requires the lowest level of resources and commitment. More than half of the U.S. firms involved in international trade do so through exporting.[27] In many cases, a firm can locate an exporting firm that can provide assistance in selling products to foreign countries, thereby avoiding significant upfront investments.[28]

American exports are making a strong comeback and have reduced the trade deficit. The United States trade deficit fell from a record $146 billion in 1987 to $99 billion in 1992.[29] In 1992, for the second year in a row, the United States ranked as the top merchandise exporter in the world, with $448.2 billion in exports.[30] Many products once considered in serious trouble domestically are selling well in foreign markets. Exhibit 6.4 lists the 20 largest U.S. exporters.

Exporting is a key to growth, especially when domestic markets are saturated. Many large and small U.S. firms are growing because of their exports. For instance, the United States is the leading exporter of food to Japan, with annual sales exceeding $10 billion.[31] General Motors markets a minivan manufactured in the United States and sold in Europe under the Opel name. GM expects to export about $750 million worth of vans by 1996.[32] Small companies also rely on exports for growth and sales. Treatment Products exports $5

Exhibit 6.4
The 20 Largest U.S. Exporters

Rank	Company	Export Sales (in millions)	Total Sales (in millions)	Exports as a Percentage of Sales
1	General Motors	$14,913	$133,622	11.2
2	Boeing	14,616	25,285	57.8
3	Ford Motor	9,483	108,521	8.7
4	General Electric	8,498	60,823	14.0
5	Chrysler	8,397	43,600	19.3
6	IBM	7,297	62,716	11.6
7	Motorola	4,990	16,963	29.4
8	Hewlett-Packard	4,738	20,317	23.3
9	Philip Morris	4,105	50,621	8.1
10	Caterpillar	3,743	11,615	32.2
11	United Technologies	3,503	20,736	16.9
12	DuPont	3,500	32,621	10.7
13	Intel	3,406	8,782	38.8
14	McDonnell Douglas	3,405	14,487	23.5
15	Archer Daniels Midland	2,900	9,811	29.6
16	Eastman Kodak	2,242	20,059	11.2
17	Raytheon	2,063	9,201	22.4
18	Compaq Computer	1,922	7,191	26.7
19	Digital Equipment	1,800	14,371	12.5
20	Lockheed	1,743	13,071	13.3

Source: "Top 50 U.S. Industrial Exporters," *Fortune* (August 22, 1994).

million in auto wax, Sharper Finish exports $3 million in laundry and ironing equipment, and Midwest Tropical exports $5.5 million in aquariums.[33]

Licensing

Licensing
An agreement in which one firm allows another firm to sell its product and use its brand name in return for a commission or royalty.

In a **licensing** agreement, one firm (the licensor) agrees to allow another firm (the licensee) to sell the licensor's product and use its brand name. In return, the licensee pays the licensor a commission or royalty. For example, a beverage company such as PepsiCo might enter into a licensing agreement with a firm in Taiwan. The Taiwanese firm would have the right to sell Pepsi products in Taiwan and would pay PepsiCo a specified percentage of the income from sales of Pepsi products. Playboy Enterprises has licensed 20 mainland Chinese sportswear boutiques operated by the Chinese government. The boutiques sell a variety of outerwear and other products with the rabbit logo.[34]

Licensing offers advantages for both licensor and licensee. The licensor can become involved in international trade with little financial risk. The licensee gains products and technology that may otherwise be too costly to produce. For the licensor, the agreement usually results in a payoff of only about 5 percent of sales. Some American executives and managers believe that licensing agreements merely give away trade secrets for a meager 5 percent of sales; after the agreement expires (usually in less than 10 years), the licensee may continue to market the product without paying the licensor.

Joint Ventures

Firms may also conduct international business through a joint venture, in this case a partnership between a domestic firm and a firm in a foreign country. Because of government restrictions on foreign ownership of corporations, joint ventures are often the only way a firm can purchase facilities in another country. For instance, after years of negotiations, McDonald's of Canada opened a restaurant in the Soviet Union. The Moscow City Council's Food Service will own 51 percent of the enterprise, a requirement under Soviet joint venture laws.

One major drawback to international joint ventures is that organizations may lose control of their operations. For example, because India does not allow foreign companies to own industries, Coca-Cola once entered into a joint venture with the Indian government. Despite the huge soft drink market in India, Coca-Cola pulled out over a decade ago rather than risk giving up majority control and its secret formula.

Strategic Alliances

Strategic Alliance An agreement in which two firms combine their resources in a partnership that goes beyond a joint venture.

A recent strategy for entering foreign markets is a strategic alliance. A **strategic alliance** occurs when two firms combine their resources in a partnership that goes beyond the limits of a joint venture. Strategic alliances have been growing in the highly competitive global marketplace at an annual rate of 27 percent since 1985.[35] IBM alone has established over 400 strategic alliances with U.S. and foreign firms. Trust is the major requirement for an effective partnership. If a firm can't trust its prospective partners, it shouldn't enter into a strategic alliance with them. Trust generally evolves over time, so firms must give strategic alliances adequate time to prosper. Ford and Mazda formed a strategic alliance nearly 15 years ago to cooperate on new vehicles and exchange expertise. Ford is now the best-selling foreign auto in Japan, and building trust over the years was a major factor.[36]

Trading Companies

Trading Company A firm that buys products in one country and sells in another without being involved in manufacturing.

Another approach to international business is to use or form a trading company to provide a link between buyers and sellers in different countries. A **trading company** buys products in one country and sells them in another without being involved in manufacturing. Trading companies take title to products and move them from one country to another. Trading companies can simplify entrance into foreign markets because they are usually favored by the foreign governments. Many major corporations such as General Electric and Sears, Roebuck have developed trading companies.

Some countries—Brazil, for one—give trading companies tax advantages. In the United States, the 1982 *Export Trading Company Act* encourages the efficient operation of trading companies, helps finance international trade, and provides limited protection from antitrust laws when conducting export activities. After the act was passed, many major companies (such as General Electric, Kmart, and Sears, Roebuck) developed their own export trading companies.

Countertrading

Countertrading
Bartering agreements between two or more countries.

Countertrading involves complex bartering agreements between two or more countries. (*Bartering* refers to the exchange of merchandise between countries.) Countertrading allows a nation with limited cash to participate in international trade. The country wishing to trade requires the exporting country to purchase products from it before allowing its products to be sold there. Agreements like this account for an estimated 20 percent of U.S. exports, or $110 billion; the use of countertrade agreements is expected to grow.[37] Countertrading provides an established trading vehicle for the former Soviet bloc and other developing and Third World countries that want U.S. goods but lack currency to pay for them.[38] Although many U.S. companies still don't use countertrading, firms will find they have no choice if they wish to compete in global markets.

Countertrading has several drawbacks. First, it's often difficult to determine the true value of goods offered in a countertrade agreement. Second, it may be difficult to dispose of bartered goods after they're accepted. These problems can be reduced or eliminated through market analysis and negotiation. Companies have been developed to assist firms in handling countertrade agreements. Despite these drawbacks, companies that choose not to countertrade may miss significant opportunities.

Direct Ownership

Direct Ownership
The purchase of one or more business operations in a foreign country.

A much more involved approach to international business is **direct ownership**—purchasing one or more business operations in a foreign country. Direct ownership requires a large investment in production facilities, research, personnel, and marketing activities. Many large companies, such as Ford, Polaroid, and 3M, own facilities outside the United States. Some well-known firms operating in the United States are actually subsidiaries owned by foreign firms. Magnavox, Pillsbury, Saks Fifth Avenue, and Baskin-Robbins are wholly owned subsidiaries of foreign multinational companies. Nonprofit organizations (such as the Red Cross) and the U.S. Army also own foreign subsidiaries or divisions.

Firms invest in foreign subsidiaries for a number of reasons. Direct ownership can reduce manufacturing costs because of lower labor and operating costs. Direct ownership also enables a firm to avoid paying tariffs and other costs associated with exporting. Additionally, by paying taxes in the host

Coca-Cola is among the world's 20 largest multinational corporations. Shown here is a Coca-Cola stand in Beijing.

country and providing employment for local residents, a foreign country can build good relations with the host government. The greatest danger of direct ownership is that a firm may lose a sizable investment because of market failure or nationalization of its interest by a foreign government. When problems arise in a foreign country, it's often very difficult and expensive to move operations out of the country.

Multinational Corporations

Global Market The entire world viewed as a large market.

Multinational Corporation A firm that operates on a global basis, committing assets to operations or subsidiaries in foreign countries.

Some corporations operate as if the world were a single **global market.**[39] This approach represents a total commitment to international business, and is used by **multinational corporations** who have assets committed to operations or subsidiaries in foreign countries. Large organizations such as Exxon, General Motors, IBM, Grand Metropolitan (a British company), and Nestle (a Swiss company) are multinational corporations. Exhibit 6.5 on page 196 lists the world's largest multinational corporations.

Products most suitable for this approach include airlines, automobiles, heavy equipment, machine tools, computers, petroleum, cosmetics, and soft drinks. KLM Royal Dutch Airliner's strategy is to use global alliances to serve airline passengers around the world.[40]

ADAPTING TO FOREIGN MARKETS

Because of differences from country to country, a firm engaged in international trade must generally adapt to foreign markets. In this section, we ex-

Exhibit 6.5
The 20 Largest Mutinational Corporations

Rank	Company	Country	Market Value (in billions of U.S. dollars)
1	Nippon Telegraph & Telephone	Japan	128.94
2	Royal Dutch/Shell Group	Neth./Britain	91.93
3	General Electric	U.S.	84.94
4	Mitsubishi Bank	Japan	77.05
5	Exxon	U.S.	75.92
6	Toyota Motor	Japan	75.06
7	AT&T	U.S.	73.87
8	Industrial Bank of Japan	Japan	73.25
9	Sumitomo Bank	Japan	67.53
10	Fuji Bank	Japan	66.99
11	Sanwa Bank	Japan	63.19
12	Dai-Ichi Kangyo Bank	Japan	59.64
13	Wal-Mart Stores	U.S.	54.01
14	Coca-Cola	U.S.	52.24
15	Sakura Bank	Japan	47.26
16	Roche Holding	Switzerland	47.26
17	Nomura Securities	Japan	45.38
18	Philip Morris	U.S.	43.19
19	DuPont	U.S.	42.01
20	Tokyo Electric Power	Japan	41.34

Source: "The Global 1000–the Leaders," *Business Week* (July 11, 1994): 56.

amine how a firm gears its product offerings, prices, distribution systems, and methods of promotion to foreign countries.

Product

In some cases, the same product developed for the U.S. market can be sold in a foreign country. Coca-Cola and PepsiCo have successfully taken their soft drinks to foreign markets without changing them. But usually products have to be altered to meet conditions in a foreign market. General Electric faced problems selling refrigerators in Japan because they were too large to fit into most Japanese homes.

In some cases, companies cannot modify existing products to fit the needs of a foreign country. They then can either develop a new product for that country or try to sell the current product in other countries. Developing new products is a costly alternative but may provide a large payoff. Colgate-Palmolive for example, developed Axion, a dishwashing paste packaged in a plastic cup, for consumers in South America who traditionally used leftover soap chips kept in a bowl to wash their dishes.

Price

The price of a product is usually different in domestic and foreign markets. The costs of foreign trade, such as taxes, tariffs, and transportation, often result in higher prices in the foreign country. Exchange rates can also influence the price of foreign goods.

In some instances, firms intentionally establish lower prices in foreign markets. The practice of selling surplus products in a foreign country at a lower price than that in the country of origin is called **dumping.** Japanese companies have been accused of dumping computer chips, television sets, and automobiles on the American market while charging Japanese customers high prices that include all research and development expenses. Zenith Electronics claims to have lost $500 million in profits over a five-year period as a result of the dumping of foreign television sets in the United States.[41]

Dumping
Selling surplus products in a foreign country at a lower price than in the country of origin.

Distribution

The task of providing products in foreign nations often presents challenges and problems. Many international business firms attempt to move and sell goods and provide services through existing transportation systems, stores, and suppliers. In some countries, however, adequate distribution systems do not exist. Then a firm must develop ways to get its products to the customers. In China, for example, manufacturers typically do not make deliveries to stores and other outlets. Both Coca-Cola and PepsiCo have invested heavily in trucks and refrigeration for store owners to use to obtain and sell Coke and Pepsi products in China.

Promotion

Many companies use the same message worldwide to inform customers about products and persuade them to buy. Uniform promotion, including advertising and publicity, enables firms to gain recognition throughout the world. But promotion often must be modified because language, laws, and culture differ from country to country. For instance, Japanese advertisements commonly use ideas that people elsewhere would consider sexist. Household appliances have been promoted with the phrase "So simple a woman can operate it." Japanese companies have issued wall calendars featuring nude women. In many countries, such promotional methods would not be acceptable.

Decisions concerning which media to use for advertising or publicity must also be adapted to different countries. Some nations do not have commercial television. Others do not have advertising space in newspapers. The circulation of magazines and newspapers also varies greatly from one country to another. In nations with a low literacy rate, radio and television advertising, if available, is more effective than print media.

SUMMARY OF LEARNING OBJECTIVES

1. ***Discuss the meaning and scope of international business.*** International business is the performance of business activities across national boundaries. Involvement in international business is increasing, with growth expected to continue.

2. ***Explain why firms become involved in international business.*** Countries cannot produce everything for themselves. Most nations specialize in the production of certain goods and services and sell any surplus to other nations. A country has an absolute advantage

if it can produce a product more efficiently than any other nation. A country that can produce one product more efficiently than other products, in comparison to other nations, has a comparative advantage.

3. ***Define the basic concepts of international business.*** *Exporting* is selling domestic goods to a foreign country; *importing* is purchasing goods from another country. A country's *balance of trade* is the difference between the amount it exports and the amount it imports. The total flow of money in and out of a country is the *balance of payments*. The *exchange rate* is the rate at which one country's currency can be exchanged for another's currency.

4. ***List the various barriers to international business.*** A nation's culture and social forces can create obstacles to international trade. The political climate of a country also influences international trade. A nation can also restrict trade through import tariffs, quotas and embargoes, and exchange controls.

5. ***Identify the ways in which international business is regulated.*** Several laws affect American firms doing business in foreign countries. These laws generally exempt U.S. firms from certain antitrust laws, prohibit bribing of foreign officials, and allow banks to participate in joint ventures. Several organizations also exist to facilitate world trade, including the General Agreement on Tariffs and Trade (GATT), the International Monetary Fund (IMF), the World Bank, and economic communities such as the European Union (EU) and the Organization of Petroleum Exporting Countries (OPEC).

6. ***Describe the different approaches firms take to conduct business internationally.*** A firm can take several approaches to international trade. Some require little commitment on the part of the firm, while others require a great deal of involvement. The approaches to international business are exporting, licensing, joint ventures, trading companies, countertrading, direct ownership, and multinational corporations.

7. ***Determine how a firm can adapt to foreign markets.*** A firm engaged in international business must generally adapt to foreign markets. Some products have to be changed to be suitable to another country. Prices of products may be set differently in various countries. In some cases, products can be distributed through existing systems, but if appropriate distribution systems do not exist, firms must develop them. Advertising and publicity often must be modified because of differences in language, laws, and culture.

KEY TERMS

International Business
Absolute Advantage
Comparative Advantage
Exporting
Importing
Balance of Trade
Balance of Payments
Exchange Rate
Fixed Exchange Rate
Floating Exchange Rate
Import Tariff
Quota
Embargo
Exchange Controls
General Agreement on Tariffs and Trade (GATT)
Economic Community
International Monetary Fund (IMF)
World Bank
Licensing
Strategic Alliance
Trading Company
Countertrading
Direct Ownership
Global Market
Multinational Corporation
Dumping

QUESTIONS FOR DISCUSSION AND REVIEW

1. Why do firms become involved in international business? What is the result of global competition? Can firms avoid competing with foreign firms?

2. In what areas does the United States have a comparative advantage? Would you expect this to change in the future?

3. Explain the difference between exporting and importing. Give examples of products that the United States exports and those it imports.

4. Why is the United States' balance of trade considered unfavorable? What must be done to make it favorable? Is this possible?

5. Describe three barriers to international business. Why is it critical to examine the cultural environment of a foreign market before engaging in international business?

6. How effective has the various legislation been in regulating international business? In what areas is more regulation needed?

7. What is an economic community? Discuss two such groups that will mean greater competition for the United States.

8. Name and explain three different approaches to international business. Under what conditions should each of these approaches be used?

9. Why do firms engaged in international business often have to adapt to foreign markets? Give an example of how products, prices, distribution methods, and promotion methods might have to be adapted to a foreign country. Under what conditions might products be standardized for all countries?

10. What is dumping? Give an example of a product that has been dumped in the United States and explain why this practice is illegal in many countries.

CASE 6.1

KFC's Recipe for Global Success

Since 1939, when Harlan Sanders developed a secret chicken recipe with 11 herbs and spices, KFC (formerly Kentucky Fried Chicken) has become known all over the world. KFC's chicken is sold throughout North America, Europe, the Middle East, Africa, Asia, the South Pacific, Latin America, and the Caribbean. World sales in 1991 totaled $6.2 billion, including $2.8 billion outside the United States.

Colonel Sanders first became involved in international business in 1956 by opening stores in Canada. By 1992 KFC had 3,424 international stores (562 owned by the company, 457 joint ventures, and 2,405 franchises). Worldwide in 1992, KFC had 8,480 stores. Its 70-restaurant operation in Mexico was expected to triple in five years. With 105 restaurants in Malaysia, KFC had 60 percent of the nation's fast-food market. KFC's 10 stores in China serve an average 1 million customers a year, four times the average in the United States.

What is KFC's secret to global success? First and perhaps most important is the worldwide acceptance of chicken. In Malaysia, for instance, annual per capita consumption of chicken has doubled during the past decade. According to Allan Huston Jr., president of KFC International, "Chicken is probably the most universally accepted source of protein. There is not a country in the world where you won't find chicken." Unlike other meats, chicken isn't forbidden by religions or cultures except among vegetarians. This acceptance presented an excellent opportunity for KFC, but it didn't guarantee success.

KFC made some early mistakes in Latin America and Europe. The company learned that opening an American fast-food restaurant abroad isn't simple. Cultural differences between countries result in different eating habits.

For instance, people eat their main meal of the day at different times throughout the world. Different menus must also be developed for specific cultures, while maintaining the core product, fried chicken. You can always find original-recipe chicken, cole slaw, and fries at every KFC outlet, but restaurants in China feature Chinese tea and French restaurants offer more desserts. Above all, KFC emphasizes consistency. Whether in Shanghai or Kentucky, the product basically tastes the same.

KFC usually enters a new foreign market by opening a single store in a large urban area on the most visible piece of real estate available. If the project fails, the land can be sold. Usually foreign stores are eat-in restaurants, compared to the take-out style generally found in the United States. Prices are usually high at first to appeal to an upscale market.

International markets offer many opportunities and challenges for KFC. The company is growing outside of the United States at nearly five times the rate of its domestic growth. While many businesses complain about the inability to compete in Japan, KFC has nearly 1,000 restaurants in Japan alone. The secret, according to Huston, is quality, such as using fresh chicken rather than frozen. Freezing chicken causes a discoloring of the bone, which bothers the Japanese. Eastern Europe also holds great promise for KFC. With two stores in Hungary, KFC is working on deals in Poland and the Czech Republic.

KFC faces several challenges. In some areas of the world, such as Malaysia and Indonesia, it's illegal to import poultry, which has led to product shortages. Another challenge is to adapt KFC's people perspective. The company has been most successful in foreign markets when stores are operated by people who understand the culture. The objective is to think like a local, not like an American company starting an American business in a foreign country.

Source: Adapted from Andrew Tanzer, "Hot Wings Take Off," *Forbes* (January 18, 1993): 74; Alan I. Kirschenbaum, "The Original Recipe for International Success," *The Lane Report* (May 1992): 17–24; Sid Astbury, "KFC Malaysia: By No Means Chickenfeed," *Asian Business* (August 1992): 8; and Heidi Dawley, "Franchising: Mexico's Arms Are Wide Open," *Restaurant Business* (March 20, 1992): 74–77.

QUESTIONS

1. Why has KFC been successful globally?
2. What approaches to international business does KFC use? What are the advantages to each approach?
3. What are some of the cultural barriers encountered by KFC in its global operations?
4. Why do you think Kentucky Fried Chicken changed its name to KFC? Does this name change have any global implications?

CASE 6.2

Nestlé Expands Globally

The Switzerland-based Nestlé Corporation, once a Swiss chocolate maker, now is the world's biggest food company and the largest producer of coffee, powdered milk, and frozen dinners. The company also became number 1 in candy after passing Mars. With the purchase of Perrier for $2.7 billion, Nestlé became the world's largest producer of mineral water with a 20 percent share of the world market. Nestlé achieved its success through intensive global expansion. Only 2 percent of its business is conducted in Switzerland; the remaining 98 percent is in other countries.

One of the first multinational corporations, Nestlé now has production facilities in more than 60 countries. Its products can be found almost everywhere around the globe. In Europe, where Nestlé's success is greatest, sales of instant coffee, mineral water, yogurt, frozen foods, cold cuts, candy, and cereal bars total roughly $10.2 billion. Sales in North America are approximately $6.7 billion for products such as Nescafe instant coffee, Carnation Coffee-mate nondairy creamer, Friskies pet food, Nestlé Crunch chocolates, and Stouffer frozen foods. Other big markets for Nestlé have been Asia ($3.1 billion in sales), Latin America ($2.4 billion in sales), and Oceania—Australia, New Zealand, and other islands of the Pacific Ocean—($.6 billion in sales). The firm spends $1.2 billion annually on advertising.

One secret to Nestlé's success is that many of its products, especially instant coffee, chocolates, and frozen foods, appeal to consumers all over the world. Coffee is even closing in on tea as the favorite drink in Japan. Frozen dinners, long a hit in the United States, have caught on in Europe. Of course chocolate tastes the same in any language. Although these products have to be adapted slightly to local tastes, they generally can be sold worldwide. Because of high research and development costs as well as high costs of marketing, Nestlé benefits greatly by offering products with global appeal. After making large investments in its products, the company has been able to move brands from one country to another with relative ease.

Nestlé's Lean Cuisine dinners provide a good illustration of how the company expands internationally. Lean Cuisine was introduced in the United States in 1981 and became a huge success. In 1985 Nestlé chief executive Helmut Maucher endorsed a plan to sell Lean Cuisine in Britain. In the beginning, before the company's British frozen-food plant reached full production, products were imported from a plant in Canada. The cost of shipping frozen dinners in refrigerated ships, in addition to paying customs taxes, was extremely high. But Maucher was patient and the venture paid off. In 1989 sales of frozen dinners in Britain reached $100 million and Nestlé achieved a 33 percent share of the market. Lean Cuisine has also been successfully introduced in France.

Nestlé has several new projects in the works. Coca-Cola Nestlé Refreshment Company, a joint venture between Coca-Cola and Nestlé, should dominate the ready-to-drink iced tea market with Nestea Iced Tea. Distribution will be handled through the Coke bottling system, while Nestlé provides the brand awareness. Nestlé also bought British confectioner Rowntree Mackintosh. Few brands have Rowntree's recognition or appeal throughout Europe, which should help Nestlé build brand awareness in national markets. Nestlé manages its own operations in Thailand, where it has 80 percent of the nation's instant coffee sales. Nestlé's most recent venture in Thailand is the launch of an iced coffee drink.

Now Nestlé is looking to what Maucher thinks is the market of the future, the Third World. Currently, 20 percent of the world's population consumes 80 percent of Nestlé's products. Maucher thinks his company's products will soon be seen in more parts of the world. The company also will look to what Maucher considers the food of the future—pasta. As he puts it, "We can't feed the world on beefsteak. Noodles will conquer the world."

Most industry experts agree that Nestlé is in the best position of any food company to expand internationally. Most of its competitors, which have been concentrating on their domestic markets, are scrambling to become involved in the profitable international trade.

Source: Adapted from Carla Rapoport, "Nestlé's Brand Building Machine," *Fortune* (September 19, 1994): 147–156; Bruce Crumley, "Nestlé Muscle May Pump Perrier," *Advertising Age* (March 30, 1992): 59; Greg W. Prince, "Coke-Nestlé Venture Finally Bears Tea," *Beverage World* (January 31, 1992): 1, 4; John Parry, "Nestlé's Name Plan," *International Management* (December 1991): 54–55; Joyce Raivat, "In Thailand, Nestlé Goes Direct to the People," *Asian Finance* (September 15, 1991): 14; and Shawn Tully, "Nestlé Shows How to Gobble Markets," *Fortune* (January 16, 1989): 74–78.

QUESTIONS

1. Would you classify Nestlé as a global corporation? Why or why not?
2. What are the advantages of Nestlé's joint venture with Coca-Cola?
3. Will competitors be able to follow Nestlé into foreign markets with the same degree of success?
4. Which environmental considerations are most important as Nestlé expands into Third World nations?

BUSINESS APPLICATION

Protecting American Executives in Foreign Countries

Because of the increasing concern over terrorism in foreign countries and a growing anti-American sentiment from some terrorist organizations, American companies have had to re-examine their policies and practices related to American executives traveling in foreign countries. Terrorist groups know that a kidnapped U.S. citizen held for political or criminal gains will bring tremendous publicity and, they hope, more leverage in negotiations. If a terrorist group is able to extract a $200,000 ransom from an American company in exchange for the release of an American captive, then U.S. companies need to carefully think through their policies.

Assume that you are the president of an American corporation who must decide how the company will respond to the threat of executive kidnappings. Respond to the following scenarios:

1. One of your executives has been kidnapped by a group demanding a ransom of half a million dollars for the executive's release.

   a. Would you pay the ransom?
   b. If yes, what might be the repercussions to your company?
   c. If not, what might be the repercussions?

2. One of your executives refuses an assignment to travel in a country known to tolerate terrorists.
   a. Would you insist that the executive travel despite the resistance?
   b. Would you consider not doing business in that country, rather than pressuring executives to enter into potentially dangerous situations?

EXPERIENTIAL EXERCISE

Deciding on International Operations

Activity:

This activity is designed for small group and classroom discussions on the issues a company might confront when considering a change in operations.

Directions:

1. Divide the class into groups of 4-7 members and ask each group to appoint a recorder/spokesperson.
2. Explain the scenario: The students are to be a manufacturing plant owner contemplating whether to close a textile mill in North Carolina and open up a replacement in Mexico. The owner believes the move may be needed to keep labor costs under control.
3. Ask each group to identify the advantages and disadvantages of moving the plant out of the United States in general and the North Carolina community in particular. What problems might surface in North Carolina when the move is announced?
4. Ask each group to identify the advantages and disadvantages of setting up the manufacturing plant in Mexico. Have each group conclude by deciding whether to move the operations from North Carolina to Mexico.
5. Ask each spokesperson to share the group's conclusions with the class and to explain the reasons for the decision on moving the plant.

NOTES

1. Adapted from Maria Mallory, "At Coke, Marketing Is It," *Business Week* (February 21, 1994): 39; Maria Mallory, "Behemoth on a Tear," *Business Week* (October 3, 1994): 54–55; Laurie Hays, "Amid Russian Turmoil, Coca-Cola Is Placing a Bet on the Future," *The Wall Street Journal* (April 6, 1993): A1, A5; Walecia Knorad and Igor Reichlin, "The Real Thing Is Thundering Eastward," *Business Week* (April 13, 1992): 96–98; and Walecia Konrad, "The Coca Kings Are Feeling a Bit Jumpy," *Business Week* (July 13, 1992): 112.
2. Lloyd Dobyns and Clare Crawford-Mason, *Quality or Else* (Boston: Houghton Mifflin, 1991), 36–37.
3. "Argentina Starts to Count Again," *Fortune* (February 22, 1993): 102–104.
4. Amy Borrus, Joyce Barnathan, Bruce Einhorn, and

Stewart Toy, "China's Gates Swing Open," *Business Week* (June 13, 1994): 52–53.
5. Louis Kraan, "The Risks Are Rising in China," *Fortune* (March 6, 1995): 179–180.
6. Sharon Moshavi, Pete Engardio, Shekhar Hattangadi, and Dave Lindorff, "India Shakes Off Its Shackles," *Business Week* (January 30, 1995): 48–49.
7. Lawrence G. Franko, "Global Competition II: Is the Large American Firm an Endangered Species?" *Business Horizons* (November–December 1991): 41–42.
8. Vern Terpstra, *International Dimensions of Marketing*, 2e (Boston: Kent Publishing, 1988), 3.
9. Rob Norton, "Strategies for the New Export Boom," *Fortune* (August 22, 1994): 124–132.
10. Kazuo Nukazawa, "Japan and the U.S.: Wrangling Toward Reciprocity," *Harvard Business Review* (May–June 1988): 42–52.
11. Nancy J. Adler, *International Dimensions of Organizational Behavior* (Boston: Kent, 1986), 10–11.
12. Philip R. Harris and Robert T. Moran, *Managing Cultural Differences* (Houston: Gulf, 1987), 189.
13. "Tires Recalled So They Don't Tread on Allah," *Lexington, KY, Herald-Leader* (July 25, 1992): A3.
14. Douglas Harbrecht, Neil Gross, and Peter Burrows, "Suppose They Gave a Trade War and Nobody Came," *Business Week* (March 29, 1993): 30.
15. Douglas Harbrecht and William Spindle, "Trying a Little Tenderness with Japan," *Business Week* (January 31, 1994): 30.
16. Pete Engardio and Bruce Einhorn, "Rising from the Ashes," *Business Week* (May 23, 1994): 44–48.
17. Douglas Harbrecht, Susan B. Garland, and Owen Ullman, "Delay Would Mean the Death of GATT," *Business Week* (December 5, 1994): 33–36.
18. Phil Davies, "Europe Unbound," *Express Magazine* (Spring 1992): 16–19.
19. Bill Javetski and Silvia Sansoni, "The Finance Vigilantes Are Closing In," *Business Week* (January 30, 1995): 46–47.
20. Ann H. Hughes, "United States and Canada Form World's Largest Free Trade Area," *Business America* (January 3, 1989): 2–5.
21. Blayne Cutler, "North American Demographics," *American Demographics* (March 1992): 38–42.
22. Gaylon White, "Run for the Border," *Express Magazine* (Summer 1991): 10–13.
23. Kenneth H. Bacon, "With Free Trade Pact About Wrapped Up, the Real Battle Begins," *The Wall Street Journal* (August 7, 1992): A1, A4.
24. Amy Borrus, "A Free Trade Milestone, with Many More Miles to Go," *Business Week* (August 24, 1992): 30–31.
25. Louis Richman, "How NAFTA Will Help America," *Fortune* (April 10, 1993): 95–102.
26. Douglas Harbrecht, William C. Symonds, Elisabeth Malkin, and Geri Smith, "What Has NAFTA Wrought? Plenty of Trade," *Business Week* (November 21, 1994): 48–49.
27. John S. McClenahan, "How U.S. Entrepreneurs Succeed in World Markets," *Industry Week* (May 2, 1988): 47–49.
28. Joseph V. McCabe, "Outside Managers Offer Packaged Export Expertise," *Journal of Business Strategy* (March–April 1990): 20–23.
29. Howard Banks, "Many Ways to Look at U.S. Trade," *Forbes* (April 12, 1993): 89–96.
30. Therese Eiken, "U.S. Exporters Keep On Rolling," *Fortune* (June 14, 1993): 130–131.
31. "Japan's Big Appetite for American Foods," *Parade* (June 7, 1992): 8.
32. Jerry Flint, "Baby Steps," *Forbes* (April 13, 1992): 92.
33. William J. Holstein and Kevin Kelly, "Little Companies, Big Exports," *Business Week* (April 13, 1992): 70–72.
34. Joshua Levine, "The Rabbit Grows Up," *Forbes* (February 17, 1992): 122–127.
35. Stratford Sherman, "Are Strategic Alliances Working?" *Fortune* (September 21, 1992): 77–78.
36. James B. Treece, Karen Lowry Miller, and Richard A. Melcher, "The Partners," *Business Week* (February 10, 1992): 102–107.
37. Shelley Neumeier, "Why Countertrade Is Getting Hotter," *Fortune* (June 29, 1992): 25.
38. Matt Schaffer, "Countertrade as an Export Strategy," *Journal of Business Strategy* (May–June 1990): 33–38.
39. Theodore Levitt, "The Globalization of Markets," *Harvard Business Review* (May–June 1983): 92–102.
40. Stewart Toy, Susan Chandler, Robert Neff, and Margaret Dawson, "Flying High," *Business Week* (February 27, 1995): 90–91.
41. Janet Novack, "It's Like a Big Balloon," *Forbes,* (July 20, 1992): 48.

International Development or Exploitation?

Charlie Brown is proud of what he has been able to accomplish with his Nike factories in Asia. Brown is Nike's general manager of China and a long-time Nike veteran, with previous stints at the company's R&D facility in Exeter, New Hampshire; Bangkok, Thailand; Pusan, South Korea; and the Beaverton, Oregon headquarters. His main office now is in Guangzhou, China, a city in the center of bustling Guandong Province, an economic free-fire zone that is home to an estimated 20,000 factories. People from all over China travel long distances to take part in the region's economic revival. As a manager, Brown is delighted with the work force. The strong Confucian tradition places a premium on hard work, rigorous discipline, and sincere respect for hierarchy.

One plant near the Nike China headquarters in Guangzhou is the Yue Yuen Factory Number Two. It produces 35,000 Nikes per day. The Yue Yuen complex actually is comprised of 12 factories making shoes for Adidas, Converse, and Reebok, besides Nike. According to Brown, the Yue Yuen factories are much cleaner and brighter than the Korean factories he had been associated with in Pusan. Workers at the Yue Yuen plant can expect starting wages of around 350 Yuan a month—about \$50. A typical work day is nine hours, and a typical work week is six days. In addition to their wages, workers also get a bed in the company dorm, three meals a day, medical care in a clinic staffed by 20 doctors, and two weeks vacation per year. Most of the workers (about 90 percent) are young peasant women who send a portion of their paychecks to their parents. The average age of the workers is 21, and no one is permitted to work prior to the age of 16. Adult women are segregated from the younger girls in the dormitories, and everyone must follow strict rules concerning fraternization with men and curfews. Brown explained that parents expect the company to enforce strict rules since most of the young female workers have never been away from home before.

When Chinese leader Deng Xiaoping decreed that what was left of the Chinese economy was open for business again, Nike immediately began negotiations to establish production facilities in China. At first, only state-run factories were available, and, given that they were beset with the inefficiencies of their communist past, things rarely went right inside the plants. Five years after Nike began to order shoes from Chinese producers, not 1 of the 12 factories had yet managed to make a white shoe. Everything was so dirty and poorly maintained that the shoes came out gray. In addition, telephones, running water, and electricity were in short supply.

Nike has moved its operations around Asia as cheap labor has shifted from country to country. But the company is not merely interested in cheap labor, it also believes that it is helping the people of the developing regions as they struggle to reach a higher level of competitiveness. As Charlie Brown described his work in China, it has improved the lot of the workers tremendously. Referring to the women who worked in the Nike China headquarters, he said, "First they began to wear matching clothes. Then the makeup appeared, and soon the application of the makeup got more professional looking. Then everybody talked about getting TVs. And then you stopped seeing the same outfit very often. Every month you see another change."

Despite Nike's belief that it is contributing to the economic development of the regions in which it does business, there has been significant criticism of Nike's Asian operations. Some of these criticisms claim that Nike is "footloose," exploiting cheap labor wherever it can be found and then leaving as soon as cheaper labor can be found elsewhere without regard for what becomes of the workers left behind.

CRITICAL THINKING CHALLENGE

One of the factors Nike considers when contracting with foreign factories to produce its shoes is the cost of labor. However, if labor cost were the only factor Nike considered the company would soon lose its competitive position. What other factors do you think are important to consider in the selection of a foreign company to produce Nike products?

Accusations of Exploitation

A few years ago, the idea of a U.S. multinational corporation worrying about foreign contract workers' rights would have been hard to believe. But as reliance on foreign factories has soared and harsh conditions have been documented by the news media, a number of firms are developing standards to cover everything from wages and safety to the workers' right to organize. David Baron, an ethics professor at the Stanford Graduate School of Business said, "This is an issue that virtually all multinationals are going to have to address."

Levi Strauss & Company, maker of brand-name apparel, makes heavy use of Asian factories. When it was faced with stinging criticism that some of the plants that produced Levi jeans had deplorable working conditions, including one company that reportedly had imported Chinese women as virtual slaves, the company responded quickly. In early 1992, Levi became the first multinational to adopt wide-ranging guidelines for its hired factories, covering the treatment of workers and the environmental impact of production. Levi even promised to inspect plants regularly and to cancel contracts with those that violated the company's rules.

Nike was drawn into the controversy surrounding the social responsibility of U.S. companies contracting with Asian factories when its practices were the subject of a story on the CBS newsmagazine *Street Stories*. David Hawkins, a young CBS news producer, worked for weeks carefully preparing the piece: shooting graphic footage, interviewing eyewitnesses and victims, and gathering evidence that supported his claims. Hawkins had produced a short investigative news spot that claimed Nike was exploiting the workers in Asian factories that made shoes. The piece ran on July 2, 1993. It was introduced by respected on-air personality Ed Bradley with a dire-sounding warning to the audience: "Prepare yourself for a shock."

Hawkins's piece focused on the "marketing hypocrisy" that he perceived in the distance between "a one-hundred-dollar pair of sneakers and a worker making those sneakers being paid a dollar-fifty a day." Hawkins had approached Nike competitor Reebok about the story, but officials there reportedly agreed with him that conditions in Asia were not good and that they had a standing commitment to change the situation. When he approached Nike, however, Hawkins was irritated that they didn't apologize for the condition of their Asian plants. Thus, his story focused on Nike despite the fact that Reebok actually made a larger percentage of its shoes in Asia.

In Hawkins's story, an American labor activist named Jack Ballinger accused Nike of exploiting the workers in Asia. The segment also reported on a strike at an Asian plant that, it was claimed, resulted in the suspension of 22 workers. Wage stubs were shown that indicated Nike was paying below minimum wage, claiming that the government looked away for fear of losing the shoe factories to another developing country in the region. The report did mention some of the benefits of working in the Nike factories, but it didn't mention the dormitories, the staff doctors, the factory mosque, or the relative cleanliness of the plants.

The *Street Stories* report ignited a powder keg of criticism directed at Nike's overseas operations. Following the airing of that report, a Portland *Oregonian* reporter went to Asia and wrote about the workers' exposure to paint and glue fumes. A columnist at the *San Francisco Chronicle* claimed the 14 cents per hour paid some of the workers making Nike shoes was typical of all their plants sprinkled throughout the Pacific Basin. In fact, the public portrayal of Nike as an imperialist profiteer became so frequent that even some Nike employees began to wonder whether it was possible that the company was in the wrong in Asia.

Knight and his top lieutenants knew that Nike's intentions in using foreign labor to make their shoes was simply to be competitive in the industry. They also knew that the company was abiding by the laws of the countries in which it operated, including minimum wage laws and labor practice laws. Knight said, "We're not gouging anybody. Our gross profits are published every quarter, and at around 39 percent we're right on the industry standard. We make our profit on the volume. A country like Indonesia is converting from farm labor to semiskilled—an industrial transition that has occurred throughout history. There's no question in my mind that we're giving these people hope. I've seen the change for decades, and this happens to be the way countries move ahead."

CRITICAL THINKING CHALLENGE

Before reading the next section, determine what you would do, as head of Nike, to respond to the media reports that Nike exploits foreign workers. What messages would you try to send, and who would you try to reach with those messages? What policies would you establish with respect to working conditions in the foreign factories?

Nike's Statement of Social Responsibility

Shortly following the *Street Stories* report, Nike public relations swung into action. They quickly learned that one of the shoe factories in Indonesia that paid higher wages than the Nike factories, and which had been cited in the *Street Stories* piece as evidence of Nike's wrongdoing, had actually started operations eight years earlier and paid higher wages due to seniority of its line workers. They also found that one of the workers who had been fired at the striking Nike plant was terminated for destroying documents at another plant. None of this had been presented in the newsmagazine's video that had touched off the controversy.

The public relations effort began with an attempt to convey the company's position on the controversy to its employees. In a long interview published in the company newspaper, Dave Taylor, vice president of production, argued that the \$1.50 earned per day by Indonesian workers making Nikes "was not \$1.50 per day." The pay rate was, in fact, 3,000 rupiah per day—enough, Taylor said, relative to the cost of living in Indonesia, to buy clothes and even save money. He admitted that Indonesian law allowed for a 90-day training period during which workers were paid below minimum wage. But, he added, after one year most were making well above the minimum.

A letter sent by Nike public relations to hundreds of news organizations and companies doing business with Nike pointed out that the 3,000 rupiah-per-month entry-level wage in Indonesia was five times higher than the monthly wage of local farmers. Nike sent its own film crews to Indonesia to produce a rebuttal video to send to news organizations. Several Indonesian workers appeared on the screen to say that they liked their jobs. One woman even reported that she had left a job with an insurance company to make better money on the Nike factory assembly line. Knight himself appeared in several sound bites in the video, referring in one to Taiwan's and Japan's huge gold reserves in the wake of economic development that was due in part to the booming shoe factories. "Twenty years from now," he said, "one of those workers you say is so abused will be your landlord."

Over the years of doing business in foreign countries, Knight and the Nike managers on the production side of the business had adopted a position similar to that used by anthropologists studying strange new cultures: cultural relativism. In essence, this position is akin to asking "Who are we to say?" when it comes to judging the labor practices of the countries in which Nike does business. Nike didn't own the factories in question, nor did the company dictate the labor and wage laws under which the factories operated. Nike's position is to stay within the laws of the country it is operating in and to make high-quality shoes.

The official position of cultural relativism was reflected in a Nike document called the "Memorandum of Understanding." The Memorandum of Understanding is essentially Nike's statement of its social responsibility. According to the Memorandum, every factory manager at every supplier company and every subcontractor had to sign a written certification that "all applicable local government regulations" regarding minimum wage, overtime, child labor laws, pregnancy and other kinds of leave, retirement, safety, insurance, and environmental practices had to be honored. Forced labor was forbidden no matter what local rules applied, as was "discrimination in hiring, salary, benefits, advancement, termination, or retirement on the basis of gender, race, religion, age, sexual orientation, or ethnic origin."

Inspections of the plants and pertinent documents was part of the deal if an Asian company wanted to make shoes for Nike. However, Nike held, if the minimum wage was artificially suppressed by an authoritarian government looking for light industry, then it was not Nike's job to dictate a just wage. In the Nike video about its plants in Asia, Nike's Dave Taylor supported this point, stating, "To say that Nike can go into a country like Indonesia with 170 million people, or to China with 1.4 billion, and make huge impact on what happens there, in labor or human rights or industrialization, is ridiculous."

In fact, history has shown that industrialization is the first step toward a modern economy. History books record the squalor of early industry in the United States, but the workers who toiled in the factories were usually better off than those on a farm or those working as domestic servants. As management theorist Peter Drucker noted, "For farmers and domestic servants, industrial work was an opportunity. It was, in fact, the first opportunity that social history had given them to better themselves substantially without having to emigrate." The improved living conditions also led to decreasing infant mortality rates and rising populations.

Nike's position on its social responsibility is, to a large extent, laissez-faire. The company doesn't attempt to shape the labor policies of the nations in which it produces its shoes. Nonetheless, there are some practices that the company has determined that it won't permit. Its Memorandum of Understanding forbids child labor, forced labor, and other practices that are generally forbidden in the United States. This approach to social responsibility allows Nike to be competitive with the other major athletic shoe makers and still be confident that it's not sacrificing all values in the name of profit.

CRITICAL THINKING CHALLENGE

Nike has responded to criticism through its Memorandum of Understanding. What else do you think the company should do to address the concern that workers in its foreign plants are being exploited? Nike's competitors readily shift their foreign operations if they can reduce labor costs without reducing the quality of the product. What do you think would be the consequences if Nike decided to respond to the "footloose" charges by staying in the same country and the same plant no matter the labor costs? What do you think the people who work in the Nike factories think about the company's foreign production policies?

Sources: Adapted from Peter Drucker, "Deep Beneath a Hurricane Tormented Sea, Social Currents at Work," *Houston Chronicle* (January 1, 1995): 1C, 4C–5C; G. Pascal Zachary, "Levi Tries to Make Sure Contract Plants in Asia Treat Workers Well," *The Wall Street Journal* (July 28, 1994): A1, A6; Donald Katz, *Just Do It* (New York: Random House, 1994).

PART 3

Management and Organization

CHAPTER 7

Fundamentals of Management

LEARNING OBJECTIVES

1. Define the term *management*.
2. Explain what is meant by the term *organizational objectives* and describe the four levels of such objectives.
3. Discuss the five functions that successful managers must perform.
4. Compare the three levels of management in terms of authority, responsibility, and accountability.
5. Identify the four core skills that managers should acquire and practice.

Jan Carlson, the president of Scandinavian Airline System (SAS), stated that "all business is show business." We heartily agree. In fact, all management is show business. That doesn't mean standing up on stage entertaining like Jerry Seinfeld or David Letterman does; it means shaping the values of others, being passionate about what one is attempting to accomplish, showing enthusiasm when helping others, and paying attention to detail. The actor in a Broadway play, like the manager of a small machine shop in Salem, OR, displays these attributes. Individuals such as Willard Marriott Jr. of the Marriott Corporation, Frank Perdue of Perdue Farms, Herb Kelleher of Southwest Airlines, and Jack Welch of General Electric recognize these attributes as the ingredients necessary to succeed in business.

In today's ever-changing and competitive business world, managers are realizing the increased importance of being a "good manager" and understanding the skills necessary to help their firms attain organizational goals. Coaching, passion, enthusiasm, and attention to detail are so important to successful management that entire sections are devoted to them in books such as *In Search of Excellence, Thriving on Chaos, Swim with the Sharks Without Being Eaten Alive, The Renewal Factor, The One Minute Manager,* and even a book written by the coach of the NBA New York Knicks, Pat Riley, *The Winner Within.*

John Welch Jr., CEO of General Electric since 1981, is the subject of yet another of these books, *Control Your Own Destiny or Someone Else Will.* Although he was once dubbed "Neutron John" for his reduction of the GE workforce from 404,000 in 1981 to 268,000 in 1992 and was once named as America's toughest boss by *Fortune,* the fact remains that under his leadership, GE's profits have risen from $1.7 billion in 1981 to over $5.0 billion in 1994.

Welch's management ideas embody today's management philosophies such as total quality management, employee teams, and worker empowerment. He emphasizes the importance of an organization's defining its vision in clear but broad terms. He believes in and has himself demonstrated the ability to make hard, tough, and quick decisions such as closing plants and downsizing the workforce to improve productivity and deal with change. He is a firm believer in direct and personal two-way communication. To encourage this type of communication, Welch implemented Work-Out, a program in which GE employees of all levels team up to find better ways of working. Another concept is "boundarylessness," which seeks to break down the barriers that divide employees such as hierarchy, job function, and geography. John Welch has set the standard for GE to "be as good as the best in the world," and his leadership has enabled GE to not only survive but also thrive in a business environment that has witnessed the decline of one-time corporate giants such as IBM and Sears.

There really is no business like show business. Not unlike how the fate of a Broadway debut depends in large part on the performance of its actors, the success of business today is more and more dependent on the skills and abilities of managers to lead, guide, and motivate the members of their organizations or departments.[1]

In order to be as good as the best in the world, a manager has to understand the customer and what motivates people. How does a manager learn about what motivates himself or herself?

There are over 20 million businesses in the United States. Of those, about 160,000 are large organizations that are in the news frequently, such as IBM, General Motors, Exxon, Procter & Gamble, and General Foods. About 5 million are medium-sized businesses, with annual sales of $500,000 to $10 million. Finally, the majority of businesses—over 14 million—are mom-and-pop operations, with an owner (manager) and one to three employees.

Every size firm—large, medium, and small—employs managers. There are managers in the Fortune 500 company and managers in the family-owned corner delicatessen.[2] Thus, millions of managers (some estimate over 30 million) perform the types of roles and responsibilities spelled out in this chapter. Managers are a vital cog in the millions of U.S. businesses trying to compete effectively in an increasingly complex global marketplace.

In this chapter, we begin by defining management and indicating its importance to the pursuit of various organizational and individual objectives. We present the managerial functions—planning, organizing, staffing, directing, and controlling—as methods managers use to obtain these objectives. We then discuss the three levels of management and the various roles managers play. The chapter concludes with a presentation of four core management skills needed by managers at each level and in each role.

WHAT IS MANAGEMENT?

Everyone seems to have an opinion about the meaning of management. Unfortunately, the opinions are usually stated in complex terms and shed little light on what management entails. Perhaps the most succinct description of management was offered by early management scholar and theorist Mary Parker Follett. She stated that management is the "art of getting things done through people." In other words, the manager coordinates the work of others to accomplish goals that might not be achievable by an individual. Thus **management** will be defined as the application of planning, organizing, staffing, directing, and controlling functions in the most efficient manner possible to accomplish meaningful organizational objectives.

Management
The application of planning, organizing, staffing, directing, and controlling functions in the most efficient manner possible to accomplish objectives.

The theme of our definition of management is that a central person (a manager such as Jack Welch at General Electric or Dennis Green, coach of the Minnesota Vikings football team) must—by using such skills as decision making, communication, and objective setting—coordinate the work activities of others to achieve organizational objectives. Research has highlighted a direct relationship between the clarity of organizational objectives and business success. The successful management team develops clear objectives and enthusiastically undertakes programs and projects to accomplish them.

A VARIETY OF OBJECTIVES

Objectives
Specific results or targets to be reached by a certain time.

Goal
A broadly stated guideline that an organization or an individual is attempting to achieve.

Mission Statement
A statement of the purpose of an organization which expresses the vision of the leaders of the organization and gives focus to its members.

Objectives are desired results or targets to be reached by a certain time. Objectives are specific, state what is to be accomplished, and indicate when it will be achieved. On the other hand, **goals** are broadly stated general guidelines that an organization or individual seeks to achieve. A college student's goal may be to earn a degree in business administration. An objective would be to earn a bachelor's degree in business administration by June 1997 with an overall grade point average of at least 3.5.

Before an objective is prepared it is important to prepare and communicate a mission statement.

1. The organization must first develop a **mission statement.** A mission statement identifies the scope and uniqueness of the organization. It serves as an expression of the vision of the leaders of an organization and also brings focus to all members of the organization. It should serve to direct the organizational goals in a clear and concise manner, while providing context and coherence to the organizational purpose. One example of a simple but far-reaching mission statement is that of British Airways: "To be the best and most successful company in the airline industry."
2. Long-range goals are developed from this statement.
3. The long-range goals are converted into specific performance objectives.
4. Objectives are then developed for each subunit in each department.
5. Within the subunits, challenging but attainable personal objectives are set.

Most organizations pursue multiple objectives. The managers developing a strategy or a program for maximizing objectives must set priorities among sometimes conflicting objectives. Retail firms such as Wal-Mart, Kmart, Sears, Roebuck, and Eckerd Drug Stores emphasize shorter-run objectives, while organizations such as the Edison public utility, Eli Lilly Research, and development laboratory teams aim at longer-term results.

Objectives are important for several reasons:

- *To focus attention on the organization's mission.* Objectives give specific purpose to the organization. Managers initiate actions designed to bring an organization's resources to bear on the objectives.
- *To help integrate the work of the organization.* Objectives provide a means for setting priorities and resolving conflict between departments and subunits.
- *To help measure an organization's performance.* Objectives provide a target to be achieved and a benchmark of how well the firm is doing.

Organizations have multiple sets of objectives. Four important levels of objectives are organizational, departmental, subunit, and individual.

Organizational Objectives

The overall objectives of a firm are the responsibility of the top management group—typically the chief executive officer and staff, with the assistance and concurrence of the board of directors. In short, they represent the thinking of the executive level of management. Top managers, however, cannot act without having a great deal of information and intelligence passed up the line from the levels below.

Departmental Objectives

The Northeast Insurance Company relies on its sales force to sell policies. In 1995 the sales team decided to set an objective of capturing at least 8 percent of the Chicago-Calumet regional market by 1999. The ambitious four-year objective means the sales department will have to increase its market share from 3.6 percent to 8 percent in only four years. An increase in market share means that someone else's business must be taken away, a hard task in the insurance industry.

Subunit Objectives

The operations department of Scott Manufacturing is divided into three teams. Each team or subunit includes technicians, operators, and material-handling personnel and has an informal leader and a team nickname—Wildcats, Pirates, and Copperheads. These teams compete to be the most productive group in the department without sacrificing product quality. Each team sets objectives for specific quantities and quality, and it outlines a plan for achieving the objectives and a set of target dates.

Individual Objectives

Dan Chubrich has been employed at Ford's Chicago assembly plant for 15 years. Chubrich's boss wants him to become certified as a quality control inspector. Chubrich wants to attend the quality control training program but has put it off for six years in a row. Whenever he planned to attend the program, some personal problem (such as too much unfinished work or a family crisis) prevented him from taking the course.

After one of his closest friends attended the program, Chubrich finally began to outline a set of objectives. He has established July as the starting date to enroll in the program. He will also have to help his boss find someone to operate his spot on the line while he attends the program. Chubrich individual objectives are somewhat different from Ford's organizational objective. However, they are just as important and challenging.

Objectives serve as targets for both managers at the top of an organization and those who work with operating employees. They are the specific guideposts around which the entire management group focuses. If the objectives are clear, challenging, meaningful, and measurable, the organization will have the standards to judge whether managers are efficiently performing the functions of management.

Today's Business World illustrates how the business leaders in one South Carolina town implemented "quality management" programs to refocus the direction of their companies.

TODAY'S BUSINESS WORLD

TQM

Quality Management as a Way of Life

Quality became a way of life for the residents of Spartanburg, SC, population 230,000, in 1983. That year the plant manager of a Monsanto Corporation plant in Spartanburg came to the local chamber of commerce for help. The plant had produced textiles until 1980 when Monsanto began manufacturing silicon wafers there. The wafers were sold in an increasingly competitive global marketplace, and the plant manager needed improved quality and productivity to compete successfully.

Chamber of commerce members decided that a far-reaching quality program based on the ideas of W. Edwards Deming could benefit Monsanto—and other area businesses as well. The chamber hired QualPro, a quality management consulting firm based in Knoxville, TN, to develop a "Quality in the Workplace" program. The program uses four-day seminars to lay out the basics of quality management. The seminars provide education and training consistent with the principles embodied in Deming's philosophy, including customer satisfaction, worker empowerment, statistical process control, continuous improvement of production processes, and transforming the role of management from being a boss into more of a leadership position.

The quality programs are still alive and well in the community, and participants have spread the concepts throughout their own companies with noticeable results. Mayfair Mills, a large textile manufacturer in Arcadia, SC, is an example. Mayfair has used the statistical tools taught in the seminars to implement an overall change in the company's philosophy, with positive results. The program has also encouraged networking through bimonthly quality dinners and monthly roundtables.

Smaller firms have been slower to embrace the program due to their lack of resources and time necessary to devote to the training involved. Still, they have incorporated the quality theme into their daily business practices. ABCO, a 125-employee textile firm, recognized in the late 1980s that growth opportunities for companies in its industry lay outside the United States. It decided to change its management style by implementing quality management teams. The company formed employee teams, and in one of the first projects, produced savings of more than $60,000 by renegotiating ABCO's contract with its steam supplier.

Although there is no way to accurately measure the program's contribution to the area's prosperity, some figures are striking. From a high of 13 percent during the 1982 recession, unemployment in the county fell to below 4 percent in the late 1980s, and rose to only a little above 5 percent in the sluggish economy of the early 1990s. Total foreign investment in the county, $1.5 billion, is the nation's highest per capita. Recently, German automaker BMW announced plans to build a $1 billion plant near the airport that serves Spartanburg and neighboring Greenville. The quality concepts have even moved beyond the workplace into the personal lives of employees. For instance, in 1991, ABCO executives encouraged all employees to reexamine their own lives just as the company was reexamining itself. Individual employees wrote their own mission statements for their private lives. Results included increased attention to family, going back to church for the first time in years, and other lifestyle changes.

The challenge in implementing quality management concepts is to get top management to accept that they need to change and then to take action to actually implement such changes. However, if the challenge can be met, the rewards—as evidenced by the positive transformation of Spartanburg—can be great. Al Bullington, president of ABCO, stated that quality management has enabled executives to focus on where their companies are going. In perhaps the strongest endorsement of the concept of quality management, Bullington says, "I've even gotten to where I enjoy coming to work." It's likely many of today's struggling companies would like to hear their employees express these same sentiments.

Source: "Where 'Quality' Is a Language," *Nation's Business* (January 1993): 57–59.

MANAGEMENT FUNCTIONS

Given our definition of management, exactly how do managers go about managing in an office, on a shop floor, or in a committee meeting? What do they do to help accomplish objectives? Management theorists (e.g., Henri Fayol, Mary Parker Follet, and Chester Barnard) have identified five primary functions of managers.[3] These functions (planning, organizing, staffing, directing, and controlling), first formally discussed over 80 years ago, still characterize the activities of most managers. Although the amount of time spent on each varies, these five categories pinpoint the variety of work performed by managers.

Planning

Former President Dwight Eisenhower once said, "Plans are nothing, planning is everything." When managers plan, they project a course of action for the future. They will attempt to perform a systematic set of business actions aimed at achieving objectives. Thus **planning** essentially means deciding in advance what is to be done. Of course, plans alone do not bring about desired results; but without a plan and a set of objectives, managerial actions are likely to produce confusion. Planning is a task that managers must do every day.

Planning
The management function of establishing objectives and developing plans to accomplish them.

The work of planning is basically mental. It requires thinking things through logically. Managers should think before acting and act in light of facts rather than best guesses.

One reason for the decline of Sears as one of the retailing giants of the decade is poor planning. For example, well into the 1980s Sears was still producing position papers that included no mention of Wal-Mart. Sears refused to consider Kmart and Wal-Mart as real competition and was left behind as they both blew right by.[4]

There are many reasons why a manager must plan. Planning helps provide the coordination needed to do the job. It helps ensure that things will get done; it can also show the manager when things may not get done and why they were not done right. Planning also helps the manager determine who will do what job, how long the job will take, and what resources are needed to get the job done. Although planning takes time and energy and involves making complex decisions, firms must plan in order to keep their competitive edge in today's changing business environment.

Organizing

Organizing
The management function of grouping people and assignments to carry out job tasks and the mission.

Organizing function not directing

The **organizing** function of management consists of grouping people and assigning activities so that job tasks and the mission can be properly carried out. The establishment of the managerial hierarchy, which we discuss later, is the foundation of the organizing function. Specific details of organizing will be discussed in the next chapter.

Staffing

Staffing
The management function of selecting, placing, training, developing, and compensating subordinates.

Selection, placement, training, development, and compensation of subordinates make up the **staffing** function. A manager's staffing activities also include the evaluation and appraisal of performance. Specific details about this function are covered in Chapter 11.

Directing

Directing
The management function of initiating action: issuing directives, assignments, and instructions.

Leadership
The process of influencing the activities of an individual or group toward accomplishing objectives. Leadership may be autocratic, democratic, or laissez-faire.

As the managerial function that initiates action, **directing** means issuing directives, assignments, and instructions. Directing also means building an effective group of subordinates who are motivated to perform. It means getting subordinates to work to accomplish objectives. Directing can be accomplished through **leadership,** the process of influencing the activities of an individual or group toward the accomplishment of an objective.

The directing function is a part of any manager's job, but the time and effort managers spend in directing vary with their position in the managerial hierarchy, the number of assigned subordinates, and the type of job activities being performed. For example, the supervisor in a McKesson's distribution center in Milwaukee spends most of the day directing subordinates, whereas the president of McKesson's spends significantly greater time in more abstract and general activities.

Generally speaking, managers use many different directing styles. Three of the most common styles are autocratic, democratic, and laissez-faire leadership.

Autocratic Leadership
A type of close supervision in which the manager delegates as little authority as possible.

Autocratic leadership, a close style of supervision, means providing subordinates with detailed job instructions. The manager structures or specifies exactly what is to be done and when the work is due. Managers using this style delegate as little authority as possible. Autocratic managers assume they should do the planning and make the necessary decisions.

Some employees respond positively to the autocratic style. Others tend to lose interest and lack initiative when working for an autocratic manager. In some cases, individuals or even groups of subordinates may actively resist and develop hostilities toward the autocratic manager.

Under certain circumstances and with specific employees, autocratic direction may be necessary. Employees with skill deficiencies, lack of experience, or certain personality traits want firm and structured direction. For example, the new employee who is unsure of the job, his or her skills, and the manager's expectations would probably respond positively to an autocratic style.

Today's managers are moving away from the old autocratic style of telling their employees what to do, how to do it, and when to do it. Instead they are focusing on involving their employees in the decision-making process. One good example is Dee Zalneraitis, the information group manager at a Massachusetts division of R.R. Donnelly & Sons, America's largest printer. Rather than spending a week or more behind closed doors at budget time, she now shows all 40 of her employees the budget and asks them how they can save money. One employee helped her balance the budget by suggesting they do away with some scheduled trips to an unreasonable, demanding customer.[5]

Democratic Leadership
A type of general supervision in which the manager consults with subordinates about job-related issues.

The opposite of autocratic direction is **democratic leadership,** or general supervision (also referred to as participative). In this style, the manager consults with subordinates about job activities, problems, and corrective actions. Managers using the general approach seek help and ideas. Democratic leadership does not lessen managers' formal authority; decision-making power still rests with them. With an experienced, skilled, and intelligent group of employees, a manager would likely benefit from using a democratic style that encourages participation.

Probably the best reason for considering the democratic style is that subordinates who participate in a job-related decision are apt to be more enthused about performing the job. Those allowed to take part in decision making generally support the final decisions enacted. They try hard to make the decision a success.

Laissez-Faire Leadership
A type of supervision in which the manager avoids power and responsibility by giving assignments and support but staying out of the group's way.

With **laissez-faire leadership,** the supervisor avoids power and responsibility. He or she exists as a contact person who provides information and guidance that can be helpful in accomplishing objectives. The laissez-faire, or free-rein, supervisor may give task assignments and offer support when requested but stays out of the group's way. Such a style may be appropriate when, for example, a person is handling more than one job at once. Louis Lenzi, a general manager at RCA, is one such manager. While working on a team of employees who developed ProScan, a successful high-end line of televisions, he also had to handle his day-to-day job of managing 37 people designing other RCA products. His trick for juggling both important duties was to show up only when he was crucially needed.[6]

TOMORROW'S BUSINESS WORLD

The New Generation of Managers

Many managers don't even like to be referred to as "managers" anymore, but prefer instead to be called "facilitator," "sponsor," or "coordinator." They are today's new nonmanager managers—products of the Baby Boom era—and they are fast replacing yesterday's executives. The traits described by these new managers are coming into vogue for a variety of reasons. Former managers are simply failing to adapt quickly enough to keep up with the global marketplace—witness the resignations of IBM Chief Executive John Akers and Westinghouse Electric's Paul Lego. The baby boomers are bringing the values of their generation, such as the need for challenging and meaningful work, into the workplace. And perhaps more fundamentally, survival of the fittest rules in today's business world. Managers who acquire broad functional expertise and are able to master skills such as team building and open communication among all levels of employees will likely be in the best position to get tomorrow's top corporate positions.

While corporate America is definitely moving in the direction of the new philosophy of management, the new managers clearly have their work cut out for them. After all, old habits do die hard; the command and control mind set of yesterday's executives is one concept that will not go down without some resistance. Further, many companies still do not know what to make of these new phenomena. One thing is clear, however: This new generation of managers holds the key not only to their own future success and advancement, but also to the future prosperity of U.S. business.

Which Kind Are You?

Old Manager	New Manager
• Thinks of self as a manager or boss	• Thinks of self as a sponsor, team leader, or internal consultant
• Follows the chain of command	• Deals with anyone necessary to get the job done
• Works within a set organizational structure	• Changes organizational structures in response to market change
• Makes most decisions alone	• Invites others to join in decision making
• Hoards information	• Shares information
• **Tries to master one major discipline, such as marketing or finance**	• **Tries to master a broad array of managerial disciplines**
• Demands long hours	• Demands results

Source: "The New Non-Manager," *Fortune* (February 22, 1993): 80–84. © 1993 Time Inc. All rights reserved.

Controlling

The managerial function of checking to determine whether employees are following plans and progress is being made, and of taking action to reduce dis-

Controlling
The management function of checking to determine whether employees are following plans and progress is being made, and of taking action to reduce discrepancies.

crepancies, is called **controlling.** The core idea of control is to modify behavior and performance when deviations from plans are discovered.

Planning, organizing, staffing, and directing are the initial steps for getting the job done. Controlling is concerned with making certain that plans are correctly implemented. Supervisors who delegate their responsibility should also take care to control, because the ultimate responsibility for the delegated work is theirs. The process of control has four basic steps:

1. Set standards for time, quality, quantity, and so on.
2. Measure performance (results).
3. Compare performance to standards.
4. Make necessary modifications.

A standard indicates to employees what is expected. Ideally standards are measurable and easy to understand. For example, a management team may set a standard for producing two acceptable units a day or for achieving industrial sales of $50,000 a month. But how are standards set for an accountant or personnel manager? Standards in these and other staff areas often are somewhat fuzzy attempts to determine the important functions in the departments.

An important part of a manager's job is to monitor performance so that problems can be pinpointed. Once managers assess performance and compare it to the standards set earlier, they can begin a course of action. Of course, too much measurement can be expensive and can alienate the people being monitored. Each person involved in the control checks needs to understand his or her importance.

Managers often develop clear standards and monitor results, yet fail to make the necessary corrections. If standards are not being met, the manager must search for the problem, find it, and correct it. In the centralized planning systems now being dismantled in Eastern Europe, managers failed to search for problems and correct them. An old Soviet story associated with the five-year plans tells of the plant manager who needed an accountant. He asked each applicant for the position, "How much is two and two?" He gave the job to the applicant who answered, "How much do you need it to be, Comrade Manager?"[7]

Adapting a result to fit the standards is the complete opposite of using control to improve performance. Aaron Cohen, Johnson Space Center director, is setting up an independent office at JSC to come up with better checks and balances as well as improved measurement techniques to judge the efficiency of the NASA space program. The implementation of this system comes in reaction to NASA's litany of problems, including the *Challenger* disaster, the nearsighted Hubble Space Telescope and the poorly designed space station, *Freedom*.[8]

The control process at Del Ray Electronics (a small firm in Florida) is spelled out in Exhibit 7.1. An important phase of organizational control is the feedback that occurs. If performance is acceptable, no modification may be needed; if performance is unacceptable, objectives will not be met, so modifications are needed.

Exhibit 7.1
Del Ray Electronics' Control Process

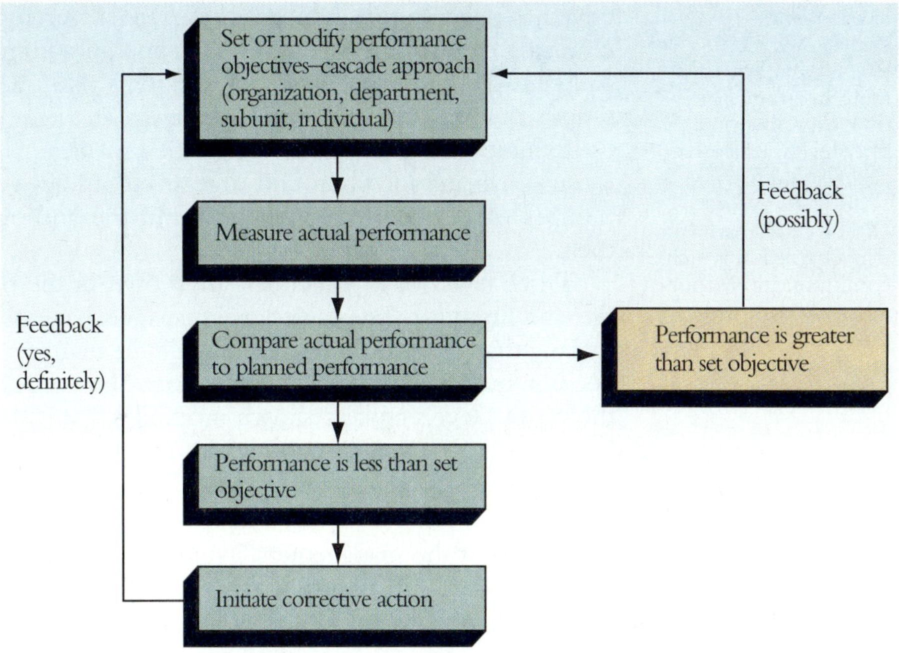

Sometimes the manager himself may be the problem. Robert Allen, CEO of AT&T, has introduced a rather unique type of feedback into the company's organizational structure. After a 1991 survey reflected that only 19 percent of AT&T's employees thought top management's statements were believable, Allen decided to have managers evaluated by their subordinates. He started by getting appraised himself, and now over 800 executives have rated their bosses and have been rated themselves. This type of "upward feedback" exists throughout the organization.[9]

Planning, organizing, staffing, directing, and controlling—these five functions must be carried out in all firms, large or small, in the United States or in Europe, profit or nonprofit. The Boston Celtics basketball team, Procter & Gamble, Ben & Jerry's Ice Cream, and Nick's Shoe Hospital all have managers who plan, organize, staff, direct, and control. As firms grow in size, they tend to have layers, or levels, of managers. At each level, these functions are carried out to some degree.

LEVELS OF MANAGEMENT

As enterprises grow from an owner to a group to a corporation, a number of managerial levels are created and they begin to take on a shape. Three distinct levels of management—executive, middle, and first-line—are usually por-

Managerial Hierarchy
The levels of management in an organization, typically three distinct levels: executive, middle, and first-line.

Chain of Command
The channel in which communication, coordination, and control flow through the various levels of management to subordinates.

trayed as a **managerial hierarchy.** This hierarchy depicts what is called a **chain of command,** or simply a channel of communication, coordination, and control. The first-line manager reports to a middle-level manager, who reports to an executive-level manager.

Exhibit 7.2 is a pyramid diagram of a managerial hierarchy. The pyramid is used for many medium- and large-sized businesses because it can show the number of managers at each level and the authority relationships among them.

Three levels of management are shown in the pyramid: executive, middle, and first-line. Executive-level managers have more authority in decision making than middle-line managers; middle managers have more authority in decision making than first-line managers. Some titles typically associated with the various levels are also shown in Exhibit 7.2.

Executive

At the top of the management pyramid sits the president or chief executive officer (Robert Allen, Jack Welch) and other managers engaged primarily in charting the overall mission, strategy, and objectives of the business. The executive management team must be skilled in planning product distribution, recruiting key personnel, and developing plans. In addition, executive-level managers often are asked to represent the organization in community activities, dealings with the government, and seminars and the like at educational institutions. They function externally for the business and are important spokespersons for everything the company is attempting to accomplish.

Exhibit 7.2
Levels of Management: The Managerial Hierarchy

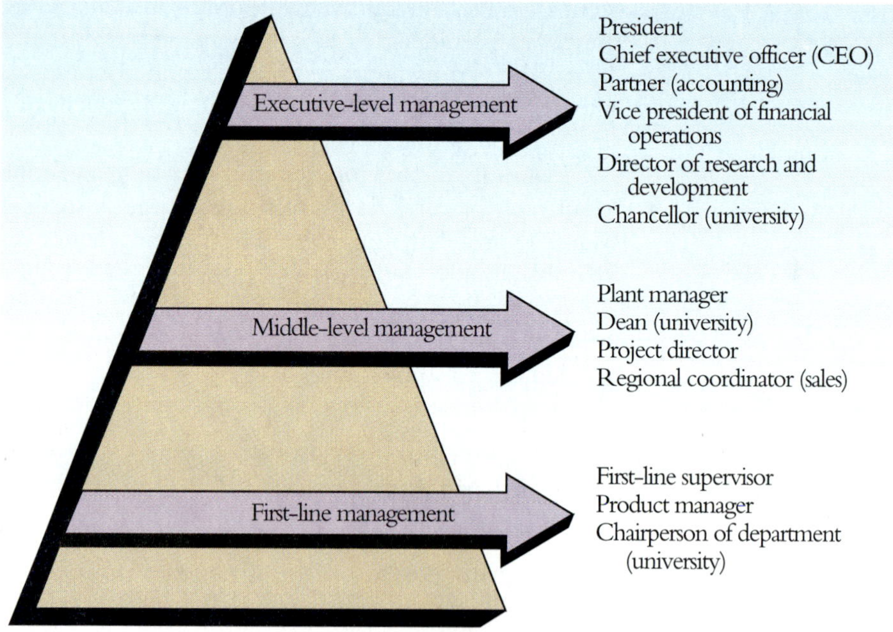

The obligations and responsibilities of executive managers in large organizations are many. Consequently, the monetary rewards are often relatively large. The pay of executive-level managers—including base salary, bonus, and other monetary considerations—is often in six figures. The effective executive is usually very mobile; each year at least one out of five moves to a new geographic location. Many executive-level managers move from one company to another. Thus the question is not *whether* the executive-level manager will move but where and when.

Middle

The middle level of the management hierarchy includes plant supervisors, college deans, project directors, and regional sales coordinators. These managers receive the broad overall strategies, missions, and objectives from executive-level managers and translate them into specific action programs. The emphasis is on implementing the broad organizational plans. Basically the middle manager is a conduit between the top policymakers (executive management) and the supervisory personnel responsible for producing products and/or services so that the company achieves its objectives.

First-Line

The third level of management, the first-line or supervisory level, is directly responsible for the minute details needed to coordinate the work of nonmanagers. Supervisors must work directly with employees and motivate them to perform satisfactorily. The supervisor in a factory, the departmental chairperson in a college, and the product manager in a marketing department must translate overall corporate goals into action plans. This management level is the link between managers and nonmanagers. Organizational objectives eventually meet the test of reality at the supervisory level.

The cornerstone that separates the three levels of managers from nonmanagers is decision making. Managers at any level, performing any managerial function and applying any management principle, must make decisions. Executive-level managers must determine the overall direction of the company. The middle manager must decide how to implement the overall plan at the supervisory level: How should the plan be communicated? How should supervisors be motivated? When should the supervisor be informed about the overall plans? The first-line supervisor must decide how to motivate employees and reward the best performers.

The world of business is constantly changing. By the year 2000, the focus of work as well as the workplace itself will be very different than today. Some trends that managers face because of the changing workplace include the following:

- The average size of companies, measured by the number of individuals it employs, will have decreased. More people will have set up businesses for themselves.

- The traditional hierarchical organization characteristic of today's industry giants will give way to a variety of organizational forms with a focus on teamwork.
- The concept of doing business will shift from making a product to providing a service.
- Workers' pay will be tied less to a person's position or tenure and more to the changing market value of his/her skills.
- Work itself will involve continuous learning and education, and the work day will move away from a nine-to-five structure.

Tomorrow's managers at all managerial levels—executive, middle, first-line—will have to rely on their expertise and diplomatic coordination skills to motivate these newly specialized employees to attain organizational goals while still making their jobs meaningful. What expertise will you be able to provide an employer? Are you diplomatic? Who has informed you about your diplomacy skills?

WHAT DO MANAGERS DO WITH THEIR TIME?

Managers at different levels in the hierarchy allocate their time in various ways. As shown in Exhibit 7.3, managers at different levels generally focus on different tasks. One study found that executive managers concentrate a sig-

Exhibit 7.3
How Managers Spend Their Time

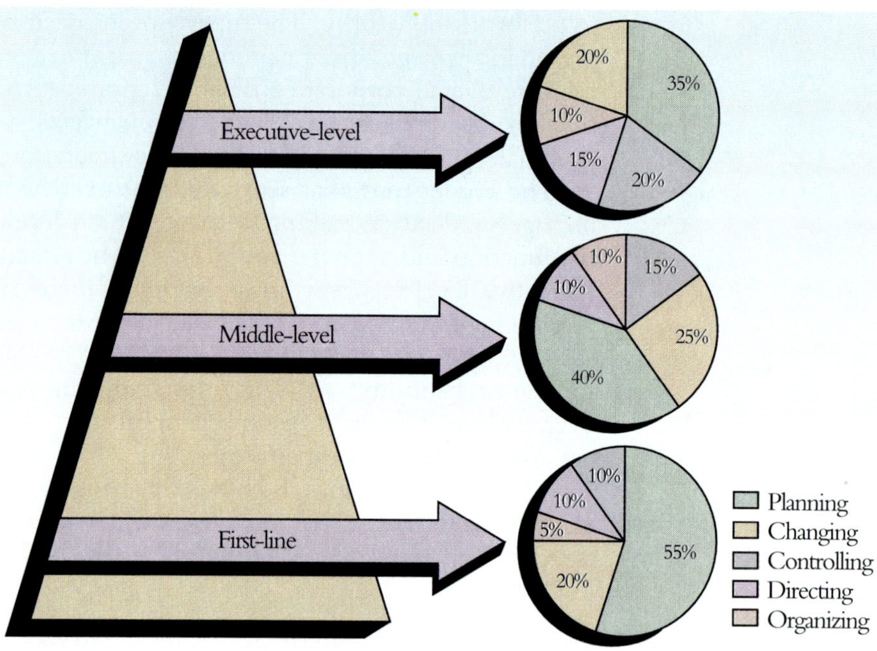

Source: Derived from *The Nature of Management Work* by Henry J. Mintzberg. Copyright © 1973 by Henry J. Mintzberg. Reprinted by permission of HarperCollins Publishers.

nificant portion of their workday on planning, managing and coping with change, and organizing; first-line managers focus primarily on directing operating employees. They spend far less time in such conceptually oriented areas as planning and in developing change programs.[10]

Another study of managerial time examined how time was used by middle-level managers in various departments.[11] Four departments were examined: production, marketing, finance, and human resource management. Four management functions were used, including planning, organizing, controlling, and a miscellaneous "other" category. The study found distinct uses of time across functions, as illustrated in Exhibit 7.4. Production, marketing, and finance managers all spend the greatest percentage of their time controlling activities. Personnel/human resource managers, however, spend the largest proportion of their time on planning activities. The diversity in time use between levels of management and functions of management has been confirmed by different researchers over the years.

Professors and consultants who have studied real-life bosses have found that a fluid time style that includes plenty of unstructured time allows good managers to stay plugged in to their organizations. One study conducted by Stephanie Winston (a New York-based expert on organizing) found that only two hours of a CEO's 9- to 10-hour working day consists of prebooked appointments. Joseph Vittoria, CEO of Avis, blocks out two to three hours of his workday just for unscheduled encounters.

However, in order to accomplish necessary tasks, managers must still set aside private time each day, even if it means having to leave the desk or office or working at unconventional hours to do so. Cosmetics tycoon Mary Kay Ashe has her own method for finding such private time. She makes a habit of rising by 5 A.M. at least six days a week to give herself an early start on the workday. Regardless of which technique a manager chooses to employ, it is clear that efficient use of time is a must in a workday that includes the number and variety of duties of today's manager.

As you read this chapter and attend to other parts of your life, you may think you're really busy. Telephone interruptions, a lack of clear objectives,

Exhibit 7.4
Middle-Level Managers' Allocation of Time

	Management Functions			
Department	**Planning**	**Organizing**	**Controlling**	**Other**
Production	17%	19%	46%	18%
Marketing	14	17	53	16
Finance	15	12	60	13
Personnel/human resources	33	26	20	21

Source: Adapted from J. Horne and T. Lupton, "The Work Activities of Middle Managers: An Exploratory Study," *Journal of Management Studies,* 1965, pp. 14–33. Reprinted with the permission of Basil Blackwell Ltd.

drop-in visitors, and meetings seem to plague managers and nonmanagers alike. However, take a peek at the fully packed schedules kept by chief executive officers of various organizations. What sets the CEO's job apart from others on the management is not the amount of time worked but the number of people and the variety of tasks that must be dealt with every day. Time demands on CEOs come from every direction—subordinates, the board of directors, customers, lawyers, consultants, civic organizations, and suppliers. Donald Schuenke, CEO at Northwestern Mutual Life Insurance, estimates that he would need to work at least 24 hours a day if he were to accept all the requests he receives from people wishing just a little of his time. In fact, he devotes about 60 hours a week to the job.

The ability to delegate work to others is one of the CEO's most important skills for managing time efficiently. Allen Rosenshine, CEO at the Omnicom Group (a holding company that controls two of the three largest U.S. advertising agencies), states, "For me, the first decision is, do I handle it or do I delegate it to somebody else and forget about it?" Delegation means giving jobs to others without always checking on them. It is tough for CEOs to give up important, crucial jobs.

Secretaries and staff assistants are an important tool in the CEO's time-management program. CEOs vary widely in the degree to which they allow secretaries to screen people, requests, and information. Most often the secretary is not an arbiter of access but rather an assistant who helps screen and schedule the bidders for the CEO's time—subject to later approval or rearrangement. Rosenshine, like a growing number of CEOs, has two secretaries. One handles typing, filing, and other clerical chores. The other helps

Busy executives often use traveling time to catch up on their office tasks.

him manage his time, both by keeping the appointment book straight and by serving as a go-between when Rosenshine can't immediately get in touch with someone.

Because CEOs must so often play important roles outside their firms, many designate special assistants to take up some of these responsibilities. Barry Sullivan, CEO at First Chicago Bank, is a trustee to the University of Chicago, a trustee of the Art Institute of Chicago, a co-chairperson of the financial advisory committee for the city, and participant in many other civic endeavors. He assigned Michael Leyden of First Chicago to help him with these demands. Now Sullivan and Leyden share the civic responsibilities.[12]

In the busy world of CEOs, there is concern about establishing objectives, applying the functions of management, performing multiple roles, and learning relevant management skills. However, there is also a lot of concern about stretching time, using it wisely, and establishing tactics to make the most of each minute.

CORE MANAGEMENT SKILLS

Regardless of what level a manager occupies within the managerial hierarchy, he or she must master and apply certain fundamental skills in order to become an effective leader of the organization or department.

Management Skill The ability to use knowledge, behaviors, and aptitudes to perform a task.

Technical Skills Skills involved in making a product or providing a service.

Human Relations Skills The ability to relate and interact with subordinates, peers, superiors, and customers or clients.

Conceptual Skills The ability to organize and integrate information to better understand the organization as a whole.

Management skill is the ability to use knowledge, behaviors, and aptitudes to perform a task. Skills are learned and developed with experience, training, and practice. Management writers have attempted to define the skills used by successful managers. Robert Katz classified management skills as technical, human relations, and conceptual.[13] **Technical skills** are those involved in making a product or providing a service. Katz points out that technical skills are especially important at the first-line management level. **Human relations skills** involve relating and interacting with subordinates, peers, superiors, and customers or clients. **Conceptual skills** are the manager's ability to organize and integrate information to better understand the organization as a whole. Conceptual skills are especially important at the executive level of management.

Henry Mintzberg provided a broader classification. He expanded the human relations skill to include three categories and the conceptual skills to include five categories. Exhibit 7.5 provides a comparison of the Katz and Mintzberg classification systems.

Studies of Management Skills

Virginia Boehm conducted an extensive study of managerial skills by assessing 1,000 managers from all levels at Sohio Corporation.[14] She wanted to determine which skills should be emphasized in selection and training at Sohio.

Boehm asked each manager to describe what skills and abilities he or she used to accomplish the job objectives. In addition each manager was rated on overall job performance. The results are summarized in Exhibit 7.6, with those skills most related to success listed first (e.g., problem solving, initiative, adaptability).

Boehm's results show that interpersonal skills were only of moderate importance in this sample. Six of the top 10 skills relate to problem solving and change. When the study was conducted, however, the company was growing rapidly. Change was therefore a fact of everyday life for managers. Under these conditions, successful managers had to possess skills to cope with managing uncertainty.

The Katz and Mintzberg classifications and the Boehm research results point to four core management skills that you will have to learn, practice, and become proficient in to be a successful manager. These skills, highlighted in Exhibit 7.7, are decision-making/problem-solving skills, communication skills, interpersonal skills, and objective/goal-setting skills. Whether we discuss a small convenience shopping store (e.g., 7-Eleven, Circle K) or an organization with thousands of employees (e.g., J.C. Penney), these skills are important.

Decision-Making/Problem-Solving Skills

Decision making and problem solving involve the type of activities listed in Exhibit 7.5: identifying problems, creatively generating alternative solutions, selecting a specific alternative, delegating authority to implement a solution, making decisions under uncertain and risky circumstances, and evaluating the success or failure of the alternative selected. These specific skill activities must be applied by managers at all levels in the management hierarchy.

Communication Skills

The majority of time a manager spends applying the functions of management is spent communicating with others via memo, speaking, listening, or use of

Exhibit 7.5
The Katz and Mintzberg Skill Categories

Katz	Mintzberg
Technical (having the required knowledge to perform job)	Technical (especially required at first-line management due to closeness to the operation)
Human relations (listening to, observing, and working effectively with people)	Human relations: Peer Leadership Conflict resolution
Conceptual (understanding the organization as a whole, and its future)	Conceptual: Information processing Decision making Resource allocation Entrepreneurial Introspection

Exhibit 7.6
Needed Managerial Skills at Sohio

Skill, Ranked by Relation to Success	Description
1. Problem solving	Looks beyond the obvious; takes practical concerns into account; determines accuracy of information and effects of alternatives.
2. Initiative	Makes up mind quickly; recognizes when decision is needed, takes charge quickly, presses for a decision; independently identifies problem areas.
3. Adaptability	Copes with change; adapts to new assignments, switches strategies rapidly, revises plans.
4. Planning	Formulates plans; imposes order in ambiguous situations; identifies key tasks and critical steps.
5. Reasoning	Organizes information; handles abstract concepts; extracts important data; identifies subtle relationships.
6. Thoroughness	Pays careful attention to detail; checks and rechecks accuracy; produces accurate work; notices even minor problems.
7. Interpersonal sensitivity	Varies his or her approach to others; adapts communication style to the audience; shows sensitivity to others; delegates when appropriate; gives recognition to the accomplishments of others.
8. Impact	Commands attention and respect; influences events; takes charge in groups; presents convincing arguments.
9. Discussion participation	Participates actively in group discussions; speaks up without being called on; expresses ideas in one-on-one meetings.
10. Quantitative analysis	Utilizes quantitative data effectively; applies extensive knowledge of quantitative techniques to work; tackles problems by using quantitative techniques.
11. Written communications	Writes concise, organized, easy-to-read reports; edits others' work substantively; writes clear and meaningful technical reports.
12. Oral communications	Makes effective formal presentations; presents oral material in an interesting way; speaks with a polished style.

Source: Adapted from V. R. Boehm and Larry M. King, "What Do Managers Really Do?" (Paper presented by V. R. Boehm at the Annual Meeting of the AACSB Graduate Admissions Council, Toronto, June 1981).

the computer.[15] Today managers are expected to give speeches, make inspirational talks to employees, and write clear memos, letters, and reports. Computers are here to stay, so managers will also have to use the computer efficiently. They don't have to be computer programmers, but they will have to know how to use computer software to make their job easier.

According to Madelyn Burley-Allen, author of *Listening: The Forgotten Skill,* a survey of Fortune 1,000 company presidents indicated that listening is a major problem for most people.[16] For example, managers report that sub-

Exhibit 7.7
Core Management Skills and Their Characteristics

Decision-Making/ Problem-Solving	Communication	Interpersonal	Objective/ Goal-Setting
Identifies problems	Writes clearly and concisely	Shows empathy	Establishes meaningful, challenging, and clear objectives
Creates feasible alternatives	Speaks effectively	Uses power and influence fairly	Sets priorities
Selects an optimal alternative	Listens carefully	Projects a positive image to others	Evaluates success of objectives/goals approach
Delegates	Has computer skills	Leads effectively	Uses objectives/goals as standards to establish reward program
Makes decisions under risk and/or uncertainty		Behaves ethically	
Evaluates alternatives used to solve problems		Resolves conflict	

ordinates' failure to receive critical information and to accept and/or carry out responsibilities is a major problem in business. Both of these failures imply deficient listening skills. With regard to all communications, listening takes about 40 percent of a manager's time (speaking is 35 percent, reading is 16 percent, and writing is 9 percent).

We tend to equate listening with hearing, but this is not correct. Good listening means being aware of what you hear, accurately receiving the information you hear, and combining the information you hear in a way that is useful to you. Your Values and Attitudes will help you determine your current level of listening skills.

YOUR VALUES AND ATTITUDES

Listening Skills

Directions: Place an X on the number that indicates how important you think the specific skill is for good listening. Then place a circle around the number to indicate your estimation of your present skill level in listening to people.

Skill areas	**High/ excellent**				**Low/ poor**
1. Regarding what the other person says as important—at least to the speaker.	5	4	3	2	1
2. Listening without interrupting.	5	4	3	2	1
3. Not rushing the other person.	5	4	3	2	1

4. Giving full attention to the other person.	5	4	3	2	1
5. Not responding judgmentally.	5	4	3	2	1
6. Adjusting to the other person's pace of speaking.	5	4	3	2	1
7. Listening objectively.	5	4	3	2	1
8. Responding both to what is said and to what is left unsaid.	5	4	3	2	1
9. Checking to be sure that the other person heard correctly.	5	4	3	2	1
10. Maintaining confidentiality.	5	4	3	2	1

Give your overall rating of the quality of your listening skills (circle one):
Very high—10 9 8 7 6 5 4 3 2 1—very low

Feedback: Both students and managers have completed the Listening Skills quiz. Based on many responses, the two skill areas in which respondents seem to be the weakest are (2) listening without interrupting and (4) giving full attention to the other person. People seem to have a knack for interrupting others and of not listening to what is being said. Any item that has an X on the 1 or 2 rating may require attention on your part. Also, an X–O gap of two or more numbers indicates a discrepancy between importance and skill level. Each of these 10 areas is extremely important.

Listening skills can be improved by:

- Talking less.
- Avoiding hasty judgments.
- Taking notes.
- Letting the person finish talking.
- Asking questions.
- Paying attention.

Students need to practice good listening skills in all of their classes. Without listening ability, learning is difficult. Are you a good listener? How can you determine your listening skill weaknesses?

Interpersonal Skills

Interpersonal relations in the work environment are the primary glue in a successful organization.[17] Talking, listening, cajoling, facilitating, and showing concern are all important in developing relationships with people. Using power and influence skillfully and serving as a referee are also crucial parts of the manager's network of interpersonal relationships. A manager's ability to empathize affects subordinates' behavior and attitudes significantly. Empathy is a skill with two main characteristics: accurately perceiving the content of another person's message and giving attention to the message's emotional components. Positive changes in behavior and attitude and interpersonal growth are associated with the superior's show of empathy in an interaction.

Effective managers know the importance of good interpersonal skills in dealing with both employees and clients.

Rick Hess, chief operating officer of M/A-Com, a Massachusetts defense company, knows the importance of interpersonal skills. He knows his employees are under a lot of stress, and, in order to make sure they avoid job burnout, he tries to stay close to them by taking them to lunch, expressing an interest in what is going on in their personal lives, and even playing softball or basketball with them one night a week.[18]

Objective/Goal-Setting Skills

The fourth skill area—setting objectives and goals—is concerned with establishing organizational, departmental, subunit, and individual objectives. Carefully set and attended-to objectives (specific targets) and goals (general targets) can affect individuals' motivation and performance. Priorities must be set and an evaluation program developed. The evaluation program must then be used as the basis for creating an equitable, timely, and clearly communicated reward system.

The four core management skills apply to managers at each level of the management hierarchy. These skills are used to perform the planning, organizing, staffing, directing, and controlling functions of management. How well managers do their jobs depends on how proficient they are in these skills; deficiency in any area diminishes the manager's chance of success. Learning, practicing, receiving feedback on, and observing (through videotaping in training programs) these skills will help shape and refine them so that optimal results are achieved.

Managers can make a difference in organizational performance. The way they work, use their skills, and apply the functions of management affects the actions of others and the accomplishments of businesses. Since managers are human, they may make mistakes, err in judgment, act unethically, and behave selfishly or insensitively. When this happens, people on the receiving end of such behavior get hurt, and objectives may be jeopardized. At other times, managerial behavior is very positive. Managers anticipate errors, help a floundering employee, create career opportunities for others, behave ethically, and act decisively. When this happens, people working with a manager blossom and gain self-confidence, and organizational objectives are accomplished.

SUMMARY OF LEARNING OBJECTIVES

1. ***Define the term* management.** Management is the application of planning, organizing, staffing, directing, and controlling functions in the most efficient manner possible in order to accomplish meaningful organizational objectives. Management is carried out by one or more managers to get things done through other people.

2. ***Explain what is meant by the term* organizational objectives *and describe the four levels of such objectives.*** Objectives are desired results or targets to be reached by a certain time. They are specific, state what is to be accomplished, and indicate when it will be achieved. Objectives are tailored to four important levels: organizational, departmental, subunit, and individual.

3. ***Discuss the five functions that successful managers must perform.*** Planning involves developing a set of actions to achieve objectives. Organizing consists of grouping people and assigning activities so that job tasks and the mission can be carried out. Staffing involves the selection, placement, training, development, and compensation of subordinates. Directing involves taking charge, initiating action, and directly motivating employees. Controlling is monitoring, or checking, employees and objectives and taking action to correct discrepancies between objectives and performance.

4. ***Compare the three levels of management in terms of authority, responsibility, and accountability.*** Executive-level managers are engaged primarily in charting the overall mission, strategy, and objectives of the business. These managers must be skilled in planning product distribution, recruiting key personnel, and developing plans. They often represent the company in the community and in dealing with the government. Middle-level managers receive the overall strategies, missions, and objectives from the executive managers and translate them into specific action programs. They function as a conduit between executive managers and supervisory personnel. First-line managers are directly responsible for coordinating the work of nonmanagers. They work directly with employees and motivate them to perform satisfactorily.

5. ***Identify the four core skills that managers should acquire and practice.*** The core skills are decision-making/problem-solving, communication, interpersonal, and objective/goal-setting skills.

KEY TERMS

Management
Objectives
Goals
Mission Statement
Planning
Organizing
Staffing
Directing
Leadership
Autocratic Leadership
Democratic Leadership
Laissez-Faire Leadership
Controlling
Managerial Hierarchy
Chain of Command
Management Skill
Technical Skills
Human Relations Skills
Conceptual Skills

QUESTIONS FOR DISCUSSION AND REVIEW

1. What is challenging about being a middle-level manager? Try to locate such a manager and ask him or her what makes the job challenging.

2. What did Dwight Eisenhower mean when he stated, "Plans are nothing, planning is everything"?

3. Can female and male managers apply each of the four core management skills discussed in this chapter with equal effectiveness? Explain.

4. Refer to the table in Tomorrow's Business World that shows the characteristics of old versus new managers. Discuss these characteristics in terms of the three leadership styles identified in the chapter.

5. Why are communication skills so necessary for success in the field of management?

6. How could a manager develop and improve his or her decision-making/problem-solving skills?

7. The need to practice good or efficient time management seems to apply to everyone. Why is it so important to managers? How can you personally improve your own time management skills?

8. Do you set individual objectives? Describe how you can improve upon the establishment of objectives and the monitoring of your progress.

9. Peter Drucker (author of numerous management books) has stated that "Every failure [of a company] is the failure of a manager." Is this a fair statement? Discuss reasons supporting your answer.

10. Find a current mission statement for a Fortune 500 company and identify how the statement affects the objectives set by each level of the organization.

CASE 7.1

Body Shop International: Practicing Management Differently

Managers are involved in objective setting, carrying out management functions, and serving as role models to operating employees. Anita Roddick is a manager, leader, and role model not only for employees but also for society in general. She and her husband started her business, "Body Shop International," in Britain in 1976 with a $6,400 loan. Roddick's company sells cosmetics. However, much of her effort is devoted to passionate environmentalism, including offering only biodegradable products, providing refillable containers, and using recycled paper for company literature.

Roddick is an environmentalist who has instilled an activism about ecology throughout her management hierarchy and employees. She has defined her business in terms of two things: social change and action, and skin care. Clearly, Body Shop is not just another chain of stores that sells shampoo, skin lotion, and hair conditioners. In 1993, the firm had 130 stores in the United States and planned to open up 50 more. Although the United States is the company's fastest growing market, this represents only a small percentage of the 900 Body Shop stores franchised around the world.

Body Shop's growth and expansion is a result of sound planning, organizing, control, and Roddick's leadership. Her product line includes Rhassoul Mud Shampoo, White Grape Skin Tonic, and peppermint Foot Lotion. The names are odd, but the packaging is simple. There are rows of shampoos and lotions in identical plastic bottles with black caps and green labels. Simplicity, no push to sell, pleasant sales personnel, and refillable containers characterize the business.

Roddick uses no marketing actions and no advertising. Can you imagine a manager making such a decision in the cosmetics business, one of the most advertising-oriented industries around? The typical Body Shop customers are members of the last part of the baby boom era who tend to distrust advertising and sales hype, demand more product information, and become loyal to companies that are socially responsible.

Roddick has carefully organized the firm's employee motivation programs. Communicating with employees is the most important skill emphasized at Body Shop. Body Shop employees receive newsletters, videos, brochures, posters, and other information. Not only does Roddick communicate about business, but she also devotes much energy to talking about the company's campaigns to save rainforests and ban ozone-depleting chemicals.

Recently, Body Shop joined with other U.S. firms including Stride Rite Shoes and Ben & Jerry's Ice Cream to form Businesses for Social Responsibility. The goal of this organization is to revolutionize how American companies operate by promoting progressive policies such as family leave and environmentally sound manufacturing. Roddick even used her U.S. stores as voter registration centers and held campaigns to encourage customers to contact their congressmen regarding domestic issues such as financial support for the elderly, homeless, and unemployed.

Roddick is passionate about managing her business in a way that is exciting, is profitable, and has a social consciousness. The effect of her management style is electric. As a role model, she wants every employee to feel the same excitement she does. She wants her employees to try to be remarkable, to be role models, to protect the environment, and to treat customers as family. All the little details of the practice of management are important at Body Shop.

Anita Roddick declares that she works not for the money, but rather to change the way business is done. Her goal is to help recreate the language of responsible business. However, are American consumers ready to accept this much social activism by corporate America? While the company reported $266 million in sales and $34 million in profit as of fiscal year-end February 1993, it also had top billing in a *Financial Times* review of the Top 10 Corporate Losers of 1992. Company shares remain depressed and company sales per square foot continue to lag behind U.S. cosmetic companies that have introduced their own lines of "natural" cosmetics such as Origins by Estee Lauder. Even if the American public is not yet ready for such a socially responsible business, a time may come when this form of management is considered a true inspiration for society. In today's "politically correct" society, the global community may be leaning toward introducing a new core management skill called environmentalism.

Source: Adapted from "What Selling Will Be Like in the '90s," *Fortune* (January 13, 1993): 63–64; Trish Hall, "Striving to Be Cosmetically Correct," *The New York Times* (May 27, 1993): C1. Also adapted from "Anita the Agitator," *Time* (January 25, 1993): 52–54; "Changing the World," *Forbes* (March 2, 1992): 83; Bo Burlingham, "The Woman Has Changed Business Forever"; reprinted with permission, *Inc. Magazine* (June 1990), © 1990 by Goldhirsh Group, Inc., 38 Commercial Wharf, Boston, MA 02110-3883.

Questions for Discussion

1. Most managers would balk at the prospect of being asked to become a social activist like Anita Roddick. Do you agree? Why?
2. How did Roddick become a role model for her employees?
3. Should companies be managed like Body Shop International? Why?

CASE 7.2

Ethical Dilemma: A Manager's Daily Concern

Managers face ethical dilemmas every single day. How they spend their time is discussed in terms of planning, organizing, and controlling. However, no category exists for decision making with an ethical orientation. Certainly planning, organizing, and controlling are important, but so is making ethical decisions that are in the best interests of people, the firm's objectives, and one's own value system. Who should be promoted? Who should be sent to the executive development seminar? Should the company hire a woman who is extremely intelligent but can't speak English very well? What about Mary's attendance record, which has been poor since her son was diagnosed as having a life-threatening disease? Each of these questions involves making decisions that managers know have an ethical overtone. Making the right decisions is not easy for any manager.

The news media give the impression that ethics is only a managerial or business-related issue. But ethics and breaches of it are a societal issue. Ethical decision making is extremely important for any manager, employee, parent, lawyer, doctor, or person who must weigh the facts and take action; each individual must decide what is ethical and what is right. Family upbringing, laws, experiences, pressures, and self-imposed anxiety all play a role in how a person deals with the ethical aspect of a decision, event, or situation.

Here are three ethical issues a manager might face. In reading them and answering the end-of-case questions, consider your own style, needs, values, and perspectives.

Nick is a district sales manager of a firm that sells men's hygiene and sports products (e.g., jock itch cream, sprays, hernia belts, athletic supporters). This successful firm has never employed a woman as a sales specialist. Now three qualified women are applying for the few vacancies in the sales force. Nick believes that legally and morally the women must be thoroughly considered for the positions. His fellow district managers believe that Nick is off-base on this issue. There are male candidates, and they can do the job well. Nick is concerned. He wants to make a good business decision, one that is best for the company and that is ethical.

Mark is a department manager. He invited four office employees out to lunch to celebrate Joyce's promotion to office manager. Each employee chipped in $15 for the lunch. The bill was paid by Mark, who placed it on his credit card. About one week after the lunch, Don, one of the luncheon participants, found out that, after collecting the money, Mark had billed the company for the entire lunch. Now Don is trying to decide how to handle this discovery.

Dana is a new account specialist working for Anders, Welboldt, and Daneke, a certified public accounting group. She has been teamed up with Rudy, an experienced CPA consultant in charge of a project. Rudy informed Carrie, the partner in charge, that a new business plan had been submitted to the client. Dana knows that Rudy did not submit the business plan. Dana does not want to be part of any project that misleads the partner. She also does not want to get Rudy into trouble. He has been a tremendous mentor and has supported her in every way possible. Deciding how to handle this dilemma is creating a lot of anxiety for Dana.

Questions for Discussion

1. Is Nick involved in an ethical dilemma, a legal dilemma, or both? Explain.
2. What should Don do to resolve his ethical quandary?
3. How can Dana keep Rudy as a friend and mentor and still solve her ethical problem?
4. Why is it said that the way daily dilemmas of a firm are handled shape the overall ethical climate of an organization?

EXPERIENTIAL EXERCISE

Setting Objectives for Your College

Activity:
Each student will develop a written list of objectives which his/her college might consider accomplishing. Since the one organization all class members and the instructor have in common is their college, this exercise will allow students to work through objective setting in an organization of familiarity. One hour of time outside of class and approximately 20 minutes of class time to review objectives will be needed for this exercise.

Directions:
1. The instructor should review the textbook chapter's material on setting objectives and relate the importance of this process to the overall success of any organization, including their college.
2. Assign each student the task of developing at least three organizational objectives for the college as a whole and at least three departmental objectives for the business department. Both sets of objectives should have short-range and long-range examples. The assignment is to be of a written nature and is to be turned in at the next class meeting.
3. On the due date of the assignment ask for volunteers to share their objectives with the class. Since some students may feel insecure sharing their work on an assignment like this, the instructor may need to call on class members in the absence of volunteers. When calling on students to participate, limit each student to only one or two objectives each. This will allow the instructor sufficient time to include a large number of participants.
4. While the students are orally sharing their objectives with the class, the instructor might wish to list the objectives on a chalkboard or overhead transparency under the categories "Organization Objectives" and "Departmental Objectives."
5. The instructor may analyze and clarify how the various organizational departmental objectives are or are not related.
6. Collect assignments and grade according to the instructor's style and standards.

BUSINESS APPLICATION

Establishing Control Guidelines for a Restaurant

Activity:

This activity is to be conducted during class and will involve reviewing the basic steps of the control process and applying such to a restaurant setting. Approximately 25 minutes of class time will be needed.

Directions:

1. The instructor should review the following four basic steps to the control process identified in the chapter:

   - Set standards for time, quality, and so on.
   - Measure performance (results).
   - Compare performance to standards.
   - Make necessary modifications.

The instructor should then explain how these four steps could be successfully applied to many organizations, including fast food restaurants.

2. Beginning with the first step of the control process, ask students to write down examples of standards the manager of a fast food restaurant might use. Indicate the standard should be numerically based if at all possible.
3. After the class has been given an opportunity to come up with a list of standards, begin calling on various students to share their list with the class. As the students are sharing their standards with their peers, the instructor might begin writing some of the standards down on the chalkboard/overhead transparency.
4. The instructor should review the list of standards obtained and lead the class in a discussion on how the manager might measure the performance (step 2 of the process).
5. After comparing performance to standards (step 3 of the process), the instructor should lead the class in a discussion on what actions might be taken if performance either is short or exceeds the standards set.

NOTES

1. Alan Farnham, "America's Most Admired Company," *Fortune* (February 7, 1994): 50–60; John Huey, "The New Post-Heroic Leadership," *Fortune* (February 21, 1994): 42–50; "Jack Welch's Lessons For Success," *Fortune* (January 25, 1993): 87–93. Books listed include Thomas J. Peters and Robert H. Waterman Jr., *In Search of Excellence* (New York: Harper & Row, 1982); Thomas J. Peters and Nancy Austin, *A Passion for Excellence* (New York: Random House, 1985); Tom Peters, *Thriving on Chaos* (New York: Alfred A. Knopf, 1987); Robert H. Waterman Jr., *The Renewal Factor* (New York: Bantam Books, 1987); Harvey Mackay, *Swim with the Sharks Without Being Eaten Alive* (New York: Morrow, 1988); Kenneth Blanchard and Spencer Johnson, *The One Minute Manager* (New York: Morrow, 1982); Pat Reilly, *The Winner Within* (New York: G.P. Putnam's Sons, 1993); Noel Tichy and Stratford Sherman, *Control Your Own Destiny or Someone Else Will* (New York: Doubleday, 1993).
2. "Annual Report on American Industry," *Forbes* (January 3, 1994): 104–176.
3. Mary Parker Follet, *Creative Experience* (London: Longmans, Green, 1924).
4. "Dinosaurs," *Fortune* (May 3, 1993): 36–42.
5. "The Non-Managers Manager," *Fortune* (February 22, 1993): 80–84.
6. Ibid., 80–81.
7. "Borderless Management," *Business Week* (May 23, 1994): 24–26.
8. "Station Foul-ups Spur Calls for Radical Change at NASA," *Aviation Week & Space Technology* (March 8, 1993): 58.
9. "Could AT&T Rule the World?" *Fortune* (May 17, 1993): 64.
10. "New Work Order," *The Economist* (April 9, 1994): 76; and Henry J. Mintzberg, *The Nature of Managerial Work* (New York: Harper & Row, 1973).
11. J. Horne and T. Lupton, "The Work Activities of Middle Managers: An Exploratory Study," *Journal of Management Studies* (January 1965): 14–33.
12. "The CEO's Secret of Managing Time," *Fortune* (June 1, 1992): 135.
13. Robert L. Katz, "Skills of an Effective Administrator," *Harvard Business Review* (September–October 1974): 90–102.
14. V.R. Boehm, "What Do Managers Really Do?" (Paper presented at the Annual Meeting of the AACSB Graduate Management Admissions Council, Toronto, June 1981).
15. Dana Weschsler Linden, "The Mother of Them All," *Forbes* (January 16, 1995): 75–76.
16. M. Burley-Allen, *Listening: The Forgotten Skill* (New York: John Wiley & Sons, 1982).
17. Noel M. Tichy and Ram Charan, "The CEO A_2 Coach: An Interview with Allied Signal's Lawrence A. Bossidy," *Harvard Business Review* (March–April 1995): 68–78.
18. Jerry Jasinowski and Robert Hamrin, *Making It in America* (New York: Simon & Schuster, 1995).

CHAPTER 8

Organizing the Business

LEARNING OBJECTIVES

1. Define the term *organizing*.
2. Describe formal and informal organizations.
3. Distinguish between line and staff authority.
4. Discuss centralized versus decentralized decision-making authority.
5. Identify what a manager can learn about an organization by reviewing an organization chart.
6. Identify the principles of organizing.
7. Compare the advantages and disadvantages of functional, product, and territorial structures.
8. Explain what types of structures combine to form a matrix organization.

Corporate America is having a love affair with work teams. In a survey of Fortune 1000 companies, the University of Southern California Center for Effective Organizations found that fully 68 percent use self-managed or high-performance teams. The teams most popular today are of two broad types: work teams, which include high-performance or self-managed teams, and special-purpose, problem-solving teams. Problem-solving teams, in particular, are very popular. The USC study found that 91 percent of American companies have used this type of team at one time or another.

Boeing, the Seattle, WA, builder of jet aircraft, has a team-based organization structure. In building its latest product, the Boeing 777, teams played a major role. Henry Shomber, a Boeing chief engineer, described the aerospace giant's corporate culture: "We have the no-messenger rule. Team members must make decisions on the spot. They can't run back to their functions for permission." This kind of freedom allowed Boeing to build the 777—which flew its first successful test flight in the summer of 1994—with fewer than half the number of design glitches of earlier programs.

When Boeing set out to design the 777 (a massive project eventually involving 10,000 employees and more than 500 suppliers), it knew it wanted an entirely team-based organization, but it wasn't sure how to make it work. In the end. Boeing created a hierarchy of teams, a structure meant to get all work teams pulling in the same direction. The goal, says Boeing President Philip Condit, "is a barrier-free enterprise where all are working to satisfy the customer."

Boeing's 777 project replaced the traditional management layers with three layers of teams. In all, there are over 200 cross-functional teams, each made up of people from departments such as engineering, manufacturing, and finance. At the top of the pyramid is a management team of the five or six top managers from each discipline who, as a group, have responsibility for the plane's being built correctly and on time. Underneath the management group is a large group of the 50 or so leaders—half each from engineering and operations, set up in 25 to 30 two-person teams—who oversee the 200-plus work teams that have responsibility for specific parts of the plane. These work teams are typically cross-functional groups of 5 to 15 workers.

The top management team holds a weekly meeting. The members of the second tier communicate with the top team through their leaders in engineering and operations and also hold meetings in which they handle major issues such as schedule delays or quality problems with suppliers. The group of 50 then returns to the work teams with solutions to big problems. While this team structure worked well to move information quickly up the organization, Boeing realized near the end of the 777 project that information wasn't moving well horizontally. To solve the problem, the company added a fourth layer of what it calls airplane integration teams—five groups, each with 12 to 15 people drawn from the work teams. These teams serve as the information conduit throughout the organization. Top management makes sure the integration teams have access to everyone in the organization.[1]

Boeing has found that the use of work teams is a successful organizational structure in the development of new airplanes. Do you think there is a lesson in Boeing's story for other types of business? Do you think service organizations can organize around teams as easily as or more easily than manufacturing organizations?

More and more firms are looking closely at their organizational structures. The decision to change an organization's structure requires an understanding of various principles of organization. The next time you visit a restaurant, a service station, or a movie theater, think about how well or poorly it is organized. Organizational structure is about relationships: authority relationships between employees, relationships among functional units, and relationships among processes. The exercise of thinking about "the organizing question" in the establishments you frequent will become more clear as you complete this chapter.

The issues and choices involved in organizational structure decisions are the subject of this chapter. First, we will discuss why businesses organize, and then we will examine some basic decisions made in organizing a business. Next, we will review the principles of organizing, followed by a discussion of the various structures for organizing a business. Finally, we will discuss the management practice of downsizing.

WHY ORGANIZE?

Organizing
The management function of assigning activities and grouping people so that the firm's objectives can be accomplished.

TQM

Hewlett-Packard had to restructure, change its system, and learn to manage workers who aren't in the office. H-P's management had to reorganize the firm to develop its world-class customer service. **Organizing** is the management function of assigning activities and grouping people (designing and developing a blueprint or structure) so that the firm's objectives can be accomplished.

When a business grows from a one-person operation to one with employees, organization becomes necessary. Any business that is more than a one-person operation requires organization. As a firm grows, it may be necessary for some employees to specialize, more interpersonal interactions may be required to accomplish complex goals, and it may be necessary to integrate diverse viewpoints to improve competitiveness. Some type of organizational structure is needed for things to run smoothly. Managers must plan and implement the way a business will be organized.

Down to her last $100 in savings, Carla Conner was sure of only one thing: She didn't want to work for someone else. So, in November 1990, Conner started her own company, C&B Industrial Safety, out of her South Florida home. Today she is working out of a 3,000-square-foot warehouse and has four full-time employees and over $700,000 in sales. Conner wants to position the company for further growth, but to do so she has to start thinking about organizational structure. When she was on her own, there was no need to think about structure—whatever needed to be done, she did it. To grow the company, however, Conner must begin to think about dividing tasks among her employees so she can take advantage of their individual strengths.[2]

In organizing a business, management (an individual or a group) usually decides what each person will do and how much authority each will have.

Organizational Structure
The arrangement of work to be done in a business.

The **organizational structure** is intended to help the business accomplish its objectives by arranging the work to be done. There is really no one best way to organize.[3] The "how to organize" decision for a particular business depends on many different factors, including size, market, personnel, competition, history, and available financial resources. Each firm believes that a particular organizational structure works best. What works for Boeing may not be what is best for its competitors. Similarly the Sears structural arrangement differs from that of Montgomery Ward, which differs from Kmart's. If there is a sound lesson about organizing, it would be: "Observe what your competitors are doing, but arrange your structure in a way that is best for your firm, its employees, and the objectives the enterprise seeks to accomplish."

ORGANIZING FUNDAMENTALS

Although differences in objectives, resources, and markets mean that different organizing strategies should be used, a knowledgeable manager will proceed with caution. Understanding the fundamentals can be helpful in earning a reasonable profit or operating a business efficiently. Reengineering is a concept that emphasizes rethinking how organizing occurs. Today's Business World illustrates how the concept works in practice.

TODAY'S BUSINESS WORLD

Reengineering Puts Focus on Business Processes

At the same time that many companies have been making a shift to total quality management (TQM), others have been using a different technique called "reengineering" to improve competitiveness. Reengineering refers to "the fundamental rethinking and radical redesign of business processes to achieve dramatic improvements in critical, contemporary measures of performance such as cost, quality, service, and speed." Leading reengineering consultants will ask companies to reconsider their fundamental reasons for being in business. Michael Hammer first brought the reengineering concept to wide attention in a 1990 *Harvard Business Review* article. In 1993 he published a book with James Champy called *Reengineering the Corporation,* which has sold more than 300,000 copies in hardcover. Hammer, who once taught at the Massachusetts Institute of Technology, is now a private consultant based in Cambridge, MA, and Champy heads his own management consulting firm, also in Cambridge. Three deceptively simple principles of reengineering have been laid out by Hammer:

- **Focus on the customer.** Everything a company does should start with the idea of adding value for the customer through better products, lower costs, greater speed, and superior service. One of reengineering's effects is to drive out practices that may be convenient or pleasant for an organization or the people who run it but have no meaning for the customer.

- **Organize around process.** "Process means that we look beyond the walls of the organization chart," Hammer says, "and we look at the value-adding work that's going on across organizational units." Order fulfillment, for example, is a single process, but many companies chop it up and parcel it out among departments isolated from one another for reasons that have nothing to do with serving the customer better.
- **Start with a clean sheet of paper.** A company should approach reengineering as if it were starting from scratch—as if the company did not exist but was going to be created in its ideal form. The idea is to scrutinize a company's practices, not just to see if they can be improved but to see if there is any reason for those practices to exist.

Companies of all sizes find benefits in the application of these three principles. The best candidates for reengineering are those firms smart enough not to believe their own propaganda—the companies that are doing well but know they could be doing much better. Such companies can enter reengineering carefully, and they can reasonably hope to emerge from it more competitive than they were before.

Reengineering is the fundamental rethinking of the purpose of a business. Think of a business that has changed fundamentally to improve competitiveness. What alternatives did the company have? Do you think it is going in the right direction now? Reengineering urges companies to focus on processes rather than functions. Think about the processes you had to go through to get registered for this class. How do you think the process might be reengineered?

Source: Adapted from Michael Barrier, "Reengineering Your Company," *Nation's Business* (February 1994): 16–22; Michael Hammer and James Champy, *Reengineering the Corporation* (New York: Harper Business, 1993).

A number of issues that managers need to consider in any type of organizing decision are discussed to illustrate that managerial action is needed to help make organizations efficient.

Clear Objectives

In Chapter 7, we said that objectives are desired results or targets. Having clearly stated, meaningful, specific, and challenging objectives is important. They give meaning to the business by determining what it is attempting to accomplish. The multiple objectives (e.g., profit, market share, human resource development) of a business provide the direction for those organizing the firm. Objectives provide the framework for hiring the type of human resources needed.

Coordination

Organizational, departmental, subunit, and individual objectives must fit together. This means the efforts of individual employees must be coordinated, or interwoven.

Coordination requires everyday, informal communication among employees. When Lee Iacocca took over Chrysler Corporation in 1978, he found little communication between the engineers and manufacturing departments. Nobody seemed to be interested in coordination. Iacocca conducted meetings in which the engineers and manufacturing technicians were required to talk and work with each other.

Any organizational structure, no matter how complicated, requires someone or some group to work continually on coordinating the activities of others. Managers and leaders can be the coordinators if they are respected and skilled in integrating the efforts of their subordinates or followers. Managers should not underestimate the effort that must go into coordination.

Formal and Informal Organizations

Formal Organization The management-designed, official structure of the business.

Two distinct organizations influence a company's employees. The **formal organization** is the one put together by management, created by those who have authority, responsibility, and accountability. At Hewlett-Packard, it was CEO Robert Walker and his associates. At IBM, CEO Lou Gerstner developed the formal reorganization plan. The formal organization is displayed in the organization chart, the graphical representation of the formal structure of the business.

Informal Organization The network of personal and social relationships that emerges when people work together.

Informal organizations exist in every business. Not planned or shown on an organization chart, the **informal organization** is the network of personal and social relationships that emerges when people work together.

Informal organizations develop because people who work together form relationships. In the past, managers tried hard—and unsuccessfully—to abolish them. Informal organization networks serve a purpose for employees. For example, a group of preretirement employees may be concerned about the pension program revision. They represent different units and are in various jobs (e.g., manager, technical, sales). Because of their common interest, they form an informal group to share information and opinions. Other informal groups begin when employees bowl, golf, play cards, or perform charity work together. These informal associations provide chances for communication between individuals from many different units of the firm. This kind of communication improves group members' understanding of each other.

Organization Chart

Organization Chart A graphic blueprint, or map, of positions, people, and formal authority relationships in the organization.

A graphical presentation of the formal structure of a business is the **organization chart.** It is similar to the blueprint of a new home. It maps positions, people, and their authority relationships. The organization chart shows authority, the location of responsibility, and to whom subordinates report. Exhibit 8.1 illustrates a simple line authority chart. Each position is represented by a box (with a title), and the flow of authority is represented by straight lines. Exhibit 8.2 shows a chart expanded to include staff authority. The legal

Exhibit 8.1
Organization Chart: Line Authority

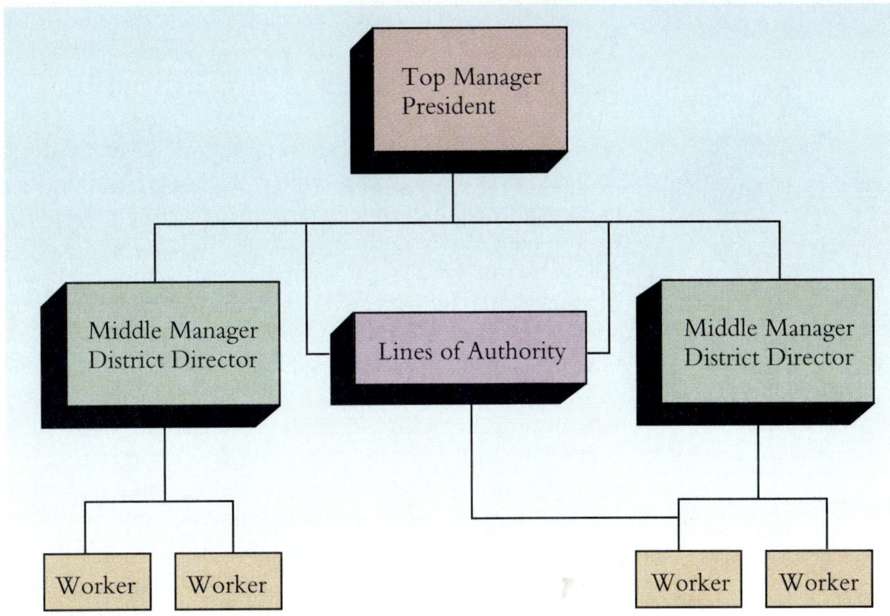

Lines of authority are pointed out as they would appear on a real organization chart.

Exhibit 8.2 *Organization Chart: Line and Staff Authority*

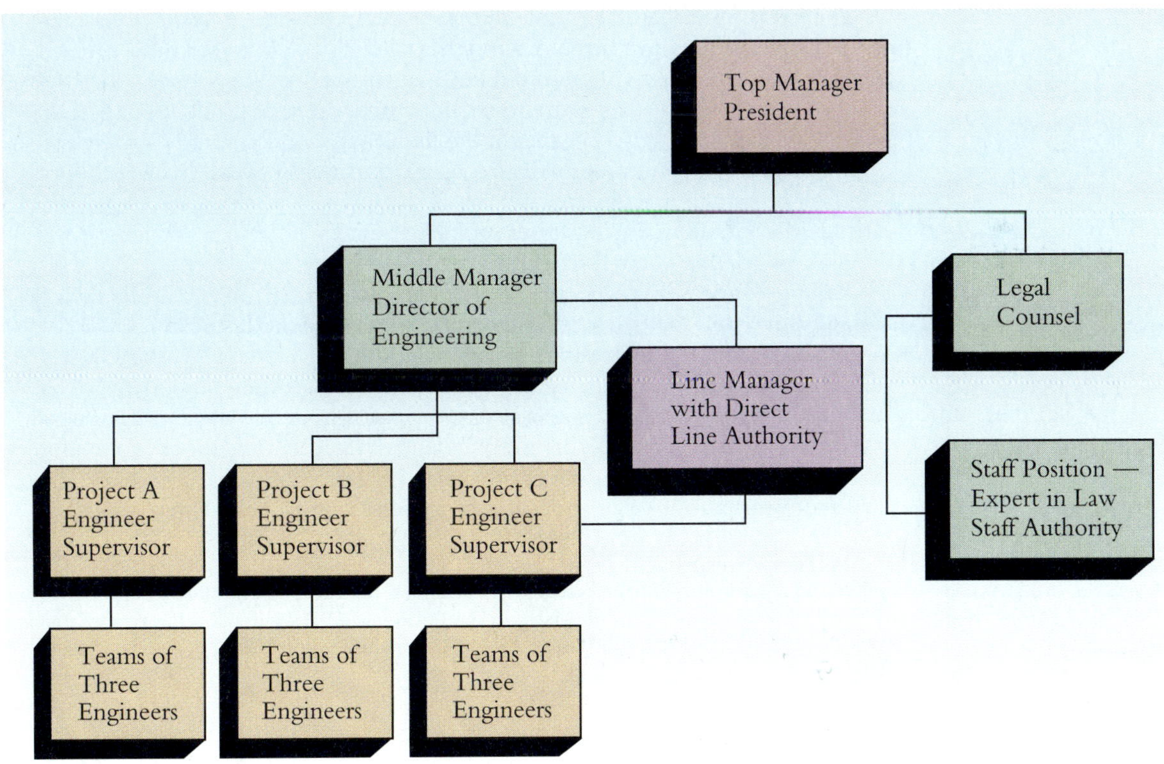

TOMORROW'S BUSINESS WORLD

Workplaces Will Be "De-Jobbed"

As we move toward the new century, signs of a radically altered workplace already abound. Even though the United States is regaining its standing in world competitiveness rankings, it is finding that recent productivity gains have not equated to job gains. In fact, three years into an economic recovery, employment has grown by just 4.8 percent compared with an average gain of 11.2 percent at similar times in previous recoveries. If the typical job-recovery pattern were still operating, more than 7 million additional new jobs would have been created. Something is happening within organizations that has changed the pattern of hiring.

What is disappearing from U.S. organizations is not just a certain number of jobs, or jobs in certain industries, or jobs in some part of the country, or even jobs in the United States as a whole. What is disappearing is the very thing itself: the job. That much-sought-after, much-maligned social entity, a job, is vanishing like a species that has outlived its evolutionary time. A century from now Americans may look back and wonder why we didn't see it happening. They will marvel at how much we came to accept the game of musical jobs as a part of life.

The modern world is on the verge of another new leap in creativity and productivity, but the job is not going to be part of tomorrow's economic reality. There still is, and probably always will be, an enormous amount of work to do; but it will not be contained in the familiar structural packages we know as jobs. In fact, many organizations today already have gone a long way toward becoming "de-jobbed."

The job is a social artifact, though it is so deeply embedded in our consciousness that most of us have forgotten its artificiality or the fact that most societies since the beginning of civilization did just fine without it. The job is an idea that emerged early in the 19th century to package the work that needed doing in the growing factories and bureaucracies of the industrializing nations.

In the future, organizations will no longer be a pattern of jobs. In place of jobs, there will be part-time and temporary work situations. The change is already occurring. Many modern organizations are built around work that needs to be done. When the work that needs doing changes constantly—as is expected in future organizations—there is no place for inflexible jobs. In a word, jobs are no longer socially adaptive, and that's why they are likely to go the way of the dinosaur.

Organizations will increasingly move toward hiring contract workers to participate in short-term projects, adding value for awhile and then moving on. What special training do you think is necessary to prepare for such a world? Is your business school preparing you for the independence and autonomy—not to mention the responsibility—that a de-jobbed workplace will require? What are some of the pitfalls for organizations that adopt the de-jobbing approach?

Source: Adapted from William Bridges, "The End of the Job," *Fortune* (September 19, 1994): 62–74; Paul Magnusson, "The Job Machine Hasn't Bounced Back with This Recovery," *Business Week* (September 19, 1994): 33; James Aley, "A Look Inside Job Churn," *Fortune* (October 3, 1994): 29.

counsel is a staff position advising the president on legal matters. The director of engineering exercises line authority over three project engineer supervisors.

Because it cannot picture informal relationships, the chart does not show exact communication patterns. A worker communicating directly with the president, for example, would represent an informal-organization activity.

Organization charts offer only a general view of the formal structure at a specific time. Every chart needs continual updating as changes in environment, personnel, resources, size, and technology occur.

Formal Authority

Formal Authority
The right to give orders.

Delegation
Giving an employee at a lower level in the organization the responsibility for a given task as well as the authority to carry it out.

The right to give orders constitutes **formal authority.** In effective organizations, managers delegate authority. **Delegation** is the process by which authority is distributed or pushed downward in an organization. The organizational structure can provide the framework for such delegation. Managers who do not have the time to perform their jobs often have failed to delegate authority properly. And subordinates who become frustrated in meeting their responsibilities may not be clear about what authority has been delegated to them.

Organizational structure determines the pattern for delegation of authority. It establishes common understanding between the manager and the employee about the degree and type of authority delegated. Two major types of

To perform their jobs successfully, managers must learn to delegate authority.

authority used in organizational structural arrangements are line and staff. Managers should understand these distinctions to know how much decision-making freedom they have.

Line Authority
Unquestioned, direct authority to make decisions and take action.

Line Authority. Each position in the managerial hierarchy has **line authority,** or direct authority over lower positions in the hierarchy. A manager with line authority is the unquestioned superior for all activities of his or her employees. At a McDonald's restaurant, the manager has authority over the salesclerks and the cooks. At the DSX electronics firm in Plano, TX, the quality control director has authority over 15 quality inspectors. He instructs, commands, and coordinates all quality inspection activities. He is in a line authority position.

Exhibit 8.1 is an illustration of line authority.

Staff Authority
An advisory authority in which a person studies a situation and makes recommendations but has no authority to take action.

Staff Authority. A person with **staff authority,** which is advisory authority, studies a situation and makes recommendations but has no authority to take action. For example, many firms have a legal department that provides counsel on legal issues important to the firm. The legal department can make recommendations about actions and their implications, but, as a staff function, it has no authority to carry out those recommendations.

The backbone of most organizational structures is line authority. Staff authority is narrower because staff expertise comes as advice, which may not be used by the line manager. In structuring a business, managers may use both line and staff authority. Exhibit 8.3 summarizes some of the advantages and disadvantages of each of these forms of authority.

Centralized Business
An organization in which all, or nearly all, authority to make decisions is retained by a small group of managers.

Centralization and Decentralization

Another important organizational consideration is the amount of authority to delegate. In a **centralized business,** only a small amount of authority is delegated. A relatively small number of managers make the decisions and hold

Exhibit 8.3
Advantages and Disadvantages of Line and Staff Authority

Advantages	Disadvantages
Line Authority	
Everything kept simple.	Neglects advisers.
Authority relationship graphically illustrated by hierarchy.	Too many decisions to make in short time period.
Close to employees so decisions can be made quickly.	Requires very skilled line managers.
Staff Authority	
Uses the best experts.	Confusing to some employees.
Frees line managers for day-to-day activities.	Creates line-staff conflicts.
Can be used as screening and training arena for future line managers.	Places staff in subservient role.

most of the power and authority. At Marie Vianett's aerobic exercise studio in Quebec, Canada, she makes all the decisions. She is the centralized and only source of authority. She hires employees and instructors, establishes the budget, provides the aerobic regimen schedule, and conducts all negotiations with the building landlord and suppliers of the aerobic exercise outfits sold in the studio.

Decentralized Business
An organization in which a significant amount of the authority to make decisions is delegated to lower-level managers.

In a **decentralized business,** authority is delegated rather than held by a small management group. The authority continuum in centralized and decentralized business is presented in Exhibit 8.4. The table includes a comparison of some advantages and disadvantages of each type of delegation.

The consulting firm McKinsey & Company reported that Toyota, which has a decentralized structure, can introduce three new cars and get market feedback in the same amount of time it takes General Motors to introduce one car. Three cars versus one car. GM managers recognized this plodding

Exhibit 8.4
The Decentralized-Centralized Continuum of Authority

Advantages	Disadvantages
Most organizations lie somewhere on a continuum from centralized to decentralized authority.	
Centralized	
Increases uniformity of policies, rules, and procedures.	Places demands and pressure on a few managers.
Helps avoid duplication of effort and use or resources.	Reduces sense of involvement.
Increases uniformity of decision.	Gives large amount of power to a few managers.
Decentralized	
Places decision making closer to the action.	Makes coordination more difficult.
Gives individual decision makers more responsibility for their actions.	Limits availability of capable managers.
Helps develop managers for the future.	Lacks uniform policies.
Decentralized operation	Centralized operation
Maximum delegation of authority	Little or no delegation of authority

reaction time and gave the Cadillac Division more autonomy to make decisions. GM decentralized decision-making power.

Some management consultants are urging American companies to adopt an approach known as the "lean enterprise." The lean enterprise is "a group of individuals, functions, and legally separate but synchronized companies."[4] This approach truly emphasizes decentralization and rapid decision making.

Organizations often move back and forth along the centralized-decentralized continuum. For years Sears was a centralized business; but in the 1950s and '60s, it changed to a more decentralized business. Then, around 1980, Sears executives declared they wanted closer control of decision making; in other words, management wanted authority centralized. In the 1990s, Sears has moved again toward a decentralized organizational structure.

An important management skill in a decentralized operation is delegation. This skill is the ability to pass on to an employee the responsibility for a given task, as well as the authority to carry it out. Can you delegate? Complete Your Values and Attitudes and learn about your delegation skills.

YOUR VALUES AND ATTITUDES

Delegation Ability

Directions: Place an X on the number that indicates how important you think the skill is for delegating job assignments or decision-making power. Circle the number that indicates how much of the skill you now possess.

Skill Areas	Very important/ significant				Not important/ little
1. Trusting the ability of other people.	5	4	3	2	1
2. Delegating meaningful, not just routine, jobs to others.	5	4	3	2	1
3. Coaching and helping others with a new job.	5	4	3	2	1
4. Sharing power and authority.	5	4	3	2	1
5. Following up to let individuals know how they are doing.	5	4	3	2	1
6. Setting reasonable goals on what is to be accomplished.	5	4	3	2	1
7. Determining others' ability to make decisions.	5	4	3	2	1
8. The challenges of the delegated job are motivational.	5	4	3	2	1

Feedback: A person with a strong orientation toward delegation would score between 33 and 40. A score of 40 would result from placing an X on the number 5 for all eight items. Being a good delegator has several payoffs for a manager. First, delegating regular, routine tasks frees the manager's time for more important tasks.

Second, employees develop and become more involved with the job because they have added responsibility. Third, having more varied tasks can break the monotony for the employee of doing the same job over and over again.

Although delegation seems simple, it requires the manager to look closely at these factors:

1. Can the employee handle delegation?
2. What will be delegated? Is it clearly stated?
3. How will the person know he or she is doing a good job, especially in terms of the delegated tasks? Are there standards of performance?
4. Is the delegator available to answer questions, coach, and provide feedback?
5. Does the employee feel good after completing the delegated task?

Instead of rushing into delegation, the manager must carefully think these factors through. The quiz points to such managerial concerns as trust, coaching, sharing of power, and building in job challenge. The quiz also highlights points that managers need to address before deciding whether delegation is a useful organizing strategy for them. Think of a time when you delegated a job or task to someone. Did you feel comfortable about delegating?

PRINCIPLES OF ORGANIZING

Are delegation of authority, organization charts, and formal and informal organizations all there is to organizing? No, some principles of organizing have been found through practice and experimentation. These principles have been considered in organizing large businesses (Sara Lee, Scott Paper, and Boeing), medium-sized businesses (Allied Champion and Castle Metals), and small businesses (Champion Forest Roofing and Mayo's Pharmacy).

Principle
A guideline that managers can use in making decisions.

Principles are guidelines for decision making; they are not laws etched in stone. Sometimes principles are used exactly as they are stated; other times they are modified or completely ignored. In general, those responsible for organizing keep a number of organizational principles in mind. Many principles are available to consider, but we have selected just a few of the more popular ones as illustrations.

Division of Labor

Division of Labor
A principle of organization that a job can be performed more efficiently if the jobholder is allowed to specialize.

Organizations of all sizes perform a wide variety of tasks. A basic principle of organizing is that a job can be performed more efficiently if the jobholder is allowed to specialize. This principle, called the **division of labor,** involves dividing a major task into separate smaller tasks. The major task of manufacturing textiles is divided into smaller tasks of weaving, finishing, and needling.

The efficiency achieved by becoming an expert in a small task can be significant. However, breaking a job into smaller and smaller tasks can be overdone. Dividing labor into small, boring jobs that offer no challenge can result in employees feeling frustrated, having low levels of job satisfaction, and seeking employment elsewhere.

In this shoe manufacturing plant, major tasks are divided into smaller tasks, thereby increasing efficiency.

Unity of Command

Unity of Command
The principle of organization that no employee should report to more than one superior.

The principle of **unity of command** states that no member of an organization should report to more than one superior. Subordinates need to know from whom they receive the authority to make decisions and do the job. Conflicting orders from different superiors should be avoided; they can cause confusion, result in contradictory instructions, and create frustration about which order to follow. This principle can be followed in an organization having only line authority. However, when a staff and line authority structure is used, the unity of command is often violated.

Scalar Principle

Scalar Principle
The principle of organization that authority and responsibility should flow in a clear, unbroken line from the highest to the lowest manager.

That authority and responsibility should flow in a clear, unbroken line from the highest to the lowest manager is called the **scalar principle.** When managerial levels are arranged in a hierarchy the importance of the scalar chain from top to bottom is obvious. Breaking the chain would result in uncertainty about authority relationships, which would in turn lead to confusion and frustration for employees.

An extension of the scalar principle is the notion that authority should equal responsibility. For example, suppose a production supervisor at Rockwell International has been assigned the responsibility to purchase new plant equipment. It would be important for this supervisor to have the authority to determine what price should be paid for the new equipment. Without this authority, how could the supervisor be held responsible for the decision?

Span of Control

Span of Control
The principle of organization that limits the number of subordinates reporting to a supervisor.

Span of control is the number of subordinates reporting to a supervisor, or boss. The **span of control** principle says there is a limit to the number of subordinates one superior should supervise. Managers using that principle often specify an exact number of subordinates. This is unrealistic, however, because some supervisors can handle more subordinates than others. The optimum span of control depends on many factors, such as the type of skill and the experience levels of subordinates, the nature of the job, the supervisor's skill in handling subordinates, the situation, and the time available to do the job.

In general, highly skilled employees require less supervision than the less skilled. This permits the manager to have a wide span of control—that is, a larger group of employees reporting to him or her. For example, a large group of highly skilled technicians in a DuPont research and development unit can be supervised by a single manager. On the other hand, an open-heart surgery team at St. Joseph Hospital in Chicago involves highly skilled employees but a narrow (also called tall or small) span of control. Exhibit 8.5 illustrates wide and narrow spans of control.

Exhibit 8.5 *Wide and Narrow Spans of Control*

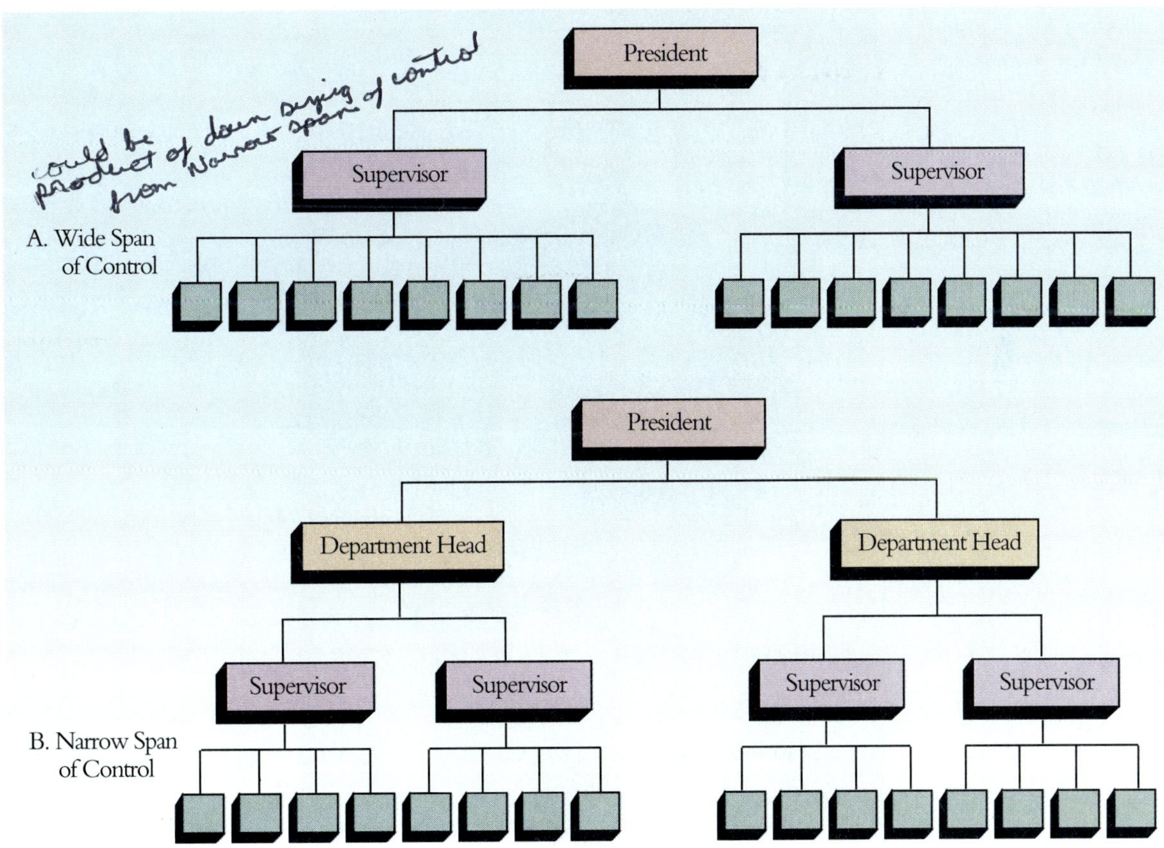

The optimum span of control depends on many factors. Rather than a universal set of numbers, managers have only general suggestions to examine the total picture—the managers, subordinates, job, resources, and time available. For example, for many years the Swedish firm Asea Brown Boveri competed in eight business segments and had developed a central management staff of over 2,000 people. When CEO Percy Barnevik arrived in 1980, he quickly reduced the staff to 200 without losing any productivity. Barnevik increased each remaining manager's span of control. Indeed, Barnevik is so convinced of his approach that he believes most organizations can pare central office staff by as much as 90 percent.[5]

HOW TO ORGANIZE A BUSINESS

A person involved in organizing a business should identify the business objectives, the types of people working for the business, the technology, and the environment in which the business operates. If you've ever been in a house

Identifying business objectives is an important first step in organizing a business.

in which the rooms are too small or poorly arranged, you know the importance of the notion that "form follows function." That principle is also important in making organizational structure decisions. People making decisions about structure need to examine the functions before selecting a form (that is, the structure).

Numerous forms, or designs, of structure are available to managers. Each way of organizing a business has advantages and disadvantages. A manager has to weigh all of these in making a selection. When the decision is made without considering disadvantages, the resulting choice may be the least effective or least suitable structure. The ones we present here are the most popular and widely used in business organizations.

Functional Structure

Functional Structure
A structure in which each unit or department has a different set of activities and responsibilities.

Each unit or department in the **functional structure** has a different set of activities and responsibilities. In a manufacturing firm, this means that engineering, manufacturing, and marketing would be separate departments. In a hospital, functional structure would include departments of nursing, housekeeping, medical records, radiology, and so forth. A functional structure for a county hospital is shown in Exhibit 8.6.

Advantages. The functional structure orients workers toward a specific set of activities. The engineer focuses on product design and improvement, and the salesperson works on selling. These functional experts become even more skilled in their areas. Research shows that the functional structure works well for a firm operating in a relatively stable (unchanging or slowly changing) environment.[6] Glass and building material companies such as Corning Glass Works, PPG Industries, and Owens-Illinois operate in a normally stable environment. Product lines change little from year to year, so the arrangement used is a functional structure.

Disadvantages. The functional structure de-emphasizes the exchange of ideas and cooperation with other departments. The boundary between, say, marketing and engineering is imaginary, but it seems like the Great Wall of China. This happens because each department is evaluated on the basis of its own performance. Knowing they will be evaluated this way, managers concentrate on departmental matters instead of overall organizational objectives.

If the business's objectives and environment require coordination across departments, the functional structure becomes an obstruction. Problems arise that have no single departmental solution. As a result, the problems go unresolved, the buck is passed, or problems are pushed up to top management.

In summary, functional structures are best suited for businesses with a relatively stable environment, such as Corning Glass Works. At Corning the organizational structure takes advantage of technical expertise. On the other hand, in an environment with numerous style changes (such as that of Liz Claiborne), a functional structure would lack flexibility and be slow in reacting. Liz Claiborne has to react quickly to fashion changes.

Exhibit 8.6 *Functional Structure in a Hospital*

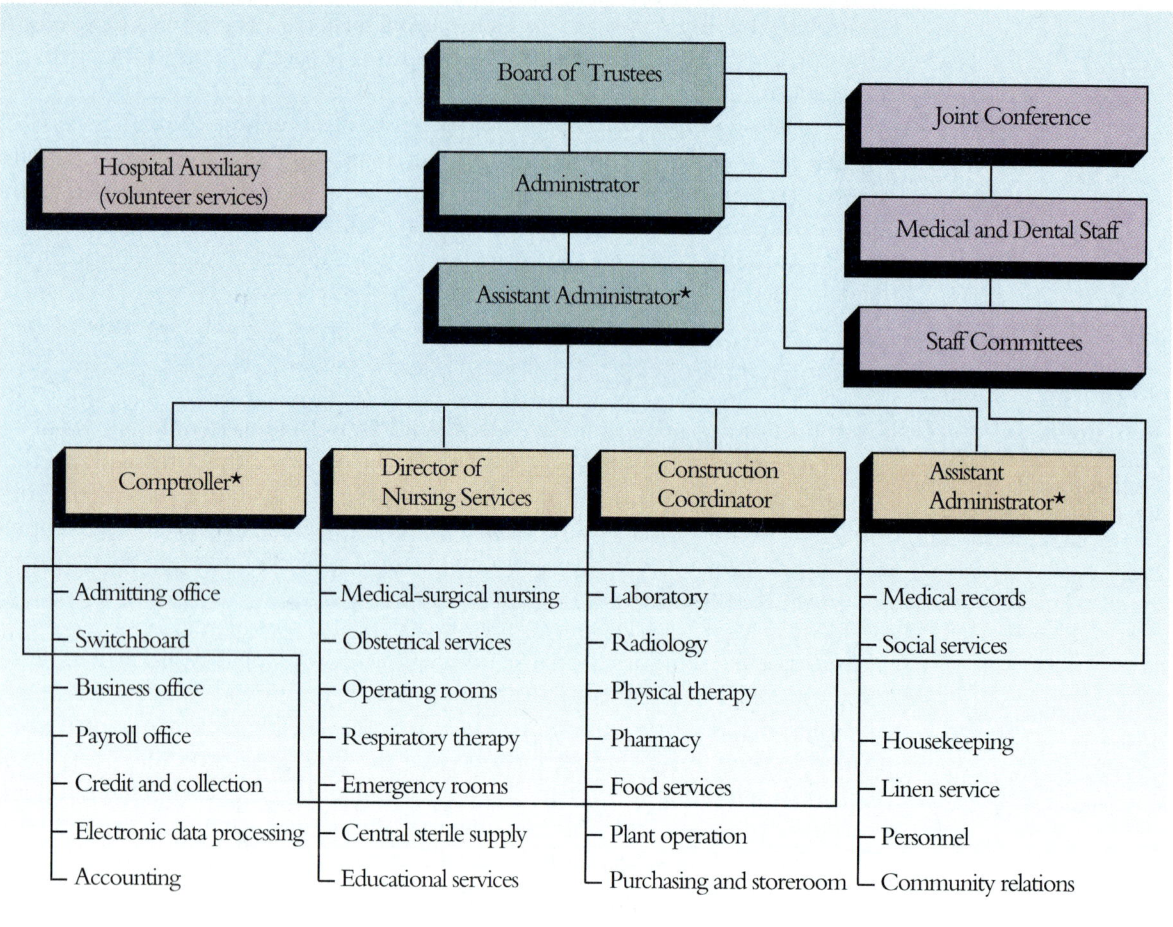

This chart reflects the line responsibility and authority in the hospital organization. However, a great part of the work of the hospital is accomplished through informal interaction between the identified services and functions. These functional working relationships are encouraged. Where there is difference in understanding or changes in procedure are required, the line organization should be carefully observed.

*Area directors.

Product Structure

Product Structure An organizational structure in which a manager is placed in charge of and has responsibility for a product or product line.

Businesses producing a wide variety of products often establish a **product structure.** The product structure was used as early as 1927 by Proctor & Gamble (P&G). A new soap product, Camay, was not selling. A young executive, Neil McElroy (who later became the president of P&G), was told to give his exclusive attention to increasing the sales of Camay. This he did by using product managers. Soon afterward P&G added other product managers.

Today many firms, especially those in the food (Pillsbury), toiletries (Gillette), and chemical (W.R. Grace) industries, use product structures. General Foods uses a product structure in its Post Division, in which separate product managers are in charge of cereals, pet foods, and beverages.

Advantages. The product structure places responsibility for a product or product line with the managers. The success or failure of Post Toasties is the responsibility of the general manager of cereals. This means product managers devote all their energy and skill toward the objectives of containing product costs, meeting schedules, and earning a profit. Instead of a department orientation, as with the functional structure, the focus is on product.

In addition the product structure encourages creativity. One study found that businesses with product structures were more successful in creating and selling new products than were businesses without product structures.[7] The product structure also is flexible enough to cope with changing environments. People have to cooperate so that the product will perform well.

Disadvantages. The price of the product structure can be high. Product managers often are not given enough authority to carry out responsibilities. They have to spend a lot of time coordinating activities so that people work together efficiently. This means less time for planning. Often they are told that they are like presidents in their product area, but in fact they are usually only referees and low-level coordinators.

Managers have also found that, compared to employees in functional structures, employees in product structures are more insecure and anxious about unemployment and personal development.[8] Perhaps this results from using product structures in relatively unstable, unpredictable environments. (Such environments reject products, even certain kinds of packages and names of products.) This unpredictability sometimes is stressful and produces anxiety because people's success depends on their product's success.

Territorial Structure

Territorial Structure An organizational structure in which units are divided on the basis of territory or geographical region.

Businesses that divide units on the basis of location are using **territorial structure.** When adjustments to local conditions, markets, or resources are important, responsibility affixed on the basis of territory has advantages.

Merchandising organizations such as JC Penny and Federated Department Stores have found territorial structure attractive. A&P, Safeway, and Kroger also use territorial division structures, coupled with centralization of certain functions (e.g., purchasing and distribution). Division managers have authority to take advantage of regional cost, resource, and competitive conditions.

Transportation companies may also be structured by territory. Low-cost airline prices have eaten into long-distance bus travel. Today the average bus trip has decreased from about 500 miles to slightly over 200 miles. This type of competition encouraged Greyhound Lines' management to change the company from a functional to a territorial structure. Greyhound now has four territorial divisions: eastern, central, southern, and western. Customer needs in Phoenix are monitored and then met by the western division, while customer needs in Chicago are observed and handled by the central division. The territorial structure helps Greyhound be more responsive to consumer needs and better able to coordinate schedules, maintenance, replacement, and employee preferences in each region.[9] Multinational corporations (MNCs) will typically use a territorial structure, dividing up the business by countries of operation. MNCs will usually appoint a "country manager," someone who is familiar with the country in which they are operating. IBM has recently abandoned that structure in favor of a product structure. Only time will tell whether that move will help its international business.[10]

Advantages. The main advantage of the territorial structure is that it allows coordination at the point of sale. This coordination can lead to more personalized and speedier service. In a territorial arrangement, customer needs can be better addressed.

Disadvantages. Some duplication of effort occurs in the territorial structure. Also, the corporation needs to hire, train, and develop managers with the broad-based ability and technical knowledge required to manage multiple functions such as sales, production, and marketing.

Matrix Structure

Matrix Structure
A functional structure combined with either a product or a project structural arrangement.

Occasionally a company utilizes a functional structure and either a product or a project structure simultaneously; that is, it combines functional structure and a second management arrangement into a **matrix structure.** The result violates the unity-of-command principle of organizing because a person works for more than one boss. The employee is assigned to both a functional department (permanent home) and a particular product or project (temporary home). Exhibit 8.7 shows a matrix structure with five functional departments and three projects staffed by employees from the departments.

Why have the matrix, when it obviously violates the principle of unity of command? Recall the weaknesses of functional and product structures. The functional structure de-emphasizes the exchange of ideas and cooperation, although it does permit specialists to interact and strive for technical excellence. The product structure is weaker at encouraging job security, although it is strong at inducing cooperation, adhering to schedules, and controlling costs. The matrix design gains the strengths of both while avoiding the disadvantages of either. Matrix structures have been used in diverse organizational types:

- Manufacturing—aerospace, chemicals, electronics.
- Service—banking, insurance, retailing.
- Professional—accounting, consulting, law.
- Nonprofit—hospitals, United Nations, universities.

Exhibit 8.7 *A Matrix Structure.*

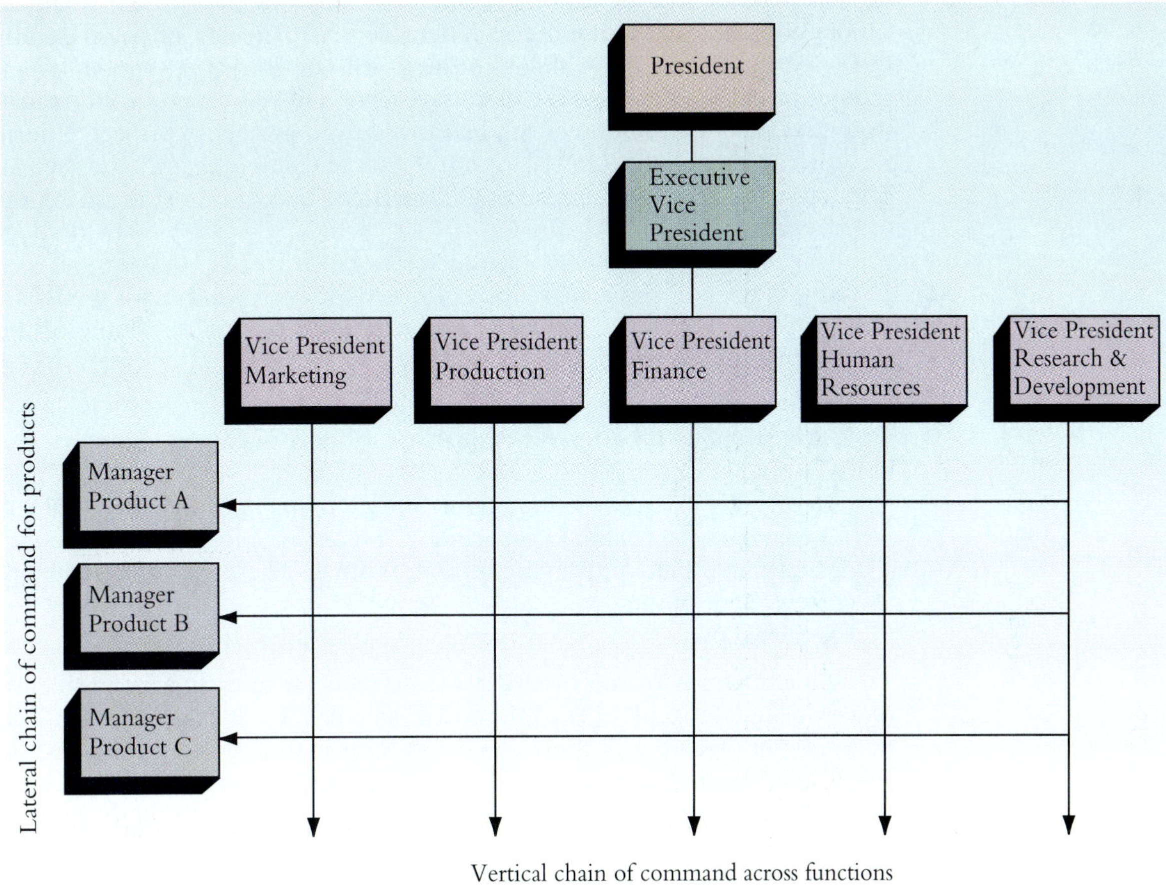

Advantages. The matrix structure responds effectively to three conditions. First, a matrix can handle a dual focus. For example, the company may need to respond to two equally important environmental pressures. Aerospace firms such as Lockheed and McDonnell Douglas must meet both technical requirements and customer cost constraints. While the manager argues for more money to improve the product technically, the product manager argues for meeting budget constraints. The dual focus of technical and cost interests is possible in the matrix structure.

Second, requirements for communication among employees may exceed the capacity of a traditional functional structure. Environmental uncertainty, work complexity, and interdependence of departments increase as a business grows and diversifies its products and markets. The functional structure does not encourage cooperation and a total team spirit. What is needed is a structure that encourages the sharing of information. The matrix gives the cross-functional benefits of a product structure while keeping the administrative controls of the functional structure.

Third, performance, cost, and time pressures require greater sharing and use of resources. Placing limited resources in only one department results in a monopolization of the resources. When talented engineers, physicists, computer specialists, and other skilled professionals are in scarce supply, several groups, projects, or units must share the talent and resources. In the matrix structure, talent and resources can be moved from project to project. Priorities for the use of the limited resources are measured against the overall business objectives and interests. The matrix makes this shifting of resources easier.

Disadvantages. If the matrix always worked for every business, it would always be used. There are, however, problems with the matrix. Some of the most frequently cited include:[11]

- Confusion about who reports to whom, and when.
- Power struggles between functional and product managers.
- Groupthink, or too much group decision making.
- "Meetingitis," or just too much time wasted in one meeting after another.
- The tendency to become "papermills." To ensure cooperation and coordination, everyone puts everything in writing. The result is a seemingly endless paper output.
- Excessive costs of having more managers to compensate.

The advantages of the matrix structure seem to outweigh its problems. Nevertheless, this type of organizational structure is not for everyone. The manager with two bosses must work very well with people. Would you be able to work with two bosses—one functional and one product? Think about some of the conflicts you might face. Suppose each wanted you to attend a different important meeting at 10 A.M. or to attend training seminars, one in Los Angeles and one in Boston, on the same date. Having more than one boss contradicts the principle of unity of command.

Multiple Structures

We have been discussing forms of structure as if they were an either/or choice. In fact a business is free to use any form or combination of structures. An example of a *multiple structure* appears in Exhibit 8.8. Sun Petroleum Products' structure shows three product divisions: fuels, lubricants/waxes, and chemicals. Each division has its own functional departments of marketing, planning and economics, supply and distribution, and manufacturing. Sun also has a number of centralized functions, such as human resources, technology, public affairs, and facilities. The multiple organizational structure enables the refineries to produce products for the three product divisions.

Advantages. Companies use multiple structures to gain the benefits of each arrangement. Perhaps the biggest advantage of the multiple structure is that it encourages management to look at the total picture of organizing. This overall view stimulates a total-company enthusiasm and a realization that each part or unit is important in accomplishing corporate objectives.[12]

Exhibit 8.8 *Sun Petroleum's Multiple Organization Structure*

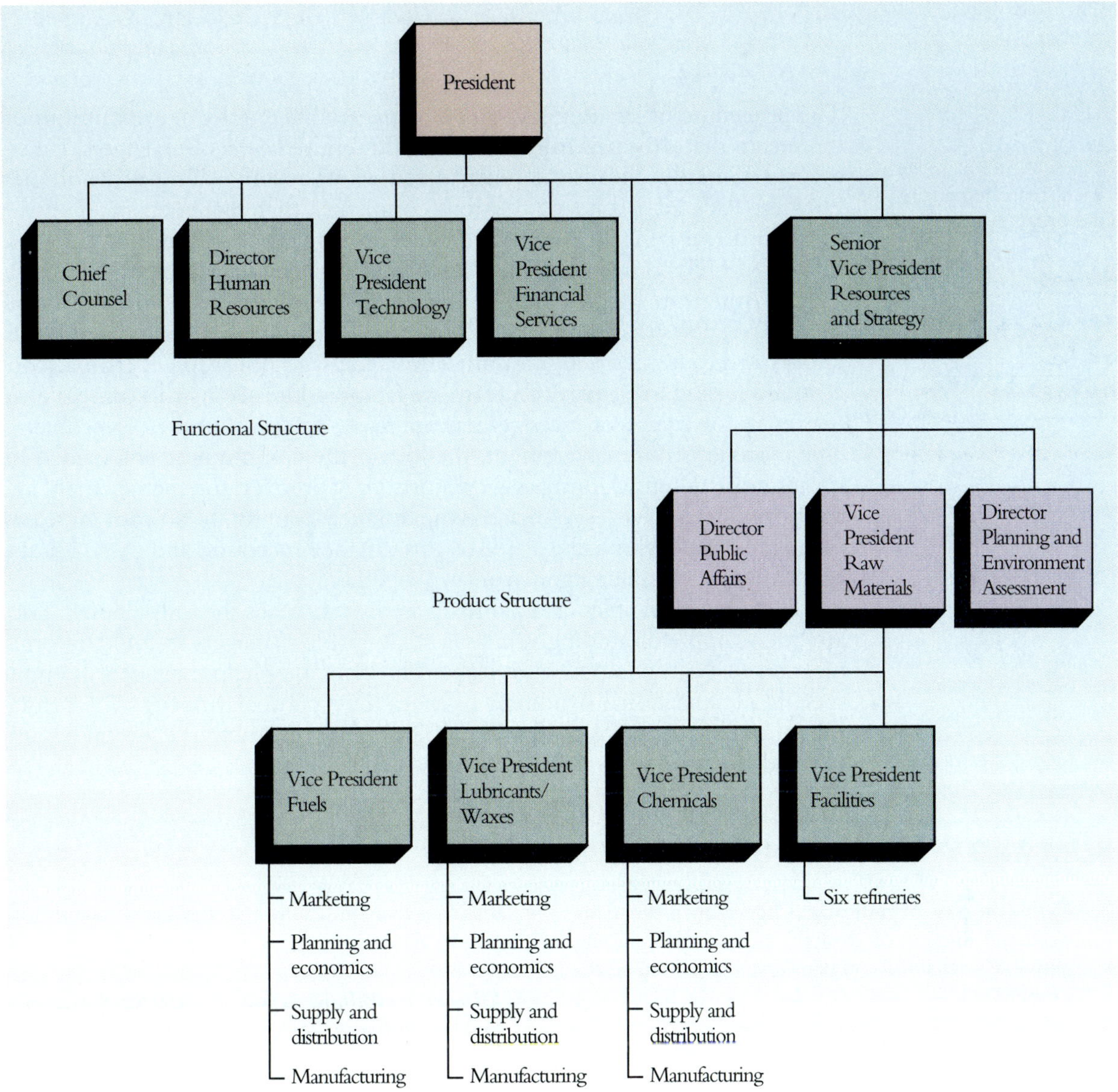

Source: Linda S. Ackerman. "Transition Management: An In-Depth Look at Managing Complex Change." Reprinted by permission of publisher, from *Organizational Dynamics,* Summer 1982 © American Management Association, New York. All rights reserved.

Disadvantages. Potential drawbacks to multiple structures, such as the one used by Sun Petroleum, are increased management overhead expenses, duplication of resources, and conflict between headquarters and product divisions. Problems in coordination of policies, programs, and resources arise often. Finally, a successful move from a single-structure arrangement to a multiple-structure system may take significant time and resources.

Downsizing

Downsizing
Cutting out entire layers of management in the organization.

The procedure of keeping levels in a managerial hierarchy to a minimum often means that **downsizing,** or cutting out entire layers of managers, is necessary. Primarily because it reorganized around networking technologies, Hewlett-Packard is one of the few companies that increased productivity through downsizing.[13] Every year since 1988 at least one-third of large and mid-sized U.S. companies have pared their workforces, according to surveys by the American Management Association. Despite this downsizing trend, the AMA reports that only 34 percent of constricting companies reported increases in productivity. Communication, message distortion, personal contact, and feeling like a part of a team are factors addressed by this principle. As the levels, or layers, of management increase, so do a number of problems. The more levels of management, the longer the communication chain. This means more potential for message distortion. Moreover, top management and the lower levels have less contact as the distance from top to bottom increases. Finally, people feel more isolated as this distance increases, and there is a loss of team spirit, of pulling and working together.

These five principles of organizing are by no means the only ones.[14] They are but a sample of guiding principles that enable managers to build an organization that can compete and adapt. The principles help managers assemble specific organizational structures to meet their particular needs. The principles of organization are the building blocks for constructing a formal organizational structure.

SUMMARY OF LEARNING OBJECTIVES

1. ***Define the term* organizing**. Organizing is the management function of grouping people and assigning activities so that the company's objectives can be accomplished.

2. ***Describe formal and informal organizations.*** The formal organization is put together by management, created by individuals who have authority, responsibility, and accountability. The formal organization is depicted in the organization chart. The informal organization is the network of personal and social relationships that emerges when people work together.

3. ***Distinguish between line and staff authority.*** Managers with line authority have direct control over lower positions in the management hierarchy. Managers with staff authority can study a situation and make recommendations, but they have no authority to take action.

4. ***Discuss centralized versus decentralized decision-making authority.*** In a centralized business, a relatively small number of managers make the decisions and hold most of the power and authority. Advantages of centralization include uniformity of policies, rules, and procedures; avoiding duplication of effort and use of resources; and uniform decisions. The disadvantages include greater pressure and demands on a few people, a reduced sense of involvement, and large amounts of power concentrated in a few people. In a decentralized business, authority is delegated to more levels of management. Decentralization places decision making closer to the action, gives decision makers more responsibility for their actions, and develops managers of the future—all

advantages. The disadvantages include more difficult coordination, possible lack of capable managers, and lack of uniformity in policies.

5. ***Identify what a manager can learn about an organization by reviewing an organization chart.*** An organization chart is a graphical presentation, or blueprint, of the the formal structure of an enterprise. The chart shows people, their positions, and their authority relationships.

6. ***Identify the principles of organizing.*** Division of labor involves dividing a major task into separate, smaller tasks to achieve greater efficiency. Unity of command means subordinates report to no more than one supervisor. The scalar principle states that authority and responsibility should flow in a clear, unbroken line from the highest to the lowest manager. An extension of this principle states that authority should equal responsibility. Under span of control, the number of subordinates who should report to a supervisor is limited.

7. ***Compare the advantages and disadvantages of functional, product, and territorial structures.*** The functional structure orients people toward a specific set of activities. As a result, they become more skilled in their areas. It works well in a relatively stable environment. However, the exchange of ideas and cooperation with other departments is lessened, and problems may arise that cannot be solved by one department. In the product structure, managers are responsible for one product or product line. They devote all their energy and skill to containing product costs, meeting schedules, and earning a profit. This structure encourages creativity. Its disadvantages include managers not having enough authority to carry out their responsibilities, the extra time required for planning, employees more insecure and anxious, and more stressful environments. The territorial structure's main advantage is coordination at the point of sale, leading to more personalized and speedier service. Disadvantages include some duplication of effort and the need to have managers who are able to perform multiple functions within their territories.

8. ***Explain what types of structures combine to form a matrix organization.*** The matrix organization is a combination of the functional structure and either a product or project structure. As a result, subordinates have a functional boss (their permanent home is in the functional unit) and a product/project boss (a temporary home).

KEY TERMS

Organizing
Organizational Structure
Formal Organization
Informal Organization
Organization Chart
Formal Authority
Delegation
Line Authority
Staff Authority
Centralized Business
Decentralized Business
Principle
Division of Labor
Unity of Command
Scalar Principle
Span of Control
Functional Structure
Product Structure
Territorial Structure
Matrix Structure
Downsizing

QUESTIONS FOR DISCUSSION AND REVIEW

1. Would a large organization such as Du Pont, Teledyne, or Shell use multiple structures? Why?

2. What skills does a manager need in an organization that uses a matrix structure to overcome the violation of the unity-of-command principle?

3. Some small-business owners claim that they don't need to worry about organizing principles of management because they are small. Do you agree with this claim? Explain.

4. Most organizations are a combination of centralized and decentralized structures. What are relevant factors for managers to think about when considering decentralizing the organizational structure?

5. Where is the scalar principle applied in the U.S. government?

6. What purposes does the informal organization serve?

7. List some significant advantages and disadvantages of the territorial structure.

8. Why is it important for a manager to be flexible in terms of how he or she structures the unit being supervised? Inflexibility can result in what types of problems?

9. Explain the difference between line and staff positions. Use an organization chart to illustrate your explanation.

10. What factors should be considered to determine the optimum span of control for a particular manager?

CASE 8.1

IBM's CEO Elects to Take Advantage of Company Size

For years International Business Machines Corporation (IBM) has been blessed with top-of-the-line senior executives and chief executive officers—Thomas Watson, T. Vincent Learson, Frank Cary, John Opel, John Akers. Now it is Lou Gerstner's turn to keep IBM at the top of the computer industry. And, from the way things have been shaping up, that is turning into an exceedingly difficult assignment.

Lou Gerstner came to IBM in 1993 when things were worse than they had ever been for dependable Big Blue. And it is not clear that he has been able to make much headway in turning the giant computer maker around. Lulled into a sense of comfort from the many years of stability, IBM leaders had assumed the company was invincible. Its vaunted mainframe business had provided the sense of security, but the rise of the personal computer abruptly changed the company's fortunes in the late 1980s. Although IBM was the leading producer of PCs, and although it had key expansion plans in place that would have allowed it to capture the shifting computer market, it didn't implement those plans. From 1987 to 1993, IBM lost $60 billion of market value. From 1990 to 1993, IBM's gross profit margin (sales minus cost of goods sold) dived 17 percentage points to less than 40 percent of sales. In 1993, IBM's gross profits were $14 billion less than in 1990—a difference equivalent to the total sales of 3M, one of the largest industrial companies in the United States. A year and a half after Gerstner took over, some people were beginning to wonder if he had the right formula to wake the sleeping giant.

When the IBM board went looking for a person to replace John Akers, they first tried to recruit several in-your-face type leaders who had led major American firms. They went after Jack Welch of General Electric and Larry Bossidy of Allied Signal. Neither man wanted the job that eventually went to Gerstner.

Despite the continuing bad profit news, there are some good signs coming out of Gerstner's IBM. The CEO has drastically reduced operating costs, holding profit margins relatively stable. He has also brought a new sense of urgency to the company. Yet, some critics contend that even these seeming successes are more a matter of luck than skill. Unexpectedly high demand for mainframe computers has given the company a temporary respite from the inevitable shift to less lucrative products. No one can predict how long the grace period will last, but it is not going to last long.

Gerstner's critics say he is moving too slowly in restructuring the company. They contend that his leadership may be too deliberate and cerebral to transform IBM's self-defeating business practices and inward-looking corporate culture in time. John Naisbitt, author of the popular book *Megatrends* and the more recent *Global Paradox,* says, "Gerstner is very, very good at what doesn't work anymore." Organizational change consultant and University of Michigan professor Noel Tichy said, "Lou hasn't made any big mistakes, but he's still putting the base camp together at the bottom of Mount Everest. In an industry moving at the speed of light, there's very little time for that." Critics fault Gerstner for being an incrementalist who relies mainly on longtime IBMers and is not fundamentally challenging the IBM way of doing business.

No matter what his critics say, Gerstner has been able to make some changes in IBM through the sheer force of his will. To force action, he frequently arbitrates disputes with snap decisions and grants sweeping authority to individuals or small committees. He has launched eight broad reengineering projects, each "owned" by a single executive.

Gerstner's most visible intellectual achievement since taking the reins at IBM is the distillation of hundreds of IBM goals into a simple list of strategic imperatives. Key points include a belief that IBM's size, scale, and technology can once again become sources of competitive advantage. For example, hoping to establish itself as a leader in computer networking, IBM is introducing a broad line of products that use state-of-the-art technology. The old business that produce most of IBM's revenue and profit—mainframe plus related software—probably will continue to shrink, and new businesses may not replace them. IBM is banking on attracting millions of customers to a new unified product line based on its PowerPC microprocessors and workplace software.

But perhaps the greatest challenge for Gerstner is creating a workable organizational structure for IBM. His sensible-sounding theory is that IBM's competitive advantage lies in its potential to offer one-stop shopping to customers seeking solutions to their technology problems. Before he arrived, IBM was moving toward a break up into 13 autonomous units that had come to be called Baby Blues: one for mainframes, one for PCs, another for disk drives, and so on. That decentralized structure appealed to the units' leaders who craved the autonomy such a structure would have provided. Many outside observers agreed that this was a good strategy, assuming that focused businesses would compete better than the monolith IBM had become. Gerstner has rejected this move, preferring to keep the company together and seek competitive advantage from its size.

Some have suggested that Gerstner should adopt a matrix structure for IBM, in which individuals may be accountable to two or more chains of command. But by involving more people in a routine decision, matrix structures can inhibit action and muddy accountability. Gerstner has tried to quiet his critics by declaring that IBM doesn't need a perfect structure. He says, "Eighty percent of the time people know what they're supposed to do without needing someone else's input." Instead of a complex set of lines and boxes, Gerstner wants a company based on teams. "Increasing teamwork is going to be complicated, but I'm not too worried. If the organization doesn't work right one way, we'll change it." Indeed, in his previous leadership post at American Express, Gerstner was known for annual reorganizations.

Maybe the more fluid organizational structure that Gerstner envisions will eventually prove successful for IBM. The stakes are high, and Gerstner likely does not have much more time to show impressive results before the vultures begin circling. When Akers was CEO it looked like IBM was headed toward the decentralized culture that would have created the 13 Baby Blues.

Questions for Discussion

1. Do you think that Gerstner's decision to hold the company together was a wise choice?
2. Suppose that Gerstner does decide to break the company into autonomous units. What do you think are some problems that are likely to go along with such a restructuring?

Source: Adapted from Stratford Sherman, "Is He Too Cautious to Save IBM?" *Fortune* (October 3, 1994): 78–90; Laurie Hays, "Gerstner Is Struggling as He Tries to Change Ingrained IBM Culture," *The Wall Street Journal* (May 13, 1994): A1, A5; Catherine Arnst, "Lou Gerstner Unveils His Battle Plan," *Business Week* (April 4, 1994): 96–99.

CASE 8.2

Many Firms Are Converting to Learning Organizations

Reorganizing. Downsizing. Coordination. Delegating. These are all attempts to organize a business to perform better, to produce more efficiently, to develop human resources. Despite these activities, some claim that even proactive steps to improve will not be enough to meet environmental demands. The command-and-control, top-down structures will not be fast enough to meet product development advances of foreign competitors, close enough to the customer to provide high-quality service, or tuned in enough to effectively manage the polyglot work force of the new century.

The evidence indicates that in the 1980s over half of the Fortune 500 companies engaged in significant restructuring. Major firms like General Motors, IBM, Sears, Roebuck, and others continue to search for the best way to organize themselves. A growing group of firms is attempting to develop themselves into what is known as learning organizations. Some major companies that have found this approach appealing include Ford, Harley Davidson, Electronic Data Systems, FedEx, Philips North America, Herman Miller, Armco Steel, and Intel. But what exactly is a learning organization?

According to David Garvin, a business professor at the Harvard Business School, "A learning organization is an organization skilled at creating, acquiring, and transferring knowledge, and at modifying its behavior to reflect new knowledge and insights." Garvin asserts that fundamental to this definition is the notion that ideas are essential if learning is to take place. Sometimes ideas are created de novo, through flashes of insight or creativity; at other times they arrive from outside the organization or are communicated by knowledgeable insiders. Whatever their source, ideas are the triggers for organization improvement. However, Garvin notes, ideas by themselves cannot create a learning organization. "Without accompanying changes in the way that work gets done, only the potential for improvement exists."

Learning organizations require changes in structure to support a learning culture. The learning organization listens to customers, suppliers, competitors, and employees. It then automatically takes action to meet challenges quickly and responsibly. In the learning organization, people continually expand their capacity to create desired results, and they are continually learning how to learn together. The learning organization, for example, would not anticipate the events in Eastern Europe, but would view the changes as opportunities to seize.

A few firms have some of the qualifications of a learning organization. Ford has designed a middle-manager training program to help managers become learning organization-oriented. In the course of a five-and-one-half day session, managers are grouped by their specialties (marketing, manufacturing, finance, etc.). They are asked to think about how their area works within the firm, how others perceive and relate to it, and how it should work. Only when colleagues from other units level with them do they find out how they come across. Groups review each other to make sure each sees clearly how it is viewed by others. Cross-department learning results from the training debates, arguments, and attention. Ford uses the term *chimney breaking* to describe the process of getting people to think beyond their own discipline.

Robert H. Waterman, in his book *Renewal Factor,* cites other means of deliberate bureaucracy busting (a form of chimney breaking): moving people from function to function; letting people roam to areas in which they have an interest; recognizing and encouraging product champions; forming teams made up of employees drawn from different disciplines. In other words, loosening up the structure, moving people around, and letting people do some things on their own. Keeping a laissez-faire distance to permit free thoughts to surface.

At Honda, for example, top managers set tough strategic objectives. There is little room for lazy, slow-thinking managers. On the shop floor, however, Honda wants everyone to learn. They want middle managers to work on multifunctional teams, to integrate what comes from the top and lower levels, and to seize opportunities to improve production and quality. Honda wants everyone to learn so that the company can use the creative talents of each. The monster bureaucracy with 22 layers—until now the American automobile company ideal—is not suited for the five managerial layers of the learning organization that Honda believes it must be to remain competitive.

The learning organization focuses on helping people become better adapted to meet the demands of the global economy.

Questions for Discussion

1. Why do you think learning is such an important part of meeting the demands of the global economy?
2. Learning, like quality, seems to be essential to organizational success. If that is the case, why do you think many companies resist changing their cultures to focus on quality or learning?

Source: Adapted from David A. Garvin, "Building a Learning Organization," *Harvard Business Review* (July–August 1993): 78–91; Walter Kiechel III, "The Organization that Learns," *Fortune* (March 12, 1990): 133–134; Peter M. Senge, *The Fifth Discipline* (New York: Doubleday, 1990); Robert H. Waterman Jr., *The Renewal Factor* (New York: Bantam Books, 1987).

EXPERIENTIAL EXERCISE

Activity:
Each student will examine an organization or organizational unit of his or her choice. He or she should contact a manager in the chosen organization and conduct a 15-minute interview. Students should briefly write up their findings and be prepared to discuss them in class.

Directions:
The interview can range over any organizational designs issues discussed in Chapter 8, but should include the following questions:

1. What is the primary purpose or mission of the unit? What functions must be performed to accomplish the mission? What customers does the unit serve with what products or services? What are the primary environmental factors that influence the unit's performance?
2. Describe the unit's primary technology, the relative uncertainty of the primary environments, and the primary information that must be processed.
3. Describe the existing organizational structure. Draw an organization chart showing both line and staff positions.
4. Which organization design studied in Chapter 8 most accurately describes the existing organizational structure?
5. Is the existing organization design appropriate for the mission of the unit given its mission, functions, customers, products/services, and environment? Justify your answer.

BUSINESS APPLICATION

Activity:
Following the discussion of various types of organizational structures, each student will develop a list of advantages and disadvantages for each type of structure. The activity will take approximately 30 minutes of class time.

Directions:
1. The instructor draws a simple organization chart focusing on the top two levels of a national retail clothing store corporation. The top level would have the CEO title written in the box, with the second level showing vice presidents with functional oriented titles, e.g., VP of Finance, VP of Human Resources, VP of marketing, and so on.
2. Ask students to write down the advantages and disadvantages of the functional type of structure for this organization. After giving students about five minutes to work on their lists, the instructor will conduct a class discussion on the functional structure by having students share their lists with the class.

3. Repeat Step 1 for the national clothing retailer, except this time a product type of structure should be used. Job titles for the second level of the chart might be VP of Footwear, VP of Coats & Sweaters, VP of Sporting Wear, etc.
4. Repeat Step 2, except have the focus be on the product structure.
5. Repeat Step 1 for the national clothing retailer, except this time a territorial type of structure will be used. Job titles could possibly include VP of Southeast Division, VP of Northeast Division, VP of Midwest Division, etc.
6. Repeat Step 2, except have the focus be on a territorial structure.
7. The instructor closes out the activity by summarizing the advantages and disadvantages of the functional, product, and territorial types of organizational structures.

NOTES

1. Adapted from Brian Dumaine, "The Trouble with Teams," *Fortune* (September 5, 1994): 86–92; Dori Jones Yang, "When the Going Gets Tough, Boeing Gets Touchy-Feely," *Business Week* (January 17, 1994): 65–67; Dori Jones Yang and Andrea Rothman, "Reinventing Boeing," *Business Week* (March 1, 1993): 60–67,.
2. Carla Conner, "Personal Growth, Professional Success," *Nation's Business* (February 1994): 6.
3. Lee Tom Perry, *Offensive Strategy* (New York: Harper & Row, 1990), 13.
4. James P. Womack and Daniel T. Jones, "From Lean Production to the Lean Enterprise," *Harvard Business Review* (March–April 1994): 93–103.
5. Tom Peters, *Liberation Management* (New York: Alfred A. Kropf, 1992), 44–55.
6. Chris Argyris, *Overcoming Organizational Defenses* (Englewood Cliffs, NJ: Prentice Hall, 1990).
7. Authur H. Walker and Jay Lorsch, "Organizational Choice: Product versus Function," *Harvard Business Review* (November–December 1968): 129–138.
8. E. Raymond Corey and Steven H. Star, *Organization Strategy: A Marketing Approach* (Cambridge, MA: Division of Research, Graduate School of Business Administration, Harvard University, 1970).
9. "Greyhound Splitting into Four to Go After Short Haul Trade," *Chicago Tribune* (April 30, 1986): 3:8.
10. Ira Sager and Gail Edmondson, "Big Blue Wants the World to Know Who's Boss," *Business Week* (September 26, 1994): 78.
11. John M. Ivancevich, Peter Lorenzi, Steven J. Skinner, and Philip B. Crosby, *Management: Quality and Competitiveness* (Burr Ridge, IL: Irwin, 1994), 271–273.
12. Charles Hampden Turner, *Charting the Corporate Mind: Graphic Solutions to Business Conflicts* (New York: Free Press, 1990).
13. James H. Donnelly Jr., James L. Gibson, and John M. Ivancevich, *Fundamentals of Management,* 9th ed. (Homewood, IL: Richard D. Irwin, 1995), 210–217.
14. Robert H. Waterman, *The Renewal Factor* (New York: Bantam Books, 1987).

CHAPTER 9

Managing Production and Operations

1. Define the production and operations management function.
2. Discuss two or three critical issues facing production and operations management.
3. Compare traditional company organization with cellular organization.
4. Describe the effects of globalization on competition and productivity.
5. Evaluate the effects of computerization on production and operations management functions.
6. Explain the importance of productivity and quality to business.
7. Review the role of the production and operations unit in safety and environmental concerns.

LEARNING OBJECTIVES

Firms in many industries are being pressured today by customer demands for both greater product variety and reduced delivery times. This combination is difficult for many companies to achieve because quick delivery is usually based on standardization, whereas product variety requires the organization to be flexible and innovative. One common response to these pressures is to begin production of expensive, specialized products prior to receiving orders. Firms using this strategy build up an inventory of unsold products that is expensive to store in a warehouse.

It is every consumer's dream, when making a major purchase, to get exactly the features that they want. Although Detroit isn't about to offer this to customers any time soon, Dell Computer, the number one marketer of PCs, is doing it today. Dell's build-to-order system has enabled the company to compete with the major computer makers since 1984 when Michael Dell got his start assembling machines in his college dorm room.

Though Dell lost $36 million in 1993, partly because of a failed third attempt to sell notebook computers, its fast-food style assembly lines for desktop machines are the envy of the industry. Compaq Computer, Dell's archrival in Houston, is restructuring its entire logistics operation in hopes of achieving similar manufacturing flexibility in 1996.

Although Dell can handle bulk orders, over 90 percent of its $2.9 billion in annual sales comes from PCs it builds for individual customers. Below is a chronology of how Dell builds a computer from customer order to delivery:

Wednesday, 10:49 A.M. (Central Time) Dave Cozzette, an accountant at Rothfos Corporation, a 20-employee coffee broker in White Plains, NY, calls in his order for a Dell Dimension PC. At Dell's order center, sales representative Cassye Ewald promises the PC will be delivered within five business days. (She estimates it will arrive sooner, but sales representatives are trained to keep customer expectations low.)

12:50 P.M. Dell's financial services unit verifies the charge with Cozzette's credit card company, and the details of his $2,700.22 order print out on the production floor across the street at Dell's factory. Laquitta Lister checks the information sheet—called a traveler—which lists the 60 items that Cozzette's computer must include, from cables to software. The order is branded with a serial number that will identify the PC for its lifetime, regardless of who owns it.

1:00 P.M. The assembly process starts with the installation of an Intel 486 DX2 chip—the brains of Cozzette's computer—onto the machine's main circuit board, known as the motherboard.

1:55 P.M. Ronda Pena applies a sticker bearing the nascent PC's serial number to the chassis then lays in the motherboard, fastening it with screws.

2:01 P.M. Anthony Garcia inserts Cozzette's fax modem, a device that can send documents created on the PC to fax machines or other computers via telephone lines.

2:10 P.M. Manuel Brito installs the floppy drive that was prepared earlier, along with a tape backup unit. It will let Cozzette make up-to-date duplicates of his hard disk files in the event his machine has a breakdown.

2:20 P.M. The power supply, a transformer that converts electrical current for use in the PC, goes into the unit, and Ronnie Hines affixes the PC's faceplate with the Dell logo subtly displayed.

2:26 P.M. Shena Galvan scans the computer's bar code to update Dell's inventory. The components that have been installed in Cozzette's PC are now listed as removed from the company's storage facility in another area of the plant.

2:27 P.M. The PC gets its first quality inspection. Steve Geil checks the traveler to make sure his co-workers have installed every component the computer should have. Then he creates a test diskette that will keep track of which software Cozzette has ordered and which components will need to be tested.

2:28 P.M. The PC powers up for the first time during a "quick test" that checks memory, video circuits, and floppy and hard disk functions. If the test diskette finds a bad sector on the hard disk—a portion that cannot properly store data—Sophia Finney will install a new hard disk. The test diskette sets the computer's clock to Central Time.

2:40 P.M. Engritt Brooks slides on the PC's hood.

2:45 P.M.–7:45 P.M. Cozzette's computer sits on a rack for an extended test called "burn in." Before it starts, Aaron Whitley plugs the PC into the factory's network. For five hours the diskette runs the PC's components through grueling tests that simulate heavy use. An indicator light hooked to the back of the PC changes color to help workers monitor the testing. Only 2 percent of the PCs fail. Finally, the test diskette uses the network to download the programs Cozzette has ordered, such as Microsoft Windows, installs them on the hard disk.

8:20 P.M. Jaye Mireles shoots a 10,000-volt charge into the PC's power supply. If the PC handles the jolt without going haywire, it earns a Federal Communications Commission Class B Certification that it is safe to use in homes and offices.

8:32 P.M. During the PC's final test, the system is hooked up to a monitor and keyboard and operated without its test diskette, just as Cozzette will use it. Lonnie Gilliland looks for glitches in the newly installed software.

8:35 P.M. Julie Goodman puts the PC through "wipe-down," which is not code language for some top-secret Dell process but a cosmetic inspection that includes scrubbing off grubby fingerprints.

8:37 P.M. Ramon Lopez puts Cozzette's computer in a box with its keyboard, manuals, and warranty papers; Darrell Arvie slaps on the Rothfos Corporation address.

9:25 P.M. Airborne Express loads the PC onto a truck. If Cozzette had called Dell a few hours earlier, his PC would have made it onto a truck before the 7 P.M. deadline for next-day delivery. Instead, he'll get it on Friday.

Friday, 10:31 A.M. (EASTERN TIME) Airborne drops off the package at Cozzette's office. He plugs in his PC, and Dell's greeting software offers its congratulations.[1]

Dell delivers customized computers practically overnight. That is the firm's distinctive competence. Why do you think other computer makers have had difficulty competing with Dell on this basis? Dell has had problems competing in the laptop computer market. What special problems do you think this market holds for Dell?

To meet the needs of their customers, businesses strive for the perfect blend of management and machine. Creating and maintaining that blend is the task of the production and operations manager. The task has not been easy. In the 1970s, double-digit inflation plus a recession dealt heavy blows to industry in the United States, along with the rest of the industrial world. Consumers could no longer afford to buy as much, so they wanted goods that would last. The cost of money soared, and financing the growth of companies became very expensive. Millions of employees lost their jobs. Vulnerable in key areas such as automotive, textiles, machine tools, and steel, the United States gradually lost its number one position in those markets to the competition—Japan, Germany, Korea, and other nations.

In order to recapture markets, top management asked production and operations managers to increase productivity, improve quality, and cut costs. Although progress has been made in all three areas, there is much work to be done to complete a turnaround. Because technology, competition, products, and worker skills have changed so much in the last 20 years, the job of the production and operations manager requires a wide range of analytical and communication skills. These managers must understand sophisticated technology, delegate tasks, and forfeit some decision-making power. Office technology used to be mechanical; now it is electronic, emphasizing computers, networks, and shared information.

This chapter will portray how production and operations managers do their jobs. We start with a description of production and operations, followed by a brief history of manufacturing. We then discuss the various responsibilities of the production and operations manager, including organizing the production process, planning site location and layout, controlling materials, purchasing, inventory, and production scheduling. Other topics covered include using technology such as computers and robots, increasing productivity while maintaining quality control, and maintaining safety for employees, consumers, and the environment. Finally, we examine some critical issues and their implications for the future.

Exhibit 9.1 *Several Types of Production*

Organization	Inputs	Production Processes	Outputs or Products (Type)
Magazine publisher	Information in various forms: written, verbal, and photo or art pictorials. Labor, energy, capital, ink, paper, tools, equipment, technology	Planning, budgeting, scheduling, design and layout, writing, editing, typesetting, art and photo preparation, management control, printing, folding, cutting, binding, shipping on time.	Magazines (nondurable goods).
Hair styling salon	Clients, hair knowledge, skills, information. Hair care supplies, tools, technology, equipment, labor, energy, capital, water.	Planning, budgeting, scheduling, materials ordering and handling, design, hair preparation, washing, conditioning, coloring, styling, meeting schedules, maintaining customer satisfaction (quality control).	Personal hair care (service).
Steel conduit manufacturer	Steel, chemicals, labor, energy, capital, tools, technology, equipment, water, location.	Planning, budgeting, scheduling, materials ordering and handling, metal processing, labor organization, employee relations and safety, quality control, forming, cooling, storage and distribution, meeting schedules.	Steel wire and pipe products (durable goods).

WHAT ARE PRODUCTION AND OPERATIONS?

Production
The total process by which a company produces finished goods or services.

Many people confuse the terms *production, operations,* and *manufacturing.* **Production** is the total process by which a company produces finished goods or services. This process might involve the work, ideas, and plans of the design engineers; the production manager, the plant manager, the plant superintendent, and their crews; and any other department actually involved with bringing forth the product. Exhibit 9.1 illustrates different types of businesses, products, and the processes involved. Production is not limited to the manufacture of goods; it applies to the service sector as well. For example, a company might produce shampoo and cream rinse for hair, which are manufactured goods; another company might operate a chain of hair salons, which provide a service. The word *production* can also be used to name the total amount of product brought forth, as in the statement "Total production increased by 20 percent in 1990."

Operations
Any function(s) needed to carry out a strategic plan, to keep the company producing.

Operations are the functions needed to keep the company producing, literally any function or series of functions enacted to carry out a strategic plan. In a firm such as Ford Motor Company, operations will usually include purchasing, materials management, production, inventory and quality control, maintenance and manufacturing engineering, and plant management. See Exhibit 9.2 for the activities managed by operations in the traditional plant.

Exhibit 9.2
The Traditional Plant

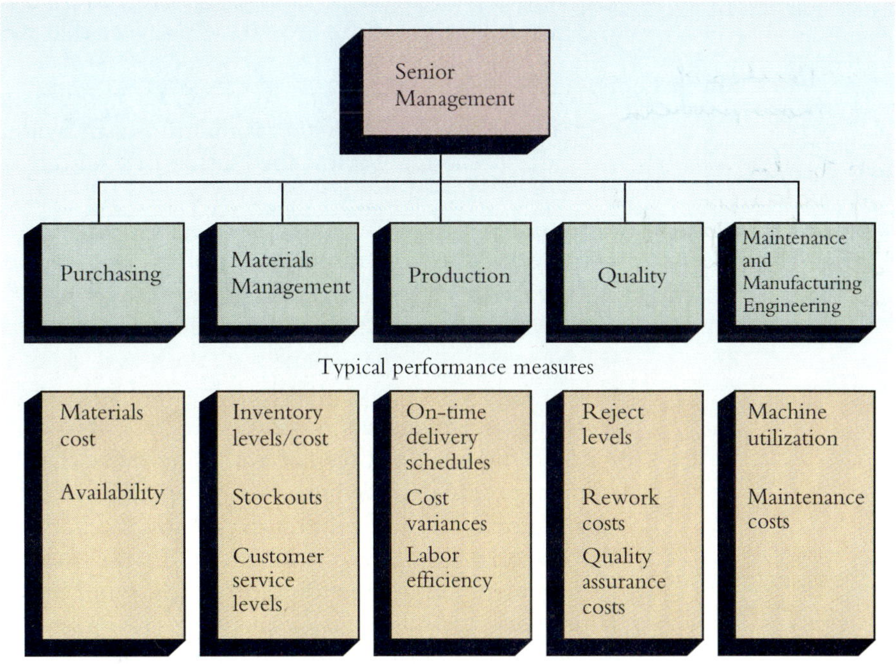

Source: Reprinted by permission of *Harvard Business Review.* An exhibit from "Manufacturing's Crisis: New Technologies, Obsolete Organizations," by Robert H. Hayes and Ramchandran Jalkumar, September–October 1988. Copyright © 1988 by the President and Fellows of Harvard College; all rights reserved.

Manufacturing
The actual processes of making products out of materials and parts. Literally, creating something by the work of one's hands.

Manufacturing refers only to the physical process of producing goods; services are not manufactured. The word *manufacturing* comes from the ancient Latin words *manu* (hand) and *facto* (create, or make)—in other words, handmade. In ancient Rome, distinguishing between machine made and handmade was not an issue; all goods were handmade. If someone sang for the Romans, it was a service; if someone crafted a brand-new jar for storing olive oil, it was a manufactured good, something created by the work of hands.

A SHORT HISTORY OF PRODUCTION AND OPERATIONS MANAGEMENT

Until the 19th century, manufacturing was done largely by hand, using only hand-operated tools. Modern industry began with (1) the use of fuel energy in manufacturing and (2) the development of mass production.

Early and Crucial Innovations

The Use of Fuel Energy. Fuel energy made it possible to use large machinery in factories; the use of large machinery made mass production possible. In the United States, the steam-powered mills of the 19th century were the first indication of the growth of industry that would follow.

Scientific Management. As the 20th century began, managers became very interested in improving production of individuals and of the total organization. Frederick Taylor, the "father of scientific management," pioneered the use of scientific methods to improve productivity.[2] The essence of his philosophy was that scientific laws govern how much a person can produce per day and that it is the function of management to discover and use these laws in the operation of productive systems.

Taylor's approach was not greeted with universal approval. Some unions feared scientific management because it was rigid; unions played almost no role in Taylor's setup of jobs, and they had little idea of Taylor's ultimate goal. In some cases, managers embraced Taylor's time study and incentive plans but ignored the need to organize and standardize the work to be done. The result was poorly designed production operations and overworked employees.[3] For example, in the steel industry, many workers unionized to fight some of the demands made by management. In the automobile industry, scientific management led to strict division of labor and the eventual collapse of competitiveness. Japanese automakers who encouraged employees to develop expertise in more than one area were more productive and had better quality.

Despite critics and inept application, Taylor's philosophy and work helped shape work-flow systems, incentive packages, and the design and arrangement of jobs. His principles of scientific management are still a part of the pro-

cedures used in production and operations. For example, the New United Motor Manufacturing Company (NUMMI), a joint venture between Toyota and General Motors, employs a new form of Taylor's scientific management.[4]

Mass Production Rapid manufacture of large quantities of goods accomplished through division of labor, specialization, and standardization.

Mass Production. **Mass production** refers to the production of a large number of standard products for sale to consumers. In the age of individual craftsmen, mass production was not used because individuals were limited in the number of goods they could produce. When fossil fuels were used to power industrial plants, it became possible to produce large quantities of products for wide distribution. Early textile mills and steel plants are good examples of mass production in action. Of course, consumers sacrificed the customized goods of the individual craftsmen, but mass-produced goods could be purchased more cheaply, and they were more widely available.

In the early 20th century several other developments made mass production more efficient: the assembly line, division of labor, and standardization of parts.

Assembly Line A production line made up of workers who each perform one specific task as the product moves past, toward completion.

The Assembly Line. Around 1913 a significant breakthrough occurred with the establishment of the moving assembly line for the manufacture of Ford automobiles. In the mass production of the early Ford cars, one worker attached the headlamps, another attached the hood, and so on. Each worker performed one function on each and every car as its chassis came down a moving conveyor belt, or **assembly line.** The belt carried work from one work-station to the next. Ford's assembly line began at the entrance to a long shed-like factory building and emerged bearing finished cars at the other end. When a finished automobile emerged at the end of the assembly line, workers had given utility to the materials used.

Use of assembly lines, such as these workers assembling light fixtures, makes mass production much more efficient.

Division of Labor. Industrial plants that mass produce goods generally use rigorous division of labor. This allows workers to focus their knowledge, skills, and concentration on a single aspect of the production process. The practice of dividing labor into discrete functions is common in manufacturing today, but it has been modified to eliminate the problem of worker boredom from repeating the same task day in and day out. Many plants today train workers to perform more than one specialized task and then rotate them to different processes. In this way, division of labor is maintained, but workers do not become bored from repeating routine behaviors. W.L. Gore Associates, the maker of GORE-TEX, for example, does not have division of labor. When a new worker is hired in the plant, he or she is told to find a place for themselves among the myriad of teams that are performing the tasks necessary to produce the final product. There are no job descriptions, no departments, and no boundaries.[5]

Ford introduced the assembly line in the early 1900s, thereby revolutionizing automobile production.

Standardized Parts. Standardization of parts was another essential factor in the development of mass production. At Ford each headlamp was exactly the same size and was connected to the same spot on identical car frames as they came down the assembly line. Thus one worker could attach headlamps over and over rather quickly and easily with a standard level of quality because the parts were standardized.

Some workers and social critics complained about the "human machines" who moved their arms and hands over and over again, in the same motions, to the rhythms of the inescapable assembly line. Comedian Charlie Chaplin even imitated and mocked them. But mass production and the assembly line were here to stay. No significant business operation could afford to ignore the technological advances they represented. Their tremendous production capacity would eventually make the United States the most productive and richest nation in the world.

Industrialization and America's Postwar Supremacy

During the 1920s, the nations of the world became increasingly industrialized and some of them increasingly competitive. Most, however, were seriously damaged by World War II. With its superior production and manufacturing achievements and the fact that its production capacity was not destroyed or badly damaged, the United States emerged from World War II the leader in production and manufacturing.

During the '50s, '60s, and most of the '70s, American goods and services were the most sought after in the world. The holds of cargo planes and ships carried American cars and trucks, mechanical and electrical parts, chemicals, commodities, wearing apparel, medicines, food products, toys, soft drinks, and recordings to every major port in the world. In the passenger compartments of the planes and ships, American services and technical know-how were being exported as well. Doctors, nurses, dentists, X-ray technicians, teachers, broadcaster, engineers, agricultural advisers, and hundreds of other specialists carried their know-how to foreign markets. Soon the workers, entrepreneurs, and governments of those markets began to respond in kind. As Europe and Japan recovered from the devastation of war, they began to rebuild their industries. They began to export goods and services, competed with each other, and created an industrial and marketing basis for competing in world markets.

Consumerism and Planned Obsolescence

In the U.S. expansion of the late '50s and the '60s, the pace of life—and the pace of production and consumption—escalated to unimagined speed. Salaries rose, prices increased, production rates climbed. By the '70s, new and unexpected pressures appeared. An uneasiness and dissatisfaction began to spread. Americans became disillusioned with leadership at national, local, and even trade and labor union levels. With disillusionment came cynicism. Manufacturers talked of planned obsolescence—goods made to last only a short period of time so consumers would have to buy again. Consumers began to question the quality of products and services and the prices charged for them. Critics also questioned the facilities being used for manufacturing; many factories were old, outdated, inefficient, and dirty.

In addition to leadership, quality, and facility problems, the pressures to produce more and faster made pride of accomplishment all but impossible. Goods and services were needed so fast that the prevailing cry was, "Never mind about the details—it's got to get out!" And, "If there's anything wrong with it, they can send it back!" And they did. In the 1940s, products might be returned once in a while; by the mid '70s, corporations maintained whole departments solely to handle returns of defective items.[6]

American Manufacturing Joins the Global Marketplace

The decline in confidence in once invincible "Made in the USA" products became a crucial issue. The manufacturing community developed a new interest in what production and operations managers do and how to improve it. Today U.S. firms are searching for new ways of manufacturing goods and delivering services.

In the United States, fears of economic decline have been linked to the nation's inability to manage production and operations efficiently over the past two decades. Critics claim that America does not produce as well as it should or as well as some other nations (e.g., Germany, Japan, and Korea) do.[7] Check your understanding by completing the Your Values and Attitudes quiz.

YOUR VALUES AND ATTITUDES

The U.S. World Market Share

Directions: The MIT Commission on Industrial Productivity published a book in 1989 entitled *Made in America.* The book emphasized that some U.S. industries and products have lost 50 percent or more of their share of world markets since 1960. Which of these industries do you think have lost 50 percent or more of their world markets?

	Yes	No		Yes	No
Automobiles	____	____	Color TV sets	____	____
Cameras	____	____	Stereo equipment	____	____
Microwave ovens	____	____	Steel	____	____
Machine tools	____	____	Copiers	____	____
Optical equipment	____	____	Commercial aircraft manufacturing	____	____

Feedback: Every checkmark should be yes, except for the manufacturers of commercial aircraft. Each of the other U.S. industries or products listed has lost 50 percent or more of the world market since 1960. The decline of the manufacturing or production part of business has been one reason why market share has dwindled.

Why does the United States need to find new manufacturing methods? Traditional mass-production methods have been changing as other countries, such as Germany and Japan, have used alternatives successfully. For example, the success of the Japanese auto industry is based on a system different from Detroit's. The Japanese make products that are different (in color, shape, weight) for each segment of the market. They have had to develop manufacturing technologies, job designs, and work flows that enable them to change production runs on assembly lines with little downtime, adapt to low-volume production of some models, and at the same time decrease the new-product development cycle. Such production innovations as just-in-time inventory, statistical process control, and quality circles originated in Japan. The Japanese emphasize quality, service, and cost.

U.S. industry today is competing globally, as companies worldwide are eyeing global market rather than relying on domestic markets. The United States must sell abroad to pay for the goods and services it purchases abroad and for the money it has borrowed from abroad. To compete successfully for foreign markets, it must explore foreign innovations and manufacturing technologies.

For decades, American businesses largely ignored technological innovations coming from foreign laboratories and companies. Most production and operations experts scoffed at Korean steel-processing procedures, Japanese inventory systems, Swedish assembly-line team concepts, and Taiwanese electronics procedures. But today more and more U.S. managers are scanning foreign projects, activities, and innovations. Importing ideas and methods of potential benefit is becoming an accepted practice.

Using a modern technique known as *benchmarking,* production and operations managers seek to identify a company that is the best in the world at some process, and then copy them. Benchmarking should not be confused with industrial espionage. Rather, it is the art of finding out, in a perfectly legal and aboveboard way, how other companies do things better than your company so you can imitate—and perhaps improve—their techniques. The American Quality Foundation and Ernst & Young report that 31 percent of American enterprises regularly benchmark their products and services. AT&T, Du Pont, Ford Motor, IBM, Eastman Kodak, Milliken, Motorola, and Xerox are just some of the major American companies that use benchmarking in their drive for quality and productivity.[8]

How to speed product development is a top priority of all managers, especially those in production and operations. Compaq, Boeing, Merck, Microsoft, Honda, 3M, and Toyota are known for their ability to develop, manufacture, and market what consumers want, when they want it, and at an affordable price. Typically these cutting-edge product developers are global, and 35–70 percent of their sales come from outside their home market.[9]

In the search for new and better manufacturing methods, production and operations managers are playing more significant roles in their organizations. As markets and technologies globalize, these managers will increasingly need to understand foreign customers' needs, preferences, and price limitations. The basis for successful global competition lies in the successful adaptation of the production and operations functions of U.S. business. Unless production and operations can restore the stature of "Made in the USA" goods and services, the economic quality of life of Americans is likely to suffer. Products that cannot compete in the global market in terms of quality and price are unacceptable for the future of business in the United States.

Production and Operations Management in the Service Sector

Most of the discussion to this point has concerned the role of production and operations management in manufacturing companies. Increasingly today, however, people are employed in the service sector of the economy. Services have been broadly defined as "anything that you can't drop on your foot." Businesses from retail sales to legal advice to health care have sophisticated operations that must be monitored, assessed, and continuously improved. Wal-Mart, for example, derives much of its competitive advantage over rivals from its sophisticated product tracking system. The retail giant's managers know almost instantly which products are selling well, thus deserving more prominent shelf space, and which items are not selling well.

United Parcel Service produces nothing, yet it has a highly developed operations function that rigorously determines the flow of packages through the system. UPS drivers are instructed how to enter and leave their trucks to maximize efficiency. Operations managers even went so far as to shave off the outside corner of drivers' seats to enable smoother exit from the vehicle.[10]

TOMORROW'S BUSINESS WORLD

Technicians Will Be in High Demand

Technological advances in modern organizations, coupled with the trend toward downsizing, has left the technician in a commanding position. As the farmhand was to the agrarian economy of a century ago and the machine worker was to the electromechanical industrial era of recent decades, the technician is becoming the core worker of the information age. Since 1950, the number of technical workers has increased nearly 300 percent—triple the growth of the work force as a whole—to over 20 million. With one out of every four new jobs going to a technical worker, the U.S. Bureau of Labor Statistics forecasts that such workers will represent one-fifth of total U.S. employment by 2004.

As corporate hierarchies collapse and the boundaries between organizations dissolve, employers are beginning to develop a new appreciation for the work technicians do. In the new economy, says Michael Arthur, a management professor at Suffolk University in Boston, it is competence rather than a place in a hierarchical pecking order that defines an employee's value. He says, "Technical occupations are becoming the new anchor for people's careers."

What are these technical careers? They cover a wide range of occupations, including computer programmers, drafters, clinical laboratory technologists and technicians, emergency medical technicians, paralegals, and many more. For example, automation has taken jobs away from many semi-skilled industrial workers. But for factory technicians who know how to operate the new computer-controlled production equipment, opportunities abound. As manufacturing consultant Tom Blunt puts it, "Employers who automate but take people out of the process are lobotomizing their factories."

Technical work is the wave of the future. Employers must offer technicians career opportunities that will keep them motivated, productive, and creative. The technical worker freed from the monotony of the old organizational structures can provide companies with new ideas and innovations that help them compete. Intellectual capital is a high-value asset to companies. Research done by Dartmouth School of Business Professor James Brian Quinn has shown that, even in manufacturing, perhaps three-fourths of value added derives from technical knowledge. In the Information Age, technical skills are the foundation of long-term organizational competitiveness.

The technical worker has suddenly become very important to many businesses. Can you think of some industries that can't benefit from technical support? What advances in technology do you think have been the most critical in lifting the technical worker's status?

Sources: Adapted from Louis S. Richman, "The New Worker Elite," *Fortune* (August 22, 1994): 56–66; Thomas A. Stewart, "Your Company's Most Valuable Asset: Intellectual Capital," *Fortune* (October 3, 1994): 68–70; John Huey, "Waking Up to the New Economy," *Fortune* (June 27, 1994): 36–46.

WHAT DOES THE PRODUCTION AND OPERATIONS MANAGER DO?

Production and operations managers are responsible for producing the goods that business needs to sell. There are many kinds of production and operations systems, just as there are many kinds of products—goods and services—wanted by people in the marketplace. Production and operations can vary in size from a single person in a very small company (e.g., a family-owned bakery such as L'Madiellenes) to thousands of employees in a huge, multinational corporation such as Procter & Gamble.

Every business's production goals focus on producing products or delivering services. Companies want to make the best products at the lowest cost, or deliver the best services that money can buy. Thus the production and operations manager must produce with effectiveness and efficiency while maintaining quality control. Richard Bodine, president of Bodine Corporation, knows about speed, efficiency, and effectiveness. He manufactures assembly lines for organizations.[11] His firm is now working on an electromechanical system that will assemble 2,400 alkaline batteries an hour. Bodine manufactures about 30 machines a year at a rate that is fast, efficient, and maintains high quality.

A production and operations manager's job is to see that the operations necessary to achieve the company's production and service goals are carried out. To do this, these managers oversee a number of company operations. The following functions are typical:

Product planning
Site location and layout
Inventory control
Purchasing and materials management
Manufacturing and production
Production control

Quality control
Plant management

In moderate-sized firms, the production and operations manager is often a vice president who reports directly to top management; managers or supervisors representing the functions listed above report to the production and operations manager.

Production and operations managers have *product planning* responsibilities, such as preparing forecasts, schedules, and budgets in collaboration with top management, finance, and marketing. In start-up operations, they oversee site location and layout. They also oversee the hiring, training, and development of personnel for departments involved with production and operations. Working with all other departments in the company—especially marketing, physical distribution, warehousing, and shipping—is important as well.

Organizing the Production Process

Chapter 8 presented different ways to organize businesses, depending on needs, types of production, strengths and weaknesses of company managers, and the like. Titles vary also. The inventory control manager in one company may be called the purchasing and inventory control manager in another company. Knowing the exact titles and type of organization in place enables managers to have appropriate expectations and communicate effectively. Production and operations managers must fit into different types of organizations.

Traditional Organization. The organization chart shown in Exhibit 9.3 follows the most traditional form. It gives each manager a specific area of authority and responsibility; however, it also sometimes pits managers against each other. For example, if a purchasing manager has budgeted $50,000 for a quantity of a specific part and the inventory control manager must order them on a rush basis for $60,000, the purchasing manager's responsibility and authority are subordinated to the inventory manager's needs.

Exhibit 9.3 shows typical departments in this type of organization and some common measures used in judging departmental performance. For example, the quality manager's performance would be appraised on the basis of costs, defect levels, and rework costs.

Companies that use an assembly-line approach to producing goods have typically been structured according to a job-shop design. Under this design, separate departments or divisions are responsible only for making a specific part and then sending it out the door to the next department. Machines that were similar to one another would all be grouped together in a job shop. Anything that needed mill work would be sent to the mill shop. Anything that needed grinding would be sent to the grind shop. This often led to lengthy travel distances for some parts that were sent to many different shops. In addition, because the product or sub-assembly was handled by so many different shops, the potential for error and the introduction of defects was increased. The more defects produced, the greater the cost to the company in terms of rework, lost customers, or worse. To eliminate some of the problems with the job-shop design, some firms have been using a cellular design.

Exhibit 9.3 *Traditional Organization: Manufacturing Firm*

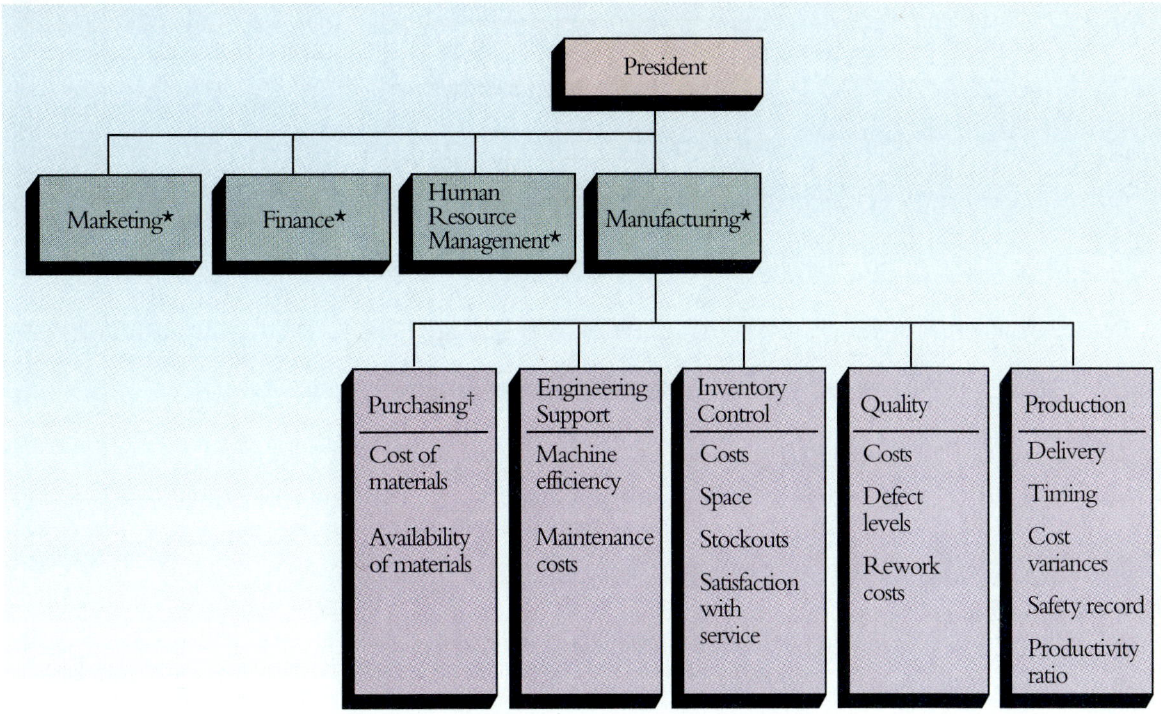

*Each function would have a complete structure if chart were presented in full.
†Examples of performance measures are shown below each departmental grouping.

Cellular Organization. In the past decade, more and more companies have begun to use a cellular organization. In this type, workers cooperate in teams, or cells, to manufacture total products or subassemblies. Each cell is responsible for the quality and quantity of its products. Each has the authority to make adjustments to improve performance and product quality. Exhibit 9.4 illustrates how, in the cellular arrangement, machines are arranged to handle all of the operations needed to assemble the products. The parts follow a path through each cell to final assembly.

The basic difference between the cellular and the traditional organization is that workers in the cells are all responsible for their output. The linear competitiveness of the traditional structure is avoided. Instead each individual is pressured to perform so that the group will succeed. Cells tend to be tightly self-monitoring and self-correcting. In a cellular organization, companies tend to have much smaller staffs overall, with middle management positions reduced and lean management numbers at the top. Sony has been pioneering a new form of cellular manufacturing that takes a page from the craft workshops of the past. In a snail-shaped shop known as the "spiral line," Sony workers assemble entire cameras by themselves, doing everything from soldering to testing. Output per worker on the experimental line is 10 percent

Exhibit 9.4
Cellular Manufacturing Layout

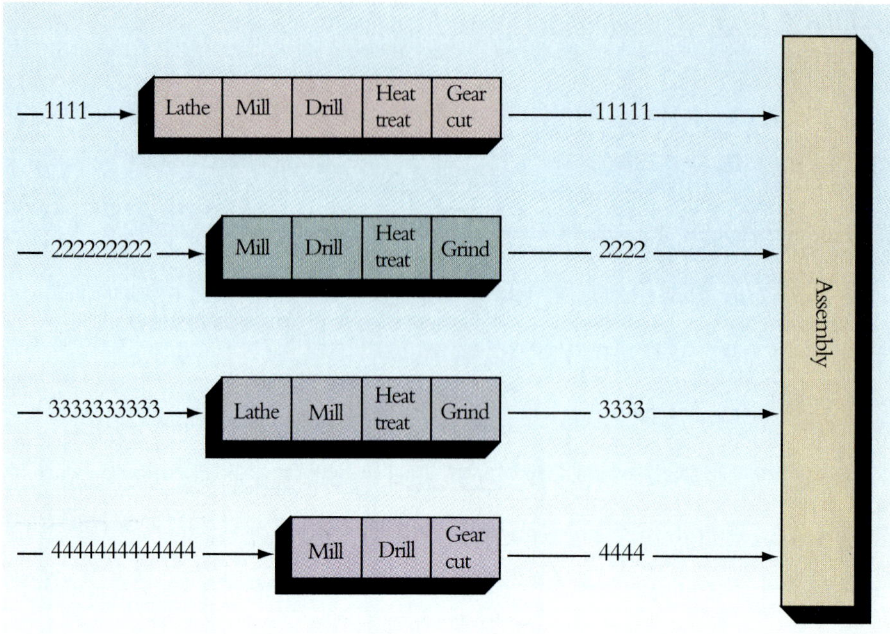

Source: Reproduced from D. Fogarty and T. Hoffman, *Production and Inventory Management,* page 472, with the permission of South-Western Publishing Co.

greater than the conventional assembly line. According to one consultant who helped Sony develop the spiral line, "there is no future in conventional conveyor lines. They are a tool that conforms to the person with the least ability."[12] Cummins Engine Company's use of a cellular design is described in Today's Business World.

Planning Site Location and Layout

When a company starts up or opens a new branch, the production and operations manager is heavily involved in planning the site location and layout. Company officers, engineers, and heads of departments add their ideas and lists of requirements.

Site Selection. A site may be bought or leased, with or without a building already in place. If the site is to be leased, all managers involved will make their plans and submit their needs to a commercial or industrial real estate broker. The broker will then submit a list of properties available in the area within the price range required. Sites may come with a "build to suit" lease

TODAY'S BUSINESS WORLD

Cellular Manufacturing Improves Quality and Productivity

For most of this century, factories were laid out according to process, with like machines located near like machines. This layout is known as the *job-shop design*. In other words, jobs of a similar nature are all done in the same shop. Under such a layout, batches of parts or unfinished product shuffle from one department to another. A major drawback to this design is convoluted flow paths.

To eliminate the time-consuming flow paths of the job-shop design, many manufacturers today use an alternative known as *cellular manufacturing*. Cellular manufacturing groups machines according to a process. Some processes require multiple machines to complete, and a cellular design will put these machines together to complete the process in one plant location. In that way, the lengthy flow paths of the job-shop design are eliminated.

Another benefit of the cellular approach is that workers receive training on more than one machine. In each cell, a worker can be trained to operate all of the machines that are required to complete the process. This gives workers stronger insight into the product and its manufacture. It also enables them to make stronger contributions to the company's quality improvement efforts. A worker who is familiar with the entire system is better able to recommend improvements than one who is only familiar with a small fraction of the system.

TQM

Cummins Engine Company is a notable example of a manufacturer that switched from the job-shop to the cellular design. This change helped the maker of heavy-duty diesel engines for trucks and tractors become more flexible and responsive to customer needs. Facing declining market share in the early 1990s, the company knew its primary competition was from foreign companies that were better able to tailor their production to meet individual needs of customers. Following a switch to cellular manufacturing, Cummins has rebounded in its global competitiveness. Productivity in 1993 shot up from 150 engines per day to 180, and the company recently reopened a plant in Indiana that had been shuttered. From 1985 to 1993, sales per employee increased 63 percent. Besides cellular manufacturing, the company lists worker training, worker quality groups, worker management, teamwork, and worker suggestions as the keys to its turnaround.

Cellular manufacturing replaces the standard assembly line approach to manufacturing. By placing people in cells where the product is produced from start to finish, travel distances are cut, quality is improved, and productivity is increased. What do you think are some barriers to converting a plant to a cellular design? Large manufacturing firms are more likely to use a cellular design than smaller firms. Why do you think smaller manufacturers have been reluctant to adopt this design?

Source: Adapted from Stephanie M. Rehta, "Cell Manufacturing Gains Acceptance at Smaller Plants," The *Wall Street Journal* (September 15, 1994): B2; Ravi Venkatesan, "Cummins Engine Flexes Its Factory," *Harvard Business Review* (March–April 1990): 120–127; "Rust Belt Resurgence," *Challenges* (February 1994): 7; Kevin Kelly, "A CEO Who Kept His Eyes on the Horizon," *Business Week* (August 1, 1994): 32.

or may be a turnkey location, in which the building and interior facilities are already completed.

The type of business dictates the kind of facility. Service sector businesses will often require small office facilities in heavy traffic areas convenient to customers or to the electronic communications and other services the business itself requires. Heavy industry, on the other hand, requires vast space near ship or rail transportation, often beside bodies of water that can be used for cooling operations as well as transportation to market. Most if not all of the factors in Exhibit 9.5 will be considered in the production and operations manager's plan for site location.

Some site choices may be based on the overriding advantages of one factor, such as availability of labor or market, or the low cost of land. In recent years, for example, many American companies have chosen to locate in Mexico because of the low costs of facilities, land, and labor. Clothing manufacturers have settled in Korea and Taiwan because of the abundant supply of cheap labor. Another production site growing in popularity is eastern Europe. Major changes in the business climate and a large untapped market have made the former Soviet Union, Poland, Hungary, and other central and eastern European countries intriguing options for joint ventures and new plants.

Site Layout. Just as it dictates the kind and location of facility, the type of business will determine the layout of the site selected. Different kinds of production require varying space for assembly lines, workstations, or other specific arrangements for the work layouts.

Exhibit 9.5
Site Selection Factors

- Economies of cost or other economic advantages for land, buildings or units, taxes, insurance, and so on.
- Nearness to related industries and suppliers, warehouse, or service operations.
- Availability of appropriate labor force, considering such factors as average educational level, quality, and cost.
- Availability of economical transportation for materials and supplies as well as for finished goods.
- Nearness to market for goods.
- Air and water conditions.
- Nearness to plentiful and economical energy sources.
- Climate and environment in line with needs for the kind of industry and amenable for employees' lifestyle.
- Ample space for planned needs of business and for later expansion.
- Nearness to such employee needs as housing, schools, mass transportation, religious facilities, day care, shopping, and recreational facilities.
- Community receptiveness.

The manager must plan the layout in detail before the site is chosen. The plan must account for the needed square footage, work areas, office and conference areas, storage, and shipping needs. To draw up specific plans, managers use templates, models, drawings, and the latest computer techniques.

Managing Materials, Purchasing, and Inventory

Materials management, purchasing, and inventory control cover the planning, ordering, and internal storage and distribution of the supplies and materials needed for production. Other names used for these areas include material handling, procurement, supply room management, and inventory management. You will encounter many variations.

Some variations also occur in the way authority and responsibility are organized. In some companies, the purchasing department purchases all goods or services bought from outside sources. In others the purchasing function covers only those materials and supplies used in the actual production process.

In large companies, the materials manager may oversee the functions of purchasing and inventory control, or inventory control may be part of production control, depending on its scope. Inventory control may handle only inventory of components and subassemblies, or it may cover all inventories—of supplies, raw materials, components and subassemblies, and even finished products.

In recent years, two important systems have been created to handle materials management and inventory control. Just-in-time (JIT) inventory control and materials requirements planning (MRP) have greatly refined the degree to which materials and inventory control can be managed and scheduled.

Just-in-Time
A system for decreasing inventory by using suppliers who agree to deliver the fewest possible items at the latest possible moment to keep production moving smoothly.

The **just-in-time (JIT)** inventory control approach was developed by Taiichi Ohno at Toyota Motor Company of Japan.[13] "Just-in-time" aptly names a production system in which operations (purchase orders, movement of materials, etc.) occur just at the time they are needed. As a result, very little inventory is carried. Under Ohno's JIT system, Toyota factories carry very little inventory. When parts are needed they are delivered from other Toyota plants or from outside suppliers.

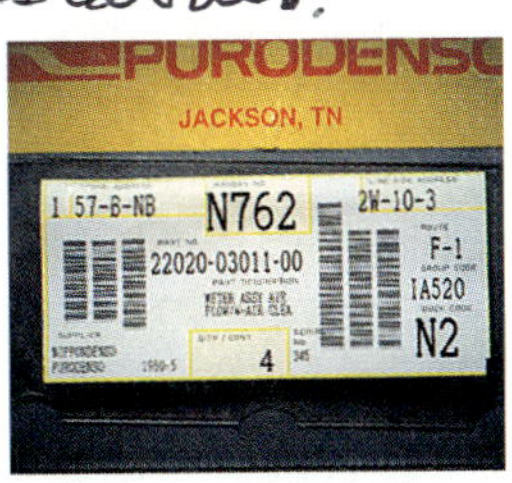

Example of a kanban that accompanies a bin of parts.

The Toyota system is called *kanban*. Kanban is the Japanese word for the piece of paper enclosed in clear plastic that accompanies each bin of parts. When a worker on the line takes a part from a new bin, the kanban is removed and routed back to the supplier. This signals the need to place a new order for a bin of parts.

An efficient JIT system can result in low inventories of purchased parts and raw materials, work in process, and finished goods. It saves warehouse and work area space as well as lowering the costs of carrying large inventories. Reducing inventory can also expose other production problems. A sometimes tardy supplier can be covered if the firm carries a large inventory. Smaller inventories spotlight the efficiency of all sources. A delinquent supplier will be replaced.

Just-in-time systems have been more common in Japan where groups of companies have traditionally associated in tight supplier-manufacturer relationships known as *keiretsu*. In these relationships, companies will mutually invest in one another to increase their commitment. American companies have been establishing closer ties to suppliers through electronic technology known as *electronic data interchange,* or EDI. EDI is a direct electronic link where manufacturers are able to begin the order cycle directly on the supplier's computer. This eliminates costly and time-consuming paperwork and also facilitates the tracking of orders.

Since JIT systems have little finished-goods inventory, machine breakdowns are very costly. Thus careful attention to maintaining efficient equipment becomes a top priority. Machines must be in tip-top working order to fulfill the JIT demands. A top-quality repair team that can move into immediate action must be available if JIT is to work effectively.

Materials Requirements Planning
A computerized forecasting system used to plan ordering of parts and materials for manufacturing.

Materials requirements planning (MRP) is a computer-driven system for analyzing and projecting materials needs and then scheduling their arrival at the work site at the right time. MRP works closely with the master production schedule and takes into account such variables as lead time in ordering.

MRP focuses on "getting the right materials to the right place at the right time." In most cases, making "right" decisions requires a computer to handle all of the materials and components involved. The MRP program analyzes data from inventory, the master production schedule, and the bill of materials. The output includes inventory status, planned order timing, and changes in due dates because of rescheduling.

MRP is used in companies involved in assembly operations. Firms that produce large volumes of tools, generators, turbines, appliances, and motors are particularly attracted to MRP. It is also very useful in companies that order a high number of units.

Together JIT and MRP provide a system that saves time and dollars. They have helped managers control the amount of inventory required to keep production moving smoothly. With JIT and MRP, suppliers of parts and subassemblies can plan in much closer time tolerances. In very large operations, such as the Detroit automobile assemblies, nearby suppliers are actually hooked up by computer to follow the progress of assembly-line work. From this vantage point, their trucks can arrive very nearly at the moment the materials are needed. Lead times on orders are greatly reduced, and costs of storing inventory drop sharply.

Controlling Production: Scheduling

The production manager is responsible for the main goal of the company: producing goods or delivering services. In the case of the production of goods, the production or manufacturing manager must be concerned with volume, production sequence, and the type of product to be produced. In a service organization, the production manager is also concerned with volume and the style in which services are delivered to customers.

Three elements of management—planning, organizing, and controlling—can clearly be seen in the tasks of the production manager. In the case of manufacturing, for example, planning the use of labor, facilities, and materials for fulfilling the production schedule is a complex, ongoing task. The manager will usually have more than one product to plan for, with the resultant needs for changes in materials, production processes, energy, and labor.

Master Production Schedule. A *master production schedule* must be created. It will show when the manager plans to produce each product and in what quantities. The production manager is responsible for meeting the dates, quantities, and cost commitments on the schedule. The master schedule will affect the efforts and success of every department in the company. Therefore it should also reflect the needs of the finance, marketing, shipping, and all other departments.

Production managers must plan for flexibility in order to be able to change from one process to another on short notice. They may use a number of tactics to meet emergencies or make changes in the plan. Requesting overtime, hiring temporary workers, cross-training workers so they can do more than one job, and many other methods are available.

PERT Chart
Program evaluation and review technique that tracks a project's progress and enables management to make optimal allocation of resources.

PERT Charts. Flexibility as well as adherence to schedule can be achieved with the use of the program evaluation and review technique **(PERT) chart.** PERT developed in the 1950s from the joint efforts of Lockheed Aircraft, the U.S. Navy Special Projects Office, and the consulting firm of Booz-Allen & Hamilton. They were working on the Polaris missile project and wanted to provide the United States with an advantage over the Soviet Union in time of completion.

An important part of PERT is the construction of a chart, a graphical system for tracking the events that must take place in order to accomplish a task. A PERT chart is one of the most effective tools of modern management. To create one, five steps are followed:

1. Break the project to be accomplished into events, or completed actions; label each with the amount of time needed to do it.
2. List the first event of the task.
3. List the event that follows the first one; draw a line with an arrow from the first event to the next one, showing the sequence. (If two events follow, draw arrows to both events to show that one event leads to two—or more—events.)
4. Chart all the events needed to complete the project in the same way, to completion.
5. Label the arrows with the amount of time it takes to complete each activity.

Exhibit 9.6 presents a PERT chart for the assembly of an engine. The interdependency of the events is spelled out in the column of prerequisites. That

Exhibit 9.6
PERT Chart

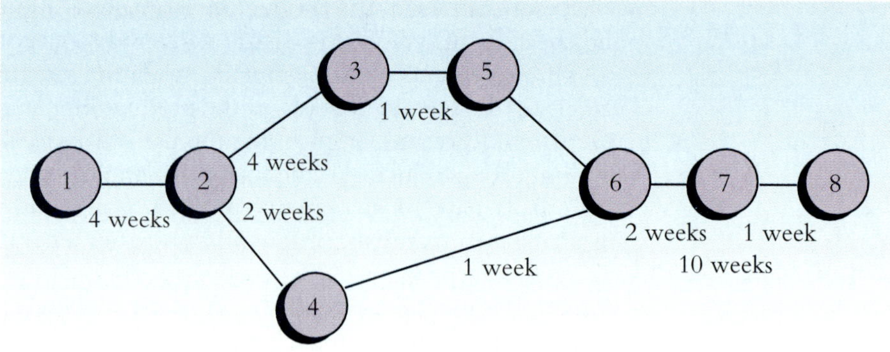

Activity			Event	
Arrow	Description	Prerequisite	Circle	Description
1–2	Develop engineering specifications		2	Specifications completed
2–3	Obtain test models	1–2	3	Test models obtained
2–4	Locate suppliers of component parts	1–2	4	Suppliers located
3–5	Develop production plans	2–3	5	Plans completed
5–6	Begin subassembly 1	3–5	6	Subassembly 1 completed
4–6	Place orders for component parts	2–4	6	Component parts received
6–7	Begin subassembly 2	5–6 and 4–6	7	Subassembly 2 completed
7–8	Begin final subassembly	6–7	8	Engine completed

Source: James H. Donnely Jr., James L. Gibson, and John M. Ivancevich, *Fundamentals of Management,* 9e (Burr Ridge, IL: Irwin, 1995), 584–585.

is, the development of the production plan, circle 5, requires that activities 1, 2, and 3 be completed. To reach the final assembly event, all seven other events must be completed.

When the chart is completed, the longest path from start to completion of the project (in time needed to complete the activities) is called the *critical path.* Path 1–2–3–5–6–7–8 will require 12 weeks, while path 1–2–4–6–7–8 will require 10 weeks. Thus path 1–2–3–5–6–7–8, as the longest, is called the critical path.

The PERT chart can be used to track exactly where a product is in its development and what needs to be done next to keep it on its path. Bottlenecks can be identified, and managers can organize employees in that part of the operation to devise ways to improve the process and reduce or eliminate the problem. For example, if the third event in a sequence always involves a delay, the production manager can form a team of employees from that process who can identify ways to improve productivity. By involving the employees in the improvement process, the manager is using the people closest to the process who probably have the best knowledge of how it works and how it can be improved.

The PERT chart is only as good in planning as the ability of its users to identify all of the steps in a chain of events. Because it helps break down the production tasks into clearly separate segments, PERT also helps to identify needs and uses for computerized manufacturing programs, temporary workers, and overtime techniques. This breakdown is very helpful in the current climate of rapid change in production techniques, numbers of products, and kinds of new products. The public presents an ever-ready market for newer, more appealing products; getting the products to the consumer is up to the the production staff. In the recent past, companies could expect to bring out a new product line or new models in the line no more frequently than every year. Now, in many industries, new products are inserted into the master schedule—and from there into the marketplace—as fast as they can be designed. With the increased capability offered by computerized design and engineering, that is very fast indeed.

USING TECHNOLOGY

Increased production is not achieved only through efficient planning. Computers have added flexibility and speed to the production process.

Computer-Aided Design, Engineering, and Manufacturing

Computer-Aided Design (CAD) The use of computers to draw plans for a product.

Computer-Aided Engineering (CAE) The use of computers to plan engineering processes and test designs.

Computer-aided design (CAD) and **computer-aided engineering (CAE)** have made possible the development of millions of new designs. Designs can be drawn, extended, contracted, added to, or taken from—all within the computer. Engineers can test designs for function and stress and try out variations without the cost or risk of building models or samples. Drafters using CAD can perform many of these tasks once the initial design has been developed. The computer does much of the calculation and the drawing, in two or three dimensions as needed.

CAD has been used to design buildings, ships, and even potato chips. Frito-Lay used CAD to design its O'Grady's double-density ruffled potato chip. An improperly designed chip is not attractive, may be too brittle and break into small pieces, or may not be suitable for using with dips.[14]

Computer-Aided Manufacturing (CAM) The use of computers to guide or control the actual production of goods.

Computer-aided manufacturing (CAM) includes the use of computers for controlling the operation of traditional, modified, and electronic machines, including robots. In Japan the Fujitsu plant in Akashi was using robots effectively in the 1980s. The plant specializes in sheet-metal manufacture, producing more than 100,000 parts each month for 1,500 different products. The production order, specifying the parts, the number, and the materials to be used, is given to the main computer. The computer then selects the most efficient way to make the parts and creates a layout for the automated shear machines and punch presses to follow. The Fujitsu plant is estimated to be 40 percent more productive with the CAM system, saving approximately $10,000 worth of material a month.

Robotics

Robot
A computerized, reprogrammable, and multifunctional machine that can manipulate materials and objects in the performance of particular tasks.

repetitive + dangerous things can use robots well

In the United States, the automotive industry is the best-known user of **robots** for manufacture. Robots paint, sand, test, and weld car parts; robots track individual cars on the assembly line and perform dozens of repetitive, exacting, unwieldy, or dangerous tasks.[15]

In 1988 approximately 51 percent of robots in operation in the United States were used in the automotive industry. As of 1995, however, only about 26 percent of the robots in operation were in the automotive industry as increased robot use swept into the service sector and other areas. However, robots still play a significant role in automotive production and will probably continue to do so.

The Moskvitch car factory in Moscow, showing the use of robots in automobile manufacturing.

The ability to manipulate other objects makes a robot unique compared to other kinds of computerized machinery. Robots also can perform the same tasks, such as welding a piece in place over and over again, hundreds and hundreds of times, without becoming tired or being endangered, as the human worker would be in the same function. Robots are therefore used especially in situations that are too repetitive or dangerous for human beings. For example, a robot can be more efficient, consistent, and cost effective than its human counterpart in the task of opening and closing a car door thousands of times. In applying acid to the surface of metal parts, a robot can perform at a constant pace for thousands of hours without danger or exhaustion.

From the early, simple machines (e.g., automated mail delivery carts) to the sensor-monitored "intelligent" machines of today, robotics has made a rapid ascent indeed. An estimated 33,000 robots are currently at work in American industry, most of them in the automotive, appliance, aerospace, chemical, electronics, food processing, home furnishings, pharmaceuticals, and textiles manufacturing areas. Technologies such as machine vision and tactile sensing promise to expand robot use in service industries such as education, health care, security, and training and development.

Flexible Manufacturing Systems

Flexible Manufacturing Systems (FMS) The use of computers to change from one production process to another in order to produce different goods.

Robots and other computerized machines programmed to switch fairly easily from producing one kind of product to another can be grouped in **flexible manufacturing systems (FMS).** Parts and materials flow to the operation by automated equipment, and finished products are removed automatically. Their flexibility allows FMS to be used in just-in-time inventory control projects as well as for small batches of customized parts or products without raising costs drastically.[16]

The National Bicycle Industrial Company, a subsidiary of Japanese electronics giant Matsushita, has used FMS with great success. Robots, computers, and people work together to turn production on a dime.[17] With 20 employees and a design-smart computer, the firm can produce any of 11,231,862 variations of 18 models of racing, road, and mountain bikes in 199 different color patterns and about as many sizes as there are people. Production doesn't start until an order is placed. But within two weeks, the customer is riding his or her personalized bike.

National Bicycle designs and manufactures the bicycle to fit the size, shape and strength of the customer. The bicycle store sends the specifications, by mail or fax, to the firm. A computer operator punches the data into a microcomputer. The bicycle is bar coded for *one* customer. The bar code is fed into the computer that instructs a robot where on the frame to build or what color the bicycle should be painted. The customer's name is imprinted on the frame. The personalized, flexibly manufactured bicycles sell for $545 to $3,200, compared with $250 to $510 for standard bicycles.

IMPROVING QUALITY

Computers, JIT systems, production schedules, and robots are all used in production and operations to improve quality, cost, service, and productivity. Improvements in productivity and quality have long-term effects on the success of business.

The term *quality* and its implications are now very important throughout the industrialized world. Germans brag about the quality of their automobiles. The Swiss praise the quality of their watches. The quality of Italian marble and tile work sets the standard for everyone in that industry. At times quality refers to workmanship or an evaluation (e.g., the "Good Housekeeping Seal of Approval"). From the consumer's perspective, quality is best defined as "perceived excellence." It is how a person views the product or service.

The perception of quality generally depends on how well the product or service meets or exceeds the customer's specifications and requirements. A consumer makes decisions about quality by evaluating one or more of its dimensions. Exhibit 9.7 illustrates eight such dimensions, including performance, features, durability, and aesthetics. In judging the quality of a Ford Taurus or an Oldsmobile Aurora, a car buyer may compare the vehicles on performance, features, serviceability, aesthetics, and perceived quality before making the purchase decision. Whether the buyer purchases a second Taurus or Aurora three years later will depend on how well the first car meets his or her expectations of quality. Ronald E. Goldsberry, Ford's vice president for customer service, expressed his company's emphasis on building long-term relationships: "In the past, the division's mission was to generate revenue through selling parts and taking care of service through warranties. Now we don't look at ourselves as parts, warranty and service providers. We want to provide an ownership experience so good that the customer will reward us by buying another Ford." Ford estimates that each one-point gain in owner loyalty is worth $100 million in profit.[18]

As we discussed earlier in this chapter, the quality of American goods—unquestioned before and just after World War II—slipped in the '60s, '70s, and '80s. Many reasons have been advanced for this. The postwar economic

Exhibit 9.7
Dimensions of Quality

Dimension	Example
Performance: Good/service's primary operating characteristics.	Sony TV's richness of color, clarity of sound.
Feature: Secondary, "extra" characteristics.	Hyatt Regency's complimentary breakfasts.
Reliability: Consistent performance within a specific period.	Honda Acura's rate of repair in the first year of purchase.
Conformance: Degree to which design and characteristics meet specific standards.	Apple computer's compatibility with IBM software.
Durability: Length of a good/service's useful life.	Average 17-year life of Kirby vacuum cleaners.
Serviceability: Speed, courtesy, competence, and ease of repair.	Caterpillar Tractor's worldwide guarantee of 48-hour delivery or replacement parts.
Aesthetics: Look, taste, sound, smell of a good/service.	Flavor, texture of Baskin-Robbins ice cream.
Perceived quality: Quality conveyed via marketing, brand name, reputation.	Bose's reputation in stereo speakers.

Source: James H. Donnelly, Jr., James L. Gibson, and John M. Ivanevich, *Fundamentals of Management,* 9e (Burr Ridge, IL: Irwin, 1995), 536.

boom created a seemingly ever-expanding market as demand for goods and services rose. Consumers, looking for the latest models in cars, cameras, tape recorders, and televisions, bought more and faster. Technological change accelerated and business hurried to keep pace, while workers complained they had no time or authority to maintain quality. In the midst of plenty, imperfections in the production process began to erode the confidence of consumers and the optimism of industry.

As American-made goods no longer were seen as top quality, foreign competitors' products began to gain acceptance as meeting top-quality standards. In major markets (automobiles, steel, electronics), this loss of sales cut deeply into the U.S. economy.

Greater pressure from competitors increases the importance of high quality in products. For example, foreign competitors—Japanese automakers, BMW, Daimler-Benz, and Volvo—have stimulated the improvements in quality now taking place in the American automobile industry. Meanwhile the Japanese are again redefining and expanding their notion of quality with a concept called *miryokuteki hindshitsu*: making cars that are more than reliable, that fascinate, bewitch, and delight.[19] Japanese engineers are working to give each car a special look, sound, and feel without sacrificing reliability. They call this the "second phase of quality." (The first phase of Japanese quality was inspired by American engineer W. Edwards Deming. Exhibit 9.8 highlights Deming's 14 principles of quality.)

Exhibit 9.8
Deming's 14 Points of Quality

1. Drive out fear.
2. Eliminate quotas and numerical goals.
3. Break down all barriers between departments.
4. Eliminate inspection. Learn to build products right the first time.
5. Institute a vigorous program of education and self-improvement.
6. Remove barriers that rob workers of their right to pride of workmanship.
7. Institute leadership. The aim of leadership should be to help people do a better job.
8. Eliminate slogans, exhortations, and production targets.
9. Adopt a new philosophy. This is a new economic age. Western managers must awaken to the challenge, learn their responsibilities, and take on leadership for change.
10. End the practice of awarding business based on the price tag. Move toward a single supplier for any one item. Base this long-term relationship on loyalty and trust.
11. Improve constantly and forever the system of production and service.
12. Put everybody to work to accomplish the transformation.
13. Institute job training.
14. Create constancy of purpose toward improvement of product and service to become competitive and to stay in business and to provide jobs.

Source: John Hillkirk, "On Mission to Revamp Workplace," *USA Today*, October 15, 1990, p. 4B.

American automakers have been steadily regaining domestic marketshare from foreign competitors and are also making inroads abroad. This turnaround in fortunes is in large measure due to improved quality and innovation. All told, U.S. automakers moved out 19 new models in 1995. As competition heats up, the biggest challenge will come in the 2.3 million-car family sedan market. Ford's new entries, the Contour and its Mercury Mystique sibling, along with Chrysler's Cirrus and Stratus represent Detroit's first credible challenge to Japan's biggest U.S. stronghold. The new models come close to matching the performance and quality of such Japanese standards as the Toyota Camry, Honda Accord, and Nissan Altima, but they sell for up to $7,000 less.[20]

Consumer pressure, lost market share, good business thinking, and competition, then, all motivate companies (whatever their nationality) to focus on quality. The unit in the company that controls quality is sometimes called *quality assurance (QA).*

Managing Quality Control

The quality control manager may be responsible for defining standards with exact specifications or for issuing guidelines regarding exact specifications set by an outside agency. Standards are set by agencies such as the Food and Drug Administration (FDA), the Bureau of Standards, and hundreds of other regulating groups. These standards affect the color, size, shape, taste, texture, durability, and many other properties of goods produced in the United States. From toothpaste to rocket fuel, American products are tested and standardized to a greater degree than any others in the world. Government contracts can be lost and consumer purchasing can fall rapidly if standards are not met.

The quality control manager must select or devise procedures to test the quality of products, establish troubleshooting procedures, pinpoint causes of any defects in products, and correct any problems rapidly to minimize losses. Customer complaints or returns of defective products must also be analyzed so that necessary corrections can be made.

Complaints and returns from customers can build up and result in lost customers and sales. Therefore a quality control expert must develop a system that reduces the chances that low-quality products or services get to the customers. A four-step program can help keep the perception of poor quality from being associated with the company.

Step 1: Define Quality Characteristics. The first step involves defining the quality characteristics desired by the customer or client. Examining customer preferences, technical specifications, marketing suggestions, and competitive products provides necessary information. Customer preferences are extremely significant, since repeat sales will likely depend on a reasonable degree of customer satisfaction. A Rolex customer wants accuracy, a long service life, and a stylish watch. But a Timex watch customer has other quality standards and preferences. The Timex keeps reasonably accurate time and sells at a much lower price than the Rolex. The exact quality characteristics for the Rolex and Timex watches meet, and depend on, different customer preferences.

Step 2: Establish Quality Standards. Once the quality characteristics have been defined (e.g., a Rolex or Timex), the next step is to establish the desired quality levels. Quality standards serve as the reference point for comparing the ideal to what actually is. Standards for factors such as size, color, weight, texture, accuracy, reliability, time of delivery, and support are set by management.

The cost of achieving and sustaining a specific level of quality must be estimated and compared to the cost of potential rejections. Exhibit 9.9 represents what is often called the *quality funnel principle*: the closer to the start of the production process, the lower the cost of rejection. As the product or service progresses through the process, more resources are invested; the greater the amount of resources invested, the higher the cost of rejection. The greatest cost is incurred when the customer or client is the source of rejection. In that case, the cost of processing the complaint and the cost of lost goodwill are added to the cost of resources. For example, complaints about Dell's first notebook computers were costly in the form of lost repeat sales and recalls to repair defective parts. Dell learned the hard way that superior quality is very important to modern consumers. Its first notebook computers had many defects, and their failure hurt the the company's reputation.

Exhibit 9.9
The Quality Funnel Principle

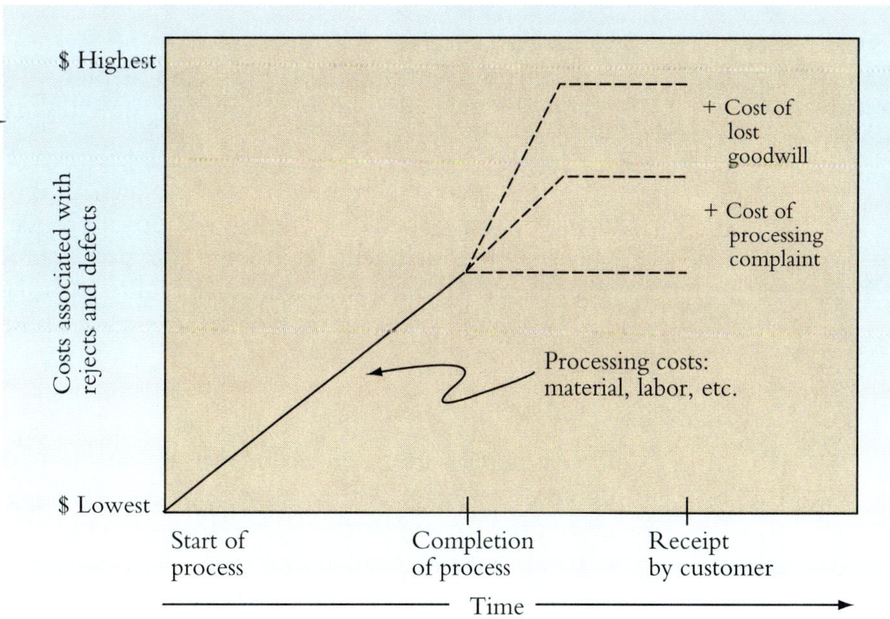

Source: Adapted from David Bain, *The Productivity Prescription: The Manager's Guide to Improving Productivity and Profits,* © 1982 McGraw-Hill, Inc. Reproduced by permission of the publisher.

Step 3: Develop the Quality Review Program. The methods for quality review, where and by whom reviews will be reported and analyzed, and other review procedures must be formalized. One important decision involves how many products will be checked for quality. Will all products be inspected or only a representative sampling? The greater the number of products inspected, the greater the costs associated with quality review. Representative sampling is less costly but creates (1) the risk that more low-quality products will get into the hands of customers, (2) a greater likelihood that customer goodwill can be tarnished, and (3) the need to decide on what number of defects or poor-quality products will be acceptable.

Sampling procedures can take many forms. Some organizations use a random spot check. A random selection of products (e.g., cars, generators, computers) is inspected for quality. When a formal random spot check is used, the results can be meaningful and can provide adequate control. Other forms of sampling plans using statistical analysis are also available.[21] In each case, the decision about which plan to use involves making inferences about the entire production, based on samples. Representative sampling presupposes that defective products will occasionally slip through the quality check network.

Step 4: Build Quality Commitment. A commitment to quality among the work force within an organization has three ingredients:

- *Quality focus.* There must be a sincere belief by employees, from top management to operating employees, that quality of all outputs is the accepted practice. Satisfying customer or client quality needs must be a goal of all employees.
- *Quality intelligence.* Employees must be aware of the acceptable quality standards and how the standards can be met.
- *Quality skills.* Employees must have the skills and abilities to achieve the quality standards set by management.

The employees' commitment to producing high-quality output is imperative.[22] It can be created with motivational programs or with programs involving job enrichment, goal setting, positive reinforcement, and team development. An approach with many adherents, participative management, involves employees in important management decisions.

Quality Circles

Quality circles are based on the belief that the people who work with the process are the best able to identify, analyze, and correct the problems in any given production situation. They are said to have begun in the United States but were expanded into a highly developed system by Japanese firms. **Quality circles** usually consist of 7 to 11 people working in a related area. They meet about once a week and discuss the flow of work, its problems, and potential solutions. Participation in the circle is voluntary, and the workers establish a moderator or team leader to lead discussions. Findings and proposals of the group are forwarded to management.

Quality Circles
Small groups of employees who meet regularly to identify, and sometimes solve, work-related problems.

Experience with quality circles suggests that several preconditions are required for success. First, those involved must be intelligent. They must know how to use statistics and work design analyses. They must know the technical aspects of the job. Second, management must trust the participants enough to provide them with confidential cost information (from competition). Third, the participants must be dedicated to working together as a team. They must have a team spirit, since groups, not individuals, are rewarded for success. Fourth, quality circles work best as part of what is called total quality control. This philosophy follows three principles:

1. The goal is to achieve a constant and continual improvement in quality year after year.
2. The focus extends beyond the actual product or service that a firm provides, to every process in the organization (e.g., finance, accounting, research and development).
3. Every employee bears the responsibility for quality improvement.

The implementation of total quality control involves the same steps used to develop the quality control system. However, the breadth of the quality focus—that every employee is responsible—and the challenge of continual improvement require extra effort.

The extra effort has paid off in the Metal Stamping Division of Irvin Industries, of Richmond, KY. After receiving quality improvement training, the firm declared that quality was a must and that each quality circle would set zero defects as a goal. Each Irvin employee has accepted the goal.[23] The quality circle improvements have resulted in many cost savings, a reduced injury rate, and increased morale.

Quality is also important in services. A plastic surgeon who performs a poor-quality surgical procedure on a patient's face can have it result in permanent disfiguration. Businesses trying to provide quality services need to use every single step of the process applied to product quality control.

Service quality is of concern at Russia's Aeroflot Airlines.[24] It has been described as the world's biggest airline. The company carries about 5 million passengers annually. Statistics and glossy promotion booklets boast of "excellent" services to and from 99 countries. In reality, Aeroflot's reputation among most Russian and Western passengers is that it provides the poorest service of any world-class airline: overbooked flights, long lines to make reservations, poor or no food service, shortages of trained flight attendants, and old equipment. The airline, to compete in the international marketplace, must totally overhaul its view of service quality and delivery.

IMPROVING PRODUCTIVITY

Productivity
A measure of output per unit of a particular input.

The rate at which goods and services are created is called **productivity.** In a healthy economy, productivity must be high and also steadily increasing. One common measure of productivity, labor productivity, is expressed in dollars of output (adjusted for inflation) per hour worked. Another important factor in productivity is technology and how it is being used by employees. Labor and technology combined generate the outputs that are priced and sold to consumers.

In the presence of increasing labor, material, and opportunity costs, uncertain world events, fast technological change, and shifting investment policies, the productivity of a company must continually increase in order for the company to stay in business. The challenge facing managers and nonmanagers in firms of all sizes is immense. Ignoring either quality or productivity improvements is likely to result in lost markets, layoffs, foreclosures, and general business decay. Consumers are demanding more quality, and companies need to improve the output per labor and technological input.

From a manager's perspective, a motivated employee works hard, sustains that pace, and is self-directed toward meeting challenging goals. Productivity improvement can only occur through such motivated employees. Thomas J. Peters and Robert H. Waterman Jr., authors of the well-known book *In Search of Excellence,* warn against falling for "the gimmicks." A quality circle program, a total quality control system, and a productivity improvement strategy all need motivated employees to implement and sustain them.

Peters and Waterman aptly point to the success of companies who have put the responsibility for quality on every employee and backed it up with management commitment to job security and meaningful profit sharing and recognition. They cite companies such as Dana Corporation, a midwestern manufacturer of propeller blades and gearboxes. Through the leadership of then-chairman Rene McPherson, Dana Corporation became the number two Fortune 500 company in returns to investors. McPherson points out:

Until we believe that the expert in any particular job is most often the person performing it, we shall forever limit the potential of that person, in terms of both his own contributions to the organization and his own development. Consider a manufacturing setting: Within their 25-foot-square area, nobody knows more about how to operate a machine, maximize its output, improve its quality, optimize the material flow, and keep it operating efficiently than do the machine operators, materials handlers, and maintenance people responsible for it. Nobody.[25]

This attitude, according to Peters and Waterman, is expressed in one way or another by the best of the American corporations. The authors define the attitude as "tough-minded respect for the individual and the willingness to train him, to set reasonable and clear expectations ... and to grant him practical autonomy to step out and contribute directly to his job."[26]

MAINTAINING SAFETY: FOR EMPLOYEES, PRODUCTS, AND THE ENVIRONMENT

A productivity and quality improvement strategy and motivated workers are key ingredients for business success. However, these can be diminished if the company shows little regard for the environment or sacrifices safety. It is important to improve productivity and quality without jeopardizing the well-being and future of the employees or the environment.

Employee and Product Safety

Chapter 4 has a detailed discussion of safety and social responsibility. Here we will view these issues in relation to the operations and production areas, where many of the most potentially hazardous materials, processes, and products are found. Although safety is a part of the responsibility of every employee in the work force, corporate responsibility for safety is most often delegated to the production and operations manager. Employee safety is mandated by a number of government regulations and laws; the production and operations manager is responsible for the implementation of these regulations in the plant. Compliance costs time, work, and money that must be provided for in schedules and budgets. Production and operations managers should realize that unsafe practices and contamination of the environment can implicate them and their failure to practice sound management.

Johnson & Johnson, maker of bandages and other health care products, is intent on being known as the number one firm in safety.[27] When any workplace accident causes death or a fracture, injury, or burn resulting in at least one lost day of work, the head of the company unit involved must file a written report to top management within 24 hours. The head must then travel to company headquarters in New Brunswick, NJ, and personally explain to a top-level committee what went wrong. Johnson & Johnson slashed its annual lost workday incidence per 100 workers from 1.81 to 0.14 in eight years (1981–89). Corporate workers' compensation expenses now average about $50 billion annually.[28] It pays to be as safe as possible.

Not only must employees have safe working conditions, the goods produced must be safe for the consumers who ultimately buy them. Product safety is the specific responsibility of the quality control department. Growing consumer consciousness of the issue has increased efforts to make products that are accident-proof. Automatic testing devices tug and pull plastic eyes and noses on toy rabbits to make sure they will not come off in the mouths of eager two year-olds. Medicine bottles are made tamperproof, and sharp products such as paring knives bear brightly colored labels to prevent consumers from cutting themselves accidentally.

Production in the United States is the most highly regulated in the world. Compliance, a production cost, has become increasingly expensive; research and development, testing, and fulfillment functions also add to the cost of production. The increased expenditures show that most companies and employees at all levels have begun to take safety issues seriously: Consumer accidents receive greater attention and investigation today than they did a decade ago.

Monsanto, the United States' fourth-largest chemical producer, has developed a program to help clean up the environment. Their pledge is reproduced in Exhibit 9.10.

Exhibit 9.10
The Monsanto Pledge

- Reduce all toxic releases, working toward a goal of zero.
- Ensure that no Monsanto operation poses undue risk to employees and communities.
- Work to achieve sustainable agriculture through new technology and practices.
- Ensure groundwater safety—making our technical resources available to farmers dealing with contamination, even if our products are not involved.
- Keep our plants open to our communities, bringing the community into plant operations. Inform people of any significant hazard.
- Manage all corporate real estate to benefit nature.
- Search worldwide for technology to reduce and eliminate waste from our operations, with the top priority being not making it in the first place.

Source: *Business and Society Review* (Spring 1990): 66.

Globalization of Environmental Pollution

In recent years international concern has focused on some alarming issues. The atmosphere's ozone layer is thinning. World climate is changing as a result of deforestation of large areas such as the Amazon rainforest. The Chernobyl nuclear accident released radiation on people hundreds of miles from its source, which is now enclosed in a giant sarcophagus-like enclosure.[29] In addition to workers and consumers, our very environment is at risk from the dangers of industry. Major corporate safety issues are chemical casualties, air/water/land pollution, waste disposal, site location and maintenance, and general environmental protection from products or by-products of industry.

Industry will continue to come under pressure to produce more, yet do it safely, cleanly, and efficiently. As globalization in all areas emphasizes the limitations and the vulnerability of our ecosystem, production managers all over the world will continue to be challenged to find new and better ways to produce.

THE CHALLENGE FOR PRODUCTION MANAGERS

If the problems of and pressures on production and operations management are unprecedented, perhaps so too are the opportunities for positive solutions. Most of these solutions have become possible as a result of the electronics revolution. It has been said that if the first Industrial Revolution multiplied the power of production 100 times, the second Industrial Revolution—empowered by the microcomputer—has increased it thousands of times.

Today, with the aid of CAD, CAE, CAM, and a wealth of other computer-based management tools, managers can plan, forecast, design, do research, and modify an infinite number of systems and products without the expense of trial and error. The expansion or contraction of schedules, the addition of a different wing to an experimental airplane plan, and the modification of a chemical coating for a 300-foot antenna that must last 20 years can all be planned and tested on the computer, with great accuracy. The computer is the single most important technological change to occur in industry in the 20th century, and the change has only begun.

Microelectronics represents not only the most powerful avenue of positive change for industry but also the greatest potential arena for error. As with all forms of power, the test is in how the power is used. Already in the last two decades, we have witnessed major problems caused by error or misuse of microelectronics—from the space shuttle disaster to the failure of AT&T's electronic programs, which tied up half the country's telephone lines for nearly an entire day. A high degree of skill is needed to use the new technology well. Keeping up with technological change is, therefore, the primary challenge to the production managers of today and tomorrow.

SUMMARY OF LEARNING OBJECTIVES

1. ***Define the production and operations management function.*** *Production* refers to the total process by which a business brings forth finished goods or services. *Operations* refers to the functions needed to keep the company producing. Functions such as purchasing, materials management, production, inventory and quality control, and maintenance are included. The process and functions needed to produce and/or deliver goods or services make up the production and operations management function.

2. ***Discuss two or three critical issues facing production and operations management.*** The concept that to live well a nation must produce well is a critical issue. The United States must find a way to improve the stature, performance, and quality of manufacturing firms. Another crucial issue involves finding the skilled workers needed to work with more sophisticated production techniques and processes.

3. ***Compare traditional company organization with cellular organization.*** The traditional organization emphasizes specialists in areas linked to manufacturing. Cellular organizations have a layout in which machines are grouped into what is called a cell. Groupings are determined by the operations needed to perform work for a set of similar items. In the cellular arrangement, units are completed by a team. The layout speeds up the assembly from start to finish.

4. ***Describe the effects of globalization on competition and productivity.*** Globalization and interdependence have spurred competition. Competition not only within a country but between countries is now at a fever pitch. This competition has resulted in improved productivity. Better technology, more strategic planning, and improved management methods have contributed to increased productivity in many countries. The United States is faced with small productivity gains and must work more on skills improvement, better management, and improved quality to increase productivity more.

5. ***Evaluate the effects of computerization on production and operations management functions.*** The effects have been significant in terms of speed, efficiency, and productivity. CAD and CAE have made possible tremendous flexibility and experimentation. The computer has become a major tool that must be understood by all production and operations employees.

6. ***Explain the importance of productivity and quality to business.*** Improvements in productivity and quality have long-term effects on the success of business. Ignoring either quality or productivity improvements is likely to result in lost markets, layoffs, foreclosures, and general business decay. Consumers are demanding more quality, and companies need to improve the output per labor and technological input.

7. ***Review the role of the production and operations unit in safety and environmental concerns.*** Corporate responsibility for employee safety is often delegated to the production and operations manager. Product safety is the specific responsibility of the quality control department. Concerns about pollution, global warming, toxic wastes, and preserving the earth's forests have made these topics of debate. The production and operations unit is expected by the corporation to oversee environmental matters. Environment-friendly technologies are needed in all areas, especially manufacturing. Production and operations units will be asked to work more on minimizing pollution at the same time they are expected to contribute to a firm's profit margins.

KEY TERMS

Production
Operations
Manufacturing
Mass Production
Assembly Line
Just-in-Time (JIT)
Materials Requirements Planning (MRP)
PERT Chart
Computer-Aided Design (CAD)
Computer-Aided Engineering (CAE)
Computer-Aided Manufacturing (CAM)
Robot
Flexible Manufacturing Systems (FMS)
Quality Circles
Productivity

QUESTIONS FOR DISCUSSION AND REVIEW

1. What is the difference between operations and production? Why is it important to make this distinction?

2. What features of quality are important to you when you purchase a product or service?

3. If you were going to open a fast-food restaurant (e.g., a Burger King), what factors would be important in selecting a site and site layout?

4. Develop a PERT chart that depicts your plans for a college education. What important events should be noted?

5. Do you think the use of robots will eliminate the need for human workers? Explain.

6. What is the meaning of the statement that quality is "perceived excellence"?

7. Do you think that inventory control systems such as the just-in-time technique can be applied to the operation of a service business? Give an example of why or why not.

8. CAD, CAM, CAE, and FMS are abbreviations of innovations in production. Provide the meaning of each abbreviation and tell, in your own words, how each has affected the production function.

9. Do you think modern consumers are more or less concerned about quality than consumers of several decades ago? Why or why not?

10. Explain how a firm using cellular manufacturing differs from a traditional manufacturing organization.

CASE 9.1

American Standard Mines Its Inventory

More and more companies today are trying to lower or completely eliminate assets tied up in inventory. How do they do it? By restructuring and reengineering to improve the efficiency of operations. Achieving zero inventory requires that every order and part move at maximum pace, never stopping. Orders streak from the processing department to the plant. Flexible factories manufacture each product every day. Finished goods flow from the assembly line onto waiting trucks. Manufacturers press suppliers to cut inventories as well, since minimal stocks translate into lower raw materials prices to the manufacturer. Instead of cluttered plants or warehouses, parts and products hurtle through the pipeline. As velocity rises, inventory decreases. That's why inventory levels are such a useful yardstick for efficiency and why, in the 1990s, manufacturers with the least inventory per dollar of sales will reign as the world's best-run companies.

The current leader in squeezing inventory out of its system is American Standard, a thriving, privately held producer of Trane air conditioners, American Standard plumbing supplies, and Wabco brakes for trucks. Not long ago the company was at the brink of failure. CEO Emmanuel Kampouris salvaged the New Jersey company by lowering the need for working capital to be tied up in inventory.

To escape a hostile takeover by Black & Decker, American Standard had taken on $3.1 billion of expensive junk bond and bank debt in a 1988 leveraged buyout. Interest and principal payments of $325 million a year on the loans and bonds swallowed almost all of the company's cash flow, leaving little for capital investment. Then, in the early 1990s, all three of its markets went sour. To save the company, Kampouris raided a hoard of idle cash, inventory. In 1988 American Standard had over $725 million tied up in inventory, 25 cents per dollar of sales. Kampouris wanted all of it. He has set a goal of zero by 1996.

To achieve this goal, Kampouris mobilized 90 factories around the world. Plants from Britain to Brazil exacted vast reductions in their inventories. One of the leaders in this effort is the Trane plant located in Lexington, KY. The plant sells over $100 million a year in large air-handling units for office buildings, restaurants, and hospitals. These units are priced up to $50,000, and each is made to order. Customized units are essential to winning customers, but in the past Trane never made an order continuously from start to finish. Instead it spewed out parts in long production runs meant to keep machines running at full capacity.

Parts usually spent only a few hours or minutes on the machines, but sat in mountainous inventories for weeks. Certain very specialized parts remained stockpiled for months or years. Wheels, filters, fans, and other components littered 10 acres of blacktop indoors and outdoors. Warehouses covered enough floor space to hold three football fields. When an order came in, Trane needed an average of 15 days to find the components and assemble the final unit. Despite the vast inventories, Trane often didn't have or couldn't find the parts it needed. Those pulled from stocks often turned out to be damaged. Many items rusted on the blacktop or were damaged by forklifts and other equipment.

Paperwork moved as slowly as the parts. Customer orders meandered through six departments, including design, materials purchasing, and production planning. At each step, stacks of orders piled up in an out-box, then lumbered to the next station. Getting an order from intake to the plant took as long as 10 days.

Trane launched a campaign—called Project Steeplechase—to lower the need for working capital by increasing order handling and lowering inventory. It began with order processing. Today, representatives from order entry, design, planning, and the other functions sit side by side. Orders pass quickly from desk to desk and reach the factory floor in one to three days.

Following the same principle, the plant clustered the machines needed to produce modules that are combined to make final products. It can complete these units so quickly—in an average of 20 hours—that it starts producing most parts only after receiving an order. Inventories are dwindling.

What's left is work in process, along with small supplies of raw materials. Instead of building a new plant, Trane refitted newly empty warehouse space for manufacturing.

Questions for Discussion

1. Some experts contend that it is possible to go beyond zero inventory to negative inventory. What do you think are the arguments against this possibility?
2. Do you think there are some industries where zero inventory is simply unrealistic?

Source: Adapted from Shawn Tully, "Raiding a Company's Hidden Cash," *Fortune* (August 22, 1994): 82–89; Marshall L. Fisher, Janice H. Hammond, Walter R. Obermeyer, and Ananth Raman, "Making Supply Meet Demand in an Uncertain World," *Harvard Business Review* (May–June 1994): 83–93.

CASE 9.2

Profile of Corning Glass: How to Survive

Competition from international firms has whittled the number of American television set makers down to one—Zenith. U.S. suppliers of TV set makers had to either give up or learn how to survive in a market dominated by foreign manufacturers. American suppliers had grown up in an era in which quality was not a top priority. Soon, however, the U.S. market became hungry for high-quality TV sets.

Corning Glass closed plant after plant. Once a major supplier to American TV manufacturers, by 1985 Corning Glass was down to one color-video-glass plant in State College, PA. The global market for video glass was about \$3 billion annually. One of the early developers, Corning decided that the market was attractive enough to try to regain a foothold. The firm worked on improving quality, controlling manufacturing costs, and improving inventory control systems. Corning concluded that better management, marketing, and manufacturing would lead to survival and profitability in a highly competitive market.

Corning initiated a number of offshore joint-venture activities with Samsung in South Korea and Thompson in Europe. The firm also formed a new marketing approach, a joint venture with Asahi Glass Company, Tokyo. The Corning-Asahi venture emphasized the importance of quality. Corning Asahi Video Products Company (CAV) is a model venture where computers, quality control, and production engineering are each considered important. Asahi is famous in Japan for manufacturing and marketing a top-quality product. This theme has carried over to CAV.

The manufacturing process at CAV combines continuous and discrete parts manufacturing. At the beginning, the process is continuous as raw materials are fed into three furnaces capable of producing about 650 tons of molten glass each day. Process variables are continuously monitored to prevent "blisters," gas bubbles that cause quality problems in producing video glass.

CAV has been successful in reducing product-development time and improving manufacturability. One example of this success is the knowledge-based software that helps design molds for the glass parts. With this software, a designer can encode into the system rules about how the shape of a mold and plunger must relate to the dimensions and property of the video glass. CAV claims the software has reduced mold-design time from 10 weeks to 1.

Corning wanted to remain in the video-glass business and decided that a joint venture was important if they were to maintain a position in the industry. The CAV joint venture has been a success. At CAV, quality, improved manufacturability, and reduced product-development time are strong competitive weapons. There is much more work to be done, but so far Corning has survived international competition and flourished.

Questions for Discussion

1. Why have most American firms failed to survive international competition in an array of industries such as steel, machine tools, and TV set manufacturing?
2. What is meant by the concept that better manufacturing is needed to be successful? Use this case as an example in preparing your response.
3. What did Corning gain by joining with Asahi Glass?

Source: Adapted from John Teresko, "Corning's Rebirth of the American Dream," *Industry Week* (January 7, 1991): 44–47.

EXPERIENTIAL EXERCISE

Interviewing a Production and Operations Manager

Activity:
To gain firsthand knowledge of the duties and job environment of production and operations managers, students will identify and interview someone in that profession at their place of work. Interviews should be limited to 20 minutes.

Directions:
1. Instructors should describe the roles of production and operations managers, emphasizing that management of production and operations often involves a large number of people.
2. Develop a short list of questions in class that each student should use for an interview with a manager.
3. Encourage students to identify someone in an industry they are interested in and then arrange an interview with that person at the workplace. The interview should be arranged at a time convenient for the manager.
4. Students should complete the interviews within two weeks.
5. Each student should write a two-page report on his or her impressions of the duties of the manager, as well as his or her impression of the workplace.
6. If class time allows students should share and debate their impressions in class.

BUSINESS APPLICATION:

Selecting Site Location for Branch Campus

Activity:
In groups of three to five, students will review the factors in site selection contained in Exhibit 9.5 and apply the criteria to the process of establishing a branch campus for the college. Approximately three hours outside of class and 30 minutes in class will be needed to complete the application.

Directions:
1. The instructor reviews the textbook material on factors involved in site selection.
2. Explain to the students that if the college were to expand its operations by opening a branch campus, then considerable time would be spend studying site location.
3. Assign students the task of making a recommendation for a site selection of the college's branch campus by applying the criteria reviewed from the textbook. The work

is to be done in groups of three to five. Each group will be asked to present its findings to the class.

4. Encourage students to include additional factors not necessarily included in Exhibit 9.5.
5. On the due date of the assignment, ask the groups to make a 5- to 10-minute presentation to the class on their site selection and the rationale behind it.

NOTES

1. Adapted from Stephanie Losee, "Mr. Cozzette Buys a Computer," *Fortune,* (April 18, 1994): 113–116; David M. McCutcheon, Amitabh S. Raturi, and Jack R. Meredith, "The Customization-Responsiveness Squeeze," *Sloan Management Review* (Winter 1994): 89–99; Peter Burrows and Stephanie Anderson, "Dell Computer Goes into the Shop," *Business Week* (July 13, 1993): 138–140.
2. Samuel Huber, *Efficiency and Uplift* (Chicago: University of Chicago Press, 1964).
3. Richard B. Chase and Nicholas J. Aquilano, *Production and Operations Management,* 7e (Homewood, IL: Richard D. Irwin, 1995), 17.
4. Paul S. Adler, "Time and Motion Regained," *Harvard Business Review* (January–February 1993): 97–108.
5. Frank Shipper and Charles C. Manz, "An Alternative Road to Empowerment," *Organization Dynamics* (Winter 1992): 48–61.
6. Erwin S. Stanton, *Reality-Centered People Management: Key to Improved Productivity* (New York: AMACOM, 1982).
7. Joseph H. Boyett and Henry P. Conn, *Workplace 2000* (New York: E.P. Dutton, 1991), 23–27.
8. Jeremy Main, "How to Steal the Best Ideas Around," *Fortune* (October 19, 1992): 102–106.
9. Gary Reiner, "Lessons from the World's Best Product Developers," *The Wall Street Journal* (August 6, 1990): A12.
10. David Greising, "Quality: How to Make it Pay," *Business Week* (August 8, 1994): 54–59.
11. Gary Slutsker, "Struggling against the Tide," *Forbes* (November 12, 1990): 312–314.
12. Michael Williams, "Some Plants Tear Out Long Assembly Lines, Switch to Craft Work," *Wall Street Journal* (October 24, 1994): A1, A4.
13. William J. Stevenson, *Production and Operations Management,* 4e (Homewood, IL: Richard D. Irwin, 1993), 624.
14. Chase and Aquilano, *Production and Operations Management*: 73.
15. Mark Hornung and Richard A. Moran, *Opportunities in Microelectronic Careers* (Lincolnwood, IL: NTC Group, 1985), 27–28.
16. David M. McCutcheon, Amitabh S. Raturi, and Jack R. Meredith, "The Customization–Responsiveness Squeeze," *Sloan Management Review* (Winter 1994): 89–99; B. Joseph Pime II, Bart Victor, and Andrew C. Boynton, "Making Mass Customization Work," *Harvard Business Review* (September–October 1993): 108–119.
17. Susan Moffat, "Personalized Production," *Fortune* (October 22, 1990): 132–135.
18. Jerry Bowles, "Quality 2000," *Fortune* (September 19, 1994): Special Advertising Section.
19. David Woodruff, "A New Era for Auto Quality," *Business Week* (October 23, 1990): 84–96.
20. David Woodruff, Kathleen Kerwin, and Larry Armstrong, "Cars, Cars, Cars," *Business Week* (September 19, 1994): 30–31.
21. Sherie Posesorski, "Here's How to Put Statistical Process Control to Work for You," *Canadian Business* (December 1985): 163.
22. Allen E. Puckett, "People Are the Key to Productivity," *Industrial Management* (September–October 1985): 12–15; Philip E. Atkinson and Brian W. Murray, "Managing Total Quality," *Management Services* (October 1985): 18–21.
23. "Quality Circles: A Worthy Tool to Use Under the QIP Umbrella," *Quality Update* (Fall 1990): 26–29.

24. Anatoly Brylov, "Aeroflot Taking the Dollar Under Its Wing," *Business in the USSR* (September 1990): 38–39.
25. Thomas J. Peters and Robert H. Waterman Jr., *In Search of Excellence: Lessons from America's Best-Run Companies* (New York: Harper & Row, 1982), 249.
26. Ibid., 239.
27. Albert R. Karr, "The Corporate Race Belongs to the Safest," *The Wall Street Journal* (July 5, 1990): B1, B5.
28. Tom W. Ferguson, "Job Injury Burden Could Disable Some Companies," *The Wall Street Journal* (July 10, 1990): A17.
29. *Time* (October 23, 1989): 60–62.

Nike's Global Network of Shoemaking

Nike began as an entrepreneurial venture when Phil Knight and Bill Bowerman invested in $1,000 worth of shoes made by a Japanese company. Part of the attraction of the shoe business for both Knight and Bowerman was that it gave them the opportunity to challenge accepted beliefs about the athletic shoe business and it enabled them to pursue their vision about how an athletic shoe company should be run. Throughout its 30 years of growth into one of the most successful companies in the world, CEO Knight has tried to maintain the entrepreneurial atmosphere that has been a trademark of Nike's culture. He has fought hard to avoid layoffs and to keep Nike bureaucracy to a minimum. However, Knight hasn't always been successful at any of these efforts.

During the lean years of 1982–1986 Knight had to lay off almost 700 workers from the Beaverton World Campus. The layoffs were difficult for Knight personally, and they left the remaining Nike employees with a sense of shell shock. During the slump, Nike stock dropped from a high of $28 per share to less than $7 per share, and the company fell to number two behind rival Reebok in total sales. Falling stock prices were certainly a shock to Knight and his colleagues at Nike. Worse, however, was falling behind Reebok. The Nike feud with Reebok—and Knight's personal antipathy toward its founder and CEO, Paul Fireman—is intensive and pervasive. The rivalry is so deep that Michael Jordan once admitted that he found himself zeroing in with special intensity on NBA players who wore Reeboks.

The period known around the Nike Campus as "the transition" has left mixed sentiments. Some see it as a period of redemption, a period when the company learned to listen to the customer again. "Reebok was God's way of telling us we'd gotten off track," remarked Dave Kottkamp, Nike's international division head. Reebok had gotten big by selling shoes to the growing aerobics enthusiast market. Nike didn't make aerobics shoes, opting to stick with its strategy that shoes made for the best athletes would always be the shoes people would buy.

Nike Bounces Back

Nike rebounded from the transition largely by riding the incredible popularity of Michael Jordan and the Air Jordan line of shoes it developed around his image. The idea of the Air Jordan line was to create a "segment," a marketable package linking the shoes, colors, clothes, athlete, logo, and inspired television advertising. Eventually Air Jordan was joined by the Air Force segment, which featured players like David Robinson and Charles Barkley. This was followed by the hugely successful "Bo Knows" products designed around multisports star Bo Jackson, and the advent of the now-famous Nike slogan, "Just Do It."

In the years since the transition Nike has regained its position as the number one athletic shoe company in the world. In doing so, however, it has developed, perhaps inevitably, some unproductive bureaucracy. As Nike designer Tinker Hatfield put it, "There are too many committees, there's too much talking, and there's too much input from retailers and focus groups.

The matrix is killing brilliant insights. As enlightened as this company is, a lot of people inside it are not. They will analyze you out of doing something that comes from the gut—though creating from gut emotions is supposed to be our specialty. Sometimes I think our structure is a formula for mediocrity."

Despite the tendency to become bureaucratic as company size increases, Nike has maintained much of the brashness of a small business in the day-to-day affairs of its employees. Conversation about management mechanics, for example, runs counter to the anti-organization ethos that pervades the company. Nike employees go to great lengths not to reveal their corporate titles. The idea of "reporting to" another employee elicits a disdainful response, and the very word "supervisor" is absent from the Nike vocabulary, as is the word "fashion."

"Structure is necessary, bureaucracy is not" reads one of the many slogans listed in a draft of the Nike "values" and "brand mission." Visitors who observe the Nike creative process soon realize that the ability to influence others is a key to intracorporate success. Marketing manager Tom Hartge (pronounced "Har-chee") talks about "lobbying" various internal constituencies to get things done. People who don't "like to get in other people's faces," as one executive put it, don't do well inside Nike. A certain force of personality and basic competence at Nike gamesmanship are essential.

Near the end of 1993, however, Knight acknowledged the company was going through another lull. He said, "It's time to re-think the business. We grew from a billion-dollar business into a four-billion-dollar global organization in just a few years. Now we have to grow even larger without becoming formulaic."

But Nike had become formulaic, and many Nike insiders had formed opinions about how to reorganize the company. Several schools of thought emerged. One school attacked the company's management structure, suggesting that the matrix be turned on its side and the silos of authority be conformed to business segments (e.g., outdoor business, basketball business) instead of organizing into discrete departments like marketing and design. Another school of thought said that Nike was backsliding into its pretransition mode and needed to pay more attention to its customers. A third school of thought decried the rigidity of the current organizational forms. This school was called the "where's Phil" contingent because its basic lament was that its fiery leader's entrepreneurial explosiveness was too often absent. The leading school of thought, however, was that it was time for Knight to appoint a successor—an Air Apparent.

By February 1994, Knight was convinced that it was time to appoint a successor. After much consideration and soul searching, he appointed his 41-year-old general manager, Tom Clarke, to succeed him as president. Considering his own future with the company, Knight was philosophical, "Whatever happens, I'm still here," he said. "I would like to stay around as a kind of senior presence, as a teacher, but I'll have to learn to find that middle ground. There's a side of me that goes in for relentless pursuit and another side that tends to back away completely."

With or without Knight at the helm, designing, producing, and distributing cutting-edge athletic footwear is Nike's core competence. The process of bringing a new product to market is one that includes science, art, and entertainment. The birth of the Air Carnivore is a good example.

Critical Thinking Challenge

Succeeding a popular and charismatic leader is never an easy task. If you were Tom Clarke, what would you do to reassure employees, stockholders, and customers that Nike would continue to produce cutting-edge footwear?

The Birth of the Air Carnivore

The National Sporting Goods Manufacturing Association holds an annual Super Show at which sports apparel manufacturers display their latest products. In 1993, the Super Show was held in Atlanta in the Georgia World Congress Center.

All told, there were over 25 acres of sports apparel on display and, some experts estimate, over a billion dollars worth of business was transacted at the four-day event.

Amid the more than 8,600 different display booths was the Nike display—so lavish that it had to be brought in on four railroad cars and numerous semitrailers days in advance of the event. Nike ads dominated display walls at the Atlanta airport baggage area. Nike images lined billboards along Interstate 85 on the way into town. Special Nike shuttle buses ran between the Super Show and downtown Atlanta hotels to save participants the hassle of finding a taxi.

In the show itself, Nike had prepared a major display to promote the release of a new line of shoes. For the unveiling of the new products, Nike hosted a group of Wall Street VIPs inside a specially designed theater. They were seated on a giant carousel, the lights went down, and the turntable rotated the visitors into position. Everyone stared up at the inner face of a towering, circular projection screen that was positioned above a banner that bore the Nike slogan, "There Is No Finish Line."

After a loud drum roll a series of images appeared, each extolling the virtues of the Nike spirit and Nike products. The video concluded with a shot of CEO Philip Knight, who said, "It's a company in a position to say the future is unlimited." The lights came back on in the theater and young Nike marketing managers and dozens of athletic-looking models continued the careful choreography of the show. Smoke descended from the ceiling, aerobic dancers danced, and a rappeller came down a wall. At the precise moment, marketing manager Hartge stood before the crowd wearing a strange shoe that was colored purple, silver, black, and green. Holding up the shoe, Hartge proclaimed, "The Air Carnivore. Vegetarians beware."

The introduction of the shoe at the Atlanta Super Show was the culmination of a twelve-month, $22.6 million process of design, prototype development and testing, and market testing for the bold new Nike product. The Air Carnivore is the brainchild of 32-year-old Nike designer Bill Worthington. According to Worthington, the design process was a long, hard road, taking over seven months from concept to prototype. "It took a lot of screaming and yelling and team building inside the matrix. It took a lot of refusing to give up. I worked hard to build alliances and to counter internal skepticism over whether the consumer would be able to appreciate the technology inside this shoe or understand its personality," he said.

Deep, snaking grooves subdivide the complicated black and purple topography on the bottom of the Air Carnivore. The major innovation in the shoe is the manner in which the sole is cleaved into separate compartments called "pods." The pod concept came from the technical people in the Nike labs, as did the velcro "anti-inversion" strapping device running vertically along the outside of the shoe. The strap is designed to help athletes resist turning their ankle inward while in the air. This will help them avoid breaking bones or straining ligaments if they hit the court or pavement on the outside edge of their feet.

Another adjustable strap encloses the "anti-inversion support collar" that bracelets the ankle, and a third strap fastens over the top of the foot to eliminate the need for shoelaces. Several composites of advanced designer polymers—variously rock hard, malleable, or "high memory" substances designers have borrowed from chemists, NASA scientists, sail makers, and women's girdles or cooked up themselves—are glued or sewn to the shoe. The Air Carnivore's "upper," the soft, outer foot covering, is made of a lightweight leather-like Nike material called Durabuck, which was cooked up when Nike made a leather "Bat Boot" for actor Michael Keaton to wear in the movie *Batman*.

Despite the statement made by the bright color of the shoe, the paramount enticement is its fully loaded technological package. The Air Carnivore incorporates numerous innovations passed along to the design team from the Nike Sports Research Lab and the Advanced Product Engineering Group. The Sports Research Lab is a large open space filled with lots of computers on trolleys, automatic treadmills, exercise bikes, and closed-circuit camera systems pointing at the treadmills and bikes. One of the machines in the lab is designed to rub the bottom of a shoe for hours on end on surfaces that resemble clay tennis courts, wet boat decks made of teak, or cement basketball courts. Another machine calls for test subjects to run without shoes across a steel pressure mat that, within seconds, causes a nearby monitor to light up with a color-coded map of the subject's foot.

There are a dozen or so exercise physiologists in the Sports Research Lab. Lab director Tom McGuirk describes the physiologists' role in the production of a shoe as "defining human movement in terms of biomechanics and physiology. Our job is to translate activities into a set of performance-enhancing and injury-reducing needs. And we do a lot of work to improve end-user perception."

The Nike Sports Research Lab also gathers a vast amount of information and data about athletes and the games they play. The data are passed on to the design team for use in the creation of new products. For example, Nike designers know that Michael Jordan ran about two and one-half miles during a typical basketball game, and that he landed after an average leap at a peak force three times his body weight. After a test conducted at the University of Delaware, the Nike lab learned that Charles Barkley, because of his size, jumping ability, and landing style, came down with a force seven times greater than his weight.

Besides gathering data about human performance, the Nike labs also experiment with advanced materials. One Nike chemist stated that "We do stuff with materials they're only thinking about putting in the space shuttle." The Nike labs are also responsible for assembling the prototypes that will be shipped to the Asian factories where the shoes are produced.

CRITICAL THINKING CHALLENGE

Nike spends a lot of time and resources studying human physiology and creating new shoe technologies. Do you think most customers purchase Nikes because the shoes improve their athletic performance? Do you think Nike would be as competitive if it eliminated its research labs and sold shoes primarily based on style? What do you look for in an athletic shoe?

Production

Nike is the largest supplier of athletic shoes in the world, yet it outsources 100 percent of its shoe production and manufactures only key technical components. Athletic footwear is technology and design intensive, requiring a high degree of flexibility at both the production and marketing levels. Nike creates maximum value by concentrating on preproduction (research and development) and postproduction (marketing, distribution, and sales) activities.

Nike uses a three-tier strategy of "production partners" in working with its foreign suppliers. The first tier consists of three types of manufacturers: Developed Partners, Volume Producers, and Developing Sources. Developed Partners produce Nike's latest and most expensive "statement" products. These companies usually produce lower volumes, codevelop products, and coinvest in new technologies.

Volume Producers are above average in size (making 70,000 to 80,000 units a day, compared to 20,000 to 25,000 units for developed partners). They generally produce a specific type of footwear (e.g., basketball shoes) and are vertically integrated. Nike does no development work with them because each company may produce for seven or eight other buyers.

Developing Sources are attractive primarily because of their low labor costs and their capacity to diversify assembly locations. All produce exclusively for Nike, which has a strong "tutelage" program to develop them into higher-level suppliers. Nike tries to link Developing Sources through joint ventures with its Developed Partners. The latter assist by providing needed training, helping to finance some operations, and moving some of their own labor-intensive activities to these units.

In addition to this first tier of assembly units, Nike supports a complex network of second-tier suppliers for materials, components, and subassemblies. In Nike's third tier, some of the more specialized and technical components are made in supplier companies that Nike totally controls.

Nike manages its external suppliers through its expatriate program. All Nike expatriates are given a six-meeting preparatory course prior to their foreign assignment. Subjects include the do's and don'ts of living offshore, with special sections on the culture of the host countries. Nike expatriates become permanent personnel in each factory producing Nike footwear, functioning as liaisons with corporate R&D, headquarters, and worldwide quality assurance and product development efforts.

Distribution

Nike's distribution network has come a long way since the early days when the company's entire inventory was sold out of the trunk of Knight's 1964 Valiant. Now, Nike has a vast distribution network, including several proprietary Nike Town stores that sell Nike products exclusively. One of the critical factors of success in the athletic shoe business is technical innovation. Nike calls it design; Reebok calls it fashion. Whatever it is, the constant changes can present problems for retailers if they are not kept informed. Customers who spend up to $150 on an athletic shoe want to know what they are buying.

To help retailers stay abreast of changes in their products, Nike has formed an elite core of employees known as "Ekins" (that's "Nike" spelled backward). Ekins are shoe experts in their mid-20s who travel from store to store to talk to retailers about the technicalities of new Nike shoes. The Ekin program was begun in 1981 as a way to institutionalize the enthusiastic personal connection to retailers that Knight and Jeff Johnson had in the early days of Blue Ribbon Sports. Ekins will cover hundreds of miles in a week, stopping in at store after store to offer clinics and explain the technical details of ever more complex shoes. Nike serves over 12,000 retail outlets. Ekins are known among the retailers as hard working and driven. "The Ekins epitomize the original lust," one Ekin said. "We are that passion from the early days, and we're the eyes and ears of the company too. While others are buzzing around headquarters, we're out there with the customer."

Nike profits per pair of shoes sold at retail are close to the industry average. The retail price of Nike shoes must account for all of the production and distribution costs. For example, the Air Carnivores are manufactured at the Tae Kwang Rubber company in Seoul, South Korea. Fifteen percent of the $29.50 Nike pays for each pair of shoes produced by the company goes to paying the workers on the line. Roughly 60 percent goes to purchase components such as the synthetic leather uppers. Another 5 percent goes to indirect costs (largely the making of expensive molds), administration, and overhead, and 10 percent is built into the formula as Tae Kwang's profit.

Nike developer Kevin Paulk estimates that each pair of Air Carnivores can be "landed" in a Nike warehouse for $36.80 per pair. This price includes the manufacturing cost, the $1.40 per pair shipping costs, and $5.90 per pair to U.S. Customs in duty charges. Retail distributors pay a top price of $70 for each pair of Carnivores they put on their shelves. About $4 of the $33.20 difference between the "landed" cost and the cost to retailers is apportioned to taxes. Another $15 is set aside for paying Knight and everyone else at the Beaverton headquarters. A final profit of about $5.50 per shoe is very close to the industry average.

In addition to the 12,000 retailers, Nike distributes its products through immense, glitzy stores called Nike Town. The Chicago Nike Town store, located not far from Michael Jordan's downtown restaurant, has over 68,000 square feet and draws some 12,000 visitors every day. The store looks more like an athletic shoe and sports museum than a shoe store—with a basketball court, statues of Michael Jordan and other Nike athletes, giant tanks full of tropical fish, and vivid Nike imagery built into every wall and even the floors. The Chicago Nike Town is the area's single most popular tourist attraction. Other Nike Towns have been established in Portland, New York, San Francisco, and a dozen other cities across the nation.

Many retailers are concerned about Nike's aggressive move into upscale retailing. It is not lost upon them that if Nike grossed $33 on a $130 pair of Air Carnivores sold to the stores for $65 to $75, then by selling the shoes in its own Nike Town stores, the company stands to make another $60 to $65 per pair. Nike sales managers have assured retailers that the Nike Towns are primarily for brand building. They call them 3-D commercials. But the retailers may have something to worry about in the future. Nike design director Gordon Thompson is dreaming about the next generation of stores. He said, "Right now I'm obsessed with going beyond Nike Town. I have an idea that will take me a year or two to finish, but I think I'm stepping into a new frontier for retailing. We have to move hard into the next series of ideas to maintain our hold on what's cool—our hold on a market saturated by competitors."

CRITICAL THINKING CHALLENGE

Nike designers are determined to press into the next series of ideas in distributing products. What are some new ways that you can think of for distributing athletic footwear? Are there any industries from which Nike can get ideas?

Sources: Adapted from William M. Bulkeley, "The Latest Thing at Many Companies Is Speed, Speed, Speed," *The Wall Street Journal* (December 23, 1994): A1, A5; James Brian Quinn and Frederick G. Hilmer, "Strategic Outsourcing," *Sloan Management Review* (Summer 1994): 43–55; Donald Katz, *Just Do It* (Random House, New York, 1994); and Donald Katz, "Triumph of the Swoosh," *Sports Illustrated* (August 16, 1993): 54–73.

PART 4

Human Resources

CHAPTER 10

Human Relations and Motivation

LEARNING OBJECTIVES

1. Define the term *scientific management*.
2. Explain what the Hawthorne studies revealed about the role that groups play in motivating employees.
3. Define the term *motivation*.
4. Discuss Maslow's view of needs and motivation.
5. Compare and contrast the Theory X, Theory Y, and Theory Z approaches to motivating employees.
6. Explain why Herzberg's view of motivation is so popular with practicing managers.
7. Describe the principles of goal setting.

Some claim that one of the best motivators of a large work force is Mary Kay Ash of Mary Kay Cosmetics. She is the chairperson emeritus of a company that had sales of $198,000 in 1963 and over $625 million in 1994. She has built a sales force of 300,000, more than 6,500 of whom are driving complimentary Cadillacs and other cars. She has helped create 74 "millionaires"—salespeople who have earned commissions of $1 million or more.

Mary Kay Ash has built her empire by practicing a principle that states that the way to motivate people is through recognition. Ash advocates giving her beauty consultants (saleswomen) recognition for their accomplishments, but the company treats everyone equally. Every consultant buys the products from the company's Dallas headquarters at the same price. Resumes count for nothing. If an applicant states that she was a brain surgeon in her last job, it means nothing more or less to Ash. All that counts is the woman's work ethic and her willingness to represent the company's cosmetics positively.

There's no cap on how much a woman can earn. As her sales increase and she recruits more consultants, she advances to sales director and eventually to national sales director. At the summer sales convention and seminar in Dallas in 1993, more than 36,000 consultants attended. Color-coded suits, sashes, badges, crowns, and emblems showed how far each woman had come in the company.

Recognition from Mary Kay Ash is what the consultants seem to thrive on the most. She personally crowns four queens of the seminar—women who have excelled in sales or recruiting. She tells her own story of making it up the ladder. She was a saleswoman with Stanley Home Products, who started at the bottom and is now a multimillionaire. She was passed over for a promotion at Stanley Products and decided to quit and start her own company. She wanted to create a business that would treat women right and help build their self-esteem.

Ash's system of motivation includes extrinsic rewards such as bonuses and intrinsic rewards such as feeling good about doing the job well. Recognizing and rewarding good performance seems to improve the self-esteem of the thousands of beauty consultants at Mary Kay Cosmetics. Ash appears to understand how motivation works and the role it plays in directing the behavior of the beauty consultants. Her reward-by-recognition motivation approach works well with women and should also work well with men. Husbands who attend the conference and seminar report that they tell their employers that praise is a key to motivation that needs to be used more.

Money at Mary Kay Cosmetics is only one of the motivators. Applause, prizes, emblems, praise, and recognition also seem to be powerful motivators. Why is Ash's approach so well received by women? Is this motivational approach suited only for women?[1]

Today people all around the world—managers and nonmanagers alike—have their own definitions of motivation. Usually the definitions include one or more of the following words: *needs, drives, motives, goods, incentives, desires,* and *wants.* The term *motivation* can be traced to the Latin word *movere* (to move). In terms of the work to be performed in an organization, moving employees to accomplish desired goals is extremely important. Thus this chapter will focus on moving people to perform.

The difficulties involved in motivation have not lessened the enthusiasm or creativity of attempts to find ways to motivate employees. Each year, Mary Kay Cosmetics' beauty consultants attend conventions and seminars to be recognized, praised, and encouraged. It seems to work very well and has resulted in a highly motivated work force.

This chapter focuses on how managers specifically look at human resource management and motivation. We begin by defining scientific management and motivation and then present several need and management theories. The chapter concludes with a discussion of various ways managers can motivate their employees. In thinking about each of the methods, recall Mary Kay Ash's straightforward, unilateral approach to motivation. Its simplicity among a range of approaches is worthy of praise.

MOTIVATION AND PERFORMANCE

In any attempt to motivate, the psychology of individuals—why they behave the way they do—is important. Motivation attempts to influence or cause certain behaviors. In fact many people equate the causes of behavior with motivation. The importance of the behavior concept is spelled out in advice Ross Perot gave to General Motors: A positively motivated person behaves enthusiastically, forcefully, and with a clear purpose.

One of the most difficult tasks facing managers is motivating employees. Managers are responsible and accountable for meeting important organizational objectives. Therefore they must be concerned about the performance of employees in such important tasks as answering a customer complaint, interpreting a computer printout, or selling a graphic computer disk player to a customer. Successful business managers must create an atmosphere that motivates employees to use their skills and abilities. When a skilled employee does not perform up to his capabilities, is this a motivation problem? Yes, it probably is.

TOMORROW'S BUSINESS WORLD

Gender and the Workplace

There are experts such as John Naisbitt, author of *Megatrends* and co-author of *Reinventing the Corporation,* who believe that the changing role of women in society is the most significant change in this century. If this is the case, the role of women in the next century will be a significant factor in how organizations are managed. In various states, it is reported that women make up over 40 percent of the work force in organizations. As the next century begins, more than 80 percent of women aged 25 to 54 will be in the work force. This would mean that about 50 percent of the work force will be women.

With the significant increase of employed women, sociologists, business writers, researchers, and managers have had a field day speculating about whether men and women differ or respond in the same ways. What motivates women? What strengths do women bring to the workplace? The speculation brings a number of predictions about the next century:

- More men and women will work together as peers. It will also become increasingly common for men to be working for women and for women to be working for other women.
- Managers and executives in dual-career families may be unwilling to relocate without significant incentives and support.
- Firms will have to become more involved in expanding child care arrangements for women with children.
- There will be more part-time, flexible, shared, and work-at-home jobs created.
- Men and women will be rewarded equally when their performance is assessed to be equivalent. Equal pay for equal work will finally become a reality.

How accurate do you believe these predictions will be? Explain your conclusion.

HUMAN RESOURCE MANAGEMENT AND RELATIONS

Frederick Winslow Taylor's principles of scientific management introduced the importance of managing human resources and relations. Taylor studied workers in the Midvale and Bethlehem steel plants in 1885. His most famous experiment involved a pig iron shoveler he called Schmidt (his real name was Henry Noll). Using a time-and-motion approach and a stopwatch, Taylor studied Schmidt's every move and work activity. He presented improvements in how to handle pig iron. Schmidt increased his productivity from 12.5 long tons (a long ton equals 2,240 pounds) to 47.5 long tons per day!

Scientific Management
The scientific study and breakdown of work into its smallest mechanical elements, and their rearrangement into the most efficient combination.

This is **scientific management**—the systematic study and breakdown of work into its smallest mechanical elements, and then the rearrangement of these elements into their most efficient combination. The application of the principles of scientific management has resulted in many cases of increased or improved productivity. However, some of the principles such as introducing a high degree of specialization or routine work results in boredom and poor morale among some individuals.

The Hawthorne Studies

Hawthorne Studies
A series of experiments that found that work groups significantly affected the way workers behave and perform.

The **Hawthorne studies** were conducted from 1927 to 1932 at a Western Electric plant in Cicero, a suburb of Chicago.[2] The team of Harvard University researchers included Elton Mayo, Fritz Roethlisberger, and William Dickson. This series of experiments is the single most important event in the historical foundation of the behavioral study of employees.

In an illumination experiment, employees were divided into two groups. One group worked in a test room where the intensity of lighting was varied, and the other group worked in a room with constant lighting over the time of the experiment. When light levels were raised in the test room, production increased; when light levels were lowered, production still increased. Puzzled, the researchers decided to change working conditions. They introduced shorter rest periods, longer but fewer rest periods, and other changes. Once again, no matter what change was introduced, production still improved.

The researchers next interviewed many of the employees involved in the study, asking questions about their reactions to working conditions. The researchers found that a change in morale occurred because the employees felt more responsible. They also did not want to let down co-workers. This was a form of self-imposed pressure. They also felt good about being a part of the experiment. Labor turnover stopped, and absences were drastically reduced. An employee who had been absent 85 times in the 32 months before the experiment went for 16 months without an absence.

A second experiment, which lasted for only 16 weeks, was designed to measure the effect of group incentive plans on productivity. Although economic incentives were offered for increased productivity, the members of the group set informal production quotas that would allow most group members to work at a comfortable pace. Productivity levels were not significantly increased. The power of the informal group, not the economic incentive, controlled production.

The Hawthorne findings offered no perfect answers or specific motivation programs for managers. But the studies did show that informal groups can influence productivity. Productivity increased through self-imposed pressure in the first experiment, but it was restricted by group pressure in the second. Both experiments used highly cohesive, or tightly knit, groups.

The major difference in the two experiments was the supervisory style used. The first used general supervision. The employees stated that they had freedom and were treated well. They felt special and good about themselves. The self was recognized, and employees liked this kind of recognition. In the second experiment, a closer supervisory style was used.

There were other dissimilarities. The employees were women in the first experiment, men in the second. In the second experiment, the room in which the employees worked was set up just for the experiment and involved no researcher-introduced changes. In the first experiment, the researchers changed lighting and rest periods.

Regardless of the differences, the Hawthorne studies showed how group characteristics and type of supervision, among other things, influence motivation and productivity. The studies have been interpreted in different ways, but one message is clear. Managers attempting to create a favorable climate for motivation need to consider (1) the group, (2) helping employees improve their self-esteem, and (3) style of supervision.

The importance of helping people to feel good about themselves, to feel special, is captured in Roethlisberger's own words: "If one experiments on a stone, the stone does not know it is being experimented upon"—which makes things simple for people experimenting on stones. But a human being experimented upon is likely to know it. Therefore, attitudes toward the experiment and toward the experimenter become very important factors in determining the subjects' responses. This phenomenon is known as the "Hawthorne effect."[3]

Scientific management and the Hawthorne studies contributed insights, methodologies, and ideas to the area of human relations; that is, the study of how organizations manage their employees individually and within groups to improve productivity. The Hawthorne studies are so important in understanding motivation, groups, and productivity that the original readings are now considered classics and are required reading for scholars and researchers around the world.

MOTIVATION: WHAT IS IT?

Motivation
The way drives or needs direct a person's behavior toward a specific goal; involves the level of effort put forth to pursue the goal.

Motivation is the way in which drives or needs direct a person's behavior toward a goal. It concerns the level of effort put forth to pursue specific goals. Managers cannot observe the motivation process directly since it occurs internally. So they observe behaviors and then reach conclusions about a person's motivation. For example, Anne Anderson, a fifth grade teacher, knows that Jose and Mike have similar intelligence and ability. Jose does well in school, but Mike continually struggles with school work. She concludes that Jose is motivated but Mike is not. Why? That's the motivation puzzle Anderson must solve.

Managers become concerned about motivation when employees exhibit productivity problems, reduced commitment to quality, and resistance to management programs. Managers know it is not simple to motivate employees. In fact, managers realize they must understand how to use an array of tools (e.g., techniques, programs, rewards) to create the best motivational atmosphere possible.

Extrinsic Reward Reward external to the work itself and administered by someone else, such as a manager.

Intrinsic Reward A sense of gratification directly related to performing the job.

Punishment An undesirable consequence of a particular behavior.

Generally speaking, rewards and punishments are the tools managers use to motivate employees. Rewards can be extrinsic or intrinsic. **Extrinsic rewards** are external to the work itself; they are administered by someone else, such as a manager. Examples include pay, fringe benefits, recognition, and praise. **Intrinsic rewards** are related directly to performing the job. In this sense, they are often described as self-administered. Intrinsic rewards include feeling good about accomplishing an objective and about being able to make job-related decisions without consulting a supervisor. On the other hand, **punishment** involves taking something away from a person or administering an undesirable consequence for a particular behavior. For example, a frequently tardy worker would be punished by having his pay docked for the time missed.

Communicating and administering rewards and punishments are part of the manager's job in creating the best motivational atmosphere. Both types of rewards appear to produce higher levels of performance than punishment does.

Motivation is goal oriented. It can work this way: First, the person experiences tension created by unfulfilled needs. A need indicates a deficiency; for example, when you are hungry, you have a need for food. Second, the person starts a search to find a reasonable way to satisfy these unfulfilled needs. Third, when some of the needs are fulfilled and some of the goals are accomplished, the process begins again. Exhibit 10.1 illustrates the goal-oriented process of motivation.

Exhibit 10.1
The Process of Motivation in the Individual

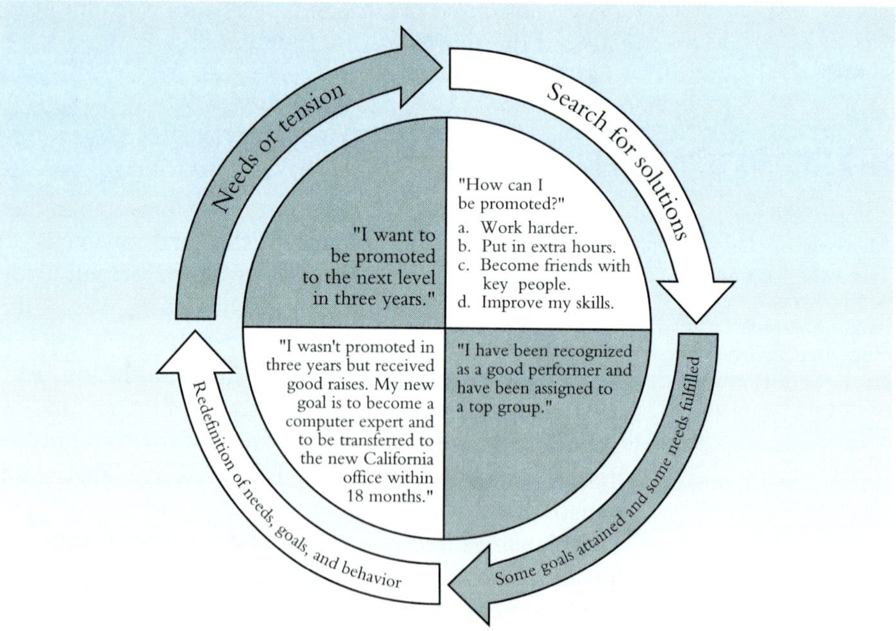

To create the atmosphere their subordinates need to perform efficiently, managers must have some grasp of the motivation process. As recognized management educator and consultant Peter Drucker stated: "No matter how authoritarian the institution, it has to satisfy the ambitions and needs of its members and do so in their capacity as individuals."[4] The rest of this chapter discusses various types of needs and how they can be used to motivate and manage employees.

THEORIES OF MANAGEMENT AND NEEDS

Maslow's Needs Hierarchy

A popular theory of human needs that helps us understand motivation is psychologist Abraham Maslow's **needs hierarchy.** He identified five basic needs that explain the internal motivation process: physiological, safety, social, esteem, and self-actualization needs.[5]

Needs Hierarchy
A motivational theory, offered by Maslow, that people have five needs arranged in a hierarchy from physiological to self-realization.

Five Need Levels. The needs Maslow identified fall into a hierarchy, or arrangement, of power to motivate behavior, as illustrated in Exhibit 10.2. Each higher-order need becomes active and motivates a person only when lower-level needs have been fulfilled. Each person is assumed to have needs in each category. Examples of job satisfiers that can fulfill the needs are also included in Exhibit 10.2.

Physiological Need
Biological needs, such as food, air, water.

Safety Need
Security need, such as the need to be financially secure and protected against job loss.

The starting point for understanding motivation is **physiological needs.** The person who is hungry or tired is thinking about food or sleep, not work. But once physiological needs are fulfilled, they lose their power to motivate. Then **safety needs** become important. For instance, workers are concerned about keeping their jobs and about being financially secure when they retire. "How safe is my job?" is a question being asked around the United States.

Around the world in late 1994 because of an economic recession many jobs were being eliminated and cut from the payroll. For example, every business day in 1994, approximately 2,000 Americans learned they would be losing their jobs.[6] Such cutbacks threaten an employee's sense of job security. Safety needs can be satisfied by the creation of seniority systems, pensions, and insurance plans. As with physiological needs, once most of the safety needs have been satisfied, the next level of needs becomes more important.

Social Need
The need to belong and to interact with other people.

Esteem Need
The need for self-respect and for respect from others.

Employees want to belong, to interact with other employees. Thus the friendly behavior of individuals in small groups within organizations is a major source of satisfaction for **social needs.** In a small group, individuals support and encourage one another; as a by-product, they get a sense of being an accepted member of the group. Once social needs have been largely satisfied, they also begin to lose their power to motivate.

The **esteem needs** are needs for self-respect and respect from others. An important part of this area is that an employee's work efforts and output be

Exhibit 10.2 *The Maslow Needs Hierarchy and Job Satisfiers*

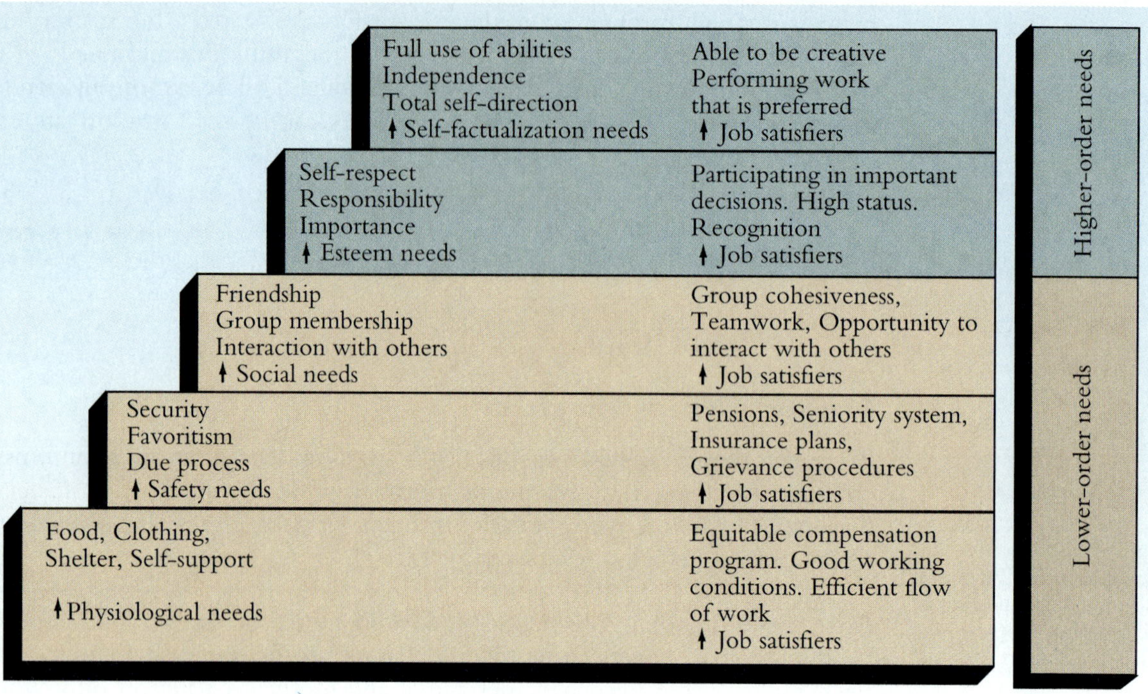

recognized and appreciated by others. When the need for esteem is strong, the individual will often set difficult goals, work hard to achieve the goals, and expect to receive recognition for these efforts. Goal accomplishment and the resulting recognition lead to feelings of self-esteem and self-confidence.

Self-Actualization Need
The need to use and display one's full range of skills and competence.

The top of the needs hierarchy is **self-actualization,** the ability to display and use one's full potential. This need takes over when an adequate level of satisfaction has been reached in the other four need levels. A person who reaches self-actualization has come close to using his or her full set of skills. Maslow noted that self-actualizing people display certain characteristics:

- They tend to be serious and thoughtful.
- They focus on problems outside themselves.
- Their behavior is unaffected and natural.
- They are strongly ethical.

Most people think of artists, composers, and scientists as seeking self-actualization. Because people work to satisfy the more basic needs, managers often overlook employees' self-actualization need.

Reaching a level of complete self-actualization rarely occurs. Certainly it is hard to achieve if other needs are not being adequately satisfied. But everyone is capable of partially satisfying the self-actualization need. Steve Jobs, one of the original founders of Apple Computer, achieved a sense of accomplishment by nurturing the personal computer concept. He had an insatiable desire to commercialize the Apple computer. He reached a state of satisfying his self-actualization needs.[7]

Of course employees differ in the intensity of their needs. Some have an intense security need that will dominate their behavior no matter what managers do. Others are more strongly influenced by esteem needs. Managers have no standard program to follow when attempting to encourage a high level of motivation. Differences in personal background, experience, and education are powerful; conditions that work for one individual may not work for another.

McGregor's Theory X and Theory Y

Although managers should try to understand needs, they often don't. Douglas McGregor, a professor of management, introduced a theory of managerial style, referred to as Theory X and Theory Y, to explain this phenomenon.[8]

Theory X
Managerial assumptions that employees dislike work, responsibility, and accountability and must be closely directed and controlled to be motivated to perform.

Theory X managers believe the average employee:

- Dislikes work and finds ways to avoid it as much as possible.
- Responds to threats of punishment or control because of the dislike of work.
- Avoids responsibility because of a lack of ambition.
- Wants to be directed and have security.

A problem with making such assumptions about people is that they can become self-fulfilling. A manager with a Theory X view of workers will probably focus on creating conditions to satisfy physiological and safety needs, closely controlling and supervising subordinates. Of course some employees respond favorably to this style, but others feel frustrated, anxious, and very much in conflict. Their goals for self-esteem and self-actualization cannot be achieved.

Theory Y
Managerial assumptions that employees want to be challenged, like to display creativity, and can be highly motivated to perform well if given some freedom to direct or manage their own behavior.

Theory Y, on the other hand, is a set of managerial assumptions that results in looser control and more delegation of authority. The Theory Y manager assumes that the average employee:

- Enjoys work and does not want to avoid it.
- Wants to achieve organizational goals through self-directed behavior.
- Responds to rewards associated with accomplishing goals.
- Will accept responsibility.
- Has initiative and can be creative in solving organizational problems.
- Is intellectually underutilized.

According to McGregor, Theory Y assumptions reflect a managerial emphasis on human growth and development instead of coercive authority.

Theory X and Theory Y represent two extremely different positions—an autocratic management style and a democratic management style. Many workers now demand Theory Y behavior from managers. They want to satisfy some of their social, esteem, and self-actualization needs on the job, and

Theory X-oriented management behavior only produces frustration and anxiety. Because of our democratic political heritage, the idea of Theory Y is more appealing to most people. On the other hand, some workers don't respond well in a Theory Y-oriented organization; some job situations call for autocratic controls. The key is the manager. He or she must review the people involved and the situation and then determine if a Theory X or a Theory Y management style will work.

Ouchi's Theory Z

The economic growth and power of Japan has garnered a lot of publicity. In the past decade, it outperformed other countries in a number of industries. This performance miracle is attributed to many factors, such as business–government cooperation, operating with relatively new (post-World War II) plants and equipment, a homogeneous ethnic population, a group-oriented culture, and even a rigorous educational system (see Exhibit 10.3).

Theory Z Management theory that draws on the characteristics of successful Japanese and American managers; emphasizes consensus management practices.

Another factor in the successes achieved by a highly motivated work force is called the **Theory Z** style of management. William Ouchi's Theory Z approach draws on characteristics of successful U.S. and Japanese management styles and organizational practices. Ouchi, a management researcher, emphasizes these characteristics of Theory Z practices:[9]

- Lifetime employment (to help satisfy physiological and safety needs).
- Consensus decision making (to help satisfy social needs).
- Individual responsibility (to help satisfy self-esteem needs).
- Careful evaluation and promotion (to build confidence and self-esteem).
- Opportunity to use skills (to help satisfy self-actualization needs).

Exhibit 10.3 *Blending American and Japanese Styles into Theory Z*

	Management Style		
Characteristic	**American**	**Japanese**	**Theory Z**
Length of employment	Relatively short-term; layoffs when business is slow.	Long term; lifetime when possible.	Retain employees in good and bad times.
Evaluation and promotion	Short-term and rapid promotions.	Longer-term and moderate promotion schedule.	Evaluate skills and promotions based on contributions, not tenure.
Decision making	Individual.	Collective, with input from all parties.	Use of a democratic process that strives for consensus.
Responsibility	Individual.	Shared by group.	Responsibility remains with key individuals.
Control	Control by use of policies and rules.	Self-control.	Informal but with an emphasis on objective facts and data.
Concern for workers	Emphasis on work itself.	Focus on entire life of workers.	Concerned with worker's life and family.

Source: A. Parasuraman, *Marketing Research*, © 1995 by Addison-Wesley Publishing Co., p. 20. Reprinted by permission of the Addison-Wesley Publishing Co., Reading, MA.

A comparison of U.S., Japanese, and Theory Z styles (see Exhibit 10.3) illustrates the blending of the first two approaches into the third.

Theory Z places a special emphasis on participative management. Employees participate in goal setting, decision making, problem solving, and designing and implementing changes. Participation, or being involved, is thought to improve employee motivation. Of course, some workers may prefer not to participate in these areas. This point should be kept in mind when an enthusiastic advocate of Theory Z and participation attempts to get everyone involved. Some people simply want to do their job and go home. Likewise some firms or jobs have a culture or atmosphere in which participation would not work. For example, in a business with only one trained scientist working in research and development, the scientist would listen to others but the experimentation and testing of new ideas would be carried out by only the one trained person.

As with Theory X and Theory Y, the Theory Z assumptions and suggestions have not been scientifically tested or evaluated. There is no solid evidence to support any of these explanations. However, each offers a perspective on the behavior of employees in organizations. And managers are interested in each perspective to help explain the differences they observe daily among their employees.

Herzberg's Two-Factor Model of Motivation

Work Motivation Model
An explanation of motivation that defines hygiene factors and motivator factors, and how they affect job satisfaction and dissatisfaction.

Hygiene Factor
External characteristic essential to avoiding job dissatisfaction.

In the 1950s, Frederick Herzberg, a social psychologist and consultant, proposed a **work motivation model** that is still very popular among business managers.[10] Herzberg surveyed accountants and engineers, asking them to describe when they felt good or bad about their jobs. He found that one set of job and personal factors produced good feelings and that another created bad feelings.

One set of factors Herzberg called **hygiene factors** (also called maintenance factors). These factors, if present and available, are essential to job satisfaction, although they cannot motivate an employee. They include:

Salary	Working conditions	Technical supervision
Job security	Status	Company policies
Personal life	Interpersonal relations	

Hygiene factors, if absent or inadequate, cause job dissatisfaction. Herzberg believes that by providing these factors, managers can prevent job dissatisfaction but cannot motivate employees to perform any better.

Motivator
Content-oriented characteristic that contributes to job satisfaction.

The second set of factors was described by Herzberg as **motivators** of on-the-job behavior. They include:

Achievement	Advancement	Growth opportunities
Recognition	The job itself	Responsibility

While hygiene factors deal with external features of the job, motivators are job-content oriented, or tied to the job itself.

Paychecks, according to Herzberg's two-factor model of work motivation, are essential to preventing dissatisfaction but cannot motivate employees to better job performance.

The employee appreciates the hygiene and motivator factors at different times. For example, the employee takes a paycheck (hygiene factor) to a bank, cashes it, and receives some satisfaction when the money is received. While actually performing the work, the employee can receive and enjoy such motivators as responsibility, recognition, and growth opportunities. These and other motivator factors make up the fabric of the job.

Omni Hotels has established a motivator-based program for its hardworking employees.[11] The Omni Service Champion (OSC) program recognizes employees who go beyond the call of duty to ensure guest satisfaction. Employees observed doing something extra to help a guest are given OSC commendations on the spot. Commendations have been given for packing luggage for a guest with a broken hand, saving someone's life at the hotel pool, or taking a taxi to another location to get something fixed for a customer. On the 1st, 5th, 10th, 15th, and 20th days of each month, the recognized employees receive the OSC medal that is worn on the uniform. At the end of the year, the three employees from each Omni hotel who received the most medals are awarded medals and cash prizes, and they attend a gala celebration to culminate the program for the year.

TQM

Hygiene factors can result in not being dissatisfied, but they are not motivational. Managers need to know this because the elimination of job dissatisfaction will not necessarily motivate employees. Exhibit 10.4 presents Herzberg's thinking on this issue. If motivation is what the manager wants to achieve, then he or she must emphasize recognition, achievement, and growth—the motivators.

Maslow and Herzberg: A Comparison

Maslow's needs hierarchy and Herzberg's work motivation model have many similarities, as Exhibit 10.5 (on page 336) shows. The lower-level needs are similar to the hygiene factors. These needs are satisfied for many employees, but some have not adequately fulfilled their lower-level needs. Then hygiene factors may be motivators. Today managers pay more attention to the higher-level needs, or motivator factors, than they did previously.

Exhibit 10.4
The Dissatisfaction-Satisfaction Relationship: An Application

Job factors	Worker dissatisfaction with the job	Neutral about the job	Satisfaction with the job
Motivators		Little or no satisfaction with motivators "I'm not being challenged by my job."	Satisfaction "My job is now really challenging me."
Hygienes	Dissatisfaction with the hygiene factors "I am dissatisfied with my working conditions."	Little or no dissatisfaction "My job is OK, I guess."	

Although Herzberg's model is popular and makes sense, it has been criticized. Some critics remind us that the original study group from which the model was developed included only engineers and accountants. These two occupational groups do not represent most employees (salesclerks, computer operators, teachers, police officers, scientists, nurses) in organizations. In response Herzberg cites studies that used nurses, supervisors, scientists, food handlers, and assemblers and found results similar to his original study. Other critics question the manner in which Herzberg collected his information. They believe that his method of asking questions influenced the way the accountants and engineers responded.

Despite these criticisms, the work motivation model is used by many managers, as it is logical and uses language that managers understand. However, it was not Maslow, McGregor, or Herzberg who really stimulated management thinking about motivation at work. It was the Hawthorne studies.

We have discussed types of needs that employees have. Your Values and Attitudes examines the Maslow needs hierarchy. Take a few minutes and complete the scale. Maslow's needs hierarchy provides a useful framework for managers.[12] Now let's talk about how managers can use their knowledge of these needs to motivate their employees and thus increase their production.

MOTIVATING EMPLOYEES

The group incentive plan in the Hawthorne studies did not motivate the employees as expected. Those and other studies show that there is no magic formula for providing employees with the interest and desire to perform well—although some programs work better than others. The manager's job is to find the best motivational trigger for his or her group and situation. For some,

Exhibit 10.5 *Similarities in the Needs Hierarchy and Work Motivation Model*

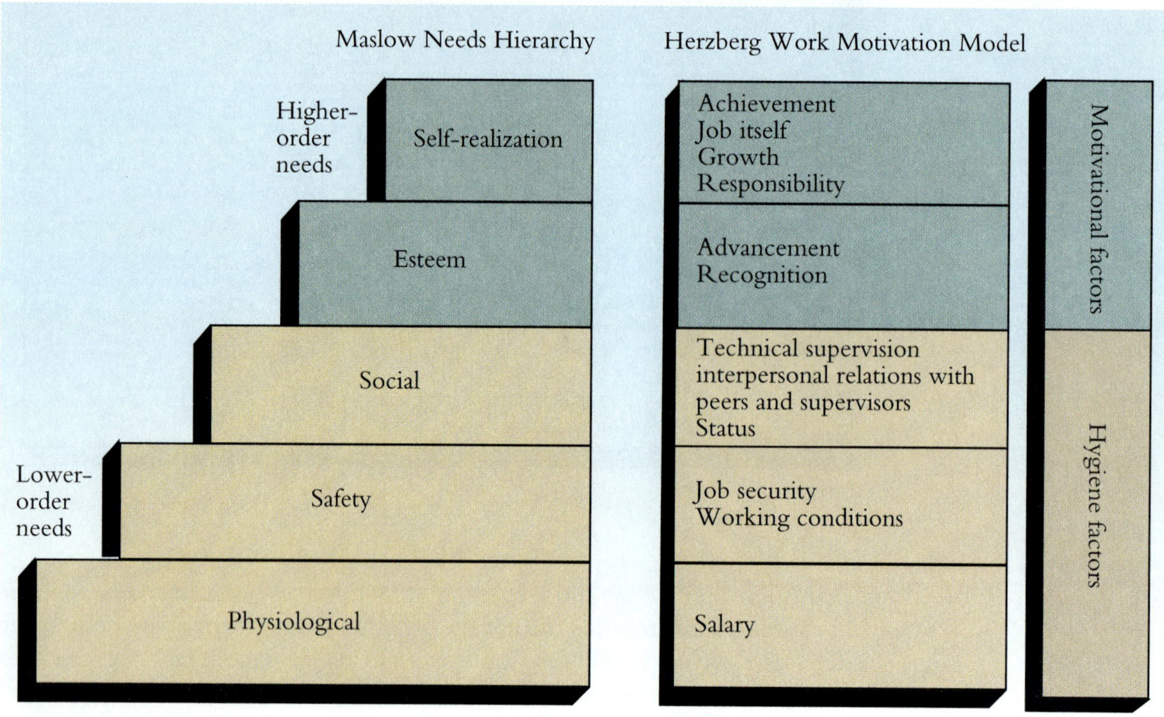

YOUR VALUES AND ATTITUDES

What Motivates You?

Directions: Circle the number under the response that best describes your own feelings about the statement. There are no right or wrong answers; the purpose of this questionnaire is simply to organize your own thoughts about your personal preferences.

	Strongly Agree	**Agree**	**Neither**	**Disagree**	**Strongly Disagree**
1. I value friendship more than almost anything else.	5	4	3	2	1
2. Just knowing I've done something well gives me satisfaction; I don't need praise from others.	1	2	3	4	5
3. Being happy is more important to me than making money.	5	4	3	2	1

	Strongly Agree	Agree	Neither	Disagree	Strongly Disagree
4. I need a lot of time by myself.	1	2	3	4	5
5. My first priority is high income and job security.	5	4	3	2	1
6. I don't believe people should waste their time pursuing dreams.	1	2	3	4	5
7. I feel disgusted if someone else gets credit for my accomplishments.	5	4	3	2	1
8. I'm more concerned with whether or not I enjoy my work than what I get paid for doing it.	1	2	3	4	5

Feedback: This quiz measures one's current motivational interests. This insight will help you understand why you view the interests of others to be similar or different.

Score your answers by filling in the numbers you have circled in the form below. Your scores will range from 2 to 10 on each of the four need scales. The four need scores correspond to the four higher-order categories of needs (or motives) identifed by Abraham Maslow. The lowest-level need category, physiological needs (food, shelter, water, etc.), is not included.

High-scale scores are 8, 9, or 10. Did you score high on more than one scale? Which ones? Do you think your scores accurately describe your own predominant motives?

Items	Scores	Need Scale
5 + 8	____+____=____	Safety, security
1 + 4	____+____=____	Belongingness, social
2 + 7	____+____=____	Self-esteem
3 + 6	____+____=____	Self-actualization

money is a key, whereas others prefer more job authority, and still others like to have clear objectives to use as targets.

In a free market society motivation is a powerful force, as described in Today's Business World.

Goal Setting

TQM

The notion that employees' motivation and performance may be enhanced by setting specific job performance goals has gained popularity in the past 20 years. As a result of research, some specific principles of goal setting have been

TODAY'S BUSINESS WORLD

A Free-Market Motivator

Joseph Schumpeter was a world class Austrian economist. At the end of World War II, Schumpeter predicted two things: Eastern Europeans would throw off communism because they need and want decent, good quality consumer goods and the West would vote in socialism because those who produced wealth within their societies would become envied. The first prediction has largely come true, and the second prediction is still percolating.

Paul Pilzer is a motivational speaker who lectures to companies such as Connecticut Mutual, Amway distributors of Yeager Enterprises, and American Airlines. He uses history and stories to outline the power of motivation. He tells the story about Boris and Igor, two serfs who lived in Russia. Each kept a goat. Boris discovered he could get more milk and prosper by treating his goat better. Pretty soon he could afford to fix the roof and buy tools he needed. But Igor was jealous. He prayed to his genie, "I want you to kill Boris's goat." Jealousy influenced the feelings and thoughts of Boris. This historical story has a connection to what is happening today in the United States, according to Pilzer.

Pilzer tells another story about the old days. Ten men are living on an island in the Pacific, pulling fish out of the ocean with fishing lines to feed their families. Then one day a missionary arrives bringing a new piece of technology called a net. Now two men can catch enough fish for everyone. What happens? Unemployment! How much? Pilzer's audience yells out, "eighty percent!" So someone gets the idea on the island to tax the two guys with the net. Pilzer believes that this story has a message about motivation and taxes. From 1930 until several years ago in the United States, taxes worked just like they did on the island in the Pacific. The people with the nets were taxed. However, on the island, some brilliant thinkers came up with the idea that one of the men wanted to be a teacher so he could do his job and be paid with fish. Another man was a good carpenter, and he was paid for his work with fish. Pretty soon all the men were working, and there was enough fish, education, and nicely constructed huts for everyone.

Pilzer uses history, storytelling, and his understanding of motivation to promote the free market and the creation of wealth. Schumpeter's second prediction five decades ago doesn't have to come true. Pilzer doesn't believe that one person's gain depends on another person's loss. He believes that wealth creation in a society of motivated men and women is possible by using logic, creative thinking, and the work ethic of people. Do you think that Pilzer has an accurate understanding of motivation?

Source: Adapted from Robert D. Hof, "The Education of Andrew Grove," *Business Week* (January 16, 1993): 60–62; Duncan Maxwell Anderson, "Unlimited Wealth," *Success* (October 1993): 21–28.

Goal Setting
The process of identifying specific levels of performance to be achieved in a certain time frame.

established.[13] **Goal setting** is the process of identifying specific levels of performance that a person seeks to accomplish in a certain time frame.

Probably the best-established goal-setting principle is that workers perform at higher levels when asked to meet a specific challenging goal than they do when simply asked to "do your best" or when no goal at all is assigned. This principle relates the effectiveness of goal setting not only to *specific* goals but also to *challenging* goals. However, when goals become too difficult, performance drops because the goals are seen as unrealistic. For example, a usually average student setting a goal to be the number one person in the class might be unrealistic.

Another interesting goal-setting concept is to involve workers in the process. Meaningful goals that employees have helped to set may enhance performance more than goals that are simply assigned by a manager. The logic is that, by participating, a person becomes more committed and develops a stronger drive to accomplish the goal.

Feedback on goal accomplishments is also important.[14] People want to know how they are doing. Whether the accomplishment concerns schoolwork, hitting a baseball, or drawing a picture, people value feedback. A study of different units in the U.S. Air Force showed that feedback and goal setting together helped improve performance for work groups as opposed to individuals.[15]

Managers can use goal setting to motivate employees. Setting specific, challenging goals and providing feedback about goal accomplishment enhance motivation and performance. Management by objectives (MBO), discussed in Chapter 7, involves the use of goal setting either throughout an organization or within units.

One excellent goal setter and goal accomplisher is Harvey Cook, the author of *Scientific Success*. He sells insurance only two days a week for seven months out of the year. He sells $4 million of insurance in the first eight days.[16] His advice: "Don't compete for number 1; compete with yourself." Cook uses a 15-minute time guide for his goals; he breaks his day into 15-minute increments.

According to Cook, a person must decide what to accomplish in each 15-minute period of the day. A salesperson's game plan might be:

- Every 15 minutes, make the three telephone calls you'll need to get one qualified appointment.
- Spend 35 minutes of selective canvassing with potential clients to get one appointment.
- Line up 16 appointments to make the 11 client presentations you need in order to close at least 10 sales every two days.

Don't just set goals to increase numbers. Use tools of motivation to improve effectiveness. Novelists such as Irving Wallace and Ernest Hemingway used reinforcement systems and goals to increase their writing productivity. Day by day they would chart the number of words they had written. That number compared to a goal scolded or encouraged the author. Hemingway accumulated words he'd written over his goal so he could reward himself with a day off. Goal setting is a powerful technique that, when combined with rewards, sanctions, and self-discipline, can be a powerful motivating force.

Job Enrichment

Job Enrichment
A motivational technique that involves incorporating variety, feedback, and autonomy in the job.

In his work motivation model, Herzberg introduced **job enrichment,** a method intended to increase the motivation and satisfaction of employees and to improve production through job design. By adding more motivators to the job, job enrichment can make work meaningful, stimulating, and challenging. The employee comes to view the job a lot like play. Don Ritcher owns an Arby's Restaurant in Chicago. He did not use authority, commands, and directives to motivate his employees to be courteous to customers, show up for work on time, help keep the restaurant immaculate, and work hard. Instead he created an achievement-oriented franchise. He permitted his workers to establish flexible work schedules to fit their needs, he instituted an "employee of the week" reward program, he held discussion meetings and allowed each employee to present opinions on how to improve business and service, and he let employees attend development seminars to improve their skills. He made working at Arby's more meaningful and interesting.

The first step in job enrichment is to determine which characteristics of a job increase motivation. Picture the golfer hitting a bag of practice balls. Such practice is meaningful because the hitting skill can be improved. The golfer is in charge of every shot attempted. Once a shot is made, the golfer receives immediate feedback on how well the ball was hit. The sense of hitting the ball well is important in determining the golfer's "psychological feelings" about practicing; it serves to motivate him or her to continue or to come back for another practice session.

The same is true for an employee doing a job. Motivational jobs contain the following characteristics:

- *Meaningfulness*—the work must be perceived as worthwhile.
- *Responsibility*—the employee must be personally responsible for any effort expended.
- *Knowledge of results*—the employee must receive, on a regular basis, feedback about how well he or she is performing.

When these conditions are present, jobholders usually feel good about the job and their contribution. These good feelings motivate employees to continue to do well. But if one of these three conditions is missing, the internal feeling (motivation) drops off dramatically.

Studies indicate that five job characteristics create good psychological feelings about a job.[17] These characteristics can be enriched by a manager. Three of the five characteristics contribute to the meaningfulness of a job:

- *Skill variety*—the degree to which a job requires activities that are challenging.
- *Task identity*—the degree to which the job requires the completion of a "whole" piece of work. For example, building an entire generator has more tasks than just placing a flywheel on the generator as it passes by on a conveyer belt.
- *Task significance*—the degree to which the job is significant to the organization or other individuals.

A fourth job characteristic leads an employee to experience more responsibility: *Autonomy* is the degree to which the job gives the worker freedom, independence, and leeway to carry out what is required. The fifth job characteristic, *feedback,* is the degree to which a worker gets information on his or her effectiveness in carrying out the job.

Such organizations as AT&T, Saab-Scania, Volvo, and General Foods have used job enrichment to motivate employees; they have redesigned or changed job characteristics for various employees or groups. But like all sound motivation programs, job enrichment must be used selectively. Management must also provide enough time for the approach to be understood. The user must consider the situation, the job, and the people involved (see Exhibit 10.6). Job characteristics that can be enriched are especially important for employees who desire enrichment. The potential consequences for these workers are spelled out in the figure. Usually, if the organization supports enrichment, more employees desire the job changes.

Quality of Work Life

Quality of Work Life (QWL)
Managerial programs that increase outcomes such as productivity or performance by better management of jobs, people, and working conditions.

The term **quality of work life (QWL)** describes a wide variety of approaches to improve the quality of human experience in the workplace. The work experience is improved to help individuals satisfy needs and accomplish goals and to give more relevance to a person's work-related contributions.[18] QWL approaches are designed to help employees feel good about themselves, their jobs, and their organizations. As such they are considered motivational.

The following dimensions have been associated with QWL:

- Adequate and fair compensation.
- Safe and healthy working conditions.
- Opportunities to develop human capacities.
- Opportunities for continued growth and job security.
- More flexible work scheduling and job assignments.
- Careful attention to work flow and job design, and worker participation in designing work.
- Attempts to achieve more and better union-management cooperation.
- Less structural supervision and more development of effective work teams.

Exhibit 10.6
Job Characteristics, Individual Differences, and Reactions

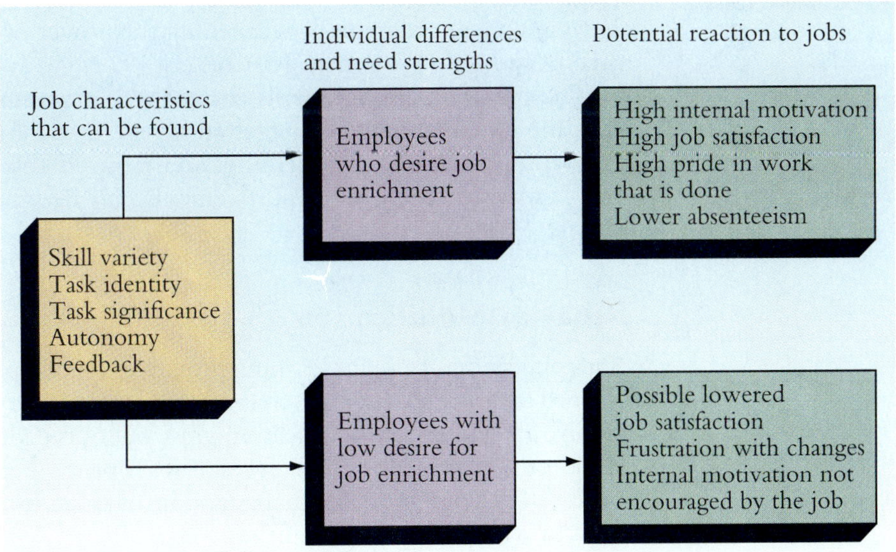

Nissan improves its employees' quality of work life by providing them with exercise equipment at the Nissan Fitness Center in Tennessee. Centers such as this one can provide a release for job stress and improve employees' physical health.

These and other QWL approaches have been used by such firms as Xerox, Nabisco, Weyerhaeuser, and Procter & Gamble. These firms have recognized that managers attempting to motivate employees need to be aware of the kinds of factors involved in the eight dimensions listed. The commitment to employee needs, goals, and satisfaction must be continual.

Despite the humanistic orientation of QWL programs, there has been some resistance. First, some managers are not convinced that the QWL programs have lasting effects on motivation or productivity. Second, the changeover to a QWL program often costs money in terms of time, people, and equipment resources; in tight economic times, such costs become threatening and unacceptable. Third, some unions have resisted QWL programs; they view these programs as weakening the power of the union in its adversarial relationship with management.

The pro and con arguments about QWL programs will continue. However, the potential benefits suggested by QWL advocates—such as improved motivation, increased productivity, and reduced costs—convince more and more managers that QWL improvements may be worthwhile in the organization.

Behavior Modification

Behavior Modification
Application of learning principles called operant conditioning.

The application of a set of learning principles called operant conditioning, developed by psychologist B. F. Skinner (1904–1990), is called **behavior modification.**[19] Behavior modification grew out of the idea that changing the attitude of a person does not necessarily improve performance. Instead the person's behavior must be changed. This is done by changing the environment in which the person behaves.

Skinner believed that the way people behave is a function of heredity, past experiences, and the present situation. Managers can control only the present situation. Therefore Skinner recommends that managers consider these two points: (1) If an act (behavior) is followed by a pleasant consequence (say, a pat on the back), it probably will be repeated: (2) if an act is followed by an unpleasant consequence (a reprimand, a harsh glare), it probably will not be repeated. The manager's job is to design the present situation so that good performance will result.

Reinforcer
A consequence of behavior that improves the chances it will or will not reoccur.

Positive Reinforcer
A consequence of behavior such as praise or other rewards that, when administered, increases the chances that the behavior will be repeated.

Negative Reinforcer
A consequence of behavior such as a reprimand that, when administered, encourages an employee to adapt more desirable behavior to avoid the unpleasant consequence.

The manager can shape the behavior of subordinates by controlling the reinforcers. A **reinforcer** is a consequence of behavior, one that can improve the likelihood that the behavior will or will not occur again. For example, praise—a **positive reinforcer**—given immediately after an employee completes a job on time may increase the occurrence of finishing work on time. Or a reprimand—a **negative reinforcer**—given immediately for not finishing on time may also increase the likelihood of work being done on time. By finishing on time, the employee creates a situation in which the supervisor will not issue a reprimand.

An interesting reinforcer-based program is used by a Chicago firm, Mediatech. Each week the firm contributes $250 to the Mediatech Employee Lottery.[20] All of the 350 full-time and 25 part-time employees in the firm's offices in New York, Los Angeles, and Chicago are eligible for the lottery. Their hopes of winning rest on the employees' last four digits of their payroll identification number. Every Monday, a different employee spins a wheel at Mediatech's headquarters. Depending on where the wheel lands, there is either a Friday afternoon drawing or the prize money rolls over until the next week. The money accumulates. The biggest winnings on a Friday so far have been $1,000. Other prizes are also given for $600, $300, and $100. Attendance on Friday has improved significantly in all of Mediatech's offices. The reinforcer (winning the lottery) increases the likelihood of coming to work.

Punishment influences behavior by presenting something distasteful or withdrawing something that is liked. For example, a manager says something rude to an employee and receives disapproval (punishment) from other managers. If the disapproval is unpleasant enough, the manager's rudeness is less likely to occur in the future. Another kind of punishment takes something pleasant away. Suppose Nick Rodman, a project engineer, is assigned temporarily to a group that is important to him. Because Rodman frequently arrives late to work for the new assignment, he is placed back in a regular work group. Rodman is not able to work with the group he likes because of his tardiness. He has been punished.

Punishment and negative reinforcement are not the same. In negative reinforcement, an act (completing work on time) that allows the person to avoid some unpleasant event (supervisor's reprimand) is reinforced when the unpleasant event is removed. In punishment, one of two things happens: (1) An unpleasant event (group disapproval) follows a behavior (rude remark), or (2) a pleasant event (being a member of a group) is taken away after a behavior (tardiness).

Managers applying behavior modification on the job must:

1. Identify the elements of a job that are observable and measurable.
2. Measure how frequently behaviors occur.
3. Positively reinforce the person when a correct behavior occurs.

These procedures have met with some success at Emery Worldwide, the air freight carrier. Emery personnel load containers with packages and ship them by air. Management had assumed that containers were always being loaded to capacity, but a check found that containers were being fully loaded only 45 percent of the time. A list of employee activities and goals for filling containers was developed. Results were recorded in terms of container use so that team results could be compared. By correcting deficiencies and providing feedback and recognition for good performance, management increased container capacity.

Like other motivation programs, behavior modification has its critics. Some view it as a technique that Skinner transferred to humans after conducting trial experiments with animals such as pigeons. They claim that employees are not pigeons and do not respond like pigeons. Another criticism is that behavior modification is too artificial. The employee who receives reinforcement should know why he or she receives a reward. In most behavior modification programs, positive reinforcers are provided without an explanation. The complexity of the work environment often leaves no time to explain their use. Finally, behavior modification has a manipulative aspect. Behavioral consequences are controlled, and people are forced to change behavior instead of changing behavior on their own initiative. This approach is not consistent with the theme that people should act freely. The need for self-actualization is not recognized, which is considered dehumanizing.

SUMMARY OF LEARNING OBJECTIVES

1. ***Define the term* scientific management.** Scientific management is the scientific study and breakdown of work into its smallest mechanical elements, and then rearrangement into their most efficient combination.

2. ***Explain what the Hawthorne studies revealed about the role that groups play in motivating employees.*** The Hawthorne studies at the Western Electric plant showed the importance of informal work groups as motivators of employees. Work groups can affect individual behavior. The studies also showed that the employees felt they were special because they were involved in the experiment. This feeling of specialness causes their work performance to improve.

3. ***Define the term* motivation.** Motivation is the way in which drives or needs direct a person's behavior toward a specific goal. It determines the level of effort a person puts forth to achieve the goal. It is an unobservable phenomenon that takes place inside everyone. Managers can readily observe a person's behavior, but they can only make assumptions about what causes the person to behave in that way.

4. ***Discuss Maslow's view of needs and motivation.*** Maslow believed that people's behavior was motivated by their desire to fulfill needs. These needs were arranged in a hierarchy from the most basic survival needs at the bottom to self-fulfilling needs at the top. The need levels are physiological, safety, social, esteem, and self-actualization. After needs on the lowest level have been satisfied, people are motivated to fulfill needs at the next highest level.

5. ***Compare and contrast the Theory X, Theory Y, and Theory Z approaches to motivating employees.*** Managers have the challenging task of identifying their

employees' needs in order to motivate them to perform better. They can also determine how their style of managing influences employee behavior. McGregor's *Theory X* manager is concerned with helping employees satisfy lower-level physiological and safety needs; such managers are more autocratic and controlling. *Theory Y* managers are concerned with fulfilling their employees' higher-level needs; their managerial style results in looser control and more delegation of authority. *Theory Z* managers emphasize lifetime employment, consensus decision making, and giving employees the opportunity to use their skills.

6. ***Explain why Herzberg's view of motivation is so popular with practicing managers.*** Herzberg's theory of motivation uses understandable managerial language and instructs managers that motivators should be used to create a more positive work environment. Motivators are conditions such as employees having increased responsibility, more advancement opportunities, and more recognition for good work.

7. ***Describe the principles of goal setting.*** Goal setting is a way to motivate employees. One principle holds that employees perform better when given specific, challenging goals than when they are given no goals at all or simply told to do their best. Workers also should be involved in the goal-setting process and should be given timely, meaningful feedback on their performance.

KEY TERMS

Scientific Management
Hawthorne Studies
Motivation
Extrinsic Reward
Intrinsic Reward
Punishment
Needs Hierarchy
Physiological Need
Safety Need
Social Need
Esteem Need
Self-Actualization Need
Theory X
Theory Y
Theory Z
Work Motivation Model
Hygiene Factor
Motivator
Goal Setting
Job Enrichment
Quality of Work Life (QWL)
Behavior Modification
Reinforcer
Positive Reinforcer
Negative Reinforcer

QUESTIONS FOR DISCUSSION AND REVIEW

1. Would the Mary Kay Ash approach to motivation work well with all women? Why?
2. Theory Z, like Theories X and Y, has not been proven scientifically. Why has Theory Z had an impact on management practices when it has not been scientifically verified?
3. Can the principles of goal setting be applied to nonwork settings such as school, family, or leisure activities? Explain.
4. What are the challenges that will face managers attempting to help motivate an increasingly diverse (e.g., ethnic, gender, age) work force?
5. Can the Hawthorne effect influence motivation negatively? Explain.
6. Why would behavior modification appeal to some managers?
7. How does goal setting work in terms of motivating an employee? A student?

8. Which motivational techniques are used by teachers? Which motivational techniques should be used by more teachers?

9. Do the principles of scientific management still apply to current managerial situations? Explain.

10. How can managers improve their ability to motivate employees?

CASE 10.1

Pay for Performance: An Application

The merit pay increases people receive are the most specific information they are given as to how well they are performing. The motivating potential of a merit pay increase is especially important if employees equate pay with performance. A pay raise can be interpreted as a reward or as a punishment.

Managers never have enough raise money to go around. Someone is always left out or believes that the system is unfair. In this case, you will serve as a manager who has a raise pool of $14,000 and must grant raises to six subordinates, all of whom have worked less than one year in the firm. You are the sole decision maker. Write down how much each person would receive and explain your decisions.

B. Nostocke: Is having adjustment problems. Performance has become worse. Nostocke is always on time, is eager to please, and works hard. Tries to serve as a resource person for a poorly trained group. Complains often about the company and its policies.

Present salary $36,300. Raise:

Comments:

A. Calero: Hard worker, good team player, has trouble correcting others. Has good background but lacks line management experience. Volunteers for tough projects.

Present salary $34,000. Raise:

Comments:

C. Babcock: Wastes time and is a big spender. Careless in comments and style. Not willing to compromise. Loses temper occasionally. Is highly skilled but doesn't seem to want to be part of a team. Likes to needle colleagues.

Present salary $32,000. Raise:

Comments:

R. Cisneros: Has trouble communicating ideas and problems. Is likable, willing to learn. Needs some training in computer skills and also in preparation of business plans. Hard worker who puts in long hours and works in miserably hot, dirty working conditions.

Present salary $34,000. Raise:

Comments:

P. Karsner: Lots of experience. Occasionally is a loafer and drags feet on projects not interested in. Creative, would like to be promoted as soon as possible. Has appeal to brighter and more skilled workers. Is not tolerant of unskilled workers.

Present salary $32,700. Raise:

Comments:

J. Webber: Is one of the most competent managers ever hired. Knows how to manage people. Every project worked on has been a success. Has ability to influence people. Is a good listener and is self-motivated.

Present salary $35,400. Raise:

Comments:

Questions for Discussion

1. Which person is the most difficult to judge in terms of allocating a merit-based raise?
2. What kind of information is provided here that gives some indication of the motivation level of these employees?
3. Should a manager discuss performance issues with the employee before making a raise decision? Explain.

CASE 10.2

The Motivation Crisis: Hitting the Wall

Many people have achieved great fame and fortune before turning 40. Mozart died five years before reaching 40. Alexander the Great conquered Asia Minor and died at 34. Michael Dell (founder of Dell Computers) was 21 when he began his march to being the head of a multibillion-dollar firm at this writing, and Tom Monaghan founded Domino's, which is now the largest home-delivery pizza chain, when he was 23 years old. When Jack Benny was in his 60s and 70s, he used to get laughs by claiming to be 39 instead of what he really was, say 74. Why did Benny pick 39?

Some consider 39 to be the last-gasp outpost of youth. In business, the goal to be president or the ambition to invent a world-renowned product may run smack into reality at 40. A 40-year-old often has a long history of work experience, including a few scars from failures.

Many 39-year-olds and even younger men and women have accomplished a lot. They may have been promoted every three or four years, and their compensation packages may be in six figures. They may also have realized that the corporate program or the management hierarchy is becoming narrow and that their opportunities are decreasing. The first 15 years in the work force are often years of advancement, recognition, autonomy, and high expectations. Motivational inspiration is all around. However, reality, burnout, fatigue, long hours, and travel are also common. By 40, motivational inspiration may be harder to find.

A few examples will highlight how self-motivation becomes a very serious concern for many people around 40 years old. Tim hit the wall at about 38 years old. He was a senior product manager at Borden's Consumer Products Division in Columbus, Ohio. He had always wanted to be president of a company. At 38 he realized that, at Borden, this wouldn't happen. His goals were being stalled. He left Borden and joined a manufacturing firm in Dayton. Today, at 44, as vice president for sales, marketing, and engineering applications for Freund Precision, he is happier and more realistic. He wants to be financially independent at 55, but he is not going to drive himself to exhaustion.

Juanita was a fast tracker when the birth of her son made her rethink her goals. The Princeton graduate had been only 34 when she stepped up to the top rung of the management ladder as president of telemarketing for Time-Life Libraries. At 36 she started to assess her life, the dizzying schedules and the frequent travel. She concluded that a person *can* have it all—but not all at the same time. By all, she meant success, power, money, recognition, time, energy, and influence. Juanita is now enjoying motherhood. When she wants to go back to managing, she will go back to work. She is confident, satisfied, and very aware of the costs and benefits of being a mother, wife, and management superstar.

About 4 million Americans turn 40 each year. Forty is the age at which reality, pyramid narrowing, and self-assessment become crucial. However, success can be measured in many ways. How a person copes depends on many things. Self-confidence, talent, resourcefulness, goals, and adaptability all count. People who love their work, have strong work ethics, and know themselves well will not be stymied by the "40" wall. The over-40 successes are the ones who, like Jack Benny, have a passion to accomplish, to achieve, and to be creative well into old age without feeling a day over 39.

Questions for Discussion

1. Can a person like Tim achieve a sense of self-actualization even though he hasn't achieved one of his major goals (becoming a president of a firm)? Explain.
2. What role does self-confidence play in terms of motivation for Juanita?
3. How did Tim and Juanita use self-assessment to their advantage in maintaining a strong degree of self-motivation?
4. What type of motivational self-assessment do you perform?

Source: Adapted from Gene N. Landren, *Profiles of Genius: Thirteen Creative Men Who Changed the World* (Buffalo, NY: Prometheus Books, 1993).

EXPERIENTIAL EXERCISE

Profiling Leaders as Motivators

Activity:
Students will review the motivational skills of leaders they have known or observed and develop profiles of such leaders. Approximately 30 minutes of class time will be needed.

Directions:
1. The instructor will review some of the motivation theories identified in the chapter.
2. Following the review of motivation theories each student is to think about a leader he/she has known or observed who was an effective motivator.
3. Each student is to write down the characteristics of the leader which contributed to being an effective motivator.
4. The instructor calls on a large number of students to individually share part of the list of personal characteristics of motivators.
5. The instructor is to write down the information shared by the students. The developing profile should be written on a chalkboard or overhead transparency.
6. At the conclusion of the exercise the instructor is to summarize the characteristics included in the profile of an effective motivator.

BUSINESS APPLICATION

Motivating Workers in Different Job Settings

Activity:
Students will participate in small group sessions analyzing motivation strategies in various types of job settings. About 40 minutes of class time will be needed.

Directions:
1. Divide the class into three groups of students, with each group electing a spokesperson/recorder.
2. Each of the three groups will develop strategies for motivating workers applicable to the job setting assigned.
   - Group 1 is to focus on motivating factory workers who are used to dull repetitious work.
   - Group 2 is to focus on sales workers in a department store.
   - Group 3 is to focus on motivating nurses in a hospital setting where turnover is high and morale is low.
3. Clarify that each group is to view the assignment from the management perspective of developing strategies to motivate workers within the particular work setting. (Allow 20 minutes for this part of the exercise).
4. Each group's spokesperson is to report the group's motivational strategies applicable to the particular setting.

5. The instructor should write the strategies on the chalkboard adjacent to the applicable setting. Following the reporting of strategies each group is to explain the rationale for selecting the particular strategies.
6. The instructor will summarize the strategies and supporting rationale provided by the groups.

NOTES

1. Adapted from Manfred F. R. Kets de Vries, "The Leadership Mystique," *Academy of Management Executive,* August 1994, pp. 73–89; Alan Farnham, "Mary Kay's Lessons in Leadership," *Fortune* (September 20, 1993): 68–77.
2. "Hawthorne Revisited: The Legend and the Legacy," *Organizational Dynamics* (Winter 1975): 66–80.
3. Ibid.
4. Peter Drucker, *Management Tasks, Responsibilities, Practices* (New York: Harper & Row, 1974), 504.
5. Abraham H. Maslow, ed., *Motivation and Personality* (New York: Harper & Row, 1954).
6. Louis B. Richman, "When Will the Layoffs End?" *Fortune* (September 20, 1993): 54–56.
7. Jeffrey Pfeffer, *Competitive Advantage Through People* (Cambridge, MA: Harvard Business School Press, 1994).
8. Douglas McGregor, *The Human Side of Enterprise* (New York: McGraw-Hill, 1960).
9. William Ouchi, *Theory Z* (Reading, MA: Addison-Wesley Publishing, 1981).
10. Frederick Herzberg, Bernard Mausner, and Barbara Snyderman, *The Motivation to Work* (New York: John Wiley & Sons, 1959).
11. Ronald Whipple, "Rewards Have Value," *Personnel Journal* (September 1990): 92–93.
12. Abraham H. Maslow, "Self-Actualizing People: A Study of Psychological Health," in *Motivation and Personality,* ed. Abraham H. Maslow (New York: Harper & Row, 1954).
13. Edwin Locke and Gary Latham, *A Theory of Goal Setting* (Englewood Cliffs, NJ: Prentice Hall, 1991).
14. Brian O'Reilly, "360-Degree Feedback Can Change Your Life," *Fortune* (October 17, 1994): 103–115.
15. R. D. Pritchard, S. D. Jones, P. L. Roth, K. K. Stuebing, and S. E. Ekeberg, "Effects of Group Feedback, Goal Setting, and Incentives on Productivity," *Journal of Applied Psychology* (April 1988): 337–358.
16. "The Science of Success: How to Develop New Performance Habits," *Success* (September 1990): 48–49.
17. J. R. Hackman and J. E. Suttle, eds., *Improving Life at Work: Behavioral Science Approaches to Organizational Change* (Santa Monica, CA: Goodyear Publishing, 1977).
18. Richard H. Axelrod, "Making Employee Participation Programs Work," *Quality Progress* (April 1994): 39–42.
19. B. F. Skinner, *About Behaviorism* (New York: Alfred A. Knopf, 1974).
20. Charles Storch, "A New Spin on Job Motivation," *Chicago Tribune* (September 23, 1990): 9E.

CHAPTER 11

Managing Human Resources

1. Define the term *human resource management (HRM)*.
2. Explain why human resource planning, recruiting, and selecting are important.
3. Describe job analysis, job descriptions, and job specifications.
4. Explain the role of the federal government in providing equal opportunities for employment to all Americans.
5. Discuss training and development programs for hourly and salaried employees.
6. Identify examples of direct and indirect compensation.
7. Discuss comparable worth.

The total quality management approach has been used in every area of business including marketing, finance, operations management, information systems, and accounting. At The Prudential Insurance Company of America the alignment of human resource systems with the company's mission and vision is now a yardstick to judge whether the firm is successful. Prudential has listed 10 human resource (HR) objectives:

1. Foster open communication.
2. Lead by example and assume personal responsibility.
3. Understand clients' needs.
4. Create an environment that's free from fear.
5. Reward and recognize individuals and teams.
6. Work toward continuous improvement.
7. Encourage education and development.
8. Emphasize teamwork and share successes.
9. Encourage innovation, creativity, and empowerment.
10. Measure performance and make decisions based on fact.

The company's revised mission is to be a world-class leader in providing relocation, real estate, human resources, and related consulting services to individuals and institutions globally while generating a satisfactory return. Above all, the company now strives to "delight its clients" and to do so with honesty, integrity, and mutual respect, realizing that its greatest asset in achieving this mission is its employees. As a learning organization, the firm states that its employees' ongoing education and development are critical to its success.

The goal of Prudential's 10 HR objectives was to recognize that the company's ongoing success is dependent on HR's ability to recognize and value each individual's unique differences and talents. The firm envisioned that a work environment supported by these 10 objectives would allow each person the opportunity to reach his or her fullest potential, and therefore directly contribute to and of course help improve the bottom line.

The firm's research suggested that the company's performance-management system was the first HR system that needed to be realigned with the company's new vision. The system had flaws in both design and execution. The biggest flaws were that it didn't clearly tie individual objectives to company objectives and that it lacked clear evaluation standards. Although people could be rated on a scale of 1 to 5 (from "needs substantial improvement" to "outstanding") in several areas such as client focus and technical ability, those performance dimensions needed further clarification.

The performance-management system underwent reconstruction. What emerged was a four-part improvement plan calling for:

1. *Systems improvements*: The plan requires feedback from three to five team members for each associate's (nonmanager's) performance evaluation. Everyone is reviewed—exempt and nonexempt—with a 360-degree feedback system. Also, managers are now responsible for coaching and counseling their direct reports (individuals) on a scheduled basis.
2. *Skills building*: A complaint about the old system was that managers, especially new managers, weren't trained on how to help employees set objectives and how to conduct

performance evaluations. Within the last several months, 700 of the company's 1,000 employees have received training in how to set objectives for themselves or for their subordinates.

3. *Education regarding the process and company expectations*: Employees are educated about how to set their job objectives based on company objectives.
4. *Management of the process*: There's now a cross-functional team responsible for managing the performance-management process—to make sure that there is continuous improvement and measurement of how the process itself is proceeding on a monthly or quarterly basis.

The new performance management system now includes setting performance objectives, ongoing communication and feedback between manager and associate, gathering associate input, client/project team input, performance review, and compensation review. The biggest difference between the company's old system and the new one is that performance management is viewed as a shared, rather than a one-sided, top-down responsibility.

For some organizations that decide to travel the total-quality road, results are immediate and measurable. Prudential Resources Management has found this to be true. Comparing its 1993 year-end results to 1991 (the year the company began its total-quality journey), it has found that:

- The number of clients it serves has nearly doubled.
- Overall client satisfaction increased almost 10 percent.
- Associate productivity jumped 5 percent.
- It increased its profits by 20 percent.

Why is Prudential's focus on tying quality objectives to HR systems so innovative? Sometimes, innovation is simply common sense put into action. However, common sense, as they say, often isn't common at all.

The fundamental key to business survival is people who are skilled to perform jobs. Nevertheless most human resource issues and problems have played second fiddle to other business decisions. Financial, production, and marketing judgments are usually made first, before people-related decisions. This second-class status is changing fast, though, as people—workers and managers—are recognized as a delicate, scarce commodity.

As many as 90 percent of all jobs in U.S. organizations will be candidates for change in the early part of the next century. The population and the work force are growing more slowly than at any other time since the 1930s. The average age of the population and work force is rising, and the pool of young workers entering the labor market is shrinking. Minorities represent a larger share of new entrants into the labor market, and more women are entering the work force. These rapidly changing demographics mean that human resource experts will work harder and longer to solve problems.

In businesses of any size—large, medium or small—human resources must be recruited, compensated, developed, and motivated. Small organizations typically cannot afford to have a separate HRM department that continually follows the progress of individuals and reviews the accomplishment of goals. Larger firms, such as Prudential, usually have an HRM department that can be a source of help to line managers. In large or small firms, with or without HRM departments, however, each manager is responsible for using the skills and talents of employees. And in either case, much of the work in recruitment, compensation, and performance appraisal must be finalized and implemented by managers.

In this chapter, we discuss the human resource management function's importance to business. We begin with human resource planning, recruitment, and selection. Laws governing recruitment and recruitment sources are discussed, as are drug and AIDS testing. We explain how a company arrives at a decision to hire a candidate for a job. In the section on training and development, we cover orientation, training, and management development, including performance appraisals. The next topic, compensation and benefits, includes direct and indirect compensation, individual and group incentives, comparable worth, benefits and services, and protection programs. The chapter concludes with a discussion of safe work environments.

THE WORK OF HRM

Human Resource Management (HRM) The process of acquiring, retaining, terminating, developing, and properly using the human resources in an organization.

Human resource management (HRM) can be defined as the process of accomplishing organizational objectives by acquiring, retaining, terminating, developing, and properly using the human resources in an organization. Accomplishing objectives is a major focus of any form of management. Unless objectives are met, the organization ceases to exist.

The success of any HRM program requires the cooperation of managers, who must interpret and implement policies and procedures. Line managers must translate into action what an HRM department provides. Without managerial support, HRM programs cannot succeed. Therefore, managers need to understand clearly how to mesh their responsibilities with those of the HRM department.

The human resource program at IBM serves the needs of the organization and facilitates the accomplishment of IBM's objectives. But this program would probably not be well suited for Apple or Compaq without modifications. Each company develops its own HRM program after considering such factors as size, type of skills needed, number of employees required, unionization, clients and customers, financial posture, and geographic location.

Acquiring skilled, talented, and motivated employees is an important part of HRM. The acquisition phase involves recruiting, screening, selecting, and properly placing personnel. Prudential and other firms are finding that acquiring the talent needed to survive is becoming more difficult; talented candidates are in short supply. If qualified individuals regularly leave a company, then that company must continually seek new personnel. This costs money and is time-consuming. Thus retention of productive people has become a major objective.

Developing human resources involves training, educating, appraising, and generally preparing personnel for present or future jobs. These activities are important for the employees' economic and psychological growth. Self-realization needs cannot be satisfied in an organization that does not have an efficient set of development activities.

The proper use of people involves understanding both individual and organizational needs so that the full potential of human resources can be employed. This aspect of human resources management suggests the importance of matching individuals over time to shifts in organizational and human needs. Exhibit 11.1 (on page 356) is an example of a human resource department in an organization large enough (usually over 1,000 employees) to have such a unit. In smaller firms, all the jobs shown in the figure are performed but usually by only one or two people. The objectives of HRM are to clarify the firm's human resource problems and develop solutions to them. HRM focuses on action, satisfying individual needs, and the future. The contribution of HRM to an organization's effectiveness is so important that managers must use the knowledge and skills of HRM specialists.

HUMAN RESOURCE PLANNING, RECRUITMENT, AND SELECTION

An organization can only be as effective as the people who operate the business. Thus, acquiring the people necessary to operate the business is the first step in any HRM program. To begin the process, managers throughout the organization need to establish human resource plans. Recruitment, selection, placement, and other employment actions stem from this planning.

Planning

Human Resource Planning
The steps taken in estimating the size and makeup of the future work force.

Human resource planning involves estimating the size and makeup of the future work force. This process helps the firm acquire the right number and kinds of people when they are needed. Experience indicates that the longer the period predicted, the less accurate the prediction. Complicating factors include changes in economic conditions, in the labor supply, and in the political environment.

Formal and informal approaches to human resource planning are used. For example, some organizations use mathematical projections. Data are collected on such topics as the supply of resources, labor market composition, demand for products, and competitive wage and salary programs. From these data and previous records, statistical procedures are used to make predictions. Of course, unforeseen events can alter past trends, but somewhat reliable forecasts can still be made.

Estimating from experience is a more informal forecasting procedure. Department managers may be asked for opinions about future human resource needs. Some managers are confident about planning, whereas others hesitate to offer an opinion or are just not reliable forecasters.

Consider the importance of human resource planning to a large firm such as Xerox, which employs over 100,000 people. Every day some new people

Exhibit 11.1 *Sample of Human Resource Department*

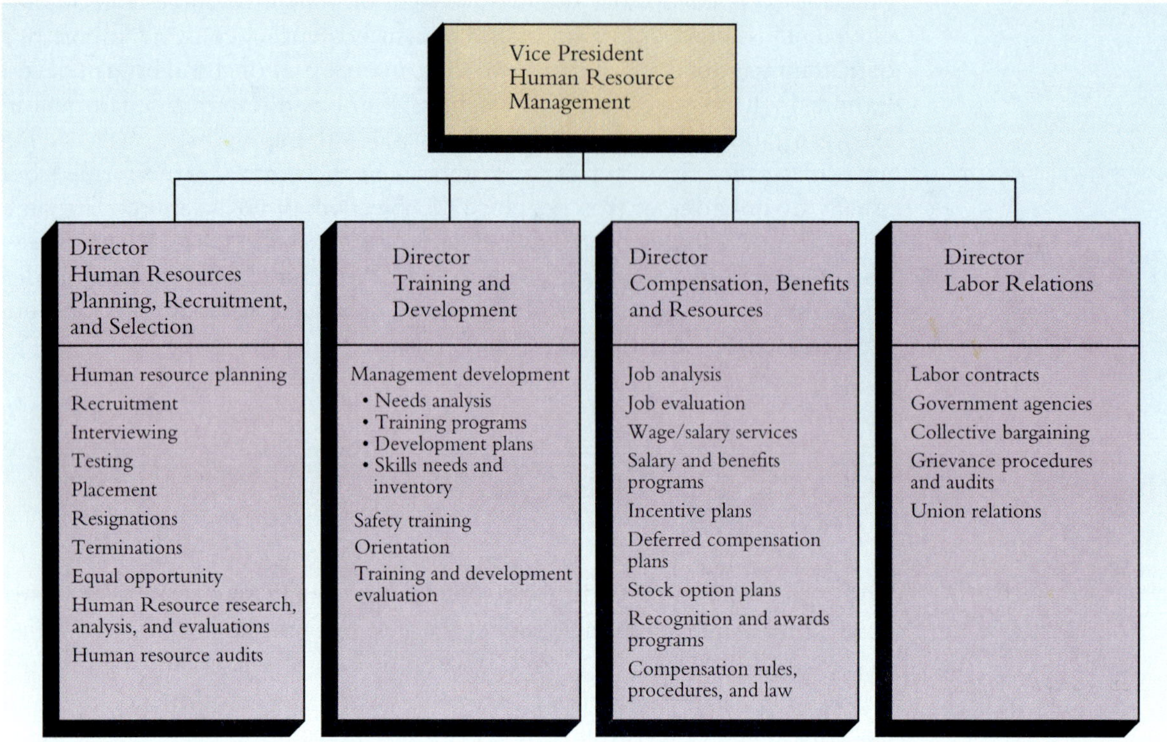

begin jobs there, while others retire or leave for other jobs. This inflow and outflow is constant. Paying attention to inflow, outflow, future plans, and competitors is vital to the effective operation of Xerox Corporation.

A small firm such as Kent Electronics of Houston, TX, also must pay attention to human resource planning. The firm employs about 300 people and plans to expand its sales by exporting to markets in Germany, Italy, Portugal, and Spain. The expansion means more employees must be hired.[2]

Although the inflow and outflow at Kent is not as frequent or as large as that at Xerox, it still must be monitored. To have the right number and type of people in the right place at the right time, a firm must engage in human resource planning. By having a sound human resource planning system, a firm can translate its objectives and plans into the number of employees needed to do the job.

Recruitment

Recruitment
Steps taken to staff an organization with the best-qualified people.

Recruitment is an essential step in staffing. Virtually every company has to perform this function.[3] The primary objective of **recruitment** is to find and attract the best-qualified applicants to fill vacancies. However, before that can be done, those involved in the recruiting process must clearly understand the position to be filled. The procedure used to acquire an understanding about a job is called job analysis.

Job Analysis
The process of determining the tasks that make up a job and the skills, abilities, and responsibilities needed to perform the job.

Job Description
A written statement that furnishes information about a job's duties, technology, conditions, and hazards; based on data from the job analysis.

Job Specification
A written statement of the human qualifications, education, and experience needed to perform a job.

Job analysis is the process of determining the tasks that make up the job and the knowledge, skills, and abilities (KSAs) an employee needs to successfully accomplish the job. *Knowledge* relates to the body of information in a subject area that is needed to adequately perform a job (e.g., knowledge of Lotus® 1-2-3® spreadsheet; knowledge of joint venture loans in Canada). The terms *skills* and *abilities,* used interchangeably, describe observable capabilities to perform a learned behavior (e.g., operating a wood lathe).

From the data gathered through job analysis, job descriptions are generated. A **job description** outlines the activities involved in performing the work and the conditions under which the jobholder will work. A statement of the qualifications, education, and experience needed for a job is called a **job specification.** Both job descriptions and job specifications must be in written form.

An efficient job analysis program provides information used to make important decisions. For example, to recruit and select effectively, the HRM department must match qualified personnel with job requirements. The job description and job specification are also used to establish proper rates of pay. A job description for an HRM manager appears in Exhibit 11.2.

Exhibit 11.2
Job Description of an HRM Manager

Job Title: Human Resource Manager

Department: HRM
Date: January 2, 1996

General Description of the Job

Performs responsible administrative work managing personnel activities of a large state agency or institution. Work involves responsibility for the planning and administration of an HRM program that includes recruitment, examination, selection, evaluation, appointment, promotion, transfer, and recommended change of status of agency employees, and a system of communication for disseminating necessary information to workers. Works under general supervision, exercising initiative and independent judgment in the performance of assigned tasks.

Job Activities

Participates in overall planning and policymaking to provide effective and uniform personnel services.
Communicates policy through organization levels by bulletins, meetings, and personal contact.
Interviews applicants, evaluates qualifications, and classifies applications.
Recruits and screens applicants to fill vacancies and reviews applications of qualified persons.
Confers with supervisors on personnel matters, including placement problems, retention or release of probationary employees, transfers, demotions, and dismissals of permanent employees.
Supervises administration of test.
Initiates personnel training activities and coordinates these activities with work of officials and supervisors.
Establishes effective service rating system, trains unit supervisors in making employee evaluations.
Maintains employee personnel files.
Supervises a group of employees directly and through subordinates.
Performs related work as assigned.

Civil Rights Act of 1964
An act that makes various forms of discrimination illegal. Title VII of the act spells out the forms of illegal discrimination.

Civil Rights Act of 1991
Increases the scope of Title VII of the Civil Rights Act of 1964. Victims are now entitled to jury trial and punitive damages.

Equal Employment Opportunity Act of 1972
A law that has specific provisions about equal opportunities for employment; provided for the establishment of the Equal Employment Opportunity Commission.

Affirmative Action Program
Program begun and carried out by a business to increase the number of women, minorities, and handicapped individuals throughout the organization.

Immigration Reform and Control Act (IRCA)
A law, passed in 1986, that places a major responsibility on employers to stop the flow of illegal immigrants into the United States by not employing unauthorized aliens.

Laws Governing Recruitment. Individuals responsible for recruiting must comply with legal requirements. For example, a certain percentage of minority group members and women must be recruited for positions that have seldom been filled by minorities. These requirements are enforced by laws administered by the Equal Employment Opportunity Commission (EEOC), as Chapter 4 mentioned. Through Title VII of the **Civil Rights Act of 1964,** the **Civil Rights Act of 1991,** and the **Equal Employment Opportunity Act of 1972,** the federal government attempts to provide equal opportunities for employment without regard to race, religion, age, creed, sex, national origin, or disability. These laws have broad coverage and apply to any activity, business, or industry in which labor disputes would hinder commerce.[4] The laws also cover state and local governments, government agencies, and agencies of the District of Columbia.

Specific provisions of the Equal Employment Opportunity Act of 1972 include the following:

It is unlawful for an employer to fail or to refuse to hire, or to discharge, any individual or otherwise to discriminate against any individual with respect to compensation, conditions, or privileges of employment because of race, color, religion, sex, age, or national origin. This applies to applicants for employment as well as current employees.

Employers may not limit, segregate, or classify employees in such a way that would deprive them of employment opportunities because of race, color, age, religion, sex, or national origin.

The EEOC has the power to file action in a federal district court if it is unable to eliminate alleged unlawful employment practices by the informal methods of conference, conciliation, and persuasion.

Employment tests may be used if they can be proved to be related to the job or promotion sought by the individual. Tests should be validated for each company. No discriminatory statements may be included in any advertisements for job opportunities.

The EEOC first attempted to encourage employers to follow the guidelines of the law. Now the EEOC is more aggressive and asks employers to prepare **affirmative action programs.** This means the employer must spell out how the company plans to increase the number of minority and female employees. If EEOC investigators believe the distribution of employees reflects discriminatory hiring policies, they can propose adjustments. The employer may then state why these adjustments can or cannot be made.

The **Immigration Reform and Control Act (IRCA)** of 1986 places a major responsibility on employers for stopping the flow of illegal immigrants into the United States.[5] The employer must:

1. Not recruit, hire, or continue to employ unauthorized aliens.
2. Verify the identity or work authorization of every new employee.
3. Not discriminate on the basis of citizenship or national origin.

The initial penalties for employers who violate the IRCA entail a cease-and-desist order along with a fine of $250–$2,000 for each unauthorized alien. Second violations result in a fine of $2,000–$5,000 per unauthorized alien. Additional violations can result in imprisonment for the employer. The IRCA requires every individual who is recruited and hired to provide acceptable documentation of his or her status. The Immigration Act of 1990 provides for 140,000 visas annually for employer-sponsored immigrants. The Act includes aliens with extraordinary ability such as outstanding scientists and researchers.

Americans with Disabilities Act (ADA) Comprehensive antidiscrimination law, passed in 1990, aimed at integrating the disabled into the American work force; prohibits all employers from discriminating against disabled employees or applicants.

An estimated 43 million Americans have some type of disability. Although many would like to work, some cannot because of discrimination. In May 1990, the **Americans with Disabilities Act** (ADA) was passed.[6] This comprehensive antidiscrimination law aims at integrating the disabled into the American work force. The ADA prohibits all employers, including privately owned businesses and local governments, from discriminating against disabled employees or job applicants when making selection decisions.

Typically, discrimination against disabled applicants takes the form of application forms and preemployment interviews that inquire into the existence of a disability rather than the ability to perform the required job activities. Title I of the ADA prohibits these and other practices that may prevent a disabled person from obtaining and maintaining employment.

To be in compliance with the ADA, business owners must make their premises accessible to the disabled by removing architectural and communication barriers. Any business undergoing renovation must give disabled persons access to restrooms, telephone, water fountains, and altered areas. Businesses that fail to comply face civil penalties of as much as $50,000 for the first violation and $100,000 for subsequent violations. Also, a disabled person can obtain an injunction against the business. Additionally, courts can award monetary damages to disabled persons victimized by discrimination.

Recruitment Sources. Internal sources of recruitment include present employees, friends of employees, former employees, and previous applicants. Firms such as Bristol-Myers, CBS, Borden, and Boise Cascade keep files on previous employment applicants. Even though these applicants were not hired, they often maintain an interest in working for a company with a good reputation and image. By carefully screening these files, some good applicants can be added to the pool of candidates.

If needed human resources are not available within the company, outside sources must be tapped. New applicants can be found through advertisements in newspapers, trade journals, and magazines. Responses to ads come from both qualified and unqualified individuals. Occasionally a company will list a post office box number and not provide the company name. This is called a *blind advertisement.* (Such an ad appears in Exhibit 11.3.) Blind ads eliminate the need to contact every applicant, even the unqualified ones. However, a blind ad does not permit the company to use its name or logo, which is a form of promotion.

To locate experienced employees, organizations can use private employment agencies, executive search firms, or state employment agencies. Most are no-fee agencies, which means the employer rather than the applicant pays the fee (if there is one). An organization is not obligated to hire any person referred by an agency, but the agency is usually notified when an applicant is hired.

Another important source for lower-level or entry-level management recruits is the college campus. Many colleges and universities have placement centers that work with organizational recruiters. The applicants read advertisements and information provided by the companies and then are interviewed. The most promising students are invited to visit the company, where other interviews are conducted.

Selection

The selection and placement of employees must comply with legal requirements. Discriminatory practices in recruiting, testing, and hiring are illegal, as stated in the Civil Rights Act of 1964 and the Equal Employment Opportunity Act of 1972.

Selection
In employment, a series of steps that starts with the initial screening and ends with a hiring decision.

The **selection** process is a series of steps that starts with the initial screening and ends with a decision to hire the person. Exhibit 11.4 is a flow diagram showing each step in the process. Preliminary interviews screen out unqualified applicants. This screening is often the first personal contact an applicant has with a company.

Exhibit 11.3
Blind Advertisement

TRAINING AND DEVELOPMENT MANAGER

A large profit-oriented company with headquarters in Houston is currently expanding its management development and training program. We seek a manager whose responsibilities will include the overall planning, development, and direction of the corporate training and development program. The qualified candidate for this position will report directly to the Vice President of Personnel Services.

The qualified candidate must have a Bachelor's degree with a minimum of 8 years directly related experience in training and development, with a demonstrated record of results in private industry. The individual must communicate effectively with different organizational levels to include working directly with high-level management and company officers.

Initial selection of qualified candidates will be based on detailed resume and any other material the candidate wishes to submit, along with salary history and salary requirements. For prompt confidential reply, send resume to:

Confidential Reply Service
Nationwide Advertising Service Inc.
Dept. 6-GC-28
5805 Richmond Ave.
Houston, TX 77057

Our client is an equal opportunity employer. M/F.

Nationwide Advertising Service, Inc., is a full-service recruitment advertising agency with 36 offices throughout the United States and Canada.

Exhibit 11.4
Typical Selection Decision Steps

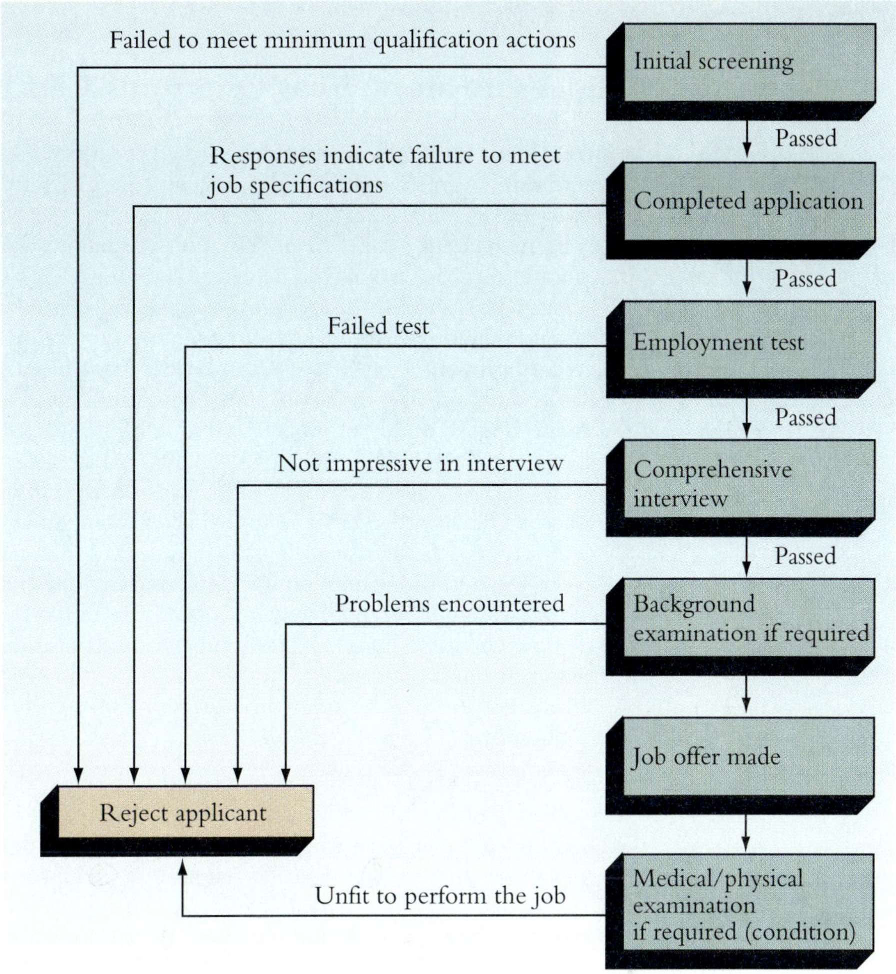

Applicants who pass the preliminary screening usually complete an application blank. The form asks for information that can be used in reaching an employment decision. Answers to the questions can even, in a general sense, *predict* job success. The appropriate questions are usually developed after a careful job analysis is completed. The application should provide all necessary information and yet be concise enough not to give a jumbled mass of unnecessary information.

Interviews occur throughout the selection process, but each includes three basic steps: (1) interviewers must acquaint themselves with the job analysis; (2) they must analyze the information on the application; (3) they need to ask questions that will add to information on the application. Every question must also be legal. Your Values and Attitudes will help you determine what is and is not lawful.

YOUR VALUES AND ATTITUDES

Do You Know What Questions Can Be Asked?

Directions: Here is a description from a preemployment interview guide. The description includes a number of unlawful inquiries made by the firm's interviewer. How many illegal inquiries can you find?

> Hi, my name is James Green. What is your name? Can you tell me a little about your background? Where were you born? We operate a very high-energy firm and like our employees to be well rested and ethical. Do you attend religious services? How frequently? We will need a complete record on your spouse. Are you married? Fine. Does your wife read and write English? Are you a citizen of the United States? Do you read or write English or any other language fluently? Have you or your wife ever been convicted of a homicide? We will need to have a name and address of a person to be notified in case of an accident. How is this person related to you? Have you ever collected workers' compensation for a previous work injury? Is there any illness that you have that may interfere with your job duties? Thank you for answering my questions.

Feedback: Well, our interviewer violated the Equal Employment Opportunity Act in several areas by making a number of unlawful inquiries. These questions should not and do not have to be answered.

Let's go through the unlawful inquiries. You should have found seven problem questions.

1. *Where were you born?* After the person is employed, you can ask if he or she can show proof of U.S. citizenship. You cannot ask the birthplace of an applicant.
2. *Do you attend religious services?* Don't even inquire about any aspect of religion.
3. *How frequently?* (Attendance at religious services: see item 2.)
4. *Does your wife read or write English?* Ask the applicant about what he or she can read or write, but ask nothing about the spouse's ability.
5. *Have you or your wife ever been convicted of a homicide?* Unless the conviction is substantially related to the job responsibilities, you shouldn't ask the question.
6. *How is this person* [the outside person to notify in case of an accident or emergency] *related to you?* You can't ask about relationship.
7. *Have you ever collected workers' compensation for a previous work injury?* You can't ask this question.

How did you do? If you only found six or less of the unlawful inquiries, you need to brush up on the law. The EEOC compliance manual published by the Bureau of National Affairs in Washington, DC, can help you conduct, and be a part of, the interviewing process.

Japanese recruiters interviewing and selecting American workers for plants operated in the United States sometimes appear puzzled by the illegality of certain questions. For example, not asking a job applicant about his or her religion, upbringing, or home life is questioned by the Japanese. "How can you learn about the applicant?" the Japanese ask. The Japanese and any other foreign employer hiring in the United States will have to comply with the law or risk being sued.[7]

Testing. For years selection tests have been widely used to screen applicants. Frequent use started with World War I, when the Army Alpha test was used to measure intelligence. Installing a sound testing program is costly and time-consuming, and it must be done by experts. Just because a test was useful for selecting sales personnel in one company does not mean it will be useful in another. Exhibit 11.5 presents the results of a Bureau of National Affairs study of firms involved in making selection decisions. The study results indicate which selection procedures are often used and which procedures are not widely used.

The advantages of a sound testing program include:

- *Improved accuracy in selecting employees.* Individuals differ in skills, intelligence, motivation, interests, and goals. If these differences can be measured and if they are related to job success, then performance can be predicted to some extent by test scores.
- *An objective means for judging.* Applicants answer the same questions under the same test conditions, so one applicant's score can be compared to the scores of other applicants.
- *Information for current employee needs.* Tests given to current employees can provide information about training, development, or counseling needs. Thus they can objectively uncover needs.

Important legal rulings and fair-employment codes have resulted in strict procedures for developing tests. The following criticisms have been directed at testing programs:

- *Tests are not infallible.* Tests may reveal what people *can* do but not what they *will* do.
- *Tests are given too much weight.* Tests cannot measure everything about a person. They can never be a complete substitute for good judgment.
- *Tests discriminate against minorities.* Ethnic minorities may score lower on certain paper-and-pencil tests. Title VII of the Civil Rights Act of 1964 prohibits employment practices that artificially discriminate against individuals on the basis of test scores.

Drug Testing. The Drug-Free Workplace Act of 1988 was passed to help keep the problem of societal drug abuse from entering organizations. The act specifies that government agencies, federal contractors, and those receiving federal funds ($25,000 or more) must actively attempt to maintain a drug-free workplace. In addition, the act requires that employees of companies regulated by the Department of Transportation and the Nuclear Regulatory Commission who hold certain jobs such as long-haul truck driving must take drug tests.

If firm get more than $25,000 in fed money, they must try to keep drug free environment

Exhibit 11.5 *Selection Devices for Different Job Classes*

	Percent of Companies					
	Any Job Category*	**Office/ Clerical**	**Production/ Service**	**Professional/ Technical**	**Commissioned Sales**	**Managers/ Supervisors**
(Number of companies)	*(245)*	*(245)*	*(221)*	*(237)*	*(96)*	*(243)*
Skill performance test/or work sample	63%	55%	19%	10%	4%	3%
Medical examination	57	43	57	47	46	45
Mental ability test	31	23	10	8	9	9
Job knowledge test	27	14	14	14	3	5
Drug test	26	21	26	22	23	21
Personality test	17	1	2	6	23	13
Assessment center test	12	**	1	3	4	10
Physical abilities test	11	1	12	2	1	1
Written honesty test	7	4	6	2	4	3
Polygraph test	5	2	4	2	5	2
Genetic screening	3	2	2	2	—	1
AIDS test	1	**	**	1	—	**
Other	2	**	1	1	1	1

Note: Percentages for each job category group are based on the number of organizations that provided data for that category, as shown by the numbers in parentheses.

* Percentages in this column show the proportion of all responding organizations that administer a preemployment test to applicants in any job category.
** Less than 0.5%.

Source: Reprinted with permission from *Recruiting and Selection Procedures*, Personnel Policies Forum Survey No. 146, p. 17 (May 1988). Copyright 1988 by The Bureau of National Affairs, Inc. (800–372-1033).

More and more employers have adopted drug and alcohol screening programs for both applicants and current employees. An American Management Association survey indicates that the percentage of firms that tested for drug abuse rose to 84 percent in 1993, up from 74 percent in 1992.[8] There are good reasons to avoid hiring substance abusers. Drug and alcohol abusers have higher rates of absenteeism and accidents. In addition, employers may be liable for negligent hiring if a drug-user employee causes an accident that injures or harms others. Forty percent of all on-the-job injuries and about half of all work-related deaths are attributed to substance abuse. Also, it has been estimated that the U.S. loses over $600 billion annually in productivity because of substance abuse.[9]

A major concern for opponents of drug testing is how the process works and how the information is used. Drug testing when conducted to eliminate drugs in the workplace is more acceptable than using a testing program to catch those doing drugs. Motorola uses a well publicized and rigid drug-testing program. Individuals who refuse the Motorola drug test are terminated immediately.[10] The company believes that a firm stand against substance abusers is necessary. Other companies are not as harsh when they identify employees that fail a drug test. These firms place the individuals failing a drug test into rehabilitation programs.

Job applicants that test positive for substance abuse are usually dropped from the pool of candidates. Companies do not want to hire substance abusers because of the cost, liability, and research findings that they have more accidents and have higher absenteeism.

The U.S. Postal Service conducted an experimental drug-testing program. More than 5,000 job candidates were tested, and 9 percent were found to be substance abusers. Second tests on a sample of specimens showed virtually no test errors; no nonusers were mistakenly identified as users. Since this was a confidential test the results were not shown to management and were not used in selection. After months of keeping records on users and nonusers, it was found that drug users had 60 percent higher absenteeism rates and were 47 percent more likely to be involuntarily discharged. The cost of testing ($11 per applicant) was minimal compared to the costs of higher absenteeism and terminations for cause that occurred when drug users were hired.[11]

A reliable and valued drug-testing program that protects the dignity of individuals being tested can be beneficial. However, there are still cases where drug testing gives false readings or the specimen is inappropriately handled. Companies need to use precise and dignified drug-testing programs so that substance abusers are correctly identified.

AIDS Testing. The human costs of acquired immune deficiency syndrome (AIDS) are incalculable. For those who suffer from AIDS and for their families, the emotional toll is terribly high. For employers AIDS presents the specter of a major economic drain. Benefits paid out for an employee with AIDS typically exceed $100,000.

The spiraling costs of caring for AIDS patients require the immediate attention of employers and insurers. Since the law states that an employer cannot discharge or refuse to hire someone with AIDS, employers need to check their health, life, and disability insurance coverage. In many federal and state courts, persons with AIDS have been extended the protection of laws for the disabled. A disability can be a reason for dismissal or refusal to hire only if it prevents the person from doing the job.[12]

AIDS victims are protected by the Rehabilitation Act of 1973. Section 504 of the act states:

No otherwise qualified individual with handicaps . . . shall, solely by reason of his handicap, be excluded from the participation in . . . or be subjected to discrimination under the program or activity receiving federal financial assistance.

The Americans with Disabilities Act now requires employees to provide reasonable workplace recommendations for an employee with HIV/AIDS.

As of June 1994 there were 401,749 reported cases of AIDS in the United States; 243,423 deaths as a result of the disease.[13] Because AIDS is a major challenge and a serious problem, organizations are now establishing guidelines for dealing with it. Some of the guidelines found in policies at IBM, Johnson & Johnson, and BankAmerica include:

- People with AIDS or who are infected with HIV, the AIDS-causing virus, are entitled to the same rights and opportunities as people with other serious illnesses.
- Employment policies should be based on the scientific evidence that people with AIDS or HIV infection do not pose a risk of transmitting the virus through ordinary workplace contact.
- Employers should provide workers with sensitive and up-to-date education about AIDS and risk reduction in their personal lives.
- Employers have the duty to protect the confidentiality of employees' medical information.

Knowledge and information in the form of a policy document can be helpful in alleviating fear and correcting misinformation about AIDS. The devastation of AIDS is well documented. It is a disease caused by a virus that breaks down part of the body's immune system. A firm's policy can't help the body fight the disease, but it provides useful information to help employees understand that AIDS victims will be treated with human dignity and concern. This important message to those with AIDS, as well as to their colleagues, says that the firm cares and wants to help.

Decision to Hire

After preliminary screening, evaluating the application, interviewing, and testing, the company may decide to make a job offer. If so, a background check is usually made. The background check verifies information by consulting references. This information may be obtained by letter, by telephone, or in person. One important group of references is previous employers; the company tries to gather information about the applicant's previous job performance. Under the Fair Credit and Reporting Act, the prospective employer must secure the applicant's permission before checking references.

When the reference check yields favorable information, the line manager and an HRM representative meet to decide what the offer will be. The offer is usually made subject to successful completion of a physical examination, which can be conducted by a company physician or by a doctor outside the organization. The objective is to screen out people whose physical deficiencies might be expensive liabilities and to place people on jobs they are physically able to handle.

TRAINING AND DEVELOPMENT

Training and development programs include orientation activities that *inform* employees of policies and procedures, *educate* them in job skills, and *develop* them for future advancement. The importance of the training and development program to the organization cannot be overemphasized. Through recruitment and placement, good employees can be brought into the company. They then need continual education and development so that both their needs and the objectives of the firm can be achieved.

Orientation

Most large companies have a formal orientation program for new employees. Although new hires usually know something about the firm, they often lack specific information about working hours, pay, parking, rules, facilities, and so on. The HRM department usually coordinates the orientation, but the immediate supervisor is the key to the process. He or she and the new employee must eventually establish a cordial relationship that will encourage communication.

Training

Training
A continual process of helping employees perform at a high level.

Training is a continual process of helping employees perform at a high level. It begins on the person's first day at work. It may occur in the workplace or at a special training facility, but it should always be supervised by training experts.

This applicant made a favorable impression during the screening, application, testing, interviewing, and reference-checking process and is now being welcomed as a new department store employee.

To be effective, a training program must accomplish a number of objectives. First, it must be based on both organizational and individual needs; training for training's sake is not the objective. Second, the objectives of training should spell out what problems will be solved. Third, all training should be based on sound theories of learning. This is the major reason why training and management development are not for amateurs. Finally, a training program must be evaluated to determine whether it is working.

Before a training program can be developed, problem areas must be pinpointed. Companies use a number of techniques to identify problems, including reviewing safety records, absenteeism data, job descriptions, and attitude surveys to see what employees think about their jobs, bosses, and the company.

Once training needs have been identified, objectives need to be stated in writing. They provide a framework for the program. Objectives need to be concise, accurate, meaningful, and challenging. There are usually two major categories of objectives—skills and knowledge. *Skill objectives* focus on developing physical abilities; *knowledge objectives* are concerned with understanding, attitudes, and concepts.

Various methods are available for reaching the skill and knowledge objectives. Such factors as cost, available time, number of persons to be trained, background of trainees, and skill of the trainees determine the method used. Some of the more widely used training methods are:

- *On-the-job training.* A supervisor or other worker may show a new employee how to perform the job.
- *Vestibule training.* This is training in a mock-up or facsimile of the actual work area.
- *Classroom training.* Numerous classroom methods are used by business organizations. The lecture—a formal, organized presentation—is one method. A conference or small discussion group gets the student more involved than the lecture method. Interactive video (IAV) lecturing is becoming a popular technique. In IAV training, employees communicate with a computer to acquire knowledge and skills.

Today's Business World displays the type of training that is being conducted in organizations.

Management Development

Management Development
The process of educating and developing selected personnel so that they have the knowledge, skills, attitudes, and understanding needed to manage in future positions.

Training is generally associated with operating, or nonmanagerial, employees; management development is associated with managerial personnel. **Management development** refers to the process of educating and developing selected personnel so that they have the knowledge, skills, attitudes, and understanding needed to manage in future positions. The process starts with the selection of a qualified individual and continues throughout that individual's career.

Companies use management development to ensure the long-term success of the organization, to furnish competent replacements, to create an efficient team that works well together, and to enable managers to reach their

TODAY'S BUSINESS WORLD

Formal Training Is a Big Business

Training magazine collected data from a representative sample of 2,496 American training executives. The table below shows what American firms are delivering in the form of training.

Types of Training	% Providing[1]	In-House Only (%)[2]	Outside Only (%)[3]	Both (%)[4]
Management Skills/ Development	91	12	18	61
Basic Computer Skills	90	21	14	55
Communication Skills	87	21	12	53
Supervisory Skills	86	18	12	56
Technical Skills/ Knowledge	82	22	6	54
New Methods/ Procedures	80	38	5	37
Executive Development	77	8	26	44
Customer Relations/ Services	76	25	9	41
Personal Growth	73	14	15	45
Clerical/Secretarial Skills	73	23	18	32
Employee/Labor Relations	67	23	12	31
Customer Education	65	28	5	31
Wellness	63	21	15	28
Sales Skills	56	15	11	30
Remedial/Basic Education	48	11	21	15

Of all organizations with 100 or more employees...

[1]Percent that provide each type of training.

[2]Percent that say all training of this type is designed and delivered by in-house staff.

[3]Percent that say all training of this type is designed and delivered by outside consultants or suppliers.

[4]Percent that say training of this type is designed and delivered by a combination of in-house staff and outside suppliers.

Experts believe that U.S. organizations will spend over $50 billion per year for formal training programs and that over 50 million individuals will receive training annually through the remainder of the 1990s. Although training is such a vital part of organizations, why is it usually one of the first areas cut when budgets are trimmed?

Source: Adapted from Gloria Cosgrove and Roy Speed, "What's Wrong with Corporate Training?" *Training* (January 1995): 53–58.

potential. Management development may also be needed because of high executive turnover, a shortage of management talent, and our society's emphasis on lifelong education and development.

Employees can acquire the knowledge, skills, attitudes, and understanding necessary to become successful managers through two types of programs: on-the-job training and formal development. On-the-job programs include:

- *Understudy programs.* A person works as a subordinate partner with a boss, with the goal of eventually assuming the full responsibilities and duties of the job.
- *Job rotation.* Managers are transferred from job to job on a systematic basis. Job assignments can last from two weeks (Caterpillar) to six months (General Electric).
- *Coaching.* A supervisor teaches job knowledge and skills to a subordinate. The supervisor instructs, directs, corrects, and evaluates the subordinate.

On-the-job development programs emphasize actual job experience. They are designed to increase the employee's skill, knowledge, and confidence.

Formal management development programs are often conducted by training units within organizations or by consultants in universities and specialized training facilities around the country. In very large corporations, full-time training units conduct regular management development courses. For example, General Electric's Advanced Management Course, designed for the four highest levels of management, lasts 13 weeks. It covers business policy, economics, social issues, and management principles. Many smaller firms send managers to development programs at universities. Publicized and well-attended programs are found at the University of Michigan, Columbia University, Duke University, the University of Houston, and Pennsylvania State University.

Performance Appraisals

Training and development also involve performance appraisals. Managers use appraisal programs to communicate expectations and to help subordinates improve personal deficiencies. Most employees want to know how well they are performing, and appraisals provide a basis for reviewing their performance. Appraisals also give employees a chance to discuss their career plans with their supervisor.

Properly handled, formal performance appraisals can help supervisors and subordinates develop mutual trust, respect, and understanding. But to do that, managers must divorce performance appraisals from the review of salary.

Perhaps the oldest performance appraisal technique is the graphic rating plan. Usually the supervisor is supplied with a printed form for each person to be rated and is asked to circle or check the phrase that best describes the individual on the particular trait. Exhibit 11.6 shows a sample rating scale.

This type of scale is easy to use but has serious disadvantages. First, scoring is difficult. Second, it doesn't tell which traits are most important. For example, is quality more important than cooperation? Third, ratings usually

Exhibit 11.6
Typical Graphic Rating Scale

Name ______________ Dept. ______________ Date ______________

	Outstanding	Good	Satisfactory	Fair	Unsatisfactory
Quantity of work: volume of acceptable work under normal conditions Comments:	☐	☐	☐	☐	☐
Quality of work: thoroughness, neatness and accuracy of work Comments:	☐	☐	☐	☐	☐
Knowledge of job: clear understanding of the facts or factors pertinent to the job Comments:	☐	☐	☐	☐	☐
Personal qualities: personality, appearance, sociability, leadership, integrity Comments:	☐	☐	☐	☐	☐
Cooperation: ability and willingness to work with associates, supervisors, and subordinates toward common goals Comments:	☐	☐	☐	☐	☐
Dependability: conscientious, thorough, accurate, reliable with respect to attendance, lunch periods, reliefs, etc. Comments:	☐	☐	☐	☐	☐
Initiative: earnestness in seeking increased responsibilities. Self-starting, unafraid to proceed alone Comments:	☐	☐	☐	☐	☐

cluster around the more positive statements. Finally, this system doesn't tell a manager how to help subordinates correct identified deficiencies.

The perfect system would be accurate, reliable, fair, informative, and designed for each key feature of a job. Furthermore, the supervisor and subordinate would know exactly what is expected in the job and that performance results are linked to preestablished criteria. Such a perfect system simply is not available. But the search has gone on for years.

COMPENSATION AND BENEFITS

In modern society, money is important both economically and psychologically. Without it a person can't buy the necessities or luxuries of life, but it is equated with status and recognition. Because money is so important, employees are quite sensitive about the amount of pay they receive and how it compares to what others in the company and in society are earning. Employees need to believe they are being compensated fairly for the work they do.

A compensation system has one objective: to create a system of rewards that is equitable to both employer and employee. The system must motivate the employee to work hard and accomplish goals. An employer views compensation in terms of cost effectiveness, fairness, and adequacy. An employee views compensation in terms of equity, security, motivation, and meaningfulness.

Direct Compensation
An employee's base pay (wages and salary) and performance-based pay (incentives).

Indirect Compensation
Federally required and state-mandated protection programs, private protection programs, paid leave, and miscellaneous benefits.

Compensation is direct or indirect. **Direct compensation** includes an employee's base pay (wages or salary) and performance-based pay (incentives). **Indirect compensation** consists of federally required and state-mandated protection programs, private protection programs, paid leave, and miscellaneous benefits. (We discuss protection programs and benefits later in the chapter.) The total (direct and indirect) compensation package is used to:

- Attract potential job applicants.
- Retain good employees.
- Motivate employees.
- Administer pay within legal regulations.
- Gain a competitive edge.

Many people take part in compensation decisions. Top management determines the total amount of the budget that goes to pay, the pay form to be used (wages versus incentive plans), and pay policies. The manager working with employees makes inputs into the pay decision. An HRM unit advises management (top and operating) on pay strategy, legal issues (regular pay, overtime pay), competition, and market conditions.

Wages

Wages
Compensation based on time worked or number of units produced.

The most common system for compensating operating or nonmanagerial employees is **wages,** based on time increments or number of units produced. Blue-collar workers have traditionally been paid at an hourly or daily rate, although some are now being paid biweekly or monthly. Hewlett-Packard has eliminated the daily rate of pay and now considers all personnel at all levels to be salaried employees—paid by the week or some longer time period.

Individual Incentives. The oldest form of compensation is the individual incentive plan, which by definition pays for performance. Individual incentive plans take several forms: piecework, production bonuses, and commissions.

Straight *piecework* means the employee is paid a certain rate for each piece produced, with no other form of compensation. A modified piecework plan works like this. The employer guarantees the employee an hourly rate for performing the expected minimum output. For production over the standard (set through work measurement studies), the employer pays so much per extra piece produced. For example, suppose the hourly rate is $5.00 and the standard of production is 10 units per hour. Management determines that paying $.50 per unit produced above the standard level is fair. Thus an employee who produces 15 units per hour (rather than the standard 10 units) would earn $2.50 more per hour, or a total of $7.50 per hour ($5.00 hourly rate + $2.50 incentive for being above standard).

Production bonus systems pay an hourly rate. A bonus—something extra—is paid when the employee, or the total output, exceeds the standard. Ruth Manufacturing Co. in Janesville, WI, has a popular bonus system. Every Friday workers get a bonus added to their paychecks.[14] The bonus is based on how much stainless-steel tubing they shipped the previous week. During the past year, an extra $1.56 an hour was tacked onto their average $10.37 hourly wage. At Ruth, the employees work together and have high morale because they like the firm and certainly appreciate their bonus.

DuPont's fibers department in Wilmington, DE, has implemented a program in which employees receive lower-than-usual merit increases. In exchange for accepting lower salaries and wages, they have the opportunity to earn bonuses as high as 18 percent of their salaries. The bonus is based on outstanding performance as measured by quantitative results.[15]

Sales employees often receive *commissions*. A commission is payment tied directly to performance standards. Straight commission, the equivalent of straight piecework, is typically a percentage of net sales.

TQM

Group Incentives. To provide broader motivation than that furnished by individual incentive plans, several group-based approaches are used. Their aim is to increase productivity and improve morale. Group incentive plans give each group member a chance to receive a bonus based on the output or performance of the group.

Scanlon Plans. A combination group incentive, suggestion, and employee participation arrangement, the Scanlon plan, has been popular in small and medium-sized manufacturing firms.[16] Such plans require management and employee involvement, interaction, and cooperation. In a Scanlon plan, named after its designer, Joseph Scanlon, each department of the firm has a production committee. Members include the supervisor and employee representatives elected by co-workers or appointed by the union. The committee receives and reviews employees' and managers' suggestions for improving work practices and procedures. The number of suggestions in a Scanlon plan company is usually double the typical suggestion-plan rate.

A Scanlon plan formula is used to calculate productivity gains resulting from the suggestions. Workers typically receive about 75 percent of the cost savings from improvements resulting from the suggestions, while the remainder goes to the firm. The savings are distributed to employees based on their wage levels.

Profit-Sharing Plans. The Gallatin glassworks factory in New Geneva, PA, used the first recorded profit-sharing plan in 1794. Today over 430,000 such plans are used by American businesses.[17] In profit sharing, an employer pays or makes available to regular employees special current or deferred sums based on profits earned in addition to their regular pay. There are three types of profit-sharing plans:

- *Cash, or current, payment.* Profits are immediately distributed quarterly or annually.
- *Deferred.* A portion of profits is credited to employee accounts, with payment made at the time of retirement, disability, or severance (when an employee leaves the company). This is the most popular plan because of the tax advantages of deferring income.
- *Combined.* This plan incorporates features of the current payment and deferred plans.

In the United States, profit sharing is the most common method firms use to provide retirement income for their employees. Advocates contend that the plans encourage better performance by employees. However, profit sharing has some potential problems. What does management do in down years, when there are no profits? Even though employees have worked hard, an ineffective advertising program or a new product from a competitor may wipe out any profits. After several difficult and lean years, employees may begin to wonder whether hard work is worth the effort. Even in good years, it is often difficult to see how hard work is significant to profits received a year away or, worse, at retirement many years later.

Lincoln Electric Plan. The majority of group incentive plans are customized to fit a particular organization. The most publicized and successful has been the Lincoln Electric plan. Lincoln Electric employees are rewarded for good performance. At Lincoln Electric, all jobs are compensated on the bonus system. The year-end bonus is intended as a sharing of the results of efficient operation based on each individual's initiative, quality, and teamwork. Lincoln has used this effective merit-rating system since 1934.[18] Needless to say, Lincoln Electric jobs are in great demand.

Job Evaluation System
A process by which the relative values of jobs within the organization are determined.

Wage Determination. In many organizations, the relative worth of a job and the wage adjustments for it are determined by using **job evaluation systems** in which a job is compared with others within the organization. Under the ranking method, all jobs are ranked from highest to lowest on the basis of skill, difficulty, working conditions, and importance to the success of the organization. The work attitudes or personalities of the current jobholders often distort rankings. In most cases, unions are not enthusiastic about job evaluation. With such a system, the union negotiator has almost no role to play.

Unions generally prefer the daily rate of pay over systems that involve piecework or incentive payments. Because time standards and records of the employee's output are not needed, a daily rate of pay is easier to understand and use than are piece rates, bonuses, or commissions. Unions also believe that a piecework system reduces the group orientation, the need for union solidarity; a worker paid on the basis of individual effort can produce at any level he or she wants to. Unions prefer to encourage group solidarity and a united front.

Many factors help determine the wage rate for a nonmanagerial job. Wages for certain jobs are affected by the supply of and demand for qualified personnel, although unions and the government may hinder these effects. Unions, for example, using strike threats and contract agreements, can prevent employers from lowering wage rates even when qualified personnel abound.

Existing wage rates in competing companies or in the community also influence wage determination. Organizations typically conduct wage surveys to assess hourly rates, piecework or other incentive rates, and fringe benefits offered by other organizations. If the wage rates of a firm are too low, it may be difficult to attract qualified personnel.

Wage and salary administration, like other areas of HRM management, has been the target of various laws. For instance, full-time employees must be paid at least the minimum wage per hour of work. Since the first minimum wage law was enacted in 1938, the rate has risen from $.25 to $4.25 per hour. In addition, the Fair Labor Standards Act of 1938 forbids the employment of minors between 16 and 18 years of age in such hazardous occupations as coal mining, logging, and woodworking.

Comparable Worth. In an effort to close the earnings gap between men and women, a growing movement has worked to have the widely accepted concept of equal pay for equal jobs expanded to include equal pay for comparable jobs. The issue is known as **comparable worth.** In *Gunther* v. *Washington,* the Supreme Court ruled five to four that a sex discrimination suit can be brought under the 1964 Civil Rights Act on the basis of "equal or substantially equal work."[19] In that case, male prison guards received significantly higher pay than female prison guards doing similar work. The county had evaluated the male prison guard's jobs and found them to have 5 percent more job content than the female jobs. However, the males were paid 35 percent more.

Comparable Worth
The concept of equal pay for jobs that require similar levels of skills, training, and experience.

The *Equal Pay Act of 1963* was designed to lessen the existing gap between male and female pay rates. Although some progress has occurred, women in general still earn about 75 percent of what their male counterparts earn. Some of this difference exists because of male- versus female-dominated occupations. There is also the fact that women have often spent less time in various jobs and because of less seniority do not receive the same salary or wage as those with more seniority.[20] Exhibit 11.7 presents the Bureau of the Census analysis on the difference between men's and women's median incomes across different occupations.

Exhibit 11.7 *A Comparison of Median Income of Male and Female Year-Round, Full-Time Workers*

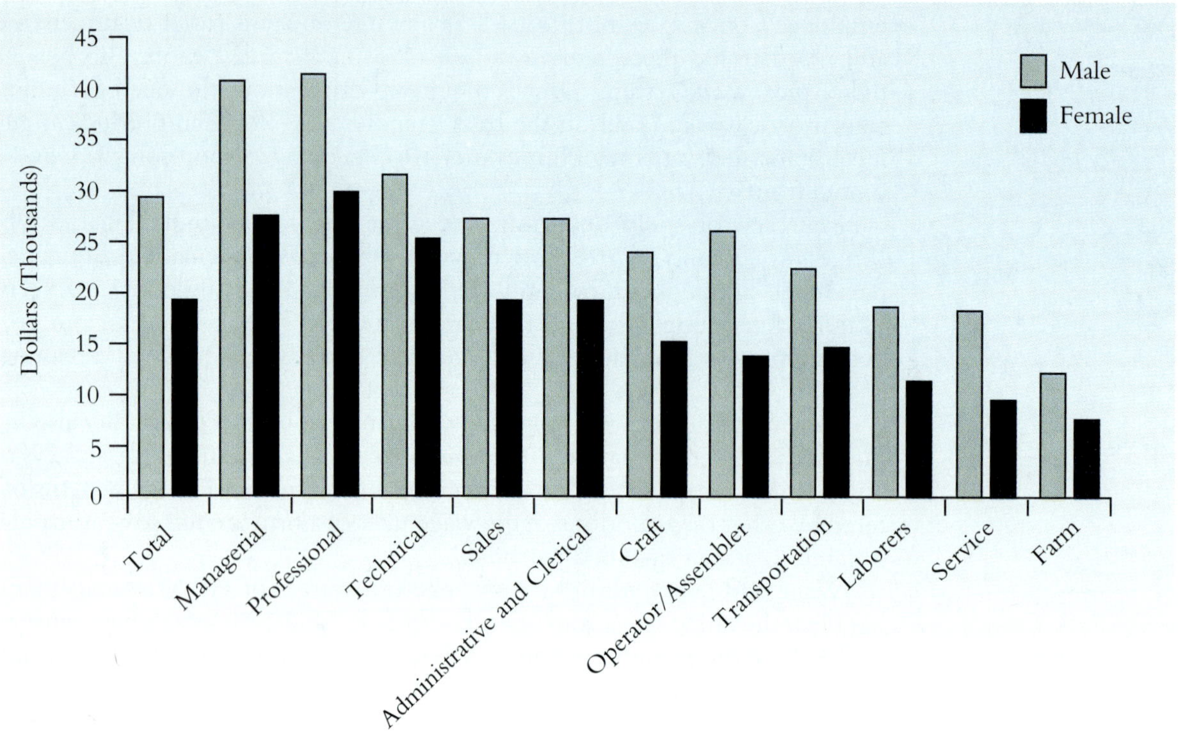

Source: U.S. Bureau of the Census, Current Population Reports, Series P-60, No. 174, *Money Income of Households, Families, and Persons in the United States: 1990* (Washington, DC: U.S. Government Printing Office, 1991).

The Equal Pay Act requires employers to eliminate pay differences for the same job. For example, if a firm is hiring a laboratory lecturer, the position must be paid the same irrespective of the sex of the job holder. If two workers, however, one male and one female, perform at different levels during a period of time they could be compensated differently based on the notion that performance is rewarded.

Using comparable worth principles requires a sound job evaluation system, regular comparison of pay across jobs, and a documented pay system. A job evaluation point system is widely used. It requires the evaluator to quantify the value of the elements of a job. For example, job knowledge may receive 20 points, quality of work 30 points, and so forth. The points are then added up and are used to rank jobs.

Salaries
Compensation based on a long time period: a week, a month, or longer.

Salaries

Employees compensated on a weekly or longer schedule are paid **salaries.** Salaried employees are assumed to be able to influence the way they perform their jobs more than can employees who are paid wages. But the approach to developing an equitable compensation system for executives is similar to that for hourly workers. Companies make comparisons, conduct surveys, and analyze supply and demand, job duties, and job responsibilities.

Hay Associates developed one method specifically for evaluating middle- and top-management positions. First, analysts evaluate each position from information provided in the job description. They consider three factors: job know-how, problem solving, and accountability. Then, through a statistical procedure, they convert evaluations for the jobs in a particular company to the Hay control standards, a special ranking system. Hay Associates publishes annual surveys showing the compensation practices of a number of companies for jobs of similar control standards. All Hay clients use the same evaluation method, so they can compare management salaries.

Benefits and Services

Benefits
Forms of indirect compensation that are financial in nature; examples include health insurance and pension fund contributions.

Services
In business, intangible products that cannot be physically possessed and that involve performance or effort; examples include teaching, nursing, air travel, tailoring, accounting, and the opera. In employee compensation, indirect compensation in the form of programs, facilities, or activities supplied by employers for employees' use.

Benefits and services are forms of indirect compensation. They are monetary and nonmonetary payments over and above wage and salary rates. **Benefits** are financial in nature (e.g., health insurance payments, contributions to a pension fund), whereas **services** are employer-supplied programs, facilities, or activities (e.g., parks, gymnasiums, housing, transportation, child care, company cafeterias) useful to employees.

To yield a return to the employer and provide something positive to employees, benefits and services must be developed and used systematically. Too often, the so-called benefits are improperly installed. The company must first determine what benefits and services employees prefer and what resources are available and then select the best package the company can afford. In developing a benefit and service package, the employer must consider two important Internal Revenue Service issues:

- Passed in 1985, the Consolidated Omnibus Budget Reconciliation Act (COBRA) ensures that terminated or laid-off employees have the option to maintain health care insurance by personally paying the premiums.
- The Tax Reform Act of 1986 has two provisions that affect indirect compensation. Essentially in 1995 it caps at $9,240 the amount of tax deferred contributions (to be paid out at a later date) employees can make into a deferred pay plan. Also the average benefits to employees not highly compensated must be at least 75 percent of the average benefits provided to highly compensated employees (top 20 percent).

The benefits and services offered to employees are significant. The average firm pays between 30 and 50 percent of its payroll to benefits. A breakdown of this payment appears in Exhibit 11.8. Indirect compensation tends to be greater on average in the manufacturing industries than it is in the nonmanufacturing industries and greater for blue-collar than it is for white-collar and service workers.

Exhibit 11.8
Employee Benefits as a Percentage of Payroll by Type of Benefit

Type of Benefit	Overall	Manu-facturing	Nonmanu-facturing
1. *Legally required payments*	8.7%	9.2%	8.6%
Social Security			
Unemployment compensation			
Workers' compensation			
2. *Retirement and savings plan payments*	6.6	5.2	7.1
Defined benefit plan			
Defined contribution plan			
3. *Life insurance and death benefits*	0.6	0.8	0.5
4. *Medical benefits*	11.1	11.3	11.1
Hospital, medical premiums			
Short-term disability			
Long-term disability			
Dental insurance			
5. *Paid rest periods*	2.3	2.0	2.4
Lunch breaks			
Wash-up time			
Travel time			
6. *Payment for time not worked*	10.4	10.4	10.4
Vacation			
Holidays			
Sick leave			
Parental leave			
7. *Miscellaneous benefits*	1.6	1.6	1.6
Discount on goods and services			
Employee meals			
Education expenses			
Total benefits	41.3%	40.3%	41.7%

Source: Reprinted with permission from Chamber of Commerce of the United States from the 1994 edition of *Employee Benefits*. (800-638-6582).

Protection Programs
Programs that assist employees and families when direct compensation is terminated and with health care expenses.

Social security
unemployment
worker's Comp.

Protective Programs. Protection programs are designed to assist employees and their families if direct compensation is terminated and to alleviate the burden of health care expenses. Public protection programs grew out of the Social Security Act of 1935. They include social security benefits, unemployment compensation, and workers' compensation.

Funding of the *social security* system is provided by equal contributions from the employer and employee under terms of the Federal Insurance Contribution Act (FICA). The average social security benefit per year for a single person is $8,376 (for a married couple, $14,136), with adjustments periodically for increases in the consumer price index.

The Social Security Act dictates that *unemployment compensation* (given when a person loses a job) be jointly administered by the federal and state governments. Because income levels vary from state to state, unemployment compensation also varies by state. With the exception of Alabama, Alaska, and

New Jersey, only employers contribute to the unemployment fund. All profit-making firms pay tax on the first $7,000 to $10,000 of wages earned by each employee. Their contribution rate, however, varies based on the number of unemployed people drawing from the fund.

To be eligible for unemployment compensation benefits, a person must:

- Have worked a set number of weeks (established by the state).
- Be available and ready to work.
- Be actively searching for a job.
- Not be unemployed due to a labor dispute (except in New York and Rhode Island).
- Not have been terminated for gross misconduct.
- Not have terminated voluntarily.

The time period that the employee receives benefits is a function of how long the person worked prior to termination; in general the standard maximum period is 26 weeks. Benefits can be extended up to 13 weeks during periods of high unemployment or when jobs are lost due to foreign competition. The benefits vary across states but are about $225 per week.

Workers' compensation benefits are provided for temporary and permanent disability, disfigurement, medical expenses, and medical rehabilitation. Several benefits, the terms of which vary by state, are provided following fatal injuries.

Private protection programs are provided by firms but are not required by law. They include such benefits as health care, income after retirement, insurance against loss of life or limb, and, in some firms, guaranteed work and pay programs.

Many firms provide child-care facilities to help meet the needs of working parents. These children are playing at the Time-Warner children's center in New York.

Another category of indirect compensation includes programs for elder care, child care, and employee services. The U.S. population 80 years old and older is expected to grow from 5 million in 1980 to over 23 million in 2040. The Travelers Companies in Hartford, CT, has established an *elder care* program to help employees with the cost of care for aging parents or dependents. Travelers has established a flexible spending account, which allows employees to deduct up to $5,000 per year in pretax dollars from their paycheck. This money can be used to cover costs of the necessary care.[21]

Until the early 1980s, the U.S. work force was largely composed of traditional family heads—husbands who worked as the employed breadwinner. Increasingly, both spouses are working for pay; dual-career couples now account for over 40 percent of the work force. One problem faced by dual-career couples and single parents is child care. Organizations, now aware of the child-care problem, address it in a number of ways. Over 8,000 firms provide day-care services, financial assistance, or referral services for child care. A growing number of firms have on-site or near-site centers.[22] Other firms allow flexible work schedules, and employees can use the time to care for sick children or for special activities such as dental appointments or meetings with school counselors.

WORKPLACE SAFETY

Another important benefit for any person is a safe work environment, as discussed in Chapter 4. The December 1984 disaster in Bhopal, India, which resulted in the deaths of 3,000 people and injury to another 300,000, emphasizes the importance of safety. Americans are also familiar with the nuclear accident at Three Mile Island (1979) and the 1986 space shuttle *Challenger* disaster. Such incidents emphasize that safe equipment, practices, and procedures are crucial benefits. Annually over 1.8 million American workers suffer crippling injuries, and over 10,000 are killed on the job.[23]

Occupational Safety and Health Act (OSHA)
Law, passed in 1970, that mandates safety and health standards for U.S. business. Provided for the establishment of the Occupational Safety and Health Administration.

Due to the efforts of unions, employees, the government, insurance companies, and society in general, the **Occupational Safety and Health Act (OSHA)** became law on April 28, 1970. The act directs the Secretary of Labor to enforce safety and health standards in over 4 million businesses and for over 57 million employees. The core of the act is the system of standards that must be met. For example, OSHA has set an industrial noise limit of 90 decibels where workers are exposed eight hours per day. OSHA puts special emphasis on improving safety in the four industries with injury rates more than double the national average, which is 15.2 disabling injuries per million employee-hours worked. These industries are longshoring, meat and meat products, lumber and wood products, and miscellaneous transportation equipment.

OSHA enforces standards through a system of inspectors, citations, and penalties. To inspect health and safety conditions, Labor Department representatives may enter any business at a reasonable time. (OSHA inspectors denied entry must obtain a search warrant before conducting an inspection.) They may also question the employer, employees, or employee representatives. Criminal penalties for violations can go as high as $70,000 and/or one year in prison. Four categories of violations can result from an inspector's visit:

- *De minimis*—a minor violation not directly job related.
- *Nonserious*—a minor violation that is job related.
- *Serious*—one in which a chance of serious injury or death exists.
- *Imminent danger*—one that threatens serious injury or death; penalty is assessed by the federal courts.

A workplace problem that has been receiving attention in recent years is secondhand tobacco smoke. In 1986 the U.S. Surgeon General issued a report that stated that 2400 to 4000 lung cancer deaths were caused annually by secondhand smoke. As a result of this report and other evidence, more and more employers are moving to restrict or abolish smoking in the workplace.[24] It is estimated that over 84 percent of employers including the federal government limit or have abolished workplace smoking.

This chapter emphasizes the importance of people and people-related issues. Increasingly organizations such as Federal Express, Liz Claiborne, American Brands, Dreyer's, and 3M are indicating that managing human resources is now mandatory in business. The recruitment, selection, development, health, and safety of employees are all part of the strategic plans of more and more organizations.

Little can be done in any organization without a motivated work force. The people doing the work, carrying out the plans, meeting the customer, finalizing the sale, working on a project theme, reviewing the purchase order, and training the recently hired engineer must be motivated. Thus, understanding people is a requirement for developing programs to encourage and sustain employee motivation, which will be covered in the next chapter.

TOMORROW'S BUSINESS WORLD

Competitive Advantage

Until a few years ago, major sources of competitive advantage were product differentiation and cost controls. Increasingly, however, quality and human resources are the key concepts. Some of the human resource issues that will play very important roles in the future include:

- Half of all available jobs will require college degrees.
- By the turn of the century 33 percent of the work force will be part-time employees.
- By the year 2000 at least half of all employees will be at least 40 years of age.
- More pay systems will be tied very closely to performance achievements.

- An increasing number of firms will offer such benefits as on-site child care, extended maternity or parental leave, elder care, referral services, and flexible work schedules.
- Group incentive programs will become very prevalent and could even pass individual incentive programs in popularity.

Since these facts about human resources are generally accepted, what changes in managerial practices that you have learned about in Chapters 7–10 do you think will likely occur in organizations?

Source: Adapted from Vicki Elliott and Anna Orgera, "Competing for and with Workforce 2000," *Human Resource Focus* (June 1993): 3–4.

SUMMARY OF LEARNING OBJECTIVES

1. ***Define the term* human resource management.** Human resource management (HRM) is the process of accomplishing organizational objectives by acquiring, retaining, terminating, developing, and properly using the human resources (people) in an organization.

2. ***Explain why human resource planning, recruiting, and selecting are important.*** Planning is an important activity that involves estimating the size and makeup of the future work force. Planning of human resources is the life-blood of the firm. Without the right people in the right place at the right time, the firm could go out of business. Recruiting is important because the best-qualified applicants must be found to fill vacancies. The company wants to have the best possible pool of applicants from which to choose. Selecting is the series of steps beginning with initial screening of candidates and ending with the decision to hire one candidate. Selecting must be done in compliance with federal laws regulating employment discrimination.

3. ***Describe job analysis, job descriptions, and job specifications.*** Job analysis is the process of determining what knowledge, skills, and abilities (KSAs) an employee needs to successfully accomplish the job. Job descriptions use the data gathered from job analysis to outline the activities involved in the job and the work conditions. Job specifications state the qualifications necessary for a job.

4. ***Explain the role of the federal government in providing equal opportunities for employment to all Americans.*** Through Title VII of the Civil Rights Act of 1964 and the Equal Employment Opportunity Act of 1972, the federal government attempts to provide equal opportunities for employment without regard to race, religion, age, creed, sex, national origin, or disability. These laws are administered by the Equal Employment Opportunity Commission (EEOC). In addition, the Immigration Reform and Control Act of 1986 (IRCA) has made employers responsible for prohibiting the recruitment and employment of unauthorized foreign-born individuals. The Americans with Disabilities Act (ADA) prohibits employers from discriminating against disabled employees or job applicants.

5. ***Discuss training and development programs for hourly and salaried employees.*** Training programs inform hourly employees of company policies and procedures, educate them in job skills, and develop them for future advancement. Management development programs for salaried employees are used to educate and develop selected personnel so that they have the knowledge, skills, attitudes, and understanding needed to manage in future positions.

6. ***Identify examples of direct and indirect compensation.*** Direct compensation includes an employee's base pay (salary or wages) and performance-based pay (incentives). Wages are compensation based on time increments or number of units produced. Salaries are compensation based on a weekly or longer schedule. Individual incentives include piecework, production bonuses, and commissions. Examples of group incentives include Scanlon plans, profit-sharing plans,

and the Lincoln Electric plan. Indirect compensation includes federal- and state-mandated protection programs, private protection programs, paid leave, and miscellaneous benefits. Benefits are financial in nature (e.g., insurance programs), and services are employer-supplied programs, facilities, or activities useful to employees (e.g., child-care services). Public protection programs include social security benefits, unemployment compensation, and workers' compensation. Private protection programs include health care benefits, income after retirement, insurance, and guaranteed work and pay programs (e.g., golden parachutes).

7. ***Discuss comparable worth.*** The concept of comparable worth is an expansion of the concept of equal pay for equal work. This has become an issue because American women working full-time earn only about 75 percent of what men earn. The idea is to rank occupations typically held by men and those typically held by women, and then assign the same pay for jobs with the same rank. Comparable worth is controversial, and its principles are difficult to practice.

KEY TERMS

Human Resource Management (HRM)
Human Resource Planning
Recruitment
Job Analysis
Job Description
Job Specification
Civil Rights Act of 1964
Civil Rights Act of 1991
Equal Employment Opportunity Act of 1972
Affirmative Action Program
Immigration Reform and Control Act (IRCA)
Americans with Disabilities Act (ADA)
Selection
Training
Management Development
Direct Compensation
Indirect Compensation
Wages
Job Evaluation System
Comparable Worth
Salaries
Benefits
Services
Protection Programs
Occupational Safety and Health Act (OSHA)

QUESTIONS FOR DISCUSSION AND REVIEW

1. Some believe that drug testing is a blatant invasion of privacy. Do you agree? Why or why not?
2. Since performance appraisals are not perfect, is it time to abolish them? Why?
3. Can a teacher's pay be tied to performance?
4. How have affirmative action programs influenced recruitment programs of businesses?
5. Is a child-care benefit for some employees fair to those employees who have no children? Who should pay for the benefit?
6. Explain the difference between direct and indirect compensation plans.
7. Are there any valid, reasonable reasons why men performing a job may receive higher pay than women performing the same job? Explain.
8. Before developing a training program, what should an organization do to identify problems?
9. Has employment law become so complex that even small firms need to have access to legal advisers on most human resource management issues?
10. Most employers do not want to hire drug and alcohol abusers. Why?

CASE 11.1

You're Darned If You Do and Darned If You Don't

Sally Yuen, director of HRM for Dough Pineapple's Maui cannery, returned to her office deep in thought. She'd just spent the last hour and a half in a lengthy and somewhat heated discussion with cannery manager Danny Sackos regarding the latest turnover crisis among cannery employees. Shrugging her shoulders, Yuen wondered if Sackos was right. Maybe the current turnover problem was her fault—well, the fault of her department anyway. According to Sackos, if she'd done a better job in selecting employees in the first place, Dough Pineapple (DP) would not be in their current mess. "You hired quitters," he argued, pointing to the high turnover among temporary *and* permanent full-time employees. But then Yuen questioned whether it really was her fault.

DP maintained a regular work force of 200 employees. Depending on the harvest, as many as 150 temporary employees were also hired. Temporary workers received higher base salaries than regular employees ($6.25 per hour). However, they were not eligible for any benefits, including vacation leave, day care, and sick leave. If they were sick, they had to take time off without pay. They also could not participate in DP's highly successful profit-sharing program and matching pension fund.

Full-time, regular cannery workers were paid $5.00 per hour ($10,400 annually). While DP's hourly rate was below the industry average of $6.00 per hour ($12,480 annually), employees more than recouped this amount in performance bonuses. To date, DP was the only canner on the islands to have a state-of-the-art incentive pay program. In fact, it was the only canner that shared organizational profits with employees at all.

Last year employees received approximately $2,000 each in bonuses. This amount was lower than usual due to a hurricane that destroyed almost all of one harvest. Since the program was implemented in 1986, bonuses have averaged $8,000 per employee. And this year they were expected to be back on target. Yuen anticipated handing out bonuses in the range of $10,000 each. Employees had the option of taking the money in one lump sum, in quarterly installments, or in even distributions throughout the next year. According to company policy, employee bonuses would be announced at the semiannual employee's meeting, to be held in six weeks.

Yuen also was proud of DP's benefits. Employee benefits as a percentage of payroll averaged 30 percent in the industry. DP's percentage was 45 percent. All full-time employees with one year's seniority (tenured) were eligible to participate in DP's extensive benefit program, which included such innovations as an on-site day-care center (Yuen's brainchild, which took her two years to get approved) and an employee assistance program, including free legal assistance. The company also matched, dollar for dollar, employee contributions to a retirement fund and offered two college scholarships annually to employees' children. Yuen was particularly proud of DP's fitness center, which could be used by tenured employees and their families. Swimming lessons were provided free of charge to family members.

Vacation days also were above the industry average. Employees with one to two years of seniority earned one-half day of paid vacation per month, three-fourths day per month with three to five years' seniority, and one day per month with more than five years' service. Personal days accrued at the same rate for tenured employees. To prevent abuse, employees calling in absent before or after a holiday or after a payday are charged with an absence of 1.5 days. Employees with less than one year's service and temporary employees are not reimbursed for absences. The failure of any employee to call in to report an absence at least four hours before his or her shift starts is grounds for disciplinary procedures.

By having a core of permanent, tenured employees, DP is assured of having enough employees to meet average production demands. By paying temporary employees base salaries slightly above the labor market average, DP has traditionally had its pick of new employees. The system was cost effective because the salaries of temporary employees were only 18 percent over the base pay for cannery employees and well under the estimated hourly rate (with benefits) for permanent tenured employees (estimated at $7.98 per hour).

With all this going for DP, Yuen wondered where things had gone wrong. Maybe Sackos was right, and she just hadn't picked the right kind of employees. Bewildered, she had her assistant, Mark George, interview some employees to see what was going on. He also prepared a report on causes of turnover at DP (see Exhibit 1).

	Reason for Leaving						
Group	**Higher Pay**	**Better Benefits**	**Supervision**	**Moving**	**Better Job**	**Job Security**	**Fired**
Permanent							
Less than 1 year	40	22	1	2	3	1	2
1–2 years	10	0	3	3	2	4	1
Over 2 years	1	0	5	4	4	2	0
Temporary							
Less than 6 months	10	45	4	3	10	17	3
6–12 months	12	23	1	0	2	32	2
Over 1 year	5	15	2	3	15	19	0

Note: An employee could list more than one reason for leaving.

According to George, the following comments are typical of the feelings of full-time permanent employees:

- "Sure, it's a great place to work, but I'm tired of those young kids walking in off the street and making more than I do."
- "I know, I know, we're eligible to get bonuses, but they just can't make up for a weekly salary—at least not when you have three kids to support."

- "I worry that things are going to be the same as last year. I hung in there and look what I got, a lousy $2,500. The bottom line is that I still made less than temporary employees and those at the other canneries. I don't like it one bit."

The following comments were typical of the views of permanent untenured workers (two years' seniority):

- "I got really steamed last month when they docked my pay for being sick. I mean, I was really sick. I hadn't gone out with the girls or anything. I was down flat in bed with the flu. Why should I work hard here if I can't even get a lousy day off when I'm sick?"
- "I've worked here seven months already, and I'm pulling my own weight around here. Know what I mean? Well, it doesn't seem right that I should be paid less than those part-timers."

Among temporary workers, the view was:

- "Yeah, we make a good rate of pay but that's not everything. My wife had to have a C-section last month. Without insurance, it cost me a bundle."
- "I work just as hard as everyone else, so why shouldn't I have the same benefits? I'm getting up there in years. It'd be nice to have a little bit set aside."

Yuen, reading these comments, felt she couldn't win for losing. Maybe the most current employee attitude survey would be of help. At least it was worth a try (see Exhibit 2). All she knew was that if they didn't come up with a strategy soon, DP would not meet its canning quotas, and the employee bonuses would be lost forever.

	Permanent			
	Less than 1 year	**1–2 years**	**Over 2 years**	**Temporary**
Pay level	2.1	2.3	2.4	3.4
Pay system	1.5	2.4	3.2	3.3
Benefits	1.0	3.2	4.1	1.1
Supervision	3.4	4.1	3.7	3.3
Job	2.4	2.7	3.1	2.3
Co-workers	3.3	4.0	4.7	2.3
Work environment	3.4	4.1	3.6	2.7

* Based on a scale of 1 to 5: 1 = Very dissatisfied; 5 = Very satisfied.

Questions for Discussion

1. What do you think about a firm that pays below-industry hourly wages and uses a bonus to make up the difference?
2. Review the DP employee attitude survey results and explain why there is a turnover problem.
3. If you were Sally Yuen, how would you solve the current HRM crisis?

Source: Reprinted by permission from *Personnel and Human Resource Management,* Fourth Edition, by Randall S. Schuler and Vandra L. Huber, copyright © 1990 by West Publishing Company. All rights reserved, pp. 356–357.

CASE 11.2

The Drug Test Dilemma

A Phoenix computer company rehired an employee who had recently been convicted of cocaine possession. The company took him back with the understanding that for the next year he would be subjected to "spot drug testing." It was also understood, of course, that if such testing disclosed use of an illegal substance, he would be fired.

Shortly thereafter the employee was injured when he fell from a ladder while painting his home. The employee was placed on disability for five weeks. When he returned, management thought it was the right time for a urine test. A security guard escorted the man to the office of a physician, who asked him to provide a sample under supervision. The employee did not refuse; he just insisted that he was unable to provide the sample. He was offered water and other liquids to drink, but nothing helped. After several hours, the doctor again requested a sample. Still the employee refused, and nothing more was said because the doctor did not believe it was appropriate to continue requesting the sample.

The next day, the doctor and the human resource manager discussed the possibility that the employee might truly be unable to provide a sample because of embarrassment or a medical disorder. The doctor said this was possible but unlikely and later expressed this opinion in writing. After reviewing employment law requirements, management decided to fire the employee for not providing a urine sample in a reasonable amount of time.

Questions for Discussion

1. Who has the burden of proof in any discharge case—the employee or the employer? Explain.
2. What are some problems with drug-testing accuracy?
3. Would you have upheld the discharge? Why?

EXPERIENTIAL EXERCISE

The Missing Money Problem

Activity:
This activity is designed for classroom discussion focusing on managerial response to money missing from the store's cash register. About 50 minutes will be needed to complete the exercise.

Directions:
1. Provide the class with a brief story, such as the following:

You (the student) are to play the role of a paint store manager who discovers that $150 is apparently missing from the cash register, as the evening receipts do not match the dollar total in the cash register. Three employees had access to the cash register that afternoon.

2. Ask each student to discuss and identify the steps to be taken by the manager. Provide about 15 minutes. Select a few students to report individual analyses.
3. Interject a new variable into the discussions at this point by saying that one of the three employees has stepped forward and admitted taking the $150. She happens to be a single mother who has previously been on welfare. Ask the students to decide what steps the manager should now take on this case. Provide about 10 minutes for further discussion.
4. Select a few students to describe their decision and underlying rationale. Allow about 10 minutes.

BUSINESS APPLICATION

Controlling Soaring Group Health Insurance Costs

Activity:
This activity is designed for small-group and classroom discussions focusing on managerial strategies for controlling the soaring costs of group health insurance. About 45 minutes should be allotted for completion.

Directions:
1. Divide the class into small groups of 4 to 7 members, asking each group to appoint a recorder/spokesperson for the group.
2. Provide the class with a brief background on the health insurance cost problem, citing aspects such as the following:
    - An employer's provision of group health insurance coverage is very important for the employee's benefit package.
    - The cost of providing group health insurance has been rising steadily and companies are closely examining strategies for dealing with these escalating costs.

- One approach to controlling insurance costs has been to attempt to reduce the employees' utilization of the insurance by trying to curb factors that contribute to poor health, such as cigarette smoking.
- Cigarette smoking contributes to increased sickness, which leads to increased use of health insurance.

3. Ask each group to discuss whether they would support a company's attempt to control group health insurance costs by requiring employees who smoke to pay higher premiums than those who do not smoke. Provide 15 to 20 minutes for discussion.

4. Ask each group's spokesperson to tell the class of the group's decision and underlying rationale. Allow approximately 20 minutes for reporting and discussion.

Note: Time permitting, the instructor may want to elicit student feedback on premium differentials for other factors contributing to sickness—for example, employees with serious health problems, family history of illness, significantly overweight people, and so forth.

NOTES

1. Jennifer J. Laabs, "Prudential Measures HR with a Total-Quality Yardstick," *Personnel Journal* (April 1995): 139–143; Elizabeth J. Hawok, "Culture and Rewards: A Balancing Act," *Personnel Journal* (April 1995): 30–37; and Patricia Jones and Larry Kahaner, *In Say It and Live It. The 50 Corporate Mission Statements That Hit the Mark* (New York: Doubleday, 1995).
2. Annual Report, Kent Electronics, 1994.
3. Daniel B. Turban and Thomas L. Keon, "Organizational Attractiveness: An Interactionist Perspective," *Journal of Applied Psychology* (April 1993): 184–193.
4. David P. Twomey, *Equal Employment Opportunity Law* (Cincinnati: South-Western, 1994).
5. David P. Twomey, *Labor and Employment Law* (Cincinnati: South-Western, 1994): 613–616.
6. Francine S. Hall and Elizabeth L. Hall, "The ADA: Going Beyond the Law," *Academy of Management Executive* (February 1994): 17–26.
7. Deborah L. Jacobs, "Japanese–American Cultural Clash," *New York Times* (September 9, 1990): 3:1.
8. "Fewer People Fail As Workplace Drug Testing Increases," *Human Resource Focus* (June 1993): 24.
9. Bill Oliver, "How to Prevent Drug Abuse in Your Workplace," *HR Magazine* (December 1993): 78–82.
10. Twomey, *Labor and Employment Law*: 605–607.
11. Larry Reynolds, "New Variations on Recruitment Prescreening," *HR Focus* (October 1994): 1, 8.
12. Clifford Pugh, "Quilting Bee Creates Comaraderie That Helps to Heal the Heartbreak," *Houston Post* (March 30, 1995): D1–D2.
13. Clifford Pugh, "The Power of the Quilt," *Houston Post* (March 30, 1995): D1–D2.
14. Cindy Zkrzycki, "Employee Bonuses Spur Productivity," *Houston Chronicle* (February 19, 1990): 4C.
15. Ira Kay, "Do Your Workers Really Merit a Raise?" *The Wall Street Journal* (March 26, 1990): A10.
16. Jay R. Schuster and Patricia K. Zingheim, "New Pay Strategies That Work," *Journal of Compensation & Benefits* (May–June 1993): 5–9.
17. U.S. Department of Labor, Bureau of Labor Statistics, "Employee Benefits in Medium and Large Firms, 1988," (August 1989): 406.
18. Carolyn Wiley, "Incentive Plan Pushes Production," *Personnel Journal* (August 1993): 86–91.
19. "Comparable Worth in Industrialized Countries," *Monthly Labor Review* (November 1992): 40–42.
20. *The Wall Street Journal*
21. Roberta Maynard, "Meet the New Law on Family Leave," *Nations Business* (April 1993): 26.
22. Judy Nixon, Marilyn Helms, and Charles White, "What Companies Are Doing About Child Care," *Journal of Compensation & Benefits* (January–February 1993): 7–24.
23. Greg LaBar, "Cutting Through the OSHA Jungle," *Occupational Hazards* (September 1993): 83–87.
24. Richard A. Wolfe and Donald F. Parker, "Employee Health Management: Challenges and Opportunities," *Academy of Management Executive* (May 1994): 22–31.

CHAPTER 12

Labor-Management Relations

LEARNING OBJECTIVES

1. Define the term *labor union*.
2. Identify the significant trends facing the labor movement today.
3. Explain why employees decide to organize unions.
4. Compare the main features of the major labor legislation.
5. List the steps in both organizing and decertifying a union.
6. Define the term *collective bargaining*.
7. Discuss what is included in a union-management contract.
8. Explain how a strike, boycott, and lockout differ.

By all rights, Caterpillar, maker of heavy-duty construction equipment, ought to be a very happy company. Two years of a consistently weak dollar have all but knocked out main competitor Komatsu of Japan. At the same time, demand for heavy equipment has been so strong that Caterpillar has more orders than it can fill without delays. As a result, the Peoria, IL, company's sales, profits, and market share are soaring.

But the company isn't happy—again. On June 21, 1994, some 14,500 angry United Auto Workers (UAW) members stalked off the job. It was the second strike against Caterpillar in two years. The first one lasted five and one-half months. Ostensibly, Caterpillar management won that strike when, led by hard-line CEO Donald V. Fites, it threatened to permanently replace striking workers. After that "victory," instead of trying to soothe workers' feelings, the company disciplined and fired union members for mostly petty actions such as wearing T-shirts that disparaged the company. These actions triggered nine local walkouts between November 1993 and the June 21 company-wide strike. One Decatur, IL, worker said that Caterpillar management's actions over that year "did more to revive the union than anything else."

The ongoing battle between Caterpillar and its workers has left workers confused and angry—both at the company and at their union. After workers returned to their jobs in 1992, union leaders tried to get them to slow production by sticking to the rule book. Members largely ignored this request, however, as productivity and quality remained stable. About all they did was wear the anti-Caterpillar T-shirts, some reading "Permanently replace Fites." The company's subsequent disciplinary actions against union members caused the National Labor Relations Board to file 89 complaints against the company. Caterpillar, for its part, denies it has broken federal labor law.

The harsh company actions drove many workers into the arms of the union. Decatur welder Nancy Waterman, for example, who hadn't been a union activist in her 18 years with the company, raised $20,000 from fellow workers to buy TV commercials telling the union's side of the story. Now, she insists, "We will last one day longer than Cat." NLRB Regional Director Glenn Zipp remarked, "There is a great sense of indignation on the shop floor about what workers feel is unjust treatment."

Underlying the bad feelings are some difficult substantive issues. Fites still insists that it's unreasonable for the UAW to demand that the company agree to the same contract the union won from farm-equipment maker Deere & Co. Fites argues that, because Caterpillar faces greater foreign competition, it needs a different pact. Although the fight isn't over wages, Caterpillar contends that its pay package is one of the richest in the nation: Including overtime, its average UAW worker earned $49,000 in 1993, plus benefits.

The union has its own concerns. With Japanese competitor Komatsu falling on hard times, it feels Caterpillar can afford to meet the union's central demand: more protection from layoffs. It points to the fact that, in the first seven months of 1994 alone, Caterpillar added 1,000 new workers.

Given Caterpillar's history of taking a tough stand against the union, many workers are nervous about a prolonged walkout. Robert Williams, a 54-year-old Caterpillar veteran five months shy of retirement, didn't cross the picket

line in 1992 but isn't sure what he'll do this time. "I'm not going to lose my pension," he says. Other workers seem equally troubled. On the second day of the strike, Caterpillar reported that one-quarter of its Peoria workers stayed on the job.

Such a bitter fight at a company that is doing so well and whose immediate prospects are so bright seems incomprehensible. But the tensions created by the hard-line management approach of CEO Fites and the demands of the union will probably ensure that this battle will go on beyond the actual strike.

American history is dotted with bitter labor disputes that result in the disruption of lives, the destruction of communities, and occasional hostility. Strikes are part of the free-market profit-and-loss system, although they could be curtailed through government intervention. Do you think it is better for government to intervene or stay out of difficult labor disputes? Do you think that organized labor has mostly helped, or mostly hindered, the free market system in the United States?[1]

Labor Union
Organization of employees who join together to protect, maintain, and improve their economic, social, and political power and well-being.

Labor unions are organizations of employees who formally join together to protect, maintain, and improve their economic, social, and political power and well-being. For centuries people have formed labor organizations known as clubs, guilds, associations, and unions. In America, labor organizations existed before the Revolutionary War. They evolved as a way to combat inhumane working conditions and practices, which were commonplace during the early stages of the Industrial Revolution. As the opening story about Caterpillar suggests, workers still use unions to fight against what they believe is unfair and unjust treatment by management.

The term *unions* has historically referred to organizations of men and women in the same trade. Today, some groups of professionals who formally join together may call themselves associations instead. For example, the American Association of University Professors and the American Nurses Association are labor organizations.

In this chapter, we first provide a brief history of the American labor movement. Next we consider trends in unionization and reasons for people to join unions. Then we examine the structure of unions and the federal regulations governing their operations. We also explore the processes of organizing and decertifying a union and of collective bargaining. Finally, we look at the elements of union-management contracts and nonunion organizations.

A BRIEF HISTORY OF THE AMERICAN LABOR MOVEMENT

Industrial Union
A union in which all members are employed in a company or industry, regardless of occupation.

Unions are of two general types: industrial and craft. **Industrial union** members are all employed in one company or industry (e.g., workers in the steel industry or the auto industry), regardless of occupation. **Craft union** members belong to one craft (e.g., carpenters, bricklayers, ironworkers) or to a closely related group of occupations.

Craft Union
A union in which all members belong to one craft or to a closely related group of occupations.

Today approximately 14 million workers belong to unions.[2] This means that about 15 percent of all employed people are in unions. To understand unions in the 1990s, let us briefly trace how they evolved.[3]

As early as 1790, skilled shoemakers, printers, and tailors organized themselves into trade unions. They made demands about minimum wages and pressured fellow workers to not accept a lesser wage. Employers did not sit idly by, however, as craftsmen attempted to unionize employees. An 1806 court ruling made it a "conspiracy in restraint of trade" for workers to combine or exert pressure on management. In effect, then, unions were illegal until 1842 when the Massachusetts Supreme Court, in *Commonwealth* v. *Hunt,* decided that criminal conspiracy did not apply if unions did not use illegal tactics to achieve their goals.

Yellow-Dog Contract
A statement signed by an employee promising not to form or join a union.

Even then employers still resisted by discharging employees who joined unions. They also forced employees to sign a **yellow-dog contract,** a statement in which the employee promised not to form or join a union. If employees who signed such contracts later joined a union, they were discharged. Employers also obtained court injunctions against strikes.

Early unions promoted social reform and free public education. Some of the more militant groups—such as the Molly Maguires from the Pennsylvania coal mines—were considered socialist or anarchist. They were involved in rioting and bloodshed, initiated by both employers and union members.

The turbulent 1870s and 1880s brought growing recognition of the labor union approach to social and economic problems. These experiences helped solidify the union movement and encouraged the development of a nationwide organization.

Knights of Labor
The first union federation that attracted members from local unions from all crafts and occupational areas.

The first union federation to achieve significant size and influence was the Noble Order of the **Knights of Labor,** formed around 1869. This group attracted employees and local unions from all crafts and occupational areas. The strength of the Knights was diluted because it failed to integrate the wide range of needs and interests of its skilled and unskilled, industrial, and craft members. Also, many workers left the Knights of Labor because they thought it was too radical.

A group of national craft unions cut their relationships with the Knights of Labor around 1886. They formed the American Federation of Labor (A. F. of L., later changed to AFL). Samuel Gompers of the Cigar-Makers' International Union was elected president. The AFL restricted its membership to skilled tradespeople. Although the AFL dominated the union scene at the turn of the century, its focus on craft unionism was not accepted by all American workers. In some places there were notable efforts to create industrial unions. For example, the United Mine Workers, the oldest major industrial union, was established around 1890. After 1900, three industrial unions emerged in the textile industry. The International Ladies' Garment Workers' Union was the strongest of the three.

In 1935 the Committee (later changed to Congress) for Industrial Organizations (CIO) was formed by John L. Lewis, president of the United Mine Workers, in cooperation with a number of presidents of unions expelled from the AFL. The CIO was formed to organize industrial and mass-production employees. At this time, the AFL began offering membership to unskilled employees also.

As shown in Exhibit 12.1, the union movement grew slowly from 1900 to 1930. The federal government's attitude toward union organizing was at different times neutral, indifferent, or opposed. But with the passage of federal laws in the 1920s and '30s that gave protection to the union organizing process, union membership began to climb. (We will discuss some of this legislation later in the chapter.) Thus, formal law helped unions grow during their formative years. From 1930 to 1947, union membership increased from 3 million to 14 million.

Exhibit 12.1
Union Membership in the United States since 1900

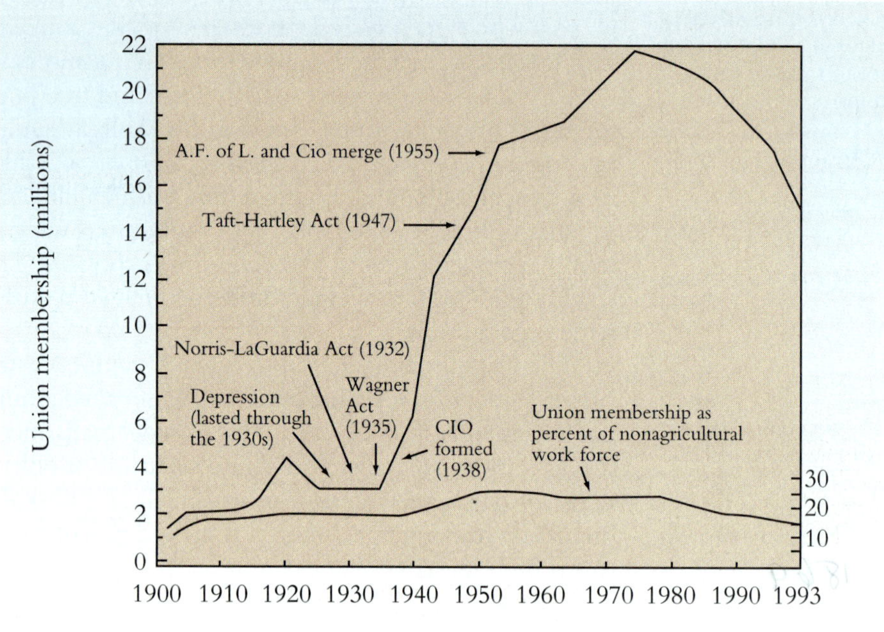

AFL-CIO
The merged body of the American Federation of Labor (craft union members) and the Congress of Industrial Organizations (industrial union members).

Competition for new union members led to bitter conflicts between the AFL and the CIO, but in 1955 they merged. The structure of the present **AFL-CIO** is shown in Exhibit 12.2. Most national and international labor unions now belong to the AFL-CIO, although a number of unions, representing over 4 million members, are unaffiliated. Such large and powerful unions as the Teamsters and the United Automobile Workers at one time broke away from the AFL-CIO, but they have now rejoined the group.

Exhibit 12.2 *Structure of the AFL-CIO*

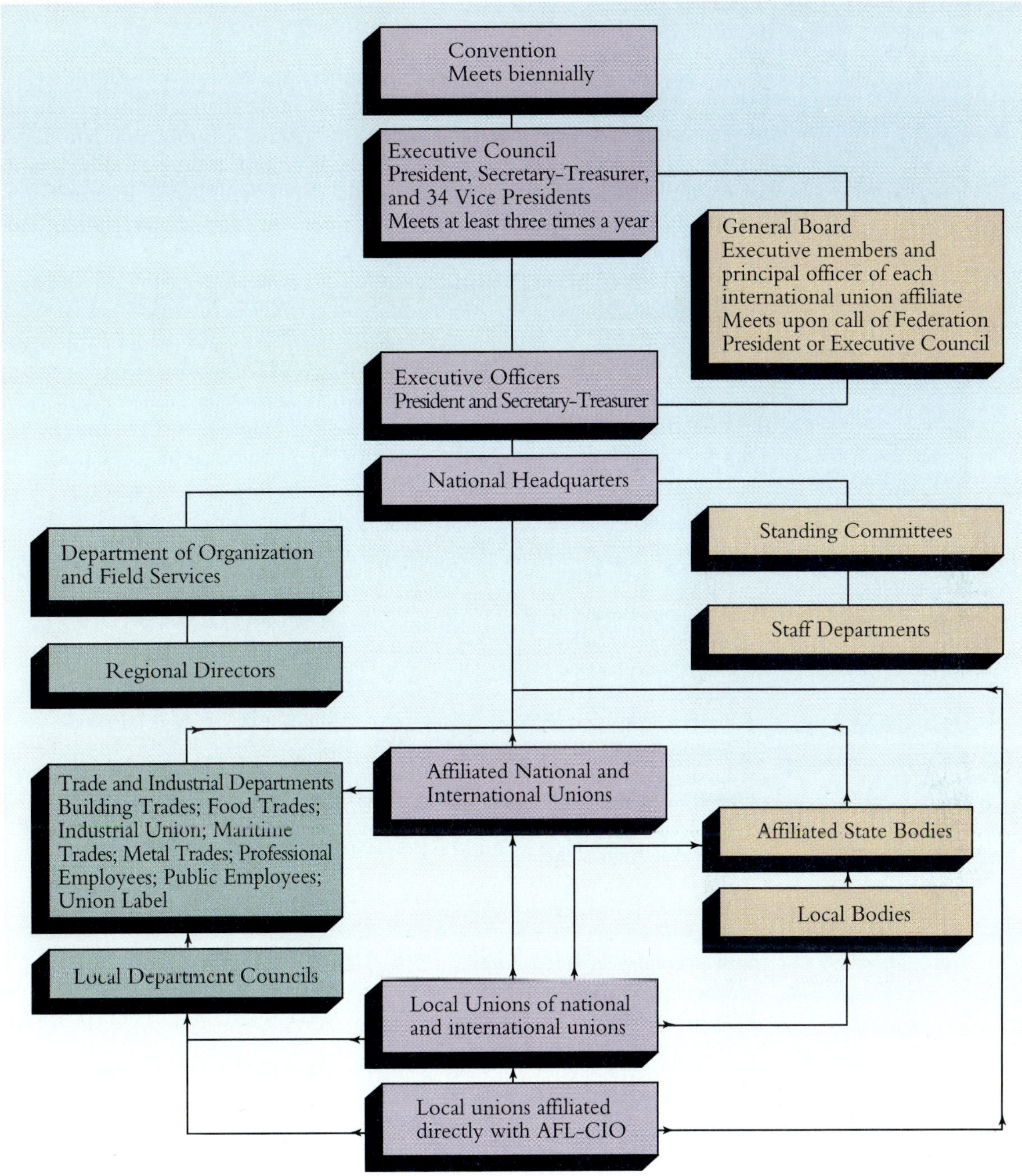

Source: Reprinted with permission, p. 2, Chart 1: Structure of the AFL-CIO, from *Directory of U.S. Labor Organizations, 1994–95 Edition*, by Courtney D. Gifford. Copyright 1994 by the Bureau of National Affairs, Inc., Washington, DC 20037.

UNIONIZATION TRENDS

The 10 largest U.S. unions and their memberships are listed in Exhibit 12.3. The two largest unions, with memberships of more than a million each, are the Teamsters and the American Federation of State, County, and Municipal Employees. Exhibit 12.4 shows the degree of unionization by industry type. For example, at least 75 percent of the blue-collar employees in transportation are unionized, whereas fewer than 25 percent of local government employees are unionized.

In the United States, union membership has been on a long downward trend. After peaking at 35 percent of the nonagricultural work force in 1954, union membership fell to 23 percent in 1980 and just 15.8 percent at the end of 1993, according to the U.S. Labor Department's Bureau of Labor Statistics. Union membership rose by 200,000 in 1993, but that followed 14 years of consecutive decline. Excluding public sector employees, U.S. unions can claim the allegiance of just 11.2 percent of the private-sector work force.[4]

Exhibit 12.3
Ten Largest Unions in the United States

Union	Affiliation	Membership
International Brotherhood of Teamsters, Chauffeurs, Warehousemen and Helpers of America	AFL-CIO	1,379,000
American Federation of State, County and Municipal Employees (AFSCME)	AFL-CIO	1,191,000
United Food and Commercial Workers	AFL-CIO	997,000
United Automobile, Aerospace and Agricultural Implement Workers of America, International Union (UAW)	AFL-CIO	840,000
Service Employees' International Union	AFL-CIO	881,000
International Brotherhood of Electrical Workers (IBEW)	AFL-CIO	730,000
United Brotherhood of Carpenters and Joiners of America	AFL-CIO	494,000
International Association of Machinists and Aerospace Workers	AFL-CIO	534,000
United Steelworkers of America	AFL-CIO	459,000
Laborers' International Union of North America	AFL-CIO	406,000

Source: *Statistical Abstract of the United States* (Austin, TX: The Reference Press, 1993), 435.

Exhibit 12.4 *Degree of Union Organization in Selected Industries*

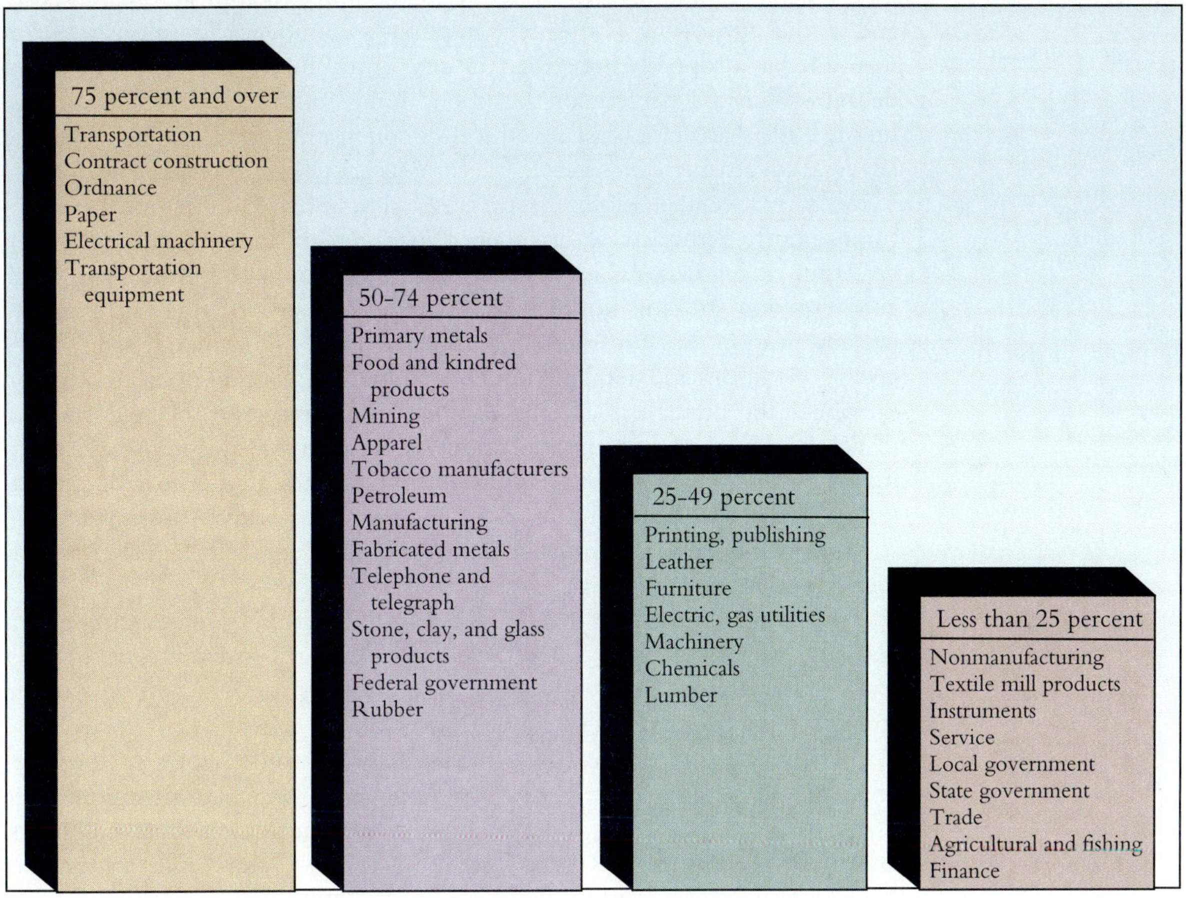

Source: Adapted from U.S. Department of Labor, Bureau of Labor Statistics (Washington, DC: U.S. Government Printing Office, 1994), 28–34 (originally prepared in 1987).

Partly out of fear that striking workers might be replaced and partly because unions recognized that employers were up against the wall, strikes at companies with 1,000 or more employees fell from 187 in 1980 to only 40 in 1991. More important, the number of elections held by workers voting to unionize their workplaces fell from roughly 4,000 a year in the early 1980s to 3,000 in 1991.[5]

Union membership and union activity have dropped over the past decade. Why? Several factors have contributed to the decline.

First, the public has been bombarded with news of irresponsible union strikes, unreasonable wage or salary demands, some union leaders' criminal activities, and featherbedding (make-work) situations. These stories are poor publicity for unions. One study indicated that the monopolistic practices of unions cost the U.S. economy $5 billion to $10 billion annually. (Other estimates point out, however, that unions increase the efficiency of the economy by the same amount. How? By reducing training expenses, job search costs, and worker turnover.) The American public's confidence in unions as an institution has dropped more than in any other enterprise in the past two decades. Only 22 percent of the public holds unions in high regard. And union leaders are rated last in ethical conduct and moral practices, behind lawyers, advertising executives, government officials, and stockbrokers.[6]

Second, several economic factors, including intense international competition, poorly equipped factories, poor management, new technologies, and government regulations, have struck hardest at unionized industries—steel, autos, oil and gas, and mining. The deregulation of trucking, airlines, and communications has contributed to the erosion of union membership. Economic conditions and deregulation have caused the layoff of millions of union members, the permanent closing of unionized plants, and the relocation of plants and offices to nonunion locations. Mergers and acquisitions have eliminated union and nonunion jobs throughout the country. The reduction in union jobs has been felt the most in the states where unionization is strongest—New York, Illinois, Michigan, Ohio, California, and Pennsylvania.

Third, management in the 1970s began to resist union organizing efforts and large wage demands. They developed programs and strategies to fight back against unions. They also built new facilities in areas with less union strength—the South and the Sunbelt.[7]

Finally, since the proportion of blue-collar jobs in the work force has decreased and the labor force is now predominantly white-collar, unions have had to redirect organizing efforts to recruit more nurses, teachers, engineers, and other professionals. Results have been spotty. White-collar employees have for years felt superior to their blue-collar counterparts. Perhaps many believe that by joining a union they would lose status, prestige, and esteem. Educational achievements, mode of dress, language, and job locations within businesses typically give the white-collar employee a more common base with management than with blue-collar employees. Also, compared to just a few decades ago, a higher proportion of women work in white-collar jobs, and women generally have been more resistant to unionization.

To sound the death knell for labor unions would be premature. Unionized workers across all industries on average earn 15 to 30 percent more than comparable nonunion workers.[8] Union advocates claim this significant difference results from union bargaining. Also, unionism has increased among government employees. The increasing numbers of better-educated, higher-status civil servants and state employees have helped improve the union's image. How much impact the image improvement will have on union membership is uncertain. But aggressive, imaginative, and fair union leadership could be effective in organizing significantly more white-collar workers. The increase in the unionization of government employees indicates that white-collar workers are listening to and watching the union message.

Another option for some unions is to purchase equity in the companies where members are employed. The United Steelworkers (USW) for example, in September 1994 formed a joint venture with a New York investment group to purchase two plants that had been shut down in 1992 by Bethlehem Steel. The union agreed to flexible work rules and pay scales that are only half what union members make at other mills. In return, workers at the new company, called BRW Steel Corporation, get a 25 percent equity stake and two seats on the board of directors—plus 800 jobs that did not exist.[9]

Organizational and recruiting efforts of unions have always varied according to changes in economic, social, and political conditions. Membership drives continue in the public sector (which includes military personnel, police, and firefighters), among professionals (teachers, medical personnel, athletes, lawyers), among employees in service industries, and among agricultural workers.

TOMORROW'S BUSINESS WORLD

Union Influence Will Continue to Decline

The reasons for the decline in unionism over the past several decades are many. Some experts link the policies of the Reagan administration to the decline in union membership. After all, he fired 11,500 striking air traffic controllers in 1981.

A more thoughtful review of the decline in union membership points to a number of demographic factors. One is a shift in the labor force away from unionized industries. The influx of young workers into the labor force from the 1960s brought in an enormous number of well-educated, highly ambitious people. On the whole, the U.S. economy has created 50 million new jobs since 1960. However, five characteristics of those jobs have distanced them from the traditional labor unions: Most of the jobs were white collar, most were in the service sector, most of the jobs were with small to medium-sized businesses, most were part-time or flexible, and most of the jobs were in the Sunbelt. Another significant factor in the decline of unionism is the rise of employer enlightenment. Most employers today are more knowledgeable about the working conditions that create a productive work force. In addition, the manner in which employers deal with employees is more constrained by law than half a century ago when unions flourished. As a result, there are few examples of the horrendous working conditions that were common in the 1930s and that built union membership.

As a result of these and other factors, the extent and influence of union power has declined steadily. Unions have responded by moving organizational activities into the service sector. While union members account for only 11.5 percent of the private work force, fully one-third of government workers are union members. Further, the unions are currently trying to create a new generation of organizers to reach the new workers in the variety of jobs they have taken on—service workers, employees of small businesses, white-collar workers. The AFL-CIO has established an Organizing Institute in Washington, DC, where it trains a cadre of young people to revive the labor movement by grass roots identification of workers' issues at plant sites.

But the way back for unions will be long and arduous. Demographics and job mobility will make it a continual challenge to increase effective representation outside of large, stable organizations like the government, large manufacturing enterprises, transportation companies, and utility firms. The weaker union structure will be the rule during the 1990s.

Unions have been an important tool for American workers to gain power in negotiating with employers. Now that unions are declining, what is a new source of employee negotiating power? Do you think that you will ever join a union? Why?

Source: Adapted from Ian Morrison and Greg Schmid, *Future Tense: The Business Realities of the Next Ten Years* (New York: William Morrow and Company, Inc., 1994); Ronald Henkoff, "Winning the New Career Game," *Fortune* (July 12, 1993): 46–49.

WHY DO PEOPLE JOIN UNIONS?

Many people ask, "Why do people unionize?" Of course, this question has no single answer. People join for different reasons. Research shows that people are attracted to unions because they are dissatisfied with what Fred Herzberg called hygiene factors (see Chapter 10): (1) pay and benefits, (2) supervision, and (3) job security. Recognizing the importance of job security, a growing group of companies have either contract specifications or a tradition to not lay off employees. Some of these companies believe that no-layoff policies mean higher productivity, increased loyalty, and retention of skilled workers. They cite research findings, especially reports issued by the Work in America Institute.

One study of nearly 88,000 clerical, sales, and technical employees at Sears, Roebuck found that the strongest predictor of unionization attempts was the employees' dissatisfaction with the supervisor.[10] What does that really mean? Is the supervisor not being fair, not being a good listener, or not being supportive? Exhibit 12.5 lists the qualities found to be important in the bond between managers and workers. They suggest that workers are satisfied with managers who possess three specific skills: technical (they know the job), administrative (they know the system), and interpersonal (they know people).

The Maslow needs hierarchy covered in Chapter 10 provides a framework for tying research findings together. Maslow portrayed humans as driven to put forth effort by the desire to satisfy needs. As research suggests, employees try to gratify important needs and wants. When needs are unsatisfied in the workplace, the union becomes an attractive tool for change. Unionization will continue to be an alternative as long as some companies fail to satisfy their employees' economic, interpersonal, and job security needs. Your Values and Attitudes will help you to discover your feelings about unions and management.

Exhibit 12.5
Factors That Determine Subordinates' Satisfaction with Supervisors

Subordinates are more satisfied with a supervisor who:

- Displays technical competence.
- Sets clear work goals for subordinates.
- Gives clear instructions.
- Clearly defines subordinates' job responsibilities.
- Backs subordinates with other managers.
- Fairly appraises subordinates' performances.
- Allows subordinates adequate time to do the job right.
- Allows subordinates adequate time to learn the job's tasks.
- Informs subordinates of work changes before they are to take place.
- Displays consistent behavior toward subordinates.
- Helps subordinates to get the job done.
- Gives subordinates credit for their ideas.
- Listens to and understands subordinates' job-related problems.
- Follows through to get the job's problems solved.
- Treats subordinates fairly when they make mistakes.
- Shows concern for subordinates' career progress.
- Congratulates subordinates for doing a good job.

Source: Adapted from V. Scarpello and R.J. Vandenberg, "The Satisfaction with My Supervisor Scale: Its Utility in Research and Practice," *Journal of Management* (Fall 1987): 447–466.

YOUR VALUES AND ATTITUDES

My Union-Management Attitude

Directions: Complete this quiz to determine your general feelings about labor (unions) and management (organizational managers). There are no correct or incorrect answers; only general impressions that you hold are of interest.

Y N 1. Do you trust management to give a fair deal on grievances, if no union (within the firm) exists?

Y N 2. Do you believe that unions have been responsible for improved working conditions in the United States over the past 40 years?

Y N 3. Do you believe that unions are democratically run?

Y N 4. Do you believe that management has fairly treated nonmanagerial personnel?

Y N 5. Do you believe that a union representative should be placed on the board of directors of a unionized company?

Y N 6. Do you believe that police officers should have the right to strike?

Y N 7. Do you believe that management would have raised wages and fringe benefits to generally high levels without union pressure?

Y N 8. Do you believe that union busting or decertification should be permitted in the United States?

Y N 9. Do you believe that management should be permitted to make promotion decisions without having to pay attention to seniority clauses (those with longer job tenure are given some preference) in a union contract?

Y N 10. Do you believe that unions treat minority employees more fairly than management treats them?

Feedback: Now assess your attitudes toward unions and management. The following answers indicate a union or management bias or attitude.

1.	Y: Management	N: Union	6.	N: Management	Y: Union
2.	N: Management	Y: Union	7.	Y: Management	N: Union
3.	N: Management	Y: Union	8.	Y: Management	N: Union
4.	Y: Management	N: Union	9.	Y: Management	N: Union
5.	N: Management	Y: Union	10.	N: Management	Y: Union

If you answered 8 of the 10 questions from either the management orientation or the union orientation, you lean in favor of that particular group. For example, if you answered all 10 questions as shown on the left (management key), the indication is that you have a strong management bias.

This is not a scientific quiz, but is used for information purposes only. Did you know that you had a bias or that you are generally neutral? Have you ever been a union member? Why did you join the union?

THE STRUCTURE AND MANAGEMENT OF UNIONS

Many unions are large organizations. They have management, leadership, and financial control problems similar to those faced by business firms. Unions' national headquarters employ staff economists, engineers, attorneys, accountants, wage and salary experts, and professional managers.

Local Union Structure

The labor movement has its foundation in the local craft union. The local directly influences the membership. Through the local, members exercise their complaints and pay the dues that support the national union.

Local union activities are conducted by officials elected by the members. Elected officers include the president, vice president, secretary-treasurer, business representative, and committee chairpersons. Elected officials of local unions often have full-time jobs in addition to their regular union duties.

Business Representative A union official who negotiates and administers the labor agreement and settles contract problems.

In many local unions, the **business representative** is the dominant person. The major responsibilities of the business representative are to negotiate and administer labor agreements and to settle problems that may arise in connection with contracts. The business representative also collects dues, recruits new members, coordinates social activities, and arranges union meetings.

Union Steward A person who represents the interests of local union members in their on-the-job relations with managers.

The **union steward** (sometimes called the *shop steward*) represents the interests of local union members in their relations with managers on the job. In the auto industry, the steward (called a *committee person*) devotes full time to solving disputes that arise in connection with the union-management labor contract.

National-Local Relationship

The constitution of the national union establishes the rules, policies, and procedures under which the local unions may be chartered and become members. Each national union exercises some control over the local unions. These controls usually deal with the collection of dues, the admission of new members by the local, and the use of union funds. The national also provides the local unions with support for organizing campaigns and strikes and for the administration of contracts. Over 100 national union organizations support about 80,000 local unions.

Managing in the Union

The job of managing a union is challenging and time consuming. Union officials need to be dedicated, willing to work long hours, able to counsel members on personal problems, and skilled in influencing people. Officers must periodically run for reelection.

Unions finance themselves through dues, fines, and initiation fees collected at the local level. But members resist high assessments. Union officials have to convince them that the union needs a sound financial base to have the power to secure favorable labor agreements. Most union members pay dues that come out to roughly two hours' wages per month; two major unions—the Steelworkers and Automobile Workers—have set their monthly dues at exactly this two-hour level. Initiation fees, paid once, tend to range from $50 to $150.

FEDERAL REGULATION OF LABOR-MANAGEMENT RELATIONS

Railway Labor Act
A 1926 law that established collective bargaining as a means for resolving labor-management disputes.

Injunction
Court order that prohibits the defendant from engaging in certain activities, such as striking.

Norris-LaGuardia Act
A 1932 law that limited the power of federal courts to stop union picketing, boycotts, and strikes; also made the yellow-dog contract unenforceable.

State and federal laws govern union-management interaction. These laws have evolved through common law and rulings by the National Labor Relations Board and the courts. They have swung back and forth like a pendulum, at one time favoring management and at another time favoring unions. Exhibit 12.6 contains a summary of the major labor-management regulations discussed in this section.

Early Labor Legislation: Pro-Labor

Railway Labor Act. The first labor legislation passed by Congress after the Clayton Act of 1914 excluded unions from the Sherman Antitrust Act of 1890 was the **Railway Labor Act** of 1926. It established the process of collective bargaining as a means of resolving labor-management disputes.

Norris-LaGuardia Act. In the 1930s, the federal government became involved in labor disputes outside the railroad industry. **Injunctions,** court decrees to stop union activities, gave employers an easy way to hinder union activities. However, in 1932 came the **Norris-LaGuardia Act** as a response to the Great Depression. This act, also called the Anti-Injunction Act, limited the power of federal courts to stop union picketing, boycotts, and strikes. The Norris-LaGuardia Act also made the yellow-dog contract (a contract, mentioned earlier, in which employees agree not to join any union) unenforceable.

Wagner Act
A law that made collective bargaining legal and required employers to bargain with the representatives of the employees. The law is also referred to as the National Labor Relations Act.

NLRB
A group that investigates cases of alleged unfair labor practices by employers and unions and holds elections to determine whether groups of employees want to be unionized.

Wagner Act. The National Labor Relations Act, better known as the **Wagner Act,** was passed in 1935. This act made collective bargaining legal and required employers to bargain with the representatives of the employees. It encouraged the growth of trade unions by restraining management from interfering with them. By restricting the activities of management, this act also forced the government to take an active role in union-management relationships. Five unfair management practices specified in the Wagner Act are summarized in Exhibit 12.7.

The power to implement the Wagner Act was given to a three-person **National Labor Relations Board (NLRB)** and a staff of lawyers and other personnel responsible to the board. The board sets up elections, on request, to determine if a given group of workers wishes to have a union as a bargaining representative. The board also investigates complaints of unfair labor practices.

Exhibit 12.6 *Major Labor-Management Regulations*

Legislation	Provisions	Coverage
Railway Labor Act (1926)	Gave employees the right to organize and bargain collectively.	Railroads. Airlines.
Norris-LaGuardia Act (1932)	Prohibited federal courts from enjoining strikes and from enforcing yellow-dog contracts.	Private-sector employment.
Wagner Act (1935)	Established the right to organize and engage in other concerted activities; declared certain employer actions to be unfair labor practices; established procedures for employees to elect a union; regulated collective bargaining; established the National Labor Relations Board (NLRB).	Private-sector employment: • Businesses • Nonprofit hospitals and nursing homes. • Private colleges and universities. • Performing arts.
Taft-Hartley Act (1947)	Established the right to refrain from the activities protected in the Wagner Act; declared certain union actions to be unfair labor practices; provided for passage of state right-to-work laws; established the Federal Mediation and Conciliation Service (FMCS); outlawed closed shops.	Same as Wagner Act.
Landrum-Griffin Act (1959)	Established standards for union treatment of union members; regulated internal union affairs.	Same as Wagner Act and Taft-Hartley Act.
Title VII, Civil Service Reform Act (1978)	Established the right to form and assist labor union; bargaining; required arbitration of impasses and grievances; prohibited strikes and other disruptions.	Federal employment (excludes some agencies, such as FBI, CIA).
The Workers' Adjustment and Retraining Notification Act (1989)	Employers with 100 or more employees or who have 100 or more employees who together work at least 4,000 hours per week excluding overtime must give employees 60 days' written notice of anticipated plant closings or other mass layoffs.	Private-sector employment.

Postwar Labor Laws: Restoring a Balance

Taft-Hartley Act A 1947 labor law that prohibits the closed shop, requires unions to bargain in good faith, and makes it illegal for a union to discriminate against employees who don't join the union.

Taft-Hartley Act. The Wagner Act was considered prolabor. To swing the pendulum back and equalize labor and management, Congress passed the **Taft-Hartley Act** (also called the Labor-Management Relations Act) in 1947. It amended and supplemented the Wagner Act and increased the size of the National Labor Relations Board to five persons (allegedly to get rid of the NLRB's pro-union bias). Taft-Hartley guaranteed employee bargaining rights and specifically forbade the five unfair employer labor practices first established in the Wagner Act. But the act also specified unfair union labor practices; the union was restrained from the practices shown in Exhibit 12.7. Finally, the act established the Federal Mediation and Conciliation Service (FMCS).

Exhibit 12.7
Unfair Labor Practices

BY MANAGEMENT:

To interfere with, restrain, or coerce employees in the exercise of their rights to organize.

To dominate or interfere with the affairs of a union.

To discriminate in regard to hiring, tenure, or any employment condition for the purpose of encouraging or discouraging membership in any union organization.

To discriminate against or discharge an employee because he or she has filed charges or given testimony under the Wagner Act.

To refuse to bargain collectively with representatives of the employees—that is, to refuse to bargain in good faith.

BY UNIONS:

To restrain or coerce employees in the exercise of their right to join or not to join a union except when an agreement is made by the employer and union that a condition of employment will be joining the union, called a union security clause authorizing a union shop.

To cause an employer to discriminate against an employee other than for non-payment of dues or initiation fees.

To refuse to bargain with an employer in good faith.

To engage, induce, encourage, threaten, or coerce any individual to engage in strikes, refusal to work, or boycott where the objective is to:

- Force or require any employer or self-employed person to recognize or join any labor organization or employer organization.
- Force or require an employer or self-employed person to cease using the products of or doing business with another person, or force any other employer to recognize or bargain with the union unless it has been certified by the NLRB.
- Force an employer to apply pressure to another employer to recognize a union. Examples include picketing a hospital so that it will apply pressure on a subcontractor (food service, maintenance, emergency department) to recognize a union; forcing an employer to do business only with others, such as suppliers, who have a union; picketing by another union for recognition when a different one is already certified.

To charge excessive or discriminatory membership fees.

To cause an employer to give payment for services not performed (featherbedding).

Landrum-Griffin Act
A 1959 labor law that requires unions and employees to file financial reports with the secretary of labor and that specifies certain activities to ensure democratic operation of the union.

Sweetheart Contract
Agreement between union leaders and management to terms that work to their mutual benefit but maintain poor working conditions for other employees.

Union Shop
A company that requires employees to join the union after being hired.

Agency Shop
A company where all employees pay union dues, whether or not they are union members.

Open Shop
A company in which employees don't have to join a union or pay dues but can decide without pressure whether to become union members.

Maintenance of Membership Agreement
Agreement that, although employees do not have to join a union, union members must maintain membership in the union over the length of the contract.

Right-to-Work Laws
State laws requiring that two people doing the same job be paid the same wages, whether or not they belong to the union.

Landrum-Griffin Act. In view of the corruption found in some unions, Congress assumed that the individual union member was still not adequately protected by the labor laws in existence. So in 1959 Congress passed the **Landrum-Griffin Act,** which is officially designated the Labor-Management Reporting and Disclosure Act. It was designed to regulate the internal affairs of unions.

This act, called the bill of rights of union members, gave every union member the right to (1) nominate candidates for union office, (2) vote in union elections, and (3) attend union meetings. Union members also gained the right to examine union accounts and records, while the union was required to submit an annual financial report to the U.S. Department of Labor. Employers had to report any payments or loans made to unions, their officers, or their members. This portion of the act was to end **sweetheart contracts,** under which the union leaders and management agree to terms that work to their mutual benefit but maintain poor working conditions for other employees.

The Issue of Job Security

One of the most important issues for workers is job security. Unions also have fought and continue to fight for their own security. To establish security, unions focus on gaining the right to represent an enterprise's workers and, where possible, to be the exclusive bargaining agent for all employees of the unit. Union job security takes several forms:

- **Union shop.** The company can hire nonunion people, but they must join the union after a prescribed period of time and pay the union dues. (Failure to join means they could be fired.)
- **Agency shop.** Employees who do not belong to the union still must pay the full union dues (assuming that the union's bargaining and agreement efforts benefit all the workers).
- **Open shop.** The workers decide whether or not to join the union. Those not joining pay no dues.
- **Maintenance of membership agreement.** Employees do not have to join a union. However, union members must maintain membership in the union over the length of the contract.

Although unions have encouraged legislation to protect their security, a number of concerns remain. First, a labor organization has no guarantee that it will not be replaced by a rival union at a later date. Second, employees still have a number of channels through which to voice their anti-union feelings and can use these to get rid of unions. Third, no government guarantee protects unions from "free riders." A free rider is an employee who decides not to be a part of the union but still gains the benefit of unionization.

The Taft-Hartley Act allows states to forbid union shops by passing **right-to-work laws.** Under these laws, two persons doing the same job must be paid the same wages, whether they belong to the union or not. Unions see this as unfair because the nonunionized employees pay no dues but share in the benefits won by the union. Twenty-one states have right-to-work laws, as shown in Exhibit 12.8.

Exhibit 12.8
Right-to-Work States

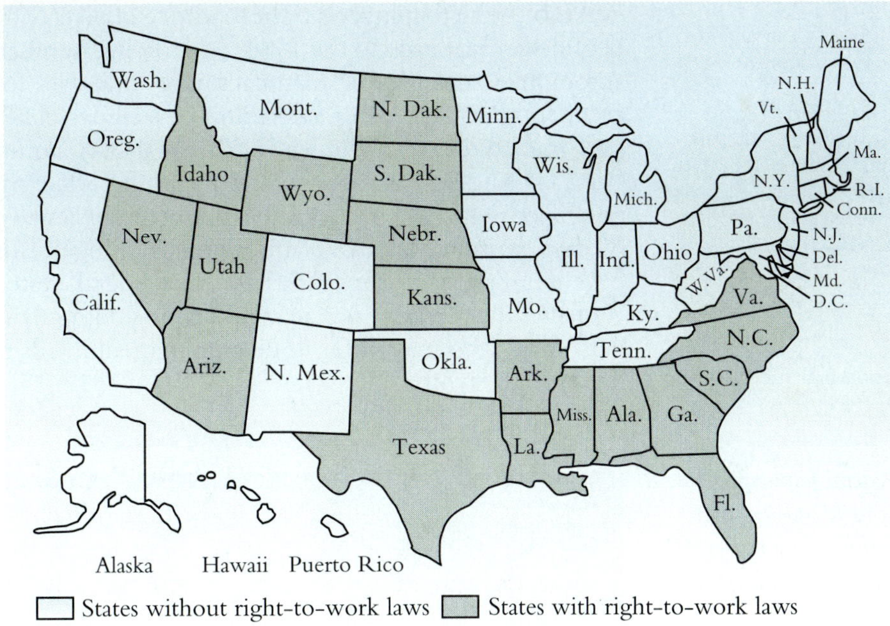

Closed Shop
A company that hires only workers who are members of the union; illegal under the Taft-Hartley Act.

A **closed shop,** prohibited by the Taft-Hartley Act, requires that a new employee be a union member when hired. The union itself provides labor to the organization. Although this type of shop is illegal, modified closed shops are still found in the construction, printing, and maritime industries. For example, an ironworkers' union hall sends out union members to construction sites on request. A nonunion worker has little chance to be sent from a union hall to a job because the union's business agent makes the assignments. Union members elect the business agent, while the nonunion members have no vote.

Recent Legislation

Title VII
Part of the Civil Service Reform Act of 1978; outlawed certain unfair labor practices and created the Federal Labor Relations Authority (FLRA); granted covered employees the right to form, join, or assist any labor organization or to refrain from such activity freely and without reprisals.

Title VII. **Title VII** of the Civil Service Reform Act of 1978, also referred to as the Federal Service Labor-Management Relations Act, did for the federal government sector what the Wagner and the Taft-Hartley acts did for employment in the private sector. Title VII outlawed certain unfair labor practices and created the Federal Labor Relations Authority (FLRA), with powers similar to the National Labor Relations Board (NLRB).

Employees covered by Title VII are granted the right to form, join, or assist any labor organization or to refrain from such activity freely and without reprisals. Employees of some federal agencies (e.g., Federal Bureau of Investigation, Central Intelligence Agency, National Security Agency, Tennessee Valley Authority) are exempted. Noncitizens working outside of the United States for federal agencies are also excluded.

WARN Act
A 1989 law that requires employers with 100 or more full-time employees to give affected employees 60 days' written notice of plant or office closing or other mass layoffs. The law is commonly known as the Plant Closing Bill.

WARN. The employee's right to notice of plant/office closing or relocation became a major issue in the 1980s. A growing number of workers in the steel, automobile, and general manufacturing industries lost their jobs because of competition, mergers, or relocation of facilities. The **Worker Adjustment and Retraining Notification Act (WARN),** commonly referred to as the Plant Closing Bill, was passed and went into effect in 1989. The act requires employers with 100 or more full-time employees to give affected employees 60 days' written notice of plant or office closing or other mass layoffs. WARN covers nonprofit organizations but not federal, state, or local governments. "Affected employees" are all workers, including managerial and supervisory personnel, who may suffer some employment loss as the result of a plant closing or mass layoff.

Federal law requires firms to give written notice to employees 60 days in advance of plant closing.

Employers violating WARN may be required to provide back pay and benefits for up to 60 days to workers laid off without proper notification. In some cases, employers may also be required to pay fines of $500 per day, up to $30,000. However, WARN allows some exceptions. A failing company actively seeking capital to prevent the plant closing or layoff is exempt, if giving notice to employees would reasonably have prevented the firm from receiving the financing. Closings due to natural disasters, such as earthquakes or floods, are also exempt from the 60-day notice requirement.

There are humanitarian arguments to support WARN. Victims of plant closures show higher rates of alcoholism, child abuse, ulcers, heart attacks, and suicides. Before WARN was passed, General Motors shut down its Fremont, CA, plant and gave the 4,000 employees only three weeks' notice. Ford closed its San Jose, CA, plant, idling 2,300 workers but giving them six months' advance notice. There were eight suicides among the laid-off General Motors employees and none among the displaced Ford workers.[11]

Critics of WARN argue that turnover, pilferage, destruction of property, and other negative behavior may occur between the time of notice and the layoff. However, research conducted in Europe and other countries with advance notice requirements reveals no evidence to support that claim.

ORGANIZING AND DECERTIFYING A UNION

The organizing drive is the process through which a group of employees attempts to establish a legally binding relationship with the employer. The process involves three steps: (1) petition for union representation, (2) determination of appropriate bargaining unit, and (3) union representation election.

The organizing drive officially begins when employees sign authorization cards that empower the union to petition the NLRB for union representation. Thirty percent of the employees must sign, per NLRB rules. But most unions will not petition the NLRB unless a majority of the workers in the group sign the authorization cards. The union must receive 50 percent plus two of the votes cast in the election that takes place later.

After they receive the petition for union representation and check its accuracy, the NLRB notifies the employer that a particular union is seeking to be the representative of a group of employees. If 30 percent of the firm's employees are on the petition list, the NLRB notifies both the employer and the employees. The employer can then recognize the union as the representative. However, if the employer does not, a formal unit determination hearing is scheduled by the NLRB. Employer and employees present facts and arguments about representation. The hearing enables the NLRB to determine (1) the employees' interest in being represented, (2) eligibility of employees to belong to the proposed unit, and (3) desires of employees as to who should or should not be a member of the proposed unit.

NLRB regional directors are empowered to decide the composition and appropriateness of the bargaining unit. After this is decided, the NLRB informs the employer and union that a bargaining unit has been formed. The NLRB then supervises a representation election. Again, the union must receive 50 percent plus two of the votes cast to win the election. When this happens, the NLRB certifies the union as the exclusive representative of the employees within the bargaining unit. If the union loses the election, the union must wait one year before trying again.

The NLRB is the referee, the guiding arm of organizing drives and elections. Its chief concern is to provide an atmosphere that permits employees to make a clear choice. The employer and union are not permitted to use threats, promises, or any means of influencing each person's free choice in the process. Exhibit 12.9 outlines employer behaviors permitted and not permitted by the NLRB.

Exhibit 12.9
Permitted and Not Permitted Employer Behaviors in Union Organizing Drives

YES: THE EMPLOYER MAY

- Discharge and discipline employees for violation of employment rules, provided the rules apply uniformly to all employees.
- Forbid the union to solicit workers during working hours and on the employer's property.
- Forbid employees to distribute union literature in working areas.
- Make speeches and speak against the union and also write letters to employees giving its position with respect to the union, as long as the speeches and letters are noncoercive and not perceived as potentially benefiting the employee if he or she does not join the union.

NO: THE EMPLOYER MAY NOT

- Prohibit union solicitation by employees during their nonworking time in work areas or nonwork areas.
- Question employees about the union or its activities, even though the questions are nonthreatening and the employees are willing to answer those questions.
- Circulate anti-union petitions or engage in any attempts to get the employees to withdraw from the union.
- Engage in any activities that change the wages, hours, terms, and conditions of employment during the term of the organizing drive.

Decertification
The process, guided by the NLRB, that results in voting out a union that has been representing employees.

Just as unions can be voted in and become the representative of employees, they can also be voted out by the same employees. The law that grants employees the right to organize also allows them to terminate the union's right to represent them. The process of voting out a union is called **decertification.** A petition must be submitted showing 30 percent employee support for the action. If there is support, the NLRB will conduct a secret ballot election to determine whether a majority of employees in the unit wish to decertify. In 1990, 587 decertification elections were held. In 170 of these elections, the employees voted to decertify the union.[12]

Employers use "union busting" consultants to help keep unions out in the first place or to decertify them when they are the representatives of employees. The consultants help managers comply with the law and use persuasive procedures to communicate better with employees. Programs developed by such consultants are usually designed to win the attention and loyalty of employees.

COLLECTIVE BARGAINING

A union certified by the NLRB becomes the collective bargaining representative of the employees. According to the Wagner Act, it is an unfair labor practice for the employer to refuse to bargain collectively with chosen representatives of a duly certified labor union. The Taft-Hartley Act states that it is an unfair practice for the representatives of a labor union to not bargain in good faith with an employer. The current national policy, then, is that employees and employers must bargain in good faith to work out employment issues and disputes.

Collective Bargaining
Negotiation of a labor contract by union and management.

Collective bargaining is a process by which the representatives of the firm meet and attempt to work out a contract with union representatives. Through this process, contractual agreements are established, managed, and enforced. *Collective* means only that representatives join in the attempt to negotiate an agreement. *Bargaining* is the process of cajoling, debating, discussing, and threatening to bring about a favorable agreement for those being represented.

Bargaining *in good faith* is the cornerstone of effective labor-management relations. It means that both sides must communicate and negotiate. Proposals are matched with counterproposals, and reasonable efforts are made to reach an agreement.

The collective bargaining process and the final agreement reached are influenced by many variables. Exhibit 12.10 identifies some of the variables influencing union and management representatives. For example, the state of the economy affects collective bargaining. The firm's representative must consider whether, based on current and expected economic conditions, the company can pay an increased wage.

Exhibit 12.10
Forces Influencing the Bargaining Process

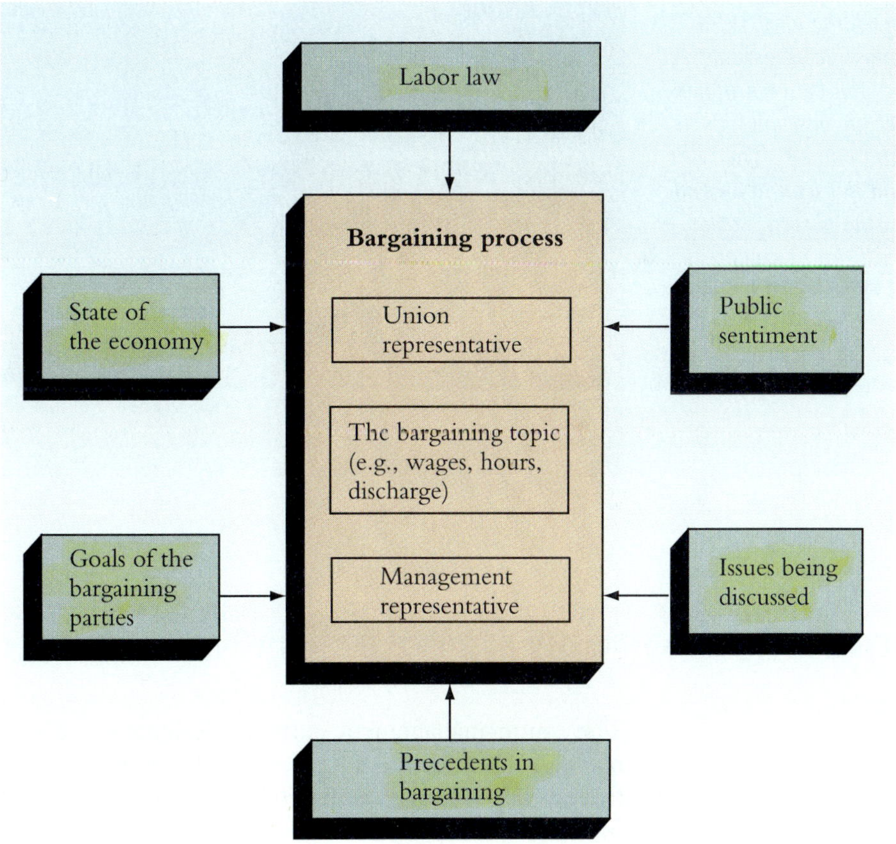

The actual process of collective bargaining involves a number of steps: (1) prenegotiation, (2) selecting negotiators, (3) developing a bargaining strategy, (4) using the best tactics, and (5) reaching a formal contractual agreement.

Collective bargaining is not always favorable for workers, however. Collective bargaining can make it difficult for the union to reach a compromise with management, even if the compromise would benefit both sides. For example, in contract negotiations with John Deere, the United Auto Workers union found itself in a difficult situation because of the inflexibility that collective bargaining entails. When John Deere asked the union to allow it to pay new workers less than the $22 per hour average pay, the union resisted. The UAW didn't want to give anything away at Deere because it was simultaneously locked in a tough battle at Caterpillar, where workers had been striking for months. In the John Deere situation, constraints on collective bargaining reached beyond Deere to another company.[13]

Baseball mediator W. J. Usury (center), with aides Herb Fishgold (left) and Tom Hickman (right), presiding at a 1994 collective bargaining session between major league baseball owners and players. The talks did not lead to an end to the players' strike until the spring of 1995.

THE RESULT OF COLLECTIVE BARGAINING: THE CONTRACT

The union-management contract designates the formal terms of agreement reached in collective bargaining. The average contract is good for two to three years and varies in length from a few pages to well over 100 pages, depending on the issues covered, the size of the organization, and the union. It must be in compliance with federal, state, and local laws.

The labor contract is divided into sections and appendixes. The sections covered in some labor agreements are listed in Exhibit 12.11. A major part of the contract is concerned with such employment issues as wages, hours, fringe benefits, and overtime.

A major task of labor and management is to jointly administer the contract. Contracts are difficult to administer perfectly because contract language requires interpretation—it is not perfect. Day-to-day compliance with contract provisions becomes an important responsibility of the first-line manager, who works closely with union members. As the representative of management, the first-line manager must discipline workers, handle grievances, and prepare for such actions as strikes.

Exhibit 12.11
Major Sections Found in Typical Labor-Management Contracts

- Purpose and intent of the parties
- Scope of the agreement
- Management
- Responsibilities of the parties
- Union membership and checkoff*
- Adjustment of grievance
- Arbitration
- Suspension and discharge cases
- Rate of pay
- Hours of work
- Overtime—holidays
- Vacations
- Seniority
- Safety and health
- Military service
- Severance allowance
- Savings and vacation plan
- Supplemental unemployment benefits (SUB) program
- SUB and insurance grievances
- Prior agreements
- Termination date
- Appendixes

*In a checkoff arrangement, the employer deducts monthly union dues from the employee's pay. The dues are then transmitted to the union.

Discipline

Most contracts state that management has a right to discipline workers. But any discipline in a unionized firm must follow legal due process. If an employee or a union challenges a disciplinary action, the burden of proof rests on the company. Often management will lose a case that is arbitrated (settled by an impartial third party), because improper disciplinary procedures have been followed.

Contracts usually specify the types of discipline and the offenses for which corrective action will be taken. Some of the infractions typically spelled out include:

- *Incompetence*—failure to perform the assigned job.
- *Misconduct*—insubordination, dishonesty, or violating a rule such as smoking in a restricted area.
- *Violations of the contract*—initiating a strike, for example, when there is a no-strike clause.

The contract should list penalties for infractions. Violators must be disciplined similarly, but inconsistent application of discipline is sometimes a problem. When one employee is reprimanded for regularly arriving at work late but another with a similar tardiness problem is discharged, discipline is being applied inconsistently.

Consistent, prompt, and reasonable discipline programs are what union and management representatives attempt to spell out in the contract. One strategy is to use a progressive program in which repeated or more serious violations result in penalties of increasing severity. The sequence of progressive discipline might be:

1. An oral caution and a note in the personnel file of the employee.
2. A written reprimand that becomes a part of the file.
3. A short, two-day to one-week suspension.
4. Demotion to the next-lower job position.
5. A long, one- to three-month suspension.
6. Discharge.

The emphasis in a progressive discipline approach should be on developing within the total work force a willingness to obey and follow rules and regulations. The goal is to encourage employees to follow rules because they want to, not because they are afraid of the progressively severe penalties. In one classic example of progressive discipline, an employee had broken many rules, but none so serious as to justify her discharge. This microfilm operator was finally fired by an Illinois firm for a hostile work attitude. Her record contained frequent notations for absenteeism, insubordination, smoking at her desk, and being absent from her workstation. A third-party judge acting as an arbitrator ruled that the firing violated a progressive discipline program. The employer cannot abruptly discharge the worker for a minor fault unless preliminary steps, such as reprimands and suspensions, have been administered in a timely manner.[14]

Grievances

Grievance
Complaint made by an employee or the union about a job, person, or condition that creates dissatisfaction or discomfort.

A complaint about a job that creates dissatisfaction or discomfort, whether it is valid or not, is a **grievance.** The complaint can be made by a single employee or by the union. All grievances should be handled correctly. Even if a complaint seems absolutely without support, management should still handle it according to formal contractual provisions.

Grievance procedures are usually followed in unionized companies, but they are also important channels of communication in nonunionized organizations. In the unionized organization, the contract contains a clause covering the steps to be followed and how the grievance will be handled. The number of steps varies from contract to contract.

Exhibit 12.12 illustrates a four-step grievance procedure used in a unionized company.

1. The employee meets with the supervisor and the union steward and presents the grievance. Most grievances are settled at this point.

2. If the grievance is not settled at step 1, a conference takes place between middle management and union officials (a business agent or union committee).
3. If the grievance cannot be settled at step 2, then a top management representative and top union officials attempt to settle the grievance.
4. If the grievance cannot be settled at step 3, both parties (union and management) turn the grievance over to an arbitrator, who makes a decision. Arbitration is usually handled by a mutually agreed upon individual or a panel of an odd number.

Although most grievances are handled at step 1, managers should follow a number of important principles: (a) take every grievance seriously; (b) work with the union representative; (c) gather all information available on the grievance; (d) after weighing all the facts, provide an answer to the employee voicing the grievance; and (e) after the grievance is settled, attempt to move on to other matters.

Exhibit 12.12
Steps in the Grievance Process

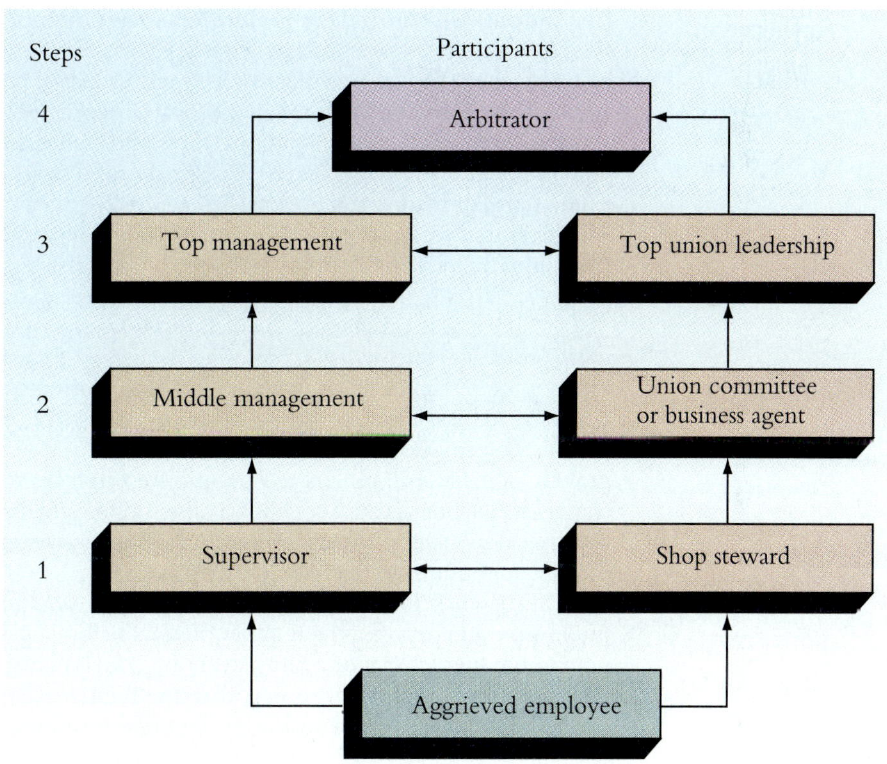

Strike
An effort to withhold employee services so that the employer will make greater concessions at the bargaining table.

Strikes

A **strike** is an effort to withhold employee services so that the employer will make greater concessions at the bargaining table. The strike, or a threatened one, is a major bargaining tool used by the unions. In 1992 there were 35 work stoppages that involved 364,000 workers, and 3,989,000 days were lost because of strikes.[15] As this book was being prepared, major league baseball players had been on strike since August 12, 1994 threatening to severely impact the 1995 season. This is their eighth strike in two decades, as Today's Business World illustrates.

TODAY'S BUSINESS WORLD

Ste-e-e-rike Has New Meaning for Major League Baseball

Major league baseball players staged their eighth strike in two decades during the summer of 1994 over an issue that many fans of the game find difficult to understand: protecting multimillion-dollar salaries from the club owners. Baseball owners claim that a fourfold increase in player salaries since 1984 has created a competitive imbalance between rich big-city teams such as the New York Yankees, with fat regional television markets to tap, and small-city teams such as the Cleveland Indians, which have few local revenue opportunities.

Decreasing revenues, mostly from less lucrative national TV contracts, have helped make at least 19 of the 28 teams unprofitable, claim the owners. For example, the New York Yankees have local TV and cable contracts that bring in about $50 million per year. With this kind of revenue, the team can afford its $46 million per year in player salaries. The Pittsburgh Pirates, on the other hand, with a much smaller market and no local TV contract, loses $1 million per month, even after slashing its payroll to $25 million. Players' representatives counter that the Pittsburgh franchise was purchased by the current owners in 1985 for $28 million, and its 1994 value is $85 million—not a bad appreciation.

To address the problem of unequal revenues and to help make owning a team more profitable, the owners are pressing the players for a salary cap that would split total league revenues 50-50 with the players. Currently, players receive 58 percent of revenues. The 1994 strike began on August 12 mostly because the players do not want to lose the 8 percent of revenues, thus slowing their explosive salary growth. The baseball players also point to research that shows there's no correlation between city size and likelihood of winning a championship. These findings, they say, don't support the owners' contention that teams with more money can buy championships in the form of star players.

The Baseball Players Association (a union) wants to increase players' minimum wage and decrease the number of years before a player can take a salary dispute to binding arbitration. The players are concerned about restrictions on what they perceive is their right to negotiate the highest salary for their services. This "right" seems to be an essential ingredient of the American free enterprise system. Shouldn't people have the opportunity to sell their services to the highest bidder? Yet, it's no secret that professional athletes in the United States earn salaries that are far beyond those of the average person. For example, the minimum wage set by the federal government for American workers is between $4 and $5 per hour. In contrast, the minimum wage for professional baseball players as set forth in their collective agreement with the owners is $109,000, and the average major league salary is over $1 million. With money like that to go around, it's likely that the strike of 1994 won't be the last time baseball players and owners feud over the way it's distributed.

Unions in major league sports have been very active during the last several decades, with strikes in major league baseball, football, and hockey. With each strike, there is controversy that the sports fan is being left out of the bargaining process. Do you think the fans should be represented in player-owner labor disputes? Do you think it is reasonable for highly paid professional athletes to strike?

Sources: Adapted from Ronald Grover, Aaron Bernstein, Zachary Schiller, "Ste-e-e-rike," *Business Week* (August 15, 1994): 26–28; Alan Truex, "Out of Control on the Road to Disaster," *Houston Chronicle* (August 21, 1994): 21B–22B; Alan Truex, "Pay Scale Plan Shows Promise," *Houston Chronicle* (August 21, 1994): 22B.

A union planning to strike needs to consider the legality of striking, the members' willingness to endure the hardships of a long strike, and the employer's ability to operate the organization without union members. The greater the employer's ability to operate the organization, the less chance the union will have of gaining its demands.

When a strike occurs, management must be able to function during the work stoppage and protect the company from strike sabotage. Employers sometimes bring in strike replacement employees to keep the firm operating.

Management should also be aware of picketing procedures. Hoping to shut down the company during a strike, the union may place members at plant entrances to advertise the dispute and discourage people from entering or leaving. Peaceful persuasion through the formation of a picket line is legal, but violence is not. Picketing may also take place without a strike to publicize union viewpoints about an employer.

Boycott
A bargaining tactic in which the union refuses to do business with a firm or attempts to get people or other organizations to refuse to deal with the firm.

Hot-Cargo Agreement
A boycott agreement between management and union that workers may avoid working with materials that come from employers that have been struck by a union.

Lockout
Management pressure tactic that involves denying employees access to their jobs.

Another type of union pressure is the **boycott.** In a primary boycott, union members do not patronize the boycotted firm. A secondary boycott occurs when a supplier of a boycotted firm is threatened with a union strike unless it stops doing business with the boycotted company. According to a 1988 Supreme Court decision, secondary boycotts are legal if they do not involve coercive tactics or picketing by the union. A special type of boycott is the **hot-cargo agreement.** Under this agreement, the employer permits union members to avoid working with materials that come from employers who have been struck by a union. This type of boycott is illegal except in the construction and clothing industries.

Management's response to these union pressures may be to continue operations with a skeleton crew of managerial personnel, to shut down the plant, or to lock the employees out. **Lockouts** are used by management to keep employees from their jobs, prevent union work slowdowns, prevent damage to property, or eliminate violence related to a labor dispute. Many states allow locked-out employees to draw unemployment benefits, thereby weakening the lockout. In practice, lockouts are more often threatened than used.

The Racketeer Influenced and Corrupt Organizations Act (RICO) was intended to be used to help keep organized crime out of labor-management business. However, a number of firms have attempted to use RICO as the basis of lawsuits to prevent or stop some union activities.[16] Desperate to end the strike violence that had engulfed Greyhound Lines, the bus firm filed a $30 million civil RICO suit accusing the striking Amalgamated Transit Union of using "coordinated criminal and extortion means" to injure the firm financially. Eastern Air Lines filed a massive $1.5 billion RICO suit accusing its machinists and pilots unions of attempting to destroy the company through racketeering, extortion, fraud, and defamation. RICO-based suits by management usually result in lengthy litigation that would seem to favor companies.

Occasionally, serious disputes between union and management do not reach the strike or lockout stages. Instead a third party becomes involved. The third party may be a fact-finding group appointed by the government or the two parties. A fact-finding group investigates the issues and makes a public report; the public statement often causes the parties to become less antagonistic or extreme. Or the third party may be a mediator or an arbitrator.

Mediator Third party to a labor dispute who tries to get union and management to reason and works at improving communication between them.

A **mediator** tries to get the two parties to reason and works at improving communication between them. Typically, mediators are full-time employees of the Federal Mediation and Conciliation Service (FMCS), a division of the U.S. Department of Labor. Under the Taft-Hartley Act, employers are required to notify the FMCS 30 days before the expiration of a contract or when new negotiating has begun. The FMCS provides experienced mediators at no cost to help the parties reach a contract agreement. The mediator does not make a decision but attempts to stimulate the parties to reach an agreement. Mediators have no power to impose a solution to the bargaining impasse.

Arbitrator Third party to a labor dispute who makes the final, binding decision about some disputed issue.

An **arbitrator** is a third party who collects information, listens to the positions taken, and (unlike the mediator) makes a binding decision. Union and management must comply with the decision. Most labor contracts provide for use of an arbitrator in grievance procedures, as shown in Exhibit 12.12. In arbitration, each party tries to persuade the arbitrator that its position is ethical, fair, accurate, and in the best interest of everyone involved. Following an arbitration hearing, the arbitrator considers the evidence and renders a decision on the case that is legally binding unless one or both parties decide to appeal the arbitrator's decision in a court of law. This rarely occurs.

The written contract usually specifies the arbitrator's selection method and scope of authority. Most contracts state that the parties shall select a mutually acceptable arbitrator from a list of available arbitrators provided by either the American Arbitration Association (AAA) or the FMCS, or from both lists.

Are unions and management cooperating more or less today than a decade ago? At the General Motors Saturn plant in Spring Hill, TN, cooperation is high. Workers have willingly spent 16 to 17 hours a day on the job building test versions of the Saturn.[17] The workers have been working closely with management to prove they can produce cares as efficiently as nonunion workers at Japanese-owned U.S. plants. While cooperation is greater in some cases, however, in others conflict, problems, and distrust still are prominent.

National Emergencies

A widespread strike or lockout or one that occurs in a crucial industry could pose a threat to the nation's economy and security. For example, if the airline, trucking, or rail industries were shut down for any length of time, such vital services as food distribution, the movement of medical supplies, or the delivery of military repair parts could be threatened.

The president of the United States can take action to resolve such strikes and lockouts. The Railway Labor Act and the Taft-Hartley Act provide the mechanisms employed in national emergency situations. For example, if there is no contract agreement and a strike or lockout could threaten the nation's welfare or security, the president can (1) direct the attorney general to obtain a court order (an injunction) preventing the strike or lockout for 80 days; (2) appoint a board of inquiry to study the impasse and make recommendations; and (3) order the FMCS to attempt to mediate the dispute.

If the impasse is still not settled by the 60th day, the inquiry board is reconvened. After the board reports the employer's final offer, the National Labor Relations Board conducts a secret ballot election among the employees. If the employees vote not to accept the offer, the attorney general must ask the federal court to dissolve the injunction. The union has a legal right to strike after this 80-day cooling-off period.

By 1995 the national emergency provisions of the law had been invoked 35 times (only twice, however, since 1972). Thirty injunctions have been issued.

NONUNION ORGANIZATIONS

Most business firms in the United States are nonunion, or unorganized. One of the largest union-free firms is IBM. In most cases, union-free firms are small and are found in right-to-work states. Union penetration is highest in the Northeast and Midwest and lowest in the South and in rural areas.

An increasing number of firms have specific union-avoidance policies and, to support these goals, develop employee relations practices: participation programs, profit-sharing plans, formal grievance systems, and all-salaried (that is, everyone is paid a salary instead of hourly wages) compensation systems.[18]

A study of nonunion organizations concluded that two types of firms—doctrinaire and philosophy-laden—can operate effectively without unions.[19] The *doctrinaire* firm wants to continue to be nonunion. It develops policies that mimic what unions have won in similar organizations. The belief is that, since the firm has good human resource policies, employees will resist union organizing efforts. The *philosophy-laden* firm has no unions because its climate of labor-management relations is excellent. Management has adopted policies on compensation, staffing, grievance handling, and discipline that it believes are correct and equitable.

SUMMARY OF LEARNING OBJECTIVES

1. ***Define the term* labor union.** Labor unions are organizations of employees who formally join together to protect, maintain, and improve their economic, social, and political power and well-being. They may also be called guilds or associations.

2. ***Identify the significant trends facing the labor movement today.*** Unions are facing declining memberships due to bad publicity surrounding union activities and union officials; economic factors, including deregulation of certain industries, plant closings, and mergers and acquisitions; management resistance; and the reduced number of blue-collar workers in the labor force. Some success in organizing white-collar workers and government employees has helped improve the image of unions.

3. ***Explain why employees decide to organize unions.*** Employees organize unions for different reasons. They may organize to try to satisfy needs for such things as pay and benefits, supervision, and job security. They may also be experiencing dissatisfaction with work-related conditions.

4. ***Compare the main features of the major labor legislation.*** The *Railway Labor Act* gave employees the right to organize and bargain collectively. The *Norris-LaGuardia Act* limited the courts' injunction power and made yellow-dog contracts unenforceable. The *Wagner Act* spelled out the right of employees to organize and elect a union, regulated collective bargaining, and listed unfair employer labor practices. It established the National Labor Relations Board (NLRB). The *Taft-Hartley Act* guaranteed employee bargaining rights, provided for passage of right-to-work laws, listed unfair union labor practices, and established the Federal Mediation and Conciliation Service (FMCS). The *Landrum-Griffin Act* specified rules for how unions were to conduct their affairs and eliminated sweetheart contracts. *Title VII* did for public-sector employees what the Wagner and Taft-Hartley acts had done for the private sector. The *Worker Adjustment and Retraining Act (WARN)* requires employers to give 60 days' written notice of plant closings or layoffs.

5. ***List the steps in both organizing and decertifying a union.*** Organizing a union involves petitioning for union representation, determining the appropriate bargaining unit, and conducting a union representation election. To decertify a union, employees must petition the NLRB, which then conducts a secret ballot election.

6. ***Define the term* collective bargaining.** Collective bargaining is the process that establishes, manages, and enforces contractual agreements between labor and management. Representatives of both sides debate, discuss, and demand better solutions for their groups. The process includes several steps: prenegotiation, selecting negotiators, developing a strategy, using negotiation tactics, and reaching a formal agreement.

7. ***Discuss what is included in a union-management contract.*** The contract represents the formal terms of agreement reached through collective bargaining by labor and management. Various sections cover the responsibilities of the parties, adjustment of grievances, rates of pay, savings and vacation plans, and arbitration procedures.

8. ***Explain how a strike, boycott, and lockout differ.*** A *strike* is an effort by employees to withhold their labor so that the employer will make greater concessions at the bargaining table. The strike—or the threat of one—is the union's strongest bargaining tool. In a *boycott,* unions try to get management to concede by not patronizing the firm. A *lockout* occurs when management closes the doors to prevent union work slowdowns, violence, or damage to property.

KEY TERMS

Labor Union
Industrial Union
Craft Union
Yellow-Dog Contract
Knights of Labor
AFL-CIO
Business Representative
Union Steward
Railway Labor Act
Injunction
Norris-LaGuardia Act
Wagner Act
National Labor Relations Board (NLRB)
Taft-Hartley Act
Landrum-Griffin Act
Sweetheart Contract
Union Shop
Agency Shop
Open Shop
Maintenance of Membership Agreement
Right-to-Work Laws
Closed Shop
Title VII
Worker Adjustment and Retraining Notification Act (WARN)
Decertification
Collective Bargaining
Grievance
Strike
Boycott
Hot-Cargo Agreement
Lockout
Mediator
Arbitrator

QUESTIONS FOR DISCUSSION AND REVIEW

1. What were the names of some of the early labor unions in the United States, and when did they form? What purposes did these early unions serve?
2. How does a worker file a grievance and win a grievance dispute?
3. Name several labor laws that have had a significant impact on the growth of labor unions in the United States. What has been the effect of these laws?
4. Why have many women been reluctant to join unions?
5. Why do employees join unions?
6. What are the unionization trends in the United States?
7. Describe the structure of major unions in the United States.
8. How do workers go about organizing and certifying a union?
9. What is collective bargaining? What variables affect the outcome of collective bargaining?
10. Besides a strike, what are other possible consequences of a dispute between management and labor? How could this dispute be resolved?

CASE 12.1

NLRB Orders Du Pont to Scrap Its Employee Participation Programs

On May 28, 1993, the National Labor Relations Board (NLRB) handed down a controversial decision in the case of *E.I. du Pont de Nemours & Company v. Chemical Workers Association, Inc.* The NLRB ruled that an Employee Participation Program (EPP) that had been organized by the company was illegal. In December 1992, the National Labor Relations Board had also ruled that EPPs formed by non-union Elkhart, IN, manufacturer Electromation were illegal. The two rulings have far-reaching consequences for most employee/management cooperation practices (*Electromation v. International Brotherhood of Teamsters*).

The Du Pont decision involved the company's use of safety and fitness committees at its Deepwater, NJ, plant. Six safety committees were established to serve a variety of purposes that included establishing safety awards and providing a means of communicating safety problems to management. One of the six committees, the Antiknocks Committee, was typical of the Du Pont employee/management committees. Its purpose was to convey employee safety complaints to management for correction. Using information gathered from employees, this committee was able to get potholes fixed, improve ventilation, and establish new procedures for handling safety garments. In one significant instance, the committee secured a new ventilated welding shop for an employee after several earlier attempts by the union had failed.

In addition to the six safety committees, the company also organized a fitness committee. This committee dealt primarily with issues related to worker fitness and recreation. Among its contributions were such activities as adding horseshoe pits and volleyball and tennis courts to the Deepwater plant's recreational facilities.

The decision to include employees on the safety and fitness committees was made in 1987. Previously, the committees had consisted solely of management personnel. In creating the EPPs, the company unilaterally changed the composition of the committees without giving the union an opportunity to bargain. Shortly after the new committee structure was announced, the union countered by filing charges with the NLRB that Du Pont had failed to bargain in good faith.

Without question, all seven of the safety and fitness committees were formed by Du Pont's management and, therefore, could also be abolished at will by the company. Furthermore, the company controlled the composition of the committees by selecting the employees from a voluntary sign-up list. The company also prescribed the number and composition of committee membership, established the organization of each committee, and specified the agenda of the meetings. Although these aspects of the seven committees are typical of many workplace employee/management groups, they are crucial to the two-part test used by the NLRB for analyzing EPPs. As specified in the Du Pont case, these apparently innocuous characteristics of EPPs are central to the NLRB's determination of unlawful employer domination of labor organizations.

In order to determine an unlawful domination of a labor organization by management, the NLRB applies a two-part test. In the first part, the NLRB must determine whether the entity in question is a labor organization. The second part is to determine whether the labor organization is unlawfully dominated by management. Under the National Labor Relations Act (NLRA), an entity is considered to be a labor organization if the following conditions are met:

- Employees participate.
- The organization exists, at least in part, for the purpose of dealing with employers.
- These dealings concern conditions of work, grievances, labor disputes, wages, rates of pay, or hours of employment.

The NLRB determined that the Du Pont committees were labor organizations and thus applied the second part of its test. Under the NLRA, a labor organization is determined to be unlawfully dominated by an employer if any one of the following conditions is satisfied:

- The employer interferes with the labor organization's formation.
- The employer interferes with its administration.
- The employer provides it with financial or other support.

The NLRB found Du Pont's committees easily met all three conditions and thus determined that they were unlawfully dominated by the employer. Consequently, Du Pont was ordered to cease and desist from dominating the operations of the seven committees.

It is difficult to imagine many EPPs that would not be declared labor organizations dominated by the employer using the two-part test of the NLRB. Additionally, since rulings have now been handed down concerning both union and nonunion workplaces, most employers fall within the precedents established by the NLRB. These decisions impose far-reaching implications on most employee/management cooperation practices currently in operation in the United States. As a further consequence of these decisions, recent employer efforts to redesign the conventional workplace and the usefulness of various EPPs is seriously curtailed. At the heart of many widely accepted management systems, such as just-in-time (JIT), total quality management (TQM), continuous improvement (CI), and team building, is the concept of employee involvement. Without such involvement and participation, most of these systems, if not all, are destined for failure, or at least to have their effectiveness diminished. The Du Pont and Electromation cases represent a legal obstacle to the implementation of EPPs. This is especially important considering the widespread use of EPPs. It has been estimated that over 80 percent of the Fortune 1000 companies have some form of EPP in place.

For companies with unions, compliance with these recent NLRB rulings can be accomplished by ensuring that the union is involved in the EPPs. Through the collective bargaining process, a union and a company may reach a legitimate agreement on specific employee participation programs. In light of the Du Pont decision, it would appear that dealing directly with the union provides the most viable alternative for a company planning EPPs.

For companies that are nonunion, however, the NLRB has apparently provided a dilemma with no easy solution. There is little doubt that unless the NLRB's ruling is overturned, most EPPs are unlikely to withstand legal challenges.

Questions for Discussion

1. Given the importance of EPPs in improving the competitiveness of companies in the global marketplace, what actions do you think employers should take with respect to the Du Pont and Electromation rulings?
2. Do you think the NLRB has gone further than the NLRA intended in curtailing the use of EPPs?
3. What do you think will happen to management techniques that require intensive employee empowerment—such as TQM—if the NLRB rulings are left unchallenged?

Source: Adapted from Ross L. Fink, Robert K. Robinson, and Ann Canty, "Du Pont v. Chemical Workers Association: Further Limits on Employee Participation Programs," *Industrial Management* (March–April 1994): 3–5; Robert K. Robinson, Ross L. Fink, and Edward L. Gillenwater, "Do Employee Participation Programs Violate U.S. Labor Laws?" *Industrial Management* (May–June 1993): 3–5.

CASE 12.2

Worker Involvement and the Law

A recent study by Princeton, New Jersey-based Princeton Survey Research Associates found a majority of U.S. workers want a stronger voice in the workplace, but not necessarily through formal union representation. Instead, of those surveyed, 63 percent favor joint employee–management committees to solve workplace issues.

Sounds good. But unfortunately, Section 8(a)(2) of the National Labor Relations Act (NLRA) prohibits companies from playing a role in encouraging any cooperative work arrangement in a nonunion setting in which terms and conditions of employment are discussed. In fact, broad interpretation of the statute by the courts has created an environment in which employers often are breaking the law if nonunion employees are given a voice in workplace issues.

Despite their illegality, the Labor Policy Association in Washington, DC, estimates that more than 30,000 employee-involvement structures exist, involving more than 80 percent of Fortune 1000 companies. But association watchdogs say that the National Labor Relations Board and the courts show no signs of bringing Section 8(a)(2) in line with today's workplace realities. In fact, an appeals court recently upheld an NLRB ruling against Electromation, Inc., in which the company was charged with violating the NLRA for having created employee–management committees. Fourteen additional employee-involvement cases are currently pending.

Situations such as these make it imperative for managers to get involved in the way labor laws work, says Ed Potter, president of the Employment Policy Foundation in Washington, DC and co-author of the book *Keeping America Competitive: Employment Policy for the Twenty-first Century*.

"Business always has worked off of other agendas," he says, "be it from civil rights groups or unions. Given the realities of the global marketplace, business should be pursuing an agenda to make it more competitive."

"The NLRB is working to make it easier for unions to gain representation rights and collective-bargaining agreements," Potter says. Furthermore, since March 1994, the NLRB has issued more injunctions against companies for unfair labor practice than it did in the entire decade of the 1980s, adds F. Stuart Keene, president of PTI Labor Research, Inc., in Houston, Texas. By comparison, the board has issued only one injunction against a union.

What all this means is that despite the probusiness Congress in Washington in 1995, executives shouldn't assume everything in the labor arena will be taken care of to the benefit of private enterprise. "Business can't stand on the sidelines any longer," Potter says. "I'm not saying business should work to get rid of certain laws—like Section 8(a)(2) of the NLRA—but that it should get involved in reengineering them.

Questions for Discussion

1. Is the study conducted by Princeton Survey Research Associates good news for labor unions? Why?
2. Why would management be supportive of joint employee–management committees to solve workplace problems in a nonunion workplace?
3. Does the political orientation of the U.S. Congress influence how labor unions are able to influence the interpretation of laws such as Section 8(a)(2) of the National Labor Relations Act? Explain.

Source: "Don't Just Sit There—Get Involved," *Personnel Journal* (March 1995): 44.

EXPERIENTIAL EXERCISE

Reviewing the Advantages and Disadvantages of Union Representation

Activity:

Students will individually analyze the advantages and disadvantages of having union representation and then share their findings with the class. About 50 minutes of class time will be needed.

Directions:

1. Ask each class member to make a list of the advantages of having a union to represent workers, and then a list of the disadvantages of union representation. Allow about five minutes for each list.
2. Ask each student to identify at least two situations at work where it would be good to have a union representing a worker. Allow five minutes.
3. Calling on several individual students to share the advantages list, the instructor should write down the responses on the chalkboard. Do the same for the disadvantages list.
4. The instructor will summarize the advantages and disadvantages on the chalkboard.

5. The instructor should now call on several students to the situations where it would be good to have union representation for the worker. The instructor should encourage class discussion.

BUSINESS APPLICATION

Public Employees and the Right to Strike

Activity:
Students will participate in small group discussions reviewing the issue of public employees having the right to strike. Allocate about 50 minutes of class time for this activity.

Directions:

1. Divide the class into groups of five to seven students, with each group electing a spokesperson/recorder.
2. Provide background information to the class that includes the following:
   - Historically, one of the most potent weapons of a union has been either to strike or threaten to strike.
   - Public employees, such as police officers and garbage collectors, have often been prohibited from striking. When the air traffic controllers went on strike during the early 1980s President Reagan fired the striking workers for breaking regulations prohibiting their going on strike.
   - If public employees are prohibited by law from striking, such laws significantly weaken the power of a union to acquire wage increases for its workers.
3. Ask each group to discuss the issue of public employees having the right to strike, with each group taking a yes or no position on the issue. (Allow about 10 minutes for this part of the exercise.)
4. Each group's spokesperson is to report the group's decision, with the instructor noting the voting decisions on the chalkboard.
5. Following the reporting of each group's vote, the instructor should ask various group members to clarify their thoughts and feelings about the issue and why the group voted yes or no.
6. The instructor will summarize the group's voting positions and underlying rationale.

NOTES

1. Adapted from Kevin Kelly, David Woodruff, and Aaron Bernstein, "Much Ado About Pettiness," *Business Week* (July 4, 1994):34–35; Bob Bouyea, "Strikers May Lose Pension Credits," *Peoria Journal Star* (August 11, 1994): A1.
2. Statistical Abstract of the United States 1993 (Austin, TX: The Reference Press, Inc., 1993), 435.
3. David P. Twomey, *Labor and Employment Law* (Cincinnati, OH: South-Western, 1994).
4. David R. Sands, "The Global Local: Can Workers of the World Unite to Reverse Union Slide?" *The Washington Times* (April 3, 1994): A12.

5. Peter Nulty, "Look What the Unions Want Now," *Fortune* (February 8, 1993): 128–135.
6. Based on Robert Hamrin, *America's New Economy: The Basic Guide* (New York: Franklin Watts, 1988), 442.
7. Shari Caudron, "The Changing Union Agenda," *Personnel Journal* (March 1995): 42–49.
8. Thomas Karier, "Unions and the U.S. Comparative Advantage," *Industrial Relations* (Winter 1991): 4.
9. Keith L. Alexander and Stephen Baker, "If You Can't Beat 'Em, Join 'Em," *Business Week* (October 24, 1994): 80–81.
10. W.C. Hammer and F.J. Smith, "Work Activities as Predictors of Unionization Activity," *Journal of Applied Psychology* (August 1978): 414–421.
11. John McLaughlin, "Union Soldiers," *Restaurant Business* (November 20, 1994): 66–72.
12. Based on a telephone conversation with the National Labor Relations Board in Washington, DC, on June 12, 1991.
13. Keven Kelly, "Why the Talks at Deere Hit Bedrock," *Business Week* (October 31, 1994): 48.
14. "Why America Needs Unions: But Not the Kind It Has Now," *Business Week* (May 23, 1994): 70–82.
15. *Statistical Abstract of the United States, 1993* (Austin, TX: The Reference Press, Inc., 1993): 435.
16. "Getting Their Dues," *The Economist* (March 25, 1995): 68–74.
17. Adapted from "The Union's Role as Co-Manager," *Fortune* (March 26, 1990): 37; "The Boardroom's Revenge," *Economist* (May 12, 1990): 72; Gregory A. Patterson, "UAW Hotly Debates Whether It Is Too Cozy with Car Companies," *The Wall Street Journal* (June 15, 1989): A1, A8; "Suddenly USX Is Playing Mr. Nice Guy," *Business Week* (June 26, 1989): 151–152; "The UAW Rebels Teaming Up Against Teamwork," *Business Week* (March 27, 1989): 110–114.
18. Micheline Maynard, "Enthusiasm Drives Saturn Workers," *USA Today* (August 31, 1990): 2B.
19. Brian Dumaine, "Why Do We Work?" *Fortune* (December 26, 1994): 196–204.

Athletes, Employees Are Nike's Most Valuable Assets

Nike's human resources consist not only of the employees whose fierce loyalty to the company is the stuff of legend, but also of the athletes who endorse the company's products. Nike is a youthful company, the average age of a Nike employee is 32. To be responsive to the diverse and changing needs of the active, intelligent, mobile people in this age group Nike has developed a novel human resources plan known as LifeTrek. LifeTrek is one of the most flexible human resources plans in any industry. The program, and a host of amenities at the company's world headquarters in Beaverton, Oregon, make Nike a great place to work. Employees have access to world-class fitness facilities, receive bonuses for riding bicycles or roller-blades to work, and have on-site child care facilities, to list a few of their favorite perks.

Nike athletes are at the center of the organization. Their place in the organization's history is immortalized in the names of the buildings at the Beaverton headquarters, in the numerous large photographs and statues that decorate the buildings, and in the commercials that have given the company its renegade identity. Nike is concerned about the interests of its athletes. Through its innovative Nike Sports Management unit, the company provides its athletes with full-service contract and endorsement management services. The unit is designed to replace that ubiquitous entity in the modern world of the highly paid athlete: the sports agent.

To tell the story of human resources at Nike, however, it is necessary to begin with the company's CEO, Phil Knight, whose presence is felt throughout the company. It is Knight's competitive spirit, and his reverence for athletes and athletic performance, that suffuses the company with its indomitable will to win. That will gives the company its swagger, and puts the "do it" in "Just Do It."

Phil Knight's Leadership Style

There are many theories about leadership and human motivation. A popular view among organizational theorists is that no single theory can account for leadership and motivation at all times or in all places. This view, known as contingency theory, asserts that leaders must be flexible, adapting their styles to the motivational needs of individual employees or to the situational context of the organization. Contingency theory contrasts sharply with other theories that treat leadership as a function of an individual leader's traits or behaviors. Despite the current popularity of contingency theory, those who subscribe to this view won't find support for their ideas in the unique leadership style of Phil Knight. Knight's leadership style is enigmatic and aloof. He doesn't change his style for anyone or any situation. Yet, he is very effective. Anyone who works for Knight is quickly struck by his elusive, intense personality. The very arrangement of the Nike CEO's office suite testifies to his elusive style.

The displays of sporting images observable throughout the Nike headquarters end suddenly at the entrance to Knight's office. Instead, the visitor to the CEO's suite atop the John McEnroe building is struck by the blond wood, black lacquer trim, and elegant wall sconces. Visitors to Knight's lush outer office are asked to remove their shoes. However, this bit of Oriental propriety is rarely an issue since Knight seldom invites anyone to his office. Instead, he meets employees and outside visitors in a private conference chamber next to his office called the Wimbledon Room.

Senior Nike managers all realize it would be pointless to try to find Knight in his outer office because he spends all his time in his inner office, a room accessible through a sliding door in the back of the outer office that most of Knight's associates of 20 years have never seen. Nike designer Tinker Hatfield is one of the only Nike employees ever to enter the inner office when he and Michael Jordan were once ushered into the strangely unbusiness-like room. As these one-time visitors have reported, the inner office is fitted with a geometric stone fireplace and delineated by redwood beams. There is a huge television, connected to a sports-grabbing satellite dish, and books and papers scattered about.

Visitors to the third floor of the McEnroe building can gaze past a sitting room where one of Knight's secretaries works and see Knight shuttling back and forth quickly, like a target in a shooting gallery. Senior Nike executives often see him moving back and forth like this, because those who need to talk to Knight before closing deals or signing off on important decisions—even the new president, Tom Clarke, who works across the central atrium; the general manager; the chief financial officer; the head of investor relations and others—tend to hang out in the hall area to see if they can catch Knight on the fly.

Requests for formal meetings with Knight are almost always denied. On the other hand, Knight appears unannounced in managers' offices all the time. If they aren't there, he has been known to read the papers on their desks. If a colleague does manage to intercept him, Knight usually avoids direct eye contact until the conversation warms up. He tends to speak in rapid-fire bursts, often punctuating phrases with a little humming noise or a laugh, as if he's already become bored by a listener's effort to catch up with his thoughts.

Knight is famous, even among employees afraid to approach him and say hello, for sponging anywhere from twenty-five cents to twenty dollars off of Nike employees and never paying it back. He is also known—ironically, in light of his otherwise competitive nature—for hating to negotiate. Knight calls the cross-table give-and-take reported each day in the world's business pages haggling: "I simply find the whole thing demeaning," he admits.

Knight manages the Nike empire by nuance—a raised eyebrow here, the jingle of keys in his pocket there, a yawn. Sage-like half-pronouncements are offered after periods of distant contemplation. In 1993, a rough-hewn line of outdoor, cement-court basketball shoes was suddenly created and brought powerfully to market by Nike because Knight, considering a similar new product from Reebok, wrote, "I think we should respond to this" on one of those little yellow Post-it notes and stuck it on a vice president's desk.

Knight believes that some of his instinct toward a low profile is genetic. But a portion of it he attributes to his mentor and former partner Bill Bowerman who taught him: Always let the performance talk for you.

CRITICAL THINKING CHALLENGE

In light of what you have learned about human motivation and leadership, what do you think are some of the strengths of Phil Knight's low-profile style? What are some of the potential pitfalls of Knight's style?

The Nike Spirit in Human Resources

Want to get a job with Nike? Forget the fancy paper and punchy verbs. Forget an eye-catching layout or typeface. When Nike reviews a job applicant's resume, it doesn't notice any of those classic standout techniques. That's because Nike relies on a computerized system that automatically stores an image of the resume and records its text with hardly a touch from a human hand. When the company needs to hire, a computer operator types in the skills needed for the position. After checking its data, the computer displays appropriate candidates' names and backgrounds on the screen. Nike receives over 40,000 job applications each year. Human resource executives praise the computer system for helping them find the right people for the right job faster, with less dependence on expensive recruiting firms.

Another sign of the changing times in Nike's human resources practices is benefits for "domestic partners"—people who live with employees but do not qualify as legal spouses or dependents. Many employers nationwide are leery of expanding their benefits at a time of rising health care costs. Companies that do provide domestic partner coverage generally argue that their move makes ethical and economic sense. For Nike, it makes competitive sense. Beginning in April 1994, Nike became the first major Oregon company to offer domestic partners the same benefits as employees' legal spouses. The policy is part of Nike's newly revamped benefits package dubbed "LifeTrek." Jim Frederick, Nike's director of compensation said, "We've always led the competition. We wanted to do that with benefits." The Nike policy covers both homosexual and heterosexual partners.

The LifeTrek package of benefits is communicated to Nike employees through an innovative set of booklets and newsletters. In 1994, these communication materials won the Best of Show award in the total benefits program category of Business Insurance's 1994 Employee Benefits Communication Awards competition. The wit and irreverence of the company are evident on the front cover of the LifeTrek benefit booklet. Very deliberately, the words "employee benefits" or "flexible benefits" don't appear. Instead, there's just the word "LifeTrek." Icons blending together on the cover, which are later used in specific chapter headings, convey the message of how benefits help employees at work and off the job.

Sexual harassment in the workplace is another issue that has received a lot of attention over the last few years. The issue leapt into public attention during the Clarence Thomas-Anita Hill hearings that were held to investigate Thomas' alleged harassment of Hill. Sexual harassment is an issue that covers a broad range of behaviors. Pats on the back, obscene jokes, and a hostile work environment created by comments or display of sexual material can all constitute sexual harassment.

Nike human resource managers deal with the issue upfront, through education of employees before any incidents occur. At the Nike plant in Greenland, New Hampshire, human resources manager Gerry Notargiacomo focuses on educating workers on sexual harassment. "It was something I felt was important to bring forward to all employees, not just management," she said. "Education needs to be brought down to the employees. They're working together on a daily basis. They need to know what the employer expects of them." The theme Notargiacomo uses is respect in the work place. "We want to ensure that our work environment is comfortable to everyone," she said.

Many companies are developing capabilities for employees to have their children cared for in on-site child-care centers. For the past several years, *Working Mother* magazine has ranked the nation's 100 leading companies on the basis of their working-mother-friendly policies. For the second time in two years, Nike was selected as one of the top 100. The company subsidizes preschool care for 160 children in the Joe Paterno Child Care Center at its Beaverton headquarters. The company also offers a Nike Tykes drop-in care center, where employees can pay for care by the hour.

Sue Levin, Nike public relations manager, noted that roughly half of the nearly 2,000 employees at the Beaverton campus are women. "When you look at the age and lifestyle of our employees, these benefits are particularly important," Levin said. "Obviously, to attract and keep quality employees, you've got to have a good program."

Employees at the Beaverton headquarters can feel a sense of relief in knowing that their children are well cared for during the day. They can also get a sense of security in the knowledge of the company's unprecedented commitment to safety and security. Contractors built the 570,000 square-foot, nine-building campus with security and privacy as priorities. Earthen berms work as a natural fence to shield the buildings from street view. Builders incorporated a high-tech electronic security system. About 50 readers of the credit-card size "keys" control after-hours access to buildings and past vehicle barrier gates. This system also protects the employees' bike lock-up area.

Nike is more than the employees that work within the privileged confines of the Beaverton headquarters. The company is also well known for the innovative ways it manages the athletes who endorse its products. The athlete is the central figure in the Nike spirit, as one would readily discern from the many statues, pictures, and other paeans to famous athletes that decorate the headquarters.

CRITICAL THINKING CHALLENGE

Nike human resource policies and procedures are published under the generic name Life-Trek. This set of policies and procedures gives employees options about what benefits will be appropriate for them. Explain why such flexible policies are becoming more prevalent in a variety of industries. Think of some ways in which flexible policies may *not* be in the best interests of employees. Besides flexibility, Nike also has some innovative programs such as the domestic partners program. What do you see as the advantages and potential problems of the domestic partners program?

Nike Sports Management

The Nike mystique has been built over the years through the efforts of hundreds of athletes in a myriad of different sports. The athletes wear Nike products in their sport, and they are made larger than life through Nike advertising. More than anyone else in the Nike family, the athlete stands at the center of the company's success. CEO Phil Knight knows the athlete is the central figure in the success of his company, that's the way he wants it. He also knows that most of the athletes that endorse Nike products have immensely complex professional lives that are made more complex by their endorsement contracts. Great athletes such as Michael Jordan make more than $30 million per year, the bulk of their money coming from endorsement contracts, not from their participation in sport.

The increasing popularity across many industries of the practice of using star athletes to endorse products began to complicate Nike's marketing strategy. Nike wanted its athletes to be athletes first, and to attach its products to that image. But some of the company's stars, like Michael Jordan, were getting so many endorsement deals that their image was becoming diluted. For example, prior to his retirement and eventual return to playing basketball for the Chicago Bulls, Jordan's endorsement "portfolio" included Gatorade, Wheaties, Chevrolet, Hanes, Ball Park Franks, Coca Cola, and McDonald's, besides Nike. This dilution of the star's image made Knight furious. None of these companies had invested in Jordan early in his career the way Nike had. Only Nike had invested the creative energy and financial resources necessary to create Air Jordan. In the vernacular of sports marketing, by 1992 Jordan's agglomeration of endorsements meant he was no longer "clean."

As difficult as it was for Nike to accept the dilution of Michael Jordan's image, the need for a change in the way Nike manages its relationship with its athletes became clear to Knight one evening as he was watching television. During one break in the action, Knight stared at his television screen and watched Andre Agassi, a Nike guy since he was a 16-year-old kid whom no other company would touch, endorsing Canon cameras. Agassi tipped down his sunglasses, looked into the camera, and with a knowing smirk, said, "Image is everything."

Knight flipped. Although he knew that Agassi was particularly precocious in his understanding of the power of image, he thought it was crazy to go public with such an analysis. Knight fumed, "This is a one-hundred-and-eighty-degree turn away from our own imagery. Here we work like crazy to convey that performance, not the image, is everything. This 'Image Is Everything' is hurting him and it's going to hurt us."

In the wake of Jordan's image dilution and Agassi's "Image Is Everything" campaign, Knight decided something had to be done to help the athletes manage their endorsements. Within several months, he created a company-owned sports management program known as Nike Sports Management.

Nike Sports Management was officially launched with the 1992 pro basketball draft when Nike agreed to pay college star Alonzo Mourning a guaranteed $16 million over five years for total control over his career. This program of "total career management" was also subsequently offered to University of Southern California basketball star Harold Miner, and to pro football player Rick Mirer. Besides helping these athletes manage their endorsement contracts, Nike Sports Management also negotiated with teams on behalf of the players.

Knight blamed the sports agents who often represented athletes in negotiations for product endorsement deals for the overselling of an athlete's image. "The agents came out at a time when someone making a hundred thousand dollars was a well paid athlete," he said. "Agents were just fringe lawyers or guys with a huge passion for a sport. From those hundred-thousand-dollar contracts, the agent got four thousand. But now you've got one-hundred-twenty-thousand-dollar agent fees for a single team contract, and for a million dollar endorsement, the agent gets up to twenty percent. The incentive to fragment an image is huge, and when you split it up too often nobody wins."

Nike athletes don't have to choose to be represented by Nike Sports Management. In fact, most don't. Nike still retains some control over the lives of these athletes through contract clauses. One clause that is placed in every Nike endorsement contract allows the company to cut and run if "the value of the consultant's endorsement is impaired by the commission of any act that shocks or offends the community, or which ridicules public morals and decency." Endorsement contracts also permit the company to drop an athlete banned from competition for using drugs.

CRITICAL THINKING CHALLENGE

Nike has been criticized by some who think the company is interfering with athletes and their relationship to the teams they play for. Certainly, being a Nike endorser gives athletes more leverage in contract negotiations with teams. What do you think will happen in the future as athletes become increasingly expensive for teams? What role do you think companies like Nike should play in the overall health of sports industries such as professional baseball, basketball, and football?

Sources: Adapted from Jerry Geisel, "With Wit and Flair, Nike, Inc., Just Does It," *Business Insurance* (November 7, 1994): 27; Fred Leeson, "Oregon Companies Make Family-Friendly List," *Oregonian* (September 14, 1994): 2D; Robert Berner, "Software Lets Computer Do the Choosing," *Patriot Ledger* (August 6, 1994): 23; Tad Shannon, "More Companies Offer 'Partner Benefits,'" *Eugene Register-Guard* (February 22, 1994): Business Section; Martha Allen, "Sexual Harassment in the Work Place Alive and Well in New Hampshire," *New Hampshire Business Review* (February 19, 1993): 1; Brenda Moss, "Access Control Workout," *Security* (December 1991): 20–21.

PART 5

Marketing

CHAPTER 13

Marketing Strategy

LEARNING OBJECTIVES

1. Explain the purpose and importance of marketing.

2. Trace the evolution of marketing.

3. Define the term *market* and distinguish between the two major types of markets.

4. Describe the steps involved in developing a marketing strategy.

5. Identify the four elements of the marketing mix.

6. Define the term *marketing environment* and list the environmental forces.

7. Describe how consumers make purchase decisions, and compare consumer buying behavior to industrial buying behavior.

8. Explain the value of marketing research and outline the research process.

A great product, a huge promotion budget, the right price—a sure formula for success. That's what the Gillette Company thought when it introduced Sensor, its new high-tech razor with twin blades independently mounted on springs.

Sensor is at the heart of Gillette's drive to regain market share lost to Bic and other companies that produce disposable razors. Gillette remains the industry leader, with 60 percent of the $2.6 billion worldwide blade and razor market, but disposable razors have a low profit ratio. Cartridge refills are much more profitable, so, Gillette hopes that Sensor will help reverse a 15-year trend toward the inexpensive disposables.

Gillette took 10 years and spent more than $200 million to develop Sensor, making it the most expensive product in the firm's history. The cartridges contain 23 parts and require laser welding and complex assembly techniques. The result is a razor blade that provides a smoother, closer shave and cartridges that are easier to clean. The complex manufacturing process also makes the Sensor cartridge difficult to copy, giving Gillette an advantage over competitors like Wilkinson Sword and Schick.

Gillette has used a single marketing strategy to sell Sensor both in the United States and abroad, since company officials believe that shaving needs are similar around the world. The problem has been that it is very hard to get consumers to change razors; those who already use cartridge systems like Gillette's Trace II keep their razors for seven to ten years. Gillette knew that getting customers to switch to the new system would be a challenge, but it believed that Sensor's close shave would make the difference.

Gillette established a $110 million advertising budget to launch Sensor. The product was first introduced to the public with $3 million worth of commercials during the 1990 Super Bowl, one of the biggest international advertising events of the year. The same spots played almost simultaneously in 19 North American and European countries.

Sensor's initial sales exceeded Gillette's wildest dreams. The firm shipped 4.5 million razors to U.S. retailers the first month. Each razor came with three sets of blades and sold for $3.75. The product immediately became one of the hottest items in the industry, with some retailers selling out in three hours. Sales of Sensor grew so fast that Gillette could not manufacture enough cartridges to meet demand. Many large drugstore chains did not receive their orders in full or on time. Replacement cartridges were unavailable in some areas of the country for several months.

To resolve the problem, Gillette stopped advertising Sensor for a few months, delayed introducing the product in Spain, Portugal, and Italy, and used razors intended for Europe to fill orders in the United States. Gillette also opened manufacturing facilities in West Berlin earlier than intended. Although some retailers were angry about shortages, Gillette anticipated that the advertising cutback would allow supply to catch up with demand.

About a year after Gillette introduced Sensor, Schick countered with a product of its own, Tracer (a flexible cartridge that follows facial contours), and backed it with a $30 million promotion campaign. Gillette, in the meantime, devel-

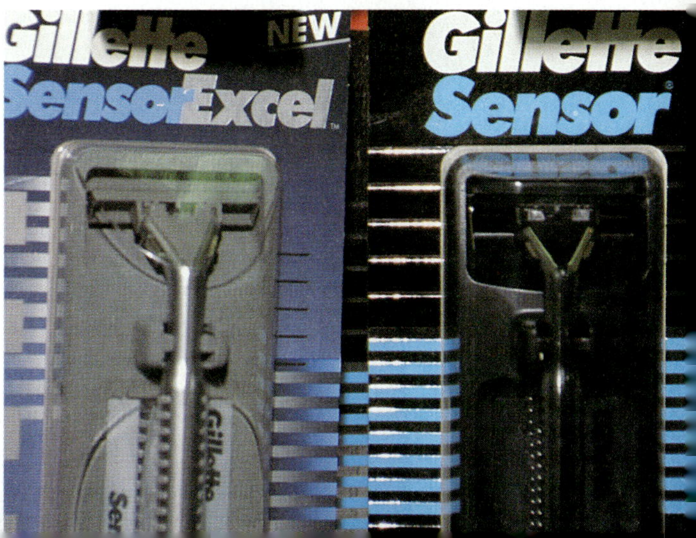

oped Sensor for Women and introduced it in 1992, and followed by Sensor Excel in 1994. Sensor Excell features a skin guard made of five flexible microfins that stretch the skin for a closer shave, and is priced higher than the original Sensor. Both companies now face a tough challenge with these new products. Schick's Tracer will have to compete against the successful Sensor, and Gillette will have to convince women to use shaving systems instead of disposable razors. Early results were encouraging for Gillette. With a radically different flat-handled design, Sensor for Women sold 7.6 million units in the first six months, more than the company had expected to sell the entire first year.[1]

What, in your opinion, is the major reason for Sensor's success? What can competitors learn from the success of Sensor?

Gillette offers a prime example of how marketing can help a firm achieve its goals. Effective marketing strategy contributes greatly to success; the lack of it can doom a business to failure. Marketing firmly links the company to customers, their needs, and their desires. Gillette has devised new products and explored new ways to reach potential customers. Those activities, all part of marketing, are based on a tried-and-true idea: Give people what they want.

In this chapter, we provide an overview of basic marketing concepts. First, we define marketing and discuss the benefits and costs of marketing activities. After briefly tracing the evolution of marketing, we introduce the marketing concept. Next we explain the steps involved in developing a marketing strategy: (1) selecting a target market and (2) designing a marketing mix (product, price, promotion, distribution) that will satisfy the needs of the target market. We also discuss the importance of understanding buyer behavior and the value of marketing research. Finally, we look at what the future holds for marketing.

AN OVERVIEW OF MARKETING

Each of you has been involved in marketing activities at one time or another. Perhaps you have tried to sell a used textbook back to the campus bookstore or to convince your parents to finance a spring vacation. You may not have known it at the time, but you were performing marketing activities.

What Is Marketing?

Marketing
The process of planning and executing the conception, pricing, promotion, and distribution of ideas, goods, and services to create exchanges that satisfy individual and organizational objectives.

When people hear the term *marketing,* many think of advertising or selling. Although those are part of marketing, the part we see most, marketing is much more. As the American Marketing Association defines it, "**Marketing** is the process of planning and executing the conception, pricing, promotion, and distribution of ideas, goods, and services to create exchanges that satisfy individual and organizational objectives."[2] This definition emphasizes the diverse activities marketers perform: deciding what products to offer, setting prices, developing sales promotions and advertising campaigns, and making products readily available to customers. Exhibit 13.1 lists several activities of the marketing team.

Marketing activities are required for many different kinds of products. The term *product* often brings to mind tangible goods—those that can be held or touched, such as compact disc players or soft drinks. But products also can be services or ideas. Hospitals offer products: health care services. The American Cancer Society offers an idea, quitting smoking, as a product. Like firms that produce tangible goods, nonprofit and service organizations and even individuals rely heavily on marketing. The Los Angeles Mission, for example, used mailers and advertisements to raise money to save the financially troubled mission.

Exchange
The process by which parties provide something of value to one another to satisfy the needs of each.

Ultimately the purpose of marketing activities is to bring about exchanges between buyers and sellers. **Exchange** consists of one party providing something of value to another party, who gives something in return.[3] Just as the "something of value" is not always a physical good, the "something in return" is not always money, as Exhibit 13.2 shows. The American Cancer Society's notion of quitting smoking to live a longer, healthier life is an intangible product, one that cannot be physically touched. For smokers who "buy" that idea, the price is the effort required to break a habit that they have found pleasurable.

Marketing Adds Value

Utility
The ability of a product to satisfy consumers' needs.

Through activities that enable exchanges to take place, marketing adds value to products. This value is **utility,** the ability of a product to satisfy a consumer need. As Chapter 9 discussed, utility is created when a firm's production function yields a product. For example, through the use of raw materials, labor, and other inputs, publishers produce newspapers and magazines. Marketing indirectly affects utility, since an organization may depend on its marketing

Exhibit 13.1
Typical Marketing Activities

Product	Pricing	Promotion	Distribution
Develop new products. Modify existing products. Test-market products. Select brand names. Package products.	Establish price objectives. Conduct cost analysis. Analyze competitors' prices. Set actual prices.	Determine type of promotion (advertising, personal selling, sales promotion, publicity). Design the advertising message. Select the advertising media (print, radio, television, billboard, specialty items). Schedule the advertisements.	Select wholesalers and retailers. Establish procedures for handling and moving products (transportation, storage, inventory control). Find the best locations for plants, warehouses, and retail outlets.

Exhibit 13.2
The Exchange Process

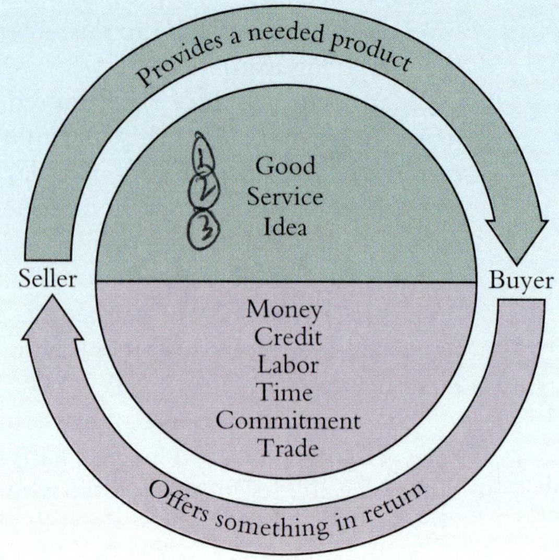

people to find out which products consumers would welcome in the marketplace.

Marketing directly creates utility in other ways. By making products available when consumers want and need them, marketing creates utility. Publishing companies print and distribute morning newspapers early so readers can read them at breakfast or while commuting to work. Making products available where consumers need or want to obtain them also creates utility. Newspapers are delivered to homes and businesses; sold in vending machines, supermarkets, convenience marts, drugstores, and bookstores; and placed in libraries. Marketing again creates utility when the ownership of a product is transferred from seller to buyer. To obtain newspapers, customers pay the publishing company for home delivery, drop money into vending machines, or pay clerks in stores.

Marketing Affects Everyone

Marketing is important to businesses and consumers alike. First, through the cost of what we purchase, each of us supports the costs of marketing. By estimate, nearly half of every dollar spent on goods and services pays for marketing activities. Most people would agree that marketing costs are worth it because the many and varied marketing activities enable us to satisfy our needs and wants. To review earlier discussions, a *need* is something required for human survival, such as food, water, shelter, and clothing; a *want* is something desired but not necessary for basic survival. Without marketing, many needs and wants would go unsatisfied because exchanges would be much harder to accomplish.

Critics contend that marketing activities stimulate the worst instincts and desires in people. In other words, they say marketing is inherently unethical. Advocates argue that marketing is driven by market forces that reflect the needs of society. Thus, marketing activities are not inherently unethical, because they satisfy consumer demands.[4] Perhaps it is difficult for you to come to grips with this issue, but we touch on it several times throughout the book.

Marketing often has special importance for students. Many of you will work in marketing—whether in sales, retailing, advertising, or another field—in a for-profit firm or a nonprofit organization. The career appendix that follows this part of the book explores various marketing careers, some of which may be new to you. How do you feel about marketing activities? Use Your Values and Attitudes to explore your attitudes; then compare your attitudes to those of your classmates.

YOUR VALUES AND ATTITUDES

How Do You Feel about Marketing Activities?

Directions: Circle the number that represents your level of agreement with each statement.

	Strongly Agree					**Strongly Disagree**
1. Marketing helps improve the quality of goods and services.	1	2	3	4	5	6
2. The number of commercials on TV is about right.	1	2	3	4	5	6
3. I would be proud to have a job in marketing.	1	2	3	4	5	6
4. Marketing people are concerned with product safety.	1	2	3	4	5	6
5. Most marketing activities are conducted ethically.	1	2	3	4	5	6
6. Advertisements portray women and minorities realistically, without stereotypes.	1	2	3	4	5	6
7. The benefits of marketing justify the costs.	1	2	3	4	5	6
8. Marketing doesn't increase materialism in our society.	1	2	3	4	5	6

	Strongly Agree					Strongly Disagree
9. Marketing doesn't encourage people to buy things they don't really need.	1	2	3	4	5	6
10. Marketing doesn't make people too concerned with how they look and dress.	1	2	3	4	5	6

Feedback: Now let's assess your attitudes toward marketing. Items circled 1 or 2 show a positive attitude; 3 or 4 suggests a middle-of-the road or neutral position; and 5 or 6 identifies a negative feeling.

Anyone considering a marketing career would want to feel positive about the different activities marketers perform. But, like consumers in general, students usually have mixed feelings about marketing. It is the most visible side of business and often one of the most controversial. Why? Are consumers generally skeptical of the purpose, methods, and results of marketing activities? Are they unfamiliar with the benefits marketing brings? To build positive attitudes toward marketing, do marketers and their organizations need to make changes in the ways goods, services, and ideas are developed, promoted, and sold?

HOW MARKETING EVOLVED

When organizations and individuals conduct marketing activities today, they usually have consumers' needs and desires clearly in mind. But that has not always been true. Beginning with the Industrial Revolution in the 19th century and the capability of mass production that resulted, most businesses had a *production orientation.* Demand for new manufactured goods was so great that producers were concerned primarily with increased production and operating efficiency rather than with consumer preferences. As goods rolled off the production line, marketing consisted of taking orders and shipping products.

By the mid-1920s, manufacturers discovered that supplies of basic consumer goods had caught up to demand; they were now producing an abundance of goods. Needing to move their products, firms developed a *sales orientation.* Marketing began to emphasize advertising and sales. Companies started using sophisticated sales techniques to increase demand for existing products, but they still did not look to the marketplace to ensure that consumers' needs and desires were met.

Not until the early 1950s did firms begin to develop a *consumer orientation.* With soldiers returning from World War II, reentering the workplace, and starting families, demand for consumer goods and services surged. So did competition among firms to meet that demand. They began to focus on satisfying consumers. One of the first companies to state a policy of customer satisfaction was General Electric. GE said that marketing should be integrated into each phase of business. The policy of customer satisfaction has become known as the marketing concept.

The Marketing Concept

At Whirlpool, the marketing department conducted a survey that showed that customers wanted a cooking range that was easy to clean. Engineers then designed a range with electronic touch pad controls, which can be cleaned with the sweep of a cloth or sponge. Industry wisdom suggested touch pads would fail, because earlier models with push buttons failed. Marketing, design, and engineering worked closely together to test consumer reactions every step of the way, and the new range succeeded where the old push-button design had failed.[5]

Marketing Concept A managerial philosophy of customer orientation with the goal of achieving long-term success.

The **marketing concept** is a management philosophy stating that an organization should strive to satisfy the needs of consumers through a coordinated set of activities that also allows the organization to achieve its objectives.[6] Thus customer satisfaction is the major force underlying the marketing concept and driving the entire company. The marketing concept calls for all departments and all members to be committed to satisfying customers. The firm must determine consumer needs and wants, develop quality products that satisfy them, make products readily available at prices acceptable to buyers (and that will allow a profit), and provide service and after-sales support.[7] If a firm can answer yes to the following questions, it is customer oriented:

- Are we easy for customers to do business with?
- Do we keep our promises?
- Do we meet the standards we set?
- Are we responsive to customer needs?[8]

Firms benefit from practicing the marketing concept. They do not waste money on developments in which customers are not interested. Also, customers pay more for products they believe will provide greater value and satisfaction, and if they are pleased with their purchase they come back and they refer business. Repeat business lowers sales costs and boosts profits; holding on to current customers is about one-fifth the cost of acquiring new ones.[9] Some marketers say the marketing concept helps set up a cycle of success: Customer satisfaction leads to loyal customers, which produces higher profits that make employees want to stay with the firm, which in turn makes for better customer service and satisfaction.

Focusing on the customer sounds like an obvious, common-sense way to run a successful business, but not all firms gear their marketing activities closely to the customer. The marketing concept is not always easy to put into practice. Top-level managers must be committed to it and must gain the commitment of other members of the organization. An organization may need to restructure departments or functions to better coordinate activities. Often a firm must be willing to forgo short-term profits for long-term customer satisfaction. And because consumer tastes and preferences constantly change, the firm must continually obtain information about customers and their needs and tailor its products to meet changing consumer preferences.

TOMORROW'S BUSINESS WORLD

The Customer Is King

"In tomorrow's business world it won't be enough to know where your customers live, what they watch and what they read," says Priscilla Ann La Barbera, associate professor of marketing in the Graduate School of Business at New York University. "You'll also need to know what they're thinking, what they want, what products they buy, what the likelihood is of their switching allegiances and what type of relationship they want with companies."

Many observers have labeled the 1990s as the decade of the customer. Managers have come to realize that the companies that are succeeding put their customers first. Books such as *Customer Satisfaction Guaranteed* and *The Service Advantage* can be found on managers' desks. Consulting firms report that customer-service work is on the rise. It almost seems as though paying attention to the customer is a new concept, but it isn't.

In the 1950s, General Motors gained a lead in customer satisfaction by designing cars to suit the needs of many different people. GM produced a variety of models and soared to a 52 percent share of the U.S. automobile market in 1962. During the 1960s and 1970s, with a growing population and little foreign competition, GM assumed that customers were satisfied and concentrated on profits. Automobile manufacturers from Japan, Germany, Sweden, and other parts of the world realized that American consumers' needs were not being satisfied and moved quickly to do the job. By 1992, GM's market share was barely 35 percent.

The automobile industry is not the only one in which the United States lost its dominance. As global competition intensified in the 1980s, the U.S. lost its preeminent position as a world leader in semiconductor, steel, and consumer electronics manufacturing. Foreign companies have also invested heavily in service industries such as banking, insurance, entertainment, and hotels. Today, firms are going back to the basics—customer satisfaction.

TQM

At MBNA, a Baltimore-based credit company, the words "THE CUSTOMER FIRST" are woven into the carpet at all four entrances; above all 350 doorways are signs saying, "THINK OF YOURSELF AS THE CUSTOMER." Phone service agents call customers who want to close an account and try to change their minds, even waiving annual fees at times. The vice president of the collection department tells his 380 employees that customers making late payments "need a hugging, not a mugging." This emphasis on the customer has helped MBNA retain 95 percent of its customers each year, while competitors keep about 88 percent.

Like MBNA, many firms try to find out what customers want and how to better serve them. Reliable Corporation, an office supply house in Chicago, monitors its own performance with a regular questionnaire to customers. According to the firm's marketing manager, the survey is based on the belief that "we could be doing better." At Embassy Suites Hotels, at least five customers are interviewed each day and their comments posted for the entire staff to see. Technicians at Du Pont now spend significant time in customers' plants to figure out new applications for Du Pont products. A Du Pont salesman in Korea once asked managers at Reebok International how his company could better serve them. As a result,

Du Pont flexible plastic tubes that were developed for the automobile industry are now built into the soles of Reebok's ERS sneakers to give them more bounce. At British Airways, service excellence, not operations, drives the business, and the airline that was once nicknamed Bloody Awful now enjoys one of the best reputations in the industry.

Source: Adapted from *U.S. News and World Report* (Special Advertising Section, 1992); Iris S. Rosenberg, "U.S. Industries Rethink the 'Role' of the Customer," *Quality Digest* (January 1993): 41–47; "Satisfaction Action Is . . . ," *Marketing News* (January 20, 1992): 4; Stephen Phillips, Amy Dunkin, James B. Treece, and Keith Hammonds, "King Customer," *Business Week* (March 12, 1990): 88–94; Patricia Sellers, "What Customers Really Want," *Fortune* (June 4, 1990): 58–68; Sharyn Hunt and Ernest F. Cooke, "It's Basic But Necessary: Listen to the Customer," *Marketing News* (March 5, 1990): 22–23; and Mark Maremount, "How British Airways Butters Up the Passenger," *Business Week* (March 12, 1990): 94.

Beyond the Marketing Concept

Does giving consumers what they want and need serve the long-term interests of society? As we move through the 1990s, the traditional marketing concept, with its consumer focus, is taking on more meaning. In addition to satisfying customers to meet company goals, many firms today also take into consideration how marketing affects society. The broader *societal orientation* means that firms are concerned with the welfare of society as well as their own interests and those of consumers.

As Chapter 4 pointed out, many firms and nonprofit organizations take active roles in dealing with issues such as scarce resources, environmental destruction, hunger, housing shortages, and illiteracy. Forward-thinking firms and their employees are involved in programs to work on such problems, as well as to help their communities, improve education, support the arts, and provide job training and opportunities for disadvantaged children and adults.

The marketing activities we discuss throughout this chapter focus on satisfying consumer needs and wants. In the next section, we look at how firms can design marketing strategies to satisfy consumers.

DEVELOPING A MARKETING STRATEGY

Marketing Strategy
A plan for selecting and analyzing a target market and developing and maintaining a marketing mix that will satisfy this target market.

To put the marketing concept into action, a firm must decide on the appropriate marketing activities to satisfy customer needs and achieve its goals. A **marketing strategy** is an overall plan for conducting marketing activities that enables an organization to use its resources and strengths to meet the needs of the marketplace. For instance, the marketing strategy at Apple Computer is to license its computer technology to makers of Macintosh clones, like Power Computing Corp., to take advantage of the growth in home and school markets.[10] Firms developing a marketing strategy follow two basic steps: (1) Select a target market and (2) design a marketing mix (a combination of product, price, promotion, and distribution) that will satisfy the needs of the target market.

Selecting a Target Market

Market
People with the authority, financial ability, and willingness to purchase a product.

Consumer Market
People who purchase products for personal use.

Industrial Market
Those who purchase products to use in the production of other products or to resell.

Organizations gear their marketing activities to reach certain customers—a market. A **market** is a group of people who need and want a product and have the ability, willingness, and authority to purchase it. Markets are divided into two broad categories: consumer and industrial. **Consumer markets** are made up of individuals who purchase products for personal use. **Industrial markets** consist of individuals or organizations that purchase goods and services so they can produce products to supply to others. Examples include manufacturers, governments, hospitals, nonprofit organizations, and stores.

Firms often sell products to both types of markets. Rossi Pasta, a family-owned business in Ohio, sells hand-rolled pasta through catalogs mailed to households (consumer) and also supplies the pasta to restaurants, supermarkets, and businesses (industrial).

Market Segment
A group of individuals with one or more similar product needs.

Consumer or industrial, most markets include numerous customers with many different needs. Businesses are rarely able to satisfy the needs of all customers in a market, so they divide a market into **market segments,** groups of individuals with one or more similar product needs. Then they decide which segment or segments to serve. Bain de Soleil Suncare offers sunscreens and lotions that provide different levels of protection to appeal to the skin types and tanning preferences of different market segments.

Target Market
A group to which a firm directs its marketing activities.

A **target market** is a group of customers—consumers or other businesses—to whom a business directs a marketing mix. The organization focuses its marketing efforts on this group and tries to meet its specific needs and preferences. Cadillac, for instance, targets affluent African Americans with television advertisements and direct mail pieces.[11] When analyzing potential target markets, marketing managers must determine whether the organization has the resources to produce a marketing mix that meets the needs of the target market and whether satisfying those needs is consistent with the firm's overall objectives. Managers must also evaluate possible markets to see how entering them would affect the firm's sales, costs, and profits. Finally, managers must consider the size and number of competitors already in that market.

Market Niche
A small, somewhat unique part of a market segment.

A more recent approach to market segmentation is targeting market niches. A **market niche** is a small, somewhat unique part of a market segment. By targeting marketing activities at a market niche, referred to as *niche marketing,* organizations can match customer needs even more precisely. Cool Cow, a cholesterol-free milk product made by Milk-Made, is attempting to carve a niche (health-conscious baby boomers) in the $19 billion U.S. liquid milk market.[12]

The 1990 U.S. census shows that racial and ethnic minority groups are growing more than seven times as fast as the non-Hispanic white majority.[13] Ethnic minorities represent nearly $600 billion in annual buying power in the United States.[14] With this increasingly diverse U.S. population, many firms are recognizing an opportunity to identify market niches with needs and wants that are not being satisfied. Today's Business World illustrates how firms are targeting customers in the age of diversity.

TODAY'S BUSINESS WORLD

Niche Marketing in the Age of Diversity

In the age of diversity, many firms are looking for smaller, unique niches in the market. When Art Vuolo was a college student, he marked road maps showing the best rock stations all the way from Michigan to Florida. Today, Vuolo publishes *RadioGuide,* a brochure that lists radio stations and their format for markets across the country. A variety of brochures are published, such as *Rock RadioGuide,* listing rock stations and formats nationwide. Even a *Rush RadioGuide* is available, detailing stations that carry the "Rush Limbaugh Show." About five million *RadioGuides* are published annually, generating $250,000 in revenue.

Bennett's MicroFridge makes a miniature microwave/refrigerator/freezer. The product is targeted at the college dormitory market, to be followed by senior citizen facilities, no-frills motels, and military barracks. Some expect the MicroFridge to become the largest-selling small appliance for the institutional market. Robert Bennett, who developed the product, said it was simply a matter of coming up with an innovative concept out of the mainstream. Although the MicroFridge does not appeal to everyone, the product makes good sense for consumers such as college students who live or work in small quarters.

Niche marketing has helped smaller firms compete with giants. Preferred Physicians Mutual Risk Retention Group is an insurance company founded in 1987 to insure anesthesiologists. By avoiding brokers' and agents' fees, Preferred Physicians offers premiums considerably lower than those of competing firms, and it is the number one firm in its specialty.

Octel Communications Corporation is another upstart firm that has dominated a market that includes giant competitors like IBM and AT&T. Octel did it by finding a niche where the large firms had failed and filling it through the use of leading technology. Only 10 years old, Octel is the leading firm in a new area of telecommunications called voice information services, technology that electronically links voice, data, and image processing over the telephone network. At any time of the day, anyone in the world with a touch-tone phone can use the technology to access computerized information sources such as corporate databases, voice mail, and e-mail. Octel's equipment is more compact and more versatile than that of its competitors.

Firms also look for niches in crowded markets. Evian is aiming its bottled water at people who want to be different and want to carry a bottle in their gym bags or even their pockets. In this crowded market, Evian doubled its sales in a single year. Giants Coca-Cola and PepsiCo are also looking for niches in the beverage market as cola sales level off. Both firms are trying to reach noncola drinkers with beverages ranging from iced tea to colorless cola.

What are some other products that could benefit from niche marketing?

Source: Adapted from John P. Cortez, "Radio Fanatic Finds Marketing Niche," *Advertising Age* (August 10, 1992): 12; Seth Lubove, "Perched Between Perrier and Tap," *Forbes* (May 14, 1990): 120; Gene Bylinsky, "How to Shoulder Aside the Titans," *Fortune* (May 18, 1992): 87–88; Brent Bowers, "Finding a Niche Based on Experience," *The Wall Street Journal* (February 6, 1992): B2.

Selecting a target market is crucial to developing an effective marketing strategy. Trying to sell a product to a group of customers who do not want or need it is bound to fail. To select a target market, firms use either the total market (or undifferentiated) approach or the market segmentation approach, as Exhibit 13.3 illustrates.

Total Market Approach
The tactic of developing one marketing mix for the total market for a product. Also called undifferentiated approach.

Total Market Approach. A firm using the **total market** (or undifferentiated) **approach** develops one marketing mix for the total market for a product. It offers one type of product with little or no variation, sets one price, establishes one distribution system, and conducts one promotional program. Producers commonly use this approach to sell staple food items like salt or sugar, many fruits and vegetables, and other products that most customers consider similar from brand to brand.

Two conditions must exist for the total market approach to be effective. A large proportion of customers in the total market must have similar a need for the product, and the company must have the resources and skills to fill that need. If customers' needs are dissimilar or if the organization is unable to develop and maintain a satisfying marketing mix, then this approach will not be effective.

Market Segmentation Approach
The division of the total market into segments, with a marketing mix directed to one of the segments.

Market Segmentation Approach. Customers in a market may have many different needs that cannot be satisfied by a single marketing mix. Then a **market segmentation approach** proves crucial. The firm divides the total market into segments and creates a marketing mix for one smaller market segment rather than for the total market (see Exhibit 13.3).

Segmenting enables a firm to apply its strengths and resources to satisfy the needs and wants of consumers. For instance, to sell cars with an undifferentiated approach—one type of vehicle for all drivers—would be difficult if not impossible. Some drivers want luxury vehicles, others prefer economy models; some crave sports cars, and others can get by only with a station wagon

Exhibit 13.3
Approaches to Selecting a Target Market

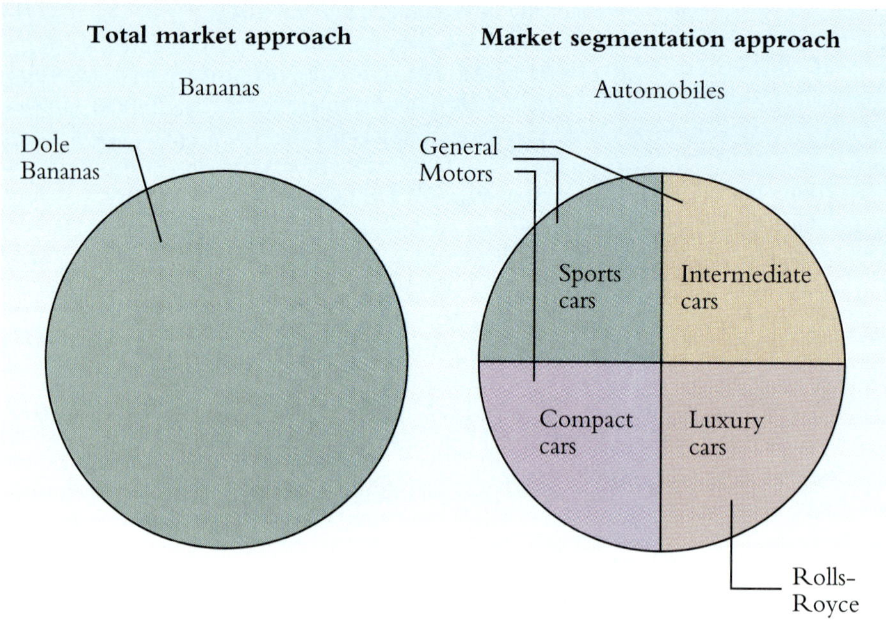

or minivan. As a result, automakers divide the total vehicle market into several segments.

Firms segment markets in one of two ways. An auto company could specialize in vehicles for one group of consumers with the *concentration approach,* as Rolls-Royce Motor Cars does with its top-of-the-line luxury vehicles. The concentration approach allows a firm to use all its knowledge, experience, and resources to meet the needs of a distinct customer group. In this way, firms with limited resources often can compete with larger firms. However, a company using this approach is dependent on a single market segment, with sales and profits tied closely to that segment's demand for the product. A drop in demand will cause a drop in sales and profits.

A firm with considerable resources and expertise may use a *multisegment approach,* directing its efforts at two or more groups by developing a marketing mix for each. General Motors produces several different vehicles intended for different groups of customers. The multisegment approach can help an organization reach more customers and increase sales in the total market. But it also can push up a company's costs, since the firm often must use more production processes, materials, and labor, as well as several different promotion, pricing, or distribution methods.

Segmentation Base
The individual or group characteristics that marketing managers use to divide a total market into segments.

To divide a market into segments, marketers use **segmentation bases** to define characteristics of individuals or groups of customers. Marketers can segment consumer markets according to geographic, demographic, psychographic, or product-related bases.

Geographic segmentation bases include city, state, region, and zip code areas as well as characteristics such as climate, terrain, and population density. A heating and air-conditioning manufacturer marketing to the entire United States, for instance, could divide the country into several regions: northeast, southeast, midwest, north, northwest, southwest, and west. Property owners living in different regions—and climates—may require different heating and cooling systems.

Demographic segmentation bases divide a market in terms of personal characteristics such as age, income, education, occupation, sex, race, social class, marital status, or family size. Such vital statistics determine in large part a person's product needs. For instance, the distribution of age groups in the United States is changing, and marketers need to understand how these changes will influence various markets. The median age of the U.S. population will be 35.7 years in 2000, up from 32.8 in 1990; over 37 million people will fall in the 45- to 54-year-old age group.[15] Demographers project that the U.S. population will increase steadily from 225 million in 1992 to about 383 million by 2050.[16] As baby boomers born between 1946 and 1964 age over this period, more than 43 percent of the population will be over 45 years old; more than 20 percent will be over 65.[17] This increase will present some major opportunities for organizations that market products for these age groups. For instance, people in their forties and fifties tend to focus on personal finances, which provides opportunities for financial services firms. In addition, music tastes vary strongly by age, education, race, and gender.[18]

The United States is becoming an increasingly diverging and diverse nation. Married couples are barely a majority of U.S. households, and nearly one-fourth of households are people who live alone.[19] The Non-Hispanic-whites share of the U.S. population is expected to decline from 75 percent in 1990 to 72 percent in 2000, and 68 percent in 2010.[20] One of the fastest-growing ethnic groups as a market segment is the American Hispanic population. Composed of Americans of Mexican, Cuban, Puerto Rican, and Central and South American heritage, this ethnic group is growing five times faster than the general population. If the Hispanic population continues to grow at its current rate, it will be the largest ethnic group in the United States by the year 2020. Businesses are beginning to tailor marketing strategies to satisfy the needs of this growing market. McDonald's, for instance, added chicken fajitas to its menu to target this segment. Miami-based Market Segment Research reported that Hispanic brand loyalty is high. Most Hispanics (62 percent) buy the same brands of food, beverage, and household items on a regular basis, and only 35 percent are lured away by sales.[21]

Psychographic segmentation bases are a person's attitudes, personality, opinions, lifestyle, interests, and motives. In recent years, many consumers have grown more health conscious and fitness oriented. Products from athletic footwear and clothing to exercise equipment and "light foods" have cropped up to appeal to those leading active or health-conscious lifestyles.

Product-related segmentation bases divide the total market according to aspects of product use, including volume of use (heavy or light, frequent or infrequent), brand loyalty, and expected benefits. For instance, bankers have segmented customers according to the benefits they're looking for. There are loan seekers, one-stop customers wanting convenience, value seekers searching for the lowest loan interest rates and no-charge checking accounts, and major investors who bank only at big-name institutions.

Many marketers believe that segmentation will become increasingly important as firms attempt to identify and reach their markets. For many prod-

Recognizing the rapid growth of the Hispanic population in the United States, businesses have begun to tailor their marketing strategies to appeal to this market.

ucts, the U.S. market, once considered fairly uniform, is slowly breaking up along regional and demographic lines, such as location, ethnic heritage, or age. Firms also segment industrial markets. Common bases include geographic location, size of customer firms, type of organization, and product usage.

Global Marketing Strategies

The world is getting smaller. Transportation and telecommunications have linked nations around the globe. Just as foreign firms like Toyota and Sony market products in America, U.S. firms like IBM and Coca-Cola, as well as smaller firms, market products throughout the world. This global boom is opening new opportunities, and many companies are developing global marketing strategies to capitalize on them. By developing marketing mixes for target markets throughout the world—or parts of the world—firms can satisfy more consumers and increase sales.

The global boom is also touching parts of the world previously closed to foreign countries. Only a few years ago it would have been hard to imagine a McDonald's or Pizza Hut restaurant in Moscow. But the former Soviet Union, Eastern Europe, Chile, and several Third World nations have abandoned communism and are welcoming free enterprise. McDonald's has even opened an outlet in Mecca, Saudi Arabia; only Muslims are allowed to enter Mecca, the holiest city of Islam.[22]

Designing a Marketing Mix

Marketing Mix
The combination of four elements—product, price, promotion, and distribution—used to satisfy the needs of the target market.

Once a firm has selected a target market, it must decide how to satisfy the needs of the target through a **marketing mix,** the combination of four elements: product, price, promotion, and distribution (See Exhibit 13.4). The marketing mix of Curtis Mathes, for example, consists of state-of-the-art television sets priced higher than most other brands, available through selected dealers, and promoted through print and television advertisements emphasizing the product's quality and dependability. Curtis Mathes targets its televisions to consumers who are willing and able to pay extra for a television and who want a strong warranty. Now let's look more closely at the marketing mix elements.

Product. As we said earlier, a product can be a good, a service, or an idea. Manufacturing a product (creating utility) is a production function. But marketing managers have the responsibility to inform the production people about products consumers would find appealing and about existing products that need to be changed or that are no longer needed. Marketers also develop brand names, packaging, and warranties. You'll read more about developing products in Chapter 14.

Exhibit 13.4
The Marketing Mix and The Marketing Environment

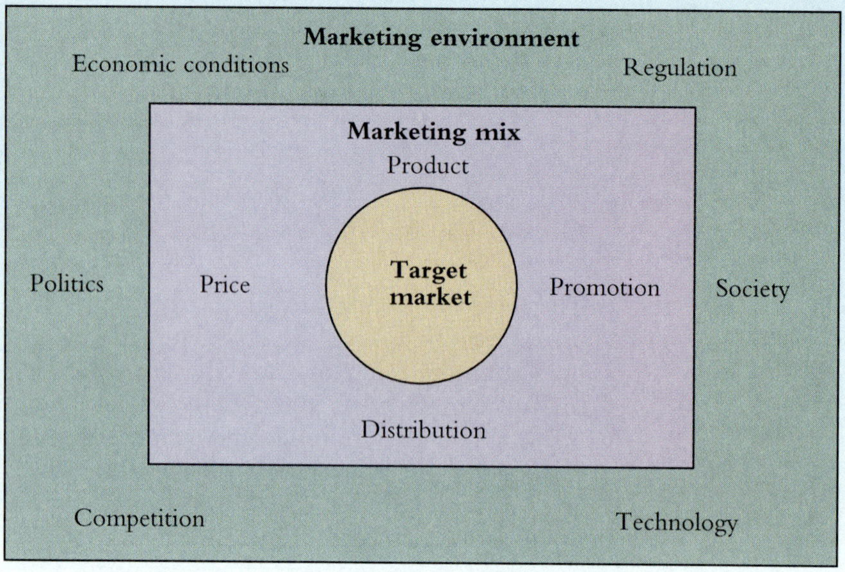

Price. Once a firm develops a product, it must set a price. Pricing requires crucial decision making because price is very visible to the consumer and is closely tied to a company's profit. Customers may not accept products priced too high; a firm may not recover its costs when products are priced too low. Chapter 14 discusses price in more detail.

Distribution. Even a terrific product, priced right, can fail if it is not available where and when the customer wants it. Distribution of products, a complex process, involves decisions about transportation, storage, and store selection. Chapter 15 gives a detailed look at distribution.

Promotion. Before they can purchase a product, consumers must know about its availability, its characteristics or benefits, and where it can be purchased. Promotion, consisting of advertising, personal selling, sales promotion, and publicity, informs or reminds the target market about a product and tries to persuade consumers to buy or adopt it. We examine aspects of promotion in Chapter 16.

The Marketing Environment and Marketing Strategy

Marketing Environment
All the forces outside an organization that directly or indirectly influence its marketing activities.

Marketing does not take place in a vacuum. Several forces outside the firm influence its marketing decisions. Economic conditions, regulation by government and industries, politics, and attitudes of society, technology, and competition from other firms combine to form the **marketing environment** (see Exhibit 13.4). These forces continually change. An organization often must adjust its marketing mix or focus on a new target market to meet changes in the marketing environment.

Economic Conditions. Economic forces in the United States and throughout the world can fluctuate rapidly and greatly influence marketing activities. Periods of slow economic growth, inflation, high interest rates for borrowers, or high unemployment may decrease consumers' ability or willingness to spend. Depending on their products and target markets, some organizations are more vulnerable than others to changes in economic conditions.

Regulation. As Chapter 5 discussed, laws and regulatory agencies bear directly on marketing decisions. Numerous federal, state, and local laws have been enacted to preserve competition and protect consumers. In addition to government agencies that enforce laws, industry associations impose self-regulation. Consumer groups like Consumer Union also serve as watchdogs, testing products, publishing ratings, and providing other information to potential customers.

Politics. Laws and government policies are determined by elected officials, who can create legislation having a favorable or an unfavorable impact on for-profit and nonprofit organizations alike. Organizations and entire industries often use lobbying to inform politicians and elected officials about issues of concern and to obtain support for favorable legislation. Legislators or federal officials who believe automobile manufacturers are trying to comply with pollution standards, for example, are less likely to impose additional restrictions.

Society. Individuals and groups in our society raise questions about business practices that they believe go against the wishes of society, as we discussed in Chapter 4. When marketing activities have the potential to harm society, special-interest groups may raise objections through publicity, consumer protests, or boycotts—refusals to buy certain products. In recent years, consumer groups who object to certain television programs have boycotted products of firms that advertise on those shows; in response some companies have pulled their advertising from the programs in question.

Competition. The actions of competitors have a big impact on a firm's marketing activities. When one organization identifies a target market and introduces a successful product, others often follow with similar offerings. Similarly, when a competing firm raises or lowers prices, improves packaging, launches innovative promotional programs, or rewrites service policies, others evaluate and often adjust their marketing strategies.

Technology. The explosion of technological innovations has deeply affected marketing mix decisions for many organizations. Dramatic developments such as the microchip, robotics, laser technology, and satellite communications offer great potential for the design, production, distribution, and promotion of products. One new trend in manufacturing, design for disassembly (DFD), has as its objective developing a product with a long-term view of how its components can be reused and disposed of safely at the end of the product's life.[23]

While they cannot control environmental forces, marketers can influence them. They can shape the political environment to some extent through lobbying, as mentioned earlier. They can use a strong promotional program of advertising, news coverage, or sponsoring a sports event to color society's attitude toward a firm or product or to minimize a controversy. A firm that can anticipate and quickly respond to the actions of society, competitors, or other environmental forces can more effectively control its destiny.

UNDERSTANDING BUYER BEHAVIOR

What makes consumers choose one brand of soft drink over another? Why do some shoppers looking for video recorders consult *Consumer Reports* and

Deciding which product to buy can be either a simple or a complex decision, depending on the product's price and its frequency of use. The decision can be influenced by marketing techniques such as advertising, free samples, and product displays.

poll all their friends, while others simply go to an electronics store and pick one out? Marketing managers study consumer behavior and consult with experts to answer such question. Understanding buyer behavior helps firms bring about satisfying exchanges. Since purchase decisions in consumer markets differ from those in industrial markets, we will discuss those two types of buying decisions separately.

Consumer Buying Behavior

Consumer Buying Behavior
The decisions and actions of individuals who purchase products for personal use.

The actions and decisions of individuals who purchase products for their personal use constitute **consumer buying behavior.**[24] The process involved in purchasing products can differ from buyer to buyer and from product to product. Exhibit 13.5 shows a decision-making continuum. Product cost and frequency of purchase influence consumer decisions. Choosing low-cost, often-used products requires little thought and quickly becomes *routine* decision making. Buyers often use *limited* decision making for products they purchase occasionally that require some consideration. To choose expensive, infrequently purchased products that involve complex thought, consumers use *extensive* decision making.

Regardless of how simple or complex the decision, consumers making purchase decisions follow a series of steps, shown in Exhibit 13.6. The buying process begins when a consumer recognizes a product need or want. Advertisement, a free sample, or a product display can trigger need recognition. The buyer then searches for information and compares alternative products. After evaluating the different options, the consumer decides on a product, uses it, and determines how well it performs or meets expectations. The consumer's level of satisfaction or dissatisfaction determines future purchases.

Exhibit 13.5
Types of Consumer Decision Making

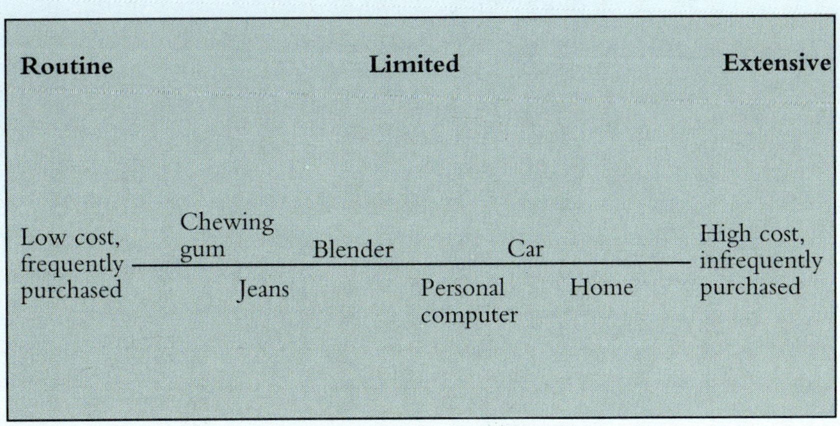

Exhibit 13.6
The Consumer Buying Process

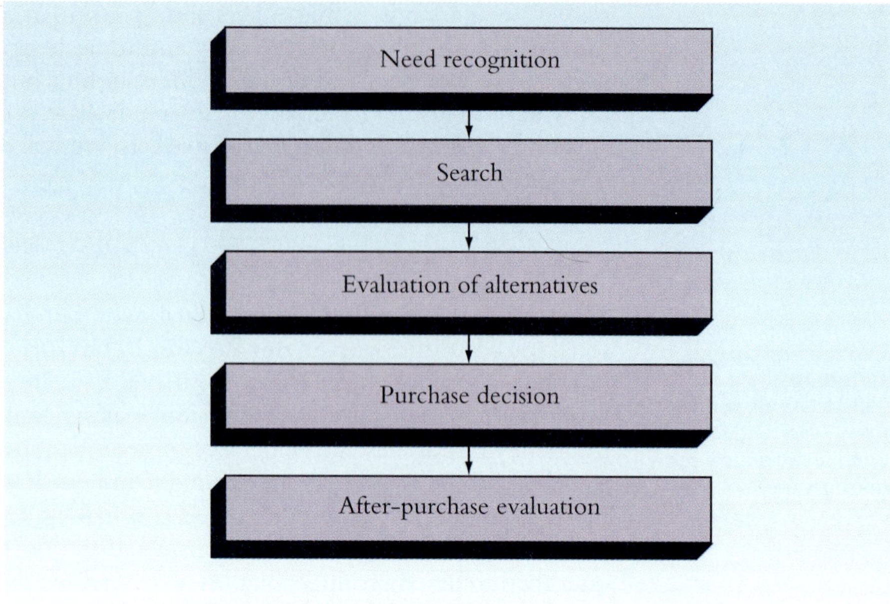

After buying a product, especially something expensive, consumers sometimes worry that they bought the wrong brand or that they should not have bought the product at all. The conflict buyers experience when they have doubts about a purchase is called *cognitive dissonance.* Consumers ask themselves whether the product should have been purchased at all or whether a different brand should have been purchased. Often firms try to reduce buyers' doubts through advertising or by providing follow-up information or service, because such doubts can decrease satisfaction after the sale.

Several factors, some within individuals and some external, affect the buying decisions of consumers. People are influenced by social factors (e.g., family members, peers), psychological factors (attitudes, personality), personal characteristics (age, education), and specific conditions that exist at the time of a purchase decision. Exhibit 13.7 explains and gives examples of factors influencing buyer behavior.

Consumer attitudes toward a firm and its products certainly affect the success or failure of its marketing strategy. For some luxury products, premium brands, and stylish services, consumer attitudes are more important—for marketing purposes—than demographics like age and income.[25] If enough consumers have strong negative attitudes toward some part of a firm's marketing mix, the firm may try to change consumer attitudes to make them more favorable. Changing negative consumer attitudes to positive ones is usually a long, difficult, and expensive task.

Organizational Buying Behavior

The purchase decision making of organizations such as manufacturers, service providers, government agencies, institutions, and nonprofit groups is referred

Exhibit 13.7 *Influences on Consumer Purchase Decisions*

Influence	Examples
Social	
Family: parents, siblings, children, grandparents.	A woman buys the same brand of dishwasher her mother always had.
Roles: as parent, spouse, child, student, employee, club member.	A young man orders flowers to send his mother on Mother's Day.
Reference groups: people such as co-workers or friends with whom a person identifies and shares attitudes and behaviors.	An accountant chooses the same kind of computer her associates use.
Social class: group of people with similar values, lifestyles, and behaviors, often classified by income, occupation, education, religion, or ethnic background.	Wealthy art lovers from all over the world come to auctions at Sotheby's in New York.
Culture: values, behaviors, and ways of doing things shared by a society and passed down from generation to generation.	Americans like soft drinks colder than Europeans do.
Subculture: group that shares values and behaviors different from those of the broader culture to which it belongs.	An American woman of Oriental background shops at a specialty food store.
Psychological	
Motive: reason or internal force that drives a person toward a goal.	A student gets a haircut before a job interview.
Perception: the way people select, organize, and give meaning to the things they see, hear, taste, smell, and touch.	A mall shopper smells cookies and stops at the cookie shop to buy some.
Attitude: a person's overall feeling about something.	A family donates money to an animal rights organization.
Learning: changes in an individual's behavior caused by experiences and information.	After a high cholesterol reading, a man cuts down on the amount of meat and fats he eats.
Personality: traits, experiences, and behaviors that make up a person.	An outgoing young woman with many friends racks up huge long-distance phone bills.
Demographic	
Personal characteristics such as age, sex, marital status, family size, race, income, education, and occupation.	A working couple take their young children to a day-care center.
Situational	
Conditions that exist when a person is making a purchase decision, such as unexpected circumstances, amount of time for the decision, or expectations for future employment.	A man who is laid off from his job puts off buying a new car.

Organizational Buying Behavior The decisions and actions of buyers in organizations.

to as **organizational buying behavior.** Buying decisions by organizations typically differ from consumer purchases in several ways. First, organizational transactions are usually much larger and less frequent than typical consumer purchases. Organizational buyers, who must meet exact product specifications, tend to be more concerned than consumers about quality and service. Buyers usually seek more information and base decisions less on emotional factors than consumers do. In small companies, one person (usually the owner) is responsible for purchase decisions; in large firms, the responsibility for buying rests with several individuals who make up a buyer center.

MARKETING RESEARCH

Throughout this chapter, we have emphasized that marketing activities should focus on customer satisfaction. No matter what its size or objectives, a firm cannot implement the marketing concept without information about customer needs. Are customers' lifestyles or preferences changing? Do some market segments still need to be reached? Who are the competitors? What product, price, distribution system, and promotional activities would enable satisfying exchanges to take place with people in the target market? To answer such critical questions, marketers must continually look at buying trends, talk to customers, and establish ways to receive feedback. Much of this communication with consumers takes place through marketing research. **Marketing research** is the systematic gathering, recording, and analyzing of information relating to the marketing of goods and services.[26]

Marketing Research The systematic gathering, recording, and analyzing of information for guiding marketing decisions.

The Need for Marketing Research

Years ago, the attitudes of many business people toward marketing research could be summarized as "If it's not broken, don't fix it." Firms conducted research in response to problems such as decreasing profits, failure to reach sales quotas, or customers lost to a competitor. But many firms today realize that research should be ongoing. Successful firms, regardless of size, continually talk to customers and study the market. As Exhibit 13.8 shows, marketing research can be proactive to prevent "breakdowns" or reactive to respond to a

Exhibit 13.8
Proactive and Reactive Research Questions

Proactive	Reactive
Are we attracting new customers?	Why are we losing customers?
How do we maintain and increase sales?	Who has surpassed us in our sales?
Are we satisfying our current customers?	How do we get lost customers back?
What new products are needed by our target market?	Can we develop a new product to keep up with our major competitor?

problem. Unfortunately marketing research conducted after serious problems emerge may be too late. Forward-looking companies take a proactive stand to keep ahead of the competition.

The Research Process

Marketing Research Process
Series of steps consisting of problem definition, research design, data collection, data analysis, interpretation, and conclusions.

The **marketing research process** consists of six steps: problem definition, research design, data collection, data analysis, interpretation, and conclusions.

Problem Definition. Trying to identify the nature and boundaries of a problem is the first step toward solving a marketing problem through a research study. The first sign of a problem is usually a deviation from normal operations, such as a failure to attain objectives. For example, if an organization's objective is to increase its share of a particular market to 15 percent but it has captured only 10 percent of the market, the organization should recognize that a problem exists. Decision makers should realize that something inside or outside the organization has blocked the achievement of the desired objective or that the objective may be unrealistic. Decreasing sales, increasing expenses, and decreasing profits are all broad indications of problems. Whatever the problem, researchers and decision makers should remain in the problem definition state until they have established precisely what they want from the research and how they will use it.

Whether research is conducted on an ongoing basis or after a problem occurs, it is critical for the marketing researcher to work closely with the marketing manager in the problem definition stage. If together they can clearly define a problem, the researcher can conduct research that will provide information the manager requires to make marketing decisions.

Research Design. After defining the research question, marketers formulate a plan for collecting information essential to the study. Depending on the type and amount of information already available, the researcher will choose one of several alternative designs.

If little is known about the question being investigated, marketers engage in *exploratory research*. They may look at company records and government or industry publications or talk to knowledgeable people inside or outside their organization. Focus group interviews, in which a researcher informally discusses an idea or issue with a small group of employees, consumers, or others, can provide helpful insights.

Sometimes organizations conduct *experimental research* to determine whether one event, circumstance, or situation causes another. For example, a publisher may distribute an issue of a magazine with different covers in different parts of the country. After a trial period, researchers investigate which cover resulted in the highest sales.

Marketers often want to know the age, sex, education, income, lifestyle, buying habits, or buying intentions of consumers. To obtain such information, they conduct *descriptive research*.

Data Collection. After settling on a research design, marketers accumulate the information that will answer the research question. Researchers sometimes rely on *secondary data*—published information available inside the firm or from government, industry, or other sources. Secondary data offer tremendous advantages. They usually can be obtained quickly at relatively little cost, which may be especially important to small firms and nonprofit organizations. Marketers generally start all research projects by looking for secondary data. Exhibit 13.9 lists common sources of secondary data.

Often secondary data are unavailable or inadequate. In such cases, marketers obtain *primary data*—information collected for the first time and specific to the study. Researchers use experiments, observation, or surveys to collect primary data.

Researchers conduct experiments either in a controlled, isolated setting (laboratory experiments) or in actual marketplace settings such as a store (field experiments). *Observation* involves watching a situation and recording relevant facts. A marketer may observe supermarket shoppers and record the purchases made. Through *surveys,* researchers question respondents to obtain needed information. Mail, telephone, and in-person surveys are becoming more and more common; you yourself probably have taken part in a consumer survey.

Because reaching all consumers in the target market (e.g., all television viewers) is often impossible or impractical, researchers collect data from a sample. A *sample* is a portion of a larger group and accurately represents the characteristics of the larger group. Companies that provide ratings for television shows may survey 1,200 viewers throughout the United States. With a sufficient sample, the researcher can use the data collected to infer important facts about the larger group.

Exhibit 13.9
Sources of Secondary Data

Internal Sources

Company reports
Sales and cost data from accounting
Reports from the sales staff
Cash register receipts

External Sources

Private publications
- *Editor and Publisher Market Guide*
- *Guide to Consumer Markets*
- Moody's manuals
- Poor's registers
- *Sales & Marketing Management Survey of Buying Power*
- Chamber of Commerce publications
- Industry reports and publications
- Computer databases available through industry associations of research organizations
- University business and economic research centers

Census data
- Census of Population
- Census of Retail Trade
- Census of Service Industries

Government publications
- *County and City Statistics*
- *Economic Indicators*
- *Statistical Abstract of the United States*
- *Survey of Current Business*

selects a *target market* and (2) designs a *marketing mix* to meet the needs of that group of people. Depending on the product and the firm's goals and resources, a firm may sell to the total market for a product or divide the total market into segments based on customers' geographic area, demographic characteristics, or psychographic aspects (such as attitudes), or on product characteristics.

5. ***Identify the four elements of the marketing mix.*** *Product* decisions require marketers to determine what would satisfy customers' need and wants. *Price* affects a customer's purchase decisions and the seller's profits. *Promotion* communicates product information to the target market. *Distribution* makes products available when and where people in the target market want them.

6. ***Define the term* marketing environment *and list the environmental forces.*** The marketing environment is the combined outside forces that influence business firms' marketing decisions. Economic conditions, regulation by government and industry, societal attitudes, political policies, actions of competitors, and technological advancements have tremendous impact on marketing activities.

7. ***Describe how consumers make purchase decisions, and compare consumer buying behavior to industrial buying behavior.*** Considering buyer behavior helps firms conduct activities that will bring about more exchanges. Consumers go through a decision-making process of recognizing a need, seeking information about a product, comparing alternatives, deciding on a product, and evaluating the product. Purchase decisions for industrial markets differ from consumer decisions because transactions are larger and less frequent and require more information.

8. ***Explain the value of marketing research and outline the research process.*** Ongoing, systematic research gives firms information they need to satisfy customers and achieve their objectives. To conduct effective and accurate studies, marketers (1) define the specific purpose of the research, (2) design a plan to collect information, (3) gather needed information, (4) analyze the information, usually by computer, and (5) interpret the information and draw conclusions to use in marketing decisions.

KEY TERMS

Marketing
Exchange
Utility
Marketing Concept
Marketing Strategy
Market
Consumer Market
Industrial Market
Market Segment
Target Market
Market Niche
Total Market Approach
Market Segmentation Approach
Segmentation Base
Marketing Mix
Marketing Environment
Consumer Buying Behavior
Organizational Buying Behavior
Marketing Research
Marketing Research Process

QUESTIONS FOR DISCUSSION AND REVIEW

1. What are some typical activities performed by marketers? How do these activities add value to products? Would consumers be better or worse off if these activities were not performed?

2. What business is each of the following organizations in: Hertz, Chrysler, Central Bank, the school you attend? What do all of these organizations have in common?

3. In today's business environment, why is it essential for companies to practice the marketing concept? Identify a firm that you feel has adapted the marketing concept, and explain why. If possible, identify one that has not.

4. Some cattle growers have formed a company to sell a new type of extra-lean beef. How would the company develop a marketing strategy?

5. Give an example of a firm using the total market approach for a product and one using the market segmentation approach. Why do you think these approaches were selected?

6. Think of a product you have purchased recently. Describe the marketing mix for the product, and compare it to the marketing mixes used for competing products. Why did this product, and specifically its marketing mix, appeal to you?

7. What is the marketing environment? How does it affect the following: environmental legislation, national health insurance, new product introductions, and global competition?

8. Trace one of your recent purchase decisions through the stages of the buying process. What were some of the ways that marketing activities helped you through each stage?

9. What are some of the differences between consumer purchases and industrial purchases? Why do we even need to make a distinction between the two for marketing reasons?

10. Explain how you think an individual or organization could benefit from using marketing research.

CASE 13.1

Disney Comes to Europe

On April 12, 1992, Euro Disney opened its gates outside of Paris. The $3.9 billion theme park and resort complex is one of Europe's largest construction projects. The French government assumed the bulk of the financial risk; Disney put up only $160 million of its own capital for the project.

Some French intellectuals are outraged at the thought of Mickey Mouse in their backyard. But the Socialist government reasoned that Euro Disney would bring in tourist dollars, create thousands of jobs, and attract many other investors to the area. Disney can be counted on to deliver a quality service that consumers will buy. In fact, Euro Disney is so extravagantly designed that some have said it surpasses Disney's parks in Florida and California. Chairman Michael Eisner himself made many of the detailed decisions, such as the placement of 35 fireplaces in hotel lobbies and restaurants, and the design of a salad bar in the back of a old pickup truck.

This eye to detail has made Disney one of the world's highest quality organizations. Emphasis on service quality starts at the top at Disney (as it does in most organizations committed to quality) and filters down to every individual in the firm, even those on clean-up duty in the parks. Ask any park attendant or ticket taker where to find the restrooms or when the next parade begins and you'll get the answer. That's why it takes four days for employees to learn how to take tickets at a Disney park.

Europe's initial response to the park that's mostly American in theme was somewhat below expectations. Disney expected 11 million visitors to Euro Disney in the first year; the park drew less than 10 million and saddled Disney with $340 million in losses for the first full year. Europe's sluggish economy and competition from Spain's World's Fair and Olympics were blamed for the rocky start.

But other problems have been noted, attributed to both cultural misjudgment and financial miscalculations. For instance, Disney failed to realize the significance of offering wine with the meals. Even after making wine available, there was not enough seating for European diners, who prefer a leisurely meal rather than fast-food restaurants. A major financial miscalculation also explains, in part, why Euro Disney continues to operate in the red: Europeans spend less per capita on food and merchandise in theme parks than Americans.

Many observers feel the attendance forecasts were optimistic, and they expect the French park to be a big success in the near future. (Disney even plans to add a Disney-MGM Studios theme park to Euro Disney by 1997.) Most of the usual Disney attractions can be found, such as Sleeping Beauty's castle and Main Street USA. Some attractions have been updated. Tomorrowland, with its 1950 images of the space age, has been replaced by Discoveryland, based on European themes by Jules Verne and Leonardo da Vinci. And despite talk of cultural differences between the French and Americans, Eisner has said that the only real difference is that visitors pay with francs. Even so, at $43 a day and $30 for children, prices are higher than competing parks in France, and some analysts feel it will be difficult for Euro Disney to make a profit. For the fiscal year ending 1994, Euro Disney continued to be a drag on profits, reporting a $353 million loss.

Questions for Discussion

1. Would you say that the Walt Disney Company practices the marketing concept? Why or why not?
2. Which approach to selecting a target market has Disney taken? Name some of the market segments Disney wants to reach.
3. What are some factors of the marketing environment that have an influence on Disney's marketing decisions? Explain.
4. How might Disney change its marketing strategy to be more successful in Europe?

Source: Adapted from Christy Fisher, "New Magic Needed for Disney Kingdom," *Advertising Age* (November 21, 1994): 4; Wentz and Bruce Crumley, "Magic Doesn't Translate During Euro Disney Visit," *Advertising Age* (September 20, 1993): 1–3, 1–23; Ronald Glover, Stewart Toy, Gail DeGeorge, and Robert Neff, "Thrills and Chills at Disney," *Business Week* (June 21, 1993): 73–74; Stewart Toy, Patrick Oster, and Ronald Glover, "The Mouse Isn't Roaring," *Business Week* (August 24, 1992): 38; Richard Turner and Peter Gumbel, "As Euro Disney Braces for Its Grand Opening, The French Go Goofy," *The Wall Street Journal* (April 10, 1992): A1, A8; and Thomas J. Peters and Robert H. Waterman Jr., *In Search of Excellence* (New York: Warner Books, 1982), 167–168.

CASE 13.2

Nissan Changes Its Marketing Strategy

Yes, Japanese automakers can make mistakes, and Nissan is living proof. Only 15 years ago it looked as though Nissan, with its sporty 240Z, was headed for greatness. In 1975, the firm passed Volkswagen as the top importer to the United States. But from 1980 to 1991, Nissan's U.S. market share fell from 5.5 to 4.7 percent, while Japan's overall market share grew from 17.7 to 26.5 percent.

Nissan's troubles came as a shock to those who think Japanese automakers can do no wrong. Much like U.S. automakers, Nissan failed to listen to its customers, thus missing changes in their needs and losing sight of important market segments like family sedans and minivans. Although its quality remains on the same level as that of major competitors, Nissan's productivity lags and its costs are higher than those of other Japanese automakers. Nissan's location in Tokyo increases overhead and puts the firm at a 10 percent cost disadvantage relative to Toyota. Higher labor costs (8 percent of Nissan's operating costs compared with 5 percent of Toyota's) add to the problem. And many observers think that Nissan's main manufacturing plants are too old to compete with the new and more efficient plants built by competitors.

Nissan broke into the U.S. market in 1958 when it began exporting the Bluebird. But it wasn't until 1968 and 1969, with the Datsun 510 and the Datsun 240Z, that the firm made a big impact in the U.S. market. Then the 1973 oil crisis put Nissan in the right place at the right time as panicked Americans abandoned their gas-guzzling vehicles. In 1983, the name Datsun was changed to Nissan to match the name of the parent company. By trading on the image of its Z cars, the firm tried to move upscale. Advertising themes turned over rapidly: "We are driven," "The name is Nissan," "Built for the human race." But none of the messages conveyed a distinctive image. Sales peaked out in 1985 at 831,000; by 1992, sales had dropped to 583,000.

Managers at Nissan know it will take a sound marketing strategy to get the firm back to where it once was. Perhaps their biggest challenge is to reestablish their mission and focus. What was once their distinctive competency, building quality economy cars, was lost when the carmaker rolled out a steady stream of new models in the late 1980s. According to Earl Hesterburg, head of the Nissan U.S. division: "We haven't been successful in the market where our competitors make their bread and butter. We have to drive traffic into dealers at the middle of the market for Altima and then let them go up to the Maxima if they choose, or down to the Sentra." The Altima, introduced in 1992, is a mid-sized family sedan built to compete with Toyota's Camry and Honda's Accord. The new Maxima, introduced in Nissan's 1995 model year, is priced at $2,500 less than the 1994 version.

It won't be easy for Nissan. John Schnapp of Boston's Mercer Management Consulting says of the challenge of introducing the Altima: "It's like trying to break into the lineup against Babe Ruth and Lou Gehrig. You've got to come up with something sensational."

Questions for Discussion

1. What specific factors contributed to Nissan's loss of market share?
2. Does Nissan have a distinctive competency? Explain why or why not.

3. What do you think is the greatest challenge Nissan will face as the firm changes its marketing strategy?

Source: Adapted from Larry Armstrong, "News from Nissan: Reverse Sticker Shock," *Business Week* (May 23, 1994): 27; Karen Lowry Miller, Larry Armstrong, and James B. Treece, "Will Nissan Get It Right This Time?" *Business Week* (April 20, 1992): 82–87; Alex Taylor, "Driving for the Market's Heart," *Fortune* (June 15, 1992): 120–121; and Clay Chandler, "Weary Nissan Now Seeks to Cooperate, Rather Than Compete, with Toyota," *The Wall Street Journal* (May 19, 1992): A8.

EXPERIENTIAL EXERCISE

The Marketing Database

Activity:
Select an organization in your area, find out who is responsible for marketing information, and phone that person to request a brief interview. A 15- to 20-minute telephone interview would also be sufficient.

Directions:
Find out what information the organization compiles in its marketing databank. How is it used? Compare the information from the organization you selected with the information gathered by other members of your class.

BUSINESS APPLICATION

Developing a Marketing Plan

Professional Management Consultants (PMC) is in the process of developing a marketing plan and is not sure just where to start the process. PMC is composed of three consultants and one clerical staff member. The company provides consulting services in the area of human resources management, assisting clients with management expertise in hiring, training, and developing employees.

PMC is concerned about a continuous decline in business and the arrival of competing consulting companies in their city. The company has limited their advertising efforts to a small ad in the yellow pages of the local telephone book. If business continues to decline at the current pace, PMC will have to cut back on their number of employees.

Questions for Discussion

1. What should be among the first steps PMC needs to take in developing a marketing plan?
2. How should PMC go about market segmentation?
3. Spending capital on expensive advertising during a time of declining business is a controversial strategy for a small organization like PMC. What type of advertising do you think should be included in a marketing plan for PMC?

NOTES

1. Adapted from Pat Sloan, "Gillette Whisks $80M into Sensor Excel," *Advertising Age* (October 10, 1994): 41; Mark Mavement, "A New Equal Right: The Close Shave," *Business Week* (March 29, 1993): 58–59; Pat Sloan, "Gillette to Launch Women's Sensor," *Advertising Age* (February 10, 1992): 36; Alison Fahey, "Schick Sharpens Razor Promotions," *Advertising Age* (February 25, 1991): 12; Keith H. Hammonds, "It's One Sharp Ad Campaign, But Where's the Blade?" *Business Week* (March 5, 1990): 30; Joshua Levine, "Global Lather," *Forbes* (February 5, 1990): 146–148; Alison Fahey, "Sensor Sensation," *Advertising Age* (February 5, 1990): 4, 49; and Keith H. Hammonds, "How a $4 Razor Ends Up Costing $300 Million," *Business Week* (January 29, 1990): 62–63.
2. "AMA Board Approves New Marketing Definition," *Marketing News* (March 1, 1985): 1.
3. Philip Kotler, *Marketing Management: Analysis, Planning and Control* 5th ed. (Englewood Cliffs, NJ: Prentice Hall, 1984), 8.
4. Robert E. Pitts and Robert Allan Cooke, "A Realistic View of Marketing Ethics," *Journal of Business Ethics* (April 1991): 243–244.
5. Sally Solo, "How to Listen to Consumers," *Fortune* (January 11, 1993): 77–79.
6. Lynne W. McGee and Rosann L. Spiro, "The Marketing Concept in Perspective," *Business Horizons* (May–June 1988): 40–45.
7. Milind M. Lele and Jagdish N. Sheth, "The Four Fundamentals of Customer Satisfaction," *Business Marketing* (June 1988): 80–94.
8. Benson P. Shapiro, "What the Hell Is 'Market Oriented'?" *Harvard Business Review* (November–December 1988): 119–124.
9. Sharyn Hunt and Ernest F. Cooke, "It's Basic But Necessary: Listen to the Customer," *Marketing News* (March 5, 1990): 22–23.
10. Kathy Rebello, "It Just May Be the Year of the Apple," *Business Week* (January 16, 1995): 84–85.
11. Cyndee Miller, "Cadillac Promo Targets African Americans," *Marketing News* (May 23, 1994): 12.
12. Cyndee Miller, "Firm Touts Milk Product as Hip Alternative to Soda," *Marketing News* (May 23, 1994): 6.
13. Judith Waldrop and Thomas Exter, "What the 1990 Census Will Show," *American Demographics* (January 1990): 20–30.
14. Leah Rickard, "Minorities Show Brand Loyalty," *Advertising Age* (May 9, 1994): 29.
15. Christy Fisher, "Boomers Scatter in Middle Ages," *Advertising Age* (January 11, 1993): 23.
16. Judith Waldrop, "New Projections Show Faster Growth, More Diversity," *American Demographics* (February 1993): 9–10.
17. Lucinda Harper, "Census Bureau Lifts Population Forecast, Citing Fertility, Immigration, Longevity," *The Wall Street Journal* (December 5, 1992): B1, B14.
18. Nicholas Zill and John Robinson, "Name That Tune," *American Demographics* (August 1994): 22–27.
19. Peter Francese, "America at Mid-Decade," *American Demographics* (February 1995): 23–31.
20. Thomas G. Exter, "The Declining Majority," *American Demographics* (January 1993): 59.
21. Christy Fisher, "Poll: Hispanics Stick to Brands," *Advertising Age* (February 15, 1993): 6.
22. "McDonald's Comes to Mohammed," *Lexington Herald-Leader* (December 15, 1994): A17.
23. Gene Bylinsky, "Manufacturing for Reuse," *Fortune* (February 6, 1995): 102–112.
24. James F. Engel, Roger D. Blackwell, and Paul W. Miniard, *Consumer Behavior* (Hinsdale, IL: Dryden Press, 1990), 3.
25. Judith Waldrop, "Markets with Attitude," *American Demographics* (July 1994): 22–33.
26. *Report of the Definitions Committee of the American Marketing Association* (Chicago: American Marketing Association, 1961).
27. Andrew Kupfer, "How American Industry Stacks Up," *Fortune* (March 9, 1992): 30–46.

CHAPTER 14

Product and Price

LEARNING OBJECTIVES

1. Define the term *product* and distinguish between consumer and industrial products.

2. Differentiate between product line and product mix.

3. Trace the process of developing new products.

4. Describe the stages of the product life cycle and explain how firms can extend the product life cycle.

5. Explain the purposes of branding, packaging, and labeling.

6. List four pricing objectives and identify three factors to consider when making pricing decisions.

7. Distinguish between cost-oriented, demand-oriented, and competition-oriented pricing methods.

8. List and explain four pricing strategies.

Switzerland-based Ciba-Geigy is the world's number five drug company, with sales of about $4.28 billion in the $200-billion-a-year pharmaceutical industry. It is an industry in which the major firms spend millions on research and development in hopes of finding new drugs that will become blockbusters. But since blockbuster medicines are rare—only about 20 now reach sales above $750 million each—Ciba-Geigy depends on effective product management rather than huge breakthroughs to secure its future.

Ciba-Geigy's best-known new product in recent years is the nicotine patch, a smoking-cessation device available with a doctor's prescription. The patch, which looks like a round Band-Aid, releases small, controlled doses of nicotine through the skin into the bloodstream over a three-month period. Ciba-Geigy received U.S. Food and Drug Administration (FDA) approval for its Habitrol patch in December 1991 and introduced it in early 1992 to immediate competition. Marion Merrell Dow had received FDA approval for its Nicoderm a few weeks ahead of Ciba-Geigy; American Cyanamid Company's Lederle division got approval for ProStep several weeks later. Warner-Lambert Company trailed the others by a few months with its Nicotrol patch. In 1992, worldwide sales of patches were about $900 million, more than double initial estimates.

A new product introduction could hardly be more intense than that of the nicotine patches. Essentially, three firms released three brands of a new prescription product within a few weeks of each other. The patches are remarkably similar, differing somewhat in the amount of nicotine contained and the services accompanying them. To gain an edge on the competition, Ciba-Geigy includes "The Habitrol Smoking Cessation Program." It consists of two brochures—one with tips for smokers and one to help their relatives and friends deal with them during withdrawal. Also included is an audio tape prepared by the American Lung Association that explains relaxation techniques and gives motivational messages.

Although only doctors can actually prescribe patches for patients, Ciba-Geigy and the other manufacturers ran aggressive advertising campaigns to get their names out to the target audience in hopes that consumers would ask for a patch by name. "It's important for pharmaceuticals to have a brand image, but with something like this, more so than most," said Doug Arbesfeld, spokesman for Ciba-Geigy in Summit, NJ. His company—and rival Marion Merrell Dow—sponsored television and radio commercials and advertisements in newspapers and leading consumer magazines such as *Time, Newsweek, U.S. News and World Report, People, Sports Illustrated,* and *Business Week.* During Habitrol's first few months on the market, Ciba-Geigy spent $9.9 million for magazine advertisements alone. Industry observers estimated the company's cost for marketing Habitrol in the first year to be as much as $35 million.

With the nicotine patches, Ciba-Geigy and its competitors are fighting for shares of a huge potential market. According to the American Lung Association, more than 51 million Americans smoke; about 18 million try to quit each year, but only 1.3 million succeed. Wall Street analysts estimate that the patch market will eventually exceed $1 billion. Immediately after the patches were put on the market, smokers flocked to them. In some areas of the country, the enormous demand caused shortages, especially of

Nicoderm, the first patch to hit the market. Within the first few months, Ciba-Geigy saw sales of Habitrol reach $110 million. The company later emerged from the pack as the leading seller with 60 percent of the market.[1]

Why are new products like the nicotine patch critical to the long-run survival of business organizations?

Ciba-Geigy's nicotine patch is more than a piece of cloth that releases nicotine. People who purchase the physical item expect a range of benefits: Reliability—a patch that works, ease of use, help dealing with withdrawal, a brand with positive image, and a product that is readily available.

For these benefits, consumers pay a price that allows Ciba-Geigy to make a profit for producing and marketing the patch. In this chapter, we discuss two of the marketing mix elements: product and price. First we define what products are and list ways to classify them. We introduce the concepts of product line and product mix. We explore the ways in which firms manage their products, including developing new ones. We describe how firms create product identification. Then we cover price by discussing pricing objectives, factors involved in pricing decisions, and methods and strategies used to price products.

WHAT ARE PRODUCTS?

Product
A good, service, or idea, including all the tangibles and intangibles provided in an exchange between buyer and seller.

A **product** consists of all the tangible and intangible characteristics provided in an exchange between a seller and a buyer. People buy a product for the benefits and satisfaction it gives. A product's characteristics include not only its physical aspects but also its function, brand name, image, packaging, warranty, and price, as well as the provider's reputation and customer service policy.

As we noted in Chapter 13, a product can be a good (an actual physical entity such as a drill bit), a service (your checking account at the bank), or an idea (the American Heart Association's advice to follow a diet low in fat and cholesterol). Sometimes a product is a blend of all three. Dinner at a fine restaurant, for example, consists not only of the tangible items, food and beverages, but also preparation, service, and the appeal of dining in that special setting. The GOP's "Contract with America" is also a product and it includes strategies to sell the public on massive spending cuts needed to finance the Republicans' promised tax cuts and balanced budget.[2]

Products are often a firm's most important link with customers, and are critical to the achievement of organizational objectives.[3] Because different products are designed for different target markets, they require various pricing, distribution, and promotion decisions. To help plan effective marketing strategies, marketers classify goods and services according to the manner in which they are purchased and used. Marketers generally divide products into two broad categories: consumer and industrial products.

Consumer Products

Consumer Product
A good or service used for personal or family consumption.

Products used by individuals for personal and family consumption are **consumer products.** Marketers classify consumer products according to customers' buying behavior, as Exhibit 14.1 shows.

Convenience Product
A frequently purchased, inexpensive item that buyers spend little effort to find and purchase.

Convenience Products. Inexpensive goods and services that consumers buy often, without much thought or effort, are **convenience products.** Milk, bread, magazines, soft drinks, and gasoline are examples. So are the routine services offered by dry cleaners and automatic teller machines. People make such purchases or go to such service providers because of habit and closeness of the outlet: They've always bought that brand; the store is nearby.

Shopping Product
An item that buyers will expend time and effort to find and purchase.

Shopping Products. Consumers will expend time, effort, and energy to find and obtain some goods and services. Buyers comparison shop for these; thus they are known as **shopping products.** Consumers gather information about different brands and styles, visit different stores, note prices, read advertisements and consumer guides, and consult family or friends. This category includes goods such as TV sets, VCRs, major appliances, and furniture and services such as dental care, legal advice, and tax preparation.

When shopping for specialty products such as stereo equipment, consumers are unlikely to accept substitutes.

Exhibit 14.1 *Convenience, Shopping, and Specialty Products*

Specialty Product
A product with one or more unique features that a group of buyers will spend considerable time and effort to purchase.

Speciality Products. Goods and services that have specific attributes desired by a particular group of consumers are known as **specialty products.** Buyers go to considerable trouble to obtain a specialty product, no matter what the price or location, and will rarely accept a substitute. Specialty products can be expensive and unique, such as a Maserati sports car or Adolfo designer dress, or less costly but still fairly uncommon, such as a certain breed of dog or tickets to a Broadway show.

Because consumers differ in their purchasing behaviors, the convenience-shopping-specialty distinction is not absolute. One customer may order food from a pizza parlor strictly because of its delivery service (convenience). Another may choose to eat there after comparing the pizza and prices all over town (shopping). Other customers may go out of their way for the super deluxe, 10-topping pan pizza available only at that restaurant (specialty). Therefore marketers classify products according to the buying patterns of the majority of consumers. Pizza thus would fall in the convenience category, based on the shopping patterns of most consumers.

Industrial Products

Industrial Product
A good or service used by an organization in producing other goods or services or in carrying out its operations.

Products used by organizations in producing goods and services or in carrying out their operations are **industrial products.**[4] Manufacturers, contractors, mining companies, utilities, government agencies, wholesalers, retailers, and institutions such as hospitals and schools buy and use a great array of goods and services to carry out their operations and produce products of their own. Industrial products often require substantial investment but have a long, useful life span, such as a robotics system in an automobile plant or a computer network for the government. Other industrial products cost much less and are purchased regularly, such as office equipment or the printing of an annual report.

Marketers sometimes find it useful to categorize industrial products into more specific classifications, such as:

- Installations, such as large storage and distribution centers or factories.
- Major equipment, including machinery and large tools essential to the production process.
- Accessory equipment, such as forklifts and small tools or office equipment and furniture.
- Component parts, usually prefinished items put into a physical product, such as cassette players installed in autos.
- Raw materials, such as minerals, sand, coal, and petroleum, which become part of physical products.
- Supplies, such as pens and paper and cleaners, which do not become part of the item produced.
- Services, either provided in-house or hired from outside the organization, such as accounting, advertising, printing, legal, and janitorial.

Classifying Services

While services are classified as consumer or industrial, other classifications are also important because of the unique characteristics of many services. Exhibit 14.2 shows the classifications marketers use for services. Marketers often find it useful to categorize services by degree of *labor intensiveness*. Services such as hair styling, education, and health care require a great amount of human labor while others, such as automatic car washes, rely heavily on machines and equipment. Labor-intensive services are especially difficult to standardize.

Another way to classify services is by degree of *customer contact*. High-contact services, such as real estate agencies, involve frequent interactions with customers. The consumer must be present for such services to be performed. Low-contact services involve much less participation on the part of the cus-

Exhibit 14.2
Classification of Services

Category	Examples
Type of market	
Consumer	Life insurance, car repairs.
Industrial	Lawn care, management consulting.
Degree of labor intensiveness	
Labor based	Repairs, executive recruiting.
Equipment based	Public transportation, air travel.
Degree of customer contact	
High contact	Hotels, health care.
Low contact	Dry cleaning, motion pictures.
Skill of the service provider	
Professional	Legal counsel, accounting services.
Nonprofessional	Taxi, janitorial.
Goal of the service provider	
Profit	Financial services, overnight delivery.
Nonprofit	Government, education.

tomer. The consumer may need to be present only to initiate the contact but not for the service to be performed. A customer goes to the dry cleaner to drop off clothes, for example, but does not have to stay while they are being cleaned.

A fourth way to classify services is by *skill of the service provider.* Some services require professionals, such as lawyers, physicians, or accountants. Other services can be offered by individuals with lower levels of skills. Consumers are more selective when choosing providers for services that require higher levels of skills.

Finally, services can be classified by the *goal of the service provider.* Not all service organizations are profit oriented. Universities, charities, libraries, and some clinics are a few examples of nonprofit service organizations.

PRODUCT LINE AND PRODUCT MIX

Decisions concerning what products to offer—the type, number, and variety—are fundamental to any organization. Often firms manufacture and sell goods or offer services that are similar in design, production, or use and are targeted to similar market segments. A group of related goods or services marketed by a firm is called a **product line.** A firm's product line can be shallow, with only one or two products, or deep, including many products. T.J. Cinnamon's product line is shallow, with a few types of sweet rolls. Boeing has a deep product line, as Exhibit 14.3 (on page 474) illustrates.

Product Line
A group of related products that are considered a unit because of marketing, technical, or use similarities.

Firms realize distinct advantages in offering related products and introducing new products within an established product line: They can use their know-how, resources, and experience to effectively produce and market new products. Similar products help promote each other. Marketers can stretch

Exhibit 14.3
Boeing's Line of Jetliners

advertising dollars by emphasizing an entire product line in an advertising campaign.

While many firms expand existing product lines by introducing new, similar items, others decide to add completely different product lines. The collection of items and services a firm offers for sale make up its **product mix.** Marketers refer to product mixes as narrow or wide, depending on how many product lines are carried.

Product Mix
The total group of products a firm offers for sale, or all of the firm's product lines.

Some companies opt for a narrow product mix, such as Mita, which has advertised that it makes only photocopiers. Others develop several product lines targeted to the same or similar markets. Fisher-Price, well known for years for its popular toys, added a line of baby furniture and equipment including high chairs, portable cribs, and car seats. Still other firms develop an extremely wide product mix consisting of multiple product lines aimed at different markets. Procter & Gamble has over twenty lines, including detergents, cleaners, analgesics, cosmetics, diapers, fragrances, paper products, and foods and beverages.[5] General Foods' many and diverse product offerings, shown in Exhibit 14.4, illustrate a wide product mix.

The decision to offer a single line of related products or many and varied product lines depends on an organization's knowledge, goals, and resources. Developing new product lines often allows a company to expand into different markets, achieve growth, and increase stability. Firms with multiple product lines often find themselves in a better position to adapt to changes in economic conditions, technology, or consumer needs.

Exhibit 14.4 *General Foods' Product Mix*

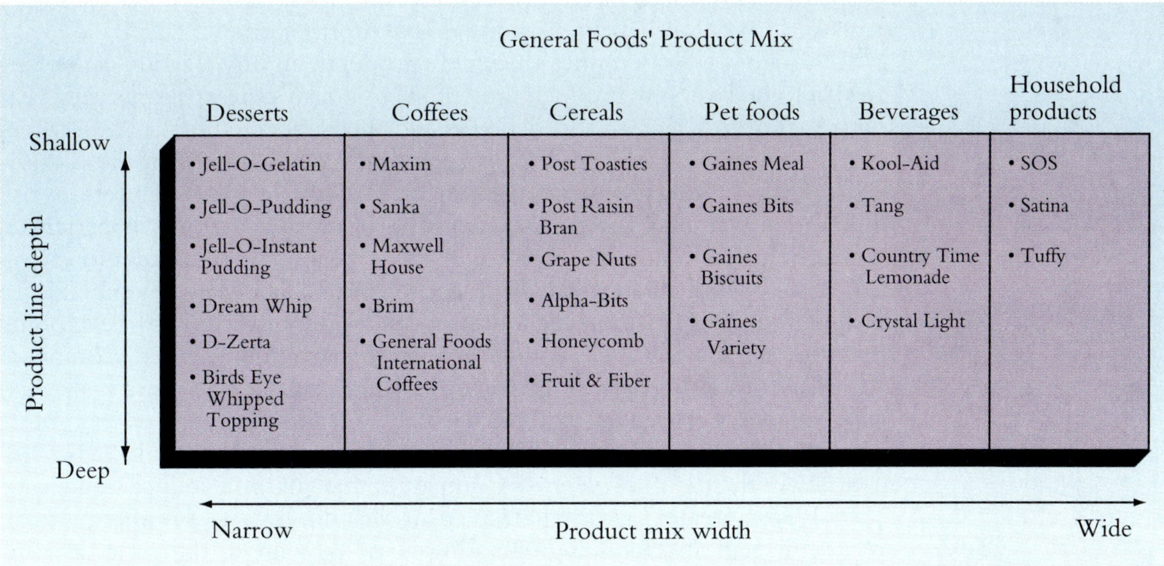

MANAGING THE PRODUCT MIX

Whether they offer a few similar products or many diverse ones, firms face numerous decisions in developing and managing their products. They must determine which to offer and must continue to develop new ones. They may need to modify products in response to competition and changing consumer preferences. Firms also must determine when to stop offering certain products.

Developing New Products

Firms spend billions of dollars each year developing new products. Boeing alone will spend over $5 billion designing a new jet, the 777. If successful, the 777, like the 747, will be a profitable machine for years to come.[6] But many of the more than 10,000 new products introduced each year fail.[7] According to a recent survey of new-product managers conducted by Group EFO, a Connecticut-based consulting firm, 8 percent of their new products survived to reach the market. Once there, 83 percent of these new products failed, which overall resulted in a 99 percent failure rate.[8] Beech Aircraft invested over $350 million in its innovative new airplane, Starship, only to stop producing the plane a few years after its introduction. The performance of the plane did not live up to expectations.[9]

Many reasons account for the high failure rate of new products. The most common reasons are lack of research, design problems, and poor timing of the product's introduction.[10] The most successful new products are superior to competitors' offerings, have been developed to meet well-defined consumer wants and needs, and enable customers to perform a unique task.[11]

Although it is risky to introduce new products, an organization cannot afford *not* to do so. New products are critical to a firm's growth for several reasons. As products age, profits decrease and their expected life span becomes shorter.[12] About 15 percent of a corporation's sales is based on new products.[13] Without new product development, even the best of organizations risk decline. For instance, the railroad industry, in recent years, has experienced an unanticipated rapid decline. By failing to explore new transportation alternatives that would better satisfy customer needs, it became vulnerable to competition from trucking and air transportation. Conversely, by developing the minivan, Chrysler beat competitors to this growing market. Combined sales of Chrysler's minivans hit a record 140,773 in the first quarter of 1994, outselling every passenger car on the road.[14] One study reported that internationally developed new products and services are expected to increase dramatically in the next five years.[15] Companies that fail to introduce new products risk even greater losses than those firms that do. In fact, as numerous firms are cutting staff and reducing operating costs, they are at the same time increasing budgets to launch new products.[16] Investing in new products during an economic downturn is a good opportunity to get ahead of competitors who are cutting back on new products. Firms cannot eliminate the risks inherent in introducing new products, but they can reduce risks through a well-planned, thorough product development process (see Exhibit 14.5). Let's examine how a firm uses a six-step process to develop new products. The process is expensive and time-consuming but it is helpful in avoiding costly mistakes.

If firms are to continue to grow, they must introduce new products periodically. The "New" Ajax is one example of a new product introduced by an established firm.

Generating Ideas. The road to a new product begins with finding ideas that fit with the organization's goals and objectives. Ideas emerge from within the firm through engineers and researchers or from outside sources such as customers, competitors, or consultants. Fewer than 10 percent of all new ideas make it into the later stages of product development.[17]

Screening Ideas. The many ideas born in the initial step must be screened to select the ones the firm will pursue. An idea may not match a firm's objectives. Others may require resources and knowledge that the firm does not have and cannot easily obtain. Such ideas will be rejected, while others are evaluated further.

Business Analysis. During this phase, the firm estimates the market potential of the product: What are the expected costs, sales, and profits? If management believes the product will make enough profit to justify the costs, the idea will advance to the product development phase.

Product Development. Here firms develop a working model of the product. In this way, they can examine the feasibility of making and offering the product on a large scale. Some ideas are rejected at this stage because the production costs are too high to bring the product to market.

Exhibit 14.5
The New-Product Development Process

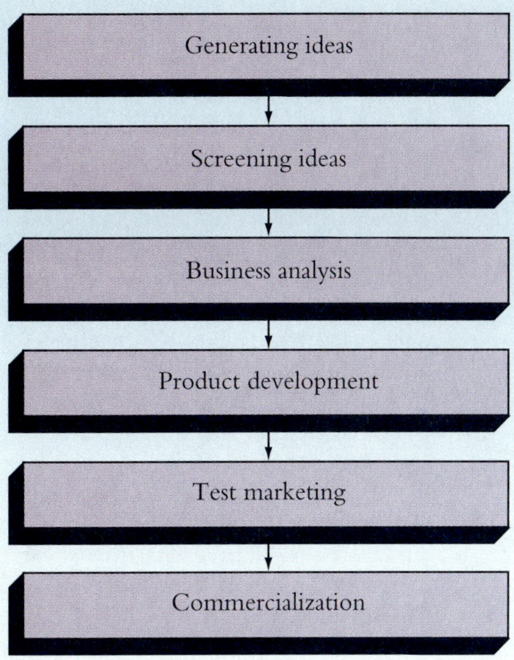

TOMORROW'S BUSINESS WORLD

TQM

Flexible Manufacturing Is the New Frontier

In their book *The Machine That Changed the World,* a group from MIT's International Motor Vehicle Program showed how Japanese automobile companies pulled ahead of their U.S. counterparts. The book's major message was that while American car companies in the 1970s and 1980s were still using production techniques developed by Henry Ford in 1913, the Japanese were using a new system of *lean production.* This system involved using less of everything, including inventory, labor, factory space, and investment. Car company executives attributed the Japanese firms' success to lower labor costs. But in 1982 Honda opened the first Japanese plant in the United States and paid U.S. wages; the new operation still had lower costs than other U.S. plants.

Since *The Machine That Changed the World* was published in 1990, the world of auto making, and that of many other products, has changed. American manufacturing firms have improved quality dramatically in recent years. In many instances, this has been accomplished by imitating ideas pioneered by the Japanese. Chrysler, for instance, after studying Honda, has cut $1 billion a year in costs. Many U.S. firms are manufacturing better-quality products with fewer workers and less inventory in less time. In many industries Japanese firms are no longer far ahead of U.S. companies. But while the quality gap has been reduced, the world's best companies are gearing up for the next frontier—flexible manufacturing.

Through a flexible manufacturing system (FMS), a single factory turns out a wide variety of products using computer-controlled robots. The idea behind this system is fairly simple. By reading the market more quickly, manufacturing many different products on the same line, and switching from one to another instantly and at lower costs, a firm can respond to customers more quickly and economically. New products reach markets more quickly, product improvements are made faster, and competitors are left to catch up. Many experts feel flexibility will be the key to competitiveness in the coming decade. Japan and the United States are racing once again, and Japan is ahead. According to Aleda Roth, a manufacturing expert at Duke University, "Most American companies are a generation behind—as far behind as they were on quality."

The Japanese take product quality as a given—a ticket into the ballpark. Without durability, conformance to customer specifications, and on-time delivery, a firm can't survive. The Japanese focus is on more and better product features, flexible factories, expanded customer service, and more new product introductions. A study conducted by the Deloitte Touche consulting firm found that Japanese companies are 25 percent more likely to emphasize leading-edge manufacturing, and have bigger investment plans for 33 of 42 advanced technologies, compared to U.S. manufacturers.

Many top U.S. companies including General Electric, Figgie International, and Motorola are working hard to develop FMS. Baxter Healthcare is testing an intravenous solutions factory that can be shipped anywhere, set up in a week, and moved anytime. Baxter can make working prototypes of complex medical instruments and ship them only 24 hours after receiving the specifications. General Motors has upgraded its Lordstown, OH, plant for flexible manufacturing. There, more cars can be built on one assembly line—450,000 a year—than anyplace else in the world. Robots and other machinery can easily be reprogrammed to build a wide mix of cars to meet changing demand. Workers have also been retrained to handle a variety of tasks instead of repeating a few rote tasks over and over.

Source: Adapted from Erie Norton, "Small Flexible Plants May Play Crucial Role in U.S. Manufacturing," *The Wall Street Journal* (January 13, 1993): A1–A2; Thomas A. Stewart, "Brace for Japan's Hot New Strategy," *Fortune* (September 21, 1992): 62–74; Bradley A. Steitz, "Detroit's New Strategy to Beat Back Japanese Is to Copy Their Ideas," *The Wall Street Journal* (October 1, 1993): A1, A10; and James B. Treece and Patrick Oster, "General Motors: Open All Night," *Business Week* (June 1, 1992): 82–83.

Test Marketing. Before full-scale introduction of a new product, a firm introduces it in selected areas chosen to represent the entire market. Test marketing can be used to monitor consumer reaction to the product and to refine the marketing mix if needed. Sometimes test marketing uncovers a weakness in the product, price, promotion, or distribution that can be adjusted before introduction to the entire market. Marketers carefully select locations to test market a product. Exhibit 14.6 lists cities often chosen as test market sites.

Commercialization. When a product shows promise in test marketing, the firm generally begins the process of production and distribution to the entire market. In some cases, the firm introduces the product in a selected geographic region (e.g., Cajun-style foods in the Southwest) and eventually moves it into other regions. Because the firm has invested so much money in its development, failure of a new product at this stage costs dearly. Thus marketers monitor commercialization carefully and attempt to make any neces-

Exhibit 14.6
Some Popular Test Market Cities in the United States

Charleston, West Virginia	Jacksonville, Florida	Portland, Oregon
Cincinnati, Ohio	Indianapolis, Indiana	Rockford, Illinois
Columbus, Ohio	Knoxville, Tennessee	Salt Lake City, Utah
Dallas-Fort Worth, Texas	Lexington, Kentucky	Springfield-Decatur-Champaign, Illinois
Des Moines, Iowa	Oklahoma City, Oklahoma	Tulsa, Oklahoma
Greensboro-Winston-Salem-High Point, North Carolina	Omaha, Nebraska	Wichita-Hutchinson, Kansas
Hartford, Connecticut	Phoenix, Arizona	

Source: "The Nation's Most Popular Test Markets," *Sales & Marketing Management,* March 1987, pp. 65–66. Reprinted by permission of Sales & Marketing Management. Copyright 1987.

sary adjustments in the product itself, the price, advertising or other promotional methods, or distribution system. The commercialization of a new product begins its life cycle.

A firm that can bring out a product faster than its competitors can enjoy a huge advantage. Several companies have taken steps to speed up the new product development process. For instance, Japanese producers of projection televisions can develop a new television in one-third the time required by U.S. firms.[18] It is becoming increasingly important that firms get it right the first time when developing products.

The Product Life Cycle

Product Life Cycle
The theoretical life of a product, consisting of four stages: introduction, growth, maturity, and decline.

Like living things, products go through several stages, known as the **product life cycle.**[19] New products enter the market during the introduction stage, they gain momentum and begin to bring a profit during the growth stage, they stabilize during the maturity stage, and finally they fade away in the decline stage. Exhibit 14.7 illustrates the four stages of the product life cycle.

Exhibit 14.7
Stages in the Product Life Cycle

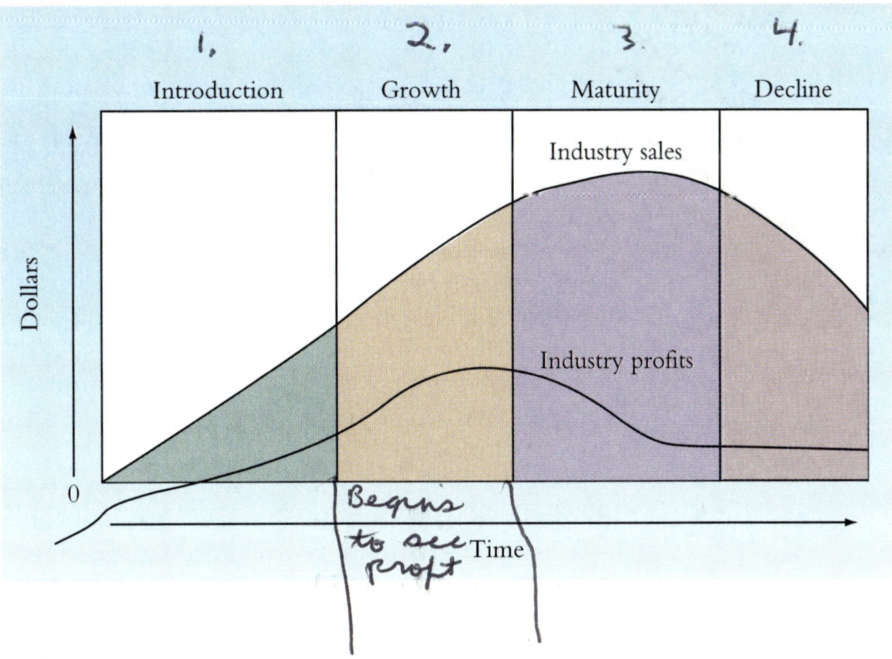

Products pass through these stages over time. For some products, the life cycle may be very short. Fad items such as cartoon-cat Garfield stick-ons for car windows may last for only a few years. Other products, such as black-and-white television sets and microwave ovens, enjoy a life cycle of several decades. Let's examine what generally occurs at each stage of the product life cycle.

Introduction Stage. In the first stage of the product life cycle, a firm makes the new product available to customers, who gradually become aware of it. Profits for a newly introduced product are negative because initial sales are low during this stage and the firm must recover its research and development expenses while it is spending large sums for promotion and distribution. Notice in Exhibit 14.7 that sales move upward from zero, but profits move from below zero. Examples of products currently in the introduction stage include liquid crystal television screens, low-calorie fat substitutes, and iced coffee.

Marketers face several challenges during a product's introduction. They must develop and carry out promotional programs to inform potential customers about the product's availability and its features. Electric vehicles, for instance, cost more than gasoline-powered ones. Marketers face a huge task in convincing car buyers to purchase electric cars, and must pick their target markets carefully.[20] Marketing managers must monitor sales, which may be slow, and make early adjustments in the product or in promotional efforts if needed. Many products don't survive the introduction stage. Have you ever heard of Campbell's Red Kettle Soups, Listerine Toothpaste, or Scott's Baby Scott Diapers? How about a graphics compact-disc player? All were brought to the marketplace, but none made it past the first stage of the product life cycle.

Growth Stage. Sales increase more rapidly during the growth stage, and the product begins to generate a profit. Competitors, seeing an opportunity, are likely to enter the market with similar products during this stage. The firm that originated the product may reduce its price as a result of new competition and decreased production costs. For instance, the prices of such growth products as compact-disc players, video cameras, and personal computers fell after manufacturers recovered their initial development costs and other firms began to introduce competing products. As prices fall, profits peak and begin to decline.

A product in the growth stage usually faces intense competition from similar offerings. Firms must rely heavily on repeat purchases for continued sales growth. Marketers therefore attempt to establish consumer loyalty to their products. They often create fresh promotional programs to emphasize the product's benefits and to encourage loyal customers to continue buying the same brand. Current growth stage products include cellular phones and facsimile (fax) machines.

Maturity Stage. During the maturity stage of the product life cycle, sales peak as profits continue to decline. As other products are introduced with new features and improvements, the product may become somewhat outdated. Color television sets and video recorders are examples of products in the maturity stage.

Intense competition from many different firms forces some products out of the market. Companies may cut prices further and increase their promotion budgets to compete for customers. They also may try product improvements, new package designs, and changes in style to encourage consumers to keep buying the product.

Decline Stage. Sales fall rapidly during the decline stage of the product life cycle. Profits also continue to fall, and sometimes additional price-cutting leads to losses. Consumers often prefer new products in earlier stages of their life cycles that provide greater satisfaction or meet different needs or wants. Electric typewriters, for example, are in decline as people increasingly use personal computers. Rotary-dial telephones are also in the decline stage.

Managers must decide at which point to eliminate a product nearing the end of its life cycle. Some products in the decline stage, such as black-and-white televisions, are not immediately eliminated. Sometimes firms generate a profit from decline-stage products by reducing promotional costs and selling to only the most profitable markets.

Extending the Product Life Cycle

Ideally firms would like their products to remain forever in the growth stage, when profits are highest. Although products eventually reach the decline stage, that some survive for decades is no accident. Firms can extend the life cycle of a product in several ways.

Increasing the Frequency of Use. Marketers commonly try to keep their product sales growing by encouraging consumers to use their goods and services more. Telephone companies, for example, run advertisements using emotional appeals to spur people to call relatives and friends more often. In some markets, Coca-Cola promotes Coke as a morning drink to replace coffee or tea. Toothbrush ads, citing dentists' recommendations, advise consumers to buy a new toothbrush more often, every two or three months.

Identifying New Users. Another way to extend a product's growth stage is to identify new target markets and promote the product to them. Oreo cookies and Frosted Flakes cereal, usually kids' fare, have been targeted to adults. Nintendo has promoted its video system to adults to expand beyond its major category of users, teenage boys.

Finding New Uses. Marketers sometimes maintain and increase sales by showing consumers other ways to use the product. For instance, Kraft has run television commercials explaining how to create a Mexican dip by pouring salsa over Velveeta cheese and putting it in a microwave.[21] Exhibit 14.8 shows how Heinz advertises its vinegar as a multipurpose household product.

Firms are acutely aware of the importance of brand names. Good names sell products. Firms often search for short names that are easy to pronounce and easy to remember, such as Sprite, Tide, or Prell. Names can suggest the product's function (L'Eggs pantyhose) or its performance (SupraLife, Energizer, and Duracell batteries). Brand names must also fit the image the company desires for its product, like the Jaguar car or Joy perfume.

Types of Brands. Brands are classified as manufacturer, private, or generic. A *manufacturer* (or producer) *brand* is owned and used by the manufacturer or service provider. Firms often use manufacturer brands to market products throughout the United States and abroad in many stores and outlets. Such brands identify who makes the products and provide the consumer with a nationally known, uniform, and widely available product such as Butternut bread, Lee jeans, or Chevrolet trucks.

A *private* (or store) *brand* is owned by a wholesaler or retailer. Examples of private brands include Sears' Die Hard and A & P's Master Choice. A firm offering private brands often can sell them at lower prices, achieve higher profits, and encourage customer loyalty. Most products sold under private brands are produced by companies that also market products under manufacturer brands. These firms find this practice profitable because they can use any excess production capacity and greatly reduce their marketing costs. For example, Whirlpool makes the refrigerators Sears sells under its Kenmore brand. The number of private label brands is growing in response to value-conscious consumers who demand higher level quality at a reasonable price.[23] Private label brands now account for about 12 percent of supermarket spending, the top products being milk and bread.[24]

Some products have no brand name at all. These are *generic products,* usually sold in simple, no-frill packages that identify only the contents. Many grocery items such as canned vegetables, cereals, crackers, and paper goods are available as generics. Generic products offer consumers an alternative to manufacturer and private brands. By using plain packages and keeping advertising to a minimum, producers and stores can sell generics at reduced prices. Sometimes, but not always, products sold as generics are not uniform in size or appearance or are of lower quality than branded goods.

Brand Loyalty. Consumers frequently buy only their favorite brands of certain products. They will not switch brands even if an alternative is offered at a lower price. *Brand loyalty* is the extent to which a consumer prefers a particular brand.

Marketers measure consumers' brand loyalty at three stages. The first, *brand recognition,* means consumers are familiar with a manufacturer's product. Buyers are more likely to choose a brand they recognize than an unfamiliar one. At the second stage of brand loyalty, *brand preference,* consumers will buy the product if it is available. At the third stage, *brand insistence,* buyers will not accept a substitute for their favorite brand.

The degree of brand loyalty varies from customer to customer and from product to product. A recent study by J.D. Powers & Associates found that older car buyers are twice as loyal to a particular make as younger customers.[25]

Firms attempt to establish brand loyalty through the product's performance, packaging, price, and advertising and other promotional efforts. Loyalty keeps consumers coming back for more. Are you a brand-loyal consumer? Your Values and Attitudes will help you find out.

YOUR VALUES AND ATTITUDES

Are You a Brand Loyal Consumer?

Directions: Test your brand loyalty to the toothpaste you use. Answer the following questions; then discuss your classmates' responses.

1. The last time you bought toothpaste, what brand did you buy?

   ____

2. Was price a major factor in your most recent toothpaste purchase?
   ________Yes ________No
3. Do you ever buy other brands of toothpaste?
   ________Yes ________No
4. Would you switch brands for a lower price?
   ________Yes ________No
5. If the store were out of the brand you bought most recently, would you buy a different brand?
   ________Yes ________No
6. Would you consider buying a new brand of toothpaste being introduced to the market?
   ________Yes ________No

Feedback: Although the quiz considered only one product, it should help you see how brand loyalty pertains to one consumer—you. If you said yes to all the questions, you are not at all brand loyal about toothpaste. If you answered no every time, you are extremely loyal. You would insist on one brand whenever you buy toothpaste. If you answered some questions yes and others no, you prefer one brand but would consider switching. You would be the target of competitors looking for customers!

Discuss with your classmates how they answered the quiz. Give possible reasons why some people are brand loyal to toothpaste while others are not. How important are differences between individuals, such as when and where they shop, financial situations, interest in finding a bargain, family shopping patterns, or willingness to try new things? Answer the questions again for other products—soft drinks, shampoo, fast food, shoes. You may find your brand loyalty varies from one product to another.

Brand Strategies. A company can use either individual branding or family branding when developing brands for its products. *Individual branding* requires creating a different brand for every product. It establishes separate identities for different products and thus helps target products to different market segments. Also, with individual branding, problems with one product seldom influence the success of other products in the line.

With *family branding,* a firm uses the same brand for most or all of its products. Many companies adopt this strategy to develop a product mix with a recognized brand name. Pepperidge Farm, for example, employs family branding. All of its breads, cookies, crackers, and desserts bear the Pepperidge Farm brand name. A company using the same brand for most or all of its products often uses similar packaging for all the products, too.

In some cases, family branding can be a liability. When Clorox introduced a new detergent, many consumers associated the product with Clorox Bleach and were afraid the detergent would not be color safe.

Packaging

Packaging The development of a container and a graphic design for a product.

Packaging involves designing a product container that will identify the product, protect it, and attract the attention of buyers. It is important to both consumers and manufacturers. Packaging can make a product easier to use, safer, and more versatile. It can also affect consumers' attitudes toward a product, which in turn affect their purchase decisions.

Plastic honey containers shaped like bears illustrate an effective use of clear packaging.

Originally, packages were designed mostly for their functional value; they protected products from damage or spoilage. Today packaging also has significance as a marketing tool. To develop an appealing package that will catch the buyer's eye, marketers consider not only function but also shape, color, size, and graphic design.

Firms work to create innovative packages to meet the needs of the consumers they want to reach. For example, after a scientific study reported that taking an aspirin a day can ward off first heart attacks, Bayer promptly designed "calendar paks." These packages contain 28 aspirins in separate blister compartments, to help buyers keep track of whether they took their daily aspirin tablet. Other innovations are Clorox's no-splash spouts on bleach containers, Armour's Golden Star Fresh Packs with deli meats individually wrapped in two-slice servings, and Wella's So Fine Shampoo Mist in a self-pressurized spray applicator that eliminates spills.

The trend toward clear bottles illustrates the many uses of packaging. Clear bottles can create an image of a product that is purer, milder, and lighter. They can be made of recycled plastic and can contain less material than thicker, opaque bottles, and they let customers see how much the package contains. A host of products are packaged in clear packages, including beverages, dish detergents, and deodorants.[26]

Packaging has become an important aspect of product safety. Since 1982, when eight Chicago-area people died from Tylenol capsules injected with cyanide, manufacturers have developed tamper-proof packages for products such as medicines, foods (peanut butter, catsup), and personal care items (toothpaste). Products available in safety-sealed packages satisfy an additional consumer need.

The impact of packaging on the environment has become another critical issue many manufacturers are facing. Packages from foods and consumer goods make up much of the tons of waste dumped into landfills each day in the United States. In response, some firms are changing packaging and products. Kellogg Company puts its cereals into boxes made from recycled paper, while manufacturers now make disposable diapers such as Pampers and Luvs with half the amount of material as before. In spite of such efforts, groups such as the Environmental Action Foundation and the U.S. Public Interest Research Group continue to criticize companies for developing wasteful packages.

Labeling

Labeling
The display of important information on a product package.

Manufacturers communicate with buyers through **labeling.** The label is the part of the package that identifies the brand and provides essential product information regarding contents, size, weight, quantity, ingredients, directions for use, shelf life, and any health hazards or dangers of improper use.

Labels also provide the means for automatic checkout and inventory monitoring. The universal product code (UPC), an electronic bar code on labels that identifies manufacturers and products, enables supermarkets and other stores to use computerized scanners at the checkout counter. Not only do scanners save time and help keep down costs, they also compile complete sales records valuable to both stores and manufacturers.

The Consumer Product Safety Commission and the Food and Drug Administration require that labels indicate warnings, instructions, and manufacturer's identification. Federal laws mandate that labels include content information and potential hazards. Manufacturers are required to be truthful in listing product ingredients on labels. Ingredients must be listed in order, beginning with the ingredient that constitutes the largest percentage of the product down to the ingredient that makes up the smallest percentage. Snack chips that contain more vegetable oil than potatoes, for example, must be labeled to show oils as the first ingredient. The Bush administration, during its final days, announced a package of nutrition-labeling rules that require food makers to adopt uniform labels for hundreds of thousands of products. The rules, which took effect in 1994, will cost the food industry $2 billion and limit health claims that can be made. However, they will also give consumers much more information about nutrition content and reduce health costs by improving nutrition.[27]

PRICING

Price
The value that buyers exchange for a product in the marketing transaction.

The price of a product is one of its most important aspects for both sellers and buyers. Many terms are used to represent price: taxi *fare,* insurance *premium,* parking *fine,* apartment *rent,* and, let's not forget, income *tax.* No matter how it is expressed, **price** represents the value consumers exchange in a marketing transaction.

Money usually is the commodity exchanged for a product that satisfies a consumer need. But sometimes money isn't involved at all; the parties exchange goods or services instead. Children trade baseball cards. Teenagers may do yard work to earn use of the family car. A retail store and a radio station may work out a deal to trade merchandise for free radio ads. Such trading, called *barter,* is the oldest form of exchange used in all societies.

The price consumers are willing to pay depends on the amount of satisfaction or utility they expect to receive from a product. A complete set of the original edition of *The Birds of America,* John James Audubon's 435 hand-colored engravings, sold in 1992 for $4.07 million, the highest price ever paid for a piece of printed Americana.[28] A buyer purchased Van Gogh's *Portrait of Dr. Gachet* in 1990 for $82.5 million.[29] And at a 1992 auction, the blue-and-white gingham dress worn by Judy Garland in *The Wizard of Oz* was sold for $48,400; an original Beatles drum skin cover brought $17,600.[30] In late 1994, William Gates, president of Microsoft, bid millions of dollars to purchase one of the 21 surviving notebooks of Leonardo da Vinci. The price of these products reflects the value consumers place on them. Today's Business World examines the pricing of sports collectibles.

TODAY'S BUSINESS WORLD

Pricing Sports Collectibles

At the Sotheby's Holdings auction house in New York, speculators have paid $2.1 million for baseball cards and other sports memorabilia. The most sought-after item was the uniform Roger Maris wore during the 1961 baseball season, when he broke Babe Ruth's home run record. Sports Heroes, a sports card brokerage firm, gave the winning bid of $120,000. Sports Heroes spent $480,095 at the auction to acquire the highest-priced items. Although the purchases were made partly to generate publicity, a company representative said that the "primary motive was return on investment."

Baseball cards in particular are in high demand among collectors. At Sotheby's a 1952 Topps card of rookie Yankee slugger Mickey Mantle went for $49,500;

the card had sold for $46,750 the previous year. A card of Jackie Robinson, the first black major league player, sold for $4,675. And a Honus Wagner card, one of only forty known to exist, sold for $451,000, compared with $220,000 the previous year.

Of course, not all sports collectibles sell at the lofty prices owners would like. Lou Gehrig's 1937 Yankee jersey still sits on a table at Christie's International PLC. Gehrig is a true baseball legend. Known as the "Iron Horse," he played 2,130 consecutive games, a record even today. He died from the muscle disease that now bears his name and left behind only a limited amount of memorabilia. It is estimated that fewer than a dozen authentic Gehrig jerseys still exist. The auction house values the jersey at $375,000 to $425,000, perhaps the highest price ever set on one piece of clothing. Yet no buyers have come forward at the current price.

Collecting trading cards remains popular today, and the card business has become a billion-dollar industry. During the 1980s, sales increased annually at a rate of 20 percent, and they continue to rise in the 1990s. The card-collecting market is still dominated by 12-year-old boys, but more and more adults are becoming speculators, and for good reason. Rookie cards of some of today's stars have increased rapidly in value. A rookie card of Cal Ripken Jr. sold at Sotheby's for $65, an increase of 117 percent from the previous year. It's hard to beat that kind of return on investment.

Would you pay that much money for a collectible item of some sort? Why or why not?

Source: Adapted from Alexandra Peers, "Speculators Take Field at Sotheby's Baseball Card Auction," *The Wall Street Journal* (March 2, 1992): C1, C18; Jennifer Pellet, "It's in the Cards," *Discount Merchandiser* (March 1992): 32–39, 71; and "Gehrig Baseball Jersey Fails to Sell at Auction," *The Wall Street Journal* (October 19, 1992): A6.

The pricing decision is crucial for marketers because price is highly visible to consumers and greatly affects purchase decisions. After noticing a product, buyers generally look at the price tag. Prices that consumers perceive as too high will prevent them from buying.

PRICING OBJECTIVES

Before establishing prices, marketing managers must decide their pricing objectives. Survival is the most fundamental one; firms will tolerate financial losses and other difficulties if needed for survival. Besides survival, firms use price to increase sales and market share, boost profits, achieve a return on their investment, and maintain their present position in the industry.

Market Share

A firm's *market share* is its percentage of the total industry sales in the geographical area where it sells its products. Maintaining or increasing market share is a common pricing objective. Many firms use market share figures to assess their performance. An increase in sales may help a company reduce production costs and achieve higher profits since it is cheaper on a per unit basis to produce more goods or offer more services. Firms sometimes lower prices to try to capture a larger share of the market. Canon, for instance, attempted to increase market share by offering basic copiers in the $1,000 to $1,200 range when the low-end copier on the market was priced around $2,000.

Profit

Of course the objective of many companies is to maximize profit. But in practice, defining "maximum profit" is difficult. No matter how profitable a firm becomes, it still may not have reached a point of maximum profit. Most firms express this pricing objective as a percentage increase over current profits. A company's pricing objective may be to increase profit by 10 percent in one year.

Return on Investment

Return on Investment (ROI) is the amount of profit earned, expressed as a percent of the total investment. ROI is sometimes more desirable as a pricing objective than is profit maximization, because it is a better measure of a firm's operating performance. For instance, the typical ROI in the automobile industry is 20 percent per year.

Status Quo

Firms wishing to maintain their present situation in the industry may establish status quo pricing objectives. A company that wants to meet (but not beat) competitors' prices, develop a favorable public image, or maintain its market share would favor status quo pricing objectives. By maintaining price stability, a firm reduces the risk it could face in a climate of price competition. For instance, when several airlines planned price hikes in the late 1980s, a few airlines lowered their air fares. Most competitors then matched the price cuts, and all the airlines lost revenues from the resulting lack of price stability.

FACTORS IN PRICING DECISIONS

A firm cannot determine a product's price without considering several factors that affect price. Managers must take into account the use of price and nonprice competition, supply and demand, and consumer perceptions of price.

Price and Nonprice Competition

Price Competition
A policy of using price to differentiate a product in the marketplace.

The pricing decision is influenced by the extent to which firms decide to use price as a competitive tool. Some rely heavily on price competition while others compete on aspects other than price. Firms competing on **price competition** generally set prices equal to or lower than competitors' prices. Car rental companies often compete based on price competition by emphasizing economy rates.

A firm competing based on price must be prepared to change prices quickly and frequently in response to competitors' price changes. One drawback to this strategy is that competitors can easily reduce their prices to counter it. Price competition is practiced by firms in many different industries, such as hotels, electronics component manufacturers, and automakers.

Nonprice Competition
A policy of emphasizing aspects other than price, such as quality, service, or promotion, to sell products.

Nonprice competition involves competing based on factors other than price, such as quality or service. This strategy is useful in building brand loyalty. Customers who prefer a brand for reasons other than price are less likely to switch to a brand that costs less. For instance, consumers who pay thousands of dollars for a Rolex watch are not likely to switch brands because of a lower price. Several firms in the athletic shoe industry use nonprice competition and emphasize the benefits and styling of their brands.

Supply and Demand

Supply
The quantity of a product that producers will sell at various prices.

Demand
The quantity of a product that consumers will purchase at various prices.

The price of a product is also influenced by the economic forces of supply and demand. The penny you pull out of your pocket is worth just that—a penny. But a coin collector may pay a great deal for a rare penny. That's the principle of supply and demand at work. **Supply** refers to the quantity of a product that producers will sell at various prices. The **demand** for a product is the quantity that consumers will purchase at different prices. For most products, quantity demanded goes up as the price goes down; quantity demanded goes down as the price goes up.

Exhibit 14.10 shows a supply and demand curve for video recorders. The curve marked *S* is a typical supply curve. The supply curve slopes upward to the right, which means manufacturers are willing to offer more VCRs for sale when they can receive higher prices. The number of items supplied increases as price increases. The demand curve, labeled *D,* slopes downward to the right. This means that consumers are willing to buy more VCRs at lower prices; the number of items demanded goes up as price goes down.

The point at which the two curves intersect is called the equilibrium point, *E* on the graph. At this point, the quantity supplied equals the quantity demanded. In our example, a manufacturer is willing to supply 20,000 VCRs at a price of $200, and consumers will buy 20,000 VCRs at $200 each. If the manufacturer makes more than 20,000 VCRs, or prices them higher than $200, not all VCRs will be sold.

Exhibit 14.10
Supply and Demand Curve: VCRs

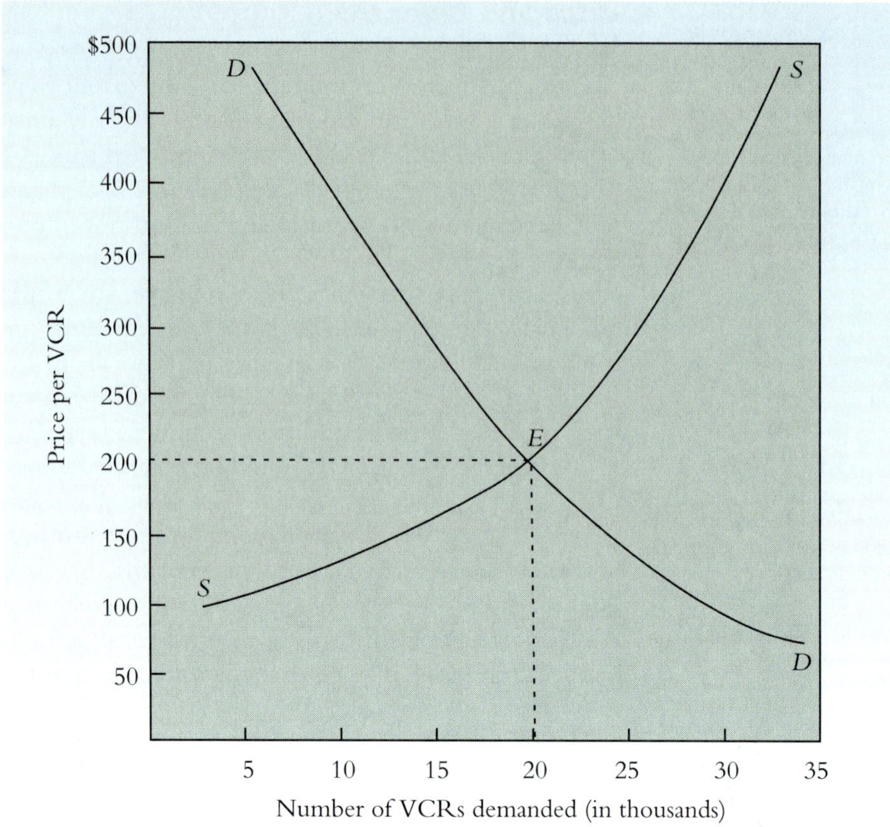

Consumer Perceptions of Price

Pricing decisions also require firms to consider consumers' perceptions of price. Price may be the top consideration in the buying decision of some consumers, while to others it may be much less important. The importance of price varies a great deal for different products and different target markets.

Buyers generally believe price is closely related to quality. For products such as wine, jewelry, and perfume, a higher price signals higher quality to the target market. In such cases, firms can use price to establish an image of product superiority. A person shopping for a diamond ring may expect a high price and be skeptical of lower-priced gems.

PRICING METHODS

After establishing pricing objectives and considering various factors that influence price, a firm decides on a **pricing method,** a procedure used to determine prices on a regular basis. When selecting a pricing method, a com-

Pricing Method
A systematic procedure for determining prices on a regular basis; considers costs, product demand, or competitors' prices.

pany takes into account the product, the market, and sales volume. The method used to price products in a hardware store carrying thousands of items must be fairly simple. On the other hand, calculating the price of a bridge or a dam would be complex. In this section, we examine three common pricing methods: cost-oriented, demand-oriented, and competition-oriented pricing.

Cost-Oriented Pricing

Cost-Oriented Pricing
A method whereby a firm determines a product's total cost, then adds a markup to that cost to achieve the desired profit margin.

Markup
In cost-oriented pricing, a percentage added to the total cost of the product to cover marketing expenses and allow a profit.

Firms such as supermarkets, department stores, and discount stores that sell numerous products often use a **cost-oriented pricing** method. They calculate prices by determining a product's total cost and adding on a percentage called the **markup.** The markup covers additional expenses incurred in marketing a product and allows the store to make a profit.

The percentage of the markup varies substantially from one product category to another but is often standardized across an industry. For instance, the markup for hardware is around 35 percent, while the markup for greeting cards is about 100 percent. How would you determine the price of a greeting card? Suppose that the total cost of producing one greeting card is 50 cents and the markup is 100 percent above costs. The price of the greeting card would be $1 (50 cents + 100 percent of 50 cents).

The major difficulty in using a cost-oriented pricing method is determining the actual markup percentage. If a firm uses a markup percentage that is too low, it underprices the product and loses potential profit. If the markup percentage is too high, the product is overpriced, and the firm may not sell enough units to cover costs.

Demand-Oriented Pricing

Demand-Oriented Pricing
A method based on the level of demand for the product.

Breakeven Analysis
A determination of how many product units must be sold at various prices for a firm to recover costs and begin making a profit.

Breakeven Quantity
The point at which the cost of making a product equals the revenue made from selling the product.

Incorporating the level of demand for the product into the pricing decision is **demand-oriented pricing.** A strong level of demand means that prices can be high. Where demand is weak, prices must be lower. The price of houses, for example, fluctuates with demand (as well as interest rates). Home prices in the San Francisco Bay area are extremely high because of the great demand for houses in a relatively small area.

In using demand-oriented pricing, firms estimate the quantities of a product that consumers will demand at various prices. A technique called **breakeven analysis** can help a manager determine how many product units must be sold at various prices for a firm to break even—to recover the costs of production and marketing and to begin making a profit. The **breakeven quantity,** the quantity beyond which profits occur, is reached when the total revenue for all units sold is equal to the total cost of all units sold. Total revenue, or all income from product sales, is obtained by multiplying the number of units sold by the selling price.

Besides total revenue, marketers must consider various business costs to calculate the breakeven quantity. *Fixed costs* are expenses that remain constant regardless of the number of units produced. Insurance, rent, and equipment are fixed costs. *Variable costs* are those that change depending on the number of units produced. Costs for raw materials and labor, for example, rise when more units are produced and fall when fewer units are produced. Fixed costs plus variable costs equal the total cost of producing a specific number of units.

Exhibit 14.11 shows how the breakeven quantity is calculated for college textbooks. A publishing company has fixed production costs of $100,000. The variable costs are $20 per book, meaning the company incurs a cost of $20 for every book produced. Suppose the textbook sells for $40. The breakeven quantity is calculated as follows:

$$\textbf{Breakeven quantity} = \frac{\textbf{Fixed Costs}}{\textbf{Price} - \textbf{Variable costs}}$$

In our example, the breakeven quantity is:

$$\frac{\$100{,}000}{\$40 - \$20} = \frac{\$100{,}000}{\$20} = 5{,}000 \text{ textbooks}$$

Exhibit 14.11
Breakeven Analysis for Textbooks

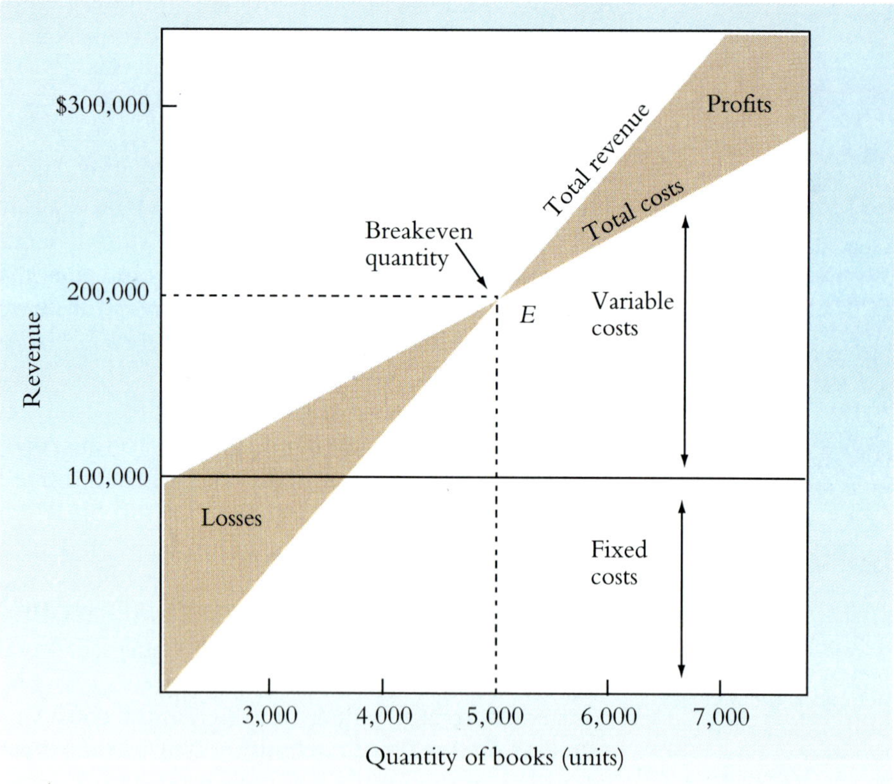

If 5,000 textbooks are sold, the publisher's total costs (both fixed and variable) will be recovered. Take another look at the graph in Exhibit 14.11. The breakeven quantity can be found where the total revenue line and the total cost line intersect. If more than 5,000 books are sold at $40, the publisher will generate a profit. Sales below 5,000 books will result in a loss.

A firm can use breakeven analysis to figure the profits and losses that would result from several different possible prices by calculating the breakeven quantity for each price. In our example, if the publishing firm reduces the price to $32, it would need to sell 8,333 books to break even. Raising the price to $48 would lower the breakeven quantity to 3,571 books. Marketers must rely on their research and experience to estimate how many units can be sold at each potential price. Then they can compare their estimated sales with the breakeven quantities to find the most appropriate price, the one at which sales will exceed the breakeven quantity and result in a profitable venture.

Competition-Oriented Pricing

Competition-Oriented Pricing A method whereby a firm sets prices on the bases of its competitors' prices rather than its own costs and revenues.

In the two pricing methods we have discussed, costs and demand are the major considerations in setting a price. In **competition-oriented pricing,** firms consider the prices charged by competitors as the major factor in setting their own prices. Competition-oriented pricing is appealing, especially to retailers, because it is simple. It involves no complex calculations; prices are simply set close to (preferably below) competitors' prices. This method is useful when a firm's pricing objective is to increase sales or market share.

Firms find competition-based pricing especially important when fierce price competition exists in the market or when competing products are very similar. Customers often use price to select a service provider, especially when services are quite comparable. If students perceive all copy shops to do work of similar quality, they are likely to select the one that charges the lowest price per copy. Likewise, if customers view all banks as similar, they will probably select the one that charges the lowest checking account fee.

PRICING STRATEGIES

Pioneer Pricing New-product pricing strategy of charging the highest possible price to regain costs quickly (price skimming) or setting the price below competitors' prices to build sales quickly (penetration pricing).

Once a firm selects a pricing method, it develops a strategy for setting and adjusting prices. We will examine four common pricing strategies: pioneer pricing, psychological pricing, professional pricing, and price discounting.

Pioneer Pricing

A firm setting a price for a new product may use **pioneer pricing.** There are two pioneer pricing strategies: price skimming and penetration pricing.

Price Skimming. Firms using price skimming charge the highest price possible during the introduction stage of the product life cycle. The purpose of this strategy is to "skim" the best buyers from the top of the market—those willing to pay a high price. When manufacturers introduced compact-disc players, they priced them fairly high. However, prices of CD players have dropped substantially since their introduction. Price skimming helps firms recover development costs more quickly and also may help to keep the quantity demanded down during product introduction, when production capacities may be limited.

Penetration Pricing. Some firms prefer to set prices low when offering a product for the first time. Penetration pricing, used to generate a large sales volume and gain a substantial market share quickly, establishes prices for new products below what competitors charge. Firms introducing consumer goods such as cosmetics, soups, or cleansers often use this strategy. One drawback is less flexibility than price skimming; raising a penetration price is more difficult than lowering a skimming price.

Psychological Pricing

Psychological Pricing
A policy that encourages purchase decisions based on emotion rather than reason; includes odd-even pricing, customary pricing, prestige pricing, and price lining.

Psychological pricing strategies encourage consumers to make purchase decisions on an emotional rather than a rational basis. Such strategies include odd-even pricing, customary pricing, prestige pricing, and price lining.

Odd-Even Pricing. Marketers sometimes try to influence buyers' perceptions of price by using certain numbers. In *odd pricing,* prices end with odd numbers, such as $98.99. This strategy assumes that buyers will perceive the product as a bargain—less than $100. The opposite strategy, *even pricing,* is used to give a product an exclusive image. Consumers may perceive a pair of slacks priced at $44 to be of higher quality than a pair priced at $43.95.

Customary Pricing. When firms price products based on tradition, they use customary pricing. Products such as candy bars, gum, magazines, and mass transit are priced according to this strategy. A company introducing a new candy bar probably would charge the same price that consumers already pay for other candy bars.

Prestige Pricing. An organization that sets an unusually high price to provide a quality image for a product uses prestige pricing. This strategy is most useful when buyers perceive a relationship between the item's price and its quality; indeed they may have second thoughts about purchasing the product if it does not cost enough. Prestige pricing is used for products such as furs, jewelry, and perfume.

Price Lining. In price lining, sellers set limited number of prices for selected lines of merchandise. These prices reflect various ranges in which consumers concentrate their purchases. For instance, a clothing store may sell a line of men's shirts for $22, $30, and $36. By holding prices constant within a certain range, price lining simplifies pricing decisions of sellers and purchasing decisions of consumers.

Professional Pricing

Professional Pricing
A policy—practiced by doctors, lawyers, and others with skills or experience in a particular field—of charging a standard fee for a particular service.

People with great amounts of training and skill in different fields use **professional pricing.** Doctors, lawyers, accountants, and many other professionals charge standard fees that reflect the expertise required to perform their jobs. For instance, a doctor may charge $30 for an office visit and $100 for a physical examination.

Price Discounting

Price Discounting
A policy of offering buyers deductions from the price of a product.

Many sellers engage in **price discounting,** offering customers deductions from the price of a product. Sellers often give cash discounts for prompt payment. A seller may specify a *cash discount* of "2/10 net 30," which means that a 2 percent discount is offered if the account is paid in 10 days and that the full balance is due in 30 days. *Quantity discounts* are provided to customers who buy on a large basis. Producers offer *trade discounts* to other sellers for performing various functions such as transporting, storing, and selling goods.

Discounts during times of lower demand are common. Because of the perishable nature of services (unused capacity cannot be stored), service providers often use price to increase demand during slow periods. Movie theaters, for instance, charge less for morning and afternoon shows than for evening shows. Some health clubs drop prices during the summer. Telephone companies reduce rates for late night or weekend long-distance calls.

Another pricing practice growing among service firms is *bundling,* which involves selling two or more services in one package for a special price.[31] An example of bundling is an airline package that includes air travel, car rental, and hotel accommodations.

SUMMARY OF LEARNING OBJECTIVES

1. ***Define the term* product *and distinguish between consumer and industrial products.*** A product consists of all the tangible and intangible characteristics provided in an exchange between a seller and buyer. The products people use for personal or family use are consumer products, classified as convenience, shopping, or specialty products. Organizations use industrial products in producing goods and services and in carrying out their operations.

2. ***Differentiate between product line and product mix.*** Firms often market a group of related products and services known as a product line. A product line of only one or two products is shallow; a deep product line contains many items. A firm's product mix is the entire collection of products it offers. Product mix width (narrow or wide) refers to the number of product lines a firm carries.

3. ***Trace the process of developing new products.*** To be successful, firms try to develop new products to satisfy consumers. New-product development consists of (a) generating ideas that fit a firm's objectives; (b) screening ideas to determine which are feasible to

pursue; (c) analyzing the costs, sales, and profits of the proposed product; (d) developing a working model of the product; (e) test marketing the product; and (f) distributing the new product to the entire market during commercialization.

4. ***Describe the stages of the product life cycle and explain how firms can extend the product life cycle.*** A product enters the market during the *introduction* stage, in which sales rise slowly and profits are low. In the *growth* stage, sales increase rapidly and the product begins to generate a profit. In the *maturity* stage, sales peak as profits decline. Sales volume falls rapidly during a product's *decline* stage. To extend a product's life cycle, a firm can modify the product's quality, functions, or style. It can find new uses for the product, identify new users, or encourage more frequent use. A product that becomes too costly for a firm is deleted from the product mix.

5. ***Explain the purposes of branding, packaging, and labeling.*** Firms identify their products through branding, packaging, and labeling. In *branding,* products are named and sometimes represented with a design called a brand. Unbranded products, called generics, are often available. *Packaging* protects products, adds to their functions, helps ensure product safety, and attracts consumer attention. *Labeling* identifies the product and brand and provides information about contents and use.

6. ***List four pricing objectives and identify three factors to consider when making pricing decisions.*** Price, the value consumers exchange for a product in a marketing transaction, is important to both buyers and sellers. Besides mere survival, a firm can use price to increase market share, increase profit, increase return on investment, or maintain the industry status quo. When making pricing decisions, a firm determines whether to compete based on price and nonprice competition and considers the forces of supply and demand and consumer perceptions of price.

7. ***Distinguish between cost-oriented, demand-oriented, and competition-oriented pricing methods.*** A firm can use any of several methods to set prices. *Cost-oriented* pricing bases price on total cost of a product plus a predetermined percentage amount called the markup. *Demand-oriented* pricing, using breakeven analysis, considers the level of demand for the product at various possible prices in order to find out how many products must be sold for the firm to recover its costs. *Competition-oriented* pricing uses prices charged by competitors as the major factor in selecting prices.

8. ***List and explain four pricing strategies.*** Various pricing strategies enable a firm to adjust the price of a product at certain times. *Pioneer pricing,* used in pricing new products, can mean setting the price high during a product's introduction to recover costs quickly (price skimming) or setting the price low during introduction to build sales and market share quickly (penetration pricing). A firm may use *psychological pricing* (odd-even pricing, customary pricing, prestige pricing, or price lining) to encourage consumers to make purchase decisions on some emotional basis. People with great amounts of training and skill use *professional pricing* to set standard fees. *Price discounting* means offering customers reductions from a product's price.

KEY TERMS

Product
Consumer Product
Convenience Product
Shopping Product
Specialty Product
Industrial Product
Product Line
Product Mix
Product Life Cycle
Product Modification
Brand
Brand Name
Packaging
Labeling
Price
Price Competition
Nonprice Competition
Supply
Demand
Pricing Method
Cost-Oriented Pricing
Markup
Demand-Oriented Pricing
Breakeven Analysis
Breakeven Quantity
Competition-Oriented Pricing
Pioneer Pricing
Psychological Pricing
Professional Pricing
Price Discounting

QUESTIONS FOR DISCUSSION AND REVIEW

1. What do marketers mean when they refer to a convenience product? A shopping product? A specialty product? Name a product for each category.
2. Are the following product lines shallow or deep—Dr Pepper soft drinks, Levi's jeans, Reebok athletic shoes? Discuss. Would you consider the following companies to have a narrow or wide product mix? McDonald's, Rolls-Royce, IBM.
3. A new product doesn't jump from the drawing board to the marketplace. What phases must it go through first?
4. Why do many new products fail? Can you name a consumer product that failed? What are some possible reasons for its failure?
5. Products we see and use every day are in different phases of the product life cycle. Name two products in each phase.
6. Choose one of the products you named in the maturity stage. What are some ways its life cycle could be extended?
7. Distinguish between manufacturer brands, private brands, and generic brands. Why would consumers select one versus the other?
8. A clothing store uses a 50 percent markup to price most of its items. What pricing method is the store using? Explain what 50 percent markup means.
9. A company that manufactures umbrellas has fixed costs of $30,000 and variable costs of $5 for each umbrella it makes. The umbrellas sell for $10 each. What is the quantity that must be sold for the company to break even?
10. Which pioneer pricing strategy is a firm likely to use when introducing an innovative new medication that stops heart attacks instantly? Why?

CASE 14.1

Product Management at Borden

The milk business founded by Gail Borden in 1857 became one of the most profitable in the dairy industry. The name Borden was synonymous with milk. But the dairy business that made "Elsie the cow" a familiar character expanded into many other businesses, ranging from sugar to fertilizer. Although dairy products accounted for more sales than any other line of products in 1979, it was still less than 30 percent of total sales. Borden's product mix included more than a dozen different product lines, including chemicals. This strategy worked for Borden (sales in 1979 were $4.3 billion), but some of the product lines were not very profitable. Additionally, an increase in prices signaled that the chemical business was reaching maturity. Borden had built chemicals into a $340-million-a-year business.

Borden realized it had too many product lines and was not paying enough attention to each. Accordingly, the firm decided to focus its marketing efforts on consumer products, especially dairy products, salty snack foods, and pasta. By 1987, Borden had sold or dropped its fertilizer, sugar, commodity chemicals, bulk cheese, and beverage lines. It placed increased emphasis on the remaining products, including grocery, dairy, and snack products.

Between 1979 and 1987, annual sales increased from $4.3 billion to $6.5 billion. Borden also increased its hold on the dairy business. With the purchase of Meadow Gold, Borden's share of the liquid milk market jumped to 10 percent. Dairy products accounted for 36.8 percent of 1987 sales. Borden continued to reinforce its brand name through advertising, portraying itself as the farm down the road that rushes the product from the cow to the market before the cream rises. This strong brand image is known in the industry as the "Borden difference." When asked exactly what this difference is, a dairy industry veteran said, "About a buck a gallon."

Between 1986 and 1991, Borden spent $1.9 billion on ninety-one acquisitions. Brands included Creamette and Prince pastas and Aunt Millie's pasta sauces, Eagle condensed milk, ReaLemon lemon juice, Wise potato chips, Cheez Doodles, Cracker Jack, Creamora coffee creamer, and Elmer's glue. In total, Borden's brands added up to $7.2 billion in annual revenues. Borden is number one or two in market share in over a dozen product lines, ranging from pasta to plastic wrap.

But fierce price wars in processed cheese, snacks, and dairy products forced CEO Anthony D'Amato to confront the problems facing Borden: ineffective marketing, poor earnings, slumping sales, and market-share losses to Frito-Lay, Eagle Snacks, and Kraft. A major problem is that Borden failed to integrate the various brands it acquired into a single, cohesive network. Whereas Borden makes 2,800 snack products alone, industry leader Frito-Lay offers only 445. One supermarket executive said, "It's really difficult to understand what business Borden is in today when you look at the number of items they have." In simple terms, Borden could not take advantage of the economies inherent in selling the same or similar products, which put the firm at a huge cost disadvantage.

In October 1992, D'Amato announced a major overhaul of the company. The plan included closing 10 plants, reducing the work force by 3,000, folding four divisions into one, and eliminating the weakest parts of the snack division. The objective was to build the parts into an efficient whole. In the past big customers such as Wal-Mart had to call five different divisions to place orders. The new integration process would serve customers better. The snack food group, for instance, was cut from 12 regional profit centers to three.

Some Wall Street analysts predicted that Borden would still have to sell one or more divisions. Early in 1994 Borden announced that many of its businesses, including dairy, food service, and snacks would be put up for sale. By late 1994, the price of Borden stock fell to below $12 a share from a high of over $35 in 1992. Acknowledging the serious problems, Borden was sold to a number of buyers through a complicated leveraged buyout. Borden shareholders received $14.25 a share in Nabisco stock. Speculation continues, with some experts predicting Borden will sell off the dairy business, which had $1.28 billion in sales in 1994.

Questions for Discussion

1. Evaluate the width of Borden's product mix and depth of its product lines.

2. Do Borden products have life cycles? How could they be extended?
3. What type of branding strategy does Borden use? Is Borden a strong brand name?
4. Why did brand acquisitions lead to a major problem for Borden? Do you think the firm is on the right track to resolve this problem?

Source: Adapted from "Borden Reports Loss Totaling $484 Million for Fourth Quarter," *The Wall Street Journal* (February 1, 1995): B3; Laura Ginn, Greg Burns, and Keith Alexander, "Elsie May Be Ailing, but KKR Is Thinking Whipped Cream," *Business Week* (September 26, 1994): 55; Elizabeth Lesly, "The Carving of Elsie, Slice by Slice," *Business Week* (January 17, 1994): 29; Seth Lubove, "Pulling It All Together," *Forbes* (March 2, 1992): 94–96; Judann Dagnoli, "Borden Joins Snack Price War," *Advertising Age* (March 23, 1992): 20; Elizabeth A. Lesley, "Borden Faces Facts: It's Time to Shed the Flab," *Business Week* (November 9, 1992): 44; Walter Guzzardi, "Big Can Still Be Beautiful," *Fortune* (April 25, 1988): 50–64; and Kevin Goldman, "Experts Say Borden Has Milked Elsie the Cow for All She's Worth," *The Wall Street Journal* (November 12, 1992): B9.

CASE 14.2

Rising Prices Leave French Winemakers' Glass Half Empty

Prices for French wines rose through the 1980s and are continuing to rise. One factor is the exchange rate. Compared with the dollar, the franc has been strong, a situation that boosts the price U.S. customers pay for French wine. Some industry analysts say that the French vintners want to take advantage of outstanding grape crops and make as much profit as possible from the resulting wines, which are in demand. Price increases for especially good vintages have been as high as 62 percent from the previous year.

Many wine importers were shocked when the price of Côte-Rotie, a red wine from France, rose to $250 for a twelve-bottle case. Eighteen months earlier, the same case had sold for $140. But many restauranteurs and importers on this side of the Atlantic refused to pay the price; instead, they started buying California wines to replace the pricey French wines. They want to buy wines their customers can afford.

When American customers switch from French to American wines, that spells trouble for France's $10 billion wine industry, which employs 700,000 people. The United States is one of the largest importers of French wines. But steady price hikes since 1985 and a slumping economy have contributed to a dramatic drop in exports of French table wine to the United States. Meanwhile, sales of California wines have doubled in the last two decades. While sales of jug wines and wine coolers are dropping, sales of mid-priced and expensive California wines continue to climb. These better vintages, called "varietals" because they are identified by the main variety of grape they contain, compete with the French imports. Many wine retailers believe that California wines offer good value for the money, but fewer see French wines that way. Sparkling wine is also becoming a more affordable alternative to high-priced French wines. Spain's champagne producers, for instance, have succeeded by improving quality while keeping prices down.

Some U.S. wine merchants say such sharp price increases are the result of greed on the part of growers, winemakers, and distributors. While some growers have taken 10 percent increases, others have raised prices 18 percent and as high as 25 percent. Added to that increase is the 2 to 3 percent for middlemen who represent these growers to the distributors. Then the distributors mark up prices another 10 to 25 percent. For superior vintages in high demand, distributors mark up prices 30 to 50 percent. To avoid paying top prices yet still trade in French wines, some U.S. buyers look for bargains and lesser-known wines of good quality.

Some French winemakers have reluctantly cut prices. Chateau Talbot, a top winemaker from Bordeaux's St. Julien region, discounted by 30 to 40 percent some 800,000 bottles of fine 1983 to 1990 wines on the wholesale market. Chateau d'Yquem sold the 1987 vintage of its fine, sweet white wine at about 50 percent less than its 1986 vintage, which sold for $133 to traders and much more in retail stores. But even after steep discounts, high-priced wine does not sell easily. The less expensive California wines, sold to consumers at $7 or less a bottle, are in great demand.

Questions for Discussion

1. When consumers purchase a product such as wine, what, other than the wine itself, are they buying?
2. Is the wine market characterized by price competition or nonprice competition?
3. Do you think consumers believe that the more a French wine costs, the better it is? If so, why do you think the French winemakers are losing their market share?
4. Which pricing objective do the French wine producers seem to have established?

Source: Adapted from E.S. Browning, "Fine French Vintages Become a Hard Sell in Slumping Economy," *The Wall Street Journal* (October 20, 1992): A1, A12; Christopher Elias, "No Whines over '89's Great Grapes," *Insight* (May 28, 1990): 38; and John Rossant, "For French Winemakers the Glass Is Half Empty," *Business Week* (February 15, 1988): 50.

BUSINESS APPLICATION

Reduce the Price or Increase the Promotion?

Judith Hardin, a 27-year-old manager of a local fast food restaurant, has been asked by the owner to make a recommendation on possible price changes. The restaurant currently charges a slightly higher price for its food than does the competition. For example, Hardin's restaurant charges $3.00 for its 1/4 pound hamburger while the competition charges $2.50 for the same menu item.

During the past two years the restaurant has been barely breaking even in its operations while the competition has done significantly better. Hardin has studied the competition's products and has been unable to determine any significant difference in actual quality, taste, or appearance between her store's food and the competition's offerings. She is now contemplating her recommendation.

Questions:

1. Before considering the option of lowering prices what other avenues might Judith Hardin explore?
2. Do you think if Hardin recommends lowering the prices to that of the competition, then the restaurant will become as profitable as the competition?
3. What other factors besides price might be contributing to the success of the competitor's restaurant?

EXPERIENTIAL EXERCISE

Identifying Examples of Product Differentiation

Activity:

Visit a grocery store and analyze the characteristics of similar products to determine examples of product differentiation.

Directions:

1. Review the concept of product differentiation whereby a company will attempt to emphasize in what manner its product is different than a competitor's product.
2. Assign each student the task of visiting a local grocery store to identify examples of product differentiation. The following aspects of the assignment may be used:
   - Students should stay within the same type of products for the comparison. For example, one brand name of mustard should only be compared to a competitor's brand name of mustard; one brand of ice cream should be compared to a competitor's brand of ice cream, etc...
   - Students should write down the product characteristics identified in the wording on the package. Also, students should write down the nonverbal characteristics, such as the shapes, sizes, and colors of packages.
   - Students should then develop a list of common characteristics and a list of differentiation characteristics.
   - Each student should examine at least three competitors' products during the comparison.
3. On the due date of the assignment the instructor should call on as many students as possible to share the findings with the class.

NOTES

1. Adapted from Patricia Winters, "Sales Spark May Be Out for Nicotine Patches," *Advertising Age* (January 18, 1993): 3, 51; Stephen D. Moore, "Ciba Finds Marketing in Its Own Kind of Blockbuster," *The Wall Street Journal* (July 14, 1992): B4; Kathleen Deveny, "Heated, If Smokeless, Competition

Rages Among Makers of Nicotine Skin Patches," *The Wall Street Journal* (March 4, 1992): B1; Scott Donaton, "Nicotine Patch Eases Cig Ad Retreat," *Advertising Age* (June 29, 1992): 12; Pat Sloan, "Consumer Craving Nicotine Patches," *Advertising Age* (March 23, 1992): 3; and Carrie Goerne, "Pharmaceutical Companies Compete Aggressively to Help Smokers Quit Habit," *Marketing News* (March 30, 1992): 8.

2. Richard S. Dunham and Mary Beth Regan, "The GOP's Designated Pitcher," *Business Week* (March 27, 1995): 66.
3. Glen L. Urban, John L. Hauser, and Nikhilesh Dholalia, *Essentials of New Product Management* (Englewood Cliffs, NJ: Prentice-Hall, 1987), 1.
4. Yoram J. Wind, *Product Policy: Concepts, Methods, and Strategy* (Reading, MA: Addison-Wesley Publishing Co., 1982), 67.
5. Jennifer Lawrence, "Marketing Giant P&E Bulks Up for the Future," *Advertising Age* (October 17, 1994): 4.
6. Dori Jones Yang and Andrea Rothman, "Boeing Cuts Its Altitude as the Clouds Roll In," *Business Week* (February 8, 1993): 25.
7. Jim Betts, *The Million Dollar Idea* (Point Pleasant, NJ: Point, 1985), 7.
8. Cyndee Miller, "Survey: New Product Failure Is Management's Fault," *Marketing News* (February 1, 1993): 2.
9. Alan Farnham, "It's a Bird! It's a Plane! It's a Flop," *Fortune* (May 2, 1994): 56–66.
10. Robert G. Cooper, *Winning at New Products* (Agincourt, Ontario: Gage, 1987), 14.
11. G. Cooper and E. J. Kleinschmidt, "Success Factors in Product Innovation," *Industrial Marketing Management* (August 1987): 215–223.
12. Thomas S. Robertson, *Innovative Behavior and Communication* (New York: Holt, Rinehart, and Winston, 1971), 11.
13. S. Hopkins, "*New Product Winners and Losers,*" Report No. 773 (New York: The Conference Board, 1980), 1.
14. Alex Taylor III, "Iacocca's Minivan," *Fortune* (May 30, 1994): 56–66.
15. "Study: Launching New Products Is Worth the Risk," *Marketing News* (January 20, 1992): 2.
16. Gariella Stern, "To Outpace Rivals, More Firms Step Up Spending on New-Product Development," *The Wall Street Journal* (October 28, 1992): B1, B7.
17. Robert D. Hisrich and Michael P. Peters, *Marketing Decisions for New and Mature Products* (Columbus, OH: Charles E. Merrill, 1984), 15.
18. George Stalk Jr., "Time—The Next Source of Competitive Advantage," *Harvard Business Review* (July–August 1988): 41–51.
19. Glen L. Urban, John R. Hauser, and Nikhilesh Dholakia, *Essentials of New Product Management* (Englewood Cliffs, NJ: Prentice Hall, 1987), 6–7.
20. David Woodruff, Gail DeGeorge, and Gregory Sandler, "The Not-So-Big Wheels Leading the Change," *Business Week* (May 30, 1994): 114.
21. Yamiko Ono, "Think Thin? Not at Kraft, Home of Velveeta," *The Wall Street Journal* (January 25, 1995): B1.
22. Jonathan Berry, "A Second Career for Some Old Warhorses," *Business Week* (May 30, 1994): 8.
23. Jeff Smyth, "A '90s Taste for Private Label," *Marketing News* (April 11, 1994): 29.
24. Marcia Mogelonsky, "When Stores Become Brands," *American Demographics* (February 1995): 32–38.
25. William R. Diem, "Bond Stronger with Age," *Advertising Age* (March 28, 1994): 5–6, 5-43.
26. Cyndee Miller, "Trendy Marketers Want Consumers to See Right Through Their Products," *Marketing News* (February 1, 1993): 1–2.
27. Rose Gutfield, "Food Label 'Babel' to Fall as Uniform System Is Cleared," *The Wall Street Journal* (December 3, 1992): B1, B7.
28. Christie Brown, "Petrels in a Storm," *Forbes* (August 31, 1992): 79–82.
29. Harris Collingwood, "Van Gogh, Gogh, Goghing, Gone," *Business Week* (May 28, 1990): 34.
30. Marcy Rivinius, "Ox Auction," *Lexington (KY) Herald Leader* (December 20, 1992): A14.
31. Joseph P. Guiltinan, "The Price Bundling of Services: A Normative Framework," *Journal of Marketing* (April 1987): 74–85.

CHAPTER 15

Distribution

1. Define the term *marketing channel* and identify the two major types of marketing intermediaries.

2. Explain how marketing channels are integrated vertically.

3. Define *wholesaling* and describe the functions wholesalers perform.

4. Define *retailing* and outline the activities retailers perform.

5. Discuss the major considerations in retail planning.

6. Explain the role of physical distribution and identify its components.

LEARNING OBJECTIVES

Compaq Computer Corporation, created in 1982, designs, manufactures, and markets its own line of computers for home and business use. Even though it is relatively new to the personal computer (PC) market, Compaq is the largest manufacturer of IBM compatibles and thus is a major competitor of IBM, one of the market leaders. Compaq's sales doubled from 1986 to 1987, and net income tripled in 1988. This growth allowed the company to exceed $1 billion in annual sales in only five years, making it among the fastest-growing companies in history.

Part of Compaq's success can be traced to a very effective distribution network. One of its largest distributors was Businessland, the nation's largest computer retailer. Businessland accounted for 7 percent of Compaq's revenue, and Compaq products made up 15 percent of Businessland's sales. Thus it came as a surprise to the industry when Compaq decided in April 1989 to stop distributing through Businessland. With that announcement, the price of Businessland stock dropped almost 10 percent. Industry analysts harshly criticized Compaq's break with Businessland as the worst decision by Compaq in a long time.

Maybe it was Compaq's worst decision. In October 1991, CEO and cofounder Rod Canion announced Compaq's first-ever quarterly loss and its first-ever layoff of 1,700 employees, or 14 percent of its work force. However, most industry observers attributed Compaq's problems to price, not distribution. Because of intense price wars, the firm's market share, revenues, and earnings had fallen faster than other competitors.[1] Although Canion blamed Compaq's problems on the recession and hoped to ride it out, chairman of the board Benjamin Rosen believed the company to be in "a crisis, almost a life-or-death situation." Canion was removed from his position.

Eckhard Pfeiffer, named CEO to replace Canion, restored the company to its lofty position nearly as quickly as it had fallen. In June 1992, Compaq announced an expanded line of PCs, including 45 newer models, bringing to 76 the total number of models. Across-the-board price cuts of up to 32 percent rocked the industry; the price of Compaq's high-quality machines became much closer to that of inferior clones. Third-quarter sales jumped 50 percent, to $1.1 billion, and earnings quadrupled to $72 million. The lower prices reduced gross profit margin 6 points, to 28 percent, but Compaq made up for the lower margins with volume. Since Pfeiffer took over, Compaq's share of the U.S. PC and workstation market has more than doubled to about 10 percent. Pfeiffer's goal is to be the number one computer maker in PC and workstation market share by 1996. In 1994, Compaq shipped 4.8 million PCs, and expects to ship more than 6 million in 1995.

With new products and increased sales, Compaq expanded its distribution network. The firm more than doubled its worldwide outlets, to more than ten thousand, by adding office supply discounters like Office Depot and Circuit City as well as computer retailers. Wal-Mart joined as a distributor in 1994. Offering a machine with a Japanese-language operating system, Compaq began a push for market share in Japan, where it has about 40 distributors.

Direct selling accounts for about 20 percent of PC sales in the United States, so Compaq also began selling some PCs by mail. Rather than establish an internal operation, the computer maker opted to sell through five separate mail-order companies. Compaq is being careful not to cut out existing channels or create demand it cannot satisfy.[1]

Where would you be most likely to purchase a PC? How does Compaq stack up against the competition?

After firms devise marketing strategies, produce products, and price them, they must get the products to the marketplace. The distribution function is important to society because it enables goods and services to reach consumers. It is vital to a firm's success. As the example in the chapter opener shows, firms use many different avenues to get products to consumers in a timely and efficient manner.

In this chapter, we examine the various activities involved in distributing goods and services. First, we explain the concept of a marketing channel of distribution and describe the types of marketing channels. Next, we explore two major distribution activities: wholesaling and retailing. Finally, we discuss the physical movement of products from producers to consumers.

MARKETING CHANNELS

Marketing Channel (Channel of Distribution)
A group of interrelated organizations that directs the flow of products to ultimate consumers.

Marketing Intermediary
An individual or organization in a marketing channel that provides a link between producers, other channel members, and final consumers of products.

A **marketing channel (channel of distribution)** is a group of interrelated organizations that directs the flow of products to ultimate customers.[2] The channel organizations that provide the link between the producer and the consumer are called **marketing intermediaries.**

The two major categories of marketing intermediaries are wholesalers and retailers. Wholesalers sell primarily to other sellers or industrial users. Wholesale transactions generally involve large quantities of goods. Retailers specialize in selling products to consumers. They generally resell products that they obtain from wholesalers. We will discuss wholesalers and retailers later in the chapter.

Functions of Marketing Intermediaries

Consumers often wonder whether products would cost less if one or more marketing intermediaries could be eliminated from the distribution system. Would cars be less expensive if customers could simply buy them straight from the manufacturer? Perhaps, but think about the practical aspects involved. How many consumers would be willing or able to go to Detroit, or maybe Japan, to buy a car? Even if manufacturers offered cars for sale by mail order, few consumers would buy a car without seeing and test driving it. Selling vehicles directly to buyers from around the United States or around the world would be impossible.

Marketing intermediaries ensure that products are available on a timely basis where they are needed. Eliminating intermediaries does not eliminate the need for their services, such as storage, record keeping, delivery and providing a product assortment. Either the manufacturer, the consumer, or some other organization has to perform these essential services. Without intermediaries, most consumer purchases would be much less efficient. Products probably would cost more, not less. Some specific functions of marketing intermediaries are summarized in Exhibit 15.1.

Exhibit 15.1
Functions of Marketing Intermediaries

Function	Description
Buying	Purchasing a broad assortment of goods from producers
Carrying inventory	Assuming the risks associated with purchasing and holding an inventory
Selling	Performing activities required to sell goods to consumers
Transporting	Arranging for the shipment of goods
Financing	Providing funds required to cover the cost of channel activities
Promoting	Contributing to national and local advertising, and engaging in personal selling efforts
Negotiating	Attempting to determine the final price of goods
Marketing research	Providing information regarding the needs of customers
Servicing	Providing a variety of services, such as credit, delivery, and returns

Types of Marketing Channels

Depending on the needs of the target market, firms utilize many different types of marketing channels to distribute products. Generally channels for consumer products are different from channels for industrial products.

Consumer Products. The four most commonly used channels for consumer products are shown in Exhibit 15.2. Channel A, the direct channel, shows the movement of products from producer to consumer. Most services are distributed through this channel, such as hair styling, dental work, and auto repair. It is not typical, however, for most consumer goods, except some products such as plants and flowers at nurseries, produce at farmers' markets, and arts and crafts items at fairs. Direct marketers like Dell Computer Corp. also use this channel; over 1 million computers were sold this way in 1994.[3]

Channel B reflects the movement of products from producer to retailer to consumer. This channel is commonly used for large, bulky items like automobiles and furniture, as well as perishable goods like fresh seafood. Bringing in another intermediary, such as a wholesaler, would add delays or unnecessary costs to the distribution of these products.

Channel C, producer to wholesaler to retailer to consumer, is the traditional marketing channel. A wide range of products, including appliances, beverages, tobacco, and most convenience goods, is distributed through this channel.

Exhibit 15.2
Typical Marketing Channels

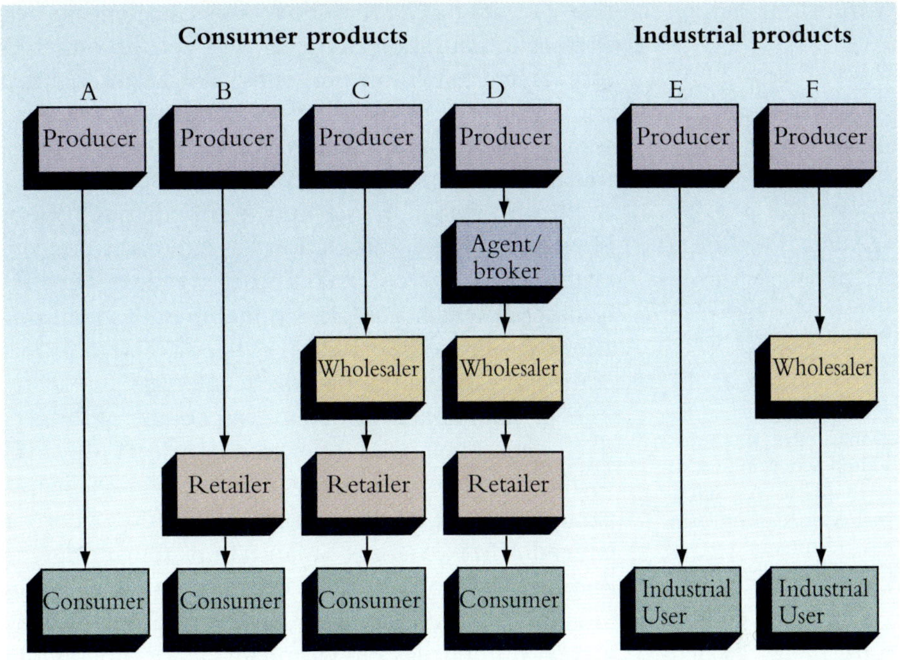

The final channel (D) for consumer products, producer to agent/broker to wholesaler to retailer to consumer, is used to distribute small, inexpensive products purchased frequently. Several wholesalers are involved in the distribution of items such as gum and candy bars that are purchased daily by millions of consumers at thousands of outlets.

Industrial Products. The common channels employed to distribute industrial products also appear in Exhibit 15.2. These channels are much shorter than the consumer channels. Most industrial products are distributed through the direct channel, producer to industrial user (channel E). For industrial products such as heavy equipment and machinery, the producer can communicate directly with the customer and provide needed and timely services such as training and repairs.

Some industrial products are distributed to customers through wholesalers (channel F). This channel is most common for accessory (smaller) equipment and supplies that are produced in large quantities but sold in small quantities. Tools and automotive parts, for instance, are sold to industrial users through wholesalers.

Vertical Integration The combining of two or more functions of a marketing channel under one management.

Vertical Integration

When one organization in the marketing channel assumes control of another, **vertical integration** takes place. For instance, movie production companies

Vertical Marketing System (VMS)
A marketing channel in which the different intermediaries are coordinated through management to improve distribution.

Corporate VMS
A marketing channel in which one organization owns successive stages of the channel.

Administered VMS
A marketing channel in which independent intermediaries use informal coordination; usually dominated by one channel organization.

Contractual VMS
A marketing channel in which intermediaries are independent but have relationships formalized through legal agreements.

Market Coverage
The number of outlets in which a product is sold.

Intensive Distribution
Market coverage in which all available outlets are used for distributing a product.

Selective Distribution
Market coverage in which only some of the available outlets are used for distributing a product.

Exclusive Distribution
Market coverage in which one outlet is used in a specific geographic area for distributing a product.

like Twentieth Century-Fox Film Corporation began purchasing television stations to gain increased control over the outlets available for its products: movies and television programs. Total vertical integration occurs when one organization controls all of the channel functions, from producer to consumer. Some oil companies, for example, own the oil wells, refineries, terminals, trucks and tankers, and service stations.

Traditionally, marketing intermediaries have operated independently. However, vertical integration has led to the concept of a planned marketing channel. A **vertical marketing system (VMS)** is a planned marketing channel in which a single channel member manages the different intermediaries to improve distribution efficiency. Vertical marketing systems have become increasingly popular in recent years.

Vertical marketing systems can be one of three types: corporate, administered, or contractual. Under a **corporate VMS,** marketing intermediaries are owned by one organization. The Sherwin-Williams Company, which makes paint and sells it in its own retail stores, uses a corporate VMS. In an **administered VMS,** channel organizations remain independent, but one member dominates the others. This organization, usually large and powerful, greatly influences the decisions of all organizations in the channel. Manufacturers such as Campbell Soup Company and Kellogg Company, for example, have extensive influence in distributing their products, including the ability to obtain adequate shelf space in supermarkets and promotional cooperation. The third type, **contractual VMS,** ties channel organizations together through legal agreements. This arrangement is popular among franchises such as McDonald's and Hallmark stores.

Intensity of Market Coverage

The characteristics of the product and the needs of the target market determine how many outlets a manufacturer will employ to cover the market. **Market coverage** refers to the number of outlets in which a product is sold.

The level of market coverage that uses all available outlets for distributing a product is called **intensive distribution.** Many convenience goods such as gum, candy bars, newspapers, bread, and soft drinks are distributed in a wide variety of locations convenient to consumers. Availability is a major factor in the sale of these items.

In **selective distribution,** only some of the available outlets are used to distribute a product. Goods such as furniture and electrical appliances are distributed selectively. Because these products are much more expensive and are purchased much less frequently than convenience goods, consumers will spend more time and will travel greater distances to shop for them.

The type of market coverage in which only a single outlet is used in a specific geographic area is called **exclusive distribution.** Infrequently purchased, expensive products are often distributed in this manner. Consumers wishing to buy a Rolls Royce, for example, would find only one dealership selling the car in their area.

WHOLESALING

Wholesaling
The marketing activities of intermediaries who sell to retailers, industrial users, and other organizational customers.

Wholesaling involves the activities of marketing intermediaries—called wholesalers—who sell to retailers, other wholesalers, or industrial users. (Wholesalers generally do not sell directly to consumers.) Wholesaling is a major segment of the economy. Nearly 478,000 wholesaling establishments conduct business in the United States, with annual sales totaling over \$2.5 trillion. About 6,219,000 people are employed in wholesaling.[4] It provides several essential services in the distribution of goods and services. Today's Business World examines how a large Japanese wholesaler responds to demand.

TODAY'S BUSINESS WORLD

Kao Responds to Demand

Kao Corporation is Japan's largest soap and cosmetics company and the sixth largest such company in the world, with annual sales exceeding \$5 billion. According to James Abegglen, chairman of Gemini Consulting–Japan, no company can match the flexibility of Kao's distribution. Goods can be delivered within 24 hours to any of 280,000 shops, whose average order is only seven items. This capability is based on a world-class information system and a wholly owned network of wholesalers. This control enables Kao to get hot-selling items on store shelves faster and to keep smaller inventories than competitors.

The objective of Kao is to maximize the flexibility of the entire firm's response to demand. This requires not only flexible manufacturing, but an information system that links all aspects of the business: sales and shipping, production and purchasing, accounting, research and development, marketing, stores' cash registers, and sales representatives' hand-held computers.

TQM

Many firms in the United States and elsewhere rely on point-of-purchase data in determining production requirements. A manager generally receives information on the previous day's sales. At Kao, managers see daily sales, stock, and production figures. They can learn about a competitor's sale within a day and make necessary adjustments. For new-product introduction, information from 216 retailers is combined with a test-marketing program called the Echo System. This system uses focus group interviews and consumer responses through calls and letters to measure customer satisfaction faster than surveys do. Within two weeks of introduction, Kao knows if a product will be successful, who's buying it, whether the packaging is effective, and what needs to be changed. Response to the factory is immediate and flexible manufacturing allows for instant changes.

The system at Kao eliminates the lag between a purchase and feedback about the purchase at the factory. It makes Kao less dependent on keeping finished-goods inventory. The system also allows the firm to smooth out production levels and increase variety without increasing stock. In 1987, Kao made 498 products and average inventory as a percent of sales was 9.2 percent. Now Kao makes 564 products and inventory is down to 8.6 percent.

Flexibility at Kao comes not only from manufacturing but from information. A flexible factory is of little use if it cannot be exploited. Kao knows what's selling and can respond to this information very quickly at the factory.

What seems to be Kao's competitive advantage?

Source: Adapted from Thomas A. Stewart, "Brace for Japan's Hot New Strategy," *Fortune* (September 21, 1992): 62–74; Masayoshi Kanabayashi, "Japan's Top Soap Firm, Kao, Hopes to Clean Up Abroad," *The Wall Street Journal* (December 17, 1992): B4; and "A Time for Mutual Respect and Understanding," *Fortune* (July 27, 1992): S16–S17.

Services Wholesalers Perform

Wholesalers are more than just conduits of merchandise. They provide a unique set of services of value to both their suppliers and their customers (retailers and other sellers).

- *Ownership.* By purchasing large amounts of goods, taking title to them, and storing them for resale, wholesalers absorb inventory costs for manufacturers.
- *Financing.* Wholesalers invest large amounts of money in inventory, extend credit to retailers, and collect payment from retailers.
- *Risk assumption.* Wholesalers take possession and ownership of products that may become obsolete or deteriorate before they are sold. In that way, wholesalers assume a great deal of risk. They also face the risk of nonpayment from retailers.
- *Promotional assistance.* Wholesalers often help promote the products they sell. They may provide retailers with displays or ideas for special promotions.
- *Information.* Wholesalers commonly employ their own sales forces, publish catalogs, and sponsor trade journals. By those means, they provide both retailers and producers with valuable information about product demand, buying trends, and prices.
- *Product assortment.* Because wholesalers usually carry an assortment of products, customers are able to order from a single source.
- *Transportation.* Wholesalers generally arrange local and long-distance shipments to customers.

Types of Wholesalers

Many different types of wholesalers offer numerous channel alternatives. Wholesalers commonly are grouped into three categories: merchant wholesalers, manufacturer-owned wholesalers, and agents and brokers (refer to Exhibit 15.3).

Merchant Wholesaler Marketing intermediary that takes ownership of goods and the risks associated with ownership.

Merchant Wholesalers. A wholesaler who takes title to products and resells them to retailers, other wholesalers, or industrial users is a **merchant wholesaler.** Most wholesalers fall into this category. They account for nearly

Exhibit 15.3 *Types of Wholesalers*

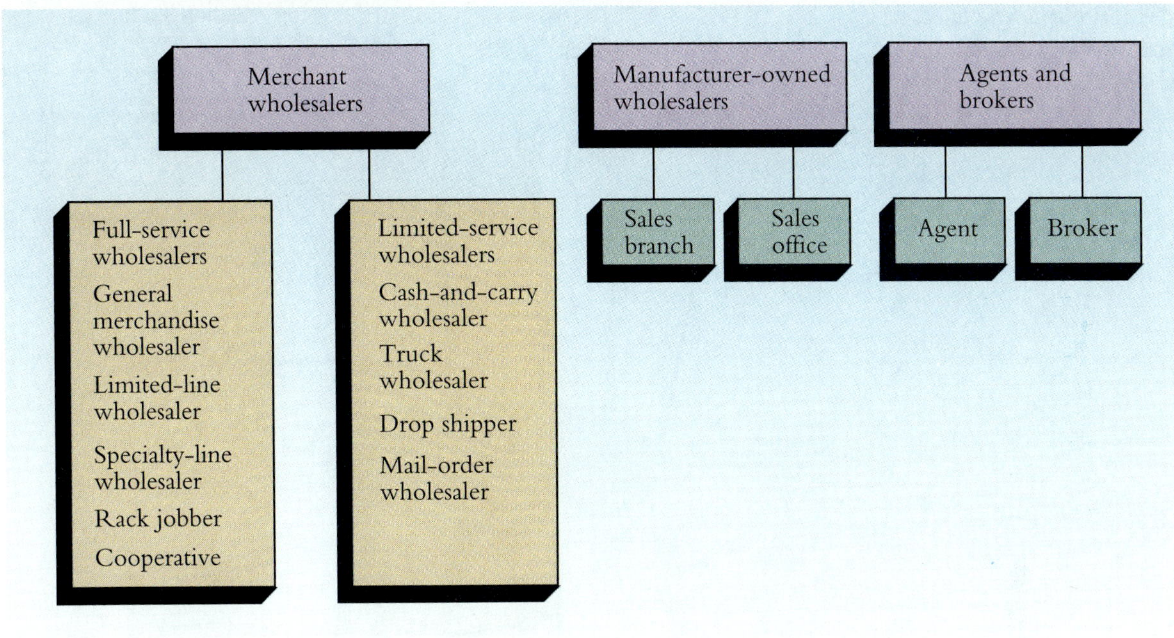

60 percent of total U.S. wholesale sales.[5] Merchant wholesalers can be either full-service wholesalers or limited-service wholesalers.

As their name implies, full-service wholesalers provide the widest range of services that wholesalers can offer, such as ownership, financing, and risk assumption. Full-service wholesalers who carry a very wide product mix are called *general merchandise wholesalers.* Those who carry only a few product lines are called *limited-line wholesalers.* For example, a general merchandise wholesaler may supply a supermarket with cosmetics, hardware, drugs, and tobacco and food items. A limited-line wholesaler may carry only a few product lines, such as tools and lighting fixtures. A *specialty-line wholesaler* usually carries a single product line, such as exotic flowers or fresh seafood. A *rack jobber* provides display units and places products on shelves. Rack jobbers serve a certain section of a store, such as bakery products, magazines, hardware, or cosmetics.

A *cooperative* is a full-service wholesaler that is owned and operated by its members. Co-ops are especially popular in the agricultural industry, where they are established by farmers to buy fertilizer in large quantities and to get better prices for their harvests than they could by selling individually. The profits earned by the co-op are divided among the members.

Limited-service wholesalers provide only a few of the services offered by wholesalers. Thus they leave some of the functions for producers or retailers to perform. *Cash-and-carry wholesalers* sell products such as construction materials to customers for cash, with customers providing transportation of the goods. *Truck wholesalers* deliver products directly to customers but offer limited services and require cash payments. They often handle perishable items

Mail order wholesalers use catalogs like the one illustrated here to sell their products.

like fresh fruit and vegetables. *Drop shippers* do not physically handle products but simply take title and negotiate sales. They commonly work in the lumber and coal industries. *Mail-order wholesalers* use catalogs to sell products such as jewelry or automobile parts to retailers and industrial customers.

Manufacturer-Owned Wholesalers. In some cases, the manufacturer owns the wholesale business. There are about 36,000 manufacturer-owned wholesalers, accounting for over 30 percent of total wholesale sales.[6] These manufacturer-owned intermediaries are either sales branches or sales offices. Except that the manufacturer owns them, **sales branches** resemble merchant wholesalers, taking title to products and reselling them. Sales branches provide services such as carrying inventory, extending credit, providing delivery, and assisting with promotion. They commonly are found in the chemical and electrical supplies industries.

Sales Branch
Manufacturer-owned wholesaler that takes title to products, assumes the risks of ownership, and provides services.

Sales Office
Manufacturer-owned sales force that sells products without maintaining an inventory.

A **sales office** is basically a sales force owned by the manufacturer. Although they do not maintain inventories, sales offices sell the manufacturer's products. Sales offices also may sell other products that complement the manufacturer's product line.

Agents and Brokers. Agents and brokers negotiate purchases for a commission but do not purchase products outright. There are fewer agents and brokers, about 42,000, than merchant wholesalers. Agents and brokers account for over 10 percent of the total sales volume of wholesalers.[7]

Agent
Wholesaler hired by a buyer or seller on a permanent basis and paid commissions.

A wholesaler hired permanently on a commission basis by a buyer or a seller is an **agent.** Agents can take possession of goods, but they do not accept legal title. By concentrating on a few products, they can provide a high level of selling effort. The major types of agents are commission merchants, manufacturers' agents, and selling agents.

A *commission merchant* receives goods from local sellers, establishes prices, and negotiates sales. For instance, in the agricultural industry, a commission merchant may take possession of a truckload of fertilizer and transport it to a central market for sale. A *manufacturers' agent* represents one or more manufacturers on a commission basis and offers noncompeting lines of products to customers. The relationship between the agent and the manufacturer is formalized by a written agreement. A *selling agent* is an independent wholesaler who sells a manufacturer's product for a commission, or fee. Manufacturers rely on selling agents to distribute canned foods, clothing, and furniture.

Broker
Wholesaler who brings together buyers and sellers on a temporary basis.

A **broker** is a wholesaler who brings together buyers and sellers on a temporary basis. Brokers are similar to agents, but they concentrate on specific commodities, such as insurance or real estate. A food broker, for example, markets food items to grocery chains, food processors, or other wholesalers. Brokers are paid a commission by the party that engages their services, such as a food manufacturer.

RETAILING

Retailing
The marketing activities involved in selling products to final consumers for personal or household use.

The side of distribution most familiar to consumers is retailing; most of us come in contact with retail stores almost daily. The marketing activity of **retailing** focuses on the sale of goods and services to the ultimate consumer for personal or household use.[8] Retailers, an essential link in the marketing channel, are often the only intermediary who deals directly with consumers. Retailers also are customers themselves, since they buy from producers and wholesalers.

Retailing is a significant part of the U.S. economy. Over 1,500,000 retailers provide a wide assortment of products to consumers and employ approximately 20 million people, with annual sales exceeding $2 trillion.[9] Many retailers, including the two largest U.S. retailers, Wal-Mart and Kmart, are also expanding globally from South and Central America to South China,

Exhibit 15.4 *Retail Sales for Major Store Types ($ in Millions)*

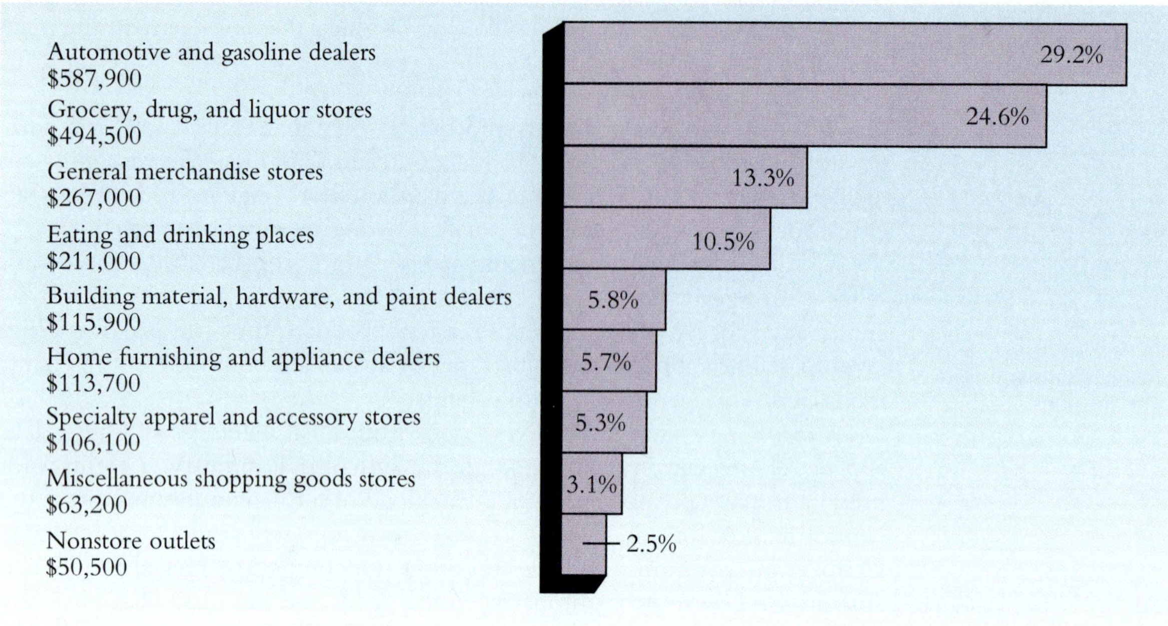

Source: *Statistical Abstract of the United States* (1994), 786.

where markets number in the billions of dollars.[10] Exhibit 15.4 shows retail sales for major store types in the United States.

Types of Retail Stores

Most retail sales take place within stores. The diverse types of retail stores include department stores, discount stores, specialty stores, supermarkets, superstores, convenience stores, warehouse showrooms, catalog showrooms, and warehouse clubs.

Department Store
A large retailer offering a wide product mix, organized into separate departments and offering a full line of service.

Department Stores. Retail stores such as Nordstrom's, Hudson's, and Macy's carry a wide variety of products. These **department stores** are organized into separate departments for such items as apparel, housewares, furniture, sporting goods, and appliances. Department stores generally offer a full line of services, including credit, delivery and personal assistance. Department stores have for a number of years lost market share to discount stores, specialty stores, and mail-order catalogs.

Discount Store
A retailer offering a wide variety of general merchandise at low prices.

Discount Stores. Stores like Wal-Mart and Target that offer general merchandise at low prices are called **discount stores.** They carry a wide assortment of products but keep services to a minimum. For example, Home Depot, the largest home-repair chain in the United States, stocks 30,000 separate items; its prices are 30 percent below those of a typical hardware store. Some discounters, like Wal-Mart, continue to grow. The retailer plans to open six stores in Argentina and five in Brazil by late 1996, Wal-Mart's first ventures in South America.[11]

Specialty Store
A retailer that offers a narrow mix of products with deep product lines.

Specialty Stores. Retailers who offer a narrow mix of products with deep product lines are called **specialty stores.** The Foot Locker, for example, offers athletic shoes, and Talbots specializes in traditional clothing and accessories for women. The Gap, specializing in selling basic apparel, tries to limit the number of styles, thereby reducing inventory and the risk of picking the wrong styles.[12]

Supermarket
A large, self-service retailer that stocks a wide variety of groceries and a limited assortment of nonfood products.

Supermarkets. Known for their large size, self-service, wide variety of food products, and limited assortment of household goods, **supermarkets** usually offer convenient locations, adequate parking, and lower prices than those at neighborhood grocery stores. Kroger, Winn-Dixie, A&P and Jewel are large supermarket chains.

Superstore
A giant retail outlet that stocks food and nonfood items as well as most products purchased on a routine basis.

Superstores and Hypermarkets. A giant retail outlet that carries food and nonfood items plus a wide assortment of other routinely purchased products is a **superstore.** With about 30,000 square feet, superstores are much larger than supermarkets (about 18,000 square feet). They emphasize low prices and one-stop shopping. After losing market share to such high-volume, low-margin, low-price stores, many supermarket chains are switching to this format.

A typical supermarket offering a wide variety of foods and household products.

An even larger retail store is the *hypermarket,* which combines the one-stop supermarket and the discount store. Hypermarkets offer more than 50,000 items, including groceries, clothing, building materials and furniture. Several retail giants such as Kmart and Wal-Mart have developed hypermarkets but with little success. The hypermarket concept has not caught on in the United States; many shoppers think they are too big and too remote.

Convenience Store
Small retail store with a convenient location and open for long hours.

Convenience Stores. Small retail stores characterized by convenient locations and long hours open for business are called **convenience stores.** Convenient Food Mart and 7-Eleven fall into this category. At convenience stores, the variety of food and nonfood items is limited, with prices generally higher than at supermarkets.

Warehouse Showroom
A retail store carrying a large inventory that deals in volume and provides limited service.

Warehouse Showrooms. Retail stores with sizeable inventories housed in large buildings, **warehouse showrooms** deal in volume and provide limited service. Warehouse showrooms commonly are operated by large furniture retailers.

Catalog Showroom
A form of warehouse showroom where customers select products from catalogs sent to customers' homes or available in the store.

Catalog Showrooms. A combination of catalog shopping and a warehouse showroom is found in the **catalog showroom.** Catalogs are sent to customers' homes and are also available in the store. Sample items are displayed in the store, with the merchandise kept in the warehouse. Customers can examine display items, then place orders with clerks. Customers are responsible for transporting their purchases. Service Merchandise, Zale, and Best Products are well-known catalog showrooms.

Warehouse Club
A large discount retail store offering members a broad range of name-brand merchandise at low prices.

Warehouse Clubs. Among the newest retail stores are **warehouse clubs,** large-scale, discount operations open to members only. Membership fees typically are around $25. These huge outlets, often located in industrial districts, carry a broad range of brand-name merchandise including appliances, tires, clothing, food, and beverages. Warehouse clubs usually sell items at 20 to 40 percent below prices at supermarkets and other discount stores. Prices are held down by keeping services to a minimum. Price-Costco and Sam's Wholesale Club are warehouse clubs. As their share of retail sales grow, and with over 600 warehouse clubs open in the United States, they are becoming the number-one challenge for conventional supermarkets. Some successful retailers have expanded and diversified by opening warehouse clubs in addition to their existing store types. For example, the discount chain Wal-Mart operates Sam's, the leading chain in the $39 billion club industry.[13]

With retailing making up a major part of the U.S. economy, business students frequently pursue careers in the retailing sector. Many Americans dream of one day owning and running their own retail store; some make it a reality. Use Your Values and Attitudes to help you assess your potential as a retailer.

Nonstore Retailing

As you know if you have ever bought merchandise from a catalog and had it delivered to your home or ordered items from a television shopping program,

Nonstore Retailing
Retailing that takes place outside of stores; includes in-store selling, direct marketing, and vending machines.

In-home Selling
Nonstore retailing activities that involve personal contacts with consumers in their homes.

not all retailing takes place within stores. **Nonstore retailing** includes in-home selling, direct marketing, and vending machines.

In-Home Selling. Personal contact with consumers in their homes is the essence of **in-home selling.** Salespeople may go door-to-door or telephone potential customers in advance and make appointments. Avon, Fuller Brush, and Encyclopedia Britannica are a few of the firms that sell products to consumers in their homes. As its traditional U.S. market has decreased, Avon has moved its door-to-door selling approach to emerging markets in China, Argentina, Poland, and Mexico, which are producing $1.3 billion in annual

YOUR VALUES AND ATTITUDES

Retail Aptitude

Directions: Circle the number that represents your level of agreement with each statement.

	Strongly Disagree					**Strongly Agree**
1. I am a self-starter who doesn't need a lot of guidance in getting the job done.	1	2	3	4	5	6
2. I wouldn't mind working long hours, even weekends, as long as I'm working for myself.	1	2	3	4	5	6
3. I like making my own decisions.	1	2	3	4	5	6
4. I would be willing to take a risk for the right opportunity.	1	2	3	4	5	6
5. I like to set my own schedule on a job—be my own boss.	1	2	3	4	5	6
6. I like to perform a variety of tasks, the small stuff as well as the most visible duties.	1	2	3	4	5	6
7. I would enjoy being a leader and managing other people.	1	2	3	4	5	6
8. The potential for a high salary is important to me.	1	2	3	4	5	6
9. I like working with the public.	1	2	3	4	5	6
10. I am willing to stick with a job for several years if that's what it takes to succeed.	1	2	3	4	5	6

Feedback: Your answers should give you some feel for your potential as a retail store owner and operator. If you circled 1 or 2 for most items, you probably have little interest in owning a retail business. If you circled 5 or 6 to most statements, you just may possess many of the characteristics and skills needed to be a successful retailer. Retailing is a demanding field with no guarantees. The hours are long, the responsibilities great, and problems with employees or customers inevitable. But owning your own retail store also can be rewarding both personally and financially.

sales.[14] Sales representatives of firms such as Tupperware or Mary Kay Cosmetics sell products at demonstrations given in homes or offices.

The newest method of in-home selling is television home shopping, which has grown into a billion-dollar industry. Televised home shopping services, such as the Home Shopping Network, are available 24 hours a day on some cable stations. They potentially can reach every home with a television and a cable hookup. In some instances, television shopping services employ as many as 400 to 500 operators in a room taking orders around the clock from a loyal following.

Direct Marketing Nonstore retailing that uses nonpersonal media to introduce products to consumers, who then purchase the products by mail, telephone, or computer.

Direct Marketing. Many firms promote products directly to buyers through a variety of techniques referred to as **direct marketing.** This type of nonstore retailing includes catalog sales, direct mail, telephone soliciting, and television or radio ads that include telephone numbers and instructions for ordering the items offered. Direct marketing is useful in reaching potential members of a target market. For example, some retailers, like JC Penney, mail catalogs directly to elderly consumers. The catalogs feature products targeted at those 65 and older, and offer services that this age group prefers, such as easy returns and toll-free telephone numbers.[15]

Direct marketing is one of the fastest growing forms of retailing, with yearly sales in excess of $200 billion. Many firms generate telephone orders for their products by advertising them on cable television and including toll-free numbers. Thousands of firms use catalogs to sell a huge variety of items. L.L. Bean and Spiegel exemplify firms that operate large mail-order businesses throughout the United States. Lands' End, a mail-order clothing company based in Wisconsin, has distinguished itself by providing services that range from helping callers determine sizes to an unconditional guarantee that customers can return any purchases. As competition among firms in the industry intensifies, catalog companies are becoming more specialized, are increasing their efficiency, and emphasizing service.[16]

Vending Machines. Candy, gum, snacks, soft drinks, coffee, newspapers, and other convenience goods are familiar items available in the self-service dispensers known as vending machines. In Japan even items like french fries and shrimp are sold in vending machines. Firms place vending machines in high-traffic areas of office and classroom buildings, service stations, and shopping malls. Vending machines offer the advantages of 24-hour-a-day operation with no sales staff. Their main drawbacks include the costs of frequent servicing and needed repairs, as well as the threat of vandalism. Vending machines account for less than two percent of all retail sales.

Retail Planning

Owners, whether individuals or large firms, must consider several factors when developing plans for a retail store. Major considerations include store location, atmosphere, scrambled merchandising, the wheel of retailing, and new technology.

Store Location. Deciding where to locate the store is critical in retailing. Retailers usually prefer a location with a high level of pedestrian traffic or easy access from main thoroughfares. Owners must evaluate the cost to buy or rent space, the availability of parking spaces, and the nature and image of the area surrounding the store site.

Retailers also need to consider the type of store best suited for their business. Retailers able to attract many customers often prefer a *free-standing store,* a building not attached to another. Because this store stands alone, a retailer locating there cannot rely on other stores to generate traffic.

In an *unplanned business district,* stores are located close to one another without any prior planning by retailers. Business districts in the downtown areas of cities are typical examples. Unplanned business districts also are located in suburbs and residential areas. Central business districts are located in the downtown areas of cities. Secondary business districts are bounded by at least two major streets. Neighborhood business districts are located in residential areas.

A third type of store location, the *planned shopping center,* is a privately developed facility consisting of numerous complementary stores. Through landscaping, parking facilities, and special events, shopping centers create an environment designed to attract a broad mix of consumers. Neighborhood shopping centers are made up of numerous small stores serving a residential district. Community shopping centers include larger department stores and specialty stores. Regional shopping centers, with several large department stores as well as specialty stores, serve consumers in a wide geographic area.

Atmosphere
The design of a store's physical space.

Atmosphere. The design of a store's physical space is called the store's **atmosphere.** Retailers try to develop an atmosphere that appeals to the target market. Waterfalls and plants in shopping centers, music playing in record stores, bright colors in toy stores, or crowded aisles in discount stores all create different atmospheres to draw customers and influence their shopping moods. Some banks have begun designing their branches with bright colors, moving stock tickers and "boutiques" that offer everything from home loans to travel services in an effort to liven up their atmosphere. Exhibit 15.5 lists the major components of a store's atmosphere.

Exhibit 15.5
Components of a Store's Atmosphere

Exterior	General Interior	Store Layout	Interior
Storefront	Flooring	Floor plan	Displays
Entrances	Colors	Product groupings	Merchandise display
Windows	Lighting	Department locations	Racks
Marquee	Fixtures		In-store advertising
Traffic	Scents		Mannequins
Store visibility	Aisle width		
Surrounding area	Dressing facilities		

Scrambled Merchandising
Adding unrelated products to a firm's existing product mix.

Scrambled Merchandising. To maintain or increase their sales volume, many retailers use **scrambled merchandising,** which involves adding unrelated products to a firm's existing product mix. Scrambling merchandising is rapidly gaining popularity. Gas stations, for instance, have added convenience items such as bread, ice, candy, and many grocery items. Many supermarkets, such as certain Kroger stores, now offer pharmacies, floral departments, bank branches, insurance, and photo processing.

Wheel of Retailing
The idea that retailers enter the market as low-priced, low-status businesses, evolve into high-cost establishments, and become vulnerable to new competitors entering the market.

The Wheel of Retailing. As they strive to succeed, retailers face constant changes as new stores replace established ones. A popular explanation for how retail stores originate and develop is called the **wheel of retailing,** illustrated in Exhibit 15.6. This theoretical depiction suggests that a retail business enters the market as a low-priced, low-profit, low-status store. Gradually it moves up by improving facilities and adding new services, thus increasing business costs. Over time it becomes a high-cost establishment that is vulnerable to new competitors entering the market—and the wheel turns.

The wheel of retailing can be illustrated by off-price retail chains such as T.J. Maxx and Clothestime. They attract customers by offering brand-name merchandise discounted as much as 60 percent below department store prices. In the past, the outlets were plain and offered limited services. Spurred by weak performance, department stores began to discount their prices up to 50 percent and started taking business from the off-price stores. Now some off-price retailers are imitating department stores—redesigning stores to be more

Exhibit 15.6
The Wheel of Retailing

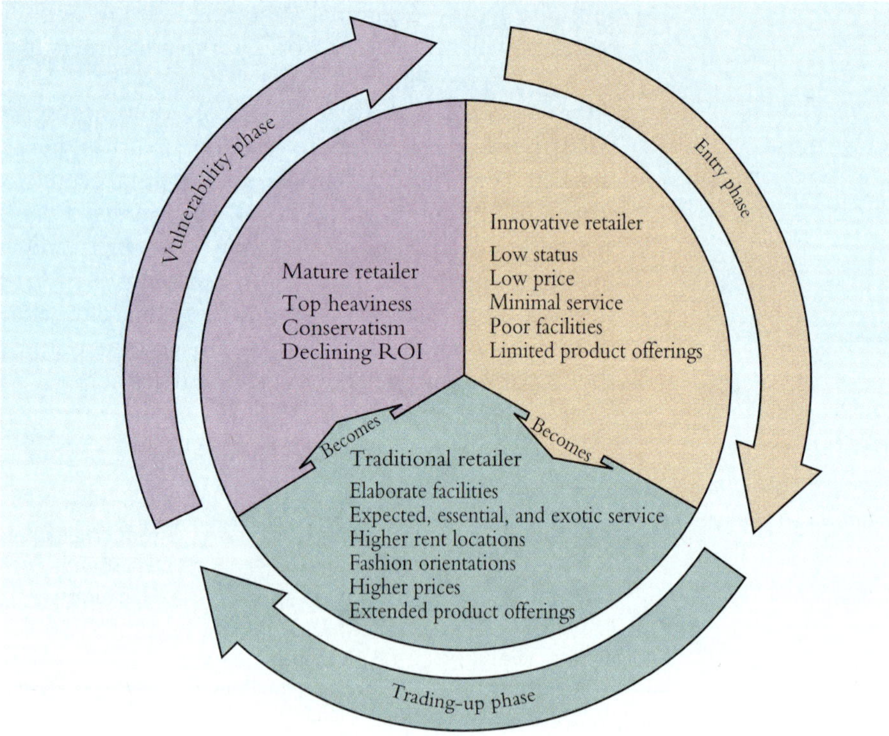

Source: Lewiston, Dale M. *Retailing*, 5e, © 1994, p. 94. Reprinted by permission of Prentice Hall, Upper Saddle River, New Jersey.

attractive, conducting advertising campaigns that emphasize quality, and promoting specific products rather than focusing on discount prices.

Technology. Recent advances in technology also have affected retailing. Cable television and video ordering systems are changing the retail environment. Anti-shoplifting tags attached to merchandise reduce thefts. Computerized checking systems speed up check-outs, reduce cashier errors, and provide valuable data for inventory planning. New developments in computerized site selection programs enable firms to make better location decisions. Such technological advances help retailers improve efficiency, reduce labor costs, minimize losses, and obtain accurate and timely information.

TOMORROW'S BUSINESS WORLD

High-Tech Retailers Dominate the Industry

The nature of retailing has changed significantly and will continue to change in the years ahead. The retail recession of 1989 to 1991 was a major hurdle through which the industry passed on the way to a new retailing environment. During that period, the industry witnessed an unprecedented number of bankruptcies. Retail sales in the 1990s will grow slowly, people will shop less, and shoppers will be more purposeful and thus more destination-oriented than during the 1980s. Consumers will be more value-conscious and less status-conscious. They will be more loyal to specific stores. Successful stores will be more attentive to their target customers. A substantial competitive advantage will go to those retailers with the resources and savvy to invest in technology. In short, a small number of large, technologically sophisticated firms are likely to dominate the industry.

The general trends taking place in the United States include the following:

- Competition will remain extremely strong and opportunities for expansion will be much reduced compared with those in the 1980s.
- There will be less growth in retail spending.
- Expansion opportunities will lie in acquisitions and mergers, the increasing diversity of the American consumer, and specific growth areas such as Florida and Washington state.
- There will be less innovation in terms of new store types and concepts.
- Innovation will focus on improving the profitability of existing stores, shopping stores, shopping centers, and distribution systems.
- The focus on existing stores and shopping centers will take two major forms—the application of information technology and systems to achieve greater efficiency and to cut costs, and smarter store-level marketing, employing electronic point-of-sale systems and consumer research.
- More retailers will rely on outsourcing—contracting with other firms outside of the company—for a variety of technology functions, including operations systems. Technology will also be used to improve customer service by identifying merchandise that is on sale and by determining product availability from the warehouse or another store.
- Strong systems will enable retailers to improve customer service by reducing transaction time, enhancing inventory replenishment, and freeing employees to concentrate on the needs of customers rather than on paperwork. Technology will also allow stores to reduce costs, improve distribution efficiency, and engage in *micromarketing*—satisfying the needs of a diverse customer base.

• Retailers are also expected to add more store brands, which are already resulting in higher margins, attracting an increasing number of consumers, and providing a way for stores to differentiate themselves from competitors.

Source: Adapted from "Retailers Hungry for Store Brands," *Advertising Age* (January 11, 1993): 20; "Technology Trends in Retail: An Executive Overview," *Chain Store Age Executive* (October 1992): 6–10; Ira Kalish, "After the Dust Settles: Retailing in the 1990s," *Chain Store Age Executive* (August 1992): 10A–12A; and David Rogers, "An Overview of American Retail Trends," *International Journal of Retail & Distribution Management* (1991): 3–12.

PHYSICAL DISTRIBUTION

Physical Distribution Those activities that involve the movement of products through marketing channels from manufacturer to consumer.

Physical distribution includes the activities that enable the movement of products through marketing channels from manufacturer to customer. Physical distribution activities, which are essential marketing functions providing customers with the goods they want, where and when they want them, include establishing customer service standards, selecting transportation modes, designing and operating warehouse facilities, handling products, and managing inventory. These activities are becoming more critical than ever in this era of total quality management; goods that move are better than goods that sit, and constantly moving goods have become a competitive advantage for modern firms.[17] These activities are strongly interrelated. For instance, a modern warehouse facility may reduce handling costs. However, if it is not properly located, it can increase transportation costs. Firms thus need to plan and integrate their physical distribution activities.

Service Standard A specific, measurable goal relating to physical distribution activities.

Physical distribution begins with a consideration of customers' needs. Improving customer service is a major priority. Some marketers examine the activities performed by competing firms and develop service standards that meet or exceed those of competitors. **Service standards** are specific, measurable goals relating to physical distribution activities. Because on-time delivery is important to customers, for example, a company may set a service standard to "deliver all orders within 24 hours." When a firm such as Federal Express guarantees overnight delivery, it must develop physical distribution activities that will achieve this service standard. Federal Express transports packages via airplane in most cases, since shipping by truck or railroad could not meet the overnight deadline.

Transportation

Transportation Shipping goods to customers by railways, airlines, trucks, waterways, and pipelines.

Transportation, shipping goods to customers, is a critical physical distribution activity. To ship goods, firms generally choose one of the five major modes of transportation: rail, air, truck, water, and pipeline. Firms that transport products, through any means, are called *carriers*.

When selecting a transportation mode for products, marketing managers look at important factors such as cost, delivery speed, number of locations served, reliability, range of products carried, loss and damage records, and fuel efficiency. Exhibit 15.7 ranks the different transportation modes according to these factors. Exhibit 15.8 compares the share of shipping mileage and shipping revenue for each transportation mode.

Rail. Railroads carry about 37 percent of all products and account for 10 percent of shipping revenue. Railroads are fairly cost and fuel efficient and can reach a large number of locations. A wide range of products such as coal, grain, chemicals, lumber, and automobiles can be transported by rail.

Exhibit 15.7
Ranking the Transportation Modes

	1*	2	3	4	5
Lowest Cost	Water	Pipeline	Rail	Truck	Air
Delivery Speed	Air	Truck	Rail	Water	Pipeline
Number of Locations Served	Truck	Rail	Air	Water	Pipeline
Dependability	Pipeline	Truck	Air	Rail	Water
Range of Products Carried	Rail	Truck	Water	Air	Pipeline
Losses and Damages	Pipeline	Water	Air	Truck	Rail
Fuel Efficiency	Pipeline	Water	Rail	Truck	Air

* 1 = highest ranking

Source: Donald J. Bowersax, David J. Closs, and Omar K. Helferich, *Logistical Management*, 3e (New York: Macmillan, 1986), 166; and Carl M. Guelzo, *Introduction to Logistics Management* (Englewood Cliffs, NJ: Prentice-Hall, 1986), 46.

Exhibit 15.8
Shipping Mileage and Revenue of Transportation Modes

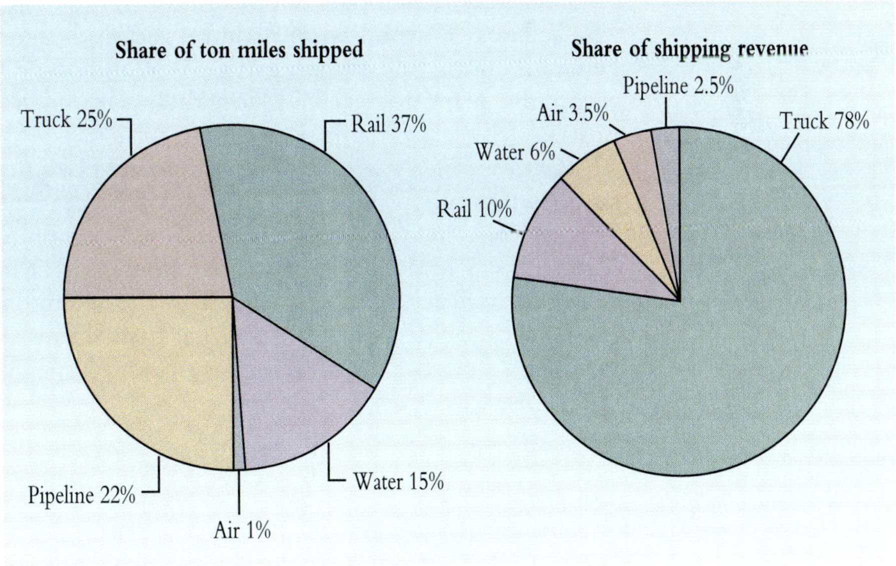

Source: *Statistical Abstract of the United States* (1994): 627.

Air. Air transport, the most expensive means of transportation, accounts for only 1 percent of all products transported. Yet the use of air transit is growing rapidly. The need to deliver some items quickly, such as fresh flowers, perishable foods, technical instruments, and emergency parts, justifies the high cost.

Trucks. Trucking dominates the transportation industry, with a 78 percent share of shipping revenue. Although trucks account for only a 25 percent share of ton miles shipped, they often carry the most profitable products, such as clothing, paper goods, computers, fresh fruit and vegetables, and livestock. Trucks are the most flexible mode of transportation. They can travel anywhere there are roads and can provide door-to-door service.

Water. Barges and cargo ships are the least costly means of transportation; they also are among the slowest and least dependable. Another limitation is, of course, that only cities with ports can be served. In spite of these drawbacks, water transport accounts for about 15 percent of ton miles shipped. Products commonly transported on waterways include petroleum, chemicals, and iron ore.

Pipeline. The major products shipped via pipelines are oil, processed coal, and natural gas. Pipelines have increased in importance as the demand for oil and natural gas has increased. Pipelines account for 22 percent of ton miles shipped and 2.5 percent of shipping revenues.

Warehousing

Warehousing
The physical distribution activities involved in receiving, storing, and shipping goods.

Another important aspect of distribution is the design and operation of storage facilities. **Warehousing** includes various responsibilities involved in receiving, storing and shipping goods. Warehouses accept delivered goods, record the quantities received, store them, coordinate shipments, and dispatch orders.

Private warehouses are owned and operated by firms who wish to distribute their own products. Usually they are companies that carry large inventories. For example, Spec's Music, a Miami-based firm with music and video outlets throughout Florida, has its own warehouses. It carries huge inventories and can quickly process orders and deliver fast-selling items to the stores. *Public warehouses* provide storage on a rental basis. Firms that do not wish to own warehouses or that need extra space on a temporary basis often use public warehouses.

Order Processing

Order Processing
The receipt and preparation of an order for shipment.

Order processing refers to the receipt and preparation of an order for shipment. Efficient order processing procedures can reduce the time needed for delivery and thus help firms satisfy their customers.

Processing begins when a customer places an order by mail, telephone, or computer. Typically the order is forwarded to the warehouse and the credit department. Clerks can fill an order quickly if the item is in stock and the customer's credit rating is approved. For items not in stock, an order is placed at the factory. Finally, the product is packaged and shipped.

Materials Handling

Materials Handling
The physical handling of products during transportation and warehousing.

The physical handling of a product during transportation and while it is in the warehouse is termed **materials handling.** Firms institute materials handling procedures that make maximum use of warehouse space, minimize the number of times a product is handled, and reduce damage to merchandise.

The use of containerization and freight forwarders has improved the ability of organizations to handle materials. *Containerization* is packing goods within a strong container that is easy to transfer between train, truck, ship, and airplane. Containerization reduces damage, theft, insurance costs and materials handling time, thereby reducing the cost of distribution. *Freight forwarders* combine small shipments from several firms. They arrange for the merchandise to be picked up from the shipper and delivered to the buyer.

Inventory Management

Inventory Management
The process of developing and maintaining stocks of products that customers need and want.

Inventory management is the process of developing and maintaining products that are in demand by customers. Efficient inventory management, an important aspect of physical distribution, can help a firm achieve its profit goals. A business should design its inventory system so that the number of products sold and the number of products in stock can be determined at specified checkpoints. One method could involve tearing off a code number from each product sold so that the correct sizes, colors, and models can be tabulated and reordered. In many larger stores, such as Toys "Я" Us and Wal-Mart, checkout terminals or cash registers are connected to central computer systems to allow instantaneous updating of inventory and sales records.

Good inventory management balances the cost of holding a large inventory with the cost of losing sales because of shortages, or stock-outs, of certain products. One inventory management technique used to achieve this balance is *just-in-time (JIT) inventory,* popularized in Japan. Companies using JIT maintain smaller inventories by ordering more often and in smaller quantities, just in time for production. The results, when JIT is used properly, include better-quality products, quicker production time, and reduced operating costs, all of which increase competitiveness.

Distributing Services

Service firms are generally limited in their channels of distribution since services are produced and consumed at the same time and the customer is present to initiate the contact. Through employees, service providers usually perform services directly for customers with no use of intermediaries. Health care professionals at clinics, for instance, perform physical examinations and medical tests for clients.

Distribution can separate a service from the seller, however. Bank credit cards allow the intangible service of credit to be separated from the financial institution. Through bank credit cards, organizations such as restaurants, gas stations, retailers, supermarkets, and even fast food outlets can distribute credit to consumers. Some service businesses have developed innovative methods of distribution. The communications industry offers cellular phones for cars, insurance companies sell policies through vending machines at airports, entertainment firms sell tickets to concerts through computers in stores, and banks allow customers to have paychecks deposited directly in accounts and to pay bills by automatic withdrawal.

SUMMARY OF LEARNING OBJECTIVES

1. ***Define the term* marketing channel *and identify the two major types of marketing intermediaries.*** A marketing channel is a group of interrelated organizations that directs the flow of goods from producer to consumer. Marketing intermediaries, organizations that provide the link between producers and consumers, are vital because they create place, time, and possession utility. The major types of intermediaries are *wholesalers* and *retailers*.

2. ***Explain how marketing channels are integrated vertically.*** Vertical integration occurs when one organization takes control of another member of the marketing channel, often by purchasing it. Distribution efficiency may be improved with a vertical marketing system (VMS), a planned marketing channel in which one channel member manages all intermediaries. The three types of vertical marketing systems are corporate, administered, and contractual.

3. ***Define* wholesaling *and describe the functions wholesalers perform.*** Wholesaling consists of the activities of marketing intermediaries who sell to retailers, other wholesalers, or industrial users. Wholesalers provide several services, including ownership, financing, risk assumption, promotional assistance, information, product assortment, and transportation. The major types of wholesalers are merchant wholesalers, manufacturer-owned wholesalers, and agents and brokers.

4. ***Define* retailing *and outline the activities retailers perform.*** Retailing activities consist of the sales of goods and services to consumers for personal or household use. Retailing activities can take place in stores or through the nonstore retailing methods of in-home selling, direct marketing, and vending machines.

5. ***Discuss the major considerations in retail planning.*** Retail planning, crucial to success in the retail sector, involves several important considerations. Store *location* is a critical decision since it influences shopper traffic. The *atmosphere,* or design of the store's physical space, must be appealing to the target market. Retailers also must decide whether or not to use *scrambled merchandising,* which means adding unrelated products to a store's existing mix. Another consideration is the *wheel of retailing,* which suggests that new stores constantly emerge to replace established stores. Recent advancements in *technology* also have an impact on retail planning.

6. ***Explain the role of physical distribution and identify its components.*** Physical distribution activities accomplish the physical movement of products through marketing channels from manufacturer to customer. Physical distribution activities include establishing customer service standards, selecting transportation modes, designing and operating warehouse facilities, handling products, and managing inventory.

KEY TERMS

Marketing Channel (Channel of Distribution)
Marketing Intermediary
Vertical Integration
Vertical Marketing System (VMS)
Corporate VMS
Administered VMS
Contractual VMS
Market Coverage
Intensive Distribution
Selective Distribution
Exclusive Distribution
Wholesaling
Merchant Wholesaler
Sales Branch
Sales Office
Agent
Broker
Retailing
Department Store
Discount Store
Specialty Store
Supermarket
Superstore
Convenience Store
Warehouse Showroom
Catalog Showroom
Warehouse Club
Nonstore Retailing
In-Home Selling
Direct Marketing
Atmosphere
Scrambled Merchandising
Wheel of Retailing
Physical Distribution
Service Standard
Transportation
Warehousing
Order Processing
Materials Handling
Inventory Management

QUESTIONS FOR DISCUSSION AND REVIEW

1. Is it possible—or desirable—to eliminate the intermediary in the distribution of goods to consumers? Explain your answer.
2. What types of marketing channels are used to distribute consumer products? To distribute industrial products?
3. Have you ever purchased a product directly from a producer (channel A)? Name some products that manufacturers or producers sell directly to consumers.
4. Distinguish between intensive, selective, and exclusive distribution. Give examples of products distributed by each method.
5. Wholesalers perform a variety of services in product distribution. What are those services? Whom do they benefit?
6. How do full-service wholesalers and limited-service wholesalers differ? Give two examples of each type.
7. Give some examples of instances when you've made purchases through nonstore retailing. What advantages does nonstore retailing offer sellers? Buyers?
8. Choose one of your favorite retail stores and describe its atmosphere. Why is store atmosphere important in retail planning?
9. What can the wheel of retailing teach someone who is starting a retail business?
10. List the various forms of transportation and the advantages and disadvantages of each.

CASE 15.1

Kmart Tries to Get Back on Track

Kmart, the pioneer discount retailer that experienced rapid growth in the 1970s, seems to have lost its momentum. The price of its stock has fallen, earnings are flat, and sales growth is slow. Trouble comes from stiff competition from Wal-Mart and newer retail outlets, changes in consumer buying habits, the chain's image, and its dated distribution system. Marketing expert Joseph E. Antonini, Kmart CEO since 1987, had been leading the drive to get the giant company back on track.

To compete with the increasingly popular specialty retailers that offer a huge selection of merchandise in one or two categories, Kmart developed Builders Square and purchased OfficeMax and Sports Authority. To ward off the threat from hypermarkets and warehouse clubs, which force down the usual profit margins of discount stores, Kmart started American Fare (an Atlanta hypermarket) and purchased Pace Membership Warehouse Inc. Pace has since gone out of business, with most of the stores sold to Wal-Mart's Sam's Clubs.

But these specialty retailers were not the answer to Kmart's problems. Management had to improve the 2,300 core Kmart stores, which produce 80 percent of the firm's sales. Antonini was strongly pressured to sell some of these specialty stores and focus on the slumping core discount business. An important first step was to upgrade merchandise and image. Even in discount stores, shoppers increasingly want quality. So stores like Kmart and Wal-Mart need to keep a delicate balance between convincing customers that prices are low and making people feel the stores are too cheap.

Experts say Wal-Mart excels at attending to the details that influence shopper's attitudes. Some say Wal-Mart's simple logo in white letters on a brown background conveys a warm, inviting message, which is carried further by the greeters inside the stores. Kmart followed suit by changing its logo and placing employees near the door to answer questions. Its highly recognizable logo of bright red "K" and cool turquoise "mart" grabbed attention and signaled low prices but gave the impression the store hadn't changed in decades. So Kmart adopted a simpler logo with red letters on a gray background.

Antonini hired actress Jaclyn Smith and decorator Martha Stewart to design and promote better-quality apparel and housewares and professional golfer Fuzzy Zoeller to promote sporting goods. The heavily advertised Martha Stewart promotion has been especially successful, but almost one-third of Kmart's stores were too small to carry the housewares line properly. Antonini earmarked $1.3 billion to enlarge and remodel 700 of the company's oldest outlets to feature wider aisles, bolder displays, and taller, deeper shelves. The roomy new design will make items available where customers can get them instead of in the stockroom.

Kmart officials also lowered prices on 8,000 items to be more competitive. But lowering prices reduced Kmart's profit margins and made some goods, such as health and beauty aids, so popular that the chain's distribution system couldn't keep them in stock. A flawed distribution system hampered Kmart outlets. Even when inventory was piled high in warehouses, stores were not always able to keep popular items on the shelves—a serious failing that can lose customers. In response, Kmart installed a $1 billion computer system that monitors store sales and automatically reorders fast-selling merchandise. Antonini expected the computer system—similar to Wal-Mart's—to greatly improve Kmart's distribution.

Kmart raised cash by selling majority shares in its specialty businesses OfficeMax, Borders-Walden bookstores, and Sports Authority. But problems continue, as the retailer reported its eighth consecutive quarter of lower earnings in early 1995. Under pressure from large institutional investors, Kmart's board of directors forced Antonini to resign in March 1995.

Kmart has had other distribution problems. Like those of many other U.S. retailers, the giant discounter's dealings with suppliers have often resulted in misunderstanding and mistrust between the two parties. For example, when vendors called on Kmart buyers, the buyers would make demands about delivery dates, advertising assistance, or buying back unsold merchandise. The result was that the buyer and seller could not agree on the true cost of the goods. In contrast, some U.S. retailers (including Wal-Mart) are now trying to be more straightforward and cooperative with vendors. Their buyers go to a manufacturer with specifications, quantities, and shipment dates; payment is made when the manufacturer ships the goods.

Questions for Discussion

1. What type of retailer is Kmart? What types of retailers are its major competitors?
2. What are some factors that contributed to Kmart's decline in sales, growth and profit?
3. What is Kmart's strategy to regain its market position?

Source: Adapted from Christina Duff and Bob Ortega, "Loss Leader: How Wal-Mart Outdid a Once-Touted Kmart in Discount-Store Race," *The Wall Street Journal* (March 24, 1995): A1, A4; Avid Woodruff and Judith H. Dobrzynski, "Revolt? What Revolt?" *Business Week* (June 20, 1994): 42; and Leah Rickard, "Kmart Sacrificing Specialty Lambs," *Advertising Age* (August 22, 1994): 4.

CASE 15.2

Luxottica Group SpA of Italy

Luxottica Group SpA of Italy is the world's largest maker and distributor of eyeglass frames. It sells more than 12 million pairs of frames a year, with nearly half bought by consumers in the United States.

Luxottica emphasizes middle- and upper-end frames costing $70 or more and controls such expensive designer eyewear labels as Giorgio Armani, Yves St. Laurent, and Byblos. Fashion frames, costing $170 and up, represent 38 percent of Luxottica's sales—up from zero in 1987.

In the United States, Luxottica sells its frames through 28,000 retailers—national eyewear chains such as LensCrafters and Pearle Vision Centers as well as small optical shops. The company's nondesigner frames, available in hundreds of styles and retailing for $40 to $120 a pair, are sold through Wal-Mart's eyeglass centers. The lower-priced frames make up about 70 percent of Luxottica's revenues.

Italy's largest manufacturer, marketer, and distributor of eyeglass frames had simple beginnings. The firm is headquartered in the small town of Agordo in the Dolomite Alps of northern Italy. Founder and chairman Leonardo Del Vecchio, Italy's top individual taxpayer, was sent at age 7 to an orphanage by his widowed mother who could not support her five children during World War II. He worked his way through design school as an apprentice in a factory that made tooling and molds for such products as automobile logos, jewelry, and eyeglass frames. In 1958 at age 23, Del Vecchio used his savings to open a shop in Milan to make molds for plastic eyeglass frames and bridges and other metal parts. In 1961, with financial backing from two major customers, he moved his shop to Agordo and started Luxottica. In 1969 Del Vecchio began making eyeglass frames under his own brand and a year later bought out his partners. A skilled craftsman, he realized that vertical integration in his industry could bring considerable profit. He says, "For ten years I sold parts. One day I said, 'I'm stupid. I'm sending parts to manufacturers. Why don't I industrialize this?'"

Del Vecchio therefore set to work eliminating intermediaries in production. Now besides making frames, Luxottica designs its own machinery and makes its own tools, which gives it a three- to six-month lead time over competitors. The company spends between $10 and $15 million a year on new machinery and another $3.5 million a year on research and development in such fields as plastics compounding and basic chemistry. Computers speed frame design and manufacture and help the company take designs from concept to market in 60 days. To take advantage of new trends in the fashion industry, Luxottica designers add more than a hundred new frame styles each year. The company's offerings of plastic and metal frames include about 700 styles.

Luxottica's integrated manufacturing lowered costs and increased quality. But it was the company's distributors who greatly benefited from the increased efficiency, since they controlled pricing to retailers. During the 1980s Del Vecchio began buying out distributors.

Luxottica owns distributors in Germany and Canada and has a stake in all of its international distributors. To keep his company growing, Del Vecchio formed a joint venture with Japanese eyewear maker Charmant to distribute frames in Japan. Unlike most of its competitors, Luxottica owns its U.S. distributor. This strong distribution system enables the Italian manufacturer to provide excellent service to all customers, not only the large chains but also opticians. Luxottica fills orders overnight, and in some cases within two hours. Delivery time, formerly days or weeks, was reduced after the company reorganized its U.S. sales staff and started equipping retail customers with computer software that checks Luxottica stock and places orders. Service has helped build strong loyalty among opticians, who rarely carry much inventory, and a good reputation among large customers.

Luxottica's competitive edges have meant phenomenal growth and profitability in recent years. The company reported 1994 sales of $504 million. It is considered one of the better-performing growth stocks on the New York Stock Exchange. The company's profit margin is 13 percent on a worldwide net revenue of $44 million. To illustrate just how good that figure is, rival Safilo Group, which markets the Ralph Lauren Polo eyewear line, earns 8 percent on revenues of $197 million.

Although manufacturing and distributing to its many customers remains very profitable, Luxottica has decided to also move directly into retail sales of eyewear. It reached an agreement in April 1995 to purchase U.S. Shoe Corp. which owns LensCrafters. (U.S. Shoe's footwear and apparel divisions will be sold off.) Del Vecchio wants to increase sales of high-fashion eyewear in the United States and feels that retail chains like LensCrafters, which offer large selection and fast service, are the future of eyewear retailing. LensCrafters will also give Luxottica an outlet for sales of sunglasses, a product Del Vecchio identifies with future growth.

Questions for Discussion

1. What gives Luxottica such a competitive edge over rivals?
2. Which marketing channel is used to distribute Luxottica frames to consumers?
3. Describe the distribution intensity of Luxottica products.
4. Would Luxottica's vertical integration give it an advantage or disadvantage in managing channel relationships?

Source: Adapted from Maureen Kline, "Italy's Luxottica Seeks Footing in Retail Eyewear Market," *The Wall Street Journal* (April 18, 1995): B4; Bill Saporito, "Cutting Out the Middleman," *Fortune* (April 6, 1992): 96; Gene Marcial, "Italian Eyeglasses the U.S. Loves," *Business Week* (May 12, 1992): 91.

BUSINESS APPLICATION

From the Chicken House to the Dairy Aisle

Chuck Jennings has been the owner and operator of a chicken farm in rural Florida for the past eight years. He inherited the farm from his father and has worked in the chicken and egg business for many years. The vast majority of the income generated by the chicken farm comes from the sale of eggs to various intermediaries. The remaining income comes from the sale of the chickens themselves.

Jennings has been examining options for expanding the business and is considering the possibility of performing some of the intermediary or middleman functions. He thinks he may be able to increase his company's overall profits from egg sales by providing transportation of the eggs from the farm to supermarkets and convenience stores. Jennings has started making a list of tasks he will have to do in order to assume the role of middleman.

Questions:

1. What are five things Chuck Jennings must be able to do in order to expand into the middleman role?
2. What are some of the risks that might be associated with such a change?
3. If he decides to assume the middleman role, how might the company gradually phase in the expansion?

EXPERIENTIAL EXERCISE

Channels for Organizational Markets

Marketing channels for organizational markets are not readily visible to consumers. To learn more about the channels that organizational buyers use to obtain products, choose a firm located near you and find out some of the main products it uses. (You could choose your college or university and select some of the products that it purchases.)

Contact a purchasing agent for the organization. Ask him or her to outline the marketing channels through which the products flow and to name all the intermediaries, from the producer to the buyer's organization.

NOTES

1. Adapted from Gary McWilliams, "At Compaq, a Desktop Crystal Ball," *Business Week* (March 20, 1995): 91–97; Stephanie Losee, "How Compaq Keeps the Magic Going," *Fortune,* (February 21, 1994): 90–92; Peter Burrows, "Compaq: Ready to Rumble," *Business Week* (August 22, 1994): 29; Peter Burrows, "Compaq: Turning the Tables on Dell?" *Business Week* (March 27, 1993): 87.
2. Louis W. Stern and Adel I. El-Ansary, *Marketing Channels,* 3e (Englewood Cliffs, NJ: Prentice-Hall, 1988), 3.
3. Peter Burrows, "The Computer Is in the Mail (Really)," *Business Week* (January 23, 1995): 76–77.
4. *Statistical Abstract of the United States,* (1992), 771.
5. *Census of Wholesale Trade,* (1987), 1–3.
6. Ibid.
7. Ibid.
8. J. Barry Mason and Morris L. Mayer, *Modern Retailing: Theory and Practice,* 5e (Homewood, IL: Irwin, Inc., 1991), 5.
9. *Statistical Abstract of the United States,* (1992), 396, 760.
10. Carla Rapoport and Justin Martin, "Retailers Go Global," *Fortune* (February 20, 1995): 102–108.
11. Mike Galetto, "Wal-Mart Sustains L. America Push," *Advertising Age* (March 20, 1995): 25.
12. Russell Mitchell, "The Gap Dolls Itself Up," *Business Week* (March 21, 1994): 46.
13. Wendy Zellner, "Why Sam's Wants Businesses to Join the Club," *Business Week* (June 27, 1994): 48–53.
14. Veronica Byrd and Wendy Zellner, "The Avon Lady of the Amazon," *Business Week* (October 24, 1994): 93–96.
15. Helen Mundell, "Direct Marketers Discover the Elderly," *American Demographics* (June 1994): 18–26.
16. Julie Tilsner, "Strategies for the New Mail Order," *Business Week* (December 19, 1994): 82–85.
17. Ronald Henkoff, "Delivering the Goods," *Fortune* (November 28, 1994): 64–78.

CHAPTER 16

Promotion

1. Explain the role of promotion in marketing and list five promotional objectives.
2. Describe the major types of advertising and the purpose of each.
3. List the steps involved in planning an advertising campaign.
4. Differentiate among the three types of salespeople and their functions.
5. Outline the personal selling process and describe each step.
6. Explain the purpose of sales promotion and list common activities of consumer sales promotion and trade sales promotion.
7. Describe how firms use publicity.
8. Identify factors that influence a firm's promotion mix.

On the ski slopes of the United States, business has been flat for more than a decade. Since 1980, 25 percent of U.S. ski resorts have closed. The industry's annual growth, 15 percent at its peak, is now about 3 percent. Vermont's Sugarbush Resort, for example, attracts 300,000 skiers a season, down from 425,000 a decade ago. What happened? Single, free-spending skiers of the baby boom generation married, had children, and started using their disposable income toward a home and kids instead of expensive vacations. The recession and large number of layoffs in the early 1990s also took a tool on travel. Now the U.S. resorts are trying to get old skiers back and attract new ones with promotion marketing to specific niches—children, oldsters, families, Europeans.

Hoping to get children hooked on skiing—and parents skiing longer—some resorts are remaking themselves as family destinations. Ski resorts think families are worth going after. A survey by a Boulder, CO, research firm showed that from 1991 to 1992 there was a 12 percent increase in the number of skiers who usually ski with family members. The number of children who ski has increased 18 percent since 1987, according to the United Ski Industries Association. Ski schools throughout the United States have experienced great demand for children's classes.

Ski resorts are adding family entertainment and designating certain slopes where fast and reckless skiers are not welcome. Ski instructors are taking courses on how to teach children, and people trained in child psychology are managing children's centers at resorts. Vail and Beaver Creek in Colorado built children's ski areas—resembling Indian villages and mining towns. Breckenridge Spa made its Kids' Castle four times larger. Alpine Meadows in California is doubling the space in its two children's centers. Snowmass in Colorado emphasizes its ski in/ski out lodging, which means easy access to the slopes for skiers with children. This feature helped Snowmass earn the rating of number one family resort by two ski magazines in 1992.

Smuggler's Notch Resort, in Burlington, VT, promotes itself as a prime family spot. Its "Family Club Smuggler's Ski Week" package includes lodging, lift tickets, ski lessons, cross-country skiing, parties, ice skating, swimming, and tennis. For very small children, the resort has a petting zoo, a sliding hill, and a playground. Smuggler's offers nighttime sledding, family games each evening until 9 P.M., and a weekly torchlight parade and fireworks. Teenagers have a large influence over where a family goes to ski, so the resort provides pizza parties, snow soccer, volleyball tournaments, and dances. Parents can enjoy nightly entertainment after 9 P.M., plus the weekly Parents' Night Out, when children get dinner, do crafts, and watch a movie until 10 P.M.

Catering to families has its drawbacks, however. First, there is the perception of having less challenging slopes. Although the resorts have tried to change that image, some hard-core skiers avoid any place that calls itself a family spot. Second is the problem of cost: Ski vacations are very expensive. To keep families coming, nearly all resorts offer discount lift tickets for children; some, including Purgatory/Durango in southwest Colorado, let them ski free when they are with a paying adult.

Other resorts are looking abroad for new skiers. For several years, Breckenridge Spa, an upscale lodge in Colorado, has been targeting foreign skiers, especially the British, who provide 40 percent of its revenue. The spa provides a currency exchange, British newspapers, and an afternoon tea with cucumber sandwiches and scones. Breckenridge executives find that compared with Americans, foreign visitors tend to stay two weeks rather than one and spend nearly twice as much—about $250 a day rather than $150. The resort hopes to increase its foreign business from the current 8 percent to 10 percent. Breckenridge has joined with Keystone, Copper Mountain, Arapahoe Basin, and other resorts to form a marketing consortium called Ski the Summit. The consortium began promoting to foreign skiers a few years ago. U.S. resorts also are working to lure Japanese skiers. Hunter Mountain in New York offers a hillside sushi bar; Park City, UT, has trail signs in Japanese.

Some industry experts question the long-term value of flashy promotional activities that may bring only one-time visitors to the slope. Many ski resort marketers are trying to design their promotional mixes to keep customers coming back. At Sunday River Skiway in Bethel, ME, President Leslie B. Otten conducts simple promotional programs with a clear aim: to turn first-time customers into lifetime buyers. Service begins in the parking lot, where attendants hand out maps and direct newcomers to an orientation center. For $33 a lesson, first-time skiers receive two hours on the slopes with an instructor plus free use of skis, poles, and boots ($18 otherwise), a free lift ticket (worth $33), and the chance to sign up for two more lessons at the same rate. Students who complete three lessons get a coupon for a fourth day of free skiing. They also can buy poles, skis, and boots at the resort's cost.

Sunday River's learn-to-ski program doesn't make any money, but it does bring skiers back. Before the promotion started in 1985, only 20 percent of the resort's first-time visitors returned. Now more than 75 percent do. Gross revenues have increased from $6 million to $18.3 million. "We want to stay on the top of people's minds," Otten says. "When we started here (in 1980) we tried to grow by stealing customers from other ski slopes by featuring lower prices, longer hours, or more services. That works for a while, but this is better."[1]

Why are ski resorts catering to families? Do you think promotional activities are useful to these resorts?

Promotion
The communication of favorable, persuasive information about a firm or product in order to influence potential buyers.

The communication of positive, persuasive information about an organization or its products with the intent of directly or indirectly influencing exchanges is called **promotion.**[2] As the opening example illustrates, firms use a variety of promotional methods to communicate favorable messages to consumers or other audiences. Promotional messages can inform consumers about organizations and products and influence them to make a purchase or adopt a special cause or belief.

In this chapter, we discuss the role of promotion and promotional objectives and introduce the concept of promotion mix. Next we discuss several types of advertising, major advertising media, and advertising campaign planning. Then we discuss personal selling, the roles of salespeople, and the personal selling process. We explain the use of sales promotion and various sales promotion activities. We provide an overview of publicity. Finally we describe the strategies and other factors that go into promotion planning.

THE ROLE OF PROMOTION

The fourth element in the marketing mix, promotion, supports product, pricing, and distribution decisions. It is critical to the success of any firm. Before deciding what type of promotional program to conduct, a firm needs to establish its objectives.

Promotional Objectives

Firms set promotional objectives that will help meet their broader marketing and organizational objectives. Promotional programs can be built around a single objective or multiple objectives.

Informing. The basic objective underlying all promotion is providing information. Firms want to tell potential customers about themselves as well as what products are available, where they can be purchased, and for what price. A new restaurant, for example, may advertise in local newspapers or magazines and on radio and television stations, distribute coupons in the mail, invite the newspaper restaurant critic to review and publicize it, rent billboards, and buy a listing in the telephone directory.

Increasing Sales. Aside from providing information, encouraging prospective customers to purchase products is the most common promotional objective, since sales mean survival and success for firms. Using advertisements, coupons, and other promotional methods, firms attempt to persuade customers to try new products, remind them of the benefits of products that have been on the market awhile, and reinforce their choice of particular brands.

Stabilizing Sales. Firms also rely on promotional activities to reduce or eliminate substantial variations in demand throughout the year. Companies marketing seasonal products may step up promotional efforts during slow times of the year to use production facilities and distribution systems most effectively.

Positioning the Product. Often a firm uses promotion to position a product as different or superior to competing products. Positioning means emphasizing certain product features to create a specific image for the product and add to its appeal. Firms often rely on advertising to position products.

Building a Public Image. Sometimes a company wants to develop a certain image through promotion. Publicity and, to a lesser extent, advertising provide effective vehicles for image building. Mobil, for example, sponsors programs on public television stations to provide quality entertainment for viewers and to foster goodwill toward the corporation.

The Promotion Mix

Promotion Mix
The combination of advertising, personal selling, sales promotion, and publicity used to promote a specific product.

To inform, influence, and remind customers in their target markets or the general public, firms use personal selling (person-to-person approach) and advertising, sales promotion, and publicity (nonpersonal approaches). How these four elements are combined to promote specific products is called the **promotion mix** (see Exhibit 16.1 on page 539).

A promotion mix may contain any or all of the four elements, depending on the firm's objectives, promotional strategy, product characteristics, and target market characteristics. Later in the chapter, we explore how the promotion mix is developed; now let's examine the four promotion mix elements.

Exhibit 16.1 *The Promotion Mix*

Advertising

Sales promotion

Publicity

Personal selling

ADVERTISING

Advertising
A paid form of nonpersonal communication to a target audience through a mass medium such as television, newspapers, or magazines.

Any paid form of nonpersonal communication to a target audience through a mass medium such as television, newspapers, or magazines is **advertising.** Of all promotional activities, consumers are most familiar with advertising. We see and hear many advertisements every day. Organizations and individuals spend nearly $130 billion on advertising in the United States each year.[3] Exhibit 16.2 will give you an idea of how much money large companies can spend to advertise their products to consumers.

Advertising can be quite expensive, especially using national media with immense audiences. For instance, the cost of a 30-second commercial during the 1995 Super Bowl was $1 million.[4] Since some 40 million American households watch the game each year, advertisers such as PepsiCo, Anheuser-Busch, Nike, and other companies believe the exposure their products receive from these advertisements makes the cost worthwhile. The average cost of making a national commercial is $222,000.[5] Firms often find advertising to be cost effective, however. It can reach a vast number of people at a low cost per person. It is also quite flexible, since advertisers can choose outlets to reach audiences of any size or demographic makeup. Ads can be repeated as often as sponsors wish.

Types of Advertising

An advertiser can use any of several different types of advertising, depending on its promotional objectives. Companies advertise brands, industries advertise products, and firms or individuals advertise themselves, their activities,

Exhibit 16.2
Expenditures by Leading U.S. Advertisers

	Company	Annual Advertising Expenditures ($ in millions)
1	Procter & Gamble Co.	$2,397
2	Philip Morris Companies	1,844
3	General Motors Corp.	1,539
4	Sears, Roebuck and Co.	1,311
5	PepsiCo	1,039
6	Ford Motor Co.	958
7	AT&T Co.	812
8	Nestlé SA	794
9	Johnson & Johnson	762
10	Chrysler Corp.	762

Source: Advertising Age (September 28, 1994): 4.

and their beliefs. We will examine three major categories of advertising: primary-demand, selective (brand), and institutional.

Primary-Demand Advertising
Advertising used to create demand for all products in a product group.

Primary-Demand Advertising. At times organizations want to create or increase demand for all products in a product group. In this case, they use **primary-demand advertising.** The Florida Department of Citrus, for instance, sponsored the advertisement shown in Exhibit 16.3 (on page 542) to persuade consumers to buy and drink more orange juice. The ad promotes the product without mentioning any particular brand or producer.

Selective (Brand) Advertising
Advertising used to sell a specific product or brand.

Selective Advertising. Most often a firm wants to create selective demand, or demand for a specific brand of product rather than for other, competing products. **Selective (brand) advertising** makes up the majority of advertising; marketers of virtually all goods and services use it in their promotion mixes. Over \$3.5 billion is spent each year to advertise automobiles, \$1.4 billion to advertise food, and over \$1 billion to advertise entertainment and media.[6]

Sometimes a firm compares its brand of product to another in advertisements. *Comparative advertising* identifies competitors and claims the superiority of the sponsor's brand. Selective advertising has grown in popularity during the last decade. A study conducted by Research Systems Corporation found comparative advertising most effective when it involved indirect comparative claims made by new products.[7] Libby's used the advertisement in Exhibit 16.4 (on page 542) to compare its Juicy Juice with seven competing products.

Institutional Advertising
Advertising used to build goodwill and create a favorable public image.

Institutional Advertising. When an organization desires primarily to build goodwill and create a favorable public image rather than promote a specific product, it employs **institutional advertising.** Consider the advertisement in Exhibit 16.5. In an understated manner, the ad shows how a unique plastic manufactured by DuPont helps disabled people such as Vietnam veteran Bill Demby get on with their lives. Advertisements like these can be inspirational to readers and viewers and enhance the public image of the sponsoring company.

A form of institutional advertising used to address a public issue is called *advocacy advertising.* Firms, industry groups, nonprofit organizations, and even individuals use advocacy advertising to explain controversial topics and influence public opinion. After President Clinton accused the drug industry of taking excessive profits, the Pharmaceutical Manufacturing Association began a \$500,000 advertising campaign proclaiming the benefits of prescription drugs to be worth the price.[8]

Exhibit 16.3 *Primary-Demand Advertising*

Exhibit 16.4 *Comparative Advertising*

Exhibit 16.5 *Institutional Advertising*

TOMORROW'S BUSINESS WORLD

The Media Puzzle Is Completed

Who can forget how the Persian Gulf was televised live throughout the world on Cable News Network? And the image of O.J. Simpson driving down an L.A. freeway in his Ford Bronco, with a gun pointed to his head? Without a doubt, the way we receive news "on demand" from around the world has changed dramatically. But the news is only one piece of the evolving media puzzle, and few know exactly what this puzzle will look like when it is completed sometime in the next century.

What is clear is that advances in technology, easing of regulatory restrictions, and opening of once-closed foreign markets to information and pop culture are changing this media puzzle—and it will take years and billions of dollars to complete. It will include news on demand, a vast array of movies, a live concert from Singapore, interactive shopping services, your favorite sporting event that you missed last week, a video message from your doctor reporting the results of your test, a birthday greeting from your parents, and more. These changes can be seen in a variety of disparate developments, such as a U.S. federal judge allowing Bell Atlantic to compete with cable in the video business and remote villages in China receiving MTV via satellite.

What is taking place is a major shift—the old order is falling. Old industry boundaries that clearly identified separate fields such as local telephone service, long distance, cable television, broadcast networks, computer hardware and software, publishing, entertainment, and electronic games are disappearing. And the world's telecommunications and media giants are rushing to be part of the new order.

Source: Adapted from Pat Widder, "Everyone Wants Piece of Multimedia Puzzle," *Chicago Tribune* (September 19, 1993): C1, C8.

Advertising Media

Advertising Media
Advertising outlets, including newspapers, television, direct mail, radio, magazines, and outdoor displays.

The different outlets that present advertisements are called **advertising media.** The most commonly used are newspapers, television, direct mail, radio, magazines, and outdoor displays. Exhibit 16.6 shows the advertising dollars spend for each medium and the percent of total advertising dollars each expenditure represents.

Media Plan
Selection of specific media in which advertisements will be run and when they will be run to reach the target markets.

To obtain the greatest benefit from these media expenditures, advertisers must develop an effective **media plan** which selects the specific media (particular newspapers, radio and television stations, and so on) to be used and the dates and times that advertisements will appear. The marketer or skilled media planner developing the media plan tries to communicate with the largest number of persons in the target market per dollar spent on media.

In developing the media plan, the planner must decide which kinds of media to use. The strengths and weaknesses of the major advertising media, shown in Exhibit 16.7, influence this decision.

Exhibit 16.6
Annual Advertising Media Expenditures

Medium	Expenditure: Millions of Dollars	Expenditure: Percent of Total
Newspapers		
National	$ 3,620	2.6%
Local	28,405	20.6
Total	32,025	23.2
Magazines		
Weeklies	2,850	2.1
Women's	2,009	1.4
Monthlies	2,498	1.8
Total	7,357	5.3
Farm publications	243	0.2
Television		
Network	10,209	7.4
Cable (national)	1,970	1.4
Syndication	1,576	1.1
Spot (national)	7,800	5.7
Spot (local)	8,435	6.1
Cable (non-network)	594	0.4
Total	30,584	22.1
Radio		
Network	458	0.3
Spot (national)	1,657	1.2
Spot (local)	7,342	5.3
Total	9,457	6.8
Yellow Pages		
National	1,230	0.9
Local	8,287	6.0
Total	9,517	6.9
Direct mail	27,266	19.8
Business papers	3,260	2.4
Outdoor		
National	605	0.4
Local	485	0.4
Total	1,090	0.8
Miscellaneous		
National	12,759	9.2
Local	4,522	3.3
Total	17,281	12.5
Total		
National	80,010	57.9
Local	58,070	42.1
Grand total	$138,080	100.0%

Source: Reprinted with permission from *Advertising Age* (May 2, 1994): p. 4.

Newspapers. Newspapers make up the largest category of the advertising media. Spending for newspaper advertising exceeds $30 billion each year, with more than half of that amount purchased by retailers. Firms can advertise in newspapers distributed locally, regionally, or internationally. Newspapers offer good coverage for firms of any size, because there is at least one newspaper in every local market and many people read the newspaper every day. Newspapers are well suited for immediate needs since they can run advertisements with little lead time. Advertisers can choose ads of any size, from a few lines in the classified section to full pages or separate supplements.

Because they reach diverse audiences, newspapers do not always allow advertisers to target their audience precisely. The life span of newspapers is very short since readers usually discard them quickly, although readers can clip or refer back to ads if they wish. Also, the quality of the paper is generally low, and the use of color is limited.

Television. Another large medium, television, receives about 22 percent of advertising expenditures. Advertisers spend in excess of $30 billion each year on television commercials. Automobile manufacturers alone spend a total of $2 billion to advertise their vehicles on television.

Perhaps television's greatest advantage is that it allows creative use of action, color, and sound to an extent not possible in any other medium. Television advertising also offers the capability of reaching vast audiences, since 98 percent of U.S. homes have at least one TV set. Firms can advertise nationally on a major network, regionally through cable networks, or locally through local stations.

The major drawback of network television advertising is the high cost. A 30-second commercial can cost as much as $300,000 for a popular show. To keep costs down, many advertisers now use 15-second ads, with networks running more of these shorter ads during a commercial break. When so many air during a program, they may not have as much impact on viewers. At any rate, TV ads have an extremely short life, which prompts creators to use special effects, unusual sounds, music, humor, and distinctive characters to encourage viewers to remember advertisements and products.

Another difficulty with TV ads is determining exactly what audience actually sees the commercials. Viewers in public places such as hotels, airports, restaurants, or stores are not counted. In homes, commercials play to empty rooms when viewers take breaks. Many viewers change channels when commercials begin, a habit called "zapping" that is made easier by today's remote controls and cable systems with 80 or more channels. Some rating systems estimate that zapping cuts a prime-time commercial's audience by 10 percent or more.

Empty rooms and zapping can mean that television advertisers do not get the audience they paid for. Commercials during TV spots, for example, get zapped heavily on weekends, when viewers switch between two or more games; such ads have lost over half of the audience. On the other hand, some-

Exhibit 16.7 *Strengths and Weaknesses of Advertising Media*

Medium	Types	Strengths	Weaknesses
Newspapers	Daily Weekly Special	Accessible to almost everyone; national geographic flexibility; short lead time; frequent publication; favorable for cooperative advertising; merchandising services	Not selective for socioeconomic groups; short life; limited reproduction capabilities; large advertising volume limits exposure to any one advertisement
Magazines	Consumer Business National Local Regional	Socioeconomic selectivity; good reproduction; long life; prestige; geograpic selectivity when regional issues are available; read in leisurely manner	High absolute dollar cost; long lead-time
Television	Network Local CATV	Reaches large audience; low cost per exposure; uses audio and video; highly visible; high prestige; geographic and socioeconomic selectivity	High dollar cost; short life of message; size of audience not guaranteed; amount of prime time limited
Radio	AM FM	Highly mobile; low-cost broadcast medium; message can be quickly changed; can reach a large audience; geographic selectivity; socioeconomic selectivity	Provides only audio message; has lost prestige; short life of message; listeners' attention limited because of other activities while listening
Direct mail	Letters Flyers Catalogs Samples Coupons Price lists	Little wasted circulation; highly selective; circulation controlled by advertiser; few distractions; personal; stimulates actions; use of novelty; relatively easy to measure performance; hidden from competitors	Expensive; no editorial matter to attract readers; considered junk mail by many; criticized as invasion of privacy
Outdoor displays	Painted buildings and vehicles Posters Billboards Electric spectaculars	Allows for repetition; low cost; message can be placed close to the point of sale; geographic selectivity; operable 24 hours a day	Message must be short and simple; no socioeconomic selectivity; seldom attracts readers' full attention; criticized for being traffic hazard and blight on countryside
Transit	Buses Taxicabs Subways	Low cost; frequency of message; "captive" audience; geographic selectivity	Limited audience; low impact; does not secure quick results

times advertisers get more than they pay for. The ads ending one "CBS Evening News" program, for instance, were viewed by twice as many people as the show's first commercial because thousands of viewers had tuned in for the next show, "Wheel of Fortune."

Direct Mail. Thousands of organizations send catalogs, advertisements, flyers, brochures, and fund-raising materials to homes, offices, or stores of target individuals. Over 19 percent of all advertising expenditures—about $27 billion—goes for direct mail, the third-largest advertising medium in the United States.

For direct mail to be effective, the material must reach the target group through up-to-date mailing lists. Advertisers can develop or purchase mailing lists that will reach nearly any target market imaginable, although selective mailing lists are expensive to buy. Direct mail's effectiveness is easily determined by the response: customers' orders or donations to fund-raising organizations. Even banks use direct mail. Targeting certain neighborhoods or high-income customers, some banks now mail catalogs explaining brokerage services, credit cards and loan offers along with applications, toll-free numbers, and even coupons for free checks. Direct mail, traditionally considered one of the less expensive forms of advertising, is becoming more costly as postal rates rise. Many firms are trimming mailing lists to include only their best customers or prospects.

Radio. About 7 percent of all money spent on advertising goes for radio ads. Radio serves a large and varied audience. Homes in the United States have nearly 500 million radios! Because of the wide variety of programming that caters to numerous interests—such as talk shows, all news, hard rock, classical music, jazz, oldies, easy listening, or foreign language broadcasts—advertisers can easily pinpoint target audiences. Spending on radio advertising has grown significantly because of its low cost and its ability to reach precisely defined target audiences.

Radio advertisements have the disadvantage of an extremely short life. Messages are limited because radio relies only on the sense of hearing. Listeners may keep radios turned on for background music or mere noise and ignore the advertisements.

Magazines. The last decade has seen a dramatic increase in the number of magazines being published. Expenditures for magazine advertising also have grown in the last several years. They now account for about 5 percent of total advertising volume. The top five magazines, by total advertising revenues, are *TV Guide, People, Time, Sports Illustrated,* and *Reader's Digest.*[9]

The sheer number and tremendous variety of magazines give advertisers the opportunity to target nearly any audience. Publications with huge circulations (*Reader's Digest, Time, Good Housekeeping*) allow advertisers to reach large general audiences. National magazines now can offer more local advertising by publishing several regional editions. Smaller, specialized magazines such as *Golf Digest, Apartment Life,* or *Cincinnati Magazine* reach more precise market segments.

Magazines offer the unique capability of high-quality color reproduction, a valuable asset in promoting many products. They also provide a more permanent message than do the other media, since subscribers often keep issues in their homes or workplaces for weeks or months and pass them along to friends. Magazine ads are not suited for immediate messages; they take a long time to produce and may be dated by printing time. Also, advertising in a widely circulated publication can be quite expensive.

Outdoor Displays. Billboards, posters, and other outdoor displays account for about 1 percent of advertising expenditures. Outdoor displays are inexpensive and useful in high-traffic areas. Their main disadvantage is that only a brief message can be communicated. Many people criticize outdoor displays along highways and roads for detracting from the beauty of the natural

The large number of magazines published in the United States means that advertisers can target a wide variety of consumer markets, both regional and national.

scenery. Nevertheless, the outdoor industry has been growing for several years, and increased spending on outdoor boards is expected to continue.[10]

The advertising media expose consumers to thousands of commercial messages each day. Advertising experts say that with the rapid growth of ads—ad "clutter"—consumers may actually remember only a fraction of these messages, perhaps only 1 percent. To grab consumers' attention, advertisers are turning to alternative media and are using traditional advertising media in new ways, as Today's Business World illustrates.

TODAY'S BUSINESS WORLD

Advertising: Here, There, and Everywhere

Like it or not, advertisements are everywhere: on the backs of buses, on the sides of tractor trailers, under scoreboards at sporting events, and in restrooms of restaurants, stores, and even planes. At supermarkets and drug stores, shoppers are bombarded with electric signs, closed-circuit radios playing commercials in aisles, and video recorders showing how to use products. At theaters and on videotapes, commercials sometimes crop up before the movie starts. It seems as though whenever there is a space, an advertisement is filling it.

Advertisers are constantly looking for new ways to get their messages to target audiences. Traditional media like television and magazines are especially cluttered. On the major networks (ABC, NBC, CBS) nonprogramming time per hour averages 12 minutes and 35 seconds; on five leading cable networks, 13 minutes and 50 seconds; on the Fox network, 14 minutes and 16 seconds; and on independent stations, 14 minutes, 33 seconds. The 1995 Super Bowl (on NBC) lasted approximately 3 hours and 25 minutes. During this time, there were 24 breaks and 68 commercials. Television clutter has increased the extent to which viewers switch channels. Clutter is also evident in magazines in the form of heavy inserts, scent strips, gatefolds (fold-out advertisements attached to front or back covers), and "printaculars," spectacular print advertisements.

To break through the clutter, advertisers are using traditional media in new ways. Some billboards now sport elaborate lights and music. One for a Southern California hospital featured a huge inflatable heart with fans inside simulating beating motions. On television, both General Electric and Shearson Lehman Hutton have experimented with different sounds—buzzes, hums, and weird music—to catch the public ear. Magazines feature pop-ups and computer chips that play Christmas carols.

Advertisers also are relying on alternative media, everything from matchbook covers to blimps. Although the use of nontraditional media represents a small part of total advertising dollars, it is growing fast. Americans spend billions of dollars each year to buy T-shirts that advertise consumer goods, movies, and political or social causes. Human billboards—people wearing huge popcorn bags—have handed out Smartfood cheese popcorn in Chicago. Jeep and Hardee's have advertised on Baltimore parking meters. Ski lifts carry lip balm and tanning lotion ads. Campbell Soup Company once put fish recipes calling for its soup on the back of Roman Catholic church bulletins during Lent. Do consumers really notice these advertisements? It's estimated that although the average consumer is exposed to up to 5,000 advertisements each day, he or she recalls only 1 percent of them. Nevertheless, to the enjoyment of some and the dismay of others, these unusual advertisements will continue to make their way into our lives.

Is there too much advertising? If so, how can this situation be corrected?

Source: Adapted from Kevin Goldman, "Barrage of Ads in Super Bowl Blurs Messages," *The Wall Street Journal* (February 3, 1993): B6; Joe Mandese, "Study Finds Shows with Worst Clutter," *Advertising Age* (February 17, 1992): 3, 61; Richard Phalon, "Walking Billboards," *Forbes* (December 7, 1992): 84–85; "Clutter Suffers Zap Attack," *Advertising Age* (March 30, 1992): 38; and Scott Hume, "Bounty in Most Unusual Places," *Advertising Age* (August 27, 1990): S1–S15.

Developing Advertising Campaigns

Firms go to considerable effort and expense to design, create, and evaluate advertisements that will accomplish their promotional goals. To lure overseas business, American Express launched a $100 million campaign that featured 60 advertisements seen in nearly 30 nations.[11] Developing an effective advertising campaign generally takes these steps:

- Identify the target audience of the advertisements.
- State the objectives to be accomplished (increase sales, build awareness, and so on).
- Determine how much money to spend.
- Develop an *advertising platform* consisting of the points to be emphasized to consumers (such as Maytag's dependability, Budget Rent A Car's low prices).
- Outline a media plan, indicating specific media in which advertisements will be run and when they will be run to reach the target markets.
- Create the actual advertisement.
- Place the advertisements with the media.
- Through sales or research, evaluate the effectiveness of the ads (see if the objectives were met).

Some firms handle their own advertising through in-house staff that plan, design, and create advertisements and place them with the media. Others use specialists outside the organization. An *advertising agency* is a business that specializes in planning, producing, and placing advertising and offers other promotional services for clients. Agencies, ranging from small firms handling local and regional advertising to large firms with national and international clients, can offer expertise and production facilities unavailable in many firms. Newspaper, radio, and television companies also offer advertising assistance, as do freelance writers, artists, and producers. Small firms often find that these sources can provide needed assistance at a reasonable cost.

PERSONAL SELLING

Personal Selling Person-to-person communication with one or more prospective customers in order to make a sale.

The oldest form of promotion, personal selling, is unique among the promotion mix elements because, as its name says, it is personal. **Personal selling** is communicating person-to-person with one or more prospective customers for the purpose of making a sale.[12] At one time or another, all of us have encountered personal selling. Has a car salesperson ever taken you on a test drive? Or maybe a salesperson helped you during a recent clothing purchase. These activities are highly visible because they are aimed at consumers. Yet they represent only a fraction of the situations involving personal selling. More than four times as many personal selling activities are directed toward industrial customers than toward consumers.

Personal selling is an important part of the promotion mix for many firms. Successful salespeople, such as this furniture salesperson, know the products they sell and communicate effectively with customers.

For many firms, personal selling is a critical element in the promotion mix. In the United States, companies spend more each year on personal selling than they spend on any other promotional method. Personal selling is also the most costly component of the promotion mix. The average cost of making a sales call on an organizational customer is over $250, about $220 for service customers, and $210 for consumer-goods customers.[13] Approximately 11 million people are employed in sales jobs in the United States, compared with half a million in advertising.[14]

Salespeople play an important role in the success of many firms. The best are highly trained professionals who before and after the sale help buyers satisfy their wants and needs. They know the product and effectively communicate their knowledge to buyers face-to-face. They also keep track of new products and competitors' activities. At IBM, salespeople are not only expected to bring in more revenue and profit, they are expected to act as sophisticated consultants selling both IBM and non-IBM technology to solve business problems.[15] Sales representatives often can reap substantial financial rewards; a highly skilled salesperson can earn more than $100,000 a year.

Types of Salespeople

Firms employ different types of salespeople for various selling situations, depending on such factors as type of product, price, number of customers, and channels of distribution used. We will examine three common types of salespeople: order getters, order takers, and support salespeople.

Order Getter
A salesperson who recruits new customers and increases sales to current customers.

Order Getters. A salesperson responsible for selling products to new customers and increasing sales to current customers is an **order getter.** Order getters engage in *creative selling.* They size up a customer's needs and convey product information in a thorough and persuasive manner. Creative selling is especially important when customers are carefully weighing alternatives in making their purchase, when they are not aware of product features and benefits, or when the product is a new one. Many industries, including insurance, computers, appliances, and heavy machinery, employ order getters.

Order Taker
A salesperson who processes repeat sales and maintains positive relationships with customers.

Order Takers. The person who receives and processes orders for repeat sales, with the objective of maintaining positive relationships with customers, is an **order taker.** The major function of order takers is to ensure that customers have the right amount of products they need when and where they need them. Order takers include salespeople who handle telephone and mail orders in a sales office and salespeople in retail stores. Other order takers handle routine sales of products such as milk, potato chips, bread, and beverages. They call on stores to check stock, inform managers of inventories, and make deliveries.

Support Salespeople
Salespeople who assist in selling by locating potential customers, educating them about products, building goodwill, and providing after-sales service.

Support Personnel. Firms commonly employ **support salespeople** to assist in selling, primarily to locate potential customers, educate them about products, build goodwill, and provide service after sales. Support people must often help sell industrial products.

Producers of technical industrial products such as computers, chemicals, steel, and heavy equipment rely on *technical salespeople* to provide information and service to current customers. Technical salespeople usually need formal education in engineering or science because they instruct customers in how a product is designed or made, how to install it, or how to use it.

Manufacturers often employ *missionary salespeople* to encourage retailers and other sellers to purchase their products. Missionary salespeople commonly represent pharmaceutical and medical supply companies to promote their products to physicians, hospitals, clinics, and pharmacies.

Trade salespeople help customers, especially retail stores, promote products to their own customers. They may set up displays of a manufacturer's product, demonstrate products to customers, give out samples, and restock shelves. Trade salespeople often work for food producers.

Chances are good that some of you reading this book will become salespeople. In the United States, roughly 1 of every 15 workers performs a sales-related job. Did you ever wonder what makes a successful salesperson and whether you might share some of those characteristics? Your Values and Attitudes can help you find out whether you have what it takes to sell.

YOUR VALUES AND ATTITUDES

Do You Have What It Takes for Sales?

Directions: Circle the number that represens your level of agreement with each statement.

	Strongly Disagree					**Strongly Agree**
1. If I didn't have direct supervision in my job, I would work just as hard anyway.	1	2	3	4	5	6
2. I am willing to work long hours.	1	2	3	4	5	6
3. I enjoy trying hard to please people.	1	2	3	4	5	6
4. I am organized and plan my daily schedule to make the most of my time.	1	2	3	4	5	6
5. I can be flexible if the situation requires it.	1	2	3	4	5	6
6. When under pressure, I try to remain calm and solve the problem.	1	2	3	4	5	6
7. I can speak to groups of people.	1	2	3	4	5	6
8. I don't think being late for appointments is a good idea.	1	2	3	4	5	6

	Strongly Disagree					Strongly Agree
9. I listen carefully to others in conversations and ask them questions about themselves.	1	2	3	4	5	6
10. I think solving a problem or completing a task I'm interested in is exciting.	1	2	3	4	5	6

Feedback: Pinpointing the sort of person who's destined for success in sales is impossible; after all, there are as many styles of selling as there are products to be sold. But those who succeed in the field share certain characteristics. If you think those qualities include being pushy, manipulative, or sneaky, think again. In fact these stereotypes generally come from salespeople who are failing.

Sales achievement requires three basic qualities. The first is *ego drive,* the desire to succeed, to win a yes, that keeps people doing the hard work required to get there. Ego drive also helps salespeople, who are largely independent, motivate and manage themselves. The second quality is *empathy,* the ability to listen and understand what someone else is thinking and feeling. Top salespeople know what questions to ask and how to interpret answers. Third, salespeople need to possess *ego strength,* the ability to take rejection and to persevere during slumps. If you find it painful when someone tells you no, don't go into sales!

How you answered the quiz questions should give you an idea of whether you have the qualities needed by effective salespeople. If you circled 1 or 2 to most of the questions, you probably don't have the interest or characteristics for sales. If you circled 3s or 4s, you might make a good salesperson if you really want to work at it and learn. If you circled 5 or 6 to most questions, you have many of the qualities shared by successful salespeople. You are hard working, emotionally mature, dependable, independent, and knowledgeable.

Sales Positions in the Future

As we have noted, the nature of personal selling is changing. The major thrust of this change is focusing on the customer. Many firms are recognizing that the key element to improving quality is continual focus on the customer. As a result, salespeople are being asked to do a great deal more listening and questioning of the customer.[16] Many salespeople are selling to diverse racial and ethnic groups, and understanding differences and similarities is vital for success.[17] The resulting relationships between salespeople and their customers take many forms; salespeople may act as partners, consultants, advisers, or problem solvers. We will refer to this emerging trend in general as *smart selling.*

Successful selling in the 1990s and beyond will depend on a salesperson's ability to build a relationship with the customer. Additionally, successful salespeople will have to be willing to work with others to satisfy customer problems. Eastman Kodak has begun to evaluate its sales representatives on how well they coordinate with co-workers to help a customer.[18] Whereas salespeople were once viewed as somewhat independent and may have even had an incentive to compete with each other, they will not be operating solo in the future. Everyone from the product designers to the financial officers will be part of the selling team.[19]

This new type of sales position poses many challenges for sales managers. Experienced salespeople may not relate to a "team" approach to selling. But as customers find they have more and more quality products from which to choose, firms must focus their selling approaches on the customer. U.S. factories can now produce six million more cars and trucks a year than the public can buy. Even though the quality gap between U.S. and foreign producers has been virtually eliminated, Chrysler announced a "Customer One" program. The purpose of the program is to teach salespeople how to meet the needs of customers, as opposed to using the hard-sell approach typically employed by automobile dealers.[20]

Selling in the 1990s will mean convincing customers that a firm can give them the most value for the least money. This approach requires a sincere and concentrated focus on the customer. The successful salesperson will concentrate less on selling and more on contributing to the success of the customer.[21]

The Selling Process

Selling Process
A series of steps salespeople perform, consisting of prospecting, preparing, approaching, presenting, answering objections, closing, and following up.

A salesperson's work is outlined in the steps that take place in the **selling process** (see Exhibit 16.8). Of course, not all salespeople perform their jobs in exactly the same way, and an individual salesperson may alter tactics for different situations. But the ultimate goal of the selling process is a long-term relationship with the customer. In the current highly competitive business environment, many firms are discovering that keeping current customers is more economical than finding new ones.[22] Customer loyalty is invaluable to a firm's long-range success.

Prospecting. Locating potential customers is called prospecting. Salespeople find prospects through many sources, including current customers, trade

Exhibit 16.8
Steps in the Selling Process

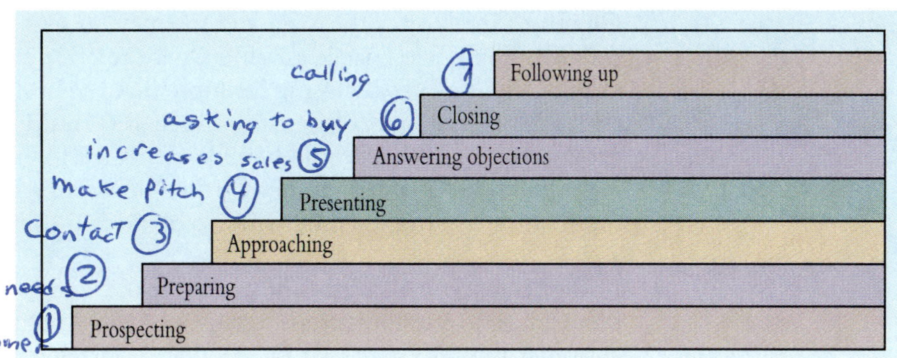

directories, business associates, telephone directories, newspaper or magazine articles, or public records. At this stage in the selling process, the salesperson tries to identify as possible customers those who have a need for the product and the financial ability and authority to purchase it.

Preparing. Sales calls require some preparatory research. A salesperson attempts to find out about the prospect's needs, attitudes about available products and brands, and personal characteristics, as well as the products and brands currently used. Knowing as much as possible about the prospect allows a salesperson to tailor the approach and presentation specifically for that prospect and that situation.

Approaching. The third step involves making the initial contact with, or approaching, a prospect. A salesperson's approach makes the all-important first impression with a potential customer. Adequate preparation and knowledge increase a salesperson's chances of making a good first impression. In approaching the prospect, a salesperson may mention a referral from an acquaintance or business associate or remind the prospect of a previous meeting. Salespeople may make the call "cold"—without the prospect's prior knowledge or an appointment.

Presenting. The next step is actually presenting the promotional message to the potential customer. During the presentation, a salesperson points out the product's features and benefits and emphasizes any advantages the product offers over competitor's products. When possible, salespeople encourage potential customers to hold, touch, or use products to experience them personally and reinforce significant points of the presentation. A salesperson also needs to ask the client questions and listen carefully to determine the client's needs and focus the presentation on those needs.

Answering Objections. After presenting, the salesperson gives a prospect sufficient opportunity to ask questions or raise objections. By answering objections, the salesperson increases the likelihood of a sale. This step gives the salesperson a second chance to tell the major benefits of the product or service and point out additional features, guarantees, service, and so forth.

Closing. In closing the sale, the salesperson ask the prospect to buy the product. Some salespeople ask directly if the prospect is ready to make a purchase. Others use trial closing to imply that the customer will buy the product. A salesperson can ask questions such as, Would you like us to finance the car for you? or When would you like delivery? to encourage customers to finalize the purchase. Sometimes salespeople offer prospects a chance to try the product for a period of time with no obligation to buy.

Following Up. A salesperson would make a critical mistake to assume that the selling process ends after the sale. To follow up, a salesperson contacts the customer to make sure that the product was delivered and installed properly (if needed) and to ask if it is performing as expected. When a problem exists, an effective salesperson assists the customer in resolving it. Providing service after a purchase encourages future sales and helps build a long-term relationship.

SALES PROMOTION

Sales Promotion An activity that offers customers or marketing intermediaries direct incentives for purchasing a product.

cupons rebates samples contests ect...

Sales promotion is a paid form of nonpersonal communication that provides direct incentives to customers, salespeople, and marketing intermediaries for purchasing a product. Methods such as coupons, contests, and displays can get consumers excited about a product, motivate salespeople to be enthusiastic, and stimulate dealers to be interested and involved in distributing it. Sales promotion activities, generally short-term, offer the advantage of immediacy; firms can implement them and obtain results quickly. Firms use sales promotions occasionally or year-round to support their personal selling, advertising, and publicity programs.

Sales promotion is big business in the United States. Over 300 billion coupons are distributed in the United States each year.[23] In this section, we will examine the major categories of sales promotion: consumer and trade.

Consumer Sales Promotion

Consumer Sales Promotion Activities—including coupons, rebates, samples, gifts, premiums, trading stamps, contests, and sweepstakes—directed to consumers to increase sales.

Firms that market consumer products frequently use **consumer sales promotion,** activities that encourage customers to buy certain brands or to shop at a particular store. Companies are shifting marketing dollars from advertising to consumer sales promotion.[24] The most common consumer sales promotion methods are coupons, rebates, samples, gifts, premiums, trading stamps, contests, and sweepstakes. Firms may use one or more of these methods in a promotional campaign. For example, Texaco offered a coupon, a rebate, and a sweepstakes in a single-page ad in a campaign for Havoline motor oil.

Coupon A sales promotion technique that reduces the price of a product by a stated amount at the time of purchase.

Coupons. Manufacturers and retailers provide special price reductions for consumers through **coupons.** The reduction may be a specified amount ranging from a few cents to several dollars, or a certain percentage to be deducted from the price of a product. Manufacturers and retailers often use coupons to encourage consumers to try new products. Some try coupons to reverse a decline in sales of a product. Sometimes a firm will distribute coupons as a defensive tactic when a competitor introduces a new product or begins a new sales promotion program. Firms distribute more than 300 billion coupons every year in the United States through newspapers, magazines, direct mail, store displays, and other methods; customers redeem about 5 percent of these.

Rebate
An extra discount or refund given to consumers who buy a product and supply proofs of purchase.

Rebates. Firms may offer customers who buy a product and send in proof of their purchase an extra discount or refund in the form of a **rebate.** Rebates range from a small percentage of the purchase price to the full purchase price. Firms typically use rebates both to motivate consumers to try new products and to provide incentives for purchasing established products. Manufacturers offer rebates for all types of products, from convenience items such as toothpaste to big-ticket goods such as cars.

Free Sample
A free package or container of a product given as a sales promotion technique.

Free Samples. An effective way to encourage consumers to get familiar with a product is to provide them with a **free sample** of the merchandise. Companies may mail or deliver samples to homes, give them out in stores, or distribute coupons for free products. While providing samples is the most expensive method of consumer sales promotion, it generally works best to induce buyers to try new products.

Premium
A gift given to customers for purchasing a certain product.

Trading Stamps
Tokens given out by retailers based on the amount of purchase; redeemable for gifts.

Premiums and Trading Stamps. Many firms offer a **premium,** or gift, to customers as a bonus for purchasing a certain product. Banks, for example, often offer household items to customers who open new accounts. To attract customers to a particular store, retailers sometimes give customers **trading stamps** based on the dollar amount spent. Customers can save the stamps and exchange them for merchandise. Trading stamps such as S&H Green Stamps were once widely distributed by grocery stores but have been lost their popularity in recent years.

Contest
A sales promotion method in which consumers compete for prizes on the basis of some skill.

Sweepstakes
A sales promotion method in which consumers enter a drawing for prizes.

Contests and Sweepstakes. Contests and sweepstakes probably generate more excitement than do other promotional methods. To stimulate sales, firms offer consumers the chance to win free trips, vacation dream houses, cars, cash, and merchandise. In a **contest,** consumers compete for prizes based on some skill. Food manufacturers, for example, often sponsor cooking contests in which contestants use certain products to create new recipes. In a **sweepstakes,** consumers send in their names to enter a drawing for prizes. Sweepstakes cost considerably less than contests and attract many more participants.

Trade Sales Promotion

Trade Sales Promotion
Activities a firm directs to wholesalers, retailers, or salespeople to encourage them to stock or sell its products.

A manufacturer often uses **trade sales promotion** activities to encourage wholesalers and retailers to stock and promote its products or salespeople to increase sales. Common methods of trade sales promotion are point-of-purchase displays, trade shows, trade allowances, premium or push money, and sales contests.

Point-of-Purchase Displays
Promotional materials such as signs, posters, and freestanding shelves used in retail stores.

Point-of-Purchase Displays. Manufacturers or wholesalers provide and set up signs, posters, freestanding shelves, and other specialized materials to use as **point-of-purchase displays** in retail stores. For example, a large, inflatable plastic Green Giant may stand atop the frozen vegetable case in a supermarket to grab attention and promote that brand. A display may contain the product being promoted. For example, PepsiCo has supplied refrigerators bearing the Pepsi name to retailers carrying its products. Displays can be very effective in increasing sales, as many buying decisions (two-thirds by some estimates) are made in the store.[25]

Video players with videotapes provided by manufacturers are among the newest point-of-purchase displays. Department stores, for instance, play videos on how to tie scarves and how to put together clothing separates for a complete outfit.

Trade Show
A temporary exhibit where manufacturers display products to potential customers and gather names for a list of prospects.

Trade Shows. Sellers in an industry gather at **trade shows** to exhibit their merchandise. There manufacturers display and demonstrate products to potential customers and gather names of prospects. Industries representing food, fashion, furniture, computers, toys, and many other products hold trade shows each year, usually in large cities. While most trade shows are conducted by manufacturers for retailers, some also are designed for a consumer audience, such as shows featuring home building and interior decorating products, or boats and recreational vehicles.

Manufacturers displaying their products at this electronics trade show find it an effective way to identify and meet potential customers.

Trade Allowance
A discount a manufacturer gives for performing certain functions or making purchases during a specified time period.

Trade Allowances. A manufacturer may give retailers and wholesalers a **trade allowance,** a discount for performing certain functions or for making purchases during a specified time period. For instance, a firm could offer price reductions to retailers to encourage them to stock a product and pass the savings on to consumers. A retailer also may earn a discount for setting up a special display to promote a manufacturer's products.

Premium or Push Money. Firms often conduct sales promotion activities for their own salespeople and those representing distributors and other sellers. To encourage salespeople to push a product, a firm may provide additional compensation in the form of **premium or push money.** While expensive, using premium or push money can boost commitment from salespeople when personal selling is a major part of the promotion mix.

Premium or Push Money
Additional compensation provided to salespeople to encourage them to sell a product.

Sales Contests. Conducting a contest for the people who sell and distribute its products is another method a firm could use to increase involvement and create excitement. In a **sales contest,** a firm may offer prizes to salespeople, distributors, and retailers who meet certain sales goals in a specific time period. A sales contest with a desirable prize, such as a trip to an exotic vacation spot, can increase participation and sales throughout the channel of distribution. The results may be only temporary, however, and the cost of prizes may be high.

Sales Contest
A competition designed to stimulate sales efforts by salespeople, distributors, or retailers.

PUBLICITY

Publicity FREE
A nonpersonal form of communication transmitted in news story form and not paid for directly by a sponsor.

Public Relations
A set of communications activities designed to create and maintain a favorable public image for a firm.

Like advertising and sales promotion, **publicity** is a nonpersonal form of communication. But it is transmitted by a mass medium in news story form and is not paid for directly by a sponsor. Publicity is actually part of **public relations,** a set of communications activities designed to create and maintain a favorable public image for a firm. Superman generated a great deal of publicity when he was killed off by his editor at Time Warner's DC Comics in 1992, selling 3.5 million copies at $1.25 each—one of the best-selling comic books ever.[26] Many organizations, industries, and individuals conduct ongoing public relations campaigns to demonstrate social responsibility.

Publicity Approaches

Firms attempt to gain publicity for several purposes. They may want to increase awareness of their products, to build a positive image with the general public, to gain recognition for employees and their accomplishments, to encourage others to participate in community projects, or at times to counter negative events or news stories.

Companies use several vehicles to obtain publicity. The *news release* is a brief report—a page or two—that announces an organization's national, regional, or local events. Firms distribute news releases widely and include the names of people within the firm for media representatives to contact for more information. A *feature article* is a longer, more detailed story about a firm, its products, or its people. It may run as long as 3,000 words and include photographs or illustrations. Firms usually submit a feature article to a specific magazine or newspaper. A *captioned photograph,* a picture along with a short explanation, can be effective in informing consumers about new products or stores. Another option is sending an *editorial film* or tape to broadcast media for inclusion in news programs. To release important or timely news, a firm may invite media representatives to a *news conference* to make announcements, hand out supplemental materials, and answer questions.

Another approach gaining use is *sponsorship* of events, programs, or even people such as amateur athletes or teams. Besides publicity, sponsorship can involve advertising and sales promotion activities such as samples and contests. Each year thousands of firms sponsor sporting events, arts festivals, public radio and television programs, and public interest advertisements. Companies paid as much as $15 million to be major sponsors of the 1994 World Cup soccer tournament.[27] At least 400 large U.S. corporations have developed event marketing departments with separate budgets; others hire consultants to manage sponsorship for them. Smaller firms often work with local government and community organizations to sponsor events.

Using Publicity Effectively

Positive publicity provides many benefits for an organization. A newspaper or magazine article or television or radio broadcast can reach large and diverse audiences at no direct cost to the firm. News and feature stories can reach people who pay no attention to advertisements. Since publicity is provided by independent media, it has a great deal of credibility. Are you not more likely to believe a news story about a new product than an advertisement paid for by the seller?

Publicity also poses several limitations. A firm exerts little or no control over a message—its content, placement, timing, or whether the media transmits it at all. News editors may have different ideas of what is news than do members of an organization seeking publicity. A news story may run on the late news show and reach only a fraction of potential viewers. Or it may be cut to a line or two in a newspaper column full of corporate news. Publicity does not always enhance a firm's image. At times the media people report negative events and criticize a firm's activities, policies, or products.

To foster positive and effective publicity, a firm must conduct well-planned, regular efforts. Many firms employ individuals or departments to handle ongoing publicity efforts, while others rely on advertising or public relations firms or freelance writers or consultants. Personnel trained in communications can supply the media with newsworthy, well-written publicity releases, handle media requests, and build cooperative relationships with reporters, editor, news directors, and other media "gatekeepers."

DEVELOPING THE PROMOTION MIX

A firm marketing several products often uses several promotion mixes simultaneously. When designing the promotion mix for a product, marketers first consider their promotional objectives (discussed earlier in the chapter). They also consider promotional techniques known as push and pull strategies, as well as product characteristics, including type of product, stage of product life cycle, and target market characteristics.

Promotional Strategies

Push Strategy Promotion of a product to wholesalers or retailers in the marketing channel, who in turn promote the product to consumers.

Pull Strategy Promotion of a product directly to consumers to stimulate strong consumer demand.

In developing promotional programs, marketers decide whether they want to use a push strategy or a pull strategy. With a **push strategy,** the firm promotes a product to wholesalers or retailers in the marketing channel, who in turn promote the product to consumers (see Exhibit 16.9). Personal selling often is used with this strategy to "push" the product to wholesalers and retailers.

In the **pull strategy** (also shown in Exhibit 16.9), by contrast, a firm promotes a product directly to consumers so that they will seek the product in retail stores and ask managers to stock it. In effect, customer demand "pulls" the product into stores. To implement a pull strategy, marketers usually use advertising and sales promotion to stimulate consumer demand for the prod-

Exhibit 16.9
Push and Pull Strategies

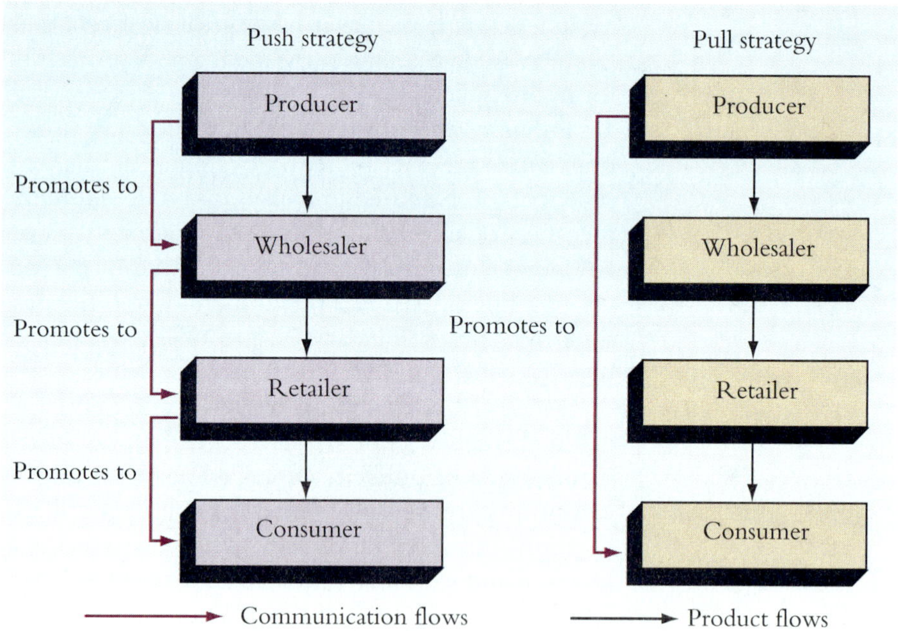

uct. While a firm often focuses on either a push or pull strategy, it could use both at the same time.

Product Characteristics

Various aspects of a product influence a firm's selection of promotion mix elements. Consumer and industrial products require different promotion mixes to meet the needs of those markets. Services often require unique considerations. For all products, firms must take into account the current product life-cycle stage and numerous characteristics of the targeted customers.

Type of Product. Firms selling industrial products generally emphasize personal selling techniques in their promotion mix, adding advertising, sales promotion, and publicity to support the personal selling efforts. For consumer products, advertising is the primary element. Firms offering consumer convenience products promote them heavily with advertising and sales promotion. Those selling consumer shopping and specialty products add personal selling to the mix so that salespeople can provide information and advice about high-priced or unfamiliar products such as appliances, cars, or computers.

Marketers of services face specific considerations when planning promotional activities. As intangible products, services cannot generally be defined in terms of physical attributes. Therefore, when service firms advertise, they use cues that provide physical representation of the service offered. Common cues are the physical facility or the employees. Carnival Cruise Lines portrays its ships as resorts on water, complete with pools, casinos, and restaurants. As Exhibit 16.10 shows, insurance companies use cues—Allstate's good hands, State Farm's good neighbors, The Travelers' umbrella, and Prudential's rock—as physical representations of their protection, stability, and concern. Such symbols make the service more tangible to consumers and build an image of the provider that the consumer will, it is hoped, retain.

Services also are based on human performances—as in rock concerts, legal advice, or dental care—which are even more difficult to define in tangible terms. Marketers need to emphasize not only the actual service but all the benefits the customer is buying.[28] For many services, personal selling becomes especially useful; it provides the interaction between service personnel and consumers that is so valuable in marketing intangible products.

Publicity, with its lower cost and generally higher credibility compared to advertising, is an important promotion element for service firms. Health providers often receive publicity by sponsoring fairs in which medical personnel perform cholesterol screening, blood pressure checks, and vision and hearing tests free for the public. Service firms may also use sales promotion, such as coupons, rebates, and free first-time visits. Some sales promotion activities are not feasible for service providers; many services cannot be displayed, and providing a free sample requires giving away the entire product.

Product Life Cycle. A firm introducing a new product, either industrial or consumer, usually advertises heavily to make potential customers aware of it

Exhibit 16.10
Promotion of Services with Physical Symbols

Physical symbols help make services like insurance more tangible to consumers and also build an image for the provider.

and encourage them to try it. Personal selling and sales promotion also prove valuable for many products in the introduction stage. For consumer convenience products in the growth and maturity stages, advertising usually continues to dominate the promotion mix. For industrial products in the growth and maturity stages, however, firms often concentrate on personal selling supported by sales promotion activities. When a product reaches the decline stage, marketers cut back on promotion, especially advertising. Instead they rely on personal selling and sales promotion to obtain a few more sales.

Target Markets. The size, geographic distribution, and demographic characteristics of a firm's target market greatly influence the choice of promotion elements. Personal selling will likely be an important element for the target market that has a limited number of potential customers, while advertising and sales promotion usually dominate the promotion mix designed to reach millions of people at a low cost per person. Similarly, personal selling is generally more practical when a firm's customers are concentrated in a small area; advertising and sales promotion, which are much more flexible, can be easily geared to markets in any geographic region whether small and precisely defined or large.

A target market's demographics—age, income, education, social class, occupation—also influence the promotion mix. A firm marketing to teenagers would emphasize advertising, especially on television, but rely less on personal selling, sales promotion, or publicity. A firm targeting educated, financially well-off consumers aged 35 and older would use personal selling, advertising, and perhaps publicity but not consumer sales promotion activities, since coupons, refunds, and sweepstakes are more important to lower- and middle-income families.

SUMMARY OF LEARNING OBJECTIVES

1. ***Explain the role of promotion in marketing and list five promotional objectives.*** Organizations use promotion to communicate favorable, persuasive information about themselves or their products, to influence buyers to make a purchase, or to foster goodwill. Promotional objectives may include informing, increasing sales, stabilizing sales, product positioning, or building a public image. To meet these objectives, a firm develops a combination of advertising, personal selling, sales promotion, and publicity—called the promotion mix.

2. ***Describe the major types of advertising and the purpose of each.*** Virtually all organizations use advertising to present messages to target markets. *Primary-demand advertising* helps create demand for a product group; *selective,* or *brand, advertising* builds demand for a specific brand; *institutional advertising* helps create a favorable public image. The media used most often are newspapers, television, direct mail, radio, magazines, and outdoor displays.

3. ***List the steps involved in planning an advertising campaign.*** When firms plan their advertising, they identify the target market, define their objectives, determine the budget, develop a platform, establish a media plan, create the advertisement, and evaluate the effectiveness of the campaign. Some companies have employees to handle their advertising, while others use advertising agencies or other specialists.

4. ***Differentiate among the three types of salespeople and their functions.*** Personal selling involves person-to-person communication with one or more prospective buyers. Firms employ *order getters* to sell products to new and current customers, *order takers* to process repeat sales and maintain good relationships with customers, and *support salespeople* to sell, educate customers, and provide service.

5. ***Outline the personal selling process and describe each step.*** Salespeople perform a series of steps in the selling process: prospecting (locating potential customers); preparing (learning about prospects and their needs); approaching (making the first contact and a good first impression); presenting (explaining product benefits and demonstrating the product); answering objections (encouraging questions and emphasizing product benefits); closing the sale (asking the prospect to buy); and following up (finding out if the product satisfies the customer's needs and providing service).

6. ***Explain the purpose of sales promotion and list common activities of consumer sales promotion and trade sales promotion.*** Sales promotion encourages sales through direct inducements to customers, salespeople, and marketing intermediaries. Coupons, refunds, samples, premiums, trading stamps, contests, and sweepstakes can get consumers interested in a product. Trade sales promotion methods—point-of-purchase displays, trade shows, trade allowances, premium or push money, and sales contests—help motivate salespeople and distributors and increase their involvement in product sales.

7. ***Describe how firms use publicity.*** Publicity can increase awareness of products and help build a positive image with target markets or the general public. Sponsors do not pay directly for publicity, which is transmitted through mass media. News releases, feature articles, captioned photographs, editorial films or tapes, and press conferences facilitate publicity. Many firms sponsor events, programs, and public

interest advertising to gain recognition, target specific markets, and increase sales.

8. ***Identify factors that influence a firm's promotion mix.*** When planning a promotion mix, a marketer considers the firm's promotional objectives, whether to use a push or pull strategy, the characteristics of the product and target market, and the stage of product life cycle.

KEY TERMS

Promotion
Promotion Mix
Advertising
Primary-Demand Advertising
Selective (Brand) Advertising
Institutional Advertising
Advertising Media
Media Plan
Personal Selling
Order Getter
Order Taker
Support Salespeople
Selling Process
Sales Promotion
Consumer Sales Promotion
Coupon
Rebate
Free Sample
Premium
Trading Stamps
Contest
Sweepstakes
Trade Sales Promotion
Point-of-Purchase Displays
Trade Show
Trade Allowance
Premium or Push Money
Sales Contest
Publicity
Public Relations
Push Strategy
Pull Strategy

QUESTIONS FOR DISCUSSION AND REVIEW

1. Distinguish between the three major types of advertising, listing specific situations when each should be used.
2. Why should a firm use institutional advertising? Give an example of a recent institutional advertisement—its sponsor, its message, and where it appeared.
3. Identify two strengths and two weaknesses of each major advertising medium: newspapers, television, direct mail, radio, magazines, and outdoor displays.
4. How would a firm go about conducting an advertising campaign?
5. What is an advertising platform? Give an example with two current advertising media: newspapers, television, direct mail, radio, magazines, and outdoor displays.
6. Name the different types of salespeople. Give examples of situations in which you have interacted with each of these types of salespeople, and why they were effective.
7. Consider a recent purchase you made in which a salesperson assisted you a great deal. Describe the interaction in terms of the steps of the selling process.
8. Distinguish between consumer sales promotion and trade sales promotion. What consumer sales promotion methods influence you to purchase products?
9. Tell some of the advantages and disadvantages of publicity. Give a recent example of a firm receiving favorable publicity and an example of one receiving unfavorable publicity.
10. Contrast the promotion mixes of two competing products that you are familiar with. Why do the promotion mixes vary considerably?

CASE 16.1

Does Sex Still Sell?

When an *Advertising Age* survey asked college students to rank print ads, a favorite was one for Calvin Klein's Obsession cologne that showed a nude couple, the man standing with his back to the camera and the woman draped over him. "Sexy ads always do well on the college level," says the president of a firm called College Market Consultants. "They grab attention on two levels, the conscious level as a consumer and the subconscious level as well."

Like Calvin Klein, many advertisers use sex to pitch products. Sexy ads attract the attention of consumers who may otherwise never look at a product. They give consumers the impression the product is daring or sensual. Advertisers believe many consumers purchase clothing, cosmetics, and fragrances in hopes of becoming more sexually appealing. Firms with smaller advertising budgets sometimes use attention-grabbing, sexy ads to compete with larger competitors.

Using sex in advertising is an old idea that has varied according to media standards and public acceptance. Magazines have run more risque ads, while network television has been more cautious. But barriers are constantly falling. In 1986, Fruit of the Loom television commercials showed men's underwear—but not with men wearing them. Then years later, TV celebrities Ed Marinaro, Patrick Duffy, and James DePaive appeared in network commercials wearing only their Fruit of the Looms.

Some advertisers stretch the boundaries beyond previous limits. For its Jovan Musk ads in 1988, Beecham used footage by Adrian Lyne, who directed the movies *Fatal Attraction* and *9 1/2 Weeks*. Network censors twice ordered cuts before approving the ads. Beecham made use of the resulting publicity and actually placed ads in *TV Guide* and *USA Today* so viewers would know when the commercials would air. The firm's marketers appeared on talk shows to discuss the Musk ads and Beecham products. One executive said the publicity was worth about $13 million, equal to the company's advertising expenditure. He claimed that Jovan's commercials are just images on the screen and do not promote sex but simply reflect typical intimate relationships. Although Beecham advertises heavily on MTV, with its audience of mostly 18- to 24-year-olds, the company says it has acted responsibly.

With the U.S. population getting older, baby boomers settling down with families, and the threat of AIDS, advertising now reflects contemporary attitudes toward sex roles. Ads now show women as equal sexual partners rather than sex objects. Print and television ads for Revlon's Charlie cologne, for example, featured a fashionable woman patting her male companion's rump. Other firms now use advertisements that suggest sensuality rather than show explicit images. For Iron cologne for men, Coty TV commercials show an attractive man pulling on a T-shirt and spraying on the cologne and a woman in a simple dress coming into the room and kissing his neck.

Even political advertising has exploited sex. Nicargua's Sandinista youth party used sexy ads to enlist young people to join the party and vote. Posters directed to first-time voters showed two pairs of naked legs pressed together and jeans and a crumpled rose on the floor, with the slogan, "It's beautiful the first time when you do it with love."

Using sex in advertising can pose drawbacks. Consumers may become so obsessed with the fantasy the ad creates that they forget about the product. Also, many consumers are turned off by sensual ads. Nearly one-third of Americans often find sexual references or images in advertising offensive; women are more likely than men to be offended. Americans do not always accept the amount of nudity that appears in European advertising. After the

German firm that markets Nivea moisturizing lotion featured a naked woman profiled against the sky in ads appearing in *Vogue, Harper's Bazaar,* and *Ladies Home Journal,* U.S. readers objected; the firm substituted a more demure photograph. And Chicago stores refused to be identified at the end of a commercial for Sansabelt pants in which a woman says, "I always lower my eyes when a man passes, to see if he's worth following."

Questions for Discussion

1. What promotional objectives do you think firms may have when they use sex in advertising?
2. Why have the ways in which advertisers use sex in ads changed?
3. What are some of the problems with using sex in advertising?

Source: Adapted from Doris Walsh, "Safe Sex in Advertising," *American Demographics* (April 1994): 24–30; "Jovan's Steamy New Ads Pick Up Where Its Other Sizzlers Left Off," *Marketing News* (June 20, 1988): 1–2; Michael Perreca, "Key to 'Successex,' *Product Marketing* (June 1988): 19; "Sandinistas Lure Youth Vote with Sex, Not Wars," *Lexington (KY), Herald-Leader* (February 20, 1990): A5; Joshua Levine, "Fantasy, Not Flesh," *Forbes* (January 22, 1990): 118–120.

CASE 16.2

Unique Selling at Body Shop International

Anita Roddick, who ran a restaurant and an eight-room hotel in her hometown of Littlehampton, England, was looking for something new to do. She came up with the idea of producing and selling shampoos, skin creams, and other body lotions made from fruit and vegetable oils rather than animal fats. Through marketing, she would capitalize on selling "natural" cosmetics to aging boomers—like herself—who generally distrust advertising and sales hype, demand product information, and are loyal to socially responsible companies.

With her idea and a $7,000 loan, Roddick hired a local chemist to develop animal-fat-free lotions. She opened her first shop in Brighton, and Body Shop International was born. Today more than 700 Body Shop stores operate around the world. Of the 78 U.S. stores, 64 are franchised.

Body Shop has not used traditional advertising, but relies on in-store selling and promotion to communicate with customers. "Ninety-nine percent of Fortune 500 chief executives have never walked into a Body Shop," said Faith Popcorn, a consultant with Brain-Reserve, "yet this is what business will be like. And it is so contradictory to the way we are used to marketing."

Body Shop's strategy is to give the customers product information rather than a sales pitch, and rely on its socially conscious image. Salespeople are expected to develop a forthright relationship with customers, tell them about the history of lotions, and provide product information. Leaflets offer tips for skin care, and a manual containing product information is available in each store. Pamphlets scattered throughout stores also tell customers about Body Shop's recycling program, whereby customers can bring in used Body Shop bottles and get them refilled. Roddick also uses the stores to push Body Shop's social agenda, a variety of causes including "Save the Whales" and Amnesty International. With her long-running social campaign, Roddick intends for her company to demonstrate what she calls the new business consciousness.

Body Shop International prides itself on its knowledgeable staff. Courses in product ingredients teach salespeople about properties, structures, and sources of cosmetics. Employees are taught to serve the needs of customers from different cultures. Training is also available to help franchises and partnership shop owners get involved in community projects. Work-force training efforts are measured by employee attitude.

Roddick also displays slogans and messages around stores to motivate employees. One of her favorites is "If you think you're too small to have an impact, try going to bed with a mosquito." Even Body Shop trucks are used as rolling billboards for pithy slogans.

Not everyone is impressed with Body Shop's approach to selling products. The British press has become especially critical of Roddick and her husband. A London daily, the *Independent,* wrote: "They represent causes attractive to the liberal conscious. Yet this goodness is used, remorselessly, to sell vanity products. You wash your hair in global concern. And it is debatable whether the wizened peasants on the walls are dignified or patronized."

Although there may be some debate about Body Shop's approach, most agree that selling in general will incorporate some aspects of it in the decade ahead.

Questions for Discussion

1. Do you think Body Shop uses relationship selling? Explain.
2. How does environmental consciousness fit into Body Shop's strategy?
3. How does the Body Shop train and motivate salespeople?
4. Do you think it is appropriate to use environmental concern in selling products?

Source: Adapted from Charles Siler, "Body Shop Marches to Its Own Drummer," *Advertising Age* (October 10, 1994): 4; Philip Elmer-Dewitt, "Anita the Agitator," *Time* (January 25, 1993): 52–54; Rahul Jacob, "What Selling Will Be Like in the '90s," *Fortune* (January 13, 1992): 63–64; Jean Sherman Chatzky, "Changing the World," *Forbes* (March 2, 1992): 83–87; and Barbara Dutton, "What Price Knowledge," *Manufacturing Systems* (August 1992): T, E3.

BUSINESS APPLICATION

High-Pressured Selling

John Garbarino has recently been hired as an auto salesman at one of the larger dealerships in the area. Garbarino is anxious to do a good job, but finds himself facing his first dilemma on the job.

As a part of his sales training, Garbarino was told to try to get customers to buy the most expensive cars with a lot of features, even if the customer could not afford such a high-priced vehicle. So when customers are greeted by Garbarino they are supposed to be ushered to the more expensive models right away.

Also, Garbarino has been advised to lie, if necessary, in order to make a sale. As his sales trainer said, "Only tell little 'white lies,' not outright fraud." For example, if a customer appears to want a certain car but is indecisive, Garbarino is supposed to say that another customer had seen the car earlier in the day and is planning to come back for a final look tonight. Even if there is no other customer about to buy the car, Garbarino is expected to go ahead and state that such is the case.

Garbarino feels uncomfortable with these sales tactics and is not sure what to do at this point.

Questions:

1. Do you see anything wrong with leading customers to autos they cannot afford?
2. Does the telling of a white lie constitute an ethical problem with you?
3. What would you do if you were John Garbarino?

EXPERIENTIAL EXERCISE

Approached by a Salesperson

Activity:

Class discussion about various approaches used by salespersons and students' responses to each. About 20 minutes of class time will be needed.

Directions:

1. The instructor reviews the steps of the selling process, with particular emphasis on the steps of approaching and presenting.
2. The instructor asks students to recall a time when a negative approach was used by a salesperson.
3. Several students should be called on to share their experiences. The instructor should ask each student to specify the particular behavior of the salesperson that was so negative.
4. The instructor asks students to recall a time when a positive approach was used by a salesperson. Several students should be called on to share the specifics of their positive experiences.

NOTES

1. Adapted from Sandra Dallas and Gary McWilliams, "Going to Extremes—to Lure the Hot Dogs Back," *Business Week* (March 13, 1995): 100; Mark Maremount, "Do Snowy Slopes Mean Dead Fish?" *Business Week* (March 15, 1993): 99; Marj Charlier, "U.S. Ski Resorts Stress Family Values," *The Wall Street Journal* (November 20, 1992): B1, B8.
2. William P. Dommermuth, *Promotion: Analysis, Creativity, and Strategy* (Boston: Kent Publishing, 1984), 4.

3. Joanne Lipman, "As Industry Feels Spring of Hope, a Forecaster Cools His Optimism," *The Wall Street Journal* (June 3, 1992): B5.
4. Jeff Jensen, "Some Sponsors Pass In-Game Ads," *Advertising Age* (January 23, 1995): 8.
5. Joe Mandese, "Cost to Make TV Ad Nears Quarter-Million," *Advertising Age* (July 4, 1994): 3, 6.
6. R. Craig Endicott, "AT&T Tops Spending Despite Ford Rush," *Advertising Age* (May 11, 1992): 56.
7. Leah Rickard, "New Ammo for Comparative Ads," *Advertising Age* (February 14, 1994): 26.
8. John Fairhall, "Drug Industry Takes Aim at Profiteering Allegations," *Lexington (KY) Herald-Leader* (March 8, 1993): A1, A6.
9. *Advertising Age* (June 20, 1994): 42.
10. Riccardo A. Davis, "Competition Ignites Outdoor Spending," *Advertising Age* (April 11, 1994): 32.
11. Jon Berry, "Don't Leave Home Without It, Wherever You Live," *Business Week* (February 21, 1994): 76–77.
12. Carlton A. Pederson, Milburn D. Wright, and Barton A. Weitz, *Selling: Principles and Methods,* 9e. (Homewood, IL: Irwin, 1988), 11.
13. "Hey, Where's My Survey of Selling Costs?" *Sales & Marketing Management* (March 1991): 42–45.
14. Lawrence B. Chonko and Ben M. Enis, *Professional Selling* (Boston: Allyn and Bacon, 1993).
15. Ira Sager, "The Few, the True, the Blue," *Business Week* (May 30, 1994): 124–126.
16. Kerry Rottenberger and Richard Kern, "The Upside-Down Deming Principle," *Sales & Marketing Management* (June 1992): 39–44.
17. Steve Rubin, "How to Sell Across Cultures," *American Demographics* (March 1994): 56–57.
18. Patricia Sellers, "How to Remake Your Sales Force," *Fortune* (May 4, 1992): 98–103.
19. Christopher Power, Lisa Driscoll, and Earl Bohn, "Smart Selling," *Business Week* (August 3, 1992): 46–48.
20. Bradley A. Stertz, "For LH Models, Chrysler Maps New Way to Sell," *The Wall Street Journal* (June 30, 1992): B1–B2.
21. Susan Caminiti, "Finding New Ways to Sell More," *Fortune* (July 27, 1992): 100–102.
22. Rahul Jacob, "Why Some Customers Are More Equal Than Others," *Fortune* (September 19, 1994): 215–224.
23. Tim Triplett, "Report of Couponing's Death Has Been Greatly Exaggerated," *Marketing News* (October 10, 1994): 1, 2.
24. Jonathan Barry and Lori Bongiorno, "Wilma! What Happened to the Plain Old Ad?" *Business Week* (June 6, 1994): 54–58.
25. Leah Rickard, "Displays Show Pulling Power," *Advertising Age* (February 21, 1994): 34.
26. Laura Zinn, "It's a Bird, It's a Plane—It's a Resurrection," *Business Week* (April 12, 1993): 40.
27. Ronald Grover and Greg Burns, "The World Cup of 'Ambush Marketing,'" *Business Week* (May 2, 1994): 37.
28. Betsy D. Gelb, "How Marketers of Intangibles Can Raise the Odds for Customer Satisfaction," *Journal of Services Marketing* (Summer 1987): 11–18.

Nike Marketing Links Products to Athletic Prowess

In 1954, a silhouette of a cowboy smoking a cigarette was just the outline of a cowboy smoking a cigarette. Six years later, after blanketing the advertising landscape with the cowboy image, Marlboro cigarettes were linked to the image by most Americans. In turn, Marlboro cigarettes became linked to the idea of the romantic, individual, rugged freedom of America's frontier past. This process of linking an image or set of ideas to a product is known as branding. Branding can transform brownish sugared water into Coca-Cola—"The Real Thing." The most powerful brands today all have used marketing techniques to enhance products with some of the compelling characteristics of people. Well-marketed products become brave, sexy, or modern. Nike creates its brand image through a carefully crafted link between star athletes and its shoes. One current Nike ad campaign features Dennis Hopper as a slightly eccentric fan who worships the shoes worn by his athlete heroes. No mention is made of the technology in the shoes, and in most commercials the products are only briefly shown. Each commercial concludes with a shot of the Nike swoosh, leaving no doubt about the image one is buying into when purchasing a Nike product.

Marketing and advertising specialists who serve the most powerful brands—Coca-Cola, Apple, Ford, Nike, and others—are often the most intellectually aggressive and culturally conversant members of a given business. American marketers in particular have taken the art of product promotion to the level of a science that blends economics, psychology, sociology, statistics, and other disciplines. Making marketing into a science doesn't mean that the art has been taken out of it. To the contrary, the intense competition fueled by increasingly well-informed marketers has speeded the evolution of promotion techniques.

Nike marketing combines athletes and an almost fanatical dedication to sport and fitness above all else. The company has a sophisticated marketing program that guards its image carefully. Despite the fact that marketing has made Nike one of the most recognized brands in the world, Nike CEO Phil Knight doesn't hold marketing in high regard.

Nike's View of Marketing

Knight was not necessarily being flip when he remarked one evening to reporters that "marketing's just getting people to buy things." Bill Bowerman, Nike cofounder, was equally succinct when he likened marketing to a certain substance produced by bulls. Cannily, Bowerman observed that the bull substance also makes good fertilizer.

Bowerman is old enough and Knight entrepreneurial enough to realize that true economic success is won by those who place something in the world that wasn't there before. The two are certain they have done that with Nike, so that intimating that their success is due largely to marketing makes both men squirm. Sometimes Knight looks into the business environment modern marketing has made—where the perspiration of certain country-and-western singers is scooped into a bottle and sold as perfume, where a county coroner's office markets T-shirts bearing an image of the chalk line police draw on the ground around murder victims—and he doesn't like what he sees.

"I think that the term 'marketing'—just the process of bringing resources to bear on selling something—isn't necessarily that wonderful a thing," Knight said. "The way I relate to marketing is as sociology. What Nike does well is interpret what people are doing, what they are interested in, and we've been lucky enough to align ourselves completely with what we perceive. In this day and age, the act of trying to sell somebody something they don't need is a wickedly difficult proposition. For us, marketing is building awareness around the products and reminding people what we do."

Advertising was always a touchy subject inside Nike, because Knight was known to believe that the whole process was phony. Athletes, to Knight, were the real ticket. Real athletes in real shoes that enhanced their performance should be all that is necessary to draw the public to Nike products because of the honesty of the process. Bowerman referred to advertising and marketing as "salesmanship." In 1986, Nike job applicants were warned that if they ended up being interviewed by Knight, they should omit the words "advertising," and "marketing" from their conversation.

Nike first began to place some of its advertising with Wieden & Kennedy in 1980. When they met, Knight's first words to Dan Wieden were "I'm Phil Knight, and I hate advertising." But by the late 1980s, Nike's relationship with the much-decorated ad shop was the stuff of Madison Avenue legend. Nike had actually transferred much of its advertising to the much larger firm of Chiat/Day in 1983. Chiat/Day had, in fact, created the first Air Jordan commercial. But, by 1986, Nike and Wieden & Kennedy were a team, and soon thereafter the W&K offices in Portland sported a basketball court complete with bleachers. The Nike anti-establishment philosophy soon became the basis of the managerial culture of the ad agency.

Knight was now saying that perhaps the running boom had been only the advance wave of a much larger health and fitness revolution to which Nike had never attached itself in a fundamental way. In a meeting at W&K, Dan Wieden spoke to Nike brass about a generalized strain of guilt shared by Americans who had let health and fitness issues slide or had managed to so complicate their lives that exercise and health had never become part of their routines. Wieden said Nike should address the sense of ennui he perceived in the culture. "What we need to convey," Wieden said, "is just go ahead, just fuck it." But the overhead that came up on the screen said it a different way. Everyone in the room looked at the words "Just Do It," and most of them were impressed.

In 1993, a year in which Nike was one of the first three companies to be inducted into the American Marketing Association Hall of Fame (with Coke and Absolut Vodka), Nike spent $250 million promoting products and the Nike brand. Brands considered for the Hall of Fame had "to show sustained success, represent innovative and trailblazing marketing, and have had a dramatic impact on our lifestyle, becoming enshrined as American icons." Knight told a *Harvard Business Review* reporter that "We had determined that we wanted Nike to be the world's best sports and fitness company and the Nike brand to represent sports and fitness activities."

Critical Thinking Challenge

Both Knight and Bowerman have expressed their disdain for marketing, despite the fact that Nike is one of the most effective marketers in the world. How do you explain their attitude in light of Nike's marketing success? Nike marketing is not as driven by segmentation as some other companies. This could cause the company to miss emerging or hidden consumer segments. What market segments do you think might emerge over the next five years that could be very lucrative to the athletic shoe industry?

The Birth of an Advertising Campaign

In 1986, following the first round of companywide layoffs, Nike still dominated the running-shoe market. The new Air Jordan line had opened with a bang but was suddenly slumping badly, in part because Michael Jordan had broken his foot early in the season and would miss 64 games. The long-thought-to-be-dead Converse was cutting into Nike sales, and Nike shoes were still relatively invisible in health clubs and on the aerobic dance scene.

Nike designers were working feverishly to try to address the latest fitness vogue—cross training. Cross training is based on the theory that participation in a variety of sports and exercises enhances performance and lowers the chance of injury. In the fall of 1986, John McEnroe played in the Volvo Tennis Tournament in Los Angeles wearing a grayish, relatively high-sided shoe with a big strap across the top. This was the world's introduction to the Nike Air Cross Trainer. Customers immediately flocked to athletic shoe stores hoping to purchase a pair of the strange shoes they had seen on McEnroe. But customers were searching for *tennis shoes,* and when they were told that the shoes McEnroe wore were not tennis shoes but rather cross trainers, they were confused. As with many other Nike innovations built for athletes, the premise of cross-trainers was not clear to the American public.

Enter onto the scene Jim Riswold, an ad copywriter with W&K. Although Riswold was 30 years old, many who knew him said they were still waiting for him to turn 13. Riswold's Portland house is cluttered with a collection of toys and other artifacts connected to Warner Brothers and his childhood hero, Bugs Bunny. Riswold is also a bona fide sports nut in the manner of a somewhat hyperactive adolescent boy. He spent seven years as an undergraduate at the University of Washington. Riswold initially earned a BA in history. However, instead of going on to law school as he had planned, he stayed on and earned another BA in philosophy, intending to pursue graduate studies in the discipline. Realizing that his inability to read or speak German would impair his intended research into certain 19th-century German philosophers, Riswold decided to seek a third BA, this one in communications.

In 1979, Riswold had a part-time job working for the Seattle SuperSonics professional basketball team. Eventually this led to a full-time job with the ad firm employed by the Sonics. Riswold figured he'd stick with advertising until he figured out what he really wanted to study during his next pass through school. But then he heard about a tiny ad agency in Portland that was looking for a writer. Riswold submitted his résumé, and he soon moved to Oregon to work for Wieden & Kennedy. Records show that he was the agency's sixth employee.

In a meeting with Nike designers in late 1986, Riswold said, "You know, I've been thinking about these next cross-trainers you want to move out next year. If you're thinking about hooking the shoes up with a guy, this Bo Jackson kid's a natural." Riswold was assigned the job of creating a way to connect Bo Jackson—who would never actually play his sports in cross-trainers—with the new category of shoes. Riswold's first attempt was a photographic concept for billboards and walls that depicted the powerful bare-chested torso of the athlete clad in football shoulder pads. Bo also held a baseball bat across the back of his neck like a yoke.

Jackson won the 1985 Heisman Trophy as a senior football player at Auburn University. At first, Knight was less than pleased that Riswold had, without his approval, agreed to a $100,000 endorsement deal with a kid from Alabama who could have played high-profile pro football but opted instead for a backwater minor league baseball career. But a year later Knight's anger was allayed as Jackson was playing major league baseball with the Kansas City Royals and had committed to play at least part of the next football season with the Los Angeles Raiders.

Riswold wrote a series of commercials with Bo exercising like crazy. He rode a bike like a madman in one and worked out furiously in another. Here, the commercials clearly implied, was the ultimate cross-training athlete. Bo was ready for anything. He was intense and hungry. Yet, the commercials were tinged with irony. In the commercials, Bo was allowed to demonstrate that he understood that his endeavors bordered on the limits of mortal capacity.

The ads were judged quite good within W&K and inside Nike, but everyone involved knew that the link between the cross-trainers and Bo Jackson could be made larger. And with Nike drifting as the number two athletic shoe power behind Reebok, nothing less than explosive success would be accepted. Speaking of Nike customers, Knight said, "They need to be woken up! What we need is a way to wake them up all over again."

Riswold had always believed that the unique selling proposition—the famous USP, which, according to standard advertising and marketing practices, was the feature or design of a product that distinguished it from the competition—could under carefully crafted circumstances be the athlete, or at least the image of the athlete. The trick was to cause an athlete to rise above the mire of sports platitudes, the clichés and the canned emotions the public had come to expect. A new creative perspective on the sports hero was needed.

In February of 1988, with the Bo-on-a-bike and other cross-training spots due to premiere that coming spring, Riswold was sitting in McCormick & Schmick's, a bar and restaurant on the corner of First and Oak, a few blocks from the W&K offices. Nike and W&K employees were often known to hang out there after work to think together. Tom Clarke, then Nike vice president of marketing, and several other Nike employees were also at the bar that night. "We've got to ignite this category," said Tom Clarke. "Bo's going to be making the national highlight reels all the time. It's time for us to really light the fire." Riswold already knew Nike was prepared to risk a significant portion of its ad budget on an inspired cross-training campaign.

"Thanks for reminding me," Riswold responded to Clarke's assertion while staring into his beer. "Bo," he said. "Bo . . . Bo . . . Bo what?"

Bo Derek," someone said. "Bo Schembechler," added another, naming the football coach at the University of Michigan. "Bo Diddley," said Tom Clarke. Following this suggestion, a brief discussion was held concerning the rock-and-roll performer. Bo Diddley stories were told, and the names of his songs were tossed back and forth for several minutes, until Riswold suddenly said, "We have to change the subject. Now." Everyone knew he had an idea. Later that night, celebrating like crazy, Riswold backed the phrase "Bo Knows" out of "Bo, you don't know Diddley," the latter having come to him back in the bar.

As the commercial evolved in his mind, Riswold combined "Bo Knows" with the cavalcade images of Nike stars hailing from different sports. Inside a 60-second commercial, the cross-training implications projected by Bo really knowing football and baseball could be ironized by testimonials to his limitless power from other Nike stars. Jordan could testify that Bo knew basketball. McEnroe could say that Bo knew tennis. Riswold envisioned Wayne Gretzky testifying that Bo knew hockey, too. A bunch of outsized weightlifters on Venice Beach would attest to Bo's knowledge, and, finally, Bo Diddley himself would appear, with Bo Jackson in a Bo Diddley hat, wearing spandex workout pants and hacking on a guitar at the other Bo's legendary side! By now, Riswold was jumping up and down on his bed.

When the commercial was completed it was shown in June 1989 to a thousand Nike sales representatives at a massive conclave at the Beaverton headquarters. The reps all jumped to their feet and applauded, whistled, and cheered for five minutes after the commercial was over. Scott Bedbury, Nike director of advertising, went to Knight and proposed it was time to take one of those Knight-like risks. Knight agreed to double the investment in the "Bo Knows" spots, from $6 million to $12 million. All running shoe advertising was put on hold, as was support for the burgeoning basketball category. No money would be spent on test groups or focus groups that might help measure the power of the commercial. All the money available and the entire back-to-school selling season would be hung on Bo.

On the morning of the July 1989 baseball All-Star game, a full-page ad in the national newspaper *USA Today* announced that anyone missing the Nike commercial in the top of the fourth inning would be sorry. As fate would have it, Bo played in the All-Star game that night and hit a home run in his first at bat. A plane flew over the stadium trailing a "Bo Knows" sign. Smaller "Bo Knows" signs and "Bo Knows" hats were unveiled in the stands by Nike people spaced throughout the crowd. And then the commercial aired in the "A" spot just as planned.

Fate again smiled on Nike. After the commercial ran, Jackson was the first batter up in the bottom of the fourth inning. He singled to right and went on to win the games' MVP award. As he watched everything fall into place that All-Star evening, Riswold said, "God is a Bo Jackson fan."

The "Bo Knows" commercial wasn't planned to run again for several weeks to coincide with the back-to-school sales season, but it was shown close to 20 times during those weeks anyway. It appeared on evening news spots about Bo and his brilliant new commercial. It ran on the network morning news shows and on the syndicated *Entertainment Tonight.*

As soon as the selling of Bo's shoes began, Nike quickly dominated 80 percent of the new cross-training shoe market. Sales of the shoes rose from $40 million after John McEnroe had introduced the shoes to more than $400 million at the height of the Bo frenzy. By the end of 1991, Bo Jackson was the second most famous athlete in the world. Nike's "Bo Knows" marketing campaign turned out to be well worth Knight's risk.

Critical Thinking Challenge

Nike sales are pushed higher through the use of innovative advertising that links Nike products to *images* of athletes. The images are not necessarily accurate or true. Bo Jackson was not able to play all the sports his commercials said he "knows." Do you think there are any ethical issues that arise concerning this form of advertising? Discuss. What do you think Nike sales would be like if government restricted advertising so that only technical specifications of products could be conveyed in messages? What do you think American culture would be like?

Source: Adapted from Donald Katz, *Just Do It* (Random House, New York, 1994); Matthew Grimm, "Nike Vision," *Brandweek* (March 29, 1993): 18–25; Geraldine E. Willigan, "High-Performance Marketing: An Interview with Phil Knight," *Harvard Business Review* (July/August 1992): 90–101.

PART 6

Financial Management

C H A P T E R 17

Money and Banking

LEARNING OBJECTIVES

1. Define *money* and state its functions and characteristics.
2. Identify the elements that make up both the M1 and M2 money supplies.
3. Compare the different types of financial institutions.
4. Explain how the federal government is involved in money and banking in the United States.
5. Discuss how the Federal Reserve System controls the supply of money and credit.
6. Identify the major changes occurring in banking and the impact of technology.

For the past 30 years, the financial industry has become ever more consolidated. Many industry experts believe that as many as 50 percent of the existing commercial banks today will not be around in another 10 years. In 1992 and 1993, there were almost 400 banking industry mergers each year. Joel P. Friedman, a bank specialist with Andersen Consulting, predicts that with the regulatory barriers to interstate banking falling fast, we are likely to see 10 to 20 national banks, as well as 50 to 100 large regional banks created by the year 2000.

According to Richard Florida of Carnegie Mellon University's Heinz School of Public Policy, the United States built a uniquely decentralized banking system after the Depression and World War II, but now we are seeing "a blowing out of the boundaries between these separate entities because of increased global competition." He points to two major trends in banking: *economies of scope*—banks going into related businesses—and *economies of scale*—merging and acquiring. "The bigger you are, the more acquisitions you can make," says H. Rodgin Chone of Sullivan & Cromwell. BankAmerica, the nation's second largest bank next to Citicorp, appears to be following these two trends. BankAmerica is currently shifting some of their business efforts into a related business called *wholesale banking* which serves corporate customers; and in 1992 BankAmerica had the largest bank merger in history with the $4 billion purchase of Security Pacific.

Consolidations may be profitable for the banking industry, but the results will ultimately affect employees and consumers. Employees who face layoffs from mergers are obvious victims. For example, when San Diego Trust & Savings Bank was acquired by First InterState, full-time teller jobs started being phased out in lieu of more cost-effective part-time tellers. Retail branch customers often complain of post-merger service decline. For instance, 5,000 residents in Julian, CA, only had one branch bank, HomeFed Bank. When Great Western Bank acquired all of HomeFed Bank's branches in 1993, it also decided to close the branch in Julian. As a result, the 5,000 residents have to travel 30 miles to the nearest branch bank and ATM.

With such an extremely powerful drive to consolidate, no financial institution, no matter how large or small, is completely safe from mergers or takeovers.[1]

Why is the banking industry contracting so rapidly?

The healthy functioning of a modern mixed economic system—whether it will have economic growth or decline, prosperity or recession, employment or mass unemployment—depends largely on what is happening with money. Money is an important commodity to all of us. With it, we can purchase many of the things that we need to survive. In the United States and other great industrial and economic powers such as Japan and Germany, we associate money with banks; therefore banks and other banklike institutions (such as credit unions and savings and loans) are also very important to us. We depend on them to keep our savings safe, to make it possible for us to pay our bills with a check, and to lend us money for the major purchases we need to make. We also depend on banks to keep our economy healthy by serving the financial needs of business.

In this chapter, we study money and banking. First we discuss the need for a common element for exchanges and how money serves as this common element, or medium. Then we consider the functions and characteristics of money and how the money supply is measured. Next we discuss financial institutions: commercial banks, other banking institutions, and nonbanking institutions. A discussion follows on the government's role in the monetary system and banking, including the Federal Reserve System and government regulation. Finally, we look at the future of banking and discuss the technological changes we see already.

MONEY AND EXCHANGE SYSTEMS

One of the things taught in economics is that individuals cannot efficiently produce for themselves everything they need to survive. You cannot grow all your own food, sew your own clothes, construct your own home, build your own car, or teach yourself business. You depend on others to provide some of these things for you. As we noted previously, one way you can get these things is through bartering, that is, exchanging something you have (other than money) with someone else to get the other things you need. For example, if you were a carpenter, you might build something for a tailor if he would make you a suit.

You might think that this type of exchange does not occur anymore, but actually bartering does still occur. For example, many radio stations and television stations exchange commercial time with companies for merchandise: One may offer commercial time to a car dealer in exchange for an automobile to give away as part of a radio station listener sweepstakes. As we prepared this book, bartering was still used when Eastern European countries transacted business with international partners. Because the economic isolation of these countries causes a lack of sufficient hard currency in their central banks, a significant amount of bartering still takes place: Florida phosphate for Polish sulfur, Russian merchant ships for Pepsi Cola extract, and Rumanian glass and textiles for General Electric turbines.[2]

While bartering works, it is not very efficient. If you are a carpenter, you cannot build something for everyone you want something from. You could not, for example, go build a step for a grocer every time you needed a carton of milk. After a while, the grocer wouldn't need any more steps, and you would be tired of building steps. And, if every time you wanted to get a carton of milk you had to find a grocer who needed a step built, you would waste a great deal of time looking for one. It would be better if you could receive some common item for building steps and the grocer could receive a similar common item for selling milk.

Money
Anything commonly accepted as a means of paying for goods and services.

Money is this item. **Money** is anything that is commonly accepted as a means of paying for the goods and services individuals need and want. Money enables us to function in society and to have the things we need to survive—things such as housing, food, clothing, transportation, heat, and water.

Money has not always been the coins and paper bills known to us. Throughout history various things of value have been used as money. For example, in many parts of the ancient world, salt was used as money because it was rare and necessary to life. Among many early American cultures, furs or pelts were used as money. Eventually valuable metals became the most common type of money; in fact, gold coins were used as money in the United States as recently as 1933.

Currency, which is dollar bills and coins, fits most of the definition of money. However, checks are accepted payment for purchases, and checking account deposits are considered money and not currency. To define money as currency would be considered too narrow for most economists.

FUNCTIONS OF MONEY

Money has three basic functions. It serves as a medium of exchange, as a measure of relative value, and as a store of value (see Exhibit 17.1).

As a medium of exchange, money enables two individuals to exchange without having to barter; that is, the carpenter doesn't have to build a step for the grocer every time he wants a carton of milk. The carpenter can build steps or anything else for anybody, receive money for his services, and use the money to purchase milk from the grocer. The grocer can in turn use the money received from the carpenter and others to purchase a suit from the tailor.

As a measure of relative value, money allows two dissimilar items to be purchased on a similar basis. It is in terms of money that we think of value. How many cartons of milk should the grocer pay for a suit? If asked that question, you might ask, How much is a carton of milk worth? and, How much is the suit worth? You would want to define the exchange in terms of the relative value of the two items and would use the value in dollars (money) to determine how many cartons of milk it should take to buy a suit. Money helps us think of different things in terms of a common value base.

Exhibit 17.1
Functions and Characteristics of Money

Functions	Characteristics	
Medium of exchange	Acceptance	Durability
Measure of relative value	Divisibility	Stability
Store of value	Portability	Scarcity

As a store of value, money makes it possible for us to hold onto the value over time. If the grocer would have to hold the value of his milk in milk, he could not hold it for long because it would spoil. However, if he sells the milk and gets money for it, he can hold the money until he wishes to purchase something.

Of course, other things can serve as stores of value. Some people collect antiques, stamps, or baseball cards and keep these things as stores of value because they will likely increase in value over time. While the value of these and other items is important, money has one distinct advantage over them: It is highly liquid. That is, it can be obtained and disposed of quickly and easily. You don't have to find someone to buy it first. We will cover liquidity in more detail in our discussion of the money supply.

Characteristics of Money

As noted before, a number of significant problems surface when we try to exchange steps for milk. Some forms of money also cause problems. For example, the inhabitants of one South Pacific Island used huge stones, weighing as much as 90 pounds, for money. This certainly made everyone aware of how much money each of them had, since these stones were very visible. But if one of the inhabitants wanted to purchase something really only worth one-fourth of a stone, how could they divide the stone? And if they decided to buy something from an individual on the other side of the island, how did they get the stone to that individual? Clearly, to be useful as a medium of exchange, money needs to have certain characteristics: acceptability, divisibility, portability, durability, stability, and scarcity.

Acceptibility. To be useful, money must be accepted by the general population it is meant to serve. You may have heard the expression "That isn't worth a continental dollar." The expression refers to the continental currency issued during the American Revolution. This currency was issued in such large amounts and with so little backing that it was virtually useless for purchasing goods. These dollars were not an effective medium of exchange.

Divisibility. If you wanted to buy a single candy bar for 25 cents, you would pay the grocer with a quarter or give her a dollar and receive three quarters as change. If the dollar was not divisible, you would have to buy four candy bars or allow the grocer to make a large profit from the exchange. The American dollar is easily divisible. It can be divided into pennies (100), nickels (20), dimes (10), quarters (4), or half dollars (2). This ability makes it an easily used medium of exchange, since it can be used to purchase items of any monetary value. All money needs this characteristic of divisibility.

Portability. Not surprisingly, paper currency and coins are the most common forms of money throughout the world. They are easily transported from one location to another. Dollar bills fold easily and store in a wallet, and coins are easily carried in a pocket or change purse. This makes money easy to take with us and use when we want to make an exchange. Those natives in the South Pacific could not fold their 90-pound rocks and tuck them into their pockets to go shopping.

Durability. Money must be durable. It cannot act effectively as a store of value if it does not last. If a society used milk as money, a lot of sour money would appear in a short period of time. Paper money and coins are very durable; they last a long time. The average dollar is in circulation for 18 months and may be folded several thousand times. While it is true that coins are more durable, they are not as portable as paper money, and so both are used. Paper money maximizes portability, and coins make the paper money easily divisible.

Stability. To maintain acceptability, money needs to be relatively stable. People lose faith in money when its value is not stable. Inflation is a major concern for governments. When inflation runs extremely high, people begin to lose faith in their currency as a medium for exchange and as a store of value. They begin to abandon their currency and demand gold coins, or they may begin to store their wealth in items such as real estate and precious metals. Furthermore, when inflation runs extremely high, as it has in recent years in many Latin American countries, people abandon their currency and return to the barter system or use another country's money. (The U.S. dollar, the German mark, and the Japanese yen enjoy wide use.) Neither of these solutions benefits the economy of the affected country. The barter system is not economically efficient and therefore tends to stunt economic growth, and other currencies are usually not available in sufficient quantities to allow for a normal, healthy economy.

Scarcity. By scarce we do not mean that money needs to be rare or in very limited supply, like rare stamps. Rather we mean that the supply cannot be unlimited. Money cannot grow on trees and everyone cannot have all they want, or it would have little value. For this reason, governments go to great lengths to prevent counterfeiting of their currency. Currency in the United States is produced by the U.S. Treasury Department; production of money by anyone else is a serious crime. Governments also go to great lengths to make duplication of currency difficult. Some countries use highly colored paper, while others use highly watermarked paper. The United States uses special paper with small red and blue silk threads imbedded in it. This makes counterfeiting the currency difficult and avoids the watering down of its value.

THE SUPPLY OF MONEY

To measure the money supply, we measure the amount of money in the economy. However, what to measure is a problem. Should someone's home be considered money? After all, it can be sold for cash. An individual's car? Boat? Or should the money supply include only cash?

Liquidity
A measure of how quickly an item can be converted to cash.

To understand the money supply in the United States, you have to first understand the concept of liquidity. **Liquidity** is a measure of how quickly an item can be converted to cash. Obviously the most liquid item is cash itself, since it does not need to be converted. However, many other items approach cash in liquidity because they function as cash in many transactions. These items include demand deposits, against which checks can be written or from which funds can be withdrawn; time deposits, from which funds can be withdrawn; and money market funds, which can be immediately sold for cash.

When measuring the U.S. money supply, we look at it at various levels, each including items that are less liquid than the items included in the previous level of the money supply. For our purposes, the first two levels of the money supply are the most important. These two levels are referred to as M1 and M2 (see Exhibit 17.2).

Exhibit 17.2
The Total Money Supply, May 1994 (seasonally adjusted in billions of dollars)

Currency	$ 338
+	
Demand Deposits	386
+	
Travelers' Checks & Other Checkable Deposits	420
=	
Total M1	**$1,144**
+	
Time Deposits & Money Market Accounts★	2,447
=	
Total M2	**$3,591**

★ Figure also includes overnight repurchase agreements, overnight Eurodollars, money market fund balances (general purpose and broker-dealer), savings deposits, and small time deposits.

Source: Adapted from "Money Stock, Liquid Assets, and Debt Measures," *Federal Reserve Bulletin,* (August 1994): pp A14–A15.

M1
The first level of money supply measurement; includes the most highly liquid forms of money; currency and demand deposits.

Currency
The coins and paper money spent to purchase things. Cashier's checks, money orders, and traveler's checks are also considered currency.

Demand Deposits
Bank accounts against which an account holder can write checks, withdrawing money immediately and without prior notice.

M2
The second level of money supply measurement; includes time deposits and money market accounts in addition to currency and demand deposits.

Time Deposits
Savings accounts that allow the financial institution to require notice before withdrawal or to assess a penalty for early withdrawal.

Money Market Accounts
Deposits that pay interest rates very competitive with those paid on other short-term investments; some allow a limited number of checks to be written in amounts over $500.

M1

The first level of money supply measurement, **M1,** includes the most highly liquid forms of money: currency and demand deposits.

Currency. **Currency** includes the coins and paper money spent to purchase things. Actually, even though most of us think of currency when we think of money, it represents only a small part of the total M1 money supply, about 30 percent. Cashiers' checks, money orders, and travelers' checks are also considered currency, since they can be used even in situations where the individual cashing them is not personally known.

Demand Deposits. Deposits at banks against which an account holder can write checks, withdrawing money immediately and without prior notice, are **demand deposits.** The holder can require the bank to pay another person or business (called the payee) the amount written on the check. Of course, the bank does not have to honor the demand if the holder's account doesn't have enough money to cover the amount of the check. This situation is referred to as insufficient funds.

Checks are used about 10 percent of the time in financial transactions conducted in the United States.[3] They are popular due to a number of factors. First, checks are more secure than currency. A person carrying checks does not have to worry about the loss of currency. Checks cannot be spent by anyone other than the account holder; they require the account holder's signature to be cashed. Second, they may be more convenient for paying odd amounts or large amounts. Writing one check for $187.85 is easier than counting out nine 20s, a five, two ones, three quarters, and a dime. It is also safer, since carrying large amounts of cash invites crime. Finally, checks make payment by mail easier and safer, and the canceled check gives the person making the payment a record of the transaction.

M2

The second level of money supply measurement **M2,** includes time deposits and money market accounts in addition to currency and demand deposits.

Time Deposits. Savings accounts that allow the financial institution to require notice—prior notification by the account holder—before withdrawal or that allow the financial institution to assess a penalty for early withdrawal are called **time deposits.** Time deposits, while not used for transactions or as a medium of exchange, are extremely liquid. Money can be moved from time deposit accounts to checking accounts, or cash can be withdrawn to make purchases.

Money Market Accounts. Accounts that pay interest rates very competitive with the interest rates paid on other short-term investments, such as short-term U.S. Treasury bills, are called **money market accounts.** Typically handled through banks, money market accounts pay interest based on investments in such things as U.S. Treasury bills. The number of checks that a holder can write each month from a money market account is limited, often to three.

Credit Cards

Not officially considered money, credit cards represent an individual's approval for credit. Since they can be used to draw directly against that credit, they are in a sense a medium of exchange. They represent a special credit arrangement between the cardholder and the financial institution issuing the card. Each time the cardholder uses the card, he or she in effect takes out a loan for the amount of the charge. This loan can be repaid at the end of the billing period, or (in the case of bank cards and retail credit cards) a stated minimum amount can be paid each month, with interest charged on the outstanding balance until it is repaid.

Over 1.1 billion credit cards are in circulation, or 12 per U.S. household.[4] In fact they are becoming a more and more popular medium of exchange in the industrial world (i.e., U.S., Japan, Europe). This is due in part to the increased willingness of merchants to accept credit cards and the increased desire of banks and other financial institutions to issue credit cards. Visa and MasterCard are the two largest global cards with 323.3 and 204 million outstanding cards respectively.[5]

Banks and other financial institutions want to issue credit cards because they are profitable. Credit card issuers earn money in three ways: fees charged to customers, interest from outstanding credit balances, and the "discount" charge they assess merchants on each purchase. In many cases, cardholders pay an annual membership fee, and interest charges on unpaid balances can range from 6 to 20 percent annually.[6] As a result, credit cards generate more profits than other bank services. Cobranded cards, which are those issued jointly by businesses and credit card companies, are a growing trend in the credit card business.[7] Some recent partnerships in cobranding include General Motors and Household International, Shell Oil and Chemical Bank, and Apple Computer and Citicorp.

FINANCIAL INSTITUTIONS: THEIR ROLE IN BUSINESS

Financial institutions that serve business include banking institutions—commercial banks, thrifts, credit unions—and nonbanking institutions, such as insurance companies and commercial and consumer finance companies. Before 1863 all commercial banks in the United States were chartered by banking commissions of the states in which they operated. To eliminate the abuses of some of the state-chartered banks, the National Banking Act of 1863 created a new banking system of federally chartered banks, supervised by the Office of the Comptroller of Currency, a department of the U.S. Treasury.[8] Today the United States has a dual banking system in which banks supervised by the federal government and by the states operate side by side. Insurance companies and consumer finance companies are regulated by the states in which they operate.

Commercial Banks

Commercial Bank
A profit-making institution that holds the deposits of individuals and businesses in checking and savings accounts and then uses these funds to make loans.

About 10,600 commercial banks do business in the United States.[9] A **commercial bank** is a profit-making institution that holds the deposits of individuals and businesses in checking and savings accounts and then uses these funds to make loans to individuals, businesses, and the government. Commercial banks in the United States are chartered by either the state or the federal government. While bank charters issued by states and federal government do differ, the differences are not noticeable to the individual depositor. Exhibit 17.3 shows the top 15 commercial banks in the United States, based on their assets.

Commercial banks are sometimes called full-service banks. Certainly most offer an extensive range of services. In addition to checking and savings accounts and personal and business loans, commercial banks offer bank credit cards, safe-deposit boxes, discount brokerage services, wire transfers of funds between banks, financial advice, overdraft protection (for checking accounts), travelers' checks, and trusts.

Thrifts and Credit Unions

Institutions other than commercial banks can accept deposits from customers or members and provide some form of checking account. These other banking institutions include thrifts (savings and loan associations and savings banks), and credit unions.

Savings and Loan Associations (S&Ls)
Institutions that now offer both checking and savings accounts and use the majority of their funds to finance home mortgages; sometimes called thrifts.

Savings and loan associations (S&Ls) offer both savings and checking accounts and use the majority of their funds to make home mortgage loans to consumers. They were created with the primary purpose of encouraging family thrift. Individual households could regularly place small amounts of money in these institutions and earn higher interest on their savings than they could

Exhibit 17.3
Top 15 Commercial Banks in the United States Based on Total Assets, December 31, 1993

Rank	Bank and Head Office	Assets ($ in millions)
1	Citicorp, New York	$216,574.0
2	BankAmerica Corp., San Francisco	186,933.0
3	NationsBank Corp., Charlotte, NC	157,686.0
4	Chemical Banking Corp., New York	149,888.0
5	J. P. Morgan & Co., New York	133,888.0
6	Chase Manhattan Corp., New York	102,103.0
7	Bankers Trust N.Y., New York	92,082.0
8	Banc One Corp., Columbus, OH	79,918.6
9	First Union Corp., Charlotte, NC	70,787.0
10	PNC Bank Corp., Pittsburgh	62,080.0
11	First Chicago Corp., Chicago	52,560.0
12	Wells Fargo & Co., San Francisco	52,513.0
13	First Interstate Bankroll, Los Angeles	51,461.3
14	Norwest Corp., Minneapolis	50,782.3
15	Fleet Financial Group, Providence	47,922.5

Source: Adapted from "The 100 Largest Commercial Banking Companies," *Fortune*, May 30, 1994: pp 204–205.

in banks. (With deregulation this is no longer true.) The S&Ls would in turn lend this money to individual households for the purchase of homes. At one time, over 60 percent of all residential mortgages were originated by thrifts.

Savings Banks
Depositor-owned, banklike institutions that began in New England in the early 19th century with the purpose of paying interest on deposits.

Savings banks are also called mutual savings banks because they are depositor owned. They are almost identical to S&Ls in their operation and are chartered by the individual states. While savings banks have existed for nearly 200 years in New England, they have not really caught on in other parts of the country. Today, savings banks are primarily concentrated in the New England states, New York, and New Jersey.

Credit Unions
Member-owned savings cooperatives, normally sponsored by a union, company, or professional or religious group; typically concentrate on small, short-term consumer loans.

A form of savings cooperative because they are member owned, **credit unions** are typically sponsored by a union, company, or professional or religious group. Because credit unions are member owned, and thus not profit-motivated, they typically offer no-fee or no-minimum-balance checking accounts, lower interest rates on loans, and higher interest rates on deposits.[10] While there are over 13,400 credit unions nationwide, individual credit unions tend to be rather small.[11] They have typically concentrated on savings and short-term consumer loans such as auto loans. However, with deregulation they have been able to expand their services and today offer share draft accounts (similar to checking accounts) and even provide some long-term mortgage loans.

Nonbanking Financial Institutions

Financial institutions act as sources and users of funds. Given this fact, many institutions that do not provide banking services qualify as financial institutions. These include insurance companies, pension funds, large brokerage houses, and commercial and consumer finance companies.

Insurance Companies. Insurance companies were originally created by groups (such as trade unions and religious groups) who pooled their resources to provide some financial protection for members and families should the member become disabled or die. The first life insurance company in the United States, Presbyterian Ministers' Fund in Philadelphia, was established in 1759.

Today insurance companies accept premium payments from policyholders and provide various types of protection. (Insurance will be discussed in greater detail in Chapter 20.) Insurance companies use the funds generated through premium payments to provide long-term loans to corporations, to provide commercial real estate loans, and to purchase government bonds. Property and casualty insurance companies are regulated by states and operate in a similar fashion to life insurance companies.

Pension Funds. Pension funds can be set up by a company, union, or nonprofit organization to provide for the retirement needs of its members or employees. To meet these needs, the fund uses a pool of money created by contributions of the members, the employer, or both. They invest these funds in long-term mortgages on commercial property, business loans, government bonds, and common stock in major firms. In addition, company pension funds will typically invest a portion of the fund in the company's own stock.

State, local, and federal governments have set up pension funds for their employees. A very important public pension plan is Social Security (Old Age and Survivors Insurance Fund), which covers virtually all individuals employed in the private sector. The fund was originally set up to supplement individual savings and other pension funds as a means of support for retired persons. It is administered through the federal government which collects social security funds from employers and deducts them from employee checks. These funds are used to pay benefits to the retired, the disabled, and young children of deceased parents.

However, many experts fear there will not be sufficient funds to pay future benefits. The reason for this concern is the change in the makeup of the American work force. The average age of U.S. citizens is increasing and, with the current low birth rate, will continue to increase. As a result, the number of people requiring benefits (especially retirement benefits) is increasing, while the number of people working and contributing to the fund is decreasing. This means that in the future fewer people will be paying into the social security fund and more people will be withdrawing funds from it. The result could be a serious shortfall.

Large Brokerage Houses. Brokerage firms buy and sell stocks, bonds, and other assets for their customers. They have also started to provide other financial services. Many brokerages have created accounts for their customers, such as Merrill Lynch's Cash Management Account and Paine Webber's Cash-Fund, which pay interest on deposits and allow clients to write checks, borrow money, and withdraw cash.

Commercial and Consumer Finance Companies. By issuing commercial paper (large corporate promissory notes) or stocks and bonds, **finance companies** acquire funds. They use the funds to make loans appropriate to consumer and business needs. Finance companies typically charge a higher rate of interest because of the higher risk of the loans that they make. These companies also frequently require some sort of collateral for loans. Businesses may be required to pledge their inventory as security for the loan, and an individual may have to put up an automobile or some interest in stocks as security. In recent years, finance companies such as Household Finance Corporation and General Motors Acceptance Corporation have become increasingly competitive with commercial banks. They are now often able to offer attractive loans with longer-term paybacks.

Finance Companies Institutions that offer short-term loans, typically at a higher rate, to businesses and individuals unable to obtain loans elsewhere.

As you can see, consumers have more choices for financial services than ever, and the choices are harder to make. Test your choice of bank and banking services with Your Values and Attitudes.

YOUR VALUES AND ATTITUDES

How Do Your Banking Choices Measure Up?

Directions: Assess your financial services by answering the following questions. If you cannot answer them, ask your banker. Then review the feedback to determine what changes you might make in your banking practices.

Checking account:

1. What are the fees?
2. Must you maintain a minimum balance to avoid fees or to qualify for free services?
3. What does the monthly statement look like?
4. What does the bank charge for money orders or certified checks?

Interest-paying accounts:

1. How is interest calculated?
2. Are there any restrictions on withdrawals, such as only a certain number allowed each month or a fee after a certain number?
3. Can you write checks on the account? How many per month?

Credit cards:

1. What are the annual percentage rate and the annual fee?
2. What is the grace period on the card?
3. Does the card also function as a debit card?

Feedback: After reviewing the information that follows, think about changes you might consider in your banking choices. How will these changes benefit you?

Checking accounts:

Fees vary. If no minimum balance is required, you should pay no more than 20 cents a check and $5 per month. With a required-minimum-balance account, first figure how much interest you would earn if the minimum balance were invested. If the interest you would earn is equal to or greater than the fees you would have to pay if you did not have the balance tied up, you may be better off paying the fees.

Balancing the checkbook at the end of every month is easier if the statement lists checks in numeric order rather than by date of receipt. Statements that summarize types of transactions are also helpful.

While the cost of money orders or certified checks may vary, money orders should not cost any more than you would have to pay at the currency exchange or the post office. Certified checks should run $3 to $6.

Interest-paying accounts:

For the saver, the best method for calculating interest is day of deposit to day of withdrawal. And the more often your interest is compounded, the higher the yield. Daily compounding is ideal.

Withdrawal restrictions can cause a problem for small savings accounts used as a backup to bill payments. Check for required minimum balances to avoid fees, and make sure the fees are reasonable.

Many more savings or interest-bearing accounts give check writing privileges. If the restrictions are not too great and your volume is not too high, many of these accounts make excellent alternatives to simple checking accounts.

Credit cards:

If you use your card a great deal and let your unpaid balance build up, you need a card with a lower rate of interest and no transaction fees. If you pay off your card every month, look for minimum annual fees and don't worry about the interest rate. Most banks allow a 25-day grace period before any interest is changed. Some charge interest from the day of purchase on the card. If you pay off your balance every month, look for a card with a grace period.

Debit cards, similar to credit cards, deduct funds directly from the customer's account rather than creating a loan. Once heralded as the new generation of plastic, they have not caught on nearly as well as expected. Part of the reason is the loss of the float, or the period between the time you write a check and the time the check clears your account. However, debit cards are accepted in many cases where checks would not be.

Source: "Ten Money Saving Questions for Your Banker," *Money,* March 1988, p. 100. Reprinted from MONEY Magazine by special permission; copyright 1988 The Time Inc. Magazine Company.

GOVERNMENT INVOLVEMENT IN MONEY AND BANKING

The federal government is very involved in money and banking in this country. It insures deposits in commercial banks and other banking institutions, regulates commercial banks and other banking and financial institutions, and through the Federal Reserve System controls the money supply and the flow of money through the banking system.

Insuring Bank Deposits

Before the creation of insurance funds, any bank failure resulted in almost all of the depositors losing whatever savings they had deposited with the bank. This problem was most apparent during the early years of the Depression. In 1933 nearly 4,000 banks collapsed, leaving hundreds of thousands of depositors without any way of recovering their savings. In many cases, this spelled financial ruin both for individuals and for businesses.

The Federal Deposit Insurance Corporation (FDIC) is responsible for protecting the deposits in banks. The FDIC provides $100,000 worth of insurance for depositor accounts and, perhaps more important, sets requirements for sound banking practices and regularly checks on banks to make sure these practices are being followed. Any commercial bank that is a member of the Federal Reserve System must also subscribe to the FDIC; most other banks have joined voluntarily. About 98 percent of all commercial banks are now insured by the FDIC. Up until 1989, similar protection was provided for depositors of most savings and loans by the Federal Savings and Loan Insurance Corporation (FSLIC). However, the responsibilities for protecting savings and loans have now passed to the FDIC. The National Credit Union Association (NCUA) insures deposits for federally chartered credit unions.

As mentioned above, FDIC insurance is limited to $100,000 for any depositor. However, accounts in different banks are separately and fully protected; so the number of $100,000 deposits that can be fully protected in different banks is unlimited. Joint accounts opened by one person in combination with another person or persons are all eligible for insurance coverage, even when opened in the same bank.

Bank Supervision

In addition to providing insurance, the FDIC and NCUA also set requirements for sound banking practices. Compliance is controlled through the use of bank examiners. These trained representatives of the enforcement agency regularly inspect the financial records and management practices of the financial institutions. Inspections are unannounced and occur at least once a year. Examinations almost always take at least a week to complete and may take up to several months.

Examiners look at the ability of the bank's management, level of earnings, sources of earnings, adequacy of loan security, capital, and the current level of liquidity. A bank with serious problems in one or more of these areas will be included on a "problem list." These banks are seen as candidates for failure unless problems are corrected. Examiners discuss the nature of the problems and potential actions with the management of the bank, and more frequent examinations are scheduled to ensure compliance with the examiners' recommendations.

Deregulation of the Banking Industry

Prior to 1981, the banking industry was highly regulated. The role played by each of the financial institutions within the system was clearly defined. Commercial banks were the only institutions allowed to offer demand deposit accounts. Savings banks and savings and loan associations offered home mortgage loans, and credit unions offered their members savings accounts and short-term consumer loans. The government even regulated the amount of interest each institution could pay on savings accounts.

With the high inflation of the late 1970s, this system began to fall apart. Depositors, seeking higher interest rates, began to move their deposits to money market mutual funds and other higher-yielding investments. Since the government dictated interest rates, banks could not respond to this threat. Pressure brought by the banks and thrifts resulted in a deregulation of the banking industry, and, while this did increase the competition among different types of financial institutions, it also blurred the differences between them.

The primary deregulation legislation was the Depository Institution Deregulation and Monetary Control Act (DIDMCA) of 1980. It permitted all deposit institutions to offer checking accounts; expanded the lending powers of the thrifts to nonmortgage loans, increasing the competition between commercial banks and thrifts; allowed credit unions to make mortgage loans; and eliminated the interest ceilings on all types of deposits.

The intent of the DIDMCA was to increase competition among financial institutions. It did throw many of the small thrifts into a competitive environment. The number of savings and loans declined from 4,600 in 1980 to less than 2,000 in 1994.[12] DIDMCA also increased the amount of control the Federal Reserve System had over all financial institutions.

Federal Reserve System
The 12 Federal Reserve Banks that serve as the central bank of the United States. Generally referred to as the Fed.

Federal Reserve System

The base of the commercial banking system in the United States is the **Federal Reserve System** (generally referred to as simply the Fed). The Federal Reserve System—the central bank of the United States—was established by

Alan Greenspan, Chairman of the Federal Reserve Board, which makes policy controlling the money supply and the flow of money through the U.S. banking system.

Congress in the Federal Reserve Act of 1913 to control the nation's money supply.

The Fed was originally created to help eliminate the problems brought on the economy by bank panics.[13] Since banks do not hold the deposits of their customers but rather lend these deposits out to other customers of the bank in order to earn interest, the banks are capable of giving only a small percentage of their depositors the funds in their account at any given time. When a number of depositors demand their money at one time, it creates a problem for the bank. The bank has to borrow the needed funds from other banks.

If the bank cannot quickly raise the needed funds to handle depositors' withdrawals, a bank panic may result. That is, the bank would have to close its doors until the needed funds could be collected from the borrowers. Panics can result in the failure of commercial banks and can have devastating effects on the national economy. Between the Civil War and 1907, four economic depressions in the United States began with bank panics. After the depression of 1907, Congress appointed a commission to study the problems of the banking system and recommend changes. The result of this study was the foundation of the Federal Reserve System in 1913.

The Federal Reserve System is a network of 12 district banks (Exhibit 17.4) supervised by a board of governors. This board, the Federal Reserve Board, has seven members, appointed by the president of the United States with the advice and consent of the Senate. Because members serve 14-year

Exhibit 17.4
Federal Reserve Bank Districts and Branches

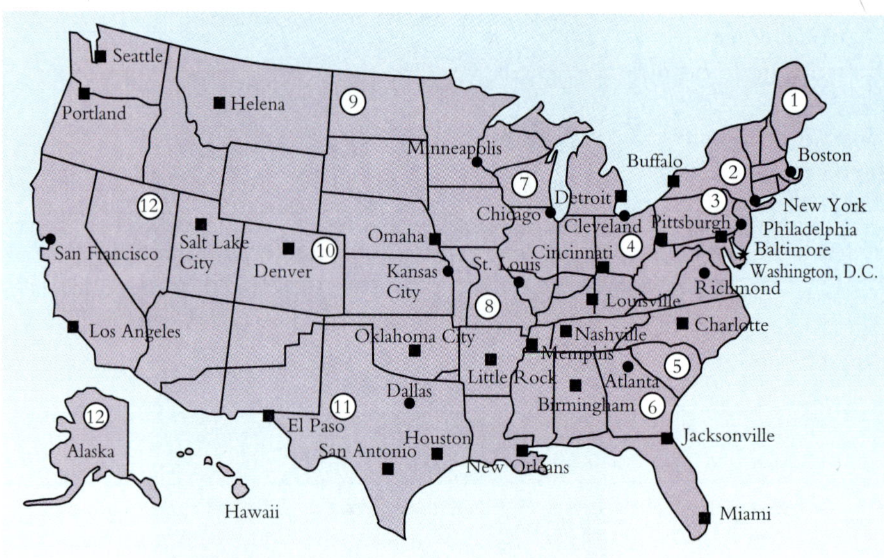

terms, with one term expiring every two years, political control is minimized. Theoretically no president should control the appointment of more than a few members of the board (although retirements and deaths can change this). The president does, however, appoint the chairman of the Federal Reserve Board every four years. Therefore the president controls the appointment of the most influential member of the board.

The organization of the Federal Reserve revolves around the 12 bank districts, each with a Federal Reserve Bank. These Reserve Banks are owned by the member commercial banks in that district. Each Reserve Bank has nine directors. Three are appointed by the board of governors; the member commercial banks elect three to represent banks and three to represent businesses. In addition to the board of governors, the Fed has a Federal Advisory Council. This council is comprised of 12 members, 1 from each of the Reserve Banks. The council advises the board of governors on policies of the Fed.

The Fed provides general direction to the 12 Reserve Banks, and it has the power to audit district bank books and coordinate their operations in the public interest. In addition, the Fed has considerable power to control the money supply. This power is discussed in the section on monetary policies later in this chapter.

The Federal Reserve performs several major functions: It manages regional and national check-clearing procedures; it controls the money supply through control of the reserve requirement, open market operations, and control of the discount rate; it regulates commercial banks; it supervises the federal deposit insurance of financial institutions belonging to the Federal Reserve System; and it provides services to the U.S. Treasury.

Check Clearing. The Federal Reserve provides national check clearing. The Federal Reserve clearinghouse handles almost all checks drawn on a bank in one city and presented for deposit to a bank in another city. Not all checks, however, are cleared through the Fed. Small banks in rural areas pay larger banks to provide the check-clearing service for them. Also, commercial banks have their own system for clearing checks written and deposited within the same city. However, checks that involve more than one Federal Reserve district are handled by the Fed. Exhibit 17.5 illustrates how a check is cleared through the Federal Reserve System.

Monetary Policies. The Fed controls the size of the money supply, both M1 (currency and demand deposits) and M2 (time deposits and money market accounts). Though the primary focus traditionally has been on M1, the Fed has recently found that the size of M2 and its effect on the money supply are more predictable. The tools the Fed uses to control the money supply include control of the reserve requirement, open market operations, and control of the discount rate.

Reserve Requirement. Each time you deposit money into your account at the bank, the bank is allowed to lend that money out to someone else. The amount lent out, however, does not equal the amount you deposited. The

Exhibit 17.5
The Path of a Check in the Fed

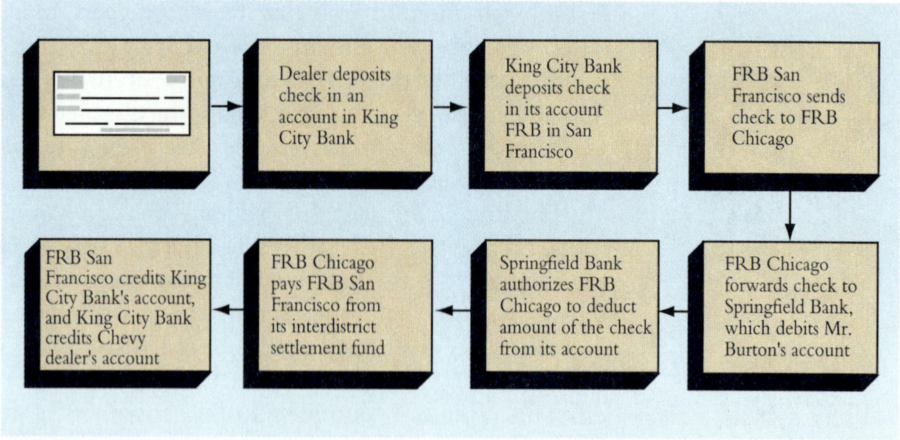

Reserve
The percentage of money from deposits that a bank must keep on hand or on deposit in the Federal Reserve Bank. Funds above this amount can be loaned out.

bank must keep a prescribed amount on hand or deposited at its Federal Reserve Bank as **reserve.** The Federal Reserve dictates the reserve requirement. Lowering or raising it can very significantly affect the money supply.

Let's say your grandmother deposits $100 of her social security benefit in her bank; this is new money into the system. If the reserve requirement is 10 percent, her bank holds $10 in reserve and lends out the rest. If the $90 lent out is deposited in another bank, that bank keeps $9 as reserve and lends out $81. This continues until all the funds are used. If full expansion were reached, the $100 your grandmother deposited would expand the money supply by $1,000. We compute this effect by dividing new deposit dollars by reserve requirement. So, if the reserve requirement were 5 percent, a new deposit of $100 would expand the money supply by $2,000 ($100 ÷ 5 percent).

Because of its dramatic effect on the money supply and because such a dramatic move will be discussed in the news and may send shock waves through corporations and Wall Street, the Fed rarely uses adjustments in the reserve requirement to regulate the money supply.

Open Market Operations. Open market operations are conducted by the Federal Open Market Committee. The FOMC consists of the seven members of the board of governors, plus five Reserve Bank presidents. The FOMC uses savings bonds, Treasury notes, and Treasury bills—the financial obligations of the federal government—to expand or contract the money supply. Open market operations involve the sale or purchase of these securities.

If the FOMC decides to purchase Treasury bills, Treasury notes, or savings bonds on the open market, the cash used to pay for the purchases is a new infusion of cash; it expands the money supply. If the FOMC decides to sell these securities on the open market, the money used by individual investors to purchase these is removed from the money supply and held by the Fed. The actual buying and selling of securities takes place between the Federal Reserve Bank of New York, on behalf of the system, and a few dozen large dealers in bonds. Open market operations are the most widely and most regularly used of the three methods for controlling money supply.

Discount Rate
The rate of interest charged to member banks when they borrow money from the Fed.

Discount Rate. If member banks need to borrow money to fulfill their reserve requirement, they may borrow it from the Fed. The rate of interest charged to member banks to borrow funds from the Fed is called the **discount rate.** Each Reserve Bank sets its own discount rate, with the approval of the board of governors. Raising the discount rate makes member banks less willing to borrow and causes them to increase the interest rate they charge their borrowers. This in turn reduces the tendency of bank customers to borrow and results in a reduction in the money supply. Lowering the discount rate has the opposite effect.

Perhaps the most important impact of the discount rate, however, is that changes in it gain a great deal of national attention. It signals how the Fed feels about the economy in general and what its future policy is likely to be relative to the money supply. The Federal Reserve increased the discount rate several times during 1994 and early 1995, and interest rates for mortgages and other types of loans also increased. Many businesspeople consider changes in the discount rate as strong indicators of economic conditions.

Supervising Banks. The Fed is responsible for regulating commercial banks. It approves requests to open a branch or merge with another bank, enforces regulations, and admits banks to membership within the system. Each of the 12 Reserve Banks examines member banks in its district.

Depository Insurance. The Federal Reserve Board also supervises the two federal depository insurance agencies: the Federal Deposit Insurance Corporation and the National Credit Union Administration. As indicated earlier in this chapter, recent occurrences in the savings and loan industry have made this an extremely important function of the Fed.

Services to the Treasury. The Fed is really the U.S. government bank. In addition to its other functions, it provides a number of services to the U.S. Treasury and to the public:

- The FRBs physically house much of the coins and paper money in circulation. They provide for the movement of paper money and coins throughout the nation and also remove worn and damaged currency from the system.
- The Fed takes care of all paperwork involved when the government sells securities such as savings bonds, Treasury bills, and other government securities.
- The Fed holds the legally required reserve accounts of member banks and acts generally as a bank for banks.
- The Fed makes sure that state member banks comply with consumer protection regulations.

THE FUTURE OF BANKING

The future of banking will develop around three important areas: (1) technological innovation and its impact on banking, (2) the further development of interstate, regional, and possibly national banks in this country, and (3) the changing impact of the world banking community.

Technological Impacts: Electronic Funds Transfer

Electronic Funds Transfer (EFT)
The transfer of funds by means of an electronic terminal, telephone, computer, or magnetic tape that orders a bank or other financial institution to debit or credit an account.

Automated Teller Machine (ATM)
Machine that dispenses cash from a customer's account, accepts deposits to the account, or performs other banking functions.

Automated Clearinghouse (ACH)
An automated clearinghouse allows payments or withdrawals to and from a bank account by magnetic computer tape.

The impact of technology on banking will be far-reaching. Some key areas developing very rapidly involve electronic funds transfer. **Electronic funds transfer (EFT)** is the transfer of funds by means of an electronic terminal, telephone, computer, or magnetic tape that orders a bank or other financial institution to debit (reduce) or credit (increase) an account. Areas showing the most promise for EFT use include automated teller machines (ATMs), automated clearinghouses (ACHs), point-of-sale (POS) systems with the use of debit cards, and in-home banking.

Automated teller machines (ATMs) allow depositors to access their accounts, and make payments, deposits and cash withdrawals 24 hours a day. Yet they were relatively slow to catch on. Early ATMs broke down frequently, and customers were reluctant to trust the machines. They worried that their account would get charged but the money wouldn't come out, or that a deposit they made wouldn't get credited. However, because of their convenience and improved reliability and because younger consumers are growing more accustomed to dealing with machines, ATMs have become extremely popular. There are almost 100,000 ATMs in the United States.[14] Nearly half of U.S. residents aged 18 to 34 use automated banking, while only 8 percent of the more reluctant over-65 group uses ATMs.[15]

With expansion of ATM networks, customers of member banks can use ATMs nationwide, always having access to their bank funds. To use an ATM, the customer inserts a plastic card supplied by the bank and then punches in a personal identification number. To access the account, the customer needs both the card and the identification number. This helps protect the accounts of customer who lose their cards.

ATMs help reduce transaction costs for banks as well as providing convenience for bank customers. Each teller transaction costs a bank an estimated \$2–\$3; each ATM transaction only costs about \$1–\$1.50.[16] It may cost an extra \$1 to \$2 to make a transaction at another bank's ATM.[17] ATMs are now available in shopping malls, supermarkets, student centers, airports, and just about every other public place.

Automated clearinghouses (ACHs) allow payments or withdrawals to and from a bank account by magnetic computer tape. Employers use ACHs to make payroll account withdrawals and transfer employees' pay directly to

A drive-up ATM allows the depositor to access his account at any time of day or night, nationwide.

employee accounts. ACHs are also becoming popular with utilities such as telephone and electric companies, who sign customers up to have their bills deducted directly from their checking accounts. The federal government is the largest ACH system user; over 50 percent of all social security payments are made through this system. Also, almost all payments for interest on Treasury notes and bills are deposited directly into the holders' accounts. However, ACH systems are expensive to implement and therefore are only efficient for large batch processing.

Point-of-Sale (POS) System
Point-of-sale system, along with EFT, allows merchants to draw money directly from a customer's bank account at the time a purchase is made.

Debit Card
A plastic card, similar to a credit card, that deducts funds directly from the customer's account rather than creating a loan.

Point-of-sale (POS) systems, along with electronic fund transfers, allow merchants to draw money directly from a customer's bank account at the time a purchase is made. These systems work through the use of a debit card. A **debit card** is very similar to a credit card except that the card does not create a loan but rather transfers funds from the customer's account to the merchant's account. Both the customer and the retail store must belong to the same bank or bank network, and the retailer must have a POS terminal.

When the customer makes a purchase using this system, the cashier enters the debit card on the POS terminal. If sufficient funds are in the customer's account, the money automatically transfers to the retailer's account through an EFT. The transaction is then complete. POS systems help reduce check processing costs and the problem of bad checks. They also help with security, since less funds need to be kept on hand in the store.

Interstate Banking

The 1927 Pepper-McFadden Act prohibited banks from having offices in more than one state unless authorized by state law. It also required that banks adhere to the branch banking laws of the states in which they operate. Since some states do not even permit branch banking within the same city, this law greatly restricted bank growth.

In June 1985, the U.S. Supreme Court ruled that interstate banking within regions (e.g., New England, the Southeast) should be allowed. This would be controlled by the states themselves, which would have to make mutually acceptable agreements that would allow banks in each region to merge across state lines. Today, all 50 states, plus the District of Columbia, permit some form of interstate banking.[18] Furthermore, the problems faced by banks in certain economically depressed areas have caused the FDIC to allow banks from other regions to buy weakened banks in order to protect the troubled banks' depositors.

As a result, a number of *superregionals* have developed in different regions of the country. Banks such as NationsBank, Banc One in Ohio, NCNB in North Carolina, and PNC Financial in Pennsylvania are operating across state lines. NationsBank has acquired a reputation as a growth-oriented superregional. As Today's Business World suggests, the driving force behind NationsBank growth is Hugh McColl, the bank's president. He is an aggressive and bold banker who plans to beat competitors.

TODAY'S BUSINESS WORLD

NationsBank Breaks Ground Across the Nation

Over the past few years Hugh L. McColl Jr., 58-year-old chairman and CEO of NationsBank Corporation, has earned a reputation for being a bargain hunter and a bold aggressive banker. He claims he has "mellowed out" over the past few years; however McColl's bold series of acquisitions within the past 10 years has fashioned more than 1,900 branches in nine states from the District of Columbia to Dallas. His skills as a clever acquirer are uncontested as he doubled the size of his bank twice since 1988. *Crains Chicago Business* states that "Mr. McColl also has done deals that have broken the traditional banking mold, from a joint venture in which New York-based brokerage Dean Witter Reynolds sells its products through NationsBank's branches to last year's purchase of Chrysler First, the automaker's consumer finance unit."

NationsBank, headquartered in Charlotte, NC, focuses on general banking, institutional banking, and financial services. Its largest branch is located in Texas and holds 27 percent of the company's total loans. The Texas branch is the third largest bank in the United States. Net income for 1993 was $1.5 billion, a 31 percent increase over the $1.15 billion it earned the year before. McColl attributes the bank's success to its diverse customers, its broad geographical reach, and varied business lines. Its major competitors include First Union, Wachovia, SunTrust Banks, Barnett Banks, J.P. Morgan, and Citicorp.

Today, McColl is set on "creating a powerful coast-to-coast conglomerate that offers everything from household accounts to global financing." Crucial to this strategy is establishing a solid base for NationsBank in Chicago, the midwest's financial center and the country's third-biggest banking market. Last year, NationsBank bought the Chicago Research & Trading Group (CRT) for $225 million. CRT happens to be one of Chicago's most prominent options trading and clearing houses. According to *The Wall Street Journal,* "as its name implies, NationsBank strives to be a force in the United States, and Mr. McColl has spoken off-and-on of expansion as far west as California."

McColl has led the crusade for interstate-banking legislation and he even threatened to withdraw membership from any type of banking association that opposed the cause. Now that Congress appears ready to remove the barriers blocking nationwide expansion of banks, McColl is already thinking further ahead about global expansion into Mexico City, Hong Kong, and Taiwan. He also plans on using CRT as a platform for international expansion by adding traders in London, Singapore and Japan. NationsBank has no desire to establish a global consumer-branch network; rather the company plans to establish foreign offices to serve U.S. corporate customers.

This banker does not sit around waiting for things to happen. McColl's aggressive attitude and behavior have made NationsBank one of the strongest superregionals in the country. What factors have contributed to McColl's success with NationsBank?

Source: Adapted from James C. Allen, "NationsBank Rides Wave of Change," *Dallas Business Journal* (April 22, 1994): 7; "NationsBank Reports 31% Increase in 1993 Profit," *Washington Post* (January 19, 1994): F2; Barbara Rose, "Knowing NationsBank," *Crains Chicago Business* (May 9, 1994): 1; and Emory Thomas Jr., "Corporate Focus: NationsBank Expansion Plans Go Beyond U.S. Borders," *The Wall Street Journal* (April 26, 1994): B4.

With regional banking possible, national commercial banking may not be too far in the future. A number of factors point to this. First, firms such as American Express and Merrill Lynch are not subject to the same restrictions as the commercial banks. Since deregulation has enabled these companies to offer checking accounts and banking services on a nationwide basis, we currently have the equivalent of national banking. Second, as a nation, we are still very mobile. On average, one out of every six families will move in any year. National banking would provide greater convenience to these customers. Finally, the disasters in the banking industry in Texas and Oklahoma brought about by the drop in the oil business indicate the need to have banks less concentrated in areas where a single industry dominates. A broader base would have helped many of the Texas and Oklahoma banks.

World Banking Community

Exhibit 17.6 presents the 15 largest banks in the world based on value of assets. In fact, of the top 15 banks in the world, 12 are Japanese. The largest bank in the United States, Citicorp, ranks 30th worldwide with $216,574 million in total assets.[19] While our focus has been on banking in this country, banking and finance obviously are global, not local, issues.

Exhibit 17.6
Fifteen Largest Banks in the World, December 31, 1993

	Bank	Country	Assets ($ in millions)
1	Fuji Bank	Japan	$583,243.2
2	Dai-Ichi Kangyo Bank	Japan	535,356.5
3	Sumitomo Bank	Japan	531,835.3
4	Sanwa Bank	Japan	525,126.8
5	Sakura Bank	Japan	523,730.6
6	Mitsubishi Bank	Japan	487,547.2
7	Norinchukin Bank	Japan	435,599.1
8	Industrial Bank of Japan	Japan	414,925.5
9	Credit Lyonnais	France	337,503.0
10	Bank of China	China	334,752.7
11	Mitsubishi Trust & Banking	Japan	330,478.7
12	Tokai Bank	Japan	328,685.4
13	Deutsche Bank	Germany	319,997.7
14	Long-Term Credit Bank of Japan	Japan	315,026.1
15	Sumitomo Trust & Banking	Japan	305,347.4

Source: Adapted from "The 100 Largest Commercial Banking Companies," *Fortune*, August 22, 1994: pp 184–185.

Any decisions made within the U.S. economy have an impact on the world economy. If the Fed decides to lower the interest rate, foreign investors can withdraw their money and invest it in banks in other countries with higher rates. Bankers look for the maximum return on their money. For this reason, they do not tend to be nationalistic in their business decisions, and the banking market becomes more and more global.

Many of the financial difficulties faced by major U.S. banks arose in part from international circumstances. First, their large investments in Third World economies for the development of oil and natural resources went sour because the market price for oil fell and many of the nations were unable to repay the loans. Second, aggressive foreign lenders have lured away many U.S. corporate borrowers; foreign sources now lend about $4 to U.S. companies for every $10 lent by U.S. banks.

Certainly, as detente continues and as previously unopened markets such as Russia, China, and Eastern Europe open up, global financing will expand even more. The 1992 formalization and lifting of trade restrictions within the European Union have led to more intense competition. The world economy is now financed by international banks. U.S. banks are just one more player in this arena—an important player, but one that must more completely understand its role in a world economy and the importance of consumers. American bankers need to compete with international banks and to win more business with smarter marketing, packages of products, and service.

TOMORROW'S BUSINESS WORLD

Consumers Bank from Homes

In-home banking is gradually developing in this country as more and more homes become equipped with computers and modems. So far, the consumer response has not been overwhelming because of a reluctance to pay a monthly charge (usually about $10) for a service that cannot accept deposits or dispense cash. Even so, nearly 25 million individuals in the U.S. use a phone-based home-banking service. These consumers tend to be more affluent and technologically comfortable than most Americans.

By using specialized phones, in-home banking is a mix between an automatic teller machine (ATM) and a phone. Consumers access their bank accounts by swiping an ATM card through the phone and entering a personal identification number. With this service, consumers can search for a billing company, pay household and credit card bills, check account balances, obtain details of recent transactions, ask for more credit, and shop for financial information services.

Several companies, such as Ameritech Corporation and Citicorp's Citibank, have formed alliances to bring home-banking to the masses. In 1994, First Chicago joined Microsoft to begin a new home-banking program. According to First Chicago banker Charles Shoemaker, "The information highways are out there. It's just a matter of connecting them." As more innovative services and technology become available, home banking may take hold in the future.

What are the advantages of in-home banking? Disadvantages?

Source: Adapted from Nicholas Bray, "Technology: Alliance Puts Credit at the Fingertips of Britons on the Go: Linkup to Allow Card Holders to Take Care of Business with Their Mobile Phones," *The Wall Street Journal* (May 25, 1994): B3; Steven Lipin, "Visa and WorldCorp Unit Join Forces to Bring Banking Home to the Masses," *The Wall Street Journal* (August 4, 1994): B5; and Pamela Sebastian, "Business Bulletin: A Special Background Report on Trends in Industry and Finance," *The Wall Street Journal* (February 24, 1994): A1.

SUMMARY OF LEARNING OBJECTIVES

1. ***Define* money *and state its functions and characteristics.*** Money is anything that is commonly accepted as a means of paying for the goods and services individuals need and want. The three basic functions of money are that it serves as a medium of exchange, making it possible for two individuals to exchange without having to barter; as a measure of relative value, allowing two dissimilar items to be purchased on a similar basis; and as a store of value, making it possible for us to hold the value over time. The desirable characteristics of money are acceptance, divisibility, portability, durability, stability, and scarcity.

2. ***Identify the elements that make up both the M1 and M2 money supplies.*** The M1 money supply consists of the most liquid forms of money. M1 includes currency (including cashier's checks, travelers' checks, and money orders) and demand deposits. The M2 money supply consists of all of the elements of M1 plus time deposits and money market accounts.

3. ***Compare the different types of financial institutions.*** The primary types of financial institutions are banking institutions, consisting of commercial banks, savings and loans, savings banks, and

credit unions, and nonbanking institutions, such as insurance companies, pension funds, brokerage houses, and commercial and consumer finance companies. Before deregulation, the differences between the banking institutions were clear and their functions distinct; now the differences are not as significant. All of them offer some type of demand deposits, and all can handle most types of loans. Nonbanking institutions, while acting as sources and users of funds, do not perform major banking services.

4. ***Explain how the federal government is involved in money and banking in the United States.*** The federal government insures bank deposits for up to $100,000 through the Federal Deposit Insurance Corporation; the National Credit Union Association insures deposits for federally chartered credit unions. The federal government had also regulated the types of accounts financial institutions could offer and the amount of interest institutions could pay in savings accounts. Deregulation has eliminated the interest ceilings on all types of deposits and has permitted all deposit institutions to offer checking accounts. Finally, the Federal Reserve System was established by Congress in 1913 to manage regional and national check clearing procedures, to control the money supply with monetary policy, to regulate commercial banks, to supervise the federal deposit insurance for banks belonging to the Federal Reserve System, and to provide services for the U.S. Treasury.

5. ***Discuss how the Federal Reserve System controls the supply of money and credit.*** The Fed controls the money supply and credit primarily through open market operations and through control of the reserve requirement and the discount rate. The reserve requirement is the percentage of deposits a bank must keep on hand. Due to the deposit multiplier effect, changes in the reserve requirement can have extreme effects on the money supply; therefore the Fed rarely uses this tool. It does use open market operations—that is, buying or selling government securities on the open market—to expand or contract the money supply. The final tool of the Fed is the discount rate, the rate banks must pay to borrow money from the Fed. By raising the discount rate, the Fed can discourage banks from borrowing and therefore from lending money, thus slowing the rate of expansion. By lowering the discount rate, the Fed can have the opposite effect.

6. ***Identify the major changes occurring in banking and the impact of technology.*** Deregulation has enabled a broad range of financial institutions to provide banking services. Technology is impacting banking through electronic funds transfers in the form of automatic teller machines, automated clearinghouses, point-of-sale systems, and in-home banking. Banks have been given the right to expand across state borders within regions, and national banking may occur in the near future. Finally, the role of foreign banks is becoming more significant, not only on the world market but also on the domestic market in the United States.

KEY TERMS

Money
Liquidity
M1
Currency
Demand Deposit
M2
Time Deposit
Money Market Accounts
Commercial Bank
Savings and Loans Associations
Savings Banks
Credit Union
Finance Companies
Federal Reserve System
Reserve
Discount Rate
Electronic Funds Transfer (EFT)
Automated Teller Machine (ATM)
Automated Clearinghouse (ACH)
Point-of-Sale (POS) System
Debit Card

QUESTIONS FOR DISCUSSION AND REVIEW

1. What is money? Why is it important for an efficient economic system? Give an example of how exchanges would occur if money were not available.

2. Explain how money functions as a medium of exchange and a measure of relative value. What are the advantages and disadvantages of using money as a store of value?

3. List the desirable characteristics of money. Why is each important to the usefulness of money within an economic system?

4. Many small governments have been overturned because they were unable to maintain a stable value for their money. Why is stable value so important? How could the lack of stability cause a revolt?

5. What is the difference between demand deposits and time deposits? Why are checks the most used method of paying for exchanges? Do you think they will remain as the most useful and frequently used method of payment?

6. Explain how the various deposit insurance funds work. If a bank were in trouble, would the Fed immediately go to payment out of the insurance funds? If not, what steps would the Fed first take?

7. What were the primary provisions of the banking act of 1980? What effect have these had on commercial banking?

8. You have been elected chairman of the Federal Reserve board of governors. Recently you have noticed that inflation is rising; you fear that the money supply might be expanding too fast. What actions might you take to alleviate this problem? Which actions would be most appropriate to take first?

9. Identify the major changes occurring in banking at this time. How will these changes affect the future of banking? How do you think a bank will operate in 2010? Do you think that U.S. banks need to become more active in the world financial market?

CASE 17.1

Attorneys Cash In on the S&L Crisis

The savings and loan (S&L) crisis during the mid-'80s has cost the United States government billions of dollars. But it is the taxpayers who will be paying hundreds and thousands of dollars to fix the mess. For example, American Savings & Loan, once the nation's largest S&L, now ranks as the most expensive failure, costing taxpayers $5.4 billion. And one man alone, Tom J. Billman, has cost Maryland taxpayers $80 million. Billman stole millions from depositors of his failed savings and loan in order to live a life of luxury—boats, villas, and mistresses.

The taxpayers have been paying for the costly actions from the crisis. But who are we actually paying? For many of the nation's law firms, the S&L crisis has been a financial dream come true. Since 1988, the federal government has paid over $4 billion in fees and expenses to private lawyers trying to recover money lost through S&Ls. In 1993 alone, more than $565 million was paid to attorneys. The top law firm to financially benefit from the S&L

crisis is Powell, Goldstein, Frazer & Murphy from Atlanta. The Resolution Trust Corporation (RTC) and the Federal Deposit Insurance Corporation (FDIC) paid over $16 million to this firm in 1993.

Some critics contend that lawyers are taking advantage of the government for the sake of profit. According to Pete Sepp of the National Taxpayers Union, "What started out as a bailout for the savings and loan industry has turned into a massive and expensive welfare program for lawyers." Sen. Joseph Lieverman claimed that he had heard stories of law firms charging excessive rates and needlessly prolonging litigation.

However, private lawyers working on the S&Ls contend that these accusations are false. "The RTC and FDIC drive a hard bargain when negotiating what each law firm will be paid," claims Rex Veal, a partner at Powell, Goldstein, Frazer & Murphy. "They insist on the lowest possible rate, which means discounts of between 10 and 20 percent off our regular rates."

According to the *Bank Bailout Litigation News,* attorneys have recovered less than $700 million for the RTC since 1988. Surprisingly, the RTC also paid out $738 million to attorneys in 1992 and 1993. Consequently, private attorneys are making more money for themselves than they are recovering for the government.

1. Do you believe that lawyers are taking advantage of the U.S. government? Why or why not?
2. Do you think the RTC and the FDIC are really "driving a hard bargain" when negotiating fees to private attorneys in light of the fact that attorneys are making so much money from the crisis? What can be done about this?
3. Assume that you are a customer at one of the failed S&Ls and you are entitled to a large amount of deposits. Also assume that one of the law firms, which has been benefiting from the crisis, is representing your case. Do your answers to questions 1 and 2 change? If so, how?

Source: Adapted from Mark Curriden, "The S&L Crisis: Lucrative Litigation," *Atlanta Constitution* (June 8, 1994): C1; James Granelli, "New Figures Rank Collapse of American S&L Costliest Ever," *Los Angeles Times* (May 20, 1994): D1; and Patty Reinert, "Will the Real Tom Billman Please Stand Up? Inside the Life and Psyche of Maryland's Top S&L Crook by the People Who Know Him Best," *Warfield's Business Record* (June 17, 1994): 1.

CASE 17.2

Debit Cards: The New Electronic Cash

Some observers say that Americans have sobered from their fling with credit and are becoming a cash society again. If this is true, then we will depend more on checks and cash than we have in the past, and credit cards will be used less. But remember, Americans still love those credit cards. Each American household owns an average of 12 plastic credit cards. The top three

U.S. issuers, Visa International, MasterCard, and American Express, have over 550 million cards in circulation.

In recent years, a special type of card, called a debit card, has been developed. The debit card differs from a credit card in that a debit card transaction actually transfers money from your bank account instead of creating a loan that you must repay. The ATM card you have from your bank is a form of debit card. When you use it to get cash, you reduce the balance in your demand deposit account by the amount of cash you get from the ATM. If you have ever forgotten to record some of your ATM cash withdrawals, your next account statement certainly showed how a debit card works. Hopefully, you saw that surprising balance and caught your error before you wrote any checks your account could not cover.

Debit cards are also now being used for retail sales. High-tech systems, such as one at Lucky Stores, a California supermarket chain, allow you to use your debit card by sliding it into a terminal at the checkout. The clerk pushes buttons to enter the amount of the sale; then you punch in your personal identification number, and the funds are transferred from your account to that of Lucky Stores. You, of course, get a receipt to remind you to enter the withdrawal in your checkbook. Other companies, such as Ameritech, are experimenting with a debit card system for pay phones. In this case, cards are offered in $2, $5, $10, and $20 denominations that can be used for local and long-distance phone calls.

While a number of these high-tech systems are in operation, some low-tech uses also hold promise. No special terminals are necessary. Your bank simply issues your debit (ATM) card with a Visa or MasterCard logo on the corner, and the card is accepted by any merchant who accepts Visa and MasterCard. The procedure for use is the same as if you were paying with a credit card, but the transaction transfers money from your account rather than creating a loan. Visa and MasterCard are aggressively courting U.S. banks because, unlike credit cards, banks are only able to issue a Visa or a MasterCard debit card, not both.

Debit cards present some problems. Banks and merchants debate who should pay for the system, retailers worry that use of debit cards will reduce impulse buying, and the costs of the system still outweigh the benefits, such as cutting down on check processing. Consumers have not rushed to adopt them, either. If you want to pay cash, consumers figure, you can do so or write a check. And if you want to use a card, you can use your MasterCard or Visa and pay it off at the end of the month. Furthermore, with instant transfer, you lose the float you have when you use a check or credit card.

Doubters feel the debit card will go the way of the Edsel. However, the industry is growing at an increasing rate. In 1993, consumers spent over $18 billion using debit cards, up from $13.36 billion in 1991.

The safeguards for debit cardholders differ from the protection given to those who pay in other ways. If a thief cashes one of your checks and you sign an affidavit of forgery, the bank will pay, says First Atlanta Corporation's Boris F. Melnikoff. If you write a check for a shirt and it turns out to be torn, the check can be stopped. If your credit card is stolen and used, you pay no more than $50; and the bank will often waive even that. If you buy a torn shirt and the store won't replace it, the bank that issued your card can wipe it off your charge.

However for most debit cards, if the card is stolen and used, you lose only $50 as long as you report the loss within two or four days, but up to $500 if you wait longer. If you let more than 60 or 90 days pass after getting the bank statement showing the fraudulent charges, all subsequent losses are yours. It's entirely up to you to get that shirt replaced. If you use a Visa or MasterCard debit card, you can get your money back on the shirt. You are given the same protection against shoddy products that you have with a credit card.

Questions for Discussion

1. Do you think that debit cards will catch on with consumers? If so, what advantages do you think will cause them to catch on? If not, why do you think people will avoid using them?
2. How do you think banks should go about promoting debit cards? Who should foot the bill for the costs of the system: banks, retailers, or consumers? Why?
3. If debit cards catch on, what do you think retail transactions will look like in the future?

Source: Adapted from "Ameritech Tests Debit Cards," *Marketing News* (January 17, 1994): 1; "Credit Cards, A Buyer's Market," *Fortune* (June 27, 1994): 13–16; Steven Lipin, "Credit Cards: Banks' Push to Sell Debit Cards Is Mostly Uphill," *The Wall Street Journal* (October 19, 1993): B1; Steven Lipin, Brian Coleman, and Jeremy Mark, "Pick a Card: Visa, American Express, and MasterCard Vie in Overseas Strategies," *The Wall Street Journal* (February 15, 1994): A1.

EXPERIENTIAL ACTIVITY

Interviewing Managers of Financial Institutions

Student groups will interview managers of various types of financial institutions and report findings to the class. Approximately one hour of homework/interview time, forty minutes of classroom time for reporting, and ten minutes of initial class time for organizing the group effort will be needed.

Directions:

1. The instructor should provide students with a brief overview of the following types of financial institutions: commercial banks, savings and loans, credit unions, and finance companies.

2. The instructor should divide the class into four small groups, with each group electing a recorder/spokesperson. Each group is to interview the manager of a financial institution as follows:

   Group 1—Manager of a commercial bank.
   Group 2—Manager of a savings & loan.

Group 3—Manager of a credit union.

Group 4—Manager of a finance company.

The interviews should include the following types of questions:

- What types of loans does your institution emphasize or specialize in? Provide some degree of proportion, such as 20% of loans in autos, 40% in residential mortgages, etc. . . .
- What types of investments or savings vehicles does your institution provide? What interest rate is your institution currently paying for each of the vehicles?
- How does your institution determine the credit rating of an applicant for a loan?
- Who is your institution's typical customer?
- Why should a customer borrow from your institution? Why should a customer open a savings account with your institution?

3. The students should report their findings in class.

BUSINESS APPLICATIONS

Finding the Best Auto Loan

Activity:

Experience the process of learning about varying interest rates on loans by contacting several lending institutions. Because students are not in the position to seek a business loan, they can gain experience by seeking an auto loan.

Directions:

1. The instructor should explain to students that interest rates on loans may vary from financial institution to institution. Not only will the institutions themselves have varying rates, but the way each institution sees a loan applicant tends to vary. For example, one bank may be willing to make a $10,000 auto loan to an 18-year-old with a part-time job, while another institution may insist on the addition of a co-signing parent or other adult before making the loan.

2. Assign each student the task of contacting several financial institutions about their conditions on making an auto loan. The following factors should be used by all students:

   - The loan is to be used for an auto loan on a three-year-old car with 40,000 miles on the odometer.
   - The auto is to be purchased for $12,500 with $2,500 to be paid up front by the buyer as a down payment and the remaining borrowed from the institution.
   - The loan may be either a four-year or a five-year loan.
   - Each student should use his/her actual age and employment status.
   - The information being sought from each financial institution should include the actual interest rate and actual monthly payments to be made for the $10,000 loan.

3. Students are to write their findings in a short homework-type paper to be turned in at the next class meeting.

NOTES

1. Adapted from Richard D. Hylton, "BankAmerica: Go Where the Money Is," *Fortune* (March 21, 1994): 70; Chris Kraul, "Merger Mania: Profits, Efficiency Fuel Frenzy of Bank Consolidations," *Los Angeles Times* (February 7, 1994): D1; and Patty Tascarella, "Banking and Beyond: Banks Are Growing in Scope and in Scale," *Executive Report* (March 1994): 23.
2. Matt Schaeffer, *Winning the Countertrade War* (New York: John Wiley & Sons, 1989), 139–154.
3. Web Bryant, "Cash Is Still King," *USA Today* (June 22, 1994): B1.
4. "Credit Cards, A Buyer's Market," *Fortune* (June 27, 1994): 13–16.
5. Steven Lipin, Brian Coleman, and Jeremy Mark, "Pick a Card: Visa, American Express and MasterCard Vie in Overseas Strategies," *The Wall Street Journal* (February 15, 1994): A1.
6. Ellen Braitman, "Dial a Deal: Credit Cards Cough It Up," *Smart Money* (August 1994): 58.
7. Bill Saporito, "What's New with Credit Cards," *Fortune* (March 7, 1994): 15–16.
8. Frederick S. Mishkin, *The Economics of Money, Banking, and Financial Markets* (New York: HarperCollins, 1994): 186.
9. "Incredible Shrinking Bank Branches," *Kiplinger's Personal Finance Magazine* (March 1995): 18.
10. Craig Shoemaker, "Higher Bank Fees Don't Equal Value," *Marketing News* (June 20, 1994): 4–5.
11. "Visa's Interlink Network Unit," *The Wall Street Journal* (March 16, 1993): A11.
12. Jerry Knight, "Fed Seeks Role Over State Banks," *Washington Post* (January 4, 1994): E1.
13. V. Bowen, *Money, Banking, and the Financial System* (St. Paul, MN: West Publishing, 1989), 161–163.
14. Thomas A. Stewart, "The Information Age in Charts," *Fortune* (April 4, 1994): 75–79.
15. Electronic Funds Transfer Association, Herndon, VA, unpublished data.
16. Ellen Braitman, "Ten Things Your Banker Won't Tell You," *Smart Money* (August 1994): 63–70.
17. "Bank ATM Fees Are Heading Up—And Up," *Kiplinger's Personal Finance Magazine* (April 1995): 18.
18. Anonymous, "Industries: The Fewer the Better—As Their Numbers Diminish, the State's Banks Get Bigger and Stronger," *Business–North Carolina* (February 1995): 55.
19. "The 100 Largest Commercial Banking Companies," *Fortune* (August 22, 1994): 184–185.

C H A P T E R 18

Financial Management

LEARNING OBJECTIVES

1. Define *finance* and explain its role within the firm.

2. Identify the reasons firms need cash and why financial management is important.

3. Discuss the different sources of funds available to a firm.

4. Compare the different types of short- and long-term financing.

5. Identify the specific duties of the financial manager.

6. Explain the role of working capital management and capital budgeting in the ongoing success of the firm.

General Electric's Kidder Peabody Group is running on life support these days. GE has invested hundreds of millions of dollars into Kidder to improve its deteriorating financial situation. Kidder's problems emanated from its huge $12 billion inventory of mortgage-backed bonds (securities created by pooling home mortgages). With the rise of interest rates, the market for mortgage bonds has come to a shocking halt. Adding to the bear market in mortgage bonds, two other developments are haunting Kidder. First, some of Kidder's key traders have recently left the company. Second, the Securities Exchange Commission and the New York Stock Exchange have begun conducting an investigation into 'the firm as a whole' over allegedly phony trading by former Kidder government-bond chief Joseph Jett.

All of these factors left Kidder as one of the most highly leveraged firm on Wall Street. At the end of fiscal year 1993, Kidder had equity capital of just $778 million, against assets of $73 billion, which translates to a leverage ratio of about 94—more than twice that of its nearest Wall Street rival.

GE poured nearly $400 million into Kidder early in 1994 and certainly had the capability to carry Kidder in the future if the need should arise. For instance, in 1993 GE had $6.6 billion in operating earnings, more than 15 times Kidder's record operating earnings of $439 million. "GE has been fully supportive of Kidder Peabody in good times and tough times," states Dennis D. Dammerman, GE's senior vice president and chief financial officer.

"We're in trouble without GE, no question about it," a senior Kidder executive says. The Kidder situation became so bad that many industry experts compared it to the collapse of Drexel Burnham Lambert—with one major difference: the help of its parent. Drexel once dominated the bond market, in its case junk bonds. But Drexel experienced problems when the market lost its liquidity and the company later found itself with huge inventories of unsalable bonds. Drexel ultimately failed in 1990 because, unlike Kidder, it was unable to get financing. GE finally reached its limit also. In early 1995, GE sold its interest in Kidder Peabody to the PaineWebber Group Inc. In the $670 million acquisition, PaineWebber retained about 1,000 former Kidder brokers.[1]

Many firms don't have the luxury of a parent company with deep pockets such as GE. What actions can these kinds of companies take to improve financial difficulties?

Every business needs capital to start, run, maintain itself, and grow. Money fuels business. If businesses are successful, they will make money. But, successful or not, they will use it. They need money to purchase equipment, inventory, land, and buildings, as well as to pay the utilities, employees' wages, taxes, and rent. Without the necessary cash, a business cannot survive. A well-funded business can lose money for a long time and hold on; but without the cash needed to pay its bills and creditors, it will not last long. It will be forced into bankruptcy.

In this chapter, first we define finance and the role of the financial manager. Then we look at the uses of money for a firm—what the specific costs of running a firm are. Next we discuss the sources of money—where firms can go to get the funds they will use. Finally we examine the management of the firm's finances, including the management of working capital, capital budgeting, and the use of financial controls.

DEFINING FINANCE

Finance
The study of money within the firm; the business function responsible for finding funds, managing them, and determining their best use.

Since a firm must have a sufficient supply of cash, the area of cash management requires special attention. Management must determine the firm's cash needs for both the short and the long term and then find sources to provide the necessary cash. This responsibility for cash management within the firm is management's finance responsibility.

Finance is the study of money within the firm. It is the functional area with the responsibility for finding funds for the firm, managing those funds,

The computer is a useful tool for the financial manager in developing the financial plan and tracking the flow of funds into and out of the business.

and determining their best uses. The financial manager is the individual responsible for the finance function. While some firms do not formally appoint a financial manager, the financial management tasks must still be performed, and one of the managers or owners will handle these tasks. In this text, when we refer to the financial manager, we are referring to the individual who is responsible for the finance function, regardless of the person's title.

To be effective, the financial manager has to develop and follow a financial plan. A number of tasks must be performed:

1. Project the month-by-month flow of funds out of the business.
2. Project the month-by-month flow of funds into the business.
3. Compare the monthly inflows to the monthly outflows and
   a. If excess funds exist, find ways to generate revenue from these.
   b. If funds are short, adjust inflows or outflows if possible and/or look for other sources of funding.
4. If other funding sources are needed, analyze the alternatives to find the most efficient source.
5. Establish a system to monitor and evaluate the results of this process.

The importance of effective cash management makes finance a crucial subject for all business managers. Your Values and Attitudes will help you see how effective you might be as a financial manager.

YOUR VALUES AND ATTITUDES

Look Before Leaping

Directions: Assume that you are interested in buying a business. You believe that you have the intelligence, energy, and skills to be successful. Review the following list of points. Then write down what things you will do to be sure that the business is right for you.

- Profits
- Cash flow
- Business records
- Financial statements
- Industry trends
- Inventories
- Supplier relationships
- Employees
- Customers

Check your steps or ideas with the feedback report, which just wants you to be cautious. The list, compiled by Western States Business Consultants, is not intended to be negative; it encourages caution. How many points that you raised correlate with the feedback pointers?

Feedback: When buying a small business:

1. *Determine exactly why the company is for sale.* People sell businesses for a lot of reasons, many of them good. But if you are buying, you need to know why they are selling. Avoid getting stuck with someone else's lemon.
2. *Ensure that a seller hasn't made a business look more attractive than it is.* You not only want to know what the owner says profits and cash flow are like, but you should also take the time to do estimates of these yourself. Survey the area, look at competition, check payroll and expense numbers, and talk to suppliers. Be happy with your projection—not the seller's.
3. *Hire an experienced lawyer to review all business records.* You can't do it all. An experienced lawyer can review records, check on unusual liabilities, and advise you on how to write the sales contract to protect yourself against past or hidden costs or liabilities.
4. *Tie financial statements to historical tax returns to spot deviations.* This is another opportunity to check what is being said against reality. If an individual will not give you tax records for the business, be suspicious.
5. *Analyze major developments and trends within the company and the industry.* This serves two purposes: It helps you make some kind of long-term forecast for the business and forces you to familiarize yourself with the nature of the business and competition. If long-range prospects are not good or you cannot understand the nature of the business, back out.
6. *Verify inventories and supplier relationships.* Take a physical inventory of goods and make sure it matches reported inventories. Spot-check invoices to verify costs. Call some suppliers, at random, to determine potential credit problems or past-due bills.
7. *Check key personnel to determine if the sale will trigger employee benefits or loss of major customers or contracts.* In a lot of selling firms, the customers are loyal to the salesperson they work with rather than to the company they are buying from. If a key salesperson would leave because of the sale, you may lose significant accounts. Also, severance agreements, golden parachutes, and the like may be activated by the sale. Explicitly inquire about these.

PLANNING FOR CASH FLOW

One common mistake made by new businesses is the failure to plan for sufficient start-up capital (the money needed to start a business). As a result, these businesses start with little chance of success. Insufficient capital can also be a problem for long-established firms. Cash needs change over time, and having sufficient capital for continued operations is a concern even for these firms. For example, Chrysler Corporation had to seek federal loan guarantees in 1979 to stay in business, and Braniff Airlines declared Chapter 11 bankruptcy in 1989, asking for court protection from the creditors they were unable to pay due to insufficient funds.

To avoid problems, a firm must plan its cash flow; it has to know what its cash needs will be. By developing a detailed financial plan, management helps ensure the long-run success of the firm. We discuss details of the financial planning framework in this section.

Projecting Month-by-Month Outward Flow of Funds

The month-by-month flow of funds out of the business represents the firm's use of funds. A financial manager sitting down to project the firm's use of funds needs to consider such areas as the cost of daily operations, the cost of the firm's credit service, the purchase of inventory, the purchase of major assets, debt repayment, and dividend payments.

Cost of Daily Operations. When a new business is formed, the owners generally have considered the cost of purchasing land, building a building, buying a cash register, purchasing a delivery van, or paying state and federal licensing fees. However, many of the costs of daily operation are not considered as start-up costs. The costs of payroll, utilities, rent, taxes, and interest on loans all have to be paid. In a new business, which has little if any revenue at first, these costs have to be paid out of a cash reserve (extra cash held to pay debts). If this cash reserve, needed to cover daily expenses until revenues are sufficient to cover them, is not figured into the start-up capital, the firm will run out of funds as soon as its first bills come due.

So the firm must plan to have sufficient cash reserves to pay rent, utilities, wages, interest expense, taxes, and the other short-term expenses of doing business.

Cost of Credit Service. Most firms cannot do business on a strictly cash basis. Typically they provide customers with some form of credit to gain new customers and to encourage larger purchases.

A firm that provides credit must maintain accounts receivable (the amount of money owed to a business from customers who purchased its goods or services). As long as the credit remains outstanding, as long as the receivable has not been received, it cannot be counted as part of the firm's cash flow. The firm does not have the use of those funds to purchase the goods and services it needs to remain in business.

Since much of the firm's assets can be tied up in accounts receivable at any given time, customers who are slow to pay greatly impact the short-term cash needs of the firm. For this reason, most firms "date" their accounts receivable; that is, they keep track of how many days a particular receivable has been outstanding. Accounts that have been outstanding for the longest period of time get special attention from the financial manager.

The financial manager may follow a policy of sending a friendly reminder to customers whose accounts are over 30 days past due and a more stern reminder to customers whose accounts are over 60 days past due. Finally, a strong reminder with a threat of ending all credit privileges may be sent to accounts over 90 days past due.

Such measures may seem harsh; but if the firm does not receive the money owed by customers, it may have to go to outside sources for the needed funds.

These outside sources may charge interest. Therefore the firm loses in two ways: it has to pay interest for the funds it needs, plus it cannot earn the interest it might have earned if the timely payment of the receivables had generated excess funds. Many of these problems can be avoided if the firm performs careful credit checks prior to granting customers credit.

Cost of Inventory. A firm that hopes to survive in a competitive environment has to provide for its customers' needs. It cannot afford to be out of products that its customers demand. If it does not maintain sufficient inventory, it may eventually find itself out of customers. Maintaining sufficient inventory to satisfy your customers' needs requires considerable expenditure of funds.

Inventory needs are further complicated by the fluctuations in demand that occur in various businesses. A retail business such as Wal-Mart will have to build up its inventory for the Christmas season, when sales are the highest, and then hold down inventory levels in January and February, when sales are much lower. A farmer must purchase his inventory of seed and fertilizer all at one time but can expect no income from his crops until they are harvested. A vegetable canner will have to purchase the vegetables for canning when the vegetables are harvested; yet while the inventory will have to be purchased and canned all at one time of the year, sales of that inventory will be stretched over the entire year. A detergent manufacturer, on the other hand, will experience a relatively stable product demand and material supply and therefore will experience much less fluctuation in inventory needs than the other firms mentioned. Exhibit 18.1 shows the different demand cycles discussed above and their effect on cash flow.

Purchase of Major Assets. While major assets such as land, buildings, and equipment have to be purchased by a firm when it first opens, these same assets must be periodically replaced and upgraded. And as business increases, additional assets may be required. A firm may need to open a second plant, purchase another delivery truck, or buy additional machinery. The company may also want to plan for the future by purchasing land for future expansion when the real estate market is most favorable. All of these represent major expenditures and therefore major uses of company funds. If these expenditures are not planned for, the company may have to borrow unnecessarily or at high rates of interest to get the needed funds. Or the firm may have to forgo the purchase of new equipment, expansion of the plant, or purchase of delivery equipment.

One factor cited when businesses from Japan and other nations took over so much of the United States' steel business was the failure of U.S. steel corporations to recapitalize. That is, they did not upgrade their plants and machinery, and the older equipment became obsolete and inefficient. With new plants and equipment, manufacturers from other countries were able to produce steel more efficiently and therefore sell it at lower prices than U.S. steel manufacturers. Obviously it is important for companies to plan for the replacement of equipment as better equipment becomes available and to plan for growth.

Exhibit 18.1
Effect of varying demand cycles on cash flow.

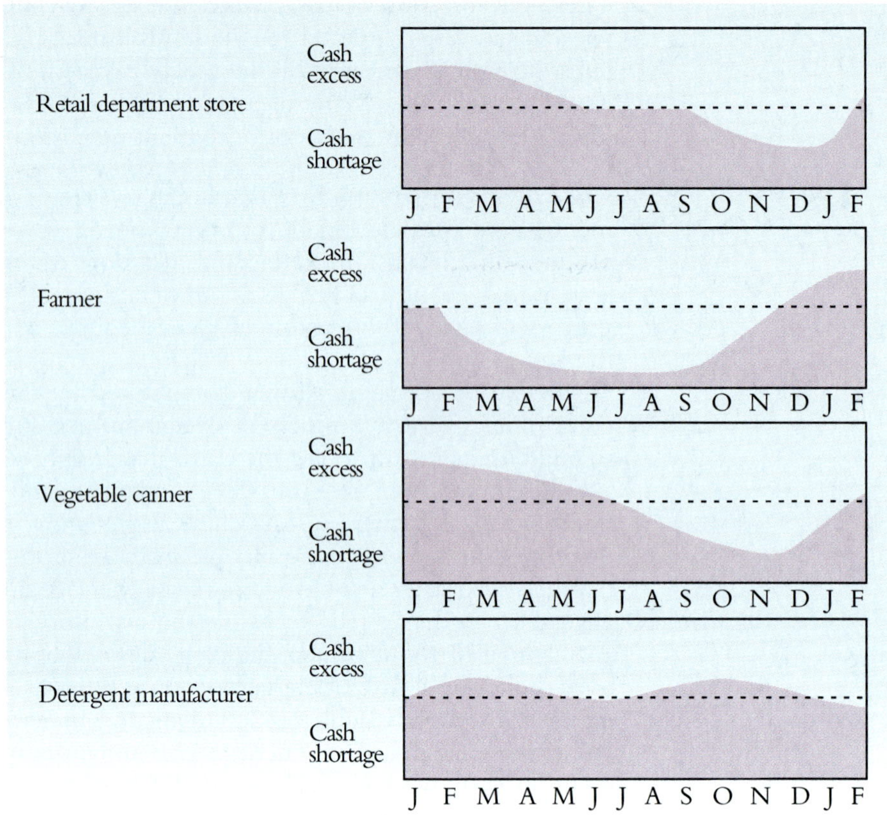

Payment for Debt. Most firms need to borrow money at some time or another. They may borrow to make major purchases or to get over a particularly tight cash period during the year. The use of debt will be discussed in the next section; however, the financial manager has to consider the payment of interest and principal on any outstanding debt as a use of funds and needs to add this debt service into the calculation for funds usage.

Payment of Dividends. Dividends are payments made to the shareholders of the firm as a form of earnings on their stocks. While stock usually does not require the payment of dividends, most firms pay dividends in order to keep their stock attractive to potential investors and to show that the firm is financially sound. As a use of funds, the payment of dividends must be planned for.

The firm needs funds for many reasons. However, the firm is also able to get funds from many different sources. Some of these sources are internal and therefore have no interest cost or repayment. Others are external and therefore cost interest and require repayment. In the next section, we examine where a firm can get money and look at the advantages and disadvantages of the various sources of funds.

Projecting Month-by-Month Flow of Funds Into the Business

The finance function in a business is responsible for acquiring the funds needed by the business. Sound financial management involves determining how much money is needed for various time periods and the most appropriate sources of these funds. Obviously the most appropriate place to get funds for the daily running of the business—that is, for expenses such as payroll, taxes, utilities, and rent—is from the revenue generated by the business. To determine the amount of outside financing needed, financial managers project the internal revenues the firm can expect on a month-to-month basis. They do this by estimating sales volume. If credit sales are involved, then the rate of payment on accounts receivable must also be estimated, since the company will not receive the cash from a credit sale until the receivable is paid. Managers should also consider any interest income expected from the investment of cash reserves and other excess funds.

Comparing Monthly Inflows to Monthly Outflows

Comparing expected income to expected expenditures will yield three possible outcomes. First, the two can match perfectly, and no action need be taken (highly unlikely). Second, expected expenditures for the month can exceed expected income, and additional funds must be found to cover the shortfall (discussed in a later section). Third, expected income for the month can exceed expected expenditures, and the company will have excess funds. The next section examines how firms generate revenue from excess funds.

GENERATING REVENUE FROM EXCESS FUNDS

If expected income for the month exceeds expected expenditures, the firm must decide how to use the extra funds. Firms may decide to expand the business, or may use the funds to make highly liquid investments.

Expansion

A company with substantial excess funds may want to consider expansion of current operations through an increase in production capacity, the addition of new sales outlets, or some other form of expansion. The firm might want to look at acquiring another firm. In 1993, U.S. firms completed $241.5 billion in mergers and acquisitions, the third highest year on record.[2]

In the 1970s and early 1980s, R.J. Reynolds Tobacco Company underwent considerable expansion through acquisition. The company had excess funds and felt the acquisitions would produce good long-term revenues; also it needed to reduce its dependency on the tobacco industry, since tobacco sales were declining. However, a company that uses its excess funds in this way has to be aware that it is hurting its *liquidity,* or the ability to generate cash quickly from internal sources. In 1987 RJR was bought by Kohlberg Kravis Roberts & Company for $29.6 billion and now finds itself mired in debt and unable to challenge Philip Morris, which has gone on the attack to increase market share.

High-Liquidity Investments

To protect liquidity, a company has alternatives that will produce interest income and still allow the firm access to its cash almost immediately. The first of these is an interest-bearing checking account. While this does give some interest income, the yield is typically low compared with other liquid market alternatives.

The most popular placement for excess funds is in marketable securities. These securities can easily be converted into cash, giving a high level of liquidity. They pay relatively high rates of interest for a liquid investment. The three most commonly used marketable securities are U.S. Treasury bills, commercial paper, and certificates of deposit.

Treasury Bill
A loan to the U.S. Treasury that typically has a maturity date of three or six months. Often called a T-bill.

Treasury bills are short-term loans to the U.S. Treasury and have maturity dates of one year or less.[3] They are sold each week by the Treasury to the highest bidder. The maturity date is the date on which the principal must be repaid to the purchaser. Treasury bills (often called T-bills) are considered to be virtually risk free and therefore are one of the most popular marketable securities. However, since they are only issued in minimum amounts of $10,000 or more, they are not for the small investor. Beyond the minimum,

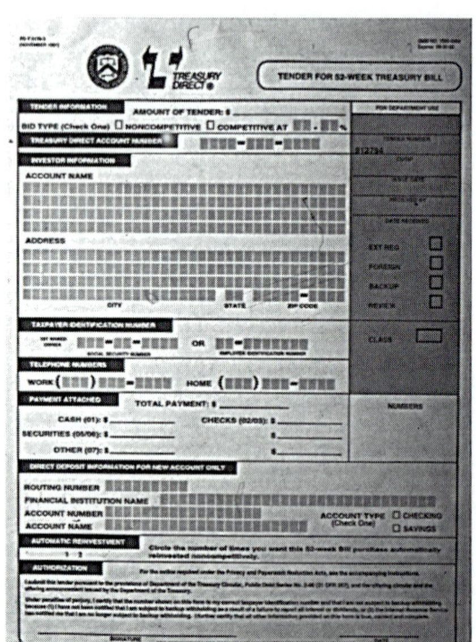

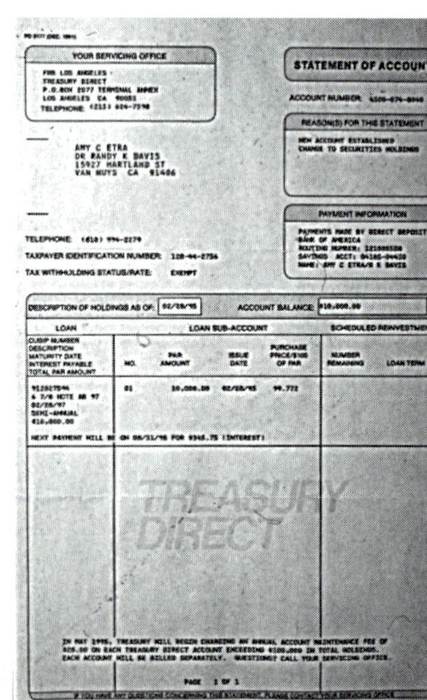

Treasury bill application (left) and statement (right).

T-bills can be sold in $1,000 increments; for instance, you could buy an $11,000 T-bill.[4]

Commercial Paper A short-term loan to a major corporation with a high credit standing.

Commercial paper is a short-term note that represents a loan to a major corporation with a high credit standing. The maturity date on commercial paper may run from three days to nine months. While commercial paper carries more risk than T-bills and is not as liquid, it does pay the purchaser a higher rate of interest. Commercial paper is normally issued in amounts of $25,000 to $100,000. In recent years companies such as Marriott Corporation and Westinghouse Electric Corporation have had problems selling commercial paper and have turned to banks for their short-term financing.[5]

Certificate of Deposit (CD) Interest-bearing note issued by a commercial bank or brokerage firm.

Certificates of deposit (CDs) are notes issued by a commercial bank or brokerage firm. The size of a CD runs from $100 to $100,000. The smaller CDs are usually available with very long maturity dates (generally 10 years); the larger CDs ($100,000) can be purchased for periods as short as 24 hours. The more common CDs are issued for 7 to 31 days, 3 months, 6 months, 18 months, and 42 months. CDs issued by banks can be redeemed early; however, early redemption results in a substantial interest penalty.

FINDING EFFICIENT SOURCES OF FUNDS

Often the firm will find that projected expenditures exceed projected revenues for a given period, making it necessary to seek funds from other sources. The financial manager must determine the most efficient source, given the firm's needs at that time. Generally managers match the source of funds to the type of need. That is, for a short-term need, short-term sources should be used. If the need is long-term, then long-term sources should be used.

Debt Capital Funds obtained through borrowing.

Equity Capital Funds provided in exchange for some ownership in the firm.

The two major sources of funds for a business are debt capital and equity capital. **Debt capital** is simply funds obtained through borrowing. **Equity capital,** on the other hand, does not require repayment. These funds come from the current owners of the firm or from outsiders who provide capital in exchange for some other ownership in the firm. According to *The Wall Street Journal,* equity capital is "the fuel that powers the firms on Wall Street."[6] Sources of equity capital include *retained earnings,* or earnings that the owners do not pay to themselves but rather leave in the firm as an additional investment; additional contributions of the owners, additional money from the owners' personal sources; investments by outsiders in a privately owned firm, adding new partners to bring in new capital; and stock issues to the general public, stock sold to the public for capital. Exhibit 18.2 compares debt and equity capital.

Short-Term Financing: Debt Capital

Short-term financing is used to obtain money to finance current operations, with repayment required within one year. The finance manager spends the

Exhibit 18.2
Characteristics of Debt and Equity Capital

Debt Capital	Equity Capital
Repayment is designated.	No repayment required.
Interest is an expense.	Dividends can be an expense but are optional.
Interest paid may be deductible.	Dividends are not a deductible expense.
Can place claim against firm's assets.	Has only secondary claim against assets.
Does not directly affect management power.	Can challenge corporate control.
Lenders may constrain management.	Shareholders typically will not block management.

most time obtaining short-term financing, generally when funds needed for day-to-day operations are not sufficient. Short-term financing can come from several different sources: trade credit, family and friends, commercial banks, commercial paper, and internal funds management.

Trade Credit
Credit given by suppliers for the purchases the firm makes from these suppliers.

Trade Credit. The most widely used source of short-term financing is trade credit. **Trade credit** is credit given to a firm by the trade—that is, by the suppliers the company deals with. For example, when Kroger purchases a carload of green beans from Del Monte, Kroger does not pay for the green beans at the time that they receive them. Del Monte gives the beans to Kroger on credit, with the understanding that Kroger will pay for the beans according to the terms of the invoice.

Invoice terms are usually stated in numbers, such as "2/10 net 30" (as Chapter 14 noted). Interpretation: The buyer can take a 2 percent discount if the invoice is paid within 10 days; if the discount is not taken, the full bill is due in 30 days. The financial manager pays close attention to such discount terms, as they represent considerable savings.

You might see 2 percent as not very much, but think about it. If the firm pays the bill 20 days before the bill is due, it saves 2 percent of its cost. Twenty days is about 1/18 of a year (365 ÷ 20). If the buyer firm were to save 2 percent every 20 days, it would save 2 percent about 18 times a year, for an annual return of just over 36 percent. Thus, if necessary, borrowing money for 20 days in order to pay the bill and gain the discount would be a wise decision as long as the annual interest rate on the loan is less than 36 percent.

Family and Friends. When funds are only needed for a short time, friends and family will often help a small business. However, such borrowed funds bring an extra risk; if things do not work out and the business goes sour, not only the business may be lost but the friend or the family relationship as well. If money is borrowed from family or friends, it should be handled the same as any other loan. An agreement should be prepared specifying the agreed-upon terms of interest and payment and then paid back just as if it were a bank loan.

Commercial Banks. As an alternative source of short-term funds, commercial banks generally make more sense than relatives or friends. The commercial banker can better help with any cash flow problems and give sound advice. Developing a close relationship with a local banker is a good idea. Once you select one, send him or her your financial statements and meet regularly to discuss your business. Establishing a close and open relationship with the bank will pay off in the long run because the banker will pay closer attention to your business and alert you to potential problems. Also, when you need emergency funds, the banker will be more willing to help out, since you have developed a trusting relationship.

Unsecured Loan
A loan issued on the good credit of the borrower and requiring no collateral.

Bank loans come in many different forms. **Unsecured loans** are loans based solely on the good credit of the borrower. They require no collateral. New businesses have great difficulty getting unsecured loans. Generally banks will require some form of collateral to guarantee the loan.

Secured Loan
A loan backed with some form of collateral.

Secured loans are backed by collateral, by something valuable. For example, First American Bank offers car loans for as little as 6.9 percent when the automobile is used as collateral.[7] The collateral reduces the risk for the banker. If the borrower fails to repay the loan, the lender may take possession of the collateral. It may be property, equipment, inventory, or accounts receivable. Using accounts receivable as collateral for a loan is called pledging. The cash received for the accounts receivable goes to the banker instead of being retained in the company.

Line of Credit
A preapproved amount the holder may borrow in whole or in part, provided that the bank has sufficient funds.

Revolving Credit Agreement
A line of credit guaranteed by the bank.

A borrower who has a good relationship with the bank may be able to open a **line of credit.** This means the bank preapproves the borrower for a specified amount of credit, usually unsecured. Provided the bank has the funds available, the borrower may borrow up to that amount without having to apply for a loan each time funds are needed. As the customer's credit record with the bank lengthens and the business matures, this line of credit is often increased. However, a line of credit does not guarantee that the loan will be available. A **revolving credit agreement** guarantees that the bank will honor your line of credit up to the stated amount. A revolving credit agreement generally requires payment of a fee.

Factoring
The sale of accounts receivable to a bank or other lender, generally at a considerable discount.

A relatively expensive form of short-term credit is **factoring.** Rather than pledging its accounts receivable to a financial institution as collateral, a firm actually sells the accounts receivable to the institution—at a discount.[8] The seller receives less than the full value of the accounts receivable. For example, a bank may only pay $7 for each $10 of receivables. This protects the bank from any uncollectible accounts and allows it to make a tidy profit. Firms do not generally like to use factoring; it is expensive and sends a message to suppliers and creditors that the company may be in financial trouble. Today's Business World tells the story of one company that is considering using factoring.

TODAY'S BUSINESS WORLD

From the Football Field to the Software Industry

Fran Tarkenton, star quarterback for the Minnesota Vikings football team during the 1970s, is now earning fame with KnowledgeWare, a small software company that develops tools for computer programmers. Tarkenton founded Tarkenton Software during the off-season while he played football in 1980. Tarkenton Software sold products to corporations using IBM mainframe computers. In 1986, he merged his company with another small one to form KnowledgeWare, which quickly became one of the country's biggest software companies. By 1991, KnowledgeWare had sales of $125 million and was on its way to dominating the mainframe market.

However, there was just one snag: Mainframes were beginning to be replaced by networks of personal computers. And KnowledgeWare did not have any products at the time to help software programmers design client-server' applications to link network PCs. In 1992, the firm began acquiring smaller companies with client-server tools, but revenues dropped to $117 million. KnowledgeWare fired more than 130 workers, experienced a plunge in the price of its stock, posted a $26 million loss, and briefly closed its doors the summer of 1993. Coincidentally, Tarkenton also increased his salary and bonus by 68 percent to $457,000 that same year.

In 1994, the company experienced a $13 million negative cash flow, but received $15 million from investors and reported a modest profit every fiscal quarter. "Even though revenues are going up, once you rip out acquisitions and consulting fees they don't have a lot of fresh money going into the bottom line," says Edward Acly, a software analyst with International Data Corporation. Charles Phillips, a PaineWebber analyst who has followed the company for several years, predicts that KnowledgeWare will soon begin factoring receivables as a sign of its cash squeeze.

"Factoring is a fancy term for a basic concept that has been around for centuries," said M.A. Connon, CFS, president of Worldwide Factoring Services. "It is simply the buying and selling of accounts receivables in the form of invoices. Factors are investors who buy account receivables, and they will pay cash now for the right to receive future payment on your invoices." According to Mace Edwards, publisher of the Edwards Directory of American Factors, "Factoring firms financed at least $62 billion in receivables in 1993, up from $46 billion in 1987."

KnowledgeWare's officials are playing down the cash flow problems and say they don't plan to factor receivables to increase working capital. Tarkenton claims that Phillips is "confused" about KnowledgeWare's intentions about factoring receivables. He also dismisses industry experts' fears that "there may not be a KnowledgeWare in the next year and a half." Tarkenton claims that "Football is a great game if you win, but it's fast and furious. Software is the same way. It's great when you're winning."

Do you think KnowledgeWare can improve its cash flow problems through factoring? Why or why not?

Source: Adapted from Anonymous, "Factoring: An Old Little-Known Solution to Cash Flow Problems," *Garden Island* (June 1, 1994): D1; Udayan Gupta, "Financing Small Business: Factoring and Venture Firms' Roles in Financing Grow," *The Wall Street Journal* (April 18, 1994): B2; and Timothy L. O'Brien, "KnowledgeWare's Tarkenton Scrambles to Survive: Former Football Star's Software Company Struggles with Cash Crunch," *The Wall Street Journal* (June 3, 1994): B2.

Floor planning is another option in bank financing. In some industries, such as automobiles and major appliances, borrowers will assign the title to their inventory to the bank as collateral for short-term loans. As the inventory is sold, borrowers pay off the loan, plus interest, to the lender.

Internal Funds Management. Whenever possible, a firm should attempt to get its needed funds from internal sources. Frequently a close review of the balance sheet and accounting ratios will reveal possible sources of funds that have been overlooked. For example, overdue accounts receivable may be collected more quickly, or a discount may be offered for earlier payment. Inventory may be reduced, since every dollar of excess inventory that is reduced represents one less dollar needed from outside sources. (Of course the manager always has to remember the need to provide adequate inventory for customer demand.) Costs may also be cut and expenses reduced to free up more dollars. A good financial manager will work hand-in-hand with accountants to ensure that funds are not tied up in noncash assets.

Long-Term Financing

A firm planning its finances should plan for long-term needs as well as short-term needs. Successful companies constantly refocus on their long-term goals and objectives. If the firm has an objective to maintain a certain level of growth, it must provide the funds to pay for that growth.

Wal-Mart had $12 billion in sales in 1993 and $14 billion was expected in 1994.[9] Although the growth rate had slowed, the company planned on adding 135 new stores in 1995.[10] Because Wal-Mart has always been profitable, funds are always available, mostly from internal sources. Forward planning has helped make Wal-Mart one of the 10 most admired corporations in America.

If a company knows its objectives, it needs to look at possible sources of long-term capital to help it accomplish those objectives. The principal questions are, What sources of capital are available? and What sources best fit the company's needs?

Because they involve the purchase of fixed assets and the expansion of the organization, decisions involving long-term financing usually take place at the highest company levels. In large firms, this may involve the chief executive officer (CEO) and the financial vice president as well as the board of directors. In smaller firms, it generally involves the owners.

Debt Capital. Debt capital can also be used for long-term financing. The interest rates are generally higher than for short-term financing because the lender has to incur the risk of loss for a longer period of time.

Loans. Long-term debt financing can often be used once a firm has established a rapport with a bank or other financial institutions, such as an insurance company or pension fund. For a smaller business the U.S. Small Business Administration (SBA) can often be a good source of loans. The SBA actually participates in two types of loans: direct loans and guaranteed loans. *Direct loans* are generally given to higher-risk businesses, usually at lower interest rates than banks would charge. However, these loans are gradually being phased out. The more frequent method of loan support used by the SBA is the *guaranteed loan.* In this case, the loan actually comes from a private lender, and the SBA guarantees as much as 90 percent of the loan value.[11] This guarantee enables many small-business owners, who might not otherwise be able to get loans, to borrow the funds needed for their business. The SBA has recently developed a new program called "micro loans" of up to $25,000 to help small businesses get started.[12]

Promissory Note
A legally binding promise of payment that spells out the terms of the loan agreement.

Most long-term loans have 3- to 7-year terms, though some may extend to 15 or 20 years. For these loans, the business signs a *term loan agreement.* This agreement is a **promissory note,** which requires the borrower to repay the loan according to a schedule of specified installments at either a fixed (remains constant) or flexible (changes as market conditions change) rate of interest.

Most long-term loans require some form of collateral, such as real estate, machinery, equipment, or stock. Typically, when determining the interest rate for such loans, the bank looks at the length of time the loan is for, the type of collateral, the firm's credit rating, and the general level of market interest.

Bond
An agreement between a firm and an investor with specific terms spelled out in an indenture.

Bonds. Another form of long-term debt financing is a **bond.** This IOU is usually held by an investor and stipulates periodic interest payments (usually every six months) and payment of the principal at maturity (usually 10 years or more). Bonds almost always are issued in $1,000 amounts or multiples. The details are spelled out in an agreement called an *indenture* (see Exhibit 18.3).

Exhibit 18.3
Corporate Bond

Bonds, just like loans, can be secured or unsecured. A *secured bond* is backed by some form of collateral—specific property such as real estate, inventory, or long-term assets that would pass to the bondholders should the company not live up to the terms of the agreement. Unsecured bonds, or *debenture bonds,* are backed by the good name of the issuing company. Holders can make claims against the assets of a failed company only after the creditors with specific collateral have been paid.

Bonds pay interest to the bondholders, at specified intervals or on specified dates. For example, the holder of a $1,000 bond that pays 10 percent interest due April 1 and October 1 could expect to receive $50 on each of these two dates.

Junk Bond
A low-grade bond that carries a very high risk.

Generally, the lower the quality of the bonds (higher risk of loss due to the heavy debt of the issuing corporation or a poor credit record), the higher the interest paid to the bondholders. This only makes sense, since no one would buy a low-quality bond without receiving a sufficient premium over the normal amount paid on higher-quality bonds. The term **junk bond** designates a low-grade bond issued by financially weak companies with no solid collateral, to fund internal expansion or corporate acquisitions and buyouts. These bonds, with a very high interest rate, have become popular in financing takeovers and leveraged buyouts. Junk bonds became big businesses largely because of one firm, Drexel Burnham Lambert. Michael Milken, a senior vice president, pushed junk bonds, and they accounted for over $14.5 billion of Drexel's $500 billion in corporate bonds outstanding. Drexel went out of business in 1990 and Milken, accused of involvement in an insider trading scandal, was convicted and began serving a 10-year prison sentence in March 1991.

A firm that sells bonds must repay its debt to the bondholders. The point at which payment is due is known as maturity. The amount due at maturity can be huge, since bonds usually fund major expansions or asset purchases. To ease their payment burden, companies sometimes issue *serial bonds,* which mature at different intervals from the date of issue. This way, the company pays off the debt in portions. A *sinking fund* may also be used. The sinking fund requires that the company set aside a certain sum of money each year to "sink" the bond debt. The company may then pay off a portion of the bonds each year or accumulate the funds until the bonds mature.

Two special types of bonds sometimes issued by corporations are callable bonds and convertible bonds. *Callable bonds* give the company the right to purchase back its bonds early. This might be desirable if the interest rates have fallen since the bonds were issued and the company wants to issue new bonds at a lower rate of interest. Callable bonds generally carry a slightly higher rate of interest than noncallable bonds, and the company usually pays a premium (an amount over the normal interest rate) to the holder when the bonds are called.

Convertible bonds may be paid off with the stock in the company. The amount of stock is indicated in the indenture terms. The decision to accept stock or money is left up to the individual bondholder.

Leverage
The use of long-term debt to raise needed cash.

Leverage. The use of long-term debt to raise needed cash is sometimes referred to as **leverage.** The borrowed cash acts like a lever to increase the purchasing power of the owner's investment. Exhibit 18.4 shows the different rate of return on the owner's investment generated when leverage is used versus when leverage is not used. Bill's Inc. used a $50,000 owner's investment and a $50,000 bond issue to raise $100,000. Jane's Inc. sold 10,000 shares of common stock at $10 per share to raise $100,000. Both companies earned $20,000 before interest and taxes. After Bill's pays the $5,000 in interest on the bond issue, it makes a 30 percent return (15,000 ÷ 50,000) on the investment of $50,000. Jane's, however, returns only 20 percent ($20,000 ÷ 100,000) to its stockholders.

Leverage works to maintain higher rates of return on owners' investments and allows the owners to create a larger firm for the same investment. As long as earnings exceed interest payments on the borrowed funds, the firm should be all right. However, leverage also means a continued obligation to service the debt and any significant downturn in sales could threaten survival. The ability to generate additional cash through debt would be limited, leaving few outside sources of funds. The required interest payments would represent a larger percentage of total sales. Current creditors and suppliers may become worried if the balance sheet does not look healthy. Suppliers may demand cash payments for merchandise, increasing the size of any cash flow shortages. The judicious use of leverage can help increase owners' returns, but too much debt can create massive problems for a company.

Equity Capital. As we discussed earlier, equity capital is funds from owners of the firm. The funds can be contributed by current owners or by outsiders who receive some share of ownership in the company in return. The five forms of equity capital are retained earnings, additional contributions by

Exhibit 18.4
Effect of Leverage

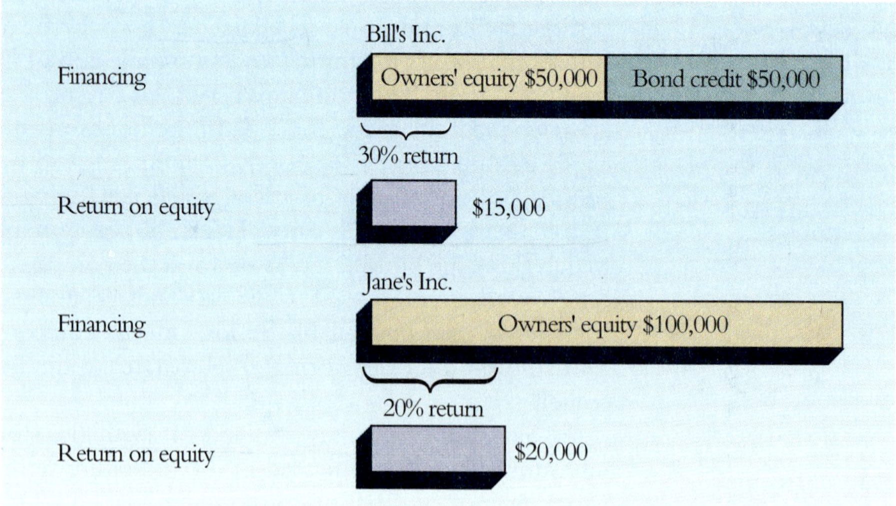

the current owners, the sale of partnerships in privately held firms, venture capital, and the sale of stock issues to the general public.

Retained Earnings. Retained earnings are profits the owners have chosen to leave in the company rather than pay out in the form of dividends to shareholders. While this method of financing growth is extremely safe, it limits the amount of cash that will be available and may cause long delays before expansion can occur.

Contributions. The current owners of the firm can increase their contributions to the firm. While this also tends to be a safe method for financing growth, the funds of current owners are often limited, which means slower growth. Outside investors may have more funds to spend, but they may demand some control over the operations of the company.

Venture Capital
Funds provided by individuals or organizations to new firms with high potential for growth: the investor receives a share of the ownership and frequently a share of control.

Sale of Partnerships. If the current owners of the firm do not have extra funds to contribute to the firm, additional partners can be sought. The additional partners contribute funds to the firm and in return receive a share of the ownership.

Venture Capital. One popular form of financing for new, small, or struggling businesses is **venture capital.** Venture capitalists provide funds for such a firm (provided they see potential for rapid growth) and in exchange receive a share of the ownership and frequently a share of control.

As a firm grows, the owners may offer stock for sale to the public as a means of raising capital. Shown here is a typical scene on the floor of the New York Stock Exchange.

Public Sale of Stock. As a company grows, its need for funds also grows. Typically, at some point, debt financing, retained earnings, and owner contributions no longer meet these needs. Then the owners have to consider selling shares of ownership in their company. These shares of ownership are called stocks. As evidence of ownership, a shareholder receives a stock certificate (see Exhibit 18.5). Each certificate shows the name of the shareholder, the number of shares of stock owned, and the special characteristics of the stock. Many stocks will also show a par value, a small, arbitrary value bearing no relation to the market value of the stock.

After making a request to the secretary of state of the state in which incorporation is sought (in some states, to the attorney general), the original incorporators and the board of directors of the corporation set a maximum number of shares into which the company can be divided. This represents all the shares of stock that can be sold at any time and is called the *authorized stock.* Typically a company does not place all the authorized stock up for sale at one time but rather sells only a portion of the shares. The shares sold are called *issued stock,* and unsold shares are *unissued* stock.

When a company sells stock, it gives a portion of the ownership of the firm to outsiders. However, shareholders do not directly run a firm. They elect a board of directors to represent them. Each shareholder has a number of votes equal to the number of shares owned and uses these votes to elect the members to the board of directors. Shareholders may also vote on mergers, acquisitions, and takeovers.

The company also may pay *dividends* to shareholders. Dividends are a distributed portion of the firm's earnings. The company is not required to pay

Exhibit 18.5
A Mobil Corporation stock certificate that is issued to those individuals who purchase stock. It is something tangible that the shareholder possesses to indicate his or her ownership in the company.

dividends; many do not, or they distribute only a small portion of the earnings in dividends in order to conserve cash for growth, research, and similar types of expenditures. Chapter 19 discusses stocks, as well as bonds and other investments, in greater detail.

MANAGING THE FINANCES OF THE FIRM

Financial managers are responsible for maintaining the proper flow of funds. They help manage the use of funds and find the appropriate sources of funds. They also invest excess cash to earn additional income for the company. In performing these duties, the financial manager has to manage the company's working capital, develop capital budgets, and develop appropriate financial controls.

Managing Working Capital

If a firm's current liabilities (obligations that must be paid within a year) are subtracted from its current assets, the result is the value of working capital. Working capital represents the amount of capital available for the day-to-day running of the firm. Sufficient working capital is obviously important to the effective management of a firm's operations.

In managing current assets, the financial manager needs to concentrate on three assets: cash, accounts receivable, and inventory. The primary concern with cash is that it should never be left idle; it should always be working. Funds not immediately needed should be invested and earning interest. At the very least, an interest-earning checking account should be used. Investment possibilities were discussed earlier in this chapter.

Float
The amount of money not yet withdrawn from the company's checking account even though checks have been written.

Float is the amount of money that has not yet been withdrawn from the company's checking account even though the checks have been written. If you have a checking account, you may notice that when you balance it at the end of the month, some of the checks you have written have not yet cleared. Therefore the balance on your statement is greater than the balance in your checkbook. The difference is float. The same is true for businesses. In a large company such as General Motors, this may represent billions of dollars and significant potential earnings. Actions taken by the Federal Reserve System and advances in electronic payment systems have resulted in float being less significant today than in the past. However, float still occurs, with three primary components (sources): mail float, processing float, and check-clearing float.[13]

Accounts receivable are really promises of cash from customers of the firm. Until this cash is in hand, the firm has only the promise. One task of the financial manager is to speed up the collection of accounts receivable as much as possible. This, of course, must be done without offending customers and with the understanding that, in many cases, providing credit is necessary to sales.

In managing accounts receivable, the financial manager needs to date accounts receivable so that overdue accounts are flagged immediately and appropriate letters are sent or some other action is taken. The financial manager also wants to speed up the conversion of received payments into cash in the company's account. Once received at the office, they must be processed and then sent to the bank. This means that the cash may not be credited to the company's account for two more days. To speed this up, many companies have a lockbox, a post office box used as a mailing address. The bank collects payments directly from the lockbox several times a day and immediately starts to process and credit payments to the customer's account. The business receives a summary of payments and can then credit the customers' accounts.

Inventory is an investment in future sales. Until sold, however, it represents a cash use for the firm. The financial manager needs to continuously review inventory levels to pinpoint any excess inventory and work with production and marketing to alleviate the condition. Of course, understanding inventory's importance to sales, the financial manager will also work with production and marketing to make sure sufficient inventory is available to satisfy customer needs.

Many inventory models use computer programs and company information to determine the best level of inventory for different levels of sales. These models also help determine the best time to order additional inventory and the amount of inventory to order. The auto industry has begun working more closely with its suppliers to reduce the lead time needed for deliveries. The goal is to achieve just-in-time (JIT) deliveries, or deliveries of materials that arrive at the plant just when they are actually needed for production (see discussion of JIT in Chapter 9).

The management of current liabilities was covered earlier in this chapter. As we discussed, taking advantage of cash discounts offered by suppliers generally makes sense.

Developing Capital Budgets

Capital budgets represent the funds allocated for future investments of the firm's cash. These may be plant expansion, equipment improvement, acquisitions, or other major expenditures. The process of **capital budgeting** involves comparing and evaluating alternative investments.

Capital Budgeting
The budgeting of funds for future, generally major, investments of the firm's cash; investments are generally ranked on the basis of the return potential.

Capital investments are generally long-term investments and therefore involve long-term sources of funds. When evaluating different capital projects, the financial manager looks not only at the amount of money required to do the project but also at the incremental cash flow the project will produce. These cash flows are looked at to determine when the project will have paid for itself (generated sufficient cash to pay for the initial investment) and what the long-term rate of return will be.

Determining the long-term rate of return can be difficult because it depends on factors such as customer response, competitive reactions, the state of the economy, and other environmental factors. Therefore, benefits are difficult to gauge in advance. Managers generally look at the most likely circumstances and try to estimate returns based on these. However, this does not always work. Case 18.2 at the end of this chapter shows how risky the future can be.

Developing Financial Controls

Financial controls mean that once cash flow projections, capital budgets, and so on are established, they must be reviewed to make sure that the actual results match projected results. Without review, there is little reason to do the budgeting in the first place. If you set a budget for a particular capital project—for example, building an extension onto the current plant—the estimated returns for that project are based on the budgeted costs. If the project comes in over cost, then the returns will be less, and some other project may have proved to be a better investment. When comparing actual and projected results, the financial manager must look for deviations. If they occur, the reasons must be found and corrective action taken. Financial planning is only worthwhile if financial controls are put in place that ensure that the financial plan is followed.

In this chapter, we have discussed the financial management of the firm. The next chapter looks at firms as investments.

TOMORROW'S BUSINESS WORLD

Small Business Owners Meet Investors on the Computer

Venture capital funds are on the rise and interested potential investors are increasingly seeking opportunities with small businesses that don't qualify for loans from traditional sources. "Electronic highways" will soon be linking entrepreneurs with potential investors through on-line databases. The new computer databases will identify individual and corporate investors, as well as their areas of interest, and then the investors will be matched against a database of capital seekers based on the amount of financing they need.

Matching investors with potential investments has always been a time-consuming, tedious task. Although matching services won't be "perfect" replacements for the protracted discussions involved in financing, the service should help both parties at least narrow their search. Also, the new systems should make financing efforts more efficient by saving time and money. New Jersey entrepreneur Maben Smith has his mind set on developing the first electronic database to bring investors and entrepreneurs together. Perhaps by the year 2000, Smith's idea will catch on—providing quality information on businesses that need money and businesses that are for sale.

Do you believe that computers will do a better job of matching investors with entrepreneurs than a human can do? Why or why not?

Source: Adapted from Udayan Gupta, "Financing Small Business: A Capital Idea: Entrepreneur Sets Up On-Line Database," *The Wall Street Journal* (May 1, 1994): B2; Deena Higgs Nenad, "Chatsworth Manufacturer Wins Venture Capital Derby," *Los Angeles Business Journal* (March 28, 1994, Sec. 2): 2; and Rickie Windle, "New Program Starting: Financing for Small Business," *Austin Business Journal* (May 9, 1994): 1.

SUMMARY OF LEARNING OBJECTIVES

1. ***Define* finance *and explain its role within the firm.*** Finance is the study of money within the firm. It is also the functional area with responsibility for managing corporate funds. To function, the firm must have adequate funding, and the finance department manages these funds by developing and monitoring the firm's financial plan. This plan should include balancing the monthly inflows and outflows of funds, determining liquid investments for excess funds, finding efficient outside sources for funds, and properly monitoring and controlling the process.

2. ***Identify the reasons firms need cash and why financial management is important.*** Firms need cash to fund the cost of daily operations, to handle the cost of the firm's credit service, to handle the cost of the firm's inventory, to purchase major assets, to service the firm's debt, and to pay dividends. Financial management is important to this process because the financial manager not only determines the future uses of funds but also identifies the most efficient sources of these funds. The financial manager makes it possible for the firm to function uninterrupted and efficiently.

3. ***Discuss the different sources of funds available to a firm.*** The firm has several sources of funds. The most obvious is the revenue generated from daily operations. When additional cash is needed, the firm should use short-term sources for short-term needs and long-term sources for long-term needs. Short-term sources of funds include debt capital; trade credit; family and friends; commercial bank loans (secured and unsecured), lines of credit, factoring of accounts receivable, and floor planning; commercial paper; and internal funds management. Long-term sources include long-term loans, bonds, and equity financing. Equity capital includes retained earnings, additional contributions of current owners, the sale of partnerships, and the sale of public stock issues.

4. ***Compare the different types of short- and long-term financing.*** For short-term financing, unsecured commercial bank loans may be preferred, but are often difficult to get. Many businesses must secure the loan with some form of collateral, a situation that ties up the property used as collateral until the loan is paid off. Loans from family and friends can be a problem, unless they are handled as a legal loan obligation complete with written and agreed-upon terms. Trade credit should always be used if available, since this is like an interest-free loan. Commercial paper will generally only be available as an option to large companies. Factoring accounts receivable poses a danger because it is expensive and negatively impacts the reputation of the firm.

   For long-term sources, long-term loans are perhaps the easiest to execute, although they may require relatively high rates of interest. For small amounts, they make sense. Bonds are better for larger amounts, due to the more favorable terms, although only larger firms can issue these. The firm needs to prepare for the date the bonds come due. Long-term debt financing also provides leverage. Equity financing has the advantage of not requiring interest or repayment; however, it reduces the return of profits to current owners and may require some sharing of ownership responsibility.

5. ***Identify the specific duties of the financial manager.*** The financial manager is responsible for maintaining

the proper flow of funds. To accomplish this, he or she must manage uses of funds, help find sources of funds, find appropriate investments for excess cash, and manage the company's working capital and capital budgeting processes. The financial manager must also develop appropriate financial controls.

6. ***Explain the role of working capital management and capital budgeting in the ongoing success of the firm.*** Working capital is the current assets minus the current liabilities of the firm. The current assets of cash, accounts receivable, and inventory must be managed. Cash must always be earning interest income, accounts receivable should be collected quickly, and inventory should be kept to the minimum needed to satisfy customer demand. Accounts payable should generally be paid in time to take advantage of cash discounts. Otherwise payment should not be made until the last possible day.

   Capital budgets represent the funds allocated for future investments of the firm's cash. These investments include plant expansion, equipment improvement, or other major expenditures. The capital budget has limited funds, so all proposed capital expenditures must be evaluated to determine which will provide the best return.

KEY TERMS

Finance
Treasury Bill
Commercial Paper
Certificate of Deposit (CD)
Debt Capital
Equity Capital
Trade Credit
Unsecured Loan
Secured Loan
Line of Credit
Revolving Credit Agreement
Factoring
Promissory Note
Bond
Junk Bond
Leverage
Venture Capital
Float
Capital Budgeting

QUESTIONS FOR DISCUSSION AND REVIEW

1. Why does a manager need to understand the concept of cash flow?

2. What is the difference between short-term and long-term financing?

3. What sources of funds would a new-business owner count on to sustain the business?

4. If you were opening a new business, what should you consider relative to needed start-up capital? Be as specific as possible.

5. List the steps in the financial planning process. Explain why each of these steps is necessary.

6. Explain internal funds management. How can it be used to generate funds?

7. What is a corporate bond? What are the different types of bonds discussed in the text? Are there any concerns a firm should have when it issues bonds? If so, what are they?

8. What are the responsibilities of the financial manager of the firm?

9. Name the different types of equity financing. What are the advantages or disadvantages of each?

10. Why would a lender decide to offer unsecured loans rather than demand collateral?

CASE 18.1

Raisin Cookies in the Bucket

Phar-Mor, the once-soaring Midwestern discount retailer, is currently operating in bankruptcy protection after disclosing that it was the target of a fraud and embezzlement scheme by some of its top executives. The losses stemming from internal fraud now total about $1 billion. At one time, Phar-Mor drew several big-name investors and was touted by the late Sam Walton as "the rival that most worried him." In fact, Phar-Mor didn't earn a penny of profit in the five years before it filed for bankruptcy protection in August 1992.

It all started with an inside executive scheme that involved fraudulently manipulated general journal entries to improve Phar-Mor's reported income. The entry amounts were tracked in a "subledger," a term coined by Stan Cherelstein, Phar-Mor's controller. The subledger was used to track false amounts that were recorded on Phar-Mor's balance sheet at any given time. The financial scam stemmed from what was called "cookies in the bucket." "Cookies" meant positive journal entries, such as reserve accounts, which could be used to cover up future problems, or "the bucket." Journal entries were manipulated to reduce expenses and to increase assets or reduce liabilities. As of June 30, 1988, the cookies account included 27 items ("raisins") and a negative balance and partly served to increase Phar-Mor's reported $2.1 million profit.

While there were not actually two sets of books, there were accounting records that allowed the perpetrators to tell the difference between the fraud versus the true state of affairs. This trickery went undetected by the board of directors and CEO for several years. Inventories were inflated and there was no way for anyone to visually detect the difference. Fraudulent asset account balances were "moved" to store inventory account balances at the end of each fiscal year and at the end of each quarter. To hide, or reduce, the false asset amounts, advance payments from exclusivity contracts were used.

The scandal was revealed in July 1992 when David Shapira, chairman and co-founder, was informed of an $80,000 Phar-Mor check written to a travel agency. The check was used to provide travel for several Phar-Mor executives to various World Basketball League games. Shapira immediately launched an investigation of financial misdealings within the company. He had already been growing suspicious about unusual numbers found on the so-called "David Report," which included the "doctored" financial statements prepared to hide the scandal from him.

Federal examiners investigated Phar-Mor and found that the accounting records were consistently manipulated for six fiscal years from 1987 to 1992. They reported that the number and magnitude of the manipulations increased over time; Phar-Mor's true financial condition and growth were grossly overstated. For example, in 1992, Phar-Mor reported a $22 million profit when they actually experienced a $238 million loss. The fraud was difficult to detect because several members of executive management were involved. Furthermore, Phar-Mor's accounting and management systems and procedures were not coordinated and lacked the internal controls necessary to prevent fraud. Finally, the examiners also found misstated financial statements presented to Shapira and others to conceal the fraud.

Michael Monus, former president of Phar-Mor, was indicted on 129 counts including bank fraud, mail fraud, fraud by wire, engaging in a monetary transaction involving criminally derived property and filing false income tax returns. Patrick B. Finn, former controller of Phar-Mor, pled guilty to counts similar to Monus, and was sentenced to two years and nine months in prison and fined $7,000.

1. Why were the fraudulent actions so difficult to detect?
2. Why are internal controls important to financial management?
3. What kinds of internal controls can financial management implement to detect fraud?

Source: Adapted from "Summary Discussion and Overview of the Federal Examiner's Investigation and Report on Phar-Mor," *Business Journal of the Five-County Region* (January 20, 1994): 3; Thomas Olson, "Inside the Phar-Mor Scam," *Pittsburgh Business Times & Journal* (January 24, 1994): 1; and Gariella Stern, "One Messy Store: Chicanery at Phar-Mor Ran Deep," *The Wall Street Journal* (January 20, 1994): A1.

CASE 18.2

Small Business Buyers Learn Hard Lessons

When Ron Blackstone quit his corporate job four years ago to buy a Wendy's Restaurant on Chicago's South Side, he had lofty dreams. The former sales manager envisioned making millions, creating jobs in the surrounding inner-city neighborhood, and branding into other lucrative businesses. But those dreams swiftly turned into an enduring nightmare that shows how easy it is to get burned when buying a business. Another Wendy's opened close to Blackstone's store. That competition and the loss of patrons when a nearby disco closed soured sales, he says, and losses have totaled $350,000 so far.

Purchasing a small business can be one of the most treacherous experiences in an entrepreneur's career. Financial flash fires such as Blackstone's misfortunes occur all the time. Buyers of small businesses also are likely to make costly mistakes because they frequently don't know where to get information or what questions to ask. The result is often a rushed purchase and, more than likely, regret.

"It's horrible how buyers get so carried away following their dream that they'll drop their savings on any deal that promises to make them boss," says Wally Stabert, president of the Institute for Certified Business Counselors in Eugene, OR.

Bernard Liebowitz, a psychologist who counsels small-business owners, states, "Some get caught up in the aura of a business's success. They will believe anything the seller tells them.... Others, imbued with past successes, convince themselves they can work miracles with someone else's troubled concern."

Daniel Imasdounian bought a nameplate company eight years ago. He says he should have known the seller wasn't disclosing everything when the seller's wife refused to part with the firm's record of receivables. Disregarding his instincts, he signed the deal anyway. Ugly surprises followed: a $2,500 court claim from unpaid suppliers, overdue tax bills of $6,600, and $15,000 in bills from other suppliers the seller had promised to pay. He sued the sellers and eventually won in court, but the process sapped his energy for running the business.

Carolyn Draper ran into a problem with a manager that stayed after she bought a delivery service three years ago. When sales dropped several months later, she grew suspicious. Visiting the company unexpectedly one midnight, she discovered the manager running his own delivery service, shipping packages for customers the company had lost.

Adele Rosecrans ran into cash flow and credit problems with her small distributor business in 1994. But because she did not own at least 51 percent equity in her business at the time she did not qualify as a woman-owned business. She learned that this factor disqualified her from several opportunities for financial assistance from her bank and the Small Business Administration.

The Banawans invested $200,000 in a Charlotte, NC, day-care center and discovered that you had better know both the laws and the bureaucracy. Just a few days after the purchase, a local welfare agency that had contracted with the previous owners for the care of 22 children pulled the children out. The Banawans had not obtained their own license to run a day-care center, and the previous agency's contract was not transferable. The center lost $31,000 before the Banawans could correct the situation.

Even the environment can be a problem, as Austin Fernandes discovered when he purchased a commercial lot for real-estate development last year. Checking records in the local county assessor's office, he discovered two empty underground storage tanks left from a gas station that had been there years earlier. Federal and state laws require an owner to remove unused tanks and clean up any damage they caused. His bill could run anywhere from $25,000 to $50,000, possibly wiping out his initial investment. He has sued the sellers and brokers in a California state court but has no guarantee he will win.

Questions for Discussion

1. Should a person starting a business have help from a lawyer? Why?
2. What type of cash flow analysis should Ron Blackstone have conducted prior to purchasing his Wendy's?
3. What kind of financial controls are needed for any business?

Source: Adapted from Barbara Marsh, "Buyers of Small Businesses Find It's Easy to Get Burned," 1989; "Running a Small Business, and Living to Tell the Tale," *Syracuse Business* (June 1994): 2.

BUSINESS APPLICATION

Researching a Financial Management Topic

Activity:

Each student will write a three- to five-page paper on a financial management topic. Five to six hours of homework time will be needed to prepare the paper.

Directions:

1. After reviewing the financial management material from the textbook the instructor assigns students the task of researching a particular aspect of financial management and writing a three- to five-page paper on the topic. Suggested topic might include the following:
    - bond market operations in general
    - junk bond market in particular
    - factors involved in a line of credit
    - using the float
    - comparing debt capital with equity financing
    - U.S. government-backed finance vehicles: CDs, T-Bills, etc ...
2. The students should be encouraged to research the topic from an application point of view. That is, how would utilizing the topic chosen impact a company's financing decisions?
3. The instructor collects the papers on the due date and grades accordingly.

EXPERIENTIAL EXERCISE

Identifying Conditions for Borrowing

Activity:

A business may be so new or so small that it cannot borrow money. The owner may have to borrow the needed money himself or herself. Develop a list of conditions for borrowing money through consumer loans or credit cards.

Directions:

1. The instructor reviews the advantages and disadvantages of using credit to purchase items rather than using cash.
2. The instructor assigns each student the task of developing a list of conditions under which using credit might be considered. The instructor might wish to prompt students with the following questions:
    - How do you know who to borrow from?
    - How much debt is too much?
    - What is a reasonable interest rate to pay?
    - How long a repayment schedule is advisable?
    - How much is a reasonable monthly payment?
3. The instructor might wish to take about 20 minutes of class time to have students share their lists of conditions with the class.

NOTES

1. Adapted from Laura Jereski and Michael Siconolfi, "On the Ropes: Kidder Peabody Gets Infusion from GE, but Problems Mount," *The Wall Street Journal* (June 15, 1994): A1; "PaineWebber Takes Control of Kidder, Peabody & Co.," *The Wall Street Journal* (January 31, 1995): C21. Terence P. Pare, "GE Monkeys with Its Money Machine," *Fortune* (February 21, 1994): 81–87; and Michael Siconolfi, "GE Expresses Support for Kidder Unit Following Report of Its Financial Woes," *The Wall Street Journal* (June 16, 1994): C18.
2. Bryan Walpert, "Mergers and Acquisitions Activity Picks Up on Struggle of Reinvigorated Economy," *Warfield's Business Record* (May 20, 1994): 5.
3. Steven T. Goldberg, "Where to Get the Best Yields Now," *Kiplinger's Personal Finance Magazine* (April 1995): 48–55.
4. Georgette Jasen, "Treasurys Are Good Buys Amid Interest Rate Gains," *The Wall Street Journal* (May 10, 1994): C1.
5. Steven Lipin, "Woolworth to Retire Commercial Paper Amid Uneasiness About Its Finances," *The Wall Street Journal* (April 11, 1994): A-2.
6. Michel Siconolfi and Anita Raghavan, "CS First Boston to Get $400 Million Infusion from Parent," *The Wall Street Journal* (May 10, 1994): C1.
7. Max Jarman, "First American Serves Unique Niche," *Arizona Business Gazette* (February 17, 1994): 6.
8. "Factoring: An Old Little-Known Solution to Cash Flow Problems," *Garden Island* (June 1, 1994): D1.
9. Bill Saporito, "And the Winner Is Still ... Wal-Mart," *Fortune* (May 2, 1994): 62–70.
10. Ibid.
11. Michael Selz, "SBA May Cut the Portion of a Loan It Guarantees to Bridge Budget Gap," *The Wall Street Journal* (January 26, 1995): 32.
12. Anne B. Fisher, "Raising Capital for a New Venture," *Fortune* (June 13, 1994): 99–101.
13. Charles Moyer, James R. McGuigan, and William J. Kretlow, *Contemporary Financial Management* (St. Paul, MN: West Publishing, 1995), 618–619.

CHAPTER 19

Investments

LEARNING OBJECTIVES

1. Differentiate between *common stock* and *preferred stock*.
2. Identify the major types of investors.
3. Discuss five investment objectives and identify appropriate investments for each objective.
4. Explain various investment options.
5. Describe the investment exchanges.
6. Explain the investment process and the role of the stockbroker.
7. Identify the principal regulations dealing with investment markets.

Socially responsible investing, or socially conscious investing, is a philosophy that states that where people invest their money is an expression of their values and philosophy. Whereas traditional investors seek the highest return consistent with the amount of risk they are willing to take, socially responsible investors consider both the money they make and the amount of good that they do.

The movement toward socially responsible investing began during the Vietnam War when dissenters did not wish to profit from the war. The trend continued to grow and was especially evident with the boycott of U.S. businesses active in South Africa. Political issues such as these have caused investors to become more conscious of potential conflicts. And thus, investors tend to seek opportunities that will do more good than harm. Today, social responsibility in business continues to receive quite a bit of attention since it has almost surfaced as public policy. The Domini Social Index lists over 400 companies that have passed multiple social tests. Industry experts contend that this list is quite parallel to the Standard & Poor's 500 index.

Some examples of businesspeople and companies involved with the socially responsible movement in investing: Vermont National Bank offers a "Socially Responsible Banking Fund" whereby all accounts and investments have a socially responsible dimension. Mary Burak, a Merrill Lynch broker, tailors socially conscious investments to her clients. "It could be anything from a church group not wanting to invest in anything related to birth control pills or abortion, to the environment, to how companies treat their workers, or are there any women on the board of directors," she said. Sunoco is pledging to balance its efforts between economic growth and environmental protection by opening its doors to activists as well as investors. Richie Lowry, at Good Money Publications, prepares handbooks, newsletters, and guides that contain information on socially concerned investors. His belief is that "over and over, good companies win, hands down."[1]

Do investors with a socially responsible philosophy sacrifice return on their investments?

When people think of investments, they often think of the stock market. As the previous chapter pointed out, corporations use stocks and bonds and other securities as a means to finance long-term capital expenditures. Understanding the workings of financial markets is important to firms that may, at some point, depend on them for the very livelihood of the firm. These markets are equally important to individuals, who may improve their own financial security through careful investment.

Even the most casual observer has become more familiar with the stock market in the last couple of years. The insider trading scandals, federal investigations, 401K plans where we work, and the video *Wall Street* have helped make us more aware. But the details of the market often escape us. This chapter will familiarize you with the stock market and how it works, as well as with other investment markets.

We begin by reviewing the use of stocks and bonds as a source of long-term financing for corporations. Then we take a look at who invests in the market and the expanding role that institutional investors play. Next we discuss the objectives different investors may have. We examine the various investment options available, the exchanges on which investments take place, and the methods used to make investments. Finally, we identify the major regulations affecting the securities markets.

USE OF SECURITIES FOR LONG-TERM FUNDING

Securities
Documents that can be bought or sold and that reflect ownership or debt.

In Chapter 18 we discussed the use of **securities** (documents, such as stocks and bonds, that can be bought or sold and that reflect ownership or debt) as a means to provide long-term funding for the firm. A firm's use of securities for funding is generally referred to as either debt capital (bonds) or equity capital (stocks). In this chapter, we examine the use of securities markets in greater detail.

Firms can, of course, use the securities market to invest funds and thereby increase income by making money from the invested funds. However, companies also commonly use security markets as a means of getting cash when funds are short.

Use of Bonds

Companies issue bonds to investors for several reasons. They may give the firm a favorable interest rate, permit a long period for payback, or allow a firm to borrow more than it could from traditional commercial sources. Regardless of the reasons, bonds are an extremely common method of long-term financing. Using bonds allows the firm to maintain complete management control, since bondholders have no vote in decision making. Also, interest paid to bondholders is a deductible expense. Managers must consider, however, that bonds increase a firm's debt, interest is a legal obligation, and the face value of the bonds must be repaid at maturity.

Use of Stocks

The sale of stock means a company has decided to create needed funds by selling some ownership in the firm itself. Offering stock has advantages: Shareholders never have to be repaid, there is no legal obligation to pay dividends, and the sale of stock can improve the balance sheet. Of course, firms do give up some control to voting shareholders. They must pay dividends out of after-tax profits. And managers sometimes become so focused on shareholders that they change decisions to satisfy them.

A firm can issue two types of stock: preferred stock and common stock. In each case, the evidence of the purchase is called a stock certificate. (See Exhibit 18.5 for an example of a stock certificate.)

Preferred Stock
Stock that has preference over common stock in the payment of dividends and in claims against the assets of the firm, but does not confer voting rights.

Preferred Stock. The fact that it has preference over common stock in the payment of dividends and in any claim against the firm's assets gives this stock its name: **preferred stock.** Preferred stock dividends must be paid before any common stock dividends can be paid. And if the firm is liquidated, the holders of preferred stock will have to be paid out of the proceeds of the sale of the firm's assets before any holders of common stock would be paid. Payments would include both dividends owed and the value of the stock itself.

The dividend on preferred stock is generally fixed. It is typically based on some percentage of the par, or face, value of the preferred stock. For example, if a preferred stock has a par value of \$50 and pays a 6 percent dividend, the annual dividend would be \$3 (.06 × \$50).

Some preferred stock is *cumulative*. It simply accumulates unpaid dividends until they are all paid. If a company decided not to pay dividends one year because of a cash crunch, preferred stock rights to dividends would accumulate until dividends were paid. If an individual had one share of 8 percent, \$100 par value, cumulative preferred stock and the company did not pay dividends one year, the individual would be entitled to \$16 the second year—assuming dividends were paid in the second year—and would be entitled to payment before any common stock dividends could be distributed. Preferred stock also is sometimes convertible; it can be converted to common stock at a price specified at the time the preferred stock is purchased. Because preferred stock offers these extra benefits, holders of such stock are typically not entitled to vote for the board of directors or on other corporate matters.

Common Stock
Stock that confers voting rights but not preferential rights of dividends or claims against the assets of the firm.

Market Value
The price at which a share of common stock is currently selling.

Book Value
The value of common stock relative to the value of the company.

Common Stock. Why would anyone want to buy common stock when it offers no guarantees? Because **common stock** gives shareholders a vote in corporate matters, an opportunity to realize greater growth in the value of their investment, and the possibility of greater income return since the dividend rate is not fixed. Common stock does not guarantee any dividends or entitle holders to any share in the assets until all other creditors have been paid.

Common stock has two values: a market value and a book value. The **market value** of the stock is the price at which the stock is currently selling. The **book value** is the value of the stock relative to the value of the company. Book value is obtained by subtracting the value of all liabilities and preferred stock from the value of all assets, and dividing the result by the number of shares of common stock outstanding.

Making a Stock or Bond Offering

Stock and bond offerings appear daily in the form of simple announcements in business newspapers such as *The Wall Street Journal* (see Exhibit 19.1). Potential investors can find a stock offering price per share and where to obtain

Exhibit 19.1
Bond Offering

This announcement is not an offer to sell or a solicitation of an offer to buy any of these securities. The offering is made only by the Prospectuses and related Supplement, copies of which may be obtained in any State in which this announcement is circulated only from such of the several underwriters as may lawfully offer these securities in such State.

March 14, 1995

$300,000,000

BFI®

Browning-Ferris Industries, Inc.

$7\frac{7}{8}$% Senior Notes due March 15, 2005

Price 99.693%

Lehman Brothers

CS First Boston

Goldman, Sachs & Co.

J.P. Morgan Securities Inc.

Morgan Stanley & Co.
Incorporated

Prospectus
A statement used by potential investors that gives information about a firm, its management, its operations, the purpose for the stock issue, etc.

Investment Banker
A financial specialist who handles the sale of new stock or bond offers.

a copy of the **prospectus,** a statement containing information about the firm, its management, its operations, the purpose for the stock issue, and other information that might be helpful to a potential buyer. The bond-offering announcement gives similar information for bonds. It states the interest and due date and whether the bonds are convertible.

While a corporation can market its own bond or stock issue, **investment bankers** usually handle the sale of new stock or bond offers. Some better-known investment bankers include Bear, Stearns & Company, Smith Barney, and the investment bank division of Merrill Lynch & Company. The investment banker advises the issuer on the timing, pricing, and appropriate size for the offering, and purchases the total issue from the company at a discount. For example, an investment banker may purchase a $5-per-share stock offering for $4.50 per share. The investment banker may then sell the shares to other underwriters, who will sell them to the public.

WHO INVESTS IN THE SECURITIES MARKET?

The securities market sees two major types of investors: institutional and private. *Institutional investors* are professional investors who invest for large groups or organizations such as pension funds, insurance companies, mutual funds, and universities. Institutional investors have come to dominate the trading on Wall Street. They represent 75 to 80 percent of all trading, although private investors still hold approximately 60 percent of the stock. Institutional traders have had far-reaching impacts on the nature of the market—for example, in the crash of October 1987, when institutional traders flooding the trade floor with orders made such a large drop occur so quickly.

The securities market still has room for private investors, however, and many participate. About 40 million people own corporate shares of stock, but in a market much trickier than it used to be. In the early 1980s, the market was rising and making money in it was relatively easy; now investors must take greater care to make a profit. Yet stocks remain a good investment. Since 1927, even including the crashes of 1929 and 1987 and the downturn of the mid-'70s, the securities market has provided an average annual return of 6.6 percent after adjustment for inflation.

The mix of investors is changing. Today, as many women as men participate in the securities market. The average age of traders has been constantly dropping, and the median age of shareholders is now 44, down from 53 in 1975.[2] Some amateur investors do quite well in the market. The National Association of Investors Corporation (NAIC) claims that the nation's 10,288 investment clubs underperformed the Standard & Poor's 500 stock index in 11 years, but they outperformed it in 23 years.[3]

Many individuals invest in the market. What motivates them to purchase stocks and other securities? What are their reasons for making investments of any kind? The next section discusses some of the motivations individuals have for making investments.

WHY INDIVIDUALS INVEST IN SECURITIES

People's reasons for investing in the market can be quite diverse. Their objectives typically fall into one of five categories: growth, income, security, liquidity, and deferment of taxes.

Growth

Many people see the market as a way to increase their personal wealth. They are interested in getting capital gains from price appreciation. *Capital gains* are the profit you make when you sell an investment for more than you paid for it. If you bought a stock for $5 and sold it a year later for $10, you would have realized a $5 profit, a $5 capital gain.

Investors who have gain as their objective will invest in growth stocks (young or rapidly expanding companies), real estate, precious metals, or, in some cases, collectibles. Collectibles are items that increase in value because they are rare, such as stamps, coins, or baseball cards. Growth stocks may not pay dividends since fast-growing companies prefer to plow money back into the company to finance growth rather than pay dividends. However, because high-growth stocks are often young or rapidly expanding companies, they typically carry greater risk than other stocks. Such companies do not have the long record of success that more mature corporations have.

Income

Blue-Chip Stock
Stock issued by large, well-capitalized companies that consistently pay dividends.

Many individuals look to investments in securities as a means of producing additional income. They want to receive a steady, reasonably predictable flow of income. Investors desiring steady income may look at Treasury bills, corporate bonds, and some common stocks, such as utilities or blue-chip stocks. **Blue-chip stocks** are stocks issued by large, well-capitalized companies, such as Campbell Soup and Coca-Cola, that have paid consistent dividends.[4] These stocks return fairly high levels of income. Obviously the opportunities for income vary greatly; a certificate of deposit insured by the federal government may pay 5 percent interest, whereas some highly speculative corporate bonds (junk bonds) may return 12 percent or 15 percent interest. The factor that dictates the difference in return is the level of risk.

Security

Rate of Return
The dollar value of the interest earned or dividend received divided by the market value of the security.

The more concerned an individual is about losing an investment, the farther away that person should stay from speculative investments. Typically the higher the risk, the higher the rate of return. The **rate of return** is the dollar value of the interest earned or dividend received from a security, divided by the market value of the security. This concept is sometimes referred to as the risk/return trade-off: Investors must be willing to assume a certain level of risk in order to accomplish higher rates of return, either in growth or income. Those interested in security may invest in highly secure investments such as savings bonds, certificates of deposit, or Treasury bills.

Liquidity

Some investors need to keep their money as liquid as possible; that is, they need to be able to get the cash out of their investment at any time. Those who desire liquidity will not want to choose an investment with a value that fluctuates very much in the short run. If an investor who chose such a stock needed to get the money out when the stock's value was low, the unfortunate timing of the need would mean the loss of a great deal of money. For example, an individual investing \$10,000 in a stock selling for \$10 at the time of purchase would own 1,000 shares of stock. If the price of the stock dropped to \$9 and the investor had to sell it to get cash, the sale would bring only \$9,000, for a \$1,000 loss.

People who want liquidity need to invest in stable investments, those with little fluctuation. As noted in Chapter 18, marketable securities such as blue-chip stocks and Treasury bills are excellent investments for liquidity and provide a reasonably high rate of return.

An Individual Retirement Account (IRA) is one means of deferring taxes on investments

Tax Deferment or Avoidance

Investors may want to put off paying taxes on a portion of their income, and some investment vehicles do allow tax deferment. Other people want some of their income to be tax free. Many municipal bonds and government securities are not taxed. Municipal bonds typically do not require the payment of any federal income tax on the income they provide. Some federal government securities do not require the payment of any state or local income tax on their income. However, the Supreme Court has given Congress the right to tax these if it chooses to do so. Because such securities are currently tax free, they typically have a slightly lower rate of return than fully taxable investments.

CHOICES FOR INVESTMENT

The principal investment choices are stocks, bonds, government securities, certificates of deposit, money market funds, mutual funds, and commodities. Real estate and collectibles also are options, but here we will concentrate on investing in the intangible property listed above.

Stocks

Bull Market
A market state in which stock values are generally rising and investors are generally optimistic.

Bear Market
A market state in which stock values are generally declining and investors are generally pessimistic.

Round Lot
A stock purchase of 100 shares.

Odd Lot
A stock purchase of less than 100 shares.

Margin Trading
Purchasing more stock shares than a given amount of money would buy because a portion of the shares are bought on credit.

Although, as explained above, the two types of stocks are common stock and preferred stock, we will focus here only on common stock. Stock investments are typically made through the stock exchanges (discussed in the next section). As you know, stock prices change regularly. We hear daily and even hourly reports of how many points up or down the market is.

Over time the market tends to rise and fall as the economy expands and contracts. During boom years, the market is usually bullish. In a **bull market,** share values are generally going up. During recessions the market typically becomes bearish. Share values generally decline in a **bear market.** Of course these are general trends. Some stocks may go down in a bull market either because of the nature of their industry, such as oil in the 1980s, or because the company's performance is questionable. Likewise some stocks can go up in price during a bear market. Investors must understand several terms referring to the purchase of stock; we will discuss these terms now.

Lot Purchases. Stocks are typically purchased in quantities called **round lots,** which are 100-share lots of stock. An individual who wants to buy stock in a smaller quantity will be purchasing in **odd lots.** Odd lots are then distributed to the various odd-lot purchasers. Odd lots are generally more expensive to trade.

Margin Trading. When buying a stock, an investor can pay the full price for the stock at the time of purchase or can buy the stock on margin. **Mar-**

gin trading means that the investor does not pay the full price for the stock but rather puts down a portion of the price and borrows the remainder from the broker. The broker retains the stock as collateral and charges interest on the loan. *Margin*—the percentage of the purchase price required in cash—is under the control of the Federal Reserve Board and can change; the current margin rate of 50 percent has been in effect for a number of years.

Margin trading enables an individual to leverage a purchase. For example, a person investing $1,000 could ordinarily buy 200 shares of a $5 stock. With a 50 percent margin, that same $1,000 investment can purchase 400 shares. If that person bought 400 shares on margin at $5 and the price went up to $6 after one year, he or she would make $400 profit minus the interest paid on the margin loan. If the investor had not bought on margin, the profit would have been $200 (see Exhibit 19.2). Investors must take care when buying on margin; if the stock value falls, the losses double.

Stock Options. If you see a car you think you might want to buy and you want to make sure it is not sold to someone else, you might put a $100 deposit on the car. This deposit would give you the right to purchase the car at the specified price within some time period, say five days. If at the end of five days you decided you did want the car, you could get it for the price you originally offered, regardless of what other offers the dealer may have received or whether the price of identical cars had gone up. If after five days you decided not to purchase the car, you would lose the $100 deposit.

Exhibit 19.2
The Leverage in Margin Trading

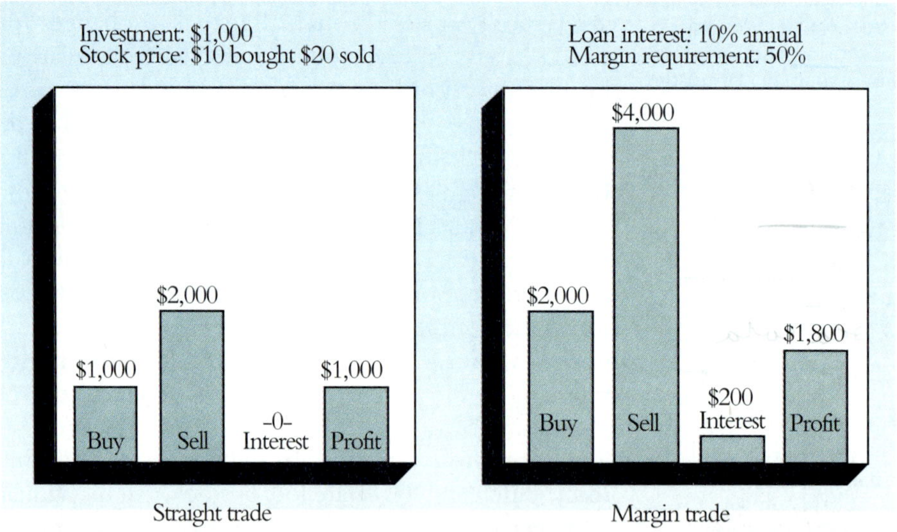

Straight trade: Individual purchases 100 shares of stock. Sale of stock later at $20 represents $1,000 gain and $1,000 profit.

Margin trade: Individual purchases 200 shares of stock using 50% margin requirement. Sale of stock at $20 represents a gain of $2,000, and this less the interest cost of $200 on the margin loan represents a profit of $1,800.

Stock Option
The purchased right to buy or sell shares of stock at a predetermined price within a specified time period.

Stock options work in the same way. A **stock option** is the purchased right (similar to the deposit on a car) to buy or sell shares of stock at a predetermined price, provided the purchaser does so within a specified time. If the stock goes up in price, you may exercise your option and purchase the stock at the predetermined price and then immediately sell it at a profit. If the stock goes down in price, you may choose to let your option expire and forfeit the price you paid for the option.

Put Option
An option to buy stock shares at market price and sell at a specified price.

Call Option
An option to buy stock shares at a specified price and sell at market price.

Two types of options are available: put options and call options. A **put option** allows you to sell at a predetermined price (you purchase the stock at market price). A **call option** allows you to purchase a stock at a predetermined price and then sell it at market price. If you bought a put option for a stock at $10 and the stock went to $12, you would have to purchase the stock at $12 to exercise your put at $10, and you would lose $2 per share. On the other hand, if you had a call option for that same stock, you could buy the $12 stock at $10 and make $2 a share.

Options are cheaper than buying actual stocks, but they are riskier. If you choose not to exercise your option, you lose it and the money you paid for it. When you buy stock, you receive the stock and can wait for the market to shift.

Reading Stock Quotations. Exhibit 19.3 will help you understand how to read stock quotations. It reproduces a stock quotation from *The Wall Street Journal.* Other sources of stock quotations include *Investor's Business Daily, USA Today,* and most major daily newspapers.

Exhibit 19.3 *Reading Stock Quotations*

52 Weeks Hi	52 Weeks Lo	Stock	Sym	Div	Yld %	PE	Vol 100s	Hi	Lo	Close	Net Chg
26 3/8	17 1/2	GablesResdntl	GBP	1.80	9.4	...	285	19 1/2	19 1/8	19 1/4	− 1/4
23 1/2	11 3/4	GaleyLord	GNL		...	11	883	12 1/2	12 3/8	12 1/2	...
36	28 1/8	Gallaghr AJ	AJG	1.00f	2.9	17	80	34 1/2	34 1/2	34 1/2	− 1/4
8 3/4	4 1/4	Galoob Toys	GAL		...	4	453	6 3/8	6 3/8	6 1/2	− 1/4
16	10 1/2	Galoob Toys pf			...	...	26	15	14 7/8	15	...
57 3/4	46 1/8	Gannett	GCI	1.36	2.6	16	1747	53	52 1/8	52 3/4	− 1/8
49 3/8	28 7/8	Gap Inc.	GPS	48	1.5	14	2667	31 5/8	30 7/8	31 3/8	+ 1/4
27 1/8	19 3/8	GaylrdEntn	GET	.32b	1.2	37	926	27	25 7/8	27	+ 7/8
20 3/4	16 1/2	Geminill	GMI		...	...	150	18 7/8	18 3/4	18 7/8	+ 1/8
11 7/8	10	Geminill pf		1.83e	16.8	...	62	11	10 7/8	10 7/8	− 1/8
15 1/2	9 7/8	GenCorp	GY	.60	4.7	dd	1348	13	12 3/4	12 3/4	− 1/8
53 1/2	41 3/4	Genentech	GNE		...	48	1099	50 1/2	50 1/8	50 3/8	+ 1/8
22 1/2	18 3/4	GenAminv	GAM	1.65e	8.4	...	122	19 3/4	19 5/8	19 5/8	− 1/8
35 7/8	10	GenData	GDC		...	dd	4410	20 3/8	19 1/4	19 1/2	− 7/8
47 1/2	38	GenDynam	GD	1.40	3.0	12	1066	46 5/8	45 3/4	46 1/4	− 1/2
56	45	GenElec	GE	1.64	3.1	19	21635	52 7/8	52 3/8	52 3/4	− 1/4
22 5/8	19 1/4	GenlGrowProp	GGP	1.64	7.8	32	86	21	20 7/8	21	...
7	3 3/4	GenHost	GH	stk	...	15	580	6 1/8	6	6 1/8	− 1/8
16 3/8	9 3/4	GenHouse	GHW	.32	2.2	18	38	14 3/4	14 5/8	14 3/4	− 1/8
34 5/8	21 1/4	GenInstrCp	GIC		...	16	11108	31 5/8	30 1/2	31 5/8	+ 3/4
61 7/8	49 3/8	GenMills	GIS	1.88	3.1	18	2464	61 1/2	60 5/8	61 1/2	+ 1/2

High and low price for year

Company name abbreviated

Pf = preferred stock all other is common

Company symbol

Annual dividend paid

Change since last trading day

Last price for day

High and low for day

Number of shares traded in a day (in hundreds)

Price-earnings ratio

Yield = $\frac{\text{Dividend}}{\text{Current price}}$

Price/Earnings Ratio
The current market price of a stock divided by the annual earnings per share.

Notice the shaded stock Gannett, a company that owns newspapers. Starting from the left column, we see that the highest price paid for this stock in the last 52 weeks was 57¾, or $57.75, and the lowest price for the same period was 46⅛, or $46.125. The symbol used on the stock tapes follows the name of the stock. The next column is the annual dividend; in this case, shareholders received $1.36 per share annually. This is followed by the yield percentage, the percentage of the closing stock price that the dividend represents. The next column shows the **price/earnings (P/E) ratio**, the closing stock price divided by the annual earnings per share (total earnings divided by the number of shares outstanding). The P/E ratio is the most common measure of a stock's value.[5] The price/earnings ratio for Gannett is 16. In March 1995, the S&P 500 had a price/earnings ratio of 16.2. Analysts generally agree that companies well above that mark merit investment consideration.[6] You can use this number to find the earnings per share by dividing the closing price of the stock by the price/earnings ratio (in this case, 52 3/4 ÷ 16 = $3.30 per share).

The remaining columns summarize the activity for that day. First the volume of shares traded is shown in 100s. Price information is next: The highest price paid that day for a share of stock was $53, the lowest was $52.125, and the closing (end of trading day) price was $52.75. This was a drop of 12.5 cents from the closing price of the previous day (net change). Reading stock quotes seems difficult at first but it gets easier with experience and practice. Pick a stock, make an imaginary investment in it, and see how you do for 30 days.

Bonds

As Chapter 18 explained, bonds are debts owed by the issuer to purchasers of the bonds. They typically pay the holder a set rate of interest on a semiannual basis.

Corporate Bonds. Bonds are initially offered and sold at a specified price, typically $1,000 or multiples of $1,000. However, once a bond is on the market, the actual selling price may vary. Bondholders do not have to keep their bonds until maturity; in fact very few do. As with stocks, bonds can be sold to other investors. The difference is that the selling price of a bond results primarily from changes in the interest rate and the value of the corporation.

Assume you bought a $1,000 bond that would return an annual interest of 10 percent, or $100. Assume also that the interest rate on similar bonds goes up to 12.5 percent. Obviously investors will not want to buy your bond for $1,000 to earn a return of 10 percent when they can get similar bonds for $1,000 that will return 12.5 percent. You may be able to sell your bond for a price that would enable the buyer to in effect earn 12.5 percent. In this case, paying $800 for the $1,000 bond that yields 10 percent interest ($100) would produce the equivalent yield ($100 ÷ $800 = 12.5 percent). Therefore, your bond might sell for approximately $800, a price determined by interest rate changes.

The value of the corporation also affects the price. Bonds are rated on the likelihood that the corporation will be able to pay the interest and the principal as indicated. Very high quality bonds are rated AAA according to Standard & Poor's or Aaa according to Moody's, and very low quality bonds are rated C.[7] The amount of interest a bond must earn for the person holding it is dictated by the rating as well as the market interest rate. In our example, if the bond you held was B-rated, it might have to return a 15 percent rate to be acceptable. This means your bond would probably sell for \$666.66 (\$100 ÷ \$666.66 = 15 percent).

Default
Failure to pay the interest on a debt instrument.

Defaults on Bonds. When a corporation fails to make an interest payment on a bond it has issued, it is said to have defaulted. Bonds in **default** are rated D, the lowest rating. Bonds in this rating are priced based on the likelihood that the company will be able to make future payments. If that is not likely, the price is based on the salvage value of the bond—its likely share from the sale of the firm's assets.

Reading Bond Quotes. Look at the bond quotation from *The Wall Street Journal* in Exhibit 19.4. Notice the shaded listing for Ann Taylor, a retailer. The numbers next to "AnnTaylr" read 8¾ 00, which means that this bond was issued to pay an annual interest rate of 8¾ percent and has a maturity date of 2000. The next number, 9.1, is the current yield of the bond. In this case, the bond is actually paying 9.1 percent of its current selling price in interest. The next number indicates the volume of trading: 75 of these bonds were traded on this day. The close number, 96½, represents the price these

Exhibit 19.4
Reading Bond Quotations

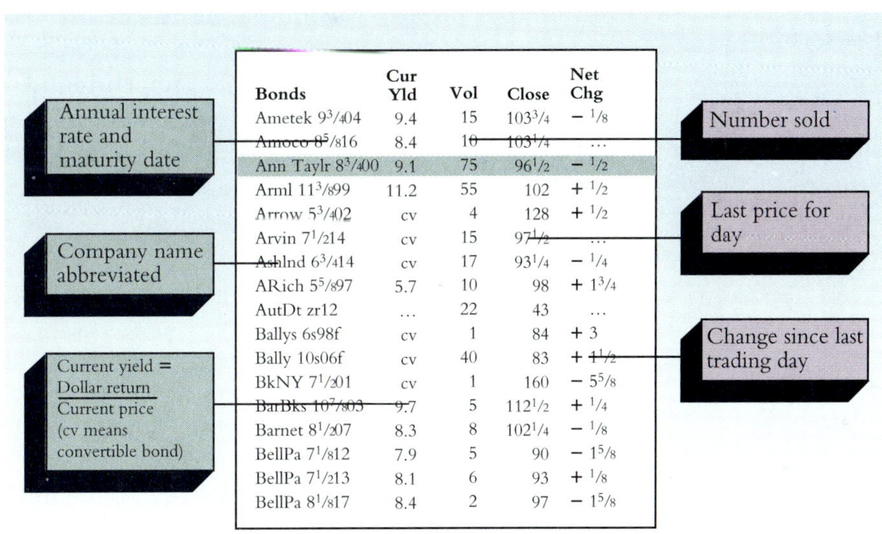

Bonds	Cur Yld	Vol	Close	Net Chg
Ametek 9¾04	9.4	15	103¾	− ⅛
Amoco 8⅝16	8.4	10	103¼	...
Ann Taylr 8¾00	9.1	75	96½	− ½
Arml 11⅜99	11.2	55	102	+ ½
Arrow 5¾02	cv	4	128	+ ½
Arvin 7½14	cv	15	97½	...
Ashlnd 6¾14	cv	17	93¼	− ¼
ARich 5⅝97	5.7	10	98	+ 1¾
AutDt zr12	...	22	43	...
Ballys 6s98f	cv	1	84	+ 3
Bally 10s06f	cv	40	83	+ 1½
BkNY 7½01	cv	1	160	− 5⅝
BarBks 10⅞03	9.7	5	112½	+ ¼
Barnet 8½07	8.3	8	102¼	− ⅛
BellPa 7⅛12	7.9	5	90	− 1⅝
BellPa 7½13	8.1	6	93	+ ⅛
BellPa 8⅛17	8.4	2	97	− 1⅝

bonds were selling for at the end of the trading day. Bond prices are quoted in 100s, and bonds are issued in denominations of $1,000. Thus the actual selling price for each bond is 10 times the stated closing price; this bond was trading for $965 at the close of the day. The final entry tells us that the current price is down $5 from the previous day's closing price.

Government Securities. The U.S. government finances its projects primarily through taxes. However, just as in business, these funds do not always come in when needed, so borrowing becomes necessary. Another reason for government borrowing is to finance the deficit.

The government finances most of its borrowing with Treasury bills (T-bills). These mature in 91 to 364 days and do not pay interest but rather are sold at a discount and then redeemed at full face value at maturity. The return to the buyer is equal to the difference between the full face value and the discounted selling price.

The government also issues Treasury notes and Treasury bonds. These finance long-term debt. Treasury notes mature in 1 to 10 years, and the bonds mature in 30 years. These securities pay a fixed amount of interest, generally about 1 percent less than the rate of interest on high-quality corporate bonds. In February 1994, the Fed adopted a "neutral" monetary policy which sent the interest rates on bonds up more than a full percentage point.[8] The interest on U.S. government securities is exempt from all state and local income taxes.

Many other agencies issue debt securities to finance their operations. Some of the better known include the Government National Mortgage Association (Ginnie Maes) and the Federal National Mortgage Association (Fannie Maes).

Municipal Bond
Bonds issued by state, towns, and other municipalities to finance schools, hospitals, roads, and other civic projects.

Municipal Bonds. **Municipal bonds** are issued by states, towns, and other municipalities to finance schools, hospitals, roads, and other civic projects. The interest earned on municipal bonds currently is exempt from federal income tax (although a recent Supreme Court ruling makes it possible for Congress to tax these); in many cases, they are free from state and local income taxes.[9] Because of their tax-exempt status, municipal bonds pay a lower rate of interest than many other securities do.

Certificates of Deposit

A certificate of deposit (CD) is really a time deposit that pays a higher-than-average rate of interest to the investor (see Chapter 18). CDs, insured by the federal government, are very secure. But an investor can suffer a substantial interest penalty if the certificate is not held until its maturity date. A person who purchases CDs through brokers can sometimes avoid an interest penalty for early withdrawal because the CDs can be resold to other investors. In this case, they are treated in much the same way as bonds.

Mutual Funds

Mutual Fund
A fund formed by a group of individuals, who pool their money to invest in securities, and usually handled by a professional investment manager.

Individual investors sometimes find it difficult to participate in the market. The idea behind **mutual funds** is that a group of investors can pool their money and invest in securities. These funds are generally formal organizations, and the investments are usually handled by a professional investment manager. The fund may buy stock, bonds, government securities, commodities, or other investments. The net asset value per share of a mutual fund is calculated by adding up the values of all the securities held by the fund and dividing the number of mutual fund shares outstanding.

In early 1995, there was approximately $1.6 trillion invested in mutual funds in the United States.[10] Mutual funds are sold by brokers, and many banks now also sell mutual funds. Because the fees earned on sales of mutual funds is a stable base of income compared to lending, banks are expected to continue selling mutual funds in the future.[11] Some mutual funds may also be purchased directly from the managers of those funds.

Mutual fund quotes are provided in *The Wall Street Journal* and many other newspapers. Exhibit 19.5 shows a portion of *The Wall Street Journal's* quotations for mutual funds sold by Fidelity Investments. The first column shows the investment objective of the fund, the first number is the net asset value per share. Using the Blue Chip fund as an example, the net asset value per share is $26.39. The second number represents the offer price and includes the maximum sales charge that would be paid at purchase; the offer price is $27.21. The third number is the change in the net asset value since the last trade day, up one cent. Notice that some of the funds have NL in the offer-

Exhibit 19.5 *Reading Mutual Fund Quotations*

Net asset value (NAV) per share = Net asset value of fund / Number of shares

Name of fund abbreviated

	Inv. Obj.	NAV	Offer Price	NAV Chg.
AgTF r	HYM	11.24	NL	−0.05
AMgrin	S&B	10.57	NL	...
A Mgr	S&B	13.87	NL	−0.02
AMgrGr	S&B	12.69	NL	−0.02
Balanc	S&B	12.49	NL	−0.02
BluCh	GRO	26.39	27.21	+0.01
CA In	ISM	9.77	NL	−0.06
CA TF	MCA	11.07	NL	0.06
Canad	ITL	15.15	NL	−0.05
CapAp	CAP	15.82	16.31	−0.14
Cpinc r	BHI	8.95	NL	−0.02
CngS	G&I	165.03	NL	+0.42
Contra	GRO	31.25	32.22	...
CnvSc	S&B	15.77	NL	−0.01
Destl	GRO	15.13	NA	−0.05
Destll	GRO	25.69	NA	−0.08
DisEq	GRO	18.54	NL	...
DivIntl	ITL	11.13	NL	...
DivGth	GRO	12.89	NL	+0.01
EmGr r	MID	17.68	18.23	+0.03
EmrMkt r	ITL	13.69	14.11	−0.20
Eq Inc	EQI	31.31	NL	−0.05

Change in NAV since last trade day

Offer price = NAV + sales charge Or if no load it equals NAV

ing price column; this means that there is no load or sales charge so the price is the same as the net asset value.

Commodities

Commodities
Large-volume items, such as raw materials, precious metals, and agricultural products, in which individuals can invest.

Commodities include raw materials, precious metals, and agricultural products such as wheat, corn, and cattle, that can be traded in large volume at a commodities exchange. The major exchanges are located in Chicago. Two types of trading occur at the exchange. The first is spot market trading, where actual merchandise is purchased at the time of the sale. The second is futures market trading, where the purchase is made for future delivery, sometimes up to a year or more later. The Commodity Research Bureau develops indexes (CRB indexes) of spot market and futures prices.[12]

The Chicago Mercantile Exchange trading floor, where most of the nation's highly speculative futures trading takes place.

Commodities trading is highly speculative. The market is driven by weather, rumor, political climate, the economy, and almost any other environmental condition you can think of. Because the market is volatile—changing rapidly—getting caught in a shifting market and losing a great deal of money is easy.

Exhibit 19.6 shows the quotation system for commodities from *The Wall Street Journal.* The pricing method used and the size of a contract appear at the top of the quotation. In the case of corn, the price is in cents per bushel, and the purchase contract represents 5,000 bushels.

Exhibit 19.6 *Reading Commodities Quotations*

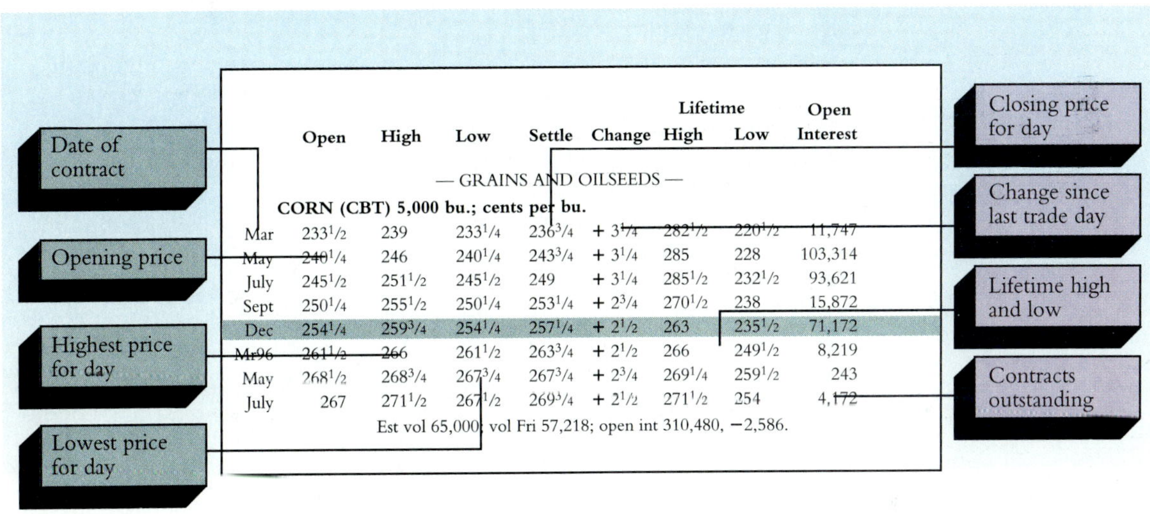

— GRAINS AND OILSEEDS —

CORN (CBT) 5,000 bu.; cents per bu.

	Open	High	Low	Settle	Change	Lifetime High	Lifetime Low	Open Interest
Mar	233 1/2	239	233 1/4	236 3/4	+ 3 1/4	282 1/2	220 1/2	11,747
May	240 1/4	246	240 1/4	243 3/4	+ 3 1/4	285	228	103,314
July	245 1/2	251 1/2	245 1/2	249	+ 3 1/4	285 1/2	232 1/2	93,621
Sept	250 1/4	255 1/2	250 1/4	253 1/4	+ 2 3/4	270 1/2	238	15,872
Dec	254 1/4	259 3/4	254 1/4	257 1/4	+ 2 1/2	263	235 1/2	71,172
Mr96	261 1/2	266	261 1/2	263 3/4	+ 2 1/2	266	249 1/2	8,219
May	268 1/2	268 3/4	267 3/4	267 3/4	+ 2 3/4	269 1/4	259 1/2	243
July	267	271 1/2	267 1/2	269 3/4	+ 2 1/2	271 1/2	254	4,172

Est vol 65,000; vol Fri 57,218; open int 310,480, −2,586.

The date of the contract, in the first column, states the date when the actual product will be delivered. Then the quotation shows the open, high, low, and closing (settle) prices for the day. The final columns show the change in price since the last trade day, the lifetime high and low, and the open interest in each contract—that is, the number of contracts outstanding. Notice that the closing price of corn for December was 257 1/4; because corn is priced in cents per bushel, that translates to \$2.5725 per bushel. Thus the market value of a contract is \$12,862.50, since each contract involves 5,000 bushels.

Commodities trading is extremely risky. It requires great expertise and should be conducted only by professionals. Most people who speculate in commodities lose money, as Today's Business World suggests.

TODAY'S BUSINESS WORLD

Taking Chances with Commodities

When Carol J. Loomis learned that Hillary Rodham Clinton made profits of \$100,000 a year through her 1970s experience as a commodity trader, Loomis understood why she would never rise to the White House. Although Loomis had a fling in commodities she did not become a mistress of the game. Unlike Clinton, Loomis claims she "crashed and burned, ignominiously."

When she was in her early 30s, Loomis put up a starting stake of \$1,000. She was working as a writer for *Fortune* and she wanted to become educated about commodities trading in order to prepare an article. "Though I owned stocks, the closest I'd been to commodities to that point was the corn fields around my hometown of Cole Camp, MO," she said. So, she met with a Merrill Lynch broker, Andrew Smith, to open an account. Smith told her that trading commodities was not the same game as trading stocks, and as a result she would have to talk to the branch manager, Walter McKeag.

Loomis considers the meeting with McKeag as her "D-Day for commodities." He advised her that commodities trading is a tough racket and it's easy to lose money. Therefore, he instructed her to get a letter of permission from her husband before she could open the account. Loomis was quite shocked, but she secured the letter immediately.

Like Clinton, Loomis made money on her first trade. On June 8, 1961, Loomis bought a March 1962 futures contract for 5,000 bushels of wheat at \$2.02375 per bushel. On October 3, 1961, she sold it for \$2.07125 for a profit of \$215.50. Instead of walking away with her profits, she continued trading for almost six more years and nearly 52 transactions. In addition to wheat, Loomis traded corn, cotton-seed oil, soybean oil, rye, eggs, silver, soybeans, and even Clinton's favorite—beef cattle. Unlike Clinton, who played the long side, Loomis chose to be a shortseller in cattle and lost \$1,222.

Loomis experienced other losses during the next six years. For example, in 1962, while on a trip to Europe with her husband, she found a \$500 margin call on corn awaiting her at her hotel in Florence. She called her broker and told him to sell her out. This resulted in a \$731.50 loss. One of her biggest losses was in January 1967 when she decided to sell silver short—four May contracts, each for about \$1.335. For five months, her silver contracts sunk toward the low price of \$1.2929. On May 18, the price of May contracts suddenly shot up to \$1.36. A rise in commodity prices signals that the economy is steaming. She decided to pursue a "hold" strategy and come up with a large margin check. The prices continued to shoot up higher and she ultimately lost \$13,176 on the four contracts.

After her silver disaster, Loomis mentally joined "Commodities Anonymous" and decided to just stay with stocks. Since then, she has been doing fine in the market. When her friends tell her that they are speculating with commodities, she says, "Get out." She also claims that if Clinton had consulted her before taking the plunge, she would have said, "Don't do it. You'll be sorry."

If you had $10,000 to invest, would you take your chances in the commodities market? Why or why not?

Source: Adapted from Susan E. Kuhn, "Commodity Prices Spell Inflation Danger," *Fortune* (June 27, 1994): 104–110; Carol J. Loomis, "Confessions of a Female Commodities Trader," *Fortune* (May 2, 1994): 58–59; and David McNaughton, "Trying to Hedge Their Bets," *Atlanta Constitution* (April 2, 1994): C1.

Financial Futures

Financial Futures
A future that requires the purchaser to buy or sell a specific financial instrument.

Another avenue of trading is financial futures. Like commodity futures, **financial futures** require the purchaser to buy or sell a specific financial instrument, such as stocks or Treasury bonds, for a set price at a specified date. Most of these are purchased on margin, and since margin requirements on financial futures are lower than the margin requirements on stocks, the potential risk is magnified.

WHERE INVESTMENTS ARE HANDLED

Stock Exchange
An organization of individuals who buy and sell securities to the public.

For the most part, security transactions occur on or through an organized exchange. A **stock exchange** is simply an organization of individuals who buy and sell securities to the public. While this is usually a physical location, it does not have to be. The largest stock exchange in the United States is the New York Stock Exchange (NYSE). More than 75 percent of all trading is done at the NYSE. The American Stock Exchange (AMEX), also located in New York, is much smaller. Both are national exchanges that handle stocks for companies from all over the United States. Securities of international firms may be listed on foreign exchanges such as those in London, Paris, Frankfurt, and Tokyo.

In addition to the national and foreign exchanges, regional exchanges include Chicago, Philadelphia, Boston, and Pacific. Regional exchanges primarily list the stocks of firms within their own market area, although some national firms also list on regional exchanges.

Over-the-Counter (OTC) Market
An electronic network of several thousand brokers who communicate trades through NASDAQ.

Many stocks are not listed on any of the major or regional exchanges. These stocks are traded through the **over-the-counter (OTC) market** and handled through an electronic network of several thousand brokers who communicate trades through the National Association of Securities Dealers Automated Quotation System (NASDAQ). Besides stocks—some of which are very well known, such as Coors and Apple—the OTC market handles most corporate and U.S. government bonds as well as many city and state government bonds. NASDAQ quotes are given in *The Wall Street Journal* on a daily basis. There are no trading floors with the NASDAQ, rather firms and individuals use telephones and computers to buy and sell stocks in their own accounts.[13]

Commodity Exchange
An organization that specializes in buying and selling commodities.

Commodity exchanges specialize in the buying and selling of commodities such as agricultural goods and precious metals. The Chicago Board of Trade is the largest commodity exchange; the Chicago Mercantile Exchange is the second largest. These exchanges operate similarly to stock exchanges.

THE INVESTMENT PROCESS

The investment process typically involves several steps. An investor usually works with a stockbroker to decide which stock to buy, the broker places the order, and the investor follows the movement of the purchased stock and the market in general by reading market indicators.

Contacting a Broker

Stockbroker
An individual licensed to act on behalf of an investor in the buying and selling of securities.

The first step in investing in stocks or bonds is to contact a **stockbroker,** an individual licensed to act on an investor's behalf in buying and selling securities. Stockbrokers are listed in the Yellow Pages under Stock and Bond Brokers. The stockbroker acts as a financial intermediary and in many cases as an investments adviser. When dealing with stockbrokers, clients need to make their investment objectives known. Your broker needs to know whether you are looking for growth or income, the risk you are willing to take, the level of liquidity you want to maintain, and whether you are looking for tax deferment or tax avoidance. With this understanding, the stockbroker can recommend the types of securities you should consider and, for stocks and bonds, recommend specific company securities. Your Values and Attitudes will help you prepare to meet with a stockbroker.

YOUR VALUES AND ATTITUDES

How Much Risk Are You Willing to Accept?

Directions: Circle the number that represents your level of agreement with each statement.

	Strongly Disagree				Strongly Agree
1. In making an investment, one of my major goals is to protect my initial principal.	1	2	3	4	5
2. Buying stock would worry me because the price could drop at any time.	1	2	3	4	5

	Strongly Disagree				Strongly Agree
3. The loss of money through an investment would be very upsetting to me.	1	2	3	4	5
4. I prefer investments that are insured, like savings accounts.	1	2	3	4	5
5. I don't consider myself much of a gambler.	1	2	3	4	5
6. I like a sure thing.	1	2	3	4	5

Feedback: In terms of investment decisions, do you consider yourself a risk taker or a risk averter? Items circled 1 or 2 suggest that you are a risk taker; 3 or 4 suggest a moderate risk position; and 5 suggests a risk averter.

Though this is a fairly simple exercise, anyone selecting a stockbroker should assess their risk position. The stockbroker should be specifically instructed as to how much risk an investor is willing to assume. This also means that you make yourself aware of the risk associated with different types of investments. Sometimes stockbrokers are blamed for problems that were a result of misconceptions of risk associated with various types of investments. Do you know what risk factors are associated with the various types of investments?

Ordering

Market Order
An order that authorizes a broker to purchase stock at the current market price.

Limit Order
An order to purchase stock only if the price is at or below a specified limit.

Once you have decided to purchase a particular stock to meet your goals, your broker can place the order for you through the appropriate stock exchange. Let's say you want to purchase some Rockwell stock, which is trading at around 39.[14] You think the stock is going to go up, so you place a market order with your broker. A **market order** authorizes the broker to purchase at the current market price. If you want to make sure you do not pay more than a certain price, you can place a limit order. Under a **limit order,** the broker would purchase the stock only if the price were at or below the price you had specified as the limit. Of course you would typically place the order for round lots of 100 shares to minimize transaction costs.

To place the order, the stockbroker contacts the firm's member on the floor of the New York Stock Exchange (Rockwell is listed on the NYSE). The New York representative goes directly to the location on the floor of the exchange where Rockwell is traded and attempts to make the purchase. Provided someone is offering (selling) at the time, the purchase will be made; otherwise the order will be held to wait for someone to offer to sell. The same process is followed if you decide to sell, except that you would place a sell order.

Reading the Market Indicators

Several indicators provide information on the condition and direction of the stock market. As we noted previously, investors can get current information on certain stocks in the stock listings of local newspapers or national newspapers such as *The Wall Street Journal* and *Investor's Business Daily*. Those papers feature a number of articles every day concerning the financial markets. Investors should also watch what is happening to the economy in the United States and in the world and be aware of any special activity in any industry. Most of all, investors should consult with their brokers, whose job it is to keep their customers informed.

Broad indicators of stock market activity are also available. The most well known of these is the Dow Jones Industrial Average, which is really three different indexes based on the market prices of 30 industrial, 20 transportation, and 15 utility stocks. The Dow Jones index indicates the total value of one share of each stock (adjusted by a factor that takes into account the effect of stock splits and changes in the firms that make up the average). The "Dow," as it is commonly called, includes firms such as Sears, Roebuck and McDonald's as well as General Motors and Boeing. Exhibit 19.7 lists the stocks that currently make up the Dow Jones Industrial Average. The Dow is the most widely reported index of the stock market's activities and can sometimes cause panic, as in October 1987 when it dropped over 500 points in a single day of trading. Many people believe the Dow is too narrowly defined since it represents a relatively small number of large blue-chip companies. Another index, Standard & Poor's, is more broadly based, developed from the market performance of 400 industrial, 40 financial, 40 utility, and 20 transportation stocks.

Exhibit 19.7 *Dow Jones Industrial Average Companies as of March 1, 1995.*

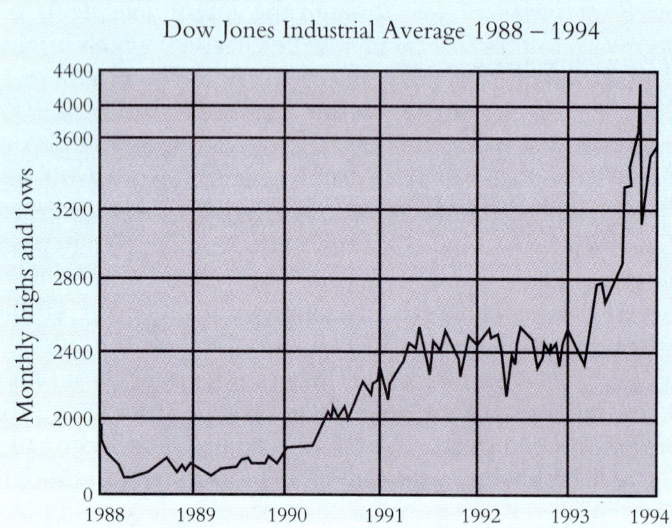

30 firms used to compute the Dow Jones Industrial Average

Allied-Signal, Inc	The Goodyear Tire & Rubber Co.
ALCOA	IBM Corp.
American Express Co.	International Paper Co.
AT&T	McDonald's Corp.
Bethlehem Steel Corp.	Merck & Co., Inc.
The Boeing Co.	J.P. Morgan
Caterpillar	Philip Morris, Inc.
Chevron Corp.	The Proctor & Gamble Co.
The Coca-Cola Co.	Sears Roebuck & Co.
Disney	Texaco, Inc.
Du Pont	3M
Eastman Kodak Co.	Union Carbide Corp.
Exxon Corp.	United Technologies Corp.
General Electric Co.	Westinghouse Electric Corp.
General Motors Corp.	F.W. Woolworth Co.

The original list published in 1896 had only 12 stocks, many of which no longer exist. The original list consisted of:

American Cotton Oil	Laciede Gas
American Sugar	National Lead
American Tobacco	North American
Chicago Gas	Tennessee Coal and Iron
Distilling and Cattle Feeding	U.S Leather Preferred
General Electric	U.S. Rubber

TOMORROW'S BUSINESS WORLD

Individuals Invest in Cyberspace

With 132 million personal computers in use worldwide combined with the constantly improving network system for moving electronic information, the use of on-line services is expected to explode by the year 2000. At present, almost 4 million Americans subscribe to one of the Big Three on-line computer services—Anerica Online, CompuServe, and Prodigy. Today people shop by phone and pay bills through the computer and modem. The latest trend is that people are taking more control of their finances and becoming more active in their investments. Individuals are starting to be their own brokers by managing their personal financial portfolios through on-line financial services.

Charles Schwab & Co. introduced StreetSmartE, the first on-line trading software program for individual investors. This program allows investors to enter trade orders on-line, retrieve real-time quotes and access up-to-date information on their personal accounts, retrieve independent investment research, and use tools to help manage their portfolios. America Online and CompuServe provide on-line investing through Quick & Reilly and E★Trade, as well as sources for solid company research and information. Prodigy started a service called the PC Financial Network that provides discounted on-line trading, portfolio tracking, and financial discussion groups. Reality Technologies developed an on-line personal investing service called Reuters Money Network that lists the latest quotes—only 15 minutes behind the stocks listed by NASDAQ, AMEX, and NYSE, as well as bonds, CDs, mutual funds and money markets.

Investing through the information highway is creating excellent opportunities for those who wish to bypass traditional brokerage firms. The future looks bright as the on-line investing services continue to grow.

Do you think on-line investing services will eventually take the place of traditional brokers? Why or why not?

Source: Adapted from John J. Keller, "Technology (A Special Report): Chasing the Gold," *The Wall Street Journal* (November 15, 1993): R20; Adrienne Redd, "Reality Technologies Aids Do-It-Yourself Investors," *Eastern Pennsylvania Business Journal* (April 4, 1994): 6; Tom Taggart, "Schwab Introduces StreetSmartE for MacIntosh," *PR Newswire* (July 5, 1994); Rick Tetzeli, "Is Going On-Line Worth the Money?" *Fortune* (June 13, 1994): 104–108.

REGULATION OF SECURITIES MARKETS AND TRANSACTIONS

Blue-Sky Laws
State laws that prevent corporations from issuing worthless securities; also require stockbrokers to be licensed and securities to be registered.

Both the issuance and trading of securities are regulated by state and federal laws. State laws, often called **blue-sky laws,** prevent corporations from issuing worthless securities to unsuspecting investors. These laws also require stockbrokers to be licensed and securities to be registered before they can be sold.

At the federal level, the most significant legislation is the *Securities Act of 1933*. This act protects the public from interstate sales of fraudulent securities. It requires a firm to provide full disclosure of information that might affect the value of its securities. This information is filed in a registration with the Securities and Exchange Commission (SEC). In addition, every prospective buyer of newly offered securities must be given a prospectus. As we noted earlier, the *prospectus* is a summary of the registration statement filed with the SEC and contains information about the firm and any information that would be helpful to a potential investor. The SEC does not judge the merit of individual securities, however, so the buyer should pay careful attention to the information in the prospectus.

The SEC was established by the *Securities Exchange Act of 1934.* It is a five-member commission appointed by the president with the consent of the Senate. Based on this act, all corporations whose securities are listed on national securities exchanges must file registration statements with the SEC. They must also update their registration statements with annual reports.

The National Association of Securities Dealers (NASD) was created by the *Maloney Act* (1938), an amendment to the Securities Exchange Act. The NASD was created as a private trade organization to regulate the OTC market. The SEC, however, does maintain final authority over the OTC market. Mutual funds were brought under the jurisdiction of the SEC by the *Investment Company Act of 1940.*

Investors receive some protection through regulation, but they are not protected against losses caused by the failure of a company. An investor who purchases a stock takes on the risk of company failure. The situation may differ, however, when funds are left with a brokerage house. The *Securities Investor Protection Act of 1970* established the Securities Investor Protection Insurance Corporation. The corporation, which is not a government agency, provides insurance protection for investors who suffer losses resulting from fraud or from a broker going out of business while still owing investors money. Investors are protected for up to $100,000 in cash losses and up to $400,000 in losses of securities.

SUMMARY OF LEARNING OBJECTIVES

1. ***Differentiate between* common stock *and* preferred stock.** Preferred stock has preference over common stock in the payment of dividends and in claims against the firm's assets. Holders of preferred stock are generally not entitled to vote. Common stock is voting stock. The holders of common stock have no guarantees of return and their rights to assets of the firm are subordinate to the rights of creditors and holders of preferred stock.

2. ***Identify the major types of investors.*** There are two major types of investors: institutional and private. Institutional investors are professionals who invest for large groups such as pension funds and insurance companies. Private investors are individuals who invest in the market on their own behalf.

3. ***Discuss five investment objectives and identify appropriate investments for each objective.*** Investor objectives include *growth,* which can be satisfied with high-growth stocks, real estate, precious metals, and collectibles; *income,* best gained with Treasury securities, bonds, utilities, and blue-chip stocks; *security,* best satisfied with nonspeculative investments such as savings bonds, certificates of deposit, or T-bills; *liquidity,* which requires the use of marketable securities such as T-bills and stocks; and *tax deferment or avoidance,* which means using government or municipal bonds.

4. ***Explain various investment options.*** Investment choices include *stocks* (including stock options, the purchased right to buy or sell stock at a fixed price); *bonds,* loans to corporations and governments; *government securities,* secure loans to the government; *mutual funds,* pooled funds for investment by many investors; and *commodities,* items people will later purchase, such as gold, corn, and cattle.

5. ***Describe the investment exchanges.*** A stock exchange is an organization of individuals who buy and sell securities to the public. The largest is the New York Stock Exchange. Others include the American Stock Exchange and the regional exchanges at Chicago, Philadelphia, Boston, and Pacific. Over-the-counter (OTC) stocks are traded on the NASDAQ. Commodity exchanges are similar to stock exchanges but deal in commodities.

6. ***Explain the investment process and the role of the stockbroker.*** Stockbrokers are individuals licensed to act on investors' behalf in the buying and selling of securities. The stockbroker not only places trades but also advises on trades. The process of making a securities trade involves the investor discussing the trade with the broker, placing a market order or a limit order, and the broker relaying the order to the appropriate exchange. The broker's representative then goes to the appropriate area on the stock trading floor and places the order.

7. ***Describe the principal regulations dealing with investment markets.*** The states have *blue-sky laws* that prevent corporations from issuing worthless stock. On the federal level, the most significant legislation is the *Securities Act of 1933,* which requires full disclosure of information about the firm to prospective buyers. The *Securities Exchange Act of 1934* established the Securities and Exchange Commission (SEC) and requires any corporation whose securities are listed on the national exchanges to file registration statements with the SEC. The National Association of Securities Dealers (NASD) was created by the *Maloney Act* in 1938; mutual funds were brought under the SEC's jurisdiction by the *Investment Company Act of 1940.*

KEY TERMS

Securities
Preferred Stock
Common Stock
Market Value
Book Value
Prospectus
Investment Banker
Blue-Chip Stock
Rate of Return
Bull Market
Bear Market
Round Lot
Odd Lot
Margin Trading
Stock Option
Put Option
Call Option
Price/Earnings Ratio
Default
Municipal Bond
Mutual Fund
Commodities
Financial Futures
Stock Exchange
Over-the-Counter (OTC) Market
Commodity Exchange
Stockbroker
Market Order
Limit Order
Blue-Sky Laws

QUESTIONS FOR DISCUSSION AND REVIEW

1. Why do companies use bonds to secure long-term financing? What are the advantages to using bonds as opposed to issuing stock?

2. If you had $1,000 to invest in stock, would you invest it in preferred stock or common stock? Why?

3. If you had $10,000 to invest in any single investment or combination you wanted, what would you choose? Why? Would any conditions, environmental or economic, change your decision?

4. Do you think the stock market is still a healthy place for small investors, or have the large investors made it too treacherous? Explain your answer.

5. If you have $5,000 to purchase stock shares and you buy 100 shares of Acme at $50 a share, how much money will you make on the sale of the stock if the stock price goes up to $60 in one year? How much money would you make if you used margin trading to increase your potential investment, if the cost of the margin loan were 10 percent per year?

6. What are stock options? What is the difference between a put option and a call option? If you buy stock options on a stock that is currently trading for $10 and that you expect to go up in value, should you buy put options or call options? Why?

7. In the stock quotation in Exhibit 19.3, what was the final selling price for the day for General Dynamics? What was the price/earnings ratio for General Mills? If you had to choose one of the stocks on that page to purchase, which would you choose? Why?

8. Assume that you buy a $1,000 bond that will yield 8 percent. A year later, when you want to sell that bond, similar bonds are yielding 10 percent. How much will you be able to sell your bond for? If similar bonds were yielding 6 percent, what would you be able to sell the bond for?

9. Describe the process you would go through to invest in the stock market. If you invested, would you place a market order or a limit order? Why?

CASE 19.1

Banks Jump on the Mutual Fund Bandwagon

At first, the gradual shift of money away from bank certificates of deposit (CDs) and into mutual funds was a threat to banks across the nation. But with the record-low returns on CDs and passbook savings accounts yielding about 2–3 percent in recent years, many banks have started selling mutual funds. "It's a drive to retain business," says Kenneth H. Thomas, an independent banking analyst in Miami. "As long as interest rates stay low, banks can't sit back and wait anymore." With sluggish loan demand and shrinking profit margins, banks can earn attractive amounts of fee income by selling securities. According to a recent Consumer Bankers Association survey, banks charge sales fees averaging between 0.7 and 4 percent on sales of mutual funds.

Almost all of the major banks are selling mutual funds today. Most of these funds are established ones from well-known investment companies. The number of mutual funds sold in banks increased from 884 in 1992 to 1,535 in 1994. Overall there were over 6,000 different mutual funds that consumers could choose from in 1994.

Some of the larger banks sell their own proprietary funds, which are managed by the bank itself and underwritten by another firm. Current banking regulations prohibit a bank from being its own sponsor or distributor of mutual funds. NationsBank Corporation is the second largest fund manager among U.S. banks. They are training at least 1,000 of their brokers to sell 41 different mutual funds worth over $72 billion.

But there is a growing concern over banks' involvement in the sale of mutual funds. U.S. Representative Henry Gonzalez, D-Texas, and chairman of the House banking committee, is pushing for increased regulation in this arena. Many are fearful that unknowing customers will lose all of their savings in their mutual funds accounts. Unlike savings accounts, which are federally insured by the FDIC for up to $100,000 per account, mutual funds are not insured. "The problem you run into is some customers, even though you tell them these are investments, still think that because the bank sells them, they must be insured," says E. Warren Smith, president of First Security Bank of Tennessee.

Rather, mutual funds expose investors to potential losses since they are subject to the fluctuations of the stock and bond markets. For example, in 1994, the Fidelity Asset Manager and Fidelity Puritan Fund each lost 4.48 percent and 0.54 percent respectively following a general market downturn.

In February 1994, the Office of the Comptroller of the Currency (OCC) developed guidelines for bank examiners for making sure that bank customers are aware of potential risks involved in investing in mutual funds. The guidelines say examiners should:

- Criticize banks that sell mutual funds with names that are similar to the bank's name.
- Examine the way banks choose the mutual funds they offer.
- Make sure banks disclose that mutual funds are not FDIC insured, are not guaranteed by the bank, and carry risk that the principal may be lost.
- Ensure that disclosures are featured in all written and oral sales presentations and advertising materials.
- Check to make sure that investment products recommended by bank employees are suitable for the individual customers.
- Make sure that a bank officer has been given responsibility for resolving customer complaints.

Questions for Discussion

1. Are the differences between commercial banks and investment banks narrowing?
2. What effect will the sale of mutual funds have on smaller banks?
3. Do you think the OCC precautions will always be necessary? Why or why not?
4. Do you think the OCC precautions will help clear up any existing confusion about mutual funds? Why or why not?

Source: Adapted from Pamela Moore, "Risky Business—Aggressive: Banks Pursuing Mutual-Fund Sales," *Winston-Salem Journal* (April 25, 1994): 13; Gwen Moritz, "Banks in Mutual Fund Business for Good," *Nashville Business Journal* (March 21, 1994): Sec. 2, 37; Alex Pham, "Really Getting Credit for Saving: Fidelity Card Program Helps Users Buy Mutual Funds," *Boston Globe* (May 19, 1994): 43; Sharon Harvey Rosenbert, "Banks Accelerate Mutual Fund Offerings," *Miami Daily Business Review* (January 26, 1994): 1; and Joanna Sullivan, "Slack Loan Demand, Thinning Margins Prompting Banks to Peddle New Products to Their Customers," *Baltimore Business Journal* (June 3, 1994): 15.

CASE 19.2

Too Many Credit Cards Cause Too Much Debt

For Elmer Hedgpeth, love and credit proved a near-ruinous mix. Caught up in a whirlwind romance with a California woman, the 63-year old Phoenix resident lived what he wistfully calls a "fantasy, the kind you dream about" for nearly three years. The once-thrifty former postal worker and his friend frequently ventured forth on spur-of-the-moment trips to Los Angeles, Las Vegas, and Salt Lake City.

At first, paying the bills with his eight credit cards wasn't a problem because Hedgpeth regularly drew a cash advance on one card to make payments on another. But then he hit the credit ceilings on all eight cards. With \$19,000 in charges, minimum monthly payments of \$2,000, and an after-tax monthly income of \$1,000, he couldn't meet the payments. He had to sell his car to help whittle down the debt, and the companies settled for partial repayments. Perhaps worst of all, the romance quickly faded. "About the only way one of these gals will look at a guy is if you've got money," he laments.

But have credit card issuers deserted him? Hardly. "I keep getting solicitations in the mail for credit cards," he says with disbelief. "I've gotten about three or four, but I just threw them out."

The problem is that the institutions appear to be addicted to offering credit, just as addicted as some people are to using credit cards. They are attracted by the cards' profit potential: The 2.5 to 3 percent that many issuers earn on their outstanding card debt is alluring to bankers who are doing well to chalk up a 1 percent return on total assets. And with the pool of potential new cardholders dwindling in the saturated market, some credit card executives believe that time is running out before a recession cuts consumer spending and boosts credit card defaults.

As a result, many card issuers are mailing out blanket solicitations and, except for the highest credit risks, are ignoring or easing their own credit standards. The issuers are simply hoping that the less creditworthy consumers they are wooing won't turn out to be deadbeats. Unfortunately the financial health of many card issuers and many new cardholders is increasingly at risk.

As one credit counselor states, "Most Americans over 25 are inundated with credit, and now the credit community is starting to go after high school seniors and college freshmen." The problem continues to grow. Deregulation has allowed a host of new competitors, including Sears, General Electric, and Merrill Lynch, to buy special-purpose credit card banks. With an estimated 1.1 billion Visa, MasterCard, American Express, and Discover cards in their pockets, Americans aren't lacking for credit. But they are having problems paying off their accounts. Only about one-third of all card holders pay off their entire balance every month.

Questions for Discussion

1. Do you think there is a problem with the way banks are issuing credit cards? Explain.
2. Whose responsibility do you think it is to protect consumers from debt problems?
3. Are constraints needed on who can have access to credit? If so, who should initiate them? What kinds of constraints?

Source: Adapted from Rodney Ho, "The Rebate Debate: Credit Cards' Incentives Could Be a Bonus or a Trap," *Atlanta Constitution* (June 27, 1994): E1; Steven Lipin, Brian Coleman, and Jeremy Mark, "Pick a Card: Visa, American Express and MasterCard Vie in Overseas Strategies," *The Wall Street Journal* (February 15, 1994): A1; John Meehan, "Picking a Path Through the Plastic Jungle," *Business Week* (August 6, 1990): 84–85; "How to Choose a Credit Card," *Consumer Reports,* (May 1990): 315; and Robert Guenther, "Credit-Card Issuers Ease Their Standards to Get New Accounts," *The Wall Street Journal* (May 22, 1989): A1.

BUSINESS APPLICATION

Finding the Handle on Controlling Debt

Allan Chang is a 19-year-old college sophomore who is contemplating how to deal with his debt problems. Chang has run up a lot of credit purchases in the past two years which have resulted in his not having enough money to pay his monthly bills.

During the past three months Chang has not paid his Visa bill or his car payment. When the letters from the Visa bank and the auto loan bank come in the mail each week Chang simply doesn't open them. The last two communications from these two banks have been discarded in the trash.

Chang is trying to stay in college, but is finding this increasingly difficult to do with his mounting bills. He has contemplated taking another loan to "consolidate all his bills into one."

Questions:

1. What will be the outcome of Chang not paying his Visa bill for the past three months?
2. What will be the outcome of Chang not paying his auto loan payment for the past three months?
3. Should Chang take out another loan to consolidate his bills?
4. How can Chang get a handle on his debt problem?

EXPERIENTIAL EXERCISE

What Would You Do with $10,000?

Activity:

Learn about the various ways individuals could invest $10,000.

Directions:

1. The instructor opens the exercise by explaining that each student has won a moderate sum in a local lottery. There is enough money to pay the taxes and pay off any outstanding debts and future education expenses. Beyond that there is $10,000 available for investment purposes.
2. Each student should complete Your Values and Attitudes on page 660 and then contact a broker in person or by phone and discuss the investment possibilities for the money.
3. After talking with the broker, students should make notes as to the questions the broker asked and suggestions that were made.
4. Classroom discussion should lead to a list of guidelines for the new investor.

NOTES

1. Adapted from Richard Andrews, "Investing with an Eye on the Dual Bottom Line," *Vermont Business Magazine* (February 1994): 37; Art Edelstein, "Social Responsibility Growing as a Business Necessity," *Vermont Business Magazine* (February 1994): 43; and Marilyn Joyce, "Sun Co.'s Campbell Takes Pledge to Protect Environment CERESly," *Philadelphia Business Journal* (January 28, 1994): B4.
2. *Fact Book* (New York: New York Stock Exchange, 1989).
3. Herbert Lockwood, "Rank Amateurs Perform Well in Investments," *San Diego Daily Transcript* (February 9, 1994): A1.
4. Susan Kuhn, "Blue-Chip Stocks Offer Value in a Volatile Market," *Fortune* (July 25, 1994): 29.
5. Ken Sheets, "When 'P' and 'E' Spell Profits," *Kiplinger's Personal Finance Magazine* (March 1995): 129–130.
6. John B. Thomas, "P/E Ratios Driven by Variety of Factors, Carry Variety of Meanings," *Indianapolis Business Journal* (May 23, 1994): B10.
7. Kristin Davis, "A Measure of Trust," *Kiplinger's Personal Finance Magazine* (April 1995): 73–77.
8. Vivian Brownstein, "New Threats to the Expansion," *Fortune* (July 25, 1994): 56–64.
9. Shelley Neumeier, "It Is Time to Look Again at High-Quality Bond Funds," *Fortune* (August 8, 1994): 29–30.
10. Susan E. Kuhn, "Time to Sell Your Mutual Fund?" *Fortune* (March 6, 1995): 98–112.
11. James Aley, Justin Martin, Shelley Neumeier, Ann Salmple, and John Wyatt, "The Outlook for U.S. Industries," *Fortune* (July 25, 1994): 66–77.
12. Susan Kuhn, "Commodity Prices Spell Inflation Danger," *Fortune* (June 27, 1994): 104–110.
13. Steve Fainaru, "Can This Stock Exchange Be Saved?" *Boston Globe* (February 13, 1994): 77.
14. "NYSE Thursday Composite Trading for the 1,900 Most Active New York Stock Exchange Issues," *USA Today* (September 2, 1994): B5.

C H A P T E R 20

Risk Management and Insurance

LEARNING OBJECTIVES

1. Define *risk* and explain the difference between speculative and pure risk.

2. Analyze the strategies of risk avoidance and risk reduction.

3. Recognize the strategies of risk coverage and explain the difference between assumption and transference of risk.

4. Explain how insurance works and how the law of large numbers affects it.

5. Identify the major sources of insurance.

6. Discuss the role of insurance for businesses and identify the major types of business insurance.

7. Describe insurance programs provided by employers for their employees.

The burning flames lit the night sky so much that the two boys saw the fire from their home several miles away. Their father was working in the burning Riverside Mills. The two boys and their mother raced to the scene, and after much searching, they found their father. The next morning, the family saw their business, their dreams, and their future plans in ruins. Worst of all—there was no insurance. Even a small fire insurance policy would have protected against financial losses to the building and its contents. Financial experts contend that many people fail to get adequate insurance.

"A fire was the last thing on my mind after I got the business up and running," said Jim Brennan, then 29. "I thought about giving up on the whole idea." But Brennan and his wife, Patti, decided to give another business a second thought. A successful business could help make a down payment on their house, begin a college education fund, allow more family time, and perhaps even provide after-school jobs for the two boys when they got older.

In September 1989, the Brennans withdrew $2,000 from their savings accounts to open a wheelchair repair store. The new venture was successful for four months. Then, the business was wiped out by another fire. The fire destroyed the tools, parts, records, wheelchairs that belonged to the customers, and even part of Brennan's spirit. Since all of his records and receipts were destroyed, he had no way of verifying what was lost in the fire. He contacted suppliers and retailers to see if they had copies of his records so he could apply for a loan from the SBA. Some had them, but many did not.

Brennan also faced serious cash flow problems. One of the biggest was the reimbursements from Medicare and Medicaid, the state and federal insurance that pays for much of the work he did. Often his reimbursements came in nearly four months after he had delivered a wheelchair.

After four years of struggling after the fire, Brennan's business is a little better than break-even. Although the small business pays his family bills, Brennan has yet to draw a salary. "It's been worth it, but we struggled for a long time," he said, "We are still struggling to make it work."[1]

What kind of advice about insurance do you think Brennan would give to other entrepreneurs?

People who live and conduct business on the Atlantic Coast know a hurricane could hit their area at some point and that property damage or personal injury would be likely. Similarly, people who live and conduct business in California know that they could experience a serious earthquake that could cause damage to their property or injury to themselves.

This chapter is about risk and how it affects business. We begin with a discussion of risk and the types of risk that businesses face. We then look at the various strategies a firm can follow to deal with risk. A discussion of insurance as a strategy for transferring risk follows. The chapter ends with a discussion of the types of insurance available to businesses and their employees.

THE NATURE OF RISK

Risk
The possibility of suffering an injury or loss.

Speculative Risk
Risk involving the chance of making a profit or taking a loss.

Pure Risk
The threat of a loss with no chance of profit.

Risk is simply the possibility of suffering an injury or loss. It is the direct result of uncertainty, the fact that in many cases we cannot know what the future holds. A large retailer who, after careful analysis, decides to purchase a piece of property and build a store cannot be certain what the future of that store will be. Perhaps the location will be perfect and the store will do well. Perhaps traffic will be rerouted to a new superhighway and business will be poor. For any number of reasons, the location may or may not work out. The retailer speculates that it will and that his choice is correct. This is called **speculative risk**—risk involving the chance of making a profit or taking a loss.

Speculative risk is necessary in business. Each time a businessperson makes a decision regarding a purchase, an advertisement, a promotional program, a new product, or anything else, the hope is that the decision will lead to additional profit. But there is also the possibility that the decision will lead to a loss.

Often managers face risks with no chance of profit; the best they can hope for is to break even. This is **pure risk**—the threat of a loss with no chance of profit. The residents and businesses in Charleston and San Francisco face pure risk from the possibility of a hurricane or earthquake. These are considered pure risks because the danger is one-sided; the firm does not profit from escaping the risk, it only avoids loss.

DEALING WITH RISK

Exhibit 20.1 summarizes the methods of dealing with risk. Good managers try to reduce speculative risk through careful study and planning. The more information that goes into making a decision, the less likely it is that the decision will lead to a loss—and the lower the speculative risk. A business can handle the presence of pure risk in two different ways. The company can *manage* risk, or it can *cover* risk.

Exhibit 20.1 *Methods for Dealing with Risk*

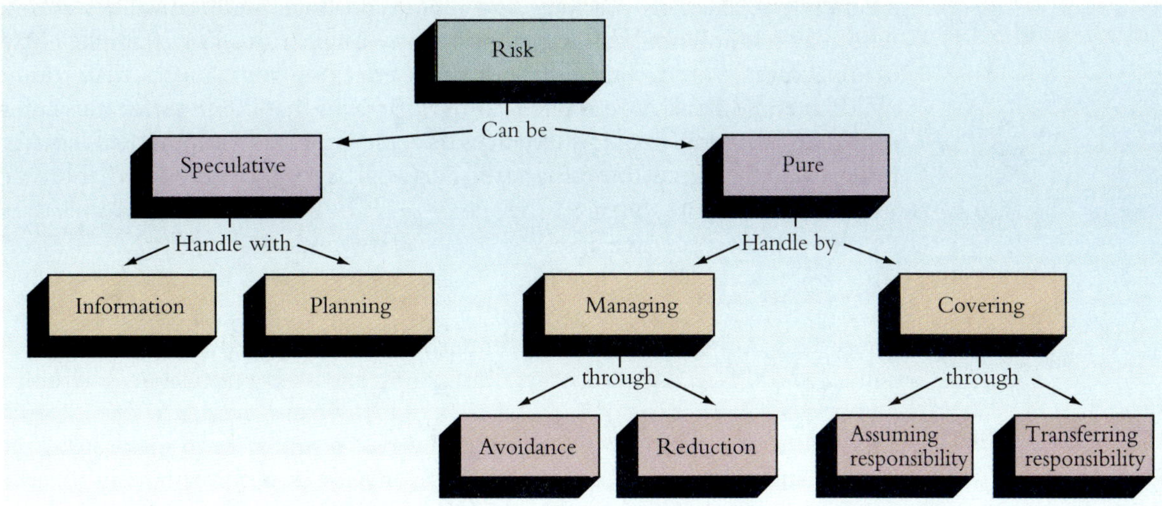

Managing Risk

Risk Management
Minimizing the amount and cost of pure risk a company will face.

In **risk management,** a firm tries to minimize the amount of pure risk it will face and the cost. To manage risk, a firm can follow one of two strategies: risk avoidance and risk reduction.

Risk Avoidance
A risk management strategy of not taking on or of getting out of risky ventures.

Risk Avoidance. One way to handle risk is through **risk avoidance**—eliminating the source of it. An individual who thinks that the risk of a plane crash is too great can avoid that risk by never getting on an airplane. A student who hears that a particular professor grades very hard can avoid the risk of failure by not taking that professor's classes. Companies can decide to avoid risks by not developing new products that may be hazardous to some individuals or by dropping certain lines of business where the dangers are too great.

Risk avoidance is not always possible. Many firms cannot afford to drop major lines or get out of certain businesses. Furthermore, firms unwilling to develop and sell new products are rarely leaders in their industry.

Risk Reduction
A risk management strategy of using loss prevention programs and other management programs.

Risk Reduction. If a firm cannot avoid risk, it should at least aim for **risk reduction,** or reducing the level of risk and the level of liability. Loss prevention programs can help accomplish this. A company needs to follow programs to lower the likelihood of fire, employee accidents, damage to company equipment, product liability suits, and other risks.

For example, to help reduce the chance of fire or the amount of fire damage, the company can install a sprinkler system, designate areas for employee smoking, and regularly inspect the plant for potential fire hazards. In order to avoid employee injury, a company can require employees to wear protective gear, it can install safety shields on dangerous machinery, and it can provide nonskid floor surfaces. To avoid product liability suits, the company has to carefully test all of its products and review products with consumer panels who may see potential dangers the company might miss. For example, a toy manufacturer would want to avoid sharp edges on toys, pieces that young children could swallow and choke on, plastic bags that could suffocate young ones, and potentially toxic substances. Retailers can reduce potential liability losses by reducing customer hazards such as glass displays, crowded aisles, or overstocked shelves.

Covering Risk

Regardless of the success of its programs to avoid and reduce risk, the company will still face financial risks. Eliminating all risk is impossible. Therefore companies must act to cover the chance of losses from accidents, fires, storms and other risk situations. In covering pure risk, a firm tries to make sure that it has a sufficient cash reserve to pay for any losses without having to take funds away from daily operations and thus possibly interrupt business. A company can cover these risks by either assuming the risks itself or transferring it to an insurance company.

Risk Assumption. When a company assumes the risk itself, it sets aside a portion of its own income to cover future losses. The company takes a certain percentage of its earnings and creates an insurance cash reserve. The money is invested in marketable securities so that it earns interest while still being available to cover pure risk losses. This method is referred to as **self-insurance** because the company is insuring itself against large potential losses by saving its own money to cover them. Today's Business World describes how one company has saved money through self-insurance.

Self-Insurance
Method by which companies assume risk by putting aside cash reserves to cover their potential future losses.

TODAY'S BUSINESS WORLD

Self-Insured Workers' Compensation Proves Successful

The Cherokee Construction Company, a small business specializing in putting up and taking down scaffolding, changed the way it pays workers' compensation claims. Instead of paying premiums directly to an insurance company, which then pays medical claims and reduced wages to injured workers, Cherokee went "self-insured" and started paying its own claims in 1991. As a result, Cherokee's workers' compensation expenses in 1993 were 72 percent less than comparable insurance premiums.

According to an employee at Cherokee Construction, "Going self-insured not only saves the company money, but seems to do another thing in our employees' eyes: make them more aware of safety." Employees somehow know that their claims won't be turned over to an insurance company that has "tremendously deep pockets" but instead will be paid by the very company they work for. This kind of knowledge not only increases awareness of safety, but enhances the bottom line as well.

Cherokee also takes a more active approach to medical treatment for its 100–200 employees compared to traditional insurance companies. For example, Cherokee may pay for surgeries or recommended physical therapy that insurance companies may not wish to cover.

According to Buck Gladden III, assistant general manager of Cherokee, "The benefits are twofold: In a shorter amount of time, the company gets a highly skilled worker back on the job, and the worker gets back to a full-time salary." Also because it is now guarding its own profit margins instead of the insurance company's profit margins, Cherokee is in a position to aggressively fight cases it suspects are fraud attempts.

Typically, insurance companies that write workers' compensation insurance prefer doing business with large companies. This is because these companies tend to pay larger premiums. As a result, smaller businesses have a difficult time finding insurance companies willing to sell them workers' compensation policies. Bill Young, executive vice president of Associated General Contractors, adds that some companies "are so small no insurer wants to fool with them." In the future, we will see small businesses becoming self-insured either by becoming a self-insured employer or by joining other businesses in forming a self-insured group fund.

What are some additional benefits a company may experience by self-insuring itself?

Source: Adapted from Bill Lewis, "Self-Insurance Clears Workers' Comp Muddle," *Memphis Business Journal* (May 23, 1994): 3; Bill Lewis, "Workers' Comp Self-Insured Pool Formed," *Nashville Business Journal* (May 23, 1994): 1; and Ellyn Toney, "Self-Insurance Savings," *Morning Advocate* (April 17, 1994): A1.

Self-insurance has become increasingly popular, partly because insurance companies will not provide coverage for high-risk ventures and partly because the costs of insurance have risen so dramatically that companies are finding self-insurance a less expensive alternative. Self-insurance was expected to go from about 25 percent of the property and casualty insurance business in 1984 to about 50 percent in 1995.

Generally self-insurance makes more sense for larger firms than for smaller ones, despite small firms' difficulties qualifying for commercial insurance. According to nationwide trade studies, nearly 80 percent of companies with 1,000 employees or more self-insure.[2] The larger company with many plants knows there is little likelihood of fires occurring in all of them at one time, and the risk of a fire in any one of the plants can be measured and protected against. The small company cannot afford to set aside the funds to cover such a large potential loss.

Transferring Risk. When a company cannot afford to cover losses with its own funds, it must turn to an outside organization for protection. It transfers

Insurance
A written contract that transfers the risk of loss from the insured to the insurer.

the responsibility for risk by purchasing insurance. **Insurance** is a written contract, taken with the insuring company, that transfers the risk of loss to the insurer according to the terms of the contract. However, not all risks are insurable. If an insurance company would have difficulty calculating the likelihood that a loss would occur because of some risk, it is reluctant to insure against that risk. Risks of this type are generally referred to as *uninsurable risks*. For example, while insurance can be purchased to insure against losses from floods, insurance cannot generally be purchased to protect against a drought, even though droughts can have devastating effects on farmers' livelihoods. Other things that cannot generally be insured against are political changes, changes in the economy, war or insurrection, strikes, or losses resulting from changes in the marketplace.

Insurable Risk
A risk for which an acceptable level of loss can be calculated and that meets the requirements set by the insurer.

While these and many other risks are not generally insurable, many risks can be covered. An **insurable risk** is one for which likelihood of loss can be calculated and one that meets the requirements set by most insurance underwriters to be insurable. To determine whether a loss is insurable or not, insurance companies generally use a specific set of guidelines.

1. *The individual policyholder must have an insurable interest.* This simply means you must actually suffer the loss to be the beneficiary of the insurance. You cannot insure your neighbor's car against theft and then collect if his car is stolen. However, you can insure the life of your spouse or a close friend and collect the benefits if he or she should die, because in this case you would have suffered a loss, even though not a financial one.

Actuary
An insurance employee who predicts the likelihood of future events based on their occurrence in the past.

2. *The likelihood of loss needs to be predictable.* Insurance companies employ actuaries to predict the likelihood of losses. **Actuaries** predict the likelihood of future events, based on mathematical models and historical records. They can predict the likelihood of a particular plant in a particular city suffering a damaging fire, or the likelihood of a car being stolen, given the neighborhood the owner lives in. By knowing the likely number of such losses and their average size, insurance companies can calculate the amount of money that must be charged to insure such losses. Without this predictability, the insurance company would not know how much to charge for its services.

3. *The amount of loss must be financially measurable.* Some losses, like the loss of a life, are not easily measured. For such losses, insurance policies are written in specific amounts. For example, a life insurance policy may pay $100,000 to the spouse when the insured person dies. Other policies, where losses and the likelihood of losses are more easily measured, may pay for the amount of the loss. Most auto insurance, for example, pays for the repair of a damaged vehicle or the market value of the vehicle, whichever is less.

4. *The losses must be fortuitous (accidental).* Insurance companies will not pay for losses created by the policyholder. If you intentionally set fire to your home, for example, your property insurance will not cover the loss.

5. *The risk should be dispersed.* In order to cover risks and pay for the losses incurred, insurance companies count on collecting premiums from a great number of people who suffer no losses. This is called the law of large numbers (discussed in the next section). The idea is that if the risk is all in one area, all of the insured may suffer the same loss at the same time. For example, claim payments for 1992's Hurricane Andrew were a record $23 billion.[3] Many insurance companies would be bankrupt if they only provided insurance in the Miami area.

6. *The insured must meet certain standards to qualify.* In recent years, insurance companies have started to charge smokers higher rates for life and health insurance. When occupations are risky, such as firefighting, some insurance companies will not insure people in those occupations; others charge a higher rate. Individuals with heart problems may not be insured. In all such cases, the insurance company has the right to set standards in order to limit the risk of loss.

HOW INSURANCE WORKS

Premium
A fee paid to the insurance company for protection.

Law of Large Numbers
Uses the probability of a specific loss occurring, the likely cost of that loss, and the number of individuals covered to calculate the premiums charged each insured individual.

When you purchase insurance, you buy an *insurance policy*. This is your contract with the insurance company. It states what losses the insurance company will cover. To get this coverage, you pay the insurance company a fee, called a **premium.** The amount of the premium is based on the **law of large numbers.** Insurers use the probability of a specific loss occurring, the likely cost of that loss, and the number of individuals covered to calculate the premiums charged to each individual insured. Of course the insurance company needs to include a charge to cover its operating expenses and provide a reasonable profit.

A simple example may help to explain this process. Say that an insurance company is going to insure automobiles against theft. In a particular city, they know that they will insure 30,000 automobiles. Furthermore they know from actuarial information that approximately 300 of these vehicles will be stolen and that the average loss will be $6,000. With this information, the company can calculate that it should expect to pay out $1.8 million in claims (300 × $6,000). If the insurance company spreads these losses over all 30,000 policyholders, the premium for each policyholder would be $60 ($1.8 million ÷ 30,000). The insurance company would also increase the individual premium amounts to pay for its operating expenses and allow for reasonable profit.

The law of large numbers explains insurance premiums in part. But not all 30,000 individuals present the same level of risk. One person's car may be a foreign luxury car (a popular target of professional thieves) while another may contain a burglar alarm. Each owner is not at equal risk. When insurance companies calculate premiums, they do take the level of risk into consideration. That is why older people pay higher premiums for a life insurance policy than do younger people. On the other hand, because they have more accidents, younger drivers pay higher auto insurance premiums than older drivers.

Deductible The amount of loss that the insured agrees to cover before insurance coverage begins.

In addition to charging certain policyholders higher premiums, insurance companies also use deductible clauses to help control their costs. A **deductible** in a policy is the amount of loss the insured assumes; the insurance company is responsible only for losses that exceed that specified amount. Therefore, if a person insures a car with a policy that includes a $150 deductible, that individual would have to pay the first $150 of each loss and then the insurance company would begin to pay. Deductibles can help reduce premiums, but insured individuals must also remember that they are not insured for the deductible portion of losses.

INSURANCE SOURCES

The size of the insurance industry shows the importance of insurance in managing risk. There are over 500 conventional insurance companies in the United States that share annual premiums of more than $300 billion each year.[4] However, the largest amount of insurance is provided not by private firms but by public sources.

Public Sources of Insurance

The federal government and certain state agencies may provide insurance for individuals or businesses. Public insurance is available to cover losses from such risks as unemployment, retirement, and work-related accidents and injuries causing disability, among other things.

Social Security. Initiated under the Social Security Act of 1935, social security is perhaps the best-known form of public insurance. The official title of the program is Old-Age, Survivors, Disability, and Health Insurance. Under this program, more than 90 percent of the U.S. working population and their dependents are eligible for retirement benefits, life insurance, health insurance, and disability income insurance.

As Chapter 5 noted, social security is financed through a tax taken out of employees' paychecks. Employers pay an equal and matching amount of tax to the federal government to help cover benefits.

The benefits of social security include:

- Payments for death, including a small lump-sum payment and continuing payments to dependent children and spouses who care for those children.

- Income payments for disability if the disability is total and expected to last at least 12 months.
- Retirement benefits.
- The Medicare program pays hospital and medical payments for eligible persons age 65 and over.[5]

Unemployment Insurance. Every state has some form of unemployment insurance. Benefits differ from state to state, but generally the program provides some weekly payments (usually for 29 to 39 weeks) to replace a portion of lost wages and offers job counseling, training, and placement services to help workers find new jobs. These insurance programs are funded by payroll taxes paid by employers.

Workers' Compensation. Every state requires that employers provide some form of workers' compensation insurance. This insurance guarantees payment of wages and salaries (generally equal to about one-half to two-thirds of the employee's weekly salary) as well as medical costs and rehabilitation services to employees injured in the workplace. These programs also provide benefits to the worker's family in the event that the worker dies from a work-related injury, accident, or condition. The employer alone pays the premiums for workers' compensation insurance.

Other Insurance. In addition to the programs mentioned above, the federal and state governments and their agencies provide many other forms of in-

Every business is required by law to carry workers' compensation insurance to provide benefits to employees injured on the job.

surance. For example, we learned in Chapter 17 that deposits in banks, thrift institutions, and credit unions are insured by government agencies. Other agencies, such as the Federal Housing Administration, provide insurance on mortgages and other government-insured loans. The National Flood Insurance Association offers flood insurance, and federal crime insurance is provided in some high-crime areas, since private insurance coverage is unavailable or cost prohibitive.

Private Sources of Insurance

Private insurance companies can be either stock companies or mutual companies.[6] A *stock company* is an investor-owned, profit-making company. The shareholders own the company, and profits are returned to them in the form of dividends. A mutual company is a nonprofit cooperative owned by its policyholders. Profits are returned to the policyholders in the form of dividends or reduced insurance premiums.

TYPES OF INSURANCE BUSINESSES NEED

A business can purchase many types of insurance to protect itself against losses. Insurance can be purchased to cover losses that arise from damage to property, injury to an individual, or damage to another's property. Insurance can also be purchased to protect a company from loss of income. Finally, insurance can be purchased to protect a company's employees. The most common types of insurance a company purchases for its employees are health and life insurance.

Property Insurance

Companies can experience property losses from many different sources. Sometimes the cause is unusual, as in the case of the Sealtest truck full of ice cream headed from the Sealtest plant in Saginaw, MI, to Detroit. Driving down Interstate 75, the truck driver misjudged a bridge overpass and rammed the top of the semitrailer into it, peeling back the top of the trailer and wedging it under the bridge. By the time a wrecking crew was able to remove the truck three hours later, the ice cream had melted into a sweet, gooey lake in the middle of the road. Sealtest experienced losses from the damage to the trailer and the loss of the ice cream. The company has to insure itself against such losses of property.

Property Insurance Protection for losses due to physical damage to or destruction of property or for property loss due to theft.

Property insurance protects a company against financial losses resulting from physical damage to or destruction of property or property loss as the result of wind, fire, flood, theft, vandalism, and accidents. Losses from these perils can be sizable; any of them might be sufficient to ruin a business without some form of insurance.

A business can purchase property insurance under one of two options: replacement-cost coverage or depreciated-value coverage. A company that purchases *replacement-cost coverage* will pay higher premiums, but the insurance will pay for the replacement of the insured item with a new item. So, replacement-cost coverage on a truck would allow the insured company to purchase a new truck. *Depreciated-value coverage* assumes that property used for some period of time is worth less because the owner has received some use, thus reducing its value. Under this policy, if the owner's 1992 Dodge van was totaled in an accident, the owner would receive the fair market price of a 1992 Dodge van as settlement for the claim.

Besides damage to property, a business can sustain a financial loss because of dishonesty on the part of outsiders or employees or the nonperformance of contracted work. The potential hazards of employee theft and pilferage and shoplifting by outsiders are great. According to a recent study, shoplifting is responsible for an average loss of 6.6 percent of sales (losses from shoplifting and costs of detection and prevention).[7] Insurance offers various ways of dealing with this problem. One way, a *fidelity bond,* protects an employer from losses resulting from employees' dishonest acts, such as embezzlement, forgery, or theft. Banks, loan companies, and other firms commonly use fidelity bonds to cover employees who handle company funds. Of course, in addition to insuring against this risk, wise businesses invest in a strong security program, which can pay big benefits in risk reduction.

A large construction firm contracts with a smaller subcontractor to complete some roof work on a new factory it is building. When the subcontractor starts the job but fails to finish, the large construction contractor loses $5,000 a day in late construction penalties and must pay a crew to complete the work subcontracted out. In order to insure against such losses, a firm can take out a *surety bond.* A surety bond is a contract written by a third party, usually an insurance company. It protects the party that has contracted to have work done from loss due to nonperformance by the contracted party. All public construction projects must be covered with surety bonds that guarantee the performance of every contract. The insurance company holding the bond is then required to pay damages if the contracted work is not completed.

Businesses may also need title insurance and credit insurance. Purchasers of real estate often obtain *title insurance* to protect against losses that could occur because of a defect in the title to the property. With title insurance, they do not need to look through legal records to find the true owner of the property and any claims against it. *Credit insurance* offers firms protection against some losses from the insolvency of customers to whom they have extended credit. Credit insurance especially benefits firms who conduct business internationally, since it covers losses for nonpayment because of political reasons as well as bankruptcy of foreign firms.

Business firms also need to protect themselves against financial losses resulting from crime. Three types of crime insurance are available: *burglary insurance,* which covers losses due to the taking of property by forcible entry; *robbery insurance,* which covers losses from the unlawful taking of property from another person by force or threat of force; and *theft insurance,* which covers losses from theft of any kind.

Liability Insurance

Liability Insurance
Covers losses from injury to another individual or from damage to other people's property.

Liability insurance covers losses resulting from injury to another individual or from damage to other people's property. When the Sealtest truck in the above example hit the bridge, it not only damaged the truck and the ice cream but did structural damage to the bridge. State highway department officials inspected the bridge the next day and determined that the cost to repair it would be $40,000. A claim for this amount was then filed against Sealtest. This is a liability claim. Unlike property claims, liability claims are made to reimburse injured individuals or repair the damaged property of other people. The damage to the truck and the ice cream is a property claim, but the damage to the bridge (which belongs to the state) is a liability claim.

Liability claims can run quite high, even into millions of dollars; however, most liability policies place limits on the amount that will be covered for liability claims. For this reason, many homeowners and businesses purchase umbrella liability insurance, which extends the amount of coverage limits to $1 million or more. This additional coverage provides a larger umbrella of protection for the business should a claim be filed.

Malpractice Insurance
Protects professionals (doctors, lawyers, etc.) from losses due to injury caused by the improper handling of their responsibilities.

Malpractice insurance is a form of liability insurance that protects professionals from losses resulting from claims of malpractice—the improper handling of their responsibilities. Doctors, lawyers, accountants, market researchers, and even college professors find themselves the target of malpractice lawsuits. A malpractice suit claims that a party was injured in some way through the improper practice of a professional. For example, a young boy goes into a doctor's office after suffering a severe cut on the wrist. The doctor administers an anesthetic and stitches the cut closed. Three days later,

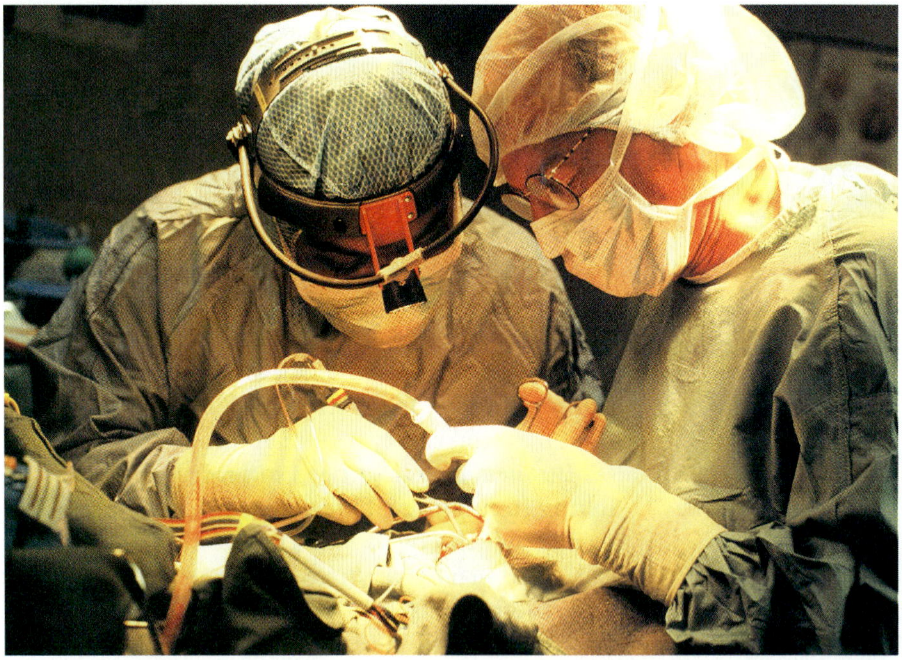

Physicians' need to purchase malpractice insurance to protect against lawsuits accounts for a significant portion of the nation's healthcare costs.

the boy loses all feeling in the hand, and the hand becomes paralyzed. The boy's parents, claiming that the doctor's failure to perform his duties properly (malpractice) led to the paralysis of the boy's hand, sue the doctor. Malpractice suits have increased in recent years, presenting a growth in the need for malpractice insurance. Nationwide costs due to medical malpractice liability are at least $15 billion a year.[8]

Product Liability Insurance
Covers losses for injuries caused by the use of a company's products.

Firms are finding it increasingly necessary to carry **product liability insurance,** which protects against claims for damages resulting from the use of a company's products. As with malpractice liability, in recent years product liability claims have increased in number, and the size of monetary awards to claimants has risen dramatically. Such claims can sometimes be carried to an extreme, and as a result legislation was introduced in Congress in 1995 to limit the size of punitive awards.

Product liability is a serious issue for firms. To stay competitive and successful, businesses must be innovative; yet innovative items are the ones most susceptible to liability claims. Companies who manufacture and market high technology and medical products are especially vulnerable. Between 1965 and 1985, for instance, the number of vaccine manufacturers declined by more than half. Since 1986 only one manufacturer has produced vaccines against measles, mumps, rubella, and rabies. Some universities refuse to license patents to small companies, fearing suits will name them as codefendants, and product development in small aircraft and reproductive technologies has slowed dramatically.[9]

The number and amount of liability claims and the resulting huge increases in insurance premiums have brought about a major crisis in the insurance industry and in business in general. Many small businesses find it very hard to obtain liability coverage. Areas having particular difficulty include day-care centers, medical practices, commercial fishing boats, and municipalities. Many companies have had to abandon products because they could not get insurance or the cost of coverage was too high. In fact, one survey showed that a number of companies have canceled introductions of new products because they were concerned about the potential liability. The problem threatens the availability of many needed products and services, such as day care and certain types of medical services, and has forced huge increases in the prices of others, such as childhood vaccines, where 95 percent of the price is the result of liability insurance and claims.[10]

Protection Against Income Losses

In addition to the common areas of property and liability, companies insure themselves against loss of income resulting from an uncontrollable interruption in business and, a related area, loss of the needed expertise of a key employee.

Many types of insurance protect a company against loss of income due to interruption of its business. A company that suffers a destructive fire loses more than property. Employee salaries, rent, utilities, and interest will likely

The loss of a key employee could be devastating to a business, especially a small business.

still need to be paid, but with the business unable to function, where will the funds come from? If there is no source for these funds, the business could be forced into bankruptcy. Three common forms of insurance used to reduce these losses are business-interruption insurance, extra-expense insurance, and contingent business-interruption insurance. **Business-interruption insurance** provides funds to cover the ongoing expenses of the business when a fire or some other disaster forces the business to shut down temporarily. The policy benefits pay for ongoing expenses and protect the business from further action by its creditors.

Business-Interruption Insurance
Covers the ongoing expenses of a business forced by disaster to shut down temporarily.

Extra-expense insurance provides the funds to pay for extra expenses when the business has to reopen in temporary quarters, rent needed equipment, or subcontract some of its work to other firms. *Contingent business-interruption insurance* protects against losses caused by an interruption of needed supplies. This coverage is different from business-interruption insurance. It only applies when the insured's business is injured because of the interruption of a key source of supply, perhaps a major supplier who has experienced a fire.

In addition to protecting income, many firms protect themselves from losses of income resulting from the loss of important personnel. These policies, called *key-employee insurance,* can be purchased by a company to protect itself against the impact of the death of a key employee, one whose expertise or skills are necessary to the smooth and successful running of the business. The assumption is that the loss of the key employee would cause the policyholding firm to lose the income that the key employee would have produced until a suitable replacement can be found.

Employee Insurance Policies

Besides carrying various types of property and liability insurance, most companies purchase insurance for their employees. They do this partly to be good employers and provide benefits and partly to be competitive with other employers in securing the best personnel to fill positions in the company.

As we stated previously, employers pay for some forms of insurance coverage because the law requires it. Employers have to pay half the cost of social security premiums and must provide money to the state for unemployment insurance. All 50 states also require employers to carry acceptable workers' compensation coverage. Beyond these required programs, most employers provide additional insurance for their employees. The two most popular types are health insurance and life insurance.

Health Insurance. Health insurance provides coverage for losses due to sickness or accidents. More than 160 million Americans have some form of employer-provided health insurance. However, according to a study by the Employee Benefit Research Institute, 20 to 30 percent of employees at firms that employ fewer than 100 people are without health insurance.[11] Employer spending for health insurance is an especially hefty expense for smaller businesses, usually about 10 to 20 percent of their payroll.[12] Many firms are trying to reduce health care costs by restricting options available for employees.[13]

Health Insurance Sources. Most employers provide their employees with some form of health and accident insurance as part of a fringe benefit package. Employers make coverage available through group policies. Rather than having an individual policy, an employee is insured as a member of a particular group: employees of the firm. In addition to such private group programs, most health care insurance providers also sell individual policies, though usually at a higher cost to the insured. The federal and state governments also provide health insurance for the elderly and the poor through the Medicare and Medicaid programs. Some 1.6 million people are covered by Medicaid.[14]

The costs of health care continue to rise, even as health insurance is being provided to a larger and larger portion of the population. One way to help reduce your personal cost of health care is to become more aware of your own health. Your Values and Attitudes will help you check your awareness of certain foods that can cause health problems in the long run.

The primary sources of employee health insurance are private insurance companies, including Blue Cross/Blue Shield, health maintenance organizations, and preferred provider organizations. Numerous private insurance companies, such as the Travelers Insurance Group, write private health insurance policies, primarily on a group basis. Perhaps the best known health

YOUR VALUES AND ATTITUDES

Do You Know About Your Health?

Directions: Answer the following questions about foods and health. Then compare your answers with those below.

1. Is cholesterol found in vegetables and vegetable oils, animal products, or all foods containing fats?
2. Which is higher in calories: saturated fat or polyunsaturated fat? Or are they both the same?
3. Is a food labeled cholesterol-free low in saturated fat or high in saturated fat? Could it be either?
4. Is a product containing vegetable oil low in saturated fat, high in saturated fat, or either?

Feedback: Here are the correct answers to the questions. The percentages in parentheses indicate the number of people surveyed who answered each question wrong. These percentages are high, considering the amount of nutritional information available these days in a variety of sources.

1. Cholesterol is found in animal products only (53 percent).
2. Saturated and polyunsaturated fats have the same caloric content (40 percent).
3. Cholesterol-free food can be either high or low in saturated fat (49 percent).
4. Vegetable oils can be either high or low in saturated fat (42 percent).

insurance program is Blue Cross/Blue Shield, a group of 69 nonprofit plans that provide insurance coverage to many U.S. households.[15]

Health Maintenance Organization (HMO) An organization that provides extensive medical care and services for members, based on a prepaid monthly fee.

Health maintenance organizations (HMOs) provide extensive health services and benefits for members, based on a prepaid monthly fee. Employees do not pay for health care services as they are administered; instead these services are provided by the HMO. The HMO hires its own physicians and health care specialists on a prepaid yearly income per patient.[16] Many HMOs own their own hospitals. Federal law requires employers to offer HMO plans to employees as an alternative to a group insurance plan when HMO plans are available in the area.

Preferred Provider Organization (PPO) A form of health care coverage that offers employers reduced premiums; employees must choose physicians and hospitals from the PPO's list of approved providers.

As HMOs have taken a larger portion of the health care business and health care costs have continued to rise, major insurers such as Blue Cross/Blue Shield have begun to develop special programs such as HMO Blue.[17] The **preferred provider organization (PPO)** is another form of health care coverage. Negotiating lower prices with certain physicians and hospitals, the PPO develops an approved list of providers—preferred providers. Thus it reduces the cost of premiums for health care packages offered to employers.

Point-of-Service (POS)
A new form of health care coverage that combines the benefits of an HMO and a PPO; the insured has the option of consulting with the plans' doctors (for a co-payment) or choosing their own doctors (paying a larger percentage of the claim).

A developing form of health coverage is the **Point-of-Service (POS)** plan. A POS is a hybrid of an HMO and a PPO.[18] A POS has a gatekeeper primary-care setup like an HMO and requires a co-payment from enrollees when they consult one of the member doctors. Enrollees who choose to move outside the plan will pay a larger percentage of the medical claim.[19]

Types of Health Insurance. Health insurance covers a wide variety of medical expenses. Most health insurance programs can be grouped into one of five general categories:

1. *Hospitalization plans.* These plans—Blue Cross/Blue Shield is one—pay the major portion of the cost of a hospital stay. Most base fees on a semiprivate room. Usually the plans cover the same portion of all drugs, lab fees and services provided while the insured is in the hospital.

2. *Surgical and medical plans.* These plans specifically cover surgical expenses. They pay the cost of surgery, the fees of medical specialists, and the physician's care while the insured is in the hospital. Generally these policies have designated maximum benefit amounts.

3. *Major medical insurance plans.* Such plans protect against catastrophic loss from a serious injury or lengthy illness. They cover all medical expenses not covered under hospitalization insurance or surgical and medical insurance. The typical policy requires a deductible payment before medical expenses are covered. A typical policy deductible might be $150 per person or $450 per family. Many major medical policies pay 80 or 90 percent of the total medical expense up to a maximum, often $250,000.

4. *Dental and vision insurance plans.* These plans have become popular in recent years, after getting off to a slow start in the 1960s. The plans pay a fixed percentage of an insured's expenses for dental work, eyeglasses, and some contact lenses. A typical plan may pay 70 percent of all expenses up to a maximum of $1,000, after which all expenses are paid.

5. *Mental health insurance plans.* These plans pay for psychiatric and/or psychological counseling. Once the deductible has been paid, the insured is eligible for benefit payments that generally range from 50 percent to 80 percent of the covered cost of treatment.

One other type of specialized health insurance, *disability insurance,* protects against loss of income while an employee is disabled as a result of accident or illness. The policy usually pays the disabled worker weekly or monthly payments after a specified waiting period.

While many companies offer all of the above programs, others offer only parts of the coverage. The most popular plans combine the hospitalization, surgical and medical, and major medical plans.

Life Insurance. In addition to health insurance coverage, many firms also provide their employees with life insurance. Unlike other forms of insurance, life insurance deals with a risk that is certain: The likelihood of dying is 100 percent. The uncertainty is when. Life insurance provides financial protection to the family of the policyholder. In the event of the policyholder's death, the family receives a benefit equal to the value of the policy. (Most policies are voided, however, if the policyholder commits suicide within the first year the policy is in force.) The individual or individuals designated to receive the benefits of a life insurance policy are referred to as the *beneficiaries*.

The appropriate amount of life insurance to purchase is a matter of personal need, depending on family responsibility. Most life insurance experts recommend that an adult with a family purchase at least four to five times his or her annual salary. However, most people have insurance worth no more than two years' financial protection.

Most firms purchase some types of insurance for their employees, including life insurance and health insurance.

Group Policies. As with health insurance, life insurance policies can be purchased on a group or individual basis. These policies can be purchased for almost any amount. Typically the smallest policies are $1,000, while the policies of some executives may have benefits of many millions of dollars. The size of life insurance policies are limited only by the amount of premiums individuals can or will pay. For larger policies, a physical examination is usually required to ensure the good health of the purchaser.

Group life insurance is frequently purchased by businesses as a benefit for their employees. Policies can be purchased on a participating basis, where the employee contributes part of the cost, or a nonparticipating basis, where the employer pays the full fee. Since group life insurance is written under a master policy, employees generally are not required to have a physical. Because group life insurance is usually more affordable than individual life insurance, taking advantage of it when it is available makes sense.

Earlier we described one unique form of life insurance, key-employee insurance. This insurance is purchased on the life of an executive of a company, with the company designated as beneficiary. Firms purchase such insurance to help make the transition when a key executive dies suddenly.

Term Insurance Life insurance that covers an individual for a specified number of years but has no value when the term is over.

Types of Life Insurance. Life insurance protection for a specified number of years is called **term insurance.** It protects for the term of the policy but has no value at the end of the term. If the covered individual does not die before the end of the policy term, the policy simply expires. While policies can be written for any length of time, most terms range from 5 to 20 years. Policies generally have a renewal option. The premium increases with each higher age range, and most policies do not cover individuals past age 65. Term insurance often offers the most economical way for young families to obtain the insurance protection they need for a number of years while they develop financial security through investments and savings.

A special kind of term insurance, *credit life insurance,* pays off a loan or installment contract if the insured dies. Individuals buying a home often purchase credit life insurance, which protects both the family and the lender. The value of the insurance decreases as the loan is repaid.

Whole Life Insurance Provides a combination of insurance and savings and stays in force for the life of the insured.

Whole life insurance, more expensive than term insurance, provides a combination of insurance and savings. Whole life policies generally stay in force for the entire life of the insured, as long as premiums are paid. In whole life policies, the premium (based on the original age of the insured) remains constant for the life of the policy unless the policy is changed.

Whole life policies accumulate value much like a savings account. The beneficiary receives the stated face value of the policy in the case of the insured's death. Because of the savings element of the whole life policy, the policy also has a cash value. This cash value grows larger as the policy is in force longer. The policyholder can take out low-interest loans against this cash value or, at retirement, can take out the accumulated value either in one lump-sum payment or in annual payments.

The high inflation rates of the 1970s and early 1980s brought corresponding high interest rates. Many people decided to avoid insurance and instead invest their money in mutual funds, money market certificates, and other higher-paying investments. Faced with a decreasing customer base, insurance companies devised alternative investment vehicles for their customers. One such vehicle is the variable life policy. Like whole life insurance,

Variable Life Insurance
Allows the policyholder to determine where the cash value of a policy should be invested.

variable life insurance pays a death benefit and accumulates cash value over the life of the policy. But it differs in that the policyholder decides how any cash value should be invested: in bonds, stocks, money market funds, or any other form of investment. Whether the cash value accumulates quickly or slowly depends on the ability of the policyholder to invest the funds. Usually the death benefit is guaranteed.

Universal Life Insurance
Combines term insurance with a tax-deferred savings account earning interest at bond market rates.

Another type of policy that insurance companies created to attract policyholders was the universal life policy. **Universal life insurance** combines term insurance and a savings account. The savings account, a tax-deferred account, earns interest at bond market rates. If the insured dies, the base policy amount plus any accumulated earnings are paid to the beneficiaries. Otherwise the accumulated earnings can be paid directly to the policyholder. One advantage of universal life policies is flexibility. The policyholder can adjust the amount of premium paid (as long as it covers the cost of their term insurance portion) as well as borrow from the policy, take out accumulated earnings, or leave the earnings with the policy to continue to accumulate for retirement.

As you can see, individuals have many life insurance options. The question of what insurance is best is not easy to answer. Many investment experts recommend buying term insurance and investing the savings. With policies such as universal life paying money market rates, achieving a high level of earnings and security at the same time is possible. When choosing the type and amount of insurance to buy, people must consider their age, health, family size, children's ages, savings or investment plans already in place, the income your family would need in the event of your death, whether college education will need to be funded, and the cost of insurance. A qualified insurance agent can help answer many of these questions. Since agents are paid on commission, however, consumers should have some knowledge of the types of policies and options available.

TOMORROW'S BUSINESS WORLD

Paperless Insurance Claims

If you have ever filed a medical insurance claim, you probably remember lots of paperwork, long waits, endless photocopying, and possibly many phone calls. Today, most transactions are processed by personnel based on paper claims filed by patients and providers. The insurance industry is looking into reducing the hassle, however, by applying information technology already used by banks, airlines, and retailers. Electronic filing of health care claims appears to be the wave of the future. Not only will such a system be easier for consumers, but it should save costs. Health care costs are skyrocketing; the filing of claims and other related paperwork related to medical care already costs about $10 billion a year.

The National Electronic Information Corporation is an insurance industry consortium that has already activated a new network to process health information electronically in nine states. This network allows medical personnel to verify the insurance coverage of patients insured by member companies through personal computers. "They can inquire on-line to see if you're covered and what the status of your benefits are," says Kenneth J. O'Donnell, the group's president and CEO. "In 20 seconds, they will have your coverage information in their offices." This type of network is expected to handle up to 100 million transactions a year by 1996.

Today, these systems are available in California, Texas, Florida, Illinois, Ohio, Virginia, New York, New Jersey, and Connecticut. Eventually, residents in all 50 states should have opportunities to file claims electronically. Furthermore, it is possible that patient medical data will be available through these types of networks as well.

Although the concept of moving to an electronic system appears efficient and cost-effective, does the system protect the rights of privacy for the consumer?

Source: Adapted from Janet L. Fix, "Video Technology Offers Face-to-Face Banking," *USA Today* (August 31, 1994): B4; Raquel Santiago, "Healthcare Costs Choking Smaller Firms, Survey Finds," *Crain's Cleveland Business* (June 6, 1994): 1; and Ron Winslow, "Insurers Activate Nine-State Network to Process Health Data Electronically," *The Wall Street Journal* (September 7, 1993): B4.

SUMMARY OF LEARNING OBJECTIVES

1. ***Define* risk *and explain the difference between speculative and pure risk.*** Risk is the possibility of suffering an injury or loss; it is the direct result of uncertainty. Speculative risk involves the chance of making a profit or taking a loss. Business owners take speculative risks when they decide to open a new store or run a promotion. Pure risk is the threat of a loss with no chance of profit, such as the risk of a natural disaster.

2. ***Analyze the strategies of risk avoidance and risk reduction.*** Risk management can involve avoiding risk or reducing risk. A firm follows a strategy of risk avoidance by eliminating the source of risk, such as when it decides not to produce a new item because the risk of lawsuits is too high. A firm follows a strategy of risk reduction when it acts to reduce the likelihood of loss. For example, it may put in sprinklers to lower the risk of fire and may conduct regular fire inspections.

3. ***Recognize the strategies of risk coverage and explain the difference between assumption and transference of risk.*** When a firm decides to cover risk, it finds a way to reserve sufficient funds to cover the financial losses that may occur, without interrupting the ongoing business. A firm can assume risk by setting aside a portion of the company's profits to cover future losses. Or it can transfer risk to an insurer, who will take the risk in exchange for a regular premium payment.

4. ***Explain how insurance works and how the law of large numbers affects it.*** Insurance works on the basis that risks can be predicted by actuaries who use past data to predict future likelihoods. The law of large numbers is used to calculate the necessary premiums. With knowledge of the probability of loss, the likely cost of each loss, and the number of individuals covered, an insurance company can calculate its needed premiums.

5. ***Identify the major sources of insurance.*** The major sources of insurance are public and private sources. Public sources include federal and state agencies that, through employers, provide coverage for retirement, disability and unemployment compensation, and some health insurance. Private sources can be either stock companies (profit-making) or mutual companies (nonprofit cooperatives).

6. ***Discuss the role of insurance for businesses and identify the major types of business insurance.*** Insurance transfers some of the financial responsibility for risk to the insurance company, thus making it possible for a business to continue to function when a major loss occurs. Businesses will typically purchase insurance to cover property, liability, income, and personnel losses. In addition, most businesses purchase insurance to cover health and life insurance benefits for employees.

7. ***Describe insurance programs provided by employers for their employees.*** Most companies provide two types of insurance for employees: health and life. Health insurance can be provided through a group plan administered by a private firm, a health maintenance organization (HMO), or a preferred provider organization (PPO). Life insurance, also usually provided through a group plan, is generally term insurance, although many other forms of life insurance are available.

KEY TERMS

Risk
Speculative Risk
Pure Risk
Risk Management
Risk Avoidance
Risk Reduction
Self-Insurance
Insurance
Insurable Risk
Actuary
Premium
Law of Large Numbers
Deductible
Property Insurance
Liability Insurance
Malpractice Insurance
Product Liability Insurance
Business-Interruption Insurance
Health Maintenance Organization (HMO)
Preferred Provider Organization (PPO)
Point-of-Service (POS)
Term Insurance
Whole Life Insurance
Variable Life Insurance
Universal Life Insurance

QUESTIONS FOR DISCUSSION AND REVIEW

1. What is risk? Do you think companies face more speculative risk or more pure risk? What strategies can they follow to help control speculative risk?

2. Describe the strategies of risk management. Give specific examples of ways firms might be able to practice risk management.

3. What is the difference between risk assumption and risk transference? What kinds of firms should practice risk assumption? Risk transference?

4. Name some types of uninsurable risks. Why are these generally considered uninsurable?

5. What guidelines do insurance firms follow when they decide whether or not a risk is insurable? Why do you think they follow these?

6. Explain the law of large numbers. In a town of 50,000 homes with a single insurer, what will premiums be if there is a likelihood of 500 fires per year and the average loss from a fire is expected to be $30,000?

7. What insurance is provided through public sources? How are employers tied in to this responsibility?

8. What types of insurance do businesses need? What kinds of insurable losses can businesses suffer?

9. What kinds of health insurance might employers provide for employees? Name the sources of this insurance.

10. List the different types of life insurance. Briefly describe each. What type of life insurance would you prefer? Why?

CASE 20.1

Health Insurance Fraud: The New White-Collar Crime

After spending the last decade or so catching the crooks involved with the savings and loan institutions, the Federal Bureau of Investigation (FBI) is now focusing its white-collar investigation efforts into health care fraud. "We're looking at every area of the health care industry where fraud can be committed," says James G. Conway, FBI special agent.

Fraud in the health care industry in the 1990s is what bank fraud was to the 1980s. Commonly cited estimates identify that insurance companies pay up to $100 billion a year in fraudulent claims. These costs ultimately get passed down to the policyholders, raising the cost of insurance by nearly 10 percent or more. It is estimated that 10 percent of insurance claims involve some kind of fraud, but the numbers could range as high as 25 percent in some areas, according to Colleen Cassidy, lead investigator for the National Insurance Crime Bureau.

Health care fraud can take many different forms. Some of them include falsified billing of insurance companies for operations never performed, charging for brand-name prescriptions when generics were actually used, charging for a specialist's services when none were performed, kickbacks to the makers of medical equipment for buying from a particular company, charging for refilled prescriptions when the prescriptions haven't been refilled, kickbacks and false test results by medical laboratories, inflated bills to cover bribes to decision makers, and podiatrists billing for expensive medical procedures when they're actually only clipping toenails.

But, as FBI agents and other investigators are becoming more aware of the types of crimes, they are also cracking down with major busts. For example:

- Ten people were arrested in connection with setting up licensed medical clinics that handled bogus insurance claims from staged car wrecks.
- Psychiatrist Ronald F. Hollander is serving a two-year prison sentence for treating one member of various families and then billing Blue Cross for treatment of other family members he never even met.
- David Harow, a podiatrist, billed an insurance company for performing surgical procedures on three bones in a patient's foot. Harrow received a six-month prison sentence and a $150,000 fine when the x-rays showed that he only operated on one bone.
- Executives from The North American Health Insurance Coordinators were charged with filing false claims on behalf of some unorthodox Mexican medical clinics. The clinics were treating American cancer patients with "coffee enemas" and "mudpacks."

Questions for Discussion

1. How can consumers become more aware of fraudulent health insurance practices?

2. What kinds of checks and balances can be set in place to avoid health care fraud?
3. Should insurance companies start charging higher premiums to finance investigations into health insurance fraud? Why?

Source: Adapted from Chris Payne, "FBI's White-Collar Force Now Targeting Health Care Crooks," *Houston Business Journal* (June 3, 1994): 4; Judy Rakowsky, "Medical Fraud Targeted in Mass.," *Boston Globe* (March 21, 1994): 13; and Greg Steinmetz, "Ex-Cop Hunts Down Petty Insurance Cheats," *The Wall Street Journal* (December 28, 1993): B1.

CASE 20.2

The Risk of Computer Viruses

As the business sector, and indeed all of our society, becomes more dependent on computers, concern about computer security grows. According to *Business Week,* roughly $1 trillion is transferred every day via computer networks. Yet a knowledgeable person can, with relative ease, access a computer system and cause serious damage.

One of the most recent computer problems firms face is called a "computer virus." A virus is a type of computer program that is intentionally hidden in other computer programs. When a program with a virus comes into contact with other programs, the virus attacks the other programs. Some viruses can destroy every bit of information on a computer. Businesses also face the problem of losing highly confidential data to computer hackers. These individuals break into computer systems and steal information or damage programs.

Computer viruses and computer hackers present a huge potential risk to firms. They have shut down entire computer systems in some large companies. Computer viruses and other computer crimes cost businesses more than $20 billion each year. Unfortunately, business firms do not back up information daily on a tape system. More typically, firms back up their systems once or twice a week.

In Massachusetts, State Senator Cheryl Jacques is urging support for a bill that would establish criminal penalties for computer hackers that vandalize computer data and software. Under her proposed bill, illegal access to computer systems would carry a fine of up to $1,000 or a sentence of up to 30 days in prison. Those who engage in "malicious vandalism" such as using viruses to destroy a program could be sentenced to up to 10 years in prison or up to 2 1/2 years in jail with a fine of as much as three times the value of the property that was destroyed.

Fortunately, business firms can now obtain insurance coverage for losses from computer crime. Although some policies specifically cover computer viruses, many others were drafted before computer viruses became a problem. These policies generally insure all risks of direct physical loss or damage, unless something is specifically excluded. The issue then becomes whether or not the damage caused by a computer virus is a physical loss. In some cases, insurance companies have maintained that information lost on a computer is not physical property and thus is not covered by a traditional all-risk policy.

Many insurance companies are beginning to use policy language that deals specifically with the loss of computer information. In this way, the insured understands what is covered and the insurance company can avoid a large, unexpected loss. Courts have held that information stored on the computer is tangible property in tax cases. In property insurance cases, they may handle the destruction of computer information the same way. Destruction of valuable information, therefore, could result in a catastrophic loss that is covered under an all-risk policy unless there is limiting language.

Questions for Discussion

1. Why is computer crime a risk to businesses?
2. Why is there a problem in determining whether or not the destruction of information by a computer virus is covered under an all-risk policy?
3. How can insurance firms protect themselves against unexpected losses from computer viruses?

Source: Adapted from Doug Abrahms, "Computer Ethics Campaign Launched," *Washington Times* (January 22, 1994): B2; Jonathan Kalstrom, " 'Televaulting' Provides Another Backup Method," *Minneapolis-St. Paul City Business* (May 13, 1994): 15; Sarah A. McNaught, "Penalties Sought Against Hackers," *Boston Globe* (April 13, 1994): 43; John Mezzacappa and Karen M. Cooke, "Computer Viruses and the All-Risk Policy," *Best's Review* (July 1990): 80–82; and Evan I. Schwartz, Jeffrey Rothfeder, and Mark Lewyen, "Viruses? Who You Gonna Call? 'Hackbusters,' " *Business Week* (August 6, 1990): 71–72.

EXPERIENTIAL EXERCISE

How Much Life Insurance Does a College Student Need?

Activity:

Students will review life insurance needs through small-group discussions. The activity will involve approximately 30 minutes.

Directions:

1. The instructor reviews the general purpose of life insurance and touches on the various types of policies.
2. The instructor divides the class into small groups of 5-7 students, with each group electing a spokesperson.
3. Each group will discuss the life insurance needs of two unrelated students. Students will make recommendations on the amount and types of life insurance coverage needed in each situation.
   - Student 1: 19 years old, lives at home with parents, has no dependents, works 20 hours per week for minimum wage, and owns a used car with a $5,000 loan outstanding.

- Student 2: 26 years old, married with one small child, works full-time in a job paying $25,000 per year, owns a home with a $60,000 mortgage, wife does not work outside the home, and owes $2,000 on a VISA credit card and $6,000 in car loans.

4. After giving each group about 15 minutes to review the two cases and make recommendations, the spokesperson of each group should share the group's recommendations with the class.

BUSINESS APPLICATIONS

Calculating the Patient's Portion of the Medical Bill

Activity:

Students will calculate the patient's portion of a medical bill using two different scenarios. Approximately 30 minutes of class time will be needed.

Directions:

1. The instructor should explain how a deductible works and the way the insurance company figures the co-insurance coverage.
2. Each student should calculate the amount of the medical bill the patient would be responsible for in two approaches to coverage.
    - Background: Samantha Reynolds breaks her leg sliding into second base during a softball game. The medical bills from her accident are as follows:
        1. Ambulance bill: $150
        2. Emergency room: 250
        3. Doctor's fee: 500
        4. Miscellaneous: 300
    - Under Scenario 1, Reynolds is able to use her Preferred Provider Organization (PPO) coverage for all of the bills, with the PPO coverage being based on a $200 deductible and 90% co-insurance coverage.
    - Under Scenario 2, Reynolds is not able to use her PPO coverage and must therefore use the standard insurance with a $300 deductible and 70% co-insurance.
3. After giving students approximately 10 minutes to calculate the answer for each scenario, the instructor should call on several students to provide their answers.

NOTES

1. Adapted from Jonathan Clements, "Harsh Realities Call for Financial Safety Net," *The Wall Street Journal* (October 22, 1993): C1; William H. Cunningham, Ramon J. Aldag, and Stanley B. Block, *Business in a Changing World,* (Cincinnati: South-Western Publishing Co., 1996); and John Kostrzewa, "Small Business Comeback: Jim Brennan Battles Back from Costly Fire," *Providence Journal-Bulletin* (January 30, 1994): F1.
2. Bonar Menninger, "Self-Insurance Under Fire," *Kansas City Business Journal* (February 25, 1994): 1.
3. "The Outlook for 22 Industries," *Fortune* (January 10, 1994): 48–56.
4. Leslie Scism, "Managed Care Thrives as Smaller Insurers 'Rent' HMOs; Cost-Conscious Employers Are Forcing Changes as Washington Deliberates," *The Wall Street Journal* (April 28, 1994): B4.
5. Jay Fitzgerald, "Growth-Minded HMOs Target

Medicare Clients," *Boston Business Journal* (January 20, 1995): 1.

6. Barnet D. Wolf, "Insurer Brings New Chief Executive Officer on Board," *Columbus Dispatch* (June 8, 1994): H1.
7. Scott Dawson, "Consumer Responses to Electronic Article Surveillance Alarms," *Journal of Retailing* (Fall 1993): 353–362.
8. Dan Quayle, "Rule of Law: How Come No One's Talking About This Health Reform?" *The Wall Street Journal* (April 13, 1994): A13.
9. Ronald Bailey, "Legal Mayhem," *Forbes* (November 14,1988): 97–98.
10. Ann Reilly Dowd, "Fixing Clinton's Health Care Plan," *Fortune* (April 4, 1994): 83–85.
11. William Kristol, "Pricing Health Care: How to Oppose the Health Plan—And Why," *The Wall Street Journal* (January 11, 1994): A14.
12. Raquel Santiago, "Healthcare Costs Choking Smaller Firms, Survey Finds," *Crain's Cleveland Business* (June 6, 1994): 1.
13. "We're Losing Health-Care Choice Now," *The Wall Street Journal* (March 10, 1994): A-19.
14. Steve Prestegard, "The Big Two: A Look at the Fox River Valley's Two Dominant Health Care Systems," *Marketplace Magazine* (January 31, 1995): 36.
15. Carol J. Loomis, "The Real Action in Health Care, *Fortune* (July, 11, 1994): 149–157.
16. Edmund Faltermayer, "Health Care: More Americans Are Switching to HMOs," *Fortune* (January 10, 1994): 34.
17. "Blue Cross/Blue Shield: Long Committed to Reform," *New Jersey Business* (February 1994): 52.
18. David Smith, "USAble Dominates HMO and PPO Markets in Arkansas," *Arkansas Business* (January 30, 1995): Sec. 2, p. 7.
19. Jim Harris, "UAMS Seeks to Compete: Medical Center Looks at Managed Care to Survive as Health Industry Reforms," *Arkansas Business* (February 14, 1994): 1.

Nike Uses Information Technology to Work Smart

Network Nike

What kind of answer would you expect to get if you asked the manager of Information Systems Technology Development at Nike to explain what networking means to his firm? Given that technologists love technology, you wouldn't expect the answer to be: "The real network is the network of people. The employees, our associates, our affiliates." But that's what Sam Rollins, head of the 55-person technology development group at Nike, firmly believes. Rollins is responsible for ensuring that Nike's systems and technology infrastructure is flexible enough to keep up with the fast-moving company and its people. That's a tall order. Nike's information network links some 10,000 people in more than 80 countries.

Technology at Nike is used to facilitate the efforts of three types of Nike teams: silo, process, and ad hoc. Rollins said, "We're very much a team company because we do a lot of things based on relationships forming. We're consensus and collaborative driven."

Silos are more or less traditional organizational structures, such as information services, marketing, and customer service. Rollins's group, for example, is one of five in the information systems (IS) silo, the other four being application development, computing services, support services, and architecture and planning.

Process teams, typically composed of people from multiple silos, are headed by project managers who coordinate projects across silos. Delivering footwear, for example, is a process that starts with the research and development silo and goes all the way through to sales and distribution.

Ad hoc teams are formed to address specific projects or needs and are later disbanded. These teams include anyone who has appropriate expertise, so they may cut across silos and process teams.

As Rollins pointed out, Nike's IS network allows his development group to "sew the company together electronically around the world. We can communicate with Thailand as quickly as we can with the building across the lake." Information technology allows teams to form more quickly because they are able to communicate more quickly. As Rollins put it, "Where it used to take me a day to send information to 50 people, now I can have responses back in 15 minutes."

The network that supports Nike teams worldwide is a large routed Internet. Company locations are typically outfitted with local area networks (LANs). The LANs are linked via a private network configured in a hub-and-spoke scheme, with the Beaverton, OR, headquarters serving as both the U.S. hub and the point of contact for the overseas hubs. The European hub is in the Netherlands, right outside of Amsterdam, and the Asian hub is in Hong Kong. Latin America and Canada are supported from Beaverton.

Of the Nike locations around the world, approximately 60 are on the private network, while the rest dial into the closest hub. The network supports Internet protocol (IP) traffic. A separate frame relay unit is used to support sales agencies around the United States and that network is interfaced to the backbone for E-mail and other services.

Besides providing a channel that enables teams to communicate, the global Internet opens doors of opportunity. For example, the European Community's economic reforms that are opening country borders on the continent are also enabling Nike to centralize its European inventory. The company is consolidating 30 warehouses throughout Europe into a single new one in Laakdal, Belgium. "We were going to buy a mainframe, put it in that warehouse, and run an inventory system there," Rollins said. "Then we realized we didn't have to, that we had enough capacity on our mainframe and—for an incremental upgrade to the network—could run it from Beaverton. We didn't have to hire a new operations staff."

With the network in place, Rollins says, one of Nike's main goals is to capitalize on the infrastructure by making sure everyone has access to it. "We're trying to drive down the cost of computing power so we can get it into the hands of more people," Rollins said. "We look at standardizing tools, standardizing configurations, and negotiating contracts that let us get the cost down to where it is no longer a value choice."

As part of this effort to "democratize" computing power throughout the organization, Nike is striving to separate software from hardware so it can use multivendor products and avoid being locked into any one platform. "Finding software that runs on the widest variety of machines really frees us up to pick and choose versus buying a package that only runs on one vintage machine of a certain size," Rollins said.

Nike is also working to ensure that data are not tied to any single application. This will help reduce costs and further aid the democratization process. Rollins said, "We're defining data as part of the infrastructure rather than being owned by a particular application." This approach makes it easier for employees to share critical data, provide access to data, and develop applications that need to use the data. To accomplish this on a global basis, Nike will replicate some of the data and centrally warehouse the rest. "We just embarked on an information warehouse concept," Rollins said. "We brought in the technology, and we're going to take about a year just to architect the data."

Since it's built on the Internet, the information warehouse will serve as the repository for Nike employees all over the world. "If you're in Thailand, France, or sitting here in the main headquarters building, you get the data from the same spot," Rollins said.

In terms of more traditional collaborative work tools, Nike relies on E-mail, videoconferencing, and a tool called *Folio Views*. "E-mail is one of the most dramatic tools for changing the culture of a company because it changes the communications pattern," Rollins said. "It's more informal, more rapid. As long as people get used to reading E-mail and just deleting it, not printing it, it changes the culture."

Both E-mail and videoconferencing were used extensively in the formation of Nike Europe. Teams in Oregon and in Europe collaborated on the development of information systems using these technologies. Since then, the use of videoconferencing throughout the company has mushroomed. Rollins said, "We now use it for all kinds of things in Europe. It facilitates the teams."

Folio Views is another tool that has proven useful for information distribution. As Rollins explained, this tool "allows you to put information up on the system and let people retrieve it." For example, Nike used the tool to create the fiscal 1995 business plan. Instead of nine divisions copying the 40-page reports and distributing them by hand, the plans were gathered and posted using *Folio Views*. Users could then read the document and respond using E-mail or that "old-fashioned" tool commonly known as the telephone. Where Nike would previously only have been able to turn around various iterations of the plan five times during the planning process, the bulk of which takes place from September through November, *Folio Views* made it possible to turn the document twice a day when needed.

Ultimately, Rollins sees Nike adding multimedia capabilities to its list of collaboration tools, which would make it possible to deliver things such as text, images, CAD designs, and full-motion video to desktops. "The product development process is what will drive us to digital media," Rollins said. "We use paper to move the image of products around as we develop them today. We move it across the headquarters campus. Across the country. Across the world. We have design centers in Europe and Asia that we collaborate with, and ultimately, we'll want to move those images electronically."

Rollins's goal is to make his technology development group's efforts as transparent to the company as possible. In the spirit of the team, Rollins says his group's job is to "facilitate collaboration across the company and bury the technology so it frees up more and more time for people to focus on getting things done."

CRITICAL THINKING CHALLENGE

Nike's global information network is designed to democratize the company's computing power. What does that mean? Sharing information broadly within the company will bring productivity gains and cost reduction. What are some of the ways in which information technology can help achieve those ends? Can you think of some ways in which information technology poses a problem for the company?

Working Smart at Nike

In this fast-paced age of information, many companies are developing competitive advantage around their internal management information systems. No longer the sole province of "techno-nerds" with plastic pocket liners, computers have taken up permanent residence on the desks of most corporate employees. Some companies have taken technology even further, providing field employees with computing power previously reserved only for those with direct connections to a mainframe. Hand-held computers with radio-frequency connections to corporate networks enable people to be productive while they are away from the office.

Nike's sales staff uses its hand-held computers to dazzle retailers. As Mike Roth, owner of the Essex House of Fashion on Market Street in downtown Newark, NJ, put it, "Nike has equipped all the sales reps with these unbelievable computers that can show me a whole line of shoes on the screen. The rep can spin the shoes around, change them into all the colors they'll come in, and he can even show me the commercials that will run to support the shoes on TV."

This extensive information network helps Nike move shoes out the door at the retail end of its business. Store managers, linked to Nike by computer, can have their orders overnighted to anxious customers by Federal Express. Roth said, "I can call Nike up on a Wednesday and tell them I need fill-ins of a hot model, and by the weekend they'll come in. No other company can do that." Emphasizing the positive impact of this information system on sales, Roth noted, "I've sold 30 percent more Nikes each year since they went into overdrive back in 1986."

Nike works smart in other ways as well. For example, the company outsources the handling of its mail to Metropolitan Presort, Inc., a Portland-based presort mailing company. Metropolitan processes 115 million pieces of mail per year, or about a half million for each working day. Besides Nike, its clients include U.S. Bank, First Interstate Bank, Legacy Health Systems, and Portland Public Schools. Nellie Musser, senior operations supervisor for Nike, said that 90 percent of the company's 2.5 million pieces of annual mail is processed by Metropolitan.

Metropolitan processes mail using optical character recognition (OCR) scanners that read the address on each piece of mail. The machine then develops a bar code that encodes that information and affixes it to each piece. Bar code readers then are able to sort the mail by ZIP code. In this way, the company achieves routing efficiency. The mail from multiple companies can be merged when headed for the same ZIP code.

Comingling its mail with other companies' mail is especially important to Nike, which sends invoices and other mail to remote ZIP codes all over the country and wouldn't otherwise be able to take advantage of the best discounts.

Communication with employees, desktop design, and handling day-to-day business functions are just some of the ways Nike uses information systems to work smart. Nike even has its own radio station—KAOS—to broadcast news and sports information to employees at the

Beaverton headquarters. As the future creates new competition and new challenges for the shoemaking company started out of the trunk of Phil Knight's car, technology and information systems will likely continue to play a major role in Nike's success.

CRITICAL THINKING CHALLENGE

Nike sales reps are able to demonstrate new lines of footwear to retailers on hand-held computers. This advance in capability has proven to be an effective marketing tool, but will almost certainly be outstripped by a new generation of technology that is more effective. What capabilities do you think that "next generation" will provide to Nike sales reps?

Sources: Adapted from John Dix, "Fast Breaks at Nike," *Network World* (April 4, 1994), pp. 18–22; Donald Katz, *Just Do It*, (New York: Random House, 1994); and Kendra Hogue, "Metropolitan Presort Becomes the Baron of Bar-Coding," *The Business Journal-Portland*, (December 6, 1993), p. 15.

PART

7

Accounting and Information Systems

C H A P T E R 21

Accounting Practices and Principles

1. Explain the purpose of accounting and its importance to a firm's managers, creditors, and investors.

2. Differentiate between financial and managerial accounting.

3. List the steps in the accounting cycle.

4. State the accounting equation, define its elements, and describe its relationship to double-entry bookkeeping.

5. Explain the purpose of the balance sheet and identify its major elements.

6. Explain the purpose of the income statement and identify its major elements.

7. Explain the purpose of ratio analysis and list the major financial ratios.

LEARNING OBJECTIVES

Quality has been a buzzword for many American and worldwide manufacturers since the mid-1980s. One issue that has not yet been adequately addressed, however, is how to account for quality. Accounting for quality involves two primary calculations:

1. Measuring quality costs in dollar terms.
2. Determining the economic soundness of implementing quality techniques.

In simple terms, quality can be measured as the dollar value of the effort it takes to rework or scrap imperfectly (or defectively) manufactured items. Organizations typically define a quality tolerance, or allowable defect rate, for the products they are manufacturing. When the defect rate of a production run exceeds this quality tolerance level, rework costs are necessary to fix or remanufacture the product. The time and effort spent reworking defects increases the amount of total production costs for the firm. Hence, quality costs are a necessary component of manufacturing costs for a firm.

Determining the economic soundness of projects to improve quality is often the task of the accountant, as discussed earlier in the book. Common techniques used to improve quality include total quality management (TQM), quality circles, computer-aided design (CAD), computer-aided manufacturing (CAM), and retooling or replacing manufacturing machinery. Before a quality technique is undertaken, an economic soundness review should be conducted.

Cost/benefit analysis is one of the most common methods used to determine economic feasibility. The cost (or expense) of implementing a quality technique are measured against the benefits that would be gained from the implementation. If the benefits outweigh the costs, then the project is said to be economically feasible and the project may be undertaken. If the opposite is true, then the project is generally not pursued.

Costs are measured as the total amount of funds expended to place a quality technique into service. They may include equipment, labor, and supplies. Benefits, on the other hand, are harder to measure, depending on whether they are tangible or intangible. Tangible benefits such as productivity gains, lower warranty costs, and lower product returns and allowances can be quantified fairly easily in terms of dollars. Intangible benefits are more difficult. Customer satisfaction with manufactured products would be an example of an intangible benefit. It is virtually impossible to place a dollar value on the concept of customer satisfaction, but no firm can be successful without it.

To illustrate cost/benefit analysis, let us assume that the Susan Corporation is considering a project to place a machine into operation that will improve quality. The machine costs \$300,000 and the labor necessary to operate the machine totals \$150,000 over a five-year period. It is estimated that the machine will lower warranty costs by \$150,000 over the five-year period and will decrease customer returns of defective products by \$100,000. Productivity is also estimated to increase with the implementation of the new machine. The benefits gained from increased productivity are approximated to be \$250,000 over the period. Hence, the costs of

placing this machine into service to improve quality total $450,000, while the tangible benefits of implementation are $500,000. In this situation the benefits are greater than the costs. According to cost/benefit analysis the recommendation to Susan Corporation would be to place the machine into service.[1]

Why is it important to include intangible benefits in the cost/benefit analysis for implementing quality techniques? Explain.

Accounting is an old profession. Business transactions have been recorded and analyzed for centuries. But only in the last 50 years or so has accounting been given the importance and respect accorded other professions.

Accounting is more than bean counting—or killer whale counting. Today accounting is the language of business: Anyone who aspires to a business career must, to some degree, speak that language. Corporations run on their numbers, and accounting plays an increasingly important role in business decisions. And with the economic unification of Europe in 1992 and increasing opportunities in global business, international accounting has gained importance.[2] (See Case 21.1.)

In this chapter, we examine how businesses use accounting information. We first define accounting and discuss the various uses and users of accounting information. We describe the professional certifications that accountants may attain and differentiate between public and private accountants. We then explain the accounting cycle, the accounting equation, and double-entry bookkeeping. Next we present the basic financial statements and their components. Finally we show how business firms interpret the financial statements through the use of ratio analysis.

WHAT IS ACCOUNTING?

Accounting
The process of identifying, measuring, and communicating economic information to permit informed decisions by users of the information.

The American Accounting Association defines **accounting** as "the process of identifying, measuring, and communicating economic information to permit informed judgments and decisions by users of the information."[3]

Accounting can be divided into two categories: financial accounting and managerial accounting. These categories differ according to the people they are designed to serve. Financial accounting is intended primarily for use by external decision makers (such as investors, creditors, and the Internal Revenue Service). Managerial accounting is mainly used by internal decision makers such as company managers.

Accounting information interests investors, creditors, managers, unions, and governmental organizations. Current investors use it to review the past performance of the company in which they have invested and to determine whether to maintain, increase, or liquidate their investment. Potential investors use it to help them make investment decisions. Creditors use financial information to evaluate credit applicants.

Company managers are the most common users of accounting information. They must have reliable information to make decisions about allocating company resources, through the use of budgets, information that can be used to predict the consequences of alternative business strategies. Managers also use accounting information to compare actual financial results with expectations. By reviewing financial data regularly, management can react swiftly when results deviate too much from expectations.

Unions review company financial information to help determine wage and benefit demands in salary negotiations. Governmental organizations rely on accounting information when establishing a company's tax liability. Exhibit 21.1 lists the various users of accounting information and some of the purposes for which the information is used.

Exhibit 21.1
Users and Uses of Accounting Information

User	Typical Uses
Current investors	Evaluate the income generated by a company and its components. Evaluate the cash flow generated by a company. Evaluate management's performance.
Potential investors	In addition to the above, determine a company's future growth potential and the risk of investing in the company.
Creditors	Evaluate a prospective borrower's ability to make principal and interest payments.
Managers	Make resource allocation decisions. Compare actual financial results with budgeted plans. Measure managerial performance.
Unions	Review a company's financial condition before negotiating wages and benefits.
Government agencies	Determine a company's tax liability.

TYPES OF ACCOUNTANTS

Public Accountant
Works for a firm that provides accounting services to companies, other organizations, and the general public on a fee-for-service basis; typical areas of service include auditing, tax consulting, and management consulting.

In the United States today, more than a million people work as accountants and several million more work in accounting-related careers. Accountants can be classified by the type of certification they achieve, as either a certified public accountant (CPA) or a certified management accountant (CMA). They are also classified as public or private accountants.

Public Accountants

A **public accountant** works for an accounting firm that provides accounting services to companies, other organizations, and the general public on a fee-for-service basis. Public accounting firms vary in size from the very largest, known as the Big 6, to sole-practitioner firms. The Big 6 have thousands of employees and offices throughout the world. Public accounting firms typically provide three areas of service: auditing, tax consulting, and management consulting.

Audit
A CPA's examination of a company's financial statements to determine the fairness of the statements in accordance with generally accepted accounting principles.

Auditing, the oldest area of practice, remains the largest for many firms. An **audit** is a CPA's examination of a company's financial statements in order to express an opinion about the fairness of those statements in accordance with generally accepted accounting principles. When a company wants to borrow funds from a bank or have its stock listed on a stock exchange, it must present statements regarding its financial affairs. Because these statements are prepared by independent auditors, those interested in the information know it has been presented fairly and accurately.

A rapidly growing area of practice is *tax consulting and preparation.* Public accounting firms help devise strategies to minimize the tax liabilities of their client companies. In many instances, the accounting firm will prepare or review the company's tax returns.

The third major area of practice for public accounting firms is *management consulting.* Activities in this area typically vary from one firm to another. Some examples include computer systems analysis, design, and implementation; employee benefits and compensation consulting; risk management services; and litigation support.

CPA
Designation for accountants who pass a rigorous examination, have accounting experience, and are licensed by the state; may be public or private accountants; qualified to conduct audits of companies' financial statements.

Exhibit 21.2 illustrates the United States net revenues of each of the Big 6 public accounting firms and how these revenues are derived from the three areas of service: auditing, tax, and management consulting. The Big 6 are international public accounting firms who audit most of the major corporations in the world.

Certified Public Accountants. Certified public accountants (CPAs) are licensed by the state in which they practice. Licensing requirements vary by state, but generally a CPA must meet certain educational requirements and

Exhibit 21.2 *Breakdown of Net U.S. Revenues for Big 6 Accounting Firms by Service Area*

					Revenue by Practice Mix		
Big 6 Firm	U.S. Net Revenue ($ millions)	Auditing	Practice Mix Tax	Mgt Consulting	Auditing ($ millions)	Tax ($ millions)	Mgt Consulting ($ millions)
Arthur Andersen & Co.	$2,680.1	35.2%	19.9%	44.9%	$ 943.40	$533.34	$1,203.36
Ernst & Young	2,281.0	51%	23%	26%	1,163.31	524.63	593.06
Deloitte and Touche	1,955.0	54%	23%	23%	1,055.70	449.65	449.65
KPMG, Peat Marwick	1,800.0	53%	27%	20%	954.00	486.00	360.00
Coopers & Lybrand	1,557.0	58%	18%	24%	903.06	280.26	373.68
Price Waterhouse & Co.	1,367.0	45%	27%	28%	615.15	369.09	382.76

Source: Adapted from *Public Accounting Report,* March 31, 1993, p. 1. Reprinted with permission of Public Accounting Report. Copyright 1995, Strafford Publications, Inc., Atlanta, GA (800)926-7926.

pass a rigorous, four-part examination developed by the American Institute of Certified Public Accountants (AICPA). In most states, two years of accounting experience are required. Today approximately 400,000 CPAs practice in the United States.[4]

CMA
Designation for accountants who pass a rigorous examination, have accounting experience, and are licensed by the state; may be public or private accountants but cannot conduct audits of corporate financial statements.

Certified Management Accountants. **Certified management accountants (CMAs)** must meet educational and experience requirements similar to those for a CPA. They take a five-part examination developed by the National Association of Accountants. Over 11,000 CMAs operate in the United States.[5] Both CPAs and CMAs are employed in public accounting; however, only a CPA can conduct an audit as to the fairness of a company's financial statements.

Private Accountants

Private Accountant
Accountant in any position not included in public accounting; may work in management accounting, government accounting, or academia.

The title **private accountant** includes all positions not in public accounting. Private accounting can be divided into management accounting, government accounting, and academia. Management accounting describes accounting positions within a company. The private accountant is employed by a single business, whereas a public accountant may have many clients. Government accounting positions can be at the federal, state, or local level. Accountants in academia teach and conduct research at the college and university level.

In this discussion, we mention only some of the career opportunities available to those interested in accounting as a profession. How much do you know about the accounting field? Your Values and Attitudes will help you assess your knowledge and perceptions of accounting.

THE ACCOUNTING CYCLE

Accounting Cycle
The steps—analyzing, recording, posting, and preparing reports—by which the results of business transactions are communicated.

A primary purpose of accounting is to communicate the results of business transactions. The accounting cycle was developed to accomplish this goal. The steps in the **accounting cycle** include analyzing, recording, posting, and preparing financial statements.

The accountant first *analyzes* business transactions to determine which should be recorded and at what amount. Typically accountants only record transactions that can be measured and verified with some degree of precision. For example, the purchase of a truck can be accurately measured and easily verified. The resignation of a key company official, also a business transaction, would not be recorded. Although such an event may represent an economic

YOUR VALUES AND ATTITUDES

Are You Up on Accounting?

Directions: Below are some statements about job opportunities in accounting and the different types of accountants. Circle the number that represents how strongly you agree or disagree with each statement.

	Strongly Disagree				Strongly Agree
1. Accountants tend to be employed in very boring jobs.	1	2	3	4	5
2. There is little opportunity to move out of accounting because other departments do not want "bean counters."	1	2	3	4	5
3. Accountants do not make enough money.	1	2	3	4	5
4. Because accountants deal primarily with numbers, they do not need good people skills.	1	2	3	4	5
5. The opportunities for women in accounting are not as good as those for men.	1	2	3	4	5
6. The only accountants with professional certifications are CPAs.	1	2	3	4	5
7. A CPA is independent with respect to his/her client.	1	2	3	4	5
8. A CMA is independent with respect to his/her client.	1	2	3	4	5
9. CPAs are limited to jobs in public accounting.	1	2	3	4	5
10. CMAs in public accounting can express an independent audit opinion on a company's financial statements.	1	2	3	4	5

Feedback: If you tended to agree with the first four statements, you need to learn some basic facts about the accounting profession. Whether it is auditing a multinational company such as IBM or working for the FBI as an agent, opportunities abound for accountants to move out of the accounting area and into other departments. Most departments view the financial training accountants receive as an excellent background for all areas of business. Also, opportunities for women within the accounting profession today are every bit as good as they are for men. Most larger CPA firms actively recruit, hire, and promote qualified accountants who happen to be women. Women make up more than 50 percent of the enrollment in many accounting programs in schools around the country.

The last five questions deal with types of accountants. CPAs are entrusted with the public welfare when they undertake audits of financial statements; the primary responsibility of CMAs is to their employers. CPAs are extensively employed outside of public accounting. More AICPA members are engaged in private practice than in public accounting. Another fundamental difference between CPAs and CMAs is that only a CPA can express an audit opinion on a company's financial statements.

loss to a company, it is difficult to determine what the amount of the loss would be.

Journal
A book or computer file in which business transactions are recorded chronologically.

originily recorded

Transactions are then *recorded* chronologically in a **journal.** A journal may be either a book (in a manual accounting system) or a file (in a computerized accounting system). Each entry contains the date of the transaction, its description, and debit and credit columns. Transactions are recorded in the firm's general journal or in specialized journals. A *general journal* is a book or file in which transactions are recorded in the order they occur. As businesses expand, they may adopt *specialized journals* to record particular types of business transactions (for example, credit sales or cash disbursements).

Account
Record of all transactions affecting a particular financial statement element.

General Ledger
A book or computer file summarizing all accounts of the business.

Financial Statement
Document presenting a company's financial position, results of operations, and cash flow during a stated period of time.

Businesses need to know the balances of various financial statement elements (assets, liabilities, owners' equity, revenues, and expenses) at any point in time. **Accounts** are used to summarize all transactions that affect a particular financial statement element. A business maintains separate accounts for each of its assets, liabilities, equities, revenues, and expenses. All transactions affecting an account are *posted* (recorded) from the general journal or specialized journals to the account. All the accounts of a business are summarized in the **general ledger.**

The final step of the accounting process is *preparing* financial statements. **Financial statements** present a company's financial position, results of operations, and flow of cash during a particular period of time. The financial statements that are prepared include the income statement, balance sheet, statement of cash flows, and statement of retained earnings. They can be prepared for any time interval, but they are always prepared annually. Investors, creditors, company managers, and others interested in a firm's financial position all rely heavily on financial statements. Exhibit 21.3 on page 714 illustrates the steps in the financial accounting cycle.

THE ACCOUNTING EQUATION

Accounting Equation
Assets = Liabilities + Owners' Equity, indicating a company's financial position at any point in time.

The **accounting equation** indicates a company's financial position at any point in time. On its framework rests the entire accounting process. According to the accounting equation, a company's assets equal its liabilities plus owners' equity, thus:

Assets = Liabilities + Owners' Equity

Exhibit 21.3
Financial Accounting Cycle

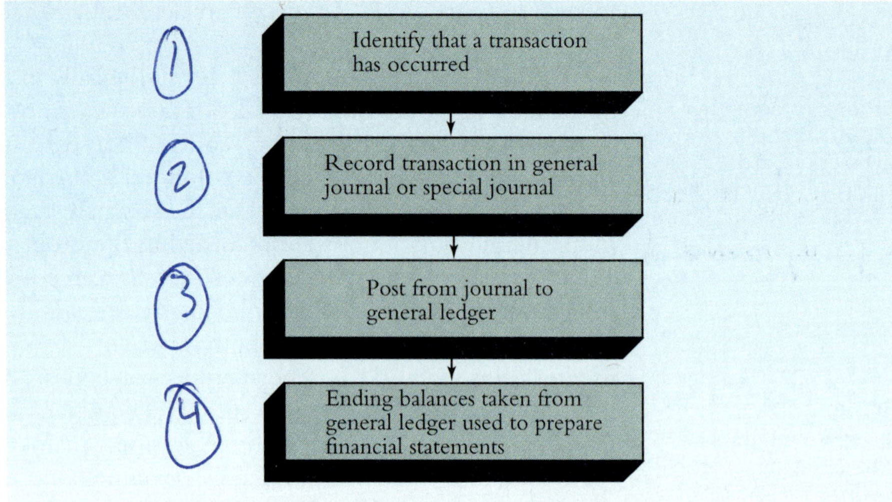

Asset
Anything of value owned by the business and used in its operation.

Liability
Debts owed by a business to its creditors.

Owners' Equity
Claims of owners, partners, and shareholders against the firm's assets; the excess of assets over liabilities.

Revenue
Inflows of assets resulting from the ongoing operation of the business.

Expenses
Costs incurred to produce revenues.

Net Income
The excess of revenues over expenses; also called the bottom line.

Any recorded business transaction can be analyzed in terms of its effect on the accounting equation. Also, business transactions must be recorded to maintain the equality of this equation. This equality is reflected in the balance sheet, one of the financial statements a firm is required to prepare.

Assets are anything of value owned by the business and used in conducting its operations. Examples include cash, investments, inventory, accounts receivable, and furniture and fixtures. **Liabilities** are debts owed by the business to its creditors, including obligations to perform services in the future. Liabilities include accounts payable and notes payable (for example, when a firm uses credit to purchase machinery or inventory), wages payable to employees, and taxes payable. **Owners' equity** represents the claims of the owners, partners, and shareholders against the firm's assets. It is the owners' claim on the firm's assets, or the excess of assets over all liabilities.

Revenues are inflows of assets resulting from the ongoing operation of a business. Businesses generate revenues by sales of goods and services, interest earned on investments, rents, royalties, and dividends. **Expenses** are costs incurred to produce revenues. Expenses include the costs of goods sold (the goods or services that the firm used to generate revenues), salaries, utilities, taxes, advertising, and interest payments. Revenues and expenses are components of owners' equity. Revenues result in an increase, while expenses result in a decrease in owners' equity. **Net income,** or the bottom line, is the excess of revenues over expenses. Net income, a chief barometer of business performance, is closely watched by investors, creditors, and company managers.

Double-Entry Bookkeeping

Debit
An entry that records an increase in assets, a decrease in liabilities, or a decrease in owners' equity; recorded on the left side of a journal or ledger entry.

Credit
An entry that records a decrease in an asset, an increase in a liability, or an increase in owners' equity; recorded on the right side of a journal or ledger entry.

Double-Entry Bookkeeping
A method of recording business transactions in which offsetting debits and credits keep the accounting equation in balance.

Every business transaction is analyzed to determine whether it increases or decreases a firm's assets, liabilities, owners' equity, revenues, and expenses. Debits and credits are bookkeeping entries that reflect business transactions. **Debits** are used to record increases in assets, decreases in liabilities, or decreases in owners' equity. Debits are recorded on the left side of an entry in the journal or ledger. **Credits** are used to record decreases in assets, increases in liabilities, or increases in owners' equity. Credits are recorded on the right side of entries made in the journal and ledger.

The terms *debit* and *credit* can be confusing. Whether debits and credits *increase* or *decrease* accounts depends on the type of account being debited or credited. The important point to remember is that debit means left side of a journal or ledger entry, and credit means right side.

Double-entry bookkeeping enables the firm to keep the accounting equation in balance. In **double-entry bookkeeping,** each business transaction is recorded with two or more offsetting entries in which the total amount of debits must equal the total amount of credits. Exhibit 21.4 shows an example of journal and ledger entries for the Music Box, a hypothetical retail establishment specializing in compact-disc players and other stereo equipment.

The Music Box's books are kept by Laura Baker, the owner. The accounts shown on the journal page in the upper portion of Exhibit 21.4 represent the company's sources and uses of funds. These accounts are then summarized in the ledger accounts, which are shown in the lower portion of the figure.

On September 1, Laura Baker contributed \$40,000 cash in return for capital stock to get the company started. This transaction increased the firm's assets and the owners' equity. The Cash account is debited (to show an increase in assets), and the Capital Stock account is credited (to show an increase in owners' equity).

Assets	=	**Liabilities**	+	**Owners' equity**
\$40,000	=	**\$0**	+	**\$40,000**
(Cash)				**(Capital Stock)**

On October 2, a sale was made. A customer paid \$2,000 cash for a CD player/stereo system. The journal entry records a debit (to show the increase in cash) and a credit (sales increase equities, and credits are used to show increases in owners' equity).

Exhibit 21.4
Sample Journal and Ledger Entries

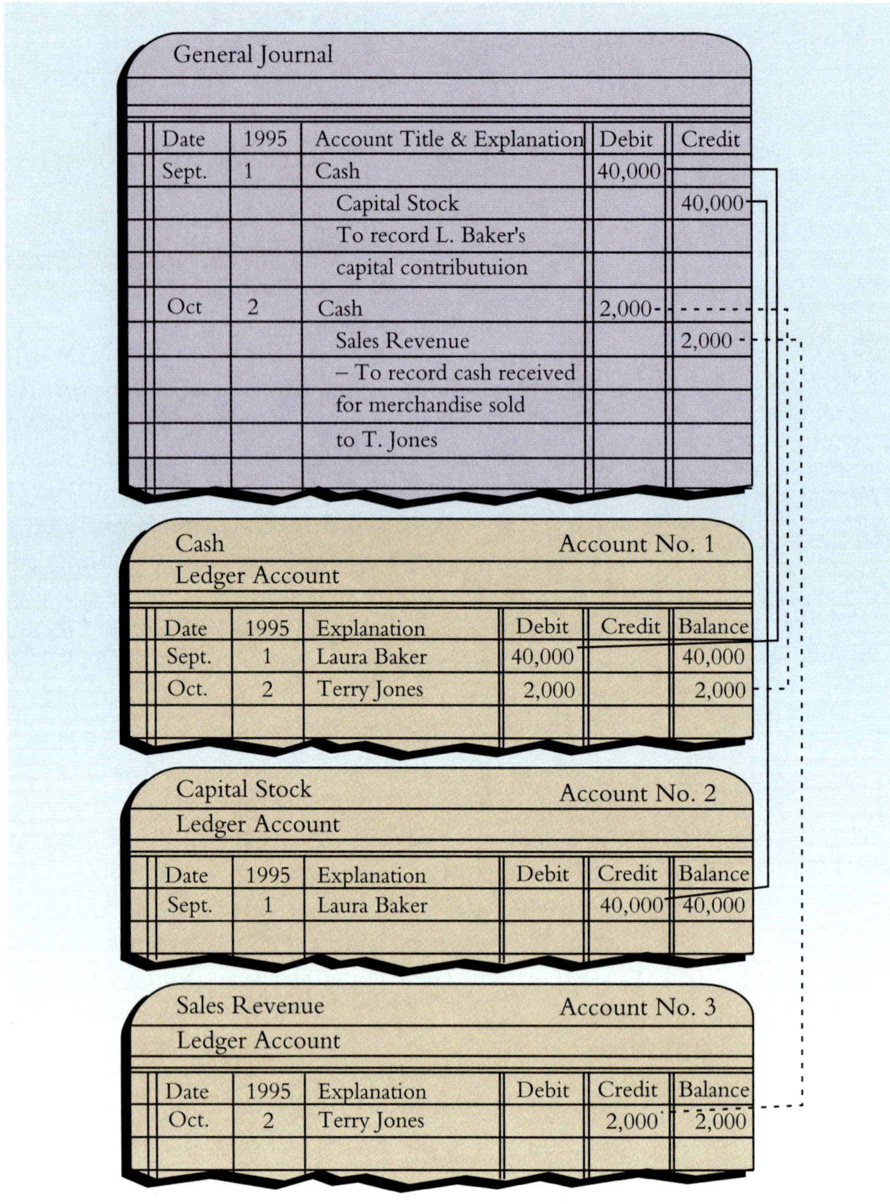

Assets	=	**Liabilities**	+	**Owners' equity**
\$2,000	=	**\$0**	+	**\$2,000**
(Cash)				**(Sales Revenue)**

As you can see, double-entry bookkeeping keeps the accounting equation in balance.

FINANCIAL STATEMENTS

We already know that one accounting cycle step is to summarize a firm's transactions in various financial statements. Every business prepares a balance sheet and an income statement. Many businesses also prepare a statement of cash flows. A fourth financial statement, the statement of retained earnings, is beyond the scope of this chapter and is mentioned here only so you know it exists.

The numbers and accounts appearing in the financial statements are drawn from the general ledger. The elements of the accounting equation (assets, liabilities, and owners' equity) are reflected in the balance sheet. Revenues and expenses are shown on the income statement. These two statements indicate solvency and profitability for those interested both inside and outside the firm.

Solvency relates to a firm's ability to pay its debts, while profitability describes a firm's ability to generate revenues. The information presented is meant to give users of the financial statements a true picture of how the company is performing. Sometimes it does not, outlined in Today's Business World.

TODAY'S BUSINESS WORLD

IBM Undertakes an Aggressive Accounting Strategy

The woes of IBM have been well documented in the popular business press. Since the mid-1980s, IBM has suffered from increased competition and a questionable business strategy throughout the 1970s and early 1980s. In 1992, IBM reported a \$5 billion loss and a decrease in market value by more than \$70 billion since its peak in 1987. These business trends forced IBM to cut back its work force from the 1986 peak of 406,000 to 300,000 in 1992. Most of this trimming was in the form of layoffs, used for the first time in half a century, and early retirements. At the same time, IBM began to adopt aggressive accounting policies.

IBM undertook an accounting strategy that many experts feel was designed to make its financial numbers appear more favorable by pushing bad financial news into the future. None of the accounting moves were illegal, and most were disclosed to the public, but the tactics were uncharacteristic for IBM which has generally been regarded as financially conservative. Thornton O'Glove, an accounting expert and former publisher of the *Quality Earnings Newsletter,* described it this way: "Since the mid-1980s, IBM has been borrowing funds from the future to bolster today's profits."

Many accounting practices used in businesses are discretionary in nature, meaning that there may be two or three different acceptable methods to account for an item, and the management must decide which method fits the company's profile. Conservatism, in an accounting context, is defined as choosing the accounting method that will not inflate profits or assets.

In IBM's case, there were three accounting practices that were cited as disturbing. First, IBM was placing revenue on the books as soon as its products were shipped to dealers for sale or to IBM warehouses prior to shipment to dealers, even though these dealers had the right to return the products. IBM was booking sales too quickly, thereby reporting revenues it might never receive. This procedure is far more aggressive than the accounting practices used by most companies. Secondly, IBM recorded long-term lease contracts as revenue, placing the total revenues to be earned from long-term lease contracts on the income statement in the year they were signed, even though IBM was to be paid rental fees over the life of the lease. Chief external auditor Donald Chandler from Price Waterhouse disagreed with these two accounting choices and penned a 20-page memo voicing his opinions.

The third aggressive accounting policy used by IBM related to the cost side of operations. IBM adopted a more liberal accounting policy regarding huge investments that allowed the company to defer many investment costs into the future. IBM defends its accounting practices and says they were undertaken for business reasons. These aggressive accounting policies may have boosted IBM's profits more than investors realize, but "Big Blue" is unwilling to say by how much.

How comparable are different company's income statements and balance sheets if alternative methods are acceptable for accounting for certain items? Discuss.

Source: Adapted from Michael W. Miller and Lee Berton, "As IBM's Woes Grew, Its Accounting Tactics Got Less Conservative," *The Wall Street Journal* (April 7, 1993): A1:6; Carol J. Loomis, "Dinosaurs?" *Fortune* (May 3, 1993): 41.

The four financial statements mentioned are part of the annual report, which is a main source of information for stockholders. In a recent study, stockholders were asked what information they used in making investment decisions. Annual reports, which contain more information than just financial statements, and statements of cash flow were found to be more useful than in prior years, while income statements were seen as less useful. This study shows a trend toward individuals making more investment decisions based on company information provided mainly by financial statements and annual reports and relying less on the advice of stockbrokers.[6]

Balance Sheet
A financial statement that indicates a firm's financial position at a particular point in time; reflects a firm's solvency, or its ability to pay its debts as they come due. Also called the statement of financial position.

Balance Sheet

The **balance sheet,** or statement of financial position, lists the assets, liabilities, and owners' equity of the firm. Items on the balance sheet are recorded at their historical costs, the original transaction cost. The balance sheet does not reflect accounts at their liquidation or fair market value, today's values. A balance sheet indicates the firm's financial position at a particular moment in time (the date of the balance sheet). This financial statement reflects a firm's solvency, or its ability to pay debts as they come due. The balance sheet for the Music Box for the year ending December 31, 1995, is shown in Exhibit 21.5.

Assets. Assets (items of value to the company) can be classified on the basis of *liquidity,* or how quickly they can be turned into cash. Assets are usually listed on the balance sheet in the order of their liquidity. Commonly included are current and fixed assets.

Exhibit 21.5
Balance Sheet

THE MUSIC BOX
Balance Sheet
At December 31, 1995

Assets			
Current assets:			
Cash		$ 62,000	
Accounts receivable	$53,000		
Less: Allowance for doubtful accounts	3,000	50,000	
Inventory		85,000	
Total current assets			$197,000
Plant assets:			
Store equipment	30,000		
Less: Accumulated depreciation	5,000	25,000	
Furniture and fixtures	70,000		
Less: Accumulated depreciation	10,000	60,000	
Total plant assets			85,000
Total assets			$282,000
Liabilities			
Current liabilities:			
Accounts payable		$ 50,000	
Long-term liabilities:			
Notes payable in 2000		150,000	
Total liabilities			$200,000
Owners' Equity			
Capital stock		$ 40,000	
Retained earnings		42,000	
Total owners' equity			82,000
Total liabilities and owners' equity			$282,000

Current Assets
Cash plus items that can or will be converted to cash and used within one year.

Usually listed first, **current assets** include cash and items that can or will be converted to cash and used within one year. These are the most liquid of a firm's assets. The Music Box's current assets are:

1. *Cash* ($62,000)—cash on hand and bank funds that management has immediate access to when needed.
2. *Accounts receivable* ($50,000)—amounts owed to the store by customers who made purchases on credit. Because the manager believes that not all of this amount will be collected, an allowance for doubtful accounts is included to reflect this possibility ($53,000 – $3,000).
3. *Inventory* ($85,000)—merchandise (CD players, stereos, speakers, etc.) on hand for sale to customers.

Plant Assets
Relatively permanent assets that a firm expects to use for more than one year.

Depreciation
Procedures for spreading the cost of a plant asset out over the course of its useful life.

Relatively permanent assets that a firm expects to use for periods longer than one year are called **plant assets.** Long-term assets include such items as land, buildings, machinery, vehicles, and furniture and fixtures. Except for land, all these assets are considered depreciable because they wear out and must be replaced. **Depreciation** divides the cost of a plant asset over the course of its useful life. This procedure gives a more accurate idea of the total cost involved in a firm's operations. The Music Box's plant assets include:

1. Store equipment ($25,000)—office computers, display models. This amount was obtained by deducting accumulated depreciation from the assets' cost ($30,000 – $5,000).
2. Furniture and fixtures ($60,000)—office furniture, display cases, cabinetry, and lighting. Again, the cost of these items was reduced to reflect accumulated depreciation ($70,000 – $10,000).

Liabilities. As we have already noted, liabilities are debts the business owes to its creditors. Businesses list liabilities on the balance sheet in the order in which they are due to be paid. Two types of liabilities show on the balance sheet: current and long term.

Current Liabilities
Financial obligations of a firm that will be repaid within one year.

Working Capital
Measure of a firm's ability to meet short-term obligation; computed as current assets minus current liabilities.

Financial obligations of the firm that will be repaid within one year are classed as **current liabilities.** Current liabilities for the Music Box include accounts payable ($50,000). These accounts reflect the portions of inventory and supplies that were purchased on credit. Dun & Bradstreet reported in the fourth quarter of 1993 that companies were settling their accounts payable at a faster rate than previously.[7]

Because current liabilities must be repaid within one year, they could create a financial crunch for a firm with inadequate cash reserves or other liquid assets. So firms pay close attention to the relationship between current assets and current liabilities. **Working capital,** the difference between current assets and current liabilities, reflects the firm's ability to meet its short-term obligations. For the Music Box, working capital amounts to $147,000 ($197,000 – $50,000).

Long-Term Liabilities
Amounts owed by a business that must be repaid more than one year from the balance sheet date.

Amounts owed that must be repaid more than one year from the balance sheet date are called **long-term liabilities.** For the Music Box, long-term liabilities include notes payable ($150,000) in 2000. Notes payable are debts owed to banks who are usually the primary lenders of money. Walt Disney

Company owed debts to 60 banks because it had borrowed over $3.4 billion to help fund the EuroDisney project.[8]

Owners' Equity. Owners' equity represents the claims of the owners, partners, and shareholders against the firm's assets. It is the excess of assets over liabilities and includes both capital stock and retained earnings. One of the ways that businesses raise capital to operate is by issuing capital stock and selling shares of ownership to stockholders. Laura Baker invested $40,000 to get the Music Box off and running, so this amount becomes the capital stock entry on the balance sheet.

In May 1994, Kmart Corporation announced it would offer four new series of capital stock. The offerings were expected to raise between $600 and $900 million of capital for Kmart.[9]

Retained Earnings
A firm's accumulated net income minus dividends to shareholders.

A firm's profits can either be distributed as dividends to shareholders or retained and reinvested in the firm. **Retained earnings** are a firm's accumulated net income minus dividends to shareholders. They help a firm grow and expand by providing the means to invest in land or buildings or expand the items carried in inventory. The Music Box has retained earnings of $42,000.

As you can see in Exhibit 21.6, the balance sheet illustrates the accounting equation in that assets ($282,000) equal liabilities ($200,000) plus owners' equity ($82,000).

Income Statement

Income Statement
A financial statement showing a firm's revenues, expenses, and net income over a period of time; indicates profitability, the ability to generate income. Also called earnings statement or statement of profit and loss.

The **income statement** (sometimes called an earnings statement or statement of profit and loss) lists a firm's revenue, expenses, and net income over some *period* of time, typically a year. (Recall that the balance sheet indicates the firm's financial position as of a particular *moment* in time, the balance sheet date.) The firm's profitability, its ability to generate income, is determined by comparing revenues to the expenses incurred in producing these revenues.

In addition to indicating a firm's profitability (or unprofitability), the income statement focuses on overall revenues and costs, giving managers the big picture of the firm's operations. It also provides data for the ratio analyses used by managers to get the little picture of day-to-day operations. (Ratio analysis is discussed later in the chapter.)

The income statement for the Music Box for the year ending December 31, 1995, appears in Exhibit 21.6. On the income statement, all expenses are deducted from revenues to determine net profit (or loss), the net income. For the Music Box,

Revenues − Expenses = Net income
$720,000 − $712,000 = $8,000

Revenues. As mentioned earlier, sales of products or services, interest, rents, royalties, and dividends generate revenues. The Music Box earned a gross revenue of $740,000 on the sale of compact-disc players, stereos, CDs, and

Exhibit 21.6
Income Statement

THE MUSIC BOX
Income Statement
For the Year Ended December 31, 1995

Revenues:			
Gross revenue		$740,000	
Less: Sales returns and allowance		20,000	
Net revenue			$720,000
Cost of goods sold:			
Beginning inventory		70,000	
Purchases during year		605,000	
Cost of goods available for sale		675,000	
Less: Ending inventory		85,000	
Cost of goods sold			590,000
Gross profit			130,000
Operating expenses:			
Selling expenses:			
Sales salaries	$35,000		
Advertising	3,000		
Total selling expenses		38,000	
General and administrative expenses:			
Administrative salaries	35,000		
Rent	10,000		
Utilities	2,500		
Insurance	2,000		
Depreciation–equipment	15,000		
Total general expenses		64,500	
Total operating expenses			102,500
Income from operations			27,500
Interest expense			15,000
Income before taxes			12,500
Income tax expense (at 36 percent)			4,500
Net income			$ 8,000

other merchandise during the year. This figure minus returned and defective merchandise yielded a net revenue (also called net sales) of $720,000.

Cost of Goods Sold. This section of the income statement itemizes the cost of the goods or services that generate revenues for the firm. Here's how the Music Box determines cost of sales. Inventory on hand at the beginning of the year was $70,000. To this amount is added the cost of new inventory purchased during the year ($605,000). This calculation results in the firm's cost of goods available for sale, $675,000. From this figure deduct the ending (unsold) inventory amount ($85,000) as of the income statement date. The resulting amount, $590,000, represents the cost of sales for the Music Box.

Firms determine gross profit by subtracting the cost of sales from net revenue. The Music Box had a gross profit of $130,000 ($720,000 – $590,000).

Operating Expenses
All costs of doing business except the cost of goods sold.

Selling Expenses
Costs incurred in marketing and distributing a firm's goods and services.

General and Administrative Expenses
Costs incurred in the overall management of the business.

Operating Expenses. A firm's **operating expenses** include all the costs of doing business except the cost of goods sold. **Selling expenses** are the costs incurred in marketing and distributing the firm's goods or services. For the Music Box, selling expenses include salespeoples' salaries ($35,000) and advertising ($3,000). **General and administrative expenses** arise from the overall management of the business. For the Music Box, they include Laura Baker's salary ($35,000), rent ($10,000), utilities ($2,500), insurance ($2,000), and depreciation on equipment ($15,000), for a total of $64,500.

Net Income or Loss. Net income (or net loss) is the bottom line, the firm's profit or loss over a period of time. It is literally the bottom line of the income statement. Net income (or loss) is determined by subtracting all expenses from revenues.

Income from operations is determined by deducting total operating expense from gross profit. In our example, $130,000 minus $102,500 yields income from operations of $27,500. We must then deduct interest expense ($15,000) and income taxes ($4,500) to arrive at the bottom line, a net income of $8,000 for the Music Box.

Statement of Cash Flows

The last financial statement to be presented in this chapter is the statement of cash flows. In November 1987, the FASB made the statement of cash flows a requirement (as are the balance sheet and income statement) for all companies listed on an organized stock exchange. The statement of cash flows is the most complicated of the primary financial statements, and we will not give a detailed analysis here.

Statement of Cash Flows
Financial statement showing the flow of cash into and out of a business during a period of time.

The **statement of cash flows** shows the flow of cash into and out of a business during a period of time. This statement indicates net cash flow (either inflow or outflow) from operating, investing, and financing activities. Cash flow from *operating activities* measures the cash results of the firm's primary revenue-generating activities. (In the case of the Music Box, cash flow from operations represents net cash flow from merchandising activities.) *Investing* activities include buying fixed assets, buying stock in other companies, and selling stock held as an investment in another company. *Financing* activities include issuing new stock, paying dividends to shareholders, borrowing from banks, and repaying amounts borrowed. The statement of cash flows also shows the net change in cash for the period.

As a summary of the effects on cash of all the firm's operating, financing, and investing activities, the statement of cash flows allows managers to see the results of past decisions. The statement may, for example, indicate a great enough cash flow to allow the firm to finance projected needs itself rather than borrow funds from a bank. Or management can examine the statement to determine why the firm has a cash shortage, if that is the case. Investors and creditors can use the statement of cash flows to assess the firm's abilities to generate future cash flows, to pay dividends, and to pay its debts when due, as well as its potential need to borrow funds.

ANALYZING FINANCIAL STATEMENTS

Once financial statements have been prepared, managers, creditors, and investors are interested in interpreting them. Managers' analyses of the financial statements primarily pertain to *parts* of the company, allowing them to plan, control, and evaluate company operations. Creditors and investors focus on the company as a *whole* to decide whether the company is a good credit or investment candidate.

Financial statement analysis compares (or finds relationships in) accounting information to make the data more useful or practical. For example, knowing that a company's net income was $50,000 is somewhat useful. Knowing also that the prior year's net income was $100,000 is more useful. Knowing the amounts of the company's assets and sales is better yet. To this end, several types of financial statement analysis have been developed. In this chapter, we will discuss the technique of ratio analysis.

Ratio Analysis

Ratio Analysis Method of analyzing financial information by comparing logical relationships between various financial statement items.

Ratio analysis examines the logical relationships between various financial statement items. Items may come from the same financial statement or from different statements. The only requirement is that a logical relationship exist between the items.

The dollar amounts of the related items are set up as fractions and called *ratios*. Comparing company ratios to industry standards can indicate areas in which the company is successful—and those in which the company is below standard. Trends in a company's performance are also easily spotted by comparing ratios from the current period to ratios from earlier periods.

Approximately 200 ratios are currently used by credit managers, bankers and financial and investment analysts. Only a handful of these ratios are useful in interpreting a company's financial standing, and many more may give misleading information. The ratios presented in this chapter—liquidity, activity, profitability, and debt—are some of the useful ratios.[10]

It is important to note that different industries have distinct standards for ratio adequacy. What is an adequate ratio for a company in one industry may not be adequate for a different company in another industry. Beware of judging a ratio solely on the basis of a universal standard; ratios should be viewed against industry norms. For instance, the banking industry and manufacturing industry would differ significantly in terms of current assets. Banks carry an enormous amount of liquid current assets, while manufacturing firms have a much more even division of current and long-term assets. So a comparison of a bank and a manufacturing firm in terms of any ratio that contains current

Exhibit 21.7
Comparative Balance Sheet

THE MUSIC BOX
Comparative Balance Sheet
December 31, 1995 and 1994

	1995	**1994**
Assets		
Current assets:		
Cash	$ 40,000	$ 62,000
Accounts receivable	70,000	50,000
Inventory	110,000	85,000
Total current assets	220,000	197,000
Plant assets:		
Store equipment	25,000	25,000
(net of accumulated depreciation)		
Furniture and fixtures	50,000	60,000
(net of accumulated depreciation)		
Total plant assets	75,000	85,000
Total assets	$295,000	$282,000
Liabilities		
Current liabilities:		
Accounts payable	$ 55,000	$ 50,000
Long-term liabilities:		
Notes payable	150,000	150,000
Total liabilities	205,000	200,000
Owners' Equity		
Capital stock	40,000	$ 40,000
Retained earnings	50,000	42,000
Total owners' equity	90,000	82,000
Total liabilities and owners' equity	$295,000	$282,000

assets would not be realistic. Exhibits 21.7 and 21.8 present the figures that will be used in this section to compute ratios.

Liquidity Ratio
Measure of a firm's ability to pay its short-term debts as they come due.

Liquidity Ratios. A firm's ability to pay its short-term debts as they come due is measured by **liquidity ratios.** (Recall that liquidity is a measure of how quickly an asset can be converted to cash.) Highly liquid firms can more easily convert assets to cash when needed to repay loans. Less liquid firms may have trouble meeting their obligations or obtaining loans at low cost. Two common liquidity ratios are the current ratio and the quick (acid-test) ratio.

Exhibit 21.8
Comparative Income Statement

THE MUSIC BOX
Comparative Income Statement
December 31, 1995 and 1994

	1995	1994
Net revenue	$800,000	$720,000
Cost of goods sold	640,000	590,000
Gross profit	160,000	130,000
Operating expenses:		
Selling expenses		
Sales salaries	39,500	35,000
Advertising	4,000	3,000
Total selling expenses	43,500	38,000
General and administrative expenses		
Administrative salaries	39,500	35,000
Rent	15,000	10,000
Utilities	6,000	2,500
Insurance	2,000	2,000
Depreciation	15,000	15,000
Total general expenses	77,500	64,500
Total operating expenses	121,000	102,000
Income from operations	39,000	27,500
Interest expenses	15,000	15,000
Income before taxes	24,000	12,500
Income tax expenses (at 40 percent)	8,640	4,500
Net income	15,360	8,000

Current Ratio
The measure of a firm's ability to pay its current liabilities from its current assets; computed by dividing current assets by current liabilities.

2:1 is good assets to liabilities

We have already said that working capital is the excess of current assets over current liabilities. The **current ratio,** which is current assets divided by current liabilities (two balance sheet items), indicates a firm's ability to pay its current liabilities from its current assets. Thus the ratio shows the strength of a company's working capital.

$$\textbf{Current ratio} = \frac{\textbf{Current assets}}{\textbf{Current liabilities}}$$

Current ratios for the Music Box for 1994 and 1995 are computed as follows:

$$\textbf{1994: } \frac{\textbf{197,000}}{\textbf{50,000}} = \textbf{3.94 to 1}$$

$$1995: \frac{220{,}000}{55{,}000} = 4 \text{ to } 1$$

The current ratio is excellent in both years. Generally a ratio in excess of 2 to 1 is considered favorable. In 1995 the Music Box's current ratio increased slightly to 4 to 1, meaning it had $4 of current assets for every $1 of current liabilities.

Quick Ratio
The measure of a firm's immediate liquidity; computed by dividing quick assets by current liabilities. Also called acid-test ratio.

The **quick ratio,** also called the acid-test ratio, divides quick assets by current liabilities. It measures more immediate liquidity by comparing two balance sheet items. Quick assets do not include inventory because to convert inventory to cash, merchandise must be sold and a receivable collected. *Quick assets* are cash or those assets the firm expects to convert to cash in the near future. For the Music Box, the quick ratio is computed as follows:

$$\text{Quick ratio} = \frac{\text{Quick assets}}{\text{Current liabilities}}$$

$$1994: \frac{112{,}000}{50{,}000} = 2.24 \text{ to } 1$$

$$1995: \frac{110{,}000}{55{,}000} = 2 \text{ to } 1$$

The Music Box's quick ratio has deteriorated slightly.

Activity Ratio
Measure of how efficiently assets are being used to generate revenues.

Accounts Receivable Turnover
The number of times per year that the average accounts receivable is collected; computed by dividing net sales by average net accounts receivable.

Activity Ratios. How efficiently the firm uses its assets to generate revenues is measured by **activity ratios.** These ratios indicate how efficiently a firm uses its resources. A common activity ratio is accounts receivable turnover. **Accounts receivable turnover** is the number of times per year that the average accounts receivable is turned over (collected). An income statement item (net sales) is compared to a balance sheet item (accounts receivable). We calculate this ratio by dividing net sales by average net accounts receivable.

The allowance for doubtful accounts is first deducted to arrive at net accounts receivable. *Average* net accounts receivable is computed by adding the accounts receivable amounts at the beginning and end of the year, then dividing by two. For the Music Box, we determine this figure for 1995 by adding the beginning amount (which is 1994's ending amount, $50,000) to the ending amount ($70,000) and dividing by two to reach $60,000.

Accounts receivable turnover for the Music Box is computed as follows:

$$\textbf{Accounts receivable turnover} = \frac{\textbf{Net sales}}{\textbf{Average net accounts receivable}}$$

$$\textbf{1995: } \frac{\textbf{800,000}}{\textbf{60,000}} = \textbf{13.3}$$

The Music Box, then, is collecting its accounts receivable 13 times per year on average.

We can also look at accounts receivable turnover by computing the number of days it takes for each credit sale to be converted to cash. In other words, how many days does it take credit customers to pay their bills? This measure, referred to as the *number of days sales in receivables,* is computed as follows:

$$\textbf{Number of days sales in receivables} = \frac{\textbf{Number of days in year}}{\textbf{Accounts receivable turnover}}$$

$$\textbf{1995: } \frac{\textbf{365}}{\textbf{13.3}} = \textbf{27.4 days}$$

This means that the Music Box's accounts receivable are collected in 27 days on average. Because the Music Box's credit terms for its customers are for payment to be made within 30 days, this ratio indicates that customers are indeed paying for their credit purchases within the required time. Thus the company's accounts receivable policies are considered to be of good quality.

A larger ratio, say 50 or 60 days, would indicate that credit customers are slow in paying their bills; thus they would be using the Music Box as a source of interest-free credit (the company does not charge interest on past-due accounts).

Profitability Ratio Ratio that measures a firm's financial performance by comparing earnings to sales or investments.

Profitability Ratios. A company's overall operating success—its financial performance—is measured by **profitability ratios.** These ratios measure a firm's success in terms of earnings compared to sales or investments. Over time these ratios can indicate how successfully or unsuccessfully management operates the business. Two common profitability ratios are return on sales and return on equity.

Return on Sales
Measure of a firm's profitability, or its ability to generate income; computed by dividing net income by net sales.

Return on sales measures a firm's profitability by comparing net income and net sales, both income statement items. It is computed by dividing net income by net sales. For the Music Box,

$$\textbf{Return on sales} = \frac{\textbf{Net income}}{\textbf{Net sales}}$$

$$\textbf{1994: } \frac{8{,}000}{720{,}000} = \textbf{1.1 percent}$$

$$\textbf{1995: } \frac{15{,}360}{800{,}000} = \textbf{1.9 percent}$$

These ratios show a quite low profit per dollar of sales. Retail establishments average around 5 percent. However, return on sales did increase from 1.1 percent in 1994 to 1.9 percent in 1995. This trend may mean the company is becoming more profitable.

Return on Equity
Measure of the return the company earns on every dollar of owners' and shareholders' investments; computed by dividing net income by equity.

Return on equity measures the return the company earns on every dollar of shareholders' (and owners') investment. Investors are very interested in this ratio; it indicates how well their investment is doing. We compute return on equity by dividing net income (an income statement item) by equity (a balance sheet item). For the Music Box,

$$\textbf{Return on equity} = \frac{\textbf{Net income}}{\textbf{Equity}}$$

$$\textbf{1994: } \frac{8{,}000}{82{,}000} = \textbf{9.8 percent}$$

$$\textbf{1995: } \frac{15{,}360}{90{,}000} = \textbf{17.1 percent}$$

For every dollar invested in 1994, the Music Box earned nearly 10 cents. This return on equity is not good. A return of 9.8 percent is not much better than what can be earned on a bank certificate of deposit. Stock investments carry more risk, so they should offer higher returns. The 17 percent return on equity in 1995, a substantial improvement, is a better return for the risk assumed by investing in stocks.

Debt Ratio
Measure of a company's ability to pay its long-term debts.

Debt Ratios. We measure a company's ability to pay its long-term debts by **debt ratios.** These ratios try to answer questions such as (1) Is the company financed mainly by debt or equity? and (2) Does the company make enough to pay the interest on its loans when due? Potential investors and lenders are very interested in the answers to such questions. Two ways to answer them are the debt to equity ratio and the times interest earned ratio.

Debt to Equity Ratio
A measure of a firm's leverage; computed by dividing total debt by owners' equity.

The **debt to equity ratio** measures a firm's leverage as the ratio of funds provided by the owners to funds provided by creditors, both balance sheet items. For the Music Box,

$$\textbf{Debt to Equity} = \frac{\textbf{Total Debt}}{\textbf{Owners' Equity}}$$

$$\textbf{1994: } \frac{\textbf{200,000}}{\textbf{82,000}} = \textbf{2.44}$$

$$\textbf{1995: } \frac{\textbf{205,000}}{\textbf{90,000}} = \textbf{2.28}$$

Total debt includes current liabilities and long-term liabilities. The debt to equity ratio demonstrates the risk incurred by the owners of the firm. The higher the debt to equity ratio is, the greater the chance that the firm will be unable to meet its obligations. The Music Box's ratio seems high, but there is no ideal debt to equity ratio. Examining other firms in the Music Box's industry should give a better picture of how the Music Box stands with regard to debt to equity.

Times Interest Earned Ratio
The measure of how many times during the year a business earns the amount of interest it must pay; computed by dividing income before interest and taxes by interest expense.

Creditors need to know whether a borrower can meet interest payments when they come due. The **times interest earned ratio** compares cash received from operations with cash paid for interest payments. It measures how many times the firm earns the amount of interest it must pay during the year. This ratio is calculated by dividing income before interest and taxes ("Income from operations" in Exhibit 21.8) by interest expense, two items on the income statement. For the Music Box,

$$\textbf{Times interest earned} = \frac{\textbf{Income before interest and taxes}}{\textbf{Interest expense}}$$

$$1994: \frac{27{,}500}{15{,}000} = 1.83$$

$$1995: \frac{39{,}000}{15{,}000} = 2.6$$

These ratios for the Music Box are improving. The higher the ratio, the more likely that interest payments will be made. Low ratios mean a company may have trouble making its interest payments to its creditors. The Music Box's ratios would probably be considered unsatisfactory.

TOMORROW'S BUSINESS WORLD

Technology and the Accounting Function

Accounting has not been immune to the advancement of new technology. The advent of computers, especially the personal computer (PC), has led to more efficient and effective processing of accounting information. Expert systems and neural networks are the latest additions on the new technology locomotive.

An expert system is a computer program that thinks like an expert through the use of artificial intelligence. Development of an expert system program is accomplished by recording the thoughts of an expert going through the decision-making process. These thoughts are then coded by means of a programming language to form an expert system.

The expert system consists of four major components. A knowledge base contains facts about specific tasks and the rules for applying those tasks. These rules are known as heuristics and are simply rules of thumb (i.e. if this happens, then do this, etc.). What rules to apply and when to apply them is the job of the inference engine. It is said to "drive" the expert system. Communication between the user and the expert system is governed by the user interface, a piece of software that questions the user if sufficient information has not been provided to make a decision. Lastly, an explanation facility is provided that explains why the system has asked a particular question or what reasoning was used to arrive at a particular solution. The solutions of expert systems are not always implemented. Rather, they may be used as a second opinion to verify decisions made by personnel.

Expert systems have been used fairly extensively in accounting. Tax expert systems have been developed that can test the consequences of corporate reorganization on taxes, solve problems involving legal concepts, select tax shelters, give advice on projects that will help taxes, and accomplish tax planning. Auditing has been another area in which the use of expert systems has flourished. Expert systems are now used by auditors to train new personnel, assist in the development of audit programs, plan audits, determine the size of audit samples, measure the audit risk involved in an engagement, detect errors in accounting systems, and observe the effectiveness of internal controls. New systems are continually being developed to improve all areas of accounting.

As with everything else, expert system technology has evolved. One of the latest advancements in technology is neural networks, which rely on complex pattern matching rather than rules of thumb to provide advice or make decisions. The networks search for specific patterns that exist in a situation and examine other situations to see if the same pattern exists. By conducting pattern matching, neural networks are able to find solutions to complex problems.

KPMG, Peat Marwick, one of the Big 6 public accounting firms, has developed a neural network to predict bankruptcy. By examining the characteristics of a firm that has gone bankrupt, the network can search for these same characteristics (patterns) in other firms to see if they are likely to go bankrupt. Identifying patterns that accompany fraud have also allowed neural networks to help auditors detect fraud in audit engagements. Neural networks are able to process a number of pieces of data and discover the existence of patterns in this data, something auditors have not been able to do with statistical analysis.

A number of different types of neural networks exist, each serving a distinctive purpose. Prediction networks predict the value of an item based on a pattern of characteristics. Classification networks are used to classify an item into specific groups, again based on the existence of characteristics that match a pattern for the group. Data filtering networks are used when the data entered into the system is imperfect. Optimization networks help find the optimal solution to complicated problems.

Both expert systems and neural networks are programmed using artificial intelligence. Expert systems are based on rules of thumb developed by recording the thought processes of a human expert going through the decision-making process. Neural networks rely on complex pattern matching to solve complicated problems. Neural networks also have the ability to learn, because they rely on matching patterns of characteristics, while expert systems have the ability to explain the reasoning involved in arriving at a particular decision.

If computers can solve problems just like experts, will the proliferation of new expert systems and neural networks cause experts to become obsolete? Why or why not?

Source: Adapted from R. Steve McDuffie, Debra Oden, and Eugene Porter, "Tax Expert Systems and Future Development," *The CPA Journal* (January 1994): 73; Harlan L. Etheridge and Richard C. Brooks, "Neural Networks: A New Technology," *The CPA Journal* (March 1994): 36–55.

SUMMARY OF LEARNING OBJECTIVES

1. ***Explain the purpose of accounting and its importance to a firm's managers, creditors, and investors.*** Accounting identifies, measures, and communicates financial information about a company to its managers and outside parties to improve their decisions about allocating company resources and to evaluate the results of those decisions. Creditors examine a company's financial records to decide whether a firm is a good credit risk. Investors need to know whether a firm is a good investment candidate and, if so, how their investment is doing.

2. ***Differentiate between financial and managerial accounting.*** Financial and managerial accounting are

the two categories of accounting. They are defined according to the users of the accounting information. Financial accounting is intended primarily for use by external decision makers (i.e. investors and creditors), while managerial accounting is mainly used by internal decision makers (i.e. managers).

3. ***List the steps in the accounting cycle.*** The accounting cycle is the way accountants communicate the results of financial transactions. First they *analyze* business transactions to determine which can be measured and verified with some precision. These transactions are then *recorded* chronologically in a journal. Next these journal entries are *posted* in the general ledger, which summarizes all the company's accounts. In the final step, the accountant *prepares* financial statements.

4. ***State the accounting equation, define its elements, and describe its relationship to double-entry bookkeeping.*** The accounting equation states that assets equal liabilities plus owners' equity. Assets are anything of value owned by the company and used in the process of conducting business. Liabilities are creditors' claims against a company's assets. Owners' equity is the owners' claim against the company's assets.

   This equation is always kept in balance. Double-entry bookkeeping uses two entries (a debit and a credit) to record each transaction, thus keeping the accounting equation in balance.

5. ***Explain the purpose of the balance sheet and identify its major elements.*** The balance sheet indicates a firm's financial position at a particular *moment* in time and reflects a firm's solvency, or its ability to pay debts as they come due. The major elements of the balance sheet are those of the accounting equation—assets, liabilities, and owners' equity.

6. ***Explain the purpose of the income statement and identify its major elements.*** The income statement reflects a firm's profitability, or its ability to generate income. It indicates a firm's financial position over a *period* of time. All expenses are deducted from net revenue, thus giving the bottom line: the firm's profit or loss for the period of time covered by the income statement.

7. ***Explain the purpose of ratio analysis and list the major financial ratios.*** Accountants use ratio analysis as another method of interpreting a company's financial information. Ratio analysis examines the logical relationships between various financial statement items. Comparing a company's ratios to those of other companies in the same industry gives an indication of how well the firm is doing according to industry standards. Comparing the company's ratios for the current period to those of previous periods may indicate trends (positive or negative) in the company's performance. The major categories of financial ratios are liquidity, activity, profitability, and debt.

KEY TERMS

Accounting
Certified Public Accountant (CPA)
Public Accountant
Audit
Certified Management Accountant (CMA)
Private Accountant
Accounting Cycle
Journal
Account
General Ledger
Financial Statement
Accounting Equation
Asset
Liability
Owners' Equity
Revenue
Expenses
Net Income
Debit
Credit
Double-Entry Bookkeeping
Balance Sheet
Current Assets
Plant Assets
Depreciation
Current Liabilities
Working Capital
Long-Term Liabilities
Retained Earnings
Income Statement
Operating Expenses
Selling Expenses
General and Administrative Expenses
Statement of Cash Flows

Ratio Analysis
Liquidity Ratio
Current Ratio
Quick Ratio
Activity Ratio
Accounts Receivable Turnover
Profitability Ratio
Return on Sales
Return on Equity
Debt Ratio
Debt to Equity Ratio
Times Interest Earned Ratio

QUESTIONS FOR DISCUSSION AND REVIEW

1. Accounting is the process of identifying, measuring, and communicating information. How does this differ from strictly recording business transactions (the purpose of bookkeeping)? Explain.
2. What different types of information would external decision makers need vs. internal decision makers? Why?
3. How does a public accountant's job differ from a private accountant's? Explain the differences.
4. If the primary objective of accounting is to communicate information to those who need to make decisions, how does the accounting cycle help to achieve this purpose?
5. How might accounting information be useful in business? Provide details.
6. How does the fundamental accounting equation reflect double-entry bookkeeping?
7. On the balance sheet assets are listed at the price paid to acquire them. How informative will this asset valuation be 10 years down the road? Is there a better system available to value assets? Why or why not?
8. How would the statement of cash flows help users of financial statements assess the liquidity of a company? Explain.
9. What types of ratios would be common in analyzing the financial statements of banks, retailing firms, manufacturers, and service industry firms? Why?
10. There has been recent debate that the reported success of Japanese companies has been exaggerated. If the basis for the contention that Japanese companies are outperforming their United States counterparts is strictly ratio analysis, why may this exaggeration be occurring? Provide details.

CASE 21.1

Harmonization of International Accounting Standards

As the business world moves toward a global economy, the accounting profession is moving with it. As Bertil Edlund, former president of the International Federation of Accountants, noted, "The global accounting profession is becoming a reality." For example, there is an important role to be served by accounting in Eastern Europe and the former Soviet Union as countries move toward free market economies. In particular, efforts need to be directed at harmonizing the accounting standards that will govern these new market economies. The International Accounting Standards Committee (IASC) is the standard-setting body commissioned with the development of international accounting standards. While the IASC may have somewhat limited jurisdiction, it can play an influential role in reshaping new market economies.

The IASC was organized in 1973 by the United States, Canada, and the United Kingdom to internationalize accounting standards. The committee consists of representatives from the professional accountancy organizations of 75 countries and has issued 31 International Accounting Standards (IASs) over the past 20 years. These IASs have served as an invaluable model for countries such as China in developing their own accounting standards.

Why is harmonization of international accounting standards so important? With the proliferation of multinational corporations, trade blocs, and international capital markets the need for a set of global accounting standards to help govern firms in preparing financial statements is necessary. Multinational corporations such as Coca Cola, Exxon, and Goodyear, just to name a few, need to be able to prepare comparable financial statements for every segment of their business operations. Such comparability between business segments and between similar firms of different national origin will not only improve decision making, it will also reduce the cost of having to restate financial information for various regulatory bodies or others.

The trend toward the establishment of trade bloc agreements has been another driving force in the setting of harmonized global accounting standards. There has already been a trade bloc established in Europe (European Union), and the North American Free Trade Association (NAFTA) includes the United States, Canada, and Mexico. Other trade blocs are expected in the Pacific Rim and South America. This increase in international trade has forced accountants to begin dealing with the problems of measurement and reporting of financial information across national boundaries. These problems result from different national accounting systems as well as differences in economic systems, users, legal systems, etc.

The European Union has initiated accounting harmonization with the passage of the Fourth and Seventh directives. The Fourth directive highlights the rules governing the format of financial statements by establishing minimum standards companies have to follow in preparing their financial statements. It introduces a semblance of consistency and detail. Meanwhile, the Seventh directive deals with harmonizing group accounting policies. The politics of the situation have not allowed full harmonization efforts to be completed in Europe. The existence of vague options regarding certain accounting practices and differences in economic environments and terminology have held up despite the process of harmonization.

The increased competition in global capital markets has also been cited as a reason for harmonizing international accounting standards. Cross-border financing has grown rapidly, and worldwide users of financial statements demand quality information for the purpose of making investment and lending decisions. Harmonized accounting standards are necessary to provide this quality information and for the efficient operation of international capital markets. Comparison of investment opportunities is essential if the markets are going to continue to operate effectively. For instance, if an investor is examining companies from France and the United States as investment opportunities, the financial performance of the companies must be compared on a level playing field. Harmonization of international accounting standards would make this possible by forcing companies to use similar accounting practices to report financial transactions.

Multinational corporations, trade blocs, and international capital markets require harmonized accounting standards to operate effectively. Harmonization of accounting standards would enable users of financial information to compare financial statements and obtain high-quality, reliable information. Total conformity may never be achieved for global accounting standards because of the differences that govern each country's accounting policies and economic and legal systems. However, steps toward accounting harmonization must be taken as the business world moves toward a global economy.

Questions for Discussion

1. Why is it necessary for the accounting profession to become involved in trying to harmonize accounting standards? Provide details.
2. The whole argument regarding harmonizing accounting standards revolves around the issue of presenting comparable information to the users of financial statements. What benefit is served by providing this information? Explain.
3. With all the differences in accounting practices worldwide do you feel that it is possible to develop a true set of international accounting standards? Why or why not?

Source: Adapted from Robert S. Roussey, "The Changing World of International Accounting and Auditing," *Internal Auditor* (April 1994): 54; Gene Barret, "Is Accounting Becoming the First Truly International Profession?" *Australian Accountant* (February 3, 1993): 16; Dan Elnathan and Sandra Kirlich, "Accounting Harmonization in Regional Trade Blocs," *Business Forum* (Winter 1992): 49; Cameron Weber, "Harmonization of International Accounting Standards," *The National Public Accountant* (October 1992): 40; Arthur Wyatt and Joseph Yospe, "Wake-Up Call to American Business: International Accounting Standards Are on the Way," *Journal of Accountancy* (July 1993): 80–85.

CASE 21.2

Creative Accounting in Hollywood

After Art Buchwald convinced a judge that the hit movie *Coming to America* was actually his idea used without his permission, he was awarded a percentage of the net profits. Little did Buchwald know that the real battle had only begun. The Paramount picture starring Eddie Murphy already had grossed $325 million, making it one of the top movies of the 1980s. But Paramount claims the film lost money. So Buchwald and his lawyer, Pierce O'Donnell, now must convince the court that the film was indeed profitable.

Buchwald and others are questioning Hollywood studios over "net profit" contracts. Such contracts, a long-standing tradition in Hollywood, entitle actors or writers to a percentage of a film's profits. Over the years, however, net profit contracts have resulted in little money for the profit participants, regardless of a movie's success. How do studios manage to avoid paying actors and writers their share of the profits? The secret lies in the way they define net profit.

The studio takes about 40 to 50 percent off the top; this is the studio's gross. In the case of *Coming to America,* Paramount took $151 million from the $325 million the film grossed. Then the deductions begin. First the studio deducts about 35 percent of its gross as a "distribution fee" for putting the movie in theaters. Paramount deducted $53 million for *Coming to America.* Next, the studio deducts "distribution expenses" for making prints, storing reels, advertising and marketing, and other direct costs of distribution. Paramount deducted $40 million for distribution expenses.

These deductions still left Paramount with a hefty amount of money, about $58 million. From this amount, Paramount deducted the cut of the *gross players,* $22 million. The costs of producing the film, referred to in the film industry as *negative costs,* are deducted next. Paramount deducted $50 million, including 15 percent for the film's star, Eddie Murphy, and 22 percent for studio overhead. Finally, $6.5 million was deducted for "interest expense." According to the accountants, the film lost $20.5 million. Only at this point do net profits begin to accumulate.

Buchwald is not the only person to sue over a net profit contract. Jane Fonda sued Universal for a greater share of the profits from *On Golden Pond* and received an undisclosed settlement. James Garner received a settlement of about $12 million from Universal for the television series "The Rockford Files." Garner's contract entitled him to 37.5 percent of the net profits, but he had been paid less than $250,000. Universal paid Garner rather than tell a jury how his cut could be so low. According to the Los Angeles office of Laventhol & Horwath, an accounting firm that conducts many profit participation audits, nearly every audit it conducts leads to both additional claims and additional payment by the studios.

Attorney O'Donnell believes the only way to change the system is through litigation. O'Donnell plans to argue that Hollywood's net profit contracts are basically a monopoly against talent and that studios produce false accounting statements. By attacking the studios' books, O'Donnell thinks he can prove there are indeed net profits to distribute.

Questions for Discussion

1. If you were an actor or writer of a large Hollywood production and were given the choice between a percentage of gross revenue or percentage of net income (profit), which would you choose? Why?
2. If a movie like *Coming to America* can make $325 million of gross revenue and report a $20.5 million net loss, how much information do you feel the net profit/loss figure provides? Explain.
3. Do you think writers and actors who have signed net profit contracts have a legitimate complaint? Why or why not?

Source: Adapted from Dana Wechsler, "Profits? What Profits?" *Forbes* (February 19, 1990): 38–40; Robert Wolfe, "Counting the King's Gold," *American Film* (May 1990): 13–14; "There's No Business Like Show Business," *U.S. News & World Report* (January 22, 1990): 14.

BUSINESS APPLICATION

Calculating Financial Ratios

Following you will find a balance sheet and income statement for XYZ Company, a plastics manufacturing firm operating in Las Vegas. The company began operation on January 1, 19x1 (this means that all accounts have a $0 amount at the beginning of 19x1) and the balance sheet and income statement provided are dated December 31, 19x2. Your task is to analyze the success of the company by evaluating various financial ratios.

Directions:

1. Calculate the following ratios for years 19x2 and 19x1 (to two decimal places) and provide an explanation of what the ratio means for both years using the data given in the balance sheet and income statement provided:

   Current Ratio
   Quick Ratio
   Accounts Receivable Turnover
   Return on Sales
   Return on Equity
   Debt to Equity Ratio
   Times Interest Earned Ratio

   Provide an explanation of the overall health of XYZ Company based on the analysis performed.

2. Industry averages for plastic manufacturers have been calculated for 19x2 and 19x1. They are as follows:

	19x2	19x1
Current Ratio	2.0	2.1
Quick Ratio	1.0	1.0
Accounts Receivable Turnover	6.5	7.0
Return on Sales	3%	2.5%
Return on Equity	20%	20%
Debt to Equity Ratio	1.0	1.5
Times Interest Earned Ratio	75.0	75.0

Interpret the financial ratios calculated in requirement 1 by comparing them to the industry averages for plastics manufacturers. What extra information is provided by the industry averages? Discuss.

Question for Discussion:

Can an accurate analysis of corporate performance be made strictly with financial ratios of the firm or are the industry averages necessary? Explain.

Balance Sheet
December 31,

	19x2	19x1
ASSETS		
Cash	$76,200	$77,300
Accounts receivable (net)	201,700	189,100
Inventories	164,000	159,100
Total current assets	441,900	425,500
Plant Assets	289,000	276,500
TOTAL ASSETS	$730,900	$702,000
LIABILITIES		
Accounts payable	$81,100	$80,200
Notes payable	114,900	111,300
Total current liabilities	196,000	191,500
Long-term liabilities	144,400	189,350
OWNERS' EQUITY		
Capital stock	100,000	100,000
Retained Earnings	290,500	221,150
Total owners' equity	390,500	321,150
TOTAL LIABILITIES AND OWNERS' EQUITY	$730,900	$702,000

Income Statement **For the Year Ended December 31,**	**19x2**	**19x1**
Net sales	$1,486,400	$1,478,200
Cost of goods sold	1,000,300	994,800
GROSS PROFIT	486,100	483,400
Selling, general and administrative costs	356,600	354,800
OPERATING INCOME	129,500	128,600
Other income	1,000	1,300
Income before interest and taxes	130,500	129,900
Interest expense	1,900	2,100
Income before taxes	128,600	127,800
Taxes	59,250	59,900
NET INCOME	$69,350	$67,900

EXPERIENTIAL EXERCISE

Informativeness of the Annual Report

Firms listed on any major stock exchange, such as the New York and American, generally prepare an annual report for investors and potential investors. The annual report contains a set of audited financial statements along with other pieces of financial and operating information that can be used to make investment and/or credit decisions.

In this chapter, we have examined the process of accounting which leads to the identification, measurement, and communication of financial information. This project will attempt to show that the information on the face of the financial statements is only a portion of the accounting information available to decision makers. A significant amount of financial and operational information is contained in other locations within the annual report and in the notes to the financial statements.

In order to complete this project, it will be necessary for you or your group to obtain a recent copy of an annual report. Annual reports may be acquired easily in a variety of ways. First, companies of interest can be phoned or written directly (phone numbers and addresses of most public companies can be obtained from business directories located in your local or school library). Second, some libraries may actually have original or microfilmed copies of annual reports on hand. In this case, copies can be made at little expense. Third, your local stockbroker may have access to annual reports or may be willing to direct you on how to obtain one.

Once you have obtained the annual report examine it carefully and become familiar with it. Then answer the following questions:

With regard to the balance sheet:

1. For which year(s) is(are) the balance sheet(s) prepared?
2. What items are listed as current assets? What are their amounts?
3. What cost allocation methods are used on inventories?
4. Are fixed assets aggregated (listed together) or listed separately? What items are listed as fixed assets? What are their amounts?
5. What depreciation methods are used to allocate costs on fixed assets?
6. What other assets are listed on the balance sheets? What are their amounts?
7. If intangible assets are present, for how many years are they amortized?
8. What items are listed as current liabilities? What are their amounts?
9. What is the amount of long-term debt (or liabilities)?
10. What additional information is present for debt or liabilities?
11. How many different types of stock are present on the balance sheet? How many shares of each have been issued?
12. What other information is present in the annual report pertaining to stock?
13. Do Assets = Liabilities + Stockholders' (Owners') Equity? What is the amount of each?

With regard to the income statement:

14. What is the company's business?
15. Do they operate any place but the United States? If so, where?
16. What items are listed under revenue? What are their amounts?
17. What types of expenses does the company have? What are the amounts for these expenses?
18. What is the company's operating income? What is income prior to taxes? What is net income?
19. How much did the company pay in taxes?
20. What other information is provided on taxes?
21. What was the income per share of common stock?

With regard to the statement of cash flows:

22. What are the three categories present in the statement of cash flows?
23. What was the amount of depreciation and amortization?
24. Did accounts receivable increase or decrease? By how much?
25. Did accounts payable increase or decrease? By how much?
26. Did the company purchase or sell any equipment? For what amount?
27. Did the company purchase or sell any land? For what amount?
28. Did the company issue any stock? How much?
29. Did the company repurchase any of their own stock (in the form of treasury stock)? How much?
30. Was there an increase or decrease of cash? How much?

Question for Discussion

Do you feel supplemental information (information not presented on the face of the financial statements) would be presented if it were not required by the Financial Accounting Standards Board (FASB)? Explain.

NOTES

1. Michael Stanleigh, "Accounting for Quality," *CA Magazine* (October 1992): 40–42.
2. Gene Barrett, "Is Accounting Becoming the First Truly International Profession?" *Australian Accountant* (February 1993): 16.
3. American Accounting Association, *A Statement of Basic Accounting Theory* (Evanston, IL: American Accounting Association, 1966), 1.
4. American Institute of Certified Public Accountants, April 25, 1995.
5. Institute of Management Accountants.
6. Marc J. Epstein and Moses L. Pava, "Profile of an Annual Report," *Financial Executive* (January/February 1994): 60.
7. "Businesses Are Paying Bills a Little Faster, Dun & Bradstreet Says," *The Wall Street Journal* (March 10, 1994): A8:5.
8. Stewart Toy, "Is Disney Headed for the Euro-Trash Heap?" *Business Week* (January 24, 1994): 52.
9. "Kmart Plans Offerings for Units in Autumn," *The Wall Street Journal* (May 3, 1994): C20:3.
10. James E. Kristy, "Conquering Financial Ratios: The Good, the Bad, and the Who Cares?" *Business Credit* (February 1994): 14.

C H A P T E R 22

Management Information Systems

LEARNING OBJECTIVES

1. Explain why business managers need computers in this age of information.

2. Trace the evolution of computers.

3. Identify the different types of computers and the components common to all.

4. Outline the capabilities of computers.

5. Define *management information system (MIS)* and explain how an MIS is used.

6. List trends in computer development and use and in management information systems.

Hewlett-Packard (HP) is a worldwide manufacturer of computer components. It is also one of the best. The company is considered a standard setter in the laser printer market. Continuous improvement and a focus on quality have been cited as reasons for HP's success in the highly competitive world of computers.

During the late 1970s, the computer market began to thrive because of the increase in lower-cost computer components, mainly from abroad. Hewlett-Packard began, at this point, to look at manufacturing costs and their association with productivity. A study conducted by the company indicated that 25 percent of its manufacturing costs were due to poor-quality workmanship. This statistic is from a company who was generally regarded as having a good reputation for producing high-quality components. Evidently, HP was wasting large amounts of money on identifying and correcting problems, rather than focusing on quality control.

HP decided that the procedure of total quality control (TQC) would be implemented into the manufacturing process in an effort to reduce the high amount of rework costs. The approach to TQC at HP was borrowed from the Japanese, after first learning about the procedure via a joint venture with a Japanese firm. When implementing TQC, each activity in the organization is viewed as a process that can be measured and improved. Further, quality is defined, with regard to TQC, as whatever satisfies a customer. The goal that HP hoped to achieve by implementing TQC was a reduction in the product failure rate by a factor of 10 during the decade of the 1980s.

The results of implementing TQC were immediate. One division of HP, which manufactures magnetic disk drives, increased the reliability of their products by 170 percent over a two-year period. Similar results were experienced on a company-wide basis. Productivity increased by 15 percent annually from 1986 to 1990 and $800 million in warranty costs were carved away from overall manufacturing costs. Further, through streamlining of operations, inventory decreased from 20.5 percent of revenues in 1979 to 16 percent in 1990. As far as reducing product failures by a factor of 10, HP fell just short. Overall, however, the company was ecstatic about the benefits that TQC introduced. Improvement in quality was one of the reasons that Hewlett-Packard increased sales by 24 percent and doubled profits to $1 billion in 1993.

These benefits have been great, but HP realizes that the only way to maintain an increase in the success of TQC is to continually improve upon the quality of their products. In an industry like computers, where there is high competition, one of the ways a company can distinguish itself from its competitors is to manufacture higher quality products, while maintaining or reducing the prices charged to consumers. Continuous improvements in manufacturing along with the introduction of new, high-quality products should keep HP as a top manufacturer in the computer industry and on the road to excellence.[1]

The procedure of total quality control (TQC) obviously helped a manufacturing firm like Hewlett-Packard. Can this same procedure help a company in the retail or service business? Some experts feel that it is more difficult to apply TQC to service businesses. Why do you believe that this is what some experts think?

Computers are firmly entrenched in our society, particularly in the workplace. They perform tasks from the most mundane to the most complex. They store libraries of information in a tiny space. By quickly transmitting and analyzing important information, computers help business managers make complicated decisions. And unlike humans, computers are available 24 hours a day, seven days a week. They never complain, take vacations, or ask for a raise (although they do break down occasionally).

In this chapter, we introduce computers and management information systems. First we look at how the information explosion has increased the importance of computers in business. Then we examine the evolution of computers, explain the different types of computers, and distinguish between hardware and software. Next we investigate the many uses of computers in business. A discussion of management information systems follows. Finally we examine the future of computers and management information systems.

THE AGE OF INFORMATION

Businesses today have access to more information than ever before. The abundance of newspapers, journals, magazines, television and radio programs, business and government reports, and seminars has led many commentators to label this the Age of Information. Information will be the main catalyst for growth in the global economy of the 1990s.[2] But the sheer volume of information available presents a real challenge to business managers. Obviously every manager cannot use all available information. The challenge is to collect, store, process, report, and use the most relevant information to make more effective decisions.

Data
Facts, figures, and statistics concerning people, objects, events, and ideas.

Information
Data with meaning attached.

Computers help firms meet this challenge. They assist managers in converting **data**—facts, figures, and statistics concerning people, objects, events, and ideas—into useful information. Thus **information** is data with meaning attached. The figure 1,000,000 is a piece of data, but if the term *sales* and a dollar sign are attached, Sales $1,000,000, it becomes a piece of information.

Are you ready to cope in the Age of Information? Choosing and using information through computers may seem complicated, but each one of us must be prepared. Even traditional manual jobs such as working on cars have been affected by computers.

Although workers and customers find computers frustrating at times, computers are truly friends to business. Of course, when computers are blamed for a late flight, an incorrect bill, or the wrong grade in a college course, human error is actually the cause. The next section traces the evolution of computers and provides an overview of the different types of computers as well as computer hardware and software. Before you read further about computers, complete Your Values and Attitudes and assess your readiness to work in the Age of Information.

YOUR VALUES AND ATTITUDES

Living in the Age of Information

Directions: Many of us have thought at times that computers complicate our lives. In some ways, perhaps they do. But computers are, of course, here to stay. Let's see how you react to that fact. For each statement, circle the number that shows your level of agreement.

	Strongly Disagree					Strongly Agree
1. I think computers have helped businesses serve customers better.	1	2	3	4	5	6
2. I would like a job in which I use computers.	1	2	3	4	5	6
3. Computer courses are very helpful to students.	1	2	3	4	5	6
4. I like the idea of paying bills through a computer.	1	2	3	4	5	6
5. Computers have helped improve day-to-day life.	1	2	3	4	5	6

Feedback: If you strongly agree with the statements (circled 5 or 6 for most), you have accepted computers. You may realize they offer new challenges and can help businesses improve operations and service. If you circled 3 or 4 for most statements, you seem skeptical about computers. You may recognize their benefits but see the changes they've brought as too widespread or too quick. Finally, strong disagreement with the statements indicates a low tolerance for computers. You may prefer to avoid them if you can. If you are considering a career in business, avoiding them will be difficult if not impossible. Are computers now essential to conducting business? What do you think?

INTRODUCTION TO COMPUTERS

Computer
An electronic device used to input, store, and process data and to output them as useful information.

A **computer** is an electronic device used to input, store, and process data and to output data as useful information. Universities, for instance, can enter into a computer the grade reports on thousands of students from hundreds of courses, store the information, process grades in a matter of seconds, and print out individual student grade reports ready to mail. Students can receive their grades a few days after classes conclude. Before computers, the process could take weeks.

The Evolution of Computers

Electronic computers have evolved through five generations. The first generation (1946–1958) began with the introduction of the ENIAC (electronic numerical integrator and calculator). This massive computer, weighing over 30 tons, operated with 18,000 glass vacuum tubes. Primitive by today's standards, these tubes were extremely hot and burned out frequently—an average one every seven seconds. Computer operators stood by with baskets of replacement tubes.[3] During this period, computers were used primarily for scientific purposes. However, business firms also began to realize the value of computers in processing data. The ENIAC, with all its limitations, was a major start for the electronic computer era.

Transistor A small switch that controls electrical current; characterized by second-generation computers.

Integrated Circuit Small silicon chip containing dozens of tiny transistors and connections; used in third-generation computers.

The second generation of computers (1959–1964) was characterized by the use of the **transistor,** a small switch that controls electrical current. Transistors were much faster than vacuum tubes and produced less heat. With transistors, smaller, more powerful computers could be built at less cost than the first-generation computers. Businesses, even medium-sized and small ones, began using the computer to process an increasing number of business applications.

The third generation (1965–1977) began with the introduction of **integrated circuits,** small silicon chips containing dozens of tiny transistors and connections. Integrated circuitry resulted in much faster, smaller, and more reliable computers. Faster input and output methods and increased data storage facilities were developed during the third generation. More and more business firms began to rely heavily on computers. Remote terminals, typewriter-like machines located away from the computer but connected to it by telephone lines, made access to the computer possible from separate offices or even distant cities.

Large-Scale Integrated (LSI) Circuit Superchip that contains thousands of small transistors; fourth-generation innovation that made personal computers possible.

Very Large-Scale Integration (VLSI) Superchip circuitry, resulting from extremely compact transistors and circuits assembled on a single silicon chip; marked start of fifth generation of computers.

Artificial Intelligence A developing technology that allows computers to solve problems involving imagination, abstract reasoning, and common sense.

The fourth generation (1971 to present) started with **large-scale integrated (LSI) circuits.** These *superchips,* a mere cubic inch in size, contain thousands of small transistors. LSI technology enabled the development of personal computers, which are so common and so valuable today. Mass production of computer chips led to lower prices for small home and business computers. Increased storage capabilities in these small computers gave business firms the means of storing vast amounts of data.

Computer technology is now entering a fifth generation, as a result of **very large-scale integration (VLSI).** VLSI circuitry consists of a superchip created from extremely compact transistors and circuits assembled on a single silicon chip. A developing technology called **artificial intelligence** allows computers to solve problems involving imagination, abstract reasoning, and common sense. Computer scientists are trying to empower computers to behave as though they could think, by perceiving and absorbing data, reasoning, and communicating in ways similar to human behavior.

Types of Computers

Depending on their needs and resources, organizations use one of three types of computers: mainframes, minicomputers, or microcomputers. The largest

Mainframe
The largest and fastest type of computer, with the greatest storage capacity

and fastest computer, with the greatest storage capacity, is the **mainframe.** Large businesses and government units use mainframes to process and store vast amounts of data. Most mainframes today can be used by many people in several different locations at the same time. Because of their incredible speed and capacity to serve many users, mainframe computers are very expensive. Increasing price competition among mainframe vendors, however, is likely to lower prices.[4]

Supercomputer
A computer formed by connecting multiple mainframes.

Some large businesses and government agencies connect multiple mainframes together to form **supercomputers,** the fastest computers available. Some supercomputers can make billions of calculations in one second with 20-digit accuracy.[5]

Minicomputer
A smaller, slower version of the mainframe computer.

A **minicomputer** is a smaller, slower version of the mainframe. Many smaller firms rely heavily on minicomputers that cost much less than mainframes. Most minicomputers are the size of a desk, yet can perform most of the operations accomplished by mainframes.

Microcomputer
A personal computer, including a cathode ray tube and a keyboard.

A **microcomputer,** or personal computer (PC) is smaller, less powerful, and less costly than a minicomputer. Microcomputers include a cathode ray tube (CRT), which is a visual display device that shows data on a monitor and a keyboard like that of a typewriter. Designed for use by one person, PCs are self-contained units that usually fit on a desk or table and can be moved. They can be purchased for $2,000 or less. Microcomputers are popular for use in homes and professional offices as well as in corporations of all sizes. There are over 70 million personal computers used throughout the world.[6]

Laptop computers are even smaller versions of microcomputers. As the name says, they fit on a person's lap and are convenient for use while traveling. Laptop and the even smaller notebook computers are the computer industry's fastest-selling machines. Industry experts predict that in 1995 one out of every four computers purchased will be a laptop. This increase in the popularity of laptops is a result of the increased power now available with these portable computers. Laptops are now as powerful as a regular-sized PC.[7]

Computer Hardware

Hardware
The physical devices that make up a computer system.

The physical devices that make up a computer system are called **hardware.** Exhibit 22.1 diagrams the basic hardware of a computer, including the input device, the central processing unit, and the output device.

Input Device
The hardware used to enter data into and make requests of the computer.

Through an **input device,** a user enters data into a computer and makes requests of the computer. The most common input device is a keyboard for typing data or requests. Other input devices are disks, magnetic tapes, punch cards, optical scanners such as those that read universal product codes in supermarkets, the movable mouse, and voice recognition devices.

Central Processing Unit (CPU)
The electronic hardware that performs the computer operations and controls the entire system.

The **central processing unit (CPU),** the heart of the computer, controls the entire computer system. The CPU includes the electronic hardware that performs the computer operations and consists of three components.

Main Memory
The part of the computer central processing unit that stores data and instructions.

Arithmetic-Logic Unit
The part of a computer's central processing unit that performs computations.

Control Unit
The part of a computer's central processing unit that guides the operations of the computer.

Output Device
The hardware that displays the computer's requests or processed data.

Software
A sequence of instructions that a computer can carry out.

Main memory stores data, instructions, and other information the computer needs to operate. If something is not in a computer's main memory, the CPU cannot process it. Memory is measured in *bytes*; one byte is the same as one character—a numeral or letter of the alphabet. For example, computers containing 640KB (kilobytes) of main memory have the capacity to store 640,000 characters. The **arithmetic-logic unit** performs the computations. Data that need to be added, subtracted, multiplied, or divided are moved from the main memory to the arithmetic-logic unit. After the calculations have been performed, the resulting data are moved back into main memory. The **control unit** guides the operations of a computer. It directs the sequence of operations, interprets coded instructions, and sends needed data and instructions to the other units.

The **output device** is the hardware that displays the computer's requests or processed data. The most commonly used output devices are the display screen and the printer, which produces a paper printout (called hard copy). Other output devices include disks, magnetic tapes, graphic plotters, and even the spoken word.

Computer Software

Computers cannot think. They can operate and perform calculations only by following precise instructions devised by people. **Software** is the term for the instructions that tell the computer hardware what to do.

Software can be broken down into three categories: operating systems, programming languages, and applications. The operating system allows the user to communicate with the system. It serves as an interface between the person using the computer and the computer. Two well-known operating systems are Windows 3.1 and OS/2 Warp. Programming languages consist of a set of codes that the computer interprets as instructions. When a collection

Exhibit 22.1
Basic Computer Hardware

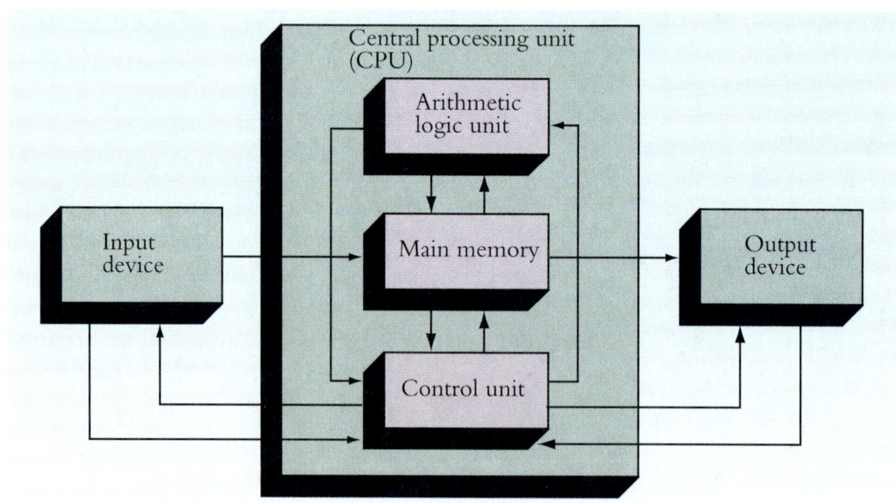

TODAY'S BUSINESS WORLD

The Advent of the PC Spells Trouble for IBM

Until the late 1970s, the computer industry was based on large machines. These large machines fell into two categories, mainframes and minicomputers. Mainframes and minicomputers were expensive and only the largest corporations could afford to pay for them. International Business Machines, IBM, was able to dominate the market during these early days. It had gained what was considered to be a monopoly position in the computer industry.

In the early days of the computer industry relatively few machines were being sold. As late as 1980, less than 10,000 mainframes and 105,000 minicomputers were sold each year. A large percentage of these were IBM machines. The complexity of the product encouraged many computer manufacturers to opt for vertical integration. This strategy enabled them to develop and manufacture most of the computer components in-house. They also created their own software to run on the machines. Hence, customers usually purchased all of their computer components from a single supplier. Decision makers in many organizations decided that if they were going to be forced to purchase computer equipment from one supplier they might as well purchase from the largest no matter what the cost. IBM, as the leader, grew quite large. In 1980, IBM accounted for 38 percent of computer industry revenues and 60 percent of the industry's profits.

Beginning in 1981, the personal computer (PC) market began to grow. In trying to seize a piece of the PC pie, IBM quickly began manufacturing PCs. IBM abandoned its strategy of vertical integration and arranged to purchase microprocessors and operating system software from Intel and Microsoft.

At first, IBM profited greatly from the PC market, becoming the leader in sales. Small software companies began writing programs for the IBM PC which further increased demand. However, because IBM did not exclusively contract with Intel and Microsoft, firms such as Compaq were able to clone IBM machines with Intel and Microsoft parts. Competition grew in the marketplace because these IBM clones could run the same software and perform the same activities that the IBM PCs could. Price became the main differentiating factor. Since the clones were cheaper than the IBM machines, IBM's hold on the PC market began to dwindle. Other manufacturers jumped into the sales mix, driving down prices and collapsing the market. At the same time, the increasingly powerful processing capabilities of PCs severely pierced the mainframe and minicomputer market that IBM once ruled. A new industry had been spawned, and IBM was being left behind.

Since 1985, IBM's market share in the computer market (hardware, software, and services) has dropped from 30 percent to less than 19 percent. Although IBM's PC market share is growing, some experts feel IBM still relies too much on the mainframe and minicomputer market, and they predict a continuing decline in revenues. The trend toward PC networks and away from bulky mainframes and minicomputers has forced IBM to change its strategic focus and begin to develop new products to try to regain its lost market share. IBM is now determined to give customers what they want, although that may mean suggesting a competitor's components to integrate with an IBM system.

The computer market has come full circle. From the days of large computer manufacturers selling all components for a large cost, today's market features thousands of firms specializing in computer components and competing on the basis of quality and price. It will be interesting to see if IBM can adjust to the marketplace and regain what it has lost. IBM was once the "king of the hill" in the computer market. Can it make the needed changes to regain its standing as the major factor in the computer market? Explain.

Source: Adapted from David C. Charbuck, "Cassandra Strikes Again," *Forbes* (February 14, 1994): 45; "The Computer Industry Survey," *The Economist* (February 27, 1993): 5–6; Carol J. Loomis, "Dinosaurs?" *Fortune* (May 3, 1993): 36–40.

Computer Program A detailed set of instructions written in a computer language.

of instructions are linked together logically they form a **computer program.** Widely employed programming languages for business include Visual Basic and C++. Application software includes such programs as spreadsheets, word processing, and graphics and are addressed in detail in the next section. Without software, computer hardware is useless.

Businesses sometimes develop their own computer software for specific tasks. For instance, many firms employ computer programmers to write special programs for payroll, billing, inventory control, and other functions. The programmer must analyze the problem and outline a series of logical steps that will provide a solution. Developing software can be both time-consuming and expensive and often is not practical for small firms, which generally do not have programmers on staff. Therefore many firms purchase ready-made software, available from a multitude of companies. Ready-made software can handle a variety of business applications and often costs less than developing computer programs from scratch. Ready-made software is also instantly available, whereas developing a computer program can take months or even years.

Much of today's computer software is "user friendly," meaning that people can use it without a great deal of technical training. User-friendly software communicates by using menus. A menu lists a number of commands that usually can be executed with the assistance of a mouse or by typing in the first letter of the command. Complex computer programs used in the United States, for example, allow users to issue commands in English rather than a computer language. This breakthrough in software development brought computers into the daily lives of many more people at work, school, and home.

The newest software technology is the CD-ROM. In this medium software is stored on a compact disc very similar to the type used in your stereo system. CD-ROM technology is able to store volumes of data and information. A current application for CD-ROM technology is interactive learning aids for home use and all levels of schooling. Retail sales for at-home learning programs were $147 million in 1992 and by 2000 are expected to be $1 billion annually.[8]

A wide variety of computer software business applications is available for purchase, and the number is growing rapidly.

COMPUTERS AND BUSINESS

Computers are a valuable asset to and often a necessity for business firms. In this section, we examine various capabilities of computers and common business applications.

Computer Capabilities

Computers possess virtually unlimited capabilities. Computer technology changes so rapidly that new uses for computers are being discovered every day. Computer hardware and software today can satisfy almost any business need. Let's look at some of the ways firms commonly use computers.

Word Processing
Creating written documents with a computer.

Word Processing. Computers, in particular the micro or personal computer (PC), have revolutionized **word processing,** which consists of creating documents such as letters, reports, newsletters, memos, and books. In fact, compared to computers, typewriters have become outdated office equipment. Through the computer keyboard, an individual enters documents and instructions into computer memory to be stored on magnetic disk. Material stored on disk can be accessed and altered easily and kept for later use. For instance, a manager can write memos, letters, and reports, store them on disk, and print them when needed. Many word-processing programs (e.g., MS Word®, WordPerfect®), perform functions such as checking spelling and grammar, suggesting alternate words, and inserting graphics such as lines, boxes, diagrams, and illustrations.

Spreadsheets
Electronic accounting ledgers generated by computer software.

Spreadsheets. Many firms use computer software to generate electronic accounting ledgers as **spreadsheets.** A manager or accountant can use computerized spreadsheets to organize data into rows and columns and to perform mathematical calculations. Popular spreadsheet software such as Lotus® 1-2-3®, Quattro Pro®, and Excel® are used to generate balance sheets, develop sales projections, and estimate profits.

Computer Graphics. Computer programs can also translate data into graphs or figures. Computer graphics are useful to display financial information and to make comparisons between companies or performance in different years. Graphics software, including CorelDraw, Illustrator, and Designer, add clarity and emphasis and are extremely valuable in both written reports and oral presentations. Exhibit 22.2 on page 753 illustrates some of the graphics capabilities of computers.

Desktop Publishing
Producing printed materials using computer software that can do page layouts and formats, insert graphics, and print with high quality.

Desktop Publishing. The computer can also be used to produce high-quality printed materials. With **desktop publishing** software, such as PageMaker and Ventura Publisher, the user can design page layouts and formats comparable to magazines and books, and insert graphics, including illustrations, wherever needed. Desktop publishing enables individuals and firms of any size to produce high-quality reports, brochures, and newsletters at much less than the price charged by a printer. Desktop publishing is done using a powerful color laser printer, now available for less than $1,000.

Presentation Graphics. Another use for the computer is valuable to businesses as well as schools and colleges. Using presentation graphics software, such as PowerPoint and Freelance Graphics, the personal computer can produce full-color text and graphic screens for overhead projection. Using LCD technology, the computer can be used to display moving presentations.

Business Applications

Firms use computers to perform a variety of tasks quickly, efficiently, and accurately. The most common business applications of computers are payroll, record keeping, inventory control, scheduling, order processing, and electronic mail.

Payroll. Many companies generate their payroll with computers. For most, calculating employees' pay is complicated. They must make deductions for taxes, insurance, profit-sharing programs, and even parking fees and contributions to charity. Employee pay can be calculated in several ways, including

Exhibit 22.2
Examples of Computer Graphics

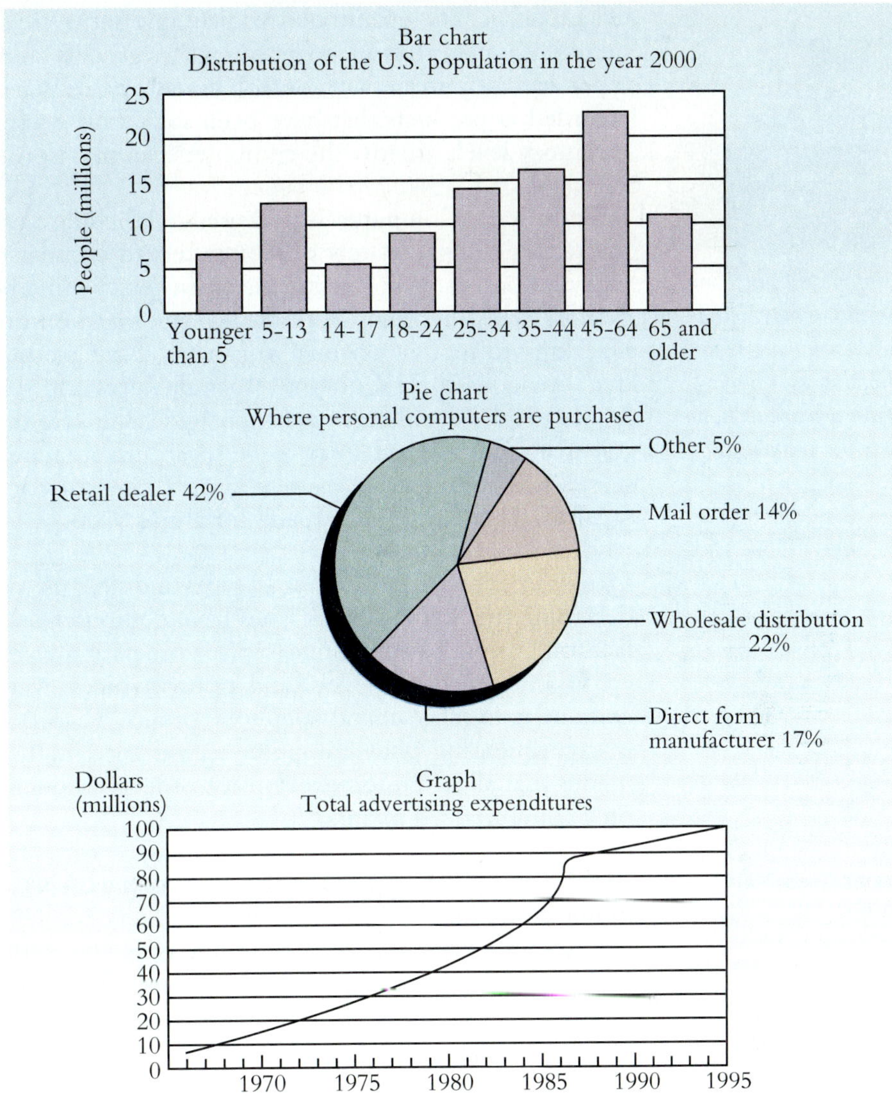

salary, sales, bonus, commission, and hourly wages plus overtime. Computers can make the many calculations required to meet a payroll in a matter of seconds.

Record Keeping. Computers are valuable for maintaining and updating records such as payroll and personnel files, customer lists, accounts receivable, and accounts payable. Business owners and managers can easily maintain accounting and financial records on a computer. With computer record keeping, firms can update records and generate financial statements on demand.

Inventory Control. Another common application of computers in business is inventory control. Many firms use programs to keep track of inventory and place orders when inventory drops to a certain level. These programs can also tell a manager the quantity and dollar amount of inventory at any time. The optical scanners that are so prevalent in grocery and department stores are types of computers that control inventory. UPC codes are scanned and recorded as products that have been sold, thus decreasing inventory. When inventory levels are low the computers can place orders for more items.

Laptop and notebook computers have made it easy for businesspeople to access data and perform work at home or while traveling.

Scheduling. Computers can be used to schedule a variety of activities. Manufacturing companies rely on computers to construct production schedules, while a number of businesses use them to schedule personnel activities such as work schedules, employee breaks, and vacation time. Recent technology is seeking to replace personal organizers that have become so popular in today's society. Apple Computer manufactures and sells the Apple Newton® MessagePad, a hand-held, pen-operated computer that serves as a scheduler, calendar, and notepad. A message regarding an appointment written on the screen will automatically be placed on a calendar contained within the MessagePad. The MessagePad retails for about $700.[9]

Order Processing. Firms of all types and sizes use computers to process orders. Supermarket checkout lanes have computerized registers. Large manufacturing firms use computers to place orders at a warehouse, check customer credit and inventory levels, and print invoices. Many catalog retailers use computers to fill mail and telephone orders. Taco Bell, a fast-food franchise, is experimenting with computer technology in the form of touch-screen menus that allow customers to place orders by touching the item they want on a computerized menu.[10]

Local Area Network (LAN)
A system of telecommunications links that connects all computers in one firm directly, without telephone lines.

Electronic Mail
A computer network used to relay messages from one user to another instantly.

Electronic Mail. A **local area network (LAN)** is a system of telecommunications links that connects all computers in one company directly, without telephone lines. Because computers in the network can communicate with one another, members of a firm can send information back and forth instantly. Through **electronic mail (e-mail),** a user can send a letter or memo to another designated user or to several. Electronic mail software keeps track of all communications sent and alerts the sender that the message has been received. Replies can be routed to the sender. Some software companies are increasing the ease with which electronic mail can be accessed by allowing users to employ a mouse to click on menus to receive their messages.[11]

MANAGEMENT INFORMATION SYSTEMS

Because of the information explosion, managers making decisions must regularly confront an abundance of facts and figures and determine which information is most useful. Many organizations design management information systems to provide managers with the necessary information to make intelli-

Management Information System (MIS) A combination of computers and procedures for providing information that managers use in making decisions.

gent decisions. A **management information system (MIS)** combines computers and regular, organized procedures to provide the information managers use in making decisions.

MIS Functions

A management information system is used to collect data, store and process data, and present information to managers (see Exhibit 22.3). This section discusses each of these functions.

Database An integrated collection of data stored in one place for easy access and information processing.

Collect Data. We have emphasized the massive amount of information available to organizations—personnel records, information about competitors, sales data, accounting data, information about customers, and so on. The first function of an MIS is to determine the information needed to make decisions and to organize it into a database. A **database** is an integrated collection of data stored in one place for efficient access and information processing.

Data can be obtained from sources within and outside the organization. Generally most data collected for an MIS come from internal sources, such as company records or reports and information compiled by managers themselves. External sources include trade publications, customers, and consultants.

Store and Process Data. Once created, a database must be stored and processed in a form useful to managers. Data are generally stored on magnetic tape or hard disks when mainframe computers are used and on hard disks or floppy disks when minicomputers or microcomputers are used. The data can be loaded into the computer in seconds for easy access by the user.

Exhibit 22.3
Functions of an MIS

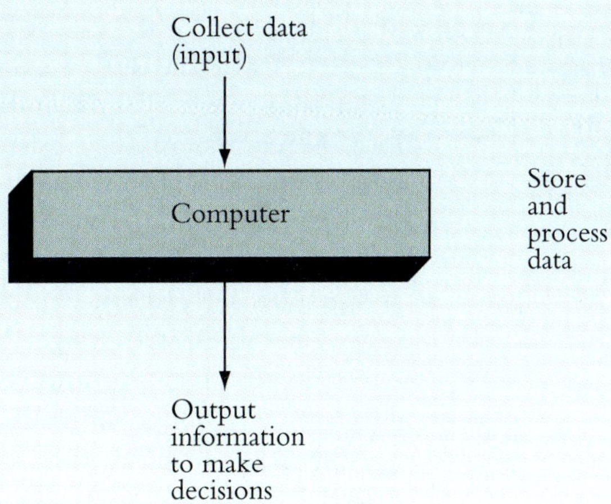

Data for an MIS must be current, which requires periodic updating of the database. A computer operator or programmer can update the database manually by loading the appropriate tape or disk into the computer, locating the data to be changed and making the necessary changes. Systems also are available to automatically update data. In this case, the database is permanently connected to the MIS, and the computer automatically makes changes as new data become available.

Once data are stored in the MIS, managers can use the data for decision making. Some data can be used in the form in which they are stored. But more often, data must be processed to meet specific information needs of managers. **Data processing** involves mechanically transferring raw data into some specific form of information. Business firms process both text, such as reports, and numerical data, such as sales figures. The MIS provides data and information necessary to help managers make decisions.

Data Processing Mechanically transferring raw data into some specific form of information.

MIS are developed by following a set of steps known as the Systems Development Life Cycle (SDLC). The steps or phases include planning, analysis, design, and implementation. Planning consists of examining the MIS and the overall and system goals of the organization to make sure they are in congruence with one another. The analysis phase explores the strengths and weaknesses of the current system. Users are interviewed to gather their viewpoints and suggestions for improvements in the system. With this feedback from the analysis phase, a new system can be designed that corrects the problems of the old system. Next, the new system must be implemented and placed into operation.

A **database management system (DBMS)** is a computer software program that helps firms manage their data files. Such programs change information stored in data files, add new information, and delete information no longer needed. DBMS software can also be used to sort and merge files, process data, and print reports. Some database programs used frequently are Borland's Paradox and dBASE software, Lotus Approach, Microsoft Access, and FoxPro.

Database Management Systems (DBMS) Computer software that helps firms manage various data files.

Present Information to Managers. Processed data must be put in a form useful to managers. Verbal information can be presented in text format in the form of reports, outlines, lists, articles, or books. Numerical information can be presented in table or graph format. As noted earlier, computer programs can offer numerous graphic options.

The most commonly used computer graphics are bar charts, pie charts, and graphs (see Exhibit 22.2). A *bar chart* uses vertical or horizontal bars to represent values, with longer bars representing greater values. A *pie chart* is a circle divided into portions, or "slices," each representing a different item. The size of each slice shows the proportion of that item to the total. Bar charts and pie charts help visualize the relative size or importance of various information. A *graph* is used to plot data, illustrating how information changes over time.

Computer Networks

Computer Network
A collection of computers connected so that they can function individually and communicate with each other.

A management information system can include multiple computers connected to each other. A **computer network** is a collection of computers connected in a manner that allows them to function individually and communicate with each other. Computer networks usually include a mainframe or minicomputer as the foundation of the system. Other mainframes, minicomputers, or microcomputers can communicate with the mainframe or minicomputer or with each other. Networks link computers within an office, across the country, or even worldwide—in which case the computers are linked by telephone lines or satellites. Hanna Industries International, for example, uses a computer network to manage 30 car washes and to communicate with five branch offices (see Exhibit 22.4). By 1995 the company plans to link 5,000 car washes on the network.[12]

The Internet is the world's largest computerized network. It links 20 million people and more than 1.5 million computers around the world. The number of Internet users is increasing by almost 10 percent per month.[13] The Internet is a collection of networks and on-line services linked together to form a "supernetwork." Three of the largest on-line services are Compuserve, Prodigy and America Online. These three services are linked to a number of different networks that allow users, for a fee, to access information on a number of topics.

Once users enter the Internet, they are able to communicate with people and companies throughout the world, as well as access home shopping, stock market information, the Library of Congress, travel information, and news, just to name a few. All of these opportunities are available to the computer user at home with a connection into the Internet by means of a modem. A

Exhibit 22.4
Hanna Industries' Computer Network

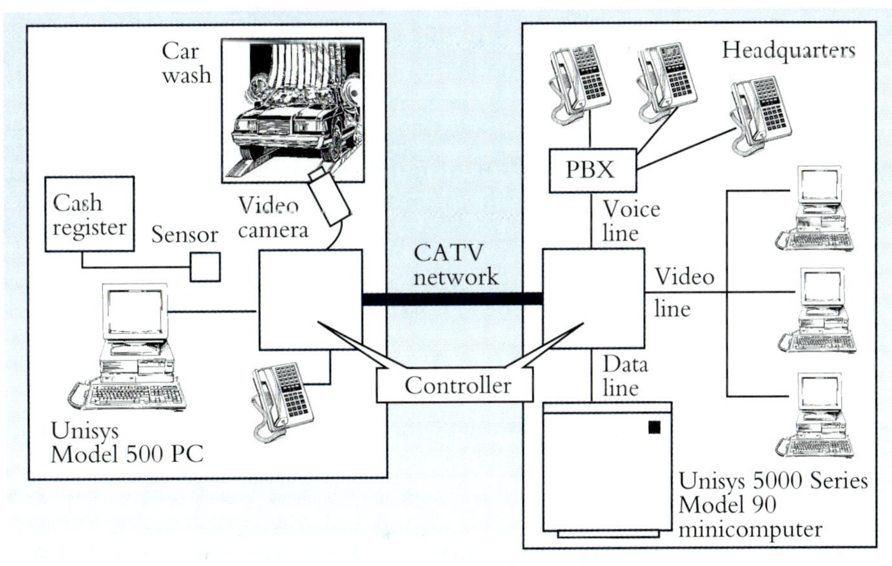

Source: Hanna Car Wash International, Portland, Oregon.

modem uses telephone lines to connect a computer in one location to a computer or network in another location. Internet and World Wide Web are part of the Information Superhighway that many hope will link computer users to all types of educational, business, and entertainment opportunities.

With the increase in popularity of laptop (notebook) computers in the business environment, new wireless network technology is being developed using radio frequencies.[14]

Decision Support Systems

Decision Support System (DSS)
A system that enables managers to instantly access information on past and current performance.

A **decision support system (DSS)** is an interactive information system that enables managers to gain instant access to information in a less structured format than an MIS. DSS software combines corporate information on past performance with what is currently taking place, allowing managers to work with large amounts of data not available otherwise.[15] Through a DSS, managers can obtain information about the firm, competitors, and the business environment. For instance:

- The healthcare industry is using a DSS for monitoring revenues, costs, and profits for individual services, as well as scheduling nurses and deploying emergency vehicles.
- Gillette uses a DSS to check market position and daily sales activity in three divisions.
- One fast-food chain uses a DSS to tell how many customers ordered french fries with hamburgers on the previous day.
- Firestone Tire & Rubber uses a DSS to pinpoint lagging areas and to control costs.
- Phillips Petroleum uses a DSS to manage operations and monitor economic and political news influencing the oil business.[16]

Executive Information System (EIS)
A user-friendly decision support system designed for executives that requires little computer knowledge and provides instant high-quality displays.

An **executive information system (EIS)** is a user-friendly DSS designed specifically for executives. An EIS is easy to use and requires no knowledge of the computer. By moving a mouse or merely touching the screen, the user directs the computer to provide information. Executive information systems use big-screen, high-quality monitors and produce full-color displays. An EIS allows top-level managers to ask questions and receive immediate answers in the form of graphs, charts, and reports.

TRENDS IN COMPUTERS AND MANAGEMENT INFORMATION SYSTEMS

The amount of information available to managers will continue to increase dramatically in the future. The ever-growing volume of information will make computers even more crucial to firms. The business sector's use of computers to process information is expected to grow rapidly. Virtually no business firm, regardless of size, will be able to function efficiently without one. Some experts even point to a "paperless" society in which computers will be used for nearly all letters, memos, reports, and other business correspondence.

The amount of computer power a dollar can buy has grown a thousand times every two decades, and this rate shows no sign of slowing.[17] The trend toward smaller, faster, and less costly computers will also continue. Engineers are packing more and more functions onto a single computer chip without increasing the power the chip burns up.[18] Notebook-size computers are already available.

One problem in making computers even smaller, however, is the keyboard. Some companies are developing computers that convert handwritten text into data and so eliminate the need for a keyboard.[19] The future will also bring computers with greater capabilities of recognizing the human voice.[20]

Smaller, portable computers such as laptops are changing the way people in business use computers. Laptops now are as essential as a briefcase or suitcase for many business travelers. Salespeople, reporters, writers, managers, and others use the small computers to work on airplanes and commuter trains and in hotels and to communicate with co-workers in other places. Salespeople often have computers in their cars for quick access to information from their managers. Computers in Federal Express vans and trucks help couriers keep track of letters and packages being shipped.

Expert System
Computer software that imitates human thinking.

Because of the ever-increasing power of computers, management information systems are also becoming more sophisticated. **Expert systems** (discussed in Chapter 21) are computer programs that imitate human thinking and offer advice or solutions to complex problems in much the same way that a human expert does. For instance, people use expert systems to plan shipping schedules, provide financial advice to investors, and help managers respond to the actions of competing firms. Accountants are using expert systems to solve tax return problems. These systems have made it much easier to file tax returns.[21]

A number of other trends in computers and MIS have evolved over time. As companies have become more decentralized, with managers rather than executives making decisions, computing has moved away from the mainframe environment and into distributed data processing, where each department within the organization is now able to process its own data. Because of this decentralization, users are beginning to develop their own programs and systems to provide information they need for decision making.

Another trend increasing in popularity is outsourcing of computing activities. Activities such as payroll are now commonly being outsourced to companies that specialize in them. By allowing another entity to perform these rather simple computing tasks, the company is able to focus on processing activities more likely to lead to the generation of profits.

Computers have increasing significance in our lives, not only for work but also for personal and family use and for play. Eventually they may be as common in homes as microwave ovens. The profusion of computers will enable business firms to explore still more computer applications, such as placing orders, paying bills, and performing bank transactions through personal computers in homes or offices. Tomorrow's Business World examines how voice-activated technology is becoming increasingly common with personal computers.

TOMORROW'S BUSINESS WORLD

Tomorrow's Business World

From HAL the computer in *2001: A Space Odyssey* to computers on the starship Enterprise, Hollywood has, for a number of years, depicted computers as capable of responding to directions by the spoken word. Technology has finally caught up with Hollywood. Multiple packages of speech recognition software are now available to consumers. These packages range in price from $169 to $6,000. Computer experts expect a continuing increase in the sales of voice recognition equipment. Voice Information Associates, a voice technology consultant, expects annual sales to reach $159 million in 1992. These sales are projected to quadruple by 1996, and by the year 2000 sales should exceed the $1 billion barrier.

Research on speech recognition technology began in 1971. Speech recognition in computers is based on mathematical calculations that originally could only be handled by large, fast mainframes. Only recently have personal computers become powerful enough to manage these calculations. Early attempts at speech recognition technology created machines that could recognize only tiny vocabularies. Today, machines equipped with lower-priced software can interpret about 200 commands, while more expensive packages can recognize up to 50,000 words. Teaching these machines words used to entail many hours of reading words into a microphone. Today's machines, however, can be trained in as little as five seconds per command. Unfortunately all of the problems have not yet been conquered, as current users of speech recognition machines must pause between words to allow the equipment to digest what is said. Experts expect that within five years the technology will have advanced to the point where computers will be able to understand continuous speech.

Practical applications for speech recognition technology are now being explored. Operating a personal computer by using verbal commands, without a keyboard or mouse, is one such example. This application opens the world of computers to many people with physical disabilities who are not otherwise able to operate a computer, and individuals with minimal or no keyboard skills. The telephone industry has begun to blend speech recognition technology into its operations by allowing customers to converse directly with company computers. Collect calls are one such application. Computerized voices are currently aiding customers in placing their collect calls. Airlines are interested in replacing clerks with computers to answer customer's questions and issue tickets. Speech recognition technology is also being applied in the medical profession. A base of medical knowledge is now being used, with the help of computers, to aid doctors in checking symptoms and enhancing the accuracy of diagnoses.

The applications for speech recognition technology seem endless. If voice recognition technology is now arriving, can computers that speak to users be far behind? Could a computer that speaks be used to teach this course? Discuss.

Source: Adapted from Gene Bylinsky, "At Last! Computers You Can Talk To," *Fortune* (May 3, 1993): 88–91.

The growth of computer technology has drawbacks. Computer crime, for instance, has gained much attention in recent years. People have used access to computer records to steal money and tamper with records in business firms and government agencies. Another serious threat to computer users is the *computer virus,* a computer program that copies itself endlessly to other programs and destroys stored data in the process. One virus spread across the Internet and paralyzed about 6,000 computers in businesses, universities, and government laboratories. A number of software programs now exist to detect and combat viruses. Experts estimate that yearly damage from computer crime in the United States runs anywhere from $500 million to $5 billion. Some suspect it is much higher because only a small percentage of computer crimes are reported and fewer still are prosecuted. According to the National Computer Security Association, a company's own employees are guilty of 25 percent of the computer abuse that occurs in the United States. This figure ranks behind only human error.[22]

Improper use of the computer's tremendous capability to compile information can violate people's right to privacy. Some businesses have been accused of keeping large data files on individuals and then releasing the data unethically. For example, firms sometimes sell their customer database to others who may use it to solicit business. Selling customer lists has led to an increase

Exhibit 22.5
An Example of Where the Information Industry Is Heading

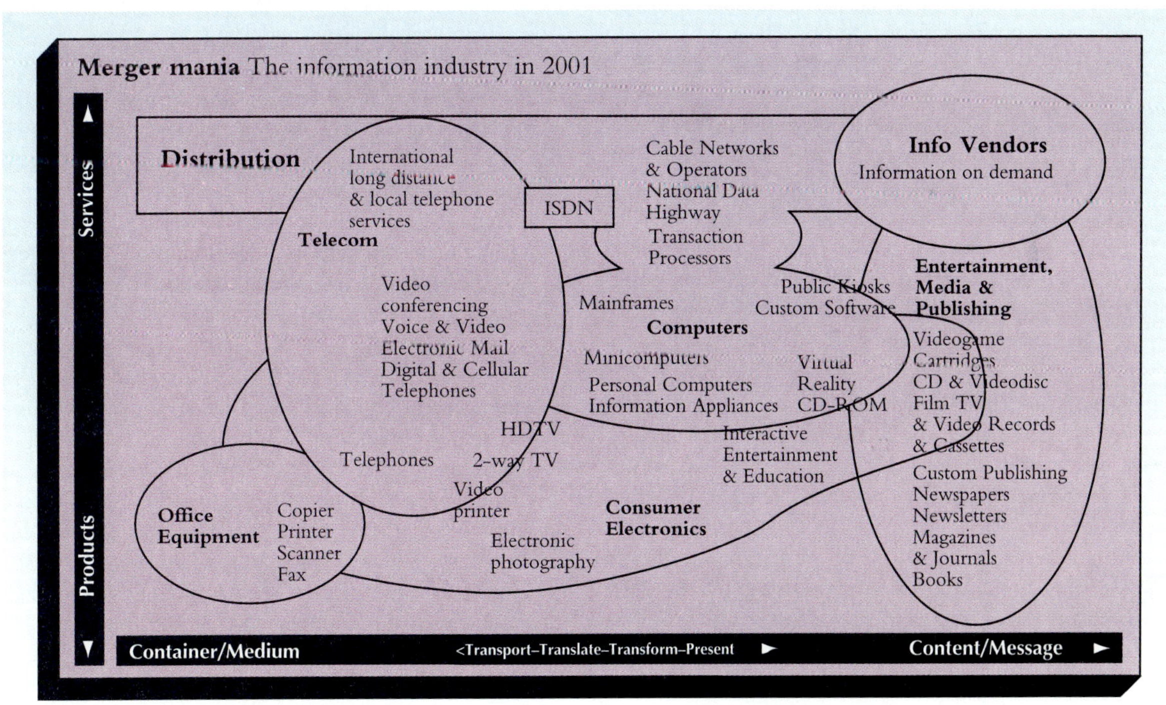

Source: "The Computer Industry Survey," *The Economist* (February 27, 1993).

in junk mail and telephone solicitations. In many cases, computers actually make telephone calls and play recordings to try to sell products or solicit donations.

Computers have become a major part of our lives. Without them, we would have fewer of the conveniences to which we have grown accustomed. When used properly, computers can increase business efficiency, assist managers in decision making, and even save lives. Computers will continue to play an increasing role in the world of business and in society, as Exhibit 22.5 illustrates.

SUMMARY OF LEARNING OBJECTIVES

1. ***Explain why business managers need computers in this age of information.*** Managers today have access to more statistics, facts, and predictions than ever before. Computers enable businesses to convert all these data into useful information. With computers readily available and affordable, business firms are taking advantage of their capabilities and becoming increasingly dependent on them.

2. ***Trace the evolution of computers.*** Through an evolution of five generations, computers have become smaller, faster, less costly, and capable of more functions and greater storage. The first generation consisted of enormous computers operating with vacuum tubes. The second was marked by transistors. The third began with integrated circuits. The fourth generation resulted from large-scale integrated (LSI) circuits contained on tiny superchips. The fifth and current generation is developing through very large-scale integration (VLSI) and the study of artificial intelligence.

3. ***Identify the different types of computers and the components common to all.*** Three different types of computers can meet the needs and resources of firms. The largest and fastest, *mainframe,* are also the most expensive. *Minicomputers* are smaller, somewhat slower, less costly versions of the mainframe. *Microcomputers,* which include a display screen and keyboard, are adaptable, affordable, and adequate for use in homes and businesses. All computers consist of physical devices called *hardware,* including an input device, central processing unit (CPU), and output device. *Software,* sets of instructions called computer programs, is needed to tell the computer exactly what to do.

4. ***Outline the capabilities of computers.*** Computers possess vast capabilities to help users perform many functions with accuracy, speed, and efficiency. Computers excel in word processing, spreadsheets, graphics, and desktop publishing. Businesses commonly use computers for payroll, record keeping, inventory control, scheduling, order processing, electronic mail, and relationship marketing.

5. ***Define management information system (MIS) and explain how an MIS is used.*** A management information system is a combination of computers and procedures for providing regular, timely information that managers use in making decisions. Through an MIS, a firm can collect data from internal and external sources, store and process data, and present information in a form useful to managers.

6. ***List trends in computer development and use and in management information systems.*** The continuing information explosion will prompt business firms to make even greater use of computers and management information systems. Computers will become faster, smaller, and more portable; management information systems will become increasingly sophisticated to further aid decision making. As more and more personal computers enter homes, they will increase in importance for personal and family use as well as for work. Along with the growth of computers has come a trend toward more computer crime, including invasion of privacy.

KEY TERMS

Data
Information
Computer
Transistor
Integrated Circuit
Large-Scale Integrated (LSI) Circuit
Very Large-Scale Integration (VLSI)
Artificial Intelligence
Mainframe
Supercomputer
Minicomputer
Microcomputer
Hardware
Input Device
Central Processing Unit (CPU)
Main Memory
Arithmetic-Logic Unit
Control Unit
Output Device
Software
Computer Program
Word Processing
Spreadsheets
Desktop Publishing
Electronic Mail
Management Information System (MIS)
Database
Data Processing
Database Management System (DBMS)
Computer Network
Local Area Network (LAN)
Decision Support System (DSS)
Executive Information System (EIS)
Expert System

QUESTIONS FOR DISCUSSION AND REVIEW

1. The abundance of information can be beneficial to managers who are trying to make decisions. Is it possible to have too much information? Why or why not?

2. Through the evolution of five generations of development computers have become more powerful and smaller. What is the sixth generation likely to hold?

3. There has been substantial debate by those who develop systems as to which should be developed first, hardware or software. What is your opinion? Support your opinion.

4. There are a number of security concerns involved with any computerized system. Discuss some of these concerns.

5. In terms of computers, small businesses have different needs than large corporations. What are some applications that small businesses might find for computers?

6. Management information systems provide *all types* of information that managers may need for decision making, while accounting information systems provide *financial* information for every category of decision maker. Is there any overlap in the contents of these two information systems? Explain.

7. The systems development life cycle (SDLC) is a blueprint for helping firms develop effective systems. What characteristics might be included in an effective system? Discuss.

8. What advantages does a firm gain by utilizing a computer network? Can you think of any disadvantages? Explain.

9. Expert systems can provide assistance in making decisions by simulating the decision processes of experts. Can you think of ways that expert systems could be developed to help in medicine? Insurance? Banking? Manufacturing? Others? Discuss.

10. The benefits of the computer's ability to process data is difficult to measure, but there are some potential hazards. What are they?

CASE 22.1

Software: Over-the-Counter or Custom Designed?

An abundance of software has been developed in recent years for virtually all computers, ranging from large mainframes to desktop and laptop microcomputers. Such a wide choice presents a dilemma for business firms: Which type is better for the business, over-the-counter products purchased through local computer stores or software specifically developed for the firm's needs? The answer to this difficult question depends on the firm's size, budget, computer knowledge, and needs.

According to the manufacturer of Marketbase, a database management system, over-the-counter products have several advantages. First, the product is available immediately, without the wait for custom software to be designed. In many instances, managers can solve problems right away rather than waiting until it may be too late. Second, ready-made software costs less than the custom-designed variety. Companies are currently spending $10 billion a year for over-the-counter software packages and an additional $20 billion on customized software. The market for customized software is quite lucrative.

Many companies have used commercial software successfully. Consumer products companies often use software developed by A.C. Nielsen. It tracks sales by regions and highlights important changes, analyzing data collected monthly from 3,000 supermarkets. For instance, it can provide data on how many 32-ounce jars of Prego spaghetti sauce with mushrooms were sold in a specific store during a given week. Information Resources has developed software that summarizes important trends in sales data collected monthly from 2,400 supermarkets. Firms in diverse industries find other software products such as Lotus® and dBASE® useful for a variety of business applications, including accounting and inventory control.

The major drawback to over-the-counter software is that these programs assume all businesses are basically the same. Some firms with unique requirements or problems will not find suitable software available. In other cases, firms use a less-than-ideal commercial software program and end up compromising some aspect of their business. Many firms, especially those with larger computer systems, prefer tailor-made software.

Questions for Discussion

1. What considerations are necessary in deciding whether to purchase or design software? Discuss.
2. Another possible option for software is to purchase a package over-the-counter and then have it tailored for use in a particular business. What are the pros and cons of using this type of software? Explain.
3. Why would a firm design its own software?

Source: Adapted from "Software Engineering: Made to Measure," *The Economist* (January 23, 1993): 79; Jeffrey Rothfeder, Jim Bartimo, Lois Therrien, and Richard Brandt, "How Software Is Making Food Sales a Piece of Cake," *Business Week* (July 2, 1990): 54–55; Michael Finley, "Tailor-Made or Off-the-Shelf," *Marketing News* (April 24, 1989): 1–2; Keith H. Hammonds, Deidre A. Depke, and Richard Brandt, "Software: It's a New Game," *Business Week* (June 4, 1990): 102–106.

CASE 22.2

United States Invasion of the Japanese Personal Computer Market

While the United States has dominated the worldwide personal computer (PC) market, U.S. computer manufacturers have not been able to penetrate the Japanese market. In 1992 Japan had a $6 billion PC market, but U.S. manufacturers only accounted for 15 percent of total sales. Apple Computer led the way with sales of 2.2 million PCs, capturing approximately 8.3 percent of the market and third place among sales in Japan. Conversely, the world's largest computer company, IBM, and IBM-compatible manufacturers Compaq and Dell together have only accounted for 6 percent of PC sales.

A combination of high prices and incompatibility of PC equipment have created a sluggish Japanese market. PC sales worldwide rose by double-digit levels in recent years, while Japanese sales actually decreased. The number of PCs per capita in Japan is half that of the United States, and technological developments have been slow. Perhaps the major problem has been incompatibility. Japanese computers must be able to manage the Japanese alphabet, the *kanji,* which is an alphabet of symbols, not letters as in the western alphabet. The problem lies in designing computers and operating systems that are powerful enough to handle *kanji* characters.

Improvements are being made. Microsoft developed a new version of Windows that gives IBM-compatible computers more power. An earlier version of Windows sold only 440,000 copies in Japan because it was unable to handle *kanji* characters. The newer version, however, Windows 3.1J, has corrected this flaw and seems to be a success. Within two days, 65,000 orders for the new operating system were taken and Microsoft expected to sell over a million copies of the operating system its first year.

The introduction of this new operating system is likely to increase the demand for PCs manufactured in the United States. IBM alone expects *PC sales* in Japan to top the 200,000 unit level, which would be an improvement of 34 percent over its 1992 sales. This improvement is expected despite competition from United States manufacturers such as Dell and Compaq who produce IBM-compatible machines. Dell has contracted with Japanese retailers in an effort to make its machines more readily available. The company has also opened toll-free order lines which have been busy since the day they opened. Apple Computer, which does not produce an IBM-compatible PC, has set as a goal to double annual sales to $1 billion by 1995.

Hardware manufacturers are not the only businesses benefiting from this U.S. invasion of the Japanese PC market. American software companies are also beginning to flood into Japan. The number of companies now operating in Japan is 86, up 50 percent from 1992. This influx of software manufacturers is due to the large expectations for Windows in Japan. Many U.S. software companies are also competing with their Japanese counterparts by slashing prices. Microsoft and Lotus have cut prices and other software manufacturers are expected to follow.

Japanese computer manufacturers have answered the bell by cutting prices and developing new technology to try to ward off this American onslaught. It is doubtful whether the market share which the Japanese once held will ever be seen again. Many feel that the introduction of competition from U.S. manufacturers into the Japanese PC market has made the market better. It will be interesting to see how this competition will affect the market.

Questions for Discussion

1. Discuss the advantages and disadvantages to Japan of introducing competition into the Japanese PC marketplace.
2. What are Japanese PC manufacturers likely to do to combat the invasion of U.S. personal computers in the Japanese marketplace? Discuss.
3. Do you feel with the breakthrough of U.S. personal computers and software, such as Windows and Lotus, into the Japanese market that this will open the door for future computer technology? Explain.

Source: Adapted from Brenton R. Schneider, "U.S. PCs Invade Japan," *Fortune* (July 12, 1993): 68–73.

BUSINESS APPLICATION

Information Systems Applications

For this class assignment students will work in pairs. Students are asked to identify computerized information systems applications in particular businesses. The instructor should assign different types of retail (e.g., clothing, sporting goods, hardware, toy, and grocery), manufacturing (e.g., automobiles, chemicals, plastics, pharmaceuticals, and office equipment), and service (e.g., law firm, hospital, bank, hotel, and insurance company) companies to the pairs of students.

Students should be given approximately 15 minutes to record different examples of computerized applications that may be used in their particular business. Remember first to focus on the main goal of the organization in order to identify applications for the business.

As the students share their applications, the instructor will record the information on the blackboard for further discussion. Recording the information on the blackboard will help summarize the different kinds of applications that may be used in a particular line of business.

EXPERIENTIAL EXERCISE

Using Information Systems in Business Operations

This project entails learning about information systems actually in use in real-world businesses. After students are placed into groups of 5-6, each group should identify and interview the person or people in charge of a computerized information system in a local business (i.e., retailing, manufacturing, or service).

Here is a list of sample questions concerning information systems that might be used in the interview:

1. Who are the users of the information produced by the information system?
2. What type of hardware does the information system consist of? Who was the vendor? Were there any problems with the selection of the hardware?
3. What type of software does the information system consist of? Who was the vendor? Were there any problems with the selection of the software?
4. What were the steps involved in developing the information system? Did the company use the systems development life cycle (SDLC)? Why or why not? Were there any problems with the implementation of the information system?
5. For what types of applications is the information system used?
6. Does the information system employ networks? In what capacity?
7. Do decision support systems help managers make decisions? How?
8. What security features are in place to protect the information system?
9. What types of new technology are currently employed in the information system?
10. In terms of information requirements, what does the future hold?

Do not feel that these are the only questions that need to be asked. These questions are meant to serve as a starting point for group members.

Once the interview has been completed, the group should use the notes taken during the interview to prepare a presentation of 10-15 minutes (suggested) for the class.

NOTES

1. Ricard Teitelbaum, "Hats Off! It Was a Heck of a Year," *Fortune* (April 18, 1994): 212; John A. Young, "Quality Lessons from Hewlett-Packard," *Manufacturing Engineering* (January 1992): 14, 16.
2. Floyd Kemske, "Brains Will Replace BTUs," *Information Center* (June 1990): 22–24.
3. "Soldiering into the Modern Computer Era, 1943," *The Wall Street Journal* (June 16, 1989): B1.
4. "Mainframe Vendors Scramble to Respond," *Datamation* (January 1, 1993): 68.
5. John W. Verity, "Supercomputers: Brute Strength—and a Sensitive Issue," *Business Week* (April 30, 1990): 83.
6. Lawrence J. Magid, "After 10 Years, PCs Continue to Evolve," *Los Angeles Times* (August 8, 1991): D3.
7. James Kim, "PC Makers Push Portables as Performance Alternatives," *USA Today* (August 8, 1994): B1.
8. Paul M. Eng, "The Learning Revolution," *Business Week* (February 28, 1994): 81.
9. "Apple's Improved MessagePad," *Byte* (May 1995): 131.
10. Myron Magnet, "Good News for the Service Economy," *Fortune* (May 3, 1993): 49.
11. Edward Baig, "Ready to Cruise Internet?" *Business Week* (March 28, 1994): 180–181.
12. Paul Desmond, "Car Wash King Oversees Empire via Integrated Network," *Network World* (November 14, 1990): 58–61.
13. Baig, "Internet"
14. Richard A. Shafter, "Marconi Lives," *Forbes* (February 28, 1994): 107.
15. Sandy Butters and Sean Eom, "Decision Support Systems in the Healthcare Industry," *Journal of Systems Management* (June 1992): 28–31.
16. Butters and Eom, "Decision Support Systems"; Christopher Elias, "An 'Executive' Newcomer Takes Its Place in the Office," *Insight* (July 11, 1988): 38–40.
17. Michael W. Miller, "Computers May Get Vast Ability to Blend Data, Images, and Sound," *The Wall Street Journal* (June 7, 1989): A1, A4.
18. Kathleen K. Wiegner, "Speed Demons," *Forbes* (January 9, 1989): 134–137.
19. Rebecca Gallun, Cynthia D. Heagy, and Howard C. Lindsey, "How CPAs Use Computers," *Journal of Accountancy* (January 1993): 39–40.
20. Gene Bylinsky, "At Last! Computers You Can Talk To," *Fortune* (May 3, 1993): 88–91.
21. Stephen R. McDuffie, Steven M. Flory, and Neil J. Humphreys, "Using Expert Systems to Expand Your Accounting Practice," *Massachusetts CPA Review* (Summer 1993): 11–13.
22. Doug Harper, "Computer Crime May Be Close to Home," *Industrial Distribution* (February 1994): 41; Gayle Hanson, "Computer Users Pack a Keypunch in a High Tech World of Crime," *Insight* (April 15, 1991): 8–16.

GLOSSARY

A

Absolute Advantage When a country can produce a product more efficiently than any other nation.

Account Record of all transactions affecting a particular financial statement element.

Accounting The process of identifying, measuring, and communicating economic information to permit informed decisions by users of the information.

Accounting Cycle The steps—analyzing, recording, posting, and preparing reports—by which the results of business transactions are communicated.

Accounting Equation Assets = Liabilities + Owners' Equity, indicating a company's financial position at any point in time.

Accounts Receivable Turnover The number of times per year that the average accounts receivable is collected; computed by dividing net sales by average net accounts receivable.

Activity Ratio Measure of how efficiently assets are being used to generate revenues.

Actuary An insurance employee who predicts the likelihood of future events based on their occurrence in the past.

Administered VMS A marketing channel in which independent intermediaries use informal coordination; usually dominated by one channel organization.

Administrative Law Regulation affecting business, passed by state and federal administrative agencies.

Advertising A paid form of nonpersonal communication to a target audience through a mass medium such as television, newspapers, or magazines.

Advertising Media Advertising outlets, including newspapers, television, direct mail, radio, magazines, and outdoor displays.

Affirmative Action Program Program begun and carried out by a business to increase the number of women, minorities, and handicapped individuals throughout the organization.

AFL-CIO The merged body of the American Federation of Labor (craft union members) and the Congress of Industrial Organizations (industrial union members).

Agency A legal relationship between two parties who agree that the agent will act on behalf of the principal.

Agency Shop A company where all employees pay union dues, whether or not they are union members.

Agent Wholesaler hired by a buyer or seller on a permanent basis and paid commissions.

Allocation The process of choosing how resources will be used to meet a society's needs and wants; includes the distribution of products to consumers.

Americans with Disabilities Act (ADA) Comprehensive antidiscrimination law, passed in 1990, aimed at integrating the disabled into the American work force; prohibits all employers from discriminating against disabled employees or applicants.

Arbitrator Third party to a labor dispute who makes the final, binding decision about some disputed issue.

Arithmetic-Logic Unit The part of a computer's central processing unit that performs computations.

Artificial Intelligence A developing technology that allows computers to solve problems involving imagination, abstract reasoning, and common sense.

Assembly Line A production line made up of workers who each perform one specific task as the product moves past, toward completion.

Asset Anything of value owned by the business and used in its operation.

Atmosphere The design of a store's physical space.

Audit A CPA's examinations of a company's financial statements to determine the fairness of the statements in accordance with generally accepted accounting principles.

Autocratic Leadership A type of close supervision in which the manager delegates as little authority as possible.

Automated Clearinghouse (ACH) An automated clearinghouse allows payments or withdrawals to and from a bank account by magnetic computer tape.

Automated Teller Machine (ATM) Machine that dispenses cash from a customer's account, accepts deposits to the account, or performs other banking functions.

B

Balance of Payments The total flow of money into and out of a country.

Balance of Trade The difference (in dollars) between the amount a country exports and the amount it imports.

Balance Sheet A financial statement that indicates a firm's financial position at a particular point in time; reflects a firm's solvency, or its ability to pay its debts as they come due. Also called the statement of financial position.

Bear Market A market state in which stock values are generally declining and investors are generally pessimistic.

Behavior Modification Application of learning principles called operant conditioning.

Benefits Forms of indirect compensation that are financial in nature; examples include health insurance and pension fund contributions.

Blue-Chip Stock Stock issued by large, well-capitalized companies that consistently pay dividends.

Blue-Sky Laws State laws that prevent corporations from issuing worthless securities; also require stockbrokers to be licensed and securities to be registered.

Bond An agreement between a firm and an investor with specific terms spelled out in an indenture.

Book Value The value of common stock relative to the value of the company.

Boycott A bargaining tactic in which the union refuses to do business with a firm or attempts to get people or other organizations to refuse to deal with the firm.

Brand A name, sign, symbol, or design a company uses to distinguish its product from others.

Brand Name The part of a product's brand that can be spoken.

Breach of Contract The failure of one party to live up to a contractual agreement.

Breakeven Analysis A determination of how many product units must be sold at various prices for a firm to recover costs and begin making a profit.

Breakeven Quality The point at which the cost of making a product equals the revenue made from selling the product.

Broker Wholesaler who brings together buyers and sellers on a temporary basis.

Bull Market A market state in which stock values are generally rising and investors are generally optimistic.

Business The exchange of goods, services, or money for mutual benefit or profit.

Business Ethics The evaluation of business activities and behavior as right or wrong.

Business Representative A union official who negotiates and administers the labor agreement and settles contract problems.

Business Trust A business used to hold securities for investors; allows the transfer of legal title to a property of one person for the use and benefit of another.

Business-Interruption Insurance Covers the ongoing expenses of a business forced by disaster to shut down temporarily.

C

Call Option An option to buy stock shares at a specified price and sell at market price.

Cancellation Provision The contract provision giving a franchisor the power to cancel an arrangement with a franchisee.

Capital Budgeting The budgeting of funds for future, generally major, investments of the firm's cash; investments are generally ranked on the basis of the return potential.

Capital Resources Goods produced for the purpose of making other types of goods and services; includes current assets (short-lived) and fixed capital (long-lived).

Capitalism A type of economic system characterized by private ownership of capital, competition among businesses seeking a profit, and consumer's freedom of choice.

Catalog Showroom A form of warehouse showroom where customers select products from catalogs sent to customers' homes or available in the store.

Central Processing Unit (CPU) The electronic hardware that performs the computer operations and controls the entire system.

Centralized Business An organization in which all, or nearly all, authority to make decisions is retained by a small group of managers.

Certificate of Deposit (CD) Interest-bearing note issued by a commercial bank or brokerage firm.

Chain of Command The channel in which communication, coordination, and control flow through the various levels of management to subordinates.

Charter A state's written agreement giving a corporation the right to operate as a business.

Civil Rights Act of 1964 An act that makes various forms of discrimination illegal. Title VII of the act spells out the forms of illegal discrimination.

Civil Rights Act of 1991 Increases the scope of Title VII of the Civil Rights Act of 1964. Victims are now entitled to jury trial and punitive damages.

Closed Shop A company that hires only workers who are members of the union; illegal under the Taft-Hartley Act.

CMA Designation for accountants who pass a rigorous examination, have accounting experience, and are licensed by the state; may be public or private accountants but cannot conduct audits of corporate financial statements.

Code of Ethics A statement spelling out exactly what an organization considers ethical behavior.

Collective Bargaining Negotiation of a labor contract by union and management.

Commercial Bank A profit-making institution that holds the deposits of individuals and businesses in checking and savings accounts and then uses these funds to make loans.

Commercial Paper A short-term loan to a major corporation with a high credit standing.

Commodities Large-volume items, such as raw materials, precious metals, and agricultural products, in which individuals can invest.

Commodity Exchange An organization that specializes in buying and selling commodities.

Common Law The body of law created by judges through their court decisions.

Common Stock Stock that confers voting rights but not preferential rights of dividends or claims against the assets of the firm.

Comparable Worth The concept of equal pay for jobs that require similar levels of skills, training, and experience.

Comparative Advantage When a country can produce one product more efficiently and at a lower cost than other products, in comparison to other nations.

Competition-Oriented Pricing A method whereby a firm sets prices on the basis of its competitors' prices rather than its own costs and revenues.

Computer An electronic device used to input, store, and process data and to output them as useful information.

Computer Network A collection of computers connected so that they can function individually and communicate with each other.

Computer Program A detailed set of instructions written in a computer language.

Computer-Aided Design (CAD) The use of computers to draw plans for a product.

Computer-Aided Engineering (CAE) The use of computers to plan engineering processes and test designs.

Computer-Aided Manufacturing (CAM) The use of computers to guide or control the actual production of goods.

Conceptual Skills The ability to organize and integrate information to better understand the organization as a whole.

Conglomerate Merger A merger involving firms selling goods in unrelated markets.

Consumer A person who purchases a good or service for personal use.

Consumer Buying Behavior The decisions and actions of individuals who purchase products for personal use.

Consumer Market People who purchase products for personal use.

Consumer Product A good or service used for personal or family consumption.

Consumer Sales Promotion Activities—including coupons, rebates, samples, gifts, premiums, trading stamps, contests, and sweepstakes—directed to consumers to increase sales.

Consumerism Activities of individuals, groups, and organizations aimed at protecting consumer rights.

Contest A sales promotion method in which consumers compete for prizes on the basis of some skill.

Contract A legally enforceable, voluntary agreement between two or more parties.

Contractual VMS A marketing channel in which intermediaries are independent but have relationships formalized through legal agreements.

Control Unit The part of a computer's central processing unit that guides the operations of the computer.

Controlling The management function of checking to determine whether employees are following plans and progress is being made, and of taking action to reduce discrepancies.

Convenience Product A frequently purchased, inexpensive item that buyers spend little effort to find and purchase.

Convenience Store Small retail store with a convenient location and open for long hours.

Cooperative (Co-op) An organization in which people collectively own and operate a business in order to compete with bigger competitors.

Copyright Protection of an individual's exclusive right to publish and sell original written materials.

Corporate VMS A marketing channel in which one organization owns successive stages of the channel.

Corporation A business that is a legal entity separate from its owners.

Cost-Oriented Pricing A method whereby a firm determines a product's total cost, then adds a markup to that cost to achieve the desired profit margin.

Countertrading Bartering agreements between two or more countries.

Coupon A sales promotion technique that reduces the price of a product by a stated amount at the time of purchase.

CPA Designation for accountants who pass a rigorous examination, have accounting experience, and are licensed by the state; may be public or private accountants; qualified to conduct audits of companies' financial statement.

Craft Union A union in which all members belong to one craft or to a closely related group of occupations.

Credit An entry that records a decrease in an asset, an increase in a liability, or an increase in owners' equity; recorded on the right side of a journal or ledger entry.

Credit Unions Member-owned savings cooperatives, normally sponsored by a union, company, or professional or religious group; typically concentrate on small, short-term consumer loans.

Cultural Diversity Differences between and within cultures.

Currency The coins and paper money spent to purchase things. Cashier's checks, money orders, and traveler's checks are also considered currency.

Current Assets Cash plus items that can or will be converted to cash and use within one year.

Current Liabilities Financial obligations of a firm that will be repaid within one year.

Current Ratio The measure of a firm's ability to pay its current liabilities from its current assets; computed by dividing current assets by current liabilities.

D

Data Facts, figures, and statistics concerning people, objects, events, and ideas.

Data Processing Mechanically transferring raw data into some specific form of information.

Database An integrated collection of data stored in one place for easy access and information processing.

Database Management Systems (DBMS) Computer software that helps firms manage various data files.

Debit An entry that records an increase in assets, a decrease in liabilities, or a decrease in owners' equity; recorded on the left side of a journal or ledger entry.

Debit Card A plastic card, similar to a credit card, that deducts funds directly from the customer's account rather than creating a loan.

Debt Capital Funds obtained through borrowing.

Debt Ratio Measure of a company's ability to pay its long-term debts.

Debt to Equity Ratio A measure of a firm's leverage; computed by dividing total debt by owners' equity.

Decentralized Business An organization in which a significant amount of the authority to make decisions is delegated to lower-level managers.

Decertification The process, guided by the NLRB, that results in voting out a union that has been representing employees.

Decision Support System (DSS) A system that enables managers to instantly access information on past and current performance.

Deductible The amount of loss that the insured agrees to cover before insurance coverage begins.

Default Failure to pay the interest on a debt instrument.

Delegation Giving an employee at a lower level in the organization the responsibility for a given task as well as the authority to carry it out.

Demand The quantity of a product that consumers will purchase at various prices.

Demand Deposits Bank accounts against which an account holder can write checks, withdrawing money immediately and without prior notice.

Demand-Oriented Pricing A method based on the level of demand for the product.

Democratic Leadership A type of general supervision in which the manager consults with subordinates about job-related issues.

Department Store A large retailer offering a wide product mix, organized into separate departments and offering a full line of service.

Depreciation Procedures for spreading the cost of a plant asset out over the course of its useful life.

Deregulation The process of reducing government involvement in the regulation of business, by eliminating legal restraints on competition.

Desktop Publishing Producing printed materials using computer software that can do page layouts and formats, insert graphics, and print with high quality.

Direct Compensation An employee's base pay (wages and salary) and performance-based pay (incentives).

Direct Marketing Nonstore retailing that uses nonpersonal media to introduce products to consumers, who then purchase the products by mail, telephone, or computer.

Direct Ownership The purchase of one or more business operations in a foreign country.

Directing The management function of initiating action; issuing directives, assignments, and instructions.

Discount Rate The rate of interest charged to member banks when they borrow money from the Fed.

Discount Store A retailer offering a wide variety of general merchandise at low prices.

Division of Labor A principle of organization that a job can be performed more efficiently if the jobholder is allowed to specialize.

Domestic Corporation An enterprise organized under the laws of one state or country and doing business within that state or country.

Double Taxation Taxing a corporate owner's money twice by taxing it as income of a corporation and as dividends of the individual owner.

Double-Entry Bookkeeping A method of recording business transactions in which offsetting debits and credits keep the accounting equation in balance.

Downsizing Cutting out entire layers of management in the organization.

Dumping Selling surplus products in a foreign country at a lower price than in the country of origin.

E

Economic Community An organization that facilitates the movement of products among member nations through the creation of common economic policies.

Economic System The accepted process by which labor, capital, and natural resources are organized to produce and distribute goods and services in a society.

Economics The study of how a society chooses to use scarce resources to produce goods and services and to distribute them to people for consumption.

Electronic Funds Transfer (EFT) The transfer of funds by means of an electronic terminal, telephone, computer, or magnetic tape that orders a bank or other financial institution to debit or credit an account.

Electronic Mail A computer network used to relay messages from one user to another instantly.

Embargo A total ban on certain imports and exports.

Endorsement A person's signature on the back of a negotiable instrument, making it transferable.

Entrepreneur A person who takes the risks necessary to organize and manage a business and receives the financial profits and nonmonetary rewards.

Equal Employment Opportunity Act of 1972 A law that has specific provisions about equal opportunities for employment; provided for the establishment of Equal Employment Opportunity Commission.

Equal Employment Opportunity Commission (EEOC) A federal agency whose purpose is to increase job opportunities for women and minorities.

Equity Capital Funds provided in exchange for some ownership in the firm.

Esteem Need The need for self-respect and respect from others.

Ethics The principles of behavior that distinguish between right and wrong.

Exchange The process by which parties provide something of value to one another to satisfy the needs of each.

Exchange Controls Restrictions on the amount of a certain currency that can be bought or sold in a nation.

Exchange Rate The rate at which one country's currency can be exchanged for that of another country.

Exclusive Distribution Market coverage in which one outlet is used in a specific geographic area for distributing a product.

Exclusive Handling A form of control in which a franchisor requires the franchisee to purchase only supplies approved by the franchisor.

Executive Information System (EIS) A user-friendly decision support system designed for executives that requires little computer knowledge and provides instant high-quality displays.

Expenses Costs incurred to produce revenues.

Expert System Computer software that imitates human thinking.

Exporting Selling domestic-made goods in another country.

Express Warranty Oral or written assurances made by the seller regarding a product.

Extrinsic Reward Reward external to the work itself and administered by someone else, such as a manager.

F

Factoring The sale of accounts receivable to a bank or other lender, generally at a considerable discount.

Federal Reserve System The 12 Federal Reserve Banks that serve as the central bank of the United States. Generally referred to as the Fed.

Finance The study of money within the firm; the business function responsible for finding funds, managing them, and determining their best use.

Finance Companies Institutions that offer short-term loans, typically at a higher rate, to businesses and individuals unable to obtain loans elsewhere.

Financial Futures A future that requires the purchaser to buy or sell a specific financial instrument.

Financial Statement Document presenting a company's financial position, results of operations, and cash flow during a stated period of time.

Fixed Exchange Rate An unvarying exchange rate set by government policy.

Flexible Manufacturing Systems (FMS) The use of computers to change from one production process to another in order to produce different goods.

Float The amount of money not yet withdrawn from the company's checking account even though checks have been written.

Floating Exchange Rate An exchange rate that fluctuates with market conditions.

Foreign Corporation A business incorporated in one state or country and doing business in another state or country.

Formal Authority The right to give orders.

Formal Organization The management-designed, official structure of the business.

Franchise The right to use a specific business name (Pizza Hut, Subway, H & R Block, Blockbuster, Masterworks International) and sell its goods or services in a specific city, region, or country.

Free Enterprise A system in which private businesses are able to start and do business competitively to earn profits, with a minimal degree of government regulation.

Free Sample A free package or container of a product given as a sales promotion technique.

Functional Structure A structure in which each unit or department has a different set of activities and responsibilities.

G

GATT An international organization formed to reduce or eliminate tariffs and other barriers to international trade.

General and Administrative Expenses Costs incurred in the overall management of the business.

General Ledger A book or computer file summarizing all accounts of the business.

General Partnership A partnership in which at least one partner has unlimited liability; a general partner has authority to act and make binding decisions as an owner.

Global Market The entire world viewed as a large market.

Goal A broadly stated guideline that an organization or an individual is attempting to achieve.

Goal Setting The process of identifying specific levels of performance to be achieved in a certain time frame.

Green Marketing Efforts by firms to move beyond the law to provide environmentally sound goods and services in areas ranging from conservation to pollution control.

Grievance Complaint made by an employee or the union about a job, person, or condition that creates dissatisfaction or discomfort.

Gross Domestic Product (GDP) A measure of the economic activity within the physical borders of a country.

H

Hardware The physical devices that make up a computer system.

Hawthorne Studies A series of experiments that found that work groups significantly affected the way workers behave and perform.

Health Maintenance Organization (HMO) An organization that provides extensive medical care and services for members, based on a prepared monthly fee.

Home-Based Business Business in which an individual works or conducts activities out of the home. About 22 percent of the total work force now works out of the home.

Horizontal Merger A merger involving competitive firms in the same market.

Hot-Cargo Agreement A boycott agreement between management and union that workers may avoid working with materials that come from employers that have been struck by a union.

Human Relations Skills The ability to relate and interact with subordinates, peers, superiors, and customers or clients.

Human Resource Management (HRM) The process of acquiring, retaining, terminating, developing, and properly using the human resources in an organization.

Human Resource Planning The steps taken in estimating the size and makeup of the future work force.

Humanistic Philosophy A set of moral principles focusing on individual rights and values.

Hygiene Factor External characteristic essential to avoiding job dissatisfaction.

I

IMF An international financial organization that lends money to countries to conduct international trade.

Immigration Reform and Control Act (IRCA) A law, passed in 1986, that places a major responsibility on employers to stop the flow of illegal immigrants into the United States by not employing unauthorized aliens.

Implied Warranty Warranty legally imposed on the seller; ensures that the seller owns the products and that they will serve the purpose for which they are sold.

Import Tariff A duty, or tax, levied against goods brought into a country.

Importing Purchasing goods made in another country.

In-Home Selling Nonstore retailing activities that involve personal contacts with consumers in their homes.

Income Statement A financial statement showing a firm's revenues, expenses, and net income over a period of time; indicates profitability, the ability to generate income. Also called earnings statement or statement of profit and loss.

Incubator A facility in which fledgling businesses can share space, costs, services, and information while their firms grow and become strong.

Indirect Compensation Federally required and state-mandated protection programs, private protection programs, paid leave, and miscellaneous benefits.

Industrial Market Those who purchase products to use in the production of other products or to resell.

Industrial Product A good or service used by an organization in producing other goods or services or in carrying out its operations.

Industrial Union A union in which all members are employed in a company or industry, regardless of occupation.

Informal Organization The network of personal and social relationships that emerges when people work together.

Information Data with meaning attached.

Injunction Court order that prohibits the defendant from engaging in certain activities, such as striking.

Input Device The hardware used to enter data into and make requests of the computer.

Insider Trading The practice of buying and selling stock on the basis of information gained through positions or contacts with others that is not available to other investors or the general public.

Institutional Advertising Advertising used to build goodwill and create a favorable public image.

Insurable Risk A risk for which an acceptable level of loss can be calculated and that meets the requirements set by the insurer.

Insurance A written contract that transfers the risk of loss from the insured to the insurer.

Intangible Personal Property Property represented by a document or other written statement.

Integrated Circuit Small silicon chip containing dozens of tiny transistors and connections; used in third-generation computers.

Intensive Distribution Market coverage in which all available outlets are used for distributing a product.

International Business The performance of business activities across national boundaries.

Intrapreneur An entrepreneurial person employed by a corporation and encouraged to be innovative and creative.

Intrinsic Reward A sense of gratification directly related to performing the job.

Inventory Management The process of developing and maintaining stocks of products that customers need and want.

Investment Banker A financial specialist who handles the sale of new stock or bond offers.

J

Job Analysis The process of determining the tasks that make up a job and the skills, abilities, and responsibilities needed to perform the job.

Job Description A written statement that furnishes information about a job's duties, technology, conditions, and hazards; based on data from the job analysis.

Job Enrichment A motivational technique that involves incorporating variety, feedback, and autonomy in the job.

Job Evaluation System A process by which the relative values of jobs within the organization are determined.

Job Specification A written statement of the human qualifications, education, and experience needed to perform a job.

Journal A book or computer file in which business transactions are recorded chronologically.

Junk Bond A low-grade bond that carries a very high risk.

Jurisdiction The right and power of a court to interpret and apply laws and make binding decisions.

Just-in-Time A system for decreasing inventory by using suppliers who agree to deliver the fewest possible items at the latest possible moment to keep production moving smoothly.

Just-In-Time Inventory An inventory management technique whereby firms maintain smaller inventories by ordering more often and in smaller quantities, just in time for production.

K

Knights of Labor The first union federation that attracted members from local unions from all crafts and occupational areas.

L

Labeling The display of important information on a product package.

Labor Resources The human talent, skills, and competence available in a nation.

Labor Union Organization of employees who join together to protect, maintain, and improve their economic, social, and political power and well-being.

Laissez-Faire Leadership A type of supervision in which the manager avoids power and responsibility by giving assignments and support but staying out of the group's way.

Landrum-Griffin Act A 1959 labor law that requires unions and employees to file financial reports with the secretary of labor and that specifies certain activities to ensure democratic operation of the union.

Large-Scale Integrated (LSI) Circuit Superchip that contains thousands of small transistors; fourth-generation innovation that made personal computers possible.

Law A standard or rule established by a society to govern the behavior of its members.

Law of Large Numbers Uses the probability of a specific loss occurring, the likely cost of that loss, and the number of individuals covered to calculate the premiums charged each insured individual.

Leadership The process of influencing the activities of an individual or group toward accomplishing objectives. Leadership may be autocratic, democratic, or laissez-faire.

Leverage The use of long-term debt to raise needed cash.

Liability Debts owed by a business to its creditors.

Liability Insurance Covers losses from injury to another individual or from damage to other people's property.

Licensing An agreement in which one firm allows another firm to sell its product and use its brand name in return for a commission or royalty.

Limit Order An order to purchase stock only if the price is at or below a specified limit.

Limited Partnership A partnership with at least one general partner, and one or more limited partners who are liable for loss only up to the amount of their investment.

Line Authority Unquestioned, direct authority to make decisions and take action.

Line of Credit A preapproved amount the holder may borrow in whole or in part, provided that the bank has sufficient funds.

Liquidity A measure of how quickly an item can be converted to cash.

Liquidity Ratio Measure of a firm's ability to pay its short-term debts as they come due.

Local Area Network (LAN) A system of telecommunications links that connects all computers in one firm directly, without telephone lines.

Lockout Management pressure tactic that involves denying employees access to their jobs.

Long-Term Liabilities Amounts owed by a business that must be repaid more than one year from the balance sheet date.

M

M1 The first level of money supply measurement; includes the most highly liquid forms of money; currency and demand deposits.

M2 The second level of money supply measurement; includes time deposits and money market accounts in addition to currency and demand deposits.

Macroeconomics The study of inflation, unemployment, business cycles, and growth focusing on the aggregate relationships in a society.

Main Memory The part of the computer central processing unit that stores data and instructions.

Mainframe The largest and fastest type of computer, with the greatest storage capacity.

Maintenance of Membership Agreement Agreement that, although employees do not have to join a union, union members must maintain membership in the union over the length of the contract.

Malpractice Insurance Protects professionals (doctors, lawyers, etc.) from losses due to injury caused by the improper handling of their responsibilities.

Management The application of planning, organizing, staffing, directing, and controlling functions in the most efficient manner possible to accomplish objectives.

Management Development The process of educating and developing selected personnel so that they have the knowledge, skills, attitudes, and understanding needed to manage in future positions.

Management Information System (MIS) A combination of computers and procedures for providing information that managers use in making decisions.

Management Skill The ability to use knowledge, behaviors, and aptitudes to perform a task.

Managerial Hierarchy The levels of management in an organization, typically three distinct levels: executive, middle, and first-line.

Manufacturing The actual processes of making products out of materials and parts. Literally, creating something by the work of one's hands.

Margin Trading Purchasing more stock shares than a given amount of money would buy because a portion of the shares are bought on credit.

Market People with the authority, financial ability, and willingness to purchase a product.

Market Coverage The number of outlets in which a product is sold.

Market Niche A small, somewhat unique part of a market segment.

Market Order An order that authorizes a broker to purchase stock at the current market price.

Market Segment A group of individuals with one or more similar product needs.

Market Segmentation Approach The division of the total market into segments, with a marketing mix directed to one of the segments.

Market Value The price at which a share of common stock is currently selling.

Marketing The process of planning and executing the conception, pricing, promotion, and distribution of ideas, goods, and services to create exchanges that satisfy individual and organizational objectives.

Marketing Channel (Channel of Distribution) A group of interrelated organizations that directs the flow of products to ultimate consumers.

Marketing Concept A managerial philosophy of customer orientation with the goal of achieving long-term success.

Marketing Environment All the forces outside an organization that directly or indirectly influence its marketing activities.

Marketing Intermediary An individual or organization in a marketing channel that provides a link between producers, other channel members, and final consumers of products.

Marketing Mix The combination of four elements—product, price, promotion, and distribution—used to satisfy the needs of the target market.

Marketing Research The systematic gathering, recording, and analyzing of information for guiding marketing decisions.

Marketing Research Process Series of steps consisting of problem definition, research design, data collection, data analysis, interpretation, and conclusions.

Marketing Strategy A plan for selecting and analyzing a target market and developing and maintaining a marketing mix that will satisfy this target market.

Markup In cost-oriented pricing, a percentage added to the total cost of the product to cover marketing expenses and allow a profit.

Mass Production Rapid manufacture of large quantities of goods accomplished through division of labor, specialization, and standardization.

Master Limited Partnership (MLP) A partnership that sells units traded on a recognized stock exchange.

Materials Handling The physical handling of products during transportation and warehousing.

Materials Requirements Planning A computerized forecasting system used to plan ordering of parts and materials for manufacturing.

Matrix Structure A functional structure combined with either a product or a project structural arrangement.

Media Plan Selection of specific media in which advertisements will be run and when they will be run to reach the target markets.

Mediator Third party to a labor dispute who tries to get union and management to reason and works at improving communication between them.

Merchant Wholesaler Marketing intermediary that takes ownership of goods and the risks associated with ownership.

Merger Combining two or more business enterprises into a single entity.

MESBIC Minority-enterprise small-business investment company. Such a company is owned and operated by established industrial or financial concerns, private investors, or business-oriented economic development organizations.

Microcomputer A personal computer, including a cathode ray tube and a keyboard.

Microeconomics Involves the study of household decision making on what to buy, business pricing decisions, and how markets allocate resources among alternatives.

Minicomputer A smaller, slower version of the mainframe computer.

Mission Statement A statement of the purpose of an organization which expresses the vision of the leaders of the organization and gives focus to its members.

Mixed Economy An economy in which both the government and private business enterprises produce and distribute goods and services.

Money Anything commonly accepted as a means of paying for goods and services.

Money Market Accounts Deposits that pay interest rates very competitive with those paid on other short-term investments; some allow a limited number of checks to be written in amounts over $500.

Moral Philosophy The set of principles that dictate acceptable behavior.

Motivation The way drives or needs direct a person's behavior toward a specific goal; involves the level of effort put forth to pursue the goal.

Motivator Content-oriented characteristic that contributes to job satisfaction.

Multinational Corporation A firm that operates on a global basis, committing assets to operations or subsidiaries in foreign countries.

Municipal Bond Bonds issued by state, towns, and other municipalities to finance schools, hospitals, roads, and other civic projects.

Mutual Fund A fund formed by a group of individuals, who pool their money to invest in securities, and usually handled by a professional investment manager.

N

Natural Resources Resources that nature provides in limited amounts, including crude oil, natural gas, minerals, timber, and water.

Need for Achievement A strong desire to succeed, to grow, to accomplish challenging tasks.

Needs Hierarchy A motivational theory, offered by Maslow, that people have five needs arranged in a hierarchy from physiological to self-realization.

Negative Reinforcer A consequence of behavior such as a reprimand that, when administered, encourages an employee to adapt more desirable behavior to avoid the unpleasant consequence.

Negotiable Instrument A written promise to pay a specified sum of money; it can be transferred from one person or firm to another.

Net Income The excess of revenues over expenses; also called the bottom line.

NLRB A group that investigates cases of alleged unfair labor practices by employers and unions and holds elections to determine whether groups of employees want to be unionized.

Nonprice Competition A policy of emphasizing aspects other than price, such as quality, service, or promotion, to sell products.

Nonprofit Corporation An enterprise (e.g., university, charity, church) that is not driven by a profit-seeking motive.

Nonstore Retailing Retailing that takes place ouside of stores; includes in-store selling, direct marketing, and vending machines.

Norris-LeGuardia Act A 1932 law that limited the power of federal courts to stop union picketing, boycotts, and strikes; also made the yellow-dog contract unenforceable.

O

Objectives Specific results or targets to be reached by a certain time.

Occupational Safety and Health Act (OSHA) Law, passed in 1970, that mandates safety and health standards for U.S. business. Provided for the establishment of the Occupational Safety and Health Administration.

Occupational Safety and Health Administration (OSHA) A federal agency with the primary purpose of ensuring safe working conditions.

Odd Lot A stock purchase of less than 100 shares.

Open Shop A company in which employees don't have to join a union or pay dues but can decide without pressure whether to become union members.

Operating Expenses All costs of doing business except the cost of goods sold.

Operations Any function(s) needed to carry out a strategic plan, to keep the company producing.

Order Getter A salesperson who recruits new customers and increases sales to current customers.

Order Processing The receipt and preparation of an order for shipment.

Order Taker A salesperson who processes repeat sales and maintains positive relationships with customers.

Organization Chart A graphic blueprint, or map, of positions, people, and formal authority relationships in the organization.

Organizational Buying Behavior The decisions and actions of buyers in organizations.

Organizational Structure The arrangement of work to be done by a business.

Organizing The management function of grouping people and assignments to carry out job tasks and the mission.

Output Device The hardware that displays the computer's requests or processed data.

Over-the-Counter (OTC) Market An electronic network of several thousand brokers who communicate trades through NASDAQ.

Owner's Equity Claims of owners, partners, and shareholders against the firm's assets; the excess of assets over liabilities.

P

Packaging The development of a container and a graphic design for a product.

Partnership A business owned by two or more people.

Patent The exclusive right of an inventor to make, use, or sell the registered product.

Personal Selling Person-to-person communication with one or more prospective customers in order to make a sale.

PERT Chart Program evaluation and review technique that tracks a project's progress and enables management to make optimal allocation of resources.

Physical Distribution Those activities that involve the movement of products through marketing channels from manufacturer to consumer.

Physiological Need Biological needs, such as for food, air, water.

Pioneer Pricing New-product pricing strategy of charging the highest possible price to regain costs quickly (price skimming) or setting the price below competitors' prices to build sales quickly (penetration pricing).

Planned Economy An economy in which the government owns the productive resources, financial enterprises, retail stores, and banks.

Planning The management function of establishing objectives and developing plans to accomplish them.

Plant Assets Relatively permanent assets that a firm expects to use for more than one year.

Point-of-Purchase Displays Promotional materials such as signs, posters, and freestanding shelves used in retail stores.

Point-of-Sale (POS) System Point-of-sale system, along with EFT, allows merchants to draw money directly from a customer's bank account at the time a purchase is made.

Point-of-Service (POS) A new form of health care coverage that combines the benefits of an HMO and a PPO; the insured has the option of consulting with the plans' doctors (for a co-payment) or choosing their own doctors (paying a larger percentage of the claim).

Pollution Contamination of air, water, and land.

Positive Reinforcer A consequence of behavior such as praise or other rewards that, when administered, increases the chances that the behavior will be repeated.

Power of Attorney A legal document authorizing an agent to act on behalf of the principal.

Preferred Provider Organization (PPO) A form of health care coverage that offers employers reduced premiums; employees must choose physicians and hospitals from the PPO's list of approved providers.

Preferred Stock Stock that has preference over common stock in the payment of dividends and in claims against the assets of the firm, but does not confer voting rights.

Premium A fee paid to the insurance company for protection.

Premium A gift given to customers for purchasing a certain product.

Premium or Push Money Additional compensation provided to salespeople to encourage them to sell a product.

Price The value that buyers exchange for a product in the marketing transaction.

Price Competition A policy of using price to differentiate a product in the marketplace.

Price Discounting A policy of offering buyers deductions from the price of a product.

Price/Earnings Ratio The current market price of a stock divided by the annual earnings per share.

Pricing Method A systematic procedure for determining prices on a regular basis; considers costs, product demand, or competitors' prices.

Primary-Demand Advertising Advertising used to create demand for all products in a product group.

Principle A guideline that managers can use in making decisions.

Private Accountant Accountant in any position not included in public accounting; may work in management accounting, government accounting, or academia.

Product A good, service, or idea, including all the tangibles and intangibles provided in an exchange between buyer and seller.

Product Liability Area of tort law that holds business firms responsible for negligence in design, manufacture, sale, and operation of their products.

Product Liability Insurance Covers losses for injuries caused by the use of a company's products.

Product Life Cycle The theoretical life of a product, consisting of four stages: introduction, growth, maturity, and decline.

Product Line A group of related products that are considered a unit because of marketing, technical, or use similarities.

Product Mix The total group of products a firm offers for sale, or all of the firm's product lines.

Product Modification The changing of one or more of a product's features as a strategy to extend its life cycle.

Product Structure An organizational structure in which a manager is placed in charge of and has responsibility for a product or product line.

Production The total process by which a company produces finished goods or services.

Productivity A measure of output per unit of a particular input.

Professional Pricing A policy—practiced by doctors, lawyers, and others with skills or experience in a particular field—of charging a standard fee for a particular service.

Professional Service Organization An organization of professional people, organized under professional association laws and treated as a corporation for tax purposes.

Profit The difference between business income (revenue) and business expenses (costs); the selling price of a product minus all costs of making and selling it, including taxes.

Profitability Ratio Ratio that measures a firm's financial performance by comparing earnings to sales or investment.

Progressive Tax Form of taxation in which the percentage of income paid in taxes increases as income increases.

Promissory Note A legally binding promise of payment that spells out the terms of the loan agreement.

Promotion The communication of favorable, persuasive information about a firm or product in order to influence potential buyers.

Promotion Mix The combination of advertising, personal selling, sales promotion, and publicity used to promote a specific product.

Property Insurance Protection for losses due to physical damage to or destruction of property or for property loss due to theft.

Prospectus A statement used by potential investors that gives information about a firm, its management, its operations, the purpose for the stock issue, etc.

Protection Programs Programs that assist employees and families when direct compensation is terminated and with health care expenses.

Proxy A written statement, signed by a shareholder of a corporation, allowing someone else to cast his or her number of votes.

Psychological Pricing A policy that encourages purchase decisions based on emotion rather than reason; includes odd-even pricing, customary pricing, prestige pricing, and price lining.

Public Accountant Works for a firm that provides accounting services to companies, other organizations, and the general public on a fee-for-service basis; typical areas of service include auditing, tax consulting, and management consulting.

Public Relations A set of communications activities designed to create and maintain a favorable public image for a firm.

Publicity A nonpersonal form of communication transmitted in news story form and not paid for directly by a sponsor.

Pull Strategy Promotion of a product directly to consumers to stimulate strong consumer demand.

Punishment An undesirable consequence of a particular behavior.

Purchasing Power Parity (PPP) The adjustment of relative prices. A relative market basket of consumer goods is compared to the same market basket in terms of the currencies of the two countries.

Pure Risk The threat of a loss with no chance of profit.

Push Strategy Promotion of a product to wholesalers or retailers in the marketing channel, who in turn promote the product to consumers.

Put Option An option to buy stock shares at market price and sell at a specified price.

Q

Quality Circles Small groups of employees who meet regularly to identify, and sometimes solve, work-related problems.

Quality of Work Life (QWL) Managerial programs that increase outcomes such as productivity or performance by better management of jobs, people, and working conditions.

Quick Ratio The measure of a firm's immediate liquidity; computed by dividing quick assets by current liabilities. Also called acid-test ratio.

Quota A limit on the amount of a product that can leave or enter a country.

R

Railway Labor Act A 1926 law that established collective bargaining as a means for resolving labor-management disputes.

Rate of Return The dollar value of the interest earned or dividend received divided by the market value of the security.

Ratio Analysis Method of analyzing financial information by comparing logical relationships between various financial statement items.

Real Property Real estate (land and anything permanently attached to it, such as houses, buildings, and parking lots).

Rebate An extra discount or refund given to consumers who buy a product and supply proofs of purchase.

Recruitment Steps taken to staff an organization with the best-qualified people.

Recycling Reusing materials such as paper, plastic, glass, and aluminum to make other products.

Reinforcer A consequence of behavior that improves the chances it will or will not reoccur.

Reserve The percentage of money from deposits that a bank must keep on hand or on deposit in the Federal Reserve Bank. Funds above this amount can be loaned out.

Retailing The marketing activities involved in selling products to final consumers for personal or household use.

Retained Earnings A firm's accumulated net income minus dividends to shareholders.

Return on Equity Measure of the return the company earns on every dollar of owners' and shareholders' investments; computed by dividing net income by equity.

Return on Sales Measure of a firm's profitability, or its ability to generate income; computed by dividing net income by net sales.

Revenue Inflows of assets resulting from the ongoing operation of the business.

Revolving Credit Agreement A line of credit guaranteed by the bank.

Right-to-Work Laws State laws requiring that two people doing the same job be paid the same wages, whether or not they belong to the union.

Risk The possibility of suffering an injury or loss.

Risk Avoidance A risk management strategy of not taking on or of getting out of risky ventures.

Risk Management Minimizing the amount and cost of pure risk a company will face.

Risk Reduction A risk management strategy of using loss prevention programs and other management programs.

Robot A computerized, reprogrammable, and multi-functional machine that can manipulate materials and objects in the performance of particular tasks.

Round Lot A stock purchase of 100 shares.

S

S Corporation A corporation with 35 or fewer owners that files an income tax return as a partnership to take advantage of lower tax rates.

Safety Need Security need, such as the need to be financially secure and protected against job loss.

Salaries Compensation based on a long time period: a week, a month, or longer.

Sales Branch Manufacturer-owned wholesaler that takes title to products, assumes the risks of ownership, and provides services.

Sales Contest A competition designed to stimulate sales efforts by salespeople, distributors, or retailers.

Sales Law Body of law involving the sale of products for money or on credit.

Sales Office Manufacturer-owned sales force that sells products without maintaining an inventory.

Sales Promotion An activity that offers customers or marketing intermediaries direct incentives for purchasing a product.

Savings and Loan Association (S&Ls) Institutions that now offer both checking and savings accounts and use the majority of their funds to finance home mortgages; sometimes called thrifts.

Savings Banks Depositor-owned, banklike institutions that began in New England in the early 19th century with the purpose of paying interest on deposits.

Scalar Principle The principle of organization that authority and responsibility should flow in a clear, unbroken line from the highest to the lowest manager.

Scientific Management The scientific study and breakdown of work into its smallest mechanical elements, and their rearrangement into the most efficient combination.

Scrambled Merchandising Adding unrelated products to a firm's existing product mix.

Secured Loan A loan backed with some form of collateral.

Securities Documents that can be bought or sold and that reflect ownership or debt.

Segmentation Base The individual or group characteristics that marketing managers use to divide a total market into segments.

Selection In employment, a series of steps that starts with the initial screening and ends with a hiring decision.

Selective (Brand) Advertising Advertising used to sell a specific product or brand.

Selective Distribution Market coverage in which only some of the available outlets are used for distributing a product.

Self-Actualization Need The need to use and display one's full range of skills and competence.

Self-Insurance Method by which companies assume risk by putting aside cash reserves to cover their potential future losses.

Selling Expenses Costs incurred in marketing and distributing a firm's goods and services.

Selling Process A series of steps salespeople perform, consisting of prospecting, preparing, approaching, presenting, answering objections, closing, and following up.

Service Standard A specific, measurable goal relating to physical distribution activities.

Services In business, intangible products that cannot be physically possessed and that involve performance or effort; examples include teaching, nursing, air travel, tailoring, accounting, and the opera. In employee compensation, indirect compensation in the form of programs, facilities, or activities supplied by employers for employees' use.

Services Intangible products that cannot be physically possessed and that involve performance or effort.

Sexual Harassment Unwelcome advances and requests for sexual favors that affect a person's performance, and a hostile work environment in which employees are subjected to sexual comments, jokes, or materials.

Shopping Product An item that buyers will expend time and effort to find and purchase.

Small Business One that is independently owned and operated and is not dominant in its field of operation.

Small Business Administration (SBA) An independent agency of the federal government created in 1953 to protect the interests of small-business owners.

Small-Business Investment Company (SBIC) A privately owned and operated company licensed by the SBA to furnish loans to small firms.

Social Audit A systematic review of an organization's performance of social responsibility activities.

Social Need The need to belong and to interact with other people.

Social Responsibility The awareness that business activities have an impact on society, and the consideration of that impact by firms in decision making.

Software A sequence of instructions that a computer can carry out.

Sole Proprietorship A business owned and managed by one individual.

Span of Control The principle of organization that limits the number of subordinates reporting to a supervisor.

Specialty Product A product with one or more unique features that a group of buyers will spend considerable time and effort to purchase.

Specialty Store A retailer that offers a narrow mix of products with deep product lines.

Speculative Risk Risk involving the chance of making a profit or taking a loss.

Spreadsheets Electronic accounting ledgers generated by computer software.

Staff Authority An advisory authority in which a person studies a situation and makes recommendations but has no authority to take action.

Staffing The management function of selecting, placing, training, developing, and compensating subordinates.

Standard of living A measure of how well a person or family is doing in terms of satisfying needs and wants with goods and services.

Statement of Cash Flows Financial statement showing the flow of cash into and out of a business during a period of time.

Statute A law created by a federal, state, or local legislature, treaty, or constitution.

Statutory Law As a body, the laws enacted by federal, state, and local governments, constitutions, or treaties.

Stock Exchange An organization of individuals who buy and sell securities to the public.

Stock Option The purchased right to buy or sell shares of stock at a predetermined price within a specified time period.

Stockbroker An individual licensed to act on behalf of an investor in the buying and selling of securities.

Strategic alliance An agreement in which two firms combine their resources in a partnership that goes beyond a joint venture.

Strict Product Liability Legal concept that holds manufacturers responsible for injuries caused by products regardless of whether negligence was involved.

Strike An effort to withhold employee services so that the employer will make greater concessions at the bargaining table.

Supercomputer A computer formed by connecting multiple mainframes.

Supermarket A large, self-service retailer that stocks a wide variety of groceries and a limited assortment of nonfood products.

Superstore A giant retail outlet that stocks food and nonfood items as well as most products purchased on a routine basis.

Supply The quantity of a product that producers will sell at various prices.

Support Salespeople Salespeople who assist in selling by locating potential customers, educating them about products, building goodwill, and providing after-sales service.

Sweepstakes A sales promotion method in which consumers enter a drawing for prizes.

Sweetheart Contract Agreement between union leaders and management to terms that work to their mutual benefit but maintain poor working conditions for other employees.

Syndicate Two or more businesses joined together to accomplish specific business goals; a popular form in underwriting large amounts of corporation stocks.

T

Taft-Hartley Act A 1947 labor law that prohibits the closed shop, requires unions to bargain in good faith, and makes it illegal for a union to discriminate against employees who don't join the union.

Tangible Personal Property Physical items, such as goods and equipment.

Target Market A group to which a firm directs its marketing activities.

Tax A payment for the support of government activities, required of organizations and individuals within the domain of the government.

Technical Skills Skills involved in making a product or providing a service.

Term Insurance Life insurance that covers an individual for a specified number of years but has no value when the term is over.

Territorial Structure An organizational structure in which units are divided on the basis of territory or geographical region.

Theory X Managerial assumptions that employees dislike work, responsibility, and accountability and must be closely directed and controlled to be motivated to perform.

Theory Y Managerial assumptions that employees want to be challenged, like to display creativity, and can be highly motivated to perform well if given some freedom to direct or manage their own behavior.

Theory Z Management theory that draws on the characteristics of successful Japanese and American managers; emphasizes consensus management practices.

Time Deposits Savings accounts that allow the financial institution to require notice before withdrawal or to assess a penalty for early withdrawal.

Times Interest Earned Ratio The measure of how many times during the year a business earns the amount of interest it must pay; computed by dividing income before interest and taxes by interest expense.

Title VII Part of the Civil Service Reform Act of 1978; outlawed certain unfair labor practices and created the Federal Labor Relations Authority (FLRA); granted covered employees the right to form, join, or assist any labor organization or to refrain from such activity freely and without reprisals.

Tort A noncriminal (civil) injury to other persons or their property or reputation; results from intentional acts or negligence.

Total Market Approach The tactic of developing one marketing mix for the total market for a product. Also called undifferentiated approach.

Trade Allowance A discount a manufacturer gives for performing certain functions or making purchases during a specified time period.

Trade Credit Credit given by suppliers for the purchases the firm makes from these suppliers.

Trade Sales Promotion Activities a firm directs to wholesalers, retailers, or salespeople to encourage them to stock or sell its products.

Trade Show A temporary exhibit where manufacturers display products to potential customers and gather names for a list of prospects.

Trademark A name or symbol, registered with the U.S. Patent and Trademark Office, that guarantees the owner exclusive rights to its use.

Trading Company A firm that buys products in one country and sells in another without being involved in manufacturing.

Trading Stamps Tokens given out by retailers based on the amount of purchase; redeemable for gifts.

Training A continual process of helping employees perform at a high level.

Transistor A small switch that controls electrical current; characterized second-generation computers.

Transportation Shipping goods to customers by railways, airlines, trucks, waterways, and pipelines.

Treasury Bill A loan to the U.S. Treasury that typically has a maturity date of three or six months. Often called a T-bill.

U

Uniform Commercial Code (UCC) Comprehensive statutory laws designed to eliminate differences between state laws governing business.

Union Shop A company that requires employees to join the union after being hired.

Union Steward A person who represents the interests of local union members in their on-the-job relations with managers.

Unity of Command The principle of organization that no employee should report to more than one superior.

Universal Life Insurance Combines term insurance with a tax-deferred savings account earning interest at bond market rates.

Unlimited Liability Obligation of investors to use personal assets, when necessary, to pay off debts to business creditors; a disadvantage of sole proprietorships and partnerships.

Unsecured Loan A loan issued on the good credit of the borrower and requiring no collateral.

Utilitarian Philosophy A set of moral principles focusing on the greatest good for the largest number of people.

Utility The ability of a product to satisfy consumers' needs.

V

Variable Life Insurance Allows the policyholder to determine where the cash value of a policy should be invested.

Venture Capital Funds provided by individuals or organizations to new firms with high potential for growth; the investor receives a share of the ownership and frequently a share of control.

Vertical Integration The combining of two or more functions of a marketing channel under one management.

Vertical Marketing System (VMS) A marketing channel in which the different intermediaries are coordinated through management to improve distribution.

Vertical Merger A merger in which a firm joins with its supplier.

Very Large-Scale Integration (VLSI) Superchip circuitry, resulting from extremely compact transistors and circuits assembled on a single silicon chip; marked start of fifth generation of computers.

W

Wages Compensation based on time worked or number of units produced.

Wagner Act A law that made collective bargaining legal and required employers to bargain with the representatives of the employees. The law is also referred to as the National Labor Relations Act.

Warehouse Club A large discount retail store offering members a broad range of name-brand merchandise at low prices.

Warehouse Showroom A retail store carrying a large inventory that deals in volume and provides limited services.

Warehousing The physical distribution activities involved in receiving, storing, and shipping goods.

WARN Act A 1989 law that requires employers with 100 or more full-time employees to give affected employees 60 days' written notice of plant or office closing or other mass layoffs. The law is commonly known as the Plant Closing Bill.

Wheel of Retailing The idea that retailers enter the market as low-priced, low-status businesses, evolve into high-cost establishments, and become vulnerable to new competitors entering the market.

Whistle-Blower An employee who informs superiors, the media, or a government regulatory agency about unethical behavior within an organization.

Whole Life Insurance Provides a combination of insurance and savings and stays in force for the life of the insured.

Wholesaling The marketing activities of intermediaries who sell to retailers, industrial users, and other organizational customers.

Word Processing Creating written documents with a computer.

Work Motivation Model An explanation of motivation that defines hygiene factors and motivator factors, and how they affect job satisfaction and dissatisfaction.

Working Capital Measure of a firm's ability to meet short-term obligation; computed as current assets minus current liabilities.

World Bank An international organization that lends money to underdeveloped and developing countries for development.

Y

Yellow-Dog Contract A statement signed by an employee promising not to form or join a union.

COMPANY INDEX

N

O

P

R

S

T

U

V

W

X

Y

Z

NAME INDEX

H

I

J

K

L

M

N

O

P

SUBJECT INDEX

C

D

E

M

N

O

P

Q

R

T

PHOTO CREDITS

For permission to reproduce the photographs on the pages indicated, acknowledgment is made to the following:

Page		
Page	2	© Ralph Mercer/Tony Stone Images
	3	AP/Wide World Photos
	12	© C. Boylan/Unicorn Stock Photos
	24	© Mike Malyszko/FPG International
	36	© Ralph Mercer/Tony Stone Images
	44	AP/Wide World Photos
	50	© Mike Malyszko/FPG International
	63	Courtesy of Farmland Industries
	71	© James Porto/FPG International
	75	Courtesy of the Greater Houston Partnership
	87	© SuperStock International, Inc.
	91	The Bettmann Archive
	114	© Michael Simpson/FPG International
	117	© Bill Losh/FPG International
	124	© SuperStock International
	128	Courtesy of Dupont
	133	© Jean Higgins/Unicorn Stock Photos
	149	© Michael Nelson/FPG International
	155	© Richard B. Dippold/Unicorn Stock Photos
	168	© Aneal Vohra/Unicorn Stock Photos
	175	© Charles Thatcher/Tony Stone Images
	179	AP/Wide World Photos
	189	AP/Wide World Photos
	195	© Alon Reininger/Unicorn Stock Photos
	210	Leo d Wys Inc./De Wys/TPL
	211	Reuters/Bettmann
	226	© Robert Llewellyn/SuperStock International
	232	© Willie Hill/FPG International
	241	© Ed Honowitz/Tony Stone Images
	249	© Ron Chapple/FPG International
	254	© Jeff Greenberg/Unicorn Stock Photos
	256	© Charles Gupton/Tony Stone Images
	273	© Tom Carroll/FPG International
	279	© Mitch Kezar/Tony Stone Images
	280	The Bettmann Archive
	296	© Vladimir Pcholkin/FPG International
	322	© Gary Buss/FPG International
Page	334	SuperStock International
	342	© Jim Pickerell/Tony Stone Images
	351	© Ted Horowitz/The Stock Market
	367	© Jeff Greenberg/Unicorn Stock Photos
	379	AP/Wide World Photos
	390	© Arthur Gurmankin/Unicorn Stock Photos
	391	AP/Wide World Photos
	408	© Chip Henderson/Tony Stone Images
	412	AP/Wide World Photos
	434	© Micheal Simpson/FPG International
	435	© Jim Shippee/Unicorn Stock Photos
	448	© Robert E. Daemmrich/Tony Stone Images
	452	© Jim Shippee/Unicorn Stock Photos
	467	© Eduardo Garcia/FPG International
	470	© Don Smetzer/Tony Stone Images
	471	Courtesy of White Hen Pantry, Inc.
	471	Courtesy of Sony Electronics Inc.
	471	Courtesy of Ferrari North America
	474	Courtesy of The Boeing Company
	476	© Jim Shippee/Unicorn Stock Photos
	482	Courtesy of Heinz USA
	483	Courtesy of AT&T
	483	The Chicago Cubs insignia depicted in this publication is reproduced with the permission of Major League Baseball Properties
	483	Courtesy of New York Life Insurance Company
	483	Courtesy of Texas Instruments Incorporated
	483	Courtesy of General Mills, Inc.
	483	Courtesy of Levi Strauss & Co.
	483	Courtesy of LEGO Systems, Inc.
	483	Courtesy of Chrysler Motors
	483	Courtesy of Fuji Photo Film U.S.A., Inc.
	486	© Gail Shumway/FPG International
	505	© Jim Corwin/Tony Stone Images
	514	Courtesy of Richardson Seating Corporation
	517	© Ron Chapple/FPG International
	536	© Scott Markewitz/FPG International

Page 539 Courtesy of PepsiCo and Scott Wanner/Journalism Service
542 Courtesy of the State of Florida, Department of Citrus, Processed Advertising, 1994–1995
542 Courtesy of the Nestlé Foods Corporation
542 Courtesy of DuPont
548 Reuters/Bettmann
551 © Don Smetzer/Tony Stone Images
559 © Tom Campbell/FPG International
564 Courtesy Travelers Insurance
578 © Shaun Egan/Tony Stone Images
593 © Mark Reinstein/FPG International
599 © Chronis Jons/Tony Stone Images
611 © John Darling/Tony Stone Images
613 © Pelton and Associate/H. Armstrong Roberts

Page 620 © Amy Etra/PhotoEdit
626 Courtesy of Mobil Corporation
629 © Chris Minerva/FPG International
630 Courtesy of Mobil Corporation
641 © Ralph Mercer/Tony Stone Images
648 © Michael Newman/PhotoEdit
656 Camerique/H. Armstrong Roberts
672 © Brian Blauser/Tony Stone Images
681 © Tony Freeman/PhotoEdit
684 © Stephan Simpson/FPG International
686 © Aneal Vohra/Unicorn Stock Photos
690 © Billy E. Barnes/PhotoEdit
706 © Jon Riley/Tony Stone Images
707 © Ron Chapple/FPG International
742 © Superstock, Inc.
751 © David Young-Wolff/PhotoEdit